AFGHANISTAN

AFGHANISTAN

A History from 1260 to the Present

Jonathan L. Lee

REAKTION BOOKS

For Andrew, Stephen and Grace

Published by
REAKTION BOOKS LTD
Unit 32, Waterside
44–48 Wharf Road
London N1 7UX, UK

www.reaktionbooks.co.uk

First published 2018

Printed and bound in Great Britain
by Bell & Bain, Glasgow

A catalogue record for this book is available from the British Library

ISBN 978 1 78914 010 1

Contents

LIST OF CHARTS

LIST OF TABLES

LIST OF MAPS

TRANSLITERATIONS

W HEN USING Persian terminology I have given preference to the Kabuli (Dari) dialect rather than Iranian Persian since the former is the official language of Afghanistan. The commonly accepted Dari meanings for technical terms have also been preferred to their Iranian usages.

I do not differentiate between the several Arabic consonants which are included in the Persian alphabet since Afghans do not do so in their pronunciation, hence 's', 'z', 't' refer to various Arabic characters. Where the final 'h' (*heh*) is silent it is not transliterated (hence *Maimana* not *Maimanah*; *daula* not *daulah*), though I have used accepted English forms where they exist, for example *mullah* rather than *mullā*; *caliph* not *khalīfa*; *shaikh* not *shaykh*; Kandahar not Qand(a)har. However, I have preferred *wazīr* to the anglicized *vizier* and the Mongol transliteration of Chinggis Khan rather than Genghis Khan.

Standard Arabic transliterations for Islamic theological terms are retained (for example, *hadith*, *sunna*), as are official titles of Afghan, Indian, Pakistan, Turkish and other organizations and institutions, such as Wolusi Jirga not Wulusi Jirga; Darul Uloom rather than Dar al-'Ulum. American English is only used in official titles (for example, Minister of Defense) or when quoting from sources such as the State Department or CIA archives.

For stylistic purposes, in the main text, transliterations of foreign and technical terms do not distinguish between long and short vowels, but they are differentiated in the Glossary. The following rules apply:

Consonants

English consonants correspond to their nearest Persian equivalent pronunciations. There are three Persian consonants not found in standard English. They are transliterated as follows: *qāf* = *q* (IPA /q/) (*qānūn*, *qāzī*); *ghain* = *gh* (as in French, 'Français'); and *khe* = *kh* (Scottish 'lo*ch*'). In Iranian Persian *qaf* is pronounced *gh* but in Dari as *q*, and *waw* as a consonant as *w* rather than *v* (for example, *wilāyat* not *vilāyat*), though Safavid is preferred to Safawid since this was a Persian dynasty. The consonant *jeh* = *zh* ('azure').

Vowels and diphthongs of Kabuli Persian (Dari)

Long vowels: *ā* ('call'); *ē* ('eight'); *ī* ('ski'); *ō* ('boat'); *ū* ('do')

Short vowels: *a* ('bat'); *e* (' bell'); *i* ('bit'); *o* ('hot'); *u* ('cut')

Dipthongs: *ai* ('pie'); *au* ('now'); *ui* ('chewy')

The glottal stop *ain* is represented by ' (for example, 'Abd al-Rahman; Shi'a), the *hamza* as ' (for example, 'Aman Allah).

The Persian relational marker, or *ēzāfa*, is written as *–i* after a consonant and *–yi* after a terminal vowel (for example, Deh-i Sabz; Khirqa-yi Sharif).

Dates

Unless otherwise stated all dates are CE (AD). The Hijra, or Islamic lunar calendar, is indicated with H. (for example, 1015 H.) and the Afghan/ Persian solar or *shamsī* year, which commences on 1 Hamal (21 March in a standard year), by s. (for example, 1350 s.). All three calendars operate in modern Afghanistan, though in the past the Gregorian calendar was not used by the Afghans.

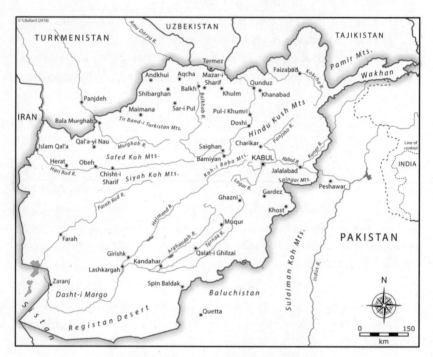

Modern Afghanistan and neighbouring states

Introduction

AFGHANISTAN IS THE fortieth largest country in the world by area, making it slightly larger than France and somewhat smaller than Texas. Administratively the country consists of 34 provinces, or *wilayat*s, which are divided into a number of sub-national districts, known as *wulswali*s. Population estimates vary considerably, since for political reasons Afghanistan has never had a comprehensive, nationwide census. According to the Central Statistics Office, Afghanistan's population in 2015/16 was 28.6 million, but other sources put the figure as high as 33 million. In addition, around 1 million Afghan refugees still live in Pakistan and some 2 million in Iran, while several hundred thousand Afghans reside, or are seeking asylum, in various European countries, North America and Australasia. According to United Nations Data, Afghanistan's population growth rate is currently more than 4 per cent per annum, which, if correct, means Afghanistan has one of the fastest-growing populations in the world. More than 40 per cent of the country's population today is under fifteen years of age.

Ethnically Afghanistan has never been cohesive and the size and percentage of the country's ethnolinguistic groups has long been a source of contention and political manipulation. According to the Polish linguistic survey conducted in the 1970s, there are between forty and fifty languages in Afghanistan belonging to seven separate linguistic groups.[1] Pushtuns, also known as Afghans or Pathans, the largest ethnic group in the country, have been the dominant political power in modern Afghanistan, but even by the most generous estimates Pushtuns make up only about one-third of Afghanistan's population. Indeed, there are more Pushtuns in Pakistan than Afghanistan. The Pushtuns consist of dozens of tribes that historically lived in the plains and mountains that straddle the modern Afghan–Pakistan frontier. Prior to European colonial intervention, this region was the original Afghanistan, that is, the land of the Afghan tribes. It consisted of the regions east of the Helmand river and stretches as far east as Jalalabad, the Kunar valley, Swat and Chitral. Southwards the Pushtun belt extended into the Pakistan provinces of Khyber Pakhtunkhwa and Baluchistan up to the banks of the Indus. At the heart of Pushtun tribal territory lies the mountains and hills of the Safed Koh, Sulaiman Koh and Spingar.

Since the foundation of the Durrani kingdom in the early eighteenth century, hundreds of thousands of Pushtuns have settled in other regions of modern Afghanistan, the result of voluntary and involuntary migration, nomad resettlement programmes and state-sponsored colonization. Today substantial Pushtun communities are located in the lower Hari Rud and Bala Murghab rivers in western Afghanistan and in and around most of the main urban centres of the northern plains from Maimana to Qunduz. Southern Kabul, Ghazni and Uruzgan provinces have also become Pushtun-majority areas due to the forcible relocation of indigenous peoples such as the Hazaras, Aimaqs and other Persian-speaking communities.

The Ghilzai and Durrani Pushtun tribes make up the largest nomadic community in Afghanistan, known as *maldar* or *kuchi*s. Since the 1970s substantial numbers of Pushtun nomads have become sedentary due to the unresolved civil war and the hostility of non-Pushtun communities in their traditional summer grazing grounds in northern and central Afghanistan. Today many former *maldar* eke out a meagre living as subsistence farmers on marginal land, some have become small-time traders, while others are lorry drivers in Pakistan's Pushtun-dominated trucking businesses.

There are probably as many Persian-speaking peoples in Afghanistan as there are Pushtuns. It is common to refer to these peoples as Tajiks, but they are far from being members of a single tribe or ethnic group, hence to lump all these peoples together under the generic label of Tajik is somewhat misleading. Historically, *Tajik* was the term used to describe the Arab Muslim invaders and not the indigenous Persian population of eastern Iran, Afghanistan or Central Asia. In Afghanistan native Persian-speakers are usually known by the generic term *farsiwan*s, though in the northern plains the term *Tajik* is more frequently employed due to the influence of Soviet ethnography. Many *farsiwan*s are simply known by their place of origin: Kabuli, Panjshiri, Kohistani, Badakhshani and so forth. Unlike Pushtuns, most *farsiwan*s are not tribal and have a diverse and mixed ethnogenesis. The only exception are the Chahar Aimaq – the Sunni Hazara, Firozkohi, Jamshidi and Taimani-Timuris – tribal people who live mainly in Badghis and southern Faryab and Sar-i Pul provinces. *Farsiwan*s are also scattered throughout the country, including Pushtun-majority regions such as the Logar valley, Nangahar and Ghazni.

Historically, Persian was the language of the court and commerce and by and large this is still the case, for while Pushtu and the Kabuli

Pushtun *maldar* in western Hazarajat. Traditionally these Ghilzai nomads spend the summer months in this region but tensions between Hazaras and the *maldar* and the civil war means many of them have abandoned their annual migration to this region.

dialect of Afghan Persian, known as Dari, are the two official languages of Afghanistan, the majority of Afghanistan's population neither speaks nor understands Pushtu. Dari, especially its colloquial form, differs significantly from literary Persian and Tehrani Persian in respect of both vocabulary and pronunciation. There are also substantial regional variations in the Persian spoken in Afghanistan.

Uzbeks are the majority population of the northern plains from the southern border of Faryab province to the eastern boundary of Qunduz, but there are sizeable populations of Turkmans, Tajiks and Pushtuns too. Uzbeki and Turkmani belong to the Altaic linguistic group, which derives from the Turco-Mongolian world of Inner Asia. Persian and Pushtu, on the other hand, are Eastern Iranian languages. A number of other smaller Turco-Mongolian groups live in northern Afghanistan, Badakhshan and the Wakhan, and include Kazakhs, Kipchaks, Kyrgyz and Uyghurs. In the Daulatabad region of Faryab province there is a small population of semi-sedentary Arabs who claim descent from the Arab Muslim invaders.[2]

Any discussion of ethnolinguistic groups in Afghanistan is complex and all maps of ethnic distribution in the country have to be regarded as rough guides only and treated with considerable caution. Apart from the mountainous regions of the southern Pushtun belt, which tend to be divided by traditional tribal boundaries, many communities, and all of Afghanistan's urban centres, are, to one degree or another, multi-ethnic. In rural communities, different ethnicities live in their own self-managing quarters, or *mahalas*, but all participate in the management of the wider community affairs.

Pushtuns, while they are affiliated by birth to a particular tribe, do not share a common ancestral or genetic origin. Tribal genealogies assert various descents, most of which are mythical and include Persian, Turkish, Kurdish, Arab, Armenian and Jewish. While Pushtu is the majority language of the Pushtu heartland on the Afghan–Pakistan frontier, many Pushtuns, especially urbanized ones, barely speak this language. In the Khushk district of Herat and along the Hari Rud settled Pushtuns speak Persian or even Turkmani as their mother tongue.

A similar situation applies to the Uzbeks, Turkmans and Hazaras. The Uzbeks are a conglomeration of Turco-Mongolian tribes who mostly settled in the region following the conquests of Chinggis Khan in the thirteenth century, while there are several Turkman tribes represented in Afghanistan. Under the influence of Western ethnology, many Hazaras today claim descent from the Mongol garrisons of Chinggis Khan or even the Mongol conqueror himself. The Hazaras certainly do have Mongol blood and heritage, and their dialect of Persian, Hazaragi, contains Mongolian-derivative vocabulary.[3] However, their ethnicity is mixed and includes genetic links to the Persianate and Turkic peoples who lived in this region before and after the Arab Muslim invasion.

Afghanistan's size and mountainous topography has always posed challenges to communications and governance and has encouraged a strong sense of regional autonomy. Despite major improvements in road communications since 2001, there is still only one sealed, all-weather road linking Kabul with the northern capital of Mazar-i Sharif and Kabul with Kandahar and Herat. In rural Afghanistan many roads are only fit for four-wheel drive vehicles and many people still rely on donkeys or horses, while the poor will walk many hours to reach local markets or obtain medical assistance.

The chain of mountains that dominates the centre of the country effectively divided the country in two and, prior to the establishment of the modern state of Afghanistan, these mountains were regarded as the frontier between India and the plains of Balkh and Central Asia. In this era, Bala Murghab, the Saighan valley north of Bamiyan, Charikar and Kabul were frontier outposts. The central highlands consist of a series of ranges that rise in height from west to east. In the northwest the limestone plateau of the Tir Band-i Turkistan stretches from Bala Murghab to east of Sar-i Pul, where it merges with the Koh-i Alburz. This chain of hills is cut through with a series of deep, narrow gorges and is one of the least explored regions of the country. The perennial springs that rise on the northern face of this limestone plateau are the main source of the rivers that irrigate the lower valleys and the Balkh plains.

To the north and south of the Hari Rud lie the Safed Koh and Siyah Koh ranges, which eventually converge with the Koh-i Baba to the east, the snow-capped tops of which dominate the skyline of the Hazarajat. The Koh-i Baba then merges into the Hindu Kush of southeastern Afghanistan and the Pamirs of Badakhshan in the northeast, mountain chains that form the western tip of the Himalayas. Another series of mountain ranges run along the Afghan–Pakistan frontier. In the southwest of Afghanistan lie the inhospitable Dasht-i Margo, the Desert of Death, and the desert of the Registan and Sistan. In the northern plains, the Dasht-i Laili, between Daulatabad and Shibarghan, is another, smaller semi-desert region.

The central highlands and the hill country of the Afghan–Pakistan frontier are bisected by ancient routes that have linked India with Inner Asia, Iran and China for millennia, routes which have been used both for trade and invaders such as Alexander the Great, Persians, Arabs, Turco-Mongolian tribes from Inner Asia, and north Indian dynasties. Travel through the central mountain chains is difficult at the best of times and from late October to April the passes and upper valleys are snowbound. In the 1950s Soviet engineers constructed a new road and tunnel through the Salang Pass, which made it possible to drive from Kabul to Mazar-i Sharif in less than a day, but the Salang too is often blocked by snow or avalanches during the winter. In the south and southeast two other historic roads cut through the mountains of the Afghan–Pakistan frontier. The southern one links Kandahar with Quetta and Baluchistan via the Khojak Pass, while in the northeast the Khyber Pass is still the only major highway between Kabul and Peshawar. Historically several other minor routes linked southern Afghanistan with the Indus plains, but today they are mainly used by local tribes, nomads, smugglers and insurgents.

To the west, north, south and southeast of the central highlands lie fertile plains that are Afghanistan's main agricultural regions. These areas are watered by rivers sourced from the melting snows: the proverb 'better

Crossing the Kham Pass between Yakaulang and Bamiyan.
Snow persists on this high plateau into early May.

Kabul without gold than without snow' can be applied to the whole of
Afghanistan, for when the snows and spring rains fail, drought inevitably follows. Apart from Nangahar and southeastern Afghanistan, very
little rain falls in the country from May to September and most rivers
have substantial seasonal fluctuations. During the peak flow period in the
spring, when the snows melt and the rains come, the rivers become raging
torrents, causing localized flooding and landslips, washing out roads and
destroying irrigation canals and diversion dams. The situation is not helped
by overgrazing and the destruction of most of the country's forests. Yet
during the low flow period of the late summer and autumn, water levels
in the lower courses of many rivers dry to a mere trickle.

All of Afghanistan's rivers are exploited to some degree for irrigation but only a few have steel control gates or concrete-lined banks and
canals. Most irrigation systems are unlined and diversion structures are
made from compacted earth or stone. Maintenance of irrigation canals
is a labour-intensive affair and local stakeholders will muster to de-silt
their canals and repair diversion structures in the spring and autumn. The
management and distribution of water within irrigation networks is in the
hands of community-appointed water bailiffs, known as *mirabs*. Another
traditional source of irrigation is underground springs that run through
underground channels, known as *karez*.

All of the country's major water-storage facilities are located in southern Afghanistan, though there are smaller, localized dams on minor rivers.

These dams provide both water for irrigation and a limited and often inter-mittent supply of electricity to adjacent urban centres. All of Afghanistan's dams and equipment are ageing and in urgent need of repair. Two of the most important dams, the Darunta on the Arghandab river and the Kajaki on the Helmand, are effectively out of government hands and are controlled by insurgents. In 2016 the Indian-funded Selma Dam on the Hari Rud was finally opened, the project having been postponed since the 1970s due to the Soviet invasion and subsequent civil war. The present government plans are for at least fifteen more major dual-use storage facilities, though where the money will come from for such an ambitious programme is anyone's guess.

Afghanistan has five major river basin systems: the Kabul, the Amu Darya, the Balkh Ab, the Murghab-Hari Rud and the Helmand-Arghandab.[4] Kabul, the capital of Afghanistan, lies on the Kabul river in a plateau that is some 2,000 metres (6,560 ft) above sea level. This city owes its position to its strategic location on the historic routes between the Indus plains, Bamiyan, Balkh and Central Asia, though the present Kabul–Jalalabad highway was constructed in the mid-twentieth century. The ancient caravan road runs further south through But Khak, the Khurd Kabul gorge, Tezin and Gandamak.

Kabul today is a sprawling city. According to UN data, more than 4.6 million people now live in the Afghan capital, which has one of the fastest urban growth rates in the world. Kabul's burgeoning population, however, is a relatively recent phenomenon. In the mid-1970s the population was probably only around 1 million and most Afghans lived in rural settlements and not urban centres. Kabul's uncontrolled growth is symptomatic of a nationwide shift to urbanization, a trend that has placed severe strains on an already inadequate urban infrastructure. Today Kabul is one of the world's most polluted cities and its streets are gridlocked with traffic.

Surrounding Kabul lie a number of fertile valleys – the Logar, the Koh Daman and Tagab – which traditionally supplied the capital with food. However, due to the capital's growing population as well as demands for luxury goods by the foreigners and the Afghan middle classes, much of Kabul's requirements are now imported from Pakistan, Iran and Dubai. The extremely fertile valley of the Koh Daman, to the north of Kabul, was once a major producer of grapes and soft fruit, while the Panjshir valley, to the northeast of the Koh Daman, is famous for mulberries. To the west of Kabul is the former royal hill station of Paghman and this, along with settlements such as Shakar Darra, which lies on the eastern face of the Paghman Range, and Gul Bahar at the mouth of the Panjshir gorge, were favourite summer picnic spots for Kabulis. During the decade of Soviet occupation and the post-Soviet era the Koh Daman and Panjshir were among the most bitterly fought-over regions of Afghanistan and became abandoned wastelands strewn with mines and unexploded ordnance. Today agricultural activity in the Koh Daman is still in the process of recovery. The Koh Daman is predominantly *farsiwan*, though Hazara settlements increase as one travels up the Ghurband valley on the Charikar–Bamiyan road. On the eastern side of the valley are a number of prosperous Pushtun settlements, while the Safis of Tagab in Kapisa province control the strategic road between Charikar and Sarobi that skirts around Kabul. Several thousand Pashais, who speak a Dardic language, live in the foothills of the Hindu Kush from Kapisa to Darra-yi Nur and the Kunar.

In the south and southeast of Kabul province Pushtun tribes, mainly Ghilzais, are the dominant ethnicity, though there are Persian-speaking settlements in the upper Kabul river, the Jalrez region and along the Logar. There are substantial iron deposits around Ghazni and one of the world's richest seams of copper is found in Mes Ainak in the Logar, though these resources have yet to be exploited. The Maidan Shahr region of Wardak province is renowned for its apples, while Ghazni, one of Afghanistan's most renowned historic cities, was the capital of the Ghaznavid dynasty (977–1186) (see Table 2). Ghazni's imposing medieval fortress still dominates the town and outside the city walls are the tombs of the Ghaznavid sultans, the remains of their palaces and two minarets.

Nangahar, on the lower reaches of the Kabul river, is the country's only subtropical, frost-free zone, which benefits from the tail end of the Indian monsoons. Jalalabad, the provincial capital of Nangahar, is a bustling commercial centre on the main road between Kabul and the Pakistan frontier, and a large volume of Afghanistan's exports and imports pass through this town. Electricity for Jalalabad comes from the Sarobi dams, while water from these storage facilities feeds into an extensive irrigation network. The Nangahar plain is intensively cultivated. Rice, olives and citrus fruit are grown here and in recent times cauliflowers have become a major export crop, while the Khogiyani district on the Surkhab river grows apricots, walnuts, almonds and grapes. Nangahar's most profitable and extensively grown crop today, however, is opium. The mountains of southeastern Afghanistan were once covered with forests of juniper and holly oak, but due to illegal logging only a small remnant now remains: only 1.3 per cent of Afghanistan's land surface is now forested – one of the lowest ratios in the world.

The Nangahar region and hinterland is almost exclusively Pushtun and influential tribes include the Afridis, Khogiyanis, Ludins, Mohmands, Safis,

The Kabul river and the Kabul–Jalalabad highway looking downstream to Sarobi. This road was badly cut up during the Soviet era but is now repaired and resealed.

Sherzads and Shinwaris. To the southwest are the Jaji and Mangal tribes of Khost, while the high, snow-capped mountains of the Hindu Kush to the east are the homeland of the Nuristanis. Formerly known as Kafiristan, these tribes were polytheists whose religion bore similarities to Vedic and ancient Indo-Aryan tradition. In the 1890s the Amir of Afghanistan invaded the area, forcibly converted its inhabitants to Islam and renamed the region Nuristan, Land of Light. Another ethnolinguistic minority, the Pashais, live at the mouth of the Kunar river and in Darra-yi Nur.

The Amu Darya river, or Oxus, as it is known in classical sources, rises in the Pamir range of northeastern Afghanistan on the border with China and Tajikistan. This is one of Central Asia's most important rivers and forms Afghanistan's northern international frontier. Due to pressure from the USSR, and more recently from Uzbekistan and Turkmenistan, Afghanistan has never exploited the Amu Darya for irrigation, though on the other side of the frontier its waters are diverted into vast canals that feed Uzbekistan and Turkmenistan's water-thirsty cotton fields. In the Wakhan, the extreme northeastern finger of Afghanistan where the Amu Darya rises, only a few Kyrgyz live and are mostly reliant on their herds. In Badakhshan only limited agriculture is possible due to long and bitter winters, but the province has considerable mineral wealth. Lapis lazuli, emeralds, rubies and other precious and semi-precious stones have been mined here for millennia and recent geological surveys indicate the province has substantial copper, iron and marble reserves. At the mouth of the Kokcha river, gold is panned by sifting the gravel through the fleece of a sheep.

Below Imam Sahib, the Amu Darya slows and widens into a fertile plain watered by the Qunduz river and its tributaries. Once a notorious malarial swamp, the region was drained in the 1940s and '50s, and up until the recent troubles Qunduz was Afghanistan's most important cotton-producing region. Qunduz was formerly known as Qataghan, after the predominant Uzbek tribe of the region, but from the late nineteenth century the government in Kabul encouraged thousands of Pushtun colonists from the south to settle in the area and apportioned them smallholdings on reclaimed marshland. In the 1920s and '30s Uzbek, Turkman and Tajik refugees from Bukhara, Ferghana, Dushanbe and other Soviet-controlled areas of Central Asia also made their home here. Qunduz is renowned for its distinctive tufted carpets, which are woven by the Uzbek women.

The Balkh plains, which spread westwards from Khulm to Maimana, are watered by rivers that rise in the Tir Band-i Turkistan and the Hazarajat, though all of them dry up before reaching the Amu Darya. The source of the Balkh Ab, the most important river of the region, is the remarkable blue lakes of Band-i Amir, north of Bamiyan. In its lower course the Balkh Ab feeds an extensive and ancient irrigation system, the Hazhda Nahr, or Eighteen Canals, which forms an inland delta that at its apex spreads from north of Aqcha to west of Mazar-i Sharif. Today only ten canals are functioning but despite neglect, poor management and increasing illegal water extraction, double cropping is still commonplace at the head of the Hazhda Nahr network and rice and cotton are grown in large quantities. The melons of this region are particularly famous for their sweetness and enormous size. Along the northern face of the Tir Band-i Turkistan lies a belt of high, loess dunes, known as *chul*, which is one of the country's most important *lalmi*, or rain-fed, wheat growing areas. Walnuts and mulberries are found in abundance in the lower valleys of this mountain range and raw silk is produced here in large quantities. In the plains to the north, marijuana and opium are widely cultivated.

There are large reserves of coal in the Tir Band-i Turkistan and there are coal mines near Darra-yi Suf and Pul-i Khumri, but mining is on a very small scale and coal is extracted using pre-industrial methods, mostly pick and shovel. Conditions for the miners are appalling, health and safety rules are virtually non-existent and there are frequent fatalities due to shaft collapses. There are oil and gas fields in the Sar-i Pul and Shibarghan areas and gas is piped to Shibarghan and Mazar-i Sharif for domestic use; in the past it also supplied a fertilizer factory south of Mazar-i Sharif. The oil is crudely refined and mainly provides fuel for water heaters, though small quantities are exported. Formerly there was a cement factory and a large-scale, state-run cotton-processing factory in Pul-i Khumri, but these are now ruined and abandoned.

Mazar-i Sharif is the largest and most important town in the northern provinces, but historically Balkh to the west was the capital of the region. In pre-Islamic times this town was known as Bactra and in the fifth century BCE (see Table 1) it was the capital of the Achaemenid province of Bactria. Bactra is mentioned in the Zoroastrian *Avesta* and local tradition claims that it was here that Zoroaster was given refuge from persecution and established his dualistic religion. Bactra was also renowned for the cult centre of Zariaspa dedicated to the goddess of the Amu Darya, Ardvi Sura Anahita. Recent French excavations at Chashma-yi Shafa, where the Balkh Ab breaks through the Koh-i Alburz, have revealed a major pre-Islamic site, including fire temples.

From the second century BCE, if not earlier, Bactra was a major Buddhist centre, and the remains of a reliquary, or *stupa*, and a monastery can be seen at the side of the modern road. To the south of the main road lies Noh Gunbad, Afghanistan's most ancient mosque. When the Arab Muslim armies conquered Bactra in the early eighth century, they renamed it Balkh and referred to it as 'Umm al-Bilad, the Mother of Cities. From the early Islamic period, Balkh was renowned as a centre of Sufism and the birthplace of many famous Sufis, including Jalal al-Din Rumi (1207–1273), whose disciples founded the Mevlevi *tariqa*, better known in the Western world as the Whirling Dervishes of Turkey. The walls, citadel and shrines that can still be seen in Balkh are mostly medieval and date from the Timurid and Tuqay-Timurid eras (see Table 3).

Mazar-i Sharif owes its rise to prominence to the founding of a major shrine by the Timurid ruler Sultan Husain Baiqara (1470–1506) (see Table 3), over what was claimed to be the last resting place of 'Ali b. Abi Talib, the cousin and son-in-law of Muhammad. In the latter half of the nineteenth century the northern plains were conquered by the Durrani kings and Mazar-i Sharif became the capital of what was known as Afghan Turkistan. Following the fall of the Communist government of President Najib Allah in 1992, many of his supporters fled to Mazar. After subsequent infighting between the *mujahidin*, thousands more people, especially Kabulis, fled north and swelled the city's burgeoning population.

Mazar-i Sharif is nowadays a multi-ethnic town but its ethos remains predominantly Turkic and it has the reputation of being the most secular urban centre in Afghanistan. It is the main transit point for the export of the region's famous tufted carpets as well as leather and *karakul* skins. Mazar-i Sharif is also one of Afghanistan's most important shrine cities and attracts thousands of pilgrims, especially during the spring New Year festival, or *Nauroz*. In the past Imperial Russia and subsequently the USSR was an important trading partner and large quantities of goods, including much of the country's fuel, pass through the frontier port and railhead of Hairatan on the Amu Darya. Uzbekistan is still an important trade partner. Recently the former Soviet railway system was extended into Mazar, opening up the possibility of overland trade with China and even Europe.

Andkhui, on the Turkmenistan–Uzbekistan frontier, is a Turkman settlement and, along with Aqcha and Qunduz, is one of Afghanistan's most important carpet-weaving centres. The Turkmans and Arabs around Andkhui also own large flocks of *karakul* or fat-tailed sheep, and breed camels and horses. There are a number of tanneries in the region and leather is an important export. Sesame seeds are grown along the lower course of the Shirin Tagab and in the Gurziwan district of Faryab, while the pomegranates of Andkhui are renowned for their sweetness. The Uzbeks of Maimana and Sar-i Pul also make fine pile carpets as well as *gilim*s. Uzbek and Turkman embroidery and traditional jewellery are highly prized on the international market, while the long-sleeved silk cloak or *chapan*, the traditional coat of the Uzbeks, is the preferred formal wear of ex-President Hamid Karzai.

The Turkmans and Uzbeks of northern Afghanistan are renowned as horse breeders, though wealthy Pushtuns, Tajiks and Aimaqs also breed and own horses. The *yabu*s are sturdy ponies capable of long journeys with heavy loads, while another strain of horse, known for their speed and agility, is bred for the traditional Turkman and Uzbek sport of *buzkashi,* in which riders, known as *chapandaz*, compete to place the carcass of a decapitated goat, or a calf skin stuffed with sand, in a goal circle. *Buzkashi* is not for the faint-hearted. Each rider carries a leather whip that they use on opponents as well as their horses. Even the horses are trained to bite opponents. All *chapandaz* enter the fray heavily padded, but even so bones are often broken and blood shed. The rewards, however, are great. *Chapandaz* who win regularly earn great fame as well as substantial sponsorship and prize money, while a good *buzkashi* horse will sell for thousands of dollars. Among the Turkmans, wrestling is also an important sport.

Throughout most of its course in Afghanistan the Murghab river, which flows into the Turkmenistan oasis of Panjdeh and Merv, runs through deep, limestone gorges and agriculture is mainly restricted to the narrow valley

Buzkashi is the traditional game of the Turkic peoples of northern Afghanistan but was adopted as a national sport under King Zahir Shah. Here two teams from Parwan and Panjshir compete for the carcass of a goat.

floors. Badghis, the plateau region between the Murghab and Hari Rud watersheds, is Afghanistan's most important pistachio-growing region, but also grows *lalmi* wheat and breeds hardy horses and ponies. It is also one of the country's most remote and inaccessible regions. Badghis traditionally was the homeland of the Chahar Aimaq tribes, but at the end of the nineteenth century thousands of Pushtuns and Hazaras were settled in this region. In the foothills of the Tir Band-i Turkistan and northern Afghanistan, many rural communities practise transhumance: between May and September they live in beehive-shaped felt tents, known as yurts or *ui*, in the upper valleys where there is pasture and water for their animals. The elderly, young children and pregnant women remain behind in the settlements to keep an eye on the houses and crops.

Herat, the major city of western Afghanistan, is situated in an extensive plain irrigated by the Hari Rud. This is an important wheat-producing region and local people proudly claim Herat has seventy varieties of grapes. Pushtun nomads winter in the lower reaches of the Hari Rud and in the spring they migrate upstream with their extensive flocks of sheep and goats and herds of camels to summer pastures around Chaghcharan. A major source of revenue for Herat is customs duties gathered at the Iran–Afghanistan frontier post of Islam Qal'a. Traditional crafts include silk weaving, a tile-making factory that has revived ancient glazing techniques, and translucent blue glassware. The region also exports fine white marble, mined near Chisht-i Sharif on the upper Hari Rud. The Herat region is strongly influenced by its historic cultural and political ties with Iran. The Iranian dialect of Persian predominates here and there is a large Shi'a minority in the region. Herat is also renowned as a centre of Sufism, while Herati musicians, including female ensembles, are much in demand for wedding parties and other celebrations.

Herat lies on the crossroads of ancient trans-Asian trade routes that link it with Persia, India, Balkh and Central Asia. Like Bactra, Herat is mentioned in the *Avesta* and was the capital of the Achaemenid satrapy of Aeria; in the sixth century CE it was the seat of an Eastern Christian, or Nestorian, bishopric and later became a Metropolitan diocese. Over the centuries Herat has suffered from frequent invasions and on numerous occasions it has been pillaged and its population slaughtered. Herat was conquered by Alexander the Great, though no monumental remains of the Hellenistic town have been found in the region. In 484 CE, the Sasanian army was virtually wiped out on the plains outside Herat by the Hephthalites, a Turco-Mongolian tribe from Inner Asia (see Table 1). In 1221 the Mongols slaughtered its population almost to the last man, woman and child, and in 1389 it was sacked by another Turco-Mongolian warrior, Timur Lang, or Tamurlaine. However, in 1405, one of Timur's descendants, Shah Rukh Mirza, made Herat the capital of the Timurid Empire (see Table 3). Together with his wife Gauhar Shad, he refined the city with mosques, *madrasas*, royal tombs, shrines and secular buildings. The Timurids were also patrons of Sufism as well as artists, calligraphers, poets and historians. Little of Herat's pre-Islamic past remains, though the imposing citadel of Qal'a-yi Ikhtiyar al-Din, named after a local ruler of the Kart Dynasty (1245–1389), is probably built on ancient foundations. Many of Herat's Timurid structures, including minarets, the Friday Mosque and the tomb of Gauhar Shad, are still standing, though some have suffered war damage.[5]

The Helmand-Arghandab river basin of south and southwest Afghanistan is the largest watershed in Afghanistan. Kandahar, the principal city of this region and the former capital of the Durrani kingdom, lies between the Arghandab and its tributary, the Tarnak, and on ancient trade routes linking Sind and the Indus with Herat, Persia and Central Asia. Kandahar also benefits from being the nearest city in Afghanistan to Karachi, the port through which most of Afghanistan's imports and exports flow, and the Pakistan railhead at Chaman.

Ahmad Shah Durrani founded the present city of Kandahar in the 1750s after Old Kandahar was levelled by the Persian conqueror Nadir Shah Afshar in 1737. The ruins of the old city lie 4 kilometres (2.5 mi.)

southwest of the modern town under the shadow of the Qaital Ridge. British excavations in the 1970s uncovered a number of Elamite cuneiform tablets and a Greek tomb inscription that relates how a certain Sophytos, having fallen on hard times, regained his family's fortunes by undertaking long sea voyages and trading with many cities. Nearby, at Chehel Zina, is a bilingual rock inscription of the Mauryan king and patron of Buddhism, Ashoka, and a Persian inscription commissioned by the founder of the Mughal Empire, Zahir al-Din Babur.

During the Mughal and Safavid era, Kandahar was a wealthy frontier town, trading with both these kingdoms mainly in locally produced wool, Indian cottons and silks. The town also made a great deal of money from recasting silver coinage. More recently Kandahar has fallen on hard times, a situation due mainly to the insecurity arising from the civil war. Kandahar and Helmand regions are still major centres of conflict and the anti-government insurgency. Wool and silk still play an important part in the local economy and the Kandahari style of embroidery adorns

As the sun begins to set, a man prays in a niche of Herat's Timurid Friday Mosque.

both men's and women's tunics. Currency exchange remains an important activity and there are goldsmiths and silversmiths in the bazaar. Small-scale industries include a fruit-canning factory and perfumery. However, the most important cash crop in the Helmand-Kandahar area is opium.

Ahmad Shah Durrani, who is known as the Father of Afghanistan, is buried in Kandahar and his tomb lies adjacent to Afghanistan's most important shrine, which contains the Khirqa-yi Sharif, or Blessed Cloak, which is said to have been worn by Muhammad himself. East of Kandahar lies a major airbase, originally built by American contractors as an international civil airport. Today more than 13,000 personnel, mostly Americans, live on this base, which is the most important centre of military operations in southern Afghanistan.

In southwest Afghanistan the provinces of Farah, Nimroz and the southern Helmand are mostly inhospitable deserts. They are sparsely populated and agricultural activity is confined mainly to the banks of the Farah, Khash and Helmand rivers and the irrigated areas around Giriskh and Lashkargah. The Sistan Desert, the triangle of land between Iran, Afghanistan and Pakistan, is criss-crossed with truck tracks, for this is a major smuggling route for opium and other high-value products between Iran and Pakistan. Zaranj and Zabul are located at the tail of the Helmand and Farah rivers, where they form shallow lakes that provide irrigation for farmers on both sides of the Iran–Afghanistan frontier. Riparian rights to these waters and the Sistan have been a source of dispute and tension between Iran and Afghanistan for more than two centuries and the dispute over the British-demarcated Sistan frontier is still unresolved.

Around 200,000 Baluch nomads live in and around Zaranj. They traditionally migrated into Iran and Pakistan-controlled Sistan, but the frontier demarcation has hindered this traditional activity. A small enclave of Brahuis, whose Dravidian language is closely related to those of south-eastern India, live in Sorabak on the southwestern tip of the Registan Desert. Before the Mongol armies destroyed the ancient irrigation system on the lower Helmand, Zaranj was an important staging post on a caravan route to southern Iran. In the early eighth century Arab Muslim armies used this town as a base for the conquest of Sind and later it was the capital of the Saffarid dynasty. Outside Zaranj is the imposing Iron Age fortress of Nadd-i 'Ali and surveys by American archaeologists in the Sistan identified dozens of other Bronze Age and Iron Age settlements. The ruins around Lashkargah and Bost, however, are of much later date, being the remains of the winter capital of the Ghurid sultans. In 2009 a new sealed road was opened linking Zaranj with the Herat–Kandahar highway and there are plans to extend this road to the Iranian port of Chabahar. The completed road will provide Afghanistan with an alternative port for its imports and exports, reducing Afghanistan's reliance on the port of Karachi in Pakistan, though security on the roads is a major problem as insurgents and bandits regularly hold up or kidnap travellers and attack security patrols.

Pushtun tribes are the dominant peoples of southern and southwestern Afghanistan. Kandahar and Girishk is the homeland of the Durrani tribes and Shahr-i Safa, on the Tarnak river between Kandahar and Muqur, was once the stronghold of the royal Saddozai clan. The other powerful Pushtun tribal confederation of southern Afghanistan is the Ghilzai. Qalat-i Ghilzai, on the Kandahar–Ghazni road, was formerly the stronghold of the Tokhi Ghilzais, though this tribe is now scattered throughout Afghanistan. In 1709 Mir Wa'is, *malik* of the Hotak Ghilzais, established an independent Afghan kingdom in Kandahar and in 1722 his son, Mahmud, occupied the Safavid capital of Isfahan and ruled southern Persia for seven years. Mir Wa'is's tomb is located in the Kokaran district of Kandahar city.

The central highlands of the Hazarajat is the domain of the Hazara peoples. Here the winters are long and harsh and the growing season short and precarious. Traditionally the Hazaras' main export was rendered sheep fat, or *roghan-i zard*, literally 'yellow fat', which was used in cooking, and a kind of thick serge coat still used by nomads in winter. Hazara *gilim*s, woven by the women, are a popular floor covering in poorer homes. Some years ago, potatoes were introduced to the region and quickly became the major crop and a staple food. Living in mountainous regions has made Hazaras men tough and strong and in the past they have worked as water carriers, porters, night soil cleaners, carters or *karachiwan*s, and wood sellers. Nowadays many young, urbanized Hazaras, both men and women, are well educated and work as translators, journalists, IT and social media specialists. Older Hazara women work in the service industry, mostly as maids and household servants. The recent surfacing and widening of the Kabul–Bamiyan road through the Ghurband valley promises to have a major impact on one of the poorest and most neglected regions of Afghanistan. There are plans to extend this highway to Herat and to widen and seal the old caravan road from Bamiyan to Doshi. If this plan is ever realized, the Bamiyan–Herat highway will substantially cut both the time and distance for travel between Kabul and Herat. The Bamiyan valley was formerly a major Buddhist centre and the whole region is dotted with Buddhist sites, as well as Kushan and Ghurid fortifications (see Table 2). Bamiyan's most famous Buddhist monuments are the giant statues of the Buddha carved into the cliff face. Blown up by the Taliban in 2001 in an act of deliberate iconoclasm, the taller of the Buddhas is now in the process of being restored. Recently the Bamiyan valley was inscribed as a UNESCO World Heritage Site.

Afghanistan had been called the Highway of Conquest, for many invaders from India, Persia, Arabia, the Asian steppes, Mongolia and even China have ruled at various eras of the region's history and have contributed to the cultural and ethnic diversity of the country. However, Afghanistan could equally be called the Highway of Commerce, for the region has been defined as much by its position on ancient trans-Asian trade routes as it has been by war or conquest. Most of the major cities and towns of Afghanistan owe their importance to their position on what is misleadingly called The Silk Road.[6] This term is misleading because there was never a single highway linking east and west, or north with south, while the transfer of goods across thousands of kilometres was the outcome of dozens of localized transactions – very much in the same way as goods are still bought and sold in weekly markets in most provincial towns of Afghanistan.

This transcontinental trade dates back to at least the third millennium BCE when there was already commercial and cultural contact between the emerging Bronze Age city-states of the Amu Darya basin, the Sistan, the Indus Valley, China, the Eurasian steppes and Mesopotamia. Items of early trans-Asian trade included gold, silver, copper, lapis lazuli, Indian ivory and probably slaves, horses and mercenaries, for the Bactrians in particular had a formidable reputation as warriors. Silk as a significant element of this transcontinental trade came much later. Equally important was the technological, ideological and cultural interchange that was a side effect of commercial activity. A Mesopotamian-style bull relief appears on a Bronze Age gold bowl from Tepe Fullol in Afghanistan, while the solid-wheeled chariots depicted on the famous royal banner from the Mesopotamian city of Ur are inner Asian in style. The Achaemenids (see Table 1) introduced irrigation techniques modelled on those of the Tigris-Euphrates, while the Akkadian goddess Nana was incorporated in the pantheon of Graeco-Bactrian and Kushan kingdoms. When Alexander the Great conquered the region in 330 BCE his followers introduced Hellenistic deities and the Greek script. Under the Seleucid and Graeco-Bactrian kingdom that succeeded Alexander's brief reign, Hellenistic, Iranian and north Indian artistic styles synthesized to produce the Gandharan culture, a style that had a profound influence on the iconography of early Buddhism. One of the most spectacular archaeological discoveries of recent times was the Hellenistic city of Ai Khanum at the confluence of the Kokcha and Amu Darya.

In the late first century BCE the Kushans (see Table 1), Yuezhi pastoralists from the Gansu region of China, displaced the Graeco-Bactrians and established their own north Indian empire. Under the patronage of the Kushans, Buddhism spread throughout eastern, central and northern Afghanistan. Christianity too established itself in the region, traditionally brought by St Thomas, the 'doubting' disciple. The Kushan

TABLE 1: Principal pre-Islamic Dynasties of Afghanistan, 555 BCE–1001 CE				
Dynasty	Dates (ruling Afghanistan)	Capital(s)	Regions ruled (in Afghanistan)	Ethnicity; comments
Achaemenid	555–330 BCE	Persepolis (Iran)	Herat (Aeria); Balkh (Bactria); Kandahar (Arachosia)	Persian (Elamite?); Zoroastrianism
Alexandrian	330–323 BCE	Babylon (intended)	all Afghanistan except the Pamirs and Hindu Kush	overthrows Achaemenids; introduced Hellenistic deities and Greek script
Seleucid	313–250 BCE	Selucia (Iraq)	Aria, Bactrian frontier with India on Hindu Kush	Hellenistic
Graeco-Bactrian	250–125 BCE	Bactra; Ai Khanum (?)	Afghanistan, excluding the Pamirs and Nuristan	Hellenistic with Persian and Indian cultic and cultural influences
Mauryan	321–185 BCE	Pataliputa (N. India)	S. Afghanistan; Helmand, Kandahar, Kabul, Jalalabad	N. Indian; Hindu then under Ashoka (268–232 BCE) Buddhist; emergence of Gandharan culture
Kushan	c. 30 CE–240 CE	Purushapara (Peshawar); Taxila (winter capital); Mathura	all Afghanistan; Kushan dynastic centres at Surkh Kotal and Rabatak	Turkic nomads from Gansu, China; patrons of Buddhism, state cults included Iranian, Indian and Mesopotamian deities; heyday of Gandharan culture
Kushano-Sasanian	230–459 CE	Bagram	all Afghanistan	Persian, Zoroastrian
Hephthalite	c. 459–670 CE	Badian (Qunduz); Balkh	N. Afghanistan; Badghis; Herat; Kandahar; Kabul	E. Iranian or Turco-Mongolian; White Huns (?)
Sasanian	496–650 CE	Estakhr; Ctesiphon	W. and N.W. Afghanistan	Persian; last Shah defeated by Arab Muslim invasion
Turki and Hindu Shahi	5th century to 1001 CE	Kapisa then Kabul	Kabul; S.E. Afghanistan	Buddhist, Hindu; overthrown by Ghaznavids

kings themselves, however, venerated a plurality of gods and goddesses. Under their rule Bactrian, an Aramaic language, replaced Greek, though Bactrian was written using a modified Greek alphabet. At the end of the third century CE, the Kushans were subjugated by the Iranian Sasanian dynasty, an event commemorated in a rock carving outside Pul-i Khumri, which depicts the Sasanian king hunting a rhinoceros. The Sasanians, who were originally priests of the goddess Anahita, imposed Zoroastrianism as the state religion of the empire, but Buddhism, Hinduism and local cults were tolerated, although Christians were sporadically persecuted. In 650 the Sasanians were overthrown by the invasion of the Arab Muslim armies and the last Shah, Yazdagird III, was killed near Bala Murghab.

The Arab Muslims established cantonments near Herat, Maimana and Balkh, and destroyed many Buddhist and Zoroastrian sites. Even so, the Islamization of Afghanistan took many centuries and was initially confined to the urban centres of the plains. Buddhists, Jews, Christians, Zoroastrians and local cults persisted, particularly in the mountainous regions of Ghur, Badghis and the Hindu Kush. In 642 Kabul was briefly occupied by an Arab Muslim army, only for it to be resoundingly defeated by the Turki Shahi, who were patrons of Buddhism. Kabul and southeastern Afghanistan was only finally Islamized in the early eleventh century by Sultan Mahmud of Ghazni (see Table 2). He also invaded Ghur and forced the people of that region to accept Islam. The Kafirs of Kafiristan, however, maintained their ancient polytheistic religion until the 1890s.

All but a tiny minority of Afghans are Muslims. Under the 2004 Constitution the country is formally designated as an Islamic Republic and since the 1920s Afghanistan's legal code has been strongly influenced by Hanafi jurisprudence, one of the four Sunni legal schools, or

The Sasanid rock relief at Rag-i Bibi near Pul-i Khumri. This remarkable relief commemorates the Sasanid subjugation of the Kushans and the conquest of northern India.

Dynasty	Dates (ruling Afghanistan)	Capital(s)	Regions of Afghanistan ruled	Ethnicity; comments
'Umayyad Caliphate	664–750	Damascus	western, north and southwestern Afghanistan	Muslim; Arab; 747 revolt of Abu Muslim led to fall of 'Umayyads
'Abbasid Caliphate	750–870	Kufa, then Baghdad	from 819 'Abbasids cede autonomy to local Muslim rulers	Sunni Muslim; Arab; strong Eastern Iranian influence
Samanid	819–992	Samarkand, then Bukhara	initially Herat, Balkh, then all of Afghanistan	shamanism, later Sunni Muslim; Persians from Balkh
Saffarid	857–901	Zaranj	Sistan; Herat; Balkh; Badghis; Ghor; Bamiyan	Sunni Muslim; Persians from Sistan; after 901 subordinate to Samanids
Ghaznavid	977–1186	Ghazni	all Afghanistan, eastern Iran and north India	Sunni Muslim; Turkic; Sultan Mahmud's *jihad* in N. India and Ghur
Saljuq	1036–1157	Rey, then Isfahan	Balkh; Herat; Ghazni (briefly)	Shamanism, later Sunni Muslims; Oghuz Turk
Ghurid	1187–1215	initially Firoz Koh (Jam), then Herat	Ghur; Bamiyan; Herat; Ghazni and N. India as far as Delhi	Sunni Muslim; Persians from Ghur; constructed Minaret of Jam; Qutb Minar of Delhi
Khwarazmian Shah	1194–1223	Gurganj, then Samarkand, Ghazni, Tabriz	most of Afghanistan	Sunni Muslim; Turkic; formerly Saljuq *ghulam*s; last Shah defeated by Mongols
Mongol Empire	1220–59	Karakorum	all of Afghanistan	Shamanism and some E. Christianity; Mongol invasion led to mass destruction and massacres

*mazhab*s. Most Afghans are deeply religious and adhere to the beliefs and practices of Islam, though many urban Afghans are not particularly regular when it comes to observing the five daily prayers. Islam, while it is rigorously monotheistic, is far from being monolithic and there are many strands of religious belief and interpretation, ranging from deistic rationalism to the puritanical exclusivism of movements such as the Taliban.

The majority of Afghans are Sunnis but the country has a sizeable Shi'a and Isma'ili minority. The Hazaras are mainly Shi'a with a smaller

TABLE 3: Principal Dynasties of Afghanistan, 1256–1858

Dynasty	Dates (ruling Afghanistan)	Capital(s)	Regions of Afghanistan ruled	Ethnicity; comments
Chaghatai Khanate	1259–1346	Almaliq	E. Afghanistan, including Kabul, Ghazni, Qunduz, Badakhshan	Shamanism, Buddhism, Christian; Mongol; after death of Chinggis Khan, empire divided between his 4 sons
Ilkhanids	1256–1333	Maragha, then Tabriz	Herat, Balkh, Zaranj, Kandahar	Shamanism, later Sunni Muslim; Mongol
Timurid	1370–1507	Balkh, then Samarkand and Herat	Herat, Balkh, Kandahar, Kabul	Sunni Muslim, Sufism and Shamanism; Turco-Mongol descendants of Timur Lang (Tamurlaine)
Shaibanid	1428–1599	Bukhara	Balkh and N. Afghanistan (briefly Herat and Kabul)	Sunni Muslim; Uzbek, descendants of Chinggis Khan
Tuqay-Timurid (Jani Begid; Astrakhanid)	1599–1785	Bukhara	N. Afghanistan from Bala Murghab to Qataghan and Khulm; Badakhshan under an independent Mir	Sunni Muslim; Turco-Mongolian descendants of Chinggis Khan and Timur Lang
Safavid	1501–1722	Isfahan	Herat, Kandahar	Shi'a Muslim; Turco-Persian
Mughal	1526–1858	Kabul, then Delhi	Kabul, Ghazni, Nangahar, Kandahar (disputed with Safavids)	Sunni Muslim; Turco-Mongolian; descendants of Chinggis Khan and Timur Lang

group belonging to the Nizari Isma'ili tradition, whose spiritual head is the Aga Khan. Herat too has a substantial Shi'a minority, while Kabul's Shi'a Qizilbash are descendants of the Safavid garrisons that were incorporated into the Saddozai kings' royal guard. Kabul is also home to a substantial Hazara Shi'a and Isma'ili community. The Pushtun tribes of Bangash, Orakzai and Turi, who live in the provinces of Paktiya and Paktika and across the Pakistan frontier in the Khurram agency, are also Shi'a. A large community of Tajik Nizari Isma'ilis live in Badakhshan and the shrine of the Isma'ili propagandist and poet Nasir Khusrau, at Yamgan, is highly venerated. Pul-i Khumri, Kayan, Doshi and the Tala wa Barfak districts of southwestern Baghlan are other major Isma'ili centres.

Sunni and Shi'a differ in both theological and certain ritual practices. However, the fundamental issue that divides them is a dispute over the succession to Muhammad. Sunnis claim this right was accorded to four Rightly Guided Caliphs. Shi'as and Isma'ilis, on the other hand, believe the succession was bequeathed to Muhammad's cousin and son-in-law, 'Ali b. Abi Talib and his descendants, known as *Imam*s. Shortly after Muhammad's death, civil war broke out over the succession, which led to the assassination of 'Ali and his son Hasan, while 'Ali's other son, Husain, was killed in battle. Subsequently the Shi'a, too, split over the succession to the *Imamate*: the Isma'ilis recognize seven *Imam*s, the Shi'as twelve. The bitterness of this early dispute is perpetuated by the Shi'as, who ritually curse the first three Caliphs during their prayers, an act that Sunnis regard as deeply insulting. The polarization is exacerbated during the month of Muharram, when Shi'as and Isma'ilis publicly mourn the death of Imam Husain in the ten-day 'Ashura' festival.

Both Sunni and Shi'a religious life revolves around the five daily prayers, the annual fast of Ramazan and the celebration of two major religious festivals, or *'Id*s. 'Id-i Ramazan marks the end of the fast, while 'Id al-Fitr, or 'Id-i Qurban as it is known in Afghanistan, takes place during the Hajj, or Meccan pilgrimage season. During this festival a sheep or calf is ritually slaughtered in commemoration of Ibrahim's (Abraham's) willingness to sacrifice his son and his salvation by the divine provision of a lamb.

Islam makes a strict distinction between what is religiously lawful and prohibited. The daily prayers, fasting and the Hajj are regarded as *fards*, or obligations required of all Muslims, while drinking alcohol or eating certain foods such as pork are deemed *haram*, or religiously unlawful and impure. All religious duties that are performed with *niyat*, sincere intent, accumulate *sawab*, or religious merit. *Sawab* offsets one's evil deeds, thoughts and actions and is reckoned in the believer's favour at the Day of Judgment. To this end, devout Muslims may perform supererogatory prayers and fasts and give *khairat*, or charitable donations, to religious institutions or the poor.

Sufism, the contemplative form of Islam, has a major influence in the religious life of Afghanistan. Sufis in Afghanistan by and large uphold the external (*zahir*) obligations of Islam while they pursue the esoteric (*batin*), inner world through a series of practices, including *zikr*, or repetitive chants, which induce trance-like states, music and hymns. Sufi devotees, or *murids*, place themselves under the authority of a spiritual guide known as a *pir*, who leads them through the various grades of initiation. The ultimate goal of a Sufi is *baqa' wa fana'*, 'negation and subsisting', in which the

Naqshbandiyya Sufis in Bukhara. Until the Soviet conquest of Bukhara in 1868, *zikr* was often performed in public spaces. In Afghanistan, since the Islamic revolution, such public performances by Sufis has been actively discouraged. However, Sufism remains an important part of many Afghans' spiritual life. Illustration from F. H. Skrine and E. D. Ross, *The Heart of Asia* (1899).

self dies as it grasps that the Oneness of God alone subsists and that the gnostic, while continuing to live in the material world, is at the same time detached from it. During *baqa' wa fana'* the adept will also experience a sense of Divine love and Sufi literature often compares the Sufi's search to that of a lover seeking the beloved. Another common metaphor for the Sufi experience is intoxication. The concept of *baqa' wa fana'* has led to some of the more extreme Sufis being accused of heresy and in the past some were even put to death.

There are three major Sufi Orders, or *tariqa*s, in Afghanistan.[7] The Naqshbandiyya, founded by Baha al-Din Naqshband (d. 1389), a native of Bukhara, established its presence in what is now Afghanistan during the fifteenth century when the Timurid rulers of Herat patronized the Khawajagan branch of Naqshbandiyya. As a result, dozens of Sufi centres, known as *khanagahs*, were set up in the Herat and Balkh regions, and the Central Asian form of Naqshbandiyya is still the predominant branch of Sufism among Uzbeks, Turkmans, Aimaqs and Heratis. The Naqshbandiyya *zikr* is unusual in that it is a silent, mental one, though around Balkh and Mazar-i Sharif there are some devotees who practise a verbalized, communal *zikr*.

In the late eighteenth century an Indian branch of the Naqshbandiyya Order, known as Mujadidiyya, established itself in southeastern Afghanistan. This *tariqa* derives its name from the teachings of Shaikh Ahmad Sirhind (1563–1624), known as Mujadid Alf-i Sani, or the Renewer of the Second (Islamic) Millennium. Shaikh Ahmad was a native of the Kabul region, but made his base in Sirhind in northern India. The Mujadidi *tariqa* is very strict in requiring all of its initiates to adhere to the external obligations of Islam and uphold the *shariʿa* while at the same time pursuing the Sufi way. The Mujadidi encounter with Hinduism in northern India made the movement particularly opposed to some of the practice of folk Islam and shrine cults, which they condemned as syncretic and un-Islamic. Following the fall of Sirhind to the Sikhs in 1763, which led to the destruction of Mujadidi institutions, some *pirs* of the movement fled north and established *khanagah*s in Kabul's Old City, Tagab, the Koh Daman, Kandahar, Ghazni and as far north as Bukhara, Badakhshan and Herat. Under the patronage of the Durrani monarch Shah Zaman, the Mujadidi Hazrat of Kabul's Shor Bazaar and the *pirs* of Tagab and the Koh Daman rose to political prominence, though subsequently the relationship between them and the crown broke down and ended in a confrontation that would change the course of Afghanistan's political history.

Kabul's historic Shor Bazaar, *c.* 1879, from the *Illustrated London News*. Due to Afghanistan's position on ancient trans-Asian highways, Afghans have always been a nation of traders and shopkeepers.

The Qadiriyya Order, founded by the Persian Sufi 'Abd al-Qadir Gilani, or Jailani, in the late eleventh century, is mostly found among Arab Muslims. In the late seventeenth century a *pir* of this *tariqa* moved to Afghanistan and many Pushtun tribes became affiliates of this Order. Later, the Gilani *pirs* intermarried with the Durrani royal house and played an important role in legitimizing the dynasty. Unlike the Naqshbandiyya, where membership is a matter of individual choice, in the Qadiriyya tradition the heads of the tribes pledge allegiance to the *pir* on behalf of their clan.

The Chishtiyya derives its name from the settlement of the same name in the upper Hari Rud, where the mausoleums of early *shaikh*s can still be seen. The Order, founded in the tenth century, was introduced to northern India by Sayyid Muin al-Din Chishti, known as Gharib Nawaz, Benefactor of the Poor. The Mughals were devotees of the Chishtis and lavished royal patronage on Gharib Nawaz's mausoleum and *langar khana* in Ajmer. Unlike other *tariqa*s in Afghanistan, the Chishtis employ music, dance, hymns and poetry in a ritual known as *sama*. Non-Muslims are also welcome to observe their rituals. The Chishtis emphasize ministry to the poor, and their *langar khana*s provide free food for the poor and vulnerable. The main Chishti centres in Afghanistan are Mazar-i Sharif, Badghis, Herat, Kabul and southeastern Afghanistan.

While many Afghans are not formally affiliated to any *tariqa*, Sufism still has a powerful influence through the medium of Persian, Pushtu and Turkic poetry, popular music and folklore. There are many freelance mystics, known as *faqir*s or *malang*s, who operate on the fringes of religious orthodoxy. Some are peripatetic, others take up residence in a local shrine, where they live off the charity of local people or sell *tawiz* – charms that protect against misfortune and illness, that provide protection in battle, or ensure good fortune in love and marriage. There are less public figures, men and women, who practise the forbidden art of *jadugari* – witchcraft, necromancy and communication with spirits.

Shrines, or *ziyarat*s, are another important element in the religious life of Afghans. These vary from major edifices to sacred trees, caves, springs or unusual geological formations. Some *ziyarat*s are dedicated to major figures of early Islam and shrines to 'Ali b. Abi Talib, known as Shah-i Mardan, King of Men, are popular and found throughout the country, even though he never set foot in Afghanistan. There are also many legends associated with Shah-i Mardan, his horse and his split-bladed sword known as *Zu'l-fiqar*. The famous shrine of Guzargah in Herat is built over the grave of Khwaja 'Abd Allah Ansari (b. 1006), a well-known exponent of Islamic jurisprudence and author of a popular devotional work, the *Munajat Nama*.

Other shrines are constructed over the graves of *shahid*s, individuals who died in the cause of Islam, while *qadamgah*s, literally footprints, commemorate visions, miracles or visitations by holy individuals. Some shrines are said to cure specific ailments. such as blindness, dog bites, madness or impotence. All *ziyarat*s are believed to be infused with *baraka*, a mystical power that can bless the devotee, ensure good fortune or even heal. Women are particularly attached to shrines, and Wednesday is observed as women's day at shrines. There are also a number of shrines devoted to women. In Balkh the shrine of Rabi'a Balkhi is dedicated to a young woman whose throat was cut by her uncle after she was found to be having an affair with a slave. The modern shrine of Bibi Nushin in Shibarghan is centred on the grave of a teenage girl who was killed because her family turned down a marriage proposal.

Despite the historic presence of Zoroastrians, Buddhists, Jews, Christians and Hindus, Afghanistan today has only a tiny minority of non-Muslim citizens. The first mention of a Christian presence in the country dates from the last decade of the second century; by the fifth century there were at least four Nestorian bishoprics in western Afghanistan, which at the time was part of the Sasanian Empire. During the Safavid and Mughal era, a few hundred Armenians established trading communities in Kabul, Kandahar, Herat and Balkh. Later Ahmad Shah Durrani brought a number of Armenians from Lahore who were skilled in casting cannon: until 1879 there was an Armenian church in Kabul's Bala Hisar. In the 1840s a daughter of one of the leaders of the Armenian community married Sardar Muhammad 'Azam Khan, who was briefly Amir of Afghanistan from 1867–8. In the mid-1890s the family of this Armenian woman were expelled by the then Amir, 'Abd al-Rahman Khan, and from this point forward they made Peshawar their home, where some trained as medical personnel in the Mission Hospital. A handful of Georgian traders are also recorded as living in Kabul, Kandahar and Herat, and early European explorers noted the grave of a Georgian bishop on the slopes of Kabul's Koh-i 'Asmayi. Over the past thirty years or so, a small, indeterminate number of Afghans have become Christians, though they mostly live in Western countries for fear of persecution and even death. Afghan Christians living in the country rarely declare their faith publicly for fear of imprisonment or execution. For the same reason Afghanistan's small Ahmadiyya and Baha'i communities rarely surface, for while these movements were born out of Islamic millenarian movements in Lahore and Shiraz respectively, followers of these faiths are regarded as apostates.

Early Arab sources record a substantial Jewish community in Maimana, which they called al-Yahudiyyan. There was also a sizeable Jewish community in the Jam region of Ghur province from around the tenth century, which survived well into the thirteenth century. A recent cache of early Jewish documents written in Persian but utilizing the Hebrew script appears to have been part of the archive of a medieval Jewish community. Until the 1930s several hundred Jews lived in Balkh, Herat and Kabul, and there were synagogues in Kabul and Herat. However, due to racial and religious prejudice as well as political factors, all Afghanistan's Jews have left. A single rabbi remains in Kabul, as caretaker of the synagogue and its Torah scrolls. Formerly there were hundreds of Hindus, mostly from Shikapur, living in many towns of Afghanistan but their numbers today are greatly reduced. The main Hindu and Sikh communities today are in Kabul, Jalalabad, Kandahar and Herat, where they trade in textiles and act as money-changers. There is at least one Hindu temple and one Sikh *Gurdwara* in Kabul.

Afghanistan's pre-Islamic heritage, however, still exerts an influence on popular culture. Pilgrims circumambulate shrines just as Buddhists once did, and the flags and banners that are commonplace at *ziyarat*s derive from Buddhist and Hindu tradition. Indeed, some shrines are built on, or adjacent to, Buddhist or other pre-Islamic sacred places. The ordeal of the *chehela khana*, during which a Sufi is confined for forty days in a sealed room or cave lit by a single candle, and with barely any food or water, is probably derived from Buddhist tradition too.

Kabul, Afghanistan's last functional synagogue. The rabbi is the last of Afghanistan's once large, indigenous Jewish community. He is seen here with the Torah scroll and prayer book.

Nauroz, or New Year festival at the shrine of Shah-i Mardan, dedicated to 'Hazrat 'Ali, the cousin and son-in-law of Muhammad, commences with the ceremony of *Janda Bala*, the raising of a ceremonial flagstaff.

Zoroastrianism and the traditions of the ancient Iranian dualistic religion also persist. Lighting lamps is a common feature of shrine cults, especially in northern Afghanistan, while the ancient Iranian New Year festival of *Nauroz*, which falls on the spring equinox, is celebrated as a national holiday. Many Afghans also celebrate *Chaharshanbe Suri*, the Wednesday before Nauroz, by jumping across fire for good luck. In Mazar-i Sharif, the celebration of Nauroz runs parallel with two other ancient pre-Islamic festivals. *Mela-yi Gul-i Surkh*, or Festival of the Red Rose, has mythic associations with Akkadian religion, the cult of Venus and Adonis, and the Armenian festival of *Vardavar*. On the morning of Nauroz a pole adorned with banners is raised in the shrine of Hazrat 'Ali. Known as *Janda Bala*, people claim to have been healed of incurable diseases during the elevation of the pole and during the forty days it remains standing in the shine. The origin of this tradition is obscure but it appears to be linked with ancient Vedic and Indo-Aryan religion. In December many families celebrate *Shab-i Yalda*, the northern hemisphere's winter solstice and the counterpart of Nauroz. Traditionally, families will stay awake all night to prevent misfortune, read the poems of Hafiz and eat red fruits such as pomegranates and watermelon.

Afghan society revolves around the extended family or clan, known as *qaum*, the primary social and political network. Afghans see themselves as part of a whole – members of a complex kith-kin network that can be countrywide and increasingly trans-national – rather than embracing the European idea of individuality and personal choice. From an early age, family members are instilled with the *qaum's* multiple identities, its histories, genealogies, its place and status in social hierarchies and ethno-cultural ties with tribal territory or a specific region, known as the *watan*.

Decision-making on important issues is not an individual matter but lies with senior males, usually father, elder brothers and uncles and, in certain circumstances, the senior women. Generally speaking, the younger and more junior an individual is in the social hierarchy the less say they have in such a process, though in more recent times younger men and women can influence decisions if they have a substantial disposable income, an influential position in government or work for a foreign organization. Family members who pursue their own personal agenda, either without consultation or in disregard of the wishes of senior *qaum* members, risk censure and sanction; in more serious situations it can lead to ostracism, disinheritance or banishment. The overriding consideration in any major decision is whether the proposed course of action will enhance the *qaum's* financial, social or political status and fortunes. Once a decision to act has been made the extended family will pool their financial resources, call in favours and debts of honour from government officials, and request distant relatives to accommodate and facilitate family members travelling to their area.

In a politically volatile and often violent society, another major consideration is how the *qaum* can ensure the security and protection of its members. This can be accomplished by marriage alliances, appointments in government, the military or with influential foreign organizations. It is not uncommon for extended families to hedge their bets by having members serving on all sides of the conflict. During the Soviet occupation of Afghanistan, for example, many Afghan families had relations serving in the Soviet-backed Communist government as well as fighting with, or financially supporting, the anti-government *mujahidin*.

Since the Taliban era Western discourse has focused heavily on women's rights in Afghanistan; indeed, following the attacks of 11 September 2001 President George Bush cited the Taliban's extremist gender policies as one justification for regime change. For some Western commentators and politicians, veiling or not veiling has become the litmus test of Afghanistan's modernity, or lack thereof, and of Islam's too. Images of women clad in the burqa, the all-encompassing, tent-like cloak traditionally worn by women in Afghanistan, regularly adorn articles on Afghanistan in the media and even academic publication, to such an extent that the burqa has become the most visible symbol of what is deemed to be the institutional oppression of Afghan women.[8]

To put this matter into its cultural context, in Afghanistan the burqa is primarily an urban phenomenon and something of a status symbol for upwardly mobile families, since the poor cannot afford the elaborately pleated and embroidered garment. Indeed, when the Taliban enforced strict veiling in public places, the poor would share one burqa between several women. In many rural areas of Afghanistan, such as the Hazarajat, the burqa is not worn. *Kuchi* women and some Turkmens also do not wear the burqa, while in Herat the Iranian-style *chadur*, or long scarf, which covers the hair but leaves the face exposed, is the most common apparel for women in public spaces.

The Taliban were not the first government to require all adult women to wear the burqa or enforce strict segregation of the sexes, for the principle of *parda*, or concealment, has been commonplace in Afghanistan since the early Islamic era. An attempt to outlaw the veil in the mid-1920s failed and there was an Islamist backlash that led to the king, Nadir Shah, imposing strict concealment and passing legislation that severely restricted women's rights. Even after the restrictions were relaxed in the 1960s and '70s, burqa-clad women were still a common sight in Kabul and most other towns. Photographs of young, unveiled, miniskirted women that appeared in the state-controlled press of this era were representative only of a tiny minority of educated state employees and students and were more government propaganda than a true representation of general realities. In 1994 the *mujahidin* government of President Rabbani also imposed strict *parda* in the wake of the fall of the secularizing Communist government and issued restrictive rules regarding female decorum. However, the *mujahidin* government stopped short of banning women from the workplace, education or the health services.

Islamic law is often blamed for this restrictive culture but customary law, known as *'adat* or *rasm wa rawaj*,[9] is equally important when it comes to determining gender roles in Afghanistan and often denies women rights that are accorded them by the *shari'a*. Under Islamic law, for example, a married woman is entitled to own property and retain control over any wealth she brings to the husband's family, while her husband is required to give her a dowry, known as *mahr*, which is usually a small plot of land. However, in many rural communities this provision is often honoured in the breach.

In Afghanistan male–female roles are more rigidly defined than in Western secular societies and the prevailing view, particularly in rural areas, is that a woman's place is in the home. In more urbanized areas, if male members of the family are confident the women will not be molested, they generally do not object to them leaving the home for social visits, shopping or work. The preference among families is for the women to work in the state sector or with foreign agencies, since the environment tends to be less of a threat. Many Afghans are keen to send their girls to school, for education is seen as a high priority. In traditional households, women have to ask their husband's or father's permission to leave the house and when they do they usually go as a group for security, or will be accompanied by a close male relative known as a *mahram*.

Most marriages are arranged by mutual agreement of the families in question. More urbanized, educated families will agree to a love match provided both parties consent to the marriage and are assured their future in-laws are of equal rank, have a good income and that the husband-to-be will treat their daughter well. In rural and tribal areas, girls are still betrothed or even married as early as ten years of age or in their early teens. Once a marriage alliance has been agreed, urbanized families will often allow the couple to have supervised visits so they can get to know each other, but they will never be left on their own. Behind the scenes, the families negotiate the dowry payments to be made by the husband's family to his future in-laws. This will always involve cash and goods. In wealthy families this can include gifts of land, fine carpets, a car or even a house. The wife-to-be's family provide her with a trousseau and other domestic items such as clothing, bedding, a sewing machine and domestic utensils. To celebrate the engagement, or *shirini khori*, literally sweet eating, there is a party and this, and the wedding feast proper, usually involves hundreds of guests. During the wedding ceremony, the bride is expected not to laugh or smile, since to do so is deemed disrespectful to her parents, since it implies she is happy to be leaving them. Traditionally weddings last three days and can be lavish affairs with many families going into debt. Once the celebrations have ended, the newly-weds usually move into the husband's family home where they will be assigned rooms of their own.

Custom dictates that wives are the first to rise in the morning and the last to go to bed. Wife beating is still not an uncommon phenomenon, and a man can theoretically divorce his wife by publicly repeating 'I divorce you' three times. Any woman who attempts to divorce her husband, however, faces a bitter, uphill struggle and even if she is eventually successful she will usually lose her children, since they are regarded as belonging to her husband's family. Levirate marriage, in which a widow is required to marry her husband's brother, is another common practice among some Afghans, but fewer Afghans than in the past marry more than one wife.

Despite the many difficulties they face, Afghan women are far from the weak, powerless victims portrayed in some Western polemics, while historians tend to forget when discussing rulers, male Islamic scholars and *pirs* that they all had wives. Women have always exercised considerable influence in the Muslim world, both in private and public. In ninth-century Balkh two of the wives of Ahmad b. Khizrawayh became renowned exponents of Islamic law,[10] and the Iraqi-born celibate mystic Rabiʿa al-ʿAdawiyya is celebrated in Farid al-Attar's famous biographies of early Sufis.[11] The Timurid queen Gauhar Shad broke with convention by founding many major Islamic institutions in Herat, while under the Durrani monarchy senior females in the royal *zanana* influenced national policy and determined the succession to the throne.

For nearly a century a number of educated Afghan women have committed themselves to the struggle for women's rights and have been very vocal, though usually out of the public eye. In Herat there are several well-known female musicians and ensembles, while some women even live as boys.[12] A few Afghan women have also fought in battle alongside their husbands, while a defeated ruler would often send his senior wife, bareheaded, to the victor to plead for mercy. A high-ranking woman who has been sexually violated may well send her veil or bloodstained clothing to a close male relative and demand he avenge the family honour. In less exalted circles, a family unable to gain the ear of a senior official will send their womenfolk to plead on their behalf or even to pour scorn on him publicly. Usually the official is so shamed by having to address women in public that he will act, if only to get rid of the nuisance. It has always been a tradition in Afghan society that punishment is only meted out to the male members of a defeated foe, and until recently women were rarely imprisoned and never executed.

Within the family, senior women gain status, power and influence by bearing children, particularly male offspring. They manage the household affairs, hold the keys of the food store, control budgets, supervise servants and organize food for family and guests. The women nurture the children and are often the ones to initiate discussion about marriage alliances for their sons and daughters. For this reason, Afghan men are often far more attached emotionally to their mothers than to their fathers. It is not unknown for an Afghan woman to deny her husband sexual relations in order to show her displeasure or to make him change his mind. There are also informal checks and balances in what still is a male-dominated world. A man who divorces his wife or beats her badly risks the wrath of his in-laws, who will have no compunction about paying the family a visit to demand he treat their daughter with dignity. If they are powerful enough and the offence serious, they may even remove the woman from the in-laws' home until the matter is settled. In cases of serious disputes, arbitrators may be appointed to reconcile the two parties and, as a last resort, in-laws may publicly shame a particularly brutal husband. Peer and family pressure, as well as the loss of face, means that divorce is not widespread and wealthy individuals, who for some reason are dissatisfied with one wife, will simply marry a second one.

Western discourse on gender issues in Afghanistan often disregards the substantial progress made in women's emancipation over the hundred or so years. It also forgets that less than a century ago in many Western nations the idea that 'a woman's place was in the home' was commonplace, nor did women have the right to own property in their own name or to vote. In Afghanistan too the struggle for women's rights has been a slow and painful process with many regressive steps. However, it is worth noting that at the beginning of the twentieth century all women had to wear the full veil in public and very few women ventured outside of the family compound. The state employed no women in the public sector, nor were there any primary schools for girls. Yet by the time President Da'ud was toppled in 1978 the state employed thousands of women in the health service, education, the civil service and in the police. There were dozens of girls' schools through-out the country, many women held tertiary degrees, had the right to vote and seats were allocated to women in parliament. Under the Communist regimes from 1978 to 1992 gender policy was even more liberal. Even the Islamizing government of President Rabbani permitted women to work and study. In this context the Taliban's harsh gender policies and brief reign was an aberration. As for the American and NATO intervention of 2001, rather than instigating a major cultural revolution for women, by and large they reinstated Islamists who held very similar views on the gender issue as the Taliban. This had made major reform of woman's rights more problematic though the presence of foreign agencies and NATO has restrained some of the more extremist ideologues embedded in the current government. Even so, institutional prejudice against women having a public role continues to surface not just in everyday life, but within state institutions.

The British colonial encounter with Pushtuns, or Pathans, on India's North-West Frontier led to much emphasis on *pushtunwali*, or *pukhtun-wali*, and these tribes' presumed state of perpetual conflict, summed up in a frequently quoted proverb, 'a Pushtun is only at peace when he is at war'. By and large, British officials inherited the Mughal prejudices, for the Mughals, like the British, were frequently at war with the Pushtun tribes.

Indeed, more than likely it was the Mughals who disparagingly summed up *pushtunwali* as *zar, zan wa zamin* – gold, women and land. Pushtuns themselves define *pushtunwali* in more positive terms, all of which are based on the principle of upholding personal and tribal honour. *Tura* is courage, especially in battle; *nang* is the defence of personal honour, but also of the weak and vulnerable; while *'izzat* is personal honour and status. Hospitality, *melmastia*, is another key value in Pushtun society since this is another means of gaining honour. The custom of *nanawatai*, sanctuary, obliges individuals to shelter and defend anyone who seeks protection and asylum, even if they are political fugitives, criminals or personal enemies. *Ghairat*, another key term, is a particularly difficult concept to define and even Pushtuns have trouble explaining it. The term involves the proactive, jealous guarding of *qaum* honour, in particular the adult male's role as 'gatekeepers' for the women. *Ghairat* is also closely linked to the concept of *namus*, the upholding of women's virtue and modesty.[13] Other values of *pushtunwali* include *badal*, the obligation of reciprocity, in particular related to revenge. However, for Pushtuns the heart of *pushtunwali* is not a list of terms or things one does, or does not do, but a way of life, for *pushtunwali* means doing, or being Pushtu.

British colonial administrators dealt mainly with the tribal, mountain-dwelling Pushtuns of the Afghan frontier where *pushtunwali* was strongly embedded and there was a tendency to regard this cultural practice as universal as well as unique to Pushtun society. Many urbanized Pushtuns do not uphold *pushtunwali* and many dislike the European tendency to focus on the negative aspects of *badal*, since it gives the impression that Pushtun society is innately lawless and 'red in tooth and claw'.[14] Some Pushtun academics even dismiss much of *pushtunwali* as a romantic construct of nineteenth- and early twentieth-century ethnology on the one hand, and the product of state-sponsored ethnocentric nationalism on the other.

Many of the features of *pushtunwali* are far from unique and are found in various degrees among other ethnolinguistic groups in Afghanistan. Uzbeks have a customary law, the *Yasa*, drawn up by Chinggis Khan in the thirteenth century. Hazaras, Nuristanis, Turkmans and Kazakhs too have their own customary law. As for the culture of reciprocal vengeance, this is mainly enforced among nomadic, rural and mountain-dwelling Pushtuns, and the idea of reciprocity for harm done is equally important among Uzbeks, Hazaras, Nuristanis and Baluch. While Western authors focus on the negative aspects of *badal* it is important to note that many Pushtuns, and other citizens of Afghanistan, have worked tirelessly to resolve disputes and vendettas by traditional conflict-resolution mechanisms.

Hospitality or *mehman nawazi*, is equally important to all Afghans. Having guests for a meal and inviting them to stay over, or providing accommodation for travellers, is both meritorious and enhances the status of both the host and guest. In rural Afghanistan travellers have the right of free board for three nights and village heads and *khan*s keep a well-appointed guest room for this purpose. Honour too is a key building block of all Afghan peoples. In Pushtu *nang* and *ghairat* are the foundation stones of *pushtunwali*, while in Persianate culture the ethics of honour are rooted in the ancient Iranian chivalric tradition known as *jawanmardi*, which is enshrined particularly in the great pre-Islamic epic the *Shah Nama*, or *Book of Kings*. *Jawanmardi* is also a central theme of the heroic sagas of the Mongols, Kazakhs and Kyrgyz.

The world of honour is rooted in the exalting of manly, warrior virtues and the pursuit of public honour. Honour can be either ascribed or achieved. Ascribed honour is derived from one's birth, blood and historic honours bestowed on the *qaum* by the state or religious institutions. Honour is achieved by valour in battle, especially in a *jihad*, generosity, hospitality, endowment of public institutions, literary achievement, public service and being a good Muslim. In Uzbek and Turkman culture, adult males also achieve honour through their skill as *chapandaz* or wrestlers. The flip side of this honour-centric world view is the need to avoid *sharm* – shame or disgrace – or a 'blackened face'. Shame covers a whole variety of negative acts, from disrespect of one's elders, to cowardice, public disgrace or

Hospitality is a foundational value in all Afghan societies. Here a family in northern Afghanistan enjoy the traditional pot of tea in their walled garden.

dismissal from high office. To be shamed, especially publicly, is one of the worst things that can happen to anyone in Afghanistan. The Pushtu proverb states that 'it is better to die with honour than to live with shame', while the Pushtu poet Khushhal Khan Khattak wrote, 'the world is shame (*sharm*), name (*nam*) and honour (*nang*) / without honour the world is nothing'.

Honour–shame cultures are by their nature both competitive and combative, since in the pursuit of honour one often attempts to shame rivals or make them lose face. Inevitably, in any contest, whether it is sports, war or dynastic power struggles, there will always be winners and losers. Anyone who gains public honour, for example, is at risk from the envy of others, for one person's gain/honour is always another's loss/shame. Since losing is shameful, and shame always has to be expunged, the loser will do all in his or her power to redeem face and name. In some cases, such as the killing of a family member, the shame is so great that honour can only be redeemed by bloodshed, for the death implies the clan is weak and unable to protect its members. Foreigners, who generally have only a superficial knowledge of Afghan culture, often find themselves unwitting victims of this honour–shame duality, since this culture is essentially alien, particularly to peoples from northern European countries. Public dressing-down (itself a strong shame phrase) of Afghan employees for incompetence, corruption or non-attendance risks incurring the wrath of the employee in question, for while the foreigner is concerned about right and wrong, the Afghan is only interested in the fact that she or he has been shamed and has lost face in front of other Afghans. Many of the so-called Green on Blue attacks, in which government security forces turn their guns on their foreign counterparts, are more often than not due to Afghans being publicly shamed by foreign officers.

Women are intricately bound up in this world of honour and shame, for *parda* is not just derived from Islamic requirements that adult women should cover their heads in public. The custom is also based on the belief that concealment is the best, and in some cases the only, way to protect a woman's virginity and hence *qaum* honour. If a woman breaks the sexual taboos she brings shame on not just herself but the family, and in some extreme cases honour can only be redeemed by her closest male relatives putting her to death, in so-called 'honour killings'. Yet despite all attempts to control and confine sexuality, Afghanistan's popular music, poetry, romances and folklore are full of stories about illicit love affairs and relate how a single glance from a woman's 'black eyes' can turn a young man literally mad with desire. Not surprisingly, such romances tend to end in tragedy.

The empires of the Iranian–Indian borderland in the mid-eighteenth century

ONE

Afghan Sultanates, 1260–1732

The fame of Bahlol and of Sher Shah too, resounds in my ears
Afghan Emperors of India, who swayed its sceptre effectively and well.
For six or seven generations, did they govern so wisely,
That all their people were filled with admiration of them.
Either those Afghans were different, or these have greatly changed.

KHUSHHAL KHAN KHATTAK

Amongst the Afghan tribes it is indisputable that where one [tribe] possesses more men than the other, that tribe will set out to destroy the other.

SHER SHAH SURI[1]

MODERN HISTORIES of Afghanistan generally regard 1747 as the founding date of the modern state of Afghanistan.[2] This is because in that year Ahmad Shah, a young Afghan of the 'Abdali tribe, who later adopted the regnal name of Durrani, established an independent kingdom in Kandahar and founded a monarchy that, in one expression or another, ruled Afghanistan until 1978. In fact the history of Afghan rule in the Iranian–Indian frontier can be traced back many centuries before the birth of Ahmad Shah. Nor was Ahmad Shah the first Afghan, or member of his family or tribe, to rule an independent kingdom.

In 1707 Mir Wa'is, of the Hotak Ghilzai tribe of Kandahar, rebelled against Safavid Persia and founded a kingdom that lasted for more than thirty years. In 1722 Mir Wa'is' son, Shah Mahmud, even invaded Persia and displaced the Safavid monarch and for seven years ruled an empire that stretched from Kandahar to Isfahan. Even after Mir Wa'is' descendants were thrown out of Persia, they continued to rule Kandahar and south-eastern Afghanistan until 1738.

In 1717, ten years after Mir Wa'is' revolt, a distant cousin of Ahmad Shah, 'Abd Allah Khan Saddozai, established the first independent 'Abdali sultanate in Herat after seceding from the Safavid Empire and for a brief period both Ahmad Shah's father and half-brother ruled this kingdom. The dynasty founded by Ahmad Shah in 1747 lasted only until 1824, when his line was deposed by a rival 'Abdali clan, the Muhammadzais, descendants of Ahmad Shah's Barakzai *wazir*, or chief minister. In 1929 the Muhammadzais in turn were deposed and, following a brief interregnum, another Muhammadzai dynasty took power, the Musahiban. This family was the shortest lived of all three of Afghanistan's 'Abdali dynasties: its last representative, President Muhammad Da'ud Khan, was killed in a Communist coup in April 1978. All these dynasties belonged to the same Durrani tribe, but there was little love lost between these lineages. Indeed, the history of all the Afghan dynasties of northern India is turbulent and their internal politics marred by feuds and frequent civil wars.

While dozens of tribes call themselves 'Afghan', a term which nowadays is regarded as synonymous with Pushtun, Afghanistan's dynastic history is dominated by two tribal groupings, the 'Abdali, or Durrani, and the Ghilzai. The Ghilzai, or Ghilji, as a distinct tribal entity can be traced back to at least the tenth century where they are referred to in the sources as Khalaj or Khallukh. At this period their main centres were Tukharistan (the Balkh plains), Guzganan (the hill country of southern Faryab), Sar-i Pul and Badghis provinces, Bust in the Helmand and Ghazni. Today the Ghilzais are treated as an integral part of the Pushtun tribes that straddle the modern Afghan–Pakistan frontier, but tenth-century sources refer to the Khalaj as Turks and 'of Turkish appearance, dress and language'; the Khalaj tribes of Zamindarwar even spoke Turkish.[3] It is likely that the Khalaj were originally Hephthalite Turks, members of a nomadic confederation from Inner Asia that ruled all the country north of the Indus and parts of eastern Iran during the fifth to early seventh centuries CE.[4] The Khalaj were semi-nomadic pastoralists and possessed large flocks of sheep and other animals, a tradition that many Ghilzai tribes have perpetuated to this day.

The Khalji Sultanates of Delhi

During the era of the Ghaznavid dynasty (977–1186), so named because the capital of this kingdom was Ghazni, the Khalaj were *ghulams*, or indentured levies, conscripted into the Ghaznavid army.[5] Often referred to as 'slave troops', *ghulams* were commonplace in the Islamic armies well into the twentieth century, the most well known being the Janissaries of the Ottoman empire. *Ghulams*, however, were not slaves in the European sense of the word. Unlike tribal levies, whose loyalties were often to their tribal leaders rather than the monarch, *ghulams* were recruited from subjugated

The minaret of the Ghaznavid Sultan Bahram Shah (1084–1157), one of two surviving medieval minarets outside Ghazni.

populations, usually non-Muslim tribes, forced to make a token conversion to Islam and formed the royal guard of the ruling monarch, or sultan. The *ghulam*s thus provided a ruler with a corps of loyal troops that were bound to him by oath and patronage and that offset the power of the sultan's tribe and other powerful factions at court.

The *ghulam*s were generally better trained and armed than any other military force in the kingdom and were the nearest thing to a professional army. Their commanders enjoyed a privileged status, often held high office and owned large estates. In a number of Muslim countries *ghulam*s eventually became so powerful that they acted as kingmakers and on occasion deposed their master and set up their own dynasty. The Ghaznavids were a case in point. Sabuktigin (942–997), a Turk from Barskon in what is now Kyrgyzstan, who founded this dynasty, was a *ghulam* general who was sent to govern Ghazni by the Persian Samanid ruler of Bukhara, only for him to eventually break away and set up his own kingdom.[6]

Given that the Khalaj in the Ghaznavid army are referred to as *ghulam*s it is very likely that they were one of many *kafir* or pagan tribes that lived in the hill country between the Hari Rud, Murghab and Balkh Ab watersheds. In 1005/6 Sultan Mahmud, the most famous of the Ghaznavid rulers, invaded, subjugated and systematically Islamized this region. As part of the terms of submission, the local rulers would have been required to provide a body of *ghulam*s to serve in the Ghaznavid army. The Khalaj soon proved their worth, repelling an invasion by another Turkic group, the Qarakhanids, and subsequently in campaigning against the Hindu rulers of northern India.

In 1150 Ghazni was destroyed by the Ghurids, a Persian-speaking dynasty from the hill country of Badghis, Ghur and the upper Murghab, and by 1186 all vestiges of Ghaznavid power in northern India had been swept aside. The Ghurids incorporated the Khalaj *ghulam*s into their army and it was during this era that they and probably the tribes of the Khyber area began to be known as Afghan, though the origin and meaning of this term is uncertain. Possibly Afghan was a vernacular term used to describe semi-nomadic, pastoral tribes, in the same way that today the migratory Afghan tribes are referred to by the generic term *maldar*, herd owners, or *kuchi*, from the Persian verb 'to migrate' or 'move home'. It was not until the nineteenth century and under British colonial influence that Afghans were commonly referred to as Pushtun or by the Anglo-Indian term Pathan.

During the Ghaznavid and Ghurid eras many Khalaj and other Afghan clans were relocated around Ghazni, others were required to live in the Koh-i Sulaiman, or in the hinterland of Kandahar, Kabul and Multan, where they were assigned grazing rights. This relocation may have been a reward for their military service, but more likely it was a strategic decision, since it meant these tribes could be quickly mustered in the event of war. By the early fourteenth century Afghans were a common feature of the ethnological landscape of southern and southeastern Afghanistan. The Arab traveller Ibn Battuta, who visited Kabul in 1333, records how the *qafila*, or trade caravan, he was travelling with had a sharp engagement with the Afghans in a narrow pass near the fortress of 'Karmash', probably on the old Kabul–Jalalabad highway.[7] Ibn Battuta damned these Afghans as 'highwaymen', but on the basis of the limited sources available it is likely these tribes expected payment for safe passage and the head of the caravan had failed to pay the customary dues. Significantly, Ibn Battuta notes that the Afghans of the Kabul–Jalalabad region were Persian-speakers, though whether they spoke Pushtu too is not recorded.

Other sources from this era portray the Afghans as a formidable warrior race. One author graphically compares them to 'a huge elephant . . . [a] tall tower of a fortress . . . daring, intrepid, and valiant soldiers, each one of whom, either on mountain or in forest, would take a hundred Hindus in his grip, and, in a dark night, would reduce a demon to utter helplessness'.[8] These Afghan *ghulams* certainly lived up to this reputation during their campaigns in India and the Ghurids rewarded their commanders with hereditary estates, or *jagirs*, in the plains of northern India. This led to a substantial migration of Afghan tribes from the hill country of what is now south and southwestern Afghanistan to the fertile, frost-free and well-watered lands of the Indian plains. Eventually the Khalaj, by this time referred to as the Khaljis or Khiljis, became so powerful that they placed their own nominee on the throne of Delhi. In 1290 they seized power and for the next thirty years ruled northern India in their own right.

The Khaljis and other Afghan tribes kept apart from their mostly Hindu subjects, living in cantonments, or *mahalas*, based on clan affiliation. Jalal al-Din Firuz, the first Khalji sultan, even refused to attend the court in Delhi and built a new capital a few kilometres away in the Afghan enclave of Kilokhri.[9] This cultural isolation was reinforced by the practice of endogamy, for the Khalji would only marry women from their own tribe. As for the Khalji tribal leaders, they showed scant respect for the authority of the sultan and there were frequent clashes between them and the crown as the former fought the monarch's efforts to curb their traditional right to the autonomous government of their tribes.[10] The Khalji were also notorious for their blood feuds, which they pursued regardless of the consequences to the body politic. Rivals even fought each other in the court and, on one occasion, in the royal presence itself. The Khalji, however, were also a formidable military power. Sultan Jalal al-Din Firuz (r. 1290–96) and his successor Sultan 'Ala' al-Din, or Juna Khan (r. 1296–1316) even defeated the invading Mongol armies on several occasions and in so doing saved northern India from the ravages they inflicted on Afghanistan, Persia and the Middle East.

The last Khalji, Sultan Ikhtiyar al-Din, was assassinated in 1320 and a Turkish dynasty, the Tughlaqs, seized power, but the Afghans remained a force in the political and military life of northern India. Between 1436 and 1531 one branch of the Khalji dynasty ruled Malwa in modern Madhya Pradesh, while thousands of Khaljis owned large tracts of land in western India and dozens of their military cantonments were scattered throughout northern India from the Punjab to Bengal. The Afghans also continued to provide high-quality troops for the Tughlaq army and some held high military office.

In 1451 Bahlul Khan, a Khalji of the Lodhi clan, deposed the then sultan and founded a second Afghan sultanate, the Lodhi Dynasty, which ruled northern India for 75 years (1451–1526). Under the Lodhis, another wave of Afghans migrated into northern India and perpetuated the tradition of living in separate cantonments and the practice of endogamy. Ludhiana, now close to the frontier between India and Pakistan, for example, derives its name from having originally been a Lodhi cantonment. The Lodhis, while Muslims, were still only semi-Islamized. After Sultan Bahlul Lodhi conquered Delhi he and his followers attended Friday prayers in the main mosque to ensure that his name was recited in the *khutba*, which was an essential act of the Friday congregational prayer service. The *imam*, or prayer leader, observing how the Afghans struggled to perform the prayers according to prescribed rituals, was heard to exclaim: 'what a strange ('*ajab*) tribe has appeared. They do not know whether they are followers of Dajal [the Antichrist] or if they are themselves Dajal-possessed.'[11]

The Mughal conquest of India and Afghan-Mughal rivalry

The Lodhi dynasty came to an abrupt end at the Battle of Panipat in 1526, when the last sultan was defeated by the Mughal armies of Zahir al-Din Babur. Babur, a descendant of both Timur Lang and Chinggis Khan, thus became the latest in a series of Turkic rulers of India whose empire included Kabul and southeastern Afghanistan. Born in Andijan in the Fergana Oasis of what is now Uzbekistan, Babur's father had ruled a kingdom that included Samarkand and Bukhara, but after his death Babur had been ousted from the region by the Shaibanid Uzbeks and fled across the Amu Darya, eventually taking Kabul from its Timurid ruler. Prior to his invasion of India, Babur had conducted a series of expeditions against the Afghan tribes of Laghman and Nangahar as well as the Mohmands of the Khyber area, and the Ghilzais of Ghazni.[12]

Following his victory at Panipat, Babur did his best to reconcile the Afghan tribes that lay across the key military road between Kabul and the Punjab. To this end he married the daughter of a Yusufzai *khan*, the most numerous and powerful tribe in the region of the Khyber Pass. Dilawar Khan Lodhi, a member of the deposed dynasty, also became one of Babur's most trusted advisers and was given the hereditary title of Khan Khanan, Khan of Khans. Other members of the Lodhi dynasty were appointed as governors or held high rank in the army. Despite this, there were numerous Afghan rebellions against Mughal rule. In 1540, following Babur's death, there was civil war between his sons and eventually Farid al-Din Khan,

A Timurid miniature
from Herat, early 16th
century, depicting a
battle scene.

of the Suri clan of the Kakar tribe, who had been a high-ranking officer under the Lodhis, ousted Babur's son and successor Humayun from Delhi, and adopted the regnal title of Sher Shah Suri. He ruled Delhi and much of northern India for fifteen years, though Humayun's brothers continued to govern Kandahar, Ghazni, Kabul and Peshawar. Humayun himself fled to Persia but after fifteen years in exile he finally regained the throne of Delhi and restored the Mughal supremacy.

Sher Shah Suri's rebellion hardened Mughal attitudes towards the Afghan tribes. Humayun's son and heir, Akbar the Great (r. 1556–1605), confiscated their *jagirs* and banned them from governorships and high military rank. Racial prejudice too ran deep, with Mughal historians regularly referring to Afghans as 'black-faced', 'brainless', vagabond' and 'wicked'.[13] The suppressions, confiscations and general prejudice caused deep resentment, for many Afghans continued to serve the Mughal empire faithfully.

One response to this disenfranchisement was the rise of a militant millenarian movement known as the Roshaniyya (Illuminated), which posed a serious threat to Mughal rule in northwestern India for almost half a century.[14] Its founder, Bayazid Ansari (b. 1525), or Pir Roshan, was from the small Ormur or Baraki tribe, whose mother tongue was not Pushtu but Ormuri. His father was a religious teacher but Ansari fell out with him and his tribe because of his unorthodox opinions. Forced to flee, he made his way into Mohmand tribal territory in the Khyber region and later made his base in the mountain country of Tirah.

From the mid-1570s onwards Pir Roshan began to claim he was the *Mahdi*, the Restorer whose appearance in the Last Days, according to Islamic teaching, would usher in the Golden Age in which all the world would be converted to Islam. After a visit to an unnamed Sufi mystic in the Kandahar area, Pir Roshan declared *jihad* on the Mughals and found strong support for his cause among the Yusufzai, Afridi, Orakzai and Mohmand tribes. The Roshaniyya movement was heterodox in its theology and was condemned by the orthodox Sunni establishment as heretical. Its many critics punning referring to the movement as the *tarikiyya*, from the Persian word for 'darkness'. At the same time the Roshaniyya had strong nationalistic overtones and one of Pir Roshan's key demands was complete independence from Mughal rule.

The Roshaniyya rebellion came at a difficult time for Akbar the Great, who was already embroiled in a civil war with his brother Hakim, governor of Lahore, as well as the conquest of Kashmir. When Akbar finally regained control of Lahore and Peshawar in 1581, he marched up the Khyber Pass and soundly defeated Pir Roshan at the Battle of Baro in Nangahar. A

The Khyber Pass, looking back towards Peshawar and the Indus plains.

short time later Bayazid died, but the revolt was perpetuated by his son Jalal al-Din, known to his followers as Jalala. In order to strengthen the Indus frontier, Akbar ordered major improvements to the road between Lahore and Peshawar, widened the mule track through the Khyber Pass to facilitate the passage of wheeled carriages and artillery, and built the massive fortress at Attock on the left bank of the Indus as a forward base for military operations against the Afghan tribes.

In 1585 Akbar's rebellious brother Hakim finally drank himself to death and the civil war petered out, leaving Akbar free to concentrate on suppressing the Roshaniyyas. To achieve this end he adopted a policy of divide and rule, securing the support of the Afghan tribes of the Indus plains who had suffered from Yusufzai raids on their villages and crops. To better manage these tribes, the Mughals dealt with them indirectly through representatives, or *maliks*, who were either chosen by the king or nominated by a tribal council or *jirga*. In return for subsidies and other royal favours, the *maliks* were required to keep their tribe loyal, maintain internal law and order and provide tribal levies when required. The *maliks* also were entrusted with collecting the tribes' annual tribute and maintaining security on the royal roads that ran through their territory. Malik Akoray of the Khattak tribe, for example, was responsible for security on the key military road from the right bank of the Indus to Peshawar.

Akbar also sent an army into the Khyber and Yusufzai hill country to suppress the rebels, but the Mughal military machine was not trained or equipped for mountain warfare. The rebel tribes lured the Mughals into the narrowest parts of the Khyber Pass, blocked the exits and proceeded to slaughter the trapped army. When a relief column tried to break through it was repulsed with heavy loss of life. A second column sent against the Yusufzais suffered a similar fate and a thousand more men died before they fought their way out of the trap. Emboldened by this success, in 1593 Jalala laid siege to Peshawar and the city was only saved at the last minute by the arrival of a relief force. Later in the same year the Roshaniyyas sacked Mughal-ruled Ghazni and sent representatives to Kandahar to seek support from the Afghan tribes in that region.

After these defeats Akbar adopted a policy of gradual attrition, knowing that he commanded far more resources in terms of manpower, artillery and cash than the Roshaniyyas. Afghan resistance slowly collapsed and, as one stronghold after the other fell, there were harsh reprisals. Yusufzai resistance was eventually broken and never again did they risk challenging the might of the Mughal empire. The Roshaniyya's legacy, however, inspired subsequent millenarian, nationalist movements among the Afghan tribes of the Indian frontier, of which the Taliban are the latest manifestation. Another legacy of the Roshaniyya was some of the earliest Pushtu poems written by Mirza Khan Ansari (d. *c.* 1630/31), a descendant of Pir Roshan.

Akbar's successor, Jahangir (r. 1605–27), adopted a more conciliatory policy to the Afghan tribes, appointing Dilawar Khan Kakar as governor of Lahore while Khan Jahan, a descendant of Pir Khan Lodhi, was given the high title of *farzand* (son). Jahangir records of this individual that:

> there is not in my government any person of greater influence than he, so much so that on his representation I pass over faults which are not pardoned at the intercession of any of the other servants of the Court. In short, he is a man of good disposition, brave, and worthy of favour.[15]

Afghan fortunes, however, suffered another blow during the reign of Shah Jahan (r. 1628–58) when Khan Jahan backed a rival candidate for the succession. Khan Jahan fled to the Punjab, where he tried to raise an army from the Afghan tribes, only for his appeal to fall on deaf ears. On 17 February 1631 Khan Jahan's revolt was crushed at the Battle of Sahindra and he, his sons and many of his Afghan followers were put to death.

Shah Jahan's successor, Aurangzeb (r. 1658–1707), continued the repressive policy against the Afghans and tried to exert more direct control over them. He imprisoned Khushhal Khan Khattak, a grandson of Malik Akoray Khattak, despite his family having served the Mughals loyally for three generations. When Khushhal Khan was finally freed after a decade of incarceration, he fled to the Afridis of the Khyber Pass and raised the banner of revolt. Aurangzeb responded by distributing large sums of gold as well as titles and gifts to the *malik*s and Khushhal's uprising collapsed. Aurangzeb even paid Khushhal's son, Bahram, to assassinate his father but, despite several attempts on his life, Khushhal Khan died of natural causes at a ripe old age.

Khushhal Khan Khattak's most important legacy, however, is his literary output and he is regarded today as one of the most famous of all Pushtu poets. His works include scathing attacks on Mughal rule and his own people for their preference for Mughal gold, rather than tribal honour and independence. A contemporary of Khushhal Khan, Rahman Baba (*c.* 1632–1706), a Mohmand, was another great Pushtu poet who was famed for his mystical verses and homilies. His verse is regarded with such veneration that 'when a [Rahman Baba] couplet is cited in Jirga, heads bow down and arguments are settled'.[16]

The rise of the Saddozais and the Mughal and Safavid struggle for Kandahar

While the Mughals fought to contain the tribes of India's northwest frontier, further west another Afghan tribe, the 'Abdalis, were emerging as a major political force under the patronage of Safavid Persia. Unlike the Ghilzai, the 'Abdalis are not mentioned in the histories until the middle of the sixteenth century and little is known about their ethnogenesis, though prior to the Mughal era one of their key strongholds was the Obeh valley in the upper Hari Rud. The *Makhzan-i Afghani*, written during the reign of Jahangir, states that the 'Abdalis fought in the army of Sultan Mahmud of Ghazni, while Mountstuart Elphinstone, the first European to attempt a systematic account of the Afghan tribes, records that the 'Abdalis claimed their original homeland was the mountains of Ghur.[17] Another tradition states that Sultan Mahmud of Ghazni rewarded the 'Abdalis for some unspecified service by granting them grazing rights in and around Kandahar.

These accounts bear an uncanny resemblance to the early history of the Khalaj and it is possible that they are an attempt to co-opt a rival tribe's history. If there is any historical basis for this claim, however, it suggests that the 'Abdalis too were probably *ghulam*s in the Ghaznavid army and, like the Khalaj, probably recruited from the non-Muslim tribes of Ghur. However, in respect of their internal management, the 'Abdalis and Ghilzais differ substantially, which suggests a somewhat different cultural background for the two tribes. The Ghilzais are referred to as Turks in early Islamic sources and at least some spoke a Turkic language as their mother tongue. In 1809 Mountstuart Elphinstone noted all the leading 'Abdalis at the Durrani court spoke Persian and dressed in the Persian manner. This, of course, was primarily due to having been ruled by the Timurids and subsequently Safavid Persia, though it may suggest that originally the 'Abdalis were a Persianate, rather than a Turkic, tribe from the central highlands of the Hindu Kush.

One of many traditions concerning the origin of the name 'Abdali is that it is derived from '*abdal*, a Sufi title accorded to individuals who have obtained a high degree of gnosis. The 'Abdalis claim that this title was due to them being *mukhlis*, or devotees, of Khwaja 'Abu Ahmad 'Abdal (d. 941), founder of the Chishtiyya Sufi Order.[18] Claiming links to a famous *pir* or a major figure of early Islam is not uncommon among the tribes and dynasties of the region, for it enhanced their spiritual and political legitimacy. However, *ghulam*s were usually affiliates of a particular Sufi Order: the Ottoman Janissaries, for example, were all initiates of the Bektashiyya

The 12th-century Ghurid mausolea of Sufi *pirs* at Chisht-i Sharif in the upper Hari Rud.
During the Mughal era the Chishtiyya Order was the most prominent Sufi movement
in northern India.

Order. Even so, it is improbable that the 'Abdalis were historically affiliated
to the Chishtiyya Order, even though its original centre, Chisht-i Sharif,
was just upstream from Obeh. Had this been the case this link would have
been perpetuated through the centuries. Instead Saddu Khan, the epony-
mous founder of the Saddozai royal line, was bound to another Sufi Order,
the Qadiriyya, which originated in Syria. From the late eighteenth century
several of the 'Abdali tribes affiliated themselves to the northern Indian,
Mujadidi *tariqa* of Naqshbandism.

The early accounts of the 'Abdalis relate mainly to the rise of the royal
Saddozai clan. According to tribal genealogies, the many 'Abdali tribes all
stem from four primary lineages, the sons of Zirak. The most senior of
these tribes, by right of primogeniture, is the Popalzai, of which the royal
house of Saddozai is a sept. The other three lineages are Barakzai, Alakozai
and Musazai. Each of these four main tribes are subdivided into dozens of
clans similar to the Scottish Highlanders or Maori *iwi*.[19]

Tribal tradition states that in or around 1558, Akko, an itinerant *darwish*,
paid an unexpected visit to a certain Salih, an impoverished member of
the Habibzai branch of the Popalzais. Salih managed to scrape together
enough food to provide for his guests and as Akko was about to leave he
told his host that he had dreamed that a lion had entered his house. The

darwish then predicted that Salih would have a son who would be as brave as a lion and earn fame for himself and his family.[20] Furthermore, the birth of this child would be a turning point in the family's financial fortunes. In due time a baby boy was born and Saleh named him 'Asad Allah (Lion of God), but his family called him Saddu, from which the Saddozai lineage derives its name. Sometime after Saddu's birth the governor of Kandahar appointed Salih as *malik* of the 'Abdali tribal confederacy and, since one of his duties was to collect the tribe's taxes and tribute, Salih soon became a very wealthy man.

Salih's rise to power was the result of a major shift in the geopolitical scene of the Indian–Persian frontier. From the early sixteenth century Kandahar, which was an important frontier town and trade emporium, was fought over by three major regional powers: Safavid Persia, Mughal India and the Shaibanid Uzbeks north of the Hindu Kush. In 1501 the head of the Shi'a Safaviyya Sufi Order in Ardabil, Azerbaijan, proclaimed himself king of Persia and took the regnal name of Shah Isma'il I. Within a decade Shah Isma'il had brought all of Persia under his authority and imposed the Shi'a rite of Islam as the state cult. The Safavid army consisted mostly of members of the Safaviyya Order and many of them were of Turco-Mongolian ethnicity: Turkman, Kurds and Chaghatais. They became known as Qizilbash, literally 'red heads', from the distinctive red cap worn by members of the Order.

North of the Hindu Kush and beyond the Amu Darya the Shaibanid Uzbeks, a tribal confederacy formed from the remnants of the armies of the Mongol conqueror Chinggis Khan, took Samarkand and sacked Balkh, Herat and Mashhad, sweeping away another Turco-Mongolian dynasty, the Timurids. Two brothers, Mukim Khan and Shah Beg Khan, whose father had been the Timurid governor of Kandahar, then established their own independent kingdom in Kandahar and Kabul. Following Zahir al-Din Babur's conquest of Kabul in 1504, Mukim fled to Kandahar and when, three years later, Babur marched against Kandahar, Shah Beg turned to the Uzbeks for military assistance. Since Babur was already fighting the Shaibanids north of the Hindu Kush, he decided he could not risk opening a second front and withdrew.

Six years later, in December 1510, Shah Isma'il routed the Uzbeks outside Merv and their leader, Uzbek Khan, was killed. Shah Isma'il then occupied Herat, while Babur spent the next decade trying to regain his father's kingdom beyond the Amu Darya. Babur eventually abandoned this quest and decided to carve out a kingdom in northern India instead. In 1520, as the first stage of this campaign, Babur besieged Kandahar. After holding out for nearly two years, Shah Beg surrendered the city in return for safe passage to Sind. Kandahar thus passed under Mughal sovereignty. Babur pushed on into India where he eventually defeated the Lodhi Sultan and established his seat of power in Delhi.

After Babur's death his son Humayun passed through Kandahar on his way to Persia following the loss of Delhi to Sher Shah Suri. Humayun was given refuge by the then Safavid ruler, Shah Tahmasp I, and in return for adopting the Shi'a rite and military assistance, Humayun agreed to cede Kandahar in perpetuity to Persia. In 1545, after fifteen years of exile, Humayun regained control of Kandahar with the aid of a Persian army, but once he was in control of the citadel Humayun reneged on his promise and threw out the Safavid garrison. Thirteen years later, in 1558, following the death of Humayun, Shah Tahmasp sent an army to attack Kandahar and demanded that the new Mughal emperor, Akbar the Great, fulfil his father's promise and cede sovereignty over the city. Since Akbar was facing a series of challenges to his power further east, he reluctantly agreed and Kandahar was incorporated as part of the Persian province of Khurasan.

'Asad Allah, or Saddu, was born around the time that Kandahar passed from Mughal to Safavid sovereignty. The appointment of his father Salih as *malik* of the 'Abdalis was undoubtedly due to this shift in the balance of power. The Safavids, while they appointed a Persian governor in Kandahar, perpetuated the *malik* system established by the Mughals as the best method of controlling the local Afghan tribes and ensuring security on the royal highways. It is more than likely Salih Habibzai was nominated as *malik* by an 'Abdali *jirga* and their choice was confirmed by the Safavid military governor of Kandahar.[21] The fact that the *jirga* chose a poor man with little influence or prestige was nothing unusual: both the Safavid governor and the 'Abdali elders had a vested interest in appointing someone with little power, since he was that much easier to control and manipulate. What is remarkable is that the 'Abdalis, who were Sunni, were not required to convert to Shi'ism, even though the Safavids always required this for the Muslim population of their empire.

Salih's appointment was confirmed by a *firman*, or royal patent, with the title of *malik* and *mir-i Afghan* or *mir-i Afghaniha*.[22] His office and its titles were hereditary, and when Salih's son Saddu succeeded him the family adopted the clan name of Saddozai. The 'Abdalis were also permitted to retain their right to autonomy and Saddu later became *kalantar* too, a position similar to that of a magistrate and one that gave him the right to adjudicate on internal disputes and punish criminals.

Such rights and privileges could only have been secured in return for substantial services to the Safavids and, given the Saddozais' subsequent history, it is likely they were a reward for 'Abdali military support against the Mughals. As we have seen, the Mughals had adopted an increasingly harsh policy towards the Afghan tribes of the Indian borderland and they, in turn, resented Mughal domination. The revolt of Sher Shah Suri, Afghan support for Khan Khanan and Akbar's rebellious brother, as well as the Roshaniyya movement, all led to further repressions until the tribes 'preferred a Shia overlord to a fellow-Hanafi who subjected them to such degradation'.[23] From the Safavid point of view the 'Abdalis of Herat and Kandahar were natural allies, for their leading men were already

Dynasty	Ethnicity	Ruled	Remarks
Ghaznavid	Turk	977–1186	Sunni Muslim: descended from a *ghulam* general of the Persian Samanid dynasty
Ghurid	Iranian	1186–1206	From Ghur in the central highlands of Afghanistan. Converted to Sunni Islam under the Ghaznavids
Mamluk ('slave')	Turk	1206–90	Successor dynasties from Ghurids to Mughal, usually referred to as the Delhi Sultanates
Khalji/Khilji	Afghan (originally Turkic?)	1290–1320	Formerly *ghulam*s in the Ghaznavid and Ghurid army
Tughlaq	Turco-Mongolian	1320–1414	1398, Timur Lang (Tamurlaine), of Central Asian Turco-Mongolian stock, sacks Delhi
Sayyid	Arab (claimed)	1414–51	Founded by Timur Lang's governor of the Punjab. The dynasty claimed descent from Muhammad
Lodhi	Afghan (Khalji)	1451–1526	Founder of this dynasty was originally governor of Lahore
Mughal	Turco-Mongolian	1526–40	Zahir al-Din Babur, its founder, originally from Ferghana. A descendant of Chinggis Khan and Timur Lang. Babur's son, Humayun, forced to flee to Persia after rebellion of his brothers and defeat by Sher Shah Suri
Suri	Afghan (Kakar)	1540–55	Farid al-Din Khan, whose regnal name was Sher Shah Suri; ruled N. India after his defeat of Humayun. Humayun's brothers continued to rule Kabul, Ghazni, Kandahar and Peshawar
Mughal	Turco-Mongolian	1555–1858	Humayun defeats Islam Shah Suri, son of Sher Shah, and reasserts Mughal power in Delhi. Mughal rule continued until it was replaced by Britain following the Sepoy Mutiny

TABLE 4: The Muslim Dynasties of Northern India, 975–1558

Persianized and spoke an 'uncouth Persian'.[24] Many 'Abdalis were also urbanized and were engaged in the overland trade with India, which was vital to the Safavid economy.

The rise of the 'Abdalis to political prominence as clients of a Persian, Shi'a monarchy has been largely airbrushed out of modern Afghan historiography and ignored by Western historians. For many Afghans, especially monarchists, it is an embarrassment, for from the early twentieth century successive governments deliberately promoted a national identity constructed on three foundations: the Durrani dynasty's adherence to Hanafi Sunnism, which was on occasion accompanied by anti-Shi'a and anti-Persian sentiment; Pushtunness and the Pushtu language; and Afghan resistance to, and independence from, the dominant imperial powers of the region, including Persia. To one degree or another all these pillars are based on fallacies and required a significant rewriting of Afghanistan's early history from school textbooks to historiography. One reason for Afghan historians favouring 1747 as the foundation of modern Afghanistan is that it avoids referring back to the previous two-and-a-half centuries of the Saddozai–Safavid alliance. It also avoids the uncomfortable fact that prior to 1747 Kandahar, which Afghan monarchists would later promote as the dynastic and spiritual capital of Afghanistan, was for many decades an integral part of the Persian province of Khurasan and that the 'Abdalis were a Persianate tribe. As one modern Afghan historian notes: 'in reality, little about the Afghan monarchy was tribal or Paxtun.'[25]

The Saddozai–Safavid alliance

When the Safavids took possession of Kandahar they inherited a prosperous region and an important urban centre that straddled a major trade and military route to northern India. As well as being an emporium for Indian cloth, spices and gemstones, Kandahar was a vital link in Persia's 'silk for silver' trade and profited substantially from foreign currency exchange and the striking of silver coinage.[26] When Zahir al-Din Babur took the city, he was amazed at the vast quantities of coins and 'white gold' – cloth and other portable goods – found in the storehouses and treasury. The French traveller François Bernier, writing in the 1650s and '60s, describes Kandahar as 'the stronghold of a rich and fine kingdom'.[27] Another European traveller of the same era noted that Kandahar was home to a large number of Hindu bankers, or *banyans*, who financed the overland trade through loans and money transfers.[28] Elphinstone, writing in the early nineteenth century, noted that 'almost all the great

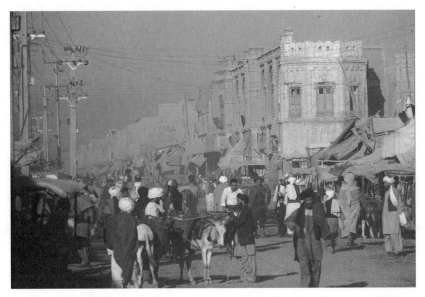

During the Mughal and Safavid era, Kandahar was a prosperous commercial centre.
The trading tradition is still strong, as shown in this 1970s image of Kandahar's bazaar.

Dooraunees' had houses in Kandahar 'and some of them are said to be large and elegant'.[29] Outside of the urban centre of Kandahar lay large tracts of fertile agricultural land irrigated by the Arghandab, Tarnak and Helmand rivers, while thousands of semi-nomadic Afghan, Kakar and Baluch tribes provided the region with meat, skins, wool and pack animals. As protectors of these military and commercial routes as well as traders in their own right, the 'Abdalis in general and Saddozais in particular became extremely wealthy.

From an early age Saddu Khan is said to have exhibited a warrior spirit. On one occasion he won an archery contest, beating the cream of Safavid marksmen in the process. Later Saddu took the oath of disciple-ship, or *ba'it*, swearing allegiance to Sayyid Najib al-Din Gailani, *pir* of the Qadiriyya Order, who is said to have presented Saddu with a *kha'lat*, or robe of honour, and the sword of 'Abd al-Qadir Gailani, *pir-i piran*, the founder of the Qadiriyya Order. These precious relics were passed down through the Saddozai line and used as symbols of their spiritual and tem-poral leadership of the 'Abdalis. Pir-i Piran's sword was eventually lost during the Sikh sack of the Saddozai stronghold of Multan in 1818, but the 'Abdalis' spiritual affiliation to the Qadiriyya Order has been perpetuated to this day. During the Soviet occupation of the 1980s, 'Abdali and other royalist tribes fought under the banner of the Mahaz-i Milli-yi Islami, whose leader, Sayyid Ahmad Gailani, was at the time *pir* of the Order.

The Safavids ruled Kandahar until 1595, when Akbar the Great, taking advantage of a war of succession that followed the death of Shah Tahmasp I, regained control of the region. The conquest was relatively peaceful, for the Safavid prince governor agreed to surrender the province to the Mughals in order to pursue his own claim to the throne of Persia. Once in charge, the Mughals stripped the pro-Safavid Saddu Khan of his privileges and appointed Hajji Jala and Malik Kalu of the rival Barakzai clan as joint *mir-i Afghaniha*s. Eventually, the struggle for the Safavid throne was resolved and the new king, Shah 'Abbas I (r. 1587–1629), set out to reassert Persian power over northeastern Khurasan, which had been overrun by the Uzbeks. In 1598 Shah 'Abbas retook Mashhad and a few months later he defeated the Shaibanid Uzbek ruler, Din Muhammad Khan, and took Herat. The following year Balkh too fell to the Safavids.

We know little about how the 'Abdalis in Herat fared under Uzbek rule but shortly after the Safavids regained control of the city. Malik Salih called a *jirga* in Herat and announced that since he was now in his eighties, he was abdicating in favour of his eldest son, Saddu. Afghan tribal assemblies dislike acting as a rubber stamp for ambitious leaders and the assembly mooted several other possible successors. One key issue was who had the right to succeed Malik Salih, for primogeniture was not traditional among the 'Abdalis. Instead the tribe followed the Turco-Mongolian model of agnatic, or patrilineal, seniority; that is, the headship passed to the next most senior male member of the clan, usually an uncle or the next oldest brother.

Despite several days of debate the *jirga* was unable to agree so Malik Salih decided to put an end to the argument by girding a *kamarband* – a sash that probably held the sword of Pir-i Piran – around his son's waist and declared Saddu as the new *mir-i Afghaniha*, whereupon the majority of the assembly reluctantly accepted this fait accompli. Saddu then made an unprecedented demand, requiring each *khan* to swear an oath of allegiance to him on the Qur'an, an action that indicates Saddu's ambitions to rule his tribe more like a prince than a *malik*. Needless to say, Hajji Jala and Malik Kalu Barakzai in Kandahar refused to accept their rival's appointment and armed clashes ensued between Barakzais and Saddozais.

Following the death of Akbar the Great in 1605, Shah 'Abbas I sent an army to regain control of Kandahar, but the Mughal garrison held out and the region remained under Mughal sovereignty until 1622, when it came to an abrupt end. In this year the then Mughal emperor, Jahangir, received a highly flattering letter from Shah 'Abbas I requesting the return of Kandahar, 'that petty country'.[30] Jahangir was not impressed, for at the end of the letter the Safavid king informed the emperor that he had already taken possession of Kandahar and expelled its Mughal garrison. Jahangir ordered an army to march against the city, but just as it was about to set out his son, Shah Jahan, rebelled and 'struck with an axe at the foot of his own dominion'. The Kandahar campaign was abandoned and the army redirected to bring the rebel prince to heel. A furious Jahangir decreed that Shah Jahan, whose regnal name meant King of the World, should henceforth only be referred to in his presence as Shah Bi-Daulat, the Stateless or Vagabond King.[31]

Saddu Khan and the 'Abdalis once again provided military support for the Safavid reconquest of Kandahar and as a reward Shah 'Abbas I heaped favours on Saddu and his tribe. The 'Abdalis were restored to their customary privileges and exempted from paying tribute, their autonomous status was consolidated and Mir Saddu was given the exalted title of *sultan*, prince. Saddu was also gifted the substantial *jagir* of Safa on the Tarrnak river, land which had probably been seized from the Tokhi Ghilzais, whose fortress of Qalat-i Ghilzai was a few kilometres away. Saddu Khan then constructed a substantial fortified palace known as Qal'a-i Safa in the hill country of Shahr-i Safa, which henceforth was the stronghold of Saddozai power.

Shortly before his death in 1627, Sultan Saddu appointed as his successor his second son, Khizr, a Sufi who spent most of his time in spiritual contemplation. He then tried to convince the *jirga* to endorse his choice by claiming he had received visions and prophesies supporting his decision. The *jirga*, though, rejected Khizr and appointed Saddu's eldest son, Maudud Khan, a battle-hardened warrior and a bully. The decision not only split the 'Abdali tribe but divided Saddu's family into two hostile factions, leading to a feud that would be perpetuated down the generations (see Chart 1).

A few months after Sultan Maudud Khan became *mir-i Afghaniha*, Khizr died from a 'mysterious illness'.[32] His family accused Maudud Khan of poisoning his brother and Khizr's wife refused to hand over the sword and *kha'lat* of Pir-i Piran, and so denied Maudud's succession any legitimacy. In response Maudud persecuted her and Khizr's family until she was eventually 'persuaded' to hand over the relics. As for Khizr, the Popalzai tribe regarded him as a *shahid*, or martyr, and referred to him as Khwaja Khizr. On occasions of great importance, the Popalzais even made offerings and prayers in his name.

Maudud's reign as *mir-i Afghaniha* was both arbitrary and repressive. One story related how one of Maudud Khan's nephews had been betrothed to an aristocratic 'Abdali woman, but when the time came for the marriage to be formalized the woman's father told Maudud's servants that he had changed his mind as he had no wish to have his daughter marry into a family of such low social status. An angry Maudud Khan sent his retainers to attack the Khan's camp and kidnap the girl, who was taken to Shahr-i Safa, where the marriage rites were performed without any member of her family being present.

The same year that Saddu Khan died the Mughal emperor, Jahangir, also passed away, followed two years later by Shah 'Abbas I. Shah 'Abbas had been so paranoid about assassination that he had had his sons blinded, so disqualifying them from the succession. A series of bloody purges followed and eventually Shah Safi I, a grandson of Shah 'Abbas, seized the throne. Shah Safi then recalled 'Ali Mardan Khan, the Kurdish governor of Kandahar, but 'Ali Mardan, realizing that this summons was tantamount to a death sentence, refused to obey the order and opened negotiations with the Mughal governor of Kabul. In 1638 'Ali Mardan surrendered the city to the Mughals and its garrison held out despite several attempts by the Persian governor of Herat to reassert Safavid authority over the region. Five years later, when the Mughal governor of Kabul rebelled, Sultan Maudud Khan marched out with the Mughal garrison in Kandahar to bring the rebel to heel, only to be killed while storming the walls of the Bala Hisar.

'Ali Mardan Khan later became the Mughal governor of Kabul and afterwards *wazir* of the Punjab. He later married a Portuguese Catholic woman, Maria de Ataides, who appears to have set aside a building in Kabul's Bala Hisar as a church, which was first used by the Jesuit missionaries attached to the Mughal court and subsequently inherited by Kabul's Armenian community. During 'Ali Mardan's era as governor of the Punjab he commissioned many major public works in Kabul and Nangahar, including the gardens at Nimla on the old Kabul–Jalalabad road and Kabul's famous Chahar Chatta bazaar.

Following Sultan Maudud Khan's unexpected death, a hastily convened *jirga* appointed Khudakka Khan, or Khudadad Khan, Khizr's eldest son, as *mir-i Afghaniha*, only for the Mughal governor of Kandahar to reject his candidacy, probably because he was deemed to be pro-Safavid. Instead the governor appointed Maudud Khan's eldest son, Shah Husain Khan. The 'Abdalis, unhappy about this interference in their internal affairs, informed the governor that: 'if any one of us sought the help of the ruler for the settlement of our mutual disputes, he no longer remained a true Afghan and was considered to be . . . an outcast'.[33] Despite this veiled threat of rebellion, the governor refused to listen and ordered Khudakka Khan to quit Shahr-i Safa. When he refused, the governor, supported by Shah Husain Khan, stormed the Saddozai stronghold and Khudakka Khan fled to Persia.

Kabul's former royal citadel, the Bala Hisar citadel, looking westwards over the Hashmat Khan lake.

Despite this success, Mughal control over Kandahar was weak and was further undermined by Shah Jahan's decision to go to war with Nazr Muhammad Khan, the Tuqay-Timurid Khan of Balkh. Though the invasion initially went well and Nazr Muhammad Khan was defeated, the Mughal lines of communication were overextended and the population refused to feed the army or pay taxes. In October 1647, faced with the prospect of a second winter of hardship, the Mughals handed Balkh back to Nazr Muhammad Khan and abandoned the province for good.

Nazr Muhammad had fled to Persia, where Shah 'Abbas II agreed to provide military support so he could regain control of Balkh. When he set out to reclaim his kingdom, he was accompanied by a substantial Persian army. While Nazr Muhammad Khan and the main army set out for Maimana, another column, supported by Khudakka Khan Saddozai, headed south and besieged Kandahar. The city finally fell in February 1649 and despite three subsequent attempts by the Mughals to regain control of the city, Kandahar and Herat remained under Safavid sovereignty. As for Shah Husain Saddozai, he made his home in Multan, 'the doorway to the kingdom of Kandahar,'[34] where he was appointed as *nawab* of the province and founded a dynasty that ruled the area until 1818. Multan thus became a haven for Saddozais fleeing the increasingly bloody power struggle between rival clan members in Herat and Kandahar. Among the prominent Saddozais born in Multan was Ahmad Shah Durrani.

The Safavids reinstated Khudakka Khan as *mir-i Afghaniha* and in a series of campaigns he extended his authority over the Zhob and Arghasan valleys, the latter being the homeland of a non-Muslim, *kafir* tribe. He also resolved a long-standing boundary dispute between the 'Abdalis and Tokhi Ghilzais of Qalat-i Ghilzai. The Band-i Sultan Khudakka and the adjacent mosque of Masjid-i Khudakka in the Arghasan valley are both said to have been commissioned by him. Sultan Khudakka Khan, though, also had a more sinister side to his nature. During the Zhob campaign he is reported to have 'wantonly and cruelly' put to death three young boys and a man who he found cowering in a hollow in fear of their lives',[35] an action that haunted him for the rest of his life. When subsequently he had a dream of a luminous figure who told him his only hope of peace of mind was to abdicate, in favour of his brother, Sher Muhammad Khan. Khudakka Khan died a few months later, around 1665, most likely from poison.

Sher Muhammad Khan's right to succession, however, was disputed by his eldest son, Sultan Qalandar, who tried to throw off the Persian yoke only to be killed a few months later during the assault on Kandahar's citadel. His uncle Sher Muhammad Khan probably died in the same battle, doubtless fighting on the Persian side, since nothing more is heard of him. Sultan Qalandar's younger half-brother, 'Inayat Khan, became the new *mir-i Afghaniha* only for the succession to be challenged by Sarmast Khan, Khudakka's youngest brother, who claimed he was the rightful heir because he was the oldest living male descendant of Saddu Khan.[36] The dispute quickly turned into open warfare that ended in the death of Sarmast Khan and the flight of his family to Multan, but the feud between the Khudakka Khel and Sarmast Khel continued and was passed on down through the generations.

'Inayat Khan's other rival was his ambitious younger brother, Hayat Khan, who sought a suitable occasion to dispose of his sibling. The opportunity eventually presented itself during a hunting expedition, when 'Inayat Khan's horse stumbled, throwing and badly injuring its rider. Hayat Khan, seizing the opportunity, ordered an Uzbek *ghulam* to kill 'Inayat Khan and he was dispatched with a single stroke of a sword. 'Inayat Khan's body was buried where it fell, but Hayat Khan's attempt to pass off his brother's death as a hunting accident failed miserably. Before the hunting party returned to Safa, news of the murder had reached the ears of their mother, Murad Bibi, a formidable woman who was accustomed to fight in battle alongside her husband. Beset with grief, she vowed to drink the blood of her son's murderer and to 'do unto this son of mine as he has done unto his brother'.[37] Clan heads pleaded with her not to demand the right of *badal*, for Hayat Khan was the last surviving male member of Sultan Khudakka Khan's line and, were he to die, the headship of the 'Abdalis, with all its power, privileges and wealth, would pass to the rival Sarmast Khel. Murad Bibi, though, was implacable and even threatened to appoint one of Khudakka's daughters as *mir-i Afghaniha*.

A woman as head of the tribe was inconceivable and in the end the heads of the clans were forced to desperate measures, appearing before Murad Bibi with their turbans around their necks like nooses, signifying their willingness to sacrifice their own lives instead of that of Hayat Khan. Confronted with this act of ritualized abasement, Murad Bibi agreed not to kill Hayat Khan on condition that he would never show his face in her presence again on pain of death, and that the actual murderer of 'Inayat Khan be handed over so she could fulfil her oath. Hayat Khan agreed to her terms and the unfortunate Uzbek *ghulam* was dragged before Murad Bibi, who slit his throat, caught the blood in a cup and drank it with every appearance of relish. His body was then thrown over the fort walls and left to be eaten by dogs. Thus Hayat Khan, having escaped with his life, became *mir-i Afghaniha* and 'honour' was satisfied on all sides.

Sultan Hayat Khan then proceeded to antagonize the Safavid governor of Kandahar by raiding and pillaging the trade *qafila*s. The final breach came when Hayat Khan attended a feast hosted by the governor, during which the guests became intoxicated. Sultan Hayat Khan and the governor began to argue over the respective merits of Afghan and Persian women and in the end they entered into a pact in which seven Saddozai women would be given in marriage to seven Persian men. The next morning, when Hayat Khan had sobered up, he called an urgent council meeting to find a way to avoid fulfilling this pledge without loss of face, for no Saddozai woman was permitted to marry outside of the clan, let alone a heretical Shi'a. A message was sent to the governor abrogating the agreement on the grounds that, as it was Afghan custom for husbands to live with their father-in-law, it was clearly impossible for any Persian man to live among the 'Abdalis. The governor responded by calling Hayat Khan's bluff and a few days later seven Persian youths arrived at Safa to claim their brides, declaring their willingness to live among the Saddozais.

Despite further crisis meetings no one could find a way out of the dilemma until Sultan Hayat Khan declared the only way was to sacrifice four of the Persian men in the name of the Chahar Yar, or Four Friends; that is, the four Caliphs who, in Sunni tradition, are regarded as the legitimate leaders of the Muslim community following the death of Muhammad. Their claim, however, is rejected by Shi'as who believe that Muhammad's cousin and son-in-law, 'Ali b. Abi Talib and his descendants, were the rightful heirs. Who came up with this grotesque solution is not stated, but given Murad Bibi's penchant for bloodthirstiness it was probably her idea. Four of the Persians duly had their throats slit and the three survivors set free and returned to Kandahar where they recounted the horrific events they had witnessed.[38] The Persian governor responded by attacking Qal'a-yi Safa but the Saddozais, commanded by Murad Bibi, defeated them with heavy loss of life. During the attack, Murad Bibi is said to have killed the Persian general with her own hands.

The increasing state of lawlessness that prevailed in the Kandahar and Helmand regions eventually led to another Persian attempt to restore some semblance of order in eastern Khurasan. In 1680 a large Safavid army arrived in Herat. One column was dispatched against the 'Abdali stronghold of Obeh, while a second division was sent to reinforce Kandahar and subsequently took Qal'a-yi Safa by storm. Sultan Hayat Khan fled to the upper reaches of the Hari Rud where he tried to prevent the Safavids taking control of Obeh, only for the lightly armed 'Abdalis to be decimated by the Persian artillery. In the aftermath of this victory the Persian general conducted a ruthless search-and-kill operation. Sultan Hayat Khan, who had been badly wounded in the battle, eventually made his way to Multan where he later married a Hindu *nautch* girl and lived off the income of a *jagir* conferred on him by the Mughal emperor. He finally died in 1729, at the age of 81 years old. What fate his mother, Murad Bibi, suffered is not recorded but the events of Hayat Khan's blood-soaked reign passed into Saddozai mythology, with members of the rival Sarmast Khel family relishing relating stories of Hayat Khan's depravity, including the scurrilous story that he allowed his son or grandson be raped by the Persian governor of Herat.[39]

Following the devastating defeat at Obeh and the loss of Safa, the 'Abdalis decided they had had enough of Sultan Hayat Khan and the Khudakka Khan lineage and appointed Ja'far Khan, the eldest surviving son of Sarmast Khan, as *mir-i Afghaniha*. Sultan Ja'far Khan sued for peace with Persia and a treaty was agreed, but Safa remained in Persian hands while Sultan Ja'far probably lived in Herat under close surveillance. However, the peace treaty did result in more than a decade of relative peace for the 'Abdali tribes, which allowed them to recover from the disasters of Sultan Hayat Khan's reign.

When Sultan Ja'far died in 1695 he was succeeded by his younger brother, Daulat Khan, who broke the peace treaty by resuming raids on *qafila*s in Girishk and Farah. After defeating two Persian forces sent against him, Sultan Daulat Khan eventually regained possession of Safa. Meanwhile in Multan, Hayat Khan's eldest son, 'Abd Allah Khan, who had married a daughter of Daulat Khan in an attempt to end the feud between the two families, quarrelled violently with his father and set out for Safa to join forces with Sultan Daulat Khan, taking with him Muhammad Zaman Khan, Daulat Khan's son.

The Hotak Ghilzai dynasty of Kandahar

Meanwhile the new Safavid monarch, Sultan Husain, made another attempt to suppress the lawless tribes in the Helmand and Kandahar region and in 1704 he appointed Gurgin Khan, a Georgian prince, as governor of Kandahar. Gurgin, whose regnal name was Giorgi, was the nominal ruler of Kartli in Georgia, but his principality had been subjugated by the Safavids and Gurgin and his Georgian *ghulams* had been forced to convert to Shi'a Islam, though in secret they continued to practise their Christian faith. Giorgi even covertly corresponded with Pope Innocent XII and after his death a crucifix and a Psalter were found on his body.

Giorgi had earned a fearsome reputation as *beglar begi* of Kirman, restoring order in this turbulent province by brute force. His mandate as military governor of Kandahar was similar: put down the raids by the Afghans and Baluch by all possible means. The Baluch rebellion was quickly snuffed out but the main threat to Giorgi's power came from the 'Abdalis and the Hotak Ghilzais. In an attempt to bring them to heel, Giorgi adopted a policy of divide and rule. He flattered Sultan Daulat Khan Saddozai by sending him valuable presents and assuring him of Persia's undying friendship, but at the same time he offered the headship of the 'Abdalis to two of his rivals, 'Izzat and Atal, who had a blood feud with the family of Daulat Khan. Giorgi then made the same offer to Hajji Amir Khan, better known as Mir Wa'is, a young but influential leader of the Hotak Ghilzais, in return for his support against the 'Abdalis.

'Izzat and Atal eventually lured Sultan Daulat Khan and his youngest son, Nazar, out of Shahr-i Safa and sent them in chains to Giorgi, who condemned them to death and handed them back to 'Izzat and Atal, who put them to a slow and excruciating death. Next Giorgi appointed Daulat Khan's eldest son, Rustam Khan, as *mir-i Afghaniha*, retaining his younger brother Muhammad Zaman Khan as a hostage for his good behaviour. The appointment was not well received by Malik 'Izzat and Malik Atal, for Giorgi had offered them the headship of the tribe. They therefore conspired with Mir Wa'is Hotaki and eventually convinced Giorgi that Rustam Khan

Saddozai was planning to rebel. He was arrested, handed over to Malik Atal and put to a long and painful death. Giorgi next appointed Malik Atal as *mir-i Afghaniha*, but only on condition he persuade the 'Abdalis to abandon Safa and camp in the open plains around Kandahar. Atal fell into the trap. Once the 'Abdalis had moved out of their fortress, Giorgi Khan, supported by Mir Wa'is Hotaki, attacked them and put them to the sword. Somehow 'Abd Allah Khan and Muhammad Zaman Khan managed to escape the bloodshed and fled back to Multan.

Having broken the back of 'Abdali resistance, Giorgi Khan now tried to do the same to the Hotak Ghilzais, only to find that Mir Wa'is was more than a match for him when it came to cunning and treachery. Giorgi arrested Mir Wa'is claiming he was planning to rebel and sent him in chains to the Safavid capital of Isfahan, fully expecting the Shah would confirm the death sentence and have Mir Wa'is executed. Mir Wa'is, though, played on the Shah's suspicions of Giorgi Khan's loyalties and eventually convinced him that it was the governor of Kandahar who was planning to rebel. Mir Wa'is then petitioned for permission to undertake the Hajj and was given royal leave to depart. It is said that when Mir Wa'is reached Mecca he prayed before the Ka'aba for deliverance from Persian oppression. That night he awoke to find his sword unsheathed, an omen that he interpreted as divine sanction for a rebellion. He then sought, and obtained, a *fatwa*, or legal ruling, which legitimized a revolt against the Safavids.

When Mir Wa'is returned to Kandahar in 1707 the Shah, convinced about his loyalty, appointed him *kalantar* of the Afghan tribes, a position traditionally held by the Saddozais. Giorgi Khan could do nothing about the decision, for to have refused to recognize the royal decree would have merely confirmed the Shah's suspicions that he planned to rebel. Mir Wa'is then craftily set out to reassure Giorgi by professing loyalty to Persia, yet at the same time rearming his Ghilzais and trying to persuade local Baluch *amir*s to join in a rebellion. He even wrote to Sultan Hayat Khan offering to share power with him in return for 'Abdali support. In response Sultan 'Abd Allah Khan went to Safa to try and raise the Saddozais and other tribes of the area.

Giorgi Khan then made matters worse by demanding Mir Wa'is' eldest daughter in marriage. This was deeply insulting to Mir Wa'is, for Giorgi was a foreigner and at heart still a Christian. Mir Wa'is repaid the insult by sending him a slave girl instead, as an indirect reminder of Giorgi's own subservient position as a *ghulam* of the Safavids. The final straw came in the spring of 1709 when the Kakars and 'Abdalis refused to pay the annual tribute and, supported by the Baluch, began to plunder the trade caravans.

TABLE 5: The Hotaki Dynasty of Kandahar and Persia, 1709–38			
Ruler	Relationship	Reign(s)	Regions/city-states governed
Mir Wa'is		1709–15	Kandahar
'Abd al-'Aziz	brother of Mir Wa'is	1715	Kandahar
Shah Mahmud	son of Mir Wa'is	1715–25	Kandahar 1722, takes Isfahan and rules as Shah of Persia
Ashraf	son of 'Abd al-'Aziz	1725–9	Isfahan
Shah Husain	son of Mir Wa'is	1725–38	Kandahar

Giorgi Khan and 1,000 of his Georgian *ghulam*s marched up the Ghazni road to bring the 'Abdalis to heel, but when he reached Deh Shaikh he was confronted with a well-entrenched force of several thousand 'Abdalis and Kakars. Giorgi tried to storm the emplacements and sent a request to Mir Wa'is to provide 3,000 Ghilzais to assist in the assault, but Mir Wa'is' levies never arrived. After fighting hard all day the exhausted Georgians failed to take the Afghan positions and withdrew to their camp to lick their wounds. Mir Wa'is then sent a message to the 'Abdalis urging them to join him in an attack on the Georgian camp, catching them off guard while they were eating their evening meal. Despite fighting bravely, the Georgians were slaughtered to the last man: among the slain was Giorgi Khan.

Giorgi Khan left an indelible mark on Afghan national consciousness and he has been depicted as a brutal and barbaric mercenary. 'Umar Khel Khan's description of him as 'a beast in the shape of a human being . . . sensual, avaricious, vindictive, cruel' is typical of the kind of invective levelled against him.[40] Afghans also like punning on the Persian version of his name, Gurjin, calling him Gurgin Khan, 'wolf-like' or 'poxy, mangy, scabby', and on his place of birth, Katli, which in its Persian form, *qatli*, can also be read as 'murderer' or 'slaughterer'. In fact Giorgi Khan was no worse than other governors and rulers of the era. The Saddozai sultans were equally repressive and Mir Wa'is and the 'Abdalis had no compunction massacring the Georgians in cold blood.

After disposing of Giorgi Khan, the combined rebel forces besieged the Qizilbash regiments who had been left to guard Kandahar. Mir Wa'is, who had no intention of sharing power with the 'Abdalis, persuaded Sultan 'Abd Allah Khan to go to Farah to confront a Persian relief force that had been sent from Herat. Once Sultan 'Abd Allah Khan was out of the way, Mir Wa'is persuaded the Qizilbash to surrender, took possession of Kandahar and expelled the 'Abdalis from the town. Mir Wa'is then legit-imized his rebellion by producing the *fatwa* he had acquired in Mecca and declared independence from Persia. For the next three decades Kandahar was ruled by the Hotaki dynasty. Sultan 'Abd Allah Khan, having defeated the Persians, returned to Kandahar only to find its gates shut against him. Lacking the military capability to take the city by storm, he returned to Safa.

The loss of Kandahar was a serious blow to the Safavids and a few months later a large Persian army commanded by Giorgi Khan's nephew, Kai Khusrau, was sent to reassert Persian authority. When the force reached Herat, Sultan 'Abd Allah Khan Saddozai pledged 'Abdali support for the campaign against Kandahar. This met with some initial success by defeating Mir Wa'is in the Helmand region, however Mir Wa'is adopted a scorched earth policy and the Persian army, unable to find sufficient food or fodder and harassed by Baluch tribesmen, was forced to retreat. As the dispirited army marched back up the road to Herat, Ghilzai and Baluch cavalry attacked and the army broke and fled. In the ensuing massacre Kai Khusrau and his brother Yese Khan, Giorgi Khan's nephews, were slain, along with Basil, a Carmelite friar who was one of three Catholic priests that had accompanied the army.

The Persian defeat secured Mir Wa'is' control over the region. When he died in 1715 he was succeeded by his brother, Mir 'Abd al-'Aziz, or 'Abd Allah. However, he was assassinated at the instigation of Mir Wa'is' son, Shah Mahmud, who then overran southeastern Persia a year after his father's death. On 8 March 1722, at the Battle of Gulnabad, Shah Mahmud defeated a much larger Persian army and laid siege to Isfahan itself. After six months the people of Isfahan were reduced to eating rats and dogs and Shah Husain was forced to go in person to Shah Mahmud's camp to surrender the city and tender his submission. Declaring that God had removed the kingdom from him as punishment for his sins, the Shah removed the royal *jigha*, the jewelled aigrette of feathers that was the Safavid equivalent of a crown, and placed it on Shah Mahmud's turban.[41] Shah Husain was allowed to remain as token head of the Persian kingdom but he was confined to the royal palace. A few years later Shah Mahmud had the Shah and most of his family put to death, but one of his sons, Shah Tahmasp, survived and eventually reached Mashhad.

Shah Mahmud Hotaki reigned for three years in Isfahan, during which time his men systematically pillaged the Persian capital and other regions under his rule and imposed swingeing taxes. One particular target of his avarice was the wealthy Armenian community of New Julfa, the Christian *mahala* of Isfahan that had been established in 1606 by Shah 'Abbas I to encourage trade with India and Europe in silk and silver. For nearly two centuries this mercantile community had been the backbone of the Safavid empire's financial liquidity and its merchants had become very wealthy indeed.

During the siege of Isfahan, Shah Mahmud had demanded 120,000 *tomans* as a ransom to prevent a general massacre of the Armenians and their women and children being sold into slavery. This was a vast sum of money, since the annual tax paid by the Armenians of New Julfa to the Safavid treasury was only 800 *tomans*. The Armenian *kalantar* of New Julfa, who was responsible for collecting taxes, declared it was impossible to find such a sum and instead gave Shah Mahmud a promissory note for 70,000 *tomans*. After the surrender of the city the cash was still not forthcoming, so Mahmud sent his men into New Julfa to seize goods and chattels equivalent to this amount. An Armenian eyewitness of these events records how the bailiffs went from house to house, removing anything of value.[42] New Julfa was thus stripped of most of its wealth and there was an exodus of Armenians to Europe, India and Russia. The overland trade with India also collapsed and even Kandahar's commercial prosperity was undermined.

Mahmud's demands also included the surrender of sixty Armenian virgins and several youths as a ransom for the lives of the rest of the community. The girls and boys were torn from their parents and handed over, but some Afghan chiefs, disgusted by Shah Mahmud's actions, returned them to their families untouched. Even so, at least twelve Armenian women ended up in the harems of Hotaki chiefs. When Shah Mahmud's men had finally ended their pillage of the *mahala*, he turned it into a ghetto by constructing a wall of exclusion around New Julfa.

Shah Mahmud's three-year reign in Isfahan was marked by many more acts of pillage and bloodshed as the Hotaki king's mental and physical health declined, exacerbated by forty days spent in solitary confinement in a Sufi cell, or *chehela khana*. The object of this Sufi exercise is to control the power of *jinn*, but in Shah Mahmud's case it was the *jinn* that ended up controlling him. The ordeal also left Mahmud with a virulent parasitic disease akin to scabies, and in an attempt to relieve the unbearable itching he lacerated his skin with sharpened fingernails. In 1725 Shah Mahmud was finally put out of his misery by an assassin hired by his cousin, Ashraf, who seized control of the western part of the Hotaki empire. In Kandahar, Mir Wa'is' heirs appointed Shah Mahmud's brother, Husain Khan, as ruler, and so the brief Ghilzai empire was divided into two rival factions.

Persian power, meanwhile, began to reassert itself under Nadir Quli Beg, a Turkman general of the Afshar tribe. In 1726, with the support of

Shah Tahmasp and the Qajar tribe, Nadir Quli took Mashhad and three years later defeated the 'Abdalis near Herat. He then attacked Ashraf Khan Hotak in Isfahan and forced him to flee to Kandahar, where he was hunted down and killed by Mir Husain Shah in revenge for the murder of his father. In December 1729 Nadir Quli entered Isfahan, placed Shah Tahmasp on the throne and was formally appointed governor of Khurasan. Shah Tahmasp even gave Nadir Quli one of his sisters in marriage.

The Saddozai Sultanate of Herat

After Mir Wa'is tricked him out of a share of the spoils of Kandahar, 'Abd Allah Khan Saddozai set his sights on establishing a kingdom in Herat, but his attempt to raise a revolt among the 'Abdalis of the Hari Rud was discovered and he was thrown into prison by the Persian governor of Herat, together with his son, 'Asad Allah Khan. Shortly afterwards, however, the Qizilbash garrison mutinied, allowing the two men to escape and flee to Obeh. 'Asad Allah Khan then overran the Hari Rud valley and occupied Maruchak on the Murghab. In the summer of 1717 he finally took Herat and struck coins in the name of Sultan Hayat Khan, since he was the most senior member of the Khudakka clan still alive. However, as Hayat Khan was by this time a very old man, he nominated 'Abd Allah Khan to be head of the Saddozai Sultanate of Herat.[43]

TABLE 6: The Saddozai Dynasty of Herat, 1717–32		
Sultan	Saddozai lineage	Reign(s)
'Abd Allah Khan	Khudakka Khel	1717–21
Muhammad Zaman Khan	Sarmast Khel	1721
Shah Qasim Khan	Zafran Khel	1721–2
Muqarrab Khan	Khudakka Khel	1722
Shah Muhammad Khan	Khudakka Khel	1722–4
Zu'l-fiqar Khan (Farah)	Sarmast Khel	1725–30
Allah Yar Khan (Maruchak)	Khudakka Khel	1725–6
Tribal elders (Herat)	various	1725–6
Allah Yar Khan, 1st reign	Khudakka Khel	1726–30
Allah Yar Khan (Maruchak)	Khudakka Khel	1730–31
Zu'l-fiqar Khan (Herat & Farah)	Sarmast Khel	1730–31
Allah Yar Khan, 2nd reign	Khudakka Khel	1731–2

Two years later a Persian army of around 35,000 men, including an artillery train commanded by European officers, set out to reclaim Herat. The two sides met at Kafir Qalʻa, the modern frontier post of Islam Qalʻa. The Persians tried to overawe the Afghans by an artillery barrage, but 'Asad Allah Khan had anticipated this move and had placed his men behind the trees of nearby orchards and in irrigation ditches. When the Persian infantry advanced they were met with withering flanking fire. After several hours of bitter fighting, a Persian gunner accidentally set fire to the powder magazine and the artillery, blinded by smoke, began to fire on their own infantry. Seeing the Persian lines in disarray, 'Asad Allah Khan ordered his cavalry to charge and the Persians turned and fled. When their general saw that the battle was lost, he mounted a barrel of gunpowder and blew himself up.

Following this victory, 'Asad Allah Khan urged his father to march on Mashhad but instead Sultan 'Abd Allah Khan ordered him to attack Kandahar, punish the Hotaks for their treachery and reclaim Safa and Arghasan. 'Asad Allah objected and the dispute between father and son became so heated that Sultan 'Abd Allah Khan asked a local dervish to mediate, only for him to declare in favour of the Kandahar campaign. In Multan, 'Abd Allah Khan's father, Hayat Khan, also lent his support to the Safa campaign, sending his son a poem in which he declared: 'in the place where there was the smell of bad blood (or humiliation) is weakness'.[44]

In an attempt to stave off the attack by 'Asad Allah Khan, Shah Mahmud Hotaki, who was also threatened by a Persian army, sent ambassadors to Herat and proposed an Afghan alliance against Persia and offered to restore Safa and Arghasan. Sultan 'Abd Allah Khan, though, demanded Shah Mahmud come in person to Herat and sue for pardon. The Hotaki ruler, however, was not prepared to undergo this humiliation and recalled his ambassadors. 'Asad Allah Khan then set out for the Helmand and in August 1720 the 'Abdali and Ghilzai armies clashed at Dilaram. The outcome of the battle remained in the balance for many hours until 'Asad Allah was shot in the back by a man who was settling an old score with Sultan 'Abd Allah Khan's family. 'Abd Allah Khan's brother-in-law, Muhammad Zaman Khan, the only surviving son of Daulat Khan, took charge of the army and retreated to Farah. The following day 'Asad Allah's body was taken to Herat and buried in the Bagh-i Rauza.

Sultan 'Abd Allah Khan was deeply affected by his son's death and for nearly a year he plunged into profound depression and neglected affairs of state. It was only in early 1721, when another Persian army was sent to take Herat, that 'Abd Allah Khan shook off his grief, rallied his troops

The old city of Herat from the citadel, Qal'a-yi Ikhtiyar al-Din.

and defeated the invaders. This time he did besiege Mashhad, only for the Saddozais to prove once again to be their own worst enemy. 'Abd Allah Khan had left Muhammad Zaman Khan, a Sarmast Khel Saddozai, and Khalu Khan Alakozai, the father-in-law of both 'Abd Allah Khan and Muhammad Zaman Khan, to oversee the affairs of Herat while he was away campaigning. The two men seized their opportunity and in May 1721 they took control of Herat, forcing Sultan 'Abd Allah Khan to return post-haste. On his approach, the guards opened the city gates and Zaman Khan and Khalu Khan took refuge in the citadel of Qal'a-yi Ikhtiyar al-Din. 'Abd Allah Khan ordered his men to set fire to the citadel gates and sent in a storming party, whereupon Muhammad Zaman, Khalu Khan and other rebel leaders surrendered and sued for mercy. Sultan 'Abd Allah Khan, however, refused to grant them clemency. Khalu Khan was beheaded on the spot and his head displayed on the citadel walls, and several other leading 'Abdali chiefs were sentenced to be crushed to death beneath millstones. Two days later Muhammad Zaman Khan, too, was put to death.

Muhammad Zaman's wife, Zarghuna, who was also Khalu Khan's daughter, was pregnant at the time. Fearing for her life and that of her unborn child, she sought *nanawatai*, or sanctuary, by sending her veil to Haji Isma'il Khan, a Ghilzai *malik*. Haji Isma'il was obligated under the Afghan code of honour to protect her and eventually smuggled Zarghuna out of Herat. She made her way to Multan and a few months later she gave birth to a son, who was named Ahmad Shah.

Meanwhile anarchy prevailed in Herat. Qasim Khan, a Zafran Khel Saddozai who had recently arrived from Multan, ingratiated himself with Sultan 'Abd Allah Khan and was appointed as his chief confidential adviser. Behind the sultan's back, however, Qasim Khan plotted to seize control of Herat. Sultan 'Abd Allah Khan was accustomed to making weekly pilgrimages to his son's grave. In October 1721 Qasim Khan engineered a 'chance' encounter with 'Abd Allah Khan in the garden, lured him into a secluded corner on the pretence of passing on confidential information, and struck him on the back of the neck with his sword, killing him instantly.

Qasim Khan then declared himself sultan of Herat with the title of Shah Qasim, but most of the heads of the 'Abdali clans refused to swear the oath of loyalty. Qasim Shah's response was a brief but bloody reign of terror. Anyone who refused to pledge allegiance was put to death on the Horse of Fortune, a crude guillotine consisting of a sloping, steel blade several metres long contained within a narrow frame. The condemned man was placed at the top of this slide with heavy stones attached to his feet and forced to slide down the 'horse'. By the time he reached the end the victim had been sliced in two from the groin upwards.

When news of Sultan 'Abd Allah Khan's murder reached Multan, Sultan Hayat Khan, who had now lost a son and a grandson to assassins, declared his intention of going to Herat to avenge their deaths, but one of his sons, Muqarrab Khan, pledged to act in his father's place and left with Hayat Khan's blessing. Unfortunately, Muqarrab Khan made the mistake of going via Kandahar, where he was imprisoned by Shah Mahmud Hotaki. Muqarrab Khan, though, appealed to Mahmud's sense of honour, declaring that the purpose of his journey was the fulfilment of *badal*. Mahmud, realizing he could only profit from the Saddozai feud, let him continue on his way. When Muqarrab arrived in Herat, most of Qasim's henchmen deserted him and he was put to death, but his execution failed to end the feud between rival members of the Saddozai clan.

Shortly after Muqarrab Khan reached Herat, Shah Muhammad Khan, a son of Sultan 'Abd Allah Khan, arrived from Multan and demanded that his uncle stand aside. The dispute eventually became so heated that in the summer of 1722 the 'Abdali *khan*s called a *jirga*, which confirmed Shah Muhammad Khan as sultan, and Muqarrab Khan returned to Multan. Shah Muhammad Khan then proceeded to alienate the very leaders who had put him in power by demanding he be invested with all the pomp and ceremony of a Safavid monarch. He was crowned with a royal *jigha* and senior members of the 'Abdali aristocracy were required to abase themselves when admitted to his presence. Shah Muhammad also insisted that his name, and not that of his grandfather, Hayat Khan, appear on the new coinage and be recited in the *khutba*.[45]

Once confirmed as Herat's new ruler, Sultan Shah Muhammad Khan marched out to attack Mashhad, but while he was away Qasim Khan's father, Sa'id Khan, organized a conspiracy to depose him. Shah Muhammad broke off the siege of Mashhad and on his return to Herat executed around a hundred leading 'Abdalis on suspicion of involvement in the plot. Two years later Zu'l-fiqar Khan, the eldest surviving son of Muhammad Zaman Khan who was governor of Farah, marched against Herat, but again the 'Abdali elders intervened and persuaded both men to step aside in favour of 'Abd Allah Khan's younger son, Allah Yar Khan. Sultan Shah Muhammad Khan, forced to abdicate, left for Multan while Zu'l-fiqar Khan returned to Farah.

When Allah Yar Khan arrived in Herat from Multan he was immediately entangled in a web of intrigue. Allah Yar Khan was a Khudakka Khel Saddozai, so Zu'l-fiqar Khan in Farah, who was from the rival Sarmast Khel lineage, refused to accept his appointment and was supported by 'Abd al-Ghani Khan, son of Khalu Khan Alakozai. For the next six months Herat became a battleground with rival factions fighting in the streets and plundering villages and trade caravans. Eventually the 'Abdali elders intervened once more and divided the sultanate between the two rivals: Zu'l-fiqar Khan retained Farah, while Allah Yar Khan was sent packing to Maruchak. What evidence there is suggests Herat was governed by a council of tribal elders.

This arrangement lasted less than a year. At the end of 1726 General Nadir Quli Khan, having radically transformed the Persian army into a professional force, took Mashhad and threatened to march on Herat. The 'Abdali leaders responded by recalling Allah Yar Khan and put him in charge of the city's defences. In October 1727 Nadir Quli overran the frontier post of Sangan, massacring its defenders and defeating a relief column, only to return to Mashhad in order to deal with a challenge to his power from Fath 'Ali Khan Qajar and Shah Tahmasp. Nadir Quli quickly put down the revolt, reducing Shah Tahmasp to a mere puppet in the process, and in May 1729 set out again to attack Herat.

In another encounter at Kafir Qal'a, during which Nadir Quli personally led a counter-charge against the 'Abdali cavalry, the Afghans were defeated. Following two further defeats, Allah Yar Khan sued for peace only to change his mind when he heard that Zu'l-fiqar Khan was marching north with a combined force of 'Abdalis and Ghilzais. The two men, though, failed to coordinate their attack and Nadir Quli picked off each force separately. Zu'l-fiqar Khan fled back to Farah while the 'Abdali *maliks* of Herat went to the Persian camp and tendered their submission. Nadir Quli presented them with robes of honour and a treaty was signed, under the terms of which Allah Yar Khan remained ruler of Herat under Persian sovereignty and pledged not to provide military assistance to the Hotaki rulers of Kandahar.[46] Much to their distaste the 'Abdali clans were also required to provide levies for the Persian army, yet surprisingly Nadir Quli Khan did not install a Persian garrison. It was a decision he soon regretted.

Shah Husain Hotaki, worried about the fall of Herat and the renewal of the Saddozai-Persian alliance, sent envoys to Herat to persuade Sultan Allah Yar Khan to revoke the treaty, proposing instead an 'Abdali-Ghilzai alliance against Nadir Quli Khan. Allah Yar Khan refused on the grounds that he could not break a treaty that he had sealed by an oath on the Qur'an. However, he had little power, and since the 'Abdali tribal leaders favoured the anti-Persian alliance, they deposed Allah Yar Khan and appointed Zu'l-fiqar Khan in his place – only for Allah Yar Khan to refuse to step down. For the next few weeks Herat was again turned into a battleground until finally Allah Yar Khan fled back to Maruchak. In April 1730 Zu'l-fikar Khan entered Herat accompanied by his nine-year-old half-brother, Ahmad Shah, and his mother, Zarguna, who had travelled from Multan to join the victory celebrations.

Zu'l-fikar Khan immediately tore up the Persian treaty and, taking advantage of Nadir Quli's absence campaigning against the Ottomans, besieged Mashhad, whereupon Allah Yar Khan joined the Persian defence of the city. When Nadir Quli heard of the siege he ordered the governor of Mashhad not to go on the offensive but to drag out the siege as long as possible so he could march to his relief. The 'Abdalis tried to starve the city into submission and laid waste all the countryside around Mashhad, but in the end it was the besiegers who ran out of food and fodder and they were forced to lift the siege.

Nadir Quli reached Mashhad in November 1730 and spent the winter preparing for a final showdown with Herat. Allah Yar Khan was shown great favour for his support and a treaty was signed restoring him to the governorship of Herat, but this time a Persian garrison was to reside in Herat's citadel. In April of the following year the Persian army marched on Herat, laying waste to the countryside as they went and driving off thousands of sheep and goats, the backbone of the 'Abdali tribe's wealth. While Herat was placed under siege, a column was dispatched to the Helmand to occupy Farah and a second force marched across the Murghab into Uzbek-held Maimana.

As the hot summer months arrived, Zu'l-fikar Khan became increasingly desperate and on 22 July 1731 he made a final attempt to break the siege, only for his men to be cut to pieces. In the flight back to the city, many more were drowned trying to cross the Hari Rud, which was in spate. Even Zu'l-fikar Khan was lucky to escape with his life. Realizing the cause was hopeless, Saidal Khan's Ghilzais, who had come to Herat along with Zu'l-fikar Khan, slipped through the Persian lines during the night along the bed of a dry irrigation canal. A few days later Zu'l-fikar Khan surrendered the city in return for a pledge of safe passage to Farah. Sultan Allah Yar Khan was reinstated but once more Nadir Khan did not insist on installing a Persian garrison.

Allah Yar Khan's reinstatement was not welcomed by many tribal leaders, while the relationship between Nadir Quli and Allah Yar Khan broke down following a misunderstanding. Nadir Quli, hearing that a large relief army was marching to Herat from Farah, sent a sizeable force to the Helmand only to find he had been sent on a wild goose chase. An angry Nadir accused Allah Yar Khan of fabricating the report in order to draw the Persian army away from Herat so that he could rebel. Sultan Allah Yar Khan denied the accusation, but despite this Nadir demanded five hundred 'Abdali leaders be sent to his camp as hostages. When the *khans* refused to comply, Allah Yar Khan offered to pay a substantial ransom but Nadir Quli rejected his offer, arrested every 'Abdali in his camp and placed Herat under siege once more. Troops were also sent against Maruchak to seize Allah Yar Khan's family and a second column was sent to occupy Obeh.

The siege dragged on through the bitter Herati winter and by February 1732, with the population starving, the 'Abdali leaders came to Nadir's camp and surrendered. Despite their broken promises, Nadir Quli spared Allah Yar Khan's life but he was not allowed to remain in power. On 27 February 1732 Sultan Allah Yar Khan, the last representative of the Saddozai sultans of Herat, left the city under safe conduct. Allah Yar Khan's involvement with Herat thus came to an end, but it was not his last encounter with Nadir Quli. Destitute, Allah Yar travelled to Delhi, where the Mughal emperor, Muhammad Shah, granted him a small pension. Seven years later Nadir Quli, now Nadir Shah, King of Persia, took Delhi and, hearing that Allah Yar Khan was in the Mughal capital, gifted him a *jagir* in Sind. But when Nadir Shah left Delhi, he took Allah Yar Khan with him and later exiled him to the Persian province of Mazandaran, where he was joined some time later by his rival, Zu'l-fiqar Khan. When Allah Yar Khan died a few years later his body was returned to Herat and buried beside his father and brother in the Bagh-i Rauza.

Farah fell soon after Herat. Zu'l-fikar Khan and his two brothers, 'Ali Mardan Khan and Ahmad Shah, fled to Kandahar where Shah Husain Hotaki threw them in prison. 'Ali Mardan died shortly after from the effects of torture and the appalling conditions in which the brothers were held, but Zu'l-fikar Khan and Ahmad Shah survived for nearly seven years, eventually being set free when Nadir Shah took the city.

The Saddozai sultanate of Herat had lasted for a mere fifteen years and was marked by a bloody power struggle between the Khudakka Khel and Sarmast Khel clans. In all seven sultans had come and gone: of these three had died at the hands of their own kinsmen, as had one heir apparent and several other clan members. Hundreds, possibly thousands, of people had been killed in the fratricidal strife that, on occasion, took place in the city itself. All of these rulers, though Afghans, were culturally more Multani, for most of them and their entourages had been born and brought up in this multicultural, Mughal-ruled city. Some had even married Hindu women. Used to the culture of the Mughal court, they regarded themselves as having a divine right to rule and regarded the 'Abdalis of Herat, Obeh and Kandahar as country bumpkins. It is not surprising, therefore, that hand-in-hand with the sibling feud between the Saddozai families, there was also a power struggle between the sultans and the local, more traditionally minded and religiously conservative 'Abdali *khans*.

Despite having feet of clay, the Saddozai sultans of Herat had a number of notable military successes against larger and better-equipped Persian armies, but both the Saddozais of Herat and the Hotaki dynasty of Kandahar found it was easier to wage war than to make peace. Neither dynasty consolidated its military successes by the implementation of what today would be called 'good governance', but instead sought quick gains and riches and often showed a lack of the most basic political acumen. As Caroe observes, 'the Ghaljis could win battles, but they could not rule', since they were 'utterly devoid of . . . statecraft';[47] a devastating critique which applied equally to the Saddozais of Herat. In the end both the Hotakis and Saddozais had only themselves to blame for their loss of power and independence.

TWO

Nadir Shah and the Afghans, 1732–47

> The whole construction is dependent on a Persian foundation. For the
> story of Mir Wais leads up to Nadir Shah, and Nadir . . . was in a very real
> sense the founder of the Durrani Empire of Afghanistan.
>
> OLAF CAROE[1]

FOLLOWING THE FALL of Herat, Nadir Quli Khan appointed one of his loyalists, Pir Muhammad Khan, as governor, backed by a substantial garrison. Some 60,000 'Abdalis were exiled to various parts of Persia and 12,000 of this tribe and a *lashkar* of Tokhi Ghilzais were conscripted into Nadir Khan's army. Over the ensuing decade, these Afghan levies earned a reputation for reckless bravery – a military experience that would prove significant when Ahmad Shah Durrani subsequently carved out his own empire. Nadir Khan persisted with the Safavid policy of appointing a *mir-i Afghaniha* to oversee the internal affairs of the tribes, but instead of giving the post to a Saddozai, he appointed 'Abd al-Ghani Khan Alakozai, whose sister, Zarguna Begum, was the mother of Ahmad Shah.

Nadir Quli did not pursue his campaign across the Helmand and attack Kandahar. Instead he marched west to combat a new Ottoman offensive. During this campaign the 'Abdali levies proved their worth, pursuing fleeing Arab horsemen at the Battle of Aq Darband near Kirkuk and putting them to the sword.[2] In 1735/6, during the winter campaign in Daghistan, when Nadir Quli was unable to take a particularly difficult stronghold, he told Nur Muhammad Khan 'Alizai, commander of the Afghan *lashkar*s, that either the 'Abdalis take the fortress or they would all be put to death. The Afghans flung themselves against the walls and despite heavy loss of life they finally broke through the defences and took control of the citadel. When the battle had ended Nadir Quli asked how he could reward the 'Abdalis for their bravery, whereupon Nur Muhammad Khan 'Alizai requested that if, or when, Nadir Quli took Kandahar, he would allow his tribe to return from exile and that he would restore Safa to the Saddozais.

The ruins of Old Kandahar and the Arghandab plains as seen from the top of the Qaital Ridge.

Nadir Quli agreed and so unwittingly laid the foundation stone of the Durrani dynasty.

Buoyed up by his victories and the peace treaty with Ottoman Turkey, on 8 March 1734 Nadir Quli finally ended Shah Tahmasp's token rule and was crowned king of Persia with the regnal title of Nadir Shah. One of his first acts was to turn the Safavid's religious policy on its head by decreeing that from henceforth the official Islamic *mazhab* of Persia was Sunnism, not Shi'ism. This decision endeared him to his Afghan troops but it alienated other powerful factions in the army, particularly the Qizilbash, as well as courtiers who had formerly served the Safavid Shahs, and the influential Shi'a religious establishment.

Nadir Shah's conquest of Kandahar and Kabul

Having made peace with the Ottomans, Nadir Shah was now free to punish the Hotaki dynasty for its ravages during its period of rule in Persia. In December 1736 Nadir Shah set out from Kirman via the shorter, Sistan route and in February of the following year the Hotaki outpost of Girishk surrendered. Nadir Shah pushed on to the Arghandab, where the 'Abdalis again proved their worth. 'Abd al-Ghani Khan 'Aliakozai, hearing the Ghilzais were planning a surprise attack on the Persian army, set out in the dead of night to intercept them. As they drew near their camp the

'Abdalis called out in Pushtu and tricked the enemy into thinking that reinforcements had arrived. Having located the camp, the 'Abdalis attacked and routed the Ghilzais.

Nadir Shah reached Kandahar in March 1737 and placed it under siege. The old city of Kandahar was a strongly fortified position dominated by the narrow Qaital Ridge and presented a formidable challenge to any army, even with artillery. Realizing that the siege was likely to be protracted, Nadir Shah constructed a new town in the plains east of the town out of the range of the Afghan guns. Nadirabad, as it was known, was a fully functioning urban space with bazaars, housing, mosques and bath houses, which made it relatively comfortable for Nadir's troops to survive what turned out to be a year-long siege, while their enemies holed up in Kandahar starved. Having sealed off Kandahar, Nadir Shah sent columns of troops to subdue key strongholds. Shahr-i Safa was the first to fall and in fulfilment of his pledge he returned it to the 'Abdalis. After a two-month siege, the Ghilzai citadel of Qalat-i Ghilzai, commanded by Saidal Khan, surrendered. As punishment for his support of the Saddozai sultans of Herat, Saidal Khan's eyes were put out. Nadir Shah then sent a column into the hill country north of Kandahar to subdue the Sunni Hazaras of Deh Zangi and Deh Kundi who had been raiding trade caravans in the area. Darwish 'Ali Khan, their chief, eventually submitted and he and many of his tribesmen were conscripted into Nadir Shah's army.

In March 1738 Nadir Shah ordered a full-scale assault of Kandahar's city walls. The first attack, led by Kurds and 'Abdalis, was beaten back, but on the second attempt they broke through the breaches and took possession of the town. Shah Husain Hotaki retreated into the citadel, but when Nadir Shah's artillery pounded its walls, he sent his sister, Zainab, and senior officers to plead for mercy and discuss terms of surrender. The following day Sultan Husain came in person and flung himself at the feet of Nadir Shah. Remarkably his life was spared, but he and his family were condemned to spend the rest of their days in exile in Mazandaran. The Hotak tribe was also exiled en masse to Sabzawar and other regions of Persia. Their homes, lands and pasturages were handed over to the 'Abdalis, who were allowed to return from exile. The Hotakis never recovered from this defeat and exile. Even though many eventually returned to the Kandahar region, they had lost most of the sources of their wealth to the 'Abdalis. Ahmad Shah and his successors also made sure the Hotak tribe were excluded from power.

The Tokhi Ghilzais were exempt from the collective punishment imposed on the Hotaks, for while they had participated in the conquest of

Persia, they had fallen out with Shah Husain Hotaki and joined forces with Nadir Shah. As a reward Ashraf Khan, a Babakrzai Tokhi, was appointed *beglar begi* of Qalat-i Ghilzai and later Ghazni. This decision was not well received by the 'Abdalis, for they coveted the Tokhi's fertile, irrigated land and resented their presence since it restrained their own power and ambitions. Over the ensuing years the 'Abdalis played on Nadir Shah's increasing fear of assassination and rebellion and eventually convinced him that the Tokhi *malik*s were planning to rebel. When Nadir Shah returned to Kandahar after the fall of Delhi, he imprisoned three senior Tokhi leaders; it was later rumoured they were walled up in their prison cell and left to die of suffocation.

It was nearly two-and-a-half centuries before a Ghilzai once again became head of state of an Afghan kingdom. Following the Marxist coup of April 1978, Nur Muhammad, a Taraki Ghilzai from the Ghazni area, become president and since then three other Ghilzais have ruled the country, however briefly: President Hafiz Allah Amin (ruled 1979) was a Kharoti Ghilzai; President Najib Allah Khan, who was President from 1987 to 1992, came from the Ahmadzai Ghilzai tribe; and Amir Mullah 'Omar, head of the Taliban (ruled 1996–2001), belonged to Mir Wa'is Hotak's tribe. Another prominent Ghilzai is Gulbudin Hikmatyar, head of the Hizb-i Islami militia, who was Prime Minister of Afghanistan during the Presidency of Burhan al-Din Rabbani.

Following the fall of Kandahar, Muhammad Zaman Khan Saddozai's two sons, Zu'l-fiqar Khan and Ahmad Shah, were freed after seven years of incarceration. This was the fifteen-year-old Ahmad Shah's second narrow escape from death, since his heavily pregnant mother had fled to Multan when his father was executed by Sultan Allah Yar Khan. Nadir Shah exiled Zu'l-fiqar Khan to Mazandaran, where he died a few years later, but Ahmad Shah was appointed to a minor position in Nadir Shah's administration and was no doubt a hostage for his elder brother's good conduct. Nadir Shah then appointed a number of leading 'Abdalis to positions of authority in and around Kandahar. 'Abd al-Ghani Khan Alakozai, who was already *mir-i Afghaniha*, became *beglar begi* of Kandahar; Nur Muhammad Khan 'Alizai, who commanded Nadir's Afghan *ghulam*s, was gifted *jagir*s and pasturing rights along the Arghandab river and in Dawar; while Hajji Jamal Khan, head of the Barakzai *ulus*, became governor of Girishk and Farah.

As for the city of Kandahar, Nadir Shah ordered it to be demolished and its population relocated to Nadirabad. However, the levelling proved too hard and much of Kandahar's ancient walls and part of its citadel were left standing. Nadir also instituted a major reorganization of the government of the Kandahar region and appointed Persian overseers, experienced in agriculture and irrigated cultivation, to improve cultivation and to reform the tax system. Other specialists supervised the cleaning and digging of new *karez*, the subterranean, spring-fed aqueducts that are such a feature of both Afghanistan and Iran.[3]

A month or so after the fall of Kandahar, Nadir Shah crossed the Mughal frontier at Muqur and marched on Ghazni, justifying his invasion on the grounds that the Mughal governor of Kabul had given protection to flee-ing Ghilzais. Ghazni quickly submitted and, as Nadir Shah continued his relentless advance, the governor of Kabul desperately pleaded with Delhi for reinforcements and cash, for his troops had not been paid for more than five years. Delhi, though, ignored his calls for help and when the Persian army arrived before the city walls, the town elders came out and tendered their submission. The garrison, however, refused to surrender so Nadir Shah

The tomb of Zahir al-Din Babur, founder of the Mughal Empire, on the western face of Kabul's Sher Darwaza hill. The marble screen is modern, constructed as part of restoration work instituted by the Aga Khan Trust for Culture.

ordered his troops to take the citadel by storm, only to find his artillery was unable to breach the Bala Hisar's walls. In the end one of the defenders' artillery pieces accidentally exploded, bringing down part of a gate tower and wall, and Nadir Khan sent in a storming party. Realizing all hope was lost, the garrison surrendered, and Kabul, which had been a Mughal possession for more than two centuries and had been Zahir al-Din Babur's first capital in northern India, was lost. One wonders how many times Babur, whose tomb lay on the other side of the Sher Darwaza hills, turned in his grave.

Nadir Shah's conquest of Delhi

Despite the loss of Kabul, Muhammad Shah, the Mughal emperor, showed stunning complacency: the only serious resistance offered as Nadir Shah advanced into the plains of Nangahar came from the Ghilzais of Laghman. After Jalalabad fell, the Mughal governor of Peshawar rallied the Khyber tribes to block the main highway through the pass only for Nadir Shah to engage a local Afghan who led a column of his army by a lesser-used route, caught the Mughal army by surprise and routed them. The fall of Peshawar finally stirred Muhammad Shah into action and he hastily assembled an army to oppose Nadir Shah's advance into the Punjab. The Mughal response, though, was too little, too late. After resting his weary troops for a month in Peshawar, in January 1739 Nadir Shah crossed the Indus and by the end of the month Lahore too had submitted.

The cumbersome Mughal force was still only 120 kilometres (75 mi.) from Delhi and in the end it was Nadir Shah who found them. On 24 February 1739 at Karnal, Nadir Shah defeated the Mughal cavalry and surrounded what was left of the army. Muhammad Shah was obliged to go in person to Nadir Shah's camp to negotiate what were in effect terms of submission. The conditions Nadir Shah demanded were harsh and included the payment of a vast tribute. Muhammad Shah baulked at such a humiliation and held out for a more face-saving deal, but after several days of futile negotiations Nadir Shah had had enough and refused the Emperor permission to leave his camp until he agreed to the terms he had demanded. Meanwhile Nadir Shah sent an advance party into Delhi to prepare for his triumphal entry into the city. The day before this took place Muhammad Shah, who had finally capitulated, was sent back to his capital with orders to prepare a suitable reception for the conqueror. On 20 March 1739 Nadir Shah marched into Delhi, his name was inserted in the *khutba* and coins were struck in his name bearing the titles Prince of the Princes of the Earth and King of Kings.

Nadir Shah had deliberately timed his entry into Delhi so that his first full day in the Mughal capital coincided with Nauroz, the start of the Persian New Year. This festival held immense symbolic significance, for both the Persians and Mughals were familiar with its ancient traditions and mythological associations. In the *Shah Nama*, the great Persian epic, Nauroz was the day when Jamshid, one of the great heroes of ancient Persia, ascended the throne of Iran and inaugurated a Golden Age. At Jamshid's coronation all the rulers of the world are said to have bowed down before him and acknowledged him as Lord of the World.[4] Nadir Shah evidently saw his conquest of Delhi in a similar light and the equation of his reign with that of Jamshid suggests a certain degree of megalomania. The conquest of Delhi did indeed earn Nadir Shah great fame, not just in the Muslim world but in Europe too, for accounts of his campaigns were read by, among others, the Duke of Wellington and Napoleon Bonaparte. Yet at the very height of his success, everything began to fall apart. Nadir Shah may have seen himself as the new Jamshid, but he failed to learn a lesson from the tragic end of this hero, for the evil Zahhak eventually slew him. Seven years after his greatest triumph, Nadir Shah too was assassinated and his empire broke up.

Even before Nadir Shah entered Delhi, reports had spread of the extortionate tribute the Persian monarch had imposed on Muhammad Shah in return for not looting the city. Delhi at the time was in the grips of an economic crisis and the merchants and middle classes, who would have borne the brunt of the exactions, were deeply resentful at this demand. The day after Nauroz, Nadir Shah tried to address the problem of shortages by ordering shopkeepers to reduce the price of grain and sending a Qizilbash guard to take control of the grain silos. The cut in the price of grain did not go down well with Delhi's shopkeepers and they gathered in large numbers outside the storehouses to protest that the price cap meant they were unable to make any profit. The situation quickly got out of hand and several of the Qizilbash were slain; it was even rumoured that Nadir Shah had been shot or poisoned. The riot continued throughout the night with Nadir Shah's troops unable to contain it and on the following morning, when Nadir Shah rode out to assess the situation, an angry crowd stoned him and his escort. Then a shot, fired from a nearby building, narrowly missed the king and killed one of his bodyguards.

The assassination attempt was the last straw. Nadir Shah climbed onto the roof of the Roshan al-Daula mosque overlooking the Chandni Chowk and ordered 3,000 of his troops to draw their swords and leave no one alive. For six hours they rampaged through the bazaar, slaughtering, raping, plundering and burning shops and houses. When Nadir Shah finally ordered an end to the bloodshed, between 20,000 and 30,000 men, women and children had perished. To add to the insult, Nadir Shah ordered the bodies to be left where they lay for several days. The massacre ended the riot but it was a watershed in Nadir Shah's reign. Up to this point he had shown remarkable restraint when he conquered towns, even sparing the lives of rebels, but the Delhi massacre marked the beginning of a more bloody era, a change that went hand-in-hand with a deterioration in Nadir Shah's mental and physical health. Towards the end of his reign Nadir Shah was increasingly paranoid and eventually trusted no one, not even his own sons, and the last years of his reign were drenched in blood.

Nadir Shah had no intention of ruling in Delhi and, having conquered the Mughal capital, he allowed the weak and ineffective Muhammad Shah to continue as token head of state. The price he had to pay, however, was very high: all Mughal territory beyond the Indus, including Peshawar, Jalalabad, Kabul and Ghazni, was ceded to Persia, while the tribute and goods acquired from the pillage of the Mughal palaces was valued at around 70 million rupees.[5] The sack of Delhi and the massacre left Muhammad Shah unable to raise sufficient revenues to pay his army or officials and so weakened the Mughal ruler that he sought the aid of the East India Company to contain revolts in Bengal. This, in turn, opened the door for the rise of British power in northern India. In the end, it was not Persia or the Afghans who benefited from Nadir Shah's invasion of India, but Great Britain.

As Nadir Shah headed back to Kabul, his Afghan levies again proved their worth by beating off the Yusufzais and the Khyber tribes who opposed his passage through the pass. Once in Kabul, Nadir Shah called on all the tribes of the area to come and formally submit to him: some 40,000 tribesmen pledged their allegiance and they were required to provide levies to replace the losses incurred during the Indian campaign. Among those who attended the Kabul *darbar* was Darwish 'Ali Khan, chief of the Sunni Hazaras of Deh Zangi, who was ordered to move his tribe to the Bala Murghab region in order to protect the frontier against Uzbek and Turkman slave raids. Badghis thus became the Sunni Hazaras' new homeland and from this point forward the tribe was reckoned as one of the Chahar Aimaq of the region.[6] Their relocation, however, led to the displacement of another Aimaq tribe, the Jamshidis, and the two tribes became sworn enemies. Later in the century Darwish 'Ali Khan's nephew, Agha-yi Sultan, founded the town of Qal'a-y Nau, which became the Sunni Hazaras' most important stronghold.

Nadir Shah's conquest of Balkh and Merv

While Nadir Shah was occupied with his India campaign, north of the Hindu Kush events were unfolding that would lead to another significant shift in the geopolitics of the region. In the summer of 1737 Nadir Shah sent his son and heir, Reza Quli Mirza, to subdue Abu'l-Hasan, ruler of the Tuqay-Timurid *wilayat* of Balkh.[7] The Persian army triumphed and Abu'l-Hasan was deposed, but the decade of Persian occupation of Balkh was an economic catastrophe for the region. Balkh produced large surpluses of grain, melons, grapes and dried fruit as well as being an important supplier of pack animals and cavalry horses, so the Persian governor proceeded to strip the region bare in order to supply Nadir Shah's military juggernaut. In 1742 alone 4,000 *kharwar*,[8] or between 1,200 and 2,240 metric tonnes, of grain were requisitioned from Balkh and thousands of men were forcibly conscripted into Nadir Shah's army; thousands more were sent to labour in western Khurasan and Merv. As a consequence Balkh was denuded of essential manpower needed for its own agricultural activities. Among the levies was a contingent of Uzbeks from Maimana commanded by Hajji Bi Ming. They later became part of Nadir Shah's royal guard, where Hajji Bi struck up a friendship with Ahmad Shah 'Abdali.

The economic hardship and resentment that resulted from Persia's ruthless exploitation of Balkh eventually coalesced around a millenarian movement led by a peripatetic dervish called Rasul, though this was probably an assumed name since *rasul* ('apostle', 'messenger') is a title applied to Muhammad and a handful of other prophets in Islam. Nothing is known about Rasul's ethnicity, but it is possible he was an 'Abdali, since he came from the Obeh region and had a considerable appeal to nomadic tribes, both Turkic and Afghan.[9]

Rasul's early years were troubled but he eventually bound himself to a dervish who taught him numerology, geomancy and sleight-of-hand tricks. There is some indication in the sources that he also associated with Hindu *sadhu*s and *yogi*s. In or around 1739 Rasul arrived in Ghazni, probably shortly after the Persian occupation, where he earned a reputation as a healer and for his knack of predicting the future. Nadir's governor, however, saw him as a threat, so in the autumn of 1741 Rasul and a band of devotees set out for Balkh, taking the Murghab route through Herat and Maimana.

When he arrived outside Andkhui, Rasul ordered his followers to tie fresh leaves to their clothes and to don green turbans prior to entering the settlement, but the Persian governor, fearing the presence of a large crowd fired with religious fervour might lead to trouble, refused him admittance.

A peripatetic *malang*, or dervish, relates the story of the martyrdom of Hazrat 'Ali to a captive audience during the New Year celebrations at Mazar-i Sharif.

Instead, Rasul set up camp outside Andkhui, more than likely in the shrine of Shah-i Mardan, where crowds flocked to him as stories of miraculous cures spread. When the governor demanded Rasul give proof of his powers in the presence of local religious and secular dignitaries, he proceeded to perform a series of wonders that persuaded his inquisitors of his genuineness. Even the governor was convinced and showered him with gifts. Soon his followers were referring to Rasul as *hazrat ishan*, a title accorded to Andkhui's most revered saint, Baba Sangu, or Baba Wali, the *darwish* who had been rewarded by Amir Timur Lang for having predicted the success of one of his military expeditions.[10]

As Rasul's fame spread, the *mutawalli*, or chief administrator of the shrine of Shah-i Mardan in Mazar-i Sharif, invited him to take up residence in the sacred precinct. Situated some 10 kilometres (6 mi.) west of Balkh, Shah-i Mardan was, and still is, the most important cult centre in northern

The entrance to the tomb of Baba Wali, Andkhui.

Afghanistan, for it is believed to be the last resting place of 'Ali b. Abi Talib, son-in-law and cousin of Muhammad. Heavily patronized by both the Timurids and Tuqay-Timurids, the shrine is particularly renowned for the miraculous healings that are said to take place during the Nauroz festival. When Rasul arrived in Balkh, the capital of the *wilayat*, thousands of people came out to see him and hailed him as Rasul-i Maddati, the Apostle of the Age, and Imam bi-Haqq, the True Imam, titles which suggest that Nadir Shah's Afshar Shi'a and Qizilbash garrisons believed Rasul was the last Imam who had finally reappeared as the *Mahdi*. On his arrival at Shah-i Mardan, Rasul took up residence in a cell that directly abutted the tomb of Hazrat 'Ali and large crowds came to visit him. It was not long before some claimed that Hazrat Ishan had healed them. When the Persian governor demanded proof of his supernatural powers, Rasul is said to have raised two decapitated men from the dead in his presence.

Certain individuals, however, saw Rasul's popularity as a means to raise a rebellion against the Persian occupation. The chief conspirator was 'Ismat Allah Beg, head of the Qipchaq tribe and his tribe's representative to the Persian authorities. In this era the Qipchaqs numbered around 120,000 households and had been at the forefront of opposition to the Persian invasion. 'Ismat Allah Beg went in person to Hazrat Ishan and placed himself and his tribe under Rasul's spiritual tutelage. He then secretly began to arm his tribe. In late 1741 the Qipchaq rebelled, defeated the Persian garrison in Balkh and besieged them in the citadel. However, in a subsequent skirmish

'Ismat Allah Beg received a life-threatening wound, so his followers took him to Hazrat Ishan in expectation of a miracle, only for Rasul's powers to fail him. 'Ismat Allah eventually died and all but the most faithful of Rasul's followers deserted him. The *mutawalli* of Shah-i Mardan, in fear of his life, allowed the government authorities to enter the sacred precinct and Rasul was seized, taken outside the sanctuary and executed.

Nadir Shah, hearing of the revolt, marched north and reduced the Qipchaq strongholds one by one. When the rebels were finally defeated, the reprisals were terrible. Some 6,500 male members of the Qipchaq tribe were selected by lot, decapitated and their heads piled into a tower of skulls. Rasul's most loyal supporter, who had gone before proclaiming him as Lord of the Age and Time, was entombed alive in this gruesome pyramid and his screams could be heard for many days and nights until death finally ended his torment. The Qipchaqs of Balkh were decimated

The resident *malang* at the Zadyan minaret and shrine, Balkh province.

and by the late nineteenth century only a few pockets of this once great tribe remained in the *wilayat*.

Following the pacification of Balkh, Nadir Shah marched down the Amu Darya and occupied the key Bukharan-held fort of Kerki, while Reza Quli took Chaharjui. Fearing the Persian army was about to march on Bukhara, 'Abu'l-Faiz, the Tuqay-Timurid Khan of Bukhara, came in person to Nadir Shah's camp and abjectly submitted. As a result Nadir Shah acquired yet more Uzbek levies for his army, commanded by Ataliq Rahim Bi, who would later found the Manghit dynasty. Khiva, too, fell. Ilbars, its Yomut Turkman ruler, was executed and thousands of Persian slaves freed, for Khiva was one of the great emporiums of the Central Asian slave trade.

Nadir Shah's conquest of Delhi also marked the rise of prominence of Ahmad Shah, who was appointed as one of the officials that drew up an inventory of the huge booty. Then in 1744, on the recommendation of Hajji Jamal Khan 'Alizai, Ahmad Shah was appointed as *kurchi bashi*, a kind of aide-de-camp, on Nadir Shah's personal staff. The following year, after Ahmad Shah showed considerable courage during another campaign against the Ottomans, Nadir Shah ordered him to raise a regiment of 'Abdalis to form part of the royal guard. Ahmad Shah assembled a force of around 3,000 'Abdalis that he called *ghazis*, a term used for warriors in a *jihad* who take a vow on the Qur'an to fight to the death. Ahmad Shah hand-picked youths of his own age and bound them to himself with an oath of loyalty. Towards the end of Nadir Shah's reign, Ahmad Shah's *ghazis* became one of his most trusted corps and were used to offset the power of Qizilbash, Afshar and Qajar commanders who the king suspected were plotting to rebel or even assassinate him.

Nadir Shah's final years and assassination

Following his campaigns in Balkh and Bukhara, Nadir Shah returned to Mashhad, where the bloodshed continued as his physical and mental health gradually deteriorated. According to Nadir Shah's personal physician, the Jesuit priest Père Louis Bazin, by 1746, the year before Nadir Shah's death, the king was unable to keep food down, suffered from chronic constipation, obstruction of the liver and dryness of the mouth. Despite being only in his forties, Nadir Shah's hair had turned white and he looked like an old man.[11] His relentless campaigning, the stress of leadership, his addiction to drink and his paranoia had all taken their toll.

Once back in Mashhad, Nadir Shah sent officials all over Persia to demand more and more cash to pay for his vast army, while his suspicion of everyone around him led to bloody repression. His son and heir, Reza Quli Mirza, was reported to have called his father an oppressor and accused him of draining Persia dry. Then a satirical verse appeared on Nadir's newly commissioned tomb, commenting that, while the king was everywhere in the world, his proper place – that is, his grave – remained empty. When on his way to Mazandaran, an assassin's bullet hit Nadir Shah on the thumb, he went to extraordinary lengths to track down the culprit. When he was finally captured the assassin was promised his life on condition he revealed who had put him up to the plot. The assassin accused Reza Quli Mirza and some of Nadir Shah's most senior military officials of being behind the conspiracy. Reza Quli vehemently denied he had any part in the plot, but despite this Nadir Shah had his son blinded and the other alleged conspirators put to death. When the surgeon presented Nadir Shah with his son's eyes, he broke down and wept, but despite this show of grief, the repressions continued unabated.

In 1744 Taqi Beg Khan, one of the king's closest confidants and commander of Fars, rebelled and Nadir Shah marched on Shiraz to besiege the city, laying waste to the country as he went. When Shiraz fell, Nadir Shah's troops pillaged the city and thousands of its inhabitants were killed, their corpses decapitated and the heads piled into a pyramid of skulls. Taqi Beg Khan was captured but, since Nadir Shah had once vowed never to put him to death, he was castrated instead and one of his eyes plucked out. Taqi Beg then had to watch with his one good eye as members of his family were executed and his favourite wife gang-raped by Nadir's soldiers. He was then dispatched to be governor of Sind, the most remote outpost of Nadir Shah's empire. Nadir's officials also extorted as much cash as possible from the Shirazis, cutting off hands, feet and noses or strangling and beating to death anyone suspected of concealing their wealth. The result was an exodus of Shiraz's mercantile community to Ottoman Turkey, Calcutta, Bombay and Madras.

Having put down the revolt with great brutality, Nadir Shah returned to Mashhad. All along his route government officials were interrogated and anyone suspected of embezzling state funds was mutilated, tortured or killed. In Mashhad even more officials were executed and a levy of half a million *tomans* placed on its inhabitants. During his visit to Isfahan at the end of 1746, Nadir Shah's officials pillaged this city too and eight merchants – Indians, Jews and Armenians – who were accused of purchasing a stolen carpet were burnt alive. Nadir Shah then issued list after list of people to be executed and demanded payment of vast sums from senior officials and provincial governors. When Nadir Shah ordered the governors of Kirman and Sistan to pay a levy of half a million *tomans*, they refused and instead raised the banner of rebellion. The revolt spread quickly and in early 1747 'Ali Quli Khan, Nadir Shah's nephew, fled to Sistan and placed himself at the head of the rebel forces. In April 'Ali Quli went to Herat, where he enlisted the support of the 'Abdalis. Behind his back, many of Nadir Shah's most senior officials, fed up with the bloodshed and fearing for their own lives, began to communicate secretly with 'Ali Quli Khan.

Matters finally came to a head in the summer of 1747, when Nadir Shah convinced himself that a section of his royal guard commanded by Muhammad Quli Khan, a member of Nadir's own Afshar tribe, was planning to assassinate him. On the evening of 19 June he summoned Ahmad Shah and several other trusted commanders to a secret meeting in his private audience tent. After communicating his fears, Nadir Shah ordered Ahmad Shah to assemble his *ghazis* at first light, and disarm and arrest Muhammad Quli's men. In the event that they offered any resistance, Ahmad Shah was ordered to kill them all.[12] Nadir Shah then retired to bed, but chose to sleep in the women's quarters with his favourite wife, Chuki, rather than in the royal tent, which was pitched some distance away. Outside the walls of the royal enclosure, the very soldiers who Nadir Shah suspected of plotting to kill him were on night duty, cutting the king off from Ahmad Shah's *ghazis*, who were camped on the outer ring of defences. Yet despite this, Nadir Shah decided not to act until daylight. It was a decision that cost him his life.

Nadir Shah dozed, fully clothed with a sword by his side, while outside the royal enclosure news of his orders to Ahmad Shah were leaked to Muhammad Quli Khan. Who passed on this information is not stated, although one source suggests it was a Georgian commander who was present at the secret night meeting.[13] Possibly it was Chuki herself, for her father, Muhammad Husain Khan Qajar, was head of one of the divisions of the royal guard. He was also implicated in the assassination attempt on Nadir Shah that had led to the blinding of Reza Quli Mirza, though he avoided execution since Nadir Shah did not want to risk a war with the powerful Qajar tribe. Even Ahmad Shah is not above suspicion, for his actions subsequent to Nadir Shah's murder were odd, to say the least.

Informed of the king's orders to disarm his troops, Muhammad Quli Khan called an emergency meeting of trusted commanders and allies who agreed to 'breakfast off [Nadir Shah] ere he should sup off them'.[14] As soon as the moon set, Muhammad Quli and three other conspirators slipped into the royal enclosure, held a knife to the throat of the eunuch guard and demanded he tell them where the king was sleeping. The terrified man pointed silently at Chuki's tent and was rewarded by having his throat slit. The noise roused Nadir Shah, who tried to reach for his sword but stumbled in the darkness. Before he could recover, a sword stroke cut the king's hand from his arm. Despite pleading for his life, Muhammad Quli severed Nadir Shah's head from his body.

Exactly what happened next is uncertain, no doubt because of the confusion that followed the assassination. It seems the conspirators began to pillage the royal enclosure while trying to keep the assassination secret, only for the news of Nadir Shah's death to spread quickly throughout the camp. Soon all law and order broke down and Bazin, who witnessed the chaos, barely escaped with his life. Ahmad Shah appears to have been unaware of what had happened, for neither he nor his ally Hajji Bi Ming and his Uzbeks did anything until daybreak, by which time the whole camp was filled with 'confusion, discord and commotion'.[15] Indeed, it appears that Ahmad Shah and Hajji Bi were surprised when the Qajar and Afshar divisions of the royal guard attacked them, no doubt to prevent them carrying out the king's orders. A bloody battle ensued but, despite being heavily outnumbered, Ahmad Shah managed to force his way into the royal enclosure, where he discovered Nadir Shah's decapitated body cradled in the lap of an old woman.

Historians mostly portray Ahmad Shah as acting in defence of Nadir Shah but there are doubts about this narrative. Ahmad Shah, like many others, must have realized that Nadir Shah's grip on power was slipping and that his mood swings and bloody repression meant he was as likely to turn on the Afghans as he had done on other regiments of the royal guard. We know that the rebellious prince 'Ali Quli Mirza was in Herat and that many 'Abdali and other chiefs had submitted to him. The prince was also in secret communication with senior military commanders at the time of Nadir Shah's assassination. 'Ali Quli may well have tried to win over Ahmad Shah and the 'Abdali *ulus* while Ahmad Shah would certainly have been aware of the positive reception 'Ali Quli Mirza had been given in Herat.

Ahmad Shah's inaction after the king was killed is therefore suspicious, as are his actions when he entered Nadir Shah's tent. Instead of treating the royal body with respect, Ahmad Shah removed the royal signet ring from the king's severed hand and stole the Koh-i Nur diamond, which was tied around his arm. This was hardly the action of a loyal commander and the theft of these two important items of regal insignia was clearly deliberate and done in full knowledge of their significance. The signet ring, after all, was the royal seal, while the Koh-i Nur, the most precious of all the Mughal crown jewels, had a long association with the Muslim dynasties of northern

The Koh-i Nur diamond before it was recut and in its originl setting with the silk sash which bound the jewel to the arm of the monarch.

India. The diamond was originally acquired by the Khalji Sultans of Delhi from a defeated Hindu Raja and became the centrepiece of the imperial crown. Later it became part of the crown jewels of the Lodhi dynasty and, following their defeat at Panipat, it was surrendered to Zahir al-Din Babur, founder of the Mughal dynasty. Subsequently Shah Jahan set the Koh-i Nur as one of the eyes of his famous Peacock Throne. For the Muslim rulers of Delhi the Koh-i Nur was a symbol of sovereignty over northern India: indeed it was said that the king who possessed this diamond would rule the world. Subsequently the Koh-i Nur was passed down the Durrani royal line until Ahmad Shah's grandson, Shah Shuja' al-Mulk, was forced to hand it over to the Sikh Maharaja, Ranjit Singh. In 1849, following the defeat of the Sikhs and the break-up of their kingdom, the East India Company acquired the diamond as booty. It was eventually recut and set into a tiara and then a circlet for Queen Victoria. It is now set in the crown formerly worn by Queen Elizabeth the Queen Mother.

Some Afghan historians have attempted to legitimize the acquisition of the Koh-i Nur by claiming it was gifted to Ahmad Shah by Nadir Shah's 'queen', presumably Chuki, as a reward for protecting her from being raped by the Persian soldiers. However, there is no contemporary evidence to support this claim. Indeed Ahmad Shah took the diamond and signet ring fully aware of their significance. The Koh-i Nur represented Muslim sovereignty over northern India, while Nadir Shah's signet ring symbolized sovereignty over Persia, two empires which for more than two-and-a-half centuries had subjugated the 'Abdali tribes of Kandahar and Herat. Ahmad Shah's acquisition of these symbols of regal power can therefore be seen as the first act in his bid to re-establish the Saddozai's sovereignty and independence and to provide legitimacy for his dynasty.

Ahmad Shah and the establishment of the 'Abdali dynasty: myth and reality

Aided by Hajji Bi Ming's Uzbeks, Ahmad Shah and the other 'Abdali *ulus* fought their way out of the Persian camp. Once they were well away from the chaos, Hajji Bi Ming set off for Maimana, intent on throwing the Persians out of Balkh. As for Ahmad Shah, he marched on Farah and Kandahar. Before the two men parted, they appear to have made a pact never to go to war with each other and allow each to carve out their own kingdom. On his deathbed, Ahmad Shah reaffirmed this pledge by telling his son and heir, Timur Shah, not to attack the Uzbeks, who were 'a hive without honey'.[16]

Ahmad Shah's next move was to establish his authority over the other 'Abdali commanders who had accompanied him. Ahmad Shah commanded around 3,000 *ghazis*, but they were outnumbered by seven other *ulus*, or clan regiments, each of which was commanded by their own tribal head. The overall commander of all the Afghan *ghulams* was the octogenarian Nur Muhammad Khan 'Alizai, whom Nadir Shah had appointed *sardar-i mulk*, or military commander, of Kandahar. Another powerful rival was Ahmad Shah's maternal uncle, 'Abd al-Ghani Khan Alakozai, Nadir Shah's *mir-i Afghaniha* who was also *beglar begi* of Kandahar. As far as Ahmad Shah was concerned, these two men were a threat to his own ambitions and had to either submit to him, or be killed.

Ahmad Shah first staged a confrontation with Nur Muhammad Khan 'Alizai by placing himself at the head of the 'Abdali regiments and refused to give way when Nur Muhammad Khan protested. Nur Muhammad Khan appealed to other commanders, only to discover he had little support and was forced to relinquish command. His life was spared, but when it came to dealing with 'Abd al-Ghani Khan, Ahmad Shah showed no mercy. Despite 'Abd al-Ghani being Ahmad Shah's maternal uncle, he ordered his *ghazis* to take him into the desert and put him to death. The outcome was that Ahmad Shah now commanded an army of some 6,000 battle-hardened Afghans and, by dint of Nur Muhammad Khan's demotion and 'Abd al-Ghani's execution, he was also de facto *mir-i Afghaniha* as well as civil and military governor of Kandahar. Long before he reached Kandahar, Ahmad Shah was king in all but name.[17]

As he advanced on Kandahar, Farah and Girishk submitted and a feeble attempt by the Persian garrison in Herat to retake them was easily defeated. When he reached Kandahar, Ahmad Shah set up camp in the Chaman-i Sanjar, probably the military parade ground of Nadirabad, and prepared the ground to be declared king. What exactly happened after Ahmad Shah reached Kandahar, however, has been obscured by an Arthurian-style legend. Indeed, few other events in modern Afghan history have been subjected to so much mythologizing. As a consequence the historical events surrounding Ahmad Khan's establishment of an independent Saddozai kingdom in Kandahar have been lost in a fog of romance that is regurgitated uncritically by both Afghan and Western historians.

According to this mythic narrative, when Ahmad Shah arrived in Kandahar he summoned all the tribal leaders to a Grand National Assembly, or Loya Jirga, to elect a king. It is claimed this assembly included all the Pushtun tribes of 'Afghanistan', as well as leaders of the Baluch, Uzbek and Shi'a Hazaras. The assembly then unanimously 'elected' Ahmad Shah as king after Hajji Jamal Khan Barakzai withdrew his candidature in the wake of the intervention of Sabir Khan, the guardian of the shrine of Sher-i Surkh, who declared that since Ahmad Shah was a Saddozai his claim to the throne was superior to any other 'Abdali. Sabir Khan, so the story continues, then placed a sheaf of wheat or barley on Ahmad Shah's turban and declared him king in front of the whole assembly.

So deeply embedded is this version of events that even Ganda Singh and Umar Kamal Khan repeat this story almost verbatim, despite admitting there is no contemporary textual evidence to support this narrative. 'Umar Kamal Khan even states that 'early chronicles . . . are unanimous that the leadership of the Afghan nation was decided on the road by younger elements of [the] Afghan contingent . . . [the] rest was formality.'[18] These 'early chronicles' include the history of Mahmud al-Husaini,[19] Ahmad Shah's official court historian, who gives a very different version of events and one that is consistent with accounts of European travellers in the late eighteenth and early nineteenth centuries.[20] The only near-contemporary Persian source that has any similarity to the later coronation myth is that of 'Abu'l-Hasan ibn Amin Gulistana, whose history was written some thirty years after Ahmad Shah's death. Yet even Gulistana portrays the meetings in Kandahar and Ahmad Shah's subsequent 'election' as a formality.[21]

According to these Persian histories, shortly after reaching Kandahar Ahmad Shah had a stroke of fortune with the arrival of a large military convoy containing the annual revenues of Sind, which amounted to as much as two *crore*, or 20 million, rupees.[22] The convoy was guarded by hundreds of Qizilbash *ghulams* commanded by Taqi Beg Khan Shirazi, Nadir Shah's governor of Sind, and included a *fil khana*, or stable of war elephants. Taqi Beg had little love for Nadir Shah, for a few years earlier he had been castrated and blinded in one eye for leading the revolt in Shiraz and then watched as members of his family were executed and his wife gang-raped. When Taqi Beg heard about Nadir Shah's assassination – Ahmad Shah probably produced the Koh-i Nur and signet ring as proof – he agreed to join forces with Ahmad Shah and was rewarded with a share of the Sind treasure. Taqi Beg then persuaded the Qizilbash garrison in Kandahar not to oppose the Afghan takeover and they too declared support for Ahmad Shah; doubtless they too were given some of the Sind treasure as an incentive. In all the Qizilbash numbered around 12,000 men and later Ahmad Shah appointed them as part of his *ghulam khana*, or royal guard. Nawab Nasir Khan, the Mughal governor of Kabul, was also in the Sind convoy, though he showed less enthusiasm initially in joining the 'Abdali enterprise and was imprisoned. A few days later he was released after he agreed to pay Ahmad Shah an annual tribute of 500,000 rupees in return for being reconfirmed as governor of Kabul under 'Abdali sovereignty.

The Sind treasure fortuitously provided Ahmad Shah with a substantial war chest that he used to buy loyalties and reward his *ghazis*. The advocacy of Taqi Beg also meant Ahmad Shah now commanded a sizeable force of at least 18,000 men as well as war elephants, the eighteenth-century equivalent of a tank corps. His position was unassailable, for this army could overawe any opposition from local Afghan and Baluch tribes. On the back of this stroke of good fortune, Ahmad Shah convened a military council of nine men, seven of whom were the commanders of Nadir Shah's 'Abdali *ulus*. The names of these seven *amirs* were Nur Muhammad Khan 'Alizai, 'Abd Allah Khan 'Ayubzai, Shah Wali Khan Bamezai, Hajji Jamal Khan Barakzai, Mus'a Khan Ishaqzai, whose nickname was Dungi, Nasar Allah Khan Nurzai and Muhabbat Khan Popalzai. The eighth member of the council represented the Tokhi Ghilzai *ulus* that had also fought in Nadir Shah's army, while the only non-Afghan representative was Nasir Khan of Kalat, an ethnic Brahui, who had also served under Nadir Shah. The object of their deliberations was to negotiate the distribution of state offices among themselves prior to a public declaration of an independent Saddozai kingdom.

Nationalist historians, as well as most European ones, claim this meeting took place in the shrine of Sher-i Surkh. Contemporary sources, however, make no mention of this location and it is certainly a myth invented in the late nineteenth or early twentieth century to support the legitimacy of the Muhammadzais, for Sher-i Surkh was the place where Hajji Jamal Khan Barakzai, founder of their dynasty, was buried. Sher-i Surkh is anyway a small single-domed shrine and unsuited for a gathering of such importance.[23] More than likely, the military council met in Ahmad

The 'shrine and sheaf' motif on a postage stamp, *c.* 1915. From the reign of Amir Habib Allah Khan onwards this motif became one of the most emotive symbols of the Durrani monarchy. On the right is the shrine and sheaf motif as elaborated under the Musahiban dynasty (1929–73).

Shah's own tent, where secrecy was guaranteed, and the *ghazi*s were on hand in case of trouble. Over a period of several days these nine military commanders haggled over their stake in the new kingdom and, in order to secure their endorsement, Ahmad Shah made a number of concessions, including a pledge that all the clans represented at the meeting would be exempt in perpetuity from taxation on their land and forcible conscription. They and their heirs would also have the right to sit on the royal tribal council. In return, the *ulus* commanders agreed to supply military levies in the event of war. Nur Muhammad Khan 'Alizai, who was still a powerful figure, was placated for his loss of rank and face by being appointed as the new *mir-i Afghaniha*.

Hajji Jamal Khan Barakzai, however, challenged Ahmad Shah's right to the throne and demanded he be acknowledged as king, for the Barakzais were the most numerous and powerful of the 'Abdali clans of the Helmand and Kandahar region. Hajji Jamal's status was also enhanced by his seniority of age, the fact that he was a substantial landowner – Nadirabad was built on his family's land – and by having performed the pilgrimage to Mecca. Ahmad Shah, on the other hand, was in his early twenties and a stranger to Kandahar, having been born and brought up in Multan. Furthermore, though he was a Sarmast Khel Saddozai, his forebears had been sultans of Herat, not Kandahar. Ahmad Shah's only acquaintance with Kandahar up to this point in time had been seven years in the local jail.

The confrontation between Hajji Jamal Khan and Ahmad Shah, though, was rooted in a historic rivalry between the two clans for, in an attempt to undermine the Saddozai–Safavid alliance, the Mughals had patronized the Barakzais. During the era of Mughal rule in Kandahar the governors had appointed a Barakzai as *mir-i Afghaniha*, and when Saddozai power shifted in Herat, the heads of the Barakzais refused to recognize the election of a Saddozai *mir-i Afghaniha* since his appointment was made by the 'Abdalis of Herat. More than likely Hajji Jamal Khan was a descendant of these Mughal-appointed *maliks*.

The dispute between the two men was only resolved after several days of heated debate. In the end Ahmad Shah swore on the Qur'an that in return for pledging his loyalty to him as king, Hajji Jamal Khan and his heirs would hold the post of *wazir*, or chief minister, in perpetuity. This meant that he would be second in rank only to the king and he would wield almost as much power, since it was the *wazir*, not the monarch, who ran the day-to-day affairs of the kingdom. Even so, the power struggle between the families of Hajji Jamal Khan and Ahmad Shah rumbled on and ended in bloodshed and civil war. Eventually Hajji Jamal's descendants deposed Ahmad Shah's family and established their own dynasty, the Muhammadzais.

Having reached agreement that Ahmad Shah was to be king, his personal spiritual adviser, Sabir Shah, offered a prayer and, in al-Husaini's words, 'took a stalk (or blade) of greenery (*giyeh sabz*) and fixed it to the cap (*kula*) of Ahmad Shah, declaring that by this token the king had been crowned'. Muhammadzai historians in the twentieth century later took up this laconic account and transformed it into an elaborate coronation myth. During the reign of Amir Habib Allah Khan (r. 1901–19), the *giyeh sabz* was transformed into a formalized sheaf of barley or wheat and became a key item of dynastic insignia, appearing on the national flag, stamps, coins and the State's official letterhead. This highly stylized sheaf bore a striking resemblance to the laurel wreath awarded to the winners of ancient Olympic competitions and the golden coronet held over the head of Roman emperors during a Triumph. In the 1940s Mir Gholam Mohammad Ghobar, in his history of Ahmad Shah, even included a romantic sketch by the famous twentieth-century Afghan artist 'Abd al-Ghafur Breshna, which depicts Sabir Shah crowning Ahmad Shah with a sheaf of gold (see p. 112),[24] while the American historian Louis Dupree speculated that the *giyeh sabz* harked back to some ancient fertility rite.[25] The wheat sheaf was given even greater potency by its use in encircling an image of the shrine of the Khirqa-yi Sharif, or Noble Cloak, Kandahar's most holy relic.[26] So deeply did this symbol become embedded in Afghanistan's nationalist consciousness that in the late 1970s the Communist government of Nur Muhammad Taraki retained it as part of the national flag, although it was recast to appear more like the Soviet sheaf that symbolized agricultural prosperity. The Taliban, though, would have nothing to do with this 'un-Islamic' symbol, but following their fall from power President Karzai rehabilitated the shrine and sheaf motif. After all, he was Popalzai, and a member of the Durrani royal lineage.

At least some of these coronation myths derive from European misunderstandings of, or lack of engagement with, contemporary sources, in particular the account of Joseph-Pierre Ferrier, a French military adventurer who travelled through Afghanistan in the mid-1840s. In his *History of the Afghans*, Ferrier recasts the nine-man military council as a general tribal assembly that met in the shrine of Sher-i Surkh. It is Ferrier too who relates how Hajji Jamal Khan graciously stepped aside in Ahmad Shah's favour and records Sabir Shah's crowning of Ahmad Shah with a wreath of barley. A more sinister reworking of Ferrier's account appears in the autobiography of Amir 'Abd al-Rahman Khan (r. 1880–1901). According to his version of events, after Ahmad Shah was crowned, the assembled elders

> all took pieces of green grass in their mouths as a token that they were [Ahmad Shah's] very cattle and beasts of burden, and throwing around their necks pieces of cloth in the shape of ropes, as a sign that they were willing to be led by him, they submitted to his rule, and gave him the powers of life and death.[27]

This perversion of the historical account, and the Pushtun concept of *nanawatai*, was designed to justify the absolutist monarchy that was the hallmark of 'Abd al-Rahman Khan's reign. In so doing, the Amir reduced the heads of all the Afghan tribes to the status of slaves or defeated enemies who, since they deserved no quarter, threw themselves on the king's mercy. The Amir graciously deigned to spare their lives, but only because they had surrendered all their rights and agreed to live like beasts of burden that could be herded or slaughtered at the whim of the monarch. Yet in the same place 'Abd al-Rahman Khan claimed that Ahmad Shah was elected by 'the accredited representatives of our nation' and that 1747 was 'the year in which the history of Afghanistan made a start in having an elected king and constitutional government to govern the country'.[28] These statements are diametrically opposed to his portrayal of Ahmad Shah's subjects as slaves and animals, and are equally absurd since Afghanistan had no

Constitution until 1923, let alone anything resembling a constitutional assembly or parliament.

All this mythologizing and sentimentality is even more ironic when one realizes that Sabir Shah's placing of the *giyeh sabz* in Ahmad Shah's cap was a jocular gesture that deliberately mocked the Safavid coronation ceremony. As he placed the stalk of greenery in the king's cap, Sabir playfully remarked that this was Ahmad Shah's *jigha*, the regal plume worn by both the Safavid and Mughal monarchs as symbol of kingship. It was a joke that all the assembled military commanders would have appreciated, for they were all too familiar with Safavid and Mughal regal regalia. At the same time Sabir Shah's action was a subtle reminder of the dangers of the new king assuming the sort of airs and graces that were hallmarks of the Safavids and, indeed, of the Saddozai *mir-i Afghaniha*s too. Ahmad Shah may have won his battle to be king, but Sabir Shah was reminding him that if he wanted to hold on to power a degree of humility and modesty would not go amiss. Subsequently all high Durrani officials in the Saddozai kingdom wore feathered *jigha*s in their turbans.

There is a further irony in the subsequent elevation of Sabir Shah to the Afghan equivalent of the Archbishop of Canterbury, for as far as the spiritual hierarchy of the 'Abdali tribe or the Kandahar area was concerned, he was not only a nonentity but an embarrassment. Faiz Muhammad Katib's famous history of the Durrani monarchy, commissioned by Amir Habib Allah Khan, for example, does not even mention Sabir Shah in his brief account of Ahmad Shah's 'coronation',[29] while al-Husaini refers to Sabir Shah as a *darwish* and a *faqir*. In fact, Sabir Shah was a peripatetic mystic who dabbled in the interpretation of dreams that, he claimed, allowed him to predict the future. In this respect Sabir Shah can be compared with Rasul, who caused such a sensation during the Nadirid occupation of Balkh. Sabir Shah was not even a Pushtun but a Punjabi from Lahore, though Ghobar and those who follow him claim he was from Kabul on the basis of a misreading of a Persian text.[30]

Sabir was born in Lahore and his birth name was Reza Shah, which strongly suggests he was a Shi'a, and in his early years he worked as a farrier or *na'lband*.[31] Sometime prior to Nadir Shah's conquest of Lahore, Reza changed his name to the more neutral Sabir and turned his hand to fortune-telling. Like many other *faqir*s of this era he attached himself to the Persian army, where his horse-shoeing skills and his alleged occult powers were much in demand.[32] It was probably while Nadir Shah was in Lahore that Sabir met Ahmad Shah, so impressing the young Saddozai that he was engaged as his personal fortune-teller, for it seems that Sabir

Abd al-Ghafur Breshna's romantic painting *The Coronation of Ahmad Shah Durrani*, 1942/3, watercolour.

Shah had told Ahmad Shah that one day he would be king. By 1747 the relationship between Ahmad Shah and Sabir Shah had grown into one of extreme intimacy, which for some went beyond the bounds of propriety. Shortly after his coronation, a courtier granted an audience with Ahmad Shah was shocked to see Sabir Shah, 'naked from head to foot with his body covered in dust', lying in the lap of the king and Ahmad Shah feeding him with his own hand from the royal plate.[33]

Ahmad Shah's 'election' as king had been agreed by a coterie of nine military commanders, which subsequently nationalist narrative reworked into a Grand National Assembly, or Loya Jirga, an assembly which, it is claimed, is an ancient and traditional Pushtun method of electing heads of state. This too has no justification in contemporary sources, as well as being a cultural fiction. Pushtun tribes do not elect kings for the simple reason that they do not have a monarchical system. Even the *malik* and *mir-i Afghaniha* structures were an external imposition by the dominant imperial powers and, though the 'Abdalis may have nominated the *mir-i Afghaniha*, their nominee had to be approved by the Safavid or Mughal governors of Kandahar. Nor did any other Afghan tribe have a say in this appointment. In a number of instances the *mir-i Afghaniha* was appointed solely by the Safavid governor, who either ignored the wishes of the 'Abdali leaders or overruled them.

Afghan tribes have a variety of traditions when it comes to nominating heads of clans and the tribe, while some only nominate such an individual for a specific purpose, such as leading the tribe into war or settling an internal dispute. Innately most Afghan tribes oppose any form of central-ized government and fiercely protect their autonomy, as the Amirs of Afghanistan have found out to their costs again and again. Notice of a tribal *jirga* is always promulgated well before time and the meeting is traditionally held in the open air in order to prevent deals being struck in secret. Every male above the age of eighteen has the right to attend and to speak his mind, while outsiders have no right of participation unless they are invited.

None of the Persian sources cited above refer to the council's deliber-ations as a *jirga*. Al-Husaini, for example, uses the generic Persian term *majlis*, 'meeting' or 'assembly', a usage that was perpetuated well into the nineteenth century, as Elphinstone noted sixty years later. The modern concept of Loya Jirga was established in successive constitutions from the 1920s onwards and has little in common with indigenous Pushtu trad-ition, but is rather the creation of Afghan monarchist-nationalists. Rather than harking back to some ancient Pushtu egalitarian tradition, the Loya Jirga is actually derived from Turkish parliamentary models and its only link with Pushtun identity is the word *loya* in the title, for even *jirga* is a Persian, not a Pushtu, term.[34]

The nine-man military council that 'elected' Ahmad Shah as king was the antithesis of a traditional Pushtun *jirga*. The issue had been more or less settled prior to Ahmad Shah's arrival in Kandahar and the council met in secret without any representation of the 'Abdali aristocracy present. Apart from a single Tokhi Ghilzai, no other Afghan tribes were invited or, indeed, welcome. Nor were there any representatives of the religious estab-lishment, the '*ulama*', present, despite their endorsement being essential to legitimize Ahmad Shah's claim to the throne according to the *shari'a*. Sabir Shah was not qualified to fulfil this role since he had no formal Islamic credentials. Put in modern terms, Ahmad Shah's assumption of kingship in 1747 was a military coup by a small clique and followed a long-standing precedent in which the commander of a *ghulam* force, taking advantage of central government weakness, would break away and set up his own independent kingdom.

Finally, the claims that when Ahmad Shah became king he adopted the regnal title of Dur-i Durran, Pearl of Pearls, and that he ordered the 'Abdali tribe to be known henceforth as Durrani are also unfounded, as is the belief that this change of name came about as a result of a dream by Sabir Shah. The title Dur-i Durran, and the change of tribal name, came many months later and was conferred on Ahmad Shah by Hazrat Mian 'Omar Baba, *pir* of Chamkani near Attock.[35]

Once Ahmad Shah had secured the endorsement of the military council that he should be king, he set out to secure the oath of allegiance from the tribal and religious elites of the region. Heralds were sent to summon these dignitaries to a public *darbar*. When they had gathered Ahmad Shah appeared before the assembly, probably already wearing a royal *jigha*, which was no doubt part of the loot acquired from Delhi or Nadir Shah's tent. The assembly was then informed that Ahmad Shah was king of an independent Kandahar, whereupon Ahmad Shah's *ghazis*, who were strategically placed around the assembly, beat their swords against their shields and declared there was no one more worthy to be king. The leaders then went forward and pledged allegiance to the Saddozai ruler. The event was so well stage-managed that there was no dissent and doubtless the presence of thousands of soldiers, artillery and war elephants convinced everyone that it was safer to submit than object.

Even so, many key regional and tribal leaders were absent from the *darbar* or deliberately did not attend. Particularly notable by their absence were the Hotak Ghilzai, mostly because their leaders had been exiled by Nadir Shah. Many other Ghilzai tribes were not represented, including the powerful Sulaiman Khel confederacy of Ghazni, Kabul and the Logar, while the Ghilzais of Kabul, Laghman and Nangahar did not attend because at the time their fealty lay with the Mughal emperor. The Kakars and Baluch of Farah and Girishk were also notable by their absence, as were representatives of the Afridis, Jajis, Mohmands, Mangals, Safis, Shinwaris, Waziris and other tribes of southern and southeastern Afghanistan and the Khyber.

One Hazara is mentioned as being present at the *darbar* but he was not, as has been assumed by a number of modern historians, a Shi'a Hazara from the Hazarajat, but Darwish 'Ali Khan, *beglar begi* of the Sunni Hazara Aimaq. As we have seen, he too had fought under Nadir Shah's banner and for a short time had been governor of Herat. Nasir Khan, *beglar begi* of Kalat, was also present at the 'swearing in', since Kalat was regarded as subordinate to the governor of Kandahar. Nasir Khan was the only non-Afghan who had a seat on the king's nine-man *majlis*. Subsequent claims that Ahmad Shah was elected by all the Pushtun tribes of Afghanistan, therefore, have no foundation in contemporary sources and this is yet one more myth that has accumulated over the years around his 'coronation'.

It is commonplace to state that Ahmad Shah's assumption of kingship marked the foundation of *modern* Afghanistan, but this too is an anachronism. As far as Ahmad Shah and his contemporaries were concerned, Afghanistan was the territory dominated by the autonomous Afghan tribes, the Pushtun tribal belt which today lies either side of the Afghan–Pakistan frontier, and a region which, in 1747, was mostly outside of Ahmad Shah's authority. In fact, Ahmad Shah and his successors had no specific name for their kingdom, a lack of which was noted by the Elphinstone Mission of 1808–9. In order to address this issue, Elphinstone arbitrarily referred to the country as the 'Kingdom of Cauboul', for by this time Kabul, not Kandahar, was the capital of the kingdom. However, he also used the term 'Afghanistan' for both the Pushtun tribal belt and the Durrani realms as a whole. Subsequently the British imperial administration in India, following Elphinstone's precedent, used Afghanistan for the whole kingdom ruled by the Durranis, even though after the Sikh and British conquest of the Punjab more than half of the original Afghanistan lay on the Indian side of the frontier.

Initially Ahmad Shah's kingdom consisted of roughly three of Afghanistan's modern provinces: Kandahar, Farah and Helmand. The Sunni Hazaras of Bala Murghab, Nasir Khan Baluch of Kalat and the Kakar tribe that controlled the passes from Kalat to Kandahar also accepted Saddozai suzerainty. Yet by the end of his reign the Durrani empire stretched from beyond Mashhad to Delhi. So the frontiers of Ahmad Shah's kingdom, both at the start and at the end of his reign, bore no relationship to the present boundaries of modern Afghanistan. As for the formal demarcation of the modern international frontiers of Afghanistan, this process took place more than a century after Ahmad Shah's death.

This is not to belittle Ahmad Shah's achievements, but rather to put them into their proper historical context. Ahmad Shah took advantage of the weakness of the Uzbek and Mughal empires and the chaos that ensued following the assassination of Nadir Shah to reassert Saddozai independence. During the course of his reign, Ahmad Shah transformed his small city-state into a major empire and laid the foundations of a monarchy that endured for nearly two-and-a-half centuries. These are remarkable achievements for a man who was not even 25 years old when he became king, achievements that do not require an aura of romanticism and myth to make them appear even greater.

THREE

Ahmad Shah and the Durrani Empire, 1747–72

An ordinary monarch might endeavour to reduce the tribes to obedience by force; but one Afghaun King has already had the penetration to discover that it would require a less exertion to conquer all the neighbouring kingdoms, than to subdue his own countrymen.

MOUNTSTUART ELPHINSTONE[1]

AHMAD SHAH SADDOZAI was in his mid-twenties when he became *padshah*, or king, but neither he nor any of the tribal council had any experience of governing a state. Ahmad Shah's solution was to adopt and adapt the Safavid models of administration and elements of the Mughal government of Multan.[2] Ahmad Shah's vision of kingship too derived from the absolutist Safavid model. In the case of the Durrani monarchy, however, it was the Sunni branch of Islam rather than Shi'ism which became the state cult of the kingdom.

Ahmad Shah 'Abdali's administration: conflicts and competition

From the very outset of Ahmad Shah's reign there were conflicts within the government about the rights and privileges of the king, tensions that were never satisfactorily resolved and eventually contributed to the break-up of his kingdom. Sixty years after Ahmad Shah's accession, the Elphinstone Mission noted that:

> there is some distinction of interests between the King and the nation, and a still greater difference of opinion regarding his legal powers; the King, the Courtiers, and the Moollahs, maintaining that he has all the authority possessed by Asiatic despots; and the people in the tribes considering him a monarch with very limited prerogatives. This produces a good deal of diversity in the actual exercise of the royal authority.[3]

The king's military-tribal council, or *majlis*, while based on the Mughal and Safavid *malik* model, differed inasmuch as the *malik*s were now located at the heart of the state, rather than on the peripheries, for the 'Abdali tribal council acted to a degree as the king's Cabinet. Since Ahmad Shah was obligated to these individuals and had agreed that their offices were hereditary, it made it extremely difficult for him to dismiss any member of the *jirga* without precipitating a rebellion. Their roles, however, were mostly honorific, for responsibilities for the performance of the duties of their offices were delegated to subordinates, usually members of their own extended family, or *qaum*. As for the civil service, it was almost exclusively in the hands of the Qizilbash, since most of the Durrani leaders were illiterate. The Qizilbash also formed the majority of the king's *ghulam khana*, or royal guard, and acted as a counterpoise to the 'Abdali *malik*s and tribal *khan*s. These complex and competing layers of government undermined effective administration, encouraged graft and contributed significantly to ethnic and sectarian tension, particularly between the Shi'a Qizilbash and members of the king's tribal council.

Another serious problem in the hastily constructed Durrani administration was Ahmad Shah's agreement to exempt the 'Abdali *malik*s and their tribes from civil and religious taxation, an exemption that was another source of tension between them and the king, especially when the treasury was empty. Other Afghan tribes and ethnic groups resented this privileged arrangement for they had to bear the burden of taxation, yet were excluded from access to high office and state patronage. The situation was not improved by Ahmad Shah adopting the tradition of auctioning the right to revenue collection to the highest bidder, an arrangement similar to the *zamindari* system in Mughal India or the Roman 'publican' one in New Testament Judaea. The winners of these auctions had a free hand to extract as much revenue as they could, provided they paid the contracted sum into the treasury. Since it was usually members of the 'Abdali tribe who won the bidding war, this was yet another source of resentment against the tribe, a bitterness exacerbated by the notorious venality of the tax gatherers who had no qualms about resorting to violence. Though their rapacity made them very rich very quickly, their exactions forced thousands of small landholders into permanent debt. Many were forced to mortgage the land or sell up, while others fled the kingdom altogether, leaving their land to be snapped up by the very individuals who had forced them into penury and exile in the first place.

Ahmad Shah, though, was not particularly concerned about this state of affairs, for he was far more preoccupied with emulating his mentor,

Nadir Shah, and pursuing military conquest rather than establishing good governance, a competent administration or a viable fiscal foundation for his kingdom. It was sufficient that money continued to flow into the state treasury and any shortfall could be supplemented by the loot and tribute acquired on his campaigns. Indeed, Ahmad Shah spent relatively little of his 25 years as king in his capital of Kandahar and for most of his reign he was campaigning thousands of kilometres from his capital, returning only in order to suppress rebellions. In all Ahmad Shah fought fifteen major military campaigns: nine in northern India, three in Persian Khurasan and three in the Uzbek appanage of Balkh, or Turkistan as it was known to the Afghans.

The revolt of Nawab Nasir Khan and Ahmad Shah's first invasion of the Punjab

A matter of weeks after being proclaimed king Ahmad Shah faced the first of many internal challenges to his authority: Nawab Nasir Khan, the former Mughal governor of Kabul, who had been allowed to return to Kabul as governor after submitting to Ahmad Shah's authority; in return he pledged to pay 50,000 rupees in tribute. However, when he attempted to raise this sum from the surrounding Ghilzai tribes, they refused to accept 'Abdali sovereignty and made it clear they would only pay taxes to their legitimate sovereign, Muhammad Shah, in Delhi. Faced with a serious Ghilzai revolt, Nawab Nasir Khan threw off the 'Abdali yoke and sent Ahmad Shah's minders back to Kandahar empty-handed. He then went to Peshawar where he recruited additional Uzbek levies and appealed to Muhammad Shah to send money and reinforcements to defend the Mughal outpost against 'Abdali aggression.

In the late autumn of 1747 Ahmad Shah, having appointed his nephew Luqman Khan as his deputy in Kandahar during his absence, marched up the Ghazni road to bring Nawab Nasir Khan to heel, only for his advance to be opposed by his erstwhile allies, the Tokhi Ghilzai, in their stronghold of Qalat-i Ghilzai. Ahmad Shah's troops stormed the citadel and five of the most senior Tokhi *maliks* were executed, so ending his fleeting alliance with this tribe.[4] An 'Abdali governor was installed and over the next decade the 'Abdalis annexed large tracts of Tokhi land in the fertile Tarnak valley.

Ghazni offered only token resistance and Ahmad Shah sent envoys to the Sulaiman Khel Ghilzais of the region to secure their support for his campaign against Nawab Nasir Khan. Taqi Khan then wrote to the Qizilbash garrison in Kabul's Bala Hisar, offering them a share of the spoils of war, appointments to offices of state and the right of self-governance

Kabul: traditional flat-roofed houses on the northern face of the Sher Darwaza
in the Chindawal area, formerly the fortified *mahala* of the Jawanshir Qizilbash.

and protection for their Shi'a faith, in return for accepting 'Abdali sovereignty. They agreed to these terms, forcing Nasir Khan to flee to Peshawar
and when Ahmad Shah reached Kabul, the Qizilbash opened the gates of
the Bala Hisar. Ahmad Shah honoured his pledge, and the Qizilbash were
assigned the walled *mahala*s of Chindawal and Murad Khaneh, while the
defection of the Kabul garrison meant Ahmad Shah had acquired several
thousand additional troops for his first campaign in northern India.

Following the fall of Kabul, Ahmad Shah sent his *sipar salar*, or
commander-in-chief, Sardar Jahan Khan Popalzai Bakhshi, in hot pursuit
of Nawab Nasir Khan. He quickly overran Jalalabad and so swift was his
advance that Nawab Nasir Khan had no time to organize a blockade of
the Khyber Pass: Jahan Khan's army marched through it unopposed, and
when he reached the Peshawar plains the Yusufzais, Afridis and Khattaks
declared for Ahmad Shah, forcing Nasir Khan to abandon Peshawar. He
eventually made his way to Delhi where he informed Muhammad Shah
that yet another invasion of the Punjab was imminent.

Once in control of Peshawar, Sardar Jahan Khan opened a clandestine
correspondence with Shah Nawaz Khan, Nawab of Lahore. Shah Nawaz
had recently deposed his brother, Yahya Khan, but Muhammad Shah had
refused to legitimize his coup, so Sardar Jahan Khan promised Nawaz
Khan that if he accepted 'Abdali sovereignty he would be confirmed as
governor of Lahore. A secret pact was drawn up between the *nawab* and

Jahan Khan but, when Muhammad Shah's *wazir* heard of the agreement, he offered to confirm Shah Nawaz as governor on condition he opposed the Afghan invasion. As a result, Shah Nawaz tore up his treaty with Ahmad Shah and marched out to confront Sardar Jahan Khan.

Shah Nawaz's sudden change of allegiance left Jahan Khan exposed. He had already crossed the Indus but had only around 8,000 men under his command and hardly any artillery, so he beat a hasty retreat to Peshawar to await the arrival of Ahmad Shah with reinforcements. Once he arrived in the city, Ahmad Shah sent envoys to Shah Nawaz but for some reason Ahmad Shah included Sabir Shah as part of this delicate mission. Instead of observing the normal diplomatic protocols and presenting himself to the governor, Sabir Shah took up residence with a local religious leader. Shah Nawaz, suspecting that the *faqir*, who was a native of Lahore, was an agent provocateur, sent trusted agents to interrogate him, only for Sabir Shah to grossly insult the Nawab. Sabir Shah and his host were thrown in prison, but when Shah Nawaz went in person to question the dervish he continued to hurl insults at him, telling the Nawab that he was a mere servant while Ahmad Shah was 'king of Khurasan' and rebuked the Nawab for breaking the treaty. After enduring several days of this invective, Shah Nawaz had had enough and ordered his executioner to pour molten lead down the dervish's throat, silencing Sabir Shah once and for all.[5]

Having disposed of the troublesome *faqir*, Shah Nawaz broke off negotiations and marched out against Ahmad Shah. Despite commanding a

The Kabul Gate, Peshawar, gateway to the Khyber Pass, late 19th-century postcard.

force far larger than the 'Abdali king, however, the Mughal army was deeply divided. The two armies met at Adina in January 1748 and even before battle commenced one of the *nawab*'s Afghan regiments defected. Ahmad Shah then sent his mounted musketeers, or *jezailchis*, to attack the massed ranks of Mughal infantry, inflicting such a great loss of life that eventually they broke ranks and fled. The Afghans poured into Lahore, looting and killing as they went and the bloodshed was only ended when Shah Nawaz's rivals were released from prison, tendered their submission and agreed to pay a tribute of 3 million rupees. As a consequence of the sack of Lahore, Ahmad Shah acquired a huge amount of booty and a vast quantity of military supplies, including siege guns and rockets. At the same time, thousands of women and children were enslaved and thousands of Punjabi men were conscripted into his army.

Among the conscripts were a number of Armenians who were experts in casting cannon.[6] One of them, whose Persian name was Shah Nazar Khan, later cast two massive siege guns for Ahmad Shah, the most famous of which was the Zamzama, or Thunderer.[7] This enormous artillery piece was more than 4 metres (13 ft) long, had a bore in excess of 21 centimetres (8 in.), and could fire a cannonball weighing more than 18 kilograms (40 lb). The gun was used in various siege situations until it was eventually captured by the Sikhs and subsequently acquired by the British, who placed it at the entrance to the Lahore Museum, where it remains to this day. Later, Rudyard Kipling, whose father was curator of the museum, featured Zamzama in the opening scene of *Kim*. As for Shah Nazar Khan, he died in Agra but several Armenian families, possibly all related to Shah Nazar, were relocated to Kabul and Kandahar where they set up artillery workshops.

Following the fall of Lahore, Muhammad Shah finally dispatched an army to halt any Afghan advance on Delhi, but Ahmad Shah bypassed this force and took the key town of Sirhind, putting most of the town's male population to the sword and enslaving its women and children. The entire treasury of the Mughal army and its heavy baggage also fell into his hands. The sack of Sirhind was carried out despite the city having a substantial Muslim population and it being the ancestral home of Shaikh Ahmad Sirhind (1564–1624), known as Mujadid Alf Sani, the Renewer of the Second Age. This Hanafi jurist, theologian and Naqshbandi *pir* had been an outspoken opponent of Muslim syncretic practices as well as Akbar the Great's unifying religious movement, *Din-i Ilahi*. At the end of the eighteenth century, members of this Mujadidi Order established *khanagah*s in the Tagab and Kohistan region north of Kabul, while another member of this *tariqa* took up residence in Kabul, where he and his descendants were known as the Hazrats of Shor Bazaar. Over the ensuing centuries these Mujadidi *pirs* played a prominent part in Afghanistan's political life, particularly as opponents of Europeanization and colonialism.

The fall of Sirhind opened the road to Delhi, which was virtually undefended, for the Mughal army was now in the rear of Ahmad Shah's advance. In Delhi itself, the reports of the massacres that had accompanied the fall of cities and towns caused panic and a mass exodus to the countryside. Ahmad Shah's advance, though, was halted unexpectedly. In March 1748 the Mughal army finally caught up with the Afghans at Manupur, defeated Ahmad Shah and forced him to retreat to Lahore. When he arrived Ahmad Shah was greeted with the news that his nephew, Luqman Khan, had rebelled, so Ahmad Shah gave the order to march on Kandahar. As soon as his army had crossed the Indus, the governor of Lahore pledged his loyalty to Delhi. A few weeks later Muhammad Shah, the Mughal emperor, passed away and was succeeded by his son Ahmad Shah Bahadur (r. 1748–54). His death precipitated a power struggle in Delhi that further undermined the Mughals' ability to resist further Afghan invasion or the rising power of the Marathas and Sikhs.

Ahmad Shah's campaigns against the Mughals, Marathas, Jats and Sikhs

Luqman Khan's revolt was quickly put down and in the autumn of 1748 Ahmad Shah set out to reassert his authority over the Punjab. After crossing the Indus, Ahmad Shah paid his respects to Hazrat Mian 'Omar Baba, *pir* of Chamkani, who blessed his campaign and bestowed on him the title of *Dur-i Durran*, Pearl of Pearls, and from this point on the 'Abdali tribe became known as Durrani. As Ahmad Shah advanced, Mir Mannu Khan, military governor of the Punjab and the general who had defeated Ahmad Shah at the Battle of Manupur, pleaded in vain with Delhi for reinforcements. In Lahore itself there was a bitter power struggle between Mir Mannu Khan and Nasir Khan, who Ahmad Shah Bahadur had appointed as *nawab*. Mir Mannu Khan decided he dared not risk confronting the Afghans in the open plains, fearing that while he was away Nawab Nasir Khan would lock him out. Instead, he reinforced the fortress and defences of Lahore, leaving the surrounding countryside to be ravaged by Sardar Jahan Khan. The Sikhs took advantage of the chaos and a small raiding party entered Lahore, helped itself to as much loot as it could find and disappeared into the surrounding jungle.

Caught between the Afghans and the Sikhs, Mir Mannu Khan sent two senior religious figures to negotiate submission to Ahmad Shah. A treaty was agreed under the terms of which Ahmad Shah was given sovereignty over all territory north of the Indus along with the annual revenues of the Chahar Mahala, or Four Districts (Sialkot, Aurangabad, Gukraj and Pasrur), which were worth 1,400,000 rupees per annum. Sovereignty over the Chahar Mahala, however, remained with the Mughal king. Having secured this highly advantageous treaty, Ahmad Shah marched back to Peshawar, passing through Dera Isma'il Khan and Dera Ghazi Khan en route. In the latter town Zahid Shah Saddozai, the great-grandson of Sultan Maudud Khan, petitioned the king to restore him to the governorship of Multan, for Mir Mannu had deposed him and installed a rival Saddozai, 'Abd al-'Aziz. Ahmad Shah referred the matter to his tribal *jirga*, who rejected Zahid Shah's petition, no doubt under pressure from the king, for he had no wish to see a potential rival from his *qaum* ruling this strategic region.

It was three years before Ahmad Shah resumed his Indian campaign, having in the interim taken Herat and mounted an unsuccessful invasion of Khurasan. His third Punjab campaign was precipitated by the failure of Mir Mannu Khan to remit the revenues of the Chahar Mahal as agreed under their treaty. In a battle in the vicinity of Lahore's Shalimar Gardens, Mir Mannu Khan was defeated and for the second time Ahmad Shah's army plundered Lahore and slaughtered its population. Mir Mannu surrendered and a second treaty was agreed that ceded partial sovereignty over Lahore and Multan to the Durrani monarch as well as all the surplus revenues of these regions. However, the right of *khutba* and coinage remained with the Mughal king. Ahmad Shah Bahadur did everything in his power to avoid confirming this treaty, but he was in no position to resist and on 13 April 1752 he put his seal on the agreement.

Ahmad Shah's next objective was the wealthy province of Kashmir, which was being torn apart by civil war. 'Abd Allah Khan, better known as Shah Pasand Khan, was sent to support the ousted governor, Mir Muqim Kanth, and quickly occupied Srinagar. Meanwhile Ahmad Shah went to Multan, where he distributed presents and gifts to members of his own lineage, but deposed the Saddozai governor and appointed 'Ali Muhammad Khan, a Khakwani Pushtun, in his place.

For the next two years Ahmad Shah was occupied with campaigns in Khurasan and Turkistan. In 1756 he returned once more to the Punjab, by which time Ahmad Shah Bahadur had been deposed and replaced by the elderly 'Alamgir II, who had spent all of his adult life as a state prisoner. Mir

Mannu Khan had also died in a freak hunting accident and 'Alamgir II had appointed his own three-year-old son as *nawab* of Lahore, a decision that precipitated yet another bloody power struggle in the Punjab capital. When Ahmad Shah's army reached the city in November 1756 its government was so divided that Lahore fell without offering more than token resistance.

Ahmad Shah then overran Sirhind, Karnal and Panipat, advanced on Delhi and sent 'Alamgir II a list of demands that included the payment of 20 million rupees, the hand of the emperor's daughter in marriage, and the secession of Kashmir and all Mughal territory north of Sirhind. While 'Alamgir and his counsellors dithered about whether to give in to these demands, in January 1757 Ahmad Shah arrived before the gates of Delhi and threatened to sack the city if his terms were not met. Eventually, senior Mughal courtiers took matters into their own hands, going from mosque to mosque ordering the *imams* to insert the name of Ahmad Shah Durrani in the *khutba*. A few days later 'Alamgir II went to Ahmad Shah's camp and acknowledged the Durrani king's sovereignty. He was allowed to remain on the throne, but the real power now lay with Ahmad Shah.

Following the submission of 'Alamgir, Ahmad Shah made a grand entrance into Delhi only to be greeted by silence and deserted streets and bazaars, for those who had not already fled the city had barricaded themselves in their houses or hid in cellars. Ahmad Shah, though, ordered his troops not to loot the city and a few days later the bazaars reopened. Ahmad Shah then reversed the long-standing Mughal policy of religious toleration, forbade non-Muslims to wear turbans and other forms of 'Islamic' dress and ordered all Hindus to wear a distinctive mark on their foreheads, probably the traditional *tikka*. Ahmad Shah also demanded the payment of millions of rupees in tribute, for he was urgently in need of the cash as his troops' pay was in arrears. The Mughal treasury, however, was empty. When the king's courtiers refused to hand over any of their wealth, Ahmad Shah sent his own tax collectors into the palaces and *hawelis* of courtiers and merchants and imposed a tax on every household in Delhi.[8] Those who refused to pay or were suspected of concealing treasure were subjected to the *falaqa,* or bastinado, and thousands died under this torture or were crippled for life. Others preferred to take poison rather than endure such torment.

Having secured control of Delhi, Ahmad Shah turned his attention to the Hindu kingdom of the Jats, which lay to the south and east of Delhi. The fortress of Faridabad fell and was put to fire and sword, but subsequently the Afghans were caught by a surprise raid and massacred. Sardar Jahan Khan retaliated by sacking Ballabhgarh and plundering the surrounding region. At the end of February 1757 Jahan Khan attacked Mathura, which in Hindu tradition is the birthplace of the god Krishna. The city's occupants were mostly non-combatants – religious mendicants, Brahmins, priests and pilgrims – but despite this Sardar Jahan Khan's troops massacred them and defiled the corpses of *sanyasis,* priests and *sadhu*s by stuffing pieces of slaughtered cow in their mouths. The city's temples were also burnt and images smashed. When Jahan Khan offered a bounty of 5 rupees for every Hindu head, thousands of men, women and children were killed and decapitated. Not even the Muslim population of the city was spared. One Muslim jeweller, in a desperate attempt to save his life, bared himself in front of a sword-wielding assailant to show that he was circumcised, but he was still slashed by the assailant's sword. One of the few survivors of the massacre later recalled how the waters of the Yamuna river, sacred to Hindus, ran red with blood for seven days after the slaughter.

The massacre at Mathura was just the beginning of Sardar Jahan Khan's blood-soaked campaign. When the nearby town of Brindaban fell, it suffered the same fate. Jahan Khan then rejected the offered ransom from the authorities of Agra, Akbar the Great's capital, as inadequate. Despite Agra's reputation as a centre of Islamic jurisprudence and the fact that the commander of the Agra garrison was a Muslim, Jahan Khan's troops went on another orgy of slaughter and pillage. Meanwhile Ahmad Shah marched on Gokul, another major Hindu cult centre, only to encounter a very different kind of Hindu devotee, for Gokul was the centre of the Nanga Sadhus, devotees of the Bakhti sect who were renowned for their martial prowess. As the army approached the town, thousands of naked, ash-smeared Nangas poured out of the city and attacked the invaders without regard for life or limb. Ahmad Shah eventually admitted defeat and Gokul was spared the fate of Mathura.

By this time the heat of the Indian summer had arrived and begun to take a toll on Ahmad Shah's troops. Provisions were in short supply, for most of the storehouses had been pillaged and the crops burnt while the Yamuna, the main source of water for the army, was so polluted by blood, corpses and the detritus of war that an epidemic of cholera and typhoid broke out. With thousands of his men dead or incapacitated, Ahmad Shah decided to return to the cooler climate of the Afghan hills. Before he left Delhi, Ahmad Shah demanded the hand of Zuhra Begam, daughter of the former Mughal king, Muhammad Shah, while 'Alamgir's daughter was married to Ahmad Shah's eleven-year-old son, Timur Shah. When informed of the arrangement, Muhammad Shah's widow declared she would rather put her daughter to death than have her wed an Afghan, but she had little choice in the matter and the marriage went ahead. Rather than abandon her daughter, she courageously decided to accompany her daughter into exile.

Ahmad Shah's army set out to return to Peshawar and requisitioned 28,000 pack animals, including hundreds of elephants, and even the cavalry horses were requisitioned to carry the booty from the campaign. On his return journey through the Punjab, however, the Sikh cavalry raided the army's flanks. When Ahmad Shah reached Jullundar Duaba he sent Sardar Jahan Khan to attack and plunder the Sikh holy city of Kartarpur, desecrating its temples and *gurdwaras* and slaughtering its inhabitants. After reaching Lahore, Ahmad Shah sent another force to attack the Sikhs' other holy city, Amritsar, which suffered the same fate.

Ahmad Shah appointed Timur Shah as governor of Lahore, with Sardar Jahan Khan as *wazir* and commander-in-chief of the garrison. Timur Mirza was not a good choice and disaffection soon spread, while the Sikhs formed an anti-Afghan alliance with the rising power of the Marathas. In December 1757 the Sikhs defeated Sardar Jahan Khan at Mahilpur and plundered Jullundar Duaba. Following a second defeat in January of the following year, the Sikhs raided the outskirts of Lahore itself and in March a joint Sikh-Maratha army overran Sirhind. Faced with the imminent fall of Lahore, Sardar Jahan Khan and Timur Mirza hastily evacuated the city but, in their haste to ford the Chenab and Ravi rivers, most of the army's baggage was abandoned and thousands drowned attempting the crossing. Those Afghans who were taken prisoner by the Sikhs were put to work cleansing the sacred tank in Amritsar.

Following the loss of the Punjab, Nasir Khan, *beglar begi* of Kalat, convinced that these defeats marked the beginning of the end of Durrani power, declared independence. Sardar Shah Wali Khan was sent to put down the revolt, but when he was defeated Ahmad Shah set out in person to deal with the troublesome governor. He eventually defeated the Baluch army but was unable to take Kalat by storm. Instead, he agreed to allow Nasir Khan to remain as governor of Kalat in return for his resubmission to Durrani sovereignty.[9]

The Kalat uprising meant Ahmad Shah was in no position to regain control over the Punjab until October 1759 and this time his campaign was given religious legitimacy by Ahmad ibn 'Abd al-Rahim, better known as Shah Wali Allah (1703–1762), one of India's leading Islamic scholars, whose teachings would inspire the Barelvi and Deobandi movements.[10] He wrote to Ahmad Shah urging him to come and save the Muslims of northern India from domination by Hindus and Sikhs. Ahmad Shah then presented

Shah Wali Ullah's letter to the *ulama* in Kandahar who formally declared the campaign against the Marathas and Sikhs to be a *jihad*. When news of Ahmad Shah's intentions to return to northern India reached the Mughal court in Delhi, however, 'Alamgir II's *wazir* put him to death, executed a number of Ahmad Shah's officials and sympathizers, and placed Shah Jahan III on the throne instead, only for him to be deposed the following year by the Marathas.

Ahmad Shah soon regained control of Lahore from the Sikhs and reinstated Timur Mirza as governor. The Rohillas of the Duaba, Muslims of Pushtun descent, then joined forces with him and he set out for Delhi, defeating the Marathas en route, and set up camp at Khizrabad. Ahmad Shah defeated the Marathas again at Barari Ghat and Sikandarabad and in March 1760 he took Aligarh. However, he had overextended himself and the Marathas, who had received substantial reinforcements from the Deccan, attacked Agra and Delhi. In early August both cities fell into their hands. A few weeks later the Marathas sacked Kunjpura and seized most of Ahmad Shah's supplies.

Ahmad Shah had been unable to prevent the fall of Agra, Delhi and Kunjpura since he was stranded on the other side of the Jamuna river, which was in flood. Finally, in late October he decided to risk the crossing anyway and was fortunate that most of his army made it across safely. The crossing caught the Marathas by surprise and Ahmad Shah was able to cut off their advanced force from the main army in Delhi and besieged them in the fort of Panipat. By early 1761 supplies had run out and Sadashiv Rao Bhau, who commanded the Maratha garrison, decided it was more honourable to die in battle than starve. On 14 January 1761 he ordered a general attack. The Marathas initially had the better of the encounter, which raged for several days, as their French artillery decimated the Rohilla while a cavalry charge almost broke through the Durrani lines. Faced with defeat, Ahmad Shah sent in the Qizilbash and his heavy cavalry reserve, backed up by a camel corps with swivel guns. Eventually the Maratha line crumpled under the onslaught. As they turned and fled, Ahmad Shah sent his cavalry in pursuit.

The Battle of Panipat was a bloody affair that left as many as 70,000 dead, while thousands more perished in the subsequent pursuit. The Afghans also systematically beheaded thousands of prisoners, including many who had surrendered. During the sack of Panipat fort, which followed the main battle, Ahmad Shah's troops decapitated every male over the age of fourteen and enslaved the town's women and children. When Ahmad Shah finally entered Panipat in triumph, he rode through its blood-soaked streets wearing a bejewelled robe resplendent with the Koh-i Nur diamond.

Panipat marked the end of Maratha power in northern India and it was Ahmad Shah's most notable military victory, but he was not able to push home his advantage and attack the Marathas' allies, the Jats. His commanders had had enough of campaigning and thousands of his soldiers had been killed or wounded. When news arrived that Hajji Jamal Khan Zargarani in Kandahar had rebelled, Ahmad Shah ordered his army to march back to Peshawar and sent a column under Shah Pasand Khan to deal with the revolt in the Durrani capital. Once again the Sikh cavalry harassed the army's flanks as it marched through the Punjab, and after Ahmad Shah had crossed the Indus, the Sikhs overran several Afghan outposts. In May 1761 a Sikh army annihilated a force led by Ahmad Shah's governor of the Chahar Mahal, and a relief army despatched from Kandahar was defeated and forced to surrender. The Sikhs then took Lahore while its governor barricaded himself in the citadel. Within just a few months after his victory over the Marathas, Ahmad Shah lost most of the Punjab to a new and even more formidable enemy, the Sikhs.

After putting down the revolt in Kandahar, Ahmad Shah returned to the Punjab, whereupon the Sikhs abandoned Lahore. In early February 1762 the governor of Malerkotla informed Ahmad Shah that the families and camp followers of the Sikh army were camped nearby. Aided by Zain Khan of Sirhind, Ahmad Shah surrounded them and ordered his troops to leave no one dressed in Indian clothes alive. The small Sikh guard formed a cordon around the defenceless camp followers and fought and died to the last man. After ten hours, Ahmad Shah finally called a halt to the slaughter. Exactly how many Sikhs lost their lives in the massacre is disputed, although Sikh historians put the number at between 10,000 and 30,000 individuals, mostly women, children, old men and camp followers. *Wadda Ghalughara*, or the Great Slaughter, is still commemorated by Sikhs to this day.

Ahmad Shah followed up this 'victory' by attacking Amritsar a few days before the Sikh New Year festival and another massacre ensued. The Golden Temple was desecrated and the dead bodies and carcases of cows thrown into its sacred lake, which was then filled up with the rubble from demolished temples and *gurdwara*s. While Ahmad Shah supervised this destruction, however, a piece of shrapnel from an explosion severed the fleshy part of his nose, leaving a gaping wound. The injury never healed and for the rest of his life Ahmad Shah wore a diamond prosthesis. Yet despite the slaughter, the Sikh army recuperated and a few months later, after Ahmad Shah had withdrawn to Kashmir to recuperate, they attacked Sirhind and Jullundar Duaba and raided the hinterland of Lahore.

After several months of convalescence, in October 1762 Ahmad Shah again attacked Amritsar on the day before the Feast of Diwali, but this time it was the Sikhs who won the day. When Ahmad Shah was informed of yet another insurrection in Kandahar, he ordered his army to march on the Durrani capital, leaving the Punjab to be once again overrun by the Sikhs. In the spring of the following year, Sardar Jahan Khan attempted to regain some of the lost territory but the tide had turned. In November 1763 Jahan Khan suffered a heavy defeat at Gujranwala and the Sikhs followed up their victory by sacking Malerkotla and Morinda. In January of the following year Zain Khan, governor of Sirhind and the man the Sikhs held responsible for the Wadda Ghalughara massacre, was also defeated and slain. The Sikhs then stormed Sirhind, slaughtered its population and burnt public buildings to the ground. In order to prevent Lahore suffering the same fate, its governor agreed to pay tribute and accept Sikh suzerainty. The Sikhs next besieged the reputedly impregnable citadel of Rohtas, which fell after four months. Sarbaland Khan Saddozai, who commanded the fortress, was taken prisoner but was reinstated after he agreed to accept Sikh suzerainty.[11] An even more disastrous blow to Saddozai power followed with the submission of Multan, with Sikh raiders penetrating as far as the hinterland of Dera Isma'il Khan and Dera Ghazi Khan.

When Ahmad Shah heard of the disasters he flew into a paroxysm of rage and wrote to Nasir Khan, *beglar begi* of Kalat, calling him to join a *jihad* against 'the accursed dogs and lustful infidels', and to 'destroy this faithless sect, and enslave their women and children'. At the time Nasir Khan was about to leave for the Hajj, but he abandoned his plans and joined the Holy War after Ahmad Shah declared that 'Jihad . . . is more meritorious that Hajj'.[12] However, when Ahmad Shah returned to the Punjab in October 1764 the *jihad* came to nothing. The advance guard was ambushed and routed by the Sikhs outside Lahore and Beglar Begi Nasir Khan was lucky to escape with his life after his horse was shot from under him. The Sikhs then retreated into the jungle, so Ahmad Shah sacked and desecrated Amritsar for the third time. The Sikhs, though, refused to be drawn into another set-piece battle and instead raided the Afghan army's flanks and attacked parties gathering fodder.

Ahmad Shah pushed on to Sirhind, plundering and destroying everything in his path, but by February 1765 his troops refused to march any further. Their pay was in arrears and Ahmad Shah's relentless campaigning had led to disaffection among the officer corps and the rank and file. Fearing a mutiny, Ahmad Shah set out to return to Lahore, but the day after fording the Sutlej river the Sikh army appeared in full strength and for the next week he fought a series of running battles with the Sikh cavalry. By the time his troops reached Lahore they were exhausted, but instead of allowing them time to recuperate Ahmad Shah ordered them to continue their march to the Indus, only for further disasters to strike. While attempting to cross the Chenab river, the army mistook the correct fording point and thousands of men were drowned or swept away. According to one observer, more lives were lost crossing the Chenab than had been lost in all of Ahmad Shah's battles with the Sikhs. Once the remnants of the Durrani army had crossed the Indus, the Sikhs once again overran the Punjab. Finally, in April 1765, the Sikhs occupied Lahore.

Eighteen months later, in November 1766, Ahmad Shah embarked on his final campaign in northern India. Initially he was victorious and in early December the Durrani army briefly reoccupied Lahore, laying siege to Amritsar. Having drawn the Afghans deep into the Punjab, the Sikhs proceeded to cut off Ahmad Shah's supply line, forcing him to confront the Sikh column that had cut off his line of retreat. Having successfully split the army in two, the main Sikh army attacked and defeated Sardar Jahan Khan, who had been left to pursue the siege of Amritsar. Despite these setbacks, Ahmad Shah insisted on marching on Delhi, but as news of his defeat spread, province after province refused to pay taxes, tribute or supply the army. Faced with another potential revolt by senior commanders, Ahmad Shah abandoned his plans and returned to Multan.

Ahmad Shah's Indian campaigns, an assessment

Despite nine punishing campaigns in northern India, in the end Ahmad Shah had little to show in terms of territorial gains beyond the Indus. Kashmir was now a Durrani principality, as were Multan, Peshawar and the Deras, but by 1767 it was the Sikhs who ruled the Punjab. Despite defeating the Marathas and Jats, Ahmad Shah's campaigns had done little or nothing to strengthen Muslim rule in northern India or prop up what was left of the Mughal empire. Rather, his invasions contributed significantly to the demise of Muslim power in northern India. In the spring of 1757 the Muslim *nawab* of Bengal had been obliged to send most of his army to defend Delhi against Ahmad Shah. Two months later, on 23 June 1757, the *nawab*'s understrength force was decimated by the East India Company's army under Robert Clive at the Battle of Palashi (Plassey), a victory that marked the rise of British imperial power in northern India. Eight years later, in August 1765, Shah 'Alam II ceded the East India Company virtual sovereignty over Bengal, Bihar and Orissa. Meanwhile in northwest India, the Sikh kingdom had ended five centuries of Muslim sovereignty over the Punjab.

The massacres and enslavement of civilians, and the desecration and destruction of Hindu and Sikh holy places, left a legacy of religious hatred in northern India and undermined the Mughal policy of religious toleration that had been a cornerstone of more than three centuries of Muslim rule in India. Ahmad Shah's invasions also had much to do in creating the Indian, and subsequently British, stereotype of the Pathans (the Indian term for Pushtuns) as cruel, bloodthirsty, religious fanatics. Ahmad Shah appeared much more interested in booty and money than in restoring Muslim supremacy in northern India, and his refusal to move his capital from the distant frontier outpost of Kandahar to Lahore or Delhi made supervision of his Indian empire more or less impossible.

Ahmad Shah's campaigns in Herat and Khurasan

As if nine hard-fought campaigns in India were not enough, Ahmad Shah set out to reassert Durrani supremacy over Herat and Persian Khurasan. His first campaign took place in 1749, between the second and third invasions of India. The main objective was to regain control of Herat, which at the time was governed by an Arab in the name of Shah Rukh Mirza, grandson of Nadir Shah, who had succeeded to the Persian throne after Nadir Shah's death. Like his grandfather, Shah Rukh made Mashhad his capital but his hold on power was tenuous, as the succession was disputed between various members of his own family and by the head of the Qajar tribe.

In the spring of 1749 Ahmad Shah, taking advantage of the political turmoil in Persia, laid siege to Herat. After several months he ordered his Durrani commanders to take the city regardless of the cost. Wave after wave of Afghans stormed the breaches, climbing over the dead and dying, until finally they broke through into the town. The remnant of the Persian garrison retreated into the citadel of Qal'a-yi Ikhtiyar al-Din and sued for peace. In order to lull their commander into a false sense of security, Ahmad Shah assured them that if they surrendered they would be spared, but under cover of darkness he sent a storming party to scale the citadel walls. The dozing guards were caught unawares and the sleeping garrison was put to the sword. Herat was once more in Saddozai hands, but rather than appointing a member of his own lineage as governor, Ahmad Shah appointed Darwish 'Ali Khan, chief of the Sunni Hazara Aimaq.

Qal'a-yi Nau, the provincial centre of Badghis and the former centre of the Sunni Hazaras, one of the Chahar Aimaq tribes. The town and region still has a large Aimaq population.

Ahmad Shah then marched on Mashhad while Sardar Jahan Khan and Nasir Khan of Kalat advanced on Turbat-i Shaikh Jam, but despite taking the strategic frontier post of Nun, Mashhad withstood all attempts by the Afghans to storm the walls. In the end Shah Rukh Mirza went in person to Ahmad Shah's camp, acknowledged Durrani sovereignty and was allowed to remain as ruler in return for payment of a substantial tribute. Ahmad Shah's next objective was Mazandaran and Gilan, where Muhammad Husain Khan Qajar and the Ghilzai chieftain Azad Khan Hotaki, a descendant of Mir Wa'is, had carved out independent fiefdoms and were threatening to attack Mashhad.[13] While Shah Pasand Khan marched into Mazandaran, Ahmad Shah set out for Nishapur, but its governor, Ja'far Khan, refused to surrender despite having only a few thousand men under his command. Ahmad Shah placed the town under siege, but a few weeks later messengers arrived to inform the king that Shah Pasand Khan had been defeated. Realizing that Muhammad Husain Khan Qajar would be marching to the relief of Nishapur, Ahmad Shah ordered his Durrani commanders to storm the walls. A sustained artillery bombardment eventually breached the city's defences but overnight the defenders dug deep, well-concealed pits behind the breach. When the storming party attacked the following morning they literally fell into the trap. In the bitter hand-to-hand fighting that ensued Ja'far Khan was slain but his eighteen-year-old nephew, 'Abbas Quli, took command, rallied his troops and threw the Afghans back from the walls. The failed assault cost Ahmad Shah dearly, for some 12,000 troops were killed and thousands more wounded.

As his army was seriously depleted, Ahmad Shah set out to return to Herat only for the icy weather to take a terrible toll on his troops, who lacked any winter clothing, and thousands perished from exposure. With Muhammad Husain Khan Qajar in hot pursuit, Ahmad Shah abandoned his artillery, baggage and most of his stores of food and fodder. When the survivors attempted to cross the frozen Hari Rud, the ice broke and many men and pack animals were drowned. Those who finally reached the safety of Herat looked more like skeletons than soldiers. Ahmad Shah's problems, though, were not over. Darwish 'Ali Khan, hearing of Shah Pasand Khan and Ahmad Shah's defeats, planned to assassinate the king once he returned to Herat. Fortunately for Ahmad Shah the conspiracy was exposed before it could be implemented. Darwish 'Ali Khan was imprisoned and in his place Ahmad Shah appointed his infant son and heir, Timur Mirza, as governor of Herat.

A year later Ahmad Shah tried a second time to subdue Nishapur. Since he lacked heavy siege guns, he ordered every mounted soldier to carry several kilograms of gunmetal. Once the siege was underway, the Armenian cannon makers melted down the metal and cast a monstrous gun.[14] Its first shot not only breached the city walls but wreaked havoc as it tore through houses and bazaars. Such was the terror this 'weapon of mass destruction' created that the city elders came and tendered their

The Hari Rud river in spate as it flows under the arches of the ancient Pul-i Malan bridge on the old road between Herat and Mashhad.

submission and opened the city gates, even though 'Abbas Quli, the governor of Nishapur, refused to surrender. What Nishapur's defenders did not know was that the cannon's first shot was also its last, for the force of the explosion had split the barrel.

Despite Nishapur having submitted peacefully, Ahmad Shah allowed his troops to plunder the city, though its inhabitants were spared on condition they took refuge in the city's main mosque and took nothing with them. The Afghans then went from house to house systematically helping themselves to anything of value. After they had finished Ahmad Shah ordered the city's defences and part of the town to be levelled. He followed up this victory by taking Sabzawar, which was also pillaged and its inhabitants slaughtered. Meanwhile Shah Pasand Khan and Nasir Khan of Kalat ravaged the rich agricultural lands of southwestern Khurasan. Finally, Ahmad Shah defeated the Qajar army and celebrated his victory by plundering Toon and Tabas and massacring their inhabitants, too.

Having secured strategic depth on his northwestern frontier, and with Shah Rukh Mirza a compliant subordinate, Ahmad Shah was free to concentrate on renewing his Indian campaign. Timur Mirza subsequently became prince governor of Lahore but he was sent back to Herat after the loss of the Punjab, a decision that no doubt pleased the heir apparent, for he lacked his father's martial spirit. Instead, Timur preferred to indulge himself in the pleasures and luxuries of his position and fathering dozens of children by his many wives. The frontier with Persia remained relatively peaceful and stable for the next two decades. In the summer of 1769, however, Ahmad Shah was forced once more to intervene when Shah Rukh Mirza's estranged son, Nasr Allah Khan, deposed his father. Ahmad Shah soon restored Shah Rukh to the throne and Timur Mirza acquired yet another wife, this time Shah Rukh's daughter.

Ahmad Shah's campaigns in Balkh, Bukhara and Merv

Ahmad Shah also set out to secure his position beyond the Hindu Kush in order to prevent a possible attack on Herat from the Khan of Bukhara.[15] His intervention in the *wilayat* of Balkh, however, was primarily in support of his former comrade-in-arms, Hajji Bi Ming of Maimana, rather than an attempt at outright annexation. Prior to the Nadirid conquest of the region, Hajji Bi had been *ataliq* of Maimana and the Chahar Wilayat, or Four Provinces – Maimana, Andkhui, Shibarghan and Sar-i Pul – which were part of the Khanate of the Tuqay-Timurid dynasty of Bukhara. Following the Persian conquest of the region, Hajji Bi had commanded a corps of

The perimeter walls of Balkh, ancient capital of what is now northern Afghanistan. These walls are mostly Timurid, though excavations have indicated pre-Islamic foundations.

Uzbeks in Nadir Shah's army, which later became incorporated into the king's personal guard, where Hajji Bi and Ahmad Shah struck up some kind of an alliance. Following the assassination of Nadir Shah, Hajji Bi fought alongside Ahmad Shah's *ghazi*s and the evidence suggests that the two men made some sort of 'gentlemen's agreement' not to attack each other.

Hajji Bi quickly regained control of the Chahar Wilayat and eventually occupied Balkh, expelling Nadir Shah's governor and subjugating the Qizilbash garrisons. All the Uzbek *amir*s, from the Murghab to Qataghan, then reaffirmed their historic allegiance to the Khan of Bukhara. In Bukhara itself, 'Abu'l-Faiz Khan was deposed by his *ataliq*, Rahim Bi Manghit, who had also served in the army of Nadir Shah. A year or so after taking control of the city of Balkh, Hajji Bi was defeated by his rival Hazara Bi of Qataghan, possibly with the support of Rahim Bi. In 1751, following Ahmad Shah's first campaign in Persian Khurasan, Hajji Bi and the *amir*s of the Chahar Wilayat came to Herat to seek Durrani support against Qataghan and complained about the oppression of Rahim Bi's officials, hinting that the presence of Bukharan officials beyond the Murghab posed a threat to the Durrani frontier post of Maruchak and Herat. In response Ahmad Shah sent 'Ata Allah Khan Turkman and a force of several thousand Qizilbash across the Murghab. In return for this military assistance, Hajji Bi agreed to pay Ahmad Shah a share of Balkh's revenues. Ahmad Shah, for his part, recognized Hajji Bi as *sahib-i ikhtiyar*, or chief collector of taxes of the region and *wali* of Balkh. There is little detail in the sources about the course of the ensuing campaign, but by the summer of 1752 Hajji Bi Ming was once more in charge of Balkh.

During this campaign Mukhlis Khan, commander of one of the Qizilbash regiments, quarrelled with 'Ata Allah Khan Turkman and was recalled, whereupon Mizrab Bi, son of Hazara Bi Qataghan, rebelled. Hajji Bi appealed once more to Ahmad Shah for help and he sent 5,000 troops north. Hajji Bi, having regained control of Balkh city, marched into Qataghan and occupied several settlements that were under the authority of the *mir* of Badakhshan. In the winter of 1752/3 Hajji Bi travelled to Kandahar where Ahmad Shah, flushed with his own victories in India, showered favour after favour on his Uzbek ally.

Three years later Hajji Bi paid a third visit to Ahmad Shah and their alliance was strengthened when Ahmad Shah stripped 'Ata Allah Khan Turkman of his position as *sipar salar* of the Durrani forces in Balkh and appointed Hajji Bi Ming in his place. After Hajji Bi had returned to Balkh, however, his enemies at the Durrani court began to accuse him of being oppressive and rapacious, so Ahmad Shah sent 'Ata Allah Khan Turkman to head a formal inquiry into Hajji Bi's affairs – hardly an impartial investigator given that Hajji Bi had only recently supplanted him. Not surprisingly, 'Ata Allah Khan 'confirmed' the reports of Hajji Bi's oppressions and as a consequence he was reinstated as *sipar salar*.

It was probably at this time that Ahmad Shah also appointed a Durrani *sardar*, Nawab Khan Alakozai, as *hakim* of Balkh. Despite this title, which is somewhat misleadingly translated as 'governor', the *hakim*'s role was primarily to represent Durrani interests in the Balkh region, in particular to tax and ensure the safety of *qafila*s travelling between Bukhara and Herat and between Bukhara and Kabul, a trade that was mostly in the hands of Pushtuns living in Bukhara. This appointment was deeply unpopular with Hajji Bi Ming and the other Uzbek *amir*s of the *wilayat*, who saw it as the first step by the Durrani monarch to assert a degree of sovereignty over their region. Nawab Khan Alakozai's position was further undermined by his rivalry with 'Ata Allah Khan Turkman, an enmity that was due in part to the fact that 'Ata Allah Khan was a Turkman and a Shi'a.

The stand-off came to a head in 1761 when Rahim Bi Manghit crossed the Amu Darya intent on reasserting Bukharan supremacy and throwing out Nawab Khan Alakozai and 'Ata Allah Khan Turkman. Aided by Izbasar, *hakim* of Shibarghan, the Bukharans took Aqcha. In an encounter near the ancient fortress of Dilbarjin,[16] some 40 kilometres (25 mi.) west of Balkh, however, Rahim Bi was defeated and retreated to the strong frontier fortress of Aqcha. 'Ata Allah Khan Turkman besieged Aqcha but failed to breach its thick walls, so he asked Hajji Bi Ming to negotiate a Bukharan withdrawal.[17] Hajji Bi sent a deputation of senior religious leaders to Rahim Bi, offering him safe passage back across the Amu Darya in return for the peaceful evacuation of Aqcha. Rahim Bi agreed to the terms and returned to Bukhara, whereupon ʿAta Allah Khan Turkman went to Shibarghan, probably to secure Izbasar's submission, only for Izbasar to go behind his back and open negotiations with Nawab Khan Alakozai. The *hakim* agreed to pardon Izbasar on condition he put ʿAta Allah Khan to death, something that Izbasar was only too pleased to do. The *sipar salar* was duly killed and peace was restored.

A few years later, there was a rebellion in Qataghan and Badakhshan. Ahmad Shah sent 6,000 troops commanded by Shah Wali Khan to deal with the situation. Shah Murad Manghit, the new Khan of Bukhara, responded by marching to Qarshi on the Amu Darya and threatened to attack Aqcha. Ahmad Shah then sent a second military division to Maimana and forced Shah Murad to negotiate. In the end Shah Murad agreed that the *wilayat* of Balkh was within the Durrani sphere of influence and the *amir*s of the region agreed to send an annual tribute, or *nazrana*, to the Durrani monarch.[18]

To seal this agreement, Shah Murad gifted Ahmad Shah one of Bukhara's most sacred relics, the Khirqa-yi Sharif, or Noble Cloak, which was reputed to have been worn by Muhammad himself. This relic not only had immense religious significance but its ownership had a political dimension, since Ahmad Shah used it to provide the religious legitimacy his dynasty lacked. As the cloak progressed from Balkh to Kandahar, Ahmad Shah made donations of *auqaf*, or tax-free lands, to various shrines, and erected *qadamgah*s to commemorate the places where it had rested during its translation. The crowds that came to perform pilgrimage to the relic in Kabul were so vast that the procession had to be halted for several days. When it finally arrived in Kandahar, Ahmad Shah ordered the *khirqa* to be placed in his own mausoleum, which was under construction, but this displeased Kandahar's ʿulamaʾ, who issued a *fatwa* declaring the cloak should not be exploited for political or dynastic ends. Consequently, Ahmad Shah built a shrine for the *khirqa* adjacent to his tomb. This in turn gave rise to the tradition that anyone seeking sanctuary within the precincts of Ahmad Shah's mausoleum was immune from arrest.

Internal challenges to Ahmad Shah Durrani

Internally Ahmad Shah faced a series of challenges to his power both from members of his own Saddozai *qaum* as well from the Durrani tribal council and senior military commanders. As a member of a minor branch of the Saddozai clan, Ahmad Shah was well aware that several members of his lineage had a superior claim to the throne and one of his first actions after escaping from Nadir Shah's camp was to have his maternal uncle, 'Abd al-Ghani Khan, put to death. Other potential claimants included Ahmad Shah's young nephew, Luqman Khan, the son of Zu'l-fiqar Khan, a boy whom Ahmad Shah had brought up like his own son following his father's death. The most senior claimant, however, was Sultan Shah Muhammad Khan, a Khudakka Khel Saddozai, who had ruled Herat from 1722 to 1724. After his enforced abdication, Shah Muhammad Khan had returned to Multan where the Mughal king had bestowed on him the title of *Amir-i Kabir* and *Mansabdar*, with the right to command 5,000 troops. Zahid Khan, the Mughal deputy governor of Multan and a descendant of Maudud Khan, Saddu Khan's eldest son, was another potential challenger. There were also several members of the minor Kamran Khel and Bahdur Khel lineage living in Multan.

The first challenge to Ahmad Shah's authority from within his own *qaum* came only a few months after he had been declared king. In the summer of 1748 rumours reached Kandahar that the king had died while fighting in the Punjab, so Muhabbat Khan Baluch, the brother and rival of Nasir Khan, *beglar begi* of Kalat, and several Durrani and Ghilzai chiefs declared Luqman Khan to be king. Ahmad Shah broke off his campaign in India and marched back to Kandahar. The leaders of the rebellion fled but Luqman Khan, who had been a pawn in the hands of ambitious men, stayed behind and sent intermediaries to plead for forgiveness. Ahmad Shah assured the emissaries that if his nephew came in person and sued for pardon he would be spared, but when Luqman Khan took his uncle at his word, he was thrown in prison. A few days later his Qizilbash guards discreetly put him to death.[19] Two years later Ahmad Shah had Shah Muhammad Khan Saddozai and two of his sons assassinated as well. The three men had travelled to Kalat, apparently in an attempt to raise an army, whereupon Ahmad Shah ordered Nasir Khan of Kalat to put his troublesome cousins to death. In the spring of 1752 Ahmad Shah also deposed the Saddozai governor of Multan and appointed a Pushtun in his place.

The most serious challenge Ahmad Shah faced from his own lineage came in early 1761. While campaigning in the Punjab, 'Abd al-Khaliq Khan, a grandson of 'Abd Allah Khan, the former Sultan of Herat, deserted the army along with two members of Ahmad Shah's tribal council, Dilawar Khan Ishaqzai and Zal Beg Popalzai. They went to the Barakzai stronghold of Girishk, announced that Ahmad Shah had been defeated and declared 'Abd al-Khaliq to be king. They then marched on Kandahar, forcing Sulaiman Mirza, Ahmad Shah's eldest son, who was in charge of the Durrani capital, to flee. Shah Pasand Khan was dispatched posthaste to put down the revolt. When he reached the outskirts of Kandahar and informed tribal leaders that Ahmad Shah was still alive, support for the rebellion evaporated. The ringleaders came to Shah Pasand's camp and sued for mercy, claiming that 'Abd al-Khaliq had deceived them, and some minor actors were pardoned. Zal Beg Popalzai and other ringleaders, however, were lured into Shah Pasand's camp and executed, despite assurances they would not be put to death. Dilawar Khan Ishaqzai fled to Herat, where Timur Mirza defied his father's order to put the rebel to death and appointed him commander of his personal bodyguard. As for 'Abd al-Khaliq, he was imprisoned but eventually escaped and made his way to Multan, only to be thrown into prison once more.[20]

One outcome of 'Abd al-Khaliq's rebellion was that Ahmad Shah decided that the military cantonment of Nadirabad was not suitable as the capital of his kingdom. Built three decades earlier as a temporary siege camp by Nadir Shah, its mud walls were crumbling and indefensible against even lightly armed troops. So Ahmad Shah ordered the construction of a completely new capital to the northeast on land confiscated from Zal Beg Popalzai.[21] It was built along traditional Central Asian lines in the form of a *chahar su*, a cruciform with a gate in each of the four walls and four streets meeting in a central covered bazaar. Ahmad Shah engaged Indian masons to lay the foundations and the town was enclosed by a wall of compacted mud, punctuated by bastions, ramparts and towers and surrounded by a wet ditch. Ahmad Shah, however, spent very little time in his capital, an absence that undoubtedly encouraged internal challenges to his leadership from the tribes of the region.

Ahmad Shah's 'election' by the nine-man military council was essentially a power-sharing agreement with the other 'Abdali *ulus* commanders. As Ahmad Shah's empire expanded, however, his increasingly autocratic style of government and relentless pursuit of conquest led to discontent within members of his *majlis*. A matter of weeks after being declared king, and shortly before he set out to deal with the rebellious Nawab Nasir Khan in Kabul, Ahmad Shah had a number of 'Abdalis trampled to death by elephants, a punishment traditionally meted out to rebels and traitors.[22]

A year later, in the autumn of 1748, Nur Muhammad Khan 'Alizai, the former head of Nadir Shah's 'Abdali *ulus* and the individual Ahmad Shah had humiliatingly supplanted in 1747, conspired to assassinate him with the help of Muhabbat Khan Popalzai, Kadu Khan, another member of the king's tribal council, and 'Osman Khan, Ahmad Shah's *topchi bashi*, or head of artillery. Their plan was to lure Ahmad Shah to a lonely place outside Kandahar and put him to death, but one of the conspirators betrayed them. Nur Muhammad Khan and the other ringleaders were arrested, taken to the same spot where they planned to assassinate the king and executed. According to Ferrier, ten men from each of their tribes were then selected at random and executed.[23] These executions created even more discontent among the tribal aristocracy, with some openly challenging the king's right to put to death Nur Muhammad Khan and other senior Durranis.

Less than a year later Darwish 'Ali Khan, head of the Sunni Hazaras and governor of Herat, rebelled, a revolt probably precipitated by Ahmad Shah's defeat in Persian Khurasan. This uprising too was quickly suppressed and Darwish 'Ali was imprisoned. When Ahmad Shah left to pursue his next campaign in India he took Darwish 'Ali with him and, since he acquitted himself honourably, he was pardoned. In 1764, Darwish 'Ali Khan rebelled again but was defeated and imprisoned for a second time.[24] In 1759 another of Ahmad Shah's allies, Nasir Khan, *beglar begi* of Kalat, also declared independence and Shah Wali Khan had to be sent to deal with this revolt. Unable to defeat the Baluch or take Kalat by storm, Ahmad Shah agreed to let Nasir Khan remain as *beglar begi* of Kalat. A few months later a certain Mir Khush Khan Durrani, 'instigated by a dervish', declared himself 'King of Afghanistan'. Once again the uprising was crushed, the *darwish* executed and Mir Khush Khan Durrani blinded.[25] Less than a year later another pretender, Hajji Jamal Khan Zargarani, set himself up as king in Kandahar and even struck coins in his name. Like other such coups, this revolt was precipitated by reports that Ahmad Shah had been killed in battle but when it was clear this was not the case, Hajji Jamal Khan Zargarani renounced his claim to the throne and 'retired', probably fleeing for his life to a remote part of the country.[26]

Ahmad Shah's relentless military campaigns, and the internal challenges he faced from his own clan and tribe, eventually took a terrible toll on his health, which was further undermined by the suppurating wound in his nasal cavity, which defied all attempts to heal it. The ulcer eventually ate into his brain and became so infested with maggots that they dropped into his mouth when he ate. By the summer of 1772 Ahmad Shah had to be spoon-fed and his speech was so incomprehensible he could only communicate by signs or notes. He finally passed away in his sleep on the night of 23 October 1772.

Ahmad Shah Durrani: historical realities and the myth of the Golden Age

As with events surrounding his coronation, the reign of Ahmad Shah has been recast and remoulded by Afghan and European historians into something that bears little resemblance to historical reality. Pushtun monarchists in the twentieth century, for example, tend to portray his reign as a Golden Age and his life as an exemplar for kings. Dubbed *Baba-yi Afghan*, Father of Afghans, Ahmad Shah is lauded as 'the idol of his nation'[27] and a king who 'possessed sublime qualities of selflessness'.[28] Even his Sikh biographer, Ganda Singh, cannot refrain from panegyric, despite all that Ahmad Shah had done to his people and the Sikh holy cities. Colonial historians have been equally profuse. According to Olaf Caroe, Ahmad Shah had a 'bold and commanding turn of natural genius'.[29] Fraser-Tytler too calls him a 'genius', who welded 'so intractable a people as the Afghans into the semblance of a nation'.[30]

Such panegyric makes an objective assessment, let alone criticism, of Ahmad Shah and his reign difficult, as well as unpopular. Ahmad Shah was certainly a great military leader and tactician, though comparing him to Sultan Mahmud of Ghazni or Zahir al-Din Babur, as Fraser-Tytler does, is going too far. After all, these two men not only won battles, but established enduring empires. Ahmad Shah's empire, on the other hand, was fleeting and was already falling apart before his death.

Ahmad Shah's military achievements are better equated to those of his mentor, Nadir Shah, for both men were more at home leading their armies into battle but were far less successful when it came to governing their kingdoms. Furthermore, the legacy of the Ghaznivids and Mughals is seen today less in terms of their military victories than the civilizations they created as patrons of the arts and architecture. The contribution of Ahmad Shah in this respect was limited. Ahmad Shah's new capital had little to commend it architecturally, while his tomb and those of his successors are copies of Mughal mausolea found throughout the Punjab. Ahmad Shah is attributed with a corpus of poetry, including some Pushtu verse, and several regnal histories were written about his reign and conquests, but by and large Ahmad Shah spent more time destroying civilizations than he did in establishing his own.

Ahmad Shah's most notable military achievement was the defeat of the Marathas at Panipat, but while this pushed them out of northern India, Ahmad Shah's campaigns did little to strengthen Muslim power in India as Shah Wali Allah had hoped, but rather contributed to the rise of an even more powerful and enduring non-Muslim power, the British East India Company. Ahmad Shah came off second best in the war against another 'infidel' power, the Sikhs, and the Afghan-Sikh war, which began during his reign, would rumble on for almost a century and eventually lead to the loss of Multan, the Deras, Peshawar and the Khyber Pass.

The makeshift nature of Ahmad Shah's civil administration created an uneasy coalition of tribal, military and sectarian factions that were thrown together by pragmatic necessity. This led to an innately unstable government riven by factionalism and Ahmad Shah's reign was plagued by internal revolts. Less than thirty years after Ahmad Shah's death, his kingdom was torn apart by internecine and clan warfare. The claim that Ahmad Shah 'welded' the Afghan tribes into a 'cohesive and powerful nation', therefore, is yet one more myth surrounding his reign.

Nor was Ahmad Shah the model of chivalric virtue that some historians claim, regardless of whether one uses the yardstick of European chivalric virtues or the Iranian values of *jawanmardi*. During the course of his Indian campaigns, Ahmad Shah and his generals presided over the massacre of thousands of civilians, including women and children, the cold-blooded beheading of prisoners who had surrendered, and the desecration and destruction of Hindu and Sikh holy places. His troops put unarmed priests and pilgrims to the sword, committed mass rape, pillaged town after town and enslaved thousands of women and children. Even Muslims were not spared. Ahmad Shah also broke oaths of pardon and safe conduct, and even had his nephew, whom he had brought up like his own son, put to death. In the words of Louis Dupree, Ahmad Shah may have 'fused but left fission in his wake'.[31]

FOUR

Fragmentation: Timur Shah and his Successors, 1772–1824

Things fall apart; the centre cannot hold;
Mere anarchy is loosed upon the world,
The blood-dimmed tide is loosed, and everywhere
The ceremony of innocence is drowned

W. B. YEATS, 'The Second Coming', 1919

AHMAD SHAH'S DEATH was neither sudden nor unexpected, yet the transition of power was far from smooth or bloodless. A few months before he died, Ahmad Shah had summoned his second eldest son, Timur Mirza, from Herat and publicly declared him as his heir apparent, a decision he made without consulting his tribal council or other government officials. The announcement consequently created a rift between the king and some of the most powerful military and tribal leaders, a faction of whom supported the claim of Ahmad Shah's eldest son and Timur's full brother, Sulaiman, governor of Kandahar (see Chart 2). Among the leading members of the Sulaiman faction were Begi Khan Bamizai, known as Shah Wali Khan, Ahmad Shah's *wazir-i 'azam*, or prime minister, and Sardar Jahan Khan, *sardar-i sardaran* of the Durrani *ulus* and Sulaiman Mirza's father-in-law. They argued that as the eldest son, Sulaiman had the superior right to the succession and urged Ahmad Shah to reverse his decision while making it abundantly clear that they were dissatisfied at not having been consulted on such a vital issue. Ahmad Shah ignored their plea, claiming that Timur was 'infinitely more capable of governing you than his brother' and accused Sulaiman of being 'violent without clemency' and out of favour with the Kandahari Durranis.[1]

Timur Shah and the Durrani revolt

The king's justification of his choice of successor, though, does not stand up to scrutiny. Timur Mirza's record as governor was poor and his military record undistinguished. He had been defeated by the Sikhs, forced to abandon Lahore and been sent back to Herat, where he spent his time in 'indolent magnificence'.[2] Timur had also defied his father by refusing to execute the fugitive rebel Dilawar Khan Ishaqzai and instead appointed him as commander of his personal guard. Yet the dying king commended Timur Mirza for not putting Dilawar Khan to death, while he condemned Sulaiman Mirza for executing the other rebels, even though he had done so in obedience to his father's orders. The king's claim that Sulaiman Mirza had alienated the tribes of the Kandahar is also disingenuous, given that two of the highest ranked Durranis in the realm supported his right to the throne.

Ahmad Shah's decision may have been due to his illness, which had affected his brain and mental state, but his choice of Timur Mirza was more likely a deliberate attempt to curtail the power of senior generals and the Durrani tribal council, whom he deemed posed a threat to the perpetuation of his dynasty. Timur Mirza was the obvious choice in this regard for he had little time for the commanders of the Durrani *ulus*, having grown up in Herat and Lahore. Apart from the Ishaqzais, Timur's military strength derived from non-Afghan tribes – the Qizilbash and the Persian-speaking tribes of Herat and Badghis, such as the Sunni Hazaras of Qal'a-yi Nau.

Unfortunately for Timur he was ruling Herat, so Begi Khan Bamizai and Sardar Jahan Khan were able to exploit their proximity to the increasingly incapacitated king to promote Sulaiman's cause. They restricted access to the king's presence and poisoned the ear of the Shah against his heir apparent, a ploy that appears to have succeeded, for when Timur Mirza heard that the king was dying and rushed to his father's deathbed, Ahmad Shah denied him an audience and ordered him back to Herat. Angered and shamed by this rebuff, when Timur reached Herat he assembled his forces for the inevitable confrontation with his elder brother.

Timur's plans, however, were stalled by the unexpected rebellion of Darwish 'Ali Khan, *beglar begi* of the Sunni Hazaras, a revolt possibly instigated by the Sulaiman faction. Darwish 'Ali Khan had formerly been Ahmad Shah's governor of Herat but had rebelled, then subsequently been pardoned, served in Ahmad Shah's campaigns in India, then rebelled once more. This time he was imprisoned but he escaped shortly before Ahmad Shah died and fled to Qal'a-yi Nau, where he raised the standard of rebellion yet again. Timur Mirza lured him to Herat, offering him a pardon and reconfirmation as head of the Sunni Hazaras provided he came and tendered his submission in person. When Darwish 'Ali arrived in Herat, however, he was executed and his nephew Muhammad Khan was appointed *beglar begi* in his place.

Kandahar, the tomb of Ahmad Shah as seen *c.* 1880.

Shah Wali Khan and Sardar Jahan Khan kept the king's death a secret by placing the body on a palanquin shrouded with thick curtains. They then left the king's mountain retreat for Kandahar, taking with them as much treasure as they could lay their hands on. As the procession made its way to the Durrani capital, Shah Wali Khan announced to everyone that the king was ill and had given strict orders that no one should disturb him, except one or two of his most trusted officials. To make the deception even more credible, Yaqut Khan, Ahmad Shah's chief eunuch, pretended to converse with the king and even brought food for the 'sick' ruler.[3]

A day's march from Kandahar Sulaiman Mirza came out to perform the customary reception of the king, only for Shah Wali Khan to inform him that his father was dead. Despite opposition from 'Abd Allah Popalzai, Ahmad Shah's *diwan begi*, and other Durrani chiefs, Shah Wali Khan proclaimed Sulaiman Mirza as king. Yaqut Khan, however, was a secret supporter of Timur Mirza and sent a confidential messenger to Herat to inform the prince of his father's death and his brother's revolt, urging him to march on Kandahar. Timur Mirza immediately set out at the head of a sizeable army and by the time he reached Farah support for Sulaiman Mirza had collapsed. In a desperate attempt to save their lives, Shah Wali Khan and Sardar Jahan Khan went to Timur's camp to plead for mercy, but their appeals fell on deaf ears. Angered by their refusal to admit him to his father's deathbed, Timur Mirza denied them the customary audience to sue for clemency. Instead he sent for his executioner and the two men, along with their sons and other members of their entourage, were put to death. Sulaiman Mirza fled to India and Timur entered Kandahar with little opposition, where the royal *jirgha* was placed on his head.

Timur Shah moves his capital to Kabul

The revolt of Shah Wali Khan and Sardar Jahan Khan was the last straw as far as Timur Shah was concerned. Ahmad Shah's reign had been blighted by a series of rebellions by Saddozai pretenders and high-ranking Durranis. Timur Shah no longer trusted these *malik*s and in order to undermine their power he decided to move his capital to the former Mughal frontier post of Kabul. This was a logical alternative, even though the Durranis had no land or historic connection with this region at this era. The tribes of Kabul, Nangahar and the Logar were mostly Ghilzais, while to the north of Kabul the Koh Daman and Kohistan were dominated by Persian-speaking agriculturalists, Shi'a Hazaras and Safis. However, Timur Shah's mother was the daughter of a Ghilzai chief from Nangahar, so Timur Shah was able to count on her tribe's military support and the fact that she was well acquainted with the politics of the region. Once installed in his new capital, Timur Shah began to recruit Tajiks, Hazaras, Safis and Ghilzais into his army in order to reduce the power of the Durranis further.

The shift of capital made strategic sense too. Nadir Shah had destroyed the citadel of Old Kandahar while Ahmad Shah's new Kandahar was

The Kabul valley looking westwards to the Paghman range. When Timur Shah moved his capital to Kabul the town was famed for its temperate climate, fruit and its many Mughal gardens.

situated on a plain and its walls were no defence against modern artillery. Kabul, on the other hand, was surrounded by high mountains and defendable passes and already had a strong Mughal citadel, the Bala Hisar, which was located on the eastern slopes of the Sher Darwaza hill. This fortress had a double line of thick, stone-faced walls punctuated by bastions, barbicans large enough for the mounting of artillery, as well as hooded fire points for musketeers.[4] The fortress itself enclosed an area of many hectares and included the Mughal governor's palace, which became the king's new residence. It also contained sufficient barracks to house a substantial garrison and various other civic buildings, including a mosque and a large bazaar. It even had its own water supply. Not far away, on the north-facing slopes of Sher Darwaza, was Chindawal, the walled *mahala* of the Jawanshir Qizilbash *ghulams*.

Kabul at this era was an important emporium for the trade between Bukhara and the Indus, and the city's revenues, derived mostly from customs duties, were somewhat higher than that of Kandahar.[5] The city was also home to a substantial number of Jews, Armenians and Hindu *baniyas*, who acted as brokers, bankers and moneylenders. Since Islamic law forbids Muslims to lend money at interest to fellow believers, these non-Muslims provided an important credit service, not just for the mercantile community but for the king, too.

Situated in a large valley some 2,000 metres (6,560 ft) above sea level, Kabul was also a far more pleasant place to live, for unlike Kandahar it was not plagued by malaria or sandfly fever. The urban sprawl, squalor and pollution that are the hallmark of modern Kabul makes it difficult to grasp that in the late eighteenth century the town was famed for its mild climate and natural beauty, a beauty enhanced by the Timurids and Mughals who had planted at least nine ornamental gardens along the banks of the Kabul river.

The change of capital meant that senior Durrani officials had to choose whether to move to Kabul or remain in Kandahar. In either case, the power of Durrani chiefs to mount a challenge to Timur Shah was undermined. The move to Kabul meant they were cut off from their tribal base, yet if they remained in Kandahar they were isolated from the centre of political power. In order to reduce the Durrani threat even further, Timur Shah recruited thousands of additional Turco-Mongolian *ghulams* and purchased six hundred Nubian slaves to swell the ranks of his *ghulam khana*. At the same time, Timur Shah wisely did not strip the Durranis of their hereditary privileges or titles and even increased their state allowances.

Dilawar Khan Ishaqzai, who had rebelled against Ahmad Shah, became commander-in-chief of the army and was accorded the title of *Madad*

Khan. In order to prevent a confrontation with the Barakzais, Timur Shah continued to honour his father's agreement with Hajji Jamal Khan, who remained as *wazir*, but he bound his family to the royal interest by marrying one of Hajji Jamal's daughters. When Hajji Jamal died, shortly after Timur Shah became king, he was succeeded by his second son, Rahimdad Khan, for Hajji Jamal Khan's eldest son, Hajji Darwish, had become a Sufi and renounced worldly ambition (see Chart 3). When Rahimdad proved unpopular with his tribe, Timur Shah dismissed him and in 1774 appointed Payinda Khan, the full brother of his Barakzai wife, and bestowed on him the title of *Sarfaraz Khan.*

Most of the other high offices of state under Timur Shah, however, were given to outsiders. Gul Muhammad Khan, Timur's *'amin al-mulk*, or chief fiscal officer, was head of the Baburis of Baluchistan, a tribe that was heavily involved in trade with India and had become exceedingly wealthy as a result. Lutf 'Ali Khan, Timur's chief collector of taxes, was a Shi'a from Turbat-i Shaikh Jam in Persia, while his religious establishment was dominated by *farsiwan*s from the Koh Daman, Kohistan and Tagab, mostly affiliates of Mujadidi *tariqa*s of northern India. His most senior religious and judicial official, Qazi Faiz Allah, was 'a Moolah of the obscure clan of Dowlut Shahee', most likely a Safi from Tagab.[6] As for the day-to-day running of the state business, this was in the hands of Qizilbash scribes and secretaries.

The rebellions of Arsala Khan Mohmand and 'Abd al-Khaliq

Despite moving his capital, Timur Shah still faced challenges from within his own Saddozai clan. The year before Ahmad Shah died, Shuja' Khan, *subadar* of Multan and a Maudud Khel Saddozai, was deposed by a Hindu and in February 1772 the Sikhs took possession of the city. Shuja' Khan appealed to Timur Shah for military assistance to recover his capital and in late 1774 Timur Shah sent Madad Khan Ishaqzai to assist in the siege of Multan. The king followed at a more leisurely pace but soon tired of life in a siege camp and returned to the comfort of Peshawar. During his stay, a plot was formed to assassinate him and place Timur's brother, Sikandar Mirza, on the throne. According to Elphinstone, the instigator of this conspiracy was Hazrat Mian 'Omar Baba of Chamkani, the *pir* who had conferred the title of Dur-i Durran on Ahmad Shah and had blessed his *jihad* against the Marathas and Sikhs.

Exactly why the *hazrat* turned against Ahmad Shah's chosen successor is unclear, but it may be that he was piqued because Timur Shah failed to honour him with a visit during his time in Peshawar. Or perhaps Timur was not particularly enamoured with an individual who represented a highly conservative version of Sunni Islam. Timur, after all, was a libertine who regularly flouted Islamic law, in particular the prohibition on drinking wine and spirits. The king's preferential treatment of the Qizilbash and his marginalization of the Durranis had probably not gone down well either with the *hazrat*. Whatever the reason, the Chamkani *pir* persuaded Faiz Allah Khan, head of the Khalil tribe, who sought revenge against Timur Shah for unspecified 'private wrongs', to depose Timur Shah.[7] He was supported by 'Asad Allah Khan, also known as Arsala Khan, who had been Ahmad Shah's governor of Sind, and Mu'iz Allah Khan, chiefs of the Mohmand tribe.[8] Even Yaqut Khan, Ahmad Shah's head eunuch, joined the conspiracy.

In January 1775 Arsala Khan persuaded the king to allow his musketeers to assemble inside Peshawar prior to being sent to join the siege of Multan. Once the Mohmands were inside the city, Arsala Khan and his 2,500 heavily armed tribesmen marched to the *arg* while Timur Shah was taking his afternoon siesta and informed the guards that the king had ordered them to parade inside the fort. While the guards' attention was diverted, Faiz Allah Khan and Yaqut Khan smashed a postern gate in another wall, killed the guards, rushed into the parade ground and attempted to break down the door of the inner keep where Timur Shah was resting.

Woken by the clamour, Timur Shah fled to the summit of the tower and signalled desperately with his turban to alert the Qizilbash *ghulams* below. The Qizilbash then attacked the Mohmands, who were so occupied with the assault on the keep that they had not bothered to set up a rearguard. Caught in the parade ground without cover, the Mohmands were either killed or arrested. Faiz Allah Khan and his son were taken alive, but despite being tortured they refused to name the other conspirators and were eventually executed. Though it is not stated, Yaqut Khan may well have suffered the same fate. Timur Shah wanted to put the Hazrat of Chamkani to death, too, but 'the whole of the Afghaun chiefs at court' pleaded with him not to do so and he remained a free man.[9]

Arsala Khan somehow escaped the carnage and fled to his mountain stronghold of Hashtnagar, where he blockaded the strategic military road through the Khyber Pass and caused considerable trouble for the Durrani king. Timur Shah was not prepared to allow such a dangerous foe to remain at large and he eventually lulled Arsala Khan into a false sense of security, publicly and privately declaring his desire to pardon the rebel and to redress the grievances of the Mohmands. An envoy was then sent to Arsala Khan bearing a Qur'an with the king's oath promising his life would be spared if he came in person and tendered his submission. Arsala Khan took Timur Shah at his word, but when he arrived in Peshawar he was arrested and his throat cut. The Mohmands and other tribes of the Khyber region were disgusted at the king's breach of his sacred oath and never forgot, or forgave, this act of treachery.[10]

Some two months after the revolt in Peshawar, 'Abd al-Khaliq Khan, a grandson of Sultan 'Abd Allah Khan Saddozai, rebelled, forcing Timur Shah to recall Madad Khan Ishaqzai from Multan and return to Kabul. 'Abd al-Khaliq had previously led a failed coup against Ahmad Shah and had fled to Multan, where he had been imprisoned by Subadar Shuja' Khan. Then after the Sikhs occupied Multan, they released 'Abd al-Khaliq on condition he raised an army to topple Timur Shah. 'Abd al-Khaliq joined forces with Muhammad Akbar Shah and Ibrahim Khan, all grandsons of Sultan 'Abd Allah Khan Saddozai, who had a long-standing blood feud with the Sarmast Khel lineage, for their father Shah Muhammad Khan and two of their brothers had been assassinated on the orders of Ahmad Shah. Nasir Khan, *beglar begi* of Kalat, along with a number of Durrani and Ghilzai chiefs, also supported the rebellion. In early March 1775 'Abd al-Khaliq marched out of Kalat intent on conquering Kandahar, only to be defeated following the defection of several Durrani chiefs. The three Saddozais were captured and sent to Kabul where Ibrahim Khan was executed, while 'Abd al-Khaliq and Akbar Shah were blinded and imprisoned in the Upper Bala Hisar. Timur Shah then ordered all the surviving male members of Sultan 'Abd Allah Khan's lineage to be hunted down and killed.

Having successfully beaten off these challenges to his power, Timur Shah concentrated his efforts on expelling the Sikhs out of Multan, but it was not until 1780 that the city was again in Durrani hands. By this time Shuja' Khan Saddozai, who had been a loyal ally of Timur Shah, was dead and his son Muzaffar Khan succeeded him as *subadar* of Multan. There were also revolts in Kashmir and Sind. While the uprising in Kashmir was put down, Sind proved to be a far more difficult proposition. In 1779 civil war broke out in the province and Timur Shah mounted a series of campaigns to bring it back under his authority, laying waste to vast areas of Sind in the process. Yet despite a few pyrrhic victories, by 1791 the Amirs of Sind were independent in all but name, though they continued to send tribute to Kabul.

Timur Shah's relations with Persia and Balkh

On the western frontier Timur Shah had to deal with a resurgent Persia, which was increasingly challenging the power of Shah Rukh Mirza, the Durrani's ally in Mashhad. On three separate occasions Timur Shah had to send troops to prevent Shah Rukh from being deposed. North of the Hindu Kush the situation was even more challenging. The change of capital meant that Timur Shah's strategic interest in the Chingissid *wilayat* of Balkh shifted from Maimana and the Chahar Wilayat to the *amir*s of Khulm and Qataghan, for Kabul's prosperity depended on the overland trade between Bukhara and India. The main caravan route north ran from Kabul through Koh Daman and up the Ghurband valley to Bamiyan. The road then followed the course of the Surkhab river down to Doshi and Khulm. A shorter, but more difficult, southern route ran via the modern town of Maidan Shah to Jalrez, Behsud and across the Hajigak and Unai passes, and met the northern route to the east of Bamiyan under the shadow of the ruined Kushan fortress of Shahr-i Zohak. These two routes were also the main invasion routes. The Salang Pass, which today is the main road north, did not exist in this era and it was only after the Soviet Union drove a tunnel through the mountains in the middle of the twentieth century that the ancient trade route to the Amu Darya shifted further east.

To protect the commerce with Bukhara and possible invasion from the north, Timur Shah forged alliances with *amir*s that controlled the Kabul–Bamiyan–Balkh road, tribes that until this time had been independent and peripheral to the Durrani monarch's strategic interests. Timur Shah also sought to secure the loyalty of the peoples of Kohistan and Tagab, for they controlled the back-door route from Nangahar to the Koh Daman. To bind these groups to the monarchy's interests, Timur Shah made a number of key marriage alliances with their leaders and appointed influential religious figures from these regions to high office.

The Shaikh 'Ali Hazaras, whose territory straddled the Shibar Pass between Bamiyan and the Ghurband and the upper reaches of the Surkhab, were one of Afghanistan's largest Isma'ili communities and posed a some-what different problem. Like the tribes of the Khyber Pass, the Shaikh 'Ali Hazaras made a great deal of money from charging *qafila*s and armies for safe passage and had no compunction raiding any convoy that refused to pay. Beyond Bamiyan another important *qafila* route to the northern plains ran via the Ajar, Saighan and Kahmard valleys, which were under the control of autonomous Tajik and Uzbek *amir*s aligned to Qilij 'Ali Beg, the Uzbek *mir* of Khulm. Further north lay Qataghan and its capital,

The ancient southern road from Bamiyan to Kabul via the Hajigak Pass, looking south from the top of the Kushan fortress of Shahr-i Zohak.

Qunduz, the fiefdom of another powerful Uzbek chief, Ataliq Murad Beg, who, while he was related to Qilij 'Ali Beg of Khulm by marriage, was the Mir Wali's greatest rival. As for the Qataghan cavalry, it had a reputation for being a formidable force.

In order to secure safe passage along these strategic highways, Timur Shah abandoned his father's alliance with the *wali* of Maimana and forged one with Qilij 'Ali Beg of Khulm, conferring on him the title of *Wali* of Balkh. Since this title had formerly been conferred on Hajji Bi of Maimana by Ahmad Shah, the loss of this position with its privileges and status did not please Hajji Bi's son and heir, Jan Muhammad, who ruled Maimana following his father's death. Jan Muhammad and the other *amir*s of the Chahar Wilayat responded by inserting the name of the 'Abd al-Ghani, Khan of Bukhara, in the *khutba* and offering the Khan military assistance to throw out the Durrani *hakim* in Balkh. Timur Shah's alliance with

Khulm was also unacceptable to Murad Beg of Qataghan and he too probably placed himself under the protection of Bukhara. Timur Shah then exacerbated the situation by sending a new *sardar* as *hakim* of Balkh.

At the time Bukhara was in political turmoil and its treasury so depleted that 'Abd al-Ghani Khan was in no position to wage war with Timur Shah, so instead the Khan intrigued with Mahmud Mirza and Firoz al-Din Mirza, Timur's sons and joint rulers of Herat.[11] In 1784 'Abd al-Ghani Khan was deposed by his *ataliq*, Murad Bi, who had formerly served in the army of Nadir Shah. Murab Bi thus founded the Manghit Dynasty of Bukhara and took the regnal name of Shah Murad Khan, as well as the title of *Amir al-Mu'minin*.

Shah Murad had great ambitions to restore the frontiers of the former Shaibanid Empire by conquering Balkh, Herat, Kandahar, Kabul and even northern India. As the first stage of this imperial dream, Shah Murad attacked and subdued Shahr-i Sabz, deposing its Shi'a governor. He then besieged Merv and, when it finally fell, Shah Murad deported all its Shi'a inhabitants, numbering several thousand families, and wrote to Timur Shah demanding he recall the Durrani *hakim* from Balkh or face an attack. Timur Shah rejected his call and in reply lectured Shah Murad about his harsh treatment of the Shi'a population of Merv and Shahr-i Sabz.

In the summer of 1788, while Timur Shah was occupied with yet another campaign in Multan, Shah Murad Khan crossed the Amu Darya and, supported by the *amirs* of the Chahar Wilayat, occupied Aqcha and expelled its small Durrani garrison. He then attacked Balkh and surrounded the remnant of the *hakim*'s troops in the citadel. Timur Shah once more recalled Madad Khan Ishaqzai from Multan and sent him with an army of 40,000 men to relieve Balkh, while the king returned to Kabul where he assembled a second army. However, shortly after Timur Shah set out for Balkh he heard the Bukharan army had fallen apart due to internal feuds that, among other things, had led to the death of one of Shah Murad's sons.[12]

In the spring of the following year the Bukharan army crossed the Amu Darya again but Timur Shah still refused to recall his *hakim*. This time he marched north with an army said to have been 150,000 strong, but the very size of this force proved a serious handicap. There were insufficient supplies in the mountains to feed such a large number of men and the artillery became bogged down and had to be manhandled over the snowbound passes. The king also refused to pay the Shaikh 'Ali Hazaras the customary fee for safe passage and he had to fight his way across the Shibar Pass and down the Surkhab river. When Timur Shah finally reached the plains of

Baghlan he was joined by the Mir Wali of Khulm, who persuaded him to first attack Qataghan, rather than relieve the beleaguered force in Balkh. Despite its size, Timur Shah's army proved no match for the Qataghan cavalry and in the end Timur agreed to allow Mizrab Bi to remain as *ataliq* in return for acknowledging Durrani sovereignty and the payment of an annual *nazrana*.

Having settled the affairs of Qataghan, Timur Shah finally marched on Balkh, but on his approach the Bukharans broke off the siege of Balkh, abandoned Aqcha and withdrew deep into the Chahar Wilayat, hoping to extend Timur Shah's already overstretched supply line. Shah Murad Khan then sent two columns of cavalry, some 30,000 strong, across the Amu Darya in the dead of night, in an attempt to trap Timur Shah's army in a pincer movement. The Mir Wali's spies, though, got wind of the plan and Timur Shah placed the whole of his army across the line of attack. In the battle that ensued some 6,000 Bukharans were killed. Shah Murad Khan sent senior religious figures to negotiate a peace deal and reconfirmed the 1768 agreement with Ahmad Shah. Timur Shah reciprocated by acknowledging Bukharan sovereignty over Shahr-i Sabz and Merv.

Timur Shah marched back to Kabul but left around 4,000 cavalry to garrison Aqcha and Balkh under the command of Muhammad Khan Qizilbash. The march across the Hindu Kush was a disaster, for winter had come early in the mountains and snow had already blocked the upper valleys and passes. Timur's men were not equipped with winter clothing and thousands died from exposure. When news of the disaster reached the *amir*s of the Chahar Wilayat, they threw off the Durrani yoke and inserted the name of Shah Murad Khan of Bukhara in the *khutba*. Thus, apart from regaining a degree of control over Balkh and Aqcha, Timur Shah had little to show for his campaign. Despite this, or perhaps because of it, Timur Shah was determined to maintain a token presence north of the Hindu Kush, even though it cost the state treasury more than half a million rupees annually.

The real winner of this Bukharan–Durrani war was Mir Qilij 'Ali Beg of Khulm. In the aftermath of Timur Shah's campaign he overran southern Qataghan, while Timur Shah reinforced his power further by conducting all his dealings with the *amir*s of the *wilayat* of Balkh solely through him. Following Timur Shah's death, the Mir Wali went to war with the Durrani *hakim* in Balkh and brought all of the region from Kahmard and Saighan in the south to Balkh and to the Amu Darya in the north under his authority. Shah Zaman was unable to do anything about this, but since the Mir Wali continued to profess his loyalty to the Durrani crown and read the *khutba* in the king's name, Shah Zaman allowed him to assume virtually all the duties of the *hakim*. In return, the Mir Wali allowed the *sardar* to remain in Balkh city as a token Durrani presence, but his lot was not a pleasant one. The local population refused to supply him or his bodyguard with food, fodder or fuel and subjected them to all kinds of verbal abuse, insults and humiliations. By the end of Timur Shah's reign, no self-respecting Durrani wanted to be posted to Balkh. The only reason the Mir Wali of Khulm did not expel the *hakim* was that he was his insurance against an attack by Bukhara, Maimana or Qataghan while Timur Shah secured 'the protection of his frontiers from the Uzbeks'.[13]

The death of Timur Shah and the civil war between Shah Mahmud and Shah Zaman

By the early 1790s the incipient weakness of the Durrani kingdom was all too evident. Kashmir had rebelled, Sind had broken away and, though the Sikhs were eventually thrown out of Multan, the decade of prolonged sieges had drained the kingdom's financial resources. Towards the end of his reign, Timur Shah become increasingly obsessed by fear of assassination, a paranoia doubtless exacerbated by the fact that he was more than likely an alcoholic. In April 1793 the king left his winter quarters in Peshawar to return to Kabul, but as he passed through the Khyber Pass his horse stumbled and the regnal *jigha* fell to the ground – an omen that he, and everyone else, regarded as a harbinger of his imminent downfall. When he arrived in Jalalabad, the king was seized by a pain in the kidneys and suffered from a severe fever, headaches and acute depression. Despite being bedridden and in great pain, Timur Shah ordered the march to Kabul to continue, but by the time his son Shah Zaman came out to meet him at Chahar Bagh, both the king and his courtiers knew that he had only a few days left to live.

Timur was only 46 years old when he died, but despite fathering dozens of sons, he had made no formal provision for the succession. Shortly before breathing his last, Timur Shah summoned his sons and senior counsellors to his bedside and declared that Shah Zaman, the eldest son of his favourite, Saddozai, wife, was to succeed him. Shah Zaman then swore that his two half-brothers, Homayun and Mahmud, would remain as governors of Kandahar and Herat respectively. Timur Shah was laid to rest in a grandiose, octagonal mausoleum that was still under construction on the right bank of the Kabul river in the centre of what had once been a Mughal garden.

TABLE 7: Saddozai Kings and Barakzai Wazirs (Sardars) of Afghanistan, 1793–1839

Ruler's name; lineage	Dates	Provinces ruled; events
Shah Zaman, son of Timur Shah	1793–1801	succession disputed by Shah Mahmud and 'Abbas Mirza 1800: executes Wazir Payinda Khan, son of Hajji Jamal Khan Barakzai 1801: Shah Zaman blinded by Wazir Fateh Khan, son of Payinda Khan
Shah Mahmud, son of Timur Shah	1801–3	contests throne with Shah Shuja' al-Mulk Fateh Khan Barakzai becomes wazir
Shah Shuja' al-Mulk, younger, full brother of Shah Zaman	1803–9	takes Kabul, imprisons Shah Mahmud 1809: Elphinstone Mission in Peshawar; Shah Shuja' defeated by Shah Mahmud 1809–10: imprisoned by Ranjit Singh 1810: flees to Ludhiana
Shah Mahmud (2nd reign)	1809–18	1817–18: Fateh Khan deposes Firoz al-Din of Herat, rebels; 1818: Fateh Khan blinded and later executed, his brothers rebel against Shah Mahmud
Shah Shuja' al-Mulk (2nd reign)	1818	Sardar Muhammad 'Azim Khan, Fateh Khan's brother, offers Shah Shuja' the throne, but quickly retracts offer
'Ayub Shah, son of Timur Shah	1818–23	placed on throne by Sardar Muhammad 'Azim Khan 1817–19: Sikhs conquer Kashmir, Multan and Peshawar 1823: 'Azim Khan defeated by Sikhs at Battle of Nowshera 1823: Shah 'Ayub deposed and exiled by Sardar Pur Dil Khan
'Ali Mirza, son of Timur Shah	1818	briefly declared king in Kabul by Dost Muhammad Khan; strangled by his half-brother, Shah Isma'il
Shah Mahmud, son of Timur Shah (3rd reign)	1818–26	Herat only; Kamran Mirza, his son, ruler in all but name
Sardar Habib Allah Khan	1823	son of Muhammad 'Azim Khan, briefly in Kabul; Kandahar under Dil brothers, the Kandahar sardars; Ghazni under Dost Muhammad Khan; Peshawar under Sardar Yar Muhammad Khan and his brothers, the Peshawar sardars
Sultan Muhammad Khan Tela'i	1823–6	rules Kabul, succession disputed by Dost Muhammad Khan
Amir Dost Muhammad Khan	1826–39	deposes Sultan Muhammad Khan; rules Kabul, Ghazni, Nangahar and Bamiyan 1839: flees after British occupation of Ghazni
Shah Kamran, son of Shah Mahmud	1826–41	ruler of Herat only

The octagonal tomb of Timur Shah. It was never completed and by the mid-1990s it was badly neglected and its vault was the haunt of heroin addicts. After 2002 the mausoleum was restored along with part of the Mughal garden in which the tomb was originally located.

Almost at once, rumours began to spread that Timur Shah had been poisoned by one of his wives. Law and order quickly broke down with rival factions fighting each other both inside and outside of the Bala Hisar. Shah Zaman's main rival was his half-brother 'Abbas Mirza, who was supported by a number of senior officials and some members of the royal household. From the enclosed quarters of the *zanana*, Shah Zaman's mother distributed vast sums of money to secure support for her son and succeeded in winning over Payinda Khan, the fourth son of Hajji Jamal Khan Barakzai. Payinda Khan, in turn, bought the loyalty of the Qizilbash and the *ghulam khana*, at the same time lulling Shah Zaman's rivals into a sense of false security by pretending to act as an honest broker between the rival factions. Once he had gained their confidence, Payinda Khan summoned a meeting of the rival claimants, but once they were all assembled the Qizilbash sealed the exits to the *qal'a* and the assembly was told no one would be permitted to leave until they swore the oath of loyalty to Shah Zaman. After five days without food and water, the princes and nobles capitulated, pledged their allegiance to Shah Zaman and were allowed to leave. 'Abbas Mirza and several of Shah Zaman's other half-brothers, however, were detained and incarcerated in the palace of the Upper Bala Hisar, which Timur Shah had turned into a state prison for members of his own clan.[14]

Shah Zaman controlled Kabul, but the Durrani leaders in Kandahar had also revolted and installed Homayun Mirza, Timur Shah's eldest son, as king, while Shah Mahmud and Firoz al-Din in Herat also submitted to the pretender. Shah Zaman sent his full brother Shuja' al-Mulk, along with Wazir Payinda Khan, to deal with this rebellion and defeated Homayun and the Durranis near Qalat-i Ghilzai. When Shah Mahmud and Firoz al-Din heard of the fall of Kandahar, they too swore allegiance to Shah Zaman, who honoured his pledge to his father and allowed them to remain governors of Herat. As for Homayun Mirza, he made his way to Kalat where he was placed under house arrest by Nasir Khan, but a year or so later he escaped, raised a ragtag army and marched on Kandahar. Shah Zaman, who was campaigning in the Punjab at the time, had to march back to deal with the rebellion but fortunately Homayun's motley band of followers deserted en masse. A few months later Homayun made a third attempt to seize the throne, only to suffer another defeat. This time Shah Zaman sent a detachment of cavalry in hot pursuit and the prince was eventually betrayed, blinded and joined the growing number of princes that had been incarcerated in the Upper Bala Hisar.

Following Timur Shah's death, several Durrani governors in northern India declared their independence and Shah Zaman spent most of his short reign either fighting members of his own extended family or in an increasingly futile attempt to defeat the Sikhs, who now controlled Lahore and the Punjab. North of the Hindu Kush, Shah Murad Manghit, the Khan of Bukhara, took advantage of the civil war to reoccupy Aqcha, defeated Muhammad Khan Qizilbash and took him and most of his men prisoner. The surviving Qizilbash retreated to the *arg* of Balkh but despite a four-month siege Shah Murad was unable to take the citadel. The Khan even paraded Muhammad Khan before the defenders and threatened to execute him if they did not surrender. When the garrison still refused to capitulate, Shah Murad had the Qizilbash commander 'barbarously executed' in the sight of his own men.[15] Eventually Shah Murad admitted defeat and sent envoys to Kabul to negotiate a truce. The former agreements were reconfirmed and the Bukharans withdrew back across the Amu Darya.

In 1796 Agha Muhammad Khan Qajar took Mashhad and put to death the Durranis' ally, Shah Rukh Mirza. Agha Muhammad then proceeded to eradicate all vestiges of Nadirid power, levelling Nadir Shah's mausoleum and digging up his bones, which were boxed and made into a footstool for the Qajar Shah. Agha Muhammad then demanded Shah Zaman surrender Herat, Farah, Girishk and Kandahar, and even laid claim to Balkh. Shah Zaman took this threat seriously and assembled an army to oppose a possible Persian attack on Herat, fearing that Mahmud Mirza and Firoz al-Din might ally themselves with Persia and march on Kandahar and even Kabul.[16] Fortunately for the embattled Shah Zaman, nothing came of the threat. Agha Muhammad Qajar withdrew from Mashhad and Nadir Mirza, another of Nadir Shah's grandsons, regained control of the city and reaffirmed his loyalty to the Durrani king.

The following year Agha Muhammad Qajar was assassinated and was succeeded by his nephew Fath 'Ali Shah. Shortly after Agha Muhammad's death, Firoz al-Din Mirza, fearing his brother planned to assassinate him, left Herat on the pretext of going on Hajj and went to Tehran, where Fath 'Ali Shah received him warmly. Meanwhile Shah Zaman decided to regain control of Herat and install a loyal governor in order to secure his western frontier against the Persian threat. Shah Zaman defeated Mahmud in a battle near Girishk and besieged Herat, but the city held out. Eventually Mahmud's mother brokered an agreement between the two siblings, under the terms of which Shah Mahmud acknowledged Shah Zaman as king in return for remaining as governor of Herat. No one, though, appears to have informed Mahmud's son, Kamran Mirza, of the peace agreement despite the fact he was leading the defence of the city. When he saw Shah Zaman's army head back down the road to the Helmand, Kamran set out in hot pursuit. Once Kamran was well away from the city, Qilij Khan Timuri, the garrison commander, rebelled and opened the gates to Shah Zaman. When Kamran heard of the fall of Herat, he and Shah Mahmud fled to Tehran.

Shah Zaman's campaign in the Punjab and the East India Company's response

In November 1796 Shah Zaman, believing that the fratricidal war had ended, set out to attack Lahore and in January of the following year he managed to regain control of the city. He was, however, out of touch with the shifting balance of power in northern India. By the mid-1790s the East India Company was increasingly the dominant power in the region and the British had no wish to see a repeat of the invasions of Nadir Shah and Ahmad Shah. Shah Zaman did not help his cause when he wrote to the Governor General suggesting that the Company join his war against the Sikhs. As far as the British were concerned, it was Shah Zaman who posed the threat to their interests while the overtones of *jihad*, implicit in every Durrani campaign in northern India, raised fears that the Durranis might form an anti-British Muslim coalition with other Muslim powers of the region. As Elphinstone later put it: 'The King of Caubul had always been the recourse of all the disaffected in India. To him Tippoo Sultaun, Vizeer Ally, and all other Mahommedans, who had a quarrel either with us or the Marattas, had long been in the habit of addressing their complaints', and 'every Mussulmaun, even in the most remote regions of the Deccan, waited in anxious expectation for the advance of the champion of Islaum'.[17]

Shah Zaman would doubtless have been flattered to think that the British regarded him as the head of this mythical Islamic coalition, but his occupation of Lahore unwittingly fuelled this paranoia. He had also given sanctuary to a dissident Mughal prince, Ahrum Bakht, who urged the king to attack Delhi. Shah Zaman was corresponding with Tippu Sultan, *subadar* of Mysore, whom the British called the Tiger of Mysore, and a ruler against whom the East India Company had already fought two wars (1766–9; 1780–84). Indeed, even as Shah Zaman crossed the Indus the Governor General was preparing for a final showdown with Mysore. French artillery and cavalry officers were training Tippu's army and Shah Zaman had at least one French artillery officer in his army. Their presence was another cause of concern, for Britain was at war with France: it was feared that France had encouraged Shah Zaman's invasion and was inciting the Muslim rulers of northern India to a *jihad* to drive out the British.

These anxieties explain the disproportionate British response to the fall of Lahore. The Bengal army was mobilized and Indian allies were called on to assist in the defence of Delhi. A British envoy was sent to Fath 'Ali Shah in Tehran with an offer of 10,000 rupees to attack Herat in the hope this would force Shah Zaman to abandon his campaign in the Punjab – an offer which came at a most opportune time since Mahmud Mirza and Firoz al-Din Mirza were raising an army for this very purpose. Supported by the Shah, the two princes occupied Farah, defeated Qaisar Mirza, Shah Zaman's son, and besieged Herat, whereupon Shah Zaman abandoned his campaign in the Punjab and return to Kabul. As soon as the Afghan army had gone, the Sikhs reoccupied Lahore.

Despite Herat's population being inclined to support Mahmud Mirza, Qaisar managed to hold out and, in an attempt to undermine Mahmud's alliance with Persia, Qaisar's *wazir* forged a letter purporting to be written by Qaisar to Mahmud's principal ally, Mir 'Ali Khan of Qa'in. The letter was drafted in such a manner as to make it appear that it was a reply to a secret communication from Mir 'Ali Khan in which he offered to assassinate Mahmud. Mahmud's spies were allowed to intercept the message and Mahmud and Kamran, completely deceived, fled for their lives in the dead of night. The following morning, when it was discovered they had taken flight, there was chaos in their camp and Qaisar Mirza, taking advantage of the confusion, attacked and routed the Persians.

Following this victory Shah Zaman resumed campaigning in the Punjab and eventually recaptured Lahore. In an attempt to divide the Sikhs, he appointed a nineteen-year-old Sikh, Ranjit Singh, as *nawab* of Lahore and returned to Peshawar. All along the road to the Jhelum river the Sikh army harried the Afghans and then, while attempting to cross the river, a sudden surge of water caused by exceptionally heavy rains high up in the catchment swept away thousands of men and supplies and bogged down the heavy artillery in the mud. When Shah Zaman and the remnants of his army reached Kandahar in late 1799 they were exhausted, but any hope the king may have had of spending the winter peacefully recuperating were quickly dashed.

The death of Wazir Payinda Khan Barakzai and the fall of Shah Zaman

Towards the end of his reign Timur Shah had become increasingly concerned at the power wielded by Wazir Payinda Khan. In an attempt to reduce his influence he appointed Fath Allah Khan, a Kamran Khel Saddozai and brother-in-law of Shuja' Khan Saddozai, as his *wazir*.[18] Better known by the title Wafadar Khan, Fath Allah Khan and his family were indebted to Timur Shah for the recapture of Multan and re-establishing his family as *subadar*s of the province. When Fath Allah Khan died in 1782 he was succeeded by his son Rahmat Allah Khan, who inherited the title of Wafadar Khan. After Shah Zaman ascended the throne he confirmed Rahmat Allah Khan as his *wazir*, an action that aroused the jealousy of Payinda Khan, who claimed he had the hereditary right to the highest office of state under the agreement made between Ahmad Shah Durrani and Hajji Jamal Khan Barakzai. He was even angrier because Shah Zaman would not have become king had it not been for his efforts in securing the support of the Qizilbash.

Shah Zaman gave Wafadar Khan a free hand and trusted him implicitly, overlooking his blatant corruption and his enmity with Payinda Khan. Wafadar Khan even went to the extent of confiscating *jagir*s gifted to Hajji Jamal Khan's family by Ahmad Shah. Matters came to a head in the winter of 1799/1800 while Shah Zaman was recuperating in Kandahar. According to the 'official' version of events, Payinda Khan and Muhammad 'Azim Khan Alakozai, supported by Nur Muhammad Khan Baburi, *'Amin al-Mulk*, Arsala Khan, the head of the Jawanshir Qizilbash, and several Durrani and Ghilzai chiefs, plotted to assassinate the king and Wafadar Khan and place Shuja' al-Mulk, Shah Zaman's younger full brother, on the throne.[19] The conspirators allegedly met at the home of a local *shaikh* under the pretext of performing *zikr*, but Wafadar Khan's spies infiltrated the meetings and informed him of their plans. Wafadar Khan then told the king what was afoot and produced witnesses who swore to the truth of the alleged conspiracy. Payinda Khan's heirs, on the other hand, claim that he and his associates were victims of a sting instigated by Wafadar Khan to bring about the Barakzai chief's downfall. Whatever the truth of these claims, Payinda Khan and other leading conspirators were arrested, beheaded and their bodies put on public display in the Kandahar *chauk*.

The execution of Payinda Khan ended the Saddozai–Barakzai alliance and Fateh Khan, Payinda Khan's eldest son, and his brothers vowed to avenge their father's death. They fled to the Persian court, where they pledged loyalty to Mahmud Mirza. When Shah Zaman set out for Lahore in the spring of 1800 to campaign against a rebellious Ranjit Singh, Mahmud Mirza and Fateh Khan went to Girishk, raised an army of several thousand Barakzais and marched on Kandahar. Shah Zaman then proceeded to make more powerful enemies. 'Abd Allah Khan Alakozai, the governor of Kashmir, had rebelled but was induced to come to Peshawar to tender his submission after having received a pledge of safe conduct, only to be arrested, tortured and executed. When his brother Saidal Khan, who commanded the defence of Kandahar, heard what Shah Zaman had done, he opened the city gates to Mahmud Mirza. Mahmud then marched on Ghazni, whereupon Shah Zaman belatedly returned to Kabul but left most of his troops and artillery in Peshawar. It was only when he reached the Afghan capital that he realized the extent of the revolt and the unpopularity of Wafadar Khan. Even the Jawanshir Qizilbash had declared for Mahmud in retaliation for the execution of Arsala Khan.

The armies of Shah Zaman and Fateh Khan finally met at the old Mughal frontier post of Muqur, between Kandahar and Ghazni. Even before battle commenced Ahmad Khan Nurzai, whose brother Wafadar Khan had imprisoned, defected to Mahmud's side and the Ghilzais around Ghazni cut off Shah Zaman's line of retreat. Panic quickly spread in the ranks and his army fell apart.

Shah Zaman, Wafadar Khan and a few faithful retainers fled to the Shinwari country, where they claimed asylum with Mullah 'Ashiq, a local *pir*. Mullah 'Ashiq welcomed the refugees, but sent a confidential messenger to Mahmud Mirza to inform him of the king's whereabouts and made sure the fugitives did not leave. When Shah Zaman found out he had been betrayed, he remonstrated with Mullah 'Ashiq about his breach of *nanawatai* and offered him treasure and other rewards in return for his freedom, only for his entreaties to fall on deaf ears. Realizing the fate that awaited him, Shah Zaman sought to deny Mahmud legitimacy by hiding the Koh-i Nur diamond in the wall of the *qal'a*, where it remained until it was recovered several years later by Shah Shuja' al-Mulk. A few days later some of Payinda Khan's sons arrived with a surgeon, who proceeded to lance the king's eyes. Shah Zaman and Wafadar Khan were taken to Kabul, where Mahmud had been proclaimed king. Fateh Khan then put Wafadar Khan and his brother to death with his own hands and Shah Zaman was confined in the palace of the Upper Bala Hisar. The ex-king later managed to escape and fled to Bukhara, but finding he was not welcome there either, he made his way to Ludhiana and joined his brother Shah Shuja'.

The change of head of state failed to end the civil war and by the time Shah Mahmud took power all semblance of central authority had broken down, with the kingdom divided into a plethora of semi-independent fiefdoms ruled by tribal *khans* and *amirs*. Shah Zaman's cause was taken up by his brother Shuja' al-Mulk, governor of Peshawar, but when he tried to oust Shah Mahmud from Kabul he was defeated. Beyond the Hindu Kush, the Khan of Bukhara made another attempt to occupy Balkh and the invasion was repulsed only with great difficulty.

In the winter of 1801 a certain 'Abd al-Rahim, who claimed descent from Mir Wa'is Hotaki, declared himself king, occupied Kandahar and besieged Ghazni, while a second army of Tokhi Ghilzais marched down the Logar to attack Kabul. In March 1802 two battles took place on the same day. In the first encounter, at Shewaki in the lower Logar, the Qizilbash massacred the Tokhis and Shah Mahmud celebrated his victory by making a pyramid from their skulls. The second encounter took place at Pul-i Sangi on the Ghazni–Kabul road, which led to the defeat and death of 'Abd al-Rahim Hotak. Having put down the rebellion, Fateh Khan ordered every Ghilzai stronghold between Kandahar and Ghazni to be demolished.

Shah Mahmud, the Persian siege of Herat and anti-Shi'a riots

Qaisar Mirza continued to cling to power in Herat for a few months after the fall of Shah Zaman, but he fled to Persia when his spies told him that his *wazir*, Afzal Khan, was planning to assassinate him. Wazir Afzal Khan then sent envoys to Firoz al-Din Mirza, Qaisar's brother, asking him to become ruler of Herat but he refused, declaring he had become a Sufi.

This excuse did not satisfy Afzal Khan, who ordered his envoys to abduct the Mirza and bring him to Herat, where he was installed as the new ruler.

Meanwhile a British diplomatic mission to the court of Fath 'Ali Shah, led by Captain (later Sir) John Malcolm, indirectly affected the situation in Herat. Malcolm's terms of reference included encouraging another Persian assault on Herat in order to neutralize Shah Zaman's threat to the Punjab, as well as to prevent a possible French invasion. By the time Malcolm reached Tehran, however, the French threat had diminished after Napoleon left Egypt. As for Shah Zaman, he was fully occupied with the civil war and maintaining his fragile hold on the throne, while Fath 'Ali Shah was more concerned about acquiring British cash and arms to combat Russian encroachments in the Caucasus. An Anglo-Persian Treaty was finally signed in January 1801 which included a pledge by Britain to provide cash and military aid to Persia 'to lay waste and desolate the Afghan dominions' and 'to ruin and humble the [Afghan] nation', in the event Shah Zaman invaded the Punjab.

Having received such encouragement, in the summer of 1803 a Persian army occupied Mashhad and ended the token Durrani control over the region. News of the loss of Mashhad precipitated a backlash from Sunni religious leaders in Kabul who incited attacks on the Qizilbash and Shi'a communities, though the fall of Mashhad was merely an excuse. The riots were more directed at curtailing the power of the Qizilbash, who by now were a major force in the kingdom. Since being instrumental in placing Shah Mahmud on the throne, the Jawanshir saw themselves as kingmakers, a power enhanced by marriage alliances with the descendants of Hajji Jamal Khan Barakzai. Wazir Payinda Khan himself had married a daughter of Musa' Khan Jawanshir, who numbered among her sons Dost Muhammad Khan, the future Amir of Afghanistan; two of Payinda Khan's sons, Nawab 'Abd al-Jabbar Khan and Muhammad 'Azim Khan, also married Jawanshir women, as did several of Payinda Khan's grandsons.

By the first decade of the nineteenth century the Jawanshir were a law unto themselves, but their involvement in the struggle for the succession fuelled sectarian and racial xenophobia. Members of the king's Durrani council had never accepted the Qizilbash as natives of their country, referring to them as Persians, although ethnically they were Turkic. All but a handful of the Qizilbash were Shi'a in a kingdom whose rulers and religious elites increasingly emphasized their Sunni credentials. Their enemies, and the enemies of Fateh Khan, claimed that if the Shah of Persia attacked Herat and Kandahar, the Qizilbash could not be trusted and would instead support the invasion.

This volatile mix of racial and religious prejudice was fertile ground for radical Sunni religious officials that Timur Shah and Shah Zaman had promoted to high office. A key member of this anti-Shiʻa, anti-Qizilbash faction was Sher Muhammad Khan Bamizai, whom Shah Zaman had appointed as *Mukhtar al-Daula*, the most senior religious office in the kingdom.[20] Sher Muhammad Khan was the son of Begi Khan Bamizai, better known as Shah Wali Khan, one of Ahmad Shah's most important generals, and the individual whom Timur Shah had put to death for his support of Sulaiman Mirza's claim to the throne. Following his father's execution Sher Muhammad Khan had fled to Kalat, where he devoted himself to Quraʼnic studies, yet ʻunder the mask of moderation, and even contempt for worldly honoursʼ, Sher Muhammad Khan ʻconcealed the highest ambitionʼ.[21] In 1794 Shah Zaman appointed Sher Muhammad Khan as commander of military operations in Baluchistan, Kashmir and the Punjab, and after Shah Zaman had been deposed he set out to undermine Shah Mahmud and Wazir Fateh Khan.

Sher Muhammad Khan found a willing ally in Sayyid Mir Ahmad Agha, a Mujadidi *pir* from Karez in the Koh Daman, whom Shah Zaman had appointed as *mir waʼis*, or head preacher of the royal mosque of Pul-i Kheshti, and *mutawalli* of Kabul's famous Ashiqan wa Arifan shrine.[22] To his disciples, however, Mir Ahmad was known simply as Khwaja Khanji.[23] In the first week of June 1803, while Fateh Khan and the Qizilbash were in Kandahar putting down another revolt, Mukhtar al-Daula publicly denounced Shiʻas in general and the Qizilbash in particular as ʻblasphemers and hereticsʼ, and condemned Payinda Khan's family for their marriage alliances with ʻhereticsʼ. He then called for the expulsion of all Shiʻas and Qizilbash from the capital, which led to violent clashes with Kabul's Shiʻa community. The rioting escalated after mourners at the funeral of a young man executed for allegedly killing a Qizilbash claimed they had been fired on by the Qizilbash, although according to Ferrier the catalyst was the abduction and gang rape of an Afghan boy by Qizilbash commanders.

Whatever the cause, Mukhtar al-Daula issued a *fatwa* of *jihad* against all Shiʻas. The following Friday, during congregational prayers, Khwaja Khanji read out the *fatwa* and whipped the congregation into a frenzy of sectarian hatred. Once prayers had ended, the mob attacked the Shiʻas and looted their homes, while a terrified Shah Mahmud barricaded himself in the Bala Hisar and sent an urgent message recalling Wazir Fateh Khan and his Qizilbash. When Khwaja Khanji and Mukhtar al-Daula realized the king was not going to suppress the rioters, they summoned their followers from the Koh Daman, Kohistan and Tagab. Thousands of Ghilzais, Safis and Kohistanis poured into the city and, under Khwaja Khanji's direction, tried to storm the Jawanshir stronghold of Chindawal, but the Qizilbash were prepared and hundreds of attackers died in well-directed fire from the walls of the *mahala*. The attackers then besieged Chindawal and fired into the houses from the Sher Darwaza heights, which dominated the Jawanshir Quarter. According to Ferrier, more than four hundred people died in the riots and the siege of Chindawal. After nearly a month of stalemate, Shah Mahmud ordered the arrest of Mukhtar al-Daula and the other ringleaders, but Sher Muhammad Khan, informed of the king's intentions, persuaded Khwaja Khanji to mount a diversionary attack on Chindawal and the Bala Hisar and he slipped out of the city.

The fall of Shah Mahmud and the accession of Shah Shuja' al-Mulk

Sher Muhammad Khan made his way to Peshawar, where he offered to help Shuja' al-Mulk depose Shah Mahmud in return for being made *wazir*. Shuja' al-Mulk agreed, marched on Kabul and on 12 July 1803 defeated Shah Mahmud, aided by the defection of a number of Durrani *sardars* and Khwaja Khanji's supporters. The day after his victory Shah Shuja' entered the Bala Hisar accompanied by Sher Muhammad Khan, who walked beside him holding the king's stirrup. The influence of the Sunni faction was immediately apparent. As the king entered the gates of the citadel, heralds

Gate of the Bazaar in Kabul, most likely the Naqqara Khana, or City Gate, leading from the Shor Bazaar into the eastern side of the lower Bala Hisar, from the *Illustrated London News*, 9 November 1878. Shah Shuja' al-Mulk would have passed through this gate following the fall of Shah Mahmud in 1803.

replaced the customary Turkic proclamation with the Durrani battle-cry *Ai Chahar Yar*, 'Oh, Four Friends', a reference to the four Caliphs who the Shi'as do not accept were the legitimate successors of Muhammad.[24] Shah Zaman was released from prison and his place taken by Shah Mahmud, though Shah Shuja' treated the deposed king with remarkable clemency, for his eyes were not put out, nor was he executed. However, Mullah 'Ashiq, the *pir* who had betrayed Shah Zaman, was hunted down and put to death and the Koh-i Nur recovered from its hiding place.

After he had secured the capital and restored a measure of law and order, Shah Shuja' sent his nephew Qaisar Mirza to Kandahar, where Wazir Fateh Khan and Shah Mahmud's son, Kamran Mirza, continued to hold out. Fateh Khan offered to submit to Shah Shuja' on condition the king restored his confiscated estates and his family's tax-free status. Shah Shuja' agreed and Fateh Khan surrendered Kandahar to Qaisar Mirza, but Kamran fled to Herat. When Fateh Khan arrived in Kabul to pledge his allegiance in person to the king, Shah Shuja' reneged on his promise, which he had only made so he could secure the surrender of Kandahar without a fight, and appointed Mukhtar al-Daula as *wazir* instead.

Fateh Khan bided his time. In the autumn of 1803, after Shah Shuja' had left to winter in Peshawar, he released the royal princes in the Bala Hisar and fled to Kandahar, where he persuaded Qaisar Mirza to join his revolt. However, when Shah Shuja' sent an army against Qaisar, the prince threw himself on his father's mercy, was pardoned and reinstated as governor of Kandahar. Fateh Khan fled to Herat but returned to Kandahar when Firoz al-Din also swore allegiance to Shah Shuja'. Qaisar Mirza threw Fateh Khan in prison, but somehow he was persuaded to set him free. Fateh Khan next went to the Barakzai stronghold of Girishk, joined forces with Kamran Mirza and marched on Kandahar. Just before battle commenced, however, Qaisar Mirza persuaded Fateh Khan to change sides yet again and Kamran Mirza was defeated. A few weeks later this alliance too broke down and Fateh Khan returned to Girishk, where he again joined forces with Firoz al-Din and Kamran. However, news arrived that a Persian army was advancing on Herat, so Firoz al-Din abandoned the campaign against Kandahar and returned home. Meanwhile Shah Shuja' had had enough of his nephew's intrigues and recalled Qaisar Mirza to Kabul.

Britain, the Napoleonic Wars and the defence of India

By 1805 Fath 'Ali Shah Qajar had become disillusioned with the Anglo-Persian alliance. Britain, which was now in an alliance with Tsar Alexander I against Napoleon's France, was no longer prepared to provide military aid to Persia in its war with Russia in Georgia. When a French ambassador arrived in Tehran in October 1805 with offers of military and financial assistance, Fath 'Ali Shah decided to pursue this alliance. The French initiative was part of Napoleon's plan to secure a safe overland route to invade India and fulfil his dream of emulating the conquests of his hero, Alexander the Great. In response to the French mission to Tehran, Fath 'Ali Shah sent an envoy to Tilsit with a letter for Napoleon, offering to join in an attack on Russia and facilitate a French invasion of India. The diplomatic exchanges led eventually to the Treaty of Finckenstein, signed in May 1807, under the terms of which France recognized Persian sovereignty over Georgia and pledged military support in return for the Shah opening the road to India and declaring war on Britain. In early December a large French military mission under General Gardane arrived in Tehran and began to train the Persian army.

Though he did not know it at the time, Gardane's position was undermined by the Treaty of Tilsit of July 1807, an agreement that 'converted, in an hour, the Emperor of France and the Autocrat of Russia into sworn friends and active allies'.[25] One outcome of this agreement was that Napoleon secretly agreed to assist Russia in its war with the Ottomans and tactically gave the Tsar a free hand in the Caucasus, a change of strategy that nullified France's pledge of military assistance to Persia against Russia. Despite this, Gardane managed to convince the Shah that only France could persuade Russia to evacuate Georgia and played on Fath 'Ali Shah's disappointment that Britain had failed to live up to its promises of military aid. British alarm increased when military officers attached to the French mission began to survey possible invasion routes to India, though Gardane's assessment of the feasibility of such a campaign was somewhat naive. According to him, the Persians and Afghans could be persuaded to unite to provide safe passage and logistical support for the French army.[26]

In response to the Franco-Persian alliance the British government in London dispatched Sir Harford Jones to Persia with plenipotentiary powers. Lord Minto, Governor General of India, convinced that the French posed an imminent threat to India, decided he could not wait until Jones arrived in India, so he sent John Malcolm to Bushire, backed by a naval squadron, to put pressure on the Shah. When Malcolm landed in Bushire he sent a letter to the Shah in Tehran, but the messenger was turned back at Shiraz, whereupon Malcolm abandoned the mission and threatened war. Sir Harford Jones's subsequent visit to Tehran was far more successful. Not only was he granted an audience with the Shah, in 1809 Fath 'Ali agreed to reaffirm the Anglo-Persian treaty after Britain promised military support against Russia and a substantial subsidy.

Lord Minto also sent Sir Charles Metcalfe to Lahore, where Ranjit Singh now ruled an independent Sikh kingdom. Metcalfe met with a much warmer reception than Malcolm had done in Persia and in April 1809 the two parties signed the Treaty of Amritsar, under the terms of which Britain formally recognized Sikh sovereignty over the Punjab, territory that the Durranis claimed as their own. Britain also tacitly allowed Maharaja Ranjit Singh a free hand when it came to conquering any territory beyond the Sutlej, including Peshawar. For the next three decades this Anglo-Sikh alliance was the keystone of Britain's policy, securing strategic depth and establishing a strong military buffer state on India's northwestern frontier. Following the signing of the Franco-Persian Treaty, in the spring of 1807 Fath 'Ali Shah resumed his campaign against Herat and occupied the frontier post of Ghuriyan. As the Persian army advanced on Herat, Hajji Firoz al-Din obtained a *fatwa* declaring the war against Shi'a Persia a *jihad*, whereupon thousands of Aimaqs, Uzbeks and Turkmans flocked to his banner. Despite being heavily outnumbered, Firoz al-Din decided to confront the Persian army in the open field. Most of his force, though, consisted of untrained *ghazi*s, devotees of Hazrat Allah Berdi, known as Sufi Islam, a Maimana-born Uzbek who in his early years had served in the Bukharan army until a vision led him to become a Sufi. In June 1807 when the two armies met near Shahdeh, Sufi Islam, seated atop a war elephant, charged the Persian lines. He and his followers, however, were surrounded and slaughtered to the last man. The corpse of Sufi Islam was skinned, tanned and sent to Fath 'Ali Shah, along with the hide of the Herati religious leader who had issued the *fatwa* of *jihad*.[27] Firoz al-Din managed to escape the massacre and fled back to Herat, but when the Persian general heard reinforcements were on their way he sent envoys to Firoz al-Din, who agreed to submit to Persian suzerainty, pay an indemnity of 50,000 rupees and send one of his sons to Tehran to be a hostage for his good behaviour.

Shah Shuja' was unable to help in the defence of Herat since by the summer of 1807 Mukhtar al-Daula and Khwaja Khanji, taking advantage of the king's absence in Sind, had rebelled and placed Qaisar Mirza on the throne. 'Ata Muhammad Khan, Mukhtar al-Daula's son, who was governor of Kashmir, also joined the revolt and even Wazir Fateh Khan deserted and made his way to Kandahar, where he pledged his loyalty to Shah Qaisar. Shah Shuja' decided to confront Mukhtar al-Daula and on 3 March 1808 the rebel army was defeated in battle outside Peshawar and Sher Muhammad

Khan along with several other ringleaders were slain. When Shah Shuja' entered Peshawar, the head of Mukhtar al-Daula was borne beside him, impaled on a spear. Shah Shuja' then marched on for Kabul, but on his approach Khwaja Khanji and Qaisar Mirza fled to the Kohistan, while Shah Mahmud made his way to Kandahar and joined forces with Fateh Khan. Kabul fell with little opposition. Shah Shuja' defeated Shah Mahmud and Fateh Khan in a subsequent encounter near Qalat-i Ghilzai, but instead of attacking Kandahar and hunting down Fateh Khan, he returned to Peshawar after hearing that a large mission from the East India Company was on its way to the Durrani winter capital.

The Elphinstone Mission and the 'Elphinstone Episteme'

The Elphinstone Mission to Peshawar was the East India Company's first formal diplomatic embassy to the Durrani court, though the Governor Generals had corresponded occasionally with Shah Mahmud and Shah Zaman. The Company had even infiltrated a native agent, Ghulam Sarwar, into the heart of Timur Shah's administration. The mission was the third initiative by Britain designed to counteract a possible French invasion of northern India and Mountstuart Elphinstone's instructions were to secure Shah Shuja' al-Mulk's agreement not to allow French or Russian surveyors to enter his kingdom. While making his way slowly to Peshawar, Elphinstone heard of Arthur Wellesley's defeat of the French forces in Portugal, which he noted in his journal as a great triumph and somewhat relieved his fears of a French invasion.

Elphinstone reached Peshawar at the end of February 1809, but his refusal to conform to the humiliating protocols enforced when ambassadors were granted an audience with the king led to a delay of nearly a month before he and the other officials were granted an audience with Shah Shuja'. A compromise was eventually worked out and the Europeans were received by Shah Shuja' with all pomp and ceremony, for the king hoped that the English would assist him against Shah Mahmud and even the Sikhs, while court officials did their best to conceal Shah Shuja' al-Mulk's fragile hold on power and the systemic weakness of the Durrani kingdom. This ploy appears to have worked, for Elphinstone reported that Shah Shuja' 'was considered as very firmly established on the throne' and dismissed the rebellions of Shah Mahmud, Fateh Khan and Mukhtar al-Daula as 'feeble'.[28] When Shah Shuja' finally met Elphinstone face-to-face he declared that their two kingdoms 'were made by nature to be united',[29] a statement that he doubtless later regretted. A treaty was eventually signed, but it failed to live up to Shah Shuja' al-Mulk's expectations. The king agreed not to allow any Frenchman or Russian to pass through his territory and, in return, Britain made a vague pledge of military aid and cash in the event of a joint Franco-Persian attack on Herat. By the time the treaty was ratified by the Governor General, however, it counted for nothing: a few weeks after the mission left Shah Shuja' was defeated and Shah Mahmud was once more king.

The real achievement of the Elphinstone Mission was its detailed survey of the ethnology, politics, geography and trade of the region between the Indus and the Amu Darya. This was effectively terra incognita since only a handful of Europeans had travelled through the region or published accounts of their journeys since the days of Marco Polo. In an attempt to fill this gap in intelligence, the mission's large entourage included a military surveyor and cartographer, a specialist on trade and commerce as well as a library of classical histories and geographies, European translations of Persian works and travel journals.

While the members of the mission waited for an audience with the king, they met and entertained officials, interviewed travellers and merchants, and made detailed enquiries about trade and invasion routes, the history of the Durranis, as well as Pushtu tribal organization and customs. In 1815 Elphinstone published a heavily edited account of his mission's work under the title of *An Account of the Kingdom of Caubul*, but a considerable amount of data, including Elphinstone's personal journal, notes and official correspondence, as well as the uncensored reports of other members of the mission, remain unpublished. Together this corpus of material was the first and most systematic study of the Durrani kingdom and remained so until the surveys of the Afghan Boundary Commission (1884–6).

Elphinstone included information derived from Persian and Arabic texts, mostly in poor English or French translations, and standard Greek and Latin accounts of the geography and history of the region. Written some two millennia earlier, these classical works had as much relevance to the contemporary ethnology, history and politics of Afghanistan and Central Asia as the histories of the Roman conquests of Gaul and Britannia had to early nineteenth-century France and England. Yet this classical and Hellenistic heritage exerted a profound influence on Europeans' perceptions of Afghanistan and Central Asia, including presumptions about the geopolitics of the region and the frontiers of India and Central Asia. Elphinstone's *Account of the Kingdom of Caubul* became a standard reference work for colonial officials and travellers, with a revised edition being printed in 1839 and 1842; it was a cornerstone of British colonial and Orientalist perceptions of Afghanistan and the Afghan tribes. The Elphinstone Mission reports, both published and unpublished, remain an important source for the early politics, history and ethnology of Afghanistan, but many scholars now take a far more critical approach to the 'Elphinstone episteme'.[30]

Elphinstone was the first British government official to employ the term 'Afghanistan' to describe the Durrani kingdom as a whole, a decision that was pragmatic and a matter of convenience, since the mission found there was no official designation for the kingdom. The bulk of the mission's reports focus on the history of the Durrani kings, Pushtun ethnology and analysis of their tribal territories. One reason for this was that there were a large number of informants available in court circles to inform about the Afghan tribes, while there were very few officials who came from other regions or who had more than a superficial knowledge of the Hazarajat, Herat, Balkh, Badakhshan, or the Central Asian Khanates. More often than not data on these more distant and remote regions was anecdotal, gleaned from one or two sources, usually merchants. The outcome was a skewed depiction of the Durrani kingdom as being more Afghan and Pushtun than it was in reality.

Elphinstone found defining the frontiers of the kingdom, and the degree of Durrani sovereignty, both confusing and complex. The realm, or *daulat*, of Shah Shuja' consisted of a plethora of autonomous fiefdoms and independent tribes, and while the king claimed sovereignty over them, in fact he had only token authority with some merely according him the right of *khutba*. One particularly problematic issue was Elphinstone's attempt to define accurately the northern frontier of this Greater Afghanistan. A close reading of the Mission's published and unpublished reports reveals much confusion and many contradictory statements on this matter, while the map Elphinstone published in his *Account* was inconsistent with his own and other mission members' findings, and differs markedly from the original, unpublished chart drawn up by Lieutenant John Macartney, the mission's official cartographer.[31]

Macartney locates all the Uzbek city-states west of Aqcha and Shibarghan, including Sar-i Pul, Andkhui, Maimana, Bala Murghab and Panjdeh, within the Khanate of Bukhara, while all territory from Talaqan eastwards is placed within the frontiers of the independent *mir* of Badakhshan. Yet Elphinstone's published map includes Talaqan, the Chahar Wilayat and the Panjdeh oasis within the Durrani kingdom. This is despite Elphinstone noting in his book that 'the only actual possession of the Afghauns in Toorkistan' in 1809 was 'the district immediately round Bulkh'.[32] Elphinstone also admits that the only Uzbek *amir* north of the Hindu Kush who accorded Shah Shuja' even token sovereignty was Qilij 'Ali Beg, the Mir Wali of Khulm, and even he only read the *khutba* in the king's name and 'did nothing else'. Elphinstone gives no reason for why he altered Macartney's map so drastically, but his decision virtually doubled the area under Durrani sovereignty between the Murghab and the Amu Darya. Possibly Elphinstone was influenced in part by his classical background and the idea that the 'Oxus' was the 'natural' frontier of Afghanistan, as it had been when Bactria was a satrapy of the Achaemenid Empire. Whatever the reason, Elphinstone's published map and its northern frontier was another element of his episteme that became embedded in imperial perceptions of the state of Afghanistan.

The mission provided an important insight into the inner workings of the Durrani court as well as biographies of influential individuals. Elphinstone also found their curiosity was reciprocated and mission members were quizzed at length on subjects ranging from Christianity to European education and astronomy. The overall impression is of an active intellectual life, with officials eager to learn more about the manners and customs of these foreigners, who were the new power in northern India. Elphinstone pompously noted the Afghans' 'extraordinary ignorance' of Britain, the British and Indian geography, a feeling no doubt reciprocated by the Afghans who were doubtless equally amazed at the foreigners' lack of knowledge of their country, customs and religion. Elphinstone's assumption about Afghan 'ignorance', though, had its comeuppance. During a discussion of the civil war that was tearing the Durrani kingdom apart, Elphinstone disingenuously asserted that 'there had not been a rebellion in our nation [that is, Britain] since 1745'.[33] Later the king's chief secretary drew Elphinstone aside and politely pointed out that he had failed to mention the revolt of the American colonies.[34]

The mission visited a number of influential religious figures including Shaikh Ewaz, a *pir* whom the king regularly consulted. When they arrived the *shaikh*, dressed in peasants' clothes, was planting flowers and fruit trees, and Elphinstone and his entourage mistook him for the gardener. After this embarrassing start, the *pir* sat the ambassador and his smartly dressed entourage down on the newly turned clods of damp soil and quizzed them on every subject under the sun, except religion. The mission also met several conservative Sunni *mullah*s, a sign of the influence of Mukhtar al-Daula, Khwaja Khanji and others, but there were also progressive and Rationalist schools of thought at court. Elphinstone was particularly impressed with Mullah 'Behramund', a regular visitor to the mission's *sarai* and an individual he describes as 'a man of genius' with 'an insatiable thirst for knowledge', who was 'well-versed in metaphysics, and the moral sciences'. The *mullah* also had a passion for mathematics and was studying Sanskrit 'with a view to discover the treasures of Hindoo learning'.[35]

Elphinstone noted the sectarian and ethnic tensions at court and, though he was probably not aware of it, the presence of the mission had exacerbated the rivalry between the anti-Shi'a party and the Qizilbash. Akram Khan 'Alizai, Shah Shuja's *wazir* and head of the Durrani tribal council, and Madad Khan Ishaqzai were the leading members of the anti-Qizilbash faction, while Mir Abu'l-Hasan Khan Jawanshir led the pro-Shi'a Qizilbash party. The recent defeat and death of Mukhtar al-Daula and the rebellion of Khwaja Khanji meant that by the time the mission reached Peshawar the Qizilbash were in the ascendant. The king even appointed Abu'l-Hasan Jawanshir as the mission's *mehmandar*, or court liaison officer, whereupon Wazir Akram Khan 'Alizai wrote to Elphinstone informing him that, since the king had not chosen him for this prestigious position, he must expect him to do all in his power to thwart the mission's aims.

The fall of Shah Shuja' al-Mulk

The king did not trust Akram Khan for he had formerly been a partisan of Shah Mahmud and Shah Shuja' suspected, rightly, that he was in clandestine correspondence with his rival. Eventually Shah Shuja' sent Akram Khan and Madad Khan Ishaqzai against Mukhtar al-Daula's rebellious son, 'Ata Muhammad Khan, governor of Kashmir, rather than dispatching them to oppose Shah Mahmud's advance on Kabul, fearing that if he did the two men would defect. The Kashmir campaign was a disaster since the king's erstwhile ally, the *mutawalli* of Muzaffarabad,[36] sent the army by a circuitous and difficult mountain route, then, when they were trapped in the high, snowbound passes and valleys, he cut off their line of retreat and annihilated the force. Akram Khan and Madad Khan managed to escape and made their way back to Peshawar, where they were lucky to avoid execution, for the king suspected them of treachery. The situation was even worse for Shah Shuja', for while his army was being slaughtered in the mountains of Kashmir, Shah Mahmud had occupied Kabul almost unopposed.

Shah Shuja' gathered the remnants of his shattered army and in June 1809 set out for Jalalabad to confront Shah Mahmud, who was now marching on Peshawar, while Elphinstone and his mission were hastily sent out of harm's way back across the Indus. A few weeks later, at Nimla on the old Kabul–Jalalabad road, Shah Shuja' was comprehensively defeated and fled. As for Wazir Akram Khan, he was killed leading a forlorn charge against the enemy ranks. Over the course of the next year Shah Shuja' made a number of attempts to regain the throne, but he eventually admitted defeat and set out for British-controlled India, only to be imprisoned by Ranjit Singh, who forced him to surrender the Koh-i Nur diamond. Shah Shuja' finally managed to escape from the Sikhs' clutches and made his way to Ludhiana, where the Governor General gave him a house and a state pension.

Shah Shuja' al-Mulk's subsequent reinstatement under British tutelage in 1839 and the disasters that followed have meant that his reputation has suffered, with European authors repeating uncritically the claim that Afghans believed he had been born under an unlucky star. Yet Shah Shuja' was far from the cowardly, ineffective quisling of imperial or subsequent Afghan nationalist discourse. Elphinstone 'found [Shah Shuja'] to possess all the good qualities ascribed to him without any one of the bad', and blamed his loss of power on the weakness of his government, the avarice of Wazir Akram Khan, and the factionalism and sectarianism at court.[37] Ferrier records of Shah Shuja' that he:

> had the reputation, and with reason, of being the most talented of the sons of Timur Shah. With great firmness of character and tried courage, it was plainly to be seen by more than one circumstance that he was not a man to support intrigues, or serve as an instrument to a party.[38]

Furthermore, Shah Shuja' appears to have realized that trying to regain control of the Punjab was a lost cause and, rather than pursuing a futile and costly war with the Sikhs, he tried to consolidate what was left of Ahmad Shah's kingdom and create a semblance of unity in a kingdom torn by dynastic, clan and sectarian feuds.

In pursuit of this objective, Shah Shuja' showed remarkable restraint when it came to dealing with rebels and personal enemies, a policy that, rather than being a symptom of weakness, should be seen more as an attempt at conciliation. He pardoned Qaisar Mirza despite him rebelling again and again, and when the king was eventually forced to remove him from the governorship of Kandahar he was imprisoned, but not executed or blinded. Shah Shuja' also declined to put out the eyes of Shah Mahmud in retaliation for the blinding of his brother, Shah Zaman. He even forgave Fateh Khan for his frequent intrigues and married one of his sisters. Yet the systemic problems that beset the Durrani kingdom in the first decade of the nineteenth century were too complex to be cured by graciousness alone and no doubt some courtiers, as well as his enemies, saw the king's attempts at conciliation as a sign of weakness.

Militarily Shah Shuja' showed far greater competency as commander than European historians have given him credit. He defeated both Shah Mahmud and Mukhtar al-Daula, though in the end he made two tactical errors that proved fatal to his cause. After having defeated Shah Mahmud, he failed to drive home his advantage by taking Kandahar and capturing Fateh Khan, while the following year he sent his army into Kashmir when it would have been better deployed against Shah Mahmud and Fateh Khan.

Shah Mahmud's second reign

The victory of Shah Mahmud meant that Fateh Khan regained his pre-eminent position as *wazir* and he used his power to dispose of personal enemies and depose key governors, appointing in their place his half-brother Pur Dil Khan, who became governor of Kandahar, while Pur Dil's three full brothers, Sher Dil, Kohan Dil and Rahim Dil, were appointed as governors of Ghazni, Bamiyan and Kalat respectively. As for Mehr Dil, Pur Dil Khan's youngest brother, he became the Amir's Foreign Minister. Later these five Dil brothers were known to British officials as the Kandahar *sardar*s. In 1811, when 'Ata Muhammad Khan, governor of Kashmir, was defeated by the Sikhs, Fateh Khan appointed his younger full brother, Muhammad 'Azim Khan, as governor of Peshawar: he and his four sons, known as the Peshawar *sardar*s, ruled this province until it too was conquered by the Sikhs (see Chart 3).

In an attempt to regain control of Kashmir, Shah Mahmud entered into an alliance with Ranjit Singh of Lahore, who demanded half the annual revenues of the province in return for military assistance. Ranjit Singh then double-crossed Shah Mahmud by persuading the king's governor in Attock to submit to his authority. When Fateh Khan tried to retake this fortress he was defeated and the Sikhs took control of the strategic ford over the Indus, which was the gateway to Peshawar. Shah Mahmud's alliance with the Sikhs antagonized the Sunni faction at court and, while the king and Wazir Fateh Khan were campaigning in Kashmir and Attock, Sayyid 'Ata and Sayyid Ashraf, members of Khwaja Khanji's circle, rebelled and placed 'Abbas Mirza, son of Timur Shah, on the throne. The Qizilbash in Shah Mahmud's army mutinied when they heard about the coup and returned to Kabul, fearing for the safety of their families. Shah Mahmud and Fateh

Khan had no choice but to break off operations against the Sikhs and return to Peshawar, where they assembled what forces they could muster and sent them post-haste to Kabul. After a series of battles on the outskirts of the capital Shah Mahmud was victorious: the ringleaders were captured and sentenced to death by being crushed by an elephant.

Khwaja Khanji escaped execution and fled to his stronghold in Kohistan. A few months later Fateh Khan's half-brother, Dost Muhammad Khan, and a corps of Qizilbash marched into Koh Daman to deal with the rebels. From his base in Charikar, Dost Muhammad laid waste to the Koh Daman, Kohistan and Tagab, burning crops and destroying orchards and vineyards. When Khwaja Khanji still refused to submit to the king's authority, Dost Muhammad used flattery, offers of a royal pardon and the prospect of a marriage alliance with the king's family. Having lured the *pir* and other leaders of Kohistan into his clutches, Dost Muhammad Khan had them all beheaded. Khwaja Khanji's two sons, however, remained at large and continued to be a thorn in the flesh for Dost Muhammad Khan and later the British.

On the Durrani's western frontier, the confrontation between Persia and Herat was renewed. In 1814, following a series of defeats by Russian forces, Fath 'Ali Shah capitulated. Under the terms of the Treaty of Gulistan, Persia surrendered all claim to sovereignty over Daghestan, Georgia, Karabagh, most of Azerbaijan and northern Armenia. Two years later, Hajji Firoz al-Din, counting on Persia's military weakness, declared Herat's independence and reoccupied Ghuriyan, only for Fath 'Ali Shah to march out against him, regain control of Ghuriyan and force Hajji Firoz al-Din to acknowledge Persian suzerainty. However, in 1818, when Fath 'Ali Shah demanded additional tribute, Hajji Firoz al-Din rebelled once more and sent his son Shah Husain to Kabul to petition Shah Mahmud for assistance.

Wazir Fateh Khan seized on Hajji Firoz's request as a golden opportunity to kill two birds with one stone: he could send an army to Herat and bring the province back under Shah Mahmud's authority, but at the same time depose Hajji Firoz and appoint one of his brothers to govern this strategic province, so extending his monopoly on power. Fateh Khan assembled an army of 15,000 men and, accompanied by Dost Muhammad Khan and the Dil brothers, reached Herat at the end of April 1818. He then tricked Firoz al-Din into allowing himself and a contingent of soldiers to enter the city. Once inside the town, Fateh Khan arrested Firoz al-Din, put a number of officials to death and opened the city gates. The soldiers poured in, plundering, raping and killing the city's inhabitants, while Fateh Khan and Dost Muhammad Khan broke into Firoz al-Din's *zanana*, tore jewels and clothing off his wives and maidservants, and raped any woman who took their fancy. Among Dost Muhammad's victims was Shah Mahmud's daughter. Once a measure of order had been restored, she sent a messenger to her father with her bloodstained pantaloons and demanded he avenge the family's honour. When her brother Kamran Mirza heard what had happened, he swore to expunge the shame but Dost Muhammad, hearing of Kamran's threat, fled for his life to Kashmir.

Once in charge of Herat, Wazir Fateh Khan expelled the Persian ambassador and brusquely told him to inform Fateh 'Ali Shah that Shah Mahmud was now the sovereign. When Shah Mahmud heard what his *wazir* had done he was terrified that Persia would use this as an excuse to annex the province, so he sent Kamran Mirza post-haste to the Shah's camp bearing a letter repudiating Fateh Khan's insulting behaviour and apologizing for the expulsion of the Persian ambassador. Meanwhile the governor of Mashhad marched out to reclaim Herat. In an indecisive battle Fateh Khan was knocked from his horse by a spent musket, whereupon his troops, thinking he had been killed, broke off the engagement and returned to Herat, while the Persian army returned to Mashhad to await the arrival of Fath 'Ali Shah with reinforcements.

Fortunately, Shah Mahmud's letter reached the Shah's camp before he arrived at Herat. Fath 'Ali agreed not to pursue the attack provided the Persian ambassador was readmitted and Shah Mahmud punish Fateh Khan. Kamran Mirza was sent to Herat with a decree dismissing Fateh Khan as *wazir* and ordering him to surrender the city. Fateh Khan, however, defied the royal command. 'I twice placed Mahmud upon the throne,' he bragged, 'and his kingdom is now in the hands of my kinsmen; who is Kamraun, therefore, that in a dream he should think of injuring me.'[39]

The death of Wazir Fateh Khan

Kamran returned to Kabul, where he gave the king an account of Fateh Khan's rebellion, his insolence, the pillage of Herat and the rape of Shah Mahmud's daughter. A furious Shah Mahmud ordered Kamran to set out for Herat immediately, take the city by any means in his power and punish the rebel Barakzai. Kamran mustered a substantial army and deceived Fateh Khan about his intentions by sending him messages claiming he was coming to convey the king's personal congratulations for his victory over Persia. When Kamran reached Herat he continued to dissimulate, treating Fateh Khan with honour and kindness and even persuading him to attend on him daily for the morning meal.

Despite Fateh Khan's advisers warning him that Kamran could not be trusted, Fateh Khan ignored them. Then one morning Fateh Khan went to breakfast with Kamran as usual only to find that all the guests were his sworn enemies. Despite this, Fateh Khan sat down and ate, but as the meal progressed the guests took it in turns to hurl abuse at him and recount the various crimes he and his family had committed against them. When Fateh Khan rose in anger to leave he was pinned to the tablecloth while 'Ata Muhammad Khan, Mukhtar al-Daula's son, thrust his dagger into the *wazir*'s eyes. He was then thrown into prison in the *arg* and a few days later his eyes were plucked out and the sockets cauterized with a red-hot iron.

After several months of incarceration, Fateh Khan was sent in chains to Ghazni to be judged in person by Shah Mahmud. When he appeared before the king and an assembly of his chief enemies, Shah Mahmud offered to spare his life on condition he ordered his brothers to come in person and swear fealty to Shah Mahmud. Fateh Khan, fearing his brothers would suffer the same fate as himself, refused and defiantly retorted that he had never sought to usurp the throne. The king retaliated by striking him with his sword, whereupon the other members of the assembly took it in turns to cut off one of Fateh Khan's limbs. Yet despite being slowly dismembered, Fateh Khan is said not to have uttered a single cry of pain. Finally, Shah Mahmud put him out of his agony and cut off his head; the mangled remains were rolled up in the blood-soaked carpet, taken out and buried.

Fateh Khan's death may have satisfied the king and his enemies' desire for vengeance, but politically the *wazir*'s execution was an act of short-sighted folly. Shah Mahmud's hold on power was fragile and Fateh Khan and his brothers controlled all the key governorships in the kingdom. When they heard of their brother's death they immediately rebelled, determined not only to depose Shah Mahmud, but to overthrow the Saddozai dynasty. Following Fateh Khan's execution, the headship of the Barakzai family, better known by its regnal name of Muhammadzai, fell to Fateh Khan's younger uterine brother, Muhammad 'Azim Khan (see Chart 3).

In an attempt to enlist support for his cause, Muhammad 'Azim Khan sought an alliance with Shah Shuja' al-Mulk, but the ex-king demanded the *sardar* pay the homage due him as king, so 'Azim Khan turned to another of Timur Shah's sons, 'Ayub Mirza, who was far more pliant. 'Make me but king,' he is reported to have said, 'and permit money to be coined in my name and the whole power and resources of the kingdom may rest with yourself; my ambition will be satisfied with bread, and the title of "king".'[40] Sardar Muhammad 'Azim Khan then renewed the war against the Sikhs in Kashmir, a decision that led to a bitter row with his half-brother, Dost

Herat, the Timurid shrine of Khwaja Abu Isma'il Ansari (1006–1088) at Guzargah. Ansari is known locally as the *pir* of Herat.

Muhammad Khan, who argued that it was more important to take Kabul and depose Shah Mahmud. Dost Muhammad Khan was eventually allowed to march on the Durrani capital with a small force of Qizilbash, while Muhammad 'Azim Khan retained the greater part of the army in Peshawar to pursue his war with Ranjit Singh.

When Shah Mahmud heard that Dost Muhammad Khan was advancing on Kabul, he quit Kandahar and set out to defend his capital, but when he reached Ghazni he heard that Kandahar had fallen to Sher Dil Khan. Undecided as to the best course of action, Shah Mahmud remained in Ghazni and sent Kamran's son Jahangir Mirza and 'Ata Muhammad Khan Bamizai to Kabul, unaware that 'Ata Muhammad was secretly in communication with Dost Muhammad Khan. He had offered to change sides on condition all of Payinda Khan's sons swore on the Qur'an not to put him to death for having put out Wazir Fateh Khan's eyes. Dost Muhammad Khan sent him the required oaths whereupon 'Ata Muhammad marched out of the Bala Hisar on the pretext of attacking the enemy lines and defected. Too late he discovered he had been tricked: when he reached Dost Muhammad Khan's camp he was bound and his eyes were gouged out with a dagger by Pir Muhammad Khan, the youngest of the Peshawar *sardar*s who had deliberately not signed the oath on the Qur'an.[41]

Dost Muhammad Khan then occupied the Lower Bala Hisar. When a well-directed shell destroyed part of the barbican of the Upper Bala Hisar, Jahangir escaped and made his way to Ghazni. Realizing all was lost, Shah Mahmud, his family and a few loyal retainers fled to Herat through the Hazarajat. In the following year, 1819, Kamran Mirza expelled his father from the *arg* and, fearing for his life, Shah Mahmud claimed sanctuary in the shrine of Khwaja Ansari at Guzargah. He later escaped to Maimana, raised an army and besieged Herat, but was unable to breach the city walls. After a stalemate that lasted several months, Kamran finally agreed to allow Shah Mahmud back into the city, but only on the condition that he relinquish all responsibility for government.

In Kabul Dost Muhammad Khan, instead of recognizing Shah 'Ayub as king as Muhammad 'Azim Khan had ordered, placed 'Ali Mirza, the son of Shah 'Alamgir II's daughter Gauhar Afraz Begum, on the throne.[42] Dost Muhammad Khan then refused to surrender Kabul, so Muhammad 'Azim Khan marched on Kabul and Dost Muhammad Khan retreated to Ghazni. 'Azim Khan decided to remain in Kabul and left his half-brother Yar Muhammad Khan as governor of Peshawar. A few months later Isma'il Mirza, Shah 'Ayub's son, encouraged by 'Azim Khan, strangled 'Ali Mirza and briefly became king.

Meanwhile the chaotic state of affairs south of the Hindu Kush encouraged the new Khan of Bukhara, Haidar Khan, to mount another attempt to reassert his authority over Balkh. In or around late 1817 or early 1818 Haidar Khan Manghit occupied Aqcha and Balkh and expelled the Durrani *hakim*.[43] Ishan Sayyid Parsa, also known as Khwaja Naqib, was appointed governor of Balkh, while his brother Ishan Sayyid Uraq was put in charge of the strategic frontier fortresses of Aqcha and Minglik.[44]

The Sikh conquest of Multan and the fall of the Saddozai dynasty

Ranjit Singh also took advantage of the civil war and in 1817 he forced Muzaffar Khan Saddozai of Multan to accept Sikh suzerainty and pay tribute. Early the following year Ranjit Singh marched into Multan with the intention of eradicating all vestiges of Saddozai power on the Indus. Despite desperate pleas for help, the Peshawar *sardar*s and other Afghan regional governors refused to send more than token assistance and so Muzaffar Khan was left to face the full force of the Sikh attack alone. As far as Ranjit Singh was concerned the conquest of Multan was more than just another military campaign: it was his opportunity to exact retribution for Ahmad Shah's pillage and desecration of the Sikh holy places and the massacre of Wadda Ghalughara. In a curious twist of fate, one of the cannons the Sikhs brought to bear on the walls of Multan was the Zamzama, the monstrous artillery piece cast by an Armenian cannon maker for Ahmad Shah Durrani, and which Timur Shah had left behind when he fled Lahore.

The Multanis fought with the desperation of those who knew the bloody fate that would befall them and their families if the Sikhs were victorious, but Ranjit Singh's army, trained and commanded by French and Italian officers, was vastly superior in men and equipment. When Muzaffarabad fell it was pillaged and its inhabitants massacred. Shujabad, named after Muzaffar Khan's father, was also besieged. Ranjit Singh himself marched on Multan and on 2 June 1818, after a siege that lasted 82 days, the Zamzama gun blew in Khizri Gate and the *akalis*,[45] the Sikh equivalent of *ghazi*s, stormed the breach. Muzaffar Khan, his five sons and one daughter joined in the defence and fought to the death. When Multan's defenders were finally overwhelmed, the Sikhs slaughtered the populace and pillaged everything in sight. Most of the Saddozai royal lineage was

Multan, once a major centre of Saddozai power and the birthplace of Ahmad Shah Durrani. When the Sikhs sacked the city its citadel was destroyed and what little remains of its walls today surround the medieval shrine of Shah Rukhn-i 'Alam, *c.* 1324.

killed and those Saddozais who survived the massacre were transported to Lahore, probably along with the sword and *khal'at* of Pir-i Piran. The following year the Sikhs took Srinagar, the capital of Kashmir, and Dera Ghazi Khan, while thousands of refugees flooded into Kabul in the wake of these conquests. In Peshawar Sardar Yar Muhammad Khan accepted Sikh suzerainty and paid tribute in return for remaining as governor. Having pushed the northern frontier of his kingdom to the mouth of the Khyber Pass, Ranjit Singh withdrew most of his troops across the Indus, leaving only a small garrison at Khairabad, the modern Nowshera.

Yar Muhammad's submission to the Sikhs was unacceptable to Sardar Muhammad 'Azim Khan, but he was unable to do anything about the situation for nearly four years. In the winter of 1822, however, he finally marched to Peshawar, where thousands of Khattak, Yusufzai and Afridi *ghazis* flocked to his banner in answer to the call of *jihad* promulgated by their *pirs* and *mullahs*. Sardar Yar Muhammad Khan had little choice but to appear to go along with his half-brother's plans, but behind his back he was in correspondence with Ranjit Singh and eventually persuaded 'Azim Khan to send him to negotiate with the Maharaja. Once in the safety of the Sikh camp Yar Muhammad Khan defected and reaffirmed his submission to Ranjit Singh. Shah Shuja' too sent levies to join the Sikh army, hoping that if Muhammad 'Azim Khan was defeated he would regain his throne.

The Afghan and Sikh armies finally met in March 1823 outside Nowshera, though Muhammad 'Azim Khan appears to have been more concerned about the safety of his treasure and womenfolk than he was about his battle strategy. Yar Muhammad Khan's defection and Shah Shuja' al-Mulk's support for the Sikhs also increased his fear of assassination. 'Azim Khan also distrusted the *ghazis* from the Khyber region for they only obeyed orders given by their *pirs*. His army too was poorly trained, armed with obsolete muskets and artillery, while the tribal levies had no military training and many of them were children, some as young as twelve, armed only with knives. Ranjit Singh, on the other hand, not only had the advantage of superior numbers but European mercenaries who drilled his troops and the artillery corps.

Initially the advantage lay with the Afghans. Muhammad Zaman Khan, another of 'Azim Khan's brothers, destroyed the Attock bridge over the Indus before the Sikhs could cross, forcing them to ford the river higher up and under fire from *jezailchis* on the opposite bank. Yet despite this, the Sikhs managed to secure a bridgehead on the right bank and the Khyber levies retreated. 'Azim Khan then made the fatal mistake of splitting his army in two. The Khyber *ghazis* were placed on the left bank of the Kabul river and formed their battle line on the isolated hill known as Pir Sabak, where they were expected to bear the brunt of the Sikh assault. Muhammad 'Azim Khan remained on the right bank, roughly in the area of Hakim Abad, with his Durrani, Ghilzai and Kohistani levies and the *ghulam khana*. This strategy appears to have been an attempt to protect his rear from attack by the Sikh garrison at Khairabad, which had already defeated an Afghan force at Jehangira. The decision to split his force, however, meant the two divisions were cut off from each other by a wide, fast-flowing river. When, during the course of the battle, 'Azim Khan tried to send reinforcements to aid the beleaguered Khyberis, the boats capsized and most of the men were drowned or swept away.

Ranjit Singh took full advantage of this tactical error and sent the *akalis* under the command of General Phula Singh to attack and contain the *ghazis*,[46] while a smaller contingent under Colonel Jean-Baptiste Ventura, a Jewish Italian mercenary who had served in Napoleon's imperial army, crossed the river to confront 'Azim Khan. After a skirmish, Ventura began to withdraw back across the river and Muhammad 'Azim, thinking the Sikhs were in retreat, ordered his cavalry to charge, only for them to be greeted by a devastating barrage from the Sikh artillery on the left bank. Muhammad 'Azim's force was ripped apart and he and his soldiers turned and fled from the field of battle.

Meanwhile the lightly armed *ghazis* managed to beat back the *akalis* and launched repeated suicidal assaults on the Sikh lines under heavy artillery fire. After hours of fierce hand-to-hand combat, the Sikh infantry began to waver, whereupon Ranjit Singh placed himself at the head of his cavalry reserve and charged. The surviving *ghazis* turned and fled, only to die under the lances and sabres of the pursuing Sikhs. As the sun set some two hundred Yusufzais, all that remained of the 20,000 tribal levies, gathered on the hill of Pir Sabak. Led by their *pir*, Muhammad Akbar, and with a cry of *Allah hu Akbar*, God is Great, they charged the Sikh lines and perished to the last man. The Sikhs followed up their victory by occupying Peshawar and plundering the countryside. Yar Muhammad Khan was reinstated as governor, but a Sikh garrison occupied the *arg*.

The Battle of Nowshera is one of the great, forgotten battles of modern Indian history, for it marked the end of Durrani sovereignty, though not government, over the region between the Indus and the Khyber and established the Sikhs as the most powerful military power in the region. Ranjit Singh's victory also had major repercussions as far as the future northwest frontier of India and Afghanistan's southeastern border, while the deaths of thousands of Khattaks, Yusufzais and Afridis weakened them militarily and made them less able or willing to oppose the Sikh occupation of Peshawar.

Muhammad 'Azim Khan fled to Jalalabad where he succumbed to an even more deadly foe, cholera. Realizing he was dying, he proclaimed his son Habib Allah Khan as the new *wazir* under the tutelage of his half-brother Nawab Jabbar Khan. The succession, though, was disputed and fighting broke out in Kabul between rival siblings. Dost Muhammad Khan and the Jawanshir Qizilbash refused to accept Habib Allah Khan's appointment, so the new *wazir* sought the aid of the Kandahar *sardar*s. As for Shah 'Ayub, his son Isma'il urged him to confiscate the dead *wazir*'s treasure and use this wealth to reassert Saddozai authority. Instead of aiding his half-brother, Pur Dil Khan, backed by Kohistani levies, occupied the Bala Hisar and in the ensuing struggle Isma'il Mirza was shot dead and the royal palaces looted. Shah 'Ayub was then paraded through the streets on the back of a donkey and treated to many other indignities. Pur Dil Khan even threatened to put Shah 'Ayub to death, but he offered to pay a ransom of one *lakh* (100,000) rupees and he was allowed to leave for India. Over the coming months hundreds of Saddozais followed him into exile, since life under the Muhammadzais was intolerable.

The exile of Shah 'Ayub marked the end of the Saddozai dynasty, for though Shah Mahmud and his son Kamran continued to rule Herat, the capital and all the other provinces from this point forward were under the authority of the sons of Payinda Khan Barakzai. In 1839 the British tried to revive the fortunes of the Saddozais by restoring Shah Shuja' to the throne, but this experiment in regime change was a hiatus that was doomed to failure from the outset and ended in his assassination.

By 1824 the civil war that commenced with the death of Timur Shah had been dragging on for more than thirty years. All semblance of central authority had broken down and most of the Durrani kingdom had been lost to the Sikhs, Persians or Uzbeks. The country and government was now in the hands of the Muhammadzais, the heirs of Wazir Hajji Khan Barakzai, and it was now their turn to try and prevent what was left of the kingdom from being absorbed by the surrounding nations and forge some form of political unity out of the chaos for which they had been partly responsible. The prospects were not good, for Hajji Jamal Khan's descendants were as divided and dysfunctional as the dynasty they displaced.

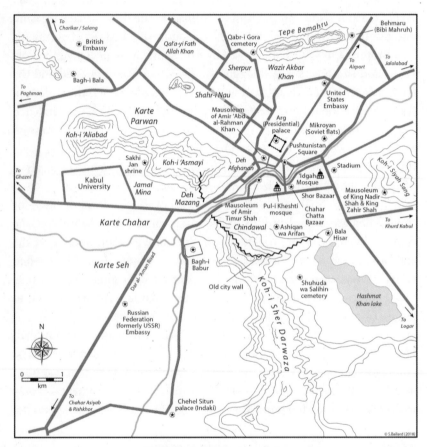

Kabul City and environs, *c.* 1970

FIVE

Afghanistan and the Indus Frontier, 1824–39

It is gratifying to reflect that while we shall consolidate the Afghan empire for our own interests we shall at the same time establish a lasting claim upon the gratitude of that people and our name will become associated with all the blessings which will flow from the restoration of security and good order.

CHARLES TREVELYAN, 1831[1]

FOLLOWING THE EXPULSION of Shah 'Ayub, Sardar Habib Allah Khan, son of Sardar Muhammad 'Azim, became titular head of Afghanistan but a few months later he was deposed by Sher Dil Khan. Faced with another civil war, this time between the heirs of Payinda Khan, the Peshawar and Kandahar *sardar*s met in Kabul and after much debate and a certain amount of bloodshed they agreed to appoint Sultan Muhammad Khan, the eldest of the Peshawar *sardar*s, as ruler of Kabul. As for Habib Allah Khan, he was compensated with the governorship of Logar and the Ghurband. The two sets of brothers deliberately excluded Dost Muhammad Khan from their deliberations and conspired to have him assassinated or blinded, but Hajji Taj Muhammad Khan, head of the Kakar tribe, warned Dost Muhammad and their plans were thwarted. Dost Muhammad Khan fled to Kohistan, while Hajji Khan Kakar sought sanctuary in the shrine of Ashiqan wa Arifan, assumed the dress of a *faqir* and declared he had renounced all worldly ambition.

The coup of Dost Muhammad Khan and internal conflicts

During his brief reign Sultan Muhammad Khan rarely ventured outside the Bala Hisar and spent his time in idle extravagance, appointing dozens of loyalists to sinecures that the country could not afford, and adorning himself in highly ornate robes, which earned him the nickname of *Sultan Tela'i*, the Golden Sultan. He also alienated the Qizilbash by supporting the Sunni-Kohistan faction, a policy that led to a number of violent attacks on Shi'as. Dost Muhammad Khan took advantage of Sultan Muhammad Khan's unpopularity to pay a secret visit to Hajji Khan Kakar and persuaded him to aid his bid for power in exchange for becoming *hakim* of Bamiyan.[2] Having secured the support of this powerful tribal leader, Dost Muhammad sent Sultan Muhammad Khan an ultimatum: quit Kabul voluntarily or be expelled by force. When Sultan Muhammad Khan failed to take the threat seriously, Dost Muhammad Khan's troops surrounded the Bala Hisar. After a few well-directed shells had been lobbed into the upper citadel, Sultan Muhammad Khan capitulated and left for Peshawar under a pledge of safe conduct. As he made his way through the Shor Bazaar, the shopkeepers lined the streets mocking him with cries of 'Welcome, Sultan Muhammad Khan, the Golden!'[3]

Sultan Muhammad Khan and the Peshawar *sardar*s were not in a position to challenge Dost Muhammad's coup, nor was Ranjit Singh prepared to support their war with Dost Muhammad Khan, for he was content to rule Peshawar through Sultan Muhammad Khan and his brothers. Anyway, the Sikhs had problems nearer home, for the Yusufzais under Pir Sayyid Ahmad were still at war with them and with the Peshawar *sardar*s, whom they damned for allying themselves with 'infidels'. In 1829 the Yusufzais even briefly occupied Peshawar, forcing Sultan Muhammad Khan to flee to Lahore. He eventually agreed to return after he pledged to govern in the name of Sayyid Ahmad, but once he had gained possession of the town he put the Yusufzai *pir* and his henchmen to death.

Dost Muhammad Khan meanwhile had to deal with a challenge from his other siblings in Kandahar. Shortly after Dost Muhammad Khan took control of Kabul, Pur Dil Khan marched on Kabul but was defeated by the Qizilbash and returned to Kandahar. A short time later Pur Dil Khan died and was succeeded by his next oldest brother, Sher Dil Khan, whose rule was undermined by a power struggle with his siblings over the succession. Having defeated his two main dynastic rivals, Dost Muhammad Khan turned his attention to restoring law and order in the capital and imposing his authority on the surrounding country. Sectarian tension continued to pose problems and in 1828 there was a particularly vicious outbreak of religiously motivated violence when a number of Achaqzais attacked Shi'as during the 'Ashura festival, which commemorates the martyrdom of Imam Husain. In an attempt to reconcile the two factions Dost Muhammad Khan appointed Hajji Khan Kakar as *wakil* for the Shi'a and Nawab Jabbar Khan to represent Sunni interests. As a sop to the Sunni lobby, Dost Muhammad Khan also outlawed gambling, dice, performances by *nautch* girls, wine making and drinking. He also scrapped the Saddozais' demeaning court protocols and reinstated the tradition of public audiences, personally arbitrating in even petty disputes. Justice, though, was swift and often arbitrary, but the fact that some sort of justice, if not actually being done, was seen to be done was welcomed by Kabulis, who had suffered from decades of anarchy and 'warlordism'. 'Is Dost Muhammad dead, that there is no justice?' soon became a popular proverb among the shopkeepers of the old city.

Another pressing issue was the chronic condition of the state revenues. Dost Muhammad Khan did not dare to risk alienating the Durranis by removing their tax exemption privileges, so instead he undertook a series of military campaigns to extend his authority over the rich agricultural areas around Kabul and in Nangahar, and to take control of the lucrative trade route between Kabul and Balkh. As each district fell, the local *amir*s and *khan*s were deposed and more often than not one of his sons was appointed as governor with a mandate to increase the amount of revenue the province paid into the state treasury.

Dost Muhammad Khan's first major campaign was aimed at extending his authority in the highly productive agricultural regions of the Koh Daman, Ghurband, Kohistan and Tagab, the *amir*s of which frequently raided trade caravans on their way to Bamiyan and looted settlements on the outskirts of Kabul. Dost Muhammad Khan adopted his now well-tried ploy of offering the rebels free pardon and monetary incentives if they came in person to Kabul and submitted, then when they were in his power he

The Koh Daman valley north of Kabul. This wide, well-watered and fertile valley was traditionally one of the main sources of food for the Afghan capital.

put them to death. Ma'az Allah Khan, or Mazu, head of the Safis of Tagab, however, remained at large. In 1829 Dost Muhammad Khan sent an army commanded by Nawab Jabbar Khan to bring him to heel, only for the campaign to end in disaster. The Safis attacked Jabbar Khan's camp during the night and in the ensuing panic his troops fled, leaving their artillery and baggage to be pillaged by the Safis. Two years later Dost Muhammad Khan set out in person to avenge this defeat. As he marched through the Koh Daman he executed or imprisoned local *maliks*, burnt and levelled *qal'as* and destroyed fields, orchards and vineyards. Mazu Khan eventually submitted and his life was spared after Hajji Khan Kakar pleaded for mercy on his behalf. A short time later Mazu Khan was shot and badly wounded by an unknown assailant: it was rumoured that the assassin was in the pay of Dost Muhammad Khan.

Lord Ellenborough's Indus policy

While Dost Muhammad Khan consolidated his control over Kabul's hinterland, in India and London a new policy was being formed that would undermine his efforts to unify the country, and lead eventually to his downfall and the occupation of Afghanistan. Following the Elphinstone Mission and the removal of the French threat of an overland invasion of India, British policy towards what was known as the Indus States had been one of non-intervention and indifference, for the Anglo-Sikh Treaty of 1809 was deemed sufficient to secure the defence of India's northwestern frontier. The Saddozais and Barakzais were embroiled in a war of succession, and the Afghans were considered to no longer pose a threat now that the Sikh kingdom acted as a buffer. Persia had ended its dalliance with France and in 1814 the Shah reconfirmed the Anglo-Persian Treaty of 1809. While Fath 'Ali Shah still cherished ambitions to regain Herat, his plans were restrained because of the Russian threat to what was left of Persian territory in the Caucasus. In 1826 Persia even went to war with Russia over the issue, only to be soundly defeated and forced to concede even more territory under the Treaty of Turkmanchi of 1828.

In 1830, however, Britain's policy of indifference was overturned by the administration of Arthur Wellesley, 1st Duke of Wellington, who appointed Lord Ellenborough as President of the Board of Control, the London-based committee that oversaw the affairs of the East India Company. Ellenborough had come under the influence of the Russophobe polemicist Lieutenant-Colonel George de Lacy Evans, who argued that Russia's territorial gains in the war with Ottoman Turkey and Iran, together with its conquests in Muslim Central Asia, posed a direct threat to British India.[4] According to Evans, Russia would only need a relatively small army of 30,000 men to invade India, since in his view Persia and the Afghan rulers would offer little resistance, and might even facilitate a Russian army marching through their kingdoms.

Evans was an armchair strategist with no personal experience of India, Persia or Afghanistan, something he shared in common with Ellenborough, though Ellenborough was subsequently appointed as Governor General of India. Ellenborough, though, was convinced by Evans's arguments, noting in his personal diary that a Russian invasion of India was 'not only practicable but easy'. 'I feel confident,' he wrote, 'we shall have to fight the Russians on the Indus, and I have long had a presentiment that I should meet them there, and gain a great battle. All dreams, but I have had them a long time.'[5]

As President of the Board of Control, Ellenborough was now in a position to turn his dreams into reality. One of his first actions was to write to Lord Bentinck, the Governor General, laying out guidelines to counteract the Russian threat. Britain, he argued, must act pre-emptively to forestall any Russian influence in the Indus States, in particular Kabul, Kandahar, Herat and Khiva, urban centres that commanded the two main invasion routes. To achieve this end, Ellenborough advocated Britain should be more aggressive in promoting its interests in the region, primarily by increasing trade with these Indus and Central Asian states.

Ellenborough's faith in the power of trade as a means to secure political influence seems somewhat strange today, but in nineteenth-century Britain commerce was seen by many politicians as a mystical, almost evangelical force by which imperial objectives could be achieved. Richard Cobden, writing not long after Ellenborough issued his 1830 Memorandum, wrote of commerce that it was:

> the great panacea, which, like a beneficent medical discovery, serves to inoculate with the healthy and saving taste for civilisation all the nations of the world. Not a bale of merchandise leaves our shores, but it bears the seeds of intelligence and fruitful thought to the members of some less enlightened community; not a merchant visits our seats of manufacturing industry, but he returns to his own country the missionary of freedom, peace and good government.[6]

Ellenborough identified with this vision, believing that trade would transfer the values of 'civilisation . . . freedom, peace and good government' to the 'less enlightened' states of Central Asia. Some 170 years later, President George W. Bush would revisit this argument, claiming that regime change followed by the implementation of free-market economics would lead to the establishment of democracy, freedom and good governance, rather than tyranny and chaos.

Ellenborough's vision, however, went much further. He wanted direct political involvement in the Indus States by employing government subsidies and other incentives to secure the loyalty of these rulers. Britain should also take a proactive approach to acquiring accurate military, political and geographic intelligence of regions that were still terra incognita. In the event Britain deemed that Russia threatened Khiva or Herat militarily, Britain, as a last resort, should unilaterally occupy Lahore, Kabul, Kandahar and Herat. Any ruler who refused to accede to British demands should be threatened with annexation or replaced by a more pliant head of state.

The problem with Ellenborough's policy was that it bore little reality to the situation on the ground and implicitly committed Britain to military intervention if its interests were threatened by rulers who did not toe the line, even if they were treaty allies. The occupation of Lahore, for example, would not only end the Anglo-Sikh alliance, which had been the mainstay of India's northwestern frontier policy since 1809, but would risk the Sikhs turning to Russia for military assistance, thus creating the very scenario Ellenborough sought to prevent. The same applied to all the other Indus States. Ellenborough's policy of 'either you are with us or with the Tsarists' was therefore a prescription for destabilization and conflict, not peace and security.

As for his vision of commercial penetration of Central Asia, Ellenborough failed to take into account the complex logistical and political problems of this trans-Asian trade. As early as 1809 Elphinstone noted that Russian goods dominated the bazaars of the Central Asian Khanates and that they were both cheap and easily transportable. St Petersburg and Bukhara had also long been on friendly terms and had regular ambassadorial contact. In 1831 Alexander Burnes, during his mission to Bukhara, noted that while there might be a demand for British woollen goods, the Uzbek Khanates beyond the Hindu Kush had very little to offer in the way of return trade. One of their main sources of income was slaves, a form of commerce British officials regarded as 'barbaric'.

In 1830 Britain had no port on the Indus, for Karachi was not then in British hands and, anyway, was just a small fishing village. All British goods bound for Central Asia therefore had to be shipped to Calcutta, unloaded, then barged up the Ganges. When they reached the river-head they had to be offloaded again and carted overland to Lahore and on to Shikapur, from where the *qafilas* left for Afghanistan and Bukhara. Not only was this a case of having to go backwards to go forwards, it was a logistical night-mare and involved substantial costs – so great in fact that, by the time the merchandise reached the Indus, the costs of transportation and customs duties would make British goods so expensive they would not be able to compete with cheap Russian merchandise. Ellenborough's solution to this problem was to turn the Indus into an Asian Thames. His dream was of ocean-going vessels of more than 200 tons sailing up the river as far as Attock, thus drastically cutting overheads and delivery times. With this in mind, he urged the Governor General to send a survey party to report on the navigability of the Indus and draw up hydrological charts.

Ellenborough's memorandum of 1830 burst 'like the biological warhead of a missile' when it landed on the Governor General's desk.[7] Bentinck and all but a handful of his most experienced military and political ad-visers showed a decided lack of enthusiasm for this romantic vision. Nor were they convinced by Ellenborough's fears of a Russian threat to India. Ellenborough, though, dismissed the opinions of individuals who knew the situation a great deal better than himself by demeaningly referring to them as 'the Indians'.[8] The new policy did not go well with British officials in St Petersburg, either, since it risked negative diplomatic and even mili-tary fallout, but they too were ignored. Though he did not know it at the time, Ellenborough's 1830 memorandum was the foundational document of what Kipling would later term 'The Great Game', a policy that influ-enced all future British imperial strategy on India's Northwest Frontier and which even today undergirds British, Pakistani, u.s. and NATO policy in the region.

The Ellenborough Doctrine and the exploration of the Indus and Central Asia

Despite their reservations about the Ellenborough Doctrine, Bentinck and his council were legally required to implement his policy since it had been approved by the Cabinet in London, although Bentinck was unaware that by the time he received his instructions, Wellington's government had fallen and been replaced by the Whig administration of Lord Melbourne. Melbourne and his Foreign Secretary, Lord Palmerston, however, were equally Russophobe and perpetuated Ellenborough's Indus policy.

So half-hearted was Bentinck about the Indus survey that he did not bother to send senior officers on the expedition. Instead he appointed a young junior officer, Lieutenant Alexander Burnes, the Assistant Political Officer in Cutch, who was on his first term in India.[9] The choice of Burnes was due mainly to the fact that three years earlier his elder brother James, a physician with no naval, nautical or hydrological training, had undertaken a medical mission to Sind and his report included a glowingly optimistic account of the navigability of the Indus. It was Dr Burnes's report that had fired Ellenborough with the vision of British merchant ships sailing up and down the length of the river. Since it was not politically expedient for it to be known that the British officers were on what was in effect an intelligence-gathering mission, the survey was disguised as a mission to the court of Ranjit Singh in order to present the Maharaja with a gift of a carriage and dray horses. When Charles Metcalfe, who had negotiated the Anglo-Sikh Treaty of 1809, heard of what was planned, he wrote to Ellenborough condemning it as 'highly objectionable . . . a trick . . . unworthy of our government'.[10]

Burnes's Indus expedition of 1830–31 included a naval surveyor, who confirmed earlier hydrological reports, discreetly compiled by British officials over the years but ignored by Ellenborough, that the Indus was a shallow, heavily braided river with shifting channels and dangerous sandbanks. It was also subject to dramatic fluctuations in depth, flow and course, which made drawing accurate nautical charts impossible. He concluded that while the Indus was navigable, it was only suitable for the local, flat-bottomed barges with shallow draught, provided they carried loads not in excess of 75 tons. Ellenborough's vision of the Indus as the Thames-in-Asia was therefore blown out of the water.

There were other difficulties. Burnes's survey caused considerable anxiety about British intentions among the rulers who had vested financial interests in the Indus trade. None of them were fooled by the public justification for Burnes's mission and they suspected, rightly, that the survey was about gathering intelligence. The Amirs of Sind did all in their power to prevent Burnes from acquiring any information about their kingdom and showed little interest in the prospects of increased trade, especially as Britain demanded they reduced customs duties. The *amirs* eventually let Burnes proceed to Lahore, but only after Ranjit Singh threatened to attack them. Then, when Burnes finally arrived at the Sikh capital, he found Ranjit Singh had little interest in the plodding, plough-pulling drays. What he wanted were thoroughbreds for his cavalry stud, so the unfortunate beasts were locked up and eventually died of heatstroke or neglect.

The Indus expedition was but one aspect of a wider political and intelligence-gathering strategy initiated by Ellenborough's memorandum.

Two more officers, both as junior as Burnes, were commissioned to draft a series of policy reports and recommendations on Afghanistan, Herat and the Khanates of Central Asia. Lieutenant Arthur Conolly was chosen because he had recently travelled overland to India through Persia, Herat and Kandahar, while his colleague Charles Trevelyan, Assistant Commissioner of Delhi, had no Central Asian experience and had only been in India a couple of years.[11] The task of fleshing out Ellenborough's policy was therefore entrusted to three men at the beginning of their Indian careers, individuals who, at best, had only a superficial knowledge of Afghanistan and Central Asia.

In drawing up their reports and recommendations, Conolly and Trevelyan appear to have overlooked the work of earlier explorers who had travelled more extensively in the region, such as William Moorcroft and George Trebeck.[12] In 1825 Moorcroft and his party had been the first modern British explorers to reach Bukhara, but they all died of fever in the plains of Balkh before they could return to India. Three years later Edward Stirling, a civil servant from Agra, travelled along the *qafila* route from Herat to Balkh via Maimana and Sar-i Pul, from where he headed south to Bamiyan and Kabul. Sir John McNeill, the British envoy in Tehran, even asked Stirling to make notes about potential Russian invasion routes only for him to encounter 'the greatest apathy' about his travels on his return to India.[13] By 1830 Stirling was living in Agra and could have provided a wealth of information for Conolly and Trevelyan, but he was never consulted. As for Moorcroft's correspondence with the Indian government, it was on file in the Calcutta archives.

Conolly and Trevelyan completed their reports in March 1831 and concluded that Russia indeed posed a military threat to India by seeking to occupy the strategic city-state of Khiva. Herat was identified as another key city, since it straddled both the northern invasion route from Khiva and the western one via Mashhad. They concurred with Evans's assumption that Persia was incapable of defending itself against Russia or acting as an Indian buffer state. Their solution was to 'reunify' Afghanistan, which, they argued, would aid commercial activity by the reduction of customs duties and improved security on the caravan route. Conolly, who had not visited Kabul, mistakenly believed Shah Kamran of Herat to be this unifying figure, and argued he would soon regain control of Kandahar and Kabul and make peace with the Sikhs.

The report concluded that in 'consolidating the Afghan empire for our own interests we shall at the same time establish a lasting claim upon the gratitude of that people', a 'singularly lofty, and dismally and naively unprophetic conclusion' that reflected more Britain's vision of its Manifest Destiny beyond the Indus than ground realities.[14] Like Ellenborough, Conolly and Trevelyan failed to evaluate properly the consequences of Britain lessening its influence in Persia, which would increase the risk of more Persian territory being annexed by Russia, and force the Shah further into the Russian camp in order to prevent the country from complete collapse. Conolly and Trevelyan's Persian policy thus increased the risk of a Russian invasion of India, rather than reduce it. As for their advocacy for a united Afghanistan, Claude Wade, the political officer in Ludhiana responsible for relations with the Sikhs, did not welcome this, nor did this policy agree with the views of Maharaja Ranjit Singh. Both men believed that a unified Afghanistan, whether ruled by a Barakzai or a Saddozai, risked renewal of the war with the Sikhs and threatened the Punjab. After all, it had been Shah Kamran's ancestor, Ahmad Shah, who first went to war with the Sikhs, while the Muhammadzais too cherished the hope that one day they would regain control over Peshawar, Kashmir and Lahore.

'Bukhara Burnes' and Britain's Afghanistan policy

When Burnes returned from his Indus survey, he recommended that he should undertake a second mission to explore the invasion routes through Afghanistan and make contact with Dost Muhammad Khan and the Khan of Bukhara. His recommendation was accepted and a second expedition was assembled disguised as a purely personal expedition undertaken by Burnes's love of exploration, but most of the rulers of the regions through which he passed suspected there was a great deal more behind his journey. If there was any doubt about the political nature of Burnes's travels, prior to setting out he met with Wade and Shah Shuja' in Ludhiana and then travelled to Lahore to see Ranjit Singh. During his stay in Peshawar, Burnes also met with the Sikh governor and Sultan Muhammad Khan Tela'i, who did all in their power to persuade Burnes not to go to Kabul. Burnes disregarded them and pushed on up the Khyber and reached the Afghan capital in April 1832, where he was hosted by Nawab Jabbar Khan.

A few days after he arrived, Burnes was amazed to hear that a *farangi* had just arrived in the Afghan capital from Bukhara. The Rev. Dr Joseph Wolff, a German Jewish convert who had been granted British citizenship, was a brilliant but eccentric Orientalist, missionary and controversialist.[15] He was a leading light of the Albury Circle, a movement concerned with the interpretation of biblical prophecy and millenarianism that was having a profound influence on British and American Evangelicalism. Wolff had

Alexander Burnes
in the costume of
Central Asia.

been commissioned by the London Society for Promoting Christianity to the Jews and had already travelled extensively throughout the Middle East, preaching to Jews and Christians and attempting to locate the lost Ten Tribes of Israel. His latest mission had taken him to Bukhara, home of a large and ancient Jewish community, but he arrived in Kabul penniless and with virtually no clothes on his back. On his way south, the *amir* of Duab had sentenced Wolff to be burnt to death for claiming to be a Muslim yet refusing to recite the *kalima*, the fundamental confession of Islam. Wolff had escaped execution only by allowing the *amir* to take all his money and pillage his baggage. Burnes persuaded Wolff to join him in Jabbar Khan's house, lent him money and sent him on his way to India, but not before he quizzed him about the road north and the political situation beyond the Hindu Kush.

As the guest of Nawab Jabbar Khan, Burnes had access to the court and had two audiences with Dost Muhammad Khan, who tried to prise from him the real purpose of his journey. He also lured Burnes into discussing the war with the Sikhs, suggested Britain join forces with him to destroy Ranjit Singh, and offered Burnes command of the army. Burnes then had a clandestine meeting with Hajji Khan Kakar, who gave him letters of recommendation for his onward journey. After three weeks in Kabul, Burnes came to the dramatic conclusion that:

> the restoration of either Shooja ool Moolk, or Kamran, is an event of the most improbable nature. The dynasty of the Sudozyes has passed away, unless it be propped up by foreign aid; and it would be impossible to reclaim the lost provinces of the empire, without a continuation of the same assistance.[16]

He then gave a favourable account of Dost Muhammad Khan and his government, and advocated that Britain pursue relations with him rather than seek to restore the Saddozais. This was not what the Indian government wanted to hear, given the state of war that existed between the Sikhs, Britain's ally, and the Muhammadzai ruler.

When it came to the Uzbek rulers north of the Hindu Kush, Burnes was far less sympathetic. He knew about the deaths of Moorcroft and his party, who were rumoured to have been poisoned by Ishan Urak, the Bukharan governor of Aqcha (though in fact they had died of natural causes), and had listened to Wolff's account of his terrifying experiences. Burnes's contempt for these petty rulers was barely concealed. After his meeting with the insomniac, slave-trading Mir Muhammad 'Ali of Saighan, Burnes wrote that he would like to 'administer a sleeping draught' to him, and declared he was 'nowise famed for justice'. His description of Murad Beg of Qataghan was a caricature of the oriental despot: 'his eyes are small to deformity; his forehead broad and frowning; and the whole aspect of his countenance is most repulsive'.[17] However, Burnes, who had an eye for the ladies, praised the beauty of the 'Torkee girls'.[18]

As Burnes and his party crossed into Bukharan territory, he noted that the Amu Darya was said to be navigable from its confluence with the Kokcha, a report that led to speculation in London about the possibility of this river, rather than the Indus, becoming a conduit for British goods. When he reached Bukhara, Burnes was obliged to reside in the citadel but was denied an audience with Nasr Allah Khan Manghit. Instead, all communication with the Khan was through his *kush begi*, the chief minister of state. Overall Burnes gave a favourable account of a city ruled solely by *shari'a* law, noting that security was so good that shopkeepers were

The citadel of Bukhara, residence of the Manghit Khans. Alexander Burnes stayed here and in June 1892 Conolly and Stoddard were beheaded in its courtyard and buried in unmarked graves.

able to leave their goods out at night without fear of theft and that the roads were not infested with highwaymen. Burnes noted that the Tsar had exchanged diplomatic missions with the Khan and that Bukhara and Russia were on friendly terms, something which the Elphinstone mission had already noted, but added, without any supporting evidence, that 'the court of St Petersburg have [*sic*] long cherished designs in this quarter of Asia'.[19]

Arguably the most dangerous part of Burnes's journey came after the party left Bukhara as they decided to travel to Mashhad through the Turkman desert, a region where *qafila*s were regularly attacked by Turkman raiders and non-Sunni Muslims enslaved. Fortunately, before leaving Bukhara the *kush begi* provided the travellers with *rahdari*s, or road passes, sealed by the Khan himself, which required everyone not to molest the *farangi*s. Even so, they had some narrow escapes. The mission eventually reached Tehran, where Burnes had an audience with Fath 'Ali Shah, before travelling to Bushire and taking ship for India. In all, he and his fellow travellers had been on the road for just over a year.

Burnes landed in Calcutta to discover that he was a celebrity and the toast of society, but this was nothing to the reception he received when he arrived in London. Lionized by the cream of London society, Burnes's opinion was sought by cabinet ministers, the Board of Control, senior army officers and even King William IV gave him a personal audience. When he

Amir Dost Muhammad Khan, founder of the Muhammadzai dynasty. His war with the Sikhs and Persia unwittingly dragged him into the sphere of British Imperial policy. His attempts to seek a rapprochement with Britain failed, mainly due to British officials' refusal to take into account the Amir's internal political difficulties. In the end, though, Britain did pursue treaty arrangements with the Amir and by the end of his reign, Afghanistan was increasingly a key element in Britain's Defence of India policy.

visited his home town of Montrose, the mayor held a public banquet in his honour. Burnes was promoted to captain, the Royal Geographical Society awarded him the Gold Medal (Burnes's portrait, showing him dressed as an Afghan noble, still dominates the staircase at Lowther Lodge, the RGS's headquarters) and the Athenaeum, Britain's most exclusive gentlemen's club, admitted him to membership without the customary ballot. Burnes also received numerous offers of marriage from well-connected families, but he knew to have taken a wife at such an early stage in his career would end his hopes of rising to the very top of his profession – and Burnes was nothing if not ambitious.

In between his round of society visits, Burnes rushed out an account of his travels that sold out on the day it appeared and eventually ran to several editions. As well as making him a small fortune, his *Travels into Bokhara* helped to fuel the celebrity status and mystique of 'Bokhara Burnes'. Nonetheless he was not enthusiastic about certain aspects of Ellenborough's policy. Burnes agreed that trade with the Central Asian states was possible and desirable, but argued for greater political involvement in the region.

Burnes also maintained that Persia still had a role to play in the defence of India, albeit a minor one, and while Khiva and Herat were also strategic-ally important, the most important urban centre was Kabul. 'The natural strength of Cabool,' he wrote, 'is the best barrier against a successful inva-sion by an Asiatic power' and 'the political state of Cabool, as a kingdom, becomes at all times an object of the deepest importance to India'.[20] Burnes therefore believed Britain should accord Dost Muhammad Khan de facto diplomatic recognition and negotiate a commercial treaty with him.

To reinforce this view, Burnes painted a rose-tinted picture of Dost Muhammad Khan and his government, emphasizing his popularity, the re-establishment of the rule of law and the Amir's own desire for good relations with Britain. On the other hand, Burnes downplayed the threat to Dost Muhammad from his siblings in Peshawar and Kandahar, as well as from Shah Mahmud and Shah Shuja'. Burnes even claimed Dost Muhammad Khan posed no threat to Sikh power in the Punjab, stating that he is 'not likely to pursue conquests abroad',[21] and advocated that Britain mediate to end the war between Sikhs and Afghans. Burnes was even far-sighted enough to grasp that when the ageing and sick Ranjit Singh died, his kingdom would be plunged into civil war that would lead to the collapse of the Sikh buffer.

Burnes provided detailed descriptions of the region and updated the political history of the Durranis, but several of his geographic and strategic assumptions were questionable and he relied heavily on the accounts of earlier travellers, some of which were still unpublished, for his description of the tribes and Afghan culture. Long before Wolff published an account of his travels to Bukhara, Burnes had picked his brains, and while in Balkh he had recovered and presumably read Moorcroft's journals, which were not made public until some years later. Burnes also took a copy of Elphinstone's *Kingdom of Caboul* with him on his travels, cutting out the illustrations and presenting them to Nawab Jabbar Khan before he left Kabul. Major D'Arcy Todd, a Royal Engineer and a member of the diplomatic mission in Tehran, was particularly critical of Burnes's data on potential invasion routes and their military capabilities, in particular his claim that a Russian army would have little logistical difficulty marching through Afghanistan.[22]

In June 1832, about a month after Burnes left Kabul, another Englishman arrived in the city. Using the name Charles Masson, he claimed to be an American citizen, though Wade's enquiries later revealed that he was actually James Lewis, a British deserter from the Bengal Army.[23] Masson briefly passed through Afghanistan in 1828 and had already travelled exten-sively in the region, but this time he decided to stay in Kabul and took up residence with one of the leaders of the city's Armenian community. Masson was a keen archaeologist and in September 1832 he accompanied Hajji Khan Kakar on his campaign against Yazdan Bakhsh of Besud and the Uzbek *amir*s of Saighan, Kahmard and Duab, during which he sketched and described the famous Buddha statues at Bamiyan. Sayyid Karamat 'Ali, the British 'native' news writer in Kabul, reported Masson's presence to Wade. After Masson returned to Kabul he wrote to Henry Pottinger, the Resident in Sind, mostly about his archaeological discoveries, and was encouraged to write regularly about the affairs in Kabul.

Wade later sacked Karamat 'Ali for allegedly forging letters to Shah Shuja' and other intrigues and appointed Masson in his place. Masson was a copious writer and keen observer, and the value of the intelligence he provided was such that Wade eventually secured a Royal Pardon for his capital offence of desertion. However, Masson's appointment as Kabul news writer was done without his prior consent, but in the circumstances Masson felt there was little choice but to accept the position, given that he was indebted to Wade for securing the pardon. Even so, Masson feared his new status in Kabul compromised him and that he would henceforth be regarded as nothing better than a spy. In fact this is exactly what happened and many of his closest friends distanced themselves from him. Masson eventually became so disillusioned with his position and with Britain's

The Saighan valley from the medieval fortress of Qal'a-yi Hanifa. Saighan was on a military and trade route between Bamiyan and Khulm. The valley was also the traditional southern frontier of the Khanate of Bukhara. Charles Masson was the first European to sketch this fortress and other monuments in the Bamiyan area.

Central Asian policy that he referred to his time as news writer as 'thral-dom'.[24] It did not help that Masson and Wade were at odds about policy, with Masson advocating for British recognition of Dost Muhammad Khan, while Wade supported the restoration of Shah Shuja', since he was already in treaty alliance with the Sikhs. Wade also manipulated Masson's reports, using selective quotes in his dispatches to the Governor General to make it appear Masson endorsed his point of view.

Hajji Khan Kakar's campaigns in the Hazarajat and Khulm

Following Burnes's visit, Dost Muhammad Khan sent Hajji Khan Kakar, who was *hakim* of Bamiyan, into the Hazarajat to subdue Yazdan Bakhsh of Behsud, who was leading a growing Hazara confederacy. Yazdan Bakhsh also controlled the road over the Hajigak Pass, a vital link in the southern road from Kabul to Bamiyan, and his subjugation was part of Dost Muhammad Khan's strategy of controlling all the commercial routes to the Amu Darya and the lucrative customs duties. Hajji Khan Kakar too had a vested interest in deposing Yazdan Bakhsh, since he was a threat to his power and revenue stream, while the Jawanshir Qizilbash supported the campaign since the Hazara *amir* had threatened to confiscate their estates in Behsud.

Dost Muhammad Khan had earlier lured Yazdan Bakhsh to Kabul under a pledge of safe conduct, despite warnings from his wife that the Amir could not be trusted. When Yazdan Bakhsh arrived in Kabul, he was imprisoned and sentenced to death, but secured a stay of execution by offering to pay a ransom of 50,000 rupees, but while these funds were being collected, Shi'a partisans in Kabul engineered his escape. Dost Muhammad vented his anger on Yazdan's wife, only to find she was more than a match for him. The daughter of the *amir* of Deh Zangi, she was a woman 'of masculine understanding and habits' and was accustomed to accompanying her husband into battle 'armed and mounted', dressed in men's clothing. She even attended tribal councils and had no compunction about giving her advice to the assembled elders.[25] When Dost Muhammad confronted her about her husband's escape, she boldly retorted: 'Oh, son of Pahinda [*sic*] Khan, art thou not ashamed to array thyself against a female?'[26] Dost Muhammad Khan responded by confining her to Chindawal, only for her to escape disguised as a man. When a posse was sent to recapture her she held them at bay with a musket and eventually rejoined her husband in Behsud.

Hajji Khan Kakar tried to convince the fugitive Yazdan Bakhsh that Dost Muhammad Khan was prepared to forgive him, but when he refused to return to Kabul, Hajji Khan forged a secret alliance with Muhammad 'Ali

Beg, the *amir* of Saighan and a notorious slave-trader who regularly raided Shi'a Hazara settlements. When Yazdan Bakhsh got wind of the pact, he expelled Hajji Khan's customs officials, confiscated the Qizilbash estates and took control of Shahr-i Ghulghula, cutting the trade routes between Kabul and Balkh in the process. With Bamiyan under siege and Hajji Khan Kakar's personal income at risk, Hajji Khan offered Yazdan Bakhsh a share of the revenues from the customs posts in the Shibar region in return for allowing his officers back into these settlements. Yazdan Bakhsh agreed, but Hajji Khan Kakar secretly continued to plot with Muhammad 'Ali Beg and increased his power base in Bamiyan by encouraging Kakar and Baluch tribesmen to settle in the valley, offering them incentives of grants of land.

In the autumn of 1832 Hajji Khan and Yazdan Bakhsh joined forces and attacked Muhammad 'Ali Beg, ostensibly to suppress his slave-trading raids, but secretly Hajji Khan Kakar was luring Yazdan Bakhsh away from his power base so he could deal with him once and for all. Following the subjugation of Saighan, Hajji Khan marched down the Kahmard valley. When they reached the remote settlement of Dasht-i Safed, Hajji Khan accused Yazdan Bakhsh of conspiring to incite a revolt among the local *amirs* and he was clapped in irons. After being subjected to all kinds of indignities, he was strangled with a bow string.

Having disposed of this troublesome Hazara, Hajji Khan marched on Khulm. Murad Beg of Qunduz then submitted to him and ceded control over Saighan, Kahmard and the Ajar valleys to Dost Muhammad Khan. Hajji Khan Kakar's advance into the plains of Balkh, however, was in defiance of the Amir's orders. Fearing his incursion might precipitate a Bukharan backlash, Dost Muhammad Khan recalled Hajji Khan and restored the territories to Murad Beg. When Hajji Khan returned to Kabul, he was disgraced and exiled to Peshawar, where he ingratiated himself with Dost Muhammad's half-brothers.

Britain, the Sikhs and Shah Shuja' al-Mulk's bid to regain the throne

Another reason for Hajji Khan's recall was a report that Shah Shuja' was planning another attempt to regain the throne. In the autumn of 1832 Shah Shuja' wrote to Lord Bentinck requesting an advance of a year's stipend to fund his campaign, but he was informed that Britain remained neutral in the dynastic conflict between the Saddozais and Barakzais. At the same time, Bentinck did not specifically disapprove of Shah Shuja' al-Mulk's plan but merely stated that the ex-king was 'master of his own actions'. Wade eventually persuaded Calcutta to advance Shah Shuja' 16,000 rupees and he was also granted the unprecedented right to purchase arms in Delhi tax-free as well as recruit Indian mercenaries for his army. Shah Shuja' al-Mulk's proclamation declaring his intention to regain the throne, however, also included a statement to the effect that his campaign had the support of the British. Ranjit Singh, too, advanced Shah Shuja' a substantial amount of money in return for a treaty, signed in March 1834 that was covertly supported by Wade. Under its terms the ex-king agreed that, in the event of him regaining his throne, he would relinquish sovereignty over all former Durrani territories between the Indus and the Khyber Pass, including Peshawar. When an anxious Dost Muhammad Khan wrote to Wade asking him whether Britain supported Shah Shuja' al-Mulk's campaign, Wade replied disingenuously that Britain 'had no participation' in the ex-king's expedition.[27]

Faced with the threat to Kandahar posed by Shah Shuja', Pur Dil Khan went to Kabul to plead for military support, a situation Dost Muhammad Khan exploited to demand concessions from the Kandahar *sardar*s that increased his power and influence. In order to secure his own defensive line in the event that Shah Shuja' or his Sikh allies attacked along the Khyber Pass, in early 1834 Dost Muhammad Khan marched into Nangahar, subdued the tribes of Bala Bagh, Laghman and Kunar, and made a formal alliance with one of the most important *khans* of the Mohmand tribe.

Shah Shuja' finally set out for Kandahar in the summer of 1834, only for his campaign to come to nothing: in early July he was defeated outside Kandahar and fled, leaving his baggage behind. When Dost Muhammad's officials searched the ex-king's effects they found several letters from Wade, addressed to Shah Shuja', that gave tacit support to his campaign. Wade claimed that they were forgeries and blamed Karamat 'Ali, the Kabul news writer, whom he accused of 'deceitful conduct', 'gross subterfuges' and 'mischievous designs', and dismissed him.[28] Wade, though, may well have written these letters in a semi-private capacity for he made no secret of his desire to see Shah Shuja' back on the throne. His correspondence, however, made Dost Muhammad Khan and many of his courtiers suspect that British officials, while publicly claiming to be neutral, covertly supported Shah Shuja' al-Mulk's restoration; an unfortunate state of affairs that would have major repercussions for future Anglo-Afghan relations.

Amir Dost Muhammad Khan and the *jihad* against the Sikhs

While Dost Muhammad Khan was in Kandahar preparing to confront Shah Shuja', the Sikhs took advantage of his absence to occupy Peshawar, depose Sultan Muhammad Khan and install a Sikh governor, Hari Singh, in his place. When Dost Muhammad Khan returned to Kabul in the autumn of 1834 he found the capital full of refugees, including Sultan Muhammad Khan Tela'i, his half-brothers and the devious Hajji Khan Kakar. They had already taken advantage of Dost Muhammad Khan's absence to stir up the Sunni, anti-Qizilbash faction who now demanded the Amir renew the *jihad* against the Sikhs and retake Peshawar. Such was the clamour for war that Dost Muhammad Khan, against his better judgement, felt he had no option but to send Hajji Khan Kakar and the Peshawar *sardars* to Jalalabad to raise the tribes of Nangahar and the Khyber.

Once his rivals were out of the way, Dost Muhammad Khan upstaged them by having himself formally proclaimed king. A private 'coronation' was hastily organized, attended by a few carefully selected officials and family members and without the usual fanfare. Towards evening Dost Muhammad Khan went to the Pul-i Kheshti mosque where Mir Mas'um, known as Mir Hajji, who had succeeded his father Khwaja Khanji as Mir Wa'is, placed 'two or three blades of grass' in the Amir's turban in what appears to have been a deliberate harking back to the coronation of Ahmad Shah Durrani.[29] Dost Muhammad Khan was declared to be *padshah*, King, and *Amir al-Mu'minim*, Commander of the Faithful. Mir Hajji concluded the ceremony by reading out a *fatwa* of *jihad* against the Sikhs, which urged every Muslim to assist 'the promotion of so righteous a cause' by giving money.

The appeal for funds, however, fell on deaf ears since, as Masson wryly remarked, 'however the Máhomedans of Kâbal were attached to their religion, they were quite as partial to their gold'.[30] Instead Dost Muhammad Khan ordered the Hindu moneylenders to pay two years' *jizya* poll tax in advance, an imposition that led many to flee back to Shikapur, taking their gold with them. Others buried their cash and property or fled to the hills. The Amir also imposed a levy of between five and ten rupees on all shopkeepers; even his wives sold or pawned their jewellery. Yet despite the threat of imprisonment and torture, the war tax raised a meagre three *lakh* rupees, while the imposition came at a terrible economic cost as the overland trade was interrupted, letters of credit were no longer issued or honoured and investment in trade caravans dropped alarmingly.

The renewal of the war with the Sikhs did not endear Dost Muhammad Khan to officials in Calcutta and reinforced Wade's advocacy for the restoration of the Saddozai monarchy. The situation was not improved when, on Masson's advice, the Amir wrote to the Governor General requesting he use his good offices to persuade Ranjit Singh to restore some of the former Durrani territories. Wade duly forwarded the letter to Calcutta but included a covering letter in which he reiterated government policy and ensured that the Amir's request received a chilly reception. Bentinck's reply was blunt: while Britain sought good relations with the Amir and his brothers, Anglo-Afghan relations were strictly commercial in nature and Britain had no intention of mediating in the dispute with the Sikhs, let alone attempting to persuade Ranjit Singh to concede any territory. Included with the letter to the Amir was one from Wade to Masson, which summarized the Governor General's communication and gave him a dressing down for encouraging Dost Muhammad Khan to write such a letter in the first place. Masson was reminded that the government position was that the Amir was solely responsible for the renewal of the war and he deserved whatever punishment the Sikhs decided to mete out. If Dost Muhammad Khan wanted to end the war with the Sikhs, Wade continued, his best course of action was to seek an unconditional peace with Ranjit Singh:

> [The Amir] committed great precipitation in bidding defiance to the Maharaja . . . If determined on hostility, he should have ascertained beforehand whether there was any person on whose aid or assistance he could depend, instead of declaring war, and finding himself left to prosecute it with no other resources other than his own, when it was too late to retrace his footsteps with credit.[31]

Dost Muhammad further undermined his cause by hinting that if Britain did not offer help he would seek the support of a 'rival power' – indeed the Amir had already written to the Shah of Persia and to St Petersburg. Wade told Masson to make it very clear to Dost Muhammad Khan that 'the threat of seeking the support of a *rival* power . . . *might* prove *more* destructive of [Barakzai] independence than *any* which they could possibly take' (Masson's emphasis).[32]

The Governor General's reply caused considerable anger among the Amir's officials, who were not used to being lectured by a foreign, infidel, power. The Amir had written in good faith and on the recommendation of the British news writer, and Masson was ostracized for several days. Furthermore, while the Governor General's letter reflected the existing policy, its arrival was poorly timed for the Amir and thousands of *mujahidin* were poised to march on Peshawar. Fortunately for Britain the *jihad* failed, but had Dost Muhammad defeated the Sikhs and marched into the Punjab, the First Anglo-Afghan War might well have been fought in 1834 on the banks of the Indus or Sutlej.

Yet even Dost Muhammad had little hope that the war would end in anything but defeat. 'He was a weak fly about to encounter a huge elephant,' he declared, 'and could but pray that God would give him victory against such overwhelming odds.'[33] The Amir even sought an augury from Hazara diviners, but his premonition proved correct. The Sikhs remained behind the safety of the Peshawar fort and Dost Muhammad Khan, unable to make any impression on its strong defences, opened negotiations. One of the envoys Ranjit Singh sent to Dost Muhammad's camp was an American adventurer, Josiah Harlan, who referred to himself as General Harlan, even though his entire military career had comprised service as a temporary medical orderly in the Burma campaign.[34] Harlan was a friend of Masson but the two men had fallen out and parted company. Harlan subsequently led an abortive attempt to place Shah Shuja' back on the throne and later spent time in Kabul, but after being implicated in a plot to assassinate Dost Muhammad Khan, he fled Peshawar and eventually entered the service of Ranjit Singh.

Dost Muhammad Khan was forced to accept the status quo and his failure to take Peshawar opened the door for his enemies. While he was away campaigning law and order broke down in the Afghan capital and when the Amir returned to Kabul his senior advisers failed to turn up for meetings. The Ghilzai then rebelled over the imposition of the war tax, while the Jawanshir Qizilbash secretly intrigued with Shah Shuja'. The security situation eventually became so bad that Masson hired armed guards and barricaded himself in his house. When Dost Muhammad asked the Kandahar *sardars* to mediate, he found out just in time that the Kandahar envoy was plotting with the Peshawar *sardars* to have him assassinated. To cap it all Masson heard that a Russian officer, Lieutenant Ivan Viktorovich Vitkevich, had arrived in Bukhara and was sending military intelligence back to St Petersburg.[35]

The Burnes Mission to Kabul and the Persian siege of Herat

Masson urged the Amir to mend his bridges with the British. Since a new Governor General, George Eden, Lord Auckland, had recently arrived in Calcutta, Masson suggested he write a congratulatory letter in the hope that Auckland would be more amenable to mediating a settlement of the Afghan-Sikh War. In his letter, written in May 1836, the Amir assured Auckland that, 'I look upon myself and country as bound to [the British Government] by the strongest ties.' He then went on to explain that the war with Ranjit Singh had not been his fault but was due to the 'reckless and misguided' conduct of the Sikhs, and renewed his request for British mediation, concluding, 'I hope your Lordship will consider me and my country as your own.' Less than three years later Auckland would take his offer rather too literally.[36]

Auckland's reply was very different in tone from Bentinck's and Masson reported that it 'excited a great sensation' among senior officials. Among other things, Dost Muhammad Khan was formally addressed by his regnal title of Amir, rather than *sardar*, which the Afghan courtiers saw as tacit recognition of Dost Muhammad Khan's legitimacy, although it is uncertain whether Auckland's use of this title was deliberate or simply an oversight by his Political Secretary, William Hay Macnaghten. The Governor General reiterated Britain's desire to improve commercial relations and the policy of non-interference in the Sikh-Afghan dispute, but left the door ajar by asking the Amir to inform him how he could assist in the matter. It was in the interest of all countries in the region, Auckland wrote, for their two nations to 'preserve unimpaired the relations of amity and concord'. Indeed, 'ere long', he planned to send a British mission to Kabul to discuss 'commercial topics'.[37] In fact, even before the Governor General's letter reached Kabul, Alexander Burnes had been appointed to head this mission.

The prospect of a British envoy coming to Kabul was seen as further evidence of a possible political rapprochement with Britain. There were other reasons to justify this belief. In early 1836 there was a serious crisis in Anglo-Sikh relations after Ranjit Singh occupied outposts in Sind, which threatened the strategic Indus port of Shikapur. Wade warned Ranjit Singh that he risked war with Britain if he tried to extend his authority into Sind, which Britain regarded as within its sphere of interest, and the Governor General even began to mobilize the army. Faced with the threat from the Sikhs, in March 1837 the Amirs of Hyderabad agreed to let their country become a British Protectorate and Ranjit Singh, realizing he had pushed his luck too far, backed down. As the threat of war receded, Wade set out to repair Anglo-Sikh relations but, as Auckland noted, Britain was now 'irretrievably involved in the politics of the countries of the Indus'.[38]

Burnes set out for Kabul in late December 1836 with the Sind crisis still unresolved, while Dost Muhammad Khan tried to take advantage of the British confrontation with Ranjit Singh to renew his war with the Sikhs. Muhammad Akbar Khan was sent against the fortress of Jamrud, which the Sikhs were constructing on the Afghan side of the Khyber Pass. He reached Jamrud in late April 1837 and, seeing no sign of the Sikhs, began to demolish the fortifications. While Akbar Khan's men were occupied with pulling down the defences, Hari Singh, who commanded the Sikh

The fortress of Jamrud, *c.* 1900. Located on the Afghanistan side of the Khyber Pass, it was originally built by the Sikhs and later taken over and modified by the British.

garrison, attacked and scattered the Afghans with heavy loss of life. Akbar Khan's army was only saved from annihilation by the arrival of his brother Shams al-Din Khan and a large body of cavalry, who charged the Sikh lines. Akbar Khan then rallied his men and pushed the Sikhs back into Jamrud, where they too were saved by the arrival of substantial reinforcements. Akbar Khan broke off the engagement and returned to Jalalabad, leaving the Sikhs in control of Jamrud, but when he returned to Kabul he claimed the victory and was given a hero's welcome. For decades after, this pyrrhic victory was celebrated annually in the Afghan capital.[39]

More to the point, the 'victory' provided the Amir with the opportunity to dispose of powerful rivals. 'Abd al-Samad Khan, his chief minister, who had failed to engage the Sikhs and whom the Amir suspected of plotting against him, was exiled to Bukhara. Hajji Khan Kakar, who had taken a substantial bribe from the Sikhs and stood aside from the fighting, was once more expelled and made his way to Kandahar, where he was welcomed by the Dil brothers. Dost Muhammad Khan later admitted that it had been one of his greatest mistakes not to have put the Kakar chief to death.

The Sikhs had beaten the Afghans but in the battle Hari Singh, Ranjit's lifelong friend, had been mortally wounded. Thirsting for revenge, the Maharaja refused to negotiate and threatened to attack Kabul, a threat Dost Muhammad Khan took very seriously, but hoped that when Burnes arrived he might agree to Britain mediating a face-saving peace. British officials, after all, had intervened to prevent a Sikh invasion of Sind, so maybe Britain would be willing to act in a similar capacity and persuade the Sikhs to withdraw from Jamrud and even come to a power-sharing agreement over Peshawar. The Amir's hopes were raised further after Wade persuaded Ranjit Singh not to carry out his threat to attack Jalalabad and Kabul, at least until Burnes had returned to India. Given the political situation, Dost Muhammad had every reason to assume that the British mission was coming to Kabul to discuss more than commercial matters, especially as Burnes's two previous expeditions had covert political and military objectives. Masson informed Burnes about Dost Muhammad's expectations long before he reached Kabul and the Amir wrote regularly to Burnes as he made his way to Afghanistan. In his replies, Burnes did little to discourage his misconceptions despite his instructions limiting his discussions to 'strictly commercial' matters. As far as Burnes was concerned, his mission was political and he was determined to seize the opportunity it presented to revive his career.

After his triumph in London, Burnes had turned down the offer of a post in Persia because he believed it was beneath him, so he had been sent to Sind as assistant to Henry Pottinger. Not only did Burnes resent this, the two men were chalk and cheese and their relationship quickly turned sour. Pottinger was an old Indian hand who had worked his way up the career ladder the hard way. As an ensign in the Indian Army he had fought in the Second Anglo-Maratha Wars (1803–5), then in 1810–11 he undertook a dangerous intelligence-gathering journey from Baluchistan to Isfahan at the height of the Napoleonic threat. Over the years Pottinger had worked tirelessly to win the confidence of the Amirs of Sind and had successfully secured British interests on the lower Indus. Yet despite more than thirty years of service in India, so far Pottinger had received little official recognition. It was not until 1839 that he was made a baronet and in 1843 he was finally appointed Hong Kong's first governor. As far as Pottinger was concerned, Burnes was an ambitious, limelight-seeking upstart whose self-confidence verged on arrogance. As for the young man's sudden fame, this hardly endeared him to a man who had spent all his life serving King and Country. Their mutual loathing eventually became so bad that they were no longer on speaking terms and Auckland had to write to both to remind them that their personal animosity must in no way affect their public duty.[40]

Burnes had been upstaged by Pottinger's successful treaty negotiations with the Amirs of Hyderabad, which had pushed British influence beyond the Indus, and Burnes was determined to outdo his superior by ending the Afghan-Sikh War, securing in the process Britain's commercial and political supremacy beyond the Khyber Pass. In the event he was successful, Burnes was certain this would not only secure him promotion but the plum position of envoy to the court of Dost Muhammad Khan. In his private correspondence Burnes confided that he saw himself as 'the humble instrument of calming a nation's fury'.[41] Even before he reached Kabul, Burnes had formulated a bizarre plan to end the Afghan-Sikh War, which involved persuading Ranjit Singh to agree that on his death all Sikh territory beyond the Indus would be returned to Dost Muhammad Khan. While in Peshawar, Burnes raised expectations further by discussing the Peshawar issue with Ranjit Singh's son and heir, who told Burnes that his father might be willing to consider letting Sultan Muhammad Khan return to govern Peshawar under Sikh suzerainty.

Burnes, however, had no authority to 'make replies' on the issue of the Afghan-Sikh War, let alone attempt to negotiate a settlement. Any political proposals made to him had to be forwarded to Calcutta through Wade and he would have to wait until he received the Governor General's formal response, which he then had to communicate to the Amir or other interested parties. This was a tortuous process for it took up to six weeks for letters to reach Calcutta from Kabul and some three months before Burnes could receive a reply, a delay that was a key factor in the breakdown of the talks. It also put Wade in a prime position to influence the Governor General and ensure that his pro-Sikh policy was maintained. This was even more important for Wade since he was doing his best to repair relations with Ranjit Singh in the wake of the confrontation over Sind. For the same reason Wade did not want Britain to seem to be too friendly to Dost Muhammad Khan, especially as the Amir was still technically at war with the Sikhs. Indeed, Wade would have been happy for the Sikhs to occupy Kabul and Kandahar. Burnes and Wade were therefore at odds over policy, but there was also an element of personal rivalry. Burnes had made no secret of his ambition to become Political Agent in Kabul, and if he secured the position Wade's monopolistic control over Afghan affairs would have been broken.

When Burnes reached Kabul on 20 September 1837, the mission was accorded full diplomatic honours and he and his fellow countrymen were borne into the Bala Hisar on the backs of elephants, while cheering crowds thronged the streets. The Amir, convinced that Burnes was on a covert political mission, held his first meeting in the most secret place he knew, his own *zanana*, with only himself and Akbar Khan present. Even when Burnes stated that his mission was strictly commercial, the Amir saw this as mere posturing and began to discuss how to resolve the war with the

Sikhs, pointing out that there could be no improvement in trans-Indus trade unless the war ended. Not only was Afghanistan on the verge of bank-ruptcy, security on the caravan routes had deteriorated to such an extent that the Hindu *banyan*s had stopped issuing letters of credit. Since the Governor General had declared himself to be the friend of both Afghans and Sikhs, the British were the obvious party to mediate in the dispute. However, they made it clear that he was not prepared to accept any peace deal that might be seen as capitulation. Dost Muhammad then suggested that allowing him to exert a degree of authority over Peshawar would be a sufficient face-saving solution.

From the outset Burnes found himself outwitted by the Amir, who cunningly linked negotiations for a commercial treaty with a resolution of the conflict with the Sikhs. Burnes, however, had no freedom of action when it came to political issues. While he made his way to Kabul, Auckland, hearing that the Amir planned to renew his war with Ranjit Singh, had sent Burnes a revised set of instructions, including informing Dost Muhammad Khan not to hold 'pretensions which he cannot maintain', particularly in respect of Peshawar. Burnes was also to advise the Amir that if he genu-inely wished to end the war he should formally apologize to Ranjit Singh, preferably by sending his son Akbar Khan to Lahore. If he did so, Britain might put in a good word about reinstating Sultan Muhammad Khan as governor of Peshawar under Sikh authority. This decision, however, would be entirely dependent on Ranjit Singh's own wishes.

Dost Muhammad Khan knew that sending his son to Lahore to beg forgiveness was not just humiliating but political suicide. While Auckland's position reflected government policy, it also demonstrated a profound lack of understanding of traditional peace-making protocols and the political dynamics of the region. For the Amir to send his son to Lahore to sue for peace and pardon was an admission of defeat as well as a tacit acknow-ledgement of Sikh sovereignty, which would make Dost Muhammad Khan effectively a vassal of Ranjit Singh. This was completely unacceptable to the Amir, the religious elites and the tribes of southern Afghanistan. As for allowing Sultan Muhammad Khan to govern Peshawar, this too was un-acceptable. 'Though of one family, and of one blood,' he informed Burnes, Sultan Muhammad Khan 'was a more fatal enemy to him . . . than the Sikhs.'[42] Burnes informed the Governor General that the Amir had rejected his proposal but, instead of waiting for the response from Calcutta, he tried to negotiate a solution to the problem, convinced that he could persuade Auckland to change his mind. In the process, Burnes raised expectations that were both unrealistic and unrealizable.

Though Burnes did not know it at the time of his first meeting, some two weeks before he arrived in Kabul, Lord Auckland wrote to Ranjit Singh, who was worried about the true object of Burnes's mission, to reassure him that Britain had no intention of making any political treaty with Dost Muhammad Khan and would 'do nothing in Cabool without [Ranjit's] consent'.[43] Auckland also informed the Maharaja that he regarded the attack on Jamrud as an act of blatant aggression by the Amir against a trusted treaty partner, and if Ranjit Singh decided to march on Kabul and punish Dost Muhammad Khan, he would not object. At least Britain would have a reliable ally beyond the Khyber. As for Dost Muhammad Khan, Auckland believed he could not be trusted, for he had written both to the Shah of Persia and the Russians seeking aid against the Sikhs, an action that was hostile to British interests. Auckland then told Burnes to inform Dost Muhammad Khan that if he were sincere about good relations with Britain he should immediately cease all correspondence with both powers.

Dost Muhammad must have been at a loss to understand why the British had bothered to send Burnes to Kabul since clearly he had no plenipotentiary powers to negotiate a solution to the dominant political issue facing him. To all intent and purposes, Burnes was just a messenger boy. In the Amir's view:

> this was not the good offices of the English which he had expected; that his hopes were quite different; that he now had a turban of muslin on his head, but on entering into friendly relations with the British he had sanguine hopes that he would have a shawl one in lieu of muslin. On the contrary, he finds the English wish to keep the old material on his head, with the obliging promise that they will not allow another power to deprive him of it. To this act of amity he attaches not much importance, as he was not afraid that any one will ever wrest it from him.[44]

Yet as a show of goodwill, Dost Muhammad halted all correspondence with Persia and Russia. He had never been that serious about a Persian alliance anyway, since that too would have been politically unacceptable to the powerful Sunni Islamist lobby. It was an alliance with Britain, the dominant power in the region, that he coveted.

In November 1837 the situation took an unexpected turn when news reached Kabul that a Persian army was marching on Herat, a campaign that Muhammad Mirza Qajar pursued in the face of strong objections by Sir John McNeill, the British envoy, in Tehran. Britain believed that

Russia was encouraging the attack as a way to extend its influence into Afghanistan and McNeill pointed out to the Shah that Kamran already accepted limited Persian suzerainty. Shah Muhammad Qajar, though, had demanded Kamran renounce the title of *Shah* and accord him the right of *khutba* and coinage, as well as pay a proportion of Herat's annual revenues into the Persian treasury. Shah Kamran refused, pointedly reminding Shah Muhammad that it had been a Persian monarch who had appointed Saddu Khan as *Mir-i Afghaniha* and bestowed on him the title of *sultan*. As a direct descendant of Saddu Khan, Kamran therefore had every right to refer to himself as *shah* and declared that 'the Afghans will never permit any other person to rule over them so long as a single Afghan remains alive in Herat.'[45]

In October 1837 Shah Muhammad Mirza marched out of Sabzawar at the head of an army of 36,000 men, intent not just on conquering Herat but also subduing Khiva, Kandahar and Kabul. The Persian attack on Herat placed Britain in an awkward position, for under the terms of the 1814 treaty Britain agreed not to intervene in any war between Persia and the Afghans. So McNeill sent his Military Secretary, Col. Stoddard, to accompany the Persian army in the hope he could eventually persuade the Shah to abandon his plans. While Stoddard was in Nishapur, Vitkevich, the Russian envoy who had recently been in Bukhara, arrived in the Persian camp and announced he was on his way to Kandahar and Kabul bearing letters from his government. Shah Muhammad then added to the paranoia about Russian intentions by grossly exaggerating the extent of Russian support, while the presence of Russians in the Persian army was seen as another sign of Moscow's involvement, though in fact these were actually Polish deserters whom Russia had asked Persia to repatriate. Once the siege of Herat was underway, a Persian envoy was sent to Kandahar to discuss an alliance with the Kandahar *sardars*.

Fortunately for Britain and Herat, Shah Muhammad Qajar was a poor general and the siege badly managed. Instead of concentrating all his resources on reducing Herat, the Shah split his army. Asaf al-Daula, governor of Khurasan, and several thousand of the Shah's best troops, along with a large number of artillery pieces, were sent into Badghis to prevent a possible attack by a Sunni Confederacy led by Sher Muhammad Khan, head of the Sunni Hazaras, and Mizrab Bi, *wali* of Maimana. Asaf al-Daula faced fierce resistance and, though he eventually took and sacked Qal'a-yi Nau, the Aimaq retreated deep into the mountains. When Asaf al-Daula pursued them, his men were trapped and ambushed in the deep, narrow gorges. With casualties mounting, Asaf al-Daula appealed for

The Tir Band-i Turkistan is cut through by deep, narrow gorges. It was terrain like this, near Ghulbiyan, in southeastern Faryab province, that the Asif al-Daula's army was trapped in during the Persian campaign against the Aimaq and Uzbek confederacy.

reinforcements. A further 3,000 men and 32 additional artillery pieces were sent to assist him and eventually Asaf al-Daula managed to occupy Ghuriyan. As he advanced on Almar, Mizrab Bi in Maimana submitted to Persian authority but the Turkmans and Aimaqs fought on, cutting the army's overextended supply line and forcing Asaf al-Daula into winter quarters in Ghuriyan. For some three months the Persian force played no part in the siege of Herat and when the bitter Badghis winter set in, hundreds of Persian soldiers and their animals died from exposure and starvation. By the time Asaf al-Daula returned to Herat in April 1838, what was left of his army was unfit for combat.[46]

By the spring of 1838 the siege of Herat had made little progress. Despite regular artillery bombardments, the city walls held and the defenders managed to beat back the Persian assaults. The siege had also taken an unexpected turn when Henry Pottinger's nephew, Lieutenant Eldred

Pottinger, who was in Herat travelling through Afghanistan in disguise, secured an audience with Yar Muhammad Khan, Kamran's *wazir*. When he announced that he was a British officer he was given charge of the city's defences.[47] Pottinger's actions at the siege of Herat made him a national hero. Dubbed the Hero of Herat, British imperial mythology claimed it was Pottinger who single-handedly ensured the city did not fall. He did indeed rally Herat's dispirited defenders and organize its defences, but his real achievement was cajoling Shah Kamran and Wazir Yar Muhammad Khan not to surrender. Pottinger's presence in Herat now meant Britain had representatives in both camps, so while Pottinger did his best to drag out the siege as long as possible, Stoddard and McNeill turned the diplomatic screws on Shah Muhammad Khan.

Initially British officials thought that Herat would fall within a matter of weeks. Meanwhile the campaign of Asaf al-Daula on the Murghab and in Maimana caused further concern. In late 1837 Dr Lord, the physician on the Burnes Mission who had travelled to Qunduz to treat Murad Beg for an ophthalmic complaint, wrote to inform Burnes of the submission of Mizrab Khan of Maimana and the *amir*s of the Chahar Wilayat, and declared that nothing now stood in the way of the Persian army occupying Balkh and Qunduz. This news came on the back of reports that a Persian envoy had arrived in Kandahar and was negotiating an alliance with Sher Dil Khan. For a while it seemed that Herat, Balkh and Kandahar were likely to fall; a scenario that the Governor General believed would open the door for Russian influence and even a possible invasion of India.

In October 1837 Burnes wrote to Sher Dil Khan warning him that Britain regarded the presence of the Persian ambassador as a hostile act, but a month later Sher Dil Khan signed the treaty anyway. Under its terms Persia agreed that on the fall of Herat it would be placed in the hands of the Kandahar *sardar*s, who would govern the province in the name of the Shah. Persia also pledged military support in the event Kandahar were attacked by Britain, Shah Shuja' or Dost Muhammad Khan. Having concluded the treaty, Sher Dil Khan sent a large force of tribal levies to assist the Persian siege of Herat. The situation became even more critical, as far as Britain was concerned, when Count Ivan Simonich, the Russian envoy at the Persian court, guaranteed the treaty, assigned a Russian artillery officer to advise the Shah on the prosecution of the siege, and even gave him money to pay his soldiers.

When Count Nesselrode, Russia's foreign minister, heard what Simonich had done, he repudiated his envoy's actions and recalled him. Nesselrode then wrote a formal apology to the British government, but by the time this news reached Burnes and McNeill the damage had been done. British officials regarded Simonich's actions as conclusive proof that Russia was behind the Persian invasion, which it was exploiting in order to extend its influence to the gates of India.[48] This assumption was reinforced when Lieutenant Vitkevich arrived in Kabul in early December bearing letters addressed to Dost Muhammad Khan from the Shah of Persia and Count Simonich. In a demonstration of good faith, the Amir showed Burnes Simonich's letters, which caused him to be even more alarmed, for the Shah urged the Amir to accept Persian suzerainty while Simonich offered to assist Dost Muhammad Khan in the event of a Sikh attack on Kabul.

Burnes now found himself caught up in a major geopolitical crisis that had not been anticipated when his official instructions had been issued. McNeill in Tehran had wide powers to deal with the situation from his end but Burnes had no such authority, yet by the time he received new instructions Herat, Balkh and Kandahar may well have fallen and the Amir, in desperation, would probably accept the offer of Russian assistance against the Sikhs. What Burnes did not know was that Asaf al-Daula's advance had stalled and news of his return to Herat did not reach him until February, for Dr Lord's letters were held up due to the winter snows blocking the passes between Qunduz and Kabul. After discussing the situation with Dost Muhammad Khan, the Amir agreed to wait three months so that Burnes could receive an official response from Calcutta to the Persian and Russian letters. Meanwhile, Vitkevich remained in Kabul, but was denied an audience with the Amir.

In the light of the information he had to hand in early December 1837, Burnes concluded that there was 'no course left' but to act immediately. Lieutenant Leech, one of his assistants, was dispatched to Kandahar with a letter urging the Dil brothers to abrogate the treaty with Persia and, in return, Burnes pledged British cash and troops to defend them against possible Persian aggression. Burnes then broke with official protocol and wrote a passionate appeal directly to the Governor General, circumventing Wade and Macnaghten, in which he justified his actions and asked Auckland to endorse his offer of financial and military assistance to the Kandahar *sardar*s. Burnes also reported that Dost Muhammad Khan had made further concessions on the Sikh question. While he was still not prepared to send Akbar Khan to Lahore, he was now willing to write apologizing for the attack on Jamrud and offer Ranjit Singh condolences for the death of Hari Singh. To compensate for this loss of face, however, the Amir requested Britain use its good offices to persuade Ranjit Singh to let one of his sons govern Peshawar under Sikh sovereignty. He even offered to pay Lahore a portion of the Peshawar revenues. Burnes wrote about this 'settlement of the Peshawar affair':

> we have, it seems to me, an immediate remedy against further intrigue and a means of showing to the Afghans that the British Government does sympathise with them, and at one and the same time satisfying the chiefs, and gaining both our political and commercial ends.[49]

Burnes was convinced Ranjit Singh would accept the terms and even offered to go to Lahore to head the negotiations.

Auckland's reply did not reach Kabul until the end of February 1838 and its contents dashed any hopes Burnes had that his actions would be approved. The offer of assistance to the Kandahar *sardars* was rejected and the Persian treaty dismissed as a fabrication, a ploy by the Dil brothers to extract concessions from Britain. As for Vitkevich's mission, this was a storm in a teacup. The Governor General then reiterated that the Amir must abandon all hope of any British mediation with the Sikhs and forget about Peshawar, since Britain had recognized it as a Sikh province. Wade had not even bothered to forward the Amir's latest proposals to Ranjit Singh. To cap it all, Burnes was reprimanded for exceeding his mandate and raising Dost Muhammad's expectations beyond anything Britain was prepared to offer.

On 22 February Burnes had his last, humiliating audience with Dost Muhammad Khan, during which he communicated the contents of Auckland's letter and confessed he had grossly exceeded his orders, misrepresented government policy and raised the Amir's hopes far too high. Dost Muhammad Khan, who had committed a great deal of time and money in order to win over the British, was bitter. Throughout the course of Burnes's mission, he declared, he had been 'either kept in the dark or misled . . . I wish no countenance but that of the English, and you refuse all pledges and promises.'[50] Britain had offered him neither '*izzat* nor *ikram* – honour or respect. Burnes then added insult to injury by trying to shift the blame onto the Amir, accusing him of being intransigent and unreasonable. When the Amir's tribal council heard the news they were incensed and their fury was exacerbated by the hectoring tone of Auckland's letter. General Harlan, who was now in the service of the Amir after having incurred the wrath of Ranjit Singh, claimed that some of Dost Muhammad Khan's advisers even wanted to put the British members of the mission to death.

Instead Dost Muhammad Khan, supported by Nawab Jabbar Khan, tried to salvage something from the wreckage. In his reply to Auckland the Amir said that even a vague pledge by Britain to protect the Amir from Persian aggression would be sufficient, or some token gesture over Peshawar. He was even prepared to accept Sultan Muhammad Khan as governor of Peshawar under Sikh suzerainty and agreed to all the Governor General's conditions to end the war. However, neither he nor his sons were prepared to abase themselves before Ranjit Singh or abjectly sue for his pardon. Burnes, though, dared not forward this final offer to Calcutta for, in the Amir's words, he had 'no powers . . . to satisfy this nation'.[51] In private, the Amir told Harlan it had been a great mistake to allow himself to be drawn into the web of Anglo-Russian intrigue.

Burnes's mission had failed and on 21 April 1838 the Amir formally received Vitkevitch. Five days later Burnes left Kabul, ordering Masson to accompany him, despite assurances from Afghan officials that he was still a friend and would not face any recriminations if he remained. Though Burnes did not know it, he and his companions were lucky to escape with their lives. The Jabbar Khel planned to ambush and kill them as they made their way through the passes to Jalalabad, but Dost Muhammad intervened and refused to sanction their assassination and so the mission reached Jamrud safely.

A few months later the Amir's faith in European diplomatic integrity received another blow when Vitkevich was recalled and revoked all offers Simonich had made. When Vitkevich finally arrived back in St Petersburg, Nesselrode snubbed him and sent an underling with the curt message that the Count 'knew of no Captain Vitkevich, except an adventurer of that name who . . . had been lately engaged in some unauthorized intrigues at Kabul and Kandahar'.[52] A furious Vitkevich returned to his lodgings, burnt his papers and put a bullet through his brain.

Burnes must bear much of the blame for the failure of his mission, for from the outset he failed to abide by his terms of reference, or at the very least adopted a very creative interpretation of them. As far as Burnes was concerned, the mission to Kabul was his opportunity to bring off a diplomatic coup that would earn him both fame and promotion, and he was naive, or arrogant, enough to believe he could persuade the bureaucrats in Calcutta to endorse his actions and recommendations. However, Auckland, rightly or wrongly, held to the official government line.

Burnes was not the only individual responsible for the debacle. His mission was the outcome of Ellenborough's aggressive Indus strategy, as well as unjustified paranoia about Russian ambitions and the degree of influence St Petersburg allegedly had over Persia. It was also naive of Auckland to believe Burnes's mission would not be viewed as political in nature. The time lag in communications between Kabul and Calcutta, as well as Burnes's restrictive terms of reference, meant he was hamstrung when it came to responding to unexpected and dramatic changes in the military and political situation. Auckland's choice of Burnes, a relatively junior officer with little diplomatic experience, as head of a mission that was always going to require delicate handling was another misjudgement. In Masson's words, the Governor General had confided in the discretion of a man who had none.[53] Henry Pottinger, Sir John McNeill or John Malcolm, all highly experienced diplomats with extensive experience of Persia and Afghanistan, would have been far better choices.

Wade's uncritical support of Ranjit Singh, his opposition to any British mediation in the Afghan-Sikh War and his preference for the restoration of Shah Shuja' further undermined Burnes's position. In the end Wade's view prevailed, but had Britain used its good offices to resolve the long-standing dispute, rather than demand what was in effect Dost Muhammad's unconditional surrender, the evidence suggests that both sides would have been more than willing to accept a compromise solution. Had this been achieved British prestige would have been significantly enhanced both in Kabul and Lahore and saved thousands of British, Indian and Afghan lives, for the failure of the Burnes Mission led to war with Afghanistan. The fallout from the failure of the mission, though, was much longer lasting. It undid the goodwill created by the Elphinstone Mission and seriously damaged Britain's image with successive rulers of Afghanistan who no longer trusted British diplomacy, which they regarded as devious, duplicitous and deceptive – a belief that endured well into the twentieth century.

When Burnes reached Peshawar, he informed Wade that he was convinced that 'consequences of a most serious nature' would result 'unless the British government applies a prompt, active, and decided counteraction' to oppose Russia. Auckland too was convinced that Britain 'ought not to suffer Persian and Russian influence quietly to fix themselves along our entire western frontier.'[54] In May 1838 Auckland called a council of war in Simla, which decided on military intervention against both Persia and Afghanistan. Vitkevich's mission, which the Governor General had previously dismissed as insignificant, was now seen to pose a direct threat to British interests and Wade's plan to restore Shah Shuja', which Auckland had rejected a few months before, was adopted as official policy. Macnaghten, Auckland's chief political secretary, was sent to meet Ranjit Singh to discuss a military alliance against Afghanistan and a new treaty. Macnaghten was also entrusted with the planning of the military campaign and a few months later he was appointed Envoy Plenipotentiary to the court of Shah Shuja'.

This was an extraordinary decision, for Macnaghten had no military or diplomatic experience but was a former High Court judge and specialist in Islamic and Hindu law. He was also an archetypal bureaucrat: punctilious, officious, a stickler for protocols, and a man who enjoyed dabbling in petty intrigues. He was not well liked by his contemporaries and many believed he should never have been entrusted with being in effect the Governor General's right-hand man. Macnaghten's wife, Frances, was even more difficult. A member of a minor Anglo-Irish aristocratic family, she had gone to India by her own admission to climb the social ladder, an ambition she achieved by the simple expedient of 'marrying 'igher and 'igher and 'igher.'[55] Her first husband, an officer in the Bombay Infantry, had died a few years after their marriage; shortly after his demise Frances accepted Macnaghten's proposal. Following his death, she returned to England where she married Thomas Taylour, 2nd Marquess of Headfort, in 1853. Ambitious, haughty, arrogant, condescending and on occasion downright offensive, she was Calcutta's answer to Barchester's Mrs Proudie.

Wade and Burnes were ordered to join Macnaghten's mission to Ranjit Singh, but Masson was not invited to join the party and remained in Peshawar. Shortly after Burnes arrived in Kabul, Masson had tendered his resignation but Auckland rejected his request and told Masson to stay on and assist Burnes. Over the following six months Masson developed a decided dislike for Burnes and his proceedings, and became increasingly critical of government policy. Now that Burnes's mission had ended, Masson once more submitted his resignation and this time it was accepted. But though Auckland assured him his services had been appreciated, Masson was not offered any new appointment. Released from his 'thraldom', Masson headed into the Yusufzai country, where he documented what turned out to be fourteen edicts of the Mauryan king, Ashoka (r. 272–235 BCE), carved into rock at Shahbazgarhi, near Mardan.

Masson anyway was recovering from a serious illness and years of arduous travel and living in Afghanistan had left him exhausted and depressed. He was also in debt and living on a pittance, for his claim for field allowance for his time in Kabul had been rejected. His disillusionment with British policy had deepened to the point of cynicism as over six months he watched from the sidelines as Burnes, Wade, Macnaghten and Auckland combined to destroy the trust and confidence he had built up with the Durrani court over the previous five years. His sense of grievance was exacerbated by having been ordered to leave the country he loved, while many of his Afghan friends no longer wanted to associate with him for fear of reprisals.

Masson was also disgusted with the personal conduct of Burnes and the other British officers during their time in Kabul, claiming that the Amir, as part of his attempt to ingratiate himself with the mission, had provided them with as many pretty women and *nauch* girls as they wanted. Burnes's many hagiographers have dismissed Masson's allegations as coming from an embittered man, but the sexual exploits of Burnes and his circle were an open secret not only to the Afghan court but to their fellow officers.[56] Indeed, Burnes's dalliance with high-ranking Afghan women during the occupation of Kabul contributed significantly to his bloody death.

After returning from his archaeological expedition and with no news of a new posting, Masson travelled to Firozpur, where an invasion force, grandiosely named the Army of the Indus, was being assembled, but deliberately avoided all contact with the 'politicals'. In Masson's view going to war with Dost Muhammad Khan was 'useless' and he mischievously claimed Auckland's decision had been due to pressure applied to him by 'the assaults of certain females, aides-de-camp and secretaries'.[57] For the next eighteen months Masson concentrated on writing his memoirs. In the summer of 1840 he was sent to Kalat, which had been sacked by the Army of the Indus the previous year, where he faced further humiliation at the hands of 'politicals'. When he paid his respects to Lieutenant Loveday, the sadistic agent in charge of the Bolan Pass, he sat on the only chair in the room and forced Masson to squat on the floor like a native. Loveday then studiously ignored him when he tried to point out the many blunders made by the Army of the Indus. Masson was even more disgusted when he took a tour of Kalat and found that this once thriving commercial centre was in ruins and his friends impoverished. Macnaghten's land and taxation reforms, designed to raise more income for Shah Shuja' al-Mulk's treasury, also created deep resentment and eventually led to a revolt. When the rebels stormed Kalat, Loveday, Masson and other British officers were taken prisoner. Masson, who lost many of his notebooks and manuscripts during the revolt, was eventually freed and sent to negotiate a prisoner exchange. The British political officer in Quetta, however, accused him of unauthorized travel in a military zone and of being a Russian spy. Masson was placed under house arrest and it was several months before he was finally released without charge.

Unable to secure redress for his imprisonment from official sources, Masson wrote a bitter account of his treatment in the Indian papers, claiming that Macnaghten was behind the persecution. Further disappointment followed. He heard that no 'respectable' publisher in England was prepared to publish his journals because they were critical of British officials and

the government's policy. His claim for compensation for wrongful imprisonment and the loss of property in the Kalat uprising was also dismissed.
In 1842 Masson returned to England to pursue his case for compensation
with the Board of Control, but he never received any redress and ended up
living on a meagre pension. He eventually published a revised version of
his memoirs but his criticism of individuals and government policy upset
many high officials. He was, after all, a commoner and a deserter, and in
the eyes of the Establishment he had no right to attack his 'betters'. Given
the way he had been treated, Masson's occasional bitter outbursts in his
published work are more than justified. In the end, though, Masson had the
last laugh for his *Narrative of Various Journeys in Balochistan, Afghanistan,
the Panjab, and Kalât* became a standard reference work for 'politicals' on
India's Northwest Frontier.

Masson's achievements were mostly overlooked during his lifetime
yet they far outweigh those of Burnes, Wade, Elphinstone or Auckland.
Masson's published work as well as his surviving journals and papers are
still an essential source for the history of Afghanistan during a crucial
period in the country's political life. His account of the inner workings of Dost Muhammad Khan's court are as important as Elphinstone's
for they provide considerable insight into complex tribal and political
inter-relationships. His unpublished journals and papers also contain
wide-ranging information about Afghanistan's geography and peoples.
As for Masson's knowledge of Afghanistan, this was equal to any of his

The Buddhist *stupa* (reliquary) and *vihara* (monastery) at Gul Darra in the Logar Valley.
One of many Buddhist monuments documented by Charles Masson.

contemporaries, while his archaeological explorations were groundbreaking. Masson almost single-handedly discovered and documented the virtually unknown Gandharan Buddhist civilization, transcribed dozens of ancient inscriptions, drew detailed sketches of a host of major monuments, including the Bamiyan Buddhas, and accumulated a vast collection of ancient coins, which have only just been catalogued in full by the British Museum. Today his pioneering work has rightly earned Masson the title of Father of Afghan Archaeology.

The Tripartite Treaty and the Simla Declaration

While Masson took no part in the military preparations against Dost Muhammad Khan, Burnes saw the invitation to join Macnaghten's mission to Ranjit Singh as a sign that he was not to be punished for his actions in Kabul. Despite admitting privately that he 'differed entirely with the Governor General' over Afghanistan, and even privately accused Auckland of 'mismanagement' of the mission,[58] Burnes endorsed the decision to place Shah Shuja' on throne when it was clear his advocacy for Dost Muhammad Khan was no longer politically acceptable. His political rehabilitation raised Burnes's expectations that the forthcoming military campaign would lead to his appointment as envoy in Kabul. He was to 'be chief', he boasted in a private letter to his brother, 'it is "*aut Caesar aut nullus*" (either Caesar or nothing), and if I get not what I have a right to, you will soon see me *en route* to England'.[59]

Burnes, however, had misjudged his own importance. In July 1838 Auckland informed him that Macnaghten was to be the envoy, yet Burnes did not carry out his threat to leave India and accepted the subordinate post of political officer after receiving a vague promise that he would succeed Macnaghten. Burnes's consolation was that Auckland informed him that London had endorsed his decision to offer assistance to the Kandahar *sardars*: 'The Home Government has pronounced me right and His Lordship wrong', he wrote exultantly, 'this is the greatest hit I have made in my life.' This was not all: Auckland's letter was addressed to Lieutenant Colonel Sir Alexander Burnes, Kt – Burnes had not only been promoted, he had been knighted as well. Wade, too, became Sir Claude Wade and the following year Macnaghten received his knighthood. Such were the rewards of failure. Needless to say there was no such honour bestowed on Masson.

Macnaghten's mission to Ranjit Singh was designed to formulate a plan for the invasion of Afghanistan, an invasion that Auckland hoped would be mostly a Sikh affair. However, it soon became clear that Ranjit Singh had no intention of his army becoming embroiled in a potentially bloody and prolonged conflict beyond the Khyber Pass. In the end, it was British and Indian troops who bore the brunt of the fighting and made up the majority of the fighting men. The plan was to march on Afghanistan on two fronts: the main army would take Kandahar, while the Sikhs and a much smaller force of mostly Indian troops would open a second front in Nangahar. On 26 June 1838 the two sides signed the Tripartite Treaty, an agreement designed to leave Afghanistan a weak and divided kingdom politically dependent on Britain and the Sikhs. In return for being restored to the throne, Shah Shuja' was required to renounce in perpetuity all claims to 'whatever territories lying on either bank of the River Indus that may be possessed by the Maharaja . . . as far as the Khyber Pass', while Herat would be ruled independently by Shah Shuja' al-Mulk's cousin and rival, Shah Kamran. Shah Shuja' was also required to pay an annual tribute of two *lakh* rupees, a payment thinly disguised as reimbursement for Sikh military assistance, and undertook not to communicate with foreign powers without the 'knowledge and consent' of both the Sikh and British governments.[60] The king retained the title of *shah* but to all intents and purposes he was a vassal of Ranjit Singh; the very scenario that Dost Muhammad Khan had rejected as too humiliating.

The treaty may have been a tripartite one but Shah Shuja' had not been consulted nor had he been asked to send envoys to participate in the negotiations. Macnaghten therefore had the awkward task of persuading the ex-king to sign an agreement made over his head. It is hardly surprising that Shah Shuja' strongly objected to the terms imposed on him. In particular, he did not wish to seem to be paying money to Ranjit Singh, for this would be interpreted as tribute. Nor did he want to cede sovereignty over the key commercial centre of Shikapur. Macnaghten, however, made it abundantly clear that it was a case of 'take it or leave it'. All Macnaghten was prepared to do was give the king his personal assurance that British officials would not exercise any authority over 'the people of Afghanistan' without the king's consent and agree that, if Shah Shuja' decided to annex Balkh, Sistan, Baluchistan and Kandahar, neither the Sikhs nor the British would stand in his way. In the end Shah Shuja' capitulated: 'half a loaf with a good name,' he quipped, 'was better than abundance without it.' On 16 July 1838 he put his seal to the treaty and by so doing signed his own death warrant.

While plans for the invasion of Afghanistan were underway, in early June 1838 McNeill informed the Shah that his acceptance of Russian support for the siege of Herat was in breach of the Anglo-Persian Treaty and told him to prepare for war with Britain. MacNeill then quit the Persian camp and returned to Tehran. In fact war had already been unofficially declared, for a month earlier Auckland had ordered a naval expedition to occupy the island of Kharg in the Persian Gulf. After McNeill left, Shah Muhammad made a final, desperate attempt to take Herat but his troops were beaten back from the breaches. In September the Shah, hearing that Kharg was now in British hands, 'consented to the whole of the demands of the British Government', and abandoned the siege.[61]

The British action had prevented Herat from falling into Persian hands, while the Russian Foreign Ministry had formally disassociated itself from the actions of Simonich and Vitkevich. Hence, despite the failure of the Burnes Mission, by the late autumn of 1838 Britain had effectively won the diplomatic war. The only distant threat that remained to India was a possible Russian occupation of Khiva. Yet despite this, the invasion of Afghanistan was not called off for it was argued that, since the Tripartite Treaty had been signed, Britain was legally bound to fulfil its terms. The plan for 'regime change' in Kabul had now assumed a life of its own.

As the Army of the Indus assembled, Auckland set out to publicly justify the intervention. On 1 October 1838 he issued the Simla Declaration, a document that would have done Orwell's Ministry of Truth proud.[62] As well as justifying the invasion, the Manifesto was a declaration of war, although Dost Muhammad Khan never received a copy of the document or any formal notification that Britain was at war with Afghanistan. The document, drafted by Macnaghten, placed all the blame for the war solely on 'the Barakzais'. The attack on Jamrud was declared to be an act of unprovoked aggression by Dost Muhammad Khan that had brought the whole region to the brink of war. Needless to say, there was no mention of the fact that the Sikhs had constructed this fort on Afghan sovereign territory. Rather, Ranjit Singh had shown the utmost restraint by agreeing to suspend hostilities to allow Burnes a chance to restore 'an amicable understanding between the two powers'.

As for the failure of the Burnes Mission, this too was blamed solely on Dost Muhammad Khan's 'unreasonable pretensions' and 'avowed schemes of aggrandisement and ambition' that were 'injurious to the security and peace of the frontiers of India'. The Amir had shown an 'utter disregard' for British interests by his 'undisguised support to the Persian designs in Afghanistan', his 'subservience to a foreign power' and his rejection of the Governor General's offer of a 'just and reasonable' settlement with the Sikhs. Furthermore the 'hostile policies' of the Barakzais meant they were 'ill-fitted, under any circumstances, to be allies of the British government or to aid her just and necessary national defence', and concluded that 'so long as Caubul remained under [Dost Muhammad's] government [Britain] could never hope that the tranquillity of our neighbourhood would be secured, or that the interests of our Indian empire would be preserved inviolate'.

As for Shah Shuja', his popularity had 'been proved . . . by the strong and unanimous testimony of the best authorities' and he would return to Afghanistan 'surrounded by his own troops'. Without the least hint of irony, the Declaration went on to declare that he would be 'supported against foreign interference . . . by a British army'. Once the 'independence and integrity' of Afghanistan was secured, British forces would then be withdrawn. In conclusion, the Governor General 'rejoiced that . . . he will be enabled to assist in restoring the union and prosperity of the Afghan people'. The Declaration was even more duplicitous, since Russia's presumed ambitions in Central Asia, which was the real reason for going to war, were barely mentioned, and then only obliquely. Lord Palmerston, the British foreign secretary, was delighted with this, for he was anxious not to raise further tensions with St Petersburg given Russia's recent military campaigns in the Balkans, the death of the Ottoman sultan and the threat posed to what was left of the Ottoman Empire from Pasha Muhammad 'Ali in Egypt.

The justifications for war contained in the Simla Declaration uncannily echo similar statements made to justify 'regime change' by the Soviet Union in 1979 and the u.s. and Britain in 2001. Here too the Afghan governments were deemed untrustworthy by dint of their hostile policies, which allegedly posed a threat to the invading nation's 'national security'. Both the Soviet Union and United States mistakenly believed that their nominee for head of state was more popular (that is, pliant) than the then incumbent and claimed that their military intervention was altruistic and would bring peace, prosperity, stability, security and good governance. They too pledged to withdraw their forces as soon as the new government had established law and order. As was the case in the First Anglo-Afghan War, all of these assumptions and assurances would prove to be fallacious.

Lord Melbourne, the prime minister, and Palmerston still had the problem of justifying military action to Parliament, where they faced a storm of criticism from the Tory opposition. Like Auckland and Macnaghten, London had suffered from the long delay in communications between London and Calcutta and dispatches arrived often months after events in Central Asia had overtaken the home government's policy.

Parliamentarians, for example, did not have a copy of the Tripartite Treaty until March 1839, while the papers related to the missions of Burnes and McNeill only began to be released in early April. This made it difficult for the Tories to determine whether, as Ellenborough put it, the Governor General's actions were just folly or a crime. Other voices raised in concern about the possibility of war in Afghanistan included the Duke of Wellington who, with a foresight Auckland lacked, stated that 'our difficulties would commence where our military successes ended'.[63] Mountstuart Elphinstone also noted that while it might be easy to occupy Kandahar and Kabul, it would be 'hopeless' to attempt to maintain Shah Shuja' on the throne.[64]

When the government finally published the Parliamentary Papers they were heavily edited, several key documents were omitted altogether and Burnes and McNeill's dispatches had been heavily redacted. The published paper, though, did not indicate where there was a lacuna and read as if nothing had been removed. This gave a highly misleading view of the events leading up to the Simla Declaration and made it impossible for parliamentarians outside of the inner cabinet to assess the situation object-ively. When unexpurgated copies of Burnes's correspondence were leaked to the *Bombay Times* there was uproar, with the Tories demanding the government publish the documents in full. Palmerston, though, hid behind the usual government excuse that it was 'not in the public interest' and appealed to Honourable and Right Honourable members not to impugn the integrity of Her Majesty's Government but to trust its judgement in such sensitive issues. Palmerston's stonewalling won the day; the Tory motions of censure were never debated and there was not even a vote in the House on whether to go to war or not.

Amir Dost Muhammad Khan's invasion of Balkh

Meanwhile in Kabul, Dost Muhammad Khan appears not to have fully grasped the implications of the withdrawal of the Burnes Mission. He was unsure if Britain would go to war and, even if Britain did, he believed hostilities would not commence until the spring of 1839 at the earliest. The Amir therefore decided to extend his authority north of the Hindu Kush and sent an army commanded by his designated heir, Akram Khan, to force Khulm and Qataghan to accept his authority. His hope was that if he succeeded, state revenues would increase, for he would control all the customs points between the Amu Darya and Kabul, as well as receive substantial additional income from tribute. The subjugation of these Uzbek states also provided the Amir with a possible safe haven in the event of an invasion of southern Afghanistan, as well as the chance of incorporating Qataghan's formidable cavalry into his army.

Saighan and Kahmard quickly submitted and Mir Muhammad Amir Beg, son of Qilij 'Ali Beg, who had succeeded his father as Mir Wali of Khulm, came into Akram Khan's camp and renewed his oath of loyalty. Following his father's death, Murad Beg of Qataghan had forced the Mir Wali into subservience, so Amir Beg anticipated that with the help of the Muhammadzais he could restore Khulm's pre-eminence. However, instead of attacking Qataghan, Akram Khan marched on Bukharan-held Balkh and forced Ishan Sudur and Ishan Uraq to accept Durrani suzereignty. Following these victories, Murad Beg of Qataghan tendered his submission too and for a few months the northern frontiers of Dost Muhammad's kingdom extended as far as Aqcha in the west to the borders of Badakhshan in the east.

In early March 1839 Dost Muhammad Khan, hearing of the advance of the British army, recalled Akram Khan only for the march back to Kabul to end in disaster. Fodder, fuel and food were in short supply, the Shibar Pass was snowbound and the troops crossed it in the teeth of a blizzard. When the survivors reached the headwaters of the Darband river, they found it was a raging torrent and, while crossing its icy and fast-flowing waters, many more men drowned or died from exposure. By the time the remnant of Akram Khan's army straggled into Kabul in early April it was no longer a fighting force. Thousands of men and pack animals had died and most of the survivors were suffering from snow blindness, frostbite and hunger. To cap it all, Akram Khan had abandoned all his artillery. These losses significantly affected Dost Muhammad Khan's ability to resist the British invasion and further undermined his position with army commanders, tribal leaders and the Qizilbash. Criticism of the Amir's policy had increased in the wake of the failure of the Burnes Mission, especially because he had offered to accept Sikh sovereignty over Peshawar, abandoned the *jihad* and failed to secure any military, financial or political advantage from the British mission. Subsequently many senior officials and military commanders openly criticized the Amir's decision to mount a winter campaign north of the Hindu Kush and questioned his judgement as commander of the army.

The Army of the Indus and the occupation of southern Afghanistan

By the time Akram Khan returned to Kabul the Southern Field Force had reached Baluchistan and was preparing to march on Kandahar. Commanded by General Sir Willoughby Cotton, this task force consisted of 9,500 troops of the Bengal and Bombay army and 7,000 mostly Indian levies recruited by Shah Shuja'. Meanwhile in Peshawar, Wade, who had been promoted to the local rank of Lieutenant Colonel, commanded some eight hundred British troops and a motley assemblage of Sikhs, Afghans and mercenaries. On paper the invasion force was formidable, but there was dissent within the chain of command and it lacked appropriate military experience and training for the Afghan campaign. Wade was so disgruntled by the minor role he had been given that he had even tendered his resignation, only for Auckland to reject it. The three most senior commanders – Fane, Keane and Elphinstone – were in their late fifties or early sixties, long past their military prime, and all were in ill health. Fane, commander-in-chief of the India Army, was so sick that he was about to return to England, but since his replacement had not arrived he was ordered to cancel his plans. Many of the most senior officers had little or no campaign experience in India and for some their last military engagement had been during the Napoleonic Wars, more than two decades earlier (see Table 8).

Disputes over areas of responsibility and personal animosities were rife. Military commanders complained that the political officers interfered with their decision-making, while political officers accused their military counterparts of exceeding their orders, acting against government policy and even incompetence and cowardice. The more junior Indian officers had fought in India and Burma, but when they tried to advise their senior commanders on strategy their advice was more often than not ignored.

This dysfunctional command structure was exacerbated by the rigid English class system. The officers of the Queen's regiment, which were composed solely of British troops, were all aristocrats while the officers of Indian regiments were mostly members of the middle or artisan classes who had been educated privately or in grammar school rather than the great English public schools. The Indian army officers had won their cadetships by dint of hard study and had worked their way up through the ranks, rather than securing commissions by virtue of an accident of birth. The Queen's officers regarded their Indian army counterparts as inferior and some even refused to obey their orders, even when they were outranked. Shah Shuja', not to be outdone, treated his subordinates 'like a pack of dogs' and insisted on arcane court protocols that offended many British officers.[65] Such were the men entrusted with the occupation of a kingdom whose tribes had one of the most fearsome martial reputations in the subcontinent and who were masters of mountain warfare.

The Southern Field Force was a slow-moving juggernaut encumbered by an entourage of some 30,000 camp followers and a vast baggage train.

Name and rank	Age	Regiment/command in 1838	Military background; campaigns
		TABLE 8: Military Backgrounds of British Commanders in the First Anglo-Afghan War	
Gen. Sir Henry Fane	60	Commander-in-Chief, India	1805–5: Peninsular and Napoleonic Wars 1835–9: Commander-in-Chief, Indian Army 1838: sick, awaiting replacement
Maj. Gen. Sir John Keane	57	Commander-in-Chief, Army of the Indus Commander, Bombay Division	1809–14: Peninsular War 1814–15: Commander, 3rd Brigade at Battle of New Orleans (a British defeat) 1831–2: Commander-in-Chief, West Indies; Governor of Jamaica 1834: Commander-in-Chief, Bombay Army 1838: in ill health
Maj. Gen. Sir Willoughby Cotton	55	Commander, Scots Guards; Operational Commander, Army of Indus Commander, Bengal Division	1797 (aged 14): expelled from Rugby as a ringleader of the Great Rebellion 1798: enlists as Ensign in 3rd Scots Guards 1805–15: Peninsular and Napoleonic Wars; Commander, 3rd Guards Regiment, Waterloo 1824–6: Commander, First Anglo-Burmese War 1831–2: Commander-in-Chief, Baptist War, Jamaica (a slave revolt) 1835: Lieutenant Governor of Plymouth
Maj. Gen. (Sir) William Elphinstone	59	succeeded Cotton as C-in-C of Army of Indus	1805–15: Peninsular and Napoleonic Wars 1815: Commander, 33rd Foot, Waterloo
Brig. William Nott	56	Commander, Bengal Brigade and 42nd Bengal Native Infantry	son of farmer, grammar school educated 1800: enlists as cadet in Bengal Regiment 1825: Commander, 20th Bengal Native Infantry
Brig. John Shelton	49	Commander, 44th Queen's Foot 1841: appointed Second-in-Command to Maj. Gen. Elphinstone	1805: enlists as Ensign, 9th (East Norfolk) Foot 1808–9: Portugal Campaign 1809: Walcheren Expedition, Netherlands 1812–13: Peninsula War; lost right arm at Siege of San Sebastian 1814: Montreal 1817: Commander, 44th (East Essex) Foot 1824–6: First Burmese War, siege of Ava
Col. Sir Robert Sale	56	Commander, 13th Queen's Light Infantry 1839–41: Commander, Bengal Infantry Second-in-Command to Maj. Gen. Cotton	1798–9: Mysore Wars 1808–9: Travancore 1810: Mauritius 1824–6: First Burmese War

Despite General Fane's appeal not to encumber the army with 'large establishments', officers had wholeheartedly embraced the adage that 'an army marches on its stomach' and were determined that if they were going to war, they would do so in style. Among the 'essentials' they took with them were fine wines, cigars, potted meats and silver tableware, eau de cologne, bath tubs and whole suites of furniture. The 16th Lancers took a pack of foxhounds, while General Cotton had a horse and buggy and requisitioned 260 camels to carry his personal baggage and that of his servants. It was not so much an army going to war as one vast imperial picnic.

Prior to the Southern Field Force setting out, Burnes and Henry Pottinger were sent to negotiate with the Amirs of Sind to secure the passage over the Indus. Before they set out, Macnaghten reminded them again that their personal animosity must not interfere with their public duty. Less than a year earlier, Pottinger had signed a treaty that made Sind a British Protectorate, assuring the *amirs* that the Indus would remain demilitarized and that Britain would not interfere in Sind's internal affairs. This treaty was now effectively torn up as the Indus became a military highway, while the *amirs'* worst fears about British imperial objectives, first precipitated by Burnes's survey, were now confirmed. Britain's amoral dealings with the Amirs of Sind were then extended to other erstwhile allies that lay along the line of advance. As Kaye, the great imperial historian of the First Afghan War, noted:

> The system now to be adopted was one of universal intimidation and coercion. Along the whole line of country which the armies were to traverse, the will and pleasure of the British Government was to be the only principle of action recognisable in all our transactions with the weaker States, which were now to be dragooned into prompt obedience. Their co-operation was not to be sought, but demanded. Anything short of hearty acquiescence was to be interpreted into a national offence.[66]

Burnes 'persuaded' the Amir of Khairpur to make his territory a British Protectorate and to cede the strategic island fortress of Bukkur, which commanded the ford over the Indus and was the gateway to Shikapur. Pottinger, meanwhile, informed Nur Muhammad Khan of Hyderabad that if he failed to comply with British demands for safe passage and assistance with supplying the army he would be 'annihilated'. Pottinger also secured a promise that in future there would be no more tolls charged to shipping or trade caravans crossing the Indus. Nur Muhammad Khan was also fined twenty *lakh* rupees for an allegedly 'treacherous' correspondence with the Shah of Persia. Nur Muhammad Khan pointed out that these demands violated the recent treaty and commented that, 'since the day that Sind has been connected with the English there has always been something new; your government is never satisfied'.[67] He had every reason to complain. Not only was Britain meant to protect him; the Amirs of Sind had been loyal allies for decades, but now they were treated as enemies and Britain exploited the presence of a large army to force them to make territorial and commercial concessions. To cap it all General Keane, hearing false rumours that Nur Muhammad Khan had gathered an army to oppose the British advance, besieged Hyderabad and humiliated the Amir by demanding he and his brothers come to his camp and submit in person. Meanwhile, British marines occupied the small fort of Karachi, securing in the process the mouth of the Indus and port access to the Indian Ocean.

Keane's attack on Hyderabad had been unauthorized and a furious Macnaghten censured Cotton and Fane for allowing the general to go on this 'wild goose chase' and demanded his recall. The generals responded by accusing Macnaghten of interfering in military strategy. In the end Macnaghten was not prepared to wait for Keane to rejoin the main army, and following another stormy meeting with Cotton, the Bombay Brigade was ordered to march on Kalat, leaving Keane and Shah Shuja' to follow later. This led to another spat, this time between Colonel Dennie, who had been left behind at Shikapur, and General Cotton, with Dennie accusing his commanding officer of dismembering the army.

The route Cotton took to Kalat was meant to be a shortcut but it led the army through a vast, uncharted desert. Despite being only late February, day temperatures rose to well over 40°c, while at night they plummeted to near freezing. The army had already denuded the region of food and fodder and the desert offered little grazing for pack animals and even less water. During the crossing thousands of animals perished and at least two officers died from thirst and heatstroke. The local tribes also robbed the mail and plundered the supply line. When the troops finally reached Dadar, at the entrance to the Bolan Pass, in March 1839, the starving animals glutted themselves on the crops of local peasants, stripping the fields like a plague of locusts.

The Bolan Pass posed an even more formidable challenge. The camels went lame on the sharp, rocky paths and the hill tribes plundered the straggling column as it marched through the narrow defile. By the time the Bengal Brigade reached Quetta it had travelled more than 1,660 kilo-metres (1,030 mi.) and was no longer an effective fighting force. With only ten days' supplies left and local rulers unable, or unwilling, to supply grain and fodder due to a poor harvest the previous year, the troops were put on half rations while the camp followers, who were left to fend for themselves, were reduced to eating fried sheepskins, clots of animal blood and roots. As morale plummeted, tempers frayed and Cotton, Keane and their subordinate officers quarrelled over policy and logistics. Privately Macnaghten admitted that the army was on the verge of mutiny, yet he showed little sympathy for its predicament. His resentment against the military command increased when Cotton informed him that army intelligence had reported that Shah Shujaʻ was extremely unpopular in Afghanistan. Cotton, Macnaghten noted, was a 'sad croaker', his favourite term of abuse for any individual who did not share his naive optimism about Shah Shujaʻ in particular and the invasion in general.[68]

Keane eventually caught up with the advanced guard in Quetta after an even more harrowing journey, for the desert was strewn with the skeletons of pack animals and during the crossing of the Bolan Pass his troops had to climb over the rotten, half-eaten bodies of sepoys and camp followers. There was some good news at least. Burnes had managed to persuade Mehrab Khan, *beglar begi* of Kalat, to provide safe passage for the army and supplies, though only after the payment of a very substantial fee. At the same time, Mehrab Khan made it clear to Burnes that in his view the whole expedition was doomed to failure.

Macnaghten, though, could not bring himself to believe that Mehrab Khan was trustworthy and even while Burnes was negotiating the treaty, Macnaghten wrote to Auckland accusing him of being an 'implacable enemy' and urged the Governor General to authorize the annexation of all the towns along the army's supply route. Auckland refused but Macnaghten eventually got his way. In early November 1839 Macnaghten again accused Mehrab Khan of duplicity and cutting the army's supply line, so the Bombay Division, on its way back to India, was sent to attack Kalat. When it fell the city was sacked, Mehrab Khan and many of Kalat's principal leaders were slain and the region incorporated as part of Shah Shujaʻ al-Mulk's kingdom. A few months later Masson recorded the devastation wrought by the army in Kalat as well as the destruction left in the wake of the army's advance through Sind.

The army's next challenge was the Khojak Pass, an even more formidable barrier than the Bolan Pass. Once again the troops had to fight their way up the narrow defile, which local Ghilzai and Baluch tribesmen had blocked with stones. On the Kandahar side of the pass Kohan Dil Khan and a force of 1,500 tribal levies were poised to attack as the army entered the plains. Fortunately for Cotton, the army did not have to fight its way into Kandahar. Hajji Khan Kakar, whom Dost Muhammad Khan had expelled from Kabul and who had joined forces with the Kandahar *sardars*, opened a secret communication with Shah Shuja', offering to change sides in exchange for the post of *Mukhtar al-Daula*, one of the most powerful positions in the kingdom. Shah Shuja' agreed and Hajji Khan Kakar promptly defected with his Kakars, whereupon Kohan Dil Khan and his brothers fled to Girishk.

On 25 April 1839 Shah Shuja' entered Kandahar unopposed and Macnaghten exultantly wrote to Auckland that the king was 'received with feelings nearly amounting to adulation', though other officers reported that there was a decided lack of public enthusiasm.[69] On 8 May the British and sepoy troops staged a grand review and the Saddozai king was formally crowned after a 21-gun salute. A flying column was sent to capture the Dil brothers but they escaped and rejected all attempts to negotiate with them, informing Macnaghten that they 'had already begun to know the value of [Britain's] political promises, and had good reason to believe that we should never adhere to them'.[70] Instead, the brothers began to gather an army to resist the occupation.

Meanwhile in Kandahar the starving troops and camp followers filled their empty bellies with local fruit and vegetables and drank water from polluted wells and streams. Soon hundreds of men were dying or incapacitated by cholera and typhoid. The Kandahar hinterland too was extremely dangerous and soldiers or camp followers who ventured too far from the cantonment risked being killed. It was not until the end of June 1839, after two months' rest and recuperation, that Keane ordered his troops to march on Kabul, though for some reason he left his heavy siege guns behind. On the same day he set out, Maharaja Ranjit Singh breathed his last and, as Burnes had predicted, his passing marked the beginning of a bitter dynastic struggle that eventually tore the Sikh kingdom apart. Keane was harassed all along the route by the irregular cavalry of Gul Muhammad, or Guru, Hotak and Sultan Muhammad Khan Tokhi, who refused to accept the customary payment for safe passage. Even had they done so, Macnaghten would have been hard pressed to find the money, for he had been so liberal with his disbursement of cash to the Durranis and Kakars that his treasury was nearly empty. The crisis was exacerbated when the Hindu *baniya*s in Kandahar refused to issue or accept bills of credit, known as *hundi*.

Dost Muhammad Khan was taken by surprise by Keane's advance, for he had expected the main attack on Kabul would be from Peshawar and that the Southern Field Force would be tasked with subduing Herat.

The Amir also assumed Keane would bypass Ghazni, since the Afghans believed the citadel was impregnable, so no reinforcements were sent, nor did Dost Muhammad Khan's son, Haidar Khan, who was governor of Ghazni, strengthen the citadel's defences. Instead, the Amir sent another of his sons, Muhammad Afzal Khan, to join the Ghilzai raiders, hoping to draw the British away from their base in Kandahar and attack them in strength at Sayyadabad, between Ghazni and Maidan Shah, cutting off their line of retreat and annihilating the invaders.

Keane, however, had no intention of leaving any fortress unsubdued in the rear of his army. Having taken the Tokhi stronghold of Qalat-i Ghilzai by storm and installed a garrison, on 21 July 1839 he arrived before Ghazni. An attack by Afzal Khan and the Ghilzais was beaten off, the grapeshot from the army's guns inflicting heavy loss of life on the lightly armed tribesmen. Some 64 prisoners were taken alive and handed over to Shah Shuja', who tried them as rebels. The Ghilzai retorted that since the king was a *kafir* and a 'friend and slave of infidels', they had every right to resist him. One prisoner even drew a knife and Shah Shuja' was only saved from serious harm when one of his bodyguards threw himself between the king and his assailant, taking the blow instead. Shah Shuja' responded by condemning them all to death and his executioner proceeded to saw off their heads with a blunt sword.

Unfortunately for the king, a British officer stumbled on the executions and a few weeks later the Bengal newspapers were full of the gory details. Keane, Macnaghten and other officers were appalled, mostly, one suspects, because of the publicity rather than at the executions themselves. As Shah Shuja' rightly pointed out, under the terms of the Tripartite Treaty and on the basis of Macnaghten's own assurances, British officials had agreed not to interfere in his internal affairs. Since he was king, he had every right to execute rebels.

The righteous anger of the press and British officials was also somewhat hypocritical. There was no such furore when a few days later Keane had several Afghan prisoners shot without due process and condemned a sepoy to be executed by firing squad after a drumhead court martial. In 1839 British military law was anyway almost as harsh as the Afghan one. Mutiny and desertion were both capital offences with the accused denied legal counsel and the guilty condemned to the firing squad, hanging or being blown from the mouth of a gun. Flogging was a regular punishment for minor misdemeanours, while under English civil law an offender could be executed for murder, burglary, counterfeiting, arson and a host of other felonies. Beheading for treason was still on the statute book, while traitors could theoretically still be hanged, drawn and quartered. As for public executions, they were an extremely popular event in Victorian Britain.

Keane did not seem to have realized how strong the fortress of Ghazni was, so when he saw its formidable walls, he doubtless regretted having left his siege guns behind. However, the General was aided by the defection of Sardar 'Abd al-Rashid, a grandson of Pur Dil Khan, who provided Keane with 'minute and correct information' about the town's defences.[71] When he identified the Kabul Gate as the weakest and least defended position, Keane ordered an immediate attack. Under cover of darkness, and with a diversionary bombardment and feint by the infantry on another section of the wall, sapping parties laid charges and blew down the gate and part of the bastion. The storming party then overwhelmed the defenders and by dawn the Union Jack flew from the top of the citadel. Ghazni had fallen in less than two days at the cost of just seventeen British lives, but more than five hundred Afghans had perished in the assault and a further hundred, including civilians, had been cut down by a cavalry charge as they fled the slaughter. When Afzal Khan heard that Ghazni had fallen he fled back to Kabul, abandoning his baggage and pack animals.

Ghazni was the high point of the Afghan campaign and was celebrated as a great victory, though imperial histories attribute its fall almost solely to the gallantry of the storming party and the two officers who led the assault, Brigadier Robert Sale and Lieutenant Colonel Dennie. Yet had not Sardar

The medieval walls of Ghazni are still impressive, but in 1839 they proved no defence against British artillery and gunpowder.

'Abd al-Rashid provided the critical information, Keane would have probably been forced into a long siege. A spat between Sale and Dennie over
military honours also marred the victory. In his dispatches Keane singled
out Sale as the hero of the hour, which incensed Dennie, and for a while
Dennie, Keane and Sale were barely on speaking terms.

While the Southern Field Force made its way to Kandahar from
Peshawar, Wade adopted different tactics to undermine Dost Muhammad
Khan. Assisted by Sardar Sultan Muhammad Khan, who arrived in
Peshawar in April 1839 and declared his support for Shah Shuja', Wade
developed a highly effective intelligence network that penetrated to the
heart of Dost Muhammad Khan's administration and family. Khan Shirin
Khan Jawanshir, head of the Jawanshir Qizilbash and commander of the
palace guard, was on Wade's payroll, as was Ghulam Khan Popalzai, whose
father had served during Shah Shuja' al-Mulk's earlier reign. He had been
recruited as a confidential news writer by Burnes's *munshi*, Mohan Lal,
during their first visit to Kabul. By the time Burnes met him again in
1838 the Popalzai chief was even more disaffected with Dost Muhammad
Khan and was 'sighing, praying and exerting himself for the restoration
of the monarchy'.[72]

Wade sent Ghulam Khan Popalzai 40,000 rupees with instructions
to raise rebellions in Kohistan and Logar, but the Amir's spy network got
wind of the plan. Ghulam Khan was arrested, but escaped disguised as a
woman concealed under a burqa. He fled to Tagab, where he was welcomed
by Shahdad Safi, son of Mazu Khan, and a short time later he was joined
by Shahzada Yahya, Timur Shah's son. He too had escaped from prison
in the Upper Bala Hisar and made his way to Peshawar, where Wade gave
him more cash and sent him to Tagab to join the rebellion.

The population of Tagab, Kohistan and the Koh Daman, however,
were reluctant to rebel, for memories of the executions and devastations
wrought by Dost Muhammad Khan's earlier campaigns were still fresh.
The situation, though, radically changed with the arrival of Mir Ma'sum,
better known as Mir Hajji, and his brother Mir Darwish, or Hafizji. These
men were sons of Khwaja Khanji, Sayyid Mir Ahmad Agha, and were the
region's most influential spiritual leaders, commanding the loyalty of thousands of devotees from Ghurband to Tagab. Mir Hajji, the elder brother,
had succeeded his father as *pir* of their sub-Order of Naqshbandiyya Sufis
and as *mir wa'is* of the Pul-i Kheshti mosque. Among other things, he
had officiated at the coronation of Dost Muhammad Khan. His younger
brother, Hafizji, was *mutawalli* of the Ashiqan wa Arifan shrine and was
married to one of Dost Muhammad Khan's daughters. Their defection was

due in part to their disaffection with Dost Muhammad's discontinuation of the *jihad* against the Sikhs, but their decision to change sides was far from idealistic, for Ghulam Khan Popalzai had offered the brothers 8,000 rupees as an incentive. Within weeks of their arrival all but a handful of the leaders of Kohistan, Tagab and the Koh Daman had declared their support for Shah Shuja'. In mid-July Ghulam Khan Popalzai set out for Kabul at the head of a substantial army.

Following the chaotic retreat from Balkh, Dost Muhammad Khan's position had become untenable. Kandahar and Ghazni had both fallen within a matter of days and Keane was now marching on the capital. In the southeast Wade had secured safe passage through the Khyber Pass while the Kohistanis were approaching the northern outskirts of Kabul. Soldiers and army officers were deserting in droves and what was left of the Amir's army was in a mutinous state. Even the Jawanshir Qizilbash refused to leave Kabul, fearing that Mir Hajji and Hafizji would take Kabul in their absence, massacre their wives and children, and plunder their houses. Khan Shirin Khan Jawanshir was already secretly corresponding with Wade and had covertly pledged support for the campaign to restore Shah Shuja' to the throne.

Faced with defeat, Dost Muhammad Khan made one last effort to reach an accommodation with the British. Shortly after the fall of Ghazni, Nawab Jabbar Khan arrived in the British camp and informed Macnaghten that the Amir was prepared to abdicate in favour of Shah Shuja' on condition that he was made *wazir*. Macnaghten, though, was not interested in negotiating and his offer was rejected outright. All he was prepared to promise was that if Dost Muhammad Khan surrendered to him in person his life would be spared and he would be sent into exile in India. Jabbar Khan replied that his brother would never agree to such a fate and threw down a challenge to Macnaghten:

> If Shah Shuja' is really a king, and come to the kingdom of his ancestors, what is the use of your army and name? You have brought him by your money and arms into Afghanistan . . . Leave him now with us Afghans, and let him rule if he can.[73]

Nawab Jabbar Khan prepared to return to Kabul but in an attempt to save face he petitioned for the release of his niece, the wife of Sardar Haidar Khan, who had been taken prisoner at Ghazni. The Afghan code of honour, he told Macnaghten, forbade waging war against women and children and the idea that women should be held as prisoners or hostages was repugnant. Macnaghten refused, but blandly assured the *nawab* that it was not the custom of the British to ill-treat any captive, particularly women. Instead Jabbar Khan was granted an audience with Shah Shuja', who was told in no uncertain terms to treat the *sardar* with kindness. Shah Shuja' played along and tried to bribe and flatter Jabbar Khan into changing sides, only for him to reject the king's offer of money and high office.

Matters would have ended here had it not been for an incident that occurred as the *sardar* left the British camp. Escorted by Mohan Lal, Nawab Jabbar Khan heard the cries of a woman in great distress from a nearby tent and insisted on investigating, only to discover that one of the female captives from Ghazni – undoubtedly a woman of rank – was being raped by a water carrier. Jabbar Khan was outraged and Lal, equally shocked, managed to secure the woman's release into the *nawab*'s custody. The water carrier was later discharged from service, but suffered no other punishment. As Jabbar Khan parted from Lal, he angrily told him that those who claimed that Britain's policy was duplicitous and hypocritical had been right all along. Britain had used him as a pawn to destroy the heirs of Payinda Khan and he compared his friendship with Britain to the *darakht-i hanzal*, or wild gourd, the leaves of which were pretty but its fruit bitter and toxic.[74] He had been the staunchest advocate of friendship with Britain, the *nawab* declared, and had hosted Burnes and other British travellers at his own personal expense, but now he had lost 'all confidence and hope' in Britain. On his return to Kabul, he would seek to redeem his honour by raising the tribes and informing them that Britain planned to exile their leaders and molest their women. So Britain's greatest ally in the Muhammadzai camp became one of her most bitter enemies. It was one more nail in the coffin of Burnes and Macnaghten.

Nawab Jabbar Khan returned to Kabul and Dost Muhammad Khan pleaded with the Qizilbash to join him and make a last stand at Sayyidabad so he could die with honour, but they still refused to leave Kabul. On 2 August 1839 the Amir discharged them from their oath of allegiance, mounted his best horse and set out for Bamiyan via the Hajigak, accompanied by Akram Khan, Nawab Jabbar Khan and other family members with their wives and children. When Keane heard of the Amir's flight, he sent Captain Outram in hot pursuit but made the mistake of sending Hajji Khan Kakar along too. According to British sources, Hajji Khan did everything in his power to delay the pursuit and Dost Muhammad had reached the safety of Saighan by the time Outram reached Bamiyan, and the pursuit was abandoned.

When Keane reached the outskirts of Kabul four days after the Amir's flight, he was surprised to find that Ghulam Khan Popalzai, Mir Hajji and Hafijzi had occupied the capital the day before – a situation that placed Ghulam Khan Popalzai and Mir Hajji in a strong position to dictate terms to the king. The following day Shah Shuja' entered Kabul mounted on a ceremonial elephant and resplendent in robes sparkling with pearls and jewels. Macnaghten, Burnes and the senior officers rode beside him in full dress uniform. As the procession wound though Kabul's Shor Bazaar and into the Bala Hisar the shopkeepers stared in sullen silence and made the occasional disparaging witticism. Further disappointment was to follow. The fine Mughal buildings that Shah Shuja' remembered from thirty years before were now in ruins and his nostalgic vision of Kabul as an earthly paradise, exaggerated by three decades of exile, were shattered. The British, though, had achieved their goal of political and military domination of the Indus States, but the battle for the hearts and minds of the Afghan population had only just begun. It was a battle that they were already losing.

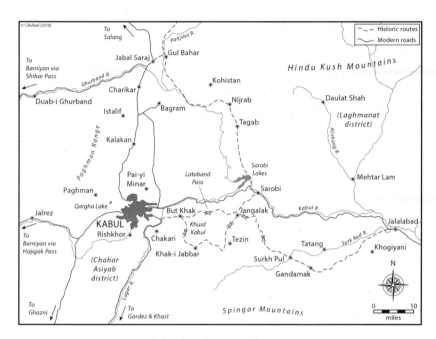

Kabul and southeastern Afghanistan

SIX

The Death of the 'Great Experiment', 1839–43

Far and near and low and louder
On the roads of earth go by,
Dear to friends and food for powder,
Soldiers marching, all to die.

East and west on fields forgotten
Bleach the bones of comrades slain,
Lovely lads and dead and rotten;
None that go return again.

A. E. HOUSMAN, 'A Shropshire Lad'

THE EASE WITH WHICH the conquest of southern Afghanistan had been accomplished created a sense of euphoria among the British military and political establishment. A jubilant Macnaghten reported in glowing terms to Auckland about the army's victories and the relatively low cost in terms of casualties. Military commanders were so confident Afghanistan had been pacified that Keane's Bombay division was sent back to India, while the Bengal army was promised that all but one brigade would return home by the end of September. News of the fall of Kandahar, Ghazni and Kabul was also greeted with exaltation in London and the prime minster, Lord Melbourne, exploited these military successes to silence Tory opposition to the war and so ensured his fragile administration was able to cling on to power for a few months longer.

Flushed with victory and the rewards and honours that inevitably followed, the army settled down in Kabul as if the country was an ocean of calm. Autumn brought a glut of fresh fruit and the officers enjoyed the pleasures of hunting, horse racing, cricket, amateur dramatics and, when winter set in, ice skating on the Hashmat Khan lake. One enterprising individual even built a sailing boat. Burnes's cellar of fine wines and spirits and his lavish entertainments quickly became the talk of the cantonment, especially since the amusements included a troupe of *nauch* girls. Several officers took things even further and began affairs with local women, some of whom were married to high-ranking Afghans, while the rank and file sought pleasure in prostitutes who had accompanied the army from India and local 'ladies of the night'. Few, if any, had any concept of the impact such liaisons might have on the army's image, let alone the potential risk to life and limb that affairs with local women entailed. Later, after the officers' wives, including the formidable Lady Macnaghten, were allowed to join their husbands in the field, these liaisons went underground, but still continued.

The occupation of Kabul and strategic misjudgements

The general aura of euphoria helped fuel Macnaghten's tendency to head-in-the-sand optimism and contributed to one of the most disastrous decisions of the war: the construction of the army's cantonment and Macnaghten's residency on a greenfield site north of the Kabul river. Located some 2 kilometres (1.2 mi.) north of the Bala Hisar, the cantonment was built on land that today includes the site of the U.S. embassy. The decision went against the recommendation of the Royal Corps of Engineers, who wanted most of the troops to be stationed behind the walls of the Bala Hisar, but Shah Shujaʻ opposed this plan, claiming that the presence of foreign forces in the royal citadel would make it appear that he was a puppet of the British. As a sop to the king, Macnaghten agreed and all repair work on the Bala Hisar's defences ceased. Instead, the Royal Engineers were put to work constructing a new cantonment and only a handful of British officers and troops remained in the citadel.

The design of the cantonment was as unsuited to the army of occupation as was its location. The ground plan – the standard one used in India – may have been adequate in a country already pacified, but it was utterly unsuited to a war zone. The eastern and western walls were more than 1.5 kilometres in length and required a great number of men to guard them, troops that would have been far better employed in combat operations. The cantonment walls themselves were so low that a mounted rider had no difficulty jumping over them. A dry ditch was added later, but only as an afterthought. The cantonment itself was surrounded by fields and orchards criss-crossed with irrigation ditches that hampered the movement of artillery, providing excellent cover for snipers as well as making it easier for thieves to infiltrate the compound.

On the northwest the cantonment was overshadowed by the twin peaks of Qalʻa-yi Musa and Tepa-yi Behmaru, which the British called the Behmaru Heights. Tepa-yi Behmaru, the eastern hill, was within *jezail* range of the northern part of the cantonment where Macnaghten's Residency was located. To the east and south lay several high-walled compounds, or *qal'a*s, and walled gardens, which too were within range of the Afghans' long-barrelled, flintlock rifles. Yet none of these fortified compounds were levelled and most were not even garrisoned. Even more extraordinary, the commissariat and munitions store were located in two of these *qal'a*s outside the cantonment walls. In Kaye's words, the cantonment 'stood, bare and defenceless, as sheep-pens, whilst the wolves were howling around them'.[1] The only thing that commended the site was that there was an abundance of water from shallow wells.

A number of officers were permitted to reside in the Old City. They included Alexander Burnes and his younger brother, who rented a house near the Qizilbash quarter of Chindawal, and Captain Johnson, paymaster for Shah Shuja' al-Mulk's troops, who rented a house near Burnes. Since Johnson thought it would be personally inconvenient to keep the regimental fund inside the Bala Hisar, he always had several *lakh* of rupees in his house. Fewer than thirty sepoys were deployed to guard these two dwellings.

Shah Shuja' al-Mulk's administration and relations with British forces

Once back on his throne Shah Shuja' proceeded to undermine the British position by alienating powerful tribes and imprisoning their leaders, including 'Amin Allah Khan Logari, who, despite being of low birth, commanded several thousand heavily armed tribesmen; 'Abd al-'Aziz Khan, a Jabbar Khel Ghilzai who was brother-in-law to Dost Muhammad Khan; and Nawab Muhammad Zaman Khan, the eldest surviving son of Payinda Khan and titular head of the Barakzais. Nawab Zaman Khan had formerly been governor of Kashmir and Jalalabad under Shah Zaman and had great influence with the Ghilzais of Tezin and Gandamak as well as the Jabbar Khel. He was lured to Kabul with promises of safe conduct underwritten by Macnaghten and told that, in return for swearing allegiance to Shah Shuja', he would be treated with due honour and appointed to an appropriate position in the new government. Instead, when he arrived in Kabul, Shah Shuja' denied Nawab Zaman Khan an audience and placed him under house arrest. Harlan, who had acted as intermediary in the negotiations, was furious and blamed Burnes for this breach of faith. Burnes retaliated by denouncing Harlan as an enemy of Britain and persuaded Macnaghten to expel him from Afghanistan. When Harlan arrived in India, he found that the Governor General had issued him with a deportation order and he had to return to America.

Hajji Khan Kakar was another powerful leader incarcerated in the Bala Hisar. Despite being a slippery schemer, it had been his defection that had secured Kandahar for the Army of the Indus without a fight. Furthermore, his Kakar tribe controlled the army's vital supply route through the Khojak Pass. Shah Shuja' had restored him to high office, but within days of the fall of Kabul Hajji Khan was imprisoned, after the British accused him of letting Dost Muhammad Khan escape. He, along with Sardar Muhammad Haidar Khan, Dost Muhammad's son, were later condemned to the ultimate humiliation: exile to India. Shah Shuja' compounded his errors by failing to reward other individuals who had played a significant role in placing him on the throne and instead appointed members of his Ludhiana circle to the highest offices of state. Among those who felt slighted were Ghulam Khan Popalzai, Mir Hajji and Hafizji, who had been responsible for raising the tribes of Kohistan and Tagab and securing control of Kabul. As Mohan Lal noted, 'the more we found the people quiet, the more steps we took in shaking their confidence'.[2]

It was not long either before conflict arose between the king and the British political establishment. Shah Shuja' maintained that no British official had any right to interfere in his internal affairs, which included the administration of justice, the appointment of military and civil officials and revenue raising. Yet despite this, Macnaghten and Burnes did their best to run the affairs of state behind the scenes by 'advising' the king on policy, securing appointments for pro-British officials and forcing the king to revoke judicial decisions. Later Burnes drew up plans for a major overhaul of revenue raising, as well as military and bureaucratic reforms. Increasingly the political and military leadership of the Army of the Indus did not even bother to consult the king or inform him of their actions, acting independently of the civil authority they themselves had established. It did not take long before Afghans realized the king and his British backers were at odds, and they skilfully played the two sides off against each other. Petitioners whose requests were rejected by the king or his *wazir* turned to Burnes, Macnaghten or senior military officers, who then put pressure on Shah Shuja' to revoke his decisions. Even Afghans who had little wish to see a Saddozai back on the throne resented the fact that the monarchy had been stripped of all but token power and that foreigners, and non-Muslims to boot, were effectively ruling the country.

The presence of some 30,000 men, women and children, which doubled the population of the Afghan capital, as well as the construction of

A bread shop, or *nanbai*, in Kabul. In Afghanistan bread, not rice, is the staple diet.

the cantonment, also created an economic crisis. The British paid labourers much higher wages than the market rate, which led to a chronic shortage of labour. Even the king complained to Macnaghten that it was impossible to hire labourers to repair the Bala Hisar's defences and its palaces and gardens. The high wages, paid in cash rather than kind as was traditional, led to an influx of labourers from the surrounding countryside, leaving fields unploughed, trees and vines unpruned and winter wheat unplanted. As the bitter Kabul winter approached, the army commissariat bought up vast quantities of grain, fodder and fuel at grossly inflated prices. The scarcity was exacerbated when landowners and shopkeepers withheld supplies in the hope that the prices would rise even higher. So large were the potential profits, most shopkeepers refused to sell their produce to local people unless they paid the same inflated prices as the British. Soon the price of bread, the staple food in Afghanistan, rose beyond the affordability level of ordinary Kabulis and the streets and bazaars of Kabul were full of people begging for crusts. Burnes responded by distributing larger amount of *nan* for free, failing to realize that by so doing his purchases were indirectly contributing to the crisis rather than solving it.

Mullah Shakar, the king's elderly *wazir*, responded by issuing an order fixing the price of wheat and bread at a price local people could afford. The *nanbais* retaliated by shutting up shop and refused to bake, so Mullah Shakar sent officials into the bazaar and forced the bakers to make bread, threatening anyone who failed to open up their shop with fines and imprisonment. The *nanbais* then complained to Burnes and Macnaghten about the king's oppression, but instead of supporting Shah Shuja', Burnes took the bakers' side, forcing the king to rescind his *wazir*'s decree and to release those *nanbais* who had been imprisoned. The bakers were thus free to charge whatever price they wanted while Shah Shuja' suffered a serious loss of face. The populace, though, blamed the occupiers. The 'universal cry throughout the whole kingdom,' noted Lal, was 'that [the British] are killing the people by starvation . . . the English enriched the grain and the grass sellers &c., whilst they reduced the chiefs to poverty, and killed the poor by starvation.'[3]

Dost Muhammad Khan and the tribal and religious opposition to the British occupation

While Macnaghten, Burnes and Shah Shuja' undermined their credibility with ordinary Afghans, resistance to the occupation began to form in the hinterland of Kandahar, Ghazni and Kabul. As a sign of the troubles to follow, in the autumn of 1839 a Ghilzai raid on the Ghazni–Kabul road led to the death of Lieutenant Colonel Herring and a punitive expedition had to be sent against Gul Muhammad Khan Hotaki and 'Abd al-Rahman Khan Tokhi.[4] Beyond the Hindu Kush, Dost Muhammad Khan was given sanctuary by the Mir Wali of Khulm and sent emissaries throughout the *wilayat* of Balkh and to Nasr Allah Khan of Bukhara appealing for them to join him in a *jihad*. The risk of local disturbances as well as a possible attack from the north by an Uzbek army commanded by Dost Muhammad Khan led to the postponement of the return of the Bengal Army until the summer of 1840, much to the troops' disgust.

Dost Muhammad Khan's appeal for Uzbek support, however, fell on deaf ears for neither the rulers of Balkh nor the Khan of Bukhara had any interest in aiding an Amir who only a year earlier had invaded their country, forced the rulers and governors of Balkh to submit to Afghan sovereignty and annexed Saighan, Kahmard and Duab. In the winter of 1839 Dost Muhammad Khan, against the advice of Nawab Jabbar Khan, decided to travel to Bukhara to appeal to Nasr Allah Khan, for the Uzbek *amir*s of the *wilayat* of Balkh still regarded the Manghit Khan as the sovereign power. Dost Muhammad Khan, along with his two eldest surviving sons, Muhammad Afzal Khan and Muhammad Akbar Khan, were initially well received by Nasr Allah Khan but it soon became clear that the Khan of Bukhara had no intention of supporting the Barakzai cause. Instead, Dost Muhammad Khan was effectively placed under house arrest. When Akram Khan and Afzal Khan made a dash for freedom and were recaptured, he and his sons were treated more like prisoners. Dost Muhammad Khan even suspected Nasr Allah Khan planned to have him and his sons poisoned.

It was not until the following summer that Dost Muhammad Khan managed to escape and made his way back to Khulm following a series of adventures, only to discover that a few weeks earlier Nawab Jabbar Khan had accepted Macnaghten's offer of amnesty and had left for Kabul with all the women and children. Despite the fact that his family was in British hands, Dost Muhammad Khan refused to give up. The Mir Wali had raised a force of some 6,000 Uzbeks and in September 1840 they marched up the Surkhab and forced the British to abandon their outposts of Ajar, Kahmard and Bajgah and fall back on Bamiyan. As a sign of what was to come, during the encounter at Bajgah half of Shah Shuja' al-Mulk's cavalry, along with all their officers, deserted while the remaining Afghan levies were captured and disarmed.

Dost Muhammad Khan followed up these successes by marching on Bamiyan but when they reached Saighan, the gateway to Bamiyan on the north, he unexpectedly encountered Colonel Dennie, who commanded a small force of Gurkhas and native cavalry. Despite being heavily outnumbered, Dennie ordered his Gurkhas to storm the enemy's position and after heavy fighting the Uzbeks turned and fled. Dennie then sent the cavalry in pursuit and most of the Mir Wali's men, as well as the deserters from Shah Shuja' al-Mulk's regiment, were slain. Following this victory Dr Lord, the political officer in Bamiyan, offered Dost Muhammad Khan honourable exile if he surrendered, only to be curtly informed that the Amir was determined to 'conquer or fall in the attempt'.[5] The Mir Wali and Murad Beg of Qataghan, however, were more willing to seek an accommodation, for the Mir Wali's army had been decimated and he feared that Dennie might push on and occupy Khulm. Dennie, though, was in no position to do so for the Bamiyan garrison was already overstretched and it was decided not to re-garrison Saighan, Kahmard or Ajar.

This did not prevent Dr Lord and Major Todd, who had replaced Pottinger in Herat, drawing up separate, and contradictory, plans for annexation of Balkh, plans that the government in London eventually

Shah Shuja' al-Mulk. By 1839 the former Saddozai king was elderly and had been in Indian exile for thirty years. Despite representing a dynasty which was discredited in the eyes of most Afghans, British officials were convinced he had popular support and restoring him to power would be easy. They could not have been more wrong.

rejected as far too costly. The threat of a British-sponsored attack by Shah Kamran, however, did force Mizrab Khan, *wali* of Maimana, to tender his submission to Shah Shuja'. The Mir Wali too opened negotiations with the king. A few weeks after his defeat, he and Murad Beg arrived in Kabul to formally pledge their allegiance to the king and undertook to deny sanctuary to Dost Muhammad Khan or any other Muhammadzai.

The desertion of Shah Shuja' al-Mulk's levies at Saighan was a blow to British expectations that the king would quickly raise an 'Afghan National Army', which would allow all foreign forces to be withdrawn within a year of the occupation. By the autumn of 1840 any such hopes had been scuppered and General Cotton told Macnaghten that the recent defections 'proved incontestably that there is no Afghan army', and he urged Macnaghten to recommend that the Governor General send reinforcements, for without them 'we cannot hold the country'.[6] An additional 2,000 troops were ordered to prepare to march to Kabul and two more Indian regiments sent to Kandahar. Despite this, Auckland still planned to withdraw all but one or two regiments by the spring of 1841.

Britain now faced the uncomfortable reality that there was little chance in the short term that Shah Shuja' could raise and train an army large or sufficiently competent enough to sustain him in power. Even had this been the case, the revenues of his kingdom were insufficient to pay for such an army. The outcome was that Britain was obliged to subsidize the king's regiments and when they proved unwilling or incapable of defeating the rising tide of revolt, British and Indian troops ended up fighting Shah Shuja' al-Mulk's wars for him. As early as May 1840 Sir John Hobhouse, President of the Board of Control, gloomily concluded, privately, that Britain faced the prospect of a 'permanent and prolonged occupation'.[7] Even Macnaghten had to accept that Shah Shuja' al-Mulk's claim that he was popular had little basis in reality. The king's power base was limited to a coterie of Durrani courtiers, mostly Popalzais, and not even the Qizilbash, who had been the military backbone of the Saddozais, could be trusted since many of their senior commanders were related by marriage to the family of Payinda Khan. Even Khan Shirin Khan, head of the Jawanshir Qizilbash, who had wholeheartedly supported the British intervention, wavered when it came to supporting Shah Shuja'. He wanted the British to annex all of southern Afghanistan, believing that only the British were capable of ruling the country effectively.

Sale's campaign in the Koh Daman and Kohistan

The defeat at Saighan and the subsequent treaty between the Mir Wali and Shah Shuja' forced Dost Muhammad Khan to abandon his attempt to raise an army in Balkh. Determined to continue to fight, he accepted an invitation from Sultan Muhammad Khan of Nijrab and Mir Hajji to join forces and lead an uprising in Kohistan and the Koh Daman. In 1839 these individuals had accepted a large sum of money from Wade to topple Dost Muhammad Khan, but a year after the occupation they were disillusioned and disappointed by the lack of reward they had received. Shah Shuja' had even reduced their allowances and demanded payment of several years' arrears of revenue. He also tried to tax their *jagirs* and nationalized *auqaf* holdings that Mir Hajji and Hafizji controlled. To add to the discontent, the king forcibly conscripted hundreds of Safis and Kohistanis into his army. As Lal remarked, 'The people of Kohistan were the warmest and stoutest friends of the Shah and of the English . . . and they were now reckoned our enemies.'[8]

Hafizji, Mir Hajji and other religious leaders of the region refused to pay tax on *auqaf*, claiming, rightly, that according to the *shari'a* it was unlawful for the civil ruler to demand revenues on land or property devoted to the support of religious institutions. When they came to Kabul to discuss the issue with Shah Shuja', he denied them permission to return home. Then, shortly after Dennie's victory at Saighan, the king imprisoned Hafizji and other religious leaders, accusing them of plotting to assassinate him. The king then 'suggested' to Hafizji that it would be good for his health if he undertook the pilgrimage to Mecca, a hint that he was more than happy to take.

Following the arrest and effective banishment of his elder brother Hafizji, Mir Hajji, who was still *mir wa'is* of the Pul-i Kheshti mosque, issued a *fatwa* denouncing Shah Shuja' as a *kafir* and legitimized a *jihad* against the king and the British. By the end of September 1840 all of the Kohistan, Tagab and Nijrab regions were in revolt and posed a serious challenge to Kabul, for this populous area could raise around 50,000 men. Since there were only two Indian regiments left to defend the Afghan capital, and with the king's forces deemed unfit for purpose, Dennie was recalled from Bamiyan and the most northern outpost of Shah Shuja' al-Mulk's kingdom from this point forward was Old Charikar in the Koh Daman.

News of the uprising in Kohistan and the Koh Daman created panic in the capital as merchants barricaded their shops, buried their treasure and sent their women and children to the safety of the surrounding country-side. General Cotton, realizing that decisive action had to be taken, ordered Lieutenant Colonel Sir Robert Sale, a veteran of the First Burmese War, to march into the region and suppress the rebellion. He was accompanied by Timur Mirza, one of Shah Shuja' al-Mulk's sons, Alexander Burnes, Mohan Lal and Ghulam Khan Popalzai, who were tasked with negotiating with rebel leaders and disbursing largesse in the form of Company rupees.

Sale encountered fierce resistance from the outset and the cost in terms of casualties was high. In his first battle at Tutam Darra, Lieutenant Edward Conolly, Arthur Conolly's younger brother, was shot through the heart, though the fort was eventually taken, burnt and levelled. Sale's next objective, Jalgah, the stronghold of Mir Masjidi, a renowned scholar of Islamic jurisprudence, was an even harder nut to crack. When Sale's men attempted to storm the walls they were repulsed with heavy loss of life, for the scaling ladders Sale had brought from Kabul were too short to surmount the *qal'a*'s walls. Even more extraordinary, Sale had not brought any siege guns with him. Fortunately for Sale, Mir Masjidi had been badly wounded in the fighting and during the night he abandoned the *qal'a*. The following morning Sale marched into an empty *qal'a* and ordered that it and the settlement of Jalgah, along with its crops, orchards and vineyards, be destroyed and burnt.

Yet Sale's storming of Jalgah was probably unnecessary, for prior to the assault Ghulam Khan Popalzai had almost secured the submission of Mir Masjidi, Mir Hajji and Khoja 'Abd al-Khaliq, head of the powerful Sayyid clan of Kohistan. The main cause of these individuals' rebellion had been the loss of their state subsidies and the king's attempt to tax *auqaf*, from which they received substantial financial benefit. Politically their loyalties lay with the Saddozai dynasty for they were indebted to Shah Zaman, Shah Shuja' al-Mulk's elder brother, for appointing them to their hereditary posts and high religious office. None of these men had any interest in Dost Muhammad Khan regaining the throne, for he had been responsible for the brutal suppression and execution of their forebears. Ghulam Khan Popalzai had even agreed to restore some of their entitlements, but his efforts to win them over were undermined when the king's *chaush bashi*, supported by Burnes, demanded Sale take 'firm' action against Mir Masjidi. So when Sale attacked and destroyed Jalgah, Mir Masjidi regarded this as an act of perfidy by the British and by Ghulam Khan Popalzai. In response, Mir Masjidi and the other *pirs* joined forces with Dost Muhammad Khan and Sultan Muhammad Khan Safi of Nijrab.

In early October 1840 Dost Muhammad Khan arrived in Nijrab and took command of the *mujahidin*. Sale, in an attempt to force the enemy to fight his force in the open field, crossed the Panjshir and began to level villages, burn crops and vineyards and ring-bark fruit trees. At the same time, his advance meant that his line of communications and supply line was overstretched. When Sale reached Kah Darra the enemy abandoned the *qal'a* after a brief skirmish, whereupon Saif al-Din, the village *malik*, along with the elders, came and tendered their submission. Yet despite this, Sale ordered all of Kah Darra's eight hundred houses to be burnt and levelled and its crops, orchards and vineyards destroyed. The grape crop, for which the area was famous and which was ready for picking, was requisitioned to feed Sale's troops. The destruction of a settlement that had peacefully surrendered, however, backfired. Saif al-Din's nephew, who commanded Shah Shuja' al-Mulk's Kohistani regiment, seeing what Sale had done to his village, deserted taking with him not just his own Kohistani troops but most of the Durrani cavalry too.

On 2 November 1840 Dost Muhammad Khan finally confronted Sale's advance at Parwan Darra. The Amir had chosen his position well and his men were well dug in on a ridge overlooking Sale's line of advance. Sale sent Captain Fraser and his Bengal Horse to attack the enemy's infantry but only a handful of Fraser's men obeyed when he gave the order to charge, leaving the British officers to charge the enemy lines alone. Dr

Lord, a physician turned political officer and finally soldier, was killed. Fraser somehow survived the charge and made it back to the British lines, but his sabre hand had been almost severed at the wrist. Dost Muhammad Khan, seeing what had happened, ordered his cavalry to counter-charge, whereupon the Bengal Horse turned and fled, and many were killed in the pursuit that followed. As a consequence of their cowardice and refusal to obey orders, the 2nd Bengal Horse was disgraced, the regiment disbanded and its name struck from the records of the Indian Army.

Sale responded by sending his infantry and Qizilbash to storm the heights. After heavy fighting and much loss of life, they finally took the ridge but the Amir withdrew in good order. During the night the Afghans reoccupied the heights, which appear to have been left undefended, and fired into the British camp in the plain below. The following day both Burnes and Timur Mirza advised Sale to abandon the campaign, for those Afghan troops that had not already deserted were on the verge of mutiny. Sale had lost hundreds of men and many more were wounded. With supplies running low, he ordered his force to return to Charikar. Once he had crossed the Panjshir river, the villages and settlements he had taken at such a great cost were quickly reoccupied.

The 'surrender' of Dost Muhammad Khan

Sale had little to show for two months of hard campaigning other than a trail of devastation. Despite this Sale claimed Parwan Darra was a victory, but he was unable to conceal the uncomfortable fact that the Indian cavalry had refused to obey orders and as a consequence several British officers had been killed or wounded. Atkinson, the army's surgeon general, called the encounter a 'disaster' and Kaye too regarded Parwan Darra as a defeat.[9] Even the ever-optimistic Macnaghten was depressed when he heard the news. Indeed, had the rebel army pursued Sale's brigade to Charikar it is likely that the defeat could have been even more disastrous, for Sale's force had suffered heavy losses and there were even fewer troops left to defend Kabul. However, even as Sale limped back to Charikar, the military and political situation was dramatically turned on its head. Early in the evening of 2 November 1840 a lone horseman, later identified as Sultan Muhammad Khan Safi, rode up to Macnaghten as he returned from his evening ride and enquired if he was the British envoy. When this was confirmed another rider came up, dismounted and grasped Macnaghten's stirrup. Much to his astonishment, Macnaghten realized the second horseman was none other than Dost Muhammad Khan.

The Amir's 'surrender' has given rise to much speculation by historians and, given the outcome of the Battle of Parwan Darra, his decision was peculiar, to say the least. Imperial historians, and even more recent ones, tend to refer to Dost Muhammad Khan's act as a surrender and offer a number of explanations that vary from the inane to the ridiculous. According to some, Dost Muhammad Khan's action was a recognition of Britain's Manifest Destiny to control, if not to rule, all the country between the Indus and the Amu Darya. Others claim that, having saved face after his defeat at Saighan, Dost Muhammad Khan was now free to surrender without loss of honour. Another absurd theory is that Dost Muhammad Khan surrendered because he had witnessed the suicidal bravery of Captain Fraser and Dr Lord, an action that convinced him that 'resistance was useless'. This, of course, ignores the fact that the Bengal Horse had refused to follow their officers into battle and then turned and fled or the fact that large numbers of Shah Shuja' al-Mulk's troops had deserted. An even less credible explanation is that the Amir was concerned about the fate of his wives and children, who were in British custody and about to be exiled to India. Yet Dost Muhammad was in no position to do anything to prevent their exile and Macnaghten had already assured them that they would be treated honourably. In fact, Dost Muhammad Khan was far more upset at Nawab Jabbar Khan's decision to accept the British offer than he was about the fate of his wives and children. He even accused his half-brother of treachery, implying that Jabbar Khan had handed over his family in exchange for a pledge that he would not be executed, imprisoned or exiled.

What is clear is that Dost Muhammad Khan was not surrendering in the manner of a defeated enemy. He had got the better of the Battle of Parwan Darra and, despite the loss at Saighan, the British had been forced to abandon Bamiyan and draw their forward defensive line at Charikar. The revolt in Kohistan had swung the military balance in Dost Muhammad Khan's favour, yet for some reason he decided to give up the struggle. Mohan Lal, who accompanied Sale's Brigade, provides the most coherent explanation for Dost Muhammad's action. According to Lal, certain unnamed Kohistani *amir*s planned to assassinate Dost Muhammad Khan and had paid a sniper to shoot him during the battle so that his death could be blamed on the British. Lal's account is supported by letters to the Amir from Sultan Muhammad Khan of Nijrab, which were found in Dost Muhammad Khan's baggage after the battle and in which the Amir is warned to take great care if he went to Tagab, for some of the *malik*s planned to betray or assassinate him. 'Abd al-Karim 'Alawi, who wrote a near-contemporary account of the First Afghan War, elaborated on the details of this plot.[10] According to him, Sale and Burnes were in secret communication with the *malik* of 'Ali Hisar, who agreed to kill or capture Dost Muhammad Khan and his two sons in return for the payment of a substantial sum of rupees.

Atkinson provides an even more intriguing slant on these events, based on confidential information provided by senior British officers. According to these sources, Macnaghten and Burnes had been intercepting communications between Sultan Muhammad Khan of Nijrab and his supporters in Kabul. In response Macnaghten forged a letter from a well-wisher to Dost Muhammad Khan, warning him that there was a plan to assassinate him during the battle. Dost Muhammad Khan, having read this communication, was convinced there was a plot against his life. The Amir, after all, had good reason to distrust the leaders of Kohistan, for twice in the past he had conducted bloody suppressions in the area and killed or executed the fathers and relatives of many of the leaders of the *mujahidin*. This explains why Dost Muhammad Khan rode away during the heat of battle without telling his sons he was leaving or where he was going. The only person he seems to have fully trusted was Sultan Muhammad Khan of Nijrab.

Dost Muhammad's options were limited. The Mir Wali and Murad Beg had signed a treaty with Shah Shuja' and would no longer provide him with sanctuary, while his experience in Bukhara convinced him that he risked death or imprisonment if he attempted to seek refuge in Balkh. His nearest point of safety, therefore, was the British cantonment in Kabul, a couple of hours' ride from Parwan Darra. The Amir had already received repeated assurances from Lord and Macnaghten that he would be treated honourably, and Dost Muhammad Khan guessed, rightly, that Macnaghten would not hand him over to Shah Shuja' for execution, although Macnaghten had originally argued that the Amir 'be shown no mercy'.[11] It is ironic that Dost Muhammad Khan reckoned that his best chance of staying alive and living to fight another day was as a prisoner of his enemy, the British, rather than claiming the protection of his own subjects.

Dost Muhammad's submission was nothing akin to surrender, since he had not been defeated at Parwan Darra and his army was in good shape. Rather, by grasping the envoy's stirrup, Dost Muhammad Khan was employing a traditional form of submission employed by high-ranking individuals. The right of *rikab giriftan*, or grasping the stirrup, was a well-established Turco-Mongolian tradition accorded to only the most senior and trusted individuals of the kingdom. To hold the king's stirrup was not just recognition of the rider's sovereignty and lordship, it was also a demonstration of the exalted rank of the one who grasped it. Atkinson rightly states that Dost Muhammad Khan's action was 'claiming . . . protection' of the British government, and in his famous sketch of the scene Dost Muhammad Khan and Macnaghten are shown shaking hands, an action that signifies both friendship between equals and agreement.[12] Akbar Khan later said that his father had 'throw[n] himself upon the honour of the British government . . . in time of need'.[13] Surrender, subjugation and humiliation were the last things in Dost Muhammad Khan's mind.

Macnaghten was elated at the unexpected turn of events for, as he noted, 'the Afghans are gunpowder and the Dost is a lighted match'.[14] 'The Dost', as he called him, was treated with due honour and housed in the Bala Hisar with only a token guard placed over his tent. His family were given permission to visit him and he was allowed to write to his sons, who were still at large. He even went out riding with an escort. During his short stay in the Bala Hisar, Dost Muhammad Khan held a parallel court under the very eyes of Shah Shuja', with even officials serving in the king's administration coming to pay their respects. The evident popularity of Dost Muhammad Khan was in direct contrast to a growing realization that Shah Shuja', despite his claims, was deeply unpopular with most of the population, nor could Macnaghten fail to observe the contrast between the two rivals. In his dispatches to the Governor General, Macnaghten painted a very different picture of the man who only two years before he had denounced and defamed in the Simla Declaration. Indeed, it appears Macnaghten developed an empathy with Dost Muhammad Khan that neither he nor Burnes ever had with Shah Shuja'. In an extraordinary admission, Macnaghten even asked the Governor General to treat the former Amir 'more handsomely' than Shah Shuja' in his exile, since 'we ejected the Dost, who never offended us, in support of our policy, of which he was the victim'.[15]

Following the submission of Dost Muhammad Khan and his subsequent exile to India, the revolt in Kohistan petered out but the resentment created by Sale's scorched earth policy continued to smoulder below the surface, awaiting a spark to reignite the flames. The Amir's son Akbar Khan remained at large and had taken refuge with his father-in-law, Muhammad Shah Khan, head of the Babakr Khel Ghilzais of Laghman, while two more of the Amir's sons, Muhammad 'Azam Khan and Sher 'Ali Khan, were in Zurmast. Yet despite the threat posed by these and other *sardars*, Macnaghten allowed Nawab Jabbar Khan and Nawab Muhammad Zaman Khan to remain in Kabul, where they secretly intrigued with the Ghilzais in an attempt to undermine Shah Shuja'.

Dysfunctional relations within the British establishment and with Shah Shuja'

Macnaghten and Burnes exploited the so-called victory in Kohistan to accuse Shah Shuja' al-Mulk's *wazir*, Mullah Shakar, of covertly inciting the revolt and eventually persuaded the king to replace him with Muhammad 'Osman Khan. This individual was the son of Wafadar Khan, Shah Zaman's *sardar-i sardaran*, and the man who had been responsible for the blinding and execution of Payinda Khan. Shah Shuja' had other reasons to distrust 'Osman Khan, for as a Kamran Khel Saddozai he was a potential rival for the throne. 'Osman Khan was also incompetent and venal, but Macnaghten turned a blind eye to these faults because, as far as the Envoy was concerned, this appointment was a great coup. Not only was 'Osman Khan an inveterate enemy of the Muhammadzais, he was a sycophant who wholeheartedly supported the British invasion and was an excellent source of inside information. Every evening the *wazir* would visit Macnaghten or Burnes, provide them with a detailed account of events at court and receive instructions for the following day. As far as Shah Shuja' was concerned, Muhammad 'Osman Khan was little better than a spy.

Macnaghten and Burnes's intervention over the appointment of the *wazir* reinforced the belief that Shah Shuja' was king in name only and that the British were ruling the country behind the scenes. Shah Shuja' did not help this perception by publicly complaining that he had no real power and sending petitioners to address their grievances to Burnes and Macnaghten. Neither of these men appeared to have grasped the real dangers such interference had for the occupation or the sustainability of the regime they had imposed in Afghanistan. Burnes, in particular, increasingly intervened in areas that were within the king's remit, drawing up plans for the reform of state finances, taxation and the country's feudal military structures. More often than not, he made these plans without bothering to consult the king or his ministers. A similar scenario took place in Kandahar, where British political officials attempted to reform the administration and drew up plans for a major overhaul of land tax, which led to tensions between British political officers and Timur Mirza, Shah Shuja' al-Mulk's son, who was governor of the region. General Nott even went as far as to flog a number of Timur Mirza's officials for allegedly looting army property. When Auckland reprimanded him, Nott flew into a rage and his relations with the Governor General and Macnaghten became increasingly bitter.

Nott's temper did not improve when he was not appointed as commander-in-chief on General Cotton's return to India, even though he was the most senior officer in the country. The reason was partly because of his fiery temper and partly because of the flogging incident. The primary reason, however, was that he was an Indian, and not a Queen's, officer. Ellenborough was even vindictive enough to claim Nott had 'not a grain of military talent'.[16] Despite reservations expressed by senior commanders the post went instead to Major General William Elphinstone, a cousin of Mountstuart Elphinstone and a friend of Lord Auckland. Auckland was convinced Elphinstone was the best man for the job, but he could not have been more wrong. His error was then compounded by appointing Brigadier General John Shelton as Elphinstone's second-in-command.

The two men could not have been more different. Elphinstone was kindly, mild-mannered and chronically indecisive. While he was only in his late fifties, he was probably prematurely senile. Elphinstone also suffered from gout and towards the end of his time in Afghanistan he could barely walk. Indeed, the reason why Elphinstone was in India in the first place was because his doctors had recommended that a warmer climate might aid his recovery. When Auckland offered him the Afghanistan command, he suggested that the 'bracing hills of Kabul might prove more congenial to your constitution than the hot plains of India'.[17]

Shelton, on the other hand, was autocratic, foul tempered and noted for personal courage in battle that verged on recklessness. During the Peninsula Campaign of 1812–13 when his arm had been shattered by a shell, Shelton is said to have remained on his horse and showed no sign of pain as the surgeon amputated his limb. Indeed, one reason for Shelton's acerbic temper was the continual pain from the stump of his amputated arm, which still had fragments of bone and shrapnel embedded in it. Even more worrying was the fact that Shelton suffered acute mood swings. When his recommendations were overruled, he would sulk in his tent, refuse to attend council meetings or even speak to Elphinstone. He also held his commander-in-chief in contempt; a degree of insubordination that Shelton would never have tolerated from the officers of his own regiment.

Shelton was also a prig. As a Queen's officer, he despised the Indian army's officers and openly expressed his lack of confidence in the fighting ability of sepoys. Given that the majority of the troops in Afghanistan were from Bengal and Bombay, Shelton was the last man to hold a senior command in this particular army. Shelton also did not command the respect of other Queen's officers or the rank and file of his own regiment, the 44th (East Essex) Foot, who dubbed him the Great Tyrant. Shelton believed that the harder you flogged your troops the better they fought, and on occasion he marched his regiment so hard that by the time they reached the battlefield they were exhausted. On at least one occasion, he had driven the 44th to the brink of mutiny. Furthermore, despite his personal bravery, Shelton lacked tactical acumen, a flaw that was starkly exposed when the military situation in Kabul began to deteriorate from the summer of 1841. His poor judgement in the stress of battle contributed significantly to the near-extermination of his regiment. For very different reasons neither Elphinstone nor Shelton was suited to direct military operations in the most complex and threat-filled theatre of war that British forces had engaged in since the American War of Independence. When the storm finally broke both men were found wanting.

Part of the problem was that Macnaghten had been constantly reassuring the Governor General that all was well and that Afghanistan was pacified. When Elphinstone and Shelton reached Kabul, Macnaghten repeated his assurances and told them there was nothing to worry about militarily. As late as August 1841 the envoy reported to Auckland that 'the country is perfectly quiet from Dan to Beersheba'.[18] When junior officers tried to warn Macnaghten that trouble was brewing and that recent victories had merely suppressed the discontent, he dismissed them as 'croakers'. Anyway, by the time Elphinstone took charge in Kabul, Macnaghten was less concerned about the situation in Afghanistan than he was about having been appointed Governor of Bombay. During his last months in Kabul, Macnaghten wanted to convince himself and the Governor General that his time in Afghanistan had been a success.

The failure of British diplomacy in Herat, Khiva and Bukhara

While the Army of the Indus settled down in Kandahar, Ghazni and Kabul, the situation in Herat imploded. After the Persian siege was abandoned, Eldred Pottinger was replaced by Major Todd, an experienced diplomat who had served under McNeill in Tehran. Todd, though, had his work cut out since Yar Muhammad Khan, Kamran's *wazir*, who was the real power in the principality, was at best difficult and at worst impossible. He was also cruel to the point of sadism and a master manipulator who skilfully played on British fears about the Russian and Persian threat to Herat to extract more and more cash in the form of subsidies and for 'special projects'. The *wazir* also covertly continued his lucrative role as middleman in the trade in Hazara and Shi'a slaves and conducted a clandestine correspondence with the Persian governor of Mashhad in violation of his treaty with Britain. In one letter, which Todd intercepted, Yar Muhammad openly declared his loathing of being subordinated to an infidel power: 'I prefer the fury of the King of Kings,' he wrote, 'to the kindness of a million English.'[19]

In January 1841 Todd's patience ran out. He had advanced Yar Muhammad Khan a substantial sum to reconquer the Persian-held frontier town of Ghuriyan, only for the *wazir* to keep the money and agree to accept Persian suzerainty in return for the peaceful surrender of Ghuriyan. Todd demanded Yar Muhammad abrogate the agreement and cease all communications with Persia. When he equivocated, Todd presented him with an ultimatum to either admit a British garrison or face outright annexation and removal from power. Yar Muhammad called Todd's bluff and rejected his demand, so Todd broke off diplomatic relations, informed the *wazir* to prepare for war with Britain and left for Kandahar. Todd's actions, though, had not been authorized and when Macnaghten heard that Todd had abandoned his post, his political career was abruptly terminated and he was ordered to rejoin his regiment. Later in the year Lord Melbourne's government approved the annexation of Herat, but nothing ever came of it for Auckland and his council vetoed the decision on the grounds of cost. Yar Muhammad went unpunished. As for Todd, he was killed four years later leading his regiment of Horse Artillery into battle against the Sikhs.

After the Persian siege was lifted, British interests shifted to the threat of a Russian occupation of the Turkman Khanate of Khiva. A few months after the British occupation of Kabul, General Perovsky, the governor of Orenburg, had marched out with 5,000 troops to attack Khiva, intent on suppressing the slave trade and freeing the Russians held captive in the Khanate. The expedition ended in disaster when much of the army perished as it attempted to cross the desert in the middle of the bitter Central Asian winter. Even so, Perovsky's campaign raised fears in London that Russia was using the suppression of the slave trade as an excuse to annex this strategic Khanate.

A few months before Perovsky's expedition McNeill sent Colonel Stoddard to Khiva to report on the situation and he eventually made his way to Bukhara, only to be imprisoned. The ostensible reason for his incarceration was that he refused to conform to the humiliating protocols that Nasr Allah Khan demanded every foreign envoy perform when granted an audience with the Khan. In fact, his imprisonment was due to the failure of Britain to recognize Bukhara's historic claim to sovereignty over the *wilayat* of Balkh. Todd and Lord, among others, had convinced Auckland that this region was historically an integral part of the Durrani kingdom, based on Bukhara's treaties with Nadir Shah, Ahmad Shah and Timur Shah, as well as European sources such as Elphinstone and his unreliable map. As far as Nasr Allah Khan was concerned, Bukhara's claim to sovereignty over Balkh was as important as the Durranis' to Peshawar, and a great deal more ancient. Britain's refusal to discuss this claim was the real reason why Stoddard was condemned to a vermin-infested prison and, ultimately, execution.

Britain regarded Stoddard's imprisonment as an insult to British power and prestige and there were calls for military action against Bukhara, despite the logistical impossibility of such a campaign and the fact that, had Britain actually gone to war with Bukhara, it would have precipitated a war with Russia – the very scenario that Britain was in Afghanistan to prevent. Instead, in June 1840 Arthur Conolly, who was with the British army in Kabul, volunteered to negotiate Stoddard's release as well as to explain British policy in Afghanistan to the Khan of Bukhara. His offer was reluctantly accepted, even though neither Macnaghten, Auckland nor even Conolly himself were optimistic about the chances of success. Conolly, though, was prepared to take the risk. He had been planning an expedition into Central Asia since 1838, he had powerful advocates in London and the fact that he was a cousin of Macnaghten's no doubt helped his cause. Furthermore, Conolly's journey presented an ideal opportunity to gather more information about invasion routes, the political situation in the Hazarajat, the Chahar Wilayat and Khiva, and the potential navigability of the Amu Darya as a possible conduit for British merchandise.

Conolly set out in the autumn of 1840 accompanied by the Khivan envoy in Kabul, an uncomfortable travelling companion since the ambassador announced to all and sundry that Shah Shuja' was a puppet and that the British hold on Afghanistan was tenuous. Conolly decided to take an extremely difficult and uncharted route that passed through Bamiyan, Yakaulang and Panjab, and then across the Tir Band-i Turkistan to Maimana. His official report provides important historical and ethnological data on a region which is still one of the least explored parts of Afghanistan. Unfortunately his personal diaries and notes have not survived.

When he arrived in Khiva, Conolly sent reports on the situation in the Khanate and mediated successfully in a dispute between Khiva and Kokand. He then persuaded Macnaghten to let him travel to Bukhara, but the timing could not have been more unfortunate. Just before he arrived in Bukhara, Nasr Allah Khan heard that the British army in Kabul had been massacred and the Khan knew that Britain was in no position to threaten him. Furthermore, Bukhara was now free to invade Balkh and reassert sovereignty without fear of military retaliation by Shah Shuja' or the British. Conolly ended up in the same dungeon as Stoddard. Nasr

Allah Khan offered to release them in return for a ransom of 10,000 gold *tilas*, but the two men refused.

Despite the harsh conditions of their imprisonment, Conolly some-how managed to smuggle out the occasional letter and kept a secret diary on the pages of his prayer book. This work remarkably survived and is a poignant testimony to his harrowing experience as well as his Christian faith, for Conolly was a member of the 'Clapham Sect', Wilberforce's evangelical, anti-slavery circle. Finally in June 1842 Stoddard and Conolly were brought into the public square, where their graves were dug before their eyes. Stoddard was the first to have his head sawn off and Conolly was offered his life on condition he converted to Islam. Conolly pointedly remarked that Stoddard had made a token conversion in an attempt to save his neck, but yet his life had been forfeited. He was prepared to die as a Christian and so the executioner beheaded him too. Despite several attempts to locate their graves in recent times, the last resting place of these two British officers has yet to be located.

The unsustainability of the British occupation and its consequences

While Conolly and Stoddard languished in a Bukharan dungeon, the British occupation of Afghanistan dragged on long after the original with-drawal date. This resulted in growing concern in Calcutta and London. The Indus campaign had tied up a total of 26,000 troops: as well as the 16,000 soldiers in Afghanistan, a further 9,000 were stationed in Sind and Baluchistan to protect the army's supply lines. Following the death of Ranjit Singh, additional troops had been sent to the Punjab frontier and yet more regiments were needed to pursue the Opium War with China, which had broken out as the Army in India marched on Kandahar. The stationing of so many troops beyond the frontiers of India raised concerns that there were insufficient forces left to deal with any revolt in the Indian heartland.

Auckland was also increasingly concerned at the burgeoning cost of the Afghan intervention. In the fiscal year 1840/41 the occupation of Afghanistan cost the Indian Exchequer more than 1 million pounds, while another half a million pounds was needed to cover the expenses of the garrisons in Sind, logistical support and the maintenance of a flotilla of barges on the Indus. The cost was such that the Indian Government was running a deficit to the tune of a million pounds and had to borrow heav-ily. This was unsustainable and in the spring of 1841 Auckland informed London that the only answer was to withdraw all but two regiments, leav-ing only one in Kabul and one in Kandahar, and withdraw all troops within a year. Shah Shuja' therefore had less than a year to fill a substantial hole in state finances and raise a minimum of 12,000 troops to replace the British army. This was an impossible task and, given the desertions of the king's troops at Saighan and Parwan Darra, what troops he already had under his command were clearly not fit for purpose.

Even before the first British soldier set foot in Afghanistan Shah Shuja' had told Wade that the rump of Ahmad Shah's kingdom did not provide sufficient revenue to cover state expenditure or pay and equip a large standing army. Once back on the throne, Shah Shuja' had tried to tax or confiscate *auqaf* holdings and tax-exempt estates, only for this to precipitate revolts in Kohistan, the Helmand, Ghazni and Qalat-i Ghilzai. In order to pacify the rebels, the new tax regime was abandoned and Britain ended up paying for most of the king's expenditure. Britain was thus caught in a cleft stick. While complete withdrawal was the preferred option, that would risk bringing about the fall of Shah Shuja' and the emergence of an anti-British government. At the same time, Britain could not continue subsidizing the Afghan government or fighting the Shah's wars indefinitely. It was a dilemma that both Soviet and NATO forces would also face during their respective occupations of Afghanistan more than a century later.

In order to save money, Auckland told Macnaghten to reduce expenditure drastically from around 1 million pounds to £30,000 by the end of 1842. Burnes and his counterparts in Kandahar then drew up plans for a major overhaul of the army and state revenues, much to the displeasure of Shah Shuja', who saw this as another example of British interference in his internal affairs. When the king tried to reimpose taxes on religious endowments and *jagirs* and demand a larger return from individuals who won the monopolies to farm customs duties and key commodities, there was fierce resistance. Among the many powerful chiefs who refused to pay were 'Amin Allah Khan Logari and Hamza Khan of Tezin. In retaliation Shah Shuja' dismissed them from their posts.

In Kandahar, the Durranis of the Helmand and Zamindawar rebelled under the leadership of Akhtar Khan, but the Afghan regiments sent by Nott to put down the uprising were defeated. Nott then sent British and Indian troops to suppress the revolt and Akhtar Khan was defeated, only for him to regroup and a few months later he besieged the British garrison of Girishk. Attempts to raise additional revenues and reports that Nott planned to garrison Qalat-i Ghilzai and exterminate the Ghilzai 'nation' led to a major uprising in the spring of 1841. The Hotaks and Tokhis flocked to the defence of Qalat-i Ghilzai and when Nott arrived at the fortress he found himself facing thousands of hostile tribesmen.

As Nott advanced on the citadel the Ghilzais attacked, whereupon Nott responded with grapeshot and disciplined musket fire, which led to great slaughter among the lightly armed Ghilzais. Despite suffering heavy losses, the Ghilzais repeatedly charged the British line until, after more than five hours, the survivors fled. For the first and last time in Afghanistan, British and Indian troops had fought a battle for which they had been trained and on their own terms.

Nott's victories in the Helmand and at Qalat-i Ghilzai reinforced Macnaghten's belief that Afghanistan was pacified and he compounded this error by grossly underestimating the strength of the rebellions. Akhtar Khan's Durranis he dismissed as a 'bag of ragamuffins', while rebellion was deemed to be second nature to the Ghilzais. 'Those who knew this country when it was ruled by the Barukzayes,' he wrote in August 1841, 'are amazed at the metamorphosis it has undergone, and with so little bloodshed.'[20] So when Henry Rawlinson, the political officer in Kandahar, warned Macnaghten that these revolts were but the beginning of more serious trouble, he was pompously rebuked for his:

> unwarrantably gloomy view of our position, and entertaining and disseminating rumours favourable to that view. We have enough of difficulties and croakers without adding to the number needlessly . . . These idle statements may cause much mischief, and, often repeated as they are, they neutralise my protestations to the contrary. I know them to be utterly false as regards this part of the country, and I have no reason to believe them to be true regarding your portion of the kingdom.[21]

Neither Elphinstone nor Macnaghten was able to see, let alone read, the writing on the wall and constantly ignored the warnings of experienced Indian officers and Afghan well-wishers. Even though Macnaghten himself admitted to Auckland that 'we are wretchedly weak',[22] more Indian troops were withdrawn and by the end of October 1841, there was just one British and one Indian regiment in Kabul, supported by a corps of Shah Shuja' al-Mulk's untried and potentially untrustworthy levies.

In order to raise the 12,000 troops that the British believed was the minimum needed to sustain Shah Shuja' on the throne, Burnes drew up plans for the reform of the kingdom's military.[23] Modelled on the British army, a completely new officer corps was to be raised based on merit rather than birth and pedigree – ironic given that the British army was as deeply entrenched in its own class system as the Afghan military. An initial force of 1,600 cavalry, known as the Janbaz, was commanded and trained by British officers but equipped at the king's expense. The Janbaz were professional soldiers who were paid a regular wage and received rewards for bravery and good conduct as well as grants of land for long service. A second corps, the Hazarbashis, commanded by Afghans, was roughly equivalent to Britain's Household Cavalry, for their primary function was to protect the king's person and defend the capital. Though it was not stated, the Hazarbashis replaced the *ghulam khana*, a fact that did not go unnoticed by the Qizilbash.

Burnes's military reforms, like his fiscal ones, struck at the heart of Afghanistan's feudal system and met with bitter resistance from vested interests whose power, wealth and status were threatened. Shah Shuja' too opposed the changes since they undermined royal patronage and reduced his ability to control and reward refractory barons. The resentment was deepened when it emerged that the Janbaz and Hazarbashis rank and file were to be recruited mainly from the Tajiks of Kohistan and the Koh Daman and the Pushtun tribes of Nangahar and the Kunar, rather than from the Durranis and Qizilbash. The officer corps too was reduced in size, and all serving military commanders were required to apply for commissions in the Janbaz and Hazarbashis. In effect, Burnes sacked every officer in the king's service. If this was not humiliating enough, these highborn nobles had to present themselves for interview to Lieutenant Trevor, Burnes's underling, and a man who held the lowest officer rank in the British army. Aristocrats, veterans of the civil war and the Sikh *jihad* who had commanded regiments of their own tribal levies now found themselves reduced to the level of petitioners who were expected to command outsiders with no loyalty to them or their tribe. To add insult to injury, Trevor was the sole arbitrator of who received a commission, since those he rejected had no right of appeal, not even to the king.

Trevor was a bad choice for a task that required the wisdom of Solomon and the patience of Job, for he had a violent temper and an evident dislike of the Durrani nobility, making no attempt to placate their anger at their loss of face. He was even stupid enough to tell the nobles that within a year or two all their kind would be unemployed and any handouts they received after then would be an act of pure charity. The greatest insult of all, though, was that the Hazarbashi officers were required to swear and sign an oath of allegiance to the king on pain of exile. Since they had already pledged their allegiance to the king when he first took Kabul, the nobles interpreted the requirement to renew their fealty as proof that both the British and the king doubted their loyalty.

The angry nobles petitioned the king to abrogate the order, only for Shah Shuja' to accuse them of being cowards who uttered idle threats. He then informed them that, since he was king in name only, they should address their complaints to Macnaghten, Burnes and Trevor. The result was mutiny. On 1 September 1841 all but a handful of the officers refused to take the new oath of allegiance, whereupon Shah Shuja' banned them from court and told them either they took the *ba'it* or face banishment. After a stand-off that lasted nearly a month, most of the officers took the oath under duress. In secret, some senior military officers began to plot to avenge themselves on Macnaghten, Burnes and Trevor, whom they blamed for instituting the reforms and their public humiliation.

Macnaghten then proceeded to alienate two other powerful factions who had supported Shah Shuja' al-Mulk's return to power. In the autumn of 1841 Macnaghten received Auckland's orders to reduce expenditure and had to find savings of several hundred thousand pounds within a matter of weeks. Convinced that the recent victories in the Helmand and at Qalat-i Ghilzai had cowed all opposition, Macnaghten decided to halve the payments made to the chiefs of Tezin and the Jabbar Khel, as well as the Kohistani *pir*s. European historians tend to depict these payments as bribes, but this is not the case. The Safavids, Mughals and the Durranis had all paid tribal *malik*s an annual subsidy in return for maintaining security on the king's highways. Indeed, it was such an arrangement between Shah 'Abbas I and Saddu Khan that led to the rise of the Saddozai dynasty. As such, these payments were for services rendered.

In September 1841 Macnaghten summoned the chiefs of Tezin and the Jabbar Khel to Kabul and informed them of the reduction in their payments, justifying his decision on the grounds that Sultan Muhammad Khan Tela'i had paid the Jabbar Khel a mere 13,000 rupees per annum. This was irrelevant as far as these chiefs were concerned, since Shah Shuja' had contracted to pay them a much higher rate and even Macnaghten admitted that these tribes had scrupulously honoured their side of the bargain and kept the Kabul–Jalalabad road open and bandit free. The dramatic cut in their payments was thus a kick in the teeth for these *khan*s, particularly as the payments were key to maintaining their own power and positions in their tribes and to buying off rivals. The loss of revenue therefore posed a serious threat to their own standing in the tribe and, given that the Kabul army's only supply route to India ran through the Jabbar Khel territory and Tezin, Macnaghten's decision was a prescription for disaster.

The *jihad* against the British occupation and the fall of Charikar

A few days after Macnaghten broke this news, and a day or so after the Durrani military elite reaffirmed their allegiance to the king, all the key actors who had suffered from these reforms and cuts in state subsidies – Durrani nobles, Ghilzai *khan*s and Kohistani *mullah*s – met in secret in Kabul and swore on the Qur'an to unite and 'annihilate' the invaders.[24] The first sign of trouble was when the Tezin Ghilzais plundered a *qafila* on its way to Kabul. A few days later the Jabbar Khel attacked But Khak, in southeastern Kabul, a settlement that was the gateway to the Jalalabad road and the Khurd Kabul gorge. Within a week the British line of supply and communication with Peshawar had been cut. Meanwhile in Laghman, Muhammad Shah Khan, the father-in-law of Akbar Khan and head of the Babakr Khel Ghilzais, secured a *fatwa* from local *mullah*s and raised the standard of *jihad*. When Shah Shuja' sent Hamza Khan, head of the Tezin Ghilzais, to negotiate with Muhammad Shah, he encouraged the Laghmani chief to continue his revolt. When Hamza Khan returned to Kabul, the king imprisoned him for treachery, inflaming his already angry tribe even further.

As Sale's Brigade was about to return to India, Elphinstone ordered him to reopen the Kabul–Jalalabad road, but since his troops were at the end of their tour of duty, Elphinstone refused to issue them with the latest percussion rifles. Instead he gave them the oldest and most worn-out Brown Bess muzzle-loading muskets, relics of the Napoleonic Wars, and a gun that one junior officer claimed was 'useless' and 'about as bad specimens of firearms as can be manufactured'.[25] Designed for the set-piece, infantry battles of the Napoleonic era, the Brown Bess was only effective at short range and was far less accurate than the Afghan *jezail*.

Sale's Brigade had to fight all the way from But Khak to Tezin and repeatedly storm the heights of the deep valleys to drive off enemy snipers. When he reached Tezin, the chief's subsidy was restored in full and he even received an unofficial apology for the 'harsh and unjust' reduction in his allowance. At Gandamak, Sale received an urgent message from Elphinstone to return to Kabul, for the Kohistan had risen in revolt. Sale's Brigade, however, was in no fit state to fight its way back to the Afghan capital. Most of its officers and hundreds of rank and file troops had been killed or wounded, they were low on ammunition and most of the baggage had been abandoned or looted. After consulting with his senior officers, Sale decided to ignore his orders and pushed on to Jalalabad, where he took possession of the principal fort and began to strengthen its defences.

While Sale battled his way down to Jalalabad, Macnaghten was congratulating himself that the Ghilzai revolt was over and that he and Elphinstone, by now incapacitated by gout, would be returning to India in a few days. So when at the beginning of November Eldred Pottinger, who was now political officer in Charikar, wrote to inform the envoy that Mir Masjidi and Sultan Muhammad Khan of Nijrab had rebelled, he failed to take the report seriously and told Pottinger that these tribes would give up once they heard news of the Ghilzai defeat at Qalat-i Ghilzai. What Macnaghten did not realize was that the Kohistan uprising was the start of the coordinated uprising agreed at the secret meeting in Kabul some six weeks earlier. Nor was it just a revolt, for Mir Masjidi too had proclaimed a *jihad*.

The outposts at Charikar consisted of two cantonments, Charikar-i Kohna, or Old Charikar, at the mouth of the Ghurband river, and Laghmani about a kilometre to the north.[26] The two garrisons were defended by around eight hundred of Shah Shuja' al-Mulk's troops commanded by Captain Codrington, consisting of Gurkhas and a small contingent of Punjabi artillerymen. Few of these men had seen any combat and most had brought their wives and children with them. When Pottinger first surveyed the outposts, he informed Macnaghten that the positions were indefensible and requested reinforcements and additional funds to strengthen their defences, but his request was denied for there was no money to spare. Macnaghten also reminded Pottinger that these posts were barracks and not fortresses. Codrington managed to stretch his budget and 'surreptitiously' added two bastions to the defences, but when the revolt broke out the barracks were only half-complete. Old Charikar did not even have a door on the main entrance and neither position had an internal water supply. Instead, drinking water came from the Ghurband canal nearby, while Old Charikar also used water from a diverted, intermittent stream that ran from the shrine of Khwaja Seh Yaran.

The first signs of the breaking storm was on 1 November 1841, when Mir Masjidi's *mujahidin* overran Aq Sarai and cut the garrison's line of retreat to Kabul. Mir Masjidi then set out for Kabul at the head of five hundred *ghazi*s, while 2,000 more men were sent to join Shah Muhammad Khan Safi, who was marching on Laghmani. The day after the fall of Aq Sarai Mir Hajji read out his *fatwa* of *jihad* from the *minbar* of the Pul-i Kheshti mosque under the very noses of Shah Shuja' and Macnaghten. Meanwhile, Old Charikar and Laghmani were surrounded by some 20,000 *mujahidin*, who outnumbered the defenders by more than twenty to one. Pottinger tried to play for time, expecting a relief column would be sent from Kabul.

Modern Charikar, gateway to the Panjshir, the Ghurband and the Salang tunnel. Old Charikar was a military outpost guarding what used to be the frontier between Mughal India and Uzbek Bukhara.

On 3 November Pottinger agreed to discuss the rebels' grievances and arranged a meeting with them in a walled orchard outside Laghmani, but when he and his assistant, Lieutenant Rattray, arrived at the meeting place they realized they had walked into a trap. Rattray was shot in the back as he fled, but Pottinger somehow managed to make it back unharmed to Laghmani, where he watched helplessly as Rattray was dispatched by a volley of bullets.

Codrington tried, but failed, to relieve Laghmani, so that night Pottinger abandoned the position and managed to reach Old Charikar without loss of life. Old Charikar was then besieged and its water supply diverted. When Codrington mounted a sortie to secure what was left of the water in the Ghurband canal, he was shot dead and Pottinger was wounded in the foot. Yet despite the lack of water, the garrison held out for more than a week and repulsed repeated assaults on the fort's walls. On 9 November a friendly *sayyid* from Istalif was allowed into the fort to inform Pottinger of the uprising in Kabul and the death of Burnes, news that dashed any hope of relief or rescue. By this time most of the officers and fighting men were dead or too badly wounded to fight, ammunition was running low and the daily water ration had been reduced to half a teacup per man. Pottinger and Lieutenant Haughton, who had taken over command after Codrington's death, decided to evacuate the fort and try to make their way back to Kabul. What Pottinger did not know was that, on the day he ordered the evacuation, Macnaghten had brokered a deal with Mir Masjidi, who agreed to allow the garrison safe passage back to Kabul in return for a payment of 60,000 rupees.

Pottinger's plan was to slip away during the night, head for the friendly settlement of Istalif and cross the plains to Pai-yi Minar and Kabul. Both Pottinger and Haughton were wounded but at least they had horses; everyone else had to walk the 80 kilometres (50 mi.) to Kabul. Pottinger split the evacuees into two columns and they managed to slip away without detection, only for the two sections to lose touch with each other in the dark. Pottinger and Haughton eventually made it to Istalif and arrived in Kabul the following morning. The rest of the force was not so fortunate. At daybreak they were overtaken on the road by the enemy cavalry and slaughtered to the last man, woman and child. The wounded, which Pottinger had left behind, were also killed when the rebels stormed the barracks. The fall of Old Charikar opened the road to Kabul and the Kohistani rebels poured into the capital where they reinforced Mir Masjidi, who had taken up a position in Behmaru. The garrison at Old Charikar had fought with exceptional bravery and held out for more than a week against overwhelming odds, yet neither they nor their officers received any recognition. Macnaghten even had the temerity to claim that the Gurkhas had 'behaved ill'.[27]

The Kabul uprising and the death of Burnes

When Pottinger and Haughton finally reached the Kabul cantonment, they found they had escaped the frying pan only to fall into the fire. Kabul was in an uproar. The uprising in the capital, which began in early November 1841, was the culmination of months of resentment at the presence of alien, non-Muslim forces on Afghan soil, British interference in the king's internal affairs and Burnes's fiscal and military reforms, which had undermined the power and wealth of both the king and his courtiers. For this reason the hatred and resentment was particularly directed at the British political establishment represented by Macnaghten, Burnes and Trevor.

It is commonplace among historians to claim the Kabul uprising of 1841 was a disorganized revolt by ordinary people and shopkeepers, but the evidence does not support this. Rather it was part of a coordinated revolt that had been sealed by an oath on the Qur'an some six weeks earlier. The chief instigator of the Kabul rebellion was 'Abd Allah Khan Achakzai, a Durrani noble and supporter of the Saddozai monarchy. Sometime just before or after the secret meeting in September, 'Abd Allah Khan had gone, Qur'an in hand, to 'Amin Allah Khan Logari and persuaded him to become the titular head of the revolt. 'Abd Allah Khan then proceeded to secure the support of a number of key Popalzai Royalists, several members of Kabul's religious establishment and the head of the Bayat Qizilbash. 'Amin Allah Khan Logari and many other leaders of the uprising had been imprisoned by Shah Shuja', dismissed from their posts or had their privileges curtailed. All of them hated the military and fiscal reforms, which they blamed on Macnaghten, Burnes and Trevor.

The conspirators' chief political objective was to restore real power to the king and the Durrani aristocracy, though they were divided over whether Shah Shuja' should remain king or be replaced by one of his sons. They were also convinced that if the British were forced to withdraw they could raise an army large enough to maintain a Saddozai monarch on the throne. In order to win over the Muhammadzais, the Royalists planned to restore the arrangement made between Ahmad Shah and Hajji Jamal Khan and appoint one of Payinda Khan's heirs as *wazir*. This political agenda was essentially unrealistic, partly because they blamed all the problems that Shah Shuja' faced on the British, and partly because the Royalists seemed unable to accept that the king had little popular following and that he was weak and ineffectual. The fact that Shah Shuja' survived at all was only because the British were fighting his battles and paying for everything from army wages to the king's civil service. Furthermore, there was little prospect that the Muhammadzais would agree to work under a Saddozai king, given the bad blood that existed between the two lineages.

'Abd Allah Khan Achakzai's revolt was also motivated by a personal vendetta against Burnes, who had demanded he honour a large debt he owed to a Hindu moneylender, which 'Abd Allah Khan had refused to repay. Furthermore, one of 'Abd Allah Khan's favourite concubines had somehow managed to escape from his *zanana* and been given sanctuary by Burnes in his house. 'Abd Allah Khan sent servants to demand her return but Burnes initially denied she was in his house and then, when it was apparent she was there, he refused to hand her over. Another woman who was pledged in marriage to 'Abd Allah Khan's brother had also fled and claimed the protection of British officers in the Old City. As far as 'Abd Allah Khan was concerned, this was a very serious matter indeed since it struck at the very heart of his and his family's *nang*, or honour. Not only had these women shamed him by fleeing, they were being protected by foreigners and invaders. Furthermore, inevitably their presence in the house of strangers raised suspicion of sexual impropriety.[28] For this reason, 'Abd Allah Khan decided his first objective was to attack the houses occupied by Burnes and Trevor, kill the hated foreigners and recover his

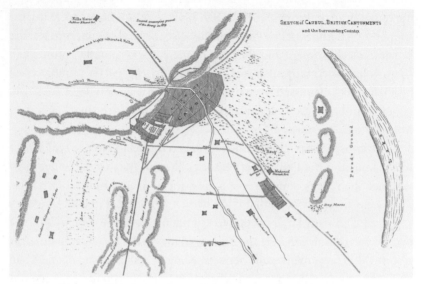

Plan of the city of Kabul, 1840, from Archibald Forbes, *The Afghan Wars, 1839–1842 and 1878–1880* (1892).

womenfolk. The fact that it was public knowledge that Trevor had thousands of Company rupees stored in his dwelling, and that both houses were protected by a small guard of sepoys, was further incentive for the attack since the treasure would provide a very useful war chest to buy loyalties and equip troops.

True to the Afghan proverb 'walls have mice, and mice have ears', news of the conspiracy soon spread. The evening before the plot was sprung Mohan Lal's spies informed him of the plan in detail and he sent an urgent warning to Burnes to increase the guard on his house. Afghan sympathizers also told Burnes that an attack was imminent and urged him to seek the safety of the Bala Hisar until the king could arrest the conspirators. Burnes, though, dismissed these warnings and refused to leave, although he did request reinforcements for the guard. These never arrived, however, leaving Burnes, Trevor and a few dozen sepoys to fend for themselves.

On the evening of 1 November 1841 Mir Masjidi rode into Kabul and announced that Kohistan had rebelled. Fearing that the Royalists had lost the initiative, 'Abd Allah Khan Achakzai decided to act. Early the following morning a band of his retainers attacked Burnes's house and set it on fire. Burnes, his younger brother and the other occupants were slain as they fled the inferno. Trevor's compound was also sacked, the sepoy guards killed and the treasury looted. Trevor, his wife and their seven children managed to escape in the nick of time to Chindawal, where they were protected by Khan Shirin Khan Jawanshir. Nawab Muhammad Zaman Khan gave

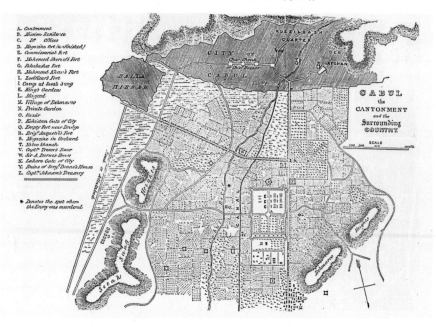

A. *Cantonment*
B. *Mission Residence*
C. *D.º Offices*
D. *Magazine Fort (unfinished)*
E. *Commissariat Fort*
F. *Mahomed Sheriff's Fort*
G. *Kababashee Fort*
H. *Mahmood Khan's Fort*
I. *Zoolficard Fort*
J. *Camp at Seeah Sung*
K. *King's Garden*
L. *Sirgenet*
M. *Village of Dehmauoo*
N. *Private Garden*
O. *Bazar*
P. *Kohistan Gate of City*
Q. *Empty Fort near Bridge*
R. *Brig.ʳ Anquetil's Fort*
S. *Magazine in Orchard*
T. *Taboo khanch*
V. *Capt.ⁿ Trevor's Tower*
W. *Sir A. Burnes House*
X. *Lahore Gate of City*
Y. *Baba or Brig.ʳ Dennie's House*
Z. *Capt.ⁿ Johnson's Treasury*

* *Denotes the spot where the Envoy was murdered*

CABUL
the
CANTONMENT
and the
Surrounding
COUNTRY.

Plan of Kabul and the British cantonment in 1841.

sanctuary to Mohan Lal and informed 'Abd Allah Khan Achakzai that, if he attempted to seize the *munshi*, he and his Barakzai clan would declare war on him.

Despite the fires, gunfire and general uproar, it was not until the following day that Macnaghten and Elphinstone were convinced that Burnes had been killed and that there had been an uprising in the Old City. This lack of action made the rebels even bolder. The Hazarbashis mutinied and attacked or killed any British officers they could lay their hands on. In the end it was Shah Shuja' who took the only decisive action, sending a corps of *ghulam*s, commanded by the Anglo-Indian adventurer and Muslim convert John Campbell, or Sher Muhammad Khan, to try and save the British officers. Campbell's men fought bravely but they suffered heavy casualties, caught in the crossfire in the narrow lanes, and were forced to retreat back to the Bala Hisar. The king then sent his eldest son, Fath Jang, to negotiate with the rebels, only for the prince to urge them to 'destroy the infidels'.[29] Shah Shuja' next ordered his artillery to bombard 'Abd Allah Khan's house, but he had already left and taken up a forward position in the *qal'a* of Muhammad Shah Bayat on the north bank of the Kabul river. Shah Shuja' was thus cut off from the main British force in the cantonment and, with the Old City and Hashmat Khan in rebel hands, the Bala Hisar was effectively besieged.

275

A city divided against itself: factionalism in the Kabul uprising

'Abd Allah Khan's attack in the old city marked the beginning of a citywide revolt in which various factions fought both the British and their rivals. 'Amin Allah Logari, 'Abd Allah Khan Achakzai and the Royalists fought on behalf of the Saddozai dynasty. Opposing them was Nawab Muhammad Zaman Khan, the eldest surviving son of Payinda Khan, who had ambitions to become Amir or at least *wazir*. One reason for his desire to topple Shah Shuja' was the fact that the king had betrayed his oath of safe conduct and had even briefly imprisoned him. Indeed, the resentment at Shah Shuja' al-Mulk's actions among senior Muhammadzais was such that some even called for the king and his sons to be put to death. The *sardars*, however, were divided as to the political future of the country. Some supported the return of Dost Muhammad Khan as Amir, while others favoured the candidacy of Nawab Muhammad Zaman Khan or one of the Kandahar or Peshawar *sardars*.

The uprising in Kohistan and the Old City took Nawab Zaman Khan and the Muhammadzais by surprise, but when trouble broke out Nawab Zaman Khan sent a messenger to Akbar Khan in Khulm, urging him to ride post-haste to Kabul. A second rider was sent to Nawab Jabbar Khan with a similar request. The day after Burnes's death, Nawab Jabbar Khan rode into the capital at the head of a large body of Jabbar Khel Ghilzais and occupied the Shah Bagh – the former Mughal garden, which today is occupied by the Presidential Palace – and a number of adjacent *qal'a*s. The Shah Bagh was a strong position located to the southwest of the cantonment, for the garden was surrounded with thick, high mud walls and controlled the road to Koh Daman and one of the fords over the Kabul river, which linked the British cantonment with the Old City. Having secured the Shah Bagh the *sardars* met to discuss the situation and appointed Nawab Zaman Khan as king. Coins were then struck in his name and the *mullah*s in Kabul were ordered to recite his name in the *khutba*. However, both Mir Masjidi and the Royalists refused to obey this order.

Even so, from the first week of November 1841 Kabul had two rival kings and currencies, while the capital was divided into four main factions. North of the Kabul river, Nawab Zaman Khan, Nawab Jabbar Khan and other Muhammadzai *sardars*, supported by sections of the Jabbar Khel and subsequently Hamza Khan of Tezin, controlled the Shah Bagh and Qal'a-yi Mahmud Khan. On the northeast side of the cantonment Mir Masjidi and his Kohistani *ghazis* controlled Behmaru, Qal'a-yi Rikab Bashi and all points north to Pai-yi Minar. In the east, the Jabbar Khel overran But

A group of Jabbar Khel Ghilzais from Khak-i Jabbar. In the 1830s and '40s the Jabbar Khel were a powerful warrior tribe who controlled the old Kabul–Jalalabad highway. Stories of their ancestors' battle with the British are still told, though the details are often garbled.

Khak and took up positions on the Siyah Sang hills. South of the Kabul river, the Old City and Hashmat Khan was held by forces loyal to 'Amin Allah Khan Logari and 'Abd Allah Khan Achakzai, backed by the Bayat Qizilbash and the *mullah*s of the Old City. As for Khan Shirin Khan and his Jawanshir Qizilbash in Chindawal, they initially adopted a neutral stance in the whole conflict.

The siege of the cantonment and the British military response

Both Royalists and Muhammadzais attempted to negotiate a face-saving withdrawal of British forces that was in their favour, while at the same time meeting with their rivals to discuss an anti-British alliance. One outcome of these discussions was that Nawab Zaman Khan agreed to recognize 'Abd Allah Khan Achakzai as commander-in-chief of all rebel forces in Kabul, though this arrangement did not last for long. In an attempt to force Macnaghten to the negotiating table, Nawab Zaman Khan's forces harassed the cantonment occupants with sniper fire and stormed the two *qal'a*s, which contained most of the army's munitions and supplies. The loss of the commissariat meant that there was only three days' supply of food and fodder left in the cantonment and the fighting men were put on half rations, while non-combatants were left to fend for themselves. By late November the situation was so desperate that horses and camels were being slaughtered for food and to reduce the number of pack animals that needed feeding.

Inside the cantonment, military and political commanders argued over how best to respond to the crisis. The situation was not helped when, the day after Burnes's death, Elphinstone's horse stumbled and fell on top of him. Already crippled by gout, Elphinstone was so badly injured – he probably suffered internal damage to his organs – that he had to order the military response from his sickbed. His tendency to dither was exacerbated by his injuries and increasingly bitter disagreements among senior officers. In the end, Shelton hardly spoke to him and often failed to turn up to meetings. To compound the problem, Elphinstone was meant to have left for India by this time and was technically no longer in command of the army. Shelton believed that it was he who was now in charge of military operations.

While the high command dithered about their plan of action, the inappropriateness of the cantonment's ground plan seriously limited the army's ability to conduct forays outside the walls, for most of the troops were tied up defending the perimeter and only one regiment could be spared for offensive operations. British forces were also split between the cantonment, the Bala Hisar and two outposts on the Siyah Sang and But Khak. Elphinstone ordered these last two positions to be abandoned and they were quickly occupied by the Jabbar Khel. Some senior officers wanted to abandon the cantonment, too, and concentrate their forces inside the Bala Hisar, a course of action that Shelton opposed on the grounds this would be tantamount to an admission of defeat.

As grain and fodder ran out there were desperate attempts to purchase supplies. Two of the leaders of Kabul's Armenian community, who owned agricultural land between the Bala Hisar and But Khak, provided some supplies. Khoja Mir, the *malik* of Behmaru and the father-in-law of Mir Masjidi, also sold flour and fodder to the cantonment at grossly inflated prices, then used the cash to finance his son-in-law's *jihad*. Mir Masjidi was not happy about this double-dealing and, shortly after his arrival in Kabul, his *ghazis* occupied Behmaru. On 10 November Shelton reluctantly agreed to try and occupy this settlement and the nearby *qal'as*. After bitter hand-to-hand fighting Shelton managed to expel Mir Masjidi's Kohistanis from Behmaru, took Qal'a-yi Rikab Bashi and Qal'a-yi Zu'l-fiqar Khan by storm, and bombarded the Jabbar Khel positions on the Siyah Sang with his artillery. Shelton's victory was greeted with relief by the beleaguered occupants of the cantonment, but while Mir Masjidi and the Ghilzai had suffered heavy losses, Shelton too had lost many men. Following the fall of Old Charikar the day before this battle, thousands more Kohistanis arrived in Kabul bringing with them captured British artillery pieces, muskets and ammunition. Reinforced, Mir Masjidi reoccupied Behmaru, cut the supplies to the cantonment and sent his *ghazis* to dig in on the summit of Tepa-yi Behmaru. Once entrenched, they fired at will down into the cantonment, making it exceedingly dangerous for anyone to venture into the open.

Despite Shelton's objections, Elphinstone ordered him and his regiment, the 44th Foot, to take Tepa-yi Behmaru and clear it of snipers. Before dawn on 23 November 1841 Shelton's men took control of the eastern slopes without meeting any opposition, then when day broke he opened fire with his single artillery piece on the Kohistanis in Behmaru village below. When the enemy fled for shelter into the houses, Shelton sent in a storming party only for them to be ambushed in the narrow lanes. Assailed on all sides from the houses and rooftops, the storming party retreated back up the hill. The noise of battle woke the Muhammadzais and Ghilzais in the Shah Bagh. Grabbing their weapons they rushed up the eastern flank of the adjacent Qal'a-yi Musa' hill and tried to storm the western side of Tepa-yi Behmaru.

Shelton now had to divide his forces, leaving one section to defend the eastern flank of the hill in case Mir Masjidi tried to storm its slopes, while he went to confront the Ghilzais and Barakzais on the western side. Exposed on the bare hillside with no cover and with the enemy out of range of their Brown Bess muskets, the 44th in their red coats were easy targets. As his men dropped like flies Shelton ordered them, inexplicably, to form two squares. This was the standard European infantry defence when faced with a cavalry charge or advancing infantry, but the worst possible option when it came to counteracting sniper fire. The battle quickly became a turkey shoot, yet despite men falling all around him, Shelton ordered them to hold their ground. For a while the enemy were held at bay with grapeshot, but the overheated gun seized and the Ghilzai swarmed up the slope. After a brief hand-to-hand struggle the 44th Foot fled back down the hill in full view of the cantonment onlookers. In the rout that followed many soldiers were killed and the death toll would have been even higher if Sardar 'Osman Khan had not ordered his men to hold their fire.

In the aftermath of this disaster, Shelton informed Elphinstone he was no longer able to mount further forays from the cantonment due to the lack of men. From this point onward, the high command's deliberations were about how best to negotiate a face-saving withdrawal and with which faction. Since this was a political matter, Elphinstone passed the buck to Macnaghten, who in turn handed it to Lieutenant Trevor, informing him that since he was now the most senior political official it was up to him to find a way out of the predicament.

Not everything had gone the rebels' way. Shelton's grapeshot had wreaked havoc among Mir Masjidi's *ghazis*, the Jabbar Khel and Muhammadzais, while a diversionary attack on the Bala Hisar by Royalist forces had been beaten off. Several key leaders of the uprising had been killed or mortally wounded, including Shah Muhammad Khan of Nijrab, 'Abd Allah Khan Achakzai (who was shot dead, probably by an assassin, in the heat of battle) and two of 'Abd Allah's sons and his brother-in-law. 'Amin Allah Khan Logari lost two of his sons, and two nephews of Dost Muhammad Khan had also been killed. Mir Masjidi, who had been severely wounded in an earlier encounter, died a few days after the battle, amid rumours that he had been poisoned. On his death, his followers left Kabul en masse and returned to the Koh Daman to bury their *pir*, leaving Behmaru almost undefended. These deaths were a serious blow to the rebel forces, but instead of exploiting this lack of leadership and going on the offensive, Elphinstone and Shelton opted for passive defence, which allowed the enemy time to regroup and bring in reinforcements.

Macnaghten's attempts to divide and rule

Macnaghten meanwhile tried to play one faction off against the other and turned to Mohan Lal to help him divide, if not conquer. Though most historians of the First Anglo-Afghan War fail to acknowledge it, it was Lal and not Burnes who was the most effective political operator in Kabul. Since his first visit to Kabul with Burnes, he had developed a highly efficient and extensive network of informants and had contacts with leaders of all the main factions. After Burnes's death Lal played a crucial role as both a mediator between Macnaghten and the rebel leaders and as an agent provocateur. It was a role Lal revelled in, for it gave him a far greater freedom of action than any native *munshi* would normally have been permitted.

While Macnaghten attempted to exploit the various dynastic, political and tribal rivalries and set one faction against the other, this was not Bengal and he was out of his depth, dealing with individuals for whom intrigue was second nature. Macnaghten's petty schemes fooled no one, instead they turned his amateurish gambits to their own advantage. Macnaghten's first object was 'Amin Allah Khan Logari. He authorized Lal to offer a reward of five *lakh* rupees for his arrest, making it clear that he would gladly see the Logari chief put to death. To undermine 'Amin Allah's position further, Lal was told to offer the headship of his Logar tribe to Yar Muhammad Khan, his long-standing rival. Yar Muhammad Khan naturally assumed that the substantial reward was the price for 'Amin Allah Khan's death and Macnaghten's assurance that 'assassination was not our custom' was taken with a very large pinch of salt.[30]

Lieutenant John Conolly, Arthur Conolly's younger brother, who was political representative to Shah Shuja' and who was living in the Bala Hisar, reinforced this misconception in a confidential letter in which he stated he would pay 10,000 rupees for the head of every rebel chief brought to him. Exactly who, if anyone, authorized Conolly to make such an offer is unclear, and he may well have been acting on his own initiative, though his offer probably reflected the view of Shah Shuja', who was eager to give more work to his underemployed executioner. Since Conolly's wishes were in line with instructions already received from Macnaghten, Lal placed a price on the heads of the rebel leaders. It is at this point in his published narrative that Lal, who is usually loquacious about his part in the First Anglo-Afghan War, becomes extremely coy about his actions. What is clear is that the rebel leaders were convinced that Macnaghten, through his political underlings, was offering to pay handsomely for the assassination of rebel leaders and was inciting their rivals to stick the knife into their ribs. It was a belief reinforced by suspicions that the assassin who shot 'Abd Allah Khan Achakzai during the Battle of Behmaru Heights had been in the pay of the British. It was also rumoured that the British had paid someone to poison Mir Masjidi. After all, this was exactly what they would have done.

On the political front Lal managed to negotiate a deal with some chiefs of the Jabbar Khel to abandon their support for Nawab Zaman Khan and to swear allegiance to Shah Shuja'. In return, Elphinstone agreed to pay them two *lakh* rupees as a down payment for supplying the cantonment with grain and fodder. Trevor was sent to make the payment, but when he reached the meeting place he was told all but one of the chiefs had reneged on the contract, so Macnaghten tore up the agreement on the grounds that the Jabbar Khel had failed to fulfil their side of the bargain. The Jabbar Khel, however, did not see the matter this way. According to them, an unnamed chief had tried to trick Trevor into giving him the cash, claiming that the other *khan*s had pulled out of the deal. As a consequence the Jabbar Khel accused Macnaghten of reneging on his promise.

While trying to undermine the Royalist cause, Macnaghten paid far less attention to Nawab Zaman Khan and the Muhammadzai *sardar*s.

Shortly after Burnes's death, Lal recommended Macnaghten send a delegation to Khulm to broker a power-sharing deal with Muhammad Akbar Khan, even to the extent of offering to restore Dost Muhammad Khan to the throne. Macnaghten rejected Lal's advice, a misjudgement that he would later regret, for the day after the debacle on Tepa-yi Behmaru Akbar Khan rode into Kabul at the head of 6,000 of the Mir Wali's Uzbeks cavalry. Nawab Zaman Khan, who had suffered particularly heavy losses in the battle, was in no position to prevent Akbar Khan taking charge of the Barakzai forces, overriding his complaint that since the *sardars* had nominated him as king, Akbar Khan had no right to usurp his authority.

Akbar Khan and Macnaghten

Nawab Zaman Khan had adopted a conciliatory approach to the British, offering to negotiate a safe withdrawal of British forces in return for the abdication of Shah Shuja' and presumably hoping for British recognition as the king or Amir. Akbar Khan, on the other hand, adopted a much harder line, for he bore a personal grudge against Burnes and Macnaghten for the humiliation his father had suffered as a result of the failure of the Burnes Mission. Now that he had the upper hand, Akbar Khan was determined to inflict equal pain and humiliation on his British adversaries. He dismissed Nawab Zaman Khan's negotiators, appointed his own trusted envoys and sent them to Macnaghten with a list of demands that were tantamount to unconditional surrender. All British forces must be withdrawn from Afghanistan as soon as practicable and all the army's artillery, muskets, ammunition and baggage must be surrendered. Before leaving, Macnaghten had to give a written undertaking that Britain would release Dost Muhammad Khan and allow him to reclaim the throne. To ensure this promise was fulfilled a number of British officers would remain as hostages and be released only after Dost Muhammad Khan reached Kabul. Shah Shuja' and his family, too, must be handed over. Akbar Khan then threatened that if the British rejected his demands he would storm the cantonment and no one within its walls could expect any mercy.

Macnaghten rejected Akbar Khan's terms outright, declaring he would rather decide the issue on the battlefield. However, Akbar Khan knew time was on his side, for the bitter Kabul winter had set in and the lack of food, fodder and fuel would eventually force the British to accept more or less any terms they were offered. Rather than storming the cantonment, Akbar Khan tightened the blockade and burnt the bridge over the Kabul river to prevent any attempt to escape to the Bala Hisar. His men then harassed the occupiers of the cantonment with sniper fire. During the last week of November there was a brief lull in fighting as Akbar Khan fell ill and the end of Ramazan was celebrated, but by this time the situation inside the cantonment was critical. Food had almost run out, camp followers were dying from starvation and exposure while the hospital, already overflowing with more than six hundred wounded soldiers, became even more overstretched as hundreds of Indians fell victim to bronchitis, pneumonia and frostbite.

In an attempt to relieve the food crisis as well as to undermine Akbar Khan, Macnaghten turned again to the Jabbar Khel, offering them the astronomic sum of two *lakh* rupees in return for food and fodder and a public oath of loyalty to Shah Shuja'. The chief, though, rejected the offer and informed Macnaghten that they had recently sworn an oath on the Qur'an to fight the infidel to the death. On 10 December 1841 there was more bad news when a letter from Nott arrived stating that he was unable to send a relief army to Kabul as the garrisons in Ghazni and Qalat-i Ghilzai were also under siege. It was now even more imperative to reach a face-saving agreement as quickly as possible before the worst of the winter weather set in and the occupants of the cantonment starved to death.

The day after receiving Nott's dispatch, Macnaghten agreed to meet with Akbar Khan, representatives of Nawab Zaman Khan's faction and the Ghilzais. He took with him a hastily drafted treaty, the terms of which differed very little from the demands made by Akbar Khan more than three weeks earlier. The agreement provided for the withdrawal of all British forces as quickly as possible, the release of Dost Muhammad Khan and British recognition of him as Amir of Afghanistan. Shah Shuja' would be 'persuaded' to abdicate and offered the choice of either staying in Kabul or leaving for India with the army. A number of officers would act as hostages and be released after Dost Muhammad Khan reached Kabul. Macnaghten even agreed to surrender most of his guns, ammunition and baggage. In return, Akbar Khan would provide food, fodder and transport and guarantee safe passage to India. To ensure this bargain was upheld, several Barakzai and Ghilzai chiefs would accompany the army as protection. At the end of the text Macnaghten slipped in an article that allowed a British Resident to reside in Kabul, a feeble attempt to save face that fooled no one, for it was evident the British had capitulated and were desperately trying to extract themselves with some degree of honour intact.

When Macnaghten began to read the text of the agreement to the assembled leaders, Akbar Khan angrily interrupted him and demanded the British leave the following day. As for safe conduct, the British had no right to demand any such undertaking, they were invaders and infidels and neither Afghan customary law nor the *shari'a* required any Muslim leader to give such a guarantee. The British had two choices: either throw themselves on his mercy, or stand and fight to the last man. Maybe as Akbar Khan spoke, he was thinking of how, not that long ago, Lord Bentinck and Auckland had presented his father with a similar ultimatum: either go to Lahore and submit in person to Ranjit Singh or risk being annihilated by the Sikhs.

Akbar Khan's outburst did not go down well with the other chiefs at the meeting. He was told in no uncertain terms to sit down and shut up, and not a word was uttered for the remainder of the reading of the treaty. When Macnaghten finished the leaders calmly debated the pros and cons of the agreement. After two hours the consensus of the *jirga* was to accept the treaty with only a few minor changes. The evacuation would commence in three days and in the meantime Lieutenant Trevor, who had accompanied Macnaghten, was to act as both a hostage and liaison officer between the two sides. The meeting ended amicably and as far as the Afghans were concerned the agreement, though not signed or sealed, was binding since it had been decided in *jirga* by all parties.

Macnaghten now had to justify what was effectively a surrender to the Governor General as well as informing Shah Shuja' of the deal, for as usual the king had not been consulted. In what was to be his last letter to Auckland, and one that was never completed, Macnaghten argued he had no choice but to accept the terms as it was essential to secure a pledge of safe passage for the army, since it was incapable of fighting its way to Jalalabad or through the Khyber Pass. Yet despite the dire situation, Macnaghten optimistically informed Auckland that 'we shall part with the Afghans as friends'.[31] When Shah Shuja' was told of the agreement he was furious and refused to abdicate or return to India, but he had little choice other than to agree to the arrangement, even though, as far as he was concerned, it was the ultimate betrayal by his British allies. The Tripartite Treaty, which he had signed just three years earlier, was now not worth the paper on which it was written. Instead his erstwhile allies planned to sacrifice him in order to save their own skins and hand him and his country over to his inveterate enemies.

Macnaghten's treaty, however, was not quite as transparent as it seemed, for he had composed it in such as way as to drive a wedge between Akbar Khan and Nawab Zaman Khan on the one hand, and the Muhammadzai *sardar*s and Royalists on the other. Initially Macnaghten's scheme appeared to be working. The day after the meeting several leaders who had attended the *jirga*, and who had no desire to see Dost Muhammad Khan return as Amir or any Muhammadzai rule the country, paid their respects to Shah Shuja'. They offered to support him remaining on the throne on condition he appoint one of Payinda Khan's heirs as *wazir*, more than likely Nawab Zaman Khan. When Lal informed Macnaghten of the meeting, the envoy replied that he would have no compunction tearing up the 11 December agreement if there were sufficient forces available to defeat Akbar Khan.

Akbar Khan, though, was astute enough to realize that the treaty had a sting in its tail and that Macnaghten was trying to undermine his position and that of his father. He saw this trick as yet further evidence of British perfidy and, convinced that Macnaghten could not be trusted, Akbar Khan cunningly set out to turn Macnaghten's scheme to his own advantage and to prove to all factions that the envoy was devious, untrustworthy and treacherous. At the same time, he saw an opportunity to put himself into an unassailable position militarily and politically.

Under the 11 December agreement, all British and Indian forces had to withdraw from the Bala Hisar to the cantonment. Once this had been completed, Akbar Khan and other leaders would be admitted to the Upper Bala Hisar to meet with Shah Shuja' and discuss his fate as head of state. Akbar Khan realized this arrangement presented him with an excellent opportunity to seize control of the strongest and best-fortified citadel in Kabul, depose or kill Shah Shuja', and defy all his rivals. To achieve this goal, Akbar Khan craftily persuaded Elphinstone to allow his men to escort the troops from the Bala Hisar to the cantonment. Elphinstone agreed without any inkling of Akbar Khan's scheme. While the evacuation was underway, Muhammad Shah Laghmani's Ghilzais tried to force their way into the citadel but Shah Shuja', possibly warned of Akbar Khan's plan, opened fire with artillery from the citadel's barbican, killing and maiming dozens of the enemy, as well as a number of sepoys. Consequently, Akbar Khan had to abandon his attempt to seize the Bala Hisar and Shah Shuja' lived to die another day.

The arrival of yet more troops and camp followers exacerbated the critical supply situation inside the cantonment. Three days later the weather took a turn for the worse with heavy snow falling throughout the night and all the following day. Eastern Afghanistan was about to experience its harshest winter for decades. By this time the agreed date for the evacuation of Kabul was passed and Macnaghten tried to delay the army's departure as long as possible in the hope that he would be able to secure sufficient supplies for the journey, as well as cut a deal with factions more willing to compromise.

Kabul in winter. Temperatures in the Afghan capital can fall as low as -20°C and heavy snow covers the ground from late November to March. The winter of 1841/2 was particularly severe and took a terrible toll on the retreating Army of the Indus.

Akbar Khan's attack on the Bala Hisar did not go down well with other factions and behind the scenes some of his rivals opened discussions with Macnaghten. On 21 December Macnaghten informed Lal that several unnamed Ghilzai chiefs, probably those he had been negotiating with before, were now prepared to supply 100 to 200 *kharwar*s of food and fodder to the cantonment during the night of the 21/22 December for a cash payment of two *lakh* rupees. In return, on the following morning the chiefs would seek an audience with the king and tender their oath of allegiance.

The agreement, though, was a double-cross. As soon as these Ghilzai chiefs had tendered their submission to the king, Lal was to inform Macnaghten, whereupon he would send a message to Akbar Khan abrogating the 11 December agreement on the grounds that neither he nor his father had the support of the people of Afghanistan. The British forces would then attack Akbar Khan in the Shah Bagh while the Ghilzais, Khan Shirin Khan's Jawanshir and Royalist forces would attack from the south. 'Do not let me appear in this matter,' Macnaghten told Lal, 'say that I am ready to stand by my engagements, but that I leave it to the people themselves.'[32]

Macnaghten's scheme was both treacherous and high risk, for while he publicly reassured Akbar Khan that Britain would abide by the terms of the 11 December agreement, behind his back Macnaghten was planning his destruction. What Macnaghten did not know was that Hamza Khan of Tezin and 'Amin Allah Khan Logari had a foot in both camps and kept Akbar Khan briefed on Macnaghten's double-cross. When Akbar Khan realized what was planned he decided to set a trap that would finally expose the envoy's treachery to all his rivals.

On the evening of 21 December Sardar Muhammad Saddiq Khan, Akbar Khan's nephew, arrived at the cantonment and was ushered into a private meeting with Macnaghten and Trevor. The conference was so secret that neither Elphinstone nor Shelton knew about it, let alone were invited to attend. Muhammad Saddiq proceeded to inform Macnaghten that Akbar Khan had changed his mind. He and his father-in-law, Muhammad Shah Khan, chief of the Babakr Khel of Laghman, were now prepared to allow Shah Shuja' to remain as king on condition that he appointed Akbar Khan as *wazir*. In return, the British garrison would be allowed to remain in Kabul until the spring thaw. The British would therefore save face and withdraw, claiming they had solved the Afghanistan 'problem'. Akbar Khan's apparent change of heart, however, came at a cost. Macnaghten would make an immediate cash payment of 30 *lakh* rupees and guarantee Akbar Khan an annual pension of four *lakh* rupees for the rest of his life. These terms were similar to ones proposed some weeks earlier by Nawab Zaman Khan and held out the prospect of unifying the two rival Muhammadzai factions and Nawab Jabbar Khan's Ghilzais. However, the deal had a sting in its tail: on the morning of the following day the British would signal their consent to this deal by joining forces with Akbar Khan and attack Qal'a-yi Mahmud Khan, the stronghold of 'Amin Allah Khan Logari and the Bayat Qizilbash. Akbar Khan even offered to bring the envoy the head of 'Amin Allah Khan in return for a suitable reward.

Akbar Khan's offer presented Macnaghten with a stark choice. He could continue with the agreement he had already made with one Ghilzai faction and join them in attacking Akbar Khan's position in the Shah Bagh, or he could change sides and, with the aid of Akbar Khan, destroy 'Amin Allah Khan and the other leaders who had been responsible for the insurrection and the death of Burnes. Akbar Khan's plot was a superb piece of cunning, for Macnaghten was caught in double check. Whichever of the two options he chose it was bound to convince all parties that he would happily betray them if he saw political advantage from doing so. The only way out was to reject Akbar Khan's plan, call off his own scheme to attack Akbar Khan and publicly reaffirm to all parties that the British government remained committed to upholding the 11 December agreement, since it had been agreed by a *jirga*.

Instead, Macnaghten fell headlong into the trap. Finally, it seemed, Akbar Khan was prepared to abandon his hard line and agree to terms acceptable to all parties – except, of course, 'Amin Allah Khan Logari and his allies in Qal'a-yi Mahmud Khan. Macnaghten then compounded his error by agreeing to sign a document presented to him by Sardar Saddiq Khan, which confirmed his assent to Akbar Khan's proposal. Akbar Khan now had documentary proof that Macnaghten was prepared to betray each and every member of the resistance and to pay one party to eliminate the other. When Akbar Khan showed them Macnaghten's signature on the document their anger knew no bounds. It was a particularly bitter blow for Nawab Zaman Khan as he had done everything in his power to negotiate an honourable compromise and restrain Akbar Khan. He had even risked his life to protect Lal and other officers from the wrath of 'Abd Allah Khan Achakzai. All this goodwill, it seemed, counted for nothing, since Macnaghten appeared to be prepared to betray him and cut a deal with his rival.

'Amin Allah Khan Logari was equally incensed for he had already agreed to join forces with the British and attack Akbar Khan. Now it seems this agreement was a trap to lure him into the open field so that the British and Akbar Khan could annihilate him. As for the Ghilzai, who were due to make a fortune by supplying fodder and food to the cantonment, for the third time in less than a month they were to be disappointed, for Macnaghten ordered Lal to inform them not to deliver the supplies and to call off the attack on the Shah Bagh. By the morning, all factions were united by anger and hatred at Macnaghten's betrayal. Akbar Khan's plan had worked to perfection and as a result he was now in control of the rebel agenda. Finally, the time had come to avenge the humiliations that Burnes, Macnaghten and Britain had heaped on his father and family over the past three years.

The assassination of Macnaghten and Trevor

It was not until early the next day that Macnaghten finally briefed his political officers and the military high command about the secret deal he had made with Akbar Khan and informed them he planned to have another meeting with Akbar Khan prior to attacking Qal'a-yi Mahmud Khan. Almost to a man, everyone condemned the envoy's actions. Lieutenant Colin Mackenzie, one of Macnaghten's aides, was astute enough to realize that the plan was a trap and bluntly warned the envoy that he had been tricked. 'A plot,' Macnaghten blithely replied, 'let me alone for that, trust me for that.'[33] General Elphinstone too was alarmed and wrote to Macnaghten asking him what guarantees he had from Akbar Khan that he was not about to be betrayed. As for Mohan Lal, he had been warned by an impeccable source that Macnaghten was walking into a trap. Mirza Khudadad, Saddiq Khan's confidential secretary who had been present at the secret meeting, was one of his many informers and during the night he risked his life to visit Lal and warn him that Akbar Khan had laid 'a deep scheme to entrap the Envoy.'[34] In response, Lal sent an urgent messenger to warn Macnaghten not to attend the meeting. He found the envoy just as he was leaving the cantonment, yet Macnaghten would not listen to the warnings and was stupid, or arrogant, enough to believe it was he who had the upper hand. So confident was he that he went to the meeting accompanied by a handful of officers and without a military escort.

Before leaving the cantonment Macnaghten requested Shelton to assemble two regiments outside the cantonment, ostensibly to act as his backup, though the real intention was that once his meeting had ended these troops would join Akbar Khan in the attack on Qal'a-yi Mahmud Khan. Shelton, despite his many faults, was nothing if not an honourable man and he was not prepared to be party to such a disgraceful trick, so he informed Macnaghten that he could not assemble a force so quickly, and anyway his men were far too busy preparing for the evacuation. In the end the regiments never appeared, which may have led Akbar Khan to believe that at the last moment Macnaghten planned to double-cross him too.

If the warning were not enough to alert Macnaghten to his precarious position, Akbar Khan's choice of meeting place should have set alarm bells ringing. The location was a small, isolated hillock beside the Kabul river, on what is today the west side of the Stadium opposite the Id Gah Mosque, a location which is still marked by a memorial plaque. When he arrived Macnaghten was surprised to find representatives of most of the rival factions present, including 'Amin Allah Khan Logari's brother and the chiefs of the Jabbar Khel, with whom he had been negotiating regarding provisions and submission to Shah Shuja'. There was also a large body of armed *ghazi*s surrounding the meeting place. When Macnaghten asked Akbar Khan why these men were present at a meeting that was meant to be highly confidential, Akbar Khan replied, 'they are all in on the secret'. Macnaghten failed to grasp the implication of these words and instead of fleeing back to the cantonment, he stretched out on the ground as if he was taking his ease.

Seeing the envoy had not taken the hint, Akbar Khan offered him a final chance to redeem himself by asking whether he was still prepared to carry out the agreement reached the night before. 'Why not?' replied Macnaghten casually, an expression which in Persian signified not uncertainty but consent. His reply was sufficient. 'Seize him', Akbar Khan cried and grabbed the envoy by his left hand. Another *sardar*, Sultan Jan, seized the envoy's other hand and together they dragged him head first down the slope. Meanwhile the British officers who had accompanied Macnaghten had their arms pinned and pistols put to their heads.[35]

Akbar Khan later claimed he had no intention of harming Macnaghten but merely planned to take him hostage. The facts, however, suggest otherwise. As Macnaghten struggled to free himself, Akbar Khan discharged a pistol into the envoy's body, one of a pair that Macnaghten had presented to him only the day before. In the confusion that followed the *ghazis* pounced on the badly wounded Macnaghten, hacking off his arms and legs and finally severing his head from his body. Lawrence and Mackenzie, two of the officers who had accompanied Macnaghten, were saved from a similar fate by the intervention of Nawab Zaman Khan, whose men fought off the *ghazis* and took them to the relative safety of Qal'a-yi Mahmud Khan. The following day he moved them into his own house. Lieutenant Trevor was not so fortunate. He was disarmed and was being taken away when Sultan Jan, who hated Trevor for having shamed the Royalist officers, rode up exclaiming 'this is the dog, Trevor' and cut him with his sword, whereupon he was dragged from his horse and hacked to death by *ghazis*. The torsos of Macnaghten and Trevor were later hung from a meat hook in the Chahar Chatta bazaar, while Macnaghten's hands were paraded in triumph through the streets of the Old City on a lance. As for Macnaghten's head, Akbar Khan had this wrapped in a sack and sent to the Mir Wali of Khulm. Three days later, what was left of the envoy's torso was thrown into a ditch near the smouldering ruins of Burnes's house.

Inside the cantonment there was confusion as to the fate of Macnaghten and his fellow officers. It was not until the following day that it was confirmed that Macnaghten and Trevor were dead and the other officers had been taken hostage. A few days later Eldred Pottinger, who was now in charge of political affairs, received a letter signed by Akbar Khan, 'Amin Allah Khan Logari and other leaders demanding that the British adhere to the terms of the 11 December agreement. Akbar Khan, however, made a number of additional demands. The army must leave immediately and all the treasure, except for funds needed for immediate road expenses, must be handed over along with all but six guns and most of the ammunition. The wives of senior officers were also to be surrendered as hostages until Dost Muhammad Khan returned to Afghanistan. In return, Akbar Khan pledged he and other leaders would accompany the army and ensure their safe passage. As for Shah Shuja', he could stay or go as he pleased, for Akbar Khan knew that the king's days were numbered.

The British withdrawal and massacres in the Haft Kotal

Pottinger objected to the humiliating conditions and urged Elphinstone to march the troops into the Bala Hisar but he was ignored, for in the wake of Macnaghten's assassination Elphinstone and Shelton had mounted what was tantamount to a *coup d'état*, placing themselves in sole charge of both military and political operations. In the end the army hung on for nearly three weeks, by which time snow lay deep on the ground and many more camp followers had died from exposure. After enduring one of the most miserable Christmas Days any British army could have ever spent, on 1 January 1842 a new treaty was signed with even harsher terms imposed on them for the withdrawal. This recognized Nawab Zaman Khan as regent and not Akbar Khan, possibly because Akbar Khan planned to accompany the army to Jalalabad. The signatories included Akbar Khan, Mir Hajji, 'Amin Allah Khan Logari and Sardar 'Osman Khan. The seals of Hamza Khan of Tezin and the *khan*s of the Jabbar Khel were notable by their absence for they had their own plans for the army as it passed through their territory. In return for the pledge of safe passage, Pottinger drew up bills on the East India Company treasury to the tune of nearly fourteen and a half *lakh* rupees, which was shared among Akbar Khan, Nawab Zaman Khan, 'Amin Allah Khan Logari, Khan Shirin Khan Jawanshir, Sardar 'Osman Khan and various Ghilzai chiefs.

Finally, on 6 January 1842, 4,500 British and Indian troops and some 11,500 camp followers set out in deep snow and icy conditions for Jalalabad. The night before they left Lady Sale had a chilling premonition of what was to come when she found the works of Thomas Campbell open at 'The Battle of Hohenlinden', a poem about a bloody, winter battle during the French Revolutionary Wars:

> Ah, few, few shall part where many meet!
> The snow shall be their winding-sheet
> And every turf beneath their feet
> Shall be a soldier's sepulchre.

The evacuation was a shambles. As soon as they left the cantonment what was left of Shah Shuja' al-Mulk's regiments deserted. The escort promised by Akbar Khan never arrived and long before the cantonment was evacuated, looters were climbing over the walls, pillaging the houses and killing stragglers. In an attempt to escape the slaughter the camp followers rushed forward to seek the protection of the rearguard, spreading panic in the process and hampering the troops. All semblance of order broke down as the column was strung out for several kilometres along the road, making its exposed and unprotected flanks easy picking for the Ghilzais and other plunderers who picked off stragglers, the sick and the wounded.

After two days the column had only managed to travel 16 kilometres (10 mi.) to But Khak, which under normal circumstances was a short ride from the Bala Hisar. In front of them lay the deep, steep-sided, U-shaped valley of the Khurd Kabul, the start of what was known as the Haft Kotal, or Seven Passes, which lay between Khurd Kabul and Gandamak. This was Jabbar Khel country, tribes whose *khans* and *maliks* felt betrayed by Macnaghten's cut in their subsidies and other broken pledges, and who were bound by a sacred oath to destroy the infidel. The retreating troops and hangers-on stood no chance and the Ghilzais picked them off from the safety of the heights above as they ran the gauntlet of the Khurd Kabul. The slaughter was terrible with no quarter given. After five days all but a handful of the 16,000 men, women and children who had set out from Kabul had been slain, or had died from exposure during the bitter nights, while the wounded and those too exhausted to continue sat by the wayside, awaiting the cold touch of a Ghilzai knife on their throat.

By the time the remnant reached Gandamak on the morning of 13 January 1842, all that remained of the army was a mere twenty officers and 45 men of Shelton's 44th Foot. Gandamak was meant to have had a garrison of the king's troops stationed there, but the survivors found only the Ghilzais waiting to greet them. Major Griffith, who had assumed command of what was left of the regiment after Akbar Khan had taken Shelton hostage a few days earlier, was offered the chance to surrender, but perhaps remembering the humiliation the regiment had suffered on Tepa-yi Behmaru, he refused. When the Ghilzais tried to disarm the soldiers a scuffle broke out that soon turned to hand-to-hand combat. By the time it was over all but three had been killed. Captain Souter, one of the survivors, was lucky. He had tied the regimental colours around his waist and the Ghilzai, thinking he was an important person who would command a substantial ransom, took him prisoner.

Around one o'clock in the afternoon of the same day a watchman on the walls of the Jalalabad fort saw a single horseman riding towards the citadel, waving his forage cap. Assistant Surgeon William Brydon, who had been attached to Shah Shuja' al-Mulk's regiments, was the sole British soldier to survive the march. Even he was more dead than alive. He had a sabre wound to his wrist and part of his skull was hanging off, yet despite losing a great deal of blood, he lived to tell his story. However, contrary to the popular imperial myth, Brydon was not the only European to survive the massacre. Early on in the retreat both Elphinstone and Shelton had been taken hostage after Akbar Khan tricked them into attending a conference and Shelton had to watch from afar as his regiment was annihilated. In all 63 European men, women and children, including Lady Macnaghten, General and Lady Elphinstone, Lady Sale and Trevor's wife and children, were held captive by Akbar Khan, while John Conolly, Eldred Pottinger and Mohan Lal remained in Kabul under house arrest. Many Muslims, both sepoys and camp followers, were spared but those that were taken prisoner were sold into slavery and their womenfolk ended up in the *zanana*s of local chieftains. Some ended up begging in the streets of Kabul, while others deserted and joined one or other of the Afghan militias.

Despite the dire situation in Kabul, Sale's Brigade had managed to beat off all attempts to storm the Jalalabad fort. When he realized that a massacre had taken place he decided to stay put to provide a refuge for any other survivors and to act as a forward base for a relief army. This was no easy matter, for a few days later Akbar Khan and his father-in-law, Muhammad Shah Babakr Khel, arrived at the head of a large army and placed the fort under siege. Yet despite overwhelming odds, Sale's small force held out until General Pollock relieved him three months later.

In Kandahar and Ghazni the situation was little better. In early November 1841 the Tokhi and Hotak Ghilzais rebelled once more, attacked Ghazni and eventually took control of the town, forcing the British forces to retreat into the citadel. Qalat-i Ghilzai too was besieged but both garrisons managed to hold out through the winter. Nott beat off an attempt to storm Kandahar and then went on the offensive, defeating a Durrani army commanded by Safdar Jan, Shah Shuja' al-Mulk's son, who had defected to the rebels. Nott also evicted thousands of men, women and children from Kandahar since he was unsure where their loyalties lay.

When news of the Kabul uprising reached Auckland he ordered reinforcements post-haste to Peshawar and Quetta, but the situation in the eastern front was complicated when the Afridis blocked the Khyber Pass and overran the fort of 'Ali Masjid. In early February 1842 Brigadier Wild tried unsuccessfully to force the Khyber so General Pollock, who commanded what was known as the Army of Retribution, decided to wait

George Alfred Croly, *Khoord Caubel Pass, 1842*, ink wash over pencil sketch. Croly was a member of Pollock's 'Army of Retribution'. His drawing shows the army as it approached Kabul and the skeletons of those who died in the retreat of 1841/2.

in Peshawar until the spring to allow additional reinforcements to be sent and for his troops' morale to improve. Finally, on 31 March 1842, Pollock marched out of Peshawar at the head of 8,000 troops. In order to clear the Khyber Pass of the Afridis and their barrier, Pollock sent the Highland regiments, with bagpipes playing, to surmount the heights. After bitter fighting, the enemy fled and abandoned 'Ali Masjid. The army met with little opposition for the rest of the march through the Khyber Pass. When Sale heard that Pollock had broken through, he marched out of Jalalabad, defeated Akbar Khan and recovered several guns that had been taken from the Kabul garrison. Finally, on 16 April 1842, Pollock arrived in Jalalabad and Akbar Khan fled to the safety of his father-in-law's tribe in Laghman.

The column sent from Quetta reached Kandahar in early May and managed to relieve the beleaguered troops in Qalat-i Ghilzai, but they were too late to save the Ghazni garrison. Faced with starvation and with their water supply cut off, Colonel Palmer, the commander, had surrendered in early March 1842 after he received a pledge of safe conduct. However, as soon as they were in the open plains the Ghilzai attacked, killing the garrison almost to the last man and taking the few surviving officers hostage. Nott eventually defeated the Ghilzai, retook Ghazni and joined Pollock in Kabul before both armies withdrew back to India.

The assassination of Shah Shuja' and the battle for Kabul

Almost as soon as British forces began the evacuation of Kabul, the various factions began to fight among themselves for supremacy.[36] Shah Shuja' was still king, though in name only, for his writ did not run beyond the walls of the Bala Hisar and he hoped against hope that the British would send a relief army to Kabul, reassert its authority and punish Akbar Khan and the other rebels. As for Akbar Khan, he left the capital to preside over the destruction of the British and then besieged Jalalabad, leaving Nawab Zaman Khan the effective ruler in Kabul. In mid-January 1842 the various factions agreed that Shah Shuja' could remain as king with Nawab Zaman Khan as *wazir* and 'Amin Allah Khan Logari as his deputy. It was a brittle compromise that lasted a matter of weeks.

Meanwhile Shah Shuja' came under pressure from Mir Hajji, who demanded he take command of the Kohistani *ghazi*s and combine with Akbar Khan to defeat Sale and confront Pollock. The king did not trust Mir Hajji and refused to leave the safety of the Bala Hisar. In early April Mir Hajji, hearing Pollock was advancing on Jalalabad, sent the king an ultimatum; either lead his *mujahidin* against the British or he would issue a *fatwa* declaring the king to be 'an infidel and friend of infidels'. Shah Shuja' capitulated, but only after Nawab Zaman Khan sent his wife to him with an oath sealed on a Qur'an, vowing to protect him from harm. Two days later Shah Shuja' left the Bala Hisar accompanied by a handful of Indian retainers, but he was waylaid by Shuja' al-Daula, Nawab Zaman Khan's son, and some sixty 'adventurers', who shot him in cold blood. For three days the king's body was left to rot in a ditch until it was finally buried in an unmarked grave near the mausoleum of his father, Timur Shah. According to Vincent Eyre, one of the British hostages, Shah Shuja' al-Mulk's assassination had been instigated by Dost Muhammad Khan, a Ghilzai chief, in retribution for an earlier attempt on Akbar Khan's life.

The king's assassination was universally condemned by the populace, especially since Nawab Zaman Khan had vowed to protect him. In an attempt to redeem his reputation, Nawab Zaman Khan disinherited Shuja' al-Daula and banished him from his presence. Shah Shuja' al-Mulk's eldest son, Fath Jang, succeeded his father, but his authority did not extend beyond the walls of the Bala Hisar, while outside the citadel walls Nawab Zaman Khan, Mir Hajji and 'Amin Allah Khan Logari fought each other for control of the Afghan capital. Shah Fath Jang demanded that Mir Hajji and 'Amin Allah Khan avenge his father's death and they attacked Nawab Zaman Khan. The latter, however, bought off Mir Hajji by handing over

John Conolly as a form of compensation, for the *pir* was angry that he had not received his rightful share of war booty. Mir Hajji then relieved Conolly of large sums of cash, forced him to sign credit notes on the Calcutta Treasury and used the cash to bribe his rivals and pay his *ghazi*s. Meanwhile 'Amin Allah Logari tried to secure the *pir*'s loyalty by granting him the right to taxes levied on the houses in the Old City.

At the end of April 1842 Nawab Zaman Khan and 'Amin Allah Khan fought another battle, this time for the right to control the revenues of Kabul's Customs House. In an attempt to restore order, Nawab Zaman Khan proposed that these revenues be apportioned to Mir Hajji instead in order to pay for the *jihad* against Pollock. 'Amin Allah Khan's response was to arrest Mir Hajji, so drawing the Kohistani *ghazi*s into the power struggle. Mir Hajji was eventually released after he pledged his loyalty to Shah Fath Jang, but he renounced his oath as soon as he was set free and joined forces with Nawab Zaman Khan. 'Amin Allah Khan Logari, outnumbered, sought refuge in the Bala Hisar but while Fath Jang agreed to give him sanctuary, he refused to allow any of the Logar chief's 4,000 armed retainers to enter the citadel. Instead they returned home and Fath Jang lost his opportunity to reinforce the Bala Hisar's defences.

A few days later the combined forces of Nawab Zaman Khan and Mir Hajji besieged the Bala Hisar, but shortly after the siege commenced Akbar Khan and Muhammad Shah arrived in Kabul with a large force of Shinwaris and Babakr Khel Ghilzais. Nawab Zaman Khan had little choice but to relinquish command of the Muhammadzai forces to Akbar Khan, who sent 'Amin Allah Khan Logari a copy of an intercepted dispatch from Calcutta ordering Pollock to retire to India. This news dashed any hope that the British would come to the king's rescue and all but a handful of the defenders in the Bala Hisar surrendered.

Shah Fath Jang, probably realizing he would be put to death, refused to capitulate despite having only a handful of Arab and Nubian *ghulam*s to protect him, so Akbar Khan sent the Babakr Khel Ghilzais to occupy the Sher Darwaza heights. They then proceeded to mount a captured British field gun on the Bala Burj, the tower that dominated the Upper Bala Hisar, and opened fired at point-blank range on the defenders. On 7 May Darwish Muhammad Khan, commander of the king's *ghulam*s, accepted the inevitable and opened the citadel gates to Muhammad Shah's Ghilzais, while Akbar Khan stood guard to prevent Nawab Zaman Khan or any of his rivals entering the citadel. Fath Jang was confined to a small room in the Upper Bala Hisar and over the ensuing weeks Akbar Khan extorted what wealth the king had left, using the proceeds to buy the loyalty of the Qizilbash and

Nawab Zaman Khan's Barakzais. Nawab Zaman Khan then did his cause little good by having a bitter row with Nawab Jabbar Khan that ended with him pulling Jabbar Khan's beard, a great insult, and accusing the *nawab* of having brought all the disasters upon the country, for it was he who had 'first brought the Feringhees into the country'.[37]

Following the fall of the Bala Hisar, Nawab Zaman Khan's followers deserted him so he appealed to Mir Hajji to recognize his right to the throne by reciting his name in the *khutba*. In reply, Mir Hajji told him he would only agree to do this provided he took charge of the *ghazis*, who had been kicking their heels at But Khak for more than three months, and march against Pollock who was now in control of Jalalabad. Nawab Shah Zaman refused and argued for negotiations instead, but Mir Hajji rejected any compromise. A few days later Akbar Khan called his own assembly of Kabul's *'ulama'* and on 29 June 1842 Mir Hajji formally proclaimed Shah Fath Jang as king-regent, pending the return of Dost Muhammad Khan, with Akbar Khan as his *wazir*. When Nawab Zaman Khan and Khan Shirin Khan Jawanshir boycotted this meeting, Muhammad Shah's Ghilzais attacked Nawab Zaman Khan, Hamza Khan of Tezin and Khan Shirin Khan, who eventually surrendered. Nawab Zaman Khan's life was spared but he and many other *sardars*, rivals of Akbar Khan, were imprisoned, as was Hamza Khan. Khan Shirin Khan was deposed as head of the Jawanshir Qizilbash and was forced to surrender Mohan Lal to Mullah Jalal Achakzai, *mir wa'is* of the Pul-i Kheshti mosque, who tortured the *munshi* and extracted large sums of money from him. Yet despite all his trials, Lal continued to risk his life smuggling out news and intelligence to Pollock's advancing army.

All would have been plain sailing for Akbar Khan had it not been for Ellenborough's decision to countermand his order to General Pollock to return to India and permitting him to march on Kabul to exact retribution for the 'outrages' committed against British officers and to rescue the hostages. When Akbar Khan heard the news, he assembled an army to oppose Pollock's advance, a force that included the British-trained Janbaz and Hazarbashi corps. Since he had already drained Shah Fath Jang of all his wealth, Akbar Khan forced him to abdicate in favour of his younger brother, Sultan Shahpur, and imposed a *jihad* tax on Kabul's shopkeepers and the Pushtun *maldar*. Akbar Khan then tried to negotiate with Pollock, using the hostages as a bargaining chip, but his approaches were rejected out of hand. Even so, the condition of the hostages' detention markedly improved and some of their looted property was restored.

General Pollock's campaign in eastern Afghanistan

On 20 August 1842 General Pollock, having ruthlessly subdued the Shinwaris, set out for Kabul. Sale, whose wife was one of the hostages, accompanied him and his experience of fighting his way through the Haft Kotal proved invaluable. Sale had raised a regiment of Afghan *jezailchis* and their firepower helped swing the battle in Pollock's favour, for Akbar Khan and the Jabbar Khel were waiting for Pollock in expectation of another massacre. As Pollock's force advanced up the road from Gandamak, the troops were constantly reminded of the fate their comrades-in-arms had suffered eight months earlier. At Gandamak, the vultures were still gorging themselves on the rotting flesh of Shelton's 44th Foot, and all along the route mounds of skeletons and decomposing bodies were strewn everywhere. Many of the corpses showed signs of mutilation and some could still be identified as the bodies of friends and comrades-in-arms. The Khurd Kabul gorge was so clogged with corpses and skeletons that the troops had to clamber over the decomposing remains.[38] The stench of rotting flesh was almost unbearable, yet there was no time to bury the thousands of dead, for Pollock's force had their hands full fighting a series of running battles.

Pollock, though, outsmarted Akbar Khan, sending his troops to storm the heights and then dispersed the enemy with bayonet charges. After two defeats and with the British force approaching But Khak, Akbar Khan fled north to the Ghurband, while Pollock occupied the Bala Hisar unopposed. Kabul itself was deserted, for most of the capital's population had fled to the Koh Daman, though the Hindu traders and moneylenders had stayed behind. A few days later General Nott arrived from Kandahar, having defeated the Ghilzais at Qalat-i Ghilzai and Ghazni. Among the trophies he brought with him were the sandalwood gates from the tomb of Sultan Mahmud of Ghazni, which he claimed had been pillaged some eight hundred years earlier from the Hindu temple of Somnath. However, Major Henry Rawlinson, the political officer at Kandahar and a Persian scholar who later distinguished himself by documenting and deciphering the Achaemenid inscriptions at Behistun, was not convinced. He was 'positively convinced' that the gates were Ghaznavid, based on the Kufic inscriptions inscribed on them.[39]

Kabul may have fallen but the hostages were still in Afghan hands. Akbar Khan ordered them to be moved from Laghman to Bamiyan, with the intention of sending them to the safety of Khulm. Fortunately for Pollock, Akbar Khan entrusted this task to Saleh Muhammad Khan, who had formerly commanded one of Shah Shuja' al-Mulk's cavalry regiments.

When Khan Shirin Khan heard he was heading to Bamiyan, he offered him a large sum of money to hand over the hostages. Saleh Muhammad accepted and set out for Kabul, while Khan Shirin Khan and his Jawanshir Qizilbash, accompanied by a number of British officers, rode out to intercept him and freed the hostages. Captivity, however, had not improved Shelton's temper and he rebuked Captain Shakespear, who had volunteered for the rescue mission, for his failure to observe the proper military protocol and present himself first to Shelton, the senior officer, when he reached their camp.

The rescue mission came too late for General Elphinstone, for in April he succumbed to his injuries and sheer exhaustion. Akbar Khan packed his body in a crude coffin and sent it to Sale in Jalalabad for burial, but the cortège was intercepted by Muhammad Shah's Ghilzais, who stripped the corpse, pelted it with stones and tried to burn it. Akbar Khan's escort managed to prevent this final insult, but they were forced to return to Laghman where the body was repacked and this time sent safely to Jalalabad. After her release, Lady Elphinstone had her husband's body exhumed and conveyed to Calcutta for a proper burial.

Another casualty was John Conolly, who died a few weeks before Pollock reached the capital from what Lal claimed was a 'sad pain at the heart caused through the public misfortunes'.[40] He was buried in the 'Mughal garden', most likely the Armenian graveyard near the Bala Hisar. John was the third Conolly brother to die as a direct, or indirect, result of the invasion of Afghanistan. Another 'loss' (as far as the Europeans were concerned) was Mrs Wade, the Anglo-Indian wife of a British sergeant killed in the retreat. Unable to endure the rigours of captivity and threatened with being sold into slavery, she converted to Islam and married a Ghilzai chief.

Having secured Kabul, Pollock sent Major General McCaskill into the Koh Daman to kill or capture the rebel leaders. His first objective was Istalif, where 'Amin Allah Khan Logari was said to have concentrated his forces, but the rebel chief had already fled. Despite the settlement being packed with thousands of displaced civilians from Kabul. McCaskill ordered his troops to attack and thousands of men, women and children were slaughtered in cold blood while the houses and bazaar were set on fire. The massacre was doubly bitter, for the elders of Istalif had provided fodder and food to the British cantonment and the *pir* of Istalif had sheltered Pottinger and Haughton the night they fled from Charikar. McCaskill's men had so much loot that they could not find enough pack animals to carry their ill-gotten gains to Kabul, so any chattels they could not transport were thrown into the fires. McCaskill then pushed on to Charikar, dealing out death and destruction as he went, but failed to kill or capture any of the rebel leaders and he was eventually recalled to Kabul.

Pollock too dealt out retribution, but since he was unable to punish the leaders of the revolt or the assassins of Burnes, Macnaghten and Trevor, he vented the collective wrath of Britain on the chieftains' qal'as and the Old City. Pollock was determined to destroy at least one major monument in the capital as a permanent reminder of the dire consequences of daring to challenge British military might. Initially he wanted to level the Bala Hisar, but changed his mind when it was pointed out that this was the residence of Shah Shuja' and the Saddozai monarchs, the dynasty on whose behalf Britain had gone to war in the first place. Instead, Pollock ordered the destruction of the Chahar Chatta, or Grand Bazaar, justifying his action on the grounds that it was in this *chauk* that the bodies of Macnaghten and Trevor had been put on public display.

His decision was an act of petty-minded vindictiveness. None of the occupants of the Chahar Chatta had had any hand in the uprising, nor had they played any part in the deaths of any British officer. Indeed, most of the residents and shopkeepers of the bazaar were Shikapuri *baniya*s, Hindus who were citizens of India and not Afghan Muslims. They had remained in Kabul since Pollock had assured them that they and their property would be protected. During the occupation they had advanced Macnaghten millions of rupees and honoured letters of credit made out to the Calcutta treasury, yet now it was these Hindus, and their homes and livelihoods, that were to suffer for the sins of others. Forced from their homes and shops at bayonet point, they were given no time to remove their goods and chattels; indeed anyone who showed the slightest signs of resistance risked being shot or bayoneted. Once the bazaar was empty, the Royal Engineers tried to pull the bazaar down, but it was so well built that they had to resort to gunpowder.

The destruction of the Chahar Chatta was an act of unwarranted cultural vandalism, for the bazaar, which Atkinson declared to be 'a gem amidst the edifices of mud by which it is surrounded', was the finest example of Mughal architecture north of the Khyber Pass.[41] Commissioned by 'Ali Mardan Khan, it was some 200 metres (650 ft) in length and flanked by two-storey buildings. At either end were two ornamented, octagonal *chauk*s, or courtyards, flanked by imposing arches, and in the centre of each was a fountain and cistern lined with white marble. The walls were adorned with naturalistic paintings of trees, fruit, birds, animals as well as mirrors, and there was at least one congregational mosque. Tragically, no

George Alfred Croly,
*The Sacking of the
Great Bazar of Caubul*,
1842, ink wash over
pencil sketch.

one bothered to make any detailed plans or sketches of the bazaar or its principal buildings prior to its destruction. Of the three drawings that exist of Chahar Chatta prior to 1843, only one provides any detail of the Mughal architecture.[42] Several other monuments were also demolished, including the Masjid-i Farangi, the Frank's Mosque, which had been constructed over the site where Macnaghten had been assassinated.

The troops sent to carry out the destruction in the Old City soon got out of hand. Burning for revenge and with the memories of the rotting and mutilated corpses of their comrades fresh in their minds, the soldiers looted and burnt shops and houses and killed anyone who stood in their way. By the time discipline was restored many of the wooden houses and shops in the Old City, some of which dated back hundreds of years, were ablaze. Only the Bala Hisar and the Qizilbash quarter of Chindawal, both of which were faced with stone and well defended, survived. When Pollock left two weeks after his arrival, the fires were still burning and the smoke could be seen as far away as the Khurd Kabul.

When Pollock withdrew, many of the Hindu *baniyas* decided to accompany the army back to India, for not only had they lost their homes and livelihoods, they feared the reprisals that would follow once the British army left. Shah Fath Jang joined the exodus, but his younger brother, Shah Shahpur, decided to stay behind, only for him to flee to Peshawar a few months later, barely escaping with his life. Other individuals who left for permanent exile included 'Osman Khan Saddozai, Nawab Zaman Khan, Saleh Muhammad Khan and Sayyid Muhammad Khan, also known as Jan Fishan Khan, the great-great-grandfather of Idris Shah, the well-known author and exponent of Westernized neo-Sufism. Most of these exiles ended up in Ludhiana, where Shah Shuja' al-Mulk's heirs and a few other prominent officials were given small pensions and *jagirs*. Most of the refugees, though, had to fend for themselves. Many lived in great poverty and were forced to do menial work or relied on the charity of American Presbyterian missionaries. In 1858 two of Shahzada Timur's sons, grandsons of Shah Shuja', were rewarded for having saved the lives of the missionaries during the 1857 Sepoy Mutiny.

The political and military fallout of the Afghan War

The political and military failures of the First Anglo-Afghan War had widespread repercussions in both India and Britain. First and foremost, Britain's imperial and military prestige suffered a major blow for even the most ardent imperial propagandists could not deny the campaign had been a disaster. Britain had been humiliated and its army had suffered its worst defeat since the American War of Independence. The fact that this defeat had come at the hands of poorly armed, factionalized, 'wild' and 'uncivilized' tribesmen rubbed even more salt into the wound. The heavy loss of life and the deaths of many senior officers also caused a crisis in India, and there were concerns that there were insufficient forces left to maintain security. To add to the woes, the cost of the war had plunged the East India Company into debt and a serious budget deficit.

Politically the occupation was equally disastrous, for its outcome was exactly the opposite of what British officials had intended. Saddozai power, already in terminal decline, was broken and never again would a Saddozai challenge the descendants of Payinda Khan for control of Afghanistan. Dost Muhammad Khan, who Britain had damned as an unfriendly and treacherous ruler, was allowed to return to Afghanistan where he quickly regained the throne and established a dynasty that would last for the next 85 years. Dost Muhammad Khan, Akbar Khan and Mir Masjidi became 'national' heroes, and by the end of Dost Muhammad Khan's reign Afghan historians were referring to him as *Amir-i Kabir*, the Great Amir. One near-contemporary Afghan even composed a turgid history of

Akbar Khan's feats employing the same poetic metre as the *Shah Nama*.[43] Today Afghan historians still portray Dost Muhammad Khan as one of Afghanistan's greatest rulers, while the Afghan capital's diplomatic quarter bears the name of Wazir Akbar Khan.

In Britain, politicians who had promoted and supported the invasion now had to face the consequences of their flawed policies. Peel's recently elected Tory government did all it could to play down the shambles, for while in Opposition they had supported the invasion. The Whigs, who were now sitting on the Opposition benches, were also reluctant to use the issue against the government for it had been their prime minister who had taken Britain into the war. As such 'both parties had more to bury than to flourish'.[44] Inevitably, the British political and military establishment closed ranks and sought scapegoats to save their own careers. Palmerston, now in Opposition, adopted his usual policy of stonewalling, refusing to admit his government's Indus policy had been a disaster and stoutly defending the decision to go to war. Disraeli, from the Tory back benches, tried to blame Hobhouse, President of the Board of Control, accusing him of 'pure trickery and fraud' for omitting or suppressing sections of the dispatches from Afghanistan.[45] Hobhouse, however, refused to be the whipping boy and mounted such a spirited defence of his position in Parliament that he won the day.

Auckland came in for the most bitter criticism, despite the fact that he had resigned as Governor General before the disaster in Kabul. However, as he was still at sea on his way back to England when the massacre took place, he was in no position to answer his critics. It was only after he landed that he heard of the destruction of the Kabul garrison and discovered that the press, politicians, the Governor General's Council as well as the Board of Control were trying to pin the blame on him. The Board of Control even wrote to London claiming that Auckland had kept them in the dark over the situation in Afghanistan. As for Ellenborough, who replaced Auckland as Governor General and whose Indus policy had led to the Afghan intervention in the first place, he publicly repudiated the actions of his predecessor. This unpleasant denunciation created such bitterness that the long-standing friendship between the Law and Eden families ended abruptly.

Remarkably, no heads rolled either in London or Calcutta and indeed the political careers of those chiefly responsible for the Indus policy and the Afghan debacle continued uninterrupted. After losing the 1841 election, Melbourne faded from political life but in 1843 Auckland became First Lord of the Admiralty; Ellenborough was appointed as the new Governor

General of India; while Palmerston, Melbourne's Foreign Minister, became one of Victorian England's greatest politicians, twice holding the office of Prime Minister. Auckland, Melbourne and Palmerston even had cities in New Zealand and Australia named in their honour.

Much of the blame for the debacle was placed on the dysfunctional political and military establishment in Kabul, in particular Elphinstone and Macnaghten and, to a lesser degree, Burnes. This was highly convenient since all three men were dead and in no position to defend themselves. Even the Afghans were blamed for having the temerity to fight for their independence and were damned as 'a faithless enemy, stained by the foul crime of assassination' and guilty of 'consummate treachery'.[46] The conclusion was clear: the Afghans had only won because they cheated. As for the chaos, anarchy and bloodshed the British left behind, Ellenborough regarded this as Divine retribution, 'the consequence of their crimes'.[47]

Over the ensuing years the Victorian imperial propaganda machine did its best to transform the humiliation into a heroic action; a scenario which in the latter half of the twentieth century would come to be known as the Dunkirk Spirit. Macnaghten's treachery was downplayed, as was the dalliance of Burnes and other officers with the wives and concubines of nobles. Instead the emphasis shifted to the heroism of the storming of Ghazi; Nott's victories over the Durranis and Ghilzai; Pottinger's defence of Herat; Sale's defence of Jalalabad and Pollock's Army of Retribution. Burnes, Lord, Arthur Conolly and Stoddard, in particular, were recast as martyrs to the Imperial cause, men who gave their lives trying, in vain, to extend the benefits of civilization to an ungrateful, 'savage' and 'treacherous' people.

So successful was this 'spin' that on the eve of going to war a second time with Afghanistan, Viscount Cranbrook, Secretary of State for India, in an address to the House of Lords, was able to dismiss the disaster of 1841/2 as 'unfortunate' (a very British understatement) to 'hear hears' from the assembled peers:

> the sufferings sustained by our troops in the [First Afghan] war . . . did not happen because the country was too weak to maintain her rights and put down all opposition by the sword, but because we were unfortunate. We were unfortunate in our political negotiators; we were unfortunate in our generals (Hear, hear). The commonest precautions were neglected, and from these causes, and not from any want of valour in the field, resulted those disasters which we all regret (Hear, hear).[48]

Two subsequent paintings helped to transform the bungled disaster into an act of Imperial heroism. William Barnes Wollen's *Last Stand of Her Majesty's 44th Regiment at Gundamuck* (1898) and Lady Butler's *Remnants of an Army* (1879), which depicts Dr Brydon's arrival at Jalalabad, both reinforce the myth of Britannia's implacable resolve. The indomitable spirit of Dr Brydon and the 44th Foot, even in defeat, is contrasted starkly with the barbarism of the Afghans and Afghanistan, symbolized by the cruel faces and knives of the Ghilzais who surround the 44th Foot, and the barren, infertile, frost-bound landscapes that are the backdrop to both paintings. In Butler's painting, composed just before British forces invaded Afghanistan for a second time, the Union Jack is shown flying defiantly, and at full mast, from the Jalalabad fort.

Seven officers faced a military tribunal to answer to the charge of 'conduct disgraceful to the character of an officer', but all were acquitted on the grounds that they were obeying General Elphinstone's orders. Only Brigadier Shelton and Colonel Palmer were subject to a full court martial. Palmer, who had surrendered Ghazni, was honourably acquitted, while Shelton faced four minor charges: ordering preparation for a retreat without authority; using disrespectful language to a superior within the hearing of troops; entering into a clandestine correspondence with the enemy; and suffering himself to be taken prisoner by not taking due care and precaution. His incompetent leadership on Tepa-yi Behmaru, his refusal to attend council meetings even when ordered to do so by a superior officer and his persistent advocacy of withdrawal were not even mentioned. Shelton was found guilty on a single and very minor charge, that of entering into a clandestine correspondence with Akbar Khan. Despite this, he was not cashiered because of his military record in the Napoleonic Wars and Shelton resumed command of his regiment, only to die in 1845 when his horse stumbled and fell on him.

The wider political fallout from the Afghan disaster raised serious concerns about the impact the defeat would have on India's Muslim population in particular. Eldred Pottinger prophetically wrote that 'if government does not take some decided steps to recover the affection of the army . . . a single spark will blow the Sepoys into a Mutiny'.[49] Another concern was the negative impact the failure of the Afghan war would have on Britain's role as a European superpower, and no doubt in the corridors of power in St Petersburg there was a great deal of smug satisfaction at Britain's bloody nose. Following the defeat, the Russian government showed far less concern about continuing its expansionist policies in Central Asia, counting on the fact that Britain would think twice before risking any further military intervention beyond the Khyber and Bolan passes. Over the next three decades, Imperial Russian forces pushed south and annexed all of the Central Asian Khanates without facing any military response from Britain. By the late 1860s Russia's frontier in Central Asia had been drawn on the Amu Darya, Afghanistan's northern border.

Militarily, Pollock and Nott's campaigns in the summer and autumn of 1842 went some way to restore British military prestige. The annexation of Sind the following year and two successful wars against the Sikhs (1845–6; 1848–9), which led to the annexation of the Punjab, helped to rehabilitate the shattered reputation of the Indian Army and pushed the northwestern frontier of British India to the Khyber. These and other victories and territorial acquisitions made it that much easier for Imperial historians to portray the First Afghan War as an exception rather than the rule.

Britain's Central Asian policy, however, was in tatters and Anglo-Afghan relations could not have been worse. The conduct of Burnes and Macnaghten reinforced Afghan distrust of British diplomacy and led to hostility to Britain per se. Britain now faced the monumental task of rebuilding trust with a ruler whom she had defamed, deposed and exiled, and a government and people who were even less willing to risk engaging with European powers or civilization.

SEVEN

The Pursuit of 'Scientific Frontiers', 1843–79

We can never feel much pity for the flesh-dealing Toorkistan, let it fall to whom it may. As a question of politics, the more the Affghans [*sic*] take the less there will be for either Russia or Persia.

HERBERT EDWARDES

[Amir Sher 'Ali Khan] should clearly realize our views of his position as a weak power between two enormously strong ones, an earthen vessel between two iron ones.

BARTLE FRERE

WHILE THE BRITISH OCCUPATION of Afghanistan was imploding, Dost Muhammad Khan had not been idle. During his exile in India he successfully petitioned for an audience with Lord Ellenborough, now Governor General, and when the Amir reached Calcutta, Ellenborough received him with great honour. Indeed his visit was more like a royal progress: he was guest of honour at balls, had a guided tour of the city and docks and an official reception was held in his honour. When Dost Muhammad Khan fell ill, the Governor General sent him to a hill station to recuperate. Dost Muhammad Khan's visit to Calcutta was far more effective in terms of winning over the future ruler of Afghanistan than the costly invasion of his country. For the first time a Durrani monarch saw for himself the extent of Britain's technological and industrial achievements and the economic and military might of its Empire. He also learnt a great deal about the English themselves, their alien civilization and religion. It was undoubtedly this experience that helped to reinforce Dost Muhammad Khan's belief that Afghanistan's survival depended on an alliance with Britain, for it was the only power capable of guaranteeing his country's frontiers against invasion by Persia or Russia.

Dost Muhammad Khan's return to Afghanistan and consolidation of his authority

Even so, Dost Muhammad Khan's time in India would have had little impact on Afghanistan's future political development if Lord Ellenborough had not decided to allow the Amir and all other exiles to return to their country without any preconditions. This was a risky strategy given that the Amir's son, Akbar Khan, had been instrumental in Macnaghten's assassination and the massacre of British and Indian troops. After all, Dost Muhammad Khan could have decided to make the most of Britain's unpopularity to renew his claim on Peshawar or invade the Punjab, especially now that in the wake of Ranjit Singh's death his kingdom had been torn apart by civil war.

Dost Muhammad Khan, however, had too much on his plate internally to risk another war with the Sikhs and anyway, two years after his return to Kabul, the British lost patience with the chaotic situation in the Punjab and sent in the army. Following a series of heavy defeats in March 1846, Maharaja Duleep Singh signed a treaty that included the payment of a heavy war indemnity and ceded Jullundar Duaba to the British. Dost Muhammad Khan must have watched the destruction of Sikh power with a great deal of satisfaction for it now no longer posed a threat to his kingdom and indirectly Britain had strengthened his own hand. Free from the threat of invasion the Amir was now able to pursue his own expansionist plans.

Dost Muhammad Khan's first priority on returning to Afghanistan was to assert his authority over a country devastated by war. Kabul was in ruins, the result of both internecine fighting and the destruction caused by the Army of Retribution. As for the rich agricultural regions of Koh Daman and Tagab, they had been devastated by Sale's scorched-earth policy. Trade, too, was at a standstill and most of the Hindu *baniya*s had fled to India, taking their wealth with them. The country was suffering from major shortages of food and fodder since most of the country's reserves had been consumed by the Army of the Indus, while the mortality rate among Afghans as a consequence of the war, both directly and indirectly, was far higher than anything the British had suffered. The use of grapeshot left many thousands more maimed for life and unable to support their families. To add to the misery, thousands of civilians had been internally displaced and many had lost everything they possessed. Such material losses had a severe impact on agricultural output as well as state revenues.

Perhaps even more destructive was the socio-political impact of the invasion. The mainly Pushtun south turned back in on itself and the power of radical and xenophobic *pirs* and *'ulama'* was reinforced. All trust in British diplomacy had evaporated and the bitter memories of Burnes's and Macnaghten's missions and intrigues and broken promises led to successive governments refusing to allow any British envoy or representative to reside in Afghanistan. This xenophobia, however, was not just an Afghan phenomenon. The deaths of Burnes and Macnaghten and the massacres and mutilation of the dead and dying gave rise to the British Imperial perception of the 'barbarity' of all Afghans, most famously 'celebrated' in the poetry of Rudyard Kipling, such as his 'The Young British Soldier':

> When you're wounded and left on Afghanistan's plains,
> And the women come out to cut up what remains,
> Jest roll to your rifle and blow out your brains
> An' go to your Gawd like a soldier.

At least from Dost Muhammad Khan's point of view Kabul was no longer a battlefield since Akbar Khan, backed by his father-in-law Muhammad Shah Babakr Khel, controlled the Bala Hisar and most of the capital. To celebrate his father's return and his resumption of the Amirship, Akbar Khan ordered the city illuminated for seven days and tribal and religious leaders were ordered to come to the capital and pledge their allegiance. Dost Muhammad Khan, in an attempt to conciliate rival factions, pardoned those who had fought against Akbar Khan or who had aided the British and appointed some of them to his inner council, included Nawab Jabbar Khan, Khan Shirin Khan Jawanshir, Hafizji and Sher Muhammad Khan Bamizai. After the British annexation of Peshawar, Dost Muhammad even gave Sultan Muhammad Khan and Pir Muhammad Khan, the last of the Peshawar *sardars*, seats in this inner cabinet. One individual who was not included in the amnesty was 'Amin Allah Khan Logari. Despite his advanced years, he spent the rest of his days in prison.

As for Akbar Khan, he was in such a powerful position that Dost Muhammad Khan had to concede to his demand that he be both *wazir* and the heir apparent, despite not being the Amir's eldest son (see Chart 4). Akbar Khan's uterine brothers, Ghulam Haidar Khan, Sher 'Ali Khan, Muhammad 'Amin Khan and Muhammad Sharif Khan, were also appointed to the highest offices of state, a decision that was not welcomed by the Amir's firstborn, Muhammad Afzal Khan, and his full brother, Muhammad 'Azam Khan. Their resentment simmered away all through Dost Muhammad Khan's reign and would eventually lead to another civil war. The Amir was less tolerant of the Kandahar *sardars*. After the withdrawal of General Nott, Kohan Dil Khan had reoccupied the city, which became a safe haven for Muhammadzai *sardar*s opposed to Dost Muhammad Khan and his family. A year or so after the Amir returned to Kabul, Kohan Dil Khan marched on the capital in an attempt to depose his half-brother, but after an inconclusive encounter near Ghazni, Kohan Dil Khan pledged his allegiance to Dost Muhammad Khan on condition he remained as the autonomous governor of Kandahar.

Dost Muhammad made it his priority to establish a more professional army and to rely less on unreliable tribal levies and *ghulam*s, a conviction strengthened by his experience of fighting the British and Indian army as well as his time in India. Wazir Akbar Khan and his brothers were required to raise and equip five regiments, totalling some 4,000 men, which became the core of a nascent national army. Many of the troops had previously belonged to the British-trained Janbaz and Hazarbashi regiments, wore European-style uniforms and were armed with muskets pillaged from, or surrendered by, the Army of the Indus. The army's munitions also included several British artillery pieces, including siege guns, and a vast store of ammunition, armaments that helped to swing the military balance in the Amir's favour.

Despite all this military equipment, the army's first campaign was a disaster. *Sardar*s Afzal Khan and Akbar Khan were sent into the Kunar to subdue the Khan of Bajur, only to abandon the campaign in the face of fierce resistance. Dost Muhammad Khan had better success with his next project, the subjugation of Bamiyan and the eastern Hazarajat. This time Akram Khan was put in charge of operations and within a matter of months the *amir*s of Behsud, Deh Zangi, Dai Kundi and Bamiyan had acknowledged the Amir's suzerainty. When Akram Khan returned to Kabul, he was laden with booty as well as a large sum of cash. In 1846, however, the Amir's attempt to impose his authority in Kohistan and raise new taxes led the region to rebel under the leadership of Ma'az Allah Khan, or Mazu Khan, who had given Dost Muhammad Khan so much trouble during his first reign, and Sahibzada Janan and Sahibzada Fath, probably leaders of the Sayyid clan. When Nawab Jabbar Khan and his Ghilzais were sent against them he was defeated, so Wazir Akbar Khan and Sher 'Ali Khan were dispatched with three of the new regiments and crushed the revolt. Mazu Khan and Sahibzada Janan died in battle, but Sahibzada Fath was captured and sentenced to be crushed to death by an elephant.

By the fourth year of his second reign, Dost Muhammad Khan's hold on power had been greatly increased, only for tragedy to strike. In September 1847 an outbreak of cholera led to the deaths of hundreds of people in

A typical house in the lower Kunar valley. The Safis and Mohmands, who are the dominant populations here, frequently caused problems for central government.

Kabul, forcing Dost Muhammad Khan and his court to flee to Chahar Asiyab, but despite this Wazir Akbar Khan succumbed to the plague. He was in his early thirties and in accordance with his last will and testament his body was sent for burial to the shrine of Shah-i Mardan in Mazar-i Sharif, a decision that led to rumours concerning Dost Muhammad Khan's ambitions to reassert his authority over this independent region. It was a fear that would soon prove to be justified.

Following Akbar Khan's death, the Amir decided it was time to break the power of Akbar Khan's father-in-law, Muhammad Shah Khan, head of the Babakr Khel Ghilzais. Muhammad Shah had played a major role in the sieges of the Kabul cantonment and Jalalabad and subsequently assisted Akbar Khan to take control of Kabul and the Bala Hisar. However, his very power was a threat and now that Akbar Khan was no longer alive to protect him, Dost Muhammad Khan set out to curtail it.

Muhammad Shah, informed by sympathizers of the Amir's intentions, fled to his stronghold of Badiabad in Laghman, while the Jabbar Khel raided caravans on the Kabul–Jalalabad road. Dost Muhammad Khan set out for Nangahar to supervise operations in Laghmanat in person, and after pacifying the Jabbar Khel by restoring state payments for safe passage, the Amir marched up the Alishang river. It took nearly two years before Badiabad fell, only for Muhammad Shah to retreat into the high mountainous region of what was then known as Kafiristan, from where he raided the plains of Nangahar and fomented revolts in Tagab, Nijrab, Gulbahar and Parwan. In 1855 Muhammad Shah Khan even captured Dost Muhammad's nephew, Shah Muhammad Khan, who was released only after the payment of a large ransom. The Babakr chief finally died, in mysterious circumstances, in early 1857, but the revolt continued to simmer away until the end of Dost Muhammad Khan's reign.[1]

In April 1848 Britain went to war with the Sikhs for a second time, whereupon Chattar Singh, the governor of Hazara, appealed to the Amir for assistance, offering to return Peshawar and the Derajat (that is Dera Isma'il Khan and Dera Ghazi Khan), to Durrani sovereignty. It was an offer Dost Muhammad Khan could not refuse and he set out for Peshawar at the head of 5,000 troops. After successfully securing the defection of the Pushtun garrison in Attock, Dost Muhammad Khan realized, too late, that he had backed the wrong horse. On 13 February 1849 British forces routed the Sikhs at the Battle of Gujarat, and when a month later Chattar Singh surrendered unconditionally, Dost Muhammad Khan beat a hasty retreat to Jalalabad.

In the wake of this victory, Britain annexed the entire Sikh kingdom, including the Punjab and Peshawar. News that the British army had reached the Khyber Pass caused panic in the Afghan capital. Fearing another invasion, Dost Muhammad Khan appealed to the Mir Wali of Khulm to provide him with sanctuary in the event that British forces once more occupied Kabul. However, by this time the long-standing alliance between the Durrani monarchy and the ruler of Khulm had broken down and the Amir was told in no uncertain terms that he was not welcome. Fortunately, Britain had no wish to risk another bloody nose in Afghanistan and they were content with the fertile Peshawar plains and controlling access through the Khyber Pass. This unexpected reprieve meant that Dost Muhammad Khan was now free to pursue his own imperial ambition, the conquest of Balkh.

The conquest of the *wilayat* of Balkh

By 1849 the situation north of the Hindu Kush was a matter of grave concern to the Amir. In early 1844, when the Mir Wali came to Kabul to reaffirm his alliance with the Amir, he brought disturbing news. Wazir Yar Muhammad Khan, who had taken control of Herat following the death of Shah Kamran, had defeated and broken up the powerful Sunni Hazaras of Qal'a-yi Nau and was preparing to invade the Chahar Wilayat. To this end, he had signed a treaty with Nasr Allah Khan of Bukhara who had agreed to

The Timurid shrine of Khwaja Abu Nasr Parsa (d. 1460), Balkh. Up until Amir Dost Muhammad Khan's annexation of the region in the mid-19th century the *wilayat* of Balkh had been under the sovereignty of the Khan of Bukhara. Khwaja Parsa was a *pir* of a Central Asian sub-order of Naqshbandiyya Sufism.

assist Yar Muhammad Khan in return for recognition of Bukharan sovereignty over all territory from Aqcha to Qataghan. Even more alarming was the claim by the Mir Wali that once Balkh had fallen, the two allies planned to march on Kabul, depose Dost Muhammad Khan and place Yar Muhammad Khan on the Durrani throne.[2]

Dost Muhammad Khan took this threat seriously and told the Mir Wali to pre-empt such a move by occupying Balkh in the Amir's name. The Mir Wali, however, was not prepared to risk a war with Herat and Bukhara and refused. It appears the Mir Wali then appealed to Dost Muhammad for military assistance but the Amir demanded as a precondition that an Afghan *hakim* reside in Khulm. Since this impinged on the Mir Wali's traditional autonomy, he rejected this demand as well, whereupon the relationship between Khulm and the Amir broke down. When he was eventually allowed to return to Khulm, the Mir Wali threw off the Durrani yoke and ordered the name of the Khan of Bukhara to be read in the *khutba*, an action that provided the excuse Dost Muhammad Khan sought to invade Balkh.

By the mid-1840s the *wilayat* of Balkh was in turmoil, beset by dynastic wars, a cholera epidemic and plagues of locusts. The economic situation was so dire that families were selling their children into slavery in order to feed themselves. The Chahar Wilayat was being torn apart by sibling rivalry in the wake of the deaths of Zu'l-fiqar Khan, *beglar begi* of Sar-i Pul, Mizrab Khan, *wali* of Maimana, and Shah Wali Khan, *hakim* of Andkhui. As rival claimants in these Uzbek *amirates* fought each other for supremacy, they sought military support from their neighbours, including Yar Muhammad in Herat and the Khan of Bukhara. When Ghazanfar Khan of Andkhui appealed for Bukharan assistance against his rival, Shah Wali Beg, Nasr Allah Khan passed him over to the Mir Wali, who joined forces with Ishan Uraq and Ishan Sudur (the Bukharan governors of Balkh and Aqcha), Shuja' al-Din, *mutawalli* of Mazar-i Sharif, and Mahmud Khan, the new *beglar begi* of Sar-i Pul. Together they subdued Hakim Khan of Shibarghan and reinstated Ghazanfar Khan, but as soon as the Mir Wali withdrew, Shah Wali Khan retook Andkhui, backed by Hukumat Khan, *wali* of Maimana, and Hakim Khan of Shibarghan.

Hukumat Khan in Maimana then appealed to Yar Muhammad Khan for military aid to depose his rival and half-brother, Sher Muhammad Khan, an appeal that provided the justification for Yar Muhammad Khan to invade. He marched on Maimana with an army of around 10,000 men, forced Sher Muhammad Khan to flee for his life and reinstated Hukumat Khan as *wali*. Ghazanfar Khan then petitioned Yar Muhammad Khan and Hukumat Khan to help him depose Shah Wali Khan, to which they agreed. Andkhui fell after a brief siege and was pillaged by the Herati troops, who slaughtered the settlement's Turkman population.

Following this victory, Yar Muhammad Khan marched on Balkh but its garrison refused to surrender. As winter was already setting in and with supplies running low, Yar Muhammad decided not to risk besieging the citadel and ordered his troops to return to Herat. Many of his soldiers, however, perished from starvation and exposure as they crossed the snowbound passes of the Murghab watershed. Despite this setback, in the following year, 1849, Yar Muhammad marched again on Maimana, but Hukumat Khan had had enough of the Heratis' depravations and refused to allow Yar Muhammad to enter his capital. Yar Muhammad Khan besieged Maimana for the next eleven months but eventually had to admit defeat and return to Herat. His rampage through the Chahar

Wilayat in the previous year, however, had weakened the ability of the rulers of Balkh and the Chahar Wilayat to resist an even more powerful and determined enemy.

While Yar Muhammad Khan attempted in vain to subdue Maimana, Muhammad Akram Khan and Ghulam Haidar Khan assembled a large army in Bamiyan. In the summer of 1849 they marched north, forcing the *amir*s of Saighan, Ajar, Kahmard and Darra-yi Suf to accept Durrani suzerainty. As the *sardar*s advanced on Doshi, the Mir Wali fled to Bukhara and by early 1850 Mazar-i Sharif and Balkh were in Afghan hands. Akram Khan then besieged Aqcha and when the fortress was taken by storm, its defenders were slaughtered and the town plundered. Ishan Uruq, Ishan Sudur and Mahmud Khan of Sar-i Pul were captured and imprisoned, though Mahmud Khan was later released. In the autumn of 1852 Akram Khan defeated both the Mir Wali and the Mir Ataliq of Qataghan, but during this campaign he caught pneumonia and died. In his place, Dost Muhammad Khan appointed his next eldest son, Muhammad Afzal Khan, as his heir apparent and military governor of Balkh.

Even though the Afghan army had secured control of Balkh and the eastern marches of Turkistan, the occupation proved to be a protracted and bloody affair. For the next forty years Durrani domination of the *wilayat* was bitterly contested by the predominantly Turco-Tajik population, who resented living under what they regarded as foreign occupation. Frequent rebellions were brutally suppressed and after each revolt the powers of the indigenous Uzbek *amir*s were further eroded and eventually swept aside. Another source of resentment was the forcible conscription of local labour for public works and the army, as well as a new and swingeing tax regime. A comparison between the Chinggisid and Afghan taxation system in Maimana dating from the mid-1880s shows that tax increases imposed under Muhammadzai rule were equivalent to a hike of between 100 and 300 per cent. In addition, many commodities that had previously been exempt were subject to state tax.[3] The burden of taxation drove many small landholders and labourers into abject poverty, while much of the wealth of the region went to constructing military cantonments, paying the army or disappeared into the pockets of Kabul's ruling elite. Hyperinflation and a series of natural disasters, including a devastating earthquake, merely added to the misery and depravation.

One of Afzal Khan's first actions as governor of Balkh was to move his capital to the military cantonment at Takhtapul, between Balkh and Mazar, which was large enough to house most of the northern army and which was deliberately located well away from the main centres of population.

As a devotee of the shrine of Shah-i Mardan, the move to Takhtapul meant Afzal Khan was able to pay a daily pilgrimage to Mazar-i Sharif and eventually this town became the administrative capital of the province. The peri-urban areas around Takhtapul, Balkh and Mazar soon became home to thousands of Pushtun migrants and colonists from the south as well as retired soldiers, who were gifted land in the fertile plains that, more often than not, had been confiscated from local Uzbeks.

The Anglo-Afghan Treaties and the frontiers of Greater Afghanistan

Britain had little interest in Dost Muhammad Khan's invasion of Balkh and the Mir Wali's appeal to British officials to ask them to intervene to prevent the annexation fell on deaf ears. In Britain's view, the conquest of Balkh was an internal matter and, anyway, Britain had its hands full with the pacification of the Punjab and had no wish to antagonize the Amir. Britain's main concern north of the Hindu Kush was the resumption of Russian military expansion into the Central Asian Khanates. A year before Wazir Akbar Khan's invasion of Balkh, Russian forces had occupied Aralsk on the Syr Darya, then in March 1854 Britain went to war with Russia in the Crimea to prevent the Black Sea becoming a Russian lake. The Crimean War did not have any direct impact on Afghanistan and the Central Asian situation, but Dost Muhammad Khan did attempt to exploit the conflict to his advantage. When the Mir Wali crossed the Amu Darya in the winter of 1854 at the head of a largely Bukharan army, the Amir appealed to the Governor General for military and financial assistance, claiming that Persia and Russia were behind the invasion.

The Crimean War also resurrected the moribund debate about the Russian threat to India and Afghanistan's strategic position in the wake of the fall of the Sikh Empire. Herbert Edwardes, Deputy Resident of the Punjab, argued that Britain should formally recognize Dost Muhammad Khan as Amir and negotiate a treaty of friendship between the two powers, thus tying him to Britain's strategic interests and turning Afghanistan into the new buffer state to replace the Sikh kingdom. In Edwardes's view, Dost Muhammad Khan's annexation of Balkh was a positive step for 'the more the Affghans take the less there will be for either Russia or Persia'.

His view eventually prevailed in Calcutta despite opposition from his immediate superior, Henry Lawrence. Lord Dalhousie, the Governor General from 1848 to 1856, wrote to the Amir suggesting a meeting to discuss putting Anglo-Afghan relations on a formal footing and in February 1855 Dost Muhammad Khan sent his son Haidar Khan to Peshawar to meet

British officials. Predictably, Haidar Khan wanted to discuss the Durrani claim to Peshawar, but when Edwardes told him that British sovereignty over the region was not negotiable, the issue was dropped. Haidar Khan's attempts to secure British recognition of the Amir's claim to Herat also failed, but when it came to the *wilayat* of Balkh, Britain and Afghanistan were of one mind, for neither party wanted to see Uzbek supremacy restored. To support the Afghan case for sovereignty over Balkh, Edwardes downplayed reports by a secret agent about the discontent at Durrani rule among the indigenous population and the oppressive nature of Afzal Khan's administration.[4]

The deliberations concluded with a landmark treaty signed on 30 March 1855 under the terms of which Britain recognized Dost Muhammad as king of Afghanistan with the treaty formally referring to him as 'His Highness'. The disappointment over the loss of Peshawar was also mitigated by Britain's implicit acceptance of Durrani sovereignty over Balkh, a timely recognition since at the time a Bukharan army had crossed the Amu Darya in support of yet another revolt in the Chahar Wilayat. Dost Muhammad Khan exploited the propaganda value of this treaty by informing the Uzbek rebels and Nasr Allah Khan of Bukhara that Britain had recognized the Amu Darya as Afghanistan's northern frontier and disingenuously claimed the Governor General might even provide military assistance for an attack on Bukhara itself.

The Anglo-Afghan Treaty encouraged the Amir to challenge his rival *sardar*s in Kandahar. Shortly after it was signed Kohan Dil Khan died, precipitating a power struggle between Rahim Dil Khan, the last surviving Dil brother, and Kohan Dil's son Siddiq Khan. Kandahar descended into chaos and when the religious establishment failed to negotiate a settlement, both factions appealed to Dost Muhammad Khan, who sent Sher 'Ali Khan to Kandahar to mediate. However, Sher 'Ali Khan took advantage of the opportunity to infiltrate his own armed retainers into Kandahar. The Amir arrived with a substantial army in November 1855 and was admitted after claiming he had come to perform the *fatiha* prayers for his dead half-brother. Once inside the town, the Amir's troops put on a show of force and the following day Dost Muhammad Khan curtly informed the Dil family he was now in charge and forced them to hand over the keys of the city gates.

Following this coup, the Amir imposed a new fiscal regime on the province, reducing the *jagir*s of powerful chiefs and demanding revenues from estates that were previously tax exempt. Dost Muhammad Khan then wrote to Dalhousie requesting that Kandahar be inserted into the treaty, but the Governor General replied that such a change was not legally possible. However, he reassured the Amir that he would interpret the terms of the treaty to include 'whatever territories may be in the Ameer's possession', provided he upheld its other stipulations.[5] In effect, Dalhousie gave Dost Muhammad Khan carte blanche to annex other regions including, by implication, Herat.

Dalhousie's liberal interpretation of the Anglo-Afghan Treaty marked a shift in British policy in respect of Herat that was due in part to the death of Yar Muhammad Khan, which had taken place shortly before the fall of Kandahar. Yar Muhammad Khan was succeeded by his son Sayyid Muhammad Khan, but when he showed signs of mental instability he was killed in a *coup d'état* led by Shahzada Muhammad Yusuf, son of Hajji Firoz al-Din, the former Saddozai ruler of Herat. Shahzada Yusuf then proceeded to remove the name of the Shah of Persia from the *khutba*, and in response a Persian army was sent to besiege the city. Eventually Firoz al-Din's *wazir*, 'Isa Khan, handed the unfortunate prince over to the Persian commander and he was sent to Tehran for execution. 'Isa Khan then promptly reneged on his promise to surrender Herat and the siege dragged on for another six months. Finally in October 1856 the Persian army took Herat by storm, put 'Isa Khan to death and replaced him with Sultan Ahmad Khan, son of Sardar Muhammad 'Azim Khan.

The siege of Herat brought Persia into conflict with Britain yet again, for Britain suspected that Russia had incited the attack. When a British naval expedition occupied the key port of Bushire, Shah Nasir al-Din Qajar capitulated and in March 1857 a new Anglo-Persian Treaty was signed. Under its terms all Persian forces were to be withdrawn unconditionally from Herat and Ghuriyan, and the Shah formally recognized Herat and Afghanistan as independent, sovereign states. A British officer, Major Taylor, was sent to Herat to ensure the terms of the treaty were upheld, while in the city he established a relief programme to alleviate the suffering of hundreds of Mashhadi Jews, who had fled to Herat after the Shah ordered they either convert to Islam or be put to death.

In response to the siege of Herat and another Bukharan incursion into the Chahar Wilayat, the Governor General gifted Dost Muhammad Khan 4,000 muskets, together with ammunition and gunpowder, and five *lakh* rupees. He also began discussions about a second, more detailed, treaty. Dost Muhammad Khan was more than happy to accept the weapons, cash and a treaty that would strengthen his own position and legitimacy. The Anglo-Afghan Treaty of January 1857 was indeed markedly more favourable to the Amir, for the preamble specifically referred to Balkh and Kandahar as being part of the Amir's kingdom and committed Britain 'to aid Ameer Dost Mohummad Khan to defend and maintain his present possessions in Balkh, Cabool and Candahar against Persia'. The Amir received additional military supplies and one *lakh* rupees per month for the duration of the Persian siege of Herat. In return, Dost Muhammad Khan agreed to follow British policy in respect of Persia and Russia and allow a native news writer, or *wakil*, to reside in Kabul. A few months later a military mission led by Major Lumsden arrived in Kandahar to oversee the disbursement of military aid.[6] Between August 1856 and October 1858 the Indian government paid Dost Muhammad Khan a total of 20.6 *lakh* rupees, the equivalent of more than a quarter of a million pounds sterling, and supplied him with an additional 4,000 muskets and ammunition free of charge. The guns and cash, however, were used mainly to put down another revolt in the Chahar Wilayat and consolidate the Amir's control over the *wilayat* of Balkh.

The signing of the Second Anglo-Afghan Treaty could not have been timelier as far as Britain was concerned. The day after it was signed there was an arson attack in Calcutta, followed a month later by the mutiny of the Bengal Infantry. The Indian Mutiny, or the First War of Independence as it is now officially designated by the Indian government, was superficially caused by the issuing of musket cartridges that were thought to have been smeared with the fat of pigs or cows. The underlying causes of the revolt, however, were far more complex. The revolt quickly spread throughout the Indian army and received support from rulers and leaders who the British had displaced.

As the mutineers rampaged through northern India, Dost Muhammad Khan came under considerable pressure from individuals within his own administration and Nasr Allah Khan of Bukhara to abrogate the Anglo-Afghan treaties, lead a *jihad* against the British and reconquer Peshawar. Nasr Allah Khan even offered to recognize Afghan sovereignty over Balkh if the Amir joined the Holy War. The Amir's second eldest son, Muhammad 'Azam Khan, along with several other members of his extended family supported the *jihad* and were backed by the Amir's chief religious adviser, Hafizji, and his powerful Islamist allies in Kabul and Kohistan. After a long and acrimonious debate, Dost Muhammad Khan judged that he had more to lose than gain from breaking the treaties and attacking Peshawar. He knew if the British crushed the uprising it would not just be the end of his reign but of his dynasty and even lead to the dismemberment of Afghanistan. The Amir therefore rejected the Bukharan proposal and dismissed the ambassador.

In his reply to the Khan of Bukhara, Dost Muhammad Khan pointed out that when he had gone to Bukhara to plead for assistance against the British invasion, the Khan not only refused to help, but treated him and his sons like prisoners. Dost Muhammad Khan then compared this treatment with the kindness and honour accorded to him in exile in India. 'I have not the slightest concern about the friendship or enmity of any foreign power,' he concluded, 'feeling assured of the British . . . What is it to me if Russia, Persia and Bokhara are my enemies on account of my friendship with England?'[7] When Henry Lawrence, the British Resident in Lahore, heard of the Amir's decision, he greeted the news as a godsend: 'it is clear that, if we had been on bad terms just now with Kabul, we should have lost, first Peshawar and then the Punjab and all India would have reeled under the blow'.[8] The news from Kabul meant that Lawrence was able to withdraw all but a token force from the Punjab and send them to suppress the Sepoy uprising.

Many of the British officers who played a major part in the suppression of the Mutiny were from the Punjab and the Northwestern Frontier and had had their first campaign experience as junior officers in the First Afghan War, where they had learnt many hard lessons. Unlike the superannuated veterans of the Napoleonic Wars who had bungled that war, this new breed of Frontiersmen's response to the Mutiny was swift, decisive and often brutal. Not only did they succeed in preventing any major uprising in the Punjab, they contributed significantly to the defeat of the Indian rebellion. Pushtun units such as the Multani Horse and the Mounted Police also played an important role in the defeat of the rebellion. The Afridis even handed over fugitive sepoys who claimed *nanawatai* to the authorities in Peshawar. In the wake of the Mutiny, India was placed under Crown rule with Queen, and later Empress, Victoria as head of state while a Viceroy replaced the old office of Governor General.

The conquest of Qataghan and Herat and the death of Amir Dost Muhammad Khan

While Britain fought for its Indian Empire, Dost Muhammad Khan set out to subjugate the Mir Ataliq of Qataghan, who had formed a military alliance with Bukhara and the fugitive Mir Wali of Khulm. The Mir Ataliq was sent an ultimatum to admit an Afghan *hakim* and to recite the *khutba* in the Amir's name. When these demands were rejected Afzal Khan assembled his forces in Khulm. The Mir Ataliq appealed to Bukhara, but although the Khan raged about the Amir's imperial ambitions and excoriated him for his refusal to invade India, Nasr Allah Khan was powerless to assist Qataghan, for he had his own problems with rebellions nearer to home. In the spring of 1859 Afzal Khan marched into southwestern Qataghan, where the predominantly Tajik population greeted him as a liberator, for Murad Beg had seized their lands and forced them to live in the *dasht*, or wastelands, and mosquito-infested marshes. When the stronghold of Dahan-i Ghuri fell after a protracted siege, the Mir Ataliq fled across the Amu Darya and by June 1859 Qunduz was in Afghan hands. Meanwhile a second column occupied Rustaq and the Mir of Badakhshan too accepted Afghan suzerainty. A year later Afzal Khan occupied Sar-i Pul, deposed Mahmud Khan and installed a Muhammadzai governor backed by a garrison. By the end of 1860 Maimana was the last independent Uzbek *amirate* left in the *wilayat* of Balkh.

In early 1862 Dost Muhammad Khan, by now in his seventieth year, set out to conquer Herat, arguably the greatest prize of all. Once again Britain viewed his campaign favourably because Persian and, more importantly, Russian ambitions would be more easily contained with Herat under direct rule from Kabul. Prior to his campaign, Dost Muhammad Khan wrote to Lord Canning, the Viceroy, reassuring him that his aim was to 'reunify' Afghanistan and that he had no intention of pushing Afghanistan's frontier further west than Ghuriyan. He then justified the Herat campaign by reminding the Viceroy that its ruler, Sultan Ahmad Khan, was implicated in a war crime, for he had been present at the murder of Macnaghten and

The tomb of Amir Dost Muhammad Khan in Guzargah, Herat. The Amir died a matter of days after he finally conquered Herat.

had done nothing to prevent his death. Vengeance, it seems, was at least one reason why Britain did not oppose Dost Muhammad Khan's annexation of Herat.[9] The fact that it had been the Amir's son who fired the shots that mortally wounded the British Envoy was conveniently forgotten. When a Russian envoy arrived in Herat and Sultan Ahmad Khan announced he planned to sign a treaty with Russia, Britain was even more willing to support the Amir's invasion.

In the late summer of 1862 the Amir occupied Farah and, after beating off a feeble attempt by Sultan Ahmad Khan to prevent his advance, his army surrounded Herat. On 27 May 1863, after an eight-month siege, Dost Muhammad Khan's troops stormed the walls, plundered the city and slaughtered its population. Sultan Ahmad Khan, though, did not live to see the fall of his city for he had died a few weeks before the final assault. Two weeks after this victory Dost Muhammad Khan too passed away and was buried in Guzargah, near the tomb of Khwaja 'Abd Allah Ansari.

The reigns of Dost Muhammad Khan: an appraisal

Dost Muhammad Khan must be reckoned as Afghanistan's luckiest ruler. Not only did he survive a series of assassination attempts and other challenges from within his extended family, he suffered heavy military defeats at the hands of both the Sikhs and the British, lost control of the Durrani winter capital of Peshawar, and was exiled to India. Yet after Britain's attempt to restore the Saddozai monarchy failed, he was freed and allowed to return to Kabul, while at the same time the empire of his old enemy, Ranjit Singh, was imploding. Britain's annexation of the Punjab in the wake of the Second Sikh War meant that Afghanistan became far more strategic as far as Britain's Defence of India policy was concerned. The outcome was two Anglo-Afghan treaties that, as well as providing the Amir with substantial military and financial assistance, gave his dynasty international legitimacy and legalized his conquests of Balkh, Kandahar and Herat. Against all odds, Dost Muhammad Khan had bounced back from one misfortune after another. By the end of his life he had pushed the frontiers of his kingdom up to the Amu Darya in the north and Ghuriyan in the west.

Internally, Dost Muhammad revolutionized local government. Instead of ruling through proxies – autonomous, hereditary rulers who paid the king a fixed amount of revenue or an annual *nazrana* in return for remaining in power – the Amir appointed his favourite sons as ministers and provincial governors, and while he had a council of advisers, all but token power was concentrated in his and his sons' hands. The shift to a central-ized autocracy was extended to the judicial system, with Dost Muhammad Khan reviving the tradition of public audiences where he adjudicated on complaints and acted as both judge and jury. To all intents and purposes, under Dost Muhammad Khan government became a family enterprise, with the country run more on the lines of an Arab sheikhdom than a European nation state, a situation that would be perpetuated until the fall of the Musahiban dynasty in 1978.

The civil war between Sher 'Ali Khan and Muhammad Afzal Khan

Dost Muhammad Khan had fathered dozens of children from his many wives and any hopes that there would be a peaceful transition of power on his death were soon dashed. Sher 'Ali Khan, the heir apparent, was recog-nized as Amir in Herat but his right to the throne was contested by his half-brother Afzal Khan, the Amir's eldest son, and Afzal's uterine brother Muhammad 'Azam Khan. The trouble began as soon as news of the Amir's death was announced, when the Khanabad garrison in Qataghan rebelled and declared support for 'Azam Khan. The Mir Ataliq of Qunduz and Mir Jahandar Khan of Badakhshan tried to exploit the conflict by attempting to regain control over Qunduz, only to be defeated by Afzal Khan's son 'Abd al-Rahman Khan.

As soon as Sher 'Ali Khan had completed the funeral rites for his father he set out for Kabul, leaving his fourteen-year-old son Ya'qub Khan in charge of Herat. Afzal Khan's younger brother, 'Azam Khan, however, made excuses for not accompanying the Amir and, once he was on the road to Kandahar, headed for Kabul by the shorter, Hazarajat route, hoping to reach the capital before his half-brother and seize control. However, when he heard that Kabul was well defended by Muhammad 'Ali Khan, Sher 'Ali's eldest son, 'Azam Khan went instead to the Logar and raised an army, but was defeated and fled to the protection of his mother's tribe in Khost. 'Azam Khan then sent envoys to ask Sher 'Ali Khan's forgiveness. When the Amir demanded he come in person to pledge his allegiance and reside in Kabul, he refused. Instead he sent his son Sarwar Khan as a hostage for his good behaviour, only for the Amir's spies to discover, in the nick of time, that Sarwar Khan was plotting to assassinate him.

Afzal Khan, governor of Balkh, also refused to come in person to Kabul and pledge his allegiance, but he did order Sher 'Ali Khan's name to be read in the *khutba* and sent gifts and letters expressing his loyalty. However, in secret he and his brother conspired to seize the throne. In the spring of 1864

The Kahmard valley north of Bamiyan straddled an important military and trade route linking Kabul with Balkh. The Ajar valley at the head of the valley was once the hunting grounds of King Zahir Shah.

Amir Sher 'Ali Khan's spies intercepted correspondence between the two brothers that implicated them in a conspiracy to depose him, and several individuals were arrested. When further compromising correspondence was discovered during searches of their homes, the Amir sent an army into Khost and 'Azam Khan fled across the frontier into India. In retaliation, Afzal Khan had himself declared Amir in Mazar-i Sharif and assembled his forces at Khanabad, preparatory to marching on Kabul.

In the spring of 1864 Sher 'Ali Khan and Muhammad 'Ali Khan marched north to confront Afzal Khan. Before he left Kabul, the Amir released Ishan Sudur and Ishan Uruq, the former Bukharan governors of Balkh and Aqcha, respectively, and sent them to Maimana after they agreed to raise support for the Amir in the Chahar Wilayat in return for a pledge to restore them to the governorship of Aqcha. In mid-May 1864 the armies of Muhammad 'Ali Khan and Afzal Khan came face-to-face at Bajgah in the Kahmard valley. Under cover of night Muhammad 'Ali's men surmounted the heights of the steep-sided valley and literally caught Afzal Khan's guards napping. When dawn broke, they fired into the enemy camp below, causing panic, and as they turned and fled Muhammad 'Ali opened fire with grapeshot. Those who escaped the slaughter fled to Duab, but when Sher 'Ali Khan ordered his troops to pursue the enemy, other *sardars* urged the Amir to seek reconciliation rather than tear the kingdom apart with civil war. Sher

'Ali agreed and sent Afzal Khan a Qur'an sealed with the royal seal, with a letter inscribed on the flyleaf offering to resolve their differences.

On the basis of the reassurance of safe conduct, and despite the warnings of his son 'Abd al-Rahman Khan, Afzal Khan went to Sher 'Ali Khan's camp and was received with the honour due to his rank. Reassured by this reception, Afzal Khan ordered 'Abd al-Rahman Khan to return to Takhtapul while he and Sher 'Ali travelled to Tashqurghan to discuss terms of peace. The talks did not progress well, for Afzal Khan insisted that Sher 'Ali Khan honour their father's dying wish and allow him to remain governor of Balkh and that 'Azam Khan be reinstated as governor of Khost and Khurram. Sher 'Ali Khan was not prepared to let his rivals have this degree of power but eventually they agreed a compromise. Afzal Khan would remain governor of Balkh, but Maimana would be placed under the jurisdiction of Herat, while Qataghan and Badakhshan would be governed by an appointee of the Amir. Afzal Khan reluctantly agreed to the deal and in August 1863 the two siblings made a pilgrimage to Mazar-i Sharif, where they swore on the tomb of Hazrat 'Ali to uphold their agreement.

Matters may well have been resolved had not 'Abd al-Rahman Khan refused to pay his respects to Muhammad 'Ali Khan, the heir apparent, claiming that since he was superior in both age and rank, Muhammad 'Ali ought to attend on him. The *sardar* then refused to go in person to swear allegiance to the Amir. When Afzal Khan failed to condemn his son's actions, Sher 'Ali Khan suspected he was using 'Abd al-Rahman Khan as a proxy to maintain his claim to the throne. After the Amir's spies intercepted letters from Afzal Khan to 'Abd al-Rahman Khan that implicated them in a plot to rebel, Afzal Khan was clapped in irons and 'Abd al-Rahman Khan was dismissed as commander of Takhtapul. Fearing imprisonment and even death, he fled across the Amu Darya to Bukhara.

Despite Afzal Khan plotting to overthrow the Amir, it was Sher 'Ali Khan who was blamed for violating his oath and many of his supporters deserted him. When the Amir returned to Kabul, yet another plot was uncovered and several conspirators were exiled to India while others fled to Kandahar where they joined forces with Muhammad 'Amin Khan, the Amir's uterine brother, who had also rebelled. In early June 1865 Sher 'Ali Khan and Muhammad 'Amin Khan fought a bloody battle at Kaj Baz, between Kandahar and Qalat-i Ghilzai, but although the Amir was victorious it came at a terrible cost, for both Muhammad 'Amin Khan and the Amir's son and heir, Muhammad 'Ali Khan, were slain.

Sher 'Ali Khan regarded these deaths as divine retribution for breaching his oath to Afzal Khan and when he reached Kandahar he abdicated.

For the next seven months Sher 'Ali Khan devoted himself to memorizing the Qur'an and mourned the death of his favourite son. Eventually his grief spiralled into depression and mental instability. On one occasion Sher 'Ali Khan jumped from a first-floor window into the garden's water-storage cistern and began searching frantically for his dead son. His servants dragged the unconscious ex-Amir from the water in the nick of time.

During the period of Sher 'Ali Khan's abdication government ground to a halt, allowing 'Azam Khan to seize the initiative. He returned to Khost, but finding little support for his rebellion, he set out for Badakhshan. Meanwhile 'Abd al-Rahman Khan crossed into the Chahar Wilayat and persuaded his uncle, Faiz Muhammad Khan, governor of Aqcha, to join him. Within a matter of weeks, the military commanders of Takhtapul, Sar-i Pul and Minglik had joined the rebellion, forcing Fath Muhammad Khan, Sher 'Ali's governor in Balkh, to flee to Kabul. 'Abd al-Rahman Khan followed in hot pursuit, taking Bamiyan without a fight and setting up camp in the mouth of the Ghurband, where the leaders of Nijrab, Tagab and Kohistan, including Hafizji and Mullah Mir Aftab, and the *malik* of Kabul's Deh Afghanan, came and pledged their allegiance.

The fall of Balkh and Bamiyan finally roused Sher 'Ali Khan out of his torpor. Having resumed the reins of government, he set out for Kabul, fearing that its governor, Wali Muhammad Khan, whose elder brother, Faiz Muhammad Khan, had already declared support for the Afzalids, was about to surrender the city. Fortunately Sher 'Ali's loyalists arrested Wali Muhammad Khan before he could change sides. Once in Kabul the Amir opened negotiations with 'Abd al-Rahman Khan and as a gesture of goodwill, he allowed Wali Muhammad Khan to leave for Ghurband, but he refused to release Afzal Khan or reinstate him as governor of Balkh. In retaliation 'Abd al-Rahman Khan marched on Kabul, which he occupied after a brief skirmish. Sher 'Ali retreated to Ghazni, but defeated 'Abd al-Rahman Khan in an encounter at Shah Gau, pushing him back to Sayyidabad. In a second battle a week later, however, 'Abd al-Rahman Khan was victorious and Sher 'Ali Khan fled to Kandahar. In May 1866 Afzal Khan was proclaimed Amir in Kabul.

The Amirships of Muhammad Afzal Khan and Muhammad 'Azam Khan

Afzal Khan's hold on power was as fragile as Sher 'Ali Khan's had been. Shortly after being declared Amir, Afzal Khan's nephew, Muhammad Rafiq Khan, and several other Muhammadzais were arrested after it was discovered he had written to Shahzada Shahpur, Shuja' al-Mulk's son, in Ludhiana, offering him the throne. Rafiq Khan was strangled by a silken cord, his body thrown over the walls of the Bala Hisar and left to be eaten by the dogs. Then Faiz Muhammad Khan, whom 'Abd al-Rahman Khan had appointed governor of Balkh, refused to swear allegiance to Afzal Khan and defeated an army sent against him.

Afzal Khan had greater success in the south. In January 1867 'Abd al-Rahman Khan took Kandahar and Sher 'Ali Khan fled to Herat. Hearing of Faiz Muhammad Khan's disaffection, Sher 'Ali decided to go to Balkh and join forces against the Pretender. As Sher 'Ali Khan marched through the Chahar Wilayat, all the Uzbek *amir*s from Bala Murghab to Badakhshan declared their support for him. When he reached Takhtapul, Sher 'Ali Khan called a grand assembly of Balkh's indigenous rulers and went with them to the shrine of Shah-i Mardan, where he pledged on the Qur'an to restore their right to self-rule in return for their support against the Muhammad Afzal Khan. He even swore that if he was victorious he would remit all taxes in the province for two years.

While Sher 'Ali Khan was consolidating his control in the north, a plague of cholera swept through Kabul and the Koh Daman, decimating Afzal Khan's army in Charikar and striking down the Amir himself. When Sher 'Ali heard that Afzal Khan was at death's door, he marched into the Panjshir across the high Anjuman Pass and set up camp in Bazarak, where *mullah*s and *malik*s from Kohistan and Tagab came and pledged their allegiance. Despite being on his deathbed, Afzal Khan ordered 'Abd al-Rahman Khan to confront the enemy. In early October 'Sher 'Ali Khan was defeated at Qal'a-yi Allahdad, near the modern settlement of Jabal Saraj,[10] and Faiz Muhammad Khan was slain when he was disembowelled by a ricocheting cannonball.

Qal'a-yi Allahdad ought to have been the decisive battle of the civil war, but the pendulum swung unexpectedly back in Sher 'Ali Khan's favour. On 7 October 1867, three days after this victory, Afzal Khan passed away and 'Abd al-Rahman returned to Kabul to lead the mourning rituals. On his arrival he was greeted with the unwelcome news that Afzal Khan had designated his brother, 'Azam Khan, as Amir, and a stand-off ensued between 'Abd al-Rahman Khan, who believed he ought to have become Amir, and his uncle. 'Abd al-Rahman Khan eventually reluctantly acknowledged 'Azam Khan's right to the succession but fearing his nephew planned to depose him, 'Azam Khan ordered him to march to Balkh and confront Sher 'Ali Khan. 'Abd al-Rahman obeyed the order, but only after an angry exchange of words.

The siege of Maimana

Following his defeat at Qal'a-yi Allahdad, Sher 'Ali Khan retired to Takhtapul where he decided to return to Herat, raise a new army and march on Kabul via Kandahar. The *amirs* of the Chahar Wilayat meanwhile were ordered to oppose 'Abd al-Rahman Khan's advance and hold out as long as possible and buy Sher 'Ali Khan enough time to take Kandahar. This was an extremely ambitious plan, but Sher 'Ali Khan gambled that 'Abd al-Rahman Khan would not set out for Balkh until the spring, for the snow had already fallen on the passes of the Hindu Kush. 'Abd al-Rahman Khan, however, surprised him and marched north immediately. Despite many of his men suffering from frostbite, in January 1868 he reached Aibak with his troops still battle ready.

Within a matter of weeks all the Uzbek *amirs* from Aqcha to Badakhshan had sworn fealty to 'Azam Khan,[11] but the *amirs* of the Chahar Wilayat refused to submit, forcing 'Abd al-Rahman Khan to march against them and so being drawn even further away from Kabul. His first obstacle was Minglik, a strong fortress on the old Balkh–Aqcha road and a citadel that was reputed to be impregnable. Its Uzbek defenders had sworn an oath to fight to the death, but the citadel's medieval construction was not strong enough to withstand the power of nineteenth-century artillery and siege guns. Following a four-hour bombardment, the main gate shattered and 'Abd al-Rahman Khan ordered his troops to fill the ditch with bales of straw and grass, which the defenders set alight. Despite this, storming parties were sent into the breaches where they were met with fierce resistance. When they finally broke into the citadel more than 1,000 defenders were slaughtered; casualties were also high on the Afghan side with some seven hundred men killed and many more wounded.

Ishan Sudur and his son Qara Sultan, along with Ahmad Khan, son of Ishan Uruq, were captured alive. Ishan Sudur and Ahmad Khan were condemned to be buried alive, but Qara Sultan was set free in order that he could tell the *amirs* of the Chahar Wilayat the fate that awaited them if they refused to submit. Instead of capitulating, however, the Uzbeks concentrated their forces in Maimana and only Mir Hakim Khan, *hakim* of Shibarghan, who had long been at odds with the other rulers of the Chahar Wilayat, tendered his submission. The alliance was sealed by the marriage of one of his daughters to 'Abd al-Rahman Khan.

'Abd al-Rahman Khan had no choice but to attack Maimana, even though his troops were on the verge of mutiny. Their wages were six months in arrears and they demanded 'Abd al-Rahman Khan pay all that was owed to them before they were once more sent into battle, so their families at least would have money to live on if they were killed. 'Abd al-Rahman Khan then weakened his army further by sending the Qataghan cavalry back to Qunduz for he suspected their loyalty. Since he did not have enough money to pay the troops or sufficient men to storm Maimana, which was strongly fortified, 'Abd al-Rahman Khan wrote to Amir 'Azam Khan requesting cash and reinforcements and called a halt until he received a reply. 'Azam Khan, however, refused his request, for the cash and troops were needed for the defence of Kabul. Indeed, 'Azam Khan ordered half of 'Abd al-Rahman Khan's remaining force to return to the Afghan capital, since Ya'qub Khan was marching on Girishk and threatening Kandahar. Yet despite weakening 'Abd al-Rahman Khan's fighting ability even further, 'Azam Khan insisted he subdue Maimana and attack Herat.

'Abd al-Rahman Khan set out for Maimana, but Husain Khan, the *wali* of Maimana, stalled his advance for a couple more weeks by sending his mother to the *sardar*'s camp and offering to pay one *lakh* of rupees if he refrained from attacking Maimana. When the cash failed to appear 'Abd al-Rahman Khan, by now in a state of profound anxiety and perplexity, marched on the city. He sent troops to storm the city walls, but they were ambushed by Turkman and Uzbek cavalry and forced to retreat. Unwilling to risk a second assault, 'Abd al-Rahman Khan placed the

The ruins of the Maimana citadel, a key town on Afghanistan's northwest frontier and once a major stopping point on the Balkh–Herat trade route. The fort was mostly pulled down in the 1940s as part of the redevelopment. In the 1970s it was the site of the local cinema and a tea house.

city under siege and ordered sappers to commence mining operations under the walls.

While the siege of Maimana dragged on, Kandahar fell to Ya'qub Khan. Amir 'Azam Khan sent a desperate message recalling 'Abd al-Rahman Khan to Kabul, but it was too late. 'Abd al-Rahman Khan, realizing that his only chance of saving his family's fortunes was to subdue Maimana as quickly as possible, march on Herat and attack Sher 'Ali. Khan ordered his troops to prepare for a second assault. Early on the morning of 17 May 1868 the mines were sprung and a storming party sent into the breach. The attackers met with stiff resistance from the defenders – even the women threw rocks down on them from the walls. After more than twelve hours they were still unable to take the town and were finally recalled. The following day Mir Husain sent Maimana's religious leaders to the *sardar*'s camp and agreed a face-saving deal, after which 'Abd al-Rahman Khan set out for Takhtapul with what was left of his shattered force.

As they marched back through the Chahar Wilayat, Turkman and Uzbek raiders swooped down, looting the baggage and killing the wounded and stragglers. By the time 'Abd al-Rahman Khan reached Takhtapul his troops were so exhausted that he ordered them into barracks to recuperate, and he himself fell seriously ill. Sher 'Ali Khan's nephew Isma'il Khan, who had accompanied 'Abd al-Rahman Khan, declared his support for his uncle, promptly deserted and headed for Kabul with his regiment. On 21 August 1868 the garrison in Kabul's Bala Hisar surrendered to Isma'il Khan after a brief siege and 'Azam Khan, who was in Ghazni at the time, fled north to Takhtapul.

A few weeks later Sher 'Ali Khan entered Kabul in triumph. 'Azam Khan and 'Abd al-Rahman Khan tried to raise another army in Wardak, but there was little support for their cause. In the winter of 1868 'Azam Khan was defeated at Shash Gau, near Ghazni, and he and his nephew fled to the Sistan and from there to Persia, where 'Azam Khan died. 'Abd al-Rahman Khan subsequently made his way to Samarkand, which was by this time under Russian rule, where he was joined by other Muhammadzais and supporters of the Afzalid cause.

Britain and the civil war in Afghanistan

The civil war of 1863–8 was a matter of considerable concern for British officials on a number of counts. In 1864 Russia had resumed its conquests of the Central Asian Khanates by occupying Kokand, and the following year Tashkent too fell. The newly conquered territories were designated

Samarkand, the tomb of Amir Timur Lang, or Tamurlaine. The Russian occupation of the city in 1868, which was followed shortly by the surrender of the Khan of Bukhara, marked the end of over half a millennium of Turco-Mongolian rule in the region.

as Russian Turkistan and Konstantin Petrovich von Kaufman (1818–1882), a general of Austrian extraction, became the territories' first Governor General. Kaufman continued the push to the Amu Darya and in 1865 took Jizakh, the gateway to Samarkand and Bukhara. Three years later, in the spring of 1868, Russian forces pushed deeper into Bukharan territory. Muzaffar Khan, who had succeeded his father Nasr Allah Khan in 1860, appealed to 'Abd al-Rahman Khan for military assistance but the *sardar* had his hands full with the siege of Maimana and turned down the request. Samarkand fell in May 1868 and Russian troops pursued the remnants of the Khan's army to the gates of Bukhara. A revolt in Samarkand, which was put down with great brutality, gave Muzaffar Khan a short stay of execution, but in mid-June Muzaffar Khan surrendered in order to spare Bukhara suffering the same fate as Samarkand. Muzaffar Khan remained as Khan, but Bukhara became a Russian Protectorate. The conquest of Bukhara meant that by the summer of 1868 Russia's Central Asia frontier had reached the Amu Darya and the northern border of Afghanistan.

The fall of Bukhara led to calls by British officials for a more interventionist policy in Afghanistan, Kalat and other frontier states, regurgitating many of the arguments used to formulate Ellenborough's Indus policy of the 1830s. By 1868, however, the Rubicon was not the Indus but the Amu Darya, or rather the Oxus, as Britain's classically educated officials anachronistically referred to it. The civil war in Afghanistan, it was argued, was an ideal opportunity for Russian interference, either by providing military assistance to a pro-Russian claimant to the throne or by outright annexation of Balkh on the grounds that it had formerly been part of the Khanate of Bukhara. This fear was exacerbated after 'Abd al-Rahman Khan and other Afzalids were given asylum in Samarkand, where Kaufman provided them with houses and pensions, openly consulted 'Abd al-Rahman Khan on Bukharan politics and even tried to persuade him to join the campaign against Muzaffar Khan.

The British government sought clarification from St Petersburg about Russian intentions in the region and received assurances that Russia regarded Afghanistan as being within the British sphere of influence and had no plans for invasion or annexation. This reassurance, however, was not as clear-cut as it seemed, for the Russian government's definition of Afghanistan was markedly different from the kingdom Britain had recognized in the Anglo-Afghan Treaties of 1855 and 1857. According to the Russian Foreign Ministry, Afghanistan was the Pushtun tribal belt of the Afghan–India frontier. As such, the kingdom did not include Balkh, Herat, the Hazarajat or even Kabul. Furthermore, since this Afghanistan included the Pushtun tribes on the Indian side of the frontier, it opened the door for Russian support of the Durrani dynasty's long-standing claims to sovereignty over all Pushtun tribal territory, as well as Kalat, Quetta and Peshawar.

The civil war also created complications in Anglo-Afghan relations. Lord Elgin, the Viceroy in 1863, recognized Sher 'Ali Khan as Amir but, in accordance with the policy of non-interference devised by Henry Lawrence, the first Resident and Commissioner of the Punjab, Britain did not provide military or financial assistance to any faction. There were problems with an influx of refugees into the Northwest Frontier and when 'Azam Khan fled to the Punjab he was closely watched, for he tried to recruit levies from the Pushtun tribes on the Indian side of the Frontier and had known ties with influential, anti-British *pirs*.

Henry Lawrence had died at the siege of Lucknow in 1857 but his younger brother, John Lawrence, survived the Mutiny and in 1864 he succeeded Lord Elgin as Viceroy. Shortly after his appointment Afzal Khan took Kabul and was declared Amir, whereupon Lawrence, in accordance with the policy of not siding with one faction in the civil war, recognized Afzal and his successor, 'Azam Khan, as Amir of Eastern Afghanistan. This decision angered Sher 'Ali Khan, who believed that, as the lawful heir of Dost Muhammad Khan, the Viceroy should recognize him as the only legitimate ruler of Afghanistan. It was only after Sher 'Ali Khan regained control of Kabul in the spring of 1868 that Lawrence accorded him recognition as Amir of all Afghanistan and, in a gesture of goodwill, sent a gift of twelve *lakh* rupees and 12,000 muskets. Shortly after the Russian conquest of Bukhara, and as one of his last acts as Viceroy, Lawrence invited Sher 'Ali Khan to India to discuss Anglo-Afghan relations, but by the time Sher 'Ali Khan arrived it was Lawrence's successor, Lord Mayo, who greeted him at Umballa (modern Ambala).

The Forward Policy and the Umballa Conference

From both the British and Afghan point of view, Lawrence's retirement came at an unfortunate time as far as Anglo-Afghan relations were concerned. During his years in the Punjab, he and his brother had developed a relationship of trust with Dost Muhammad Khan and the Anglo-Afghan treaties had mostly been due to the diplomacy of Henry Lawrence. Lord Mayo, on the other hand, was new to India and had no experience with dealings with Afghanistan or the tribes of India's Northwest Frontier. Lawrence's retirement also opened the door for advocates of a more interventionist approach to Afghanistan, known as the Forward Policy. In many ways the Forward Policy rehashed the Ellenborough Doctrine of the 1830s, which ultimately led to the First Anglo-Afghan War. Its advocates too were paranoid about Russian territorial acquisitions in Central Asia, which, they believed, threatened British power in India. To counteract such a scenario, they urged Britain to be more proactive in Afghanistan's internal affairs and bind the Amir to British interests through military aid and financial subsidies, as well as ensuring that the ruler in Kabul was pro-British. If the incumbent Amir became too friendly with Russia, interfered in tribal affairs or tried to stir up revolts on the Indian frontier, Britain should act unilaterally to protect its strategic interests. Such 'action' boiled down to the invasion, annexation and even dismemberment of Afghanistan.

This sea change in Britain's Afghanistan policy was enshrined in Sir Henry Rawlinson's 'Memorandum on the Frontiers of Affghanistan',[12] which was one of the key briefing papers in Lord Mayo's *Umballa Papers*. Rawlinson, a leading advocate of the Forward Policy, had been a junior political officer in Kandahar during the First Anglo-Afghan War and had advocated the Sikh annexation of Kabul and Jalalabad and the partition of Kandahar and Herat into two separate kingdoms. Thirty years later, Rawlinson was one of Britain's most senior Orientalists, known as the Father of Assyriology, as well as being a Member of Parliament with a seat on the London-based Council of India.

Rawlinson was convinced Russia did not intend to halt its military advances on the Amu Darya, but planned to secure political dominance in Persia and occupy Herat and Balkh as a precursor to an invasion of India. As was the case in the 1830s, Rawlinson identified Herat as the key to the defence of India and argued Britain must prevent the Russian occupation of that city at all costs, whether directly or by using Persia as a proxy. He recommended reviving the moribund Anglo-Persian alliance and pressuring Russia to formally agree a demarcation of Afghanistan's northern and northwestern frontier, a 'scientific frontier' that if violated would mean Britain would go to war with Russia in Asia and Europe. 'On no account', Rawlinson declared, must Russia be permitted to challenge the 'national dependency' of the Uzbek *amirates* of the *wilayat* of Balkh on the Amir of Afghanistan, and he criticized Lawrence for failing to provide financial and military aid to Sher 'Ali Khan. 'Interference in Afghanistan,' Rawlinson declared, 'has now become our duty.'[13] This 'interference' included negotiating a new treaty with Sher 'Ali Khan, which bound him to British interests and allowed Britain to control the country's foreign policy. A precondition of this new treaty, however, was that the Amir had to agree to the presence of a permanent British Resident in Kabul to both advise the Amir and keep an eye on Russian activities in Afghanistan and beyond the Amu Darya.

Lord Mayo, however, was not prepared to adopt such radical policies, although his successors would embrace Rawlinson's recommendations wholeheartedly. Instead Mayo's approach to the negotiations with Sher 'Ali Khan was to tread a fine line between pursuing neither 'extreme lines of absolute inaction' nor 'the worse alternative of meddling and interfering by subsidies and emissaries'. The 'safe course', he noted, lay in 'watchfulness, and friendly intercourse'.[14]

As for Sher 'Ali Khan, he accepted the invitation in the hope that his visit would bring him urgently needed financial and military assistance that would keep him in power, for though he had secured Kabul, the Afzalids were still at large in Samarkand and posed a serious threat to his control of what Rawlinson termed 'Afghan Turkistan'. Indeed, even as he made his way to India, Sardar Muhammad Ishaq Khan, Amir 'Azam Khan's son, backed by a force of Bukharan levies, had occupied Aqcha and, though he was eventually defeated, the Umballa Conference took place against a background of fear about the renewal of the civil war, possibly with Russian assistance. Sher 'Ali Khan was therefore equally anxious to secure a new treaty with Britain to replace what he termed the 'dry friendship' of the earlier ones, for in his view they were very one-sided arrangements.[15] The 1855 and 1857 treaties, after all, required the Amir to be the 'friend of the friends, and the enemy of the enemies' of the British, but there was no reciprocal commitment that Britain would be the enemies of his enemies.

Given Sher 'Ali Khan's precarious military situation, he gambled that it was worth the risk of visiting India, but at the same time he was careful that he did not appear to cede too much to Britain, for the memories of the Burnes Mission and the First Anglo-Afghan War were still raw. There were also powerful voices within the Muhammadzais and government circles who opposed too close a friendship with the old enemy. Indeed, one of the leading opponents of the Anglo-Afghan detente was the Amir's prime minister, Sayyid Nur Muhammad Khan, who was also the Amir's chief treaty negotiator and an authority on Islamic law. Another influential individual of the conservative Islamic party was Din Muhammad, known as Akhund Mishkin or Mushk-i 'Alam (Perfume of the World). Din Muhammad's grandfather was an Indian Sufi who moved to Afghanistan, probably during the reign of Timur Shah, and was gifted a *jagir* in Andar Ghilzai near Ghazni, where he founded a *langar khana* and was adopted as the *pir* of the local Sulaiman Khel tribes.[16]

Another voice raised against the Anglo-Afghan alliance was Sayyid Jamal al-Din al-Afghani, who, despite his name, was born in Asadabad in Iran.[17] Jamal al-Din was educated in the Shi'a tradition but had also dabbled in heterodox millenarian movements, including Babism and Shaikhism. Later he came under the influence of French Rationalists, leading some conservative Sunni theologians to condemn his approach to Islamic doctrine as heretical. Later in the century al-Afghani became the leading apologist for the pan-Islamic movement and he was stridently opposed to European domination of Muslim lands in general and British rule in India in particular. Politically, his aim was to revive the Caliphate and bring about the political unification of all Islamic countries as independent, sovereign states free from domination by European, 'Christian' nations.

Jamal al-Din arrived in Afghanistan at the end of the reign of Dost Muhammad Khan, using the pseudonym of Hajji Sayyid Rumi or Sayyid Istanbuli, and it was only after he was expelled from Afghanistan that he adopted the title of al-Afghani. Following the death of Dost Muhammad Khan, 'Sayyid Istanbuli' threw in his lot with Afzal Khan, since he shared his anti-British sentiments, and was a guest of Ghulam Muhammad Tarzi, a descendant of the Kandahar *sardar*s and the father of Mahmud Tarzi who, in the early twentieth century, became one of Afghanistan's most influential nationalists.

After Amir Afzal Khan's death, al-Afghani was appointed to Amir 'Azam Khan's advisory council and was described by the Kabul *wakil* as 'the most influential and leading member of the Ameer's Privy Council'. When al-Afghani urged 'Azam Khan to abandon relations with Britain in favour of Russia, British officials suspected he was a Russian agent provoca-teur.[18] When Sher 'Ali Khan took Kabul, al-Afghani stayed on in the hope he would be given a state appointment, but he was ignored. After deluging the administration with petitions, Sher 'Ali Khan finally lost patience and expelled al-Afghani from the country under armed guard in November 1868, an expulsion that more than likely was influenced by the Amir's imminent visit to India.

When Sher 'Ali Khan arrived in Umballa, the Amir and Lord Mayo struck up a personal friendship but the negotiations themselves proved problematic. Mayo's policy of balancing inaction with too much interfer-ence meant that he was not prepared to commit the British government to a treaty that might require military intervention in support of Sher 'Ali Khan or his heir in the event of the renewal of the civil war. As for the Amir, he wanted Britain to formally recognize 'Abd Allah Jan as his heir apparent and accept that his descendants alone were the rightful rulers of Afghanistan. Mayo was not prepared to agree to this either, since such a commitment threatened to drag Britain into military support for Sher 'Ali Khan against any foreign power with which he decided to pick a fight.

Mayo then disappointed the Amir further by informing Sher 'Ali Khan that Britain would not reinstate the subsidy agreed with his father under the 1857 treaty, since this had been only a temporary arrangement, not a permanent commitment. Instead the Amir was given a one-off gift of a few artillery pieces, 10,000 muskets and sixty *lakh* rupees with a vague promise that further gifts of cash and weapons might follow, but only at the Viceroy's discretion. The Amir's request for British officers to train his army was also declined, nor was Mayo willing to agree to Sher 'Ali Khan's request that Britain arbitrate Afghanistan's long-standing dispute with Persia concerning sovereignty over the Sistan.

As far as the Amir was concerned there was very little material gain from his meeting other than a one-off gift of guns and cash. Yet British demands were considerable and included stationing a permanent British envoy in Kabul, a request that caused great 'alarm' and 'agitation' among the Afghan delegation. Sher 'Ali agreed, in principle, to the idea but not immediately, and only if and when he was able to guarantee the security of these officials. Due to the sensitivity of the matter, the Amir was essentially opposed to the idea of any British Resident in Kabul, since his enemies would use his presence as a sign that he was a British puppet. Lord Mayo, realizing the delicacy of this issue, did not insist and assured him that

Britain 'would not force European officers or Residents upon him against his wish'.[19] The Viceroy even 'distinctly intimated to the Ameer that under no circumstances should a British soldier ever cross his frontier to assist him in coercing his rebellious subjects'. Mayo anyway believed there was no immediate need for a British presence in Afghanistan:

> with the friendly feelings that Shere Ali entertains towards us in consequence of the assistance in money and arms that we have given him, we may, without sending at present any European official to Cabul, exercise sufficient influence over him to keep him on the most amicable terms with us.[20]

Lord Mayo drew up an aide-memoire, signed by both parties, in which the Viceroy assured the Amir that Britain would view with 'severe displeasure any attempt on the part of your rivals to disturb your position as Ruler of Cabul'. He also expressed the hope that Sher 'Ali Khan would soon establish his 'legitimate rule over the entire kingdom' and 'transmit to your descendants all the dignities and honours of which you are the lawful possessor'.[21] Sher 'Ali Khan was disappointed at his failure to secure a more formal agreement, but as Mayo admitted his wording of the aide-memoire 'sailed very near the wind'; indeed some Ministers in London were very concerned about the vagueness of its undertakings. Mayo's actions were eventually approved, but over the following decade the degree of commitment made to the Amir in this aide-memoire was subject to much debate and disagreement in British government circles, and between the Amir and successive Viceroys. One particular problem was that the legal status of Mayo's letter was uncertain, for while it was not a formal treaty it clearly had some legal status, since both parties had signed it and the Cabinet in London had endorsed it.

As far as the British press was concerned, the Umballa Conference was a triumph for Britain, but in Sher 'Ali Khan's view it was mostly a failure. True, his expectations had been far too high, but the Amir had hoped to return to Kabul with something more substantial than a letter and a one-off gift of cash and guns. In hindsight, the Umballa Conference did not mark the beginning of a new era of improved Anglo-Afghan relations, but the start of a slow decline that would eventually lead to a complete breakdown in diplomatic relations. The problem was that each side had very different objectives. Sher 'Ali Khan needed cash and arms to defend himself against the Afzalids and had little interest in the British obsession with a Russian invasion. Britain's main interest was containing Russian military and political influence beyond the Amu Darya and securing strategic depth on India's Northwest Frontier. As far as Britain was concerned, Afghanistan was a key geopolitical kingdom, but there was little interest in the Afghan people themselves.

Back in Kabul, Sher 'Ali Khan did his best to portray his Indian visit as a diplomatic triumph. The sixty *lakh* rupees and muskets helped to suppress criticism from some quarters, but he still had to explain why he had not returned with a new treaty and lost the subsidy that his father had enjoyed. Sher 'Ali therefore disingenuously claimed that the cash and guns were the first of many similar gifts and the official statement and histories refer to the aide-memoire as an *'ahd* (treaty or covenant).[22]

It was not long after the Amir returned that he faced another serious challenge to his authority, though whether it was related to the outcome of the Umballa Conference or not is unclear. Muhammad Isma'il Khan, who had defected from the army of 'Abd al-Rahman Khan and secured Kabul in the name of Sher 'Ali Khan, was disappointed at not being rewarded with the governorship of Balkh. After a row with the Amir, he stormed out of the Bala Hisar and took refuge with the Jawanshir Qizilbash in Chindawal, occupying Qal'a-yi Madar-i Wazir in Chahardeh. When Sher 'Ali Khan threatened to turn his artillery on Chindawal, the Jawanshir surrendered the rebel *sardar*, who was exiled to India. However, Muhammad Isma'il escaped and fled to Balkh where he tried to raise another revolt. When this failed too, he threw himself on the Amir's mercy and agreed to go into exile in Lahore.

Isma'il Khan's revolt appears to have convinced Sher 'Ali Khan that the Bala Hisar was no longer a secure place for him to live in, so he commissioned a new fortified royal residence, which he named Sherpur, located under the southern slopes of the Behmaru and Qal'a-yi Musa hills. The citadel incorporated most of the ruined British cantonment and was a vast complex of barracks, administrative buildings and royal residences, surrounded by thick mud walls punctuated by bastions. Sherpur, however, was never finished and the site lacked an adequate water supply. As costs spiralled out of control, the Amir eventually abandoned the project.

Dynastic rivalries and revolts in Afghan Turkistan

Meanwhile there were growing tensions within the Amir's immediate family. When 'Abd Allah Jan was proclaimed as heir apparent in 1870, Muhammad Ya'qub Khan, the Amir's eldest son, refused to accept his father's decision. Ya'qub Khan then tried to take control of Kandahar, but was defeated and fled to Persia. The following spring he reoccupied Herat and wrote to his father demanding official recognition as its governor. Instead Sher ʿAli Khan sent an army against him, but a feud broke out between the various *sardar*s and the force broke up before it reached Herat. Sher ʿAli Khan decided it was better to concede to his son's demand and a few months later Yaʿqub Khan came to Kabul, where he received a royal pardon but failed to supplant ʿAbd Allah Jan.

While this struggle between the Amir and his two sons was taking place, another battle was raging beyond the Hindu Kush precipitated by the oppressive rule of Muhammad ʿAlam Khan, governor of Balkh. After the defeat of Ishaq Khan, Muhammad Khan purged the region of Afzalid sympathizers, executing, imprisoning and exiling hundreds of individuals, confiscating their lands and property and imposing heavy fines on districts that had supported the rebellion. The *amir*s of the Chahar Wilayat were required to attend the governor in Mazar-i Sharif every year at Nauroz and then travel to Kabul to renew their oath of alliance to the Amir in person. ʿAlam Khan also bled the province dry in order to pay for the escalating costs of Sherpur and new military bases in the province, conscripting thousands of labourers to work on these projects without pay. The fact that ʿAlam Khan was a Shiʿa, the son of a Qizilbash mother, merely added to his unpopularity. Thousands of people fled across into Russian Turkistan in order to avoid arrest or conscription, while the Uzbek *amir*s began to correspond with Ishaq Khan and ʿAbd al-Rahman Khan, offering to assist them to depose Muhammad ʿAlam Khan.

Matters came to a head in 1875 when Husain Khan, *wali* of Maimana, refused to attend the annual oath-swearing ceremony, executed several government well-wishers and ordered the name of Muzaffar Khan of Bukhara to be read in the *khutba*. Soon the whole of the western marches of the *wilayat*, from the Murghab to Aqcha, had followed suit. ʿAlam Khan tried to negotiate, but when the governor sent officials to Maimana to demand payment of back taxes, Husain Khan expelled them, along with all the government officials in the region. In the autumn of 1875 two armies were set against the *wali*, one from Balkh and the other from Herat, only to meet with fierce resistance from Maimana's defenders. Eventually in March 1876, after a siege lasting more than five months, the attackers broke through the defences, plundered and burnt the town and bazaars, and slaughtered hundreds of men, women and children.

Mir Husain Khan and other rebel leaders of the Chahar Wilayat were sent in chains to Kabul but Sher ʿAli Khan, in honour of the oath he had made in 1868, refused to put them to death. Indeed, when he heard their harrowing account of the pillage and slaughter of Maimana and 'Alam Khan's repressive reign, the Amir was appalled. When 'Alam Khan arrived in Kabul the following year to celebrate Nauroz, instead of being welcomed as a hero, the Amir ordered an audit of his accounts and placed him under house arrest. A few months later it was announced that 'Alam Khan had died. According to the official version of events, the *sardar*'s leg had been broken after his horse kicked him, and he subsequently contracted typhus and died. What actually happened was that the Amir had ordered his grooms to beat him to death during a visit to his stables. Following the assassination, Sher 'Ali Khan confiscated all of 'Alam Khan's property and appointed Shahghasi Loynab Sherdil Khan as governor of Balkh in his stead.

The Russian conquest of Khiva and the Simla Conference

Relations between Britain and Afghanistan had markedly deteriorated by the time Maimana fell. In 1870 General Kaufman initiated a correspondence with Sher 'Ali Khan, which the Amir dutifully showed to the Kabul *wakil*, who made copies and sent them to India. The Amir then followed the Viceroy's advice on how to reply. Despite this show of loyalty, Forward Policy advocates used the correspondence to claim that Sher 'Ali Khan was moving too close to Russia. Allegations about the Amir's alleged disloyalty intensified two years later when Kaufman offered to meet with Afghan officials to discuss frontier issues. At the end of 1873 Kaufman even hinted that Russia had made some kind of alliance with Afghanistan. Russophobes in the British government made much about the growing influence of Russia at the Afghan court and claimed that Sher 'Ali Khan was increasingly untrustworthy. Forward Policy advocates called for Britain to demand a formal presence in the Afghan capital and other key cities, partly to ensure the Amir toed the British line and partly to keep an eye on Russian activities in Central Asia.

Ironically, Kaufman's correspondence was due primarily to British pressure on the Russian Foreign Ministry to demarcate Afghanistan's northwestern frontier, a policy designed to prevent possible Russian military expansion up the Murghab or across the Amu Darya. This correspondence made little headway, so at the end of 1872 Britain unilaterally declared the Amu Darya from Lake Sar-i Kul, also known as Lake Victoria or Wood's Lake, in the Wakhan to Khwaja Saleh, northwest of Andkhui, to be the official northern frontier of Afghanistan. Russia eventually agreed to this boundary, but Sher 'Ali Khan was incensed, for Britain had not bothered to include him in the diplomatic exchanges or ask his opinion on the proposed frontier. Then in June 1873 Russian troops occupied Khiva and the Khan ceded exclusive navigation rights along the Amu Darya to Russia. He also surrendered sovereignty over any Khivan territory that bordered on this river. As far as Forward Policy advocates were concerned, the fall of Khiva proved Russia was not prepared to honour any de facto frontier arrangement but planned to occupy Herat, which would become the base for an invasion of northwestern India.

In May 1873, with Russian forces poised to take Khiva, Sher 'Ali Khan, alarmed at the possible Russian threat to Herat and Afghan Turkistan, imposed compulsory conscription to increase the size of his army and began to construct a series of new fortifications in the Chahar Wilayat. Sher 'Ali then wrote to Lord Northbrook, who had succeeded Mayo as Viceroy, requesting guns, ammunition and money to defend his northern frontier. Yet despite the strident demands for active intervention made by Disraeli's Conservative Opposition, Northbrook rejected the Amir's request, for the Viceroy was not convinced the fall of Khiva posed an imminent threat to India. As long as the Tsar's forces 'did not touch Persia or Afghanistan', he believed there was no need to panic, for Russia risked overextending itself. 'The more Russia extends her possessions in these parts,' Northbrooke noted, 'the more open she is to injury from us, while she has no more power to injure us than she did before.'[23]

In 1869 it had been Lord Mayo who was most concerned about the Russian threat to Afghanistan but now it was Sher 'Ali Khan who was fearful. Only four years before the *amir*s of the Chahar Wilayat had welcomed Ishaq Khan with open arms, while Herat under his rebellious son, Ya'qub Khan, was ripe for Russian interference. Northbrook's solution was to send a mission to Kabul to discuss the crisis, but the Amir declined the request and offered instead to send his prime minister, Sayyid Nur Muhammad Shah, to India. Northbrook accepted and in July 1873 the two sides met in Simla, but it was evident from the outset that Anglo-Afghan relations had deteriorated markedly since their last meeting.

Nur Muhammad Shah informed the British delegation that the Amir was angry about the Viceroy's failure to consult him over the Anglo-Russian frontier agreement and wanted a clear statement of Britain's intentions in the event of a Russian attack on Afghan territory. Nur Muhammad then pointed out that, since Britain expected the Amir to defend India's frontiers, it was only proper that Britain should contribute to the cost of the military build-up and argued that, according to the Afghan interpretation of Mayo's aide-memoire, Britain had committed itself to provide military and financial

assistance in such circumstances. Northbrook, however, rejected this interpretation and pointed out any assistance was solely at the discretion of the
Viceroy. At the same time, Northbrook assured Nur Muhammad Shah that
Britain remained committed to the territorial integrity of Afghanistan, but
in the event of an unprovoked attack military aid would only be forthcoming
after every diplomatic channel had been exhausted.

Another serious stumbling block was Afghanistan's dispute with
Persia over the Sistan. In 1869 the Amir had asked Lord Mayo to mediate
in this affair but he had declined, yet just two years later Major General
Frederick Goldsmid was sent to demarcate this frontier. The Amir agreed
to this arrangement only because he was convinced Afghanistan's claim
to the whole of the Sistan was so strong that Goldsmid would find in
Afghanistan's favour. The Shah of Persia, on the other hand, was so
angry about the demarcation that the Iranian government withdrew all
its cooperation. So in an attempt to pacify the Shah, Goldsmid adopted
the solution of Solomon and divided Sistan between the two countries,
which pleased neither the Amir nor Persia. To make matters worse, the
first intimation the Afghan government had of the Goldsmid frontier was
when Nur Muhammad Shah arrived in Simla. When Sher 'Ali Khan heard
of the proposed new border he greeted the news with 'deep mortification'
and there was a prolonged and heated debate over the matter between
the Afghan and British negotiators. Nur Muhammad Shah eventually
agreed to the Goldsmid demarcation under duress, in expectation that
the British would compensate the Amir for this substantial loss of territory and revenue by agreeing a more favourable treaty. However, Lord
Northbrook had no authority to conclude a formal arrangement, despite
the threat posed by the occupation of Khiva.

While not able to meet the Amir's expectations, Northbrook wanted
Sher 'Ali Khan to make what for him were major concessions and permit the
stationing of a permanent British Resident in his country. Nur Muhammad
Shah again declined the request, for 'the Afghans were deplorably ignorant and entertained the idea that a deputation of British Agents is always
a precursor to annexation'. He also pointed out that 'there was a strong
party in Cabul opposed to the Ameer entering into intimate relations with
the British government'.[24] Northbrook eventually concluded, on the basis
of Mayo's aide-memoire, that he could not insist on a British officer in
Afghanistan without the Amir's consent, but suggested that British officers
should demarcate the country's northern frontier and advise him on the
defences in Balkh. Given the heavy-handed way the British had handled
the Sistan frontier dispute, however, the Amir rejected this suggestion too.

In the end all Nur Muhammad Shah gained from his visit was a second Viceregal aide-memoire and verbal assurances that Britain wanted a 'powerful and independent' Afghanistan and would 'endeavour from time to time, by such means as circumstances may require, to strengthen [his rule]'.[25] This was hardly the kind of commitment the Amir had sought or needed, though some British officials claimed it was firm and clear-cut. As far as Sher 'Ali Khan was concerned, negotiations with Britain had again short-changed him, though he did receive a gift of 5,000 rifles (and a pledge of 15,000 more to follow) and a total of fifteen *lakh* rupees, five of which were compensation for Persian raids in Afghan Sistan.

Sher 'Ali Khan's disappointment is understandable. He had received a great deal more weapons and cash in 1869, while his father had been subsidized heavily during the siege of Herat in 1856–7, yet both sides agreed that the Russian threat to Afghanistan was far greater than in 1856 or 1869. Britain had defensive treaties with other nations so why not Afghanistan, especially since the country was so strategic to British interests? Instead, the Amir had lost sovereignty over more than half of the Sistan and the British government had not reinstated his father's annual subsidy, let alone committed to regular financial or military support. All the Viceroy had done was make a series of non-binding, verbal promises and assurances. Britain, it seemed, was not even prepared to assist with shoring up Afghanistan's vulnerable northern borders. The Amir's deep disappointment was reflected in his reply to the aide-memoire, which Northbrook claimed was 'somewhat sulky' and which puzzled the Viceroy. Northbrook did what he could to reassure the Amir that Britain remained committed to friendly relations but the damage had already been done.

One reason for Sher 'Ali Khan's negative reaction to the Simla Conference was due to internal developments. During the conference the Amir fell gravely ill and for most of the summer and early autumn of 1873 he was incapable of governing. As rumours spread that the Amir was on his deathbed, Sher 'Ali Khan ordered a public celebration to confirm 'Abd Allah Jan as heir apparent, only for Ya'qub Khan in Herat to refuse to hold any festivities in his half-brother's honour. Sher 'Ali decided that he had to pre-empt the possibility of civil war after his death and sent envoys to Herat with orders to persuade Ya'qub to come to Kabul, pledging that he would not be harmed or imprisoned. In early 1874 Ya'qub Khan finally came to Kabul only for the Amir to refuse to allow him to return to Herat; a few months later he placed him under house arrest. In response 'Ayub Khan, Ya'qub's uterine brother and acting governor of Herat, rebelled, though the uprising was soon crushed and 'Ayub fled to Persia.

The imprisonment of Ya'qub Khan was a cause of further tension between Britain and the Amir. Northbrook had not interfered in the appointment of 'Abd Allah Jan as heir apparent, but in his personal view Ya'qub Khan was the best candidate to ensure stability after the Amir's death. So when Ya'qub was imprisoned the Viceroy wrote to Sher 'Ali Khan asking him to honour his pledge and release and reinstate Ya'qub as governor of Herat. The Amir did not appreciate Northbrook's intervention and in reply Sher 'Ali Khan pointed out that Britain had no right to interfere in his internal affairs. Northbrook's untimely intervention led the Amir to suspect Britain had covertly encouraged Ya'qub Khan's rebellion in the belief that he would be more willing to yield to British demands.

Lord Lytton and the Forward Policy

While the Amir tried to prevent an internecine war, a change in government in Britain led to a further deterioration in the already strained Anglo-Afghan relationship. In February 1874 Disraeli's Conservatives came to power with Lord Salisbury in charge of the India Office. Both Disraeli and Salisbury were ardent supporters of the Forward Policy, with the consequence that the new administration was far more interventionist when it came to Anglo-Afghan relations and took a negative view of Sher 'Ali Khan personally and his relations with Britain in general. Even before their election victory, Salisbury had told Disraeli that Britain should insist on at least one British agent being stationed in Afghanistan. After the Conservatives came to power, this became one of the government's key foreign policy objectives. In one of his first communications to Northbrook, Salisbury questioned the whole Afghanistan policy: 'Have you entirely satisfied yourself of the truth of the orthodox doctrine that our interest is to have a strong and independent Afghanistan?' Salisbury then expressed his own 'many misgivings as to the wisdom of making the friendliness of the Ameer the pivot of our policy', claiming that one day he might well use any guns and military support Britain gave him to invade India.[26] As far as Salisbury was concerned, Sher 'Ali Khan was not just untrustworthy but potentially treacherous. Sher 'Ali Khan's correspondence with Kaufman was now used against him with Salisbury claiming, erroneously, that Sher 'Ali Khan had initiated it.

Disraeli's aggressive Afghanistan policy was influenced by wider concerns about Russia's intentions, in particular in the Balkans. A series of nationalistic uprisings against Ottoman rule in Bosnia, Herzegovina, Bulgaria and Romania had been brutally suppressed by Ottoman mercenaries. In response Russia threatened to send its army across the Danube to protect the mainly Orthodox Christian population of the Balkans from genocide. In Disraeli's view, this was merely a pretext for Russia to secure naval bases in the Mediterranean, challenge Britain's maritime supremacy and threaten its control of the newly opened Suez Canal. As the threat of war with Russia in Europe grew, Disraeli feared Russia planned to open a second front against India, either by occupying northern Afghanistan or providing military assistance to 'Abd al-Rahman Khan and the Afzalid refugees in Samarkand. Britain therefore had to ensure that it had a trustworthy ally in Kabul. Salisbury doubted Sher 'Ali Khan was the right person for this strategic objective and decided his loyalty must be tested and that Britain needed to secure 'a closer hold on the Amir'.[27]

To this end, Salisbury renewed Britain's demand for a permanent British presence in Kabul and, if possible, in Herat and Kandahar too. Northbrook strongly disagreed, arguing that such a demand was a breach of the undertaking made by Lord Mayo in 1869 and pointed out that on two separate occasions the Amir had turned down similar requests on the grounds he could not guarantee the safety of British officials. Furthermore, if Britain enforced this demand the Amir might well turn to Russia. Salisbury rejected Northbrook's view and in January 1875 he instructed the Viceroy to place a British agent 'with as much expedition as the circumstances . . . permit' at Herat and to take 'similar steps with regard to Candahar'. Kabul was not included in Salisbury's list since he now deemed it 'too fanatical to be quite safe'.[28] In the event the Amir rejected the 'request', Salisbury continued, Northbrook should send a mission to Kabul anyway with or without the Amir's consent.

Northbrook and his Council unanimously agreed that Sher 'Ali Khan would reject this demand and composed a studied rebuttal of Salisbury's position. They pointed out that the Amir had dutifully upheld the terms of the 1869 and 1873 aide-memoires, refuted Salisbury's claim that the Amir's refusal to admit a British mission was proof of disloyalty, and informed him that if the Amir was forced to allow a British presence in Afghanistan there was a high risk that the officers would be assassinated. As for Sher 'Ali Khan's correspondence with Russia, the Amir had dutifully shown all of Kaufman's letters to the Kabul *wakil*, who had forwarded copies to Calcutta and the Amir had sought the Viceroy's advice in his replies. In conclusion, Northbrook hinted both he and his Council were prepared to defy London by refusing to implement the new government policy. In a private letter, Northbrook confided that:

All those who are best qualified to form an opinion say that the Amir will strongly object to the presence of British officers in Afghanistan and this view is confirmed by his proceedings since I have been in India. We think it is very desirable to place a British officer in Herat, if it can be arranged with the cordial consent of the Ameer, but that if it is done against his will under pressure, the officer will have no real power of being of use, and his presence is as likely as not to occasion a breach some day between us and Afghanistan.[29]

Salisbury was unmoved and in response accused Northbrook and his Council of cowardice, claiming that the disaster of the First Anglo-Afghan War had 'entered like iron into their souls' and rendered them incapable of 'decisive' action. Britain's current position was 'both dangerous and humiliating', he declared, and it was time to abandon the 'stationary' policies of Lawrence and his successors. In the government's view, the Amir had already opened the door for Russia to 'make herself mistress' of Afghanistan, and 'we cannot leave the keys of the gate [of India] in the hands of a warder of more than doubtful integrity.'[30]

In the end the Indian government had no option but to implement London's policy, but in the autumn of 1875 Lord Northbrook resigned in protest, though his official letter of resignation cited only 'personal reasons'. In private, he told friends and well-wishers that he found it impossible to work with the Disraeli administration and he refused to implement its Afghanistan policy. His resignation, however, provided Salisbury with the opportunity to appoint Lord Lytton, a Conservative who shared Salisbury and Disraeli's views on Afghanistan. It was Lytton's appointment, more than anything else, that led to the final breach with Sher 'Ali Khan and drew Britain once more into war with Afghanistan.

On his way to India, Lytton stopped off in Cairo where he met with one of the leading ideologues of the Forward Policy, Sir Bartle Frere, whose supporters claimed that 'no man living possesses a more intimate knowledge of the questions concerned with our relations with Afghanistan.'[31] In fact, this was very far from the case. Frere had spent his first six years in India in Multan and Sind, but for the rest of his career he had served in Calcutta as a member of the Viceroy's Council and subsequently governor of Bombay. Frere's Frontier experience was therefore limited, with minimal involvement in Afghanistan's political affairs. However, he did have one close, though negative, connection to Afghanistan. His brother Richard had served in Sale's Brigade at the siege of Jalalabad and had died shortly

Robert Bulwer-Lytton, 1st Earl of Lytton and Viceroy of India, 1876–80. His aggressive pursuit of the Forward Policy was instrumental in provoking the confrontation with Amir Sher 'Ali Khan that led to the Second Anglo-Afghan War.

after Pollock's relief army arrived, probably from wounds received during the siege.

Frere had accompanied the Prince of Wales on his state visit to India and Salisbury commissioned him to report on Frontier affairs and British relations with the Amir. After visiting his brother's grave in Rawalpindi, Frere spent two weeks in Peshawar where he had a series of meetings with the Commissioner, Sir Richard Pollock, who refused to divulge any information of a confidential nature on Afghanistan. This infuriated Frere and in his dispatches to Salisbury he claimed, erroneously, that Pollock had no authority and that he did not have access to the Persian dispatches. When it came to 'accurate and reliable information' on Afghanistan, he wrote, the Commissioner 'had little or none and can have none under the present blind-man's bluff system', and claimed he could only make 'shrewd guesses' about the Amir's intentions.

Despite his lack of access to confidential government documents, Frere pontificated about Afghan affairs and informed Salisbury that Amir Sher 'Ali Khan's disposition was 'one of most bitter hostility' to Great Britain. He then endorsed Salisbury's position regarding stationing at least one permanent British officer in Afghanistan and added that:

If, on the other hand, the Ameer showed obvious signs of dis-
inclination to improve his relations with us, I would take it as clear
proof that hostile influence had worked more effectually than we
now suppose, that it was useless to attempt to coax or cajole him
into a better frame of mind, and we must look for alliances and
influences elsewhere than at Cabul, [we] must seek them in Kalat,
at Candahar, Herat, and in Persia, and I would lose no time in
looking out for them.[32]

The Amir must realize, Frere went on, that he was 'a weak power
between two enormously strong ones, an earthen vessel between two iron
ones'.[33] During their Cairo meeting, Frere showed Lytton copies of his
letters and recommendations to Salisbury. Lytton noted: 'There is something positively startling in the almost exact coincidence of Sir Bartle
Frere's opinions with those which, before leaving England, I put on paper
confidentially for examination by Lord Salisbury and Mr Disraeli who
entirely concurred with them.'[34] In fact there was nothing remarkable about
this 'coincidence', for Salisbury's official instructions to Lytton included
most of Frere's recommendations.

Salisbury, in a serious breach of protocol, had not bothered to telegraph
a copy of Lytton's instructions to Calcutta and left him to deliver them in
person. When the Viceroy's Council heard that Lytton was instructed to
force the issue of a permanent resident in Afghanistan as the litmus test
of the Amir's loyalty, there was a storm of protest and relations between
Lytton, his Council and other senior officials deteriorated. One member
of the Viceroy's Council later denounced him as 'the very worst Viceroy
that ever went to India', while other officials concluded it was impossible
to work under Lytton and applied for extended home leave. Despite being
'shockingly ignorant' of the situation in Afghanistan,[35] Lytton overruled
all objections and in the end did not bother to consult his Council in such
matters. Some officials concluded that the Viceroy had secret instructions
from London to pick a fight with Sher 'Ali Khan so that Britain could
have an excuse to annex or dismember Afghanistan. Lytton's opinion of
Sher 'Ali Khan did not help the situation either: in private correspondence
he called the Amir, among other things, 'a semi-barbarous sovereign', 'a
weak, barbarian chief' and 'not only a savage, but a savage with a touch
of insanity'.[36]

The Pelly Mission and the Peshawar Conference

One of Lytton's first acts as Viceroy was to order Sir Lewis Pelly, an experienced diplomat who had served in the embassy in Tehran, to travel to Kabul in order 'to ascertain the true attitude of the Amir towards the Government of India'. Lytton, though, did not bother to consult the Amir's wishes on the matter and the first intimation Sher 'Ali Khan had of the Pelly Mission came in Lytton's first official letter to him. Lytton disingenuously claimed Pelly's visit was to explain the Disraeli government's decision to declare Queen Victoria as Empress of India and to discuss 'matters of common interest between the two governments'. He then held out the prospect of a treaty that would include an annual subsidy, 'more decided recognition' of 'Abd Allah Jan as heir apparent, and 'an explicit pledge . . . of material support in case of foreign aggression'. However, while raising the Amir's hopes, Lytton deliberately omitted to inform the Amir what Britain's preconditions were for such a treaty. Furthermore, as Frere and Salisbury had recommended, Pelly's mission was more a test of the Amir's loyalty than it was about anything else. As Lytton noted, 'in the event of the Amir refusing to receive such a mission the Government of India might find themselves obliged to reconsider their whole policy towards Afghanistan, but there would be no doubt about the Ameer's estrangement'.[37]

The Amir was deeply troubled at the news of the Pelly Mission, for he was well aware how unpopular such a visit would be, particularly with the anti-British party at court. In his reply, the Amir suggested he send Nur Muhammad Shah to Peshawar to meet Pelly and reiterated the warning that he could not guarantee Pelly's safety if he came to Kabul. The Amir also pointed out that if Pelly came to the Afghan capital, General Kaufman might well demand the right to send a Russian envoy too. Sher 'Ali Khan then admitted he was far from optimistic about the outcome of a third round of negotiations, noting that the two previous meetings had failed to produce the outcome he had expected and had only led to further strains in Anglo-Afghan relations. A third conference, he warned, might make matters worse.

Lytton regarded the Amir's reply as further proof of his untrustworthiness and that he was trying to play Britain off against Russia. In a dispatch to Salisbury, Lytton claimed that the Amir's rejection of the Pelly Mission was an insult to 'the government of a great empire'. Britain, he declared, 'suffers itself to be with impunity addressed by a weak and barbarian chief who is under accumulated obligations to its protection and forbearance in terms of contemptuous disregard'.[38] Lytton therefore initially rejected the offer of a meeting in Peshawar and accused the Amir of 'hastily rejecting the hand of friendship held out to you'. He even warned Sher 'Ali Khan that if Pelly was not allowed to come to Kabul he would be obliged 'to regard Afghanistan as a State which has voluntarily isolated itself from the alliance and support of the British government'.[39]

When Lytton presented this reply to his Council three of its most senior members refused to endorse its contents, claiming that Sher 'Ali was within his rights to refuse the mission on the basis of Mayo's undertaking in his aide-memoire. Lytton, however, overruled them and sent the letter anyway, but he did agree to the meeting with Pelly to take place in Peshawar. In Kabul, meanwhile, the Viceroy's threat was seized on by the Islamic and anti-British party who claimed the mission was a deliberate provocation intended to give the British an excuse for annexing southern Afghanistan. When a Russian envoy arrived in Kabul in June 1876 Lytton saw this not just as further proof of the Amir's 'estrangement', but as a potential military threat, given that Russia was once more on the brink of war with Ottoman Turkey in the Balkans.

Sher 'Ali Khan was now caught in a difficult dilemma, with opponents of the Anglo-Afghan alliance calling for a *jihad* against India. In an attempt to mollify these critics, in August 1876 the Amir called an extraordinary council of '*ulama*', chaired by Mushk-i 'Alam, and laid before them all his correspondence with Britain and Russia. The Amir then requested them to decide, on the basis of the *shari'a*, whether or not he should agree to Pelly coming to Kabul. The Council concluded that the Amir had been correct in not allowing Pelly to enter Afghanistan but it did endorse negotiations with the British, provided they did not take place on Afghan soil.

The Amir briefed 'Ata Muhammad Khan, the Kabul *wakil*, about the Council's decision as well as his expectations for his meeting with Pelly. In October 'Ata Muhammad travelled to India where he reported that Sher 'Ali Khan was deeply disillusioned with Britain, in particular at the failure to secure a treaty in 1873. The *wakil* then listed the Amir's expectations in regard to the meeting with Pelly and how to repair the relationship. They included an undertaking by Britain that no 'Englishman' should reside in Afghanistan, least of all in Kabul; recognition of 'Abd Allah Jan as heir apparent; military support against unprovoked external aggression; and an annual subsidy. The Amir also wanted a clear statement that Britain would not interfere in Afghanistan's internal affairs. Lytton agreed, in principle, to discuss these conditions, but only if the Amir was prepared to accept a permanent British presence in Herat. He also wanted the Amir to allow British officers to demarcate Afghanistan's northern frontier and extend the Indian telegraph from Peshawar to Kabul. When 'Ata Muhammad returned to Kabul Sher 'Ali Khan reluctantly agreed to consider the issue of a British Resident. In January 1877 Sayyid Nur Muhammad Shah and other Afghan officials arrived in Peshawar, but by this time Anglo-Afghan relations had been placed under even more strain by Lytton's decision to intervene militarily in the affairs of Kalat. For several years Baluchistan had been plagued with tribal and civil war. So in the autumn of 1876 Lytton sent troops to support the Khan of Kalat and put down the revolts. The outcome was the Treaty of Jacobabad, signed in December 1876, which in Lytton's words made Britain 'virtually masters' of Baluchistan. The terri-tory became a British Protectorate and, in return for military aid to keep him in power, the Khan of Kalat agreed to allow a British garrison to be stationed in Quetta and for the Indian rail and telegraph network to be extended to Chaman, on the Afghan frontier. This was a triumph for Lytton's Forward Policy, for among other things the Viceroy believed that Quetta would become the most important intelligence-gathering centre on the Afghan frontier.

The news from Baluchistan was not well received in Kabul for the Khans of Kalat had been subordinate to, and allies of, the Durrani mon-archy since the days of Ahmad Shah. Sayyid Nur Muhammad Shah, Sher 'Ali Khan's prime minster and chief negotiator at the Peshawar Conference, was a native of Baluchistan and he was particularly angry about the treaty. As for the presence of a British garrison in Quetta and the extension of the rail and telegraph to the Afghan frontier, these were regarded as a direct threat to Afghanistan. Yet Lytton failed to understand the wider political repercussions of the Kalat intervention and expressed amazement as to how the Treaty of Jacobabad could 'injuriously affect the Amir of Kabul'.[40]

When the two sides finally met in Peshawar, it was clear to all that Anglo-Afghan relations were almost at breaking point. The discussions did not start well, for Sayyid Nur Muhammad Shah made it clear that the Amir was still not prepared to consider a permanent British pres-ence in Afghanistan. The prime minister then laid out his government's view on the obligations Britain was under because of previous treaties and the aides-memoires of 1869 and 1873. According to the Amir, Britain had already committed itself to the defence of Afghanistan against unpro-voked external aggression. Since there were Russian troop movements on the Murghab and Amu Darya frontiers, Sher 'Ali wanted Britain to provide financial and military assistance. The British view, on the other hand, was that any discussion regarding financial and military commit-ments was conditional on the Amir first agreeing to allow a permanent

British presence in Afghanistan. The result was a deadlock that lasted for three months.

While the Peshawar Conference dragged on without any resolution in sight, the threat of a Russo-Turkish War in the Balkans grew more and more likely. As far as the Disraeli government was concerned, it was even more urgent for military observers to be located inside Afghanistan, for all that lay between Russia and British India, according to Salisbury, was a 'weak' and 'barbarous' country'.[41] So when Pelly reported to Lytton that he had 'conclusive' proof that Sher 'Ali Khan was engaged in a secret agreement with Kaufman, Lytton claimed that Pelly had finally 'torn aside the impenetrable veil which has so long concealed from us the increasing, and now apparently complete, extinction of British influence at Kabul'.[42]

On 3 March 1877 Lytton wrote a detailed response to the Afghan interpretation of Anglo-Afghan agreements, a memorandum that is to the Second Anglo-Afghan War what the Simla Declaration was to the war of 1838–42. In a detailed critique of the 1855 and 1857 treaties and Mayo and Northbrook's aides-memoires, Lytton effectively annulled these agreements, arguing that none of them placed Britain under any obligation to the Amir in respect of the defence of his realm, the maintenance of Afghanistan's territorial integrity or the sustaining of his dynasty on the throne. This was especially so since 'the conduct and language of the Amir during the last four years has been one of chronic infraction, or evasion, of the first Article of the Treaty of 1855'.[43]

As far as the 1857 treaty and the aide-memoire of 1869 were concerned, these related 'exclusively . . . to special circumstances, considerations and conditions', and hence there was no right of appeal to these undertakings in the current circumstances. As far as the 1855 and 1857 treaties were concerned,

> it is as clear as anything can be, that neither the one nor the other imposes on the British Government, either directly or indirectly, the least obligation, or liability, whatever, to defend, protect, or support, the Amir, or the Amir's dynasty, against all enemies, or any danger, foreign or domestic.

The Afghan view that the aides-memoires of 1869 and 1873 had the force of 'adhs – covenants or treaties – was 'entirely erroneous' and the statement that Britain would 'view with severe displeasure any attempts on the part of [the Amir's] rivals to disturb your position' was interpreted as relating solely to the Amir's situation in 1869. Lord Mayo, he declared:

did not, and could not, thereby commit the British Government to an unconditional protection of the Amir, or to any liabilities on behalf of His Highness which were not dependent on his future conduct towards the British Government and his own subjects. In short, the plain meaning of the Viceroy's statement was neither more or less than an assurance that, so long as the Amir continued to govern his people justly and mercifully, and to maintain cordial, and confidential, relations with the British Government, that Government would, on its part, also continue to protect His Highness.

As for Northbrook's commitment to go to war on behalf of the Amir in the event of an unprovoked attack, this was merely 'a personal assurance' that 'committed the British Government to no pledges which were not carefully guarded on every side by positive conditions with which the Amir has of late evinced no disposition to comply'.

Lytton instructed Pelly to pass on this memorandum to Sayyid Nur Muhammad Shah and inform the envoy that the offer of a treaty and the terms contained in his letter of October 1876 were now withdrawn:

if His Highness sincerely desired to deserve the friendship and thereby secure the protection of the British Government, [the terms] would be cordially and unreservedly accorded to him. But His Highness has evinced no such desire; and it is a puerile absurdity to assume that, because the British Government would have viewed with severe displeasure in 1869 any attempt to disturb the throne of a loyal and trusted ally, it is, therefore, bound in 1877 to protect, from dangers incurred regardless of its advice, the damaged power of a mistrustful and untrustworthy neighbour.[44]

Pelly was also to inform Nur Muhammad Shah that Britain repudiated 'all liabilities on behalf of the Amir and his dynasty', and so in one stroke Lytton undid the work of three previous Viceroys and turned Anglo-Afghan relations back into the Dark Ages of 1838. Yet despite all this, Lytton continued to insist Britain still upheld the terms of these treaties and obligations. Furthermore, Pelly was to 'explain distinctly to the Envoy, and to place on record, in language not susceptible to misconstruction' that 'the British Government harbours no hostile designs against Afghanistan'. Furthermore, the British government

will scrupulously continue . . . to respect the Amir's independence
. . . and duly refrain from every kind of interference with tribes and
territories not its own . . . the British Government has no sort or
kind of quarrel with the people of Afghanistan. It sincerely desires
their permanent independence, prosperity, and peace. It has no
conceivable object, and certainly no desire, to interfere in their
domestic affairs. It will unreservedly respect their independence;
and, should they at any time be united in a national appeal to its
assistance, it will doubtless be disposed, and prepared, to aid them
in defending that independence from aggression. Meanwhile, the
Afghan people may rest fully assured that so long as they are not
excited by their ruler, or others, to acts of aggression upon the
territories or friends of the British Government, no British soldier
will ever be permitted to enter Afghanistan uninvited.[45]

A year later these undertakings too would be honoured in the breach and
British troops would once more march into Afghanistan 'uninvited'.

Further problems arose when the old and infirm Sayyid Nur
Muhammad Shah died before the Amir could respond to Lytton's letter.
Since the other Afghan delegates were not authorized to continue the nego-
tiations, they prepared to return to Kabul with the prime minister's body.
Lytton, hearing of Nur Muhammad Shah's demise, terminated the negoti-
ations and refused permission for the Kabul *wakil* to return to Afghanistan.
Shortly after the Afghan mission left for Kabul, Lytton appointed Captain
Louis Cavagnari, an avid supporter of the Forward Policy and a personal
friend of Lytton, as the new Commissioner in Peshawar. When Pelly was
informed of this appointment he wrote a long letter to the Viceroy endorsing the government's hard line on Afghanistan. Lytton now had an ally in
Peshawar who could counteract opposition to his policy from other senior
administrators.

The road to war and the death of Amir Sher 'Ali Khan

The Amir's worst fears were now confirmed: rather than improving
Anglo-Afghan relations, the Peshawar Conference had led to a complete
breakdown, for Britain had effectively severed diplomatic relations. To add
to the pressure on the Amir and on Britain, in April 1877 120,000 Russian
troops marched into Romania, which promptly declared independence
from Turkey. British dealings with the Amir were now more about the
potential consequences of the Russo-Turkish War and Afghanistan found

itself yet again caught up in the fallout from a European confrontation. The Russian intervention in the Ottoman-held Balkans and Caucasus raised the prospect of Britain going to war with Russia and the possibility that Russia might open a second front and occupy Herat or Afghan Turkistan.

Sher 'Ali Khan made one last attempt to mend the fence and appointed a new envoy authorized to continue the talks. The Amir also hinted he might be willing to compromise and allow a British officer to be stationed in Herat, if Britain agreed to the demilitarization of Quetta. However, when his envoy tried to cross the Indian frontier he was turned back and informed that, since the Viceroy had terminated the negotiations, there was no point proceeding any further.

The failure of the Peshawar talks and the breakdown in Anglo-Afghan relations was a matter of the deepest concern for Sher 'Ali Khan. It raised the possibility that Britain might covertly encourage a more Anglophile member of his family, such as Ya'qub Khan, to seize the throne – something that Lytton was indeed discussing with London. Furthermore, since Britain was not prepared to provide arms or cash, Afghanistan was now far more vulnerable to Russian intervention or a Russian-backed attempt by an Afzalid pretender, such as 'Abd al-Rahman Khan, to topple the Amir. Sher 'Ali Khan therefore ordered a general mobilization under the banner of *jihad*, which Lytton misinterpreted as evidence that the Amir, incited by Russia, was planning to raise the Frontier tribes and attack India. Nothing could have been further from the truth. Sher 'Ali Khan's sole concern was the defence of his own throne and kingdom against a possible Russian, or British, intervention.

In an attempt to mediate and persuade Sher 'Ali Khan to join an anti-Russian coalition, in September 1877 the Ottoman Caliph sent a mission to Kabul, only for the Amir to complain to the ambassador how, after a decade of negotiation, he had failed to secure any significant benefit from the Anglo-Afghan relationship.[46] Friendship with Britain, he declared, was 'a word written on ice' and he was no longer prepared to 'waste precious life in entertaining false hopes from the English'.[47] The Ottoman envoy could do little. He had no authority from Britain to mediate between the Amir and London and the British government treated the whole venture with some scepticism, especially as the Turks had applied to locate an Ottoman representative in Peshawar. What the Ottoman mission did accomplish, however, was the beginning of a closer relationship between Afghanistan and Turkey, which laid the foundation for a pan-Islamic movement that would play an important part in Afghan internal affairs, and in Anglo-Afghan relations, over the ensuing years.

The stand-off with Britain continued unresolved until the summer of 1878, meanwhile Turkey suffered a major defeat in the Balkans and in the Caucasus. In February 1878 Russian forces occupied Erzerum, while in the west Russian troops were a matter of a few marches from Istanbul. In response, Britain sent a fleet into the eastern Mediterranean to halt the Russian advance. On 3 March 1878 Turkey signed the Treaty of San Stefano, and by so doing lost all but token sovereignty over most of the Balkans, Armenia and Georgia. In June the six Great Powers met in Berlin to finalize the new Balkan frontiers with Britain attempting to contain Russian expansion and prevent her from securing a naval base in the eastern Mediterranean.

General Kaufman, in an effort to put pressure on Britain and influence the outcome of the Congress of Berlin, wrote to the Amir informing him that he was sending General Nikolai Stoletov to Kabul to discuss Russian-Afghan relations. A short time later another Russian officer, Colonel Nikolai Ivanovich Grodekov, crossed the Amu Darya and, in defiance of the Amir's wishes, conducted a high-profile military survey of the caravan route from Mazar to Herat via Sar-i Pul, the Shirin Tagab and Maimana.[48] Kaufman's brinkmanship created even greater concern in Britain that Russia was planning a military intervention in Afghanistan. Sher 'Ali Khan was equally alarmed and requested that Stoletov's mission be called off, but Kaufman refused and instead informed the Amir that Russia would hold him personally responsible for the safety and honourable reception of the envoy. Sher 'Ali Khan was now caught in a cleft stick. He dare not turn Stoletov back at the frontier as this would provide Russia with an excuse to invade Herat or Afghan Turkistan, yet if he received the envoy, Britain might well use his presence to justify the invasion and possible annexation of southern Afghanistan.

Sher 'Ali Khan did his best to delay Stoletov's arrival in Kabul in the hope that under British pressure the Russian Foreign Ministry would recall him, but Stoletov ignored the delaying tactics of the Amir's officials and in late July 1878 he arrived in the Afghan capital. According to the British version of events, Sher 'Ali Khan then negotiated a secret treaty with Russia, but in fact all Stoletov did was to draft a memorandum of the Amir's wish list and forward it to Kaufman for approval. What Sher 'Ali did not know at the time was that Kaufman had no authority from St Petersburg for either the Stoletov Mission or Grodekov's survey. When the British asked Count Gorchakov, the Russian Foreign Minister, who was heading Russia's delegation in Berlin, to explain his country's actions, he admitted privately that he had no knowledge of any mission to Kabul. Gorchakov ordered

Grodekov to recall Stoletov, disowned the Kabul mission and withdrew any offers of assistance or treaty made to the Amir. By the time Stoletov heard this news his mission was anyway redundant, as the Congress of Berlin had put pressure on Russia to withdraw its forces back beyond the Danube and a war between Russia and the other Great Powers was averted.

Despite the threat of war in Europe having receded, as far as Afghanistan was concerned the damage could not be undone. Lytton exploited Stoletov's mission and the alleged secret treaty with Russia as conclusive proof of the Amir's political infidelity. Before Stoletov arrived in Kabul, Lytton had written to Salisbury stating that the Amir had 'irrevocably slipped out of our hands' and was already discussing the partition or dismemberment of Afghanistan, even though only a few months earlier he had assured Sher 'Ali Khan that Britain would respect Afghanistan's independence. Lytton then ordered General Sir Neville Bowles Chamberlain to prepare to travel to Kabul to discuss the crisis and wrote to the Amir informing him that a British envoy was on his way to the Afghan capital, with or without the Amir's consent.

Tragically, the very day the Viceroy's letter reached the Afghan Foreign Ministry, 'Abd Allah Jan, the heir apparent, died and the Amir and his court went into deep mourning. As the funeral rites were in full swing and with memories of Amir Sher 'Ali Khan's slide into mental instability following the death of his other son still fresh, no official was prepared to risk their neck by showing the grief-stricken Amir the Viceroy's dispatch. Eventually, the Amir's chamberlain took his life in his hands and showed him Lord Lytton's letter. A few days later Stoletov set out to return to Samarkand, leaving two junior officers behind in Kabul.

It was almost a week before British officials heard of 'Abd Allah Jan's death, but despite this news Lytton insisted Chamberlain continue his mission to Kabul. On 30 August 1878 Lytton informed the Amir in his official letter of condolence that Chamberlain planned to leave Peshawar for Kabul on 16 or 17 September. When the courier reached Jalalabad, however, he was handed a note from the Amir informing him he was 'unfit to attend to business' and that 'the matter must be deferred until after Ramazan'.[49] The last day of Ramazan fell on 27 September and in the circumstances this was a reasonable request for postponement, but Cavagnari ordered the messenger to continue on to Kabul in defiance of the Amir, and Sher 'Ali Khan had little option but to allow him to proceed.

News of the impending arrival of a British mission led to a heated debate among the Amir's senior advisers who were unable to reach any consensus on whether to allow Chamberlain to proceed. On 16 September the commander of the Afghan border post at 'Ali Masjid wrote to Cavagnari informing him that, since he had received no instructions from the Amir regarding permitting the mission to enter Afghanistan, any attempt by British officials to cross the frontier would be resisted by force of arms. Cavagnari ignored the warning and he and Chamberlain set off up the Khyber Pass accompanied by a large armed guard, only to be turned back at the frontier. When Cavagnari informed Lytton of the Amir's message and the mission having been prevented from crossing into Afghanistan, the Viceroy telegraphed London claiming the denial of entry was an 'affront' and 'insult' to British prestige and recommended the government declare war on Afghanistan immediately. In anticipation of military action, Lytton ordered troops to the Quetta and Peshawar frontiers.

Disraeli's cabinet, however, was divided about going to war and even Salisbury feared that an invasion might be counterproductive, since it would provide Russia with the excuse it sought to abrogate the terms of the Congress of Berlin. The cabinet decided instead to give the Amir one last chance and on 2 November 1878 Lytton wrote to Sher 'Ali Khan, informing him that war was imminent and listing the various 'hostile acts' he was alleged to have committed. The Viceroy then presented him with an ultimatum. If he wished to avoid war, the Amir must send a 'full and suitable apology' for refusing entry to the Chamberlain Mission 'tendered on British territory by an officer of sufficient rank', and agree to the presence of a permanent British envoy in Afghanistan. The deadline of 20 November was set for the Amir to comply after which, Lytton declared, 'I shall be compelled to consider your intentions as hostile, and to treat you as a declared enemy of the British Government'.[50] The deadline passed without any reply. So on the following day three British columns marched into Afghan territory.

In fact, the Amir had replied to the Viceroy's ultimatum a day before the deadline, but the letter failed to reach Peshawar in time. The courier, having heard rumours that British forces had occupied 'Ali Masjid, turned back to Kabul to seek new instructions from the Amir. The Amir was extremely angry with him and ordered the postmaster in Jalalabad to ensure the letter reached Cavagnari, but it did not reach the Commissioner's desk until 30 November, ten days after the Viceroy's ultimatum had expired. By this time British forces had already occupied parts of southern Afghanistan and Cavagnari anyway dismissed the Amir's response as inadequate, even though Sher 'Ali Khan had made two major concessions to British demands. He was now prepared to allow Chamberlain to travel to Kabul and consider the stationing of a permanent British official in his country.

As far as Lytton was concerned this was too little too late, nor was it the 'clear and unequivocal submission' that Britain had demanded.

As British forces marched into southern Afghanistan, Sher 'Ali Khan decided not to oppose them and withdrew most of his troops from Kandahar and Jalalabad to Herat and Kabul. Encouraged by the promises made by Stoletov, Sher 'Ali decided to travel to St Petersburg and appeal in person to the Tsar for military assistance. To this end he released Ya'qub Khan, appointed him governor of Kabul and at the end of December 1878 the Amir set out for Mazar-i Sharif, taking with him his family and the remaining members of the Russian Mission.

Claims by imperial historians that the Amir fled in panic, or that he abdicated in favour of Ya'qub Khan or appointed him as heir apparent, however, are incorrect. Afghan histories make it clear that Sher 'Ali Khan remained as Amir and that his departure for Mazar was both deliberate and strategic.[51] However negative this decision may appear in hindsight, Sher 'Ali Khan's plan had a rationale. His army was no match for the British and his only hope was to draw the enemy deeper into Afghanistan, overstretch their supply line, and hope that the tribes would rise and make it impossible for Britain to occupy southern Afghanistan for any length of time. No doubt these tactics drew on his father's and Akbar Khan's experience in the First Afghan War, when the tribes' hit-and-run tactics had worn down the invader and eventually forced them to quit the country. As for Mazar-i Sharif, this was an ideal safe haven, for with winter already set in Sher 'Ali Khan gambled that that the invaders would not be able to cross the snowbound Hindu Kush until the spring. Furthermore, there were 15,000 government soldiers stationed in various locations in the province and the Amir planned to use the winter to raise more levies. Mazar-i Sharif was also close to the Russian frontier, which would make it easy for the anticipated gift of Russian arms to reach him. It was only after he reached Mazar-i Sharif that the Amir's strategy unravelled.

Before leaving the Afghan capital, Sher 'Ali Khan released all the surviving Uzbek *amirs* of the Chahar Wilayat whom he had imprisoned. On his arrival in Mazar-i Sharif, they went to the shrine of Shah-i Mardan, where the Amir pledged to restore them to their fiefdoms on condition they raised levies for the forthcoming war and guaranteed safe conduct for government troops to return to Takhtapul or Herat. Most of these indigenous rulers had been in jail for more than a decade, the result of the Amir breaking a similar oath. They had not only lost all faith in his promises, they saw the British invasion as an opportunity to reassert their independence. So when Muhammad Khan, the ex-*beglar begi* of Sar-i Pul, and Husain

Khan, the deposed *wali* of Maimana, arrived back in their homelands they rallied their forces, attacked the Afghan garrisons and expelled them from their territory. Thousands of Turkmans also took advantage of the chaos to raid the Chahar Wilayat, plundering settlements and enslaving an estimated 6,000 women. When the Amir tried to suppress their raids, his troops were defeated.

The survivors of the Maimana garrison eventually made their way back to Herat despite the icy conditions, starving and penniless. They demanded their arrears of pay and went on the rampage when they were told the treasury was empty, pillaging the bazaars and private dwellings. In an attempt to suppress the disorder 'Ayub Khan left Mashhad and, fortified by a gift of Persian cash, took over the government of Herat and distributed what money he had to the mutinous soldiers. The cash, however, was not enough to satisfy their demands and 'Ayub was powerless to bring them to heel.

Meanwhile, Kaufman turned down the Amir's request for an audience with the Tsar and refused to allow him to cross into Russian territory. Instead, he advised the Amir to make peace with Britain on whatever terms he could negotiate. Kaufman was already in enough trouble for his unauthorized mission to Kabul and he was not prepared to go out on a limb again. As for the Russian Foreign Ministry, it had no interest in risking war with Britain over Afghanistan.

By the time Sher 'Ali Khan reached Mazar-i Sharif he was in poor health and his condition continued to worsen. When his swollen legs turned gangrenous he and his courtiers realized death was not far away. As rumours of the Amir's imminent demise spread, a power struggle for the succession began. One of the Amir's sons, Muhammad 'Ali Khan, tried to seize control of the key garrison of Takhtapul but the troops refused to allow him to enter. Instead they mutinied, arrested their commanding officer and elected their own general. Muhammad 'Ali Khan then headed south to Deh Zangi, where he began to gather an army to attack Ya'qub Khan in Kabul. On 22 February 1879 Sher 'Ali Khan died and was buried beside Wazir Akbar Khan in a mausoleum attached to the shrine of Shah-i Mardan. Following his death, all state resistance to the British invasion collapsed and the army fell apart. The very survival of Afghanistan as a nation now hung in the balance.

Amir Sher 'Ali Khan: an appraisal

The reign of Amir Sher 'Ali Khan was a troubled one. It had begun with four years of bitter civil war during which time the country was divided into two rival states. Sher 'Ali Khan eventually triumphed but at great cost, both personally as well as to the nation as a whole. For the remainder of his reign, the Amir fought to hold the country together and to contain a growing Islamic and anti-British faction within his court as well as a series of rebellions beyond the Hindu Kush and the dispute with his son, Ya'qub Khan, over the succession. To add to his difficulties, after 1868 Afghanistan shared a common frontier with Russia while the pretenders to the throne, 'Abd al-Rahman Khan and Ishaq Khan, were living at Russian expense in Samarkand.

The Amir's solution was to seek a new and better treaty arrangement with Britain or, at the very least, an agreement that would provide him with urgent financial and military aid. Yet despite three conferences and repeated assurances by British officials that they wanted good relations with Afghanistan, the British government was not prepared to commit to any formal treaty. Lord Lytton did offer Sher 'Ali Khan the possibility of a treaty, but on terms that were both unrealistic and unacceptable, for they could well have led to the Amir's downfall. Lord Lytton made matters worse during the Peshawar Conference by interpreting all previous Anglo-Afghan agreements as a one-way street in which all the obligations were placed on the Amir and few, if any, on Britain. From the British point of view, Sher 'Ali Khan also made unreasonable demands in respect of the defence of his realm and the issue of succession. Yet by demanding the Amir should prove his loyalty by admitting the Pelly Mission and agreeing to a permanent British officer being stationed in his country, Britain cut off its nose to spite its face. Lytton must have known that the Amir would only agree to such a demand at the point of a bayonet. So instead of strengthening Anglo-Afghan ties at a time when the Russian threat to India was deemed to have risen exponentially following the conquest of Bukhara and Khiva and the Russo-Turkish War, the Disraeli government's policy actually led to the very thing Britain sought to avoid. All Lytton's aggressive imperialism succeeded in doing was to start another costly war with Afghanistan which would inflict even more misery on ordinary Afghans.

It is something of a mystery why the Umballa or Simla conferences failed to end in a treaty, or at least a renewal of the arrangement made with Dost Muhammad Khan – missed opportunities that contributed to the eventual war. Both parties had everything to gain by building on the 1855 and 1857 treaties and, given Britain's paranoia about the Russian threat to Afghanistan and India, the decision not to provide regular financial and military aid to the Amir made little sense strategically. Furthermore, had a legally binding treaty been agreed in 1869 or 1873, Lytton and the Disraeli administration would have been hard put to make the kind of demands they made in respect of a British Resident. Nor would Lytton have been able to claim Britain had no formal obligations to support the Amir, or to dismiss so easily the undertakings made by his predecessors as purely personal, temporary arrangements.

Unfortunately, historians still tend to follow the Imperial version of the causes of the Second Anglo-Afghan War, which places all the blame on the Amir's 'intransigence', in particular his correspondence with Russia and his refusal to allow Pelly or Chamberlain to visit Kabul. This view takes little consideration of the extreme difficulties the Amir was in at the time, caught as he was between two rival superpowers, each of which had designs on his country, and opposition to the Anglo-Afghan alliance from his own extended family and Islamic radicals such as Mushk-i 'Alam. It was a delicate balancing act that would have taxed the ingenuity of a far greater statesman than Sher 'Ali Khan.

The real cause of the Second Anglo-Afghan War lay with the hard-line, interventionist approach adopted by Forward Policy advocates such as Rawlinson and Frere and the bull-in-a-china-shop diplomacy of Lytton and Salisbury. Lytton's arrogant refusal to heed the advice of experienced officials who knew the Afghan situation far better than he did contributed significantly to the ultimate breakdown in relations with Sher 'Ali Khan. However, Disraeli, Lytton and Salisbury were committed to an assertion of Britain's imperial rights over a ruler who, they were convinced, was not merely fickle and devious, but a half-crazed savage.

In the end both Britain and Russia proved to be broken reeds as far as Sher 'Ali Khan was concerned and he found himself caught between the devil and the deep blue sea. *Punch*, in a famous contemporary cartoon, shows the Amir wringing his hands, with a drooling bear on one side of him and a roaring lion on the other. The caption has the Amir crying, 'Save me from my friends!' and underneath it is an ironic quotation from a leader in *The Times*: 'If at this moment it has been decided to invade the Ameer's territory, we are acting in pursuance of a policy which in its intention has been uniformly FRIENDLY to Afghanistan.'[52]

The Amir's visit to Umballa was the first state visit by a Durrani ruler to British India and exposed him and his entourage to a world of mechanization and the Industrial Revolution. This encounter led Sher 'Ali Khan to take the first tentative steps to engage with modern technology. He introduced Afghanistan's first printing press, which published the country's first Persian newspaper, *Shams al-Nahar*, and printed Persian translations of English works, mostly military manuals, as well as the country's first postage stamps. The Amir built Afghanistan's first factory, known as the *mashin khana*, which manufactured gunpowder and small arms. He established Afghanistan's first military academy, which included instruction in mathematics, geography, map reading and other sciences, and commissioned a census of Kabul city. Another notable feature of Sher 'Ali Khan's reign was the increasing use of Pushtu titles and terminology, especially in the military, for many of the army's commanders were Ghilzais from Ghazni and Wardak. However, the degree of Pushtunization that took place during Sher 'Ali Khan's reign has been somewhat overstated by Afghan historians,[53] and Persian remained the language of the court and official communications.

Sher 'Ali Khan was the first Afghan ruler known to have worn European dress and on official occasions he often appeared wearing a Russian military uniform. The Amir's adoption of foreign dress was far more controversial than it might appear, for European clothing did not conform to the strict Islamic dress code. However, by adopting European modes of dress, Sher 'Ali Khan symbolized that his sympathies lay with modernizers who sought engagement with the Western world and its technology. Furthermore, to the mid-nineteenth-century European mind, the dress code of foreign rulers and chieftains was a defining feature of whether they were treated as civilized or barbarians. For this reason chieftains from Africa to New Zealand Maori wore frock coats and starched collars rather than traditional garb, for to do so was one of the keys that opened the door to membership, though a second-class one, of Europe's Imperial club. European versus 'Islamic' or traditional dress would continue to be a point of conflict between Afghanistan's educated urban elite and conservative Islamists and rural populations well into the twentieth century.

In other aspects of social life Afghanistan under Sher 'Ali Khan remained rooted in the past. Slavery was commonplace and there was no attempt to introduce modern education, encourage literacy or provide even basic health services. Rich Afghans employed private tutors, others sent their children to be educated in India, either in the Mission schools in Peshawar and Ludhiana, or Sir Syed Ahmad Khan's Muhammadan Anglo-Oriental College at Aligarh. The religious elites, on the other hand, favoured Indian *madrasa*s, particularly the Darul Uloom at Deoband, as suitable places for their children to pursue a traditional Islamic curriculum. Known for its anti-colonial views and its focus on Hanafi jurisprudence and religious texts, Deoband would have a profound influence on succeeding generations of Afghan Islamists and '*ulama*' who would lead the opposition to attempts to introduce constitutional, educational and social reforms.

EIGHT

'Reducing the Disorderly People',
1879–1901

The whole Afghan Population is *particeps criminis* in a great national crime.

LORD LYTTON[1]

During the reign of Peter the Great . . . were not lakhs of people put to death, and launched into oblivion . . . My work is like that of those times and so I am reducing the disorderly people to a state of new order.

AMIR 'ABD AL-RAHMAN KHAN

FOLLOWING THE DEATH of Sher 'Ali Khan, Ya'qub Khan was declared Amir in Kabul and a number of *sardars* suspected of favouring the Afzalids were arrested. In Mazar-i Sharif, Sher 'Ali Khan's courtiers pledged their loyalty to Ya'qub Khan's eldest son, Muhammad Musa', who attacked and subdued the mutineers in Takhtapul, forced them to take the oath of loyalty to Amir Ya'qub and sent their leader to Kabul in chains, where he was put to death. In Herat, 'Ayub Khan too recognized his brother's succession, but many of the officer corps in Balkh and Herat favoured the Samarkand exiles. Since military discipline had all but broken down in Herat, there was little 'Ayub could do to enforce loyalty to his brother, especially as his treasury was almost empty. In an attempt to pacify the troops, 'Ayub sent an urgent message to Mazar-i Sharif pleading for more cash and issued the garrison with one month's pay, only for the troops to riot and pelt their officers with stones. Even when the cash did arrive, 'Ayub still did not have sufficient money to pay all the arrears of wages, while the regiments recently arrived from Maimana and the Murghab received nothing at all. In order to get rid of the unruly troops, 'Ayub ordered the two Maimana regiments to Kabul, promising that once there Amir Ya'qub would pay them.

The Treaty of Gandamak and Siege of the Kabul Residency

The collapse of the Afghan army meant the only serious opposition to the British columns as they advanced on Jalalabad, Khost and Kandahar came from local tribesmen. Within a matter of weeks most of southern Afghanistan had fallen and Amir Ya'qub Khan had little choice but to offer to negotiate what was in effect his surrender, in the hope that his submission would prevent the partition of Afghanistan. In May 1879 Cavagnari and Ya'qub met at Gandamak, a venue chosen deliberately by Cavagnari because of its emotive link with the last stand of Shelton's regiment in January 1842. With British forces victorious, Cavagnari was in no mood to compromise and Amir Ya'qub was presented with a series of demands that he had no choice but to accept in order to remain as head of state. They included the installation of a permanent British Resident in Kabul backed up by a substantial body of troops and the right of British troops to enter Afghanistan without the Amir's prior permission. British surveyors would also demarcate Afghanistan's northern frontier, Kabul was to be linked to the Indian telegraphic system, and Kurram, Sibi and Pishin became 'assigned districts' under British rule, a temporary arrangement that ended up as de facto annexation. The Amir also ceded the key fortress of Jamrud in the Khyber Pass and renounced any right to interfere in

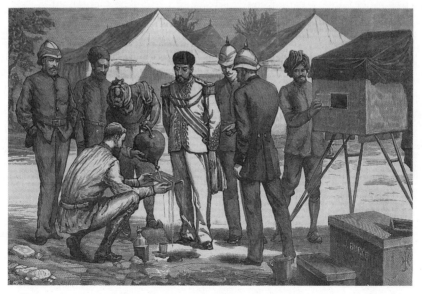

'"Fixing the Negative". The End of the Afghan War – Photographing the Ameer Yakoob Khan at Gandamak', *The Graphic*, 12 July 1879. The photographer John Burke, depicted here holding the plate, volunteered for the post of official war photographer and made a series of historic photographs of Afghanistan during the Second Anglo-Afghan War.

the internal affairs of the Afridis. In return Amir Ya'qub Khan received a meagre annual subsidy of six *lakh*s rupees and a pledge that British forces would eventually withdraw from all Afghan territory, with the exception of Kandahar.

Ya'qub Khan was in no position to argue and on 26 May 1879 he put his seal on the Treaty of Gandamak. Lytton was exultant and declared the treaty marked 'the commencement . . . of a new and better era for Afghanistan'. Such was his level of self-deception that Lytton even claimed the Afghans would 'like and respect us all the more for the thrashing we have given Sher 'Ali and the lesson we have taught Russia', and that they bore Britain no ill will for invading their country. Salisbury profusely congratulated the Viceroy on his 'great success . . . and the brilliant qualities you have displayed', while Disraeli told Lytton that it was 'greatly owing to your energy and foresight [that] we have secured a scientific and adequate frontier for our Indian Empire'.[2] Yet even before Disraeli's letter of congratulation reached India, this experiment in imperial bullying had blown up in Lytton's face.

Cavagnari was appointed as the British envoy in Kabul with the rank of major and a knighthood thrown in for good measure. He arrived in Kabul in late July 1879 where the mission was welcomed by a rendition of 'God Save the Queen' from the Amir's brass band. His escort consisted of 75 Frontier Guides, Pathans and Sikhs, commanded by Lieutenant Walter Hamilton, a great-nephew of General Sir George Pollock. Three months earlier Hamilton had earned the Victoria Cross for his bravery at the Battle of Fatehabad in Nangahar, but he never lived long enough to hear he had won Britain's highest military honour. The mission's accommodation was a crumbling *sarai* in the lower Bala Hisar. The building was never intended as a defensive position, but it was the only unoccupied place in the citadel capable of housing more than a hundred persons. According to Major General Sir Charles MacGregor, who surveyed the site later, the place was a 'rat trap'.[3] Cavagnari knew the *sarai* was indefensible, but he did not demand more appropriate quarters for he had no wish to offend Amir Ya'qub Khan.

Since most Afghan officials regarded the Treaty of Gandamak and the imposition of Cavagnari's mission as a national humiliation, they refused to pay the customary courtesy call on the envoy. As far as they were concerned, Amir Ya'qub Khan was king in name only and even Cavagnari noted that 'the people of Afghanistan are inclined to look to the British Envoy more than to their own ruler'. When the Amir sent his tax collectors into the Koh Daman, the population refused to pay until his officials had written authorization from the British envoy. As for the Afghan conscripts, they pestered the Guides asking them when Cavagnari was going to abolish the hated conscription system and allow them to return home.[4]

Cavagnari, who had less than two years' experience on the Afghan frontier, ignored these warning signs and informed the Viceroy the Afghans had been cowed and that even 'the religious element at Kabul was wonderfully quiet; in none of the mosques has a single word disapproving of the English alliance been uttered'. At the same time he noted a strong anti-Ya'qubid faction in the capital, but failed to make the connection between this party and the British occupation. Cavagnari was soon floundering in a sea of intrigue and confessed to Lytton that he was 'quite bewildered' as to whether to trust the Amir or not and he had not the 'slightest conception' about what was going on behind his back.[5] His lack of skill and experience made him easy prey for officials, who exploited the British presence to enrich themselves and further their own ambitions.

One of the most powerful of these opportunists was Sardar Wali Muhammad Khan, who had been governor of Kabul during Sher 'Ali Khan's reign. His loyalties were uncertain, for he was suspected of being in communication with 'Abd al-Rahman Khan and Ishaq Khan in Samarkand and had ambitions to become Amir himself. Despite his familial affiliation with the Afzalids, Sardar Wali Muhammad Khan had defected to the British when they occupied Kurram and Cavagnari appointed him to his advisory council, where he and his allies proceeded to destroy what little faith the envoy had in Amir Ya'qub Khan's loyalty.[6]

As Cavagnari struggled to cope with a posting for which he was eminently unqualified, in August the two mutinous regiments from Herat and a third one from Balkh arrived in Kabul, having been promised that the new Amir would pay their arrears of wages. The Herat regiments were in a particularly bad mood for they had been given only 3 rupees per head for road expenses and by the time they arrived in the capital they were starving and penniless. Their temper was not improved by the fact that the Ramazan fast had begun during their march. Within a matter of days of their arrival they clashed with the Guides, but Cavagnari ignored sympathizers when they warned that trouble was brewing.

Ya'qub Khan had no cash to pay these troops for the state treasury was nearly empty and he had not received a single rupee of the British subsidy. Lytton had told Cavagnari that if Ya'qub Khan was in need of 'prompt pecuniary assistance' it 'would not be grudged', but Cavagnari withheld payment, for he wanted Ya'qub Khan to 'recognise and admit his helplessness before offering such aid'.[7] Specifically, Cavagnari wanted the Amir to overhaul his administration, but the Amir had stalled for he was not prepared to risk angering powerful individuals by meddling with the well-established patronage system. On 2 September, in what would be his last official communication, Cavagnari cabled Lytton 'all well'. Early on the following morning General Da'ud Khan, Amir Ya'qub's commander-in-chief, ordered the Herat regiments to muster, without weapons, inside the lower Bala Hisar to receive their pay, but when they were told they would receive only two months' wages they pelted the general and their officers with stones, forcing them to seek shelter in the Amir's palace. The mutineers then tried to storm Amir Ya'qub's residence, only to be met with stern resistance from a handful of Arab *ghulams*. An unidentified person then shouted that they should ask the British envoy for their money and they rushed to the Residency. When Cavagnari refused to disburse any money, the mutineers began to stone the Guides and eventually Cavagnari ordered them to open fire, killing or wounding several attackers in the process. The deaths enraged the troops even more and they sent for reinforcements and their weapons from Sherpur. Meanwhile they looted the bazaars and the nearby arsenal. Reinforced and now armed to the teeth, the soldiers attacked the Residency with renewed vigour while *mullahs* in the Old City broke their silence and called from the minarets for everyone to come and join the attack.

The defence of the Residency, according to one Afghan eyewitness, was 'miraculous'. Despite overwhelming odds and heavy loss of life, the Guides held out for most of the day. Eventually the buildings were set alight and the attackers broke down the main door of the *sarai*, set up a field gun in the courtyard, and prepared to fire point-blank into the house where the defenders had taken refuge. Cavagnari, Dr Kelly, the mission's physician, Jenkyns, the mission's Oriental Secretary, and Lieutenant Hamilton, along with those Guides still capable of fighting, made a series of sorties to spike the gun, only to be killed or mortally wounded. The survivors were offered their lives – the Sikhs on condition they converted to Islam – but the offer was rejected and so Muslim Pathans and Punjabi Sikhs fought side by side and were slain to the last man. In the end, only two sepoys lived to tell the tale.[8]

Cavagnari's death and the massacre of his escort was a mortal blow to Lytton's Afghanistan policy and British prestige, as well as a personal tragedy as Cavagnari was a friend of the Viceroy. In his dispatch to Disraeli notifying him of the massacre, Lytton reported that: 'The web of our policy so carefully and patiently woven has been rudely shattered . . . All that I was most anxious to avoid in the conduct of the late war and negotiations has

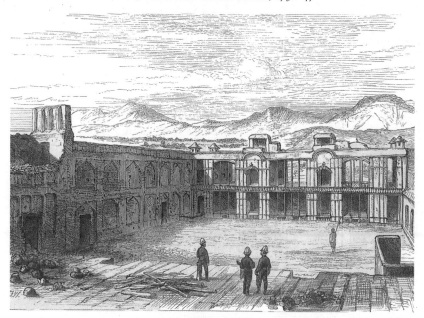

'Interior of the British Residency, looking south', *Illustrated London News*, 20 December 1879. The sketch was drawn after the massacre of Cavagnari and his escort.

now been brought about by the hand of fate.'[9] Britain now had no choice but to send troops to Kabul, despite Lytton recognizing that there was a risk of repeating the events of 1841/2. Since the Viceroy blamed Amir Ya'qub for the death of Cavagnari, rather than his, and his government's, aggressive policies, it was no longer possible for Ya'qub to remain as Amir and the search was on, in Lytton's words, for a new 'puppet ruler'. Lytton was particularly harsh in his condemnation of Amir Ya'qub, accusing him of actively inciting the mutineers, covertly calling for a *jihad* and deliberately standing back while the British officers and their escort were slaughtered. The Viceroy's accusations were based mostly on the account of Sardar Wali Muhammad Khan, a version that was highly convenient as far as Lytton and Disraeli were concerned, since it exonerated them from any blame and put all of it on the Amir. For this reason, Wali Muhammad Khan's account of Cavagnari's death became embedded within British imperial history and continues to be repeated uncritically by both popular writers and academics.

Afghan and other contemporary accounts give a very different picture about the background to the attack on the Residency. Perhaps the most telling is that given by Amir Ya'qub Khan himself in a letter to the Viceroy written a few days after the events, and which included a profound apology for the deaths. Lytton, inevitably, dismissed the Amir's account as excuse-making by a craven and devious ruler. Ya'qub Khan's account of Cavagnari's death is still ignored or not taken seriously, despite the fact that the Amir had nothing to gain from the envoy's death and everything to lose. Wali Muhammad Khan, on the other hand, penned his version of events in the hope that British would depose Ya'qub Khan and appoint him as Amir in his place.

Ya'qub, rightly, claimed he was unable to send a relief force to the Residency for he and his senior officers were besieged by the same mutinous regiments and equally feared for their lives. The troops, anyway, refused to obey any orders issued by either the Amir or his generals, but despite this Ya'qub Khan did what he could to end the siege. General Da'ud Shah was sent to attempt to restore order, only to be attacked and badly wounded. The Amir then sent one of his sons along with other sardars, Qur'an in hand, to appeal to the mutineers to negotiate, only for their pleas to be ignored. Finally Ya'qub Khan sent 'well-known Syuds and Mullahs of each clan', but they too failed to persuade the mutineers to end their attack. In the end, Ya'qub was lucky to escape with his own life.

Imperial histories depict the attack as both sudden and spontaneous, but here too Afghan accounts differ. According to Katib the mutiny was a premeditated attempt to overthrow Amir Ya'qub Khan by the anti-British, pro-Afzalid party, 'masterminded' by 'Aisha Begum, Sher 'Ali Khan's favourite wife and the mother of 'Abd Allah Jan, the recently deceased heir apparent.[10] 'Aisha Begum was the daughter of Muhammad Shah Khan Babakr Khel of Laghman, the father-in-law of Wazir Akbar Khan. Muhammad Shah had not only been responsible for keeping the British hostages following the British withdrawal in 1842, but he had played a major part in the siege of Jalalabad and in securing Kabul for Dost Muhammad Khan's party. As well as her father's history of opposition to British intervention, there was a long-standing rivalry between her and Ya'qub Khan's mother over which of their sons would become Amir. When 'Abd Allah Jan, the heir apparent and 'Aisha's only son, died unexpectedly, she lost her paramount position in the zanana to Ya'qub's mother. In an attempt to regain her power 'Aisha plotted to have Ya'qub deposed or killed in the hope that her son-in-law, Muhammad Ishaq Khan, who was in exile in Samarkand, would succeed to the throne.

'Aisha began to sell her jewellery in order to buy army loyalties, but when Amir Ya'qub heard what she was doing, he forbade her from selling any of her property. Not daunted, 'Aisha wrote secretly to British officials offering to poison Ya'qub and used what cash she had to hand to bribe senior military officers and the mutinous troops to join the plot. The two recently arrived Herat regiments were a prime target for her intrigue; not only were they penniless and starving, they had been commanded by 'Abd Allah Jan. As for the officers of the Balkh regiment, many of them were already partisans of Ishaq Khan and 'Abd al-Rahman Khan. According to Katib, the Queen had even bribed General Da'ud Shah, Ya'qub's commander-in-chief, to tell the regiments not to accept the two months' pay and rebel.

If this were the case, then it may explain Da'ud Shah's decision to muster regiments that were in a mutinous state inside the Bala Hisar rather than outside the citadel's walls. Under normal circumstances no troops, armed or otherwise, would have been allowed to enter the royal citadel for the risk they posed to the Amir was too great. General Da'ud Shah probably knew the troops would not accept just two months' pay and attack the Amir's palace, but the plot unravelled after the mutineers were beaten back from the palace walls and attacked the Residency instead. When the Guides killed and wounded several mutineers, the soldiers were more intent on avenging their comrades' deaths than they were in storming Ya'qub Khan's palace. No doubt the prospect of looting the Residency's full treasury was an additional incentive. By the time the last defender was slain and the Residency pillaged, it was dusk and the exhausted troops withdrew to break the fast and share out the booty.

General Roberts and the occupation of Kabul

Cavagnari's death made the occupation of Kabul inevitable and the Khost Field Force, commanded by General Frederick Roberts, was ordered to march on the Afghan capital. In Kabul itself Ya'qub Khan somehow managed to hold out in the Bala Hisar, even though the rest of the city was out of his control. Roberts made relatively easy progress to Kabul until he reached Chahar Asiyab, on the outskirts of Kabul, where he defeated a force of tribal levies and government forces after a sharp engagement. Amir Ya'qub Khan then came into Roberts's camp to submit and he and a number of his followers were arrested.

Lord Lytton was deeply affected by his friend's death as well as by the shattering of his Forward Policy, and his instructions to Roberts made it clear that he was on a mission of both personal and Britannic revenge. Roberts had 'perfectly unfettered . . . freedom of action' to punish any civilian or soldier implicated in the attack on the Residency. Suspects were to be subjected to 'the roughest and readiest kind' of justice and Roberts was specifically ordered not to keep any written records of the judicial proceedings. The accused had no right of appeal and the military courts Roberts set up were authorized to accept uncorroborated evidence by informers, even though it was 'highly probable . . . some comparatively innocent persons may suffer', but 'that cannot be helped'. As far as Lytton was concerned, the guilt or innocence of particular individuals was of no consequence for not only was Kabul 'the great national culprit',

> The whole Afghan population is *particeps criminis* in a great national crime; and every Afghan brought to death by the avenging arm of the British Power, I shall regard as one scoundrel the less in a den of scoundrelism . . . You cannot stop to pick and chuse [*sic*] Ringleaders. Every soldier of the Herat Regiment is *ipso facto* guilty; and so is every civilian, be he priest or layman, Mullah or peasant, who joined the mob of assassins . . . Remember, it is not *justice* in the ordinary sense, but *retribution* that you have to administer on reaching Kabul . . . Your object should be to strike terror, and to strike it swiftly and deeply; but avoid a '*Reign of Terror*'.[11]

According to Major General Sir Charles MacGregor, Roberts's aide-de-camp, 'Bobs' was just the right man for this job, for he was a 'cruel, blood-thirsty little brute'.[12] Indeed, Roberts had already shown his ruthlessness during his occupation of Khost, where he had burnt and plundered villages, ordered a cavalry officer to 'take no prisoners' and turned a blind eye to an Indian officer who executed ninety prisoners in cold blood. Unfortunately for Roberts, a journalist embedded with his division wrote an account of his actions in the British press, which led to a furore. Roberts, with Lytton's agreement, responded not by moderating his policy, but by expelling the offending correspondent.

Once in possession of Kabul, Roberts summoned government officials to the Bala Hisar and dismissed them. He then proclaimed martial law over a 16-kilometre (10-mile) radius from the capital and offered substantial rewards for information leading to the arrest of anyone implicated in the Residency massacre. All the surrounding villages were forcibly disarmed and settlements that were found to be harbouring mutineers, such as Indiki, were fined heavily. Roberts then set up a Commission of Enquiry, consisting solely of British officers, to attribute blame for the massacre; it concluded, not unexpectedly, that Amir Ya'qub Khan's 'guilt and complicity' was 'conclusive'. As a result, the Amir abdicated and he and three other senior *sardars* were exiled to India.

Others implicated in the massacre were less fortunate. Roberts erected two gallows in the ruins of the Residency where those condemned to death were hanged. In all, 87 individuals were executed, often on the flimsiest of evidence, including Sardar Muhammad Aslam Khan, *kotwal* of Kabul; Sardar Sultan 'Aziz Khan, son of Nawab Muhammad Zaman Khan and a rival of Wali Muhammad Khan; Khwaja Nazir, a prominent *mullah* from the Old City; and General Khusrau Khan, a Kafir who had converted to Islam. As for the actual ringleaders of the attack, they escaped 'justice' for most of them had fled Kabul long before Roberts arrived.

Roberts's harshness, however, eventually rebounded on him. Journalists embedded with the army wrote a series of highly critical articles about his heavy-handedness, the arbitrary nature of the courts martial and the burning of villages. After one press report alleged that some Gurkhas had burnt alive and beheaded several Afghan prisoners, the *Daily News* damned Roberts as a murderer. These press reports provided excellent political fuel for Gladstone's Liberal Opposition, who accused Disraeli of authorizing a Reign of Terror. Lytton, too, came in for his share of criticism for pushing Sher 'Ali Khan into a corner and actively seeking an opportunity to invade Afghanistan. In an attempt to save face and his career, Lytton tried to blame Roberts, only for the latter to defend his actions angrily, claiming that he had been as 'merciful and forbearing' as the circumstances permitted.[13]

Despite martial law and all the executions, the British occupation of Kabul led to both tragedy and revolt. During an inventory of the Bala Hisar's arsenal, it was discovered that a huge amount of gunpowder, rockets and other munitions were lying on the ground in a volatile state. While troops attempted to neutralize the hazard, there was a massive explosion that killed a British officer and several Gurkhas, as well as destroying part of Upper Bala Hisar. Meanwhile in the hinterland of Kabul and Ghazni, opposition to the British invasion was gathering, though Roberts dismissed the threat as 'too far away to take notice of'.[14] The resistance was divided into four main factions, all but one of which favoured the return of Ya'qub Khan or his son, Shahzada Musa'. In Wardak, Mushk-i 'Alam declared *jihad* against the British and was in an uneasy alliance with General Muhammad Jan Khan. General Ghulam Haidar Khan, a Tajik from Charkh, was gathering his forces in the Logar; in the Koh Daman, Mir Bacha Khan Kohistani and Mir 'Osman Khan, head of the Safis of Nijrab, favoured the cause of 'Abd al-Rahman Khan and the Samarkand exiles.

There were some, however, who supported the British occupation. They included the Jawanshir Qizilbash, whose commander had told Cavagnari that if the British army took Kabul they would happily slaughter every Muhammadzai they could lay their hands on. Other pro-British groups included the Hazaras of Kabul and Ghazni and the Chahar Aimaq of the

Murghab and Badghis. Even Dilawar Khan, *wali* of Maimana, wrote to Roberts tendering his submission to Britain. As marginalized and disenfranchised ethnic and religious minorities, all of these tribes hoped that Roberts would finally sweep away the Durranis and place Afghanistan under direct British rule.

The first signs of unrest came in early December 1979 when the telegraph line between Gandamak and Kabul was cut. A few days later the Logaris refused to provide the army with any more supplies. On 11 December, the 48th anniversary of Macnaghten's treaty with Wazir Akbar Khan, Muhammad Jan Khan and Mushk-i 'Alam attacked and defeated a British column at Chahardeh. A second force sent into the Koh Daman had a sharp encounter with the Safis and Mir Bacha Kohistani, but managed to return to Kabul in good order. A few days later, some 60,000 *mujahidin* poured into Kabul from all directions and occupied most of the southern, western and northern parts of the capital.

Roberts now faced a very serious situation. He had only 6,000 troops at his disposal and there was insufficient fuel or fodder to withstand a prolonged winter siege. Roberts decided to concentrate all his forces behind the Sherpur defences and evicted thousands of Hazaras who had been employed repairing the cantonment's accommodation and defences. They were quickly hunted down by Mushk-i 'Alam's *ghazis* and beaten or killed. Major General Bright, who commanded the outpost at Gandamak, was ordered to march to Kabul, but he refused for he had been attacked by Asmat Allah Khan of Laghman and was preparing for a second assault. Instead, Roberts ordered General Gough in Jalalabad to march to the relief of both garrisons.

Roberts's force managed to hold out for ten days, despite having to defend more than 4 kilometres (2½ mi.) of poorly built perimeter walls. He was helped by the fact that the Afghans failed to storm the cantonment immediately and instead looted the houses and shops of Hindu and Armenian merchants, and sacked the Qizilbash quarters of Murad Khana and Chindawal. The rebel leaders then argued over who should be declared Amir and whether Mushk-i 'Alam ought to be governor of Kabul. When Muhammad Jan Khan opened negotiations, Roberts strung him along without any intention of conceding anything and bought a few more days' grace.

Mushk-i 'Alam eventually lost patience and on 23 December 1879, the anniversary of the assassination of Macnaghten, 20,000 of his *ghazis* flung themselves against Sherpur's ramparts. Roberts, pre-warned of the assault, opened up with grapeshot and disciplined rifle fire. After repeated attempts to storm the breaches failed, Mushk-i 'Alam's *ghazis* abandoned the attack, leaving thousands of dead and dying piled up against Sherpur's walls. Roberts had won the day, but it had been a close call. The following day Gough's relief force reached Kabul and the rebels dispersed. Roberts sent the cavalry in pursuit with orders to show no quarter and any Afghan bearing arms or suspected of being a rebel was shot or cut down in cold blood.

The defeat at Sherpur ended all but desultory resistance to the British occupation. Unlike the First Afghan War, Roberts was decisive and ruthless. His army was far better equipped and could communicate almost instantly over long distances by telegraph and heliograph. Modern breach-loading rifles had replaced the old muzzle-loading Brown Bess and were far more accurate and outranged the Afghan *jezails* and muskets, still the primary weapon of the Afghan tribes and even the army. Roberts also deployed Gatling guns, an early form of machine gun. Furthermore, the Ghilzais of Tezin and the Khurd Kabul played little or no part in the siege of Kabul and the Royal Engineers had driven a new road over the Lataband Pass, which bypassed the gorges and passes of the Haft Kotal and the country of the Jabbar Khel.

After regaining control of the capital, Roberts lifted martial law and proclaimed an amnesty for rebels, though he put a price on the heads of the leaders of the uprising. Ya'qub Khan's mother was also imprisoned, charged with encouraging and financing the uprising. Wali Muhammad Khan was appointed as governor of Kabul, although when he heard the British planned to withdraw, he opted for exile in India. Roberts ordered the construction of a series of new defensive positions in and around the capital and levelled everything around Sherpur to improve the field of fire. All the buildings in the lower Bala Hisar were also levelled and the Royal Engineers drew up detailed plans for new barracks, a parade ground, a military hospital and a new road to link the eastern and western gates. The works were abandoned before any of the new buildings were erected, but all the shopkeepers, government servants, *ghulams* and other inhabitants were evicted anyway without compensation, while most of the wood, stone and other building material was used to repair Sher 'Ali Khan's half-completed Sherpur citadel. Among the buildings destroyed by the Royal Engineers were what was left of the Mughal and Saddozai palaces and Afghanistan's only Christian church, used by Kabul's small Armenian community. Later one old Armenian woman wryly noted the irony of how the church built for them by a Muslim king had been destroyed by Christians.[15] Roberts also sent a column to the Koh Daman to punish Mir Bacha Khan, whose home village of Baba Kachgar, which Sale had burnt to a cinder in 1840, was once more razed to the ground.

The return of 'Abd al-Rahman Khan

In London the political fallout from the Afghan War contributed to Disraeli's decision to call a General Election in early 1880. Lytton, in an attempt to pacify the war's more strident critics, removed Roberts from control of civil affairs and sent Lepel Griffin, Chief Secretary of the Punjab, to be Political Officer in Kabul with orders to 'set about the preparation of a way for us out of that rat trap'.[16] A few weeks later General Stewart, head of the Kandahar Field Force, replaced Roberts as commander-in-chief of the army and was ordered to march to Kabul. Stewart was the most senior officer in Afghanistan, but Roberts was furious at being cut down to size and was so embittered that he wrote to Lytton informing him he planned to resign from the army once the Afghan campaign ended.

Lepel Griffin faced the complex task of finding a ruler who was pliant enough to do Britain's bidding but who also had the support of at least some of the main Afghan factions. Roberts had surrounded himself with Muhammadzais and they naturally told Griffin that only one of their own lineage was acceptable, a claim he endorsed without question. There were, however, dozens of potential candidates and Lytton briefly toyed with splitting the country up between 'Ayub Khan in Herat, Sardar Sher 'Ali Khan, son of Mehr Dil Khan, in Kandahar and a separate Amir in Kabul. Then a dramatic change took place in the north that altered the whole equation.

When 'Abd al-Rahman Khan in Samarkand heard of the death of Sher 'Ali Khan he asked Russian officials for permission to return to Afghanistan to claim the throne, but his request was denied. After Ya'qub Khan's abdication and the British occupation of Kabul, however, the Russians had a change of mind and allowed 'Abd al-Rahman Khan to return and stake his claim to the throne. 'Abd al-Rahman Khan set out for Badakhshan, for the *mir* was related to him by marriage, but en route he made a pilgrimage to the shrine of the famous *pir*, Khwaja Ahrar, in Samarkand, where he claimed to have had a vision of the *shaikh* who told him to take his banner with him as its presence would ensure victory. Despite this act of sacred theft, 'Abd al-Rahman Khan's campaign did not start well. The *mir* tried to prevent him from crossing the Amu Darya, only for 'Abd al-Rahman Khan to outwit him and ford the river further downstream. Then, instead of heading for Faizabad, the *sardar* marched on Rustaq, crossing a high mountain pass despite deep snow. When he arrived the garrison defected. A few weeks later, following a brief battle, the Mir of Badakhshan fled to Chitral.

While 'Abd al-Rahman Khan took over Badakhshan, Sardar Ishaq Khan and his two brothers, Muhammad Sarwar Khan and 'Abd

Faizabad in Badakhshan. This town was the first provincial centre to fall
to 'Abd al-Rahman Khan.

al-Quddus Khan, crossed into the Chahar Wilayat, hoping that the
Afghan garrisons there would support them. General Ghulam Haidar
Khan, Ya'qub's governor of Balkh, however, attacked and forced them
to flee into the Dasht-i Laili. Sarwar Khan then went to Shibarghan in
disguise, hoping to persuade the garrison commander to join them.
Instead he was arrested and sent to Mazar-i Sharif, where he was brutally
tortured and eventually beheaded. Ishaq Khan and 'Abd al-Quddus Khan
fled to Maimana where they were detained, but on their way to Herat
they managed to escape. Their attempt to raise a rebellion in the Chahar
Wilayat had failed miserably.

'Abd al-Rahman Khan's bid for the throne might well have ended
at this juncture had not Ghulam Haidar Khan made a serious error of
judgement. 'Abd al-Rahman Khan had asked Sultan Murad of Qunduz for
safe passage for his men to march on Kabul, only to be refused. Ghulam
Haidar Khan responded by launching a pre-emptive attack and occupied Qunduz, whereupon Sultan Murad fled to Faizabad, threw in his lot
with 'Abd al-Rahman Khan and called on all the Uzbeks of the province
to rebel. The commander of Takhtapul, appalled at the brutal execution
of Sarwar Khan, also declared for 'Abd al-Rahman Khan. As more and
more troops defected, Ghulam Haidar Khan fled across the Amu Darya,
while his brother committed suicide. By Nauroz 1880 the whole of Afghan
Turkistan was in 'Abd al-Rahman Khan's hands.

Lepel Griffin had kept a close watch on 'Abd al-Rahman Khan's progress and in early April 1880 he sent an envoy to Khanabad to sound out the *sardar*'s potential as Amir. Griffin informed 'Abd al-Rahman Khan that he would seriously consider his claim to the throne provided he was willing to accept the arrangements his predecessors had made with Britain. 'Abd al-Rahman Khan's reply was cautious, for his followers wanted him to declare a *jihad* against the British. He had merely come 'to help my nation in much perplexity and trouble', he told Griffin, but the door was now open for more detailed negotiations.[17] In subsequent correspondence 'Abd al-Rahman Khan asked for clarification on whether Britain would demand the right to station a British envoy in the country and asked that Kandahar and, if possible, Herat be included in his realms.

Griffin, though, continued to hedge his bets. While negotiating with 'Abd al-Rahman Khan, he called the leaders of the factions that had taken part in the siege of Sherpur to attend a *darbar* in Kabul. Most of these factions favoured the return of Ya'qub Khan or his son, Musa', so they were deeply disappointed when Griffin informed them that Britain would not allow any member of Ya'qub's family to become Amir and that the Viceroy was contemplating dividing the country into three separate kingdoms. This was not what the delegates wanted to hear. When they returned back to the bases Ghulam Haidar Khan's Logaris attacked a British force near Chahar Asiyab, and when General Stewart arrived at Ahmad Khel, near Ghazni, his advance was blocked by between 12,000 and 15,000 Ghilzais loyal to Mushk-i 'Alam. A one-sided battle followed in which more than a thousand *ghazi*s were slaughtered. Among the dead on the battlefield was at least one female warrior. Following the Battle of Ahmad Khel, Griffin abandoned his attempt to win over Mushk-i 'Alam and the Ya'qubids and decided to pursue the option of 'Abd al-Rahman Khan: 'We have found in Abdul Rahman a ram caught in the thicket', he informed Lytton.[18]

By May 1880 there were many pressing reasons why Britain wanted to secure a quick settlement and withdraw. At the end of April Gladstone's Liberal Party had swept to power in a landslide victory and Lytton had tendered his resignation. His replacement, the Marquis of Ripon, had specific instructions to abandon the Forward Policy and withdraw all troops from Afghanistan as soon as practicable. Since Gladstone's government no longer made it a precondition that any candidate for the throne had to agree to a British envoy being stationed in Afghanistan, this removed the most important stumbling block as far as 'Abd al-Rahman Khan was concerned. The only point of difference was that the British wanted to retain control of Kandahar with Sher 'Ali Khan as governor, while 'Abd al-Rahman Khan wanted the former Durrani capital to be an integral part of Afghanistan.

'Abd al-Rahman Khan decided to move nearer to Kabul in case the British withdrew. In July 1880 he arrived in Charikar, where the religious leaders and elders from Panjshir, Kohistan and Tagab came and 'kissed his stirrup'. On 19 July he received a letter from Griffin, which informed him that Britain was prepared to accord him official recognition as Amir of Kabul and invited him to the capital for the inauguration ceremony. The announcement caught 'Abd al-Rahman Khan by surprise, so he convened a hasty *jirga* of as many religious and tribal leaders as he could muster and the following day they pledged their allegiance to him. Two days later Griffin publicly proclaimed 'Abd al-Rahman Khan as Amir of Kabul *in absentia*, for the *sardar* was still in Charikar.

Throughout the two decades of Amir 'Abd al-Rahman Khan's reign, British officials always maintained it was Britain who had conferred legitimacy on the Amir since, by right of conquest, sovereignty belonged to the victors. 'Abd al-Rahman Khan, on the other hand, maintained his legitimacy was based on the 'election' of 20 July 1880, which he claimed was a form of national assembly. In fact the tribal and religious leaders present at the *jirga* were mostly from the Kabul region and there were no representatives of the Durranis, Mushk-i 'Alam and his Ghilzais or the other Ya'qubids who had spearheaded resistance to the occupation. Griffin did eventually secure written pledges of loyalty to 'Abd al-Rahman Khan from a number of Ghilzai tribes around Ghazni, but 'Abd al-Rahman Khan's claim that he had been elected by the nation at large had no basis in fact.

Maiwand and Kandahar

Griffin's decision to negotiate a handover of power with 'Abd al-Rahman Khan was in part a panic reaction to a sudden change in British military fortunes in southwestern Afghanistan. Shortly after Stewart left Kandahar, the religious establishment issued a *fatwa* condemning the British-backed governor, Sher 'Ali Khan, as an unlawful ruler. 'Ayub Khan, informed of this decree, set out for Kandahar at the head of a large and well-equipped army. Sher 'Ali Khan marched out to confront 'Ayub, but when he crossed the Helmand he discovered that the Herat army was far larger than he had anticipated. Sher 'Ali appealed to Brigadier General Burrows, the garrison commander in Kandahar, to come to his aid, whereupon Burrows set out with 2,400 men, but by the time he reached Girishk most of Sher 'Ali Khan's men had defected.

Uncertain as to the location of 'Ayub's army and with supplies running low, Borrows withdrew back down the Kandahar road to Khushk-i Nakhud. On 26 July 1880 his scouts reported a small body of enemy cavalry at Maiwand. Burrows, believing that 'Ayub Khan was still on the other bank of the Helmand, ordered his troops to march to Maiwand early the next morning. Exhausted from marching in high summer under the blazing desert sun, and parched from lack of water, the troops spent the whole night striking camp. By the time they reached Maiwand they were exhausted, thirsty and many of them were suffering from heatstroke.

To his dismay, Burrows discovered that he had marched straight into 'Ayub Khan's main army, which was well dug in on high ground between his troops and the only water source. Burrows then made another serious misjudgement, sending two of his infantry regiments forward to adopt a static line of defence. Exposed and without any cover, the troops were caught in crossfire from entrenched snipers and artillery. Despite heavy losses, the regiments held their ground for more than four hours until Burrows, in an attempt to save them, ordered his cavalry to storm the trenches. When they failed to break through, he ordered the forward line to withdraw, only for the retreat to turn into panic-stricken flight. A few stood their ground and fought to the last man, but most turned and tried to flee back to Kandahar, some 80 kilometres (50 mi.) away, only to run the gauntlet of local villagers who attacked them with any weapon they could lay their hands on. In the end, more troops perished in the flight than were killed at Maiwand: in all Burrows lost more than 1,200 men, nearly half of his Brigade.

The Battle of Maiwand remains one of the cornerstones of Afghanistan's nationalist identity. Streets are named after the battle and memorials to the victory are found in Kabul, Herat and Kandahar. In Kabul's Old City, the graves of ancestors killed at Maiwand, or who died later from their wounds, are still venerated as family shrines. Maiwand also gave rise to the legend of Malalai, arguably the most famous Afghan woman of modern times, whom nationalists in the twentieth century dubbed the Afghan Joan of Arc. Malalai, so the story goes, was the teenage daughter of a poor shepherd from Khig who, along with hundreds of other women, brought water to the troops during the battle. When, in the heat of the battle, the ranks of the *mujahidin* faltered, Malalai is said to have seized the Afghan flag and rallied the soldiers with an extempore Pushtu couplet about the shame of defeat, turning defeat into victory. In some versions, the day of the battle is said to have been her wedding day.

This romantic story is very probably a later fabrication, for there is no mention of either Malalai, or any such act of heroism, in contemporary ·

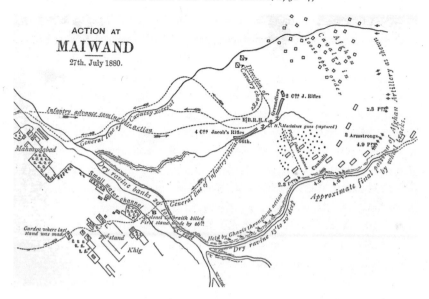

'Action at Maiwand', a British defeat and a pyrrhic victory for Sardar Muhammad 'Ayub Khan, for the defeat led to the British recognition of 'Abd al-Rahman Khan as Amir. As a result the heirs of Sher 'Ali Khan ended up in exile in India.

Persian histories. We know there were hundreds of women carrying water to the Afghan troops at Maiwand and there are references to women warriors fighting at the battles of Ahmad Khel and Chahar Asiyab. According to one eyewitness of the retreat, village women also hurled rocks and other missiles at the fleeing troops. As for Khig, this is famous in British military history as the site of the last stand of the 66th Foot. Yet while Malalai's story is most likely a myth, she is symbolic of the role played by Afghan women in resisting foreign occupation. Today many Afghan women still bear her name, for Malalai has become a symbol of Afghan women's struggle against all forms of (male) oppression and their right to a public role in society.

Lepel Griffin heard by telegram about the disaster at Maiwand the following day and he called an urgent meeting with 'Abd al-Rahman Khan to discuss an immediate handover of power and the relief of Kandahar, which was now being besieged by 'Ayub Khan. Griffin, however, had no authorization to negotiate a treaty or to agree to recognize 'Abd al-Rahman Khan as Amir of Kabul and Kandahar. Instead, he presented the Amir with a Memorandum of Obligation drawn up by Sir Alfred Lyall, India's Foreign Secretary. Known as the Lyall Agreement, this document became the foundation of all Anglo-Afghan relations during the reign of Amir 'Abd al-Rahman Khan. The memorandum was remarkable for the concessions Britain made. The precondition of a permanent British officer stationed in Afghanistan was dropped and Britain committed itself to provide the Amir military aid in the event of unprovoked aggression by another nation and to pay him an annual subsidy. These were very similar to the terms Sher 'Ali Khan had asked for at Umballa and Simla, and had the British government agreed to these terms then, there would have been no invasion of Afghanistan and both Britain and Afghanistan would have avoided the expense of going to war.

After two days of discussions, 'Abd al-Rahman Khan agreed to the terms and a few days later he arrived in Kabul to oversee the handover of power. Sherpur, the Bala Hisar and other positions were evacuated and thirty field guns, part of Sher 'Ali Khan's artillery park, were handed over, along with the contents of the Kabul treasury and a gift of ten *lakh* rupees. Roberts then paid the Jabbar Khel and the Ghilzai of Tezin a similar sum for safe passage and the troop withdrew safely with hardly a shot fired in anger. The Amir used the British cash to secure the loyalty of key individuals, in particular Ghulam Haidar Khan Charkhi, whom he appointed as his commander-in-chief. Griffin had also been patiently negotiating with Mushk-i 'Alam for several weeks and, shortly after 'Abd al-Rahman Khan entered Kabul, two of the *pir*'s sons came and pledged their father's allegiance to the new Amir. In return, Mushk-i 'Alam's eldest son became Head of Religious Affairs.

The only problem now facing the British army of occupation was the relief of Kandahar. Roberts was given charge of this task and secured safe passage through the Logar and Ghazni with the help of 'Abd al-Rahman Khan, Ghulam Haidar Khan and Mushk-i 'Alam, meeting with only token resistance. Since the situation was critical, Roberts's troops marched twice the usual daily distance and covered more than 500 kilometres (310 mi.) in 23 days, a remarkable achievement in the era before motorized transport. A second brigade commanded by Major General Pharye marched out from Sibbi in Baluchistan but it had to fight almost all the way to Kandahar. Roberts's force, however, proved more than enough. On 1 September 1880 'Ayub Khan's army was destroyed at Baba Wali, near Old Kandahar, and the siege of Kandahar was lifted. Gladstone's government was therefore able to portray the withdrawal from Afghanistan as an orderly handover of power instead of a defeat or retreat.

The relief of Kandahar transformed Roberts into one of Britain's most feted military heroes. Both Houses of Parliament passed a vote of thanks, Queen Victoria wrote him a personal letter of congratulation and a baronetcy followed soon after. Roberts abandoned his plan to resign from the army and in 1885 he became commander-in-chief of the India

Army. Fifteen years later he repeated his Kandahar exploit by leading the relief of Mafeking during the Boer War. As for 'Ayub Khan, Maiwand was a pyrrhic victory, for instead of securing him the throne, it drove Britain into a hasty deal with his cousin and rival, 'Abd al-Rahman Khan. The siege of Kandahar, however, did result in the British government deciding to abandon the plan to retain control over the area and in April 1881 the province was handed over to 'Abd al-Rahman Khan's governor.

Britain had been fortunate to escape the 'rat trap' without suffering the kind of humiliation that it experienced in the First Afghan War. Even so, the invasion was hardly a resounding success. Cavagnari and three other British officials along with their escort had been slaughtered, and the raising of the siege of Sherpur had been touch and go. The defeat at Maiwand and the siege of Kandahar were further dents to British military prestige. The intervention was the death knell for Forward Policy supporters and cost Disraeli an election, Lytton his Viceroyship and the British Exchequer £17 million, three times the original estimate. General Roberts eventually emerged as a British hero, but the real winner was 'Abd al-Rahman Khan, who finally won the struggle for the throne that had begun with the death of Dost Muhammad Khan nearly two decades before. Even so British officials claimed the gains of the Second Anglo-Afghan War outweighed the losses. Britain now had an ally on the Durrani throne who provided the strategic depth India sought against Russian aggression. The Afghans viewed the occupation in a very different light for, as Kakar rightly remarks, 'What the British gained from this and from their first Afghan war was the everlasting bad will of Afghans.'[19]

Amir 'Abd al-Rahman Khan and the suppression of dissent

After the withdrawal of British forces, the situation inside Afghanistan continued to be unstable. A few months after the British evacuated Kandahar, 'Ayub Khan took the city and 'Abd al-Rahman Khan, backed by Mushk-i 'Alam's Ghilzais, set out to confront his rival, while 'Abd al-Quddus Khan, now governor of Turkistan, was ordered to march on Herat. In September 1881 'Ayub Khan's army was soundly defeated at Chehel Zina, near Old Kandahar, and he fled into Persian territory after he heard that Herat had fallen to 'Abd al-Quddus. Meanwhile 'Abd al-Rahman Khan's troops celebrated their victory by plundering Kandahar. 'Abd al-Rahmin Akhund and Maulawi Wasi, Kandahar's most senior religious figures and the men who had issued a *fatwa* condemning the Amir's alliance with Britain, sought sanctuary in the shrine of the Khirqa-yi Sharif. 'Abd al-Rahman Khan ordered them to be forcibly removed and proceeded to slay them with his own sword on the threshold of the shrine.

The fall of Kandahar and Herat may have reunited Afghanistan but it did not end subsequent challenges to the Amir's rule. Over the next two decades 'Abd al-Rahman Khan faced more than forty major rebellions, encompassing every region and ethnic group.[20] Indeed the reign of 'Abd al-Rahman Khan was one of almost perpetual conflict, the result not so much of what he claimed was reducing a 'disorderly people to a state of new order',[21] but rather the inevitable outcome of his autocratic style of government, which was unlike anything Afghanistan had experienced under the Durrani monarchy.

During his decade of exile in Russian Turkistan, 'Abd al-Rahman Khan had come to admire the autocratic rule of the Tsars in general and Peter the Great in particular. Russia's imperial system, with its highly central-ized administration and rigid feudalism, was the antithesis of the tribal federalism that was, and still is, the hallmark of Afghanistan's political life. 'Abd al-Rahman Khan's ambition was to remodel Afghanistan along Tsarist lines by concentrating all power in his own hands, which meant destroying and dismantling all competitive power structures. Instead of just being head of state, 'Abd al-Rahman Khan wanted to be its body, mind and soul as well.[22] As one author aptly put it, 'the seat of government was the bed-room of [the Amir]'.[23]

One of the inevitable consequences of this centralizing policy was rebellion, for powerful individuals were not prepared to surrender their political autonomy, social position or hereditary privileges without a fight. As each power broker was broken, the Amir stripped them of their wealth, land or control of religious endowments, which were the basis of their power. Many were executed, often in a variety of novel ways, rival Muhammadzais were exiled and thousands were left to rot in the country's disease-infested prisons. By the end of 'Abd al-Rahman Khan's reign it was estimated that as many as 100,000 people had been executed. 'Abd al-Rahman Khan backed up his repressions with an all-pervading intelligence-gathering network. Fear reigned in every household and no one dared utter the slightest criticism of the Amir lest they were betrayed by members of their own family and ended up in prison, or were handed over to the Amir's torturers and executioners.

Following the defeat of 'Ayub Khan the Amir's first round of repression was aimed at Muhammadzais, former officials of Sher 'Ali Khan's govern-ment and supporters of 'Ayub Khan and Ya'qub Khan. One particular focus of the Amir's attention was the families of the Kandahar *sardar*s and a number of their descendants were exiled, including Ghulam Muhammad Tarzi. The Amir also arrested or executed several leaders who pledged their allegiance to him at Charikar, as well as a number of Pushtun tribal leaders who had assisted the British invasion. Over the following decade the Amir also conducted military campaigns against the Mohmands, Shinwaris and other tribes of Nangahar and Kunar, killing or exiling their leaders and replacing them with men often of no rank or status, but who were bound to the Amir by bonds of loyalty and patronage. He also introduced a new tax, known as *seh kot*, equivalent to one-third of all revenues and yields, to replace the traditional Islamic taxes of *zakat* and *ushr*.

Another target was Mushk-i 'Alam and General Muhammad Jan Khan Wardak, the two individuals who had been instrumental in the siege of Sherpur. The Amir accused them and 'Asmat Allah Khan, head of the Jabbar Khel, and Mir Afzal Khan Hotaki, a direct descendant of Mir Wais Hotaki, of plotting the restoration of 'Ayub Khan. They were arrested and subsequently poisoned in prison or put to death at night in killing fields near the Hashmat Khan lake, outside the walls of the Bala Hisar. At the end of 1885 'Abd al-Karim, Mushk-i 'Alam's eldest son, who had succeeded him as *pir*, issued a *fatwa* condemning 'Abd al-Rahman Khan as an infidel and called for the restoration of 'Ayub Khan. His Andar Ghilzais, though, were soon crushed and 2,000 heads of slain or executed Ghilzais were sent to Kabul where they were piled into a pyramid of skulls. 'Abd al-Karim and his brothers managed to escape to India, so the Amir vented his ire on the corpse of Mushk-i 'Alam, which was exhumed and burnt to ashes. As for the Andar Ghilzai, they lost all their land and wealth and were reduced to abject poverty.

'Abd al-Karim's revolt was the harbinger of a far more serious Ghilzai rebellion. In the spring of 1886 the Amir's officials attempted to fine and disarm the Tokhi and Hotak Ghilzais of Kandahar, only for them to rebel, with the support of the equally powerful Kakar tribe. In Herat the Ghilzai regiments mutinied and invited 'Ayub Khan to take control of the city, but when he crossed the Persian frontier 'Ayub's small force was defeated and he fled back to Persia. He eventually gave up any hope of regaining the throne and accepted a British offer of exile in Lahore and the Ghilzai revolt was eventually put down.

Anglo-Afghan relations and Afghanistan's northwestern frontier

After the withdrawal from Afghanistan, British officials were less concerned about the Amir's internal battles than they were about the Russian threat to

Herat and Afghanistan's poorly defined and poorly defended northwestern frontier. One particular problem was that Dilawar Khan, *wali* of Maimana, refused to acknowledge 'Abd al-Rahman Khan's suzerainty and in May 1882 he wrote to British officials asking for protection and threatened to 'apply to other quarters' if Britain did not recognize Maimana's independence. When British officials curtly replied that they regarded Maimana as an integral part of Afghanistan, Dilawar Khan accepted Russian cash and arms and by so doing turned a minor dispute into an international crisis.

In the previous year Russian forces had occupied the Akkal Oasis, the gateway to Merv and Herat, so when Maimana accepted Russian cash and military assistance, British officials feared this was a precursor to the occupation of Herat. The Amir was urged to bring Maimana back under central authority and establish a garrison in the town. To assist this campaign the Viceroy sent 'Abd al-Rahman Khan a thousand muzzle-loading muskets. In the spring of 1882 two armies from Herat and Balkh marched on Maimana, whereupon Dilawar Khan raised the Imperial Russian flag over his citadel. Yet again Maimana proved a hard nut to crack and Muhammad Ishaq Khan, governor of Balkh, unable to take the town by storm, finally agreed to a truce after Dilawar Khan agreed to make a token submission to the Amir.

The following summer Ishaq Khan tried once more to subdue Maimana, but this time he was aided by Mir Husain Khan, Dilawar Khan's uncle and dynastic rival. Maimana was besieged once more in March 1884, but when Dilawar Khan appealed to the Russians for military assistance his pleas were ignored. A few weeks earlier Russian forces occupied and annexed Merv, despite St Petersburg having assured Britain that Russia had no designs on the region. The furore that followed led to calls from Members of Parliament and the British press for Britain to declare war on Russia. A conflict was eventually avoided but as a consequence Russia was not prepared to push Britain any further by intervening in Maimana, and so Dilawar Khan was left to face the Amir's wrath alone. When Maimana finally fell it was sacked and many of its inhabitants slaughtered. As for Dilawar Khan, he was sent in chains to Kabul. Ishaq Khan then installed Husain Khan as the new *wali*, but all real power lay with the Afghan military governor, backed by a large force of government troops.

As far as Britain was concerned, the fall of Maimana could not have been more timely, for British and Russian officials were in the process of negotiating a joint demarcation of Afghanistan's northwestern frontier. A month after Maimana fell, the agreement was signed and for the next two years Russian, British and Afghan commissioners surveyed the region from Herat to the Amu Darya and drew an internationally agreed frontier. At the same time, British and Indian surveyors conducted the most extensive exploration to date of western and northwestern Afghanistan.[24] Since the frontier was poorly defined, both Russia and Afghanistan tried to claim as much territory as possible. In early 1885 Russia occupied the Zu'l-fiqar Pass, the gateway to Herat in the north, and when the Amir sent reinforcements to the area there was a very undiplomatic exchange of insults between the Afghan commander and his Russian counterpart. Britain responded by informing St Petersburg that if Russia attempted to occupy Herat or the Panjdeh Oasis, downstream from Maruchak, Britain would go to war. Yet despite this threat, on 30 March 1885 a Russian force overran the Afghan frontier post of Pul-i Kheshti and claimed Panjdeh in the name of the Tsar.

The Panjdeh Crisis brought Britain and Russia to the brink of war once more but London eventually backed down, as it was not prepared to start a European war over a small and insignificant Central Asian oasis. Instead, Britain made it clear that any further Russian incursions into Afghan territory that threatened Herat would be regarded as a declaration of war.

Ironically, 'Abd al-Rahman Khan, who was on a state visit to India at the time, showed little interest in the fate of Panjdeh and was far more concerned about possible Russian annexation of the fertile plains around Balkh and Mazar-i Sharif. The Amir even delayed granting permission to the British boundary commissioners to enter Herat in order to prepare its defences against a possible attack, much to the frustration of the Indian government. It was not until some eight months after the occupation of Panjdeh that they were granted access. In an attempt to make the city more defensible, the Amir ordered several of the city's most important Timurid buildings to be levelled, including the great *musalla* complex built by Queen Gauhar Shad, which consisted of a vast Friday mosque and *madrasa* and royal tombs.

One of the findings of the Afghan Boundary Commission that caused much alarm was the level of discontent with Afghan rule they encountered from the Murghab to Maimana. Indeed, many local people openly told the commissioners they would prefer to be ruled by Russia than the Muhammadzais. The intensity of this discontent raised serious concerns about the defensibility of a frontier that was anyway an arbitrary line that bore little relationship to traditional grazing and irrigation rights.

Afghanization and the colonization of the northern provinces

In an attempt to address this problem, Colonel C. E. Yate, one of the commissioners, proposed that the indigenous population of the region

– Aimaq, Turkman and Uzbek – be forcibly removed from the frontier and replaced by Pushtun colonists from the south. Yate called his policy Afghanization and it appealed to the Amir, for had not Peter the Great also implemented similar policies? At the same time, Afghanization killed several birds with one stone. The mostly Durrani tribes who were relocated to the region would have more loyalty to Afghanistan by dint of their ethnic and tribal links with the ruling dynasty, a bond which was reinforced by the distribution of free land, houses and grazing rights seized from displaced populations. Furthermore, the presence of large numbers of Pushtuns in the frontier meant there was a pool of military levies that could be called up in emergencies. Afghanization was also an ideal way to relocate rebellious Ghilzais as well as Kabul's urban poor, another source of trouble, and relocate them far away from the centre of power. Finally, the policy fed 'Abd al-Rahman Khan's views about the racial superiority of Pushtuns in general and the Durranis in particular.[25]

The first phase of Afghanization focused on the forcible relocation of the Aimaq tribes of the Murghab and Badghis, but was eventually extended to all regions from Maimana to Qataghan and as far south as Pul-i Khumri and the Hari Rud. In the space of some three years between 100,000 to 200,000 Pushtuns were either forcibly or voluntarily relocated from the Helmand, Kandahar, Ghazni, Nangahar and Kabul to the northern provinces, with the result that the Pushtun population of the *wilayat* rose from 4 per cent in 1884 to more than 30 per cent by the end of 1888. Probably as many, if not more, Uzbek, Turkman and Aimaqs were forcibly evicted from their homes and lands, without compensation, and dumped down on marginal lands in the foothills of Badghis, Ghur and the Tir Band-i Turkistan, the hinterland of Herat and the *dasht* around Balkh, Pul-i Khumri and Qataghan. Other tribes left the country altogether: some fled into Russian territory, others into Persian Khurasan or British India.

The new Pushtun colonists, or *naqelin*, found life in their new home far from easy. The climate and environment of northern Afghanistan was very different from what they were accustomed to, especially those tribes who came from the warmer southern plains or subtropical Nangahar. The first wave of settlers arrived at the onset of the bitter northern winter and with fodder, grain and food in short supply, the price of basic commodities soon rose steeply. As winter set in the nomads' herds, unable to break through the frozen ground, starved for lack of grazing, or died from exposure, new strains of animal diseases, predation, or from eating unfamiliar, poisonous plants. Many colonists too died of influenza, pneumonia or exposure. When summer arrived, malaria and sandfly fever took their toll, while

A group of Ishaqzai Pushtuns from Langar, a remote settlement in Badghis. These Durrani tribesmen were relocated here as part of the Afghanization programme of Amir ʿAbd al-Rahman Khan in the wake of the Panjdeh Crisis of 1885.

locusts ate the spring grass and sprouting grain. The government gave the nomads large tracts of arable land as well as grazing rights, but these tribes had no tradition of agrarian pursuits and regarded agriculture and horti-culture as demeaning. Some of their leaders even suspected Afghanization was a ploy by the Amir to undermine their leadership and force their tribe to adopt a sedentary lifestyle. After barely surviving their first winter, in the following autumn Taju Khan Ishaqzai, one of the first of the Pushtun *naqelin* to settle in the Murghab, ordered his tribe to return en masse to their traditional winter quarters in the Pusht Rud.

Tensions between *naqelin* and indigenous populations began as soon as they arrived in the area. Local populations resented the immigrants, whom they regarded as foreigners, and there were armed clashes over land ownership, water rights and grazing. The *maldar*'s tradition of allowing their flocks to roam freely was particularly resented, for the animals ate newly planted crops, fruit trees and vines, as well as fouling and blocking irrigation channels. When the local population complained to local gov-ernors, more often than not the officials sided with the colonists. To add insult to injury, the government conscripted local people to build houses and storehouses for the colonists. In the Maimana and Murghab regions thousands of local tribesmen – Uzbeks, Turkmans and Aimaq – fled across into Russian territory, formed resistance movements and began to raid government outposts and rustle the herds of colonists.

Britain was indifferent to the social impact of Afghanization and many saw it as a good thing that Pushtu tribes were located on the vulnerable Murghab and Maimana frontier. What was important for Britain was the signing of the boundary agreements in the summer of 1887. Lord Salisbury, now Prime Minister, privately confessed that he did not think the frontier convention would stand the test of time and this seemed to be the case when Lieutenant Tarnovsky, the Russian officer in charge of Panjdeh, briefly occupied Qal'a-yi Nau in 1892 in the name of the Tsar. War with Britain was averted, however, after the Russian Foreign Ministry denounced Tarnovsky as a 'madman' and recalled him to St Petersburg, where he was 'broken' and disgraced. Even so, Afghanistan's northern and northwestern frontier proved to be far more stable than its one with India and far less subject to dispute.

The demarcation, however, created great social upheaval in a region that had been plagued with unrest, war and economic decline. Panjdeh ended up on the Russian side of the frontier and in return Russia made territorial concessions further north, but the frontier was artificial and cut through customary water and grazing rights as well as split populations. When the boundary agreement was finally signed, 'Abd al-Rahman Khan closed the frontier to all traffic, a decision that was an economic disaster for Maimana, Andkhui and Bala Murghab, which traditionally traded with Merv, Khiva and Bukhara. These regions were now relegated to backwaters and went into steep economic decline.

The revolt of Sardar Muhammad Ishaq Khan

The Amir's policies increasingly alienated Sardar Ishaq Khan, governor of Turkistan, for he had to manage the many social upheavals created by the Afghanization programme and the new frontier, as well as a declining economy and simmering unrest among the indigenous population. Ishaq Khan proved to be a popular governor. His administration of justice was mild and he defied orders from the Amir that he deemed unjust or unjustified. His popularity was increased by his affiliation to the Central Asian *tariqa* of Naqshbandiyya Sufism, which was, and still is, the dominant Order in the region, and his devotion to the shine of Shah-i Mardan.

Tensions between Ishaq Khan and the Amir first emerged during the Ghilzai revolt when he refused to send additional Uzbek conscripts for the war, or more of the province's revenue to pay for the campaign. When the Amir exiled a number of political dissidents to the region, Ishaq released them, claiming there was no evidence of their guilt. By early 1888

Amir 'Abd al-Rahman
Khan, c. 1880. Towards
the end of his life he
became morbidly
obese and afflicted
with chronic bouts
of sickness which
rendered him, at
times, unconscious
and unable to govern.

'Abd al-Rahman Khan had had enough of Ishaq Khan's proceedings and
ordered all garrison commanders in the northern province to come to
Kabul; a command that they knew would probably lead to dismissal,
imprisonment or even execution. Ishaq Khan made excuses and delayed
implementing the Amir's order. In June 1888 he called a secret council of
military commanders and indigenous leaders in the hill station of Shadyan,
which agreed they could no longer tolerate the Amir's autocratic rule and
swore on the Qur'an to support Ishaq Khan's bid for the throne. The only
dissenting voice was that of Husain Khan, *wali* of Maimana, who owed his
position to the patronage of 'Abd al-Rahman Khan. His refusal cost him
his life. Mir Husain Khan had attended the Shadiyan meeting of August
1888 but refused to swear the oath of loyalty to Sardar Ishaq Khan, in part
because Maimana at the time was under the authority of the governor of
Herat and not Balkh. Furthermore, throughout his time as Na'ib of Afghan
Turkistan, Ishaq Khan had done his utmost to remove Mir Husain Khan
from office. When Husain Khan refused to support the revolt, Ishaq
Khan threw him in prison and subsequently handed him over to Muzaffar
Khan, Mir Husain Khan's nephew and son of Mir Hukumat Khan. In 1862

Mir Husain Khan had killed his half-brother, Hukumat Khan, during a struggle for the succession and now Muzaffar Khan avenged his father's death by putting his uncle to death with his own hands.

For six weeks following the Shadyan meeting, Ishaq Khan and his supporters secretly gathered their forces and somehow managed to keep the plot hidden from the Amir. They were helped by the fact that at the time 'Abd al-Rahman Khan was suffering a relapse of his long-standing and chronic illness, which led to periods of unconsciousness and on occasion rendered him unable to speak.[26] When, in early August, reports reached Mazar-i Sharif stating that the Amir was dying or already dead, Ishaq Khan decided the time was ripe to stake his claim for the throne. On 10 August 1888, during Friday prayers, Ishaq Khan's name was recited in the *khutba* and a *fatwa* issued by the *mutawalli* and *shaikh*s of the Shah-i Mardan shrine was read out that condemned the Amir and his government as a *kafir* regime. Religious leaders were then sent through the province to call the populace to join the *jihad*. Within a matter of days, Qataghan and Saighan were in rebel hands and government forces fell back to Khinjan. However, Muhammad Sharif Khan of Maimana, who had succeeded his father, Husain Khan, refused to join the rebellion and held out, supported by the Herati garrison, despite overwhelming popular support in the region for the revolt.

The rebellion caught the Amir by surprise, but despite being seriously ill he acted swiftly to prevent the revolt spreading. All of Ishaq Khan's extended family in Kabul, including his elderly Armenian mother, were imprisoned and the Amir secured his own *fatwa*, declaring *jihad* on Ishaq Khan. General Ghulam Haidar Khan, who had been instrumental in the suppression of the Ghilzai revolt, was ordered to assemble an army at Bamiyan, while in Herat 'Abd al-Quddus Khan dispatched a relief force to Maimana. Less than two weeks after Ishaq Khan had been declared Amir, Ghulam Haidar Khan took the rebel outpost of Kahmard and sent the garrison's commander, Najm al-Din Khan, Ishaq Khan's father-in-law, in chains to Kabul, where he was executed by having boiling oil poured over him. Following the fall of Kahmard, the Shaikh 'Ali Hazaras submitted and petitioned the Amir to allow them to emigrate en masse to Persia. Instead they were offered the choice of resettlement near Kandahar or Herat, or exile to India. In the end they opted to settle in Quetta rather than remaining in a country ruled by 'Abd al-Rahman Khan.

The Amir's swift military response had taken the initiative away from Ishaq Khan. He then made another tactical error by deciding not to oppose Ghulam Haidar Khan's advance. Hearing that the Herat army was already advancing on Sar-i Pul, Ishaq Khan concentrated his forces at Tashqurghan so he would be in a better position to defend Mazar-i Sharif in the event the Herat column subdued the Chahar Wilayat. This allowed Ghulam Haidar Khan to march unopposed into Doshi and, as he pushed on to Khulm, Ishaq Khan had no choice but to stand and fight.

The two armies finally met on 27 September 1888 at Ghaznigak, south of the Tashqurghan gorge. Initially the battle went Ishaq Khan's way, when a cavalry charge caused one wing of Haidar Khan's army to flee, but Sardar Haidar Khan counterattacked and the rebel army gave way. Ishaq Khan, thinking his army was in full retreat, rode off the battlefield, whereupon the rest of the army turned and fled. On 3 October Ghulam Haidar Khan marched into Mazar-i Sharif unopposed. Ishaq Khan fled across the Amu Darya with those of his supporters who were able to, and spent the rest of his days as an exile in Samarkand. Later 'Abd al-Rahman Khan had a plaque placed above the entrance of the shrine of Shah-i Mardan to commemorate his victory.

The Turkistan Atrocities

Despite being ill, 'Abd al-Rahman Khan decided to travel to Mazar-i Sharif to oversee the punishment of rebels and the pacification of the region. For the next eighteen months the Amir presided over what British officials termed the 'Turkistan Atrocities'.[27] The Amir's wrath fell not just on those implicated in the revolt but on any individual or group who might pose a threat to his power. The purges encompassed all sections of society from religious elites to the families of the former Uzbek *amirs*, the officer corps and rival Muhammadzais. Thousands were condemned to death in 'the most inhuman and fiendish' ways, many more were mutilated, blinded or crippled for life as result of being tortured.[28] Women too were tortured, others were forcibly married to Muhammadzais or condemned to imprisonment in Kabul, where their jailers and government officials systematically raped them. Even individuals who had remained loyal to the Amir were not safe and many were imprisoned or executed for allegedly supporting Ishaq Khan.

All *auqaf* in the province were nationalized, including the lands and holdings of the Shah-i Mardan shrine in Mazar-i Sharif. Hundreds of *mullahs*, *pirs* and other religious leaders were imprisoned or executed and 120 Ansaris, the hereditary guardians of the shrine of Shah-i Mardan, were taken to Kabul where they were publicly sawn in two. Traders and local landholders had their assets seized and many were tortured to reveal where they had hidden their wealth. The region's major export commodities were nationalized and merchants ordered, on pain of death, not to trade with Russia but send all their goods to India. This was yet one more blow to the local economy, for the region's famous perishable exports, in particular grapes and melons, were too fragile to be transported over such large distances. Yet not everything went 'Abd al-Rahman Khan's way. While reviewing his troops a soldier fired at the Amir from close range, but the bullet missed his head and wounded a pageboy standing nearby. The would-be assassin was instantly cut down by one of the regiment's officers. 'Abd al-Rahman Khan attributed his narrow escape to a charm he wore around his right arm.

The Kabul *wakil*, who accompanied the Amir to Mazar-i Sharif, sent regular reports to India about the situation, but officials thought he was exaggerating. When his reports continued to flood in, Colonel Warburton, the Political Agent in Peshawar, and Carl Griesbach, a geologist who was conducting a survey of mineral resources in Turkistan, were asked to investigate. Both men confirmed the *wakil*'s reports, while Griesbach gave a gruesome eyewitness account of the torture and execution of men and women.

The 'Turkistan Atrocities', as Griesbach called them, put British officials in a difficult position. By 1888 there was already much concern about the unsatisfactory nature of the Anglo-Afghan relationship, with some high officials contemplating the annexation of southern Afghanistan or its complete dismemberment. One of the chief advocates of this view was General, now Lord Roberts. In 1885 he wrote a memorandum in which he argued the policy of maintaining a united Afghanistan as a bastion against a Russian invasion of India was 'full of illusions'. Britain, he asserted, was 'living in a fool's paradise' and an expensive one at that, for the state of Afghanistan was only held together by virtue of British financial and military aid. The longer Britain propped up 'Abd al-Rahman Khan, he argued, the more difficult it would be to disengage without loss of 'dignity and prestige'. 'Abd al-Rahman Khan, he went on, ruled 'by fear alone in a kingdom divided against itself'; as for the Amir's style of government, it was 'at best, a reign of terror'.[29]

Reports of the Turkistan Atrocities eventually appeared in the Indian and British press, which led to a public outcry. Even Queen Victoria wrote to Salisbury expressing her revulsion at the Amir's conduct. In Parliament the Liberal Opposition demanded Salisbury release the correspondence related to the atrocities, but he refused on the grounds it was 'not in the public interest'. In fact, it was not in his interests, for had Warburton and

Griesbach's reports been made public Salisbury would have undoubtedly faced demands for his resignation and Britain's Afghanistan policy would have collapsed, along with its support for 'Abd al-Rahman Khan.

The situation also created a diplomatic crisis with the Russian Foreign Ministry complaining to Britain about the Amir's public allegations that Russia had encouraged Ishaq Khan's rebellion. Russia was also unhappy about the loss of trade resulting from the Amir's closure of the Russo–Afghan frontier as well as the refugee crisis, for thousands had fled across into Russian territory in order to escape persecution and the region's economic crisis. When nothing was done about these issues, the Russian Foreign Ministry lost patience and informed Britain that unless action was taken to curb the Amir's 'excesses' they would intervene militarily in order to protect the population.

Britain had invested heavily in Amir 'Abd al-Rahman Khan, but it was not prepared to invade Afghanistan and depose the Amir, or risk another civil war. By 1888 the British government had paid the Amir more than eighteen *lakh* rupees per annum and had gifted him an additional 114 *lakh* rupees, 25,000 breech-loading rifles, seventy artillery pieces and millions of rounds of ammunition. The Amir had used these weapons and cash to crush the internal revolts and keep his army and loyalists happy. The irony was that Sher 'Ali Khan had pleaded again and again for Britain to provide him with a far lower level of subsidy and military assistance, only for his request to be refused. Had Britain agreed to Sher 'Ali Khan's requests and supported him to the same degree as 'Abd al-Rahman Khan, there would have been no need to invade Afghanistan, and the country would have been ruled by a monarch whose style of government was far more benign and acceptable to both the Afghans themselves and Britain.

British relations with Amir 'Abd al-Rahman Khan

The Turkistan Atrocities were just another, albeit public, example of Britain's key ally in Asia acting against her interests. For despite the propaganda about the Amir being the protector of India, behind closed doors British officials were increasingly frustrated with relations with 'Abd al-Rahman Khan and his erratic behaviour. The heart of the issue was the lack of reciprocity. Britain believed that since it was paying for the piper it had the right to call the tune, yet again and again the Amir either played the wrong melody or refused to pipe at all. The Amir even had the temerity to accuse Britain of parsimoniousness and when Lord Lansdowne, the Viceroy, asked him for details of troop numbers and their deployment in order to assess possible additional military assistance, the Amir angrily refused to provide the information. In the widely read English version of his autobiography, the Amir was often critical of British policy and of successive Viceroys, including Lytton and Lansdowne.[30]

'Abd al-Rahman Khan also violated the Lyall Agreement by corresponding directly with Persia, Turkey, Russia and Germany, even though Britain was meant to manage Afghanistan's foreign relations. When Britain began work on extending the Indian railway to Chaman, he claimed it was like pushing a knife into his vital organs. 'Abd al-Rahman Khan even published a series of pamphlets calling for Afghans to prepare for *jihad* against Britain and Russia, accusing both countries of secretly plotting to dismember Afghanistan.

Lansdowne wrote and urged the Amir to moderate his 'provocative language' about Russia and warned him it could lead to a 'collision'. At the same time he raised the issue of the Turkistan Atrocities, though in a somewhat apologetic manner. If the reports prove correct, Lansdowne wrote, such punishments were 'abhorrent to civilisation', yet at the same time the Viceroy conceded that 'severe measures may have been necessary' against the rebels and 'energetic action' was 'most necessary'.[31] Shortly after sending this letter Griesbach and Warburton's reports reached him, so Lansdowne wrote a second, sterner letter to the Amir in which he pointed out that the atrocities were 'abhorrent to the ideals of civilised nations' and 'calculated to produce a bad impression'. The Viceroy also raised a number of other issues that had led to strains in the Anglo-Afghan detente, and hinted that if the Amir did not change his ways Britain would reconsider its unconditional support. When the Amir read the Viceroy's communications he flew into a violent rage and in a very undiplomatic reply he accused Lansdowne of addressing him in 'a dictatorial manner' and interfering in Afghanistan's internal affairs. 'Abd al-Rahman Khan then went to great lengths to defend his actions and showed not the slightest expression of regret, claiming that, like Peter the Great, he was 'reducing the disorderly people to a state of new order'.[32]

The Amir's reply was highly unsatisfactory, but Lansdowne did not pursue the matter any further and consoled himself by claiming the Amir's reply was 'temperate in tone' and that the atrocities were abating. In fact, things were as bad as ever. A few years later a similar dilemma arose during the Amir's repression of the Hazaras, which led to more mass executions, deportations and expulsions. Privately senior officials admitted it was increasingly difficult 'to justify to ourselves our actions in supporting upon the throne of Afghanistan, for political reasons, a ruler so bloody and implacable', but concluded that the only option was to 'let sleeping dogs lie'.[33] Relations would 'drift on' in the hope that the Amir would soon die and his successor would prove a more suitable ally. Fear of political instability and civil war, which might provide an excuse for Russian intervention, meant Britain felt it had no alternative but to support 'Abd al-Rahman Khan and consequently he had a free hand. The Amir had called Britain's bluff and won.

Despite the bloody repressions, the Amir failed to prevent further rebellions. In 1890 the Firozkohi Aimaq in the Murghab rebelled, followed in the spring of 1892 by yet another revolt in Maimana. Both uprisings were ruthlessly crushed and Muhammad Sharif Khan, the last Uzbek *wali* of Maimana, fled across the border and asked the Russian authorities for permission for thousands of Maimanagis to emigrate. His request was denied but Muhammad Sharif Khan continued a cross-border guerrilla war with the Afghan authorities in Maimana until he was eventually lured to Herat by a promise of an amnesty, only to be imprisoned.

The Hazara Wars

A far more serious revolt began in 1891 when the Hazaras of the western Hazarajat rebelled.[34] Discontent with Muhammadzai rule had simmered away in this region since the days of Dost Muhammad Khan. As a result of expropriation of their lands, many Hazaras had been forced to pursue menial work in Kabul and other cities, where they formed a despised underclass of day labourers. The attitude of the urban upper classes to Hazaras was exemplified by the Amir himself, who compared them to donkeys. Prejudice increased during the British occupation of Kabul in 1879–80 after the Hazaras welcomed the invaders and worked on the rehabilitation of Sherpur.

The catalyst for the Hazara revolt was the appointment of Sardar 'Abd al-Quddus Khan, a descendant of Sultan Muhammad Khan Tela'i, as governor of Bamiyan. According to the confidential *Who's Who in Afghanistan*, 'Abd al-Quddus was 'somewhat fanatical in matters of religion . . . a Tory of the most crusted type in politics, and an apostle of Afghanistan for the Afghans'.[35] The appointment of such a hard-line Sunni and Pushtun supremacist was about the worst choice to govern a region where the population was predominantly Shi'a and Isma'ilis and of Turco-Mongolian ethnicity. 'Abd al-Quddus Khan and the Muhammadzai officer corps in Bamiyan treated the Hazaras abominably, imprisoning or executing their leaders, disarming the population, helping themselves to Hazara women and imposing the Sunni rites on the region. In the spring of 1891 the Hazaras of Uruzgan had had enough and rebelled. Three brigades armed with modern British weaponry were sent into the area and quickly crushed the uprising. The Uruzgan rebellion, however, was just the start of a war that raged for more than three years. The following year Muhammad Mir 'Azim Beg of Deh Zangi and Qazi Muhammad Askara of Fouladi led another revolt in the Ghurband. In 1879 both these men had pledged their allegiance to 'Abd al-Rahman Khan and in return the Amir conferred on 'Azim Beg the title of *sardar*.

The rebels blockaded the roads from Kabul to Bamiyan, disrupted trade and communications with Mazar-i Sharif and Herat, eventually obliging 'Abd al-Quddus Khan to abandon Bamiyan. The revolt quickly spread to urban Hazaras, Hazara regiments and Kabul's Qizilbash community. 'Abd al-Rahman Khan's cynical response was to play on sectarian and racial prejudice. He secured a *fatwa* damning all Shi'as and Isma'ilis as *kafirs* and called on the Ghilzai *maldar*, who had long been at odds with the Hazaras over migration routes and pasturage rights, to lead the *jihad*. As an incentive, the Amir promised them that if they were successful he would allocate them increased grazing in the region and let them loot the Hazaras' flocks and property. He also encouraged Muhammad Husain Hazara, the rival of 'Azim Beg, to join the Holy War, offering to appoint him as head of the Hazara tribes.

The *fatwa* led to a nationwide persecution of Shi'as and Isma'ilis. Qizilbash civil servants were dismissed, their property plundered and Sunni *imam*s were put in charge of Shi'a mosques and shrines. Some urban Hazaras and Qizilbash fled to the Hazarajat to join the rebels, while many of Herat's large Shi'a community made their way to Persia, potentially internationalizing the conflict in the process. In April 1893 the Shi'a *mujtahid*s of the shrine of Imam Reza in Mashhad issued their own *fatwa* legitimizing war with Afghanistan in defence of its Shi'a population and the Shah of Persia threatened to invade. In the end nothing came of this threat, for the Shah had no wish to risk yet another confrontation with Britain over Afghanistan. Instead, he wrote a strong protest to the Viceroy. Britain, he declared, was 'friends of the Amir and not of the Afghan people', and demanded that 'Abd al-Rahman Khan be deposed.[36] Britain temporarily suspended arms shipments to the Amir, but as he was already armed to the teeth this gesture did little to prevent the persecution of Shi'as and made not the slightest difference to the outcome of the Hazara War.

By August 1892 the Hazara revolt had been crushed, despite almost suicidal resistance, and 'Azim Beg was captured and executed. When,

Hazaras gather to celebrate Nauroz at the shrine of Sakhi Jan in Kabul's Jamal Mina quarter, March 1976. The shrine is constructed on the site where the Khirqa-yi Sharif was housed during its 'translation' from Bukhara to Kandahar.

in early 1893, Muhammad Husain Hazara, sick of being the Amir's instrument of killing his own people, led a third rebellion, it too was crushed with similar ruthlessness. On the back of each victory, the Amir unleashed an even more fearful reign of terror, which many Hazaras claim was tantamount to genocide. According to some estimates more than 50 per cent of the male Hazara population died as a direct or indirect result of the wars. Thousands of women were forcibly married to Pushtuns in a deliberate attempt to destroy Hazara social and religious hierarchies. The Hazara populations of southern Uruzgan, Zawar, Ghazni and Maidan Shah were expelled and their land distributed to Muhammadzais, Ghilzai *maldar* and government loyalists. Many of them were exiled to Quetta, where Hazaras are still a major element of the city's population. All provincial, district and village leaders in the Hazarajat were appointed solely by the Amir and answerable to him alone. To add to their humiliation, Shi'as and Isma'ilis were required to pay the *jizya*, the religious capitation tax, which under Islamic law is only imposed on non-Muslims. Public celebration of Muharram, 'Ashura' and the *Ta'ziya'* Passion Play, which commemorates the death of Husain, son of 'Ali b. Abi Talib, were banned, a prohibition which remained in force until the fall of the Durrani dynasty in 1978.

The Durand Agreement and the Durand Line

The Hazara repressions led to further calls for Britain to depose the Amir, but government officials were still not prepared to risk destabilization or another invasion. Once again, wider geopolitical interests were at stake, for at the time Britain was negotiating with Russia over Afghanistan's northeastern frontier. In 1893, with the Hazara war still raging, Mortimer Durand, Foreign Secretary of India, arrived in Kabul in order to secure the Amir's agreement on the Pamir frontier and Afghanistan's border with India. This was a delicate assignment, for Durand had to persuade the Amir to cede Roshan and Shignan in return for territorial concessions on the left bank of the Amu Darya and obtain his agreement to include the barren and mountainous panhandle of the Wakhan in Afghanistan, for Britain did not wish India to have any common frontier with Russia.

The issue of Afghanistan's frontier with India was even more problematic since some of the tribes on the Indian side still regarded the Amir as their titular head and even sent him occasional tribute. Britain could not tolerate this situation, especially since the Amir continued to interfere in tribal affairs, as well as provide sanctuary for Indian revolutionaries. Britain even suspected the Amir was encouraging Pushtun religious leaders who were calling for *jihad* against British rule and that Afghan officials were turning a blind eye to the smuggling of breech-loading rifles into Tribal Territory.

The mission, though, was a success and in November 1893 the Amir signed the Durand Agreement, which included acceptance of the Wakhan–Pamir frontier and the establishment of a joint Anglo-Afghan commission to demarcate the Afghan–Indian frontier based on a rough map that Durand brought with him. Amir 'Abd al-Rahman Khan also renounced any territorial claims and 'rights of influence' over Chitral, Swat, Bajur, Dawar and Waziristan, although Afghanistan retained the Barmal region in the Kunar. As compensation, the Amir's subsidy was increased and he was allowed to import arms freely from India, an important concession given that the Hazara War was still raging.

The Durand Agreement, however, would prove to be a major cause of disagreement in future Anglo-Afghan relations and, following Partition in 1947, in Afghan-Pakistan relations too. The emergence of Pushtun nationalism in the early twentieth century went hand-in-hand with a romantic vision of the unity of all Pushtun tribes and calls for a united homeland known as Pushtunistan. This led to the legality of the Durand Line being questioned by successive Afghan administrations and Pushtun pan-nationalists, who even today denounce it as 'poorly marked', 'illegal' or 'imaginary'.[37]

According to this discourse, the Durand Agreement did not have the legal status of a treaty. Over the ensuing years a variety of arguments have been advanced to justify setting it aside, including a claim that Durand deliberately deceived 'Abd al-Rahman Khan about the actual line of the frontier, despite the fact that a map was attached to the agreement; that the Amir signed the protocol under duress; that he never actually signed it; or that he only signed the English and not the Persian text. Others assert the Amir only surrendered his right to influence over the tribes and not sovereignty. Some argue for a semantic and legal difference between 'boundary' and 'frontier', claiming that the former appears in the Durand Agreement, but the latter does not. In fact 'boundary', 'frontier' and 'frontier line' are used almost synonymously in the text of the Durand Agreement.[38] In the 1990s it was commonplace among Afghan refugees in Pakistan to assert that the Durand Agreement was only binding for a hundred years and hence after November 1993 the frontier was no longer legal under international law. This, too, is not the case for the text makes no limitations on the agreement.[39]

Such arguments are at the best disingenuous and at the worst a deliberate distortion of historical facts. 'Convention', 'Agreement' and 'Protocol' are all terms employed in legally binding international agreements concluded between sovereign states and as such the Durand Agreement, also known as the Kabul Convention, had full legal status under international law. Since the Amir personally conducted the negotiations, the claim that he was duped or misled is frankly absurd. The Amir even called a *darbar* where both he and Durand explained the terms and implications of the treaty to an assembly of Pushtun tribal and religious leaders. Copies of their speeches were then distributed to every delegate, and each one was required to set his seal on the Amir's speech. The Amir clearly knew exactly what the Durand Agreement meant, and though he was not happy with some of the concessions he made, his view was that the alliance with Britain, which brought him regular infusions of cash and arms, was more important than token sovereignty over regions that he called Yaghistan, the unruly, or ungovernable, land.

In his autobiography 'Abd al-Rahman Khan wrote of the Durand Agreement:

The misunderstandings and disputes which were arising about these frontier matters were put to an end, and after the boundary lines had been marked out according to the above-mentioned agreements by the Commissioners of both Governments, a general peace and harmony reigned between the two Governments, which I pray God may continue for ever.[40]

The idea that the Durand Agreement was only valid for a century is even more disingenuous since the preamble states the intention was 'to remove for the future, as far as possible, all causes of doubt and misunderstanding', while Clause 6 states that the articles were 'regarded by the Government of India and His Highness the Amir of Afghanistan, as full and satisfactory settlement of all the principal differences of opinion which have arisen between them in regard to the frontier'. The Amir later mused that he had 'a great fancy for a little piece of sandy desert . . . in order to bring the country in touch with the ocean',[41] either in the Persian Gulf, which, of course, was not remotely feasible,[42] or the Indian Ocean, and suggested at some point Britain might consider ceding Afghanistan a narrow corridor to the sea. This 'fancy' for a warm water port would be seized on later by Pushtun nationalists and became entwined with the polemic about Pushtunistan and the Durand Line.

Following the signing of the Durand Agreement, a joint Anglo-Afghan Commission surveyed the frontier from April 1894 to May 1896 and its officials were required to 'adhere . . . with the greatest possible exactness to the line shown in the map attached to this agreement'.[43] The commissioners held extensive consultations with tribal leaders and all parties agreed to any changes to Durand's original map. Boundary pillars were then constructed at regular intervals and their locations carefully recorded. Copies of the final demarcation, including detailed descriptions of each section of the frontier and large-scale maps, were presented to the Amir and filed in the archives of the British and Indian governments. In 1919, under the Anglo-Afghan Treaty, the Mohmand region was demarcated and further slight adjustments were made in 1921 and 1932. Both the 1919 and 1921 treaties reaffirmed the Durand Line as 'accepted by the late Ameer' and were negotiated and agreed by none other than Mahmud Tarzi, the father of Afghan nationalism.

Despite the Durand Agreement, the Amir continued to meddle in affairs across the frontier, particularly Chitral, and high officials in his government covertly encouraged 'fanatics' on the Indian side of the border. As for the Afghan tribes themselves, they paid little heed to the Durand Line, as the frontier was known, and continued to cross the border without bothering to obtain official documentation, a practice that continues to this

A Kafir wood carving
of the goddess Disani,
National Museum
of Afghanistan, as
displayed in 1971.
The Kafir images
were smashed by the
Taliban but were later
carefully restored by a
team led by Professor
Max Klimburg.

day. Given the semi-independent status of Tribal Territory on both sides
of the frontier, the region has always been a haven for smugglers, opium
traders and militant movements such as al-Qaʻida, the Taliban, Kashmiri
'freedom fighters' and more recently Daesh-ISIS.

Britain, though, gained a great deal from the Durand Agreement for
the Indian government garrisoned Gilgit, Swat and Chitral, creating a
defensive line against a possible Russian invasion through the Wakhan.
However, the demarcation did not put a stop to tribal uprisings and Indian
forces conducted a series of campaigns against the frontier tribes including
the Mahsuds (1897), Mohmands (1897–8), Waziris (1897) and the Afridis
and Orakzais (1897), all of which extended British authority and control
deeper into tribal territory.

Under the Durand Agreement, the independent mountain region
known as Kafiristan was included within Afghanistan, despite many Kafirs
regarding the Mehtar of Chitral as their titular sovereign. The Kafirs were
the largest surviving pagan enclave in the Muslim world, whose religion
and culture had strong affinities with ancient Indo-Aryan cults.[44] The
region was particularly famous for its carved wooden images of deities

and ancestral heroes and the exposure of their dead. The Kafirs were never consulted about whether they wished to become part of Afghanistan and their incorporation was the death blow to their ancient culture and religion.

Once the Hazara rebellion had ended, 'Abd al-Rahman Khan declared *jihad* against the Kafirs and in 1895 he sent two large columns into the region from the north and west. The Kafirs, who were mostly armed with bows and arrows, axes and spears, stood no chance against an army armed with breech-loading repeater rifles, artillery and machine guns. Faced with annihilation, many tribes agreed to convert to Islam in order to save themselves and their families. Those that resisted faced the full force of the Afghan blitzkrieg. Men and women were slaughtered indiscriminately and male children above the age of seven were given the choice of conversion or slavery. In a desperate attempt to save their lives, some Kafirs offered their infant daughters in marriage to the invaders, but many younger children too ended up as slaves or servants in the households of Muhammadzais, tribal leaders and other officials. Most of the Kafir tribal and religious leaders were executed, their herds seized, and their homes, temples, ancestral burial grounds and images smashed and burnt. A small number of wooden images were taken to Kabul as trophies of war, where they were later exhibited in the Kabul Museum. The region was then renamed Nuristan, Land of Light, and *mullah*s were sent into the region to oversee an Islamization programme. In 1896, to celebrate the conversion of the Kafirs, the Amir convened a grand *darbar* and took the title of *Ziya' al-Milat wa al-Din*, Glory of the Nation and Religion.

Sardar Nasr Allah Khan's state visit to Britain

Despite the controversy surrounding the Amir's internal repressions, in 1895 the British government formally invited 'Abd al-Rahman Khan to make a state visit to Britain, but since he was in declining health the Amir delegated his son, Sardar Nasr Allah Khan, to undertake the tour in his place. While in Britain Nasr Allah Khan had an audience with Queen Victoria, visited munitions factories, attended Royal Ascot races and made gifts to Muslim institutions. He continued his tour of Europe with visits to France and Italy, but rather than making him more sympathetic to Britain, the tour had a negative impact on Nasr Allah's views on European culture and its values.

Unlike his father, whose beliefs were a mixture of Islamic mysticism and outright superstition, Nasr Allah Khan was a strict and orthodox Sunni Muslim. His religious conservatism, combined with his sheltered and isolated upbringing, meant that the tour of Europe came as a profound culture shock. Nasr Allah Khan was particularly appalled at having to meet and talk to naked, that is, unveiled, women and the fact that they mixed freely with men who were not even their relatives. By the time he returned to Afghanistan, Nasr Allah Khan had developed a deep distaste of European education, social mores and modernization in general, regarding them as not just un-Islamic but irretrievably tainted with 'Christian' values. Nasr Allah's visit also failed to realize the Amir's primary objective, which was to secure the right to open an Afghan Embassy in London. His request was rejected on the ground that 'Abd al-Rahman Khan had repeatedly refused to allow a British Resident to live in Kabul. However, Nasr Allah regarded the British refusal as a personal insult, which alienated him even further from Britain.

Yet not everything was quite what it seemed. When a British military doctor examined the twenty-year-old prince, his highly confidential medical report revealed that Nasr Allah Khan and Sardar Muhammad Akram Khan, the Amir's brother-in-law, were suffering from 'chronic alcoholism', which on occasion verged on delirium tremens.[45] Consumption of alcoholic drinks is forbidden under Islamic law, but Sadar Nasr Allah Khan, his father and other members of the royal family had developed a taste for spirits during their exile in Russian Turkistan, and after becoming 'Abd al-Rahman Khan Amir had reinstituted the production of local wine and spirits, which had been banned since the days of Dost Muhammad Khan.

By the mid-1890s the Amir's health, which had never been good, had deteriorated to the point he was so unwell that he was barely able to govern for months at a time. The management of daily affairs of state fell to his son, Habib Allah Khan, whom he had been grooming as his heir apparent for several years. By 1901 it was clear the Amir had not long to live and he moved to Paghman. His last days were dreadful to behold as his body literally rotted from the feet upwards, while the stench of his gangrenous flesh was so foul that his courtiers could only remain in the Amir's presence for a few minutes at a time. He finally passed away in the autumn of 1901 and was buried the same day, without any pomp or ceremony, for his enemies had threatened to steal the corpse and dishonour it. Over the ensuing months there were a number of attempts to burn down the mausoleum.

Amir 'Abd al-Rahman Khan: an appraisal of his reign

The reign of 'Abd al-Rahman Khan was significant in the development of Afghanistan as a nation state, though his legacy has been far from positive.

During his reign the northern and southern frontiers of Afghanistan were demarcated and legitimized, but many of the fault lines that still beset the state and national identity are traceable to his reign. The northern and southern frontiers arbitrarily divided tribes and peoples who traditionally had been part of the same social and economic networks. The Durand Line did not end Afghan interference in tribal affairs, the problem of arms smuggling, or tribal revolts on the Indian side of the frontier. After Partition, Afghanistan and Pakistan disputed the Durand Line, while the issue of the frontier and the use of Tribal Territory as a safe haven for insurgents remains unresolved to this day. The repressions and forcible relocations of hundreds of thousands of people, as well as the nationalization of land and property, led to major social upheaval and economic hardship, and created deep resentment against central government that still simmers away under the surface. Afghanization also fuelled the emergence of ethnocentric nationalism and ideas of Pushtun cultural and ethnic supremacy, which exacerbated racial, sectarian and regional tensions.

'Abd al-Rahman Khan's obsession with concentrating all power in his own hands undermined state institutions and civil society, in particular regional government. As for any form of consultative assembly, he told his heirs 'never to make themselves puppets in the hands of these representatives'.[46] 'Abd al-Rahman Khan therefore had little interest in replacing the traditional structures of sub-national government, which he dismantled or rendered impotent, with any effective mechanism for local government. Kabul became the hub for everything and provincial governors, fearing imprisonment or execution, refused to act until the Amir gave his seal of approval. This centralization of power remained essentially unchanged after his death, and even after the fall of the Musahiban dynasty in 1978 this model was perpetuated by the imposition of Stalinist centralization. Today, both the Executive and Legislative branches of the Afghan government still regard the centralized state and a command economy as the preferred model of governance.

'Abd al-Rahman Khan was the first ruler of Afghanistan to employ state propaganda to justify his actions both to his own people and the world at large. During his reign he published a series of pamphlets in Persian and Pushtu and posted official proclamations in prominent places. An Indian *munshi* was commissioned to write the English version of the Amir's Persian autobiography, which was widely read in Britain and India, and which helped promote the Amir's version of Afghanistan's history.[47] In this work, 'Abd al-Rahman Khan portrayed himself as the defender of India against the Russians on the one hand, and a modern and modernizing

KASSRI - DILKUCHA KABOUL

قصر دلکشا
کابل

The Dilkusha Palace, in the *arg* complex. Amir Habib Allah Khan even had a small power station built in Jabal Saraj to provide electricity for the palace. Its British architect also constructed a clock tower which chimed the hour and quarter hours, much to the amazement of the local population.

ERK KABOUL

ارک
کابل

The walls and grounds of Amir 'Abd al-Rahman Khan's new citadel complex on the site of what used to be a Mughal garden. Amir Habib Allah Khan remodelled the *arg* and added formal gardens and other features, all in the European style.

king on the other, a benevolent father figure who was working tirelessly to bring a nation of ungrateful, ignorant and fanatical people into the modern world. As for his brutal suppressions, the Amir argued that the end justified the means.

Under the Iron Amir, as the British press referred to him, Afghanistan became a closed and increasingly inward-looking country. The British reinforced this isolation by insisting that anyone wishing to visit, or travel through, Afghanistan had to have official permission. The Amir did employ a number of Indians and a few British technicians, the latter mostly as advisers for his munitions and leather factories. Dr Alfred Gray and subsequently a British woman physician, Dr Lilias Hamilton, were appointed as the Amir's personal medical advisers, while Kate Daly, a British nurse and companion of Dr Hamilton, opened Afghanistan's first modern medical clinic. The Amir, however, refused to employ any foreign military advisers to train his army.

Contact with European culture and ideas was mostly through the Urdu and Persian press, or imported luxury goods. Visitors to the Amir's new palace, the Dilkusha, noted that the place was cluttered with expensive bric-a-brac and novelties, including mechanical toys, carriage clocks and a vast collection of European glass and tableware. Many of the women of the royal household bought the latest French fashions. Remarkably, in his advice to his heirs, which appears at the end of his autobiography, 'Abd al-Rahman Khan advocated the introduction of women's education, but only at some very distant point in the future. The Amir himself did nothing to improve the nation's medieval education system or address endemic illiteracy, other than to translate a few military manuals into Persian and Pushtu. As for Afghan scholars or officials, they were discouraged from studying abroad.

One of the Amir's grandest civil engineering projects was the construction of a new palace complex on the site of the old Shah Bagh.[48] Known today as the Presidential Palace, it was designed by a British architect and even included a clock tower. The palace was also an *arg*, or citadel, fortified with a double line of walls, punctuated by bastions for artillery and surrounded by a dry ditch. South of the *arg*, and outside its walls, lay a complex of palaces. The Bastan Sarai, originally designed to entertain guests and foreign dignitaries, eventually became the Amir's mausoleum and his son, Amir Habib Allah Khan, later added a dome and mosque. Another royal residence, the Zarnegar Palace, was pulled down in 1964 to make way for the park of the same name. The Gulistan Sarai, located between these two palaces, was the residence of the Amir's favourite wife,

Kabul, the mausoleum of Amir 'Abd al-Rahman Khan. Originally this building was the Bastan Sarai where the Amir entertained foreign dignitaries. However, shortly after his death it was almost burnt to the ground, probably by an arsonist. Amir Habib Allah Khan restored the building and transformed it into a grandiose tomb with its own mosque.

Bibi Halima, while the Amir's sons, Habib Allah Khan and Nasr Allah Khan, built private residences in Deh Afghanan. Other major building projects included Kabul's vast 'Idgah Mosque and the palaces of Shah Ara, Bagh-i Bala and Chehel Situn. The Amir also built a *haram sarai* for Bibi Halima in Babur's Gardens and the Kot-i Shah winter palace in Jalalabad. The Amir employed Indian architects for most of these buildings, which were designed mostly in a neo-Mughal style. However, a Bukhara architect was responsible for the Gulistan Sarai, while some of the architectural features in the *arg* drew their inspiration from Russian Orthodox architecture.

The Amir was convinced that Afghanistan had vast and unexploited mineral wealth, a view based on a very liberal interpretation of Griesbach's geological survey. This vision of potential riches and wealth was passed on down to successive governments until it became embedded in the national consciousness. Yet neither the Amir nor his successors did anything to exploit these resources, which would have at least made the country more financially viable. The reason for this was again due to the Amir's testament, in which he urged his heirs never to grant extraction rights to any foreign companies. The result was that most of these mineral resources remain unexploited due to lack of technological expertise and modern mining equipment.

The Amir's only serious engagement with modern technology, apart from the trinkets that littered the Dilkusha Palace, was the purchase of machinery for the manufacture of weapons, ammunition, boots and uniforms. A number of new, unsealed roads were constructed, primarily to facilitate the swift movement of troops. The Amir repeatedly rejected British offers to link Kandahar and Jalalabad into the Indian rail and tele-graph network and advised his heirs to do the same. Until recently, the only working railway in Afghanistan was a kilometre or so of track that linked the frontier port of Hairatan to Uzbekistan.

Though Amir 'Abd al-Rahman was never willing to admit it, his hold on power was due more or less solely to the fact that Britain continued to supply him with modern weapons and large sums of cash to suppress rebellions. This stability may have served Britain's geopolitical aims by creating a buffer state that protected India from a Russian invasion, but it was achieved at great cost to the Afghan people, who were forced to endure twenty years of tyranny. It also turned Afghanistan into a rentier state that was even less capable of financial self-sufficiency than it had been before. When the Amir died, Afghanistan was no longer technically in debt, but this was only because several million rupees of the British subsidy were retained in Indian banks as a strategic reserve.

Despite the fraught nature of the Anglo-Afghan relationship, as far as Britain was concerned Amir 'Abd al-Rahman Khan had done the job required of him. He had been a reasonably loyal ally who had reasserted central government's control over a country that had teetered on the edge of collapse. He had allowed Britain to demarcate Afghanistan's inter-national frontiers and so reduced the risk of a Russian invasion, as well as Afghan interference in India and tribal affairs. Afghanistan as a buffer state was thus effective, even though British military strategists knew that, had Russia decided to call Britain's bluff and occupy Herat, there was little Britain could have done to prevent it. In the end, it was diplomacy, combined with the threat of war in Europe as well as Asia, that made Russia honour the frontier protocols.

Afghanistan thus survived as a nation state, but it had been a close call. Prior to and even after the Second Afghan War, Lytton, Roberts and other senior officials had seriously debated the breakup of the country into smaller self-governing units, or even outright annexation of southern Afghanistan. In the end a united Afghanistan was deemed far less trouble and far less costly than another invasion. Maintaining 'Abd al-Rahman Khan on the throne became the keystone of Britain's Defence of India policy, and in recognition of this 'Abd al-Rahman Khan was made a Knight Grand Commander of the Order of the Star of India in 1885 and in 1893 he was elevated to a Knight of the Order of the Bath.

For many Afghans – particularly Hazaras, Uzbeks and Aimaqs – however, the Amir's legacy was far more bitter, and while Britain justified the repressive regime of the Iron Amir as a necessary evil, to those who were forced to endure his reign he was, and still is, the Bloody Amir.

NINE

Reform and Repression, 1901–19

In spite of the Amir's inclination towards modern influences, he was distrustful of any progressive political or educational institutions. There were definite limits beyond which he would not go, for suspicion and lack of faith in his own people made reform impossible. He has remained the absolute Amir.

A. C. JEWETT[1]

Two watermelons cannot be held in one hand.

AFGHAN PROVERB

IN EARLY OCTOBER 1901 Habib Allah Khan, 'Abd al-Rahman Khan's eldest son, was declared Amir. At 29 years of age, he was a relatively young head of state, but following Ishaq Khan's rebellion his father had groomed him for the succession and ensured he contracted appropriate marriage alliances with powerful tribal and religious leaders. Habib Allah Khan, however, despite being heir apparent, had not been exempt from the fear instilled by his father's reign. He had on occasion fallen foul of his father's temper and mood swings, and for a while had been under house arrest for refusing to obey his father's orders. He also suffered from a speech impediment, said to be the result of an attempt to poison him when he was a child, was prematurely obese and had inherited his father's chronic, degenerative illness, which court officials euphemistically referred to as gout.

Amir Habib Allah Khan's administration

The relatively peaceful transition of power was due primarily to a power-sharing agreement with his younger, full brother Nasr Allah Khan, who commanded the loyalty of many of the tribes of Nangahar and the Kunar. Furthermore, as head of the conservative Sunni party at court, Nasr Allah Khan was allied to influential *pir*s such as Fazl Muhammad

Sardar Nasr Allah Khan, Habib Allah Khan's uterine brother and leader of the Islamic, anti-Westernizing faction at court.

Mujadidi, Hazrat of Shor Bazaar, and Shaikh Najm al-Din Akhundzada, known as the Hadda Sahib or the Hadda Mullah. In return for not contesting the succession, Nasr Allah Khan was appointed as na'ib al-sultan, or regent, to 'Inayat Khan, the heir apparent, as well as commander-in-chief of the army, head of Treasury, Revenue and Internal Affairs, and Minister of Education. He also had responsibility for tribal affairs and established Afghanistan's first Ministry of Foreign Affairs.

Another powerful figure in Habib Allah Khan's government was Sardar 'Abd al-Quddus Khan, a descendant of the Peshawar *sardars*. He had been one of Amir 'Abd al-Rahman Khan's most effective generals and had the title of 'Etimad al-Daula, Pillar, or Confidence, of the Nation. It had been mostly due to 'Abd al-Quddus Khan that the Kabul army swore the oath of loyalty to Amir Habib Allah Khan, and it was he who brokered the power-sharing arrangement between the Amir and Nasr Allah Khan. In return, 'Abd al-Quddus was appointed as Lord Chamberlain and head of the Amir's inner council. From 1905 onwards he was also in charge of Anglo-Afghan relations.

'Abd al-Quddus Khan and Nasr Allah Khan were ideologically allied and together they rehabilitated the religious establishment, which had been persecuted and suppressed by 'Abd al-Rahman Khan, forming an advisory council of senior '*ulama*', known as the Mizan al-Tahqiqat-i Shari'at, which scrutinized all laws and decrees to ensure they conformed to Islamic law. Its chairman, Hajji 'Abd al-Razzaq, head of the Supreme Court and Nasr Allah Khan's spiritual adviser, was a graduate of the Darul Uloom seminary at Deoband. The *Mizan al-Tahqiqat* persuaded Amir Habib Allah Khan to abolish some of his father's more brutal forms of execution, since they did not conform to the Islamic penal code. The Amir also released hundreds of political prisoners and closed the fearful Siyah Chah dungeon, the disused well outside the walls of the Bala Hisar where the condemned were left to rot in the filth and darkness.

Since it was imperative that Amir Habib Allah Khan win over powerful Islamic conservative figures, the Amir invited the Hadda Mullah to Kabul, for as the spiritual head of a Qadiriyya *tariqa,* Najm al-Din commanded the devotion of many Pushtun tribes of southeastern Afghanistan and on the Indian side of the Durand Line. Najm al-Din was also a noted opponent of British rule and frequently incited the tribes of the Northwest Frontier to *jihad*. In order to secure the support of the Hadda Mullah, Amir Habib Allah Khan accorded official recognition to his spiritual authority and increased his state allowance.

Three years later, in an attempt to offset Najm al-Din's radicalism and probably on the recommendation of Mahmud Tarzi (see below), the Amir invited Sayyid Hasan Gailani, head of an Iraqi branch of the Qadiriyya Order, to settle in Afghanistan. Hasan Gailani was given a *jagir* in the Surkh Rud district of Nangahar, and the *pir* reciprocated by endorsing the Amir and the Muhammadzai dynasty's legitimacy. Indeed, the Gailani family became one of the staunchest religious backers of the monarchy, a tradition that Hasan's son and heir, Ahmad Gailani, has perpetuated to the present day.

While there was little bloodshed over the issue of the succession, Amir Habib Allah Khan faced at least one serious dynastic challenge. His stepmother, Bibi Halima, 'Abd al-Rahman Khan's favourite wife and a maternal granddaughter of Dost Muhammad Khan, resented the fact that her twelve-year-old son Muhammad 'Omar Khan, or 'Omar Jan, had been passed over in favour of the son of a Tajik concubine from Badakhshan. In a bid to topple Habib Allah Khan, Bibi Halima secured the support of a number of mid-ranking army officers, but in early 1903 the plot was discovered and 36 military personnel were executed. 'Omar Jan was stripped of all his official positions and Bibi Halima was confined to the *haram sarai* in the Bagh-i Babur for the remainder of her life. In the same year, Amir Habib Allah cracked down on religious dissent, executing Sahibzada 'Abd al-Latif Khosti, head of Afghanistan's tiny Ahmadiyya community.

The return of the Tarzi, Musahiban and Loyab families

In an act of reconciliation Amir Habib Allah Khan offered an amnesty to a number of prominent Muhammadzais exiles, including descendants of the Kandahar *sardar*s and supporters of the former Amir, Ya'qub Khan, and his brother, 'Ayub Khan. Of the returnees, three kin groups would become particularly important in determining Afghanistan's political and social direction in the twentieth century.

Shortly after Habib Allah's accession Mahmud Tarzi and his half-nephew Habib Allah Khan travelled from Damascus to Kabul to request permission to return home (see Chart 5).[2] Mahmud was a grandson of Rahim Dil Khan, the Kandahar *sardar*, while on his maternal side he was Saddozai. Mahmud's father, Ghulam Muhammad Khan, had served under both Dost Muhammad Khan and Amir Sher 'Ali Khan, but he was best known as a poet, writing under the pen name of *tarzi*, 'stylist', a *takhalus* that was adopted as the family's surname. In 1866 Ghulam Tarzi had hosted Sayyid Jamal al-Din al-Afghani and became a devoted follower of his Pan-Islamic and anti-British ideology. The Tarzis eventually moved to Kabul and, according to the family history, after Amir Ya'qub Khan was sent into exile, Mahmud Tarzi's father sent him to Charikar to tender the family's submission to 'Abd al-Rahman Khan. However, following 'Abd al-Rahman Khan's defeat of 'Ayub Khan and the fall of Kandahar, the Amir accused Ghulam Muhammad Khan of aiding the 'Ayubids and his family was imprisoned and subsequently exiled to India.

After three years in Karachi, Ghulam Muhammad accepted the invitation of Shaikh Gailani to reside in Baghdad and even had an audience with the Ottoman sultan, 'Abd ül-Hamid II. For the next two decades the Tarzi family lived in Damascus where Mahmud and his brothers and nephews were educated in Ottoman schools and imbibed the relatively liberal Levantine milieu. Mahmud grew up speaking Turkish as his first language, although he was fluent in Persian and read Urdu and some Arabic too. Turkish gave him to access to Turkish translations of French and German philosophical and literary works in an era when the Ottoman Empire was undergoing major reforms and the Young Turks were embracing an ethnocentric nationalism. In 1889 Mahmud visited Paris for the Exposition Universelle. Later he married Asma Rasmiya, daughter of

Shaikh Muhammad Saleh al-Fatal of Aleppo, *imam* of one of the main mosques in Damascus.

The era of the Tarzis' exile in Damascus was one of great turmoil as the Ottoman Empire imploded under military and political pressure from European powers, particularly Russia and Britain. By the mid-1870s Turkey was technically bankrupt and in 1881 the Ottoman government was forced to hand management of its debt to a council of European bankers, mostly French and British. Successive Russian military interventions across the Danube had led to the loss of most of the Balkans and Greece, too, had declared its independence. Cyprus and Egypt were effectively under British rule, there was unrest in the Levant and the Arabian Peninsula with the rise of Arab nationalism, while in Anatolia the Armenian National Awakening led to a series of revolts. The loss of territory led to a mass influx of internally displaced peoples to Istanbul, Damascus and other cities, which put further strain on the already overstretched Ottoman treasury. To add to the misery, there was a series of natural disasters.

The decline of Ottoman power led to a political crisis and demands for radical reform of state institutions. Between 1839 and 1876 the *Tanzimat*, or Reorganization, Period was an era of profound social and political change. Young Turks, educated in Paris, embraced the political philosophies of Rousseau, Compte, the Italian Carbonari, Marxism and even Anarchism, which in turn led to demands for the secularization of state institutions. State schools began to teach Western subjects such as natural sciences and the *madrasas* became increasingly marginalized. In 1876 Turkey adopted its first Constitution based on the Napoleonic Code, which restricted the powers of the caliph and downgraded the role of Hanafi Islamic law. To demonstrate their modernity, progressive Turks increasingly embraced both European manners and dress codes.

From the late 1880s onwards these reformers, known as Young Ottomans and later Young Turks, formed societies aimed at democratic and liberalizing reforms based on the ideals of Europe's Enlightenment. They were particularly obsessed with the notion that the natural sciences, rather than religion, were the answer to Turkey's political and social problems. Even their slogan, 'Liberty, Equality, Justice', echoed the battle cry of the French Revolution. Eventually these societies coalesced under the banner of the Ittihad ve Terakki Cemiyeti, or the Committee of Union and Progress (CUP), which later become the Party of Union and Progress (CPU). These organizations were republican in outlook and sought the disestablishment of Islam and Islamic institutions and their replacement with European-style democracy.

The Young Turks' ideology, however, was not consistent, for while they declared their support for Pan-Islamic ideals, at the same time they wholeheartedly endorsed social Darwinism, which was popular in Europe at this era, and the radical ethno-nationalism of Germany's Völkisch Movement. According to the Young Turks, Turkey was the *vatan* of the Turks, a term synonymous with the German concept of Fatherland or Homeland. As such, the Young Turks embraced an ethnocentric world view in which those who were not Turkish by birth or language were relegated to the status of minorities. This idea of Turkism and Turkishness was alien to Islamic and Ottoman understanding of citizenship. In the Ottoman Empire, non-Muslim confessional groups, known as *millet*s, had a high degree of autonomy and freedom to practise their religion. To be an Ottoman it was not essential to be a Muslim or an ethnic Turk, nor was being Greek, Armenian, Slav, an Orthodox Christian or a Jew a bar to high office. Indeed many high Ottoman officials were from the non-Muslim community while the Ottoman Christian schools provided the best education in the empire. Since the political agenda of the Young Turks was opposed to the status quo and Islamic domination of the Ottoman state, the CPU started life as an underground movement with some of its more radical members resorting to direct action and terrorism. Mahmud Tarzi grew up in this milieu of radical political and social reform. Like most educated and well-connected young men of his generation, he embraced the CPU's radicalism and its ethno-nationalism, which was grafted onto the Tarzi family's existing enchantment with al-Afghani's Pan-Islam and anti-colonialism.

In 1892, while the Tarzis were still in Damascus, the Ottoman Caliph invited Jamal al-Din al-Afghani to settle in Istanbul, following his expulsion from Egypt and Iran and several years in Paris where he published the highly polemical newspaper *al-'Urwah al-Wuthqa*.[3] Al-Afghani's expectation was that he could persuade the Caliph to endorse and embrace his Pan-Islamic vision, but this optimism was soon dashed. Al-Afghani was a virulent opponent of British rule in India, but the Ottoman government was reliant on British financial, military and political assistance in its war with Russia, and had no intention of upsetting its most important ally. Al-Afghani did not help his cause by encouraging Arab nationalist movements and conducting a polemic against Sufi *pir*s and the *madrasa* system. In 1896, after one of al-Afghani's followers assassinated Nasir al-Din Qajar, Shah of Persia, al-Afghani was placed under house arrest; the following year he died from throat cancer. Six months before his death, Mahmud Tarzi travelled to Istanbul to meet al-Afghani and, according to the Tarzi family, he was at al-Afghani's side when he passed away.

When the Tarzis returned to Kabul in early 1905, Mahmud, his brothers and nephews were culturally Ottoman rather than Afghan. Ideologically they were committed to the anti-British, Pan-Islamic agenda of al-Afghani and the social and political reforms of the Young Turks, which included a distaste for traditional Islamic leaderships, the need for rapid social and legislative transformation as well as technological modernization. To most Afghans and Europeans working in the country, Mahmud Tarzi was known as The Turk, or Mahmud Beg. After two decades of the cultural and intellectual sophistication of Damascus, Afghanistan must have been a profound cultural shock for the Tarzis. However, the very 'backwardness' of his native land made Mahmud even more convinced that Afghanistan needed its own Tanzimat revolution to bring the country out of its political, cultural and educational Dark Ages. Within a matter of months after his arrival in Kabul, Tarzi formed a group of young, like-minded reformers, which he called the Young Afghans.

The second prominent Muhammadzai family to return to Afghanistan was that of Sardar Muhammad Yusuf Khan, who were known as the Musahiban or Yahya Khel (Chart 5). Yusuf was a grandson of Sultan Muhammad Tela'i, the Peshawar *sardar* whom Dost Muhammad Khan had displaced in 1826. Like Ghulam Tarzi, he and his family had been supporters of Amir Ya'qub Khan, accompanying him into Indian exile in 1880, but they returned to Afghanistan shortly before 'Abd al-Rahman Khan's death, a pardon no doubt due to the influence of Yusuf's half-brother, 'Abd al-Quddus Khan. The Musahiban's experience of exile, however, had been very different to that of the Tarzis. Yusuf's sons and daughters were educated in Dehra Dun in northern India and spoke Urdu as their first language. During his exile Yusuf had fathered five sons by his two wives: Muhammad 'Aziz Khan, Muhammad Nadir Khan, Muhammad Hashim Khan, Shah Mahmud Khan and Shah Wali Khan. They would eventually dominate the political life of Afghanistan for a generation. Initially, however, Yusuf and his sons were appointed to mid-ranking posts in the army, with the youngest son, Shah Wali Khan, becoming head of Amir Habib Allah Khan's personal guard. Following Nadir Shah and Shah Wali Khan's successful suppression of the Mangal rebellion of 1912, Nadir Khan became commander-in-chief of the army.

The third prominent Muhammadzai returnee was Loynab Khushdil Khan, whose father, Sher Dil Khan, had first served under Dost Muhammad Khan and married one of the Amir's daughters. Subsequently Amir Sher 'Ali Khan appointed him as *Shahghasi*, or Lord Chamberlain, and governor of Afghan Turkistan.[4] The Loynabs had gone into exile with Amir Ya'qub

Khan, following General Roberts's occupation of Kabul, and had been part of the ex-Amir's entourage in Lahore. Despite this association, Amir Habib Allah Khan had married Sher Dil Khan's eldest daughter, Sarwar Sultana, or Ulya Hazrat Begum, mother of the future Amir of Afghanistan, 'Aman Allah Khan. As Amir Habib Allah Khan's favourite wife, Ulya Hazrat used her position at the top of the *zanana* pecking order to undermine 'Inayat Allah Khan's position as heir apparent and to secure the succession for her son. On their return to Kabul, Loynab Khushdil Khan and his son, 'Ali Ahmad, became members of the Amir's inner council and eventually 'Ali Ahmad became Amir Habib Allah Khan's most trusted adviser.

Habibiyya College and the start of the reform movement

In September 1902 Amir Habib Allah Khan celebrated the first anniversary of his reign with a *darbar*. The guest of honour was Najm al-Din, the Hadda Mullah, who conferred on Amir the title of *Seraj al-Millat wa al-Din*, Light of the Nation and Religion, and from this point forward Habib Allah Khan's family adopted Seraj as their family name and his era, and that of his son Amir 'Aman Allah Khan, was known as *Serajiyya*. Seraj was also frequently used in titles of state projects, publications and place names. To commemorate the *darbar* the Amir declared an annual holiday celebrated as *Jashn-i Etiffaq-i Millat*, Festival of National Unity, the first non-Islamic national day to be celebrated in Afghanistan.

Under the influence of the Mahmud Tarzi and the Young Afghans, in 1903 Habib Allah Khan inaugurated Afghanistan's first European-style school, Habibiyya College, modelled on Sir Syed Ahmad Khan's Muhammedan Anglo-Oriental Collegiate School at 'Aligarh. The curriculum broke new ground by including basic science, mathematics, history and geography as well as *Islamiyat*, Islamic Studies. This initiative was not well received by Nasr Allah Khan and his Sunni faction, especially graduates of Deoband's Darul Uloom. They opposed any secularization of education and the inclusion of subjects outside the traditional Islamic curriculum of the *madrasa*, for in their view Western science and education undermined Islamic doctrine and the *'ulama*'s monopoly over education. Furthermore, they disliked Sir Syed Ahmad's rationalist and progressive views on Islam, which they regarded as verging on the heretical, as well as his active engagement with British rule in India, a government that individuals such as the Hadda Mullah regarded as illegitimate. In order to forestall any religious backlash over Habibiyya, the Amir let Nasr Allah Khan establish state-funded *madrasa*s in key provincial centres.

A traditional *madrasa* depicted in a miniature of the famous story of Layla and Majnun: unknown artist, Herat, late 15th–early 16th century. Amir Habib Allah Khan attempted to reform the education system and curriculum, in part to reduce the power of the religious elites who controlled the *madrasas*. However, these tentative steps to modernization ran foul of conservative elements in government and within his own extended family.

Afghanistan's first tentative steps towards modernization of its educational system thus involved a delicate balancing act between Islamic conservatives and a small coterie of young, foreign-educated, urban reformers, known as *roshanfikr*s. Later in Habib Allah Khan's reign the reform movement become inextricably associated with Mahmud Tarzi, but the original impetus for change came not from Tarzi and his Turcophile Young Afghans but what Nile Green terms the Urdusphere.[5] The Urdu press was widely available in Afghanistan and read by many high officials, while Indian Muslims were employed in Afghanistan during the reigns of Amir 'Abd al-Rahman Khan and Amir Habib Allah Khan. They included architects, medical workers and supervisors of state projects. Habibiyya College's first two headmasters and its teachers were also Indians, mostly graduates of 'Aligarh, Lahore's Islamia College, or Mission schools.

In the ensuing decades, the debate over social and political reform became increasingly polarized with the Amirs battling to balance the demands for modernization and political and legal reform, promoted mainly by a younger, better-educated generation, with those of the powerful conservative Islamic lobby. The return of the exiles was partly responsible for exacerbating these fault lines as Tarzi's Turcophiles, in particular, demanded fast, radical change. Unfortunately, one of the many negative legacies of 'Abd al-Rahman Khan's reign was the belief, espoused by both Afghans and Europeans, that the only way Afghanistan could be ruled was by an absolutist monarch backed by state terror. Consequently some misinterpreted Habib Allah Khan's attempts at conciliation as a sign of weakness, while political and ideological enemies exploited his tentative reforms as a means to undermine his power and the Anglo-Afghan alliance.

Amir Habib Allah Khan and Anglo-Afghan relations

While Amir Habib Allah Khan struggled with the issue of reform, relations with Britain turned sour. The problem began with a dispute with Russia over riparian rights to the waters of the Hari Rud and Murghab, with the Russians accusing the Afghans of helping themselves to more than their fair share of water for irrigation. Then a number of boundary pillars on the Herat–Murghab frontier either disappeared or were deliberately vandalized. In an attempt to resolve these issues Sa'ad Allah Khan, the governor of Herat, negotiated directly with his counterpart across the frontier in breach of the Lyall Agreement of 1880 and the subsequent Anglo-Russian Accord of 1900. The situation was not helped by the fact that the Amir had recently divorced one of his wives, the daughter of the Herat governor.

Britain complained to the Russian Foreign Ministry about holding direct talks with the Afghan governor, but St Petersburg argued that since the dispute was not political, the governor had every right to discuss local issues with his counterpart across the frontier. Britain rejected this interpretation of the Anglo-Russian Accord since it opened the door for Russia to send agents to Herat, ostensibly to discuss riparian rights, but covertly obtaining valuable military intelligence, stirring up anti-British sentiment and encouraging the disaffected governor to rebel. Lord Curzon, the Viceroy, invited Amir Habib Allah Khan to Peshawar to discuss the Herat frontier crisis, in the hope that the Amir would agree to renew the Lyall and Durand agreements or, preferably, sign a new treaty more favourable to Britain's interests. As far as Curzon was concerned, a new Anglo-Afghan treaty was essential since it was unclear if the agreements of 1880 and 1893 were government-to-government arrangements or merely personal undertakings by Amir 'Abd al-Rahman Khan. If the latter were the case, then both treaties effectively terminated with the death of Habib Allah Khan's father.

Habib Allah Khan was not prepared to risk leaving Afghanistan, but assured Curzon that he would 'adhere firmly' to the Anglo-Afghan alliance.[6] Curzon, however, was not satisfied. In the autumn of 1903 he persuaded the Amir to allow Sir Henry Dobbs to travel to Herat, report on the frontier situation and repair the broken boundary pillars.[7] Dobbs's mission, though, was obstructed by both Russian officials and the governor of Herat, whom the British suspected, rightly, of accepting bribes from the Russians not to cooperate. In the end all Dobbs accomplished was an inspection of the broken pillars and filing an alarming report about the chronic shortcomings of Herat's defences. Tensions increased when Ernest Thornton, a British engineer working in Kabul, informed the Indian government in confidence that Russian agents had recently visited the Afghan capital and had held secret talks with the Amir.[8] Then, at the end of 1903, Russia opened the rail link between Tashkent and Turkistan and began to survey the route from Samarkand to Termez on the Amu Darya. Since Russia already had a railhead at Khushk, just across the Herat frontier, British officials feared that when the Termez line became operational, Russia would be able to move thousands of troops and munitions quickly to the Afghan frontier and mount a two-pronged invasion of Herat and Mazar-i Sharif.

This scenario was a nightmare for British military strategists as they knew Britain was powerless to prevent any Russian occupation of Herat or Afghan Turkistan. In the autumn of 1903 British military chiefs held war games in Simla, simulating a Russian invasion of India through Afghanistan. The outcome was the alarming conclusion that any army sent into Afghanistan would be defeated. The problem was the logistical impossibility of simultaneously supplying 50,000–60,000 troops in three separate armies: one to attack the Russians in Herat; a second to draw a Maginot Line on the Helmand; and a third to occupy Kandahar, Jalalabad and Kabul. It emerged that the railheads at Chaman and Peshawar did not have sufficient capacity for such a campaign and they were too far away from the theatre of war to facilitate the swift movement of so many troops and their baggage and equipment. It was also estimated there were not sufficient pack animals, not just in India, but in the whole world, to supply such an army in a region where the attrition rate of beasts of burden was the highest in the empire. When Curzon tried to address the problem and asked the Amir for permission to extend the rail network to Jalalabad and Kandahar, Habib Allah Khan, like his father before him, refused.

To add to Britain's geostrategic problems, the Dobbs mission to Herat took place with the threat of war between Russia and Japan looming in Manchuria. In early February 1904 Japan launched a pre-emptive strike on the Russian naval base of Port Arthur and so dragged Britain into a proxy war, for Britain had recently signed a treaty of mutual defence with Japan. Russia responded to the invasion of Manchuria by moving large numbers of troops nearer to the frontier with Afghanistan, a military build-up that Britain feared might be a precursor to an invasion designed to tie down British forces in India. In the first half of 1904, Britain expected Russia to win the war and hence it was even more imperative to ensure Amir Habib Allah Khan was bound to Britain's strategic interests by a new treaty. Unexpectedly, however, the Japanese were victorious and Russia's ability to invade India was undermined.

In order to keep an eye on Russian troop movements, Curzon encouraged Dobbs to drag out his mission to Herat as long as possible. When Habib Allah Khan eventually demanded his recall, Curzon sent Dobbs to Kabul, using the excuse that he needed to brief the Amir on his activities. In fact, Dobbs's primary object was to report on the political situation in the Afghan capital and to persuade the Amir to renew the Anglo-Afghan alliance. When he reached Kabul, Dobbs received a very cordial reception and the Amir, who was equally worried about the Russian threat, verbally assured Dobbs that he was willing to negotiate a renewal of the Anglo-Afghan Treaty.

In response, Curzon sent Sir Louis Dane, India's foreign minister, to Kabul with a draft treaty. Its terms embraced most of the long-standing demands of the Forward Policy, including the right of British officers to conduct military surveys of Afghanistan, the extension of the Indian railway to Kabul and the stationing of native news writers in all of Afghanistan's main provincial centres. Dane reached the Afghan capital in December 1904 and a few weeks later, in January 1905, the Russian commander surrendered Port Arthur to the Japanese. With Russian forces in retreat, troops were shifted from the Afghan frontier and sent to Manchurian. As a consequence it was no longer so vital for the Amir to sign a new treaty since the imminent threat of invasion had dissipated. Dane then proceeded to botch his mission. When he presented Habib Allah Khan with Curzon's draft treaty it was rejected by most of the Amir's inner council, including Nasr Allah Khan and 'Abd al-Quddus Khan, while Muhammad Yusuf Khan threatened to shoot the Amir if he signed it. As with all previous

Anglo-Afghan Treaties, Britain had demanded substantial concessions, while offering very little in return. Curzon's draft even restricted the Amir's right to import arms from India, for Britain continued to be concerned about the number of modern rifles that had found their way into the hands of rebellious Afghan tribes on the Indian side of the frontier.

The Amir then wrong-footed Dane by arguing that, in his view, the 1880 and 1893 agreements had been made with the nation rather than personally with his father so there was no need for a new one. He then made Dane even more uncomfortable by pointing out that if, as the Viceroy believed, these agreements were personal he was under no legal obligation to uphold his father's undertakings until a new treaty was agreed. Furthermore, he was technically an independent monarch and free to communicate directly with whatever foreign power he chose. Having driven Dane into a corner, Amir Habib Allah Khan stated his willingness to negotiate a new treaty, but Dane had to allow time for the Amir's council to draw up an official response to Curzon's draft.

Dane fell into the trap and instead of insisting the Amir negotiate solely on the basis of Curzon's draft, as per his official terms of reference, he agreed to the Amir's terms and so surrendered the initiative to the Afghans. When Dane was finally presented with the Council's counterproposals in January 1905, none of Curzon's key demands were mentioned and Dane found himself negotiating on what in effect was a completely different treaty. One of the key preconditions of the Afghan draft was for Britain to cover the cost of constructing a series of fortifications throughout northern and western Afghanistan, as well as pay for the increase in Afghan military personnel that would be required to man these outposts.

When Curzon read the Amir's draft treaty, he was furious. Not only had Dane breached his terms of reference, the Afghan demands were un-acceptable and included none of Britain's key requirements. If this were not bad enough, the Amir continued to maintain that since the British believed all former agreements had lapsed on his father's death, Afghanistan was now technically an independent sovereign state. This had serious impli-cations for Britain since Amir Habib Allah Khan would be legally entitled to reassert sovereignty over territory ceded to Britain under the Durand Agreement, as well as his right to influence over the Afridis of the Khyber and even ignore the frontier demarcations.

Curzon now faced an extremely difficult dilemma. His treaty had been drafted in order to enhance Britain's military options in the event of a Russian invasion of Afghanistan, but Dane had been suckered into letting the Afghans turn the tables on him and advance unacceptable and costly proposals that had nothing to do with the original intent of his treaty. Since Curzon was not prepared to accept the Afghan terms, he decided that no treaty was better than a bad one and instructed Dane to secure the Amir's formal acknowledgement that the 1880 and 1893 agreements were still valid. Lord Balfour, the British Prime Minster, disagreed, arguing that to recall Dane without securing a treaty would be a diplomatic humiliation. A furious row ensued that ended with Balfour ordering Curzon to instruct Dane to sign a treaty, even if it did not include any of Britain's original terms.

On 21 March 1905 Dane and the Amir signed the Kabul Treaty, which was a significant defeat for British diplomacy but marked Afghanistan's first step to becoming an independent nation. To the relief of Curzon and Balfour, the Amir reconfirmed the 1880 and 1893 treaties; in return he retained the annual subsidy and the right to import unlimited supplies of arms from India. However, while Britain continued to control Afghanistan's foreign affairs, the treaty title stated the agreement was made between Britain and the 'State of Afghanistan' and referred to the Amir as the 'independent King' of Afghanistan. For Habib Allah Khan this meant his personal status, as far as the imperial pecking order was concerned, was now that of a monarch rather than a subordinate ruler, while Afghanistan, for the first time, was indirectly accorded recognition as a nation state. Three months after the signing of the Kabul Treaty, Curzon resigned citing irreconcilable differences between himself and Balfour over Central Asian policy.

Following the failure of the Dane Mission, Britain set out to explore new ways to defend India against Russian aggression. Exploiting Russia's military weakness in the wake of its defeat by Japan, Britain opened negotiations with St Petersburg aimed at formal recognition of Afghanistan's neutrality and status as a buffer state under international law. Despite referring to him as an independent king, Britain did not bother to inform the Amir of these proceedings, nor was he consulted. Britain also strengthened its military alliance with Japan, a move designed to tie down Russian forces in Manchuria and so reduce the risk of an invasion of Afghanistan.

Amir Habib Allah Khan's state visit to India

Curzon's replacement, Lord Minto, adopted a less confrontational approach to Anglo-Afghan relations. He invited the Amir to India shortly after he arrived in India and, despite objections from Nasr Allah Khan and the anti-British, Sunni faction, Habib Allah Khan accepted. The Amir arrived in Peshawar in early 1906, and for the next three months British officials did everything in their power to impress him with British power and technological might. When he crossed the Afghan frontier, the Amir was presented with a personal cable of welcome from King Edward VII and he was greeted with a 31-gun salute, the same number accorded to the Viceroy. He attended glittering receptions in Agra and Calcutta, went on a tiger hunt, visited the Royal Mint, Calcutta's Zoological Gardens, hospitals, munitions factories and schools. During his tour of the naval dockyards he even fired a ship's gun. On his way home, he visited Aligarh College and laid the foundation stone of Islamia College in Lahore. During his speeches at these institutions, the Amir publicly endorsed the Rationalist, Pan-Islamism of al-Afghani, Sir Syed Ahmad Khan's theological liberalism and his advocacy for engagement with European culture and science. The Amir also urged the students at both institutions to embrace Western education and secular subjects as well as the study of *Islamiyat*.

Behind the scenes there was considerable discontent at the Amir's behaviour in India. His endorsement of Sir Syed Ahmad Khan's Aligarh Movement did not go down well with the more reactionary members of his entourage or in Kabul, while his cosiness with the old enemy was far from welcome, as was the Amir's attendance at mixed parties where unveiled foreign women were present. More serious was the report that Habib Allah Khan had not removed his shoes when entering the Delhi mosque for Friday prayers, a privilege accorded to royalty under British law, but a practice that was unacceptable in Islamic and Afghan custom. The discontent increased when the Amir visited the Golden Temple at Amritsar and made complimentary remarks about the Sikh faith.

Most controversial of all was the Amir's request to become a Freemason, which was an embarrassment both to British officials and the Calcutta Lodge for, by virtue of his rank, the Amir had to be initiated into all three degrees at a single session. This was a highly unusual procedure but, under pressure from the government, Prince Arthur, Grand Master of the United Grand Lodge of England, agreed to a special dispensation. The initiation itself took place in utmost secrecy, with only the Amir and a few senior brothers, all high government officials, present as witnesses.

Habib Allah Khan never explained his reasons for wanting to join what the Afghans called the *Faramush Khana*, the Forgotten, or Forgetful, House, but his initiation flew in the face of a ruling by Sunni *'ulama'*, which had declared membership of Freemasonry incompatible with Islam. Possibly the Amir believed that initiation was an affirmation of his new status as king and reformer, for most of the monarchs of Europe were Grand Masters. Furthermore, despite the Islamic proscription, many

Muslim rulers as well as intellectuals and political reformers were members of the Brotherhood, which they saw as one sign of their modernism and liberalism. Muhammad Abduh, al-Afghani's Egyptian counterpart, and leaders of Turkey's CPU, as well as Al-Afghani himself and many leading Arab nationalists, were all Freemasons. One reason for this was that the Lodge was one of the few places where revolutionaries could share in complete secrecy – hence the Persian term for the Masonic Lodge – radical views that would be treasonous or heretical in the world outside. More than likely, it was Mahmud Tarzi who encouraged the Amir to become a Freemason, for he would have been well acquainted with the Lodges in Beirut, Cairo and Damascus, which were hotbeds of revolutionary, anti-colonial and nationalist activism.[9] The first Lodge in Damascus had opened a few years before the Tarzi family arrived in Syria and counted among its membership high-ranking military and civil officials, intellectuals, Arab and Turkish nationalists and freethinkers. Indeed, it is highly probable that Tarzi and his brothers and nephews were members of one or other of the Damascus Lodges.

The discontent created by the Amir's behaviour among some of his entourage was such that during his visit to India there were rumours of a plot to assassinate him. When Habib Allah Khan returned to Kabul he faced a storm of criticism, for news of his initiation had leaked out and some religious leaders openly accused the Amir of converting to Christianity. The Amir eventually publicly admitted he had become a Freemason and so provided further fuel for his enemies. In an attempt to suppress criticism from religious elites, the Amir executed four particularly vocal *mullahs* and embarked on a countrywide tour in an attempt to win over the population.

During his tour of India, Habib Allah Khan become obsessed with all things Western and once back in Kabul he began to introduce modern technology and Western ways in a haphazard, dilettante manner. He commissioned a royal standard, presented colours to every regiment, created Afghanistan's first national flag and had a national anthem composed based on tunes from Wagner's *Siegfried*, which he had heard played while in India. Muhammadzais were 'encouraged' to adopt Western-style surnames, civil servants and government officials were ordered to attend their offices in Western dress, and the Turkish fez and the *karakul* fur hat replaced the turban.

The Amir recruited a number of foreign experts to expand manufacturing and oversee the construction of new palaces, ministerial buildings and dams. An American engineer supervised the construction of Afghanistan's first hydroelectric dam at Jabal Saraj, designed to provide electricity for

Amir Habib Allah Khan in formal dress. During his reign civil servants and courtiers were required to wear European clothes, a policy which was not popular, especially with conservative Muslims.

Kabul's *mashin khana*, government ministries and the Amir's residencies, while the Qargha Dam between Kabul and Paghman was intended to provide potable, piped water for the capital. Telegraphic links were established between the Amir's residences and government offices and between Kabul, Jalalabad, Paghman and the king's mountain retreat in Laghman. However, the Amir continued to refuse to link Kabul into the Indian telegraphic network. The Viceroy had gifted the Amir two Rolls-Royce cars, so new roads and iron bridges were constructed to allow Habib Allah

Khan and his family to drive them around the capital and surrounding countryside. The Amir also brought back cameras and became an avid photographer. His other passions were golf and tennis, and towards the end of his reign the Amir spent more and more time at these pleasures to the serious detriment of the affairs of state.

Anglo-Afghan relations and the Anglo-Russian Convention

Despite the Amir's warm reception in India, Anglo-Afghan relations took another turn for the worse in the year after he returned to Afghanistan with the signing of the Anglo-Russian Convention in August 1907. The outcome of painstaking negotiations that were precipitated by the failure of the Dane Mission, the Convention formalized Russia's and Britain's spheres of influence in Persia, Afghanistan and Tibet. Russia accepted that Afghanistan was in the British sphere of influence, provided Britain did not invade the country, and in return Britain conceded Russia's right to equal trade and to communicate directly with Afghan officials on matters of a non-political nature. This would have been something of a victory for the Amir, but yet again Britain had not bothered to inform the Amir about the negotiations or their outcome. Habib Allah Khan only heard about the terms of the Convention a month after it had been signed when Lord Minto wrote to the Amir asking for his signature on the document – for the Convention was not legally binding until Habib Allah Khan had formally signified his consent. The Amir was both humiliated and horrified when he read the terms of the Convention. Nasr Allah Khan and most of the royal council opposed the agreement and were angry that Britain had left Afghanistan out of the loop in negotiations with Russia over matters that impinged on the country's sovereignty. In the end, Habib Allah Khan delayed a formal response to the treaty for nearly a year.

Details of the Anglo-Russian Convention eventually leaked out to the wider public and fuelled a rising tide of anti-British sentiment. In May 1908 when the Hadda Mullah declared a *jihad* in support of a revolt against British rule by the Mohmands and Afridis, thousands of tribesmen flocked to Nangahar to join the campaign. Najm al-Din called on the Amir to place himself at the head of the *mujahidin* but Habib Allah Khan temporized, whereupon 'Abd al-Quddus Khan declared his intention to take charge of the army and invade India. Behind the scenes, Nasr Allah Khan had encouraged the *jihad*, turning a blind eye to the on-selling of British rifles to the rebels across the Indian frontier. A few months later the Anglo-Russian Convention was put under further strain when some

10,000 Jamshidis fled across the border to Panjdeh and proceeded to raid Afghan territory. Russian officials eventually persuaded many of them to return to Afghanistan but others, including their leaders, were given asylum in Russian Turkistan, despite the Amir's objections.

The Amir's inordinate delay in signing the Convention placed the British government in a difficult position. The revolt in the Khyber was serious, and with thousands of the Hadda Mullah's supporters crossing the Durand Line to join the uprising, British officials seriously contemplated occupying Jalalabad. However, the idea was shelved for such an action was a breach of the Anglo-Russian Convention and opened the door for Russia to occupy Balkh and Herat, a scenario that would have led to war between the two countries. Amir Habib Allah Khan too was caught in a cleft stick. He had no interest in supporting the Hadda Mullah's *jihad*, but he dared not antagonize such an influential figure, especially as he had the support of Nasr Allah Khan and the anti-British party at court. At the same time the Amir knew that he could not win a war with Britain and that it would mean the end of the 'money sent from God', as the British subsidy was known and which was essential to the country's financial solvency.[10] Furthermore, more than likely such an action would end in the British once again sending in its army to occupy Kandahar and Jalalabad.

In August 1908 the Amir finally responded officially to the Anglo-Russian Convention in a communication that ran to more than fifty pages of detailed critique. The reply, composed mainly by Nasr Allah Khan and 'Abd al-Quddus Khan, was highly critical of the agreement and pointed out that not only did it undermine Britain's commitment to guarantee Afghanistan's independence, but in the Afghan view it was a prelude to the dismemberment of the country. The Amir therefore refused to sign the Convention without significant changes. Since neither Britain nor Russia was prepared to renegotiate the treaty or make any alterations to the existing document, British and Russian officials agreed they would abide by its terms, despite the Amir's objections.

The Mashruta Conspiracy

Discontent at Habib Allah Khan's rule, his haphazard experiment in modernization and the lack of political reform led to the formation of Afghanistan's first political party in 1908. In the autumn the Amir was shown an anonymous *shab nama*, or night letter, which demanded he establish a constitutional monarchy and threatened that if he 'did not do as was requested of him, he would have to abide the consequences'.[11] The letter was written in the name of the Hizb-i Mashruta, or the Constitutional Party. This movement also went under the name of Hizb-i Sirr-i Milli, the Secret National Party and on the basis of the limited information available on this extremely secretive organization, it was probably a radical revolutionary faction embedded within the wider Constitutional movement.[12]

The Hizb-i Mashruta probably drew its inspiration from the revolt of the National Constitutional Party in Turkey a month earlier, an uprising that forced the Ottoman Sultan to reinstate the 1876 Constitution. Two years earlier, the Iranian Hizb-i Mashrutiyya had forced Shah Muzaffar al-Din Qajar to agree to Iran's first national Parliament and a Constitution modelled on that of Belgium. Amir Habib Allah Khan, doubtless aware of these revolts, had no intention of surrendering any of his absolutist powers and, fearing for his life, he ordered Mirza Muhammad Husain Khan, *kotwal* of Kabul, to hunt down the conspirators. In so doing, the Amir unwittingly provided a golden opportunity for the opponents of the reform movement to destroy both their personal and ideological enemies.

In the first week of March 1909 an unnamed informant identified the head of the Mashruta Conspiracy as Dr Abdul Ghani, headmaster of Habibiyya College, and it was alleged that he and his two brothers, who were teachers at the college, planned to poison the Amir and seize the throne. In all some three hundred people were arrested and interrogated, though many were released a few weeks later.[13] Dr Ghani, his brothers and several other Indian citizens and other leading members of the alleged conspiracy, however, spent the next decade incarcerated in an Afghan jail. The only reason Ghani and the other Indians were not executed was because they were British subjects. Those arrested included Maulawi 'Abd al-Ra'uf Akhundzada Kandahari, a highly respected exponent of Islamic law, and a well-known poet, who wrote under the *takhalus* of Khaki. He was also a direct descendant of Mullah Faiz Allah, tutor to King Timur Shah.[14] His father, 'Abd al-Rahim, had been one of the religious leaders executed by Amir 'Abd al-Rahman Khan on the threshold of the shrine of Khirqa-yi Sharif for issuing a *fatwa* condemning his government as *kafir*. In late 1905 'Abd al-Ra'uf secured permission from 'Abd al-Quddus Khan to publish Afghanistan's first private newspaper, the *Seraj al-Akhbar-i Afghanistan*, although it was closed down after one edition.[15] At the time of his arrest, 'Abd al-Ra'uf was Chief Examiner of the Royal Madrasa and *Mullah Huzur*, or Court *mullah*.

Two of 'Abd al-Ra'uf's sons were also detained. 'Abd al-Rabb Akhundzada, his eldest son, was personal spiritual adviser to Amir Habib Allah Khan and a teacher at Habibiyya College. He had been instrumental in establishing Afghanistan's first Teacher Training Institute and played a prominent part in the formation of national education policy. As for 'Abd al-Ra'uf's younger son, Maulawi 'Abd al-Wasi', or Wa'is, he was a leading light in the emerging Pushtu literary movement and an advocate of Pushtun nationalism. 'Abd al-Ra'uf, his sons and many of his family members spent nearly a decade in prison and were only freed after 'Aman Allah Khan came to power. 'Abd al-Wa'is subsequently chaired the committee that drafted the *Nizam Nama*s that formed the basis of Afghanistan's first Constitution. Other prominent individuals arrested included: a relative of the Hazrat of Chahar Bagh; a son of 'Abd al-Quddus Khan; Na'ib Habib Allah Khan, Mahmud Tarzi's nephew; Ghulam Muhammad Mosawar Maimanagi, a descendant of the Uzbek *amir*s of Maimana, who had studied in Paris and taught at the School of Fine Art; and Faiz Muhammad Katib, author of the *Seraj al-Tawarikh*.

Seven individuals were condemned to be blown from the muzzle of a gun, including Nazir Muhammad Safir Khan, a Chitrali who had been Amir 'Abd al-Rahman Khan's most confidential adviser, Keeper of the Royal Seal and head of 'Abd al-Rahman Khan's feared internal security. As Supervisor of the Royal Kitchen, Nazir Muhammad Safir was responsible for ensuring no one introduced poison into the king's food. However, at the time the conspiracy was exposed Safir Khan was already in prison, having been accused of the illegal use of the royal seal, after it was discovered he had been covertly selling arms to the Mohmand and Afridi rebels. Safir Khan's eldest son, a student at Habibiyya, was also executed, along with Maulawi Muhammad Sarwar Wasef, an Islamic scholar from Kandahar and the author of the *Seraj al-Ahkam*, a Persian version of the Ottoman Hanafi legal code commissioned by Amir Habib Allah Khan. At the time of his arrest Wasef was employed as a scribe on the *Seraj al-Akhbar*. Under torture, Wasef confessed to being the head of the movement and the author of the *shab nama*, and before he was put to death he smuggled a note to an associate declaring he was happy to sacrifice his life in the cause of freedom.

Despite all the arrests and executions, the official version of the Mashruta Conspiracy, which claimed it was an attempt to assassinate and depose Habib Allah Khan, does not stand up to close scrutiny. British intelligence could make no sense of the conspiracy.[16] They initially thought Nasr Allah Khan and 'Abd al-Quddus Khan were behind the plot, though the idea that either of these men would support a move to Constitutional government is absurd, as is the allegation that Dr Ghani, a Gujarati Indian, planned to set himself up as Amir of Afghanistan. As for Nasr Allah Khan, he tried, but failed, to convince the Amir that the British were behind the coup. Later the government claimed that the conspirators were mostly army officers, yet apart from Nazir Muhammad Safir Khan, none of the alleged ringleaders held military rank.

Most of the accused had a family history of support for the ex-Amir Ya'qub Khan and several had held high office under Amir 'Abd al-Rahman Khan. Many came from Kandahar, while the religious scholars had been educated in the royal *madrasa*, an institution set up by 'Abd al-Rahman Khan to train a body of loyal '*ulama*' and to promote the form of Islam that endorsed the monarch's policies and offset radical, independent and often anti-government religious leaders. Some of the alleged ringleaders also played an active part in educational and legal reforms and had close ties to Habibiyya College. The exception was Nazir Muhammad Safir, who ideologically was aligned to the conservative Sunni party and was an outspoken critic of Habibiyya College and the Amir's education policies. As such, Muhammad Safir was the last person to support a movement like the Hizb-i Mashruta.

The evidence suggests that the Mashruta Conspiracy was in fact a cover for something far more sinister. The night letter that precipitated the witch-hunt appears to have been timed for maximum effect, for the Amir was recovering from a severe bout of illness, one of the symptoms of which was acute paranoia. The real plotters exploited the Amir's mental state, reckoning that the assassination plot would so terrify him that Habib Allah Khan would order the arrest and execution of the conspirators without bothering to determine the truth, or otherwise, of the allegations. This is exactly what happened, and those who hatched the scheme had a free hand to suppress and discredit the reformers and destroy their personal enemies at the same time.

According to Dr Ghani's account, the appointment of Indians to run Habibiyya College created a great deal of jealously among powerful individuals at court. Further hostility had been aroused when Dr Ghani's appointment as headmaster came at the expense of another Indian medical doctor, Ghulam Nabi, who was sacked following a vicious campaign of character assassination by Ghani's two brothers. Once in charge of Habibiyya, Dr Ghani dismissed all Dr Nabi's appointees and replaced them with his own nominees. Dr Ghani then encouraged basic primary education and persuaded a number of *mullah*s to allow their mosques to be used for this purpose and even initiated a teacher training programme for these religious leaders. The Amir, impressed by the success of this programme, allocated an additional *lakh* of rupees for the expansion of the project and shortly before his arrest Dr Ghani presented Habib Allah Khan with a series of proposals that included extending primary education to every province, the establishment of a university and the opening of a vocational college. He even secured the Amir's approval to recommence publication of a newspaper, presumably 'Abd al-Ra'uf's *Seraj al-Akhbar-i Afghanistan*.

Nasr Allah Khan and 'Abd al-Quddus Khan opposed Ghani's educational plans and urged the Amir to reject his proposals, claiming they were a plot to destroy Islam and the 'Afghan way of life'. As far as Nasr Allah Khan was concerned, Habibiyya College ought to have been an exclusive *madrasa* for the Islamic education of Muhammadzais, while 'Abd al-Quddus Khan declared publicly on numerous occasions that the stability of Muhammadzai rule rested entirely on the 'utter ignorance of [Afghanistan's] subjects'.[17] Nasr Allah Khan's opposition to Ghani was also personal, for despite being Minister of Education, the Amir had overruled him and given Ghani control of a huge budget, which he was able to spend without any reference to Nasr Allah Khan.

Dr Ghani, apparently unaware of the powerful enemies he was making, pushed on with his educational programme and began paddling in even more dangerous waters. Under his leadership, Habibiyya College became a hotbed of political dissent, with students openly mocking the Amir and his courtiers as 'blundering old fools'. A number of teachers and students joined the Hizb-i Mashruta, a movement established by reform-minded Islamic scholars from Kandahar who met in secret in the Masjid-i Chob Firoshi in the Old City. To what extent Ghani knew about the existence of this clandestine movement in Habibiyya is unclear, but he did nothing to quash it or rebuke young hotheads. Instead, he decided to hold night classes to discuss 'political economy'. His objective may have been intellectual rather than political, but Dr Ghani ought to have known better than to debate such issues publicly in a country ruled for generations by paranoid autocrats. His decision to hold these lectures provided the excuse his enemies needed to act against him.

Two individuals in particular were responsible for Ghani's downfall and for fabricating, or at least exaggerating, the plot to assassinate the Amir. The first was Dr Ghulam Nabi, who had a personal vendetta against Ghani and his brothers for ousting him as headmaster of Habibiyya. In the winter of 1908 Habib Allah Khan had summoned Dr Nabi to return to Afghanistan to treat the acute pain that was one of the symptoms of his illness, for during a previous attack Dr Nabi had managed to cure the Amir. While treating the Amir, Dr Nabi also exploited his position of confidence to denounce Ghani and his brothers as radical revolutionaries and British agents provocateurs.

Ghani's other enemy was even more powerful. Mirza Muhammad Husain Khan Safi, the Amir's *Mustufi al-Mulk*, or Auditor General, was also *kotwal* of Kabul, head of Internal Security of the Eastern Provinces, and chief of the Safi tribe of Qal'a Murad Beg near Jabal Saraj, which was later renamed Husain Kot in his honour.[18] The *mustufi* commanded a substantial militia and was ideologically aligned to the Sunni party with strong links to the Hazrat of Shor Bazaar, while his family's spiritual guide, Maulana 'Abd al-Hai Panjshiri, was a graduate of the Darul Uloom at Deoband. Jewett, the American engineer employed to supervise the hydroelectric project at Jabal Saraj, described the *mustufi* as 'intriguing and unscrupulous',[19] while the Kabul *wakil* noted that he was 'extremely bigoted and conservative' with a 'natural aversion' to the Amir's 'western ways'. The *mustufi* developed a personal dislike for Dr Ghani and his educational policies, while Ghani accused Muhammad Husain Khan of being behind the cold-blooded murder of his twelve-year-old son a few years after he was imprisoned.

The *mustufi*'s sons, who were pupils at Habibiyya College, no doubt kept their father informed about Dr Ghani's proceedings, the public mocking of government officials, and the fact that some teachers and students had joined a secret political party. In order to purge these critics of the ruling family, Husain Khan Safi produced, and possibly even forged, the *shab nama*, purporting to come from the Hizb-i Mashruta, knowing that he would be entrusted with the task of hunting down the culprits. Indeed, according to Ghani, it was the *mustufi* who convinced the Amir that he and his brothers were the ringleaders of the conspiracy. So Husain Khan, with royal approval, was able to purge Habibiyya of its Indian teachers and arrest leading members of the reform movement, including religious scholars and literary figures known for their progressive views. At the same time, the *mustufi* undermined the Amir's faith in the liberalization of education, halted moves to reform the legal and social framework of the country, and disposed of personal rivals.

When it came to Nazir Muhammad Safir, he and the *mustufi* were long-standing rivals, for the *mustufi* had replaced him as *kotwal* of Kabul and head of security and was probably responsible for his imprisonment. The *mustufi* now accused his rival of being head of the Hizb-i Mashruta and Nazir Muhammad Safir was put to death, even though he had no ideological ties to any reform movement. According to Jewett's somewhat garbled account of the conspiracy, the *mustufi* concocted the plot partly out of envy and partly so he could gain control of the revenues of Kabul's Custom House.[20]

Not everything went the *mustufi*'s way for, despite his repeated attempts, the Amir refused to sign death warrants for Dr Ghani and his brothers, probably because their execution would have had serious repercussions for Anglo-Afghan relations. Nor did Habibiyya College end up in the hands of Islamic reactionaries. Instead the Amir appointed his eldest son and heir, 'Inayat Allah, as Minister for Education and Western subjects continued to be taught. The Amir, though, did crack down on political debate and dissent, disbanded his consultative council, and reverted to the autocratic tradition of his father.

One of the many unsolved questions arising from the Mashruta Conspiracy is the role of Mahmud Tarzi and his Young Afghan circle, a movement which was regarded as almost synonymous with Hizb-i Mashruta. Like many of those accused of involvement in the conspiracy, Tarzi's family had a history of support for Ya'qub and 'Ayub Khan and some of Tarzi's circle of Young Afghans were arrested, including his nephew. Tarzi later employed several of the alleged conspirators as editors on his newspaper and published their literary works. It is therefore difficult to believe that Mahmud Tarzi knew nothing about the Hizb-i Mashruta, or that he was not complicit in the alleged conspiracy to depose Amir Habib Allah Khan. One well-placed Afghan official even told Jewett that the chief conspirator was 'the son of a cousin [of the Amir's] who was exiled to Turkistan', a comment that surely refers to either Mahmud Tarzi or his nephew, since Tarzi's father was dead by this time. Evidently some officials believed Mahmud Tarzi had a leading role in the plot and in the Hizb-i Mashruta.

If, as seems highly likely, Mahmud Tarzi was a leading light in the Hizb-i Mashruta and/or the Sirr-i Milli, why was he not arrested along with his nephew, and why was his nephew not executed? Did the Tarzis betray the other conspirators in return for their lives and was Mahmud Tarzi secretly conspiring to depose Amir Habib Allah Khan? We will probably never know the answers to these questions, for the Tarzi family are highly unlikely to publish any papers that might tarnish the saint-like image accorded to him by his descendants and Afghan monarchists.

Mahmud Tarzi, the *Seraj al-Akhbar-i Afghaniyya*, and Afghan nationalism

What we do know is that the suppression of the Constitutional Party marked Mahmud Tarzi's rise to political power. During the last decade of Habib Allah Khan's reign, Mahmud and his brothers and nephew were leading lights in the field of education and journalism, as well as heading up the movement for social reform. Tarzi also used his newfound influence to secure the appointments of Turkish advisers in education, health and in the Military Academy. A few months after the suppression of the Mashruta Conspiracy, Mahmud Tarzi's political power and dynastic rights were re-inforced by the marriage of his eldest daughter to the heir apparent, 'Inayat Allah Khan, and a few years later another of Tarzi's daughters, Soraya, was betrothed to the future Amir of Afghanistan, 'Aman Allah Khan. Tarzi also became tutor to 'Aman Allah Khan, Soraya's son, the future Amir of Afghanistan, who was the most liberal and reform-minded of all Amir Habib Allah Khan's sons. The result of these and other alliances meant the fortunes of the Tarzi family became inextricably bound to the Seraj dynasty.

In October 1911 Mahmud Tarzi received official approval to revive 'Abd al-Ra'uf's newspaper, which he renamed *Seraj al-Akhbar-i Afghaniyya*.[21] The *Seraj al-Akhbar* appeared fortnightly with a print run of 3,000 and was distributed to every government department with subscriptions deducted from civil servants' salaries. Tarzi maintained that the newspaper was not an official publication, but this was disingenuous to say the least, since Tarzi received a substantial salary from the Amir and the printing was subsidized by the salaries of civil servants. Indeed officials regarded the *Seraj al-Akhbar* as a court circular.

Tarzi's stated intention was for the *Seraj al-Akhbar-i Afghaniyya* to be a 'bazaar of knowledge' and despite its relatively small circulation, the news-paper had a profound effect on educated Afghans. Over the seven years of its publication the *Seraj al-Akhbar* covered topics including literature, science, geography, economic theory, technology and philosophy as well as publishing numerous translations of European works. In the process of translation, Tarzi also introduced many foreign loan words into Afghan Persian and for many Afghans the broadsheet was their first contact with the world of European culture, literature and technology.

A number of individuals contributed to the *Seraj al-Akhbar*, included 'Abd al-Ra'uf, Loynab 'Ali Ahmad and the Pushtun poet 'Abd al-Hadi Dawai, but most of the articles were written or translated by Tarzi, and the newspaper was essentially a vehicle for Tarzi to promote his vision of Pan-Islam, nationalism and modernization. Like most Muslim reformers of his day, Tarzi argued that there was no intrinsic conflict between Islam and Western education, science and technology. This view was at odds with most of Afghanistan's religious establishment, who held to the traditional opinion that all necessary knowledge was contained in the Qur'an, *Hadith* and *Sunna*. Tarzi opposed this narrow world view and accused the religious

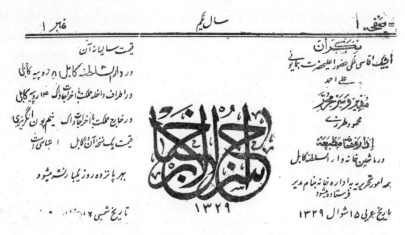

The masthead of the first edition of Mahmud Tarzi's *Seraj al-Akhbar* dated 15 Shawwal 1329, or 8 October 1911. In many ways its contents were revolutionary, and Tarzi used the publication to promote his new nationalism. However, the *Seraj al-Akhbar* was not the first newspaper to be published in Afghanistan.

establishment of holding the nation in intellectual darkness and of being proponents of superstition and obscurantism. This polemic made Tarzi and his Young Afghans powerful enemies and, rather than persuading the religious establishment to accept reform, it served to entrench them even further, for they feared that Tarzi and his circle were undermining the whole Islamic framework on which the country was founded. After all, Tarzi's ideological opponents were well aware of the radical, anti-*shari'a* agenda of the Young Turks and the *Tanzimat* era.

Arguably the most important and enduring aspect of Tarzi's political vision was his promotion of a new national identity, a polemic that subsequently earned him the title of Father of Afghan Nationalism. Tarzi's views on nationalism, however, were far from original and were mostly a recasting of the political philosophy of the Young Turks. The fundamental premise on which Tarzi's nationalism was constructed was what he termed *Afghaniyya* (plural *Afghaniyyat*) – Afghanness or Afghanism – a term coined by Tarzi but which was the Afghan equivalent of Turkism. It was this ethnocentric world view that led Tarzi to changing the name of 'Abd al-Ra'uf's newspaper from *Afghanistan* to *Afghaniyya*. Tarzi treated Afghan and Pushtun as synonymous terms and *Afghaniyya* increasingly became identified with Pushtunness and the Pushtu language, despite Pushtunness being essentially the values and identity of the hill tribes of the Afghan–Indian frontier, rather than one espoused by all those who called themselves Afghan. Some Afghan tribes, for example, including the urban Durranis, were more Persianate than Pushtun.

438

Despite this, Tarzi's *Afghaniyya* became adopted as part of the monarchy's nationalist discourse and provided an intellectual veneer to justify the Durranis' presumed divine right to rule Afghanistan, the 'Land of the Afghans'. Tarzi, after all was a Muhammadzai, who also had a Saddozai heritage. Tarzi argued that the national language, or *zaban-i milli*, for Afghans ought to be Pushtu, even though Persian had been the language of the Durrani court since the days of Saddu Khan, as well as the language of commerce and diplomacy. This polemic also ignored the fact that the vast majority of citizens of Afghanistan did not speak Pushtu, indeed for most of them it was a foreign language. However, Tarzi argued that Persian could not be the *zaban-i milli* since it was not unique to Afghanistan and it was already the official language of Shi'a Iran. Tarzi therefore demoted Afghan Persian to the status of *rasmi*, or the official language, rather than *milli*, or national one. Later in the century, in an attempt to distance Afghan Persian from its Iranian cousin, the government officially renamed the Kabuli dialect *Dari*, on the mythic grounds that it was the Persian spoken at the Mughal court. More practically, Tarzi encouraged his readers to submit articles and poetry in Pushtu and employed a Pushtu-speaker to translate works into the language. Even so, the *Seraj al-Akhbar* published very few articles in Pushtu. Ironically, the longest submission in Pushtu came from an Afghan in Turkey. In another irony, despite Turkish being his first language, Tarzi never published a single item in Uzbeki, Chaghatai or any other of Afghanistan's Turkic languages.

Tarzi's *Afghaniyya* went much further than merely promoting the revival of Pushtu literature and culture, arguing that *afghan* should be the only official designation of nationality for all citizens of Afghanistan, ignoring the fact that Afghanistan was a multicultural, multi-ethnic nation in which the majority of the population consisted, and still consists, of peoples who were not ethnically Afghan. Tarzi thus sought to impose an artificial, alien identity on all non-Afghan ethnolinguistic groups and by so doing indirectly exacerbated sectarian, regional and ethnic divisions as well as alienating large sections of the population who were reduced to the status of minorities. It was as if the British government insisted all Scottish, Welsh and Irish citizens be designated as English on their passports.

Tarzi defined national identity as consisting of four interrelated elements: Religion (*din*), which he defined as the Hanafi school of Sunnism; Patriotism (*daulat dosti*); the Fatherland (*watan*); and the Nation (*millat*), which combined all three of the other elements. Most of these terms were derived from Turkish nationalist discourse, but these terms had different nuances in Afghanistan. In colloquial Kabuli Persian, for example, *watan* is not Fatherland or Nation, but the region of one's birth (such as Panjshir, Herat, Wardak or Mazar), while the Ottoman concept of *millat*, which embraced even the empire's substantial non-Muslim populations, would have been lost on all but a small clique of educated Afghans. As for *daulat*, depending on its context, it could mean kingdom, realm, government, dynasty, or even wealth and possessions, while the term *daulat dosti*, patriotism, or literally 'love of the country', was probably coined by Tarzi himself.

Unlike Turkey in the early twentieth century, there was no sense of national identity in Afghanistan, at least in the European sense. Traditionally tribal and religious leaders swore an oath of personal fealty, or *ba'it*, to the Amir on behalf of their tribe or followers, rather than to the state or even the monarchy. As was the case in medieval Europe this oath was renewed every time a new ruler came to power, or in the wake of a major rebellion. In return, the Amir, as chief of chiefs, was expected to reciprocate by the disbursement of royal patronage and uphold the leaders' traditional right of autonomy.

As for the religious elites, they expected the Amir to rule according to Islamic law under the guidance of a council of *'ulama'*. Serious breaches of the *shari'a* were deemed sufficient justification for rebellion and the condemnation of the Amir and his government as *kafir*. Under Islamic law it is a religious obligation on the population to overthrow any ruler who has been formally condemned in this manner or who has committed serious violations of Islamic law such as the sin of *bid'a*, religious innovation or heresy. When the country went to war, the Amir did not appeal to patriotism, 'the national interest' or 'the defence of the realm', but to Islam and the oath of fealty. Traditionally, prior to any military campaign the Amir would secure a *fatwa* that gave religious legitimacy to the war. As for the army's tribal levies, their loyalty lay not with the nation, the government or the head of state, but to their tribal and religious leaders.

Tarzi's *Afghaniyya* was a jumble of inappropriate ideas cut and pasted from Turkish nationalism and showed little understanding of the fluidity of Afghanistan and Pushtun society. It was also shot through with ironies. For while Tarzi was ethnically Afghan, he neither spoke nor read Pushtu, and both his own and his father's literary output was in Persian. Rather than Pushtu being the language of the literate or of the nation as a whole, the primary native speakers of Pushtu were mostly illiterate peasants, the *maldar* nomads and the semi-independent hill tribes of the Afghan–Indian frontier. Indeed, with the exception of the remarkable output of Khushhal Khan Khattak and a few others, in the first decades of the twentieth century Pushtu was barely a written, let alone a literary, language. The emergence of Pushtu as a written language only really began following the British occupation of the Punjab, when Frontier officials were required to learn Pushtu and missionaries translated the New Testament and other religious tracts into the language. Tarzi's advocacy for Pushtu as the national language of Afghanistan, therefore, was equivalent to the British government making Welsh the national language of Britain. Yet despite this, Tarzi's *Afghaniyya* became the foundation stone of all subsequent royalist-nationalist discourse.

Many Young Afghans, like the Young Turks, went a stage further and conflated *Afghaniyya* with social Darwinism, German ideas of racial supremacy and Aryanism. Aryanism was popular in the early twentieth century and was derived from a misreading of *Sacred Books of the East*, a comparative study of the Vedas and Avesta by the German-born Orientalist Max Müller. Based on linguistic and theological similarities between these ancient Hindu and Persian sacred texts, Müller posited that there had been an ancient race, whom he called the Aryans, who lived somewhere in Central Asia and spoke a language that was the precursor to Sanskrit, Greek and Persian. According to Müller's theory, the Aryans eventually migrated south and west, bringing the Vedic religion to India and Zoroastrianism to Iran, while in Europe they were the primogenitures of the Nordic and Germanic races.

Müller's Aryan theory was later hijacked to justify the racial theories of Germany's Nazi party and other Fascist movements, but it also had a profound influence on both Turkish and Afghan nationalism as well as in India, where 'the acceptance of the Aryan theory underlined the Hindu idiom in nationalist historical writing'.[22] Indeed Tarzi probably first heard of the Aryan theory from the Indian revolutionary and refugee Mahendra Pratap, a member of the German Mission of 1915. After the mission ended, Pratap remained in Kabul and Tarzi published several of his articles in the *Seraj al-Akhbar*. Some years later, when Pratap published his memoirs of Afghanistan, he entitled it *Afghanistan: The Heart of Aryan*.

As Afghan nationalism increasingly became intertwined with Aryanism, many Afghan intellectuals began to claim that Pushtu was a proto-Aryan language. Though this theory was based on the slimmest of evidence, it allowed advocates of Pushtun to assert that their language was more ancient than Iranian Persian and that the Achaemenid dynasty, who referred to themselves as Aryan in their dynastic inscriptions, were actually Afghan. Later in the twentieth century members of the Pushtu Academy identified Balkh, ancient Bactra, as the original Aryan homeland, while some of the more radical Pushtunists claimed that the Pushtun 'race' was part of the *Herrenvolk*, or Master Race. From the 1940s onward the government began to employ the term Aryana for state institutions, including the state airline and national press. Aryana was even used as a synonym for Afghanistan itself. Another outcome of Tarzi's *Afghaniyya* was the emergence of the Pushtunistan, or Pukhtunistan, movement, which sought the political 'reunification' of the Pushtun tribes on both sides of the Durand Line. In the 1960s the establishment of Pushtunistan became official government policy, but the idea was mooted as early as 1916 by Dr Aurang Shah, one of the first Afghans to study in California, who founded the Azad Pakhtunistan Association of America.[23]

In two important respects, however, Tarzi departed from the nationalistic vision of the Young Turks. He was a staunch advocate of the monarchy and argued for the perpetuation of *shari'a* as the foundation of the state legal system. As a Muhammadzai, two of whose daughters were married to Habib Allah Khan's sons, Tarzi had a vested interest in maintaining the dynastic status quo and even the title of his newspaper, the *Seraj al-Akhbar*, was an affirmation and endorsement of the monarchy. As far as Tarzi was concerned, patriotism was not merely the love of *watan* and *din* but loyalty to the Amir, the Durrani dynasty and the monarchy in general.[24]

When it came to the role of Islamic law, Tarzi adopted a bipolar position. On the one hand he attacked Islamic leaders for their obscurantism and superstition, while on the other he maintained that the Hanafi *mazhab*, arguably the most conservative school of Islamic jurisprudence, should remain the foundation stone of Afghanistan's social and legal system. Tarzi thus endorsed the political and cultic status quo in an era when Muslim nationalists in Turkey, Iran and Arab countries were demanding root-and-branch reform of the Executive and legal systems, including a constitution based on European legal norms, the disestablishment of Islam, democratic assemblies and republicanism. According to these reformers, the autocratic nature of the monarchy and the domination of state legislation by the '*ulama*' were the two most serious hindrances to modernization. For Tarzi, however, freedom and liberty were defined primarily in terms of independence from Britain, rather than the establishment of democratic institutions or representative government.

Every edition of the *Seraj al-Akhbar* included a great deal of sycophantic praise for Amir Habib Allah Khan's modest reforms and included detailed accounts of the Amir's activities. Furthermore, with the exception of the publication of official dispatches related to the Khost uprising of 1912, the *Seraj al-Akhbar* studiously avoided any mention of political unrest or dissent. In one editorial Tarzi went as far as to claim there was not 'the slightest trace of despotism' in Afghanistan. Tarzi's monarchical patriotism even led to him rewriting Afghanistan's history as dynastic propaganda. For example, he praised the reign of Amir 'Abd al-Rahman Khan as a Golden Age, even though it was this same Amir who had imprisoned and exiled his family. As for the massacres and religious pogroms of Ahmad Shah Durrani's campaigns against the Jats and Sikhs, these were said to have been conducted in the name of freedom, national integrity and national unity.

In retrospect, Tarzi's *Afghaniyya* has been more of a curse than a blessing, as anyone who has attended conferences on Afghanistan's political future will know. To this day Afghans continue to fight bitterly over the role of Islamic law, the rights of non-Pushtun minorities, the values of Republicanism or the restoration of the Durrani monarchy, and the rights of the Executive and the Legislature. Rather than binding the nation together, Tarzi's *Afghaniyya* divided the kingdom even more against itself.

The Great War and the German Mission to Kabul

The outbreak of the First World War in August 1914 created yet another major crisis for Habib Allah Khan, who came under intense pressure from both the Young Afghans and the Islamic party to join the war on the side of Turkey and Germany. Despite these pressures, however, the Amir reassured Lord Hardinge, the Viceroy, of his determination to remain neutral, a pragmatic decision since there was tribal unrest in southeastern Afghanistan. Habib Allah Khan's decision came as a relief to Britain, but it was unpopular with senior Muhammadzais and the population at large. Tarzi used the *Seraj al-Akhbar* to argue for Afghanistan to go to war on Turkey's side and to use this as a lever to demand full independence from Britain. The *Seraj al-Akhbar*'s increasingly strident anti-British polemic eventually led to Lord Hardinge complaining to the Amir about the 'offensive matter' in the newspaper and the Amir forced Tarzi to publish an official statement about Afghanistan's neutrality. In May 1915 the Viceroy again complained to Habib Allah Khan about the 'bigoted editor of the "Siraj-ul-Akhbar"' and Tarzi was required to 'bind himself to abstain hereafter from publishing such passages . . . as may lead to an interference of peace on the frontier or in India'.[25]

Tarzi largely ignored this commitment. Following the arrival of a German mission in September 1915, he stepped up the anti-British polemic by publishing articles by Barakat Allah and Mahendra Pratap, Indian revolutionaries who had accompanied the German mission. Later he employed Barakat Allah as a subeditor on the *Seraj al-Akhbar*. Despite frequent rebukes from the Amir, Tarzi continued to publish articles hostile to British policy, so Habib Allah Khan cut Tarzi's salary, threatened him with deportation and ordered him to submit the proofs of the newspaper so the Amir could personally approve the copy prior to publication. A month or so before Habib Allah Khan was assassinated, the Amir finally suspended publication of the *Seraj al-Akhbar*.

The internal pressures on the Amir increased when both Turkey and Germany tried to persuade Afghanistan to declare war on Britain. A few months after war broke out in Europe, the Ottoman Caliph sent a member of the Turkish National Assembly to Afghanistan bearing a *fatwa* declaring *jihad* against Britain. British intelligence managed to thwart the mission before it reached Kabul, while a subsequent German-Turkish mission led by Oskar von Niedermayer became bogged down in Iran. In the summer of 1915 the German Foreign Ministry, encouraged by American-based Indian revolutionaries, sent a second mission to Kabul led by Werner Otto von Hentig.[26] When he reached Iran, Hentig joined forces with Niedermayer and despite many of their party being interned by Russian and British forces, the mission managed to reach Herat and arrived in Kabul in September 1915. On their arrival the Turkish officer in charge of Kabul's Military School formed his cadets up as a guard of honour for the mission, an action that led to his summary dismissal.

The Hentig-Niedermayer Mission was a direct challenge to the Anglo-Afghan alliance, for under the terms of the 1880 and 1893 treaties the Amir ought to have turned the mission back at the frontier. However, Amir Habib Allah Khan felt he had little choice but to allow the mission to come to Kabul since Nasr Allah Khan and his heir apparent, 'Inayat Allah Khan, along with most of his senior advisers, were in favour of entering the war on the side of Turkey. There were also strident calls from *mullahs* and other religious figures on the Afghan–Indian frontier for a *jihad* against Britain, while in the streets of Kabul people openly accused the Amir of being a *kafir* and a friend of *kafirs*. The admission of the German envoys was thus a sop to the war party, even though Habib Allah Khan had no intention of being dragged into the Great War.

The German mission was housed in the former palace of Bibi Halima in Babur's Gardens, but they were not allowed outside its walls. The Amir then deliberately delayed their formal reception, but after more than a month of kicking their heels the envoys went on hunger strike in protest. In late October Hentig and Niedermayer were finally driven to Paghman, where they had a secret audience with Amir Habib Allah Khan and his

Amir Habib Allah Khan's pavilion in the Bagh-i Babur after restoration by the Aga Khan
Trust for Culture. The German Mission was housed in this building, which was well away
from the old city with high walls surrounding its gardens.

closest advisers. During the six-hour meeting, the envoys argued the case
for Afghanistan joining Germany on the grounds of the Caliph's *fatwa*. The
Amir in return questioned the mission's credentials, declared his dissatisfaction that the Kaiser's letter was typed rather than handwritten and
criticized the envoys for being too young to be taken seriously. Though
they were probably unaware of it, the Amir planned to exploit the Germans'
presence in Kabul to extract more money and weapons from the British
and compared the mission to tradesmen trying to sell their wares. The
Amir's ploy succeeded for the Viceroy eventually increased his subsidy
by two *lakh* rupees.

In response to the Germans, the Amir pointed out the practical difficulties of declaring war on India. Not only would he lose the British subsidy,
but Afghanistan ran the risk of being partitioned by Britain and Russia,
who were now allies, and the dismemberment of the country. This scenario
had already taken place in Iran, for when the First World War broke out,
and in accordance with the Anglo-Russian Convention, Russian and British
forces had occupied northern and southern Iran respectively. The Amir
therefore demanded as a precondition of joining the war that Germany
and Turkey pay him a substantial sum in gold bullion and provide him
with guns, ammunition and troops. The meeting ended inconclusively and
the Amir postponed further negotiations until he had called an assembly

of elders and religious leaders to discuss the situation. Meanwhile negotiations continued informally with Nasr Allah Khan, 'Inayat Allah Khan
and Mahmud Tarzi, all of whom privately pledged their support for an
Afghan-German alliance.

At the end of December 1915 the Amir learnt that neither Hentig nor
Niedermayer had plenipotentiary powers, which provided Habib Allah
Khan with a face-saving solution to his dilemma. The Amir requested
Hentig to draft a treaty, knowing that the agreement was not binding
unless the German Foreign Ministry ratified it. The treaty, concluded on 24
January 1916, provided for Germany to supply Afghanistan with weapons,
ammunition, £10 million and 10,000 front-line troops. It was an arrangement that both sides knew could not be honoured, for marching a division
of German troops through occupied Iran was impossible, even if they
could be spared from the Western or Eastern Fronts. The Amir was astute
enough to demand that the provision of the weapons, cash and troops be
a precondition of declaring war on India and so he appeased the pro-war
party while at the same time maintaining Afghanistan's neutrality.

The day after signing the treaty Amir Habib Allah Khan met with
the British *wakil* and reassured him that he was determined to remain
neutral. Then, shortly before the German mission left, Nasr Allah Khan
informed Hentig that the Amir would not declare war unless the Turks
and Germans sent a fully equipped army of 20,000 to 100,000 men. Even
then, he would only attack India if Indian Muslims first rose against the
British. The Afghan-German treaty was thus essentially meaningless and
Afghanistan remained neutral throughout the First World War. Once the
German mission had left Afghanistan, the Amir purged the administration
of pro-German officials and published a leaflet arguing that all subjects
were required to obey their ruler and that the Amir alone had the authority
to declare *jihad*.

Habib Allah Khan's neutrality came as a relief to the British government, despite concerns that the Indian revolutionaries who accompanied
the German mission had remained in Kabul and formed an Indian
Nationalist Government in exile. Shortly after the German mission left,
a small group of anti-British *mujahidin* established a colony of what the
British termed 'Hindustani fanatics' in tribal territory on the Indian side
of the frontier and received covert support from high-ranking Afghan
officials, including Nasr Allah Khan. Britain was thus obliged to retain
troops on the Afghan–Indian frontier that otherwise would have been
sent to Europe. To this extent, the Hentig-Niedermayer Mission had been
successful, though it made no difference to the outcome of the First World

War. The German-Afghan Treaty of 1916, however, was yet another step in Afghanistan's move to full independence, but the most enduring legacy of the German mission of 1915–16 is the series of historic photographs taken by Hentig and Niedermayer and another member of the mission, Emil Rybitschka.[27]

The assassination of Amir Habib Allah Khan

The following year the revolutions in Russia, culminating in the Bolshevik coup of October 1917, created further cause for concern in both Afghanistan and India. On 3 March 1918 the Bolshevik government signed the Treaty of Brest-Litovsk, which ended Russia's war with Germany and the Anglo-Russian alliance. Shortly afterwards Russia plunged into civil war, which removed any immediate threat of a Russian invasion of Afghanistan, but at the same time led to fears that the Indian revolutionaries in Kabul would spread Communist revolutionary propaganda into Afghanistan and India. In the summer of 1918 Habib Allah Khan received another *shab nama*, which demanded constitutional government and threatened direct action if he failed to comply. Habib Allah Khan ignored the threat but a few days later, during celebrations to mark his birthday on 2 July, someone fired a shot at the Amir as he drove through the Shor Bazaar, but the bullet struck his car and fell harmlessly at his feet.

Habib Allah Khan once more turned to Mustufi Husain Khan to hunt down the assassins and again he used this opportunity to purge more reformers. He identified the chief conspirators as two men who were among Tarzi's closest associates: 'Abd al-Rahman Ludin and the poet 'Abd al-Hadi Dawai, who wrote under the *takhalus* of *Preshan*. Both came from Kandahar, were graduates of Habibiyya College and at the time of their arrest they were subeditors on the *Seraj al-Akhbar*. The *mustufi* even tried to implicate 'Aman Allah Khan and Dr Ghani, despite the fact that Ghani was still languishing in prison. The Amir, however, ignored these allegations against his son and refused to sign Ghani's death warrant. Ludin and 'Abd al-Hadi were also spared execution. Mahmud Tarzi once more escaped arrest, but the Amir suspended publication of the *Seraj al-Akhbar* for more than four months. 'Abd al-Rahman Ludin and 'Abd al-Hadi were freed following the death of Habib Allah Khan, and after 'Aman Allah Khan succeeded to the throne, Tarzi handed control of the *Seraj al-Akhbar* to 'Abd al-Hadi, who renamed the newspaper *'Aman-i Afghan*.

As winter approached Habib Allah Khan travelled to Jalalabad, where he hoped to escape the epidemic of influenza that was sweeping through

Kabul, leaving his younger son, 'Aman Allah Khan, in charge of the capital. In early January 1919 the Amir went on a hunting trip and in mid-February he arrived at his hunting lodge at Kalagosh, in Laghman. On the night of 19 February, an unidentified assassin slipped through the cordon of body-guards and shot the Amir through the ear at point-blank range, killing him instantly.

Habib Allah Khan's reign has been overshadowed both by his prede-cessor, 'Abd al-Rahman Khan, and his successor, 'Aman Allah Khan. Yet it was under Habib Allah Khan that Afghanistan made its first steps towards independence from Britain with the reception of the German mission. It was during his reign, too, that the country began to grapple with the complex issues of reform of the state and education and Afghanistan's first underground political party was formed. Under the influence of Mahmud Tarzi and his circle, Turkish nationalist ideas became embedded in Afghan nationalist discourse, which contributed significantly to the subsequent rise of Pushtunism, Aryanism and Pushtunistan. For the first time too, foreign literary and historical works were translated into Persian.

The Amir's reform programme, however, was tentative and limited to the educational field, with no interest in reform of the powers of the Executive. Afghanistan remained an autocracy and a country where indivi-duals who challenged the rights and privileges of the Amir, or sought a more inclusive form of government, risked imprisonment or execution. Amir Habib Allah Khan's refusal to contemplate political reform led to the suppression of the Hizb-i Mashruta, the suspension of the *Seraj al-Akhbar*, and the imprisonment and execution of leading reformers. The grow-ing ideological confrontation between modernizers and reformers, and conservative Sunnis who opposed any liberalization of education, social mores or the legal code, was a battle for the soul of the nation and one that would dominate Afghanistan's political life for the next century and which to this day has yet to be resolved.

Modernization under Habib Allah Khan meant primarily civil engin-eering and technological projects, most of which were for the convenience of the royal family and included dams, a small hydroelectric power station and road improvements. Apart from the German-built dam at Band-i Sultan, near Ghazni, all of these infrastructure projects benefited only the capital and it was as if the provinces did not exist. Construction of these civil engineering projects also led to much hardship, for labourers were forcibly conscripted and land seized without compensation. A clinic run by a Turkish doctor introduced vaccinations for the first time, but it was a drop in a very large ocean. Cholera, typhoid and other diseases remained endemic, while the influenza epidemic of 1919 led to the deaths of hundreds of thousands of Afghans, especially in Kabul.

Incompetent and untrained oversight of capital projects led to spiralling costs and extensive corruption. After eight years the hydroelectric station at Jabal Saraj was abandoned, unfinished; the Seraj al-Amirat palace at Jalalabad was so badly designed that the architect forgot to include any internal toilets; while the pipes for Kabul's potable water supply from the Qargha Dam were never laid. As for the goods produced in the state-run *machin khana*, the costs were up to four times higher than the same items imported from India. Like Habib Allah Khan's obsession with photography, golf and tennis, his engagement with modern technology was just another hobby.

TEN

Dreams Melted into Air, 1919–29

Abdur Rahman was content with repression whereas Amanullah hoped for conversion.

LEON B. POULLADA[1]

['Aman Allah Khan] admitted . . . that ever since he came to the throne he has been impelled by an uncontrollable desire to bring about the complete modernisation of his country during his own lifetime.

SIR FRANCIS HUMPHRYS[2]

AMIR HABIB ALLAH KHAN'S BODY was brought to Jalalabad the day after he was assassinated and interred on the golf course he had built for his enjoyment. On the following day, 21 February 1919, Saiyid Naqib Gailani, Hazrat of Chaharbagh, proclaimed Nasr Allah Khan as Amir with the support of Nadir Khan, Commander-in-Chief of the army, and Loynab 'Ali Ahmad Khan. 'Inayat Allah, the heir apparent, and his younger brother, Hayat Allah Khan, were powerless to prevent this putsch and they too swore allegiance to their uncle.

The accession of 'Aman Allah Khan

News of the Amir's death was telegraphed to Kabul early on the day after the murder, whereupon 'Aman Allah Khan, backed by Tarzi and the Young Afghans, took control of the Dilkusha Palace and the state treasury, and secured the support of the Kabul army by promising to substantially increase their pay. 'Aman Allah Khan then held a hastily assembled *darbar* where he was proclaimed Amir by Fazl Muhammad Mujadidi, Hazrat of Shor Bazaar, and Akhundzada Hamid Allah Safi, the Mullah of Tagab. During his inauguration 'Aman Allah Khan publicly denounced his uncle, Nasr Allah Khan, for masterminding Habib Allah Khan's assassination and condemned his half-brothers' oath of allegiance to him as treason.

450

Civil war was avoided only because the officer corps of the Jalalabad garrison declared for 'Aman Allah Khan and arrested Nasr Allah Khan, Nadir Khan and Loynab 'Ali Ahmad. Nasr Allah Khan was then forced at gunpoint to write a letter of abdication and he and the other prisoners were sent to Kabul under heavy guard. Meanwhile 'Inayat Allah Khan and Hayat Allah Khan, seeing which way the wind was blowing, drove post-haste to Kabul where they tendered their allegiance to their brother, only for them too to be arrested. When they reached the capital, Nasr Allah Khan, 'Inayat Allah Khan and Hayat Allah Khan were brought before a kangaroo court that convicted Nasr Allah Khan of plotting the Amir's assassination. He was sentenced to life imprisonment, but a few months later he was secretly put to death and his body buried in an unmarked grave on the Koh-yi 'Asmayi.[3] 'Inayat Allah Khan and Hayat Allah Khan were imprisoned but eventually released, although their role was reduced to a purely ceremonial one. Loynab 'Ali Ahmad too was set free following the intervention of his aunt, Ulya Hazrat, and despite his shifting loyalties he became a key member of Amir 'Aman Allah Khan's administration.

Nadir Khan, who was in charge of Habib Allah Khan's bodyguard the night he was slain, was exonerated by the court and reappointed as Commander-in Chief, Minister for War and Tribal and Frontier Affairs. Nadir's three brothers also suffered no penalty and retained their military rank. Later Shah Wali Khan, Nadir's youngest brother, married one of 'Aman Allah Khan's daughters. The Musahiban family escaped punishment probably because the Amir feared their imprisonment might lead to a revolt, for Nadir Khan and Shah Wali Khan were popular with the army and the tribes of Nangahar. However, 'Aman Allah Khan made sure Nadir Khan was kept as far away from Kabul as possible, dispatching him first to Khost and later to remote Qataghan.

The assassination of Habib Allah Khan and the subsequent arrests provided the Young Afghans with the opportunity they sought to dispose of their dynastic and ideological opponents. One individual who was particularly hated by the reformers was Mustufi Mirza Muhammad Husain Safi. As far as we can tell from the sources, the *mustufi* had no hand in the assassination of Habib Allah Khan and, according to his descendants, the *mustufi* tried to warn the Amir about the conspiracy in a letter before he left for his hunting trip. Unfortunately for Habib Allah Khan, he never read the note, which was recovered, unopened, in his jacket pocket after his death. The letter was then used against the *mustufi* as proof that he had had a hand in the assassination. He was condemned to death and unceremoniously hanged from a mulberry tree in the Dilkusha Palace.

The *mustufi*'s terminally sick brother, Hasan Khan, was also sentenced to death, but he died before the execution could take place. Following their deaths, the *mustufi*'s estates in Kabul, Kohistan and Jalalabad were confiscated, and his extended family were arrested and subsequently exiled to Kohistan and Qataghan.

Colonel Shah 'Ali Reza, a Qizilbash or Hazara Shi'a, became the public scapegoat for the actual murder. He had been on guard outside the tent the night Habib Allah Khan was slain and had tried to detain the fleeing assassin. However, instead of being rewarded for his loyalty, Amir 'Aman Allah Khan accused him of firing the fatal shot, claiming his father had appeared to him in a dream and denounced 'Ali Reza as his murderer. 'Ali Reza was brought before the Amir, who handed his sword to an Iraqi *ghulam*. The *ghulam* first slit the condemned man's mouth and then cleaved him in two with a single stroke of his sword.[4]

The accession of Amir 'Aman Allah Khan, however, did bring freedom for Dr Ghani, his brothers and the other Indian teachers of Habibiyya College who had been incarcerated for their alleged role in the Mashruta Conspiracy. Despite having spent nearly a decade in prison, Dr Ghani remained in Afghanistan as an adviser to the Amir and in August 1919 he was a member of the Afghan delegation at the Rawalpindi Conference.

Despite the arrests and executions, rumours continued to circulate that 'Aman Allah Khan and Mahmud Tarzi had masterminded Habib Allah Khan's assassination. Several years later, Shuja' al-Daula, Habib Allah Khan's *farash bashi*, who had been responsible for the Amir's camping arrangements, confessed to Ghulam Siddiq Charkhi that he was the assassin and even produced the pistol that he had used to shoot the Amir. Shuja' al-Daula claimed he killed the Amir to avenge a personal grievance, but the fact that 'Aman Allah Khan appointed him *kotwal* of Kabul and Director of Military Intelligence, positions previously held by Mustufi Mirza Muhammad Husain Safi, suggests that 'Aman Allah Khan or his mother, Ulya Hazrat, may have incited Shuja' al-Daula to assassinate the Amir. Mahmud Tarzi, after all, had every reason for wanting Amir Habib Allah Khan out of the way. In the last years of Habib Allah Khan's reign, Tarzi had been increasingly at odds with the Amir over his policy of neutrality during the Great War, the suppression of the Hizb-i Mashruta and the suspension of the *Seraj al-Akhbar*. Less than a year earlier, Tarzi's closest associates had been imprisoned for attempting to shoot the Amir. The succession of 'Aman Allah Khan was also a political triumph for Tarzi, for he had personally groomed the prince for kingship and he was the most reform-minded of Habib Allah Khan's sons. Tarzi became 'Aman Allah Khan's foreign minister and his chief adviser, positions that meant he was now able to influence the young and highly impressionable Amir and implement his dream of transforming Afghanistan into a modern, Europeanized, nation state.

The declaration of independence and the Third Anglo-Afghan War

On 27 February 1919, just a week after taking power, 'Aman Allah Khan held a second *darbar* where he declared he intended to rule Afghanistan as a fully independent nation and ordered the assembled tribal leaders to return home and gather their forces for a *jihad* against India. The Amir then wrote to the Viceroy in the name of 'our independent and free government of Afghanistan', a declaration that signalled the end of the Anglo-Afghan alliance.[5] 'Aman Allah Khan's declaration of independence and his subsequent war with Britain also diverted attention from the *coup d'état* and won over governors, military commanders and tribal and religious leaders who had yet to pledge their allegiance. Tarzi and the Indian revolutionaries, who had already been covertly inciting tribal unrest in the Northwest Frontier, also convinced the Amir that if he invaded India there would be a mass revolt in the Punjab, which would force Britain to recognize Afghanistan's independence and make territory concessions. It was a serious misjudgement, the first of many in a reign marred by poor political decisions.

Another reason for declaring independence and going to war was the perceived failure of Britain to reward Afghanistan for remaining neutral during the Great War. In March 1916, shortly before signing the Afghan-German Treaty, Amir Habib Allah Khan had written to the Viceroy, Lord Chelmsford, requesting a seat on any post-war peace conference, only for his petition to be rejected. Three weeks before his assassination, and with the Paris Peace Conference imminent, Habib Allah Khan again wrote to the Viceroy asking for him to recognize the 'absolute liberty, freedom of action, and perpetual independence' of Afghanistan,[6] only for his request to again be denied. By the time the Viceroy's reply reached Kabul, Habib Allah Khan was dead and it was Amir 'Aman Allah Khan, advised by Mahmud Tarzi, who replied to the Viceroy's letter. The new Amir made it clear that the continuation of the Anglo-Afghan alliance was conditional on Britain's formal recognition of Afghanistan as an 'independent and free' nation.[7] 'Aman Allah Khan then proceeded to emphasize his independence by dispatching envoys to Moscow, Turkey, various European countries and even the United States without seeking Britain's prior approval.

The death of Habib Allah Khan, 'Aman Allah Khan's declaration of independence and *jihad* against India caught British officials off guard.

In the aftermath of the November Armistice of 1918 which ended hostilities in the First World War, British diplomacy was focused on the Paris Peace Conference, which convened shortly before Habib Allah Khan's assassination. Initially the British and Indian administrations were unsure even if the Amir had formally declared war on India, and were divided on how to respond to 'Aman Allah Khan's declaration of independence. Lord Chelmsford argued for Britain to accept a degree of independence for Afghanistan but Lord Curzon, who was now Britain's Foreign Secretary, refused to compromise. The October Revolution of 1917 and the heavy losses of the First World War meant that Russia no longer posed a military threat to India, at least in the short term. Curzon, though, was wedded to the Forward Policy and reinvented the Russian threat in ideological terms as the 'Bolshevik Menace'. Lenin, he believed, was actively encouraging India's civil disobedience campaign and inciting the Amir to invade India. Curzon therefore argued that rather than cede Afghanistan any degree of independence, Britain should strengthen its control over the country's foreign affairs and severely restrict the supply of armaments in case the guns ended up in the hands of the tribes on the Indian side of the frontier. As for Amir 'Aman Allah Khan himself, Curzon regarded the new Amir as an 'irresponsible' and 'hot-headed young man' and believed the anti-British Tarzi was the real power behind the throne.[8]

Chelmsford did his best to leave the door ajar for negotiations and in his reply to the Amir's letter he sidestepped the vexed issue of independence. London's refusal to negotiate on this issue, however, encouraged the Amir to pursue his *jihad*. The threat of war with Afghanistan posed serious problems, for India was ill prepared for an invasion. All but eight battalions of regular troops had been withdrawn and sent to the Western Front or the Middle East, while stocks of rifles, artillery, ammunition, rolling stock and other military equipment were at an all-time low. Most of the battalions still in India were under strength and Pushtun levies, many recruited from Afghanistan, had replaced front-line troops on the Northwest Frontier. Furthermore, following the November Armistice, many officers had returned to Britain on long-overdue home leave.[9]

To add to the Viceroy's woes in the spring of 1919 there was serious civil unrest in the Punjab and along the Afghan Frontier, precipitated by the passing of the Rowlatt Act, which extended the draconian measures of the Defence of India Act of 1915. The severe restriction on civil liberties imposed under these Acts led to boycotts, strikes and mass protests. In response the Indian government had interned many of the leaders of the independence movement. The protests culminated in what became

DREAMS MELTED INTO AIR, 1919-29

known as the Massacre of Amritsar. On 13 April 1919 Brigadier General Dyer ordered his sepoys, which included a contingent of Pathans, to fire on a large crowd of unarmed protesters assembled in the walled garden of Jallianwala Bagh, an action that led to the deaths of hundreds of unarmed civilians, including women and children, and inflamed the situation even further.

Although most of the dead and injured were Sikhs, the Indian revolutionaries in Kabul exploited the massacre as justification of the Amir's *jihad*. On 1 May 1919 Amir 'Aman Allah Khan called another *darbar* where he read out an account of the Jallianwala Bagh massacre and claimed that most of the dead and wounded were Muslims. He then referred to the campaigns of Lawrence in Arabia and the Hijaz and the British occupation of the Ottoman cities of Jerusalem, Aleppo and Damascus, and claimed that Britain was planning the extermination of Islam and that the honour of every Muslim was violated. Having whipped his audience into a religious fervour, the Amir gave orders for the army to be moved to the India frontier.

Afghan and Western historians represent the Third Anglo-Afghan War primarily as a War of Independence, but officially it was a *jihad*. After all, Amir 'Aman Allah Khan did not have to go to war to secure independence, since he had already declared Afghanistan independent and he knew Britain was not in a position to do anything about it. The Amir, however, needed to legitimize his invasion of India by securing a *fatwa* and to this end state propaganda portrayed the war as in defence of Islam and persecuted Muslims. Once he secured this decree, however, 'Aman Allah Khan played the ethno-nationalist card, appealing to Pushtuns on both sides of the Durand Line to rise up and expel the British from the Punjab. Later the government issued proclamations to the Mohmands and Afridis 'printed in shockingly bad Pushtu which is almost impossible to translate'.[10]

The Afghan campaign consisted of a three-pronged attack. General Saleh Muhammad Khan commanded the Nangahar division which consisted mostly of Mohmand and Afridi levies. His objective was to seize control of the Khyber Pass and attack Peshawar. Meanwhile, Mahmud Tarzi and the Indian revolutionaries, with the help of the Afghan agent in Peshawar, planned an uprising in Peshawar to coincide with Saleh Muhammad Khan's advance.[11] The second front was entrusted to Nadir Khan, who was gathering an army in Khost. His orders were to occupy Waziristan and the Khurram agency, territories that Afghanistan had ceded to Britain under the Durand Agreement. However, Nadir Khan's plans were delayed by a revolt in Gardez and a decided lack of enthusiasm for the *jihad*

Pushtun tribesmen from the Khyber region. It was individuals such as these that British troops faced during the Third Afghan War.

among the frontier tribes. Memories of Nadir Khan's brutal suppression of the Mangal revolt a decade earlier were still fresh in local memories, while many of the Waziris and other tribes on the Indian side of the frontier were content with the autonomy granted by British rule and were unwilling to allow any army, Afghan or British, to march through their territory.[12]

A third division under 'Abd al-Quddus Khan was sent to Kandahar with orders to occupy Chaman, Gulistan, Pishin and the Khojak Pass. 'Abd al-Quddus took an inordinate time to reach Kandahar, however, and when he finally arrived he had to put down a revolt by religious leaders. With the help of Loynab 'Ali Ahmad Khan the rebellion was eventually suppressed, then followed this success by conducting a brief but bloody pogrom against Kandahar's Qizilbash. By the time 'Abd al-Quddus was ready to march into Baluchistan, the war had ended.

Who exactly fired the first shot in the Third Anglo-Afghan War is still a matter of dispute, at least as far as Afghans are concerned. According to the official British account, on 3 May 1919 General Saleh Muhammad Khan cut off the water supply to the British garrisons and occupied outposts on the Indian side of the Khyber Pass. Afghans, on the other hand, claim that fighting began when British airplanes bombed positions inside Afghanistan,[13] though official British accounts state the Royal Air Force was not deployed until after the Afghans invaded.

What seems to have happened was that the *ghazi*s disobeyed Saleh Muhammad's orders and launched a pre-emptive strike on British outposts, forcing the general to march across the frontier in support of the lightly armed levies. As a result, the plan to coordinate the attack on the Khyber Pass with the uprising in Peshawar was thrown into disarray. The British hastily evacuated their forward positions, but Saleh Muhammad Khan failed to drive home his advantage and, instead of storming Landi Kotal, he decided to besiege it instead. This gave the Indian government the breathing space it needed to move reinforcements up to the railhead at Landi Kotal. Meanwhile British intelligence uncovered Tarzi's plot for an uprising in Peshawar in the nick of time. The police and military sealed off the Old City, cut off its water, electricity and food supplies, and Ross-Kepel, the Commissioner, informed the rebels that the blockade would not be lifted until the ringleaders either surrendered or were handed over. Two days later the Amir's agent and other conspirators gave themselves up and the uprising petered out.

By the time the Peshawar revolt ended, thousands of troops with heavy equipment had arrived at Landi Kotal. On 11 May British forces under General Fowler attacked and defeated the Afghan army and Saleh Muhammad Khan, who had been wounded in the leg, fled to Jalalabad where he was promptly relieved of his command. General Fowler meanwhile continued his advance and, despite heavy resistance, retook Dakka, 'Ali Masjid and Jamrud. When he reached the Afghan frontier, Fowler halted to await orders to attack Jalalabad, but the invasion never took place. Instead, Dyer's battalion was sent to relieve the siege of Thal.

During Fowler's brief campaign, for the first time the Royal Air Force was deployed in Afghanistan, bombing Afghan trenches. RAF planes also bombed Jalalabad and Kabul, severely damaging Habib Allah's unfinished mausoleum and the tomb of 'Abd al-Rahman Khan. Aerial warfare was new to Afghans, indeed hardly any Afghan had even seen an aeroplane, and it had a devastating psychological impact. 'Aman Allah Khan complained to the Viceroy that this form of warfare was unjust, since it led to the deaths and injury of civilians, including women and children, while the pleas of the terrified victims of the bombing raids were a key factor in the Amir's decision to agree to a truce.

Nadir Khan's division had far greater success, at least initially. On 23 May 1919 two columns entered northern Waziristan and Parachinar, forcing the evacuation of Wana and Gomal, while the North Wazir Militia mutinied. Quick action by the commander at Parachinar foiled a pincer movement by Nadir Khan, but despite this setback he crossed the ranges into south Khurram by an extremely difficult route in an attempt to outflank the British, and appeared unexpectedly within 32 kilometres (20 mi.) of Thal. Brigadier General Eustace, who commanded the Thal

The Pakistan–
Afghanistan frontier
in Waziristan. In 1994
this frontier post was
manned by a single
official and his son.
In 1919 the invasion
of Waziristan by
Sardar Nadir Khan
led to a major uprising
among the Waziris
which took months
to suppress.

garrison, concentrated all his forces in the main fort and decided to remain
behind its walls until a relief army could reach him. He then successfully
repulsed an attempt to take the fortress by storm, inflicting heavy loss
on the Afghans. Later Nadir Khan claimed he had taken Thal, but all he
managed to do was overrun an abandoned police post nearby.[14]

Dyer's Brigade was detached from Khyber operations and sent post-
haste to relieve Eustace. His force reached the railhead at Kohat two days
after the assault on Thal. The following day, following a forced march,
Dyer arrived at Thal, and despite his troops being exhausted, he sent
them to attack the Afghan front line. Nadir Khan, caught by surprise,
was forced back into northern Waziristan. On 3 June 1919 Dyer received
a telegraph informing him that the Amir had agreed to a ceasefire and
he suspended operations. However, since the Armistice did not include
tribes on the Indian side of the frontier who had aided the invaders, Dyer

burnt and pillaged the Waziri settlement of Biland Khel. Further south, in Baluchistan, British troops pre-empted an attack by 'Abd al-Quddus Khan's Kandahar Division by occupying the Afghan frontier post of Spin Baldak.

The Third Anglo-Afghan War lasted exactly one month, though desultory fighting continued until the Armistice was signed in August. Despite subsequent propaganda by the Afghan government, its army had been soundly defeated on two fronts, while Spin Baldak was occupied by British forces. The war had been brief, but it had also been bloody. British casualties amounted to 1,751 dead or wounded. Several hundred more soldiers and camp followers died from 'the most extensive and sudden' outbreak of cholera to have occurred in the Khyber, Peshawar and Kohat Districts.[15] The body count of Afghans dead on the field of battle was 1,000, but hundreds more later died from their wounds. In all the war cost the Indian treasury around £16 million.[16]

The Afghan invasion may have been thwarted, but Nadir Khan's campaign precipitated a major uprising of the Achakzais and Waziris in Baluchistan, which Nadir Khan did all he could to encourage. The revolt began with the mutiny of Ghilzai levies recruited from Afghanistan, which forced the evacuation of forward outposts and even Fort Sandeman. Although Fort Sandeman was retaken a few days later, hostilities continued until the summer of 1919 when an outbreak of cholera decimated both British and Afghan forces.

The Rawalpindi Conference and Anglo-Afghan relations

On 24 May 1919 Amir 'Aman Allah Khan, threatened with a British occupation of Jalalabad and Kandahar, sued for peace and in early June he accepted the Viceroy's terms for an Armistice. The decision to agree to a ceasefire was not welcomed by religious and tribal leaders who were eager to continue the *jihad*, while Nadir Khan continued to covertly support the revolt in Waziristan. 'Abd al-Quddus Khan wished for the war to be perpetuated too, for he had yet to fire a shot in anger. In order to justify the Amir's decision to order a ceasefire, government propaganda claimed that Afghan victories had forced Britain to the negotiating table.

While the Amir dealt with the fallout of his failed *jihad*, British officials disagreed over how best to handle the Afghan crisis.[17] Curzon, backed by Sir Denys Bray, India's Deputy Foreign Secretary, wanted to revert to the closed frontier policy of the era of 'Abd al-Rahman Khan and maintain strict control over Afghanistan's foreign relations. Curzon also wanted the Amir to hand over the Indian revolutionaries living in Afghanistan, as well as Mahmud Tarzi and 'Abd al-Quddus Khan, for Bray was convinced these individuals had been the real instigators of the war. On the other hand, the Viceroy and Dobbs, India's Foreign Secretary, were more conciliatory and calculated that the Amir would adopt a more moderate tone in the wake of his defeat. The two sides eventually met in Rawalpindi on 26 July 1919 with the Afghan delegation headed by Loynab 'Ali Ahmad Khan, a somewhat curious choice given that a few months earlier he had supported Nasr Allah Khan's bid for power. 'Ali Ahmad was also conducting a clandestine, extramarital affair with Sahira Begum, the Amir's half-sister, a liaison that was exposed a few months later and led to 'Ali Ahmad Khan being condemned to death, though his sentence was commuted to house arrest after he agreed to marry the princess and pay a huge indemnity. The Afghan delegation included two Indian citizens: Dr Ghani, the former headmaster of Habibiyya College, now finally released from prison, and Diwan Narinjan Das, the Hindu banker who had been Amir Habib Allah Khan's Chancellor of the Exchequer. Of all the Afghan officials sent to Rawalpindi, only Mullah Ghulam Muhammad, the Minister of Commerce, represented the war party. 'Abd al-Quddus Khan, Mahmud Tarzi and Nadir Khan were all conspicuous by their absence.

Despite Dobbs's hope that the Afghans would be conciliatory, Loynab 'Ali Ahmad took an uncompromising approach, demanding the restoration of the Amir's subsidy, the payment of a war indemnity and recognition of Afghanistan's sovereignty over the whole of the Tribal Territory. Sir Alfred Grant, Britain's chief negotiator, rejected these demands and bluntly informed the delegates that the draft treaty placed on the table by Britain was the 'utmost to which his Majesty's Government is prepared to go, all we require is your acceptance or rejection.'[18] Loynab 'Ali Ahmad, however, insisted that Britain give 'some definite assurances in writing . . . as regards independence of our foreign relations'. Behind the scenes Chelmsford pleaded with London to compromise on the independence issue, arguing that an independent Afghanistan still left the country economically and militarily reliant on Britain: 'If we now surrender our hold on the shadow,' he wrote, 'we may hereafter secure the substance of real control.'[19] Eventually the Cabinet reluctantly accepted indirect recognition of Afghanistan's independence and the agreement included the phrase 'Independent Afghan Government' in the title. However, there was no mention of Afghanistan as an 'independent' or 'free' nation in the actual clauses. Instead Grant wrote a personal letter to the Amir in which he stated that the agreement 'contains nothing that interfered with the complete liberty of Afghanistan in internal and external matters . . . the said treaty and this letter leaves

Afghanistan officially free and independent in its internal and external affairs'.[20] Both sides were content with this compromise and on 8 August 1919 they signed the Rawalpindi Peace Agreement.

As far as Afghanistan was concerned, the losses outweighed the gains for, as Grant pointed out to 'Ali Ahmad, 'war tears up all previous agreements and treaties. You can claim no rights under the old treaties now and we admit no obligation under them.'[21] This meant the loss of the British subsidy, forfeiture of the balance of subsidies held in Indian banks and the repeal of the right to import arms. 'Aman Allah Khan also confirmed his acceptance of the 'Indo-Afghan Frontier as accepted by the late Amir' and agreed to allow British surveyors being sent to demarcate a disputed section of the Mohmand frontier, while Spin Baldak remained in British hands until the demarcation was completed and signed off. The agreement even included a statement blaming the war on 'Afghan aggression' and concluded with the terse declaration that 'this war has cancelled all previous Treaties'. The Rawalpindi Agreement was also defined as a personal arrangement 'because it was the Amir who made war on us', rather than with the state of Afghanistan, the issue of a state-to-state treaty being deferred 'if friendship negotiations materialise'.

The Afghan government had effectively capitulated and all they had to show for their meeting was a letter addressed personally to the Amir, which indirectly recognized the country's independence. On his return to Kabul, however, Loynab 'Ali Ahmad Khan claimed Britain had given in to all of Afghanistan's demands. Government propaganda continued to claim it had won the war and made much of the fact that Britain had tacitly recognized Afghanistan's independence. To commemorate this 'victory', 18 August was declared Afghan Independence Day, even though formal recognition of Afghanistan's independence by treaty did not take place until 1922. So successful was the government in concealing the real terms of the Rawalpindi Agreement that Amir 'Aman Allah Khan was hailed as a hero by Muslims from India to the Middle East and some, including the Hazrat of Shor Bazaar, even called for him to become the new Caliph.

The Rawalpindi Agreement marked another turning point in Anglo-Afghan relations. Britain never forgave 'Aman Allah Khan for his invasion of India and for the remainder of his reign British relations with the Amir were marred by suspicion, hostility and a certain amount of diplomatic petulance on both sides. The British government refused to refer to the Amir as 'Your Majesty' in official correspondence and a letter from 'Aman Allah Khan to King George V went unanswered. When the Afghan government sought diplomatic relations with Italy, London pompously informed the Italians they had to first recognize Britain's 'superior and predominant political influence' in the country. Tarzi's response was to call all the foreign diplomatic corps in Kabul to a meeting, where he proceeded to subject Sir Henry Dobbs, who was in Kabul trying to negotiate a new Anglo-Afghan Treaty, to a public dressing down. Curzon retaliated by refusing to meet an Afghan delegation visiting London and denied them an audience with the king. Tarzi's riposte was to write Dobbs a letter of 'studied insult' and blocked the British diplomatic mail.[22]

The Mussoorie Conference and the Khilafat Movement

The second round of negotiations aimed at a permanent settlement commenced in Mussoorie in April 1920. This time the Afghan delegation was headed by Mahmud Tarzi and included other anti-British Young Afghans, including 'Abd al-Hadi Dawai. Tarzi too adopted an uncompromising stance, demanding an unequivocal and unconditional recognition of Afghanistan's independence, the right to open embassies in London and Delhi, and Afghan sovereignty over Waziristan and other tribal territories. When Dobbs, who led the British negotiating team, rejected these demands outright, Tarzi resorted to a naive attempt at political blackmail.

A few months before the Mussoorie Conference convened, Yakov Zakharovich Suritz, a Russian envoy, had arrived in Kabul to negotiate a treaty with Afghanistan, so Tarzi claimed Moscow was offering far better terms than anything the British had put on the table. Dobbs called Tarzi's bluff and presented the Afghan delegation with a 'series of *fait accomplis* which whilst open to explanation cannot be modified and against which it would be useless for them to protest'.[23] What Tarzi did not know was that London was already negotiating with Moscow about the renewal of the Anglo-Russian Convention of 1907 and Tarzi's attempts to play Britain and Russia off against one another was doomed to failure. The negotiations were thus at an impasse and Dobbs suspended the meetings when he heard that Nadir Khan and 'Abd al-Quddus Khan had been supporting the rebel Waziris. In an attempt to break the deadlock, Dobbs made a few minor changes to the draft treaty but London rejected them as too conciliatory. Finally, in July 1920, Dobbs terminated the negotiations and wrote another aide-memoire to the Amir, in which he reassured 'Aman Allah Khan of Britain's 'sincere goodwill' and outlined the conditions under which Britain would agree to a new treaty.[24]

While the Mussoorie negotiations dragged on, 'Aman Allah Khan faced a number of internal crises. In March 1919, shortly before the outbreak of the Anglo-Afghan War, a number of Indian Muslims, mostly former pupils of Aligarh and Deoband, had formed the Khalifat Movement following the Bolshevik government's publication of the Sykes-Picot Agreement of May 1916. This highly secret deal between France, Britain and Imperial Russia divided the Ottoman provinces of the Levant and Anatolia between the three European powers in the form of what was termed 'Mandates'. The news outraged Muslim nationalists in India who were convinced the Allies planned to dismember the Ottoman Empire and the Khilafat Movement demanded that any post-war treaty with Turkey should uphold the temporal and spiritual powers of the Ottoman Caliphate. This view seemed to be confirmed when, while the Mussoorie Conference was still in session, British forces occupied Istanbul and deposed the CUP government, while King Faizal of Syria, the man who had led the Arab Revolt made famous by Lawrence of Arabia, was overthrown by French military intervention.

Tarzi raised the issue of the break-up of Ottoman Turkey during the Mussoorie Conference and tried to link a settlement of the Anglo-Afghan War with the post-war situation in the Near East, demanding any treaty with Afghanistan should include assurances that Britain would not dismember the Ottoman Empire and that the Caliph would retain his spiritual and temporal powers. Tarzi's demands were bizarre given that he was in Mussoorie to represent Afghanistan's interests and not that of his adopted country or the Arabs. His demands got nowhere and Dobbs curtly informed Tarzi that Britain's policy towards Turkey had nothing to do with him.

Tarzi's concerns reflected those of the Khilafat Movement, which was increasingly vociferous and heavily committed to the Muslim League's civil disobedience campaign in the Punjab and Northwest Frontier. Following the San Remo Conference of April 1920, which confirmed the partition of the Middle East and committed the Allies to the establishment of a Jewish Homeland in the Ottoman province of Palestine, Khilafat protests escalated. In the summer of 1920, several prominent *pirs* in Sind and the Northwest Frontier issued *fatwas* declaring British-ruled India as a *Dar al-Harb*, or House of War, and called on India's Muslims to emulate the example of Muhammad and migrate to the *Dar al-Islam*, that is, the nearest Muslim-ruled country. The *fatwas* precipitated a mass exodus of around 30,000 people into Afghanistan, known as the Hijrat Movement. The migration took place in the height of the Indian summer and many émigrés died from thirst or heatstroke before they reached the Afghan frontier; they were also plundered by Mohmands and Afridis as they passed through the Khyber Pass. Amir 'Aman Allah Khan welcomed the first wave of *muhajir*, who were housed in temporary camps at Bagram, but as more and more refugees flooded across the border the government, unable to provide for thousands of starving and hungry migrants, closed the frontier and urged them to return home. Thousands ended up stranded in no-man's-land until hunger, thirst, sickness and the rapacity of local tribes forced all but a handful of them to return home penniless. The decision by the Amir to close the frontier was a mortal blow not only to the Khilafat Movement, but to 'Aman Allah Khan's pan-Islamic credentials, both in India and in the Muslim world.

The Basmachi Movement and Afghan-Soviet relations

While the government was overwhelmed by the unexpected migration crisis in the southeast of the country, the Amir had to face the consequences of the failure of negotiations with Britain. Once back in Kabul, Tarzi began to discuss a treaty with Russia, encouraged by a personal letter to the Amir from Lenin in which he held out the prospect of 'a joint struggle against the most rapacious imperialistic government on earth – Great Britain'.[25] In September 1920 the Amir agreed to a draft treaty drawn up by Suritz, which pledged substantial financial, military and technical aid to Afghanistan in return for the opening of Soviet consulates in Ghazni, Kandahar and other Afghan cities. Suritz's draft treaty, however, had to be approved by Moscow and, since he had made far more concessions than his terms of reference allowed, the authorities in Moscow took several months deciding whether the benefits of the Soviet-Afghan Treaty outweighed the substantial financial and military commitments. While the Kremlin debated the pros and cons of this treaty, Afghan relations with Russia came under severe strain when the Amir decided to support a Muslim nationalist uprising in Russian Turkistan.

The rebellion, which the Russians disparagingly referred to as the Basmachi Movement (*basmachi* in Russian means 'brigand' or 'robber'), had its roots in Imperial Russia's conquest of the Muslim-ruled Khanates of Central Asia in the latter half of the nineteenth century.[26] The natural resentment created by living under foreign, non-Muslim occupation was exacerbated by the confiscation of vast tracts of irrigated land, which were apportioned to Russian colonists from the north. The government then shifted agricultural production from wheat, the main subsistence crop of the region, to cotton. While this provided a substantial hard-currency revenue for Moscow, it destroyed the economic self-sufficiency of indigenous farmers and created a man-made famine. Discontent increased in 1916 after the

Tsar removed the exemption from national service enjoyed by Turkistan's Muslims and forcibly conscripted them to replace Russia's losses on the Western Front. The widespread protests that followed quickly turned into a war for independence and the Russian authorities, backed by armed settlers, responded with bloody repression. Between June 1916 and October 1917 as many as one and a half million Central Asian people were killed.

The October Revolution of 1917 raised hopes that the Bolshevik government would agree to self-rule in Turkistan and the Caucasus. With Russia on the brink of collapse, Lenin adopted a policy of 'feigned benevolence', publicly holding out the prospect of self-determination until the Red Army was strong enough to crush the revolt.[27] In preparation for the showdown, Communist commissars were dispatched to the region to establish and arm local soviets. Encouraged by Lenin's promise of self-rule, in December 1917 the Turkistan Extraordinary Conference declared Turkistan an autonomous region with Kokand as its capital and over the next few months the Tatars, Kurds and Azeris followed suit. Just over a year later, however, Lenin sent thousands of troops into the region to crush the secessionist movements. The lightly armed rebels stood no chance. When Kokand fell in March 1919, more than 14,000 of its inhabitants were massacred and mosques, libraries and bazaars destroyed.

The fall of Kokand led to the formation of the Turkistan National Liberation Movement, the forerunner of the Basmachi Movement, an organization dedicated to the establishment of an independent Turkistanian state. The movement, however, was split ideologically as well as by tribal and regional differences, while its army was poorly armed and trained. Some eight months after the fall of Kokand the Red Army, backed by Russian settlers known as *Jadidi*s, besieged Khiva.[28] When the city fell in February 1920 the Khan was deposed and the region renamed the Khwarazmian Peoples' Republic. In September of the same year Bukhara was taken by storm and Muhammad 'Alim, Khan of Bukhara, fled to Ferghana and eventually to Afghanistan, where Amir 'Aman Allah Khan gave him sanctuary.

By the autumn of 1921 the *basmachi*s were on the brink of defeat, only for the situation to change dramatically with the defection of a Turkish general, Enver Pasha, who had been a leader of the Young Turk Revolution of 1908. Following the coup of 1913 he became the most powerful of the Triumvirate of army officers who ruled Turkey during the Great War, but he fled after the signing of the Armistice of Mudros, which ended Turkey's involvement in the Great War. He was then sentenced to death *in abstentia* for having ordered the mass deportation and expulsion of Armenians,

The flag of Turkistan in the Turkistan American Association, New York. The suppression of the Basmachi Movement ended hopes for an independent Turkistan but the movement itself went underground. In the 1980s 'Turkistanian' nationalism resurfaced following the break up of the Soviet Union and the civil war in Afghanistan.

which became known as the Armenian Genocide. Enver Pasha eventually made his way to Moscow, where Lenin put him in charge of military operations against the *basmachi*s and instructed him to make contact with Amir 'Aman Allah Khan and the Indian revolutionaries in Kabul in order to encourage them to foment anti-British activity in northern India.

Shortly after he reached Bukhara, Enver Pasha changed sides and declared his support for the exiled Khan of Bukhara, a decision due in part to treaty negotiations between Moscow and Mustafa Kemal, who was now President of Turkey and Enver Pasha's most bitter political enemy. Enver made his base in Ferghana and Tajikistan, where he began to refer to himself as Vice-caliph, Commander of the Islamic Forces and Son-in-Law of the Caliph. Enver appealed to 'Aman Allah Khan for assistance and the Amir covertly began to supply him with cash and arms, as well as providing his *mujahidin* with a safe haven in northern Afghanistan. In February 1922 Enver Pasha occupied Dushanbe and the following month besieged Bukhara. Moscow responded by sending thousands of additional troops, heavy armour and war planes to the area, forcing Enver Pasha to lift the siege and flee to his mountain stronghold in Tajikistan. A few months later he was killed in an encounter with a Soviet search party. The *basmachi* revolt rumbled on for several more years, but Enver Pasha's death ended any hopes of an independent Turkistan for the next seventy years.

The emergence of a Turkistanian independence movement posed one more foreign policy dilemma for 'Aman Allah Khan, as many Muslim leaders urged him to support their struggle for independence. In the summer of 1919 'Aman Allah Khan sent a mission to the Khan of Bukhara that included the Hazrat Sahib of Karokh, the Mir of Guzargah, military advisers and a gift of six artillery pieces. Two more ambassadors, accompanied by a large body of troops, were sent to Merv and Khiva, while hundreds of Afghans and Indians joined the Afghan Volunteer Force and were sent north to assist the Khan of Bukhara. The following year Nadir Khan was dispatched to Qataghan to coordinate this military assistance. However, the Amir's support was far from altruistic. In return he demanded Muhammad 'Alim Khan cede substantial territory in the Ferghana oasis, while Afghan assistance to the Khans of Merv and Khiva was tied to a pledge that they would cede the Amir sovereignty over the Pandjeh oasis.

The Dobbs Mission and the Anglo-Afghan Treaty of 1921

Moscow was well aware of the Amir's covert assistance to the *basmachi*s, even as Suritz and the Kremlin debated the pros and cons of the draft Soviet-Afghan treaty. Following the fall of Bukhara, the Soviet administration covertly set up the Central Committee of Young Afghan Revolutionaries (Jawanan-i Afghan), a movement dedicated to the overthrow of the Durrani monarchy and the establishment of a Soviet-style Republic. In Afghanistan and Britain, the fall of Khiva and Bukhara resurrected the spectre of a Soviet invasion of Balkh, so despite having agreed to the draft treaty with Russia only a matter of months earlier, 'Aman Allah Khan asked the Viceroy to send Dobbs to Kabul to renew discussions about an Anglo-Afghan treaty.

When Dobbs arrived in Kabul in early 1921 he reported the capital was seething with intrigue with Russians, Italians, Germans, Turks and French all vying for a stake in independent Afghanistan. However, despite the threat from Russia to Afghanistan's northern borders, Tarzi continued to insist Britain agree to the terms the Afghan side had demanded at Rawalpindi, which Britain had already rejected. The negotiations from the British viewpoint were complicated by the fact that their intelligence service had failed to obtain a complete copy of the Soviet-Afghan Treaty and Dobbs had only a general idea what the Russians had offered the Amir. In the end, Dobbs spent nearly a year in Kabul, during which time the Afghan government signed treaties with Turkey, Italy and Iran. Dobbs's hands were tied, for London insisted as a precondition of any formal treaty that the Amir abrogated his treaty with Russia, so when in August

1921 'Aman Allah Khan ratified the Soviet-Afghan Treaty, Dobbs broke off negotiations and prepared to leave. On the eve of his departure, the Amir intervened personally and offered to sign a statement of 'neighbourly relations' with Britain. Dobbs agreed and at the end of November the agreement was signed.

The Anglo-Afghan Treaty of 1921 was a face-saving exercise by both sides and, given the circumstances, it was the best either party could have expected. The treaty was little more than another memorandum or aide-memoire, but even so it was a landmark in Afghanistan's history since Britain formally recognized the country's independence and agreed to refer to the Amir as His Majesty in all official communications. Britain's demand that the Soviet-Afghan Treaty be revoked was dropped and the embargo on importing arms from India was lifted – with some caveats – while the Afghan government reaffirmed its acceptance of Durand's 'Indo-Afghan Frontier'. Britain agreed to formalize diplomatic relations with the opening of an Afghan Legation in London and consulates in Delhi, Karachi, Calcutta and Bombay, while a British Legation, headed by a British Minister, was to be established in Kabul. However, the Amir's annual subsidy was not reinstated and Britain's undertaking to defend Afghanistan from unprovoked external aggression was not renewed. The outcome was that Afghanistan was weakened politically, militarily and financially. Perhaps most important of all, the Amir could no longer rely on Britain to defend Afghanistan from a Soviet invasion.

Moscow took advantage of this situation. With Enver Pasha in retreat, the Soviet government expelled the Afghan representative from Bukhara and suspended financial, military and technical aid on the grounds that the Amir's support for the *basmachi*s and the Amir of Bukhara was a breach of the Soviet-Afghan Treaty. Moscow then threatened to attack *basmachi* bases in northern Afghanistan if the Amir did not close the border and cut off aid to the rebels. 'Aman Allah Khan had little choice but to comply. Nadir Khan was recalled to Kabul, the Amu Darya frontier sealed and the Afghan Volunteer Force disbanded – decisions that contributed significantly to Enver Pasha's defeat and death. As for the ex-Khan of Bukhara, he was forced to vacate his town house in central Kabul and move to a small cottage in rural Chahardeh.

The threat of a Soviet incursion was not the only reason why Amir 'Aman Allah Khan threw the *basmachi*s to the wolves, or rather the bear. Shortly after arriving in Qataghan, Nadir Khan had written to warn the Amir that Afghanistan's northern frontier was undefended and that Afghan support for a movement that demanded an independent Turco-Tajik state beyond the Amu Darya would inevitably lead to similar demands from the Turkic and Persian-speaking populations of northern Afghanistan.[29] The presence of 300,000 Central Asia refugees, including thousands of heavily armed *mujahidin* in the northern provinces, added impetus to secessionism, tilted the region's ethnic balance back in favour of the non-Pushtun population and overstretched the nation's resources.[30] The prospect of an uprising in northern Afghanistan was as much of a nightmare scenario for the Kabul government as the threat of a Russian invasion, for while pan-Islamism and pan-Afghanism may have been an acceptable government policy, pan-Turkism could not to be tolerated under any circumstances.

The failure of the *basmachi* revolt meant that most of the refugees from Central Asia never returned to their homeland. Instead, they were resettled in dozens of towns and villages in northern Afghanistan, from Maimana to Qunduz. The Afghan government's betrayal of their cause, however, was not forgotten. *Basmachi* resistance fighters passed on stories of their struggle against Communism, Russian occupation and the Red Army to their children and children's children, who continued to foster the dream of an independent Turkistan. Their presence led to the rise of an underground Turco-Tajik nationalist, or Turkistanian, movement in northern Afghanistan, which successive governments ruthlessly suppressed.

Amir 'Aman Allah Khan's administration

The influx of hundreds of thousands of refugees from India and Central Asia, the military and economic fallout from defeat at the hands of Britain, the loss of the British subsidy and military assistance, not to mention the threat posed by the Soviet army to Afghanistan's northern provinces, were more than enough for the Afghan administration to handle. Yet 'Aman Allah Khan proceeded to destabilize the country further by a programme of sweeping social and legal reforms, which were aimed at transforming Afghanistan into a modern, Europeanized nation.

One pressing issue was the need for additional revenues to cover the loss of the British subsidy, so the Amir increased taxes. Agricultural taxes, traditionally paid in kind, now had to be paid only in cash, while taxes on livestock, grazing, irrigated land and agricultural yields were increased. An income tax was introduced that was deducted at source from the salaries of civil servants, soldiers and students – in effect a pay cut. Conscription was reintroduced, and the customary exemption of the Durrani tribes and religious elites from military service abolished. The government introduced a new, standard measurement of land, the *jerib*, undertook a cadastral survey of land, a census of livestock, and standardized weights and measures. Export duties were increased and the import duty on luxury goods was raised to 100 per cent. In 1923 Afghanistan's first national budget was introduced, and double ledger accounting replaced the archaic bookkeeping system. There was a new national currency, the *afghani*, and for the first time banknotes were issued, although they proved unpopular for people felt cheated since the paper had no actual value. Cost-cutting measures included reductions or cancellation of allowances paid to Muhammadzais, religious foundations and tribal leaders as well as reductions in army pay. Another unpopular move was the introduction of a National Identity Card, the *tazkira*, without which no one could obtain a government job or register a marriage. Yet despite all these fiscal measures, Afghanistan's annual revenue was a mere £2 million.

Instead of using the additional revenue to improve the living standards of ordinary Afghans, 'Aman Allah Khan wasted vast sums on white elephant projects that benefited only his immediate family. The two most costly schemes were the hill station in Paghman and a new capital city on the outskirts of southwest Kabul. One contemporary observer described Paghman as a 'Fairyland',[31] and rightly so, for it was the place where the Amir's vision of Europe-in-Asia could be created away from hoi polloi, a haven where the royal family, ministers and hanger-ons could act like Europeans and pretend to be modern. Traditional taboos such as the *burqa* were ignored, while men mingled freely with women and played each other at mixed doubles tennis. Architecturally, too, Paghman deliberately rejected indigenous forms in favour of a pastiche of European styles. The formal gardens were dotted with Rococo fountains and Graeco-Roman statuary; the royal palace was in English colonial style; the Bahar Hotel was stolidly Germanic; and the Taq-i Zafar, or Victory Arch, which commemorated Afghan independence, was a miniature version of the Arc de Triomphe. There was even an Opera House. Robert Byron, who visited Kabul in 1934, was particularly scathing about Paghman's 'shoddy' and 'obscene' buildings:

> In each glade stands a house or office or theatre of such appalling aspect, so vilely reminiscent of a German Kurhaus and the back parts of Pimlico, that it is impossible to imagine where Amanullah could have found the architects to design them, even as a joke.[32]

Paghman's redeeming feature was its natural setting. Set high up in the headwaters of the Kabul river, the mountain air, shady trees, clear

Paghman, Amir 'Aman Allah Khan's monument to the fallen of the Third Afghan War (foreground) and the Taq-i Zafar commemorating Afghanistan's independence. Both monuments were badly damaged during the Soviet occupation and in the subsequent in-fighting between various *mujahidin* militias.

streams and panoramic views of snow-capped mountains made Paghman an idyllic place. Despite the destruction of the 1980s and '90s, Paghman is still a favourite summer retreat for Kabulis.

The new capital, known as Dar al-'Aman, designed as a capital for a modern, independent state, was even more grandiose and cost the equivalent of a whole year's revenue.[33] The project was never completed, partly because the plans covered a vast area of southwestern Kabul from Pul-i Malan to Deh Mazang and Mir Wais Mina as far south as Rishkhor, Chahardeh and the palace at Chehel Situn.[34] The new city bore the Amir's own name, but the title equally translated as House (or Door) of Peace, a term that referred to emotive Islamic terminology, such as *Dar al-'Amn*, House of Safety, and *Dar al-Islam*. Dar al-'Aman was spatially and ideologically a rejection of the past, an ideological vision that was reinforced at the entrance to the Taj Beg palace complex by the construction of the Minar-i 'Ilm wa Jahal, the Tower of Knowledge and Ignorance.

Dar al-'Aman wholeheartedly embraced European, in particular French, architectural models. The original plans were drawn up by André Godard, Director of the newly established French Archaeological Mission, who had trained as an architect. The heart of the new capital was a straight, tree-lined boulevard that stretched for 7 kilometres (4 mi.), which Byron declared to be 'one of the most beautiful avenues in the world'. Like Paris's Champs-Élysées, the avenue ended at the Taj Beg palace complex, Afghanistan's answer to the Place de la Concorde. The Amir even constructed a railway line linking Taj Beg to the Old City.

The main palace at Taj Beg was the Amir's offices and a venue for a future Parliament. The palace was vast, covering 5,400 square metres, and, at 33 metres (108 ft) high, this three-storey building dominated the skyline of southwestern Kabul. The exterior was of plain, dressed stone but the interior was lavishly decorated with marble and lapis lazuli inlay. To the west was a smaller palace built for Queen Soraya's personal use. Surrounding these palaces were formal gardens with fountains; beyond lay government offices and, quixotically, a match factory. All these buildings were utterly inappropriate. Apart from being far too large for their function, the high ceilings and stone and brick walls meant that in Kabul's bitter winters they were freezing cold, damp and dingy.

Amir 'Aman Allah Khan undertook a number of other infrastructure projects, including dams and irrigation schemes, but there was no national development plan and responsibility for individual projects was divided up between competing European nations. The French ran the postal services, secured a monopoly over archaeological exploration and established Afghanistan's first museum. France also opened the 'Amaniyya High School, where French teachers taught a French curriculum in French. German engineers constructed dams, irrigation schemes, took over construction of Dar al-'Aman, built the railway and supplied

The rusting remains of Amir 'Aman Allah Khan's trains today lie abandoned in the garden of the National Museum. The train line was never intended for public transport but was purely for the amusement of the royal family.

the rolling stock, as well as trained the army and air force. Germany too opened its own school, the 'Amani High School, where lessons were taught in German. Turks, meanwhile, dominated the Military College, ran clinics and hospitals, and had a major influence in education and constitutional reform. However, the government lacked trained professionals and there was little interest, or skill, when it came to maintaining equipment. The outcome was that Afghanistan quickly became a graveyard of rusting metal and idle factories.

The 1924 Constitution

The changes in taxation, conscription, the identity card and the cost of the Amir's palaces created much discontent, but it was 'Aman Allah Khan's decision to alter the nation's legal and social system that provoked the most bitter hostility. Shortly after taking power the Amir established a Legislative Council and Council for Religious Knowledge to reform and update the country's law. Their committees were dominated by reformers and progressive religious figures including Maulawi 'Abd al-Wasi; a Turk who had formerly been a policeman; and one of Dr Abdul Ghani's brothers. In April 1923 the council published the *Nizam Nama-yi Asasi-yi Daulat-i 'Aliyya-yi Afghanistan*,[35] which consisted of 73 Articles, or *Nizam Nama*s, that were the foundation of Afghanistan's first Constitution. The *Nizam Nama*s reflected Tarzi's and the Young Afghans' vision of reform and modernization and drew heavily on Turkish models. Islam was declared as the state religion but there was no mention of the Hanafi legal code, though the Amir was to rule 'in accordance with the principles enunciated in the Shari'a and in this Constitution'; a deliberate ambiguity that allowed the Amir to set aside Islamic law if he deemed it to be in conflict with the Constitution. Every citizen of Afghanistan was proclaimed equal, regardless of their religion or sectarian affiliations, while the discriminatory dress and *jizya* poll tax imposed on non-Muslims was abolished. There was a declaration about the freedom of the press and freedom from arbitrary arrest, while primary education was to be compulsory for everyone, including girls.

Tarzi's ethno-nationalism was embedded in the Constitution's definition of nationality, with 'Afghan' as the sole, official designation of citizenship. A Pushtu Academy was set up to promote study of the language, but the *Nizam Nama*s stopped short of proclaiming Pushtu as the national language as Tarzi had advocated. There was no legal status accorded to *pushtunwali* or other customary law, known as *'adat* or *rawaj*, and the government's decrees on marriage and the family outlawed a number of traditional practices, such as levirate marriages, the gifting of women without bride price in settlement of blood feuds, and child brides.

The Constitution provided for a State Council, with very limited legislative powers, which met once a year. Only a small number of its members were elected, the majority being appointed by 'Aman Allah Khan, others were guaranteed seats by virtue of their tribal or religious status. The Constitution significantly failed to place any restraints on the autocratic and arbitrary powers of the Amir, indeed it reinforced them by according him the exalted title of *padshah*, king, in emulation of the Iranian monarch. 'Aman Allah Khan was also formally exempt from scrutiny by the State Council and the king alone appointed the heir to the throne, government ministers, army officers and governors. He was also the supreme commander of the army and retained his prerogative of ratifying, abrogating or overruling any law or judgement made by the Council or Judiciary.

Officially, the Constitution was said to be based on the Ottoman Hanafi legal code, but the real inspiration came from Turkey's Tanzimat period, and the post-First World War secularizing reforms of Mustafa Kemal. This influence was reflected in the Persian term used for the Constitution, *Qanun-i Asasi* (Foundational Law), which was a direct translation of *Teşkilât-ı Esasiye Kanunu*, the title of Turkey's 1921 Constitution. *Mashruta*, the more usual Persian term for Constitution, was avoided due to its historic association with the anti-government movement of 1909.

Opposition to the *Nizam Nama*s was swift and vociferous. Religious elites claimed that many of their provisions were opposed to the *shari'a*, while Pushtun tribal leaders were displeased at legislation that undermined their customary law. As early as 1921 'Abd al-Quddus Khan, 'Aman Allah Khan's prime minister, had secured a *fatwa* from senior religious leaders in Kandahar condemning the whole concept of a Constitution. 'Rationally and legally,' the decree declared, 'there is only one type of government, the *khilafat-i imamat*, which is essential for the enforcement of divine law, *qanun-i asmani*, and the implementation of the political order ordained by the Almighty.' All man-made legal structures, the *fatwa* declared, bring 'corruption' and 'in the guise of civilization encourages hatred and terror'.[36]

The *Nizam Nama*s, with their evident influence of Turkey's reform movement, were therefore a cause for great alarm for conservative Sunnis, especially since Mustafa Kemal's Constitution removed sovereignty from God and placed it the hands of the nation. He had also abolished the Ottoman Caliphate and forced Sultan Abdulmejid II into exile. Under the 1924 Constitution, Turkey also abolished the supremacy of *shari'a* law and

Mustafa Kemal declared Islam was better off if it 'ceased to be a political instrument'. The disestablishment of Islam and Islamic institutions appalled Afghanistan's religious establishment, who were convinced that the king, egged on by Queen Soraya, Mahmud Tarzi and the Turcophile Young Afghans, planned a similar fate for Afghanistan.

Despite opposition to the *Nizam Nama*s, 'Aman Allah Khan pushed on regardless and in the autumn of 1923 he held a *jirga* in Jalalabad in an attempt to gain support and legitimacy for his Constitution, only for religious and tribal leaders to condemn many of its provisions. The brother of the influential Hazrat of Chaharbagh rejected many of the *Nizam Nama*s on the grounds that they did not conform to either Islamic law or Pushtun customary law and declared his opposition to compulsory, universal primary education, which he claimed undermined the *madrasa* system. Tribal leaders then complained about reductions in their state allowances, conscription, tax hikes and the new marriage laws. There were protests too in Laghman, Kandahar and Helmand, and one army battalion mutinied. When a delegation of *mullah*s from Jabal Saraj went to Kabul to complain about the presence of foreign teachers in their schools they were arrested, though they were later released following the intervention of Akhundzada Hamid Allah, the Mullah of Tagab.

While the debate over the Constitution raged, the king's relations with Britain were further strained due to cross-border activities by bandits. In April 1923 a group of Shinwaris from the Afghan side of the frontier killed two British officers in Landi Kotal, while Afridi outlaws in Kohat murdered Mrs Ellis, the wife of a British major, and abducted her seventeen-year-old daughter Molly. When the Shinwaris fled into Afghanistan, Britain demanded the king punish them or hand them over to British justice. After a delay of several weeks, the king finally arrested the Shinwaris, only for them to conveniently escape before their trial. The king's actions angered tribal and religious leaders, since they regarded the arrests as a violation of *nanawatai* as well as abject surrender to the old enemy. The Hajji Sahib of Turangzai and the Mullah of Chaknawaz, two highly influential *pir*s, then extended their personal protection to the Shinwari fugitives, whereupon Britain demanded the king re-arrest the assassins and blocked all arms shipments to Afghanistan in order to put pressure on the king. In the end 'Aman Allah Khan sent police to take the Shinwaris by force and in the clash that followed, one policeman and one of the bandits were shot dead.

The Afridi kidnappers meanwhile took refuge deep in Tirah's tribal territory. Lilian Starr, Matron of the Church Missionary Society Hospital in Peshawar, whose husband had been stabbed to death in his bed a few years earlier by an Afridi assassin, undertook the hazardous trip and managed to negotiate the release of Molly Ellis.[37] Following the success of this mission, Sir John Maffey, Chief Commissioner of the Frontier, called a *jirga* of Afridi and Orakzai leaders and threatened them with military action, whereupon they signed a declaration outlawing the bandits and surrendering some of their traditional autonomy. Britain thus exploited the murders and hostage crisis to secure greater influence over the frontier tribes, while at the same time undermining the king's credibility with tribal leaders. From this point forward 'Aman Allah Khan's relations with the Pushtun of southeastern Afghanistan, already under strain as a result of his constitutional reforms, became even more fractious.

The Islamic backlash: the Khost Rebellion and the Loya Jirga

In the spring of 1924 tribal discontent with the government's reforms finally led to a revolt among the Mangals of Khost. The catalyst for the rebellion was the actions of a government official who, in accordance with the new family law, refused to annul a marriage because the father of the woman in question had pledged her to another man while she was an infant. A certain 'Abd Allah, known as Mullah-i Lang, the Lame Mullah, declared this ruling to be against the *shari'a* and issued a *fatwa* condemning the king as a *kafir*. In a dramatic gesture, Mullah-i Lang appeared before the *jirga* bearing a copy of the *Nizam Nama*s in one hand and a Qur'an in the other and called on the assembly to decide between human and heavenly law. The king sent mediators to the area to attempt to justify the new laws, but Mullah-i Lang sent them packing, damning them as lackeys of an infidel regime. Mullah-i Lang then declared *jihad* and condemned 'Aman Allah Khan as apostate on the grounds that his Constitution rejected the eternal nature of the Qur'an. Mullah-i Lang even went so far as to claim the king had become an Ahmadiyya, a sect founded in 1889 by Mirza Ghulam Ahmad Qadiani, a Punjabi, whose followers believed he was the Mahdi and Messiah.

Rebel forces marched down the Logar valley and occupied Gardez, though government forces led by Jamal Pasha, a Turkish general, managed to halt their advance on Kabul and retook Gardez. The victory, however, was short-lived. A few weeks later, ex-King Ya'qub Khan's son 'Abd al-Karim, who was living in exile in Lahore, escaped the surveillance of the British authorities and crossed into Khost, where the rebels declared him King. They then went back on the offensive and reoccupied Gardez, wiping out one of the government's crack Turkish-led regiments in the process. At

Khost: A typical *qal'a* house with high walls surrounding a large compound and narrow windows located well above eye height for privacy and security. The Pushtun tribes of this region rebelled against King 'Aman Allah Khan's reforms but were eventually defeated.

the end of July the rebels took Hisarak, 12 kilometres (7½ mi.) from Kabul City, causing panic in the capital. Fortunately for 'Aman Allah Khan, the Mangals did not push on and attack the capital, instead they returned to Khost laden with booty.

With rebel forces a short march from Kabul, 'Aman Allah Khan called an emergency *darbar* in an attempt to try and win support against Mullah-i Lang. The government grandiosely referred to this meeting as a Loya Jirga, or Grand Tribal Assembly, a title most likely coined by Tarzi's close associate, 'Abd al-Hadi, in an attempt to appeal to Pushtun tribal sentiment.[38] In fact, like much of the official terminology adopted during 'Aman Allah Khan's reign, loya jirga was a translation of the Turkish *Büyük Millet Meclisi* (Grand National Assembly), the legislative body set up by Mustafa Kemal. Even more ironic was the fact that most of the delegates who attended the Loya Jirga were urban Kabulis or representatives of the Persian-speaking tribes of Kohistan, Tagab and the Koh Daman.

The king's intention was to secure endorsement for his Constitution and recruit levies for the war against Mullah-i Lang. However, the delegates used the opportunity to voice their complaints about taxation, conscription and the domination of education and the military by Turks. Nur al-Mashayekh Fazl 'Omar, the Hazrat of Shor Bazaar, and Akhundzada Hamid Allah, the Mullah of Tagab, the latter who had legitimized 'Aman

Allah Khan's accession, attacked the *Nizam Nama*s as un-Islamic and they and other Deobandi-trained *'ulama'* mocked attempts by the government theologians to justify the Constitution on the basis of the *shari'a*. They demanded that, as a precondition to supplying levies for war against Mullah-i Lang, a committee of *'ulama'* redraft the *Nizam Nama*s so that they would conform to their interpretation of Islamic law.

'Aman Allah Khan had little choice but to agree to their demands, whereupon the revising committee, dominated by Deobandis and supporters of Nur al-Mashayekh, proceeded to turn the Constitution on its head. They even wrote the revised criminal code in Arabic in order to emphasize the 'sanctity' of the new laws and then translated it into Persian. The changes were swingeing.[39] Afghanistan for the first time in its history officially became an Islamic state governed by the Hanafi legal code, and a council of *'ulama'* was established with executive power to review, change or veto any legislation that did not comply with the *shari'a*. The council reinstated the traditional distinctions between Muslim and non-Muslim and made personal freedom, or *azadi*, conditional on the 'strict religious observance as imposed by the *shari'a* and the state penal codes'. The judiciary was placed in the hands of religious judges, the marriage and family laws were abrogated, and girls' education was limited to attendance at a *madrasa*, but only until puberty.

Once 'Aman Allah Khan had agreed to these changes, albeit under duress, the council of *'ulama'* issued a *fatwa* denouncing Mullah-i Lang as a rebel, and the Kohistani and Tagabis returned home to assemble their forces. In effect, one faction of anti-reformist Islamizers sacrificed another equally reactionary group for their own ideological and political ends. In order to counteract Mullah-i Lang's accusations that he was an apostate, the king then executed several Ahmadiyya converts. Nothing that 'Aman Allah Khan did, however, could disguise the fact that the Loya Jirga had been a public humiliation and someone had to be blamed for the debacle. The unfortunate scapegoat was Maulawi 'Abd al-Wasi', chair of the committee that drafted the *Nizam Nama*s and whose arguments in defence of the Constitution had been excoriated by his opponents. For the second time in his life 'Abd al Wasi' was imprisoned, but once the storm had died down he was released and reinstated as head of the royal mosque at Pul-i Kheshti. Relations between him and the king remained tense, however, and he used the occasion of his Friday sermons to indirectly criticize government policies.

Reinforced by the levies from the Kohistan, in the middle of August Shah Wali Khan, who was now in charge of military operations, attacked the rebels' forward position at Karez Darwish in the Logar, while air force planes, piloted by Russians and Germans, bombed the front lines. By early October Gardez was once more in government hands, and two months later tribal leaders from Khost came to Kabul under a pledge of safe conduct to sue for peace, only for them to be thrown in jail. Mullah-i Lang and three of his sons were eventually captured and blown from the muzzles of guns. In all, a hundred rebels were executed. Shah Wali also burnt and looted more than three hundred houses in Khost. When he returned to Kabul he brought with him six hundred female captives who were distributed among various Muhammadzais as war booty. As for 'Abd al-Karim, he fled back across the Indian frontier only to be arrested by the British authorities and exiled to Burma. Two years later he committed suicide. Mullah-i Lang's rebellion had nearly toppled the king. Even though the revolt was eventually put down, 'Aman Allah Khan was weakened militarily, while his agenda for constitutional change had been hijacked by Islamizers. If this was not bad enough, in order to pay for the war the king had to increase taxation and cut public expenditure.

The Islamization of the Constitution had unexpected repercussions for Kabul's small community of European advisers. At the end of July 1924 Dario Piperno, an Italian engineer, shot dead a policeman sent to arrest him for a minor offence.[40] He was tried and sentenced to death by a *shari'a* court, only for the dead man's next of kin to waive his right to *qisas*, the right to personally execute the murderer, and accepted blood money instead, for he had no wish to 'soil his hands with the blood of a heathen'.[41] According to both Islamic jurisprudence and Pushtun customary law, once the blood money was paid, Piperno ought to have been freed. However, the king confirmed the death sentence and the following year Piperno was hanged in secret without the Italian embassy being given prior notice.

Piperno's execution was a diplomatic disaster. All the Western powers with representation in Kabul submitted formal protests, while Italy demanded an apology and the return of the blood money. When neither was forthcoming, Italy froze the bank accounts of Afghan ministers, suspended all aid and recalled its ambassador. Just as the envoy was about to leave, however, a junior official of the Foreign Ministry presented him with a letter of apology and a pledge to return the blood money, and the confrontation ended. The Piperno Affair though cost Afghanistan a seat in the League of Nations, for Britain cited his trial and execution as justification for vetoing the government's application for membership. This time the whipping boy for the king's failures was Kabul's chief of police, who was sacked.

'Aman Allah Khan's handling of the constitutional crisis, the Khost rebellion, the Piperno Affair and foreign relations demonstrated a worrying degree of political naivety and poor judgement. The king's belief that he could impose his own reformist vision on his nation simply by fiat created only discontent and rebellion, while his capitulation to ideological opponents led to disillusionment among reformers and those who wanted a more gradual process of modernization. In April 1924 Sardar Nadir Khan, the eldest of the Musahiban brothers, confided to Sir Francis Humphrys, the British Minister in Kabul, that he opposed the rapidity of the king's modernization programme, the lack of public consultation over the Constitution, cuts in military spending and the domination of the military by Turks. Shortly afterwards, Nadir Khan told the king to his face that he only owed his position to the army, whereupon an angry 'Aman Allah Khan sent Nadir Khan into what was in effect exile, appointing him ambassador to France. The breach between the Seraj and Musahiban families became permanent a year or so later when the king annulled the engagement of his sister to Nadir Khan's brother, Muhammad Hashim Khan. In response, Nadir Khan resigned his post and retired to Nice, where he was joined later by Shah Wali Khan and Muhammad Hashim Khan.

Even Mahmud Tarzi became disillusioned with his protégé. The relationship seems to have begun to fall apart after 'Aman Allah Khan overruled Tarzi and signed the Anglo-Afghan Agreement of 1921, for a few months later Tarzi was sent as ambassador to France. He was recalled in 1924, reinstated as Minister of Foreign Affairs, but Tarzi again fell out with the king over his handling of the constitutional crisis and the Piperno Affair. In 1927 Tarzi, pleading ill-health, left for Switzerland. Other reformers, who had lost hope that any significant change could be instituted under the monarchy, re-formed the Hizb-i Mashruta and anti-government *shab nama*s once more began to circulate. Another faction founded Afghanistan's first Republican Party, while the Jawanan-i Afghan, the pro-Bolshevik movement in Bukhara, established a cell in Kabul that was the precursor of Afghanistan's Communist parties.

'Aman Allah Khan eventually regained some of the ground lost to the Islamic lobby. In 1926, when a German shot an Afghan, allegedly in self-defence, his trial was conducted according to European legal procedures; he was convicted and sentenced to imprisonment, but received a royal pardon. Tarzi then privately reassured foreign diplomats that *qisas* would not be applied in the case of foreign, non-Muslim guest workers. Queen Soraya opened a girls' school in the Dilkusha Palace and eventually established a number of girls' schools outside the palace walls. 'Aman Allah

Khan also undertook a nationwide tour to promote his views on education and argue for limited female emancipation. Public criticism of *mullah*s and *pir*s increased in the state-controlled press, while Nur al-Mashayekh, the Hazrat of Shor Bazaar, was 'encouraged' to go on Hajj and not allowed to return. Instead he set up his base across the frontier in Dera Isma'il Khan, where he mobilized his Mujadidi networks and plotted the downfall of a ruler he believed had lost all legitimacy.

Afghan-Soviet relations and the occupation of Yangi Qal'a

To add to the turmoil of 1924, at the end of the year relations with the Soviet Union deteriorated, following Stalin's decision to partition Russian Turkistan into the autonomous Soviet Republics of Tajikistan, Uzbekistan and Turkmenistan. This tacit recognition by the Soviet Union of the right to self-determination for the Uzbeks, Turkmans and Tajiks of Central Asia was poorly received in Kabul, since it raised fears it would encourage nationalist sentiment in the *wilayat* of Balkh. Then the following year a long-standing dispute over the Amu Darya frontier almost led to war. For some two decades Afghanistan and Russia had disputed sovereignty over Urta Tagai, or Darqad, an island on the Panj river opposite the Afghan frontier post of Yangi Qal'a. The argument began after the main channel of the Amu Darya dramatically shifted from south of Urta Tagai to the north, a change that, according to international law, meant the island was now on the Afghan side of the frontier. Subsequently, Urta Tagai became a key staging post for *basmachi* infiltration of Tajikistan, as well as a place of refuge for White Russians and other anti-Soviet activists.

In December 1925 Moscow sent the Red Army to occupy Urta Tagai and several Afghan soldiers were killed during the operation. The Afghan press hysterically denounced the attack as an invasion and 'Aman Allah Khan seriously considered declaring war on the Soviet Union. Britain, though, went behind the Afghan government's back and eventually persuaded Moscow to accept international arbitration. When the committee decided in Afghanistan's favour, Russia withdrew its troops, but the occupation of Urta Tagai had been a sharp warning to the Afghan government of the vulnerability of its northern frontier and the possible consequences Afghanistan might face if it antagonized Moscow.

King 'Aman Allah Khan's Grand Tour

Despite the many and complex problems facing Afghanistan, both internally and externally, at the end of 1927 King 'Aman Allah Khan announced
he was to embark on a tour of India, the Middle East and Europe, which he
declared was not 'a voyage of pleasure . . . but [for] study and social exploration'.[42] Many high government officials opposed this Grand Tour since the
king planned to be absent for more than seven months, but he ignored their
concerns and appointed Sardar Muhammad Wali Khan, a career diplomat,
to act as his Viceroy.[43] Mahmud Tarzi, who was in Switzerland at the time,
wrote to the king to dissuade him from his venture, but instead 'Aman
Allah Khan ordered Tarzi to join the royal party in Italy. When the king
continued to disregard his advice, however, Tarzi returned to Switzerland
and later made his way back to Kabul.

After visiting India and Egypt, 'Aman Allah Khan's first port of call
in Europe was Italy, where he publicly declared his admiration for Prime
Minister Benito Mussolini, leader of Italy's Fascist Party, who was rapidly
turning his country into a totalitarian state. Victor Emanuel ii, Italy's king,
then appointed 'Aman Allah Khan as a *Cavaliere dell' Ordine Supremo della
Santissima Annunziata* (Knight of the Supreme Order of the Most Holy
Annunciation), the country's highest and most ancient order of chivalry.
This too was controversial, for the *Grande Collana*, as it is known, is
bestowed only on Italian citizens who were baptized Roman Catholics,
while the badge of the Order was an icon of the Annunciation surrounded
by crosses and the letters FERT, which may be interpreted as Latin for 'He
[Christ] bore [our sins]'. The Christian significance of this honour was not
lost on 'Aman Allah Khan's religious opponents, who saw the king's acceptance of this honour as further 'proof' that he was at heart an apostate, a
view reinforced when he had an audience with Pope Pius xi.

'Aman Allah Khan's next port of call was Nice, where he tried unsuccessfully to persuade Nadir Khan and the Musahiban brothers to return
home. In Switzerland the king was met by 'stolid silence' and 'Republican
simplicity',[44] but when 'Aman Allah Khan arrived in Germany he was
treated with all the pomp and ceremony of a European monarch, for with
the economy of the Weimer Republic in freefall, the German government was anxious to secure a stake in post-independence Afghanistan.
During his stay 'Aman Allah Khan signed many costly contracts with
German companies, but only because the German government agreed
to a substantial loan that could only be spent on German equipment
and armaments.

King 'Aman Allah
Khan in European
military uniform,
just prior to his
controversial
European Tour,
from the *Illustrated
London News*,
1 October 1927.

After his visit to Germany he set sail for England, where 'Aman Allah Khan was a state guest of King George V. During his time in Britain 'Aman Allah Khan flew in an aeroplane, went underwater in a submarine and visited munitions factories. The British authorities made sure the king had frequent displays of Britain's military might, just as a reminder of the risk he ran of going to war with India a second time. 'Aman Allah Khan's visit was also popular with the general public, who lined the streets to catch a glimpse of this exotic monarch and his entourage.

'Aman Allah Khan's visit to the Soviet Union was a particularly awkward leg of the journey in the wake of the confrontation over Urta Tagai and Stalin's creation of the Central Asian Republics. The situation was made more uncomfortable by the fact that the Bolsheviks were Republicans who a few years earlier had brutally executed the last Tsar and all his family. The Soviet press never referred to 'Aman Allah Khan as Tsar, or its Persian equivalent *qaisar*. Instead the reports used King's recently assumed title of *padshah,* or king, and emphasized his role as a supporter of Indian self-rule and his war against British imperialism. 'Aman Allah Khan, though, came away from Moscow disappointed, for despite the pledges made in the Soviet-Afghan Treaty, the USSR provided only token amounts of aid and military hardware.

On his way back to Afghanistan 'Aman Allah Khan passed through Turkey and Iran. In Istanbul he met with President Mustafa Kemal Atatürk and signed a treaty of friendship, which provided for 'judicial, scientific and military experts' to assist Afghanistan's 'intellectual and military progress'.[45] During a banquet held in his honour, 'Aman Allah Khan reiterated his intention to modernize Afghanistan, but failed to make any reference to the role of Islam in this process. Indeed, it seems 'Aman Allah Khan's meeting with Mustafa Kemal reinforced his determination to force Afghanistan down the same path as Turkey, despite the bruising he had received over the Constitution and marriage laws. Even when British intelligence managed to foil a plot by Nur al-Mashayekh to depose the king while he was abroad, the king failed to heed the warning.

'Aman Allah Khan's final port of call was Iran, another country that had recently experienced major constitutional and dynastic upheavals, for some three years earlier King Reza Shah had deposed the last of the Qajar kings and inaugurated his own programme of rapid Europeanization. 'Aman Allah Khan, not to be outdone, boasted to Iranian officials that he planned to effect a similar revolution in Afghanistan within a decade. His listeners were so astonished they concluded the King had taken leave of his senses.

During his Grand Tour 'Aman Allah Khan had rubbed shoulders with the world's most powerful figures and had been showered with honours, awards and honorary degrees. For many Europeans he had put Afghanistan on the political map and managed to convince at least some nations that investment in his country was good business. 'Aman Allah Khan's affability and graciousness had made him popular with the common people while the stunningly beautiful Queen Soraya was the sensation of the Season. Tragically, his tour also turned 'Aman Allah Khan's head and the technological marvels he saw everywhere only revealed the vast gap that existed between Afghanistan and Europe. This sense of inferiority was reinforced by the popular press constantly referring to Afghanistan and its people as 'backward', 'unruly' and 'primitive'. Roland Wild, the *Daily Mail* special correspondent, even mocked 'Aman Allah Khan by claiming he believed that: 'You cannot rule by law and order, by precept and principle, if you dress in the style of the jungle and the hills'.[46] By the time 'Aman Allah Khan crossed the Afghan–Iranian frontier, he seems to have become determined to pursue reform whatever the consequences. As Wild observed, 'it could not reasonably be expected that Amanullah would be infected with the germ of the West so seriously as to lose his sense of proportion. Yet that was exactly what was happening.'[47]

'Aman Allah Khan appears to have been unaware of the storm of criticism his tour had excited, not only among his religious opponents but reformers and the military hierarchy too. His praise of Mussolini's Fascist government did not endear him to those wanting a more demo-cratic government or constitutional reform, while the acceptance of the *Grande Collana* and his audience with the Pope was exploited by Islamic opponents to reinforce their claim that the king was an apostate. His visit to the Soviet Union was not particularly diplomatic given the Bolsheviks' establishment of an atheistic state, while 'Aman Allah Khan's enthusiasm for the secularizing and disestablishmentarian reforms of Mustafa Kemal and Reza Shah angered the Islamic lobby even further. Other officials, particularly in the military, were unhappy about the terms of the Turco-Afghan Treaty, which promised even more unpopular Turkish domination of both the military and education. To cap it all, Queen Soraya and other women in her entourage had discarded the veil during the European leg of the tour and worn instead the clinging, low-cut dresses that were all the fashion in the Roaring Twenties.

King 'Aman Allah Khan's reforms: the second phase

Once back home, 'Aman Allah Khan proceeded to add even more fuel to the fires of discontent. During his stopover in Kandahar the king informed local dignitaries that he planned to reinstate universal education and eman-cipate women, declaring: 'Is it not shameful that the women of Europe are more laborious and more active than the men of Afghanistan?'[48] Comparing Pushtun men unfavourably to women, especially *farangi* women, could not have been more insulting, especially since many of the assembly would have had access to the Urdu press and seen photographs of Queen Soraya in her revealing dresses. All 'Aman Allah Khan's remarks did was to exacerbate fears that the king planned a similar 'fate' for their women.

When he finally arrived in Kabul, 'Aman Allah Khan ordered a Loya Jirga to convene at the end of August 1928 and in the meantime he retired to Paghman, leaving affairs of state in the hands of Sardar Muhammad Wali Khan. Assisted by an Iranian legal expert and the Turkish ambassador, 'Aman Allah Khan then began to plan his social and legal revolution and over the following six weeks he issued a series of bizarre decrees, including requiring all visitors to government offices to wear European clothes. The king then made radical changes in his cabinet, appointing Sher Ahmad

'The Queen of Afghanistan as seen in Europe', *Illustrated London News*, 4 February 1928, a photograph of Queen Soraya without a veil and her legs bare below the knee. Images such as this published in the Indian press found their way to Kabul and were exploited by Islamic and anti-European opponents of King 'Aman Allah Khan and contributed to his downfall.

Khan Zikriya, head of the sycophantic Royalist Party, as Prime Minister, and Ghulam Siddiq Charkhi, a 'hot headed radical',[49] as Foreign Minister in the place of Tarzi. So unpopular were these appointments that most of the existing ministers resigned.

At the end of August around a thousand delegates, uncomfortably dressed in frock coats, assembled for the Loya Jirga. 'Aman Allah Khan then proceeded to outline his plans, declaring that 'the great secret of progress lies in discarding old, outworn ideas and customs, and . . . march[ing] with the times.'[50] 'Progress', according to 'Aman Allah Khan, meant changing traditional symbols of state, as well as reinstating compulsory primary education and all of the constitutional provision that had been overturned four years earlier. The black flag of the Durranis, which harked back to the banner of 'Abbasid Caliphs, was replaced by a tricolour flag consisting of three vertical stripes of black, red and green, which was modelled on the flags of France, Belgium and Italy. The Islamic motifs of a star, mosque and crossed swords were replaced by a sheaf of wheat enclosing mountains and a rising sun with a star at the apex. The *jirga*, which government ministers had ensured was loaded with royalist supporters, also passed a law on women's rights and established the Society for the Protection of Women, while the king publicly stated his opposition to veiling and *parda*. Other measures passed by the *jirga* included restrictions on the role of *mullah*s in education and the judiciary.

Despite rubber-stamping the king's proposals, many delegates were unhappy about the king's intentions and shared their concerns once back in their homes. In Kabul there were riots, which the army put down with brute force; several *mullah*s in Qataghan refused to recite the king's name in the *khutba*; while Gul Agha Mujadidi, brother of the Hazrat of Shor Bazaar, and Akhundzada Hamid Allah Safi, the Mullah of Tagab, drew up a *fatwa* condemning the king's plans, which was signed by four hundred members of the religious establishment. When Gul Agha presented the *fatwa* to the king, 'Aman Allah Khan accused the Hazrat's family of being British agents and threw them in prison.[51] The king also denied an audience to influential tribal and religious leaders from Nangahar who had travelled to Kabul to greet the king on his return and who wanted to express their concerns at his proceedings. Queen Soraya then pushed the boundaries even further, appearing in public wearing only a light veil and publishing a series of articles in the '*Aman-i Afghan* arguing that neither the Qur'an nor *Hadith* forbade women's education or demanded full veiling. *Anis*, another influential newspaper, also ran a series of strongly worded attacks on *mullah*s and *pir*s.

Dissent quickly turned to outright revolt. When 'Aman Allah Khan tried to persuade Qazi 'Abd al-Rahman, Kabul's most senior religious judge, to issue a *fatwa* legitimizing his reforms, the *qazi*, who was a *murid* of the Hazrat of Shor Bazaar, refused. When the king threatened him with execution, 'Abd al-Rahman, Gul Aga and other dissident *'ulama'* from Kohistan and Tagab fled to Khost and tried to persuade the Ahmadzais to rebel. Instead they were betrayed and arrested. Qazi 'Abd al-Rahman and three of his male relatives were publicly executed for treason in late October 1928.[52]

'Aman Allah Khan refused to back down despite the rising tide of protest. At the end of October the king held a *darbar* of his closest supporters and over four consecutive days he outlined even more radical reforms. Thursday was to be the official holiday rather than Friday, the Islamic Sabbath; everyone living in, or visiting, Kabul had to wear European clothes, and polygamy was abolished. There was to be compulsory co-education for all children, foreign-run schools were to be opened in every province and Afghan girls would be sent to study in Europe. 'Aman Allah Khan then launched a virulent attack on the religious establishment, blaming them for all the country's ills. At the conclusion of his peroration, he reiterated his opposition to *parda*, whereupon Queen Soraya and the other women present tore off their veils to rapturous applause. The king's speech and the Queen's ill-timed piece of theatre were the last straw.

The rebellions in Nangahar and the Koh Daman

A few weeks later the Shinwaris of Nangahar rebelled, citing a variety of reasons including taxation, conscription, the enforcement of Western dress, the venality of government officials and the Queen's conduct. A number of religious figures then issued *fatwas* in support of the revolt and denounced the king and his administration as *kafir*. The air force was sent to bomb rebel Shinwari villages, whereupon the Shinwaris, Mohmands and Khogiyanis joined the uprising too. By the end of November Jalalabad and most of southeastern Afghanistan was in rebel hands. Ghulam Siddiq Charkhi was sent to negotiate with the rebels, but instead they presented him with a series of demands that included the abrogation of all recent legal, fiscal and social reforms, the abolition of conscription and the restoration of the *'ulama*'s dominant role in the judiciary. The manifesto also demanded that the king divorce Queen Soraya, send her and the Tarzi family into exile and expel all Turkish advisers and foreign diplomats, with the exception of the British.[53] In response 'Aman Allah Khan secured his own *fatwa*, which asserted that, as a Muslim king, all his subjects were required to render him absolute obedience, and sent Loynab 'Ali Ahmad Khan to put down the rebels in Nangahar, in the process denuding Kabul of all but a handful of front-line regiments.

Meanwhile north of Kabul, Tagab, Kohistan and the Koh Daman were in a state of rebellion. The trouble began when the king tried to arrest the Mullah of Tagab, only for the force sent to seize him to be ambushed and defeated. In the Koh Daman, a band of robbers had been raiding the Kabul–Charikar highway for several months and holding merchants to ransom. Their leader, Habib Allah Kalakani, better known as *Bacha-yi Saqau*, or Son of a Water Carrier,[54] had served on the estate of Mustufi Husain Khan Safi as a youth, but in 1919 he had been conscripted into the army and fought under Sardar Nadir Khan in the Third Anglo-Afghan War. He subsequently fought with the *basmachi*s as a member of the Afghan Volunteer Force. In 1924 Kalakani took part in the suppression of the Khost rebellion but deserted after he claimed he and his men had not received their share of war booty. Habib Allah and his comrades-in-arms then returned to the Koh Daman where they began to rob villages and plunder caravans.[55]

The government was unable to suppress these raids and instead Ahmad 'Ali Lodi, governor of Charikar, offered Habib Allah Kalakani a royal pardon, cash and army rank if he and his men rejoined the army and helped put down the revolt in Nangahar. As a sign of good faith, the governor offered to send Habib Allah a pledge of safe conduct, but Kalakani was suspicious and demanded the king seal the pledge of pardon and safe conduct on the Qur'an. Ahmad 'Ali called 'Aman Allah Khan on the telephone link to discuss the proposal and the king instructed him to wrap up an ordinary book in a cloth to make it seem like a Qur'an, and lure Kalakani to Charikar, where he was to arrest him and send him to Kabul to be executed. What 'Aman Allah Khan did not know was that the telephone operator, a friend of Habib Allah's, eavesdropped on the conversation and warned him of the deception. Habib Allah then phoned the king himself, pretending to be the governor of Charikar, and asked what his instructions were in respect of Kalakani, whereupon 'Aman Allah Khan shouted down the line: 'Kill him, kill him!' Habib Allah Kalakani, so the story goes, then revealed his true identity, heaped abuse on the king, and vowed to march on Kabul and depose him.[56]

Habib Allah Kalakani then held a series of secret meetings with influential religious figures in Kohistan and the Koh Daman including Akhundzada 'Abd Allah Jan, Buzurg Jan and Hazrat Mujadidi of Tagab, individuals who were opposed to the king's reforms and who had close ties with the Hazrat of Shor Bazaar, the Hadda Mullah and the rebel leader-ship in Nangahar. These men agreed to Habib Allah Kalakani becoming military head of a *jihad* and issued a *fatwa* denouncing the king and his government and declaring 'Aman Allah Khan's half-brother, Hayat Allah Khan, to be King. According to one source, Hayat Allah Khan himself attended one of their secret meetings.[57]

Habib Allah Kalakani, now transformed from a marauder to a *muja-hid*, went on the offensive. In early November 1928 he occupied Sarai-yi Khoja, cutting the telegraph and electricity lines to the capital. He then besieged Jabal Seraj. After ten days Ahmad 'Ali Lodi surrendered the town, along with its arsenal and treasury, in exchange for safe passage to Kabul and a share of the cash. Habib Allah Kalakani, with a large sum of cash now at his disposal as well as a huge store of weapons, including machine guns and heavy artillery, marched on Kabul. At the end of November he occupied Qal'a-yi Murad Beg, on the outskirts of Kabul, where the rebels halted to perform the Friday prayers. During the service Shams al-Haqq Mujadidi, who led the prayers, inserted Habib Allah Kalakani's name in the *khutba* and accorded him the grandiose title of *Khadim-i Din-i Rasul Allah*, Servant of the Religion of the Apostle of God. King Habib Allah II, as he was now officially designated, marched into Kart-i Parwan and on 14 December overran the King's residence at the Bagh-i Bala, Habibiyya College, the Military College at Shahr Ara and sacked 'Abd al-Quddus Khan's personal residence. Since most of the Kabul garrison had been sent to Nangahar only a handful of regiments, mostly conscripts whose pay was months in arrears, remained in Kabul. Most of them deserted or joined the rebel army. In desperation 'Aman Allah Khan ordered rifles to be distrib-uted to ordinary Kabulis. Ahmadzai tribesmen, who were about to leave to join Loynab 'Ali Ahmad in Nangahar, promptly turned the weapons on the king's troops or sent the guns to Khost.

For nearly two weeks fighting raged in and around Kart-i Parwan with the newly built British Legation caught on the front line. While Legation staff sheltered under the billiard table and ran the gauntlet of snipers to obtain fuel from the woodshed, Humphrys, the British Minister, pipe in mouth, valiantly turned back bands of rebels and government soldiers who tried to infiltrate the Legation's grounds. By Christmas Eve the situation was such that Humphrys ordered a general evacuation, and over the next two months 586 men, women and children were flown to Peshawar in specially adapted Royal Air Force planes in what was the world's first air evacuation.[58] In late December 'Aman Allah Khan followed suit and flew his wives and children to Kandahar.

Around Christmas there was a lull in the fighting after Habib Allah Kalakani was wounded by shrapnel and withdrew to Paghman to recuperate. This was cold comfort for 'Aman Allah Khan, for a few days later the influential Mullah of Chaknawar declared his support for the Nangahar rebels and called for the king's abdication. With his back to the wall, 'Aman Allah Khan called an emergency cabinet meeting and issued a royal proclamation revoking most of his recent reforms and capitulating to the Shinwaris' demands. It seems the king hoped that by appeasing the Nangahar rebels they would agree to support him and suppress the upstart Kohistanis. After all, he had successfully used the same ploy, in reverse, to put down the Khost revolt. The Nangahar tribes, however, had no faith in a king who had lost any religious legitimacy and his feeble attempt at divide and rule failed. In January 1929 'Aman Allah Khan made further concessions, freeing the brother of Nur al-Mashayekh and other members of the Mujadidi clan and various dissidents, but it was too little, too late. Many government officials, including ministers, leaders of the reform movement and senior Muhammadzais, were already secretly cutting deals with Habib Allah Kalakani.

The fall of Kabul and the flight of King 'Aman Allah Khan

The *coup de grâce* came in mid-January 1929. An assembly of Kohistani leaders was held in Qal'a-yi Husain Kot, the family seat of Mustufi Husain Khan Safi, during which they renewed their oath of allegiance to Habib Allah Kalakani. The following day 16,000 Kohistanis poured into Kabul, brushing aside what little resistance they encountered. 'Aman Allah Khan hastily abdicated in favour of 'Inayat Khan and drove pell-mell to Kandahar, accompanied by Mahmud Tarzi and 10 million rupees in gold coin. 'Inayat Khan, however, reigned for a matter of a week or so, and even then his authority barely extended beyond the Dilkusha Palace. Outside the palace walls, government officials and even his own brothers submitted to Habib Allah Kalakani. 'Abd al-Rahim Khan Safi, brother-in-law of Mustufi Muhammad Husain Khan, who commanded 1,000 soldiers at Tepe Maranjan, also defected. As rebel forces surrounded the royal palace Humphrys, fearing a massacre, managed to negotiate safe passage for 'Inayat Khan and his wives, Tarzi's two sons and several senior officials. RAF planes flew them to Peshawar.

King Habib Allah Khan Kalakani controlled the Afghan capital, but the governors of Herat, Ghazni and Kandahar refused to swear allegiance to him. In Nangahar the Shinwari, Mohmand and Khogiyani rebels proclaimed Loynab 'Ali Ahmad Khan as King. He attempted to take Kabul but was defeated after the Khogiyanis accepted the offer of a substantial sum of money from the Mujadidis of Shor Bazaar and defected. Loynab 'Ali Ahmad fled to Peshawar, where he consoled himself with a binge-drinking spree. After he had sobered up, he made his way to Kandahar and made his peace with 'Aman Allah Khan.

'Aman Allah Khan still hoped to raise an army from his Durrani tribe, so when he heard 'Inayat Khan had fled Afghanistan he rescinded his abdication, ignoring his religious advisers' objections that this was unlawful. The Durranis, though, were reluctant to rally to the royal standard and the king doubtless had cause to regret his sarcastic remark about lazy Kandahari men. Kandahar's '*ulama*' also refused to condemn Habib Allah Kalakani as a rebel, for many of them had opposed the king's constitutional reforms from the outset and had no interest in his plan to emancipate women. Shortly before 'Aman Allah Khan's abdication, some of Kandahar's religious leaders had written to the king, complaining about new regulations that required *mullah*s to have a teaching qualification in order to teach in state schools and the issue of female education. 'Abd al-'Aziz, the king's Minister for War, tried to win their support by persuasion as well as by gifts of cash, and made sure tribal and religious leaders heard graphic accounts from refugees of the lawlessness, rape and other atrocities committed by Kalakani's followers in Kabul.

By the end of February 1929 tribal opinion had begun to swing in the king's favour. Levies from Wardak, Jalrez and the Hazarajat even defeated a force sent by Habib Allah Kalakani against Kandahar. 'Aman Allah Khan, however, failed to win over the Sulaiman Khel Ghilzais, for as *mukhlis* of Nur al-Mashayekh these clans were bound by oath to support their *pir*, who had given his blessing to the rebellion. 'Aman Allah Khan's appeal to the Viceroy to be allowed to import arms from India was also rejected on the ground that Britain was officially neutral in the conflict. An appeal for Soviet assistance by Ghulam Nabi Charkhi, ambassador in Moscow, was more successful and Moscow agreed to provide him with money, weapons and military advisers, and granted him permission to recruit levies from the many Afghan refugees living in Uzbekistan.

The return of the Musahiban brothers

'Aman Allah Khan's chance of regaining the throne was undermined even further when he heard that Nadir Khan and his brothers had landed in Bombay, where they announced they had come to liberate Afghanistan from the bandit king. Nadir Khan and Shah Wali Khan were war heroes with a strong following in the army and among the Frontier tribes. Furthermore, as descendants of the Peshawar *sardars*, the Musahiban family presented the rebels with a viable alternative to the Saraj dynasty. Nadir Khan's progress to Peshawar was something of a triumph. Large crowds greeted him at Lahore station, while the Urdu poet and Indian nationalist Muhammad Iqbal pledged his life savings for Nadir Khan's campaign. In his address Nadir Khan declared that he 'would not rest until he had seen Amanallah back on the throne',[59] but by the time he reached Peshawar he had shifted his position, claiming he only wanted to 'establish peace and liberate my people from tyranny' and it was up to the tribes to decide who became king.[60]

This change of mind was most likely due to Nadir Khan hearing from tribal and religious leaders at first hand about how deeply they resented the reforms of 'Aman Allah Khan. Since Nadir Khan needed the support of the tribes, it was politic for him and his brothers to distance themselves from 'Aman Allah Khan and his reformist circle. Nadir Khan's meeting with Sir Francis Humphrys, who had been evacuated to Peshawar, no doubt influenced this change of heart. Humphrys had developed a personal dislike for Tarzi and 'Aman Allah Khan. Doubtless he made it clear to Nadir Khan that Britain did not want to see a Seraj back on the Afghan throne, while he assured him that Britain would help a new king, 'whoever he may be', to establish himself on the throne.[61] From this point forward Nadir Khan became more outspoken in his criticism of 'Aman Allah Khan, yet refused to declare himself as king and rejected offers from envoys from Habib Allah Kalakani and Nur al-Mashayekh to join the new government. Loynab 'Ali Ahmad Khan also failed to convince Nadir Khan that, since the Nangahar tribes had elected him King, Nadir and his brothers should tender their allegiance to him too. Instead, on 6 March 1929 Nadir Khan, Shah Wali Khan and Hashim Khan set out for Khost to raise an army to march on Kabul.

The unexpected return to India of the Musahiban brothers meant it was now a race between them and 'Aman Allah Khan to retake Kabul. 'Aman Allah Khan, however, had yet to persuade the Durrani tribes or the Kandahar '*ulama*' to condemn the Kalakani regime and join him in his bid to regain control of the Afghan capital. In a desperate attempt to secure their support 'Aman Allah Khan resorted to a bold and dramatic gesture. On 24 February 1929 the king called a *jirga* at the shrine of the Khirqa-yi Sharif, which abutted the tomb of Ahmad Shah Durrani. In an impassioned speech, 'Aman Allah Khan reaffirmed his Islamic faith and damned Habib Allah Kalakani as a traitor and infidel. Then he ordered the *mutawalli* of the shrine to open the reliquary and, holding the sacred mantle aloft, he demanded of the onlookers whether God would allow a heretic or apostate to hold such a sacred object without being struck dead. This piece of theatre had an immediate impact as one leader after another came forward and renewed their allegiance, while the *'ulama'* issued a *fatwa* condemning King Habib Allah Kalakani as a usurper.

Even so it was not until early April that 'Aman Allah Khan finally set out for the Afghan capital, a move probably forced on him by news that Nadir Khan was advancing on Gardez. At the same time, Ghulam Nabi Charkhi crossed the Amu Darya with a small force intent on marching on Kabul from the north. The problem was that 'Aman Allah Khan's army was small and the bulk of his force consisted of Hazaras, who had joined the king after senior *mujtahid*s at the Shi'a's most sacred shrine in Karbala, 'Iraq, issued a *fatwa* urging them to support 'Aman Allah Khan.

'Aman Allah Khan then made a fatal mistake. Ignoring the advice of his generals, who wanted to march on Kabul down the Logar valley, the king set out for Ghazni, even though he had not secured safe passage from the Sulaiman Khel. The fact that the majority of the king's army consisted of Hazaras made the Ghilzais even more angry, for they had long been at odds with the Hazaras, partly because they were Shi'a and Isma'ili and partly because of long-standing disputes over grazing rights. 'Aman Allah Khan was harried by raiders as he marched up the Ghazni road and when he reached Muqur 7,000 Ghilzais swooped down on the straggling column. Despite the Hazaras fighting bravely, the king's army was annihilated. 'Aman Allah Khan fled to Qalat-i Ghilzai, but when it too was besieged he fled across the border to Chaman. A few days later he was joined by a heavily pregnant Queen Soraya, Mahmud Tarzi, 'Inayat Allah Khan and his wife.

The situation beyond the Hindu Kush was equally chaotic. Shortly after Habib Allah Kalakani took Kabul, forces loyal to the new government occupied Mazar-i Sharif and Qal'a-yi Jangi. 'Abd al-Rahim Khan Safi was sent north as governor of Afghan Turkistan. After appointing new civil and military officials, 'Abd al-Rahim set out for Maimana and Herat, taking most of his troops with him, only for Ghulam Nabi Charkhi, backed by Soviet planes, to seize control of Mazar and Qal'a-yi Jangi a few weeks later. The garrison in Dehdadi managed to hold out for a month before it too capitulated, whereupon Ghulam Nabi marched on Tashqurghan, forcing Habib Allah Kalakani's troops to fall back on Qunduz and Aibak.

However, Ghulam Nabi's expectation that thousands of Pushtun colonists in the *wilayat* would join his campaign proved to be a serious

Uzbek and Turkman *talibs,* or religious students, in the *madrasa* of Khalifa Qizil Ayaq, near Shibarghan. Originally from what is now Turkmenistan, in 1929 the Khalifa and his *murid*s supported Habib Allah Kalakani's Islamizing revolution.

misjudgement, since only one or two commanders around Balkh declared support for him. The Kalakanid government, meanwhile, exploited the fact that Soviet planes had bombed Qal'a-yi Jangi, and that Ghulam Nabi's force included Russian-speaking troops and officers, to declare that he was merely a figurehead for what was in effect a Soviet invasion. As a result of this propaganda, religious leaders in Mazar-i Sharif and Balkh declared a *jihad* on Ghulam Nabi. The Turkman *pir* and former *basmachi* leader, the Khalifa of Qizil Ayaq, who commanded an army of 12,000 *murid*s, retook Mazar. In Qataghan, Ibrahim Beg, the Turkish *basmachi* commander, also declared for Habib Allah, while in Kabul the Kalakani regime abrogated the Soviet-Afghan Treaty and threatened the Soviet ambassador with expulsion if his country did not withdraw its 'advisers'.

Ghulam Nabi finally came face-to-face with the Kalakanid army at Kotal-i Rabatak, between Pul-i Khumri and Tashqurghan, only for Ghulam Nabi to be defeated and flee back across the Amu Darya. His defeat and 'Aman Allah Khan's loss at Muqur ended any hopes the king had of regaining the throne. Further humiliation followed. The Viceroy refused the ex-king's request for sanctuary in India and 'Aman Allah Khan spent the rest of his life in exile in Italy where, as a Knight of the Order of the Most Holy Annunciation, he was effectively an honorary citizen. Following his death in 1960, the government allowed his body to be returned to Afghanistan and he was buried beside his father in the family mausoleum in Jalalabad. As for Tarzi, he made his home in Turkey. When he died four years later, he was buried in the cemetery of Eyüp Sultan in Istanbul.

King 'Aman Allah Khan: an appraisal

The reign of King 'Aman Allah Khan is mostly remembered for his failed experiment in social and constitutional reforms, which, as far as many Afghans are concerned, was due primarily to the intransigence and obscurantism of religious and tribal leaders. Yet at least part of the reason for the failure of his programme was the blinkered and doctrinaire approach adopted by the king, Queen Soraya, Mahmud Tarzi and the Young Afghans, who believed that what was good enough for Turkey was good enough for Afghanistan. Fired with an unrealistic vision of rapid transformation, the king, Tarzi and their supporters tried to impose the *Tanzimat* and Atatürk model on Afghanistan, even though Afghanistan and Ottoman Turkey, despite both countries being Sunni, were in almost every respect chalk and cheese.

Unlike Afghanistan, the Ottoman kingdom was built on a heritage of thousands of years of engagement with European civilization. Indeed all European powers regarded Turkey as a European rather than a Middle Eastern nation, by dint of its thousand years of Byzantine Christian heritage as well as the fact that many of the greatest cities of Graeco-Roman civilization lay within Turkey's borders. Afghanistan, on the other hand, was both spatially and ideologically isolated from Europe and European culture. What little interaction Afghanistan had with Europe was mostly negative, for its two European neighbours, Britain and Russia, were seen as alien and a threat to the country's sovereignty as well as its religious and cultural identity. Afghanistan's engagement with Europe only began in the early nineteenth century, and until the reign of 'Aman Allah Khan the only Europeans who had lived in the country, with few exceptions, were part of an army of occupation. One of the country's long-standing foreign policies was to deny Britain and other European powers any representation in the country. Britain, too, adopted a closed-door policy to Afghanistan, while Tarzi's pan-Islamic and anti-colonial polemic reinforced this introversion, even while he advocated modernization based on a model that was essentially European in origin.

In Ottoman society ethnicity or religious affiliation was no bar to high office or government service. Christians, Jews, Slavs, Greeks and

Armenians all played a major part in Ottoman commercial, intellectual and political life. This was not the case in Afghanistan. The country's tiny religious minorities were marginalized and discriminated against and, with the exception of one or two Hindus, they played little part in the country's political life. Even sectarian Muslim groups, such as Shi'as and Isma'ili, were regarded with hostility and on occasion subject to pogroms, while Tarzi's redefining of national identity along the same ethnolinguistic lines as post-Ottoman Turkey exacerbated an already existing sense of disenfranchisement among non-Pushtun groups.

As for the political and social transformation of post-war Turkey under Mustafa Kemal, this was the culmination of more than a century of struggle, yet 'Aman Allah Khan was naive enough to believe he could achieve the same degree of transformation in a decade. Turkey's revolution was led by a well-educated intelligentsia and officer corps that had studied in Christian schools and European universities or had been trained by German officers. All of them, to one degree or another, positively engaged with European culture and its political philosophies. As for Mustafa Kemal's post-war disestablishment of Islamic institutions, this was only made possible because he was a war hero who commanded the loyalty of a well-equipped and well-trained modern army. Finally, his reforms had widespread, popular support.

None of this was true of Afghanistan. King 'Aman Allah Khan was no general and he had played no active military role in the Third Anglo-Afghan War. The Afghan army was barely fit for purpose, being defeated not just by the superior technology and discipline of the British army, but by lightly armed and untrained tribal levies. The culture of intellectual enquiry that Elphinstone noted at the court of Shah Shuja' in 1808/9 had long since dissipated, or had been forced underground by state repression. As for Afghanistan's intelligentsia, they were a tiny urbanized clique of mostly Muhammadzais who were out of touch with public opinion, partly because they despised it. European ideas of education, a key driver of Turkey's 'Enlightenment', had yet to take root in Afghanistan. Habibiyya College, the first educational institution to include modern sciences and humanities in the curriculum, had been open for less than two decades and admission was restricted to a privileged few. The only education available to the majority of the population was the *madrasa*, where engagement with non-Islamic world views was more often than not actively discouraged. In 1919 probably less than 5 per cent of Afghanistan's male population was literate, and until Tarzi began his programme of translation very few Afghans had read any works by European authors. Of all the Muslim nations, Afghanistan was one of the least likely places to implement the kind of rapid revolution envisaged by 'Aman Allah Khan and the Young Afghans.

The failure of the reform movement was therefore due in part to the naivety of its advocates, combined with their lack of understanding of the processes that led to Europe and Turkey's technological, intellectual and social revolution. Government efforts to seek consensus were mostly token and the king was foolish enough to believe that his subjects would obey his decrees without question. Reformers themselves eventually despaired as the king vacillated between the pursuit of a reformist agenda and capitulation to Islamic conservatives. In the end the king's often bizarre decrees and declarations split the reform movement between those, such as the Musahiban brothers, who realized change could only be achieved as a long-term process, and the Tarzi and the Young Afghans who, like the king, believed transformation could happen overnight.

The fall of 'Aman Allah Khan is often attributed to the negative impact of his Grand Tour, in particular the appearance of an unveiled Queen Soraya; however, as we have seen, the reasons for 'Aman Allah Khan's downfall are far more complex. As Humphrys noted:

> It would be a mistake to suppose that the primary cause of King Amanullah's downfall is to be found in the resolutions which he formed during the European tour. He has admitted to me that ever since he came to the throne he has been impelled by an uncontrollable desire to bring about the complete modernisation of his country during his own lifetime.[62]

According to Humphrys it was the promulgation of the *Nizam Namas* that marked the beginning of the end for 'Aman Allah Khan, however opposition to the idea of a Constitution emerged in Kandahar as early as 1921. Arguably the fall of 'Aman Allah Khan can be traced back to his decision to invade India, for the defeat exposed the weakness of the army and undermined the king's credibility. This encouraged tribal discontent, which later coalesced around the debate about gender, the nation's Islamic identity and Europeanization. The war also broke the symbiotic relationship between Afghanistan and Britain, which led to the loss of the annual subsidy and Britain's formal commitment to maintain Afghanistan's territorial integrity. All of this indirectly weakened 'Aman Allah Khan's hold on power.

Instead of going to war, King 'Aman Allah Khan would have been far better served by following up his declaration of independence with an offer to negotiate with Britain over the issue. Britain had already indicated to his father that it was prepared to concede some form of conditional independence, and had the king given diplomacy a chance the war-weary government in London would probably have made further concessions in order to retain its strategic interests in the country. Instead 'Aman Allah Khan's unprovoked invasion antagonized Afghanistan's key ally and the most powerful nation in the world. From this point forward, British officials regarded 'Aman Allah Khan's Afghanistan as a hostile neighbour and worked behind the scenes to undermine his rule.

The loss of what the Afghans called the 'money from God' meant the country faced a severe financial crisis, especially since it became clear that no other European power was prepared to commit the same level of financial support to keep the country financially viable. Consequently 'Aman Allah Khan was forced to raise taxes, cut expenditure and borrow heavily. He then lavished vast sums on pet projects such as Paghman, Dar al-'Aman and his Grand Tour, rather than on the welfare of the nation as a whole. By 1928 'Aman Allah Khan was forced to seek foreign loans to finance these programmes but in the process he surrendered a degree of national sovereignty. A loan of £400,000 from a British banker was only secured in return for a monopoly on Afghanistan's sugar trade, another loan of 1 million francs from a French bank was secured at the rate of 7 to 8 per cent interest and only after the king offered as security all the customs revenues of Afghanistan. The German government also agreed to a short-term loan of 6 million Reichsmark, but it was conditional on the king using the money to buy German goods.

It is also a mistake to depict 'Aman Allah Khan's downfall as a clash of ideologies between a reactionary Islamic establishment on the one hand and the forces of 'modernization' and 'progress' on the other. In 1919 the Hazrat of Shor Bazaar, the Mullah of Tagab and 'Abd al-Quddus Khan, none of whom were noted for their progressive views, supported 'Aman Allah Khan's claim to the throne despite his support of Tarzi's agenda and the fact that Nasr Allah Khan, who had been declared King in Jalalabad, was a well-respected and strict Muslim. The Loya Jirga too agreed with the concept of a Constitution in principle, even though the Deobandis forced major changes to its provisions. During the rebellions of 1924 and 1928 religious leaders had divided loyalties and, apart from Nur al-Mashayekh, most religious opponents of 'Aman Allah Khan were reactive rather than proactive, only providing religious legitimacy for revolts after hostilities had commenced.

The real tragedy of 'Aman Allah Khan's reign is that many of the changes he sought for Afghanistan would have benefited the country had they been introduced gradually and on a foundation of consensus. However, one reform that was never on 'Aman Allah Khan's agenda was surrendering the monarchy's traditional autocratic powers to an elected Legislature. The token devolution of Executive power to a State Council and the lack of any effort at creating a more participatory government is one of the many ironies of the constitutional debate. It suggests that neither 'Aman Allah Khan nor his supporters had much of an idea about what constitutional government really meant or how it functioned. Even Tarzi showed little interest in any substantive reform of the Executive and wholeheartedly endorsed the country's autocratic monarchical system.

In the end 'Aman Allah Khan and his supporters had only themselves to blame for their failure. Tragically, instead of ushering in an era of progress and modernization, 'Aman Allah Khan's reign ended with the whole idea of reform being stymied and stigmatized and the administrations that succeeded him found it that much more difficult to implement change. Even today in Afghanistan the terms 'reform' and 'progress' have negative connotations of violent revolution, social upheaval, secularization and Westernization. As for gender issues such as female education, women's right to work and the *parda* system, these remain ideological minefields to this day.

Despite the collapse of 'Aman Allah Khan's attempted cultural revolution, a number of the reforms he introduced have survived. *Afghan* remains the sole official designation of nationality; the afghani is still the official currency and the *jerib* the standard measure of land. The Loya Jirga has been perpetuated and has become increasingly intertwined with myths about its roots in an ancient form of Pushtu tribal democracy. Thursday is still the official weekly half-day holiday for civil servants and all Afghans carry identity cards. 'Aman Allah Khan's tricolour flag survived, with modifications, until the fall of President Da'ud in 1978 and was rehabilitated in 2001 by President Karzai.

What is worrying about 'Aman Allah Khan's legacy is that many urbanized Afghan intellectuals, particularly Muhammadzais, continue to look back wistfully to his reign as a Golden Age that was ruined by the forces of religious fanaticism and ideological obscurantism – an anticlerical rhetoric that itself is derived from the polemic of Mahmud Tarzi. This rose-tinted vision of a 'land of lost content' prevents an objective critique of the flaws in Tarzi's nationalism and 'Aman Allah Khan's vision of reform and modernization.[63] As Ashraf Ghani perceptively wrote before his election as President of Afghanistan, 'Both ['Aman Allah Khan's] reforms and his failures have set the pattern for successive generations of Afghan modernizers, who have returned again and again to his unfinished project, only to succumb to their own blind spots and collapse in their own ways.'[64]

Unfortunately, harking back to this 'unfinished project' has become very much the theme of 'modernizers' since 2001 who, like the Young Afghans, feel they too face the forces of Islamic obscurantism. Exiles and refugees who have returned to the country, many of whom belonged to the pre-1978 Establishment under King Zahir Shah or are descendants of these officials, have done their best to turn the clock back to an era of presumed progress and democracy, which existed only in their imagination and that of their parents. Indeed, President Ghani himself is guilty of falling into the same trap. Very few have a coherent plan for the future development of Afghanistan other than continued reliance on foreign subsidies. Ironically, it is radical Islamist groups such as the Taliban that have a far clearer idea about Afghanistan's direction, even though their vision too is equally idealized and backward-looking.

ELEVEN

Backs to the Future, 1929–33

You cannot build a nation . . . any more than you can build a house by starting at the top. Amanullah tried to change the minds of people by changing their hats. He failed. I am working from the foundation. The painstaking, difficult tasks involved . . . take as much time as sending the structure into the sky.

KING NADIR SHAH[1]

T HE FLIGHT OF 'AMAN ALLAH KHAN and the defeat of Ghulam Nabi Charkhi still left Habib Allah Kalakani's government facing a variety of military challenges. Nadir Khan and his brothers were in Khost, while the Shinwaris in Nangahar still refused to submit despite their defeat, and the Safis of Tagab, aided by the Ghilzais of Laghman, briefly occupied Sarobi. Then, after 'Abd al-Rahim took Herat, ostensibly in the name of Habib Allah Kalakani, he refused to recite Habib Allah's name in the *khutba* and had it read in the name of the 'King of Afghanistan'.

The reign of Amir Habib Allah II (Bacha-yi Saqau)

In Kandahar, while supporters of 'Aman Allah Khan squabbled over who would succeed him, Ahmad 'Ali Khan Lodi, the ex-governor of Charikar, secretly contacted General Purdil Khan, commander of the Kalakanid army, and it was probably due to his intrigue that the city elders agreed to surrender, on condition the town was not plundered. On 1 June 1929, Purdil Khan marched into Kandahar unopposed and the heads of the Durrani clans pledged their allegiance to Amir Habib Allah II. The amnesty, however, did not include 'Aman Allah Khan's family or other high officials in his government. Loynab 'Ali Ahmad Khan and his two sons were hunted down. The elder son was put to death on the spot, as for 'Ali Ahmad and his other son, along with princes Hayat Allah Khan and 'Abd al-Majid Khan, Ahmad 'Ali Lodi and Maulana 'Abd al-Wasi', they were sent in chains to Kabul, where they were paraded semi-naked through the bazaar. Ahmad 'Ali Lodi was eventually released but Loynab 'Ali Ahmad Khan, 'Abd al-Wasi' and Qazi 'Abd al-Shukur were sentenced to be blown from a cannon. 'Ali Ahmad died bravely, kissing the muzzle of the gun before he was tied down and blown away. A maidservant retrieved his severed head and he was given a proper burial. Three days later Hayat Allah Khan, 'Abd al-Majid Khan and several other Muhammadzais were executed by firing squad.

In Kabul itself, anarchy prevailed, with Habib Allah Kalakani's followers raping, pillaging and murdering at will and torturing those they suspected of concealing their wealth. Schoolteachers were arrested and beaten for having taught non-Islamic subjects, all girls' schools were closed and female pupils forcibly married to Habib Allah Kalakani's henchmen. Habib Allah also revoked all treaties with foreign powers. There was little semblance of government; revenues dried up and inflation was so out of control that metal for coinage ran out, so Habib Allah resorted to leather money instead. The Islamists who had supported the rebellion rescinded 'Aman Allah Khan's reforms, took control of the justice system and set up an Islamic Regulatory Commission to oversee the implementation of Islamic law. In late April 1929 this body issued a *fatwa* condemning Shi'as and Isma'ilis as unbelievers, a decree that led to the persecution of Kabul's Hazara and Qizilbash communities and the massacre of the Shi'a inhabitants of Khushi in the Logar.

Despite the lack of anything resembling proper governance, Habib Allah Kalakani clung on to power for nine months. This was due partly to the fragmented nature of the opposition but also because the regime received direct or indirect support from the Pushtun tribes, an embarrassing fact that has been glossed over, particularly in Afghan official histories, which tend to portray the interregnum of Bacha-yi Saqau as a purely Tajik phenomenon. This, however, was not the case. The revolt in Kohistan had been encouraged by Nur al-Mashayekh, the Hazrat of Shor Bazaar, who commanded the religious loyalty of the Sulaiman Khel and other Ghilzai tribes and it had been the Taraki and other Ghilzai tribes around Ghazni that defeated 'Aman Allah Khan and forced him to flee the country. In Kandahar, the Durranis cut a deal with the new regime and stood aside as 'Aman Allah Khan's sons and senior government officials were hunted down and executed. In southeastern Afghanistan, the defection of the Khogiyanis led to the defeat of Loynab 'Ali Ahmad; subsequently even the Shinwari and Mohmand rebels accepted Kalakani's suzerainty and fought against Sardar Muhammad Hashim Khan. In the west the mainly Pushtun garrison of Herat executed 'Aman Allah Khan's governor and

Panjshiris and Koh Damanis at a local *buzkashi* competition. Habib Allah Kalakani
is still a folk hero for many of these people and Bacha-yi Saqau's army mostly comprised
of levies from this region.

opened the city gates to 'Abd al-Rahim Safi, while the majority of Balkh's
Pushtun colonists failed to support Ghulam Nabi Charkhi's attempt to oust
the usurper. Habib Allah Kalakani also received support from the Jabbar
Khel, while the tribes of Khost showed little enthusiasm initially for Nadir
Khan's campaign. Only the Safis of Tagab and the tribes of Wardak, Maidan
Shah and Ghazni offered any resistance.

The main opposition to Habib Allah Kalakani came from the Hazaras
and the Isma'ilis of Sayyid Nadir Khan of Kayan, the Aga Khan's representative. Despite several attempts to suppress the revolt, Hazara resistance
continued until the autumn of 1929 and at one point they threatened to take
Kabul. Habib Allah Kalakani even forced the leaders of Kabul's Qizilbash and
Hazara community, which included the historian Faiz Muhammad Katib,
to travel to Behsud to persuade the rebels to submit.[2] When their mission
ended in failure and the envoys returned to Kabul, they were bastinadoed
and imprisoned, treatment which probably contributed to Katib's death two
years later. The government then cynically used the *fatwa* condemning Shi'as
and Isma'ilis as *kafir*s to encourage the Sulaiman Khel to conduct a *jihad*
against the Hazaras, holding out the prospect of plunder, land and pasturage
rights. The threat of an attack by the Sulaiman Khel forced the Hazaras to
submit, but a month later they again rose in revolt and so tied down forces
that otherwise would have been deployed against Shah Wali Khan.

Throughout the spring of 1929 Nadir Khan struggled to raise more than a token force, for he had very little money and many tribal heads suspected that he planned to restore 'Aman Allah Khan to the throne. In late May Nadir Khan's fortunes appeared to have improved when the governor of Gardez, who had been appointed by 'Aman Allah Khan, declared for the Musahiban brothers, and a few weeks later Shah Wali Khan defeated a government army sent to retake the town. However, when the Jabbar Khel joined forces with the Kalakani army Nadir Khan evacuated Gardez and fled back to Jaji territory. For a while, he contemplated abandoning the whole enterprise and returning to India, but unexpectedly the situation shifted back in his favour with the defection of Nur al-Mashayekh, the Hazrat of Shor Bazaar.

The Mujadidi networks of Kohistan had supported Habib Allah Kalakani in order to dispose of the hated 'Aman Allah Khan and the Tarzis, but once Kabul was in their hands they began to cast about for a suitable Muhammadzai to place on the throne. Nadir Khan was an obvious choice and envoys from Nur al-Mashayekh visited him while he was in Peshawar, ostensibly to persuade him to join the Kalakanid government, but in secret the *pir*'s representatives urged Nadir Khan to declare himself Amir. Nadir Khan rejected the offer, nor was he prepared to announce his candidacy for the Amirship, so Nur al-Mashayekh turned to Sardar 'Omar Khan, son of Sardar 'Ayub Khan. In January 1929 Sardar 'Omar Khan eluded British surveillance and was smuggled across the border into Shinwari territory. Not much is known about 'Omar Khan's proceedings in Nangahar or whether he played any part in the Shinwari uprising, but he seems to have found little support for his cause. In June he returned to India, only to be arrested and exiled to Burma along with all remaining members of 'Ayub Khan and Ya'qub Khan's family.

At the end of May 1929 the British authorities allowed Nur al-Mashayekh to return to Afghanistan, but instead of heading for Kabul he made his base in Katawaz, not far from Nadir Khan's camp in Khost. Following Nadir's occupation of Gardez, Nur al-Mashayekh had a series of secret meetings with the *sardar*, which Shah Wali Khan later claimed were another effort to persuade the Musahiban brothers to join Habib Allah Kalakani. In fact, Nur al-Mashayekh urged Nadir Khan to distance himself from the Serajids and declare his willingness to be Amir. In return, the Hazrat promised he would secure the oath of allegiance from the Suleiman Khel. Some kind of secret arrangement was made, for in mid-June 1929 Nur al-Mashayekh issued a *fatwa* condemning Habib Allah Kalakani's regime for its violation of human rights. A few weeks later the Mujadidi *pir*s of Kabul and Kohistan called on Habib Allah to abdicate and transfer power to Nadir Khan.

Nur al-Mashayekh's *fatwa* was doubtless issued on the assumption that, since Gardez was in Nadir Khan's hands, the fall of Kabul was just a matter of time, so Nadir Khan's subsequent defeat and flight undermined the plan. Nadir Khan's relations with the Sulaiman Khel also suffered a blow when General Muhammad Siddiq, who commanded the Kalakanid army sent against Gardez, was wounded and was given asylum by 'Asmat Allah Khan of the Jabbar Khel. Nadir Khan demanded the rebel be handed over, but the Jabbar Khel chief refused. This led to an exchange of insults and an armed clash in which 'Asmat Allah Khan was captured. Nadir Khan then had further setbacks with the defeat of Shah Mahmud and Muhammad Gul Khan Mohmand at Shewaki and the failure of Muhammad Hashim Khan to persuade the Shinwaris in Nangahar to join his campaign.

As winter was approaching, Nadir Khan decided to risk one last attempt to take Kabul and sent envoys into northern Waziristan to recruit more tribal levies, ignoring British protests and threats to bomb his camp.

Shewaki, in the lower Logar valley, scene of the battle between Habib Allah Kalakani and Shah Mahmud Khan. The area is also famous for its Buddhist heritage, in particular a series of three tower-like structures, possibly way markers for pilgrims. The 37-m-high Minar-i Chakari shown here was the only one still standing in 1977. It too fell down, or was blown up, during the Taliban era.

Thousands of Waziris answered the call and it was these tribesmen, technically citizens of India, who tipped the military balance in Nadir Khan's favour. In late September Shah Wali Khan marched over the Shutur Gardan pass, skirted around Gardez and overran Khushi in the upper Logar. Two days later he defeated the garrison at Tang-i Waghjan and occupied Zargun Shahr, where he was joined by Muhammad Gul Khan Mohmand. Early on the morning of 5 October the combined force attacked the strategic post at the entrance to the Waghjan gorge and the defenders fled in disarray after a hard-fought battle. The following day Shah Wali Khan occupied Chahar Asiyab, where he split his force: Muhammad Gul Khan Mohmand was sent down the Logar to attack Hashmat Khan, while Shah Wali Khan marched on Chahardeh and Indaki to confront Habib Allah Kalakani's main army. On 8 October Shah Wali Khan and Muhammad Gul Khan Mohmand mounted simultaneous attacks on southeastern and southwestern Kabul. After a battle that raged all day, Shah Wali Khan secured the heights of Tepe Zamburak and Koh-i 'Asmayi. When Shah Wali Khan heard that reinforcements were on their way, he decided to risk a night assault and at ten o'clock on the evening of 9 October the Waziris, accompanied by the beat of drum, swarmed down the Koh-i 'Asmayi and overwhelmed the sleeping defenders. Three days later Shah Wali Khan defeated and killed General Purdil Khan at Shahr Ara.

Habib Allah Kalakani and his closest associates sought refuge behind the walls of the Dilkusha Palace and despite Nadir Khan's family being held prisoner in the palace, he ordered Shah Wali Khan to open fire with his artillery. In the bombardment that followed the main magazine exploded and started a serious fire, whereupon Habib Allah Kalakani sent his personal spiritual adviser under a white flag to negotiate safe passage in exchange for the release of Nadir Khan's family. While the negotiations were in progress, however, Habib Allah and his associates fled to Jabal Saraj, taking with them the contents of the state treasury. When Shah Wali finally entered the Dilkusha Palace, he found all but one member of Nadir Khan's family had survived (his eldest daughter, Tahira, had died in captivity). The Waziris and other tribal levies then proceeded to plunder the capital, stripping the palaces, government buildings and even foreign embassies. Afghanistan's first museum, located in the Dilkusha Palace, was looted, as were the royal archives and library. Shah Wali did manage to save some rare manuscripts and the inscription from 'Aman Allah Khan's Independence Monument, but his intervention nearly cost him his life. When he tried to stop one Waziri from looting, the looter threw a knife at the *sardar*, but the blade failed to penetrate his thick winter *postin*.

King Nadir Shah and the founding of the Musahiban Dynasty

A few days later Nadir Khan arrived in Kabul, where cheering crowds lined his route to the Dilkusha Palace. On 16 October 1929 Shah Wali Khan and Muhammad Hashim Khan assembled a group of supporters in the Salam Khana, which is now located in the grounds of the Ministry of Foreign Affairs, and finally announced he was prepared to accept the throne if this was the wish of 'popular opinion'. Two of Amir 'Abd al-Rahman Khan's surviving sons, followed by the remaining delegates, then came forward and pledged allegiance to Nadir Khan, who thus became King Nadir Shah, founder of the Musahiban, or Nadirid, dynasty.

Much of the country, however, was still out of his control and Muhammad Ghaus and the Waziris were sent into the Koh Daman to subdue it and capture Habib Allah Kalakani and other fugitives. During this campaign the Waziris went on a killing and looting spree while the Shaikh 'Ali Hazaras, not to be outdone, attacked settlements in the Ghurband and Charikar. In order to prevent further destruction, local leaders came and submitted to Nadir Shah, who pardoned many of the religious leaders who had supported Habib Allah and even appointed some to government posts. In return for clemency, however, the leaders agreed to either hunt down Habib Allah Kalakani or persuade him and his associates to surrender.

How exactly Habib Allah fell into government hands is unclear. Habib Allah himself maintained he was betrayed, but other sources state he surrendered after Nadir Shah sent him a pledge, sealed on a Qur'an, that he would not be executed.[3] Nadir Shah, though, reneged on his promise and Habib Allah Kalakani, his brother Hamid Allah, General Sayyid Husain and nine other associates were sentenced to death. There are conflicting accounts of Habib Allah Kalakani's last hours, some of which are pure fiction.[4] Some claim he was stoned to death, others that he faced a firing squad. According to contemporary Afghan accounts, Nadir Shah handed the prisoners over to his Royal Guard, who first tortured them and then each tribesman fired a single bullet in turn into the condemned men. Their mangled corpses were then hung on gallows in Kabul's main *chauk*, where they were photographed and the pictures circulated as postcards.[5]

The brutal, extrajudicial nature of these executions was condemned by many religious figures as a violation of Islamic law, while some Pushtun leaders were disgusted that the king had broken both his oath and the Pushtun code of honour. The government did its best to justify the king's action and in a special issue of *Anis* the editor argued that, while Nadir Shah could forgive personal offences against his family, he had no power to pardon traitors or those who committed crimes against the state. The editorial also claimed the executions had been approved by the '*ulama*' and by petitions from tribal elders. In his own official statement, King Nadir Shah argued their deaths were in response to popular demand: 'I have been touched by your patriotism and religious zeal. You want to take revenge from those who have brought destruction for your nation. I therefore in accordance with your request hand over to you the twelve traitors.'[6] Shah Wali Khan too claimed the executions were carried out on 'the insistence of the people and the decision of the general assembly', even though no such institution existed at the time.[7]

Having executed the leaders of the Kohistan revolt, Nadir Shah still had to regain control of northern Afghanistan, which was controlled by the remnants of Habib Allah Kalakani's forces, *basmachi* leaders and local Uzbeks, who had taken advantage of the fall of 'Aman Allah Khan to resume raids into Soviet territory and to evict thousands of Pushtun settlers.[8] In April 1929 Fazail Maqsum, a Tajik *basmachi*, overran parts of southern Tajikistan and occupied Garm, though he was later soundly defeated by a Soviet counter-attack.[9] The resumption of *basmachi* raids led the Soviet authorities to encourage the formation of Communist cells inside Afghanistan in order to destabilize the country and eventually overthrow the monarchy.

Nadir Shah's defeat of Habib Allah Kalakani was therefore welcomed by the USSR, and it was the first nation to accord the Musahiban government diplomatic recognition. Nadir Shah then set out to suppress the *basmachi*s and reassert central authority over the *wilayat* of Balkh. Ibrahim Beg, a Laqai Uzbek *basmachi* commander from Ferghana, was of particular concern for he commanded a well-trained militia and had given shelter to Habib Allah Kalakani's commanders after the fall of Kabul. Initially Nadir Shah was unable to do much about the situation since his forces were occupied with mopping up operations in the Koh Daman and southern Afghanistan. In preparation for a campaign beyond the Hindu Kush, he ordered urgent repairs to the road between Bamiyan and Doshi and wrote to Ibrahim Beg ordering him to surrender. His letter, however, was ignored.

King Nadir Shah and the suppression of the *Basmachi* Movement

In the spring of 1930 Ibrahim Beg resumed attacks across the Amu Darya.[10] The Soviet authorities eventually lost patience and sent a motorized division of three hundred troops across the Amu Darya, which overran and destroyed the *basmachi* bases of Aq Tepa and 'Aliabad, but Ibrahim Beg himself evaded capture and withdrew south into the hill country. News of the Soviet incursion into Qataghan caused panic in Kabul and Nadir Shah forced 'Alim Beg, the exiled Khan of Bukhara, to write and order Ibrahim Beg to lay down his arms and come to Kabul. Ibrahim Beg did not bother to reply to the letter and instead declared the establishment of an independent Turkistanian state in Qataghan and Badakhshan. He then proceeded to occupy Darwaz, Rustaq, Yangi Qal'a, Hazar Bagh and Khanabad.

Ibrahim Beg's secession was a direct challenge to Durrani sovereignty and one that had to be addressed as a matter of urgency. Despite continuing unrest in the Koh Daman and Gardez, in December 1930 Nadir Shah sent Shah Mahmud and Muhammad Gul Khan Mohmand with an army of tribal levies to put down the revolt in Qataghan. Their campaign did not start well, for in their first encounter with Ibrahim Beg, at Banghi Qishlaq, a few hundred of his Uzbek militia virtually wiped out the Mohmands. Shah Mahmud withdrew to await reinforcements. Meanwhile, in order to undermine support for Ibrahim Beg, he allowed the Waziri and Mohmand *lashkars* to pillage and terrorize the settlements of southern Qataghan. The reign of terror that ensued so appalled religious leaders and government sympathizers that they petitioned the king to order a halt to the raids, but Nadir Shah ignored their pleas.

In February 1931 Shah Mahmud returned to the offensive and eventually pushed Ibrahim Beg out of the area. He withdrew to Aq Tepa where he was besieged, but when provisions and ammunition began to run out Ibrahim Beg fled across into Tajikistan. He was subsequently arrested by a Soviet border patrol and several months later was put on trial, condemned to death and executed by firing squad. Following the fall of Qataghan and Balkh, 'Abd al-Rahim Safi submitted to Nadir Shah in Herat and was allowed to remain as governor, at least for a while. A few months later Nadir Shah renewed the Soviet-Afghan Treaty and in March 1936 a commercial and friendship treaty further cemented relations with Moscow.

The administration of King Nadir Shah

In order to reduce the potential for further rebellions, Nadir Shah reorganized sub-national government into a complex system of authorities designed to divide and rule. Seven major provinces, or *wilayat*s, were created centred around Afghanistan's main urban centres with their governors (*walis*) answerable directly to the Minister of the Interior. Seven additional, minor provinces, or *hukumat-i a'la*, were established, which in turn were subdivided into smaller administrative units. Urban centres with more than 10,000 residents elected their own *ra'is*, or mayor, and town councillors, but the governor had the last word when it came to these appointments. Each provincial centre also had a military head, who commanded a large garrison of front-line troops. Most of these new provincial officials and military commanders were southern Pushtuns; local people were only employed in the lower grades of the civil service.

When it came to organizing a new administration, Nadir Shah appointed his brother, Muhammad Hashim, as prime minster, while Shah Mahmud became commander-in-chief of the army and Minister of Defence. Shah Wali Khan, who had a far better claim to command the army, was marginalized and sent to London as ambassador, while Nadir's eldest brother, Muhammad 'Aziz Khan, was packed off to Moscow and later Berlin. Since the national army had virtually ceased to exist, the king initially relied on tribal levies, mostly Waziris, Mangals and Mohmands, who were then merged into a new national army. Nadir Shah did away with the traditional one-in-eight system of conscription and required every adult male to do national service for two years, although among Pushtuns it was left to the *khan*s and *jirga*s to select the cadets due for conscription, rather than government officials. The government also encouraged voluntary enlistment, and improved pay and conditions of service. In 1933 Nadir Shah opened a new military college for secondary students. Several officers were also sent to Germany and France for military training. With the help of Britain, Germany and Russia the army was re-equipped and within the space of just three years the Afghan army numbered between 40,000 and 70,000 men, with a core fighting force of 12,000, mostly Pushtuns, though there were also two Hazara regiments. Nadir Shah also established Afghanistan's first modern police force.

The distribution of army ranks and civilian positions among the king's Pushtun tribal supporters led to an influx of new and often semi-literate officials with little military training and who were ignorant of Afghanistan's bureaucratic system. The swath of new appointments caused resentment among the older generation of government servants and many found themselves out of a job. These appointments also changed the ethnolinguistic balance, particularly within the military, for most of the new recruits and their officers spoke Pushtu as their mother tongue and had little or no working knowledge of Persian. In areas where Pushtu was not spoken, some officials resorted to employing translators in order to communicate with the local populace.

Another priority for the new dynasty was to distance itself from the radical and unpopular reforms of 'Aman Allah Khan's reign. To do this

Nadir Shah adopted a far more cautious approach to change and emphasized the government's Islamic and Pushtun credentials. Nur al-Mashayekh
Fazl 'Omar, the Hazrat of Shor Bazaar, became Minister of Justice and
during the three years of his tenure he transformed Afghanistan's legal and
social order to create an Islamic state in all but name. When he retired, his
son-in-law succeeded him and continued the Islamization programme.
During the era that the Hazrat and his family were in power, many *mullah*s
and Mujadidi *pir*s became actively involved in Afghanistan's political life,
where they acted as a brake on legal, social and educational reform.

The Islamizing Constitution of 1931

In his first public statement, Nadir Shah announced that he intended
Afghanistan to be 'a progressive state' but that it would adhere staunchly to
Islamic doctrines.[11] A month after taking office he issued a ten-point policy
statement that endorsed the revisions to the 1924 Constitution. In October
1931 a new Constitution formalized Nur al-Mashayekh's Islamization project
by declaring 'Hanafi Sunnism' as the foundation of the state's legal system
and the faith of 'the population in general'. A council of religious specialists,
known as the Jam'iyat-i 'Ulama'-yi Afghanistan, was established to ensure
all legislation conformed to the Islamic law, *shari'a* courts became the basis
of the justice system and all judges were required to adjudicate solely on
the basis of Islamic jurisprudence. Nur al-Mashayekh also established the
Ihtisab, a department within the Ministry of Justice that enforced Islamic
morality and religious practices. This was backed up by an ideological
police, the al-'Amr bi'l-Mar'uf.[12] This was the first time in Afghanistan's
history that such a body had been deployed as an arm of the state.

It became compulsory for women to be veiled in any public space. All
adult women had to be accompanied by a *mahram*, or close male relative,
when they left the family compound, although the al-'Amr bi'l-Mar'uf
instilled such fear that few women ventured out. A few foreign women
married to Afghans defied the *parda* laws, but they and their husbands
faced harassment and persistent offenders risked being dismissed from
their posts and even imprisonment. There was strict press censorship and
the women's newspaper founded by Queen Soraya was banned, as were
all publications deemed to be against Islam. Foreign publications were
only permitted provided they did not contain material 'against religion
and the policy of the Afghan government'. Freedom of movement was
restricted with the reintroduction of identity cards, a Soviet-style internal
passport system, while social interaction between Afghans and foreigners

was actively discouraged. The government also arrested many leading reformers and supporters of the Seraj dynasty, who spent decades under house arrest or in jail.

Education, too, was hard hit. The 1931 Constitution made primary education compulsory up to year 6, but this effectively applied only to boys, for girls were only permitted to attend *madrasa*s, and then only until puberty. The Darul Uloom at Deoband rewrote the primary curriculum, which meant primary schools taught an almost exclusively Islamiyat curriculum based on the *Panj Ganj*, a fourteenth-century didactic text.[13] Every school and teacher was legally required not to infringe the articles of the Islamic faith and substantial state funding was earmarked for new provincial *madrasa*s. Private educational institutions were outlawed and foreign teachers restricted to teaching a limited range of subjects. Women were banned from studying abroad and those already in foreign countries were ordered to return, even if they had not completed their course of study. If any woman showed signs of reluctance to return home, threats were made against family members in Afghanistan.

The German 'Amani School was renamed Nejat College, while the French 'Amaniyya Lycée was renamed the Lycée Istiqlal.[14] Habibiyya College, however, retained its original name. These secondary institutions continued to teach elementary geography, maths, history and science, and the government opened a number of vocational institutions. However, the focus on Islamiyat at primary level meant that the new intake of secondary students were utterly unprepared for higher education. The al-'Amr bi'l-Mar'uf and internal security also kept a close watch on the colleges to ensure 'Western' influences did not undermine Islamic values and because they were suspected, rightly, of being breeding grounds for political dissent.

In February 1933 two addenda to the Constitution prohibited Afghan women from marrying foreigners; those already married to non-Muslims lost both their citizenship and all rights to property, land and inheritance. Foreign widows who had married Afghans could only resume their former nationality and return to their place of birth on condition they satisfied the religious authorities that they would not apostatize. Foreigners were forbidden from purchasing or owning land, though this provision was ignored when it came to Pushtuns from the Indian side of the Durand Line who had assisted the Musahiban's bid for the throne. They were gifted land in Balkh and other areas of northern and southeastern Afghanistan.

Despite the heavy restrictions on education, in 1932 the government opened the country's first medical school, which later became Kabul University, but it remained a male-only institution for many years and

Islamic taboos meant medical students could not dissect cadavers. The establishment of the first women's hospital posed even greater logistical and theological problems, for Afghanistan had only one semi-qualified woman doctor, yet male doctors were forbidden to see, let alone examine, female patients. The following year a French couple started a nursing and midwifery school, which covertly functioned as a girls' school, but it was more than a decade before this institution was officially recognized as the Lycée Malalai.

One of the main intents of the 1931 Constitution was to give legitimacy to the Musahiban dynasty: Article 5 stated that 'the Afghan nation in general' recognized Nadir Shah as 'a fit and worthy king' and continued with a rambling justification of why the 'crown of Afghanistan' should be 'transferred to the family of this king'. The Constitution established a National Assembly, the Majlis-i Shura-yi Milli, which consisted of 105 members all selected by, and from, the membership of the Loya Jirga. An Upper House, the Majlis-i Ayan, was composed of 44 'intelligent and farseeing' individuals, all handpicked by the king. Government ministers and the president of the National Assembly could hold sessions in camera, form secret committees and pass legislation without the consent of the full House. Furthermore, any law passed by the National Assembly 'must not contradict the true faith of Islam and the policy of the kingdom', and the king and/or the Council of 'Ulama' had the right to veto any of the Assembly's legislation. Nadir Shah referred to both Lower and Upper Houses as consultative, not legislative bodies, and they were essentially toothless institutions designed to rubberstamp legislation preapproved by the king and his brothers.

Despite the Loya Jirga having no basis in Islamic law, this assembly, which had been instituted during the reign of 'Aman Allah Khan, was retained. Under the Musahiban dynasty, however, it became an exclusively Pushtun club for government-appointed *khan*s and religious elites. The Loya Jirga appointed the National Assembly from among its own constituents and it could veto any measures passed by the Lower and the Upper House, an arrangement that provided another means whereby the Executive could circumvent any attempt by the Legislature to curtail its powers.

While the 1931 Constitution created a veneer of democracy, its intention was to reinforce the absolute powers of the king and the supremacy of Islamic law. Since many of its clauses were contradictory and could be overridden by the Council of 'Ulama' on the grounds that they were inconsistent with Islamic law, the result was an uncomfortable and ultimately unworkable duality that was perpetuated in all subsequent constitutions. Many of the provisions were honoured in the breach, especially those Articles that related to personal freedom and civil liberties. What the Constitution did do was to recast Afghanistan's national values in a Deobandi mould, a 're-sacralisation' of the state that Nadir Shah and his brothers considered an acceptable price to pay for holding on to power.[15] What this meant in practice was that the 1931 Constitution formalized an Islamization programme unprecedented in Afghanistan's history until the era of the Taliban.

'Abd al-Majid Zabuli and the centralization of the economy

When it came to the issue of reform and modernization, Nadir Shah and his successors trod carefully and concentrated on upgrading the nation's infrastructure, which was far less controversial than social or legal reforms. There were improvements in telecommunications and the postal service, new roads fit for motor vehicles and a number of large-scale irrigation and hydroelectric dams were inaugurated. One of the many issues Nadir Shah had to face was the government's empty coffers and an economy that was in tatters. He appointed 'Abd al-Majid Zabuli as Minister for National Economy to address this crisis. Zabuli, a Taraki Ghilzai, was one of the richest merchants in the country who had inherited his family's Tashkent-based import–export business. After his father's death he moved his base to Moscow, where he developed close ties with high Soviet officials. Then in 1929 he shifted operations to Berlin, where he married the daughter of a German policeman. A few months later Nadir Shah invited Zabuli to come to Kabul and draw up plans to address the country's chronic fiscal crisis.[16]

Zabuli drew up a Seven Year Plan modelled on Lenin's New Economic Policy, which placed Soviet-style state monopolistic capitalism at the heart of national economic recovery, shifting the raising of revenues from traditional taxes on land and agricultural yields to state control of, and duties on, imports, exports and other major commodities. The outcome was that over the ensuing years the state became one vast corporation that controlled all major assets and commodities. To implement what was tantamount to nationalization by the back door, Zabuli established a branch of his business empire in Kabul, the Shirkat-i Sahami-yi Afghan, usually referred to by its plural form Shirkat-i Ashami, and private individuals were offered the opportunity to invest in dozens of state-controlled *shirkat*s, or joint stock companies. In 1932 Zabuli convinced Nur al-Mashayekh to legitimize the creation of a joint stock bank, the Bank-i Milli, which paid dividends on profits, rather than charging interest on loans, since usury is forbidden under Islamic law. The bank was essentially the Shirkat-i Ashami under another name, for Zabuli was both president and its main share-holder, though the government contributed just under half of the initial capital. Zabuli then appointed senior members of the dynasty as directors. The Musahiban brothers and other Muhammadzais, as well as wealthy Afghans, reaped immense profits from their investment that were as high as 500 per cent. Many senior officials stationed abroad spent more time pursuing their personal commercial interests than performing state duties, and the line between personal and national interest became so blurred that for many officials they were two sides of the same coin.

Zabuli's fiscal policies more than tripled state revenues and, since ministers and other government officials benefited substantially from the *shirkat*s, he was given almost unlimited authority over Afghanistan's economic and fiscal affairs. The Bank-i Milli eventually controlled more than fifty state monopolies including the lucrative *karakul*, or lambskin, trade, sugar, raisins, dried fruit, rice, cotton, wool, petrol, motor vehicles and cement. Before the creation of the Da Afghanistan Bank in 1938, the Bank-i Milli also functioned as the Reserve Bank, controlling financial markets, exchange rates, foreign currency and bullion trading, and the issue of treasury drafts. Since Zabuli was also Minister of Commerce, he

Currency dealers, Herat. In Afghanistan such transactions have always been conducted through the informal *hawala* system rather than banks. Zabuli's monetary and fiscal reforms were designed to undermine this system and to exert state control over exchange rates and foreign currency dealings.

made sure that it was almost impossible for any private independent entre-
preneur to trade and merchants seeking to retain their independence faced
a Kafkaesque bureaucratic process that deterred all but the most determined. Those who persisted in trading in competition with the *shirkat*s
risked accusations of smuggling, tax evasion or even anti-government
activities. Most traders gave up the unequal struggle and either subscribed
to a *shirkat* or went out of business.

Despite Dupree praising Zabuli's 'pioneering free enterprise system'
and his 'laissez-faire economy',[17] his economic policies were the antithesis
of a free market economy and were more akin to Soviet state monopolies. They encouraged price fixing, corruption and tax evasion as well
as smuggling and a flourishing black market. The *shirkat*s concentrated
most of the nation's wealth in the hands of the ruling elite and contributed significantly to widening the already vast gap between rich and poor.
Furthermore, Zabuli's policies eventually led to a self-inflicted economic
crisis. When the bottom fell out of the international *karakul* market due
to the Great Depression, the Bank-i Milli was forced to restrict the issue
of foreign exchange, with the result that the afghani fell heavily against
the Indian rupee.

Afghanistan's Hindu, Sikh and Jewish communities were hardest hit by
the *shirkat* system, for non-Muslims were forbidden to have any share in
the joint stock companies. Historically these religious minorities had been
the backbone of the country's commercial activity, a situation that Zabuli
regarded as intolerable. Indeed, Zabuli openly stated that the *shirkat*s were
intended to 'cut off the hands of the foreigners'. Afghanistan's indigenous
Jewish community, as well as the substantial refugee Bukharan Jewish
community, who had been the main traders in *karakul*, were particularly hard hit. To add to their misery, during the 1930s Nazi Aryanism
and anti-Semitism was increasingly popular among the ruling elite of
Afghanistan. In 1933 the government accused Bukharan Jewish émigré
merchants of being fifth columnists for Moscow and Nadir Shah ordered
all Jews to relocate south of the Hindu Kush. Two years later, following
anti-Semitic riots in Herat, most of the Bukharan and indigenous Jews fled
to Kabul. Eventually all but a handful of this historic Jewish community
left for Palestine.[18]

One of the few traders wealthy enough to remain semi-independent
was 'Abd al-'Aziz Hamidi, known as Londoni, due to a visit he made to the
British capital during the reign of King 'Aman Allah Khan. 'Abd al-'Aziz's
family were originally from Kashmir, where his father had traded in
animal pelts and sheepskin *postin*s. However, while in London 'Abd al-'Aziz

realized there was a European market for *karakul* and he made a fortune exporting these lambskins. After the Bank-i Milli took over the *karakul* trade, 'Abd al-'Aziz began exporting cotton to the USSR and encouraged farmers in Qataghan and Balkh to expand the area under cotton cultivation, advancing them seed, fertilizer and farming equipment on credit. He was supported in this enterprise by the governor of Qataghan, Sher Khan Bandar, a Kharoti Ghilzai whose forebears had settled in Khanabad. In order to expand the area under cash crops, Zabuli persuaded the government to sell him large tracts of marshland around Qunduz at rock-bottom prices, which he and Sher Khan sold on, or gifted, to Durrani and Kharoti nomads from southern Afghanistan as well as Turkman refugees from Soviet Central Asia. They then drained the land and planted cotton, rice, vines and fruit trees. Within two decades Qunduz's malarial marshlands, which had been the haunt of wild boar and the now-extinct Oxus tiger, were transformed into the most productive agricultural regions of Afghanistan. Sher Khan later founded the Spinzar Cotton Company; in honour of his achievements Qizil Qal'a, the ford across the Amu Darya on the Panj river, was renamed Sher Khan Bandar.

Londoni realized his survival depended on cooperating with government enterprises and he undertook a number of joint ventures with the Bank-i Milli, constructing ginning mills, soap factories and extraction plants for cotton seed oil. However, while the local population saw little benefit from the Bank-i Milli's vast profits, 'Abd al-'Aziz made sure farmers were paid well above market prices for their produce and operated a highly effective credit scheme. He also built rural clinics, dug wells for potable water and improved sanitation. Londoni's immense efforts eventually wore him out and he died in 1938 at the early age of 55. After his death, the government nationalized the cotton trade and all the light industries he had set up.

The Musahiban dynasty and Anglo-Afghan relations

Another major challenge the Musahiban government faced was repairing the relationship with Britain, which had been badly damaged by 'Aman Allah Khan's declaration of independence and the Third Anglo-Afghan War. British officials welcomed the change of government, but they were uncertain as to what policy Nadir Shah would adopt towards India and the tribes. Nadir Shah, after all, had led the invasion of Waziristan and the attack on Thal during the Third Anglo-Afghan War. Then in 1929 he had ignored British protests and recruited Waziris from the India side of the frontier for his campaign against Habib Allah Kalakani. Once in power, Nadir Shah failed to expel Indian nationalists such as Allah Nawaz Khan, leader of the Indian Revolutionary Party, and even appointed him as an aide-de-camp.

At the same time the good relations with Britain were facilitated by Nadir Shah and Shah Wali Khan's long-standing friendship with Humphrys, Fraser-Tytler and other British diplomats who had served in the Legation in Kabul. As descendants of the Peshawar *sardar*s, the Musahiban brothers also had a historic connection with Peshawar and the Punjab and all five brothers had been brought up and educated in India. This background led the new dynasty to look to India rather than Turkey as its model for modernity and reform, and at the opening of the medical school in 1933 the guests of honour included Sir Muhammad Iqbal and Sir Syed Ross Masood, Vice Chancellor of Aligarh University. Iqbal subsequently visited Ghazni and wrote a Persian poem in which he declared:

Asia is a body of water and clay,
Of which the Afghan nation forms the heart.

As for Nadir Shah and his brothers, they were wary not to appear too close to the old enemy in case this antagonized the frontier tribes and

The British Legation building in Kabul's Kart-i Parwan, a mansion commissioned by Lord Curzon as a statement of British imperial power. In the winter of 1928/9 Legation staff found themselves on the front line and were evacuated by the RAF. In 1994 it was handed over to the Pakistan government and the following year it was burnt and looted by supporters of Jami'at-i Islami. The building has recently been bought back by the British government.

King Nadir Shah's plaque in the Bala Hisar marking the place where Cavagnari and his guides were killed in 1879. Nadir Shah publicly distanced himself from Britain but behind the scenes Anglo-Afghan relations were extremely cordial. Britain even covertly provided the Musahiban brothers with financial and military assistance.

provided further propaganda for the Serajids, who accused the Musahiban brothers of being British stooges. The Serajids had made much of the presence of aircraftsman T. E. Shaw, alias Lawrence of Arabia, in Quetta from 1926 to 1928 as 'proof' of a British conspiracy to overthrow 'Aman Allah Khan, although there is no evidence that Lawrence was involved in Afghan affairs. Nadir Shah repeatedly denied he had received any support from Britain for his campaign against Habib Allah Kalakani, though eventually he did admit to unspecified assistance, probably cash.

Shortly after Nadir Shah became king, the Viceroy sent him a congratulatory telegram expressing the hope for a renewal of 'the old friendly relations'. Full diplomatic recognition came a month later after Shah Wali Khan, who was on his way to London, verbally assured British officials in India that the new government had abandoned the aggressive, anti-British policies of 'Aman Allah Khan. However, as the Kabul Legation had been badly damaged in the fighting and required extensive repairs, the new Minister, Sir Richard Maconachie, who had been Humphrys's deputy during the 'Aman Allah era, did not return to Kabul until the following spring.

Shah Wali Khan's assurances about Frontier policy were timely as far as Britain was concerned, for in 1930 the Indian government faced the worst tribal uprising for thirty years, instigated by Fazl Wahid, the Hajji Sahib of Turangzai.[19] The Hajji Sahib, a Deobani-trained *pir* and disciple of the Hadda Mullah, had already spent several years in jail for anti-British agitation. Following his release he took refuge among the Mohmands on the Afghan side of the Frontier. From 1926 Hajji Sahib put pressure on the *malik*s of the 'assured tribes' – that is, those in receipt of British subsidies – not to accept British rupees any longer and any clan that refused this 'request' risked being raided by Hajji Sahib's *mujahidin* and their *malik*s and *khan*s assassinated. The British responded by increasing the subsidies of loyal clans, bombing rebel settlements and imprisoning Hajji Sahib's relatives and supporters. Fazl Wahid retaliated by attacking British outposts in the Khyber Pass and extended the revolt into the Tochi valley, Khurram and Waziristan.

In November 1929 a relative and associate of Hajji Sahib, Khan 'Abd al-Ghaffar Khan, or Bacha Khan, an Utmanzai Pushtun from the Peshawar region, formed a non-cooperation movement, the Khudai Khidmatgar, Servants of God, more commonly known as the Red Shirts after the colour of its followers' *pehran*s. 'Abd al-Ghaffar Khan had been educated in the Church Missionary Society (CMS) school in Peshawar. In 1920 he joined the Khilafat Movement and participated in the *Hijra* to Afghanistan, for which he was sentenced to three years hard labour. Inspired by Rev. Edmund Wigram, head of the CMS Mission in Peshawar, who had instilled in him the importance of education, 'Abd al-Ghaffar Khan established hundreds of schools throughout the Frontier and was a leading light in the promotion of Pushtu literature and Pushtun national identity. Among the institutions he founded were the Anjuman-i Islah-i Afghan (the Society for the Reform of Afghans, 1928), the Pukhtun Jirga (1927), aimed specifically at young Pushtuns, and *Pukhtu* (1928), a monthly political journal funded by the Pushtun diaspora in California. Indeed, 'Abd al-Ghaffar's contribution to education, Pushtu literature and Pushtun self-determination was far more significant and long lasting than that of Tarzi and his Young Afghan clique in Kabul.

The Khudai Khitmatgar was a left-wing socialist movement that British propaganda claimed was Bolshevik-inspired, but the movement's philosophical roots were in Pushtun identity and an Islamic version of Mahatma Gandhi's satyagraha, or pro-active, non-violent protest. Politically, 'Abd al-Ghaffar was at odds with the All India Muslim League's demand for a separate Muslim state and supported Gandhi's plan for a unified, secular India. After Partition, which Bacha Khan opposed, he demanded the establishment of an independent Pukhtunistan, a stance that led to him spending many years in a Pakistani jail, a period under house arrest and eight years of exile in Nangahar.

During the winter of 1929 'Abd al-Ghaffar established Khudai Khidmatgar committees throughout the Northwest Frontier and in April 1930 he held a mass meeting in his home village ostensibly to celebrate the anniversary of his Azad ('Freedom') School system. However, during the event the schoolchildren staged a drama that the British declared was seditious and 'Abd al-Ghaffar was arrested. When security forces moved into the Qissa Khwani bazaar in the old city of Peshawar to detain other leaders of the movement, they were confronted by thousands of angry protestors. The Deputy Commissioner tried to restore order but was knocked unconscious by a stone. A dispatch rider was lynched in the melee and an armoured car tried to recover his body by driving into the crowd, killing or injuring several protestors and inflaming the mob even more. Eventually the commander of the paramilitary force ordered his men to open fire, which led to the deaths of dozens more demonstrators. The troops were eventually forced to withdraw and negotiations took place, but it was almost a month before the authorities regained control over the Old City.

A few weeks after the Qissa Khwani Massacre, several thousand Afridis besieged the Peshawar Cantonment, but were driven off by artillery fire and RAF planes. In mid-August 1930 martial law was proclaimed throughout the Peshawar District and reinforcements shipped in. The government then sent troops, tanks and heavy artillery into the Khyber and Mohmand Agency and forced the Afridis and Mohmands to sue for peace. The Hajji Sahib of Turangzai, however, remained defiant until his death in 1937.

Despite personal appeals from tribal leaders to support the rebellion, Nadir Shah remained neutral and even denied fleeing Afridis entry to Afghanistan, a policy that won him the respect of British officials. Relations improved even further when the Afghan Foreign Ministry reaffirmed the government's acceptance of the Anglo-Afghan Treaty of 1923 and the subsequent Trade Agreement. Privately, Nadir Shah assured Maconachie that his government did not intend to intervene in Frontier affairs, although he did point out that it would be necessary on occasion to dissimulate in order to appease tribal sentiment. Afghanistan's neutrality soon brought substantial dividends. In the summer of 1930 the government, faced with revolts in the Koh Daman, Qataghan and Khost, asked Britain for a loan and weapons and was gifted 10,000 rifles and £200,000. Over the ensuing years, Britain clandestinely shipped more munitions to Kabul to help the government suppress a series of revolts.

King Nadir Shah's bilateral relations

Nadir Shah's relations with Turkey were distant and strained as the new government sought to distance itself from Tarzi's Turcophile policies. All Turkish military trainers and advisers were sent home, despite complaints from Ankara that this was in breach of the Turco-Afghan Treaty. It was not until the summer of 1930 that Turkey finally agreed to restore diplomatic relations with Afghanistan. Iran-Afghan relations remained cordial but the dispute over the Sistan frontier and riparian rights to the waters of the lower Helmand rumbled on. The biggest concern for the Afghan government, however, was the fear that Iranian nationalism might lead to rebellions among the Persianate population of Herat and western Afghanistan as well as among Afghanistan's Shi'a minority. France continued to dominate the cultural section and Nadir Shah, who regarded France as the intellectual and scientific centre of Europe, sent his son and heir Muhammad Zahir Shah to Paris for his education. Other Muhammadzais followed suit, though some preferred Germany or the USA. Italy played a minor role in Afghanistan after 1930, but the government did permit the Vatican to establish a Catholic chaplaincy inside the Italian embassy to serve the foreign community's spiritual needs.

By 1929 Germany was Afghanistan's third most important foreign stakeholder and the country's largest creditor, for the government had loaned 'Aman Allah Khan 8 million marks. The new administration had no means of paying this loan back within the agreed six-year term, so the government successfully negotiated a two-year extension. Initially, however, Afghan-German relations were complicated by a dispute over the Deutsch-Afghanische Company (DACOM), the company that had been set up to handle Germany's trade and aid to Afghanistan. DACOM had run into financial difficulties after 'Aman Allah Khan's officials insisted the value of German exports had to equal Germany's imports of Afghan goods, an impracticable demand given Afghanistan had little of value in terms of export that DACOM could sell on. After the fall of 'Aman Allah Khan, Habib Allah Kalakani had cancelled the DACOM contract, imprisoned its Afghan staff and seized all its stock, so when Nadir Shah came to power the German government refused to normalize relations with Afghanistan until the issue of compensation was settled. Nadir Shah retaliated by refusing to renew the contracts of German technicians, but eventually both sides realized they were cutting off their noses to spite their faces and in 1931 diplomatic relations were restored. By this time DACOM had gone bankrupt.

Nadir Shah and the Charkhi family

Another major cause of tension between the Musahiban dynasty and Germany was the presence of anti-government agitators in Berlin led by Ghulam Nabi Charkhi and his three brothers, Ghulam Jailani, 'Abd al-Aziz and Ghulam Siddiq, who were related by marriage to both 'Aman Allah Khan and Mahmud Tarzi. The brothers were living abroad at the time of the fall of 'Aman Allah Khan, and following Ghulam Nabi's defeat at Kotal-i Rabatak, the Charkhis sent a substantial amount of money to assist Nadir Khan's campaign, after they received assurances that Nadir Khan would restore 'Aman Allah Khan to the throne.[20] When Nadir Shah reneged on this promise the Charkhi brothers accused the Musahiban brothers of usurping the throne and embarked on a sustained propaganda campaign against the dynasty.

Nadir Shah's response was to try to lure the Charkhis to Kabul, where he could dispose of these troublesome enemies. Ghulam Jailani Khan eventually returned home and remained out of the public eye, but Ghulam Nabi and Ghulam Siddiq continued their campaign against Nadir Shah. In the summer of 1930 they met with 'Aman Allah Khan and Mahmud Tarzi in Ankara and Ghulam Nabi subsequently published an open letter to Nadir Shah demanding a plebiscite to determine who should rule Afghanistan.[21] Nadir Shah responded by stripping the Tarzis of their Afghan citizenship and renewed his efforts to lure the two remaining brothers to come to Kabul.

Nadir Shah eventually convinced Ghulam Jailani that he was genuine in his desire for a reconciliation. Jailani agreed to travel to Berlin accompanied by Shah Wali Khan, who took with him a personal letter from Nadir Shah and a pledge of safe conduct sealed on the Qur'an. Shah Wali even offered to seal the reconciliation with a marriage alliance between the two families and hinted that the reason why Nadir Shah was summoning them to Kabul was because he wanted to discuss a transfer of power to 'Aman Allah Khan.[22] It was probably the possibility of abdication that persuaded Ghulam Nabi to trust Shah Wali's promises and return home. He arrived in Kabul in October 1932 and his first meeting with Nadir Shah, witnessed by the foreign diplomatic corps, was a tense affair.[23] In the private meetings that followed it soon became evident that Nadir Shah had no intention of abdicating. Instead he demanded that Ghulam Nabi renounce his family's oath of allegiance to 'Aman Allah Khan and in return he promised him safe passage to Ankara, on condition he never returned to Afghanistan. As for Ghulam Jailani and Ghulam Siddiq, they would be appointed as ambassadors to Japan and Germany respectively. If the brothers refused to submit, however, they would have to face the consequences.

Ghulam Nabi was given a week to consider the ultimatum, but early on the morning of 8 November 1932 soldiers from the Royal Guard arrived at the family home and ordered the two brothers to attend the king immediately.[24] When they arrived, Nadir Shah angrily produced documents that he claimed proved Ghulam Nabi was behind a recent revolt in Gardez. Ghulam Nabi denied the accusation and heaped insults on the king, whereupon Nadir Khan ordered his bodyguard to club him to death with their rifle butts. Following his execution more than a hundred members of the extended Charkhi family and their retainers were thrown into jail. The king subsequently tried to give a veneer of legitimacy to this extrajudicial killing by presenting written evidence of Ghulam Nabi's alleged treason to three separate judicial bodies. Not unexpectedly, all of them found Ghulam Nabi guilty and endorsed the king's actions.

The execution of Ghulam Nabi sparked a blood feud between the Musahiban and Charkhi families that was perpetuated by Ghulam Siddiq, who had stayed behind in Berlin. In June 1933 Nadir Shah's half-brother Muhammad 'Aziz Khan, who was the Afghan ambassador in Germany, was shot dead by Sayyid Kemal, an engineering student and former pupil of Nejat High School. When he was interrogated by the Gestapo, Sayyid Kemal claimed he had acted in order to restore 'Aman Allah Khan to the throne, while the government in Kabul accused Ghulam Siddiq Charkhi of being behind the assassination. In retaliation Ghulam Jailani Charkhi, Sher Muhammad Khan Charkhi and several former ministers of 'Aman Allah Khan were executed.

'Aziz Khan's assassination strained Afghanistan's relations with Germany. The Afghan government complained that Germany had failed to protect its diplomats and was angered when Germany refused to extradite Sayyid Kemal or put him on trial. The problem was that since the crime had taken place inside the Afghan embassy, Germany had no legal jurisdiction. Eventually, in the interests of German-Afghan relations, a court sentenced Sayyid Kemal to death and he was executed in January 1935. Three months after 'Aziz Khan's assassination, Muhammad 'Azim, a teacher at Nejat High School, entered the British Legation in Kabul on 6 September 1933 and shot dead three staff members. When interrogated, Muhammad 'Azim confessed he had planned to assassinate the British Minister in the hope that Britain would depose Nadir Shah and return 'Aman Allah Khan to power.

The Musahiban Dynasty and Pushtun nationalism

The assassination of Muhammad 'Aziz Khan took place only a few months after Hitler became Chancellor of Germany. Initially his government supported the reinstatement of 'Aman Allah Khan, but 'Abd al-Majid Zabuli, who led the influential pro-German faction at court, which included 'Aziz Khan's two sons, Muhammad Da'ud and Muhammad Na'im, actively promoted closer ties with the Third Reich. Sympathy with Hitler's Germany and National Socialism ran deep within the ruling elite, due in part to the government's active promotion of Pushtun nationalism, which was increasingly conflated with ideas of racial and cultural superiority and Aryanism. One reason for the adoption of this more hard-edged version of Tarzi's *Afghaniyya* was an attempt by the Musahiban to appeal to its primary support base, the Pushtun tribes of the Afghan–Indian frontier.

One of the foremost advocates of this state-sponsored ethno-nationalism in the first decades of Musahiban rule was Wazir Muhammad Gul Khan Mohmand.[25] Despite his aristocratic Mohmand ancestry, Gul Khan was brought up in an urban, Persian-speaking milieu and only began to learn Pushtu when a student at Kabul's Military Academy, where it was a compulsory subject. Subsequently he was sent to Turkey for military training where he fell under the influence of the ethnocentric nationalism of the Young Turks. During the reign of Amir 'Aman Allah Khan, Gul Khan Mohmand became a founder member of the Pushtu Maraka, the Pushtu Society, and following the Amir's fall he played a major role in Nadir Khan's campaign against Habib Allah Kalakani, conducting military operations in Nangahar and the Logar and publishing a Pushtu broadsheet, *Da Kor Gham*, which promoted the Musahiban cause.

After Nadir Shah became king, Muhammad Gul Khan Mohmand was appointed as Minister of the Interior and Ra'is-i Tanzim, or Minister Plenipotentiary, and was entrusted with the task of bringing the country back under central authority, which he did with ruthless efficiency. He also used his position of influence to promote the state's romanticized and idealized vision of Pushtun identity. In 1932 Gul Khan Mohmand merged all of Kandahar's literary societies into a single, state-funded body, Da Pakhtu 'Adabi Anjuman, whose president was appointed by the governor of Kandahar. Five years later he incorporated this, and all other Pushtu literary societies, into the state-run Pushtu Tolana, or Pushtu Academy, which was an arm of the Ministry of Higher Education, in effect nationalizing the Pushtu literary revival and co-opting it to serve dynastic ends. Under Gul Mohmand's influence, the Pushtu Academy began to purge Pushtu of its substantial Arabic, Persian and Turkic elements, creating in the process a vocabulary that was unintelligible to most native Pushtun speakers. Later Gul Mohmand published a Pushtu dictionary and grammar as well as a small corpus of Pushtun poetry.

Muhammad Gul Khan Mohmand's Pushtunism was profoundly political and, as Caron notes, 'successfully translated the monarchy's case into a social vocabulary of masculine Pashtun [*sic*] chivalry . . . for the benefit of tribes which had always viewed the hierarchy of the state's ruling elites with suspicion'.[26] This chauvinistic romanticism was epitomized in his poem 'On Pushtu and Pushtunness', in which Gul Khan declared: 'Pushtu is essential/true nobility . . . Pushtu is salvation . . . Pushtu is dignity (or majesty) . . . Pushtu is honour . . . in Pushtu there is no dishonour or degradation . . . Pushtu is being noble and free-born, Pushtu is lordship'.[27] According to 'Abd al-Ra'uf Benawa, a founder member of the Pushtun Academy, Muhammad Gul Khan Mohmand ended the era of *gul wa bulbul*, rose and nightingale, which were the traditional themes of Persian and Pushtu poetry, while Siddiq Allah Rikhtin, a former president of the Academy, declared:

> Muhammad Gul Khan Momand [*sic*] brought about political Pashtu. His work was far more substantial than ours. He was the shadow over our heads. If he had not had so much force, we would not have been able to do so much work . . . His Pashtu was loftier than ours.[28]

In 1936 the government took this version of Pushtun nationalism to its illogical conclusion and decreed Pushtu henceforth to be the only official language of Afghanistan. The outcome was chaos. Pushtu street signs were unintelligible and very few schoolteachers spoke or read Pushtu; even when they did, students did not understand them, nor could they read the textbooks. Civil servants, threatened with dismissal, frantically tried to master the intricacies of Pushtu grammar. Even Nadir Shah, his brothers and their children had to take Pushtu lessons, for very few of the Musahibans spoke, let alone read, the language.[29] The policy was eventually abandoned as unworkable and Persian was reinstated as one of two equal national languages, but the government persisted in its promotion of its version of Pushtun identity.

Ordinary Pushtuns, who the government sought to co-opt to its agenda, were not fooled by this attempt to manipulate their identity, nor did they need a government to tell them about what it meant to be a Pushtun. This state-sponsored Pushtunism was essentially the creation of urban, Persianized intellectuals who did not speak Pushtu as their mother tongue. It bore only a superficial resemblance to the culture and values of rural Pushtuns, the *maldar*, or the Frontier tribes. In Nangahar, bards composed satirical *landai*, or epigrams, and ballads mocking the monarchy's attempt to ingratiate itself with Pushtuns, lambasting it for failing to uphold the very Pushtun virtues it claimed to espouse.

The assassination of King Nadir Shah

By 1933 the government had established a degree of stability and had secured control over most of the country, only for the reign of Nadir Shah to come to an abrupt end. On 8 November 1933, the first anniversary of the death of Ghulam Nabi Charkhi, the king held an award ceremony for Nejat students in the grounds of the Dilkusha Palace.[30] During the ceremony 'Abd al-Khaliq, a seventeen-year-old Hazara and the son of a trusted retainer of Ghulam Nabi Charkhi, stepped forward and calmly shot the king three times at point-blank range, killing him almost instantly. Despite being tortured, 'Abd al-Khaliq refused to implicate the Charkhis or anyone else, claiming he had acted solely to avenge the death of his patron. A week

King Nadir Shah's mausoleum on Kabul's Tepe Maranjan. This stark square structure shows a marked influence of the public architecture of Nazi Germany. Badly damaged in the infighting of 1993–5 (as shown), after 2002 it was restored. King Zahir Shah and his wife are also buried here.

later the Charkhi family and 'Abd al-Khaliq's relatives were forced to watch as the assassin was dismembered limb by limb by the Royal Guard. In all more than twenty persons were executed in a variety of novel ways. They included members of the Charkhi family, the principal and deputy principal of Nejat High School and several of 'Abd al-Khaliq's schoolfriends, most of whom had no idea what he was planning.[31] In addition, hundreds of suspected Serajid sympathizers were rounded up.

Nadir Shah's reign ended as it had started, with bloody extrajudicial executions. Yet despite this, Fraser-Tytler, without the slightest hint of irony, describes Nadir Shah's reign as 'a wellnigh perfect form of benevolent autocracy', while another British obituarist went as far as to claim Nadir Shah was 'the greatest ruler who had ever reigned over Afghanistan'.[32]

TWELVE

A House Divided, 1933–73

We cannot all be masters, nor all masters
Cannot be truly follow'd.

WILLIAM SHAKESPEARE, *Othello*, Act I, scene i

He who plays with lions must expect to be mauled.

ARAB PROVERB

S INCE NADIR SHAH'S ELDEST SON had died prematurely, he was succeeded by his younger son Muhammad Zahir, a shy, introverted nineteen-year-old with very little experience of government. Prime Minister Hashim Khan therefore became regent and for the next two decades ruled as king in all but name. Hashim Khan's style of government was even more autocratic than that of Nadir Shah, while Hashim Khan himself was so paranoid about assassination that he only left his house during daylight hours accompanied by a large guard. As for Zahir Shah, he spent most of the next two decades pursuing personal amusements, helping the Qizilbash artist 'Ali Muhammad Chindawali paint miniatures on the palace ceilings, playing tennis, hunting or watching *buzkashi*. As for his official appearances, these were mostly ceremonial and usually brief.[1]

Publicly the transition of power was relatively smooth, but Nadir Shah's death exacerbated a split within the two branches of the Musahiban family. Muhammad 'Aziz Khan's sons, Muhammad Da'ud and Muhammad Na'im, were both ambitious, frustrated by Hashim Khan's alliance with conservative Islamists and the lack of progress in reform and modernization. In an attempt to neutralize the threat posed by these two brothers, Nadir Shah had contracted a double marriage alliance between Da'ud and Na'im and two of his daughters. Fortunately for Zahir Shah, when his father was assassinated Da'ud was in Jalalabad, where he commanded the eastern army, and Na'im was Afghan ambassador in Rome. Nadir's younger brother Shah Wali Khan, whom many believed was the best candidate to succeed to the throne, was in France. Later, in 1935, Hashim Khan recalled Shah Wali Khan and appointed him Minister of Defence in an attempt to offset Da'ud's popularity with the military, but he and Da'ud quickly fell out and Shah Wali was sent back to France.

Hashim Khan set out to widen Afghanistan's relations with other nations. In 1934 Afghanistan joined the League of Nations and the United States formally established diplomatic relations, though initially the Afghan desk was the responsibility of the Tehran embassy. It was not until after the United States entered the Second World War that the State Department opened a Legation in Kabul in 1942. However, in 1938, with war in Europe again threatening, the American Inland Exploration Company (AIEC) became interested in Afghanistan's natural resources, particularly oil, and secured an exclusive 75-year concession to exploit the country's mineral reserves. AIEC sent a survey team into northeastern Afghanistan, which led to protests by the USSR to the Afghan government, but the survey concluded that the lack of accessibility and infrastructure made any oil or mineral extraction unprofitable and the company surrendered its concession.[2] Afghan officials, brought up in the belief instilled by Amir 'Abd al-Rahman Khan that their country had vast mineral wealth, were angered by AIEC's withdrawal, which helped foster a lack of confidence that American companies would fulfil their contractual obligations.

Afghan-German and Anglo-Afghan relations and the Second World War

Under the regency of Hashim Khan, Afghan relations with Germany became ever closer, with Zabuli urging closer ties with the Third Reich. Zabuli even went as far as to provide intelligence to the German embassy in Kabul. Hashim Khan renewed the Afghan-German alliance, secured new loans to purchase German military equipment and German technical aid to Afghanistan increased substantially. In 1935 a German mission travelled to Nuristan, ostensibly to gather botanical, linguistic and anthropological data as it was believed the Nuristanis were Aryans.[3] The following year Afghanistan sent a team to the Olympic Games in Berlin, which were attended by King Zahir Shah, Hashim Khan, Zabuli and other senior government officials. During their visit, the king, Zabuli and other senior officials had a personal audience with Chancellor Hitler and his inner circle, and during the opening ceremony all the Afghan Olympians gave the Nazi salute.[4] The outcome of this visit was a German loan of 15 million Reichsmark as well as additional commercial, educational and political agreements. In 1937 Deutsche Lufthansa began weekly flights to Kabul and in July 1939, under the Todt Agreement, an Inspector General was sent to Kabul to oversee all German projects and personnel as well as to advise the government. By the time the Second World War broke out, around three hundred German nationals were working in Afghanistan, including Abwehr agents and members of the Nazi Party.

It was only when the threat of war with Germany loomed that British officials woke up to the potential threat posed by Germany's growing influence in Afghanistan and the possibility that Germany and Italy might covertly encourage the revolt of the Hajji Mirza 'Ali, known as the Fakir of Ipi.[5] This uprising had begun in 1936 when the Fakir, a spiritual affiliate of the Hazrat of Chaharbagh, declared *jihad* against British military encroachments in Waziristan. Britain sent substantial reinforcements into the region but was unable to suppress the revolt. Hajji Mirza survived numerous attempts to kill him in RAF bombing raids, which led the British press to refer to the Fakir as the Scarlet Pimpernel of Waziristan. As far as the Fakir's followers were concerned, however, his escapes were a sign of his miraculous powers.

In 1938 the revolt was complicated by the arrival of Muhammad Sa'adi al-Jailani, known as the Shami Pir, in Southern Waziristan. Sa'adi was a Syrian from Damascus, a distant relative of Sayyid Hasan Gailani and the first cousin of Mahmud Tarzi's daughter, Queen Soraya. When Shami Pir announced he intended to march on Kabul, depose the Musahiban family and restore 'Aman Allah Khan to the throne, thousands of Waziris and Masuds flocked to his banner. He then set out for Khost, where he hoped the Sulaiman Khel, who had rebelled against the Afghan government's attempt to extract customs duties, would join him. RAF planes were sent to bomb the army and dispersed the force with heavy losses before the Shami Pir could cross the Durand Line. Sir George Cunningham then offered Jailani £25,000 to return to Syria, which he accepted and so Britain had 'a narrow escape from a disaster of the first magnitude'.[6]

The British were convinced that Germany was behind the Shami Pir's campaign, while the government in Kabul blamed Ghulam Siddiq Charkhi. There was evidence to justify both suspicions. Al-Jailani, after all, was related to both the Tarzis and 'Aman Allah Khan by marriage and had been educated in Germany, where he married a German woman. British intelligence in Damascus also reported the *pir* met regularly with Abwehr agents. More than likely the revolt was the brainchild of Werner Otto von Hentig, Germany's most effective Middle Eastern operator and the man who led Germany's first mission to Afghanistan.

British fears that Germany was involved in the Frontier uprisings led to a new diplomatic initiative aimed at drawing the Afghan government closer to British interests. In October 1938 Sir Aubrey Metcalfe, India's Foreign Secretary, flew to Kabul to discuss Frontier issues and to seek assurances from the government that it would not support the Fakir of Ipi's revolt. In return, Britain offered limited military aid and made a number of concessions on freight charges for Afghan exports in transit. Hashim Khan was grateful for the swift action by the RAF to disperse the Shami Pir's levies and Metcalfe's visit was instrumental in Hashim Khan's decision to remain neutral when war finally broke out in September 1939.

Despite Afghanistan's declared neutrality, Zabuli, backed by Da'ud and Na'im, continued to promote German interests and urged Afghanistan to join the war on Germany's side. In spring 1941 Zabuli paid a semi-private visit to Berlin where he met with Hitler and von Hentig and told the German Chancellor that he was prepared to depose King Zahir Shah and Hashim Khan and declare war on British India. In return, Zabuli asked for German planes, tanks and anti-aircraft guns so he could push the Afghan frontier to the Indus and occupy Karachi. Zabuli also asked Hitler to use his influence with the Soviet Union, which at the time was an ally of Germany, to secure undertakings that the USSR would respect Afghanistan's northern frontier.

In Kabul, German and Italian diplomats covertly supported the Fakir of Ipi and tried to persuade him to extend his revolt to other parts of the frontier. In the summer of 1941 Italian agents secretly crossed the border and met with the Fakir. A few weeks later two Germans, ostensibly conducting scientific research, were intercepted by an Afghan patrol near Charkh in the Logar. In the altercation that followed, one German was shot dead and the other badly wounded. When the patrol searched their baggage they found *lakh*s of afghanis and rupees, gold, machine guns and letters addressed to the Fakir of Ipi and other anti-British tribal leaders. Britain demanded the Afghans expel all Axis nationals and diplomats, a demand that Hashim Khan did not take lightly, for a few months earlier British forces had occupied neutral Iraq and deposed its government. British and Soviet forces, now allies following Germany's unexpected attack on Russia, had subsequently also occupied southern and northern Iran respectively. Both invasions were motivated by a need to secure vital oil supplies, but publicly the action was justified on the grounds that the Iraqi and Iranian governments had refused to expel Axis personnel. Refusal to comply with the British demand therefore raised the prospect that Afghanistan too was at risk of being occupied by British and Soviet forces.

Prime Minister Hashim Khan was caught between a rock and a hard place. He dared not risk the accusation of capitulating to Britain or Russia, yet at the same time failure to comply meant Afghanistan's territorial integrity was once more under threat from the surrounding superpowers. In an attempt to address the problem, Hashim Khan convened an emergency Loya Jirga, which was opened by King Zahir Shah dressed, inappropriately, in full German military uniform. The king and senior ministers then defended the government's policy of neutrality, but Nur al-Mashayekh, in a fiery speech, recalled Afghanistan's resistance to British domination and declared that expelling foreign residents and handing them over to Britain was both contrary to the *shari'a* and the Pushtun tradition of *nanawatai*. 'We will fight it', he declared and ended his peroration with the cry of *Allah hu-Akbar*, God is Great, a chant taken up by the whole assembly.[7] Many other anti-British speeches followed, but in the end the delegates voted to expel all non-diplomatic Axis aliens on condition Britain gave a formal pledge of safe conduct back to their home countries. However, in accordance with international law regarding neutral countries, the government refused to expel the German, Italian and Japanese ambassadors. Fearing that the USSR and Britain might invade anyway, the Loya Jirga approved compulsory conscription and a special war tax. German and Italian diplomatic staff therefore remained in Kabul and continued their intrigue with the Fakir of Ipi, but attempts to extend his revolt failed miserably. The Fakir happily took all the cash and weapons the Germans and Italians offered, but made only a few token forays against British outposts.

Following the German retreat from Moscow in the winter of 1941/2, the power and influence of the German lobby at court waned. It was further undermined when German officials in Kabul, in an attempt to tie down Soviet forces in Central Asia, tried to revive the *basmachi* militias, using agents of the ex-Amir of Bukhara. Germany recruited dozens of local agents on both sides of the Amu Darya and *basmachi amirs* reactivated their militias in northern Afghanistan. Matters came to a head in April 1943 after Britain handed the Afghan and Soviet governments a list of known German agents operating in Afghan and Russian Turkistan. The Afghan government responded by placing the ex-Amir of Bukhara and his son-in-law under house arrest and imprisoning dozens of Turkistani exiles. This action, however, did not sit well with Nur al-Mashayekh and other influential religious leaders. Akhundzada Miyan Gul of Tagab even publicly denounced the detention of the Bukharan royal family from the pulpit of the Pul-i Kheshti mosque.[8] Britain renewed its demand for the expulsion of all Axis diplomats and this time refused to back down, so Hashim

Khan called in the German ambassador and presented him with detailed evidence of his country's complicity in the Turkistan uprising. When he admitted his country's involvement, he was ordered to leave and close the embassy; in August 1943 all German, Italian and Japanese diplomats quit the country and did not return until after the Second World War ended.

Afghanistan may have remained neutral in the Second World War but during the 1930s and '40s the ideology of Germany's National Socialism was regarded with sympathy by many in government. The belief in the Aryan origins of the Pushtuns became embedded in the state's nationalist discourse. Among the many claims made by the Pushtun Academy was the assertion that the Zoroastrian *Avesta* and the Hindu *Vedas* were masterpieces of 'Pushtu' literature,[9] while Nazi anti-Semitism fuelled racial prejudice against those of Jewish descent, which eventually led to the expulsion of most of Afghanistan's Jewish population. The mythic claim that Pushtuns were part of the Aryan master race also had devastating consequences in northern Afghanistan during the era that Wazir Muhammad Gul Khan Mohmand was Minister of Interior and the military governor of Balkh.

Muhammad Gul Khan Mohmand's Turkistan policy

Gul Khan Mohmand, as we have seen, was one of the leading promoters of the state-sponsored Pushtunism. His family had also been deeply involved in the Durrani occupation of the *wilayat* of Balkh for three generations. His grandfather, 'Abd al-Karim Mohmand, took part in Muhammad Akram Khan's original invasion of Balkh in 1849, while his father had been commander of the Star Fort at Dehdadi. Muhammad Gul Khan Mohmand's involvement with the *wilayat* began in the reign of Amir 'Aman Allah Khan when he was appointed governor of Balkh and after his father died he succeeded him as commander of the Star Fort. Gul Khan Mohmand also shared Nadir Khan's anxiety about the possible repercussions of Amir 'Aman Allah Shah's policy of support for the *basmachi*s and their promotion of Turkistanian nationalism.

In 1931, following the suppression of Ibrahim Beg's nascent independence movement in Qataghan, Gul Mohmand made his base in Balkh where he oversaw the pacification of the region, imprisoning or executing *basmachi* leaders, supporters of Habib Allah Kalakani and local nationalists. In an attempt to break the secessionist movement once and for all, Gul Khan Mohmand forcibly relocated indigenous communities as well as Turkman and Uzbek refugees from Central Asia to the Helmand,

Maimana looking south showing the standard grid pattern and wide streets typical
of the rebuild of Afghanistan's northern urban centres in the 1940s.

Arghandab and Nangahar regions, confiscating their lands and property, which were sold off cheaply, or gifted, to a new wave of Pushtun
colonists from Nangahar, many of whom were members of Gul Khan's
Mohmand tribe.

From the mid-1930s Muhammad Gul Khan Mohmand inaugurated a
province-wide redevelopment of the main provincial towns, which aimed
at the eradication of emotive symbols of indigenous culture and making it
easier to control potentially rebellious populations. At the same time it was
a deliberate display of the state's power to intimidate and reduce potential
points of resistance. The key element of this project was the construction
of *shahr-i naus*, or new towns, based on a standard grid plan drawn up by
a German-Swiss architect.[10] The construction of the new towns, as one
eyewitness noted, involved 'tearing the heart out of a place and putting in
a concrete arcade of bazaar-shops instead'.[11] In the process, most of the
old medieval bazaars were levelled along with ancient city walls, citadels,
shrines, mosques, Sufi *khanaqas*, graveyards and other historic monuments, many of which had significant cultural and historical associations
with the era of Chinggisid rule.

In Mazar-i Sharif, an area of several hundred metres around the shrine
of Shah-i Mardan was completely levelled creating 'an area of desola-
tion',[12] while all of the Uzbek, Tajik and Hazara populations of Balkh,
the ancient capital of the region, were forcibly evicted and the new town

resettled mainly by Mohmands from Nangahar and the Kunar. A similar fate happened to other settlements such as Minglik, which had been one of the strategic fortresses guarding the ancient road from Aqcha to the Amu Darya. Many of the landmarks in the Balkh area, particularly those that had historic associations with Balkh's pre-Durrani history, were given Pushtu names. Government apologists justified these expulsions on the grounds that since Balkh was the *watan* of the Aryan race, it was only fitting that Pushtuns, as their direct descendants, should be the sole occupants of the Mother of all Cities.[13] Later, the government constructed a new surfaced highway between Mazar-i Sharif, Balkh and Aqcha; this ran several kilometres to the south of the ancient trade route, distancing these towns, spatially, from their ancient Islamic and pre-Islamic roots.

As a consequence of the redevelopment most of the urban centres of northern Afghanistan lost their character and charm and were replaced by vistas of concrete uniformity that were both bland and soulless. One of the few towns to escape this cultural vandalism was the abandoned settlement of Tashqurghan, which retained its covered bazaar until it was destroyed in the 1990s in a firefight between General Dostam and Hizb-i Islami.[14] The citadel of Andkhui also survived, along with two of its Timurid shrines.[15] To add insult to injury, items of value retrieved during the demolition were sold to the highest bidder or looted by high-ranking officials. At the heart of the *shahr-i naus* lay the provincial government offices, police posts, army barracks and even hotels. The wide, straight streets made policing easier, allowed for the swift movement of armoured vehicles and facilitated the control of traffic in and out of the towns. The destruction of old bazaars and many private houses forced residents and shopkeepers to rent state-owned units, which led to a substantial increase in provincial revenues. It also made taxing commercial activity easier.

The additional revenue was urgently needed, for the Second World War was an economic catastrophe for Afghanistan. Exports collapsed, particularly of the lucrative *karakul* lambskins, which led to a shortage of foreign exchange. In an attempt to secure more hard currency the government began exporting much of the country's wheat and agricultural produce, which led to internal shortages, hyperinflation and the flight of capital to India.[16] The defeat of Germany also meant the country lost one of its most important providers of financial, technical and military assistance, leaving many German-funded infrastructure projects half-finished.

The Kunar rebellion

In the winter of 1944/5 discontent led to a series of rebellions, the most serious of which was among the Safis and Mohmands of the Kunar.[17] The rebel leaders included General 'Abd al-Rahim, brother-in-law of Mustufi Mirza Husain Safi, and a son of Mir Zaman Khan Safi, known as Loya Khan, a title conferred on him by 'Aman Allah Khan.[18] The rebels appointed their own king and prime minister and in effect declared independence. In the end it took six months before the government managed to crush the Kunar revolt. When it was finally put down thousands of Safi families were exiled to the Hari Rud or the Sholgara district of Balkh. Most of the surviving members of Mir Zaman Khan and Mustufi Mirza Husain's family ended up spending years in prison, including the poet and historian Ustad Khalil Allah Khalili. He and his family were only saved from execution because King Zahir Shah, in a rare act of defiance, refused to sign their death warrants.

In the winter of the following year there was another rebellion, this time in the Hazarajat, sparked by the imposition of a tax on sheep fat, or *roghan-i zard*, the main cooking oil used in Afghanistan and a major source of income for the Hazaras. Led by Muhammad Ibrahim Beg, known as

The Sholgara valley, on the Balkh Ab, south of Balkh has such an abundance of water that rice and cotton are extensively cultivated. Following the Safi revolt of 1945, thousands of Pushtuns from the Kunar were forcibly relocated here. As the Sholgara valley lies upstream of the Hazhda Nahr canal network, which irrigates the Balkh plains, disputes over water rights are frequent.

Gau Sowar, or Cow Rider, a well-known Shi'a religious leader, the rebels briefly overran a provincial centre, killed government officials and looted the armoury. When the revolt was finally put down Ibrahim Beg was exiled to the remote district of Balkhab, but the government repealed the unpopular tax.[19]

The Premiership of Shah Mahmud Khan

In 1946 Hashim Khan, who was suffering from testicular or prostate cancer, stepped down and was succeeded as prime minister and regent by his younger brother, Shah Mahmud Khan. Shah Mahmud was more liberal in his views and his cabinet had a decidedly Leftist and Reformist leaning, with Sardar Da'ud as Minister of Defence and Sardar Na'im, his brother, appointed as ambassador to the United States of America. Shah Mahmud's Foreign Minister, 'Ali Muhammad, was a Tajik who had served under Amir 'Aman Allah Khan, while Zabuli retained his post as Minister of National Economy. Muhammad Gul Khan Mohmand lost his cabinet post, while Nur al-Mashayekh's stranglehold over the justice system was broken. Shah Wali Khan too returned to Kabul but in 1947, following a quarrel with Da'ud, he was sent as Afghan envoy to the newly created state of Pakistan. Two years later, Shah Wali was sent back to London.

U.S.-Afghanistan relations and the Helmand Valley Irrigation Scheme

Afghanistan's geopolitical situation became even more precarious after February 1947 when Britain announced it was to quit India and Lord Mountbatten made his subsequent declaration of Partition and the establishment of Pakistan. The British withdrawal caused great alarm in Kabul. For despite the government's anti-British rhetoric and the country twice being invaded by British forces, Britain had restrained Russian territorial ambitions for a century. Britain had also propped up the dynasty through subsidies and armaments, demarcated Afghanistan's international frontiers and provided the government with international legitimacy. British withdrawal from India would leave no adjacent regional European power capable of counteracting the threat to Afghanistan posed by the USSR.

Shah Mahmud's solution was to turn to the new Western superpower, the United States of America, but in so doing Afghanistan inadvertently became sucked into the Cold War. The Second World War had worked in Afghanistan's favour as far as relations with the USA were concerned. In

June 1941 an American diplomatic mission from Tehran visited Kabul and responded positively to requests for teachers, engineers and other technical experts to replace German nationals. In June the following year the State Department opened a Legation in Kabul and appointed Cornelius Engert, a Dutch-born American who was a specialist in the Middle East, as its first ambassador. Engert quickly won the gratitude of the Afghan government by arranging for the shipment to the USA of a large consignment of *karakul* and wool that had been held up in Karachi by the war.

In April 1946 Zabuli approached the State Department about the possibility of a loan of $100 million 'to finance a ten year programme of public works and to raise the standard of living', though the government planned to spend most of the money on rearming its military.[20] The loan was not forthcoming, but the following year Shah Mahmud Khan paid the first official visit of an Afghan premier to the USA and again requested financial assistance. Later in the same year Zabuli and Na'im held further discussions with State Department officials and requested military aid 'to maintain internal security' and to 'make a positive contribution in the event there is war with the Soviets'.[21]

The first American civil engineering project in Afghanistan, however, was implemented by a private company. During the reign of Amir Habib Allah Khan, the governor of Kandahar dreamed of reclaiming the 'Arachosian Corridor' in the lower Helmand, which prior to the ravages of the Mongols in the thirteenth century had been one of the most productive agricultural areas in the region. To achieve this end, the governor ordered the construction of a new intake on the Helmand river below Girishk, known as the Bogra Canal, which was designed to provide irrigation to the Musa Qal'a and Qal'a-yi Bost region.[22] In the 1930s German and Japanese engineers took over the Bogra scheme, but it was still incomplete by the outbreak of the Second World War. Zabuli was keen to revive the Helmand Valley plan, partly to increase cash cropping, but he also planned to use the new land to resettle Pushtun nomads. Since Afghanistan lacked the expertise and heavy equipment for such a major project, Zabuli turned to the California-based Morrison-Knudsen Inc. (MKI), one of the 'Six Companies' that had built the Hoover Dam. Despite MKI having no experience of working in underdeveloped countries, the company agreed to take on the task and set up a subsidiary, Morrison-Knudsen Afghanistan (MKA).

Neither Zabuli nor any Afghan minister understood the complexity of a scheme that even in a developed country would have presented major challenges. MKA did not undertake a feasibility or impact survey before signing the contract and they had virtually no knowledge of the region's hydrology or topography. From the outset the Helmand Valley Irrigation Scheme (HVIS) hit problems. MKA had to build new roads to carry the heavy equipment, construct accommodation for thousands of workers and import everything it needed from spanners to cement. The logistics were a nightmare, for all goods had to be shipped to Karachi, offloaded onto trains, transferred to Quetta, offloaded again, and trucked across the Afghan frontier.

The size of the proposed reclamation area was vast and the environment daunting. The Helmand river in its lower course runs through two inhospitable deserts, the Dasht-i Margo and the Registan, where summer temperatures exceeded 50°C (122°F). In the spring the notorious Bad-i Yak Sad-o Bist Roz, the Wind of 120 Days, blows at more than 100 km/h, whipping up sandstorms that clog irrigation ditches and strip off the thin top soil. The Helmand and Arghandab, the two rivers designated for major irrigation works, had huge variations in seasonal flow and volume. During the spring snow melt they were raging torrents that swept away control and diversion structures and canal banks, back scoured the beds of irrigation canals and deposited huge volumes of silt all down the network. Flooding and dramatic changes in the rivers' course were a regular occurrence. Yet by late summer, when crops needed water to mature, river levels could drop to a trickle, making it impossible to deliver water into the primary canals without weirs or water pumps. To add to the challenges facing MKA, by the 1940s most of the Helmand basin and Sistan was still uncharted territory.

The local population had no experience or understanding of the permanent, concrete and steel structures that MKA planned to introduce to control water flow and volume. Farmers had long ago adapted to the annual cycle of peaks and troughs, patiently repairing banks and control structures with compacted mud, stone and bricks: in Toynbee's words, 'in Afghanistan . . . Man's way of getting Nature to meet his needs has been to humour her, not to hit her over the head'.[23] Farmers inundated their fields during controlled rotations of water releases overseen by locally elected water bailiffs, or *mirabs*, and in accordance with arcane, unwritten rules. The *mirabs* were paid in kind by community stakeholders while disputes over water rights were settled by the *mirabs* and community councils, not by government officials, for the government did not legally own the water, let alone have any say in its management, once it left the main river.

MKA's scheme, on the other hand, was an attempt to beat nature into submission in the same manner as MKI had done with the Colorado river. MKA's plan was also multifaceted for it included not only the construction of in-canal concrete and steel structures, but control gates, storage

Spring cleaning on the Jui Nau canal, Herat. The maintenance of traditional irrigation systems lies with community water users under the supervision of locally elected *mirab*s. Major government irrigations schemes tended to undermine such community ownership and placed far greater power in the hands of government officials.

dams, highways, access roads and new settlements for colonists. As the scheme developed MKA also became involved in land reclamation and drainage schemes, seed distribution, tree planting, fertilizer distribution, model farms, training and capacity building for government officials, farmers and settlers, as well as cartographic, cadastral and hydrological surveys. MKA also constructed a huge, walled cantonment for dozens of its American employees.

Much of the area targeted for irrigation and reclamation was *dasht* – wasteland – and hence crown land. The government therefore saw the sale of reclaimed *dasht* and revenues from future cash crops as the means to recoup its investment. Furthermore, the scheme would allow the government to control not only the distribution of land and housing, but water allocation from the Helmand and Arghandab rivers into the primary canals by means of control gates and storage dams, for these structures were managed by government officials rather than local people. The state's intrusion into water management thus allowed the government, in the form of the Department of Irrigation, to influence the appointment of *mirab*s and potentially use the delivery of water as a weapon of political and social control. It also opened the door for corrupt practices, nepotism and profiteering. The HVIS and other major state-sponsored irrigation projects undertaken in Qunduz, Balkh and Nangahar therefore under-mined community self-management and self-reliance, leading to a far greater degree of central government control and interference.

Once MKA began to implement the programme on the ground it ran into complex, interrelated problems. Geological surveys of the area served by the Bogra Canal Extension revealed the soil was shallow with a high water table and poor drainage. The surveyors noted large saline deposits on the surface, which increased as the canal was constructed and the water table rose. MKA then discovered that the existing compacted mud diversion dam was incapable of delivering water to the tail of the network during low flow periods, so MKA decided to build bigger and better concrete struc-tures. As a consequence the costs of the Bogra scheme tripled, but this was just the beginning of MKA's woes. In an attempt to address increasing salinity, seepage, fluctuations in river level and seasonal inundations, MKA recommended the construction of two huge storage dams at Kajaki on the Helmand and Dahla on the Arghandab and proposed postponing all engineering works until a basin-wide impact survey had been completed. The estimate for these additional interventions was $63.7 million, of which $53.7 million was in foreign exchange.

By 1949 the Afghan government had paid MKA $21.3 million, yet after almost four years the Bogra Extension had still not come on line. By this time completion of the project had become a matter of national honour for the Afghan government, while the reputation of MKA and the USA too were on the line. Zabuli's personal and political credibility was at stake as the HVIS consumed most of Afghanistan's foreign exchange credits, yet the vision of Eden-in-Asia was no nearer realization. Since neither the Afghan government nor MKA dared to abandon the scheme, more and more money was poured into the project and Afghanistan became increasingly indebted.

The government approved MKA's recommendation for the storage dams but the company was told to prioritize completion of the Bogra system. In 1949 Zabuli requested a further loan of $55 million from the U.S. Export-Import Bank to cover the additional expenditure, but the bank approved only $21 million. Since this was less than half the funds needed, Zabuli scrapped the West Marja secondary canal and the geological and impact survey. MKA, feeling it was politically unacceptable to oppose the cuts, agreed, only for the downscaling to make matters worse. When water finally flowed down the Bogra network in the spring of 1950, seepage from the unlined beds led to a dramatic rise in the water table and salinity levels, which withered newly planted crops. Since the Bogra canal and diversion

Baluch tribesmen gather at the weekly market in Lashkari bazaar outside the modern town of Lashkargah and against a backdrop of ruined Ghaznavid palaces and fortifications. These ruins stretch for some 7 km (4.4 mi.) along the left bank of the Helmand river. The Helmand Valley Irrigation Scheme was inspired by a vision of rehabilitating this region which, prior to the Mongol conquest, had been a fertile oasis.

dam had been designed to carry water for two, not one, secondary canals, the scrapping of the Marja Extension led to overspilling, flooding and the degradation of in-canal structures.

As the problems mounted, Afghan officials and MKA engineers blamed each other for the cost blowout and lack of progress. Some officials even accused MKA of deliberately dragging out the scheme in order to make more and more profits. One particular bone of contention was MKA's cantonment at Lashkargah, where American employees enjoyed all the luxuries of Middle America, including air-conditioned villas, Hollywood movies, recreational facilities and cold beers. The fact that Americans were living in what for Afghans was the lap of luxury and at government expense, while outside the farmers barely made ends meet, angered both officials and local people.

While MKA struggled to fix the many complex technical issues, applications for land became bogged down in bureaucracy. Due to the reduced area of land irrigated, the government cut the acreage allocated to each settler to such a degree that the farms were no longer economically sustainable. Pushtun nomads who received grants of land had no experience of farming or water management and received only minimal training. Some *maldar* refused to sell their herds and their animals roamed freely across unfenced fields, consuming their own and their neighbours' crops. So bad did the situation become that many nomads abandoned their farms or sold them to speculators and reverted to their former way of life. There was a better success rate with the resettlement of Turkman and Uzbek refugees from Bukhara. Many of these refugees, particularly those from Ferghana, were accomplished agriculturalists and well acquainted with irrigation techniques. Even so only 15 per cent of the 10,500 acres irrigated by the Bogra canal ended up in the hands of ordinary farmers. The government took 2,000 acres for an 'experimental farm', MKA set up its own model farm and a further 6,000 acres ended up in the hands of Muhammadzais and other absentee Durrani landlords, many of whom already owned large estates in the Helmand and Arghandab.

The Dahla Dam was finally dedicated in late 1952 and the Kajaki Dam was closed off in the following spring. Their construction was a remarkable feat of engineering and MKA staff did an exceptional job under the most difficult of circumstances. However, the dams never operated as designed. Before any water was released, written authorization was needed from the Minister of Irrigation in Kabul, who in turn had to obtain the Prime Minister's signature. On numerous occasions when local officials and MKA engineers recommended water releases, Kabul denied them permission, which led to overtopping and massive, man-made floods. In the thirteen years from 1953 to 1966 the Kajaki Dam alone overtopped eleven times, turning vast areas of fertile lands into shallow lakes, drowning crops and animals, and flooding settlements. In one particularly bad year, the steel lock gates at Girishk were completely washed away.

Central government's reluctance to release the waters was due primarily to the fact that the Helmand Valley Scheme had exacerbated the long-standing dispute with Iran over riparian rights in the Helmand delta, the result of the British demarcation of the Sistan frontier in the late nineteenth century. Since then Afghan and Iranian frontier guards had often clashed and, despite Turkey's attempt at mediation, the dispute had never been resolved. Neither MKA nor the Afghan government had bothered to consult Iran before implementing the Helmand Valley scheme and Tehran strongly objected to the project since it threatened the livelihoods of its own agriculturalists. When in 1948 the crops on the Iranian side of the Sistan frontier failed, Tehran blamed Afghanistan for diverting water into the Bogra system. Tehran also protested at the construction of the Kajaki Dam.

In 1951, with the Helmand project bouncing from one crisis to another and costs burgeoning, Mahmud Khan asked the U.S. government to intervene. The State Department commissioned a survey by the Technical Assistance Group (TAG) that recommended the U.S. government assume financial responsibility for the scheme. The following year the Afghan government effectively nationalized the project by setting up the Helmand Valley Authority, later renamed the Helmand-Arghandab Valley Authority (HAVA). From this point the Helmand-Arghandab scheme was a government-to-government development project with TAG and its subsequent avatar, the United States Agency for International Development (USAID), handling the American side of the operation. MKA's involvement was gradually phased out and ended in 1959, no doubt to the relief of the company's directors and shareholders.

The involvement of the State Department meant the Helmand-Arghandab project became embroiled in the politics of the Cold War, for TAG was set up under President Truman's Point Four Program, which was designed to promote development and counteract Soviet propaganda that the Western world was not interested in the needs of underdeveloped countries. State Department funding of HAVA thus came with a political price tag, for in order to receive TAG assistance Afghanistan had to sign a Bilateral Agreement and Mutual Security Pact. In turn these agreements exacerbated divisions within Mahmud Khan's cabinet and family. When Da'ud objected to signing these agreements, he was sacked, although he was later reinstated.

In 1956 a State Department review of the Helmand-Arghandab project noted that to date MKA and the Afghan government had spent $83 million on the scheme, but after a decade of investment the financial returns were at the best modest.[24] Only around 120,000 acres of land had been reclaimed, though the additional irrigation supplied to pre-HAVA farms had led to an increase in double cropping, higher yields and better crop quality. Exports of dried and fresh fruit from the region had risen, but the costs of imports – mostly supplies for the Helmand-Arghandab scheme – had doubled in four years. The government's anticipated revenues from the scheme came in well below expectations and were insufficient to meet repayment of debt or interest on loans. Indeed, the government was running 'substantial deficits' and was increasingly indebted to the Da Afghanistan Bank as well as international donors. In all around 20 per cent of Afghanistan's national budget and well over half of all development funds were allocated to HAVA.

The report, however, noted that it was politically impossible to abandon the Helmand-Arghandab project since it was 'inextricably bound up with American prestige in Afghanistan', so the State Department committed a further $47.8 million to the programme in an attempt to fix the problems.[25]

A DC4 plane of Aryana Afghan Airlines plane at Kabul airport in the late 1950s or early '60s. The newly nationalized airline was founded in 1955 by an American commercial pilot who imported a number of war surplus Dakotas and in 1957 Pan Am took a 49 per cent stake in the company. Pan Am provided technical support and trained pilots until 1979. Many of the airline's planes were destroyed during the Soviet occupation and in the subsequent infighting following the fall of President Najib Allah.

The Helmand-Arghandab scheme was now a self-perpetuating, open-ended project driven not by realizable goals or economic and social gains, but by the need to uphold the prestige and credibility of both the USA and the Afghan government. From 1956 onwards the political dimensions of the scheme assumed an even greater importance following Prime Minister Da'ud's acceptance of a Soviet loan of $100 million. It is therefore somewhat ironic that the fiercest resistance to the American intervention from 2001 to 2015 came from the very settlements on the Bogra network that had been promised so much by the U.S.-funded scheme, only for hopes to be dashed and livelihoods destroyed by salinity, flooding and land grabs. In Afghanistan memories of old injuries never die, they merely hibernate.

This is not to say that there were not some successes for American development aid in the post-war era. MKA and USAID were responsible for the training of a generation of engineers and artisans and provided employment for thousands of labourers as well as scholarships. MKA and USAID also constructed schools and clinics, while graduates of the Cadastral Survey School drew the first maps of the country. The Kajaki and Dahla dams eventually provided hydroelectricity for Kandahar, Girishk, Lashkargah and other towns, while Kandahar's trade with Pakistan improved due to

MKA's all-weather road. From the 1950s American teachers and educators taught English, rewrote the national curriculum and paid for the printing of textbooks and primers. American aid also helped construct Kabul University, Pan Am trained Afghan pilots for the national carrier, Aryana, while Boeing supplied the country's first jet airliners.

The fall of 'Abd al-Majid Zabuli

The technical problems, escalating costs and burgeoning debt resulting from the Helmand-Arghandab scheme caused tensions between Prime Minister Shah Mahmud and Zabuli, who had committed most of the Bank-i Milli's foreign currency reserves to the project. When the scheme continued to fail to deliver the anticipated fiscal benefits, Zabuli's management of the scheme was called into question. The confrontation was fuelled by Shah Mahmud's concern that Zabuli had been given too much power and that he had politically dangerous aspirations. This anxiety was fully justified, for Zabuli, supported by Da'ud and Na'im, had increasingly dabbled in quasi-political activity by founding the Wish (or Wikh) Zalmiyan (Awakened Youth) in Kandahar, a cultural movement that promoted Pushtu and Pushtun identity. Three years later Zabuli and Da'ud established the Klub-i Milli (National Club) as the Kabul branch of the Wish Zalmiyan, which was covertly a forum for young, left-wing reformers. Zabuli also employed several radical activists, including Nur Muhammad Taraki, the future leader of the People's Democratic Party of Afghanistan. Indeed, according to Saikal, 'the entire generation of postwar politicians, including those of Marxist persuasion, grew up under Zabuli's influence'.[26]

The confrontation between the two men came to a head in the late 1940s when the Bank-i Milli refused to honour a credit note issued by the prime minister. During a stormy cabinet meeting Shah Mahmud demanded Zabuli tell him by what authority the bank dare overrule a *firman* he had signed, to which Zabuli sarcastically retorted, 'not everything is under the control of the government or under your authority'.[27] A furious Shah Mahmud called in the guards and ordered them to expel Zabuli, though after the intervention of other cabinet ministers he left of his own accord. For a while Shah Mahmud contemplated imprisoning or even executing Zabuli, but instead he packed him off to Karachi to negotiate with the Pakistan government over the issue of Pushtunistan.

When Da'ud became prime minister in September 1953, he demanded Zabuli surrender control of the Bank-i Milli's *shirkat*s to the government.

When he refused, Da'ud sent in the auditors, who discovered that Zabuli had failed to account for millions of dollars of foreign exchange, much of which had been diverted into his own, private offshore accounts. Faced with public disgrace and imprisonment Zabuli chose to go into voluntary exile; after a period in Moscow he settled in New York, where he eventually became an American citizen. He died in 1998 at the ripe old age of 102 and left 70 per cent of his immense fortune, estimated at more than $200 million in today's money, to a Trust for promoting education in Afghanistan.

The 'Liberal Parliament' and the suppression of dissent

The conflict between Zabuli and Shah Mahmud was symptomatic of a wider political and ideological struggle that was taking place. After the death of Hashim Khan, Prime Minister Shah Mahmud had set out to reduce the power of Nur al-Mashayekh and other Islamists and remove some of the restrictions imposed by Islamic law. Girls' schools were reopened, political prisoners pardoned, and restrictions on political activity and press freedom eased. It was against the background of this tentative liberalization that movements such as Wish Zalmiyan and Afghanistan's first Students' Union emerged.

Shortly after becoming prime minister, Shah Mahmud ordered new elections that allowed a far greater degree of public participation. When the results were announced, forty of the 120 members of the Wolusi Jirga represented a variety of independent, reformist groups who formed a coalition known as Jabha-yi Mardum, the People's Front. Its members were committed to breaking what they called 'the wall of silence', curbing the power of the Executive, and making ministers and the king accountable to Parliament. Known as the Liberal Parliament of 1950–51, the Legislature passed two laws that allowed greater press freedom. This led to a brief flurry of quasi-political broadsheets, all of which were critical of the government and the king, as well as attacking corruption and religious obscurantism. Most of the editors of these publications were affiliates of the Wish Zalmiyan.[28]

The new freedoms led to public demonstrations demanding reform, which more often than not led to clashes with security forces. Editors of the newspapers also ran into trouble with embedded dynastic and religious interests. Muhammad Ghulam Hasan Safi, a prominent member of Wish Zalmiyan, wrote an article accusing Nur al-Mashayekh of illegally diverting construction material designated for schools to repair the shrine of Mui

Mubarak, the Blessed Hair. He then questioned the authenticity of the relic, said to be a hair from the beard of Muhammad, and ridiculed relic cults in general. Nur al-Mashayekh riposted by accusing Ghulam Hasan of blasphemy and demanded he be stoned to death.

By the winter of 1952 Shah Mahmud had had enough of this experiment in liberalization and banned all private publications, shut down the unofficial Students' Union and jailed prominent dissidents and journalists. Those arrested included Muhammad Ghulam Hasan Safi, Babrak Karmal, a Tajik from Kamari whose family originated in Kashmir, and Mir Akbar Khyber, a Logari Ghilzai. Babrak and Mir Akbar later became leaders of Afghanistan's Parcham Communist Party. The government then called new elections and this time made sure that not a single anti-government radical returned as a Member of Parliament.

Da'ud took advantage of this brief period of liberalization to attempt to depose his uncle. On the eve of Nauroz 1951, the internal security services informed Shah Mahmud they had uncovered a coup designed to take place during the New Year celebrations.[29] The ringleader was identified as Sayyid Muhammad Isma'il Balkhi, son of Muhammad Ibrahim Beg, known as Gau Sowar, the Hazara leader who had led the 1946 uprising. Balkhi had studied in the great Shi'a centre of Najaf in Iraq, and on his return to Afghanistan established *madrasa*s in Chindawal and the Hazara *mahala* of Jamal Mina in Kabul. He also founded the underground political party Mujtami-yi Islami (The Islamic Assemblage). Balkhi's coup was nipped in the bud and the conspirators were imprisoned, but according to Khalil Khalili it was Da'ud who was the real mastermind behind the plot. In the days before Nauroz a number of prominent cabinet ministers, including Khalili, were approached by intermediaries to sound them out, while Da'ud had a secret meeting with Balkhi. It appears that Da'ud either incited the putsch or attempted to manipulate it for his own ends. If this were the case, this would account for why shortly after the plotters were arrested both Da'ud and Na'im were dismissed from the government.

The resignation of Shah Mahmud

In March 1953 Da'ud travelled to Moscow to attend Stalin's funeral, where he doubtless discussed the situation in Afghanistan with the Politburo. Soviet officials appear to have encouraged Da'ud to depose Shah Mahmud for Communist sympathizers had been imprisoned for taking part in protests and publishing anti-government articles. On his return to Kabul, Da'ud confronted his uncle and demanded he resign but Shah Mahmud refused to go. There followed a tense stand-off that lasted for several months until finally, in mid-September, the king forced Shah Mahmud's resignation, threatening to abdicate if his uncle did not step down. In his place Zahir Shah appointed Da'ud. The premiership of Muhammad Da'ud was a watershed in Afghan dynastic history, since his appointment marked the end of the reign of Nadir Shah and his brothers. Many of the second generation of the Musahiban family, as well as other Muhammadzais, had been educated in America or Europe and were dedicated reformers and modernizers. More often than not, they were part of the Wish Zalmiyan network.

Prime Minister Da'ud, Pakistan and Pushtunistan

One consequence of this change of leadership was that the state, led by Prime Minister Da'ud, promoted the creation of Pushtunistan as part of government policy. The idea of Pushtunistan was nothing new. It had been first mooted in 1916 by Dr Aurang Shah, a California-based Pushtun, who established the Azad Pakhtunistan [*sic*] Association of America. Yet

As Prime Minister, Sardar Muhammad Da'ud made it compulsory for all official maps to show Pushtunistan, as shown in this insert from a 1965 tourist map.

it was not until the declaration of Indian Independence and Partition that the issue became an increasingly important element in the Afghan government's foreign relations. Afghanistan's advocacy for the unification of all the Pushtun tribes of the Pakistan–Afghan frontier, however, led to a serious and prolonged confrontation with Pakistan.[30] Following Britain's announcement of its withdrawal from India, the Afghan government claimed a historic right to sovereignty over the Pushtun tribes on the Indian side of the Durand Line. When Lord Mountbatten, the last Viceroy of India, ordered a referendum in the Northwest Frontier Province, the vote offered only two options: to join India or Pakistan. Ghaffar Khan demanded the vote include a third option, complete independence, and when Mountbatten refused his followers boycotted the plebiscite. Shah Mahmud, on the other hand, wrote to the Viceroy petitioning for a fourth option, the right of the tribes to come under the sovereignty of Afghanistan. In reply, Mountbatten informed Shah Mahmud that under international law Pakistan legally assumed all the rights of the former imperial power, including inheriting the international frontiers as agreed under the Durand Agreement and subsequent Anglo-Afghan treaties.

When the votes from the referendum were counted just over 55 per cent of them were in favour of joining Pakistan (one wonders what chaos would have ensued had the vote been in favour of remaining part of India). Both 'Abd al-Ghaffar and the Afghan government refused to accept the result, claiming it did not represent the wishes of all Pushtuns since many of them had boycotted the plebiscite. When the issue of international recognition of West and East Pakistan was laid before the United Nations, Afghanistan voted against the motion, though a few months later the government did accord Pakistan recognition after Pakistani officials verbally promised Afghanistan that the two countries would negotiate over the management of Tribal Territory. The talks never took place and successive Pakistani administrations refused to discuss Afghan demands for a second referendum or self-determination for Pushtunistan.

A year after the founding of West Pakistan, 'Abd al-Ghaffar and other leaders of the Khudai Khidmatgar were arrested, which led to a vitriolic propaganda campaign against Pakistan by the Afghan government. On 30 June 1949 the Wolusi Jirga formally adopted the establishment of Pushtunistan as national policy and revoked all international agreements relating to the Durand Line. On the Pakistan side of the frontier an Afridi *jirga* declared an independent Pushtunistan 'from Chitral to Baluchistan and from the Khyber to the banks of the Indus', whereupon Afridis on the Afghan side poured across the border bearing the newly created

Pushtunistan flag, declaring they intended to plant it on the banks of the Indus.[31] Meanwhile, in Northern Waziristan, the Fakir of Ipi set up his own Pukhtunistan National Assembly.

Pakistan responded by sending in the army and bombing the Afridis' base, inflicting heavy casualties and dispersing the tribesmen. The Pakistan Air Force then attacked the Fakir of Ipi, only for one plane mistakenly to bomb a village on the Afghan side of the frontier and exacerbate an already tense situation. Pakistan also gave permission to Sardar Muhammad 'Amin, a half-brother of ex-Amir 'Aman Allah Khan, to set up Radio Free Afghanistan in Quetta, while in Peshawar Afghan dissidents published anti-government newspapers in the name of the Afghanistan Republican Party. Pakistan also placed severe restrictions on transit goods, which hit Afghanistan's struggling economy hard.

The Afghan government responded by breaking off diplomatic relations, though a few months later a Pakistan envoy was allowed to return to Kabul. The Afghan government, however, refused to reciprocate until Pakistan agreed in principle to discuss the issue of self-determination for Pushtunistan. In January 1950 Afghanistan established diplomatic relations with India, Pakistan's mortal enemy in the wake of the Kashmir crisis and the war of 1947–8. New Delhi reciprocated by issuing a public statement in support of Pushtunistan.[32] After Da'ud became prime minister, self-determination for Pushtunistan was a keystone of his government's regional policy, and Pushtunistan became as emotive to Da'ud's vision of Afghan national identity as Kashmir was to Pakistan. In pursuit of this chimera, however, Da'ud and his supporters were blind to the wider political implications as well as the adverse economic consequences and seemed unable to grasp that Pakistan would fight to the last to avoid the loss of something like a third of West Pakistan. The Pakistan government's position became even more implacable after the civil war with East Pakistan in 1971, which led to the creation of the independent nation of Bangladesh. As one American resident in Kabul commented, 'what Kabul is asking for is Pakistan's suicide'.[33]

The confrontation flared up once more in November 1954 when Pakistan's prime minster, Muhammad 'Ali, announced his One Unit Plan, which abolished West Pakistan's five provincial administrations, including the Northwestern Frontier Province, and replaced them with a single unitary state. Since this policy stripped the tribes of much of their traditional autonomy Prime Minister Da'ud threatened Muhammad 'Ali with 'grave consequences' if he went ahead with this reorganization. Another cause of anger in Kabul was Pakistan's decision to join the South East Asia

Treaty Organization (SEATO) in September 1954; in February the following year Pakistan also became a member of the Central Treaty Organization (CENTO), which included Turkey, Iraq and Iran.[34] These treaties were Anglo-American initiatives designed to counteract Soviet influence in Asia and the Middle East, and included mutual defence agreements as well as guarantees that contracting parties would defend the 'inviolability', 'integrity' and 'sovereign or political independence' of member states. In 1956 SEATO formally recognized the Durand Line as the international frontier of Pakistan and Afghanistan, despite protests by the Afghan government. Even more alarming, as far as Kabul was concerned, the treaties meant that the USA and Britain began to rearm Pakistan with modern weapons, including ground-to-air missiles.

Afghanistan had not been invited to join SEATO or CENTO and Afghan officials interpreted this as a sign that America and Britain were siding with Pakistan. Yet one of the reasons why Afghanistan had not been included was Da'ud's intransigence over Pushtunistan. The U.S. State Department was keen to encourage cooperation between Afghanistan, Pakistan and Iran, since it was the U.S. administration's opinion that the three nations would present a strong front against Soviet infiltration and potential aggression. To this end State Department officials urged Afghan ministers to negotiate unconditionally with Pakistan over the Pushtunistan issue, but Da'ud refused to compromise. Since the Afghan government had voted to repudiate the Durand Line as its international frontier and abrogated the Anglo-Afghan Treaties, it was not possible for both Afghanistan and Pakistan to be members of SEATO-CENTO until the dispute was resolved. The Afghan government's intransigence frustrated State Department officials who regarded the Pushtunistan issue as a 'seemingly hopeless stumbling block' and 'wasting deadlock'.[35]

Another reason for Afghanistan's exclusion from SEATO-CENTO had been the State Department's assessment, which concluded the Afghan government was unstable, the army ineffective and the country in the grip of a deepening economic crisis. In the circumstances the United States was not prepared to guarantee to defend Afghanistan from outside aggression. America had already burnt its fingers badly with the Helmand Valley Scheme and neither the State Department nor the Pentagon had any desire to put their hands any deeper into the furnace. In effect, the United States refused to assume the mantle of Britain, the former Imperial power, or become embroiled in a new Great Game with the USSR in Afghanistan. Instead, the USA opted for the pre-1830 situation with the Indus, not the Amu Darya, as their South Asian Rubicon.

Under the PDPA Communist governments Pushtunistan continued to be promoted by the state. From left to right a 1979 issue showing Pushtuns and the Pushtunistan flag; by 1982 the Pushtuns are now armed and the flag raised for war; this 1985 issue depicts the Pushtunistan flag flying in Kabul's Pushtunistan Square surrounding by tribesmen dancing the *atan*. By this time the 'Journee Nationale' also included support of Baluchistan independence.

Pakistan's prime minister, Muhammad 'Ali, ignored Da'ud's protests and went ahead with his One Unit Plan, so in March 1955 Da'ud publicly announced that 'the Afghan people do not consider Pushtunistan as part [of] Pakistan territory' and declared a State of Emergency.[36] The Pakistani consulates in Kabul, Jalalabad and Kandahar were attacked by mobs, the Pakistani flag burnt and that of Pushtunistan raised instead. Pakistan retaliated by sacking the Afghan consulate in Peshawar and reimposing transit restrictions on cross-border activity. Da'ud responded by sending tribal *lashkar*s to attack the Bajur Agency, only for them to withdraw in the face of stiff resistance from the Pakistan army. In November a specially convened Loya Jirga called for a plebiscite on Pushtunistan. The following month, during the visit of the Soviet Premier Nikolai Bulganin and Party Secretary Nikita Khrushchev, the two governments issued a joint declaration that included a call for self-determination for Pushtuns. As Pakistan and Afghanistan teetered on the brink of war, Turkey and Saudi Arabia offered to mediate, with the support of the United States. This led to a lessening of tensions and diplomatic relations were restored in the middle of 1957. The following year King Zahir Shah even paid a state visit to Pakistan.

The dispute, though, flared up again at the end of 1958 in the wake of General 'Ayub Khan's military coup. Despite being a Pushtun, 'Ayub had no time for Pushtunistan. In the crackdown that followed his declaration of martial law, 'Abd al-Ghaffar Khan and other Red Shirt leaders were once more arrested. The Afghan government demanded their release and when this was not forthcoming, 15,000 tribal irregulars marched into Bajur in September 1960 claiming they were supporting the Khan of Jandol against his rival, the Khan of Khar. Bitter fighting followed between pro-Afghan and pro-Pakistani tribal militias, while Pakistan's American warplanes bombed Afghan positions and even conducted a raid inside Afghan territory. In 1961 diplomatic relations were severed once more, the Afghan–Pakistan frontier was closed, and Prime Minister Da'ud declared he would not reopen it until Pakistan agreed to negotiation on self-determination for Pushtunistan. Pakistan retaliated by halting the annual Ghilzai migration on the grounds that they had neither Afghan passports nor Pakistani visas. Da'ud's decision to close the frontier hit Afghanistan much harder than Pakistan. Indeed his decision was as ill-timed as it could be, for Afghanistan's autumn fruit crop was about to be harvested and closure of the frontier prevented the export of grapes, melons and other perishables to Pakistan and India. In the end Aryana Airlines airlifted the grapes to India at great cost and the Soviet Union bought up the remaining crop. Da'ud, however, refused to reopen the frontier and it remained sealed for nearly four years.

Prime Minister Da'ud and Afghan-Soviet relations

The closure of the Pakistan frontier led Da'ud's government to turn to the USSR in an attempt to secure an alternative transit route for Afghanistan's imports and exports, as well as a means of rearming to counteract Pakistan's modern, U.S.-equipped army. Da'ud appears to have believed that closer ties with Moscow would lessen any possible Soviet intervention in northern Afghanistan, a threat that continued to cause anxiety in government circles. During the brief period of the Liberal Parliament, several representatives of the Turco-Tajik population of the northern provinces gained seats in the Wolusi Jirga, where they complained that most of the funds and loans for development projects were spent in the Pushtu-majority areas of southern Afghanistan. In an attempt to address this grievance, the government asked the United Nations to conduct a feasibility study into the potential exploitation of the oil and gas fields in the Shibarghan and Sar-i Pul regions. The presence of French surveyors, who were commissioned to conduct a survey, led to an immediate reaction from the Kremlin. The Afghan ambassador in Moscow was summoned to the Foreign Ministry, where he was given 'a severe tongue lashing' and presented with an aide-memoire condemning oil and gas exploration or extraction by any NATO country to be 'an unfriendly act' and a violation of the 1931 Soviet-Afghan Treaty.[37] The Afghan government was left in no doubt about the consequences of ignoring the Soviet protest or that the USSR regarded Afghanistan's northern provinces as being within its sphere of influence. The Afghan Foreign Minister went as far as to state that the Soviet aide-memoire was the 'most serious incident in [Afghanistan's] recent history'. The cabinet saved face by sending a 'firm rebuttal' to the Soviets, but the French survey team was recalled and the project shelved. Several years later the Afghan government signed an agreement with the Soviet Union to extract gas from the Shibarghan field, most of which was pumped directly across the frontier, for the gas was part payment for a massive loan that the USSR had made to Afghanistan.

Despite this unpleasant confrontation, Da'ud continued to pursue better relations with the Soviet Union. In 1955 the Afghan government signed a five-year transit agreement and accepted a loan of $3.5 million to construct grain silos and bakeries. In December of the same year the Soviet premier made the first state visit to Afghanistan, during which the two governments reaffirmed the 1931 Non-aggression Treaty and Prime Minister Da'ud announced the government had agreed to accept the USSR's offer of a low-interest loan of $100 million. The majority of this money was spent on the purchase of Soviet arms and military equipment; the remainder went on infrastructure projects, which created the greatest construction boom in Afghanistan prior to 2001 and provided employment for thousands of university graduates and labourers. Among the many civil engineering projects undertaken were the construction of the highways; the paving of Kabul's streets; hydroelectric plants; irrigation schemes; textile and cement factories; hospitals; post offices; Soviet-style housing units for government officials; and the construction of Kabul's Polytechnic. The Soviet Union also supplied buses, hospital beds, medical equipment, cars and trucks. The artificial boom also help stave off political and social unrest, at least in the short term.

The greatest engineering feat of all, however, was the construction of a new highway between Kabul and Mazar-i Sharif through the Salang Tunnel, which, when it opened in 1964, was the longest road tunnel in the world. The new highway cut hundreds of kilometres off the journey from Kabul to the northern provinces and made it possible to drive from the capital to Mazar-i Sharif in a single day. The road facilitated trade with the USSR, as well as internal trade between north and south. Following the completion of the extension of the railhead to the Afghan frontier port of Hairatan and the road–rail bridge across the Amu Darya, Afghanistan was linked into the Soviet rail network and had a reliable, alternative means of shipping goods to Europe.

The surge in Soviet aid led to an influx of hundreds of Soviet and Warsaw Pact technical and military advisers, while Army and Air Force

The Salang Tunnel's northern entrance. When completed this 2.6 km (1.6 mi.) tunnel cut travel time from Kabul to Mazar-i Sharif to a single day. However, as the tunnel mouths were built more than 3,000 m (9,842 ft) above sea level, in the winter the approach roads are often blocked.

officers, military cadets and students received scholarships to study in the USSR, where they were exposed to Communist ideology and propaganda. Da'ud, though, had a bottom line. When the USSR offered to fund the whole of the government's second Five Year Plan, estimated at around $1 billion, he politely declined the offer, for the Afghan government wanted to remain a non-aligned nation. However, from 1956 onwards Afghanistan was drawn into the Soviet sphere of influence and the government was bound to Soviet interests by virtue of its huge debt and the country's reliance on Soviet expertise and technology. Visually, Afghanistan's urban centres underwent a transformation and eventually assumed a decidedly Soviet and eastern European appearance.

Inevitably, the increased Soviet presence opened the door for the spread of Marxist–Leninist ideology, particularly among the officer corps, students and ethnic minorities. Soviet propaganda films and publications aided the spread of Communism, while in the cities of northern Afghanistan the population watched television programmes broadcast from Tashkent in Dari, Uzbeki and Turkmani. The USA and western European countries continued to assist Afghanistan, but none of them was prepared to match the level of Soviet funding. As early as the late 1950s Soviet officials believed that in Afghanistan, at least, they had won the Cold War, as one member of the Soviet oil exploration mission in northern Afghanistan pointedly told the American historian and archaeologist Louis Dupree: 'We are here for a long time . . . why don't you Americans go home? Afghanistan is our neighbour, not yours.'[38]

Da'ud's decision to accept substantial Soviet assistance was not popular with many Afghans who disliked the Soviet Union's state atheism and Communist ideology, while the religious elites opposed the liberalization of education as well as the government's secular views on social and legal matters. The close alliance with the Soviet Union was not welcomed either by the descendants of the *basmachis* and other Central Asian refugees who had fled the Russian occupation of their homelands and Stalin's Collectivization. Behind his back people jokingly referred to Da'ud as the *Surkh Sardar*, the Red Prince.

The fall of Prime Minister Da'ud

The most dramatic gesture of Da'ud's policy of social liberalization took place in August 1959 during Independence Day celebrations. In an act reminiscent of the era of Amir 'Aman Allah Khan, female members of the royal party appeared in public with their faces unveiled. Unveiling, or The Reform as it was euphemistically known, was officially voluntary but it was 'pressed rather hard', in state institutions particularly in schools, the civil service and government-run factories.[39] In Pul-i Khumri, veiled women were denied service at the state cotton mill and the traffic police fined drivers of horse-drawn carriages for taking passengers wearing the burqa. The unveiling led to an immediate backlash by Islamic conservatives who petitioned Da'ud to reinstate *parda*. Da'ud responded by challenging them to prove from the Qur'an and *Hadith* that concealment was a religious obligation, which they failed to do. Instead the Islamists resorted to direct action, holding a series of public demonstrations that quickly turned violent. In November riots in Kandahar, fuelled partly by the veiling controversy and partly by government attempts to impose taxes on Durrani landlords, led to the deaths of some sixty protestors after police opened fire on the crowd.

In the same month a poorly managed local dispute in Khost over timber rights escalated into a full-scale rebellion. Da'ud mounted a show of force and sent the army and air force, now armed with Soviet heavy weapons, to shell and bomb the rebels into submission, whereupon thousands of tribesmen fled into Pakistan's Waziristan. Da'ud later offered the rebels an amnesty but the suppression of the Khost uprising provided

Pakistan with a propaganda coup, with tribal elders giving interviews with the Pakistani press and on radio programmes in which they denounced Da'ud's government and accused it of abandoning Islam and selling out to the atheistic Soviets.

Communist sympathizers then exploited the Islamic opposition to Da'ud's social reforms in order to destroy their ideological enemies. Around the time of the Kandahar riots Babrak Karmal, who had already spent time in prison for anti-government agitation, informed Da'ud that Sibghat Allah Mujadidi, a relative of the Hazrat of Shor Bazaar, planned to assassinate the Soviet premier, Khrushchev, during his forthcoming state visit.[40] Sibghat Allah and other Islamists were arrested along with several army officers. From this point forward Da'ud developed a cooperative relationship with Babrak and other Leftists in his attempt to undermine his Islamic opponents.

By the spring of 1963 Da'ud's closure of the Pakistan–Afghan frontier had created a self-inflicted economic crisis in Afghanistan. There were shortages of essential commodities and rampant inflation. With foreign currency reserves at an all-time low, the government struggled to meet its mounting foreign debt repayments. Merchants, senior Muhammadzais and foreign diplomats urged Da'ud to negotiate with Pakistan and reopen the frontier, but he refused to back down. Finally, on 10 March 1963, Zahir Shah dismissed Da'ud and Na'im with the backing of his uncle Shah Wali Khan and General 'Abd al-Wali Khan, Shah Wali's son. The two brothers, however, were not exiled to some distant diplomatic mission, but were allowed to remain in Kabul. This was a serious misjudgement on the king's part for Da'ud, enraged at his dismissal, began to plot the downfall of Zahir Shah and developed a closer alliance with Babrak Karmal and his Marxist–Leninist allies.

The 1964 Constitution and the establishment of political parties

Dr Muhammad Yusuf, the new prime minister, was a German-educated physicist. In an attempt to make the government more inclusive and less like a family business, he appointed several technocrats and dynastic out-siders. One of Yusuf's first actions was to fly to Tehran to ask King Reza Shah to mediate in the dispute with Pakistan. A face-saving deal was eventually brokered, diplomatic relations were restored and the frontier reopened. In March 1965 Afghanistan signed a five-year transit agreement with Pakistan.

Prime Minister Yusuf went on public record that he wanted Afghanistan to develop a two-party political system and the king established a committee to revise the 1931 Constitution, a decision that the *Kabul Times* claimed was designed to put the country 'on the road to democracy'.[41] At the same time, the article emphasized the need for gradual change and cautioned against equating democracy and freedom with 'outright lawlessness' and 'anarchy'. As a sop to his religious opponents, Muhammad Yusuf had appointed as chair of the Constitutional Committee his Minister of Justice, Sayyid Sham al-din Majruh, a respected Islamic scholar whose father had been a spiritual affiliate of the Hadda Mullah. After two years of deliberation, during which the committee sought the advice of a French expert on constitutional law, the cabinet finally agreed the new Constitution in July 1964. In September of that year the king convened a Loya Jirga, for its approval was needed before the Constitution could become law, but unlike previous Loya Jirgas this session included a number of directly elected members, including a large minority of non-Pushtuns, six women and a representative of Kabul's Hindu community.

The constitutional debate in the Loya Jirga was often acrimonious and revealed how deeply the country was divided along regional, ethnic and ideological lines. Representatives of non-Pushtun communities, for example, demanded that 'Afghan' should not designate citizenship or nationality due to its duality of meaning, but they were out-voted. Islamists protested that the new Constitution marginalized the *shari'a*, for while Islam was declared to be 'the sacred religion' of the country, both the Constitution and Parliamentary legislation were given a superior role. As for judges, they could only apply the Hanafi code when the Constitution or Parliamentary legislation was unclear. Unlike the Constitution of 1931, the word '*shari'a*' appeared only twice in the new Constitution.

There was a heated debate about the Constitution's definition of liberty as 'the natural right of the human being', which 'has no limitations except the liberty of others and public interest as defined by the law'.[42] These statements were at odds with the 1931 Constitution and the conditionality required by the *shari'a*. Since the new Constitution made no specific mention of women's rights, it implied that the definition of freedom and liberty applied equally to both sexes. As such these provisions were a significant liberalization and set aside many of the restrictive provisions of the 1931 Constitution, in particular the discriminatory regulations regarding the rights of women.

The Constitution designated Afghanistan to be a constitutional monarchy, though in practice this was not the case. The Constitution perpetuated the bicameral system: the Loya Jirga and members of the Lower House, or Wolusi Jirga, being elected by 'free, universal, secret and direct election'. They even had the right to call government ministers and judges to account and impeach them. However, only a third of the Meshrano Jirga, or House of Elders, was returned by popular vote while the Loya Jirga, the third Legislative tier, could veto any changes to the Constitution. The king remained supreme commander of the armed forces, and he alone could summon or dissolve the Loya Jirga. He also appointed one-third of the members of the Meshrano Jirga, had the power to dismiss or suspend the Wolusi Jirga and could declare a State of Emergency without consulting either Parliament or the Loya Jirga. Furthermore, the monarch appointed the prime minister, high court judges, 'high-ranking civil and military officers' and 'issue ordinances'. Article 15 even declared that 'the king is not accountable'.

Another contentious issue was the succession. This was stated to be by right of primogeniture, while the queen could act as regent if the heir apparent were under age. The Loya Jirga, however, passed an amendment that 'members of the Royal House shall not participate in political parties', nor were they allowed to sit in the Lower or Upper Houses or serve as judges in the Supreme Court. This addendum was designed to deny Da'ud and Na'im the right to the throne, as well as to exclude them and other members of the Musahban family the right to a seat in Parliament or the Loya Jirga. The amendment was bitterly contested by Da'udist members of both Houses, but they were outvoted. The debate on the succession took place against a background of suspicion that Da'ud planned to mount a coup during the Loya Jirga. Zahir Shah had refused to nominate Da'ud as a delegate to the Loya Jirga and there were rumours that he planned to defy the king and turn up anyway. Dr Yusuf responded with a show of force, placing army units along the main streets of the capital, so Da'ud decided to wait for a more favourable opportunity. After eleven days of debate the Loya Jirga voted by a majority to accept the Constitution and on 1 October 1964 King Zahir Shah set his seal on the document. It was a significant victory for reformers and modernizers over religious conservatives, who had controlled Afghanistan's social and legal agenda since the era of Nadir Shah and Hashim Khan.

Under the Constitution new elections were to be held in September 1965, a process that involved a major reorganization of provincial boundaries and the creation of 29 *wilayats*, or provinces, and sub-districts known as *wulswalis*. A new law allowed limited press freedom and resulted in the publication of a plethora of private broadsheets, while political movements emerged from the shadows and prepared to register in order to contest the elections. In January 1964 the Hizb-i Demokratik-i Khalq-i Afghanistan, or

People's Democratic Party of Afghanistan (PDPA) convened its first meeting in secret. Khalq, as the PDPA was generally know, was a Marxist–Leninist Republican organization whose leaders had formerly belonged to the Wish Zalmiyan network, while the PDPA's General Secretary, Nur Muhammad Taraki, had been an employee and protégé of Zabuli.[43] Taraki later became a junior officer in the Afghan embassy in Washington and on his return to Kabul was employed as a translator for the U.S. Embassy. Taraki's deputy, Babrak Karmal, a political science graduate who had attended Kabul's Military College, had already spent time in prison for political agitation and had developed an alliance of convenience with Da'ud. Other leading lights of the PDPA included Hafiz Allah 'Amin, a Kharoti Ghilzai from Paghman and a teacher with a Master's Degree from Columbia University, and Muhammad Najib Allah, an Ahmadzai Ghilzai from Gardez who was a medical doctor. The most influential woman in the PDPA was Anahita Ratebzad, a *farsiwan* from Guldarra in the Koh Daman who had trained as a nurse in Chicago. Two years after the founding of the PDPA, Ratebzad set up a militant women's movement, the Sazman-i Demokratik-i Zanan-i Afghanistan.

Like all political parties that emerged in the 1960s, the PDPA was plagued by infighting over leadership issues and disagreements over ideology and policy. Eventually in 1967 Babrak Karmal broke away and set up his own Marxist–Leninist faction, Parcham (Flag, or Banner), which had a particular appeal to university students and ethnic minorities. Parcham's leadership included Hazaras, Uzbeks and Panjshiris, while Khalq was a mainly Ghilzai Pushtun party with a following among army and air force officers, intellectuals and urban Pushtuns in northern Afghanistan.

The Sazman-i Demokratik-i Nauwin-i Afghanistan (New Democratic Party of Afghanistan), commonly known as Sho'la-yi Jawed (Eternal Flame) after the title of its publication, on the other hand was a Maoist party whose membership was, and still is, a closely guarded secret. Its founder members were the three Mahmudi brothers: 'Abd al-Rahim, a medical doctor; 'Abd al-Hadi; and 'Abd al-Rahman, another doctor who also edited the party's broadsheet, *Neda-yi Khalq*. 'Abd al-Rahman had already spent several years in prison following a satirical attack on relic cults, had served in the Liberal Parliament and was formerly a prominent member of Wish Zalmiyan. The Mahmudis were Mohmands and had a following among Pushtuns from Balkh as well as medical and engineering students. The youth wing of Sho'la-yi Jawed, known as Sazman-i Jawanan-i Mutarraqi, the Progressive Youth Organization, was noted for its militancy and between 1963 and 1973 its members clashed violently with Islamists,

PDPA supporters and state security organs. Its leaders, Akram Yari and his brother Siddiq Yari, were Hazaras from Jaughuri whose father, 'Abd Allah Yari, had been director of the Darra-yi Shikari Highway Project. The Yari brothers' paternal uncle, Nadir 'Ali, was one of the few Hazaras to have been elected to parliament. Both 'Abd Allah and Nadir 'Ali were devoted to King Zahir Shah, who treated 'Abd Allah Yari like an adopted son – a loyalty not shared by his offspring.

Sitam-i Milli (National Oppression) was another Maoist party that split from the PDPA in 1967. Its founder, Tahir Badakhshi, was a Tajik from Badakhshan who had studied law and economics at Kabul University. He also founded SAZA, a revolutionary workers' party. Tahir opposed the government's promotion of Pushtunism and his following came mostly from ethnolinguistic minorities. One of Sitam-i Milli's key demands was greater autonomy for Afghanistan's northern provinces. Other PDPA splinter groups included Goroh-i Kar (The Workers Group) and Jawanan-i Zahmatkash (Toiling Youth).

Afghan Millat, or the Afghan Social Democratic Party, founded in March 1966, was the leading Pushtunist party. Its founder, Ghulam Muhammad Farhad, had studied engineering in Germany during the 1920s, where he had embraced the roots of National Socialism and Nazi Aryanism. The membership of Afghan Millat also included several former associates of Wish Zalmiyan. The party's policies included support for Pushtunistan, the Durrani monarchy and Pushtun domination of Afghanistan's political and cultural life.

Islamist parties, on the other hand, fought to retain Afghanistan as an Islamic state ruled by the *shari'a* and opposed the government's move towards secularism and gender liberalization. They also opposed Communist and Leftist parties and sought to revert to Nur al-Mashayekh's 1931 Constitution. By 1964 Nur al-Mashayekh had died but his successor, Muhammad Ibrahim Mujadidi, who took the title of Zia al-Mashayekh, and his relative, Sibghat Allah Mujadidi, continued the family's struggle to uphold the supremacy of Islamic law in state affairs. At the same time a new generation of politically aggressive and radical Islamic scholars was emerging, many of whom had studied at Egypt's al-Azhar Islamic University, where they had embraced the political philosophy of the Ikhwan al-Muslimin, the Muslim Brotherhood.

Founded in 1928 by Hasan al-Banna (1906–1949), an Egyptian schoolteacher, this pan-Islamic movement was a radical and militant organization that became involved in the political assassination of Egyptian leaders after the Second World War, but also engaged in social action providing material relief for Egypt's urban poor. Like al-Afghani, the Muslim Brotherhood attacked European, and particularly British, colonialism and domination of the Near East, calling for the Islamization of society and declared the Qur'an to be their only Constitution. For the founders of the Muslim Brotherhood, the state was the church and the church was the state. Many of the leaders of the Brotherhood were educated in secular institutions and were intellectuals, writers, poets and journalists, rather than members of the traditional religious elites. Such individuals and the movements they founded are usually referred to as Islamists in Western publications.

One of the leading lights of the Muslim Brotherhood was Sayyid Qutb (1906–1966), an employee of Egypt's Education Department who wrote novels in his spare time. In 1948 Qutb was awarded a scholarship to study in the American education system and during his time in Colorado he wrote his first political treatise in which he attacked American secularism and society, in particular its violence and obsession with sexuality. His political philosophy was based on the assertion that the *shari'a*, as defined by the Hanafi *mazhab*, was the only legitimate legal framework for state and society, since it was God given and represented God's eternal and irrevocable will and decrees. The *shari'a* was fundamental therefore not just to any Muslim society, but to every nation and civilization. Qutb therefore condemned all alternative forms of state and governance as *jahiliyya* – that is, the state of ignorance said to have existed in Arabia prior to the revelation of the Qur'an. For Muslims to submit to any un-Islamic form of government was not just unlawful but tantamount to a mortal sin, for they were the law of *Iblis*, the Devil. *Shari'a*ization therefore was not a matter of choice or preference but of salvific importance. Since most Muslim nations at the time he wrote were, to one degree or other, under colonial rule by European, non-Muslim, nations, Qutb called for an internal *jihad* against both European colonialism and Muslims who ruled in the name of European colonial powers. As a consequence, Qutb shifted the emphasis of *jihad*, which traditionally was a war against aggression by non-Muslim states, and redirected it to an internal political struggle against governments the Ikhwan al-Muslimin deemed were infidel regimes.

From the early 1960s onwards the Muslim Brotherhood's radicalism became increasingly popular with young Muslims, especially university students. However, its ideology was introduced to Afghanistan not by secular intellectuals but by a circle of Islamic scholars, most of whom had studied for higher degrees at Cairo's al-Azhar mosque-university. Their leader, Professor Ghulam Muhammad Niyazi, was a Ghilzai *naqil* from Pushtun Kot, outside Maimana. In 1957 he returned to Afghanistan after completing his studies at al-Azhar and was appointed Professor of Islamic Law at Kabul University. Niyazi then formed a circle of like-minded individuals, the most prominent of whom were also graduates of al-Azhar. In the late 1970s many of these men became prominent leaders of the *jihad* against the Soviet occupation, including Burhan al-Din Rabbani, a Tajik from Badakhshan, who was President of the Islamic Republic of Afghanistan from 1992 to 1996; 'Abd al-Rabb Rasul Sayyaf, a Kharoti Ghilzai from Paghman, who in the 1980s developed close ties with 'Osama bin Laden and Arab *jihad*ists; and Sibghat Allah Mujadidi, a relative of the Hazrat of Shor Bazaar. Another member of the Niyazi circle was Gulbudin Hikmatyar, a Kharoti Ghilzai from Qataghan who, unlike others in the network, had no formal background in Islamic studies. He had been educated at Kabul's Military Academy and then studied engineering at the Kabul Polytechnic. From 1993 to 1994 Hikmatyar was the nominal prime minister of Afghanistan.

The Niyazi circle had three objectives: to counteract the government's drift to Western secularism; to propagate the teachings of Sayyid Qutb and like-minded Islamists; and to develop an Islamic response to Communism and Western ideologies. Following the passing of the 1964 Constitution, which Niyazi and his circle bitterly criticized, he established the Jawanan-i Islami, or Islamic Youth Movement, which had a strong following in high schools and Kabul University. Eventually the Jawanan-i Islami came to dominate the university's unofficial Students' Union. The Harakat-i Inqilab-i Islami, the Islamic Revolutionary Movement, was another Islamist party that emerged in the 1960s. Its founder, Maulawi Muhammad Nabi Muhammadi, was a Ghilzai from Ghazni and a Mujadidi *pir*. Nabi Muhammadi was educated in the *madrasa* system and during the *jihad* against the Soviet Union in the 1980s one of Harakat's most prominent members was Mullah 'Omar, who later became head of Afghanistan's Taliban.

When the results of the elections of 1964 were announced several of these parties had representatives elected to the Wolusi Jirga. They included Babrak Karmal and Anahita Ratebzad of the PDPA, Ghulam Muhammad Farhad of Afghan Millat, Da'udist and Nabi Muhammadi. Several women gained seats in the Lower and Upper Houses and there were representatives of ethnic and religious minorities too. Almost as soon as the new session of the Wolusi Jirga convened in early 1965, the debating chamber became a battleground as Leftists, Islamists, Pushtunists, Monarchists and representatives of ethnic and religious minorities clashed. The PDPA was particularly well organized and its members staged set-piece interventions in the Chamber as well as demonstrations outside the Assembly.

When Prime Minister Yusuf sought the Wolusi Jirga's approval for his new cabinet, he faced a barrage of vituperation from PDPA members and their supporters in the public gallery. Pushtun nationalists also attacked him, for they resented a non-Pushtun being prime minister. The Wolusi Jirga then passed a motion requiring all the proposed cabinet ministers to present themselves for public scrutiny and to declare the sources of their personal fortunes. Dr Yusuf refused to comply, claiming such matters were personal, and issued his own ultimatum: confirm his new government within three days or he would resign.

The PDPA's response was swift. On the following day, 24 October 1965, Party members stormed the Chamber, refused to leave, and forced the suspension of proceedings. The following morning, the 3 'Aqrab in the Afghan solar calendar, the Wolusi Jirga went into private session while outside security forces fought PDPA supporters who tried to break into the heavily guarded building. When they failed to achieve this aim, the demonstrators broke into the nearby Habibiyya High School and tried to force the pupils to join their demonstration. A second group attempted to storm Dr Yusuf's private residence but were driven back by the guards. By the end of the day two protestors had been shot, along with a tailor who had been caught in the crossfire.[44] The following day Dr Yusuf submitted his resignation.

The new prime minister, Muhammad Hashim Maiwandwal, was an Ahmadzai Ghilzai and a well-known religious personality, journalist and diplomat who had previously served as Minister of Information under Hashim Khan. Maiwandwal, though, was an old-style monarchist and reformer in the Mahmud Tarzi mould who was deeply concerned about the increasing influence of the Soviet Union and Communism among the younger generation, which he blamed on Da'ud's decision to accept the Soviet loan and military and developmental aid. As far as Moscow and Afghanistan's Communists were concerned, Maiwandwal was an American puppet.

Like Yusuf before him, Maiwandwal had to endure several days of personalized attacks before the Wolusi Jirga passed a Motion of Confidence in his administration. In an attempt to calm the situation, Maiwandwal promised to set up a commission of enquiry to examine the students' demands and he attended the *fatiha* prayer service for the 'martyred' students, where he read a message of condolence from King Zahir Shah. At the same time, Maiwandwal ordered the closure of all schools and Kabul University for a week in order to prevent further protests and arrested leading left-wing agitators. Despite these actions protests resumed when the university reopened in early November. The students drew up a list of demands, which included punishment for security forces who had shot protestors, the release of jailed students, reductions in the pass rate for examinations, the cancellation of obligatory class attendances, and the right to form a Students' Union and political societies. When the promised enquiry came to nothing, no prisoners were released and no member of the security services prosecuted for the 3 'Aqrab killings, the students called a general strike. Maiwandwal responded by banning public demonstrations and private newspapers. The following spring, when the next academic year commenced, a new University constitution specifically forbade the formation of political parties or student movements. The king then refused to ratify a law that permitted the formation of political parties, despite both Houses having approved the legislation.

Despite the storm of protests, the royal family and Muhammadzais in general continued to believe that the king and the monarchy commanded wide popular support. Like the Romanovs before them, they failed to realize that the demonstrations and the stormy sessions in Parliament were symptomatic of widespread dissatisfaction with the dynasty's monopoly on power and the lack of any real freedoms. All the so-called New Democracy had done was to lift the lid on deeply rooted resentments that had been suppressed by decades of autocratic rule. The government, which had not the slightest idea how to deal with the situation, responded by reverting to its old, repressive ways.

At the same time, opponents of the monarchy and the status quo were divided by ideological differences, which meant there was no unified front, let alone consensus about alternative forms of governance. As u.s. Ambassador Ronald G. Neumann noted in 1970, the state-sponsored democracy tended to 'atomize the political forces in this country further, gives real power to none but keeps everybody busy and puzzled, and thus deprives the opposition of an opportunity to organize in a really dangerous fashion'.[45] The absence of cross-party cooperation, statesmanship or any concept of working for the national interest created the 'very antithesis of true freedom'.[46] Tragically, amid the turmoil, voices of moderation that sought an orderly transition to an inclusive and more democratic society were drowned out, shouted down or silenced by intimidation, not only by the government but by Islamists and Communists, too.

In November 1966 the violence reached the floor of the Wolusi Jirga itself. During an angry debate about dress code for schoolgirls, Muhammad Nabi physically attacked Babrak Karmal while 'Abd al-Rashid, Member for Pul-i Khumri, hit Anahita Ratebzad with his walking stick. Karmal and

Ratebzad, fearing for their lives, fled to the nearby Ministry of Commerce and Babrak later had to have hospital treatment for his injuries. In March the following year, during an official visit to Washington, DC, Maiwandwal prophetically informed State Department officials that Afghanistan faced an 'explosive situation . . . which might escalate into a bigger danger'.[47]

The deepening economic and political crises

While the country was in political turmoil the economy continued its downward spiral, creating even more disillusionment with government and the monarchy. By the late 1960s Afghanistan had an annual account deficit of between 500 and 600 million afghanis, due mainly to the collapse of the *karakul* trade and the closure of the Pakistan frontier. The shortages of essential foodstuffs were exacerbated when the government decided to export most of the wheat crop in order to secure the foreign currency it needed to meet repayments on the country's foreign debt. At the same time state expenditure burgeoned, for the nationalization of the *shirkat*s had tripled the number of state employees. In an attempt to raise additional revenue, the government imposed heavy duties on imports of luxury goods, but when it tried to tax livestock the Wolusi Jirga vetoed the measure.

As the deficit burgeoned, Afghanistan's international creditors became increasingly concerned about the country's liquidity, which had a negative impact on the country's credit rating and made Western countries increasingly reluctant to lend anything more than small amounts for specific projects. In 1967 American assistance was further restrained by the Conte–Long and Symington Amendments to the Foreign Assistance Act, which required U.S. foreign aid to be reduced in proportion to the sum recipient countries spent on 'sophisticated' weapons. Since the Afghan government had been buying modern Soviet tanks, MiG jets and ground-to-air missiles, the question of the legality of further American loans to Afghanistan was raised for, in the State Department's view, its military build-up was 'inordinate' and 'out of all proportion to [Afghanistan's] economic situation'. The Afghan government did not help matters when, shortly after the Conte-Symington Amendments became law, it proudly showed off its newly acquired Soviet missiles and Su-7 fighter jets during the annual Independence Day parade.

By 1967 the economic situation was so bad that Prime Minister Maiwandwal asked the State Department, during a visit to Washington, for a loan of $4.4 million to purchase American wheat and edible oil. While the U.S. administration debated whether to agree to the loan, Maiwandwal's position became increasingly untenable. Shortly after he returned home, Afghan Millat published an article based on a report in the Californian magazine *Ramparts*, in which an Afghan student at Berkeley University alleged that the CIA had tried to recruit him and other Afghan students.[48] Afghan Millat used this allegation to accuse Maiwandwal and other American-educated ministers of being in the pay of the CIA. Maiwandwal denied the allegations, but faced a barrage of hostile questions from the Wolusi Jirga. In response the government shut down Afghan Millat, which alienated influential Pushtuns and monarchists, including Da'ud and Na'im. In an attempt to support the government, Neumann persuaded the State Department to announce an emergency food aid package for Afghanistan and a loan of $12 million for a generator for the Kajaki Dam. In private Neumann noted that Maiwandwal was probably 'past saving', a judgement that turned out to be true.[49] In October 1967 Maiwandwal, who had been undergoing treatment for cancer, resigned.

In a desperate attempt to put the genie back into the bottle, King Zahir Shah appointed Nur Ahmad 'Etimadi as the new prime minister. This decision was probably one of the worst of Zahir Shah's reign. 'Etimadi was a grandson of Sardar 'Abd al-Quddus Khan and, like his grandfather, 'Etimadi was stuck in the old, autocratic model of government. He was also incompetent and his cabinet was packed with ageing Muhammadzais from the era of Hashim Khan and 'Aman Allah Khan as well as a few supporters of Da'ud, who by this time was barely on speaking terms with the king. 'Etimadi's solution to the civil unrest was repression. In the spring of 1968 transport workers and employees of state-run factories, fed up with rampant inflation and subsistence-level salaries, went on strike, whereupon college and university students staged a series of demonstrations in support of their demands. The government once more closed Kabul University and schools, only for more violent demonstrations to break out on the anniversary of the 3 'Aqrab. Student protests and strikes resumed when the new academic year began in the spring, fuelled by the announcement of new elections. When the results were announced most of the opposition factions had lost their seats and the Wolusi Jirga was packed with government loyalists. Claims that the government had rigged the election led to more protests and by June 1969 the situation was so out of hand that the government again closed Kabul's schools.

In April 1970 the ideological war between Islamists and Communists was inflamed following the publication in *Parcham* of a poem in praise of Lenin and the October Revolution, employing religious terminology traditionally reserved for panegyrics about the Prophet Muhammad. Niyazi and Sibghat

Allah Mujadidi condemned the poem as blasphemous and called on the Wolusi Jirga and the king to punish the author and *Parcham*'s editor. When their demands were ignored, Niyazi's followers took the law into their own hands, attacking known Marxists and throwing acid in the faces of unveiled women. Women's organizations responded with demonstrations demanding justice and changes to new marriage laws that endorsed polygamy.

The protests continued into the spring of 1971. In May left-wing students at Kabul's Teachers' Training College staged a sit-in. 'Etimadi ordered the security services to arrest the ringleaders, only for this to cause a riot that spread to every educational institution in the capital. In an attempt to suppress the protests, the security forces shot dead at least fifteen protestors and wounded or arrested many more. On the following day students and teachers assembled at the Maiwand Memorial in downtown Kabul to protest state violence and demand the release of prisoners and punishment for those who had fired on protestors. A second group of students assembled at the monument to Jamal al-Din al-Afghani on the university campus, intent on marching to Jadi Maiwand. 'Etimadi sent in the *Ghund-i Zarba*, the Strike Force, an elite German-trained riot squad, which proceeded to live up to its name by beating protestors 'unmercifully and indiscriminately' and attacking bystanders and shopkeepers.[50] The protestors retaliated with a hail of rocks and missiles, turning one of Kabul's main thoroughfares into a war zone. Faced with a no-confidence motion in the Wolusi Jirga, 'Etimadi threw in the towel and resigned. In the words of a senior State Department official, his government was 'lethargic', 'lacklustre', had 'died slowly' and 'achieved little'.[51]

'Abd al-Zahir, the new premier, was a Pushtun and an American-trained medical doctor, but his appointment was due primarily to the fact he was a royalist and a personal friend of the king. His cabinet too was packed with Muhammadzais, including two members of the Seraj family and, for the first time, a woman, Shafiq Ziyai, a descendant of Sardar Nasr Allah Khan. This time it took seventeen days for the Wolusi Jirga to vote in the new administration and while the debate raged in the Chamber, outside Rome continued to burn. Following the riots of 16 and 17 May students and teachers had gone on indefinite strike, and when there was no sign of the protest ending, 'Abd al-Zahir closed all of Kabul's schools. A month later he shut down the university as well, only for the students to resume their campaign when the new academic year started in March 1972. This time there were violent clashes not just between anti-government protestors and the security forces, but between Leftist and Islamist students, which led to the deaths of at least two members of Sho'la-yi Jawed.

As the government increasingly lost control of the political situation, the economic crisis was exacerbated by the worst natural disaster in living memory. From the spring of 1969 to the autumn of 1972 the winter snows and spring rains, the source of all of Afghanistan's rivers, failed. The consequences were devastating. There was insufficient water for irrigation and the water table on *lalmi* rain-fed land, the primary land for growing wheat in northern Afghanistan, dropped dramatically. Soon domestic wells began to dry up, crops failed, and fruit trees and vines withered, while domestic animals died from thirst or had to be slaughtered. The mountainous regions of western and northwestern Afghanistan were particularly hard hit, as were the Durrani and Ghilzai nomads in southwestern Afghanistan. By the spring of 1971 Prime Minister 'Abd al-Zahir admitted the country urgently needed more than half a million tons of wheat just to keep drought-affected populations alive. A survey conducted in the following year reported that nearly a quarter of a million people, or more than one-third of the population of the provinces of Herat, Faryab, Badghis, Jauzjan, Ghur and Uruzgan, were on the edge of starvation.

The government had no experience in natural disaster management and its response was patchy, uncoordinated and marred by incompetence. Eventually, in August 1971 'Abd al-Zahir swallowed his pride and petitioned the U.S. State Department for the immediate provision of 100,000 tons of wheat. Robert G. Neumann, the Austrian-born U.S. ambassador, who had spent two years in a Nazi concentration camp and knew the meaning of hunger, persuaded the State Department to double the tonnage. The World Food Programme, Canada, China, Germany, Turkey, France and the European Economic Community contributed a further 100,000 tons of wheat. Food-for-work programmes were started, fertilizer distributed and new strains of drought-resistant seed introduced. However, the USA refused a request for a moratorium on the repayment of Afghanistan's debt, citing statutory grounds. The country therefore had to continue payments despite not being able to afford to buy enough food to keep its population alive.

For the first time non-governmental organizations were allowed to supervise the local distribution of food aid, and thousands of people were saved from starvation owing to the heroic efforts of American Peace Corps volunteers and Christian relief workers. The relief effort faced immense logistical challenges as it attempted to deliver large supplies of food aid to some of the most inaccessible mountain communities in Afghanistan. The few roads into Ghur, Badghis and the Hazarajat able to take motorized vehicles were unpaved, badly maintained, extremely dangerous and barely wide enough for cars, let alone trucks. Depending on weather conditions, the journey from Kabul or Herat to the main distribution centre in Chaghcharan could take a week. At the local level relief supplies to remote communities were delivered by huge convoys of pack animals.

To add to Afghanistan's economic woes, following the outbreak of war between West and East Pakistan in December 1971, the government of West Pakistan withdrew the 100 and 500 rupee notes in order to stem rampant inflation. Consequently many Afghan exporters went bankrupt as these high denomination notes, which were commonly used when trading with Pakistan, were now valueless. From the late 1960s the government also had to deal with the influx of thousands of American and European hippies or, as Ambassador Neumann called them 'drug-frazzled freaks', who were en route to India.[52] Afghanistan was a key stopping-off place for travellers on the Hippy Trail, for it was reputed to grow the best marijuana and opium in the world.

The smoking of hashish (*chars*) and raw opium (*taryaq*) was nothing new to Afghans, who traditionally grew small amounts for domestic consumption, but the government did not regard this low-level use as a major social evil. The arrival of thousands of hippies changed all this and in response to rising demand the cultivation of marijuana and opium burgeoned. Since the opium poppy was more drought resistant than wheat, and the crop worth far more per hectare than grain or vegetables, local farmers began to switch to opium. Soon Afghan marijuana and opium began to appear on the North American and European black markets. As addiction rates rose, so did the crime rate. In an attempt to address its rising drug problem, the USA demanded that the Afghan government act to suppress opium production and USAID tried to introduce alternative cash crops, though with patchy success. The drug issue was particularly embarrassing for the USA, since the major opium-producing region was along the Bogra Canal system in the Helmand, a project built by an American company and funded by the State Department.

Both the government and foreign embassies were overwhelmed by the problems presented by the hippy trail. Many travellers died from dysentery, hepatitis or typhus or from overdoses. Addicts sold their blood, passports and possessions in order to feed their habits, others begged in the streets or turned to drug dealing, prostitution and theft. Many ended up before the courts and were jailed. Those who died were buried, often in unmarked graves, in the Qabr-i Gora, the European cemetery. The Western media's interest in the hippy trail drew attention to Afghanistan's opium production, which was deeply embarrassing for the government, since it was blamed for a problem not of its making and undermined attempts to promote middle-class and high-end tourism. As for the suppression of the opium crop, this proved politically complicated for much of the opium was grown on land owned by influential landowners, including government ministers and Muhammadzais.

In March 1972 disagreements within 'Abd al-Zahir's government led to the resignation of the Serajis, which was precipitated by the government's decision not to raise taxes. Amid rumours that the rest of the cabinet planned to quit, 'Abd al-Zahir, who had no appetite for another bruising battle with the Wolusi Jirga, decided instead to cut the salaries of civil servants and laid off state employees. The crisis of governance, however, was not limited to the Executive. When the new session of the Wolusi Jirga met, it had to be postponed due to insufficient members present to make up a quorum. The House finally convened a few weeks later, only for the session to be adjourned following a stormy debate over procedure, precipitated by King Zahir Shah calling in MPs for personal interviews and offering them state positions and other incentives in return for toeing the government line. The king even contemplated suspending Parliament, amending or suspending the Constitution and reverting to rule by royal decree. In a meeting with an American special envoy, Zahir Shah admitted that the experiment in New Democracy had perhaps been 'premature'.

At the same time the United States was unwittingly dragged into the Machiavellian world of Afghanistan's dynastic politics. In mid-March 1972 Sayyid Wahid 'Abd Allah, Director of Information at the Ministry of Foreign Affairs and a Da'udist, made an unprecedented request for a private interview with Ambassador Neumann at his own residence. When the two men met, Wahid dropped a bombshell by asking what the U.S. position would be if Da'ud returned to power. A few days later Neumann received a confidential letter, purporting to come from Da'ud himself, which asked for specific answers to four questions:

A. What is the attitude of U.S. re. Da'ud's possible resumption of power?
B. Could Da'ud/Naim count upon sympathy of USG[overnment] if Da'ud became head of government?
C. Would U.S. then continue to support Afghanistan economically and morally?
D. Will U.S. safeguard Afghan National Independence?[53]

Although these approaches indicated that plans for a coup were well under way, Neumann reassured the State Department that Da'ud's return to power was 'no more than an outside possibility' and the State Department's response to the questions was a bland statement about America's non-interference in Afghanistan's internal affairs. A few weeks later Neumann's informers told him some members of the royal family supported Da'ud's return to power and that Shah Wali Khan was attempting to reconcile the king and Da'ud – for the cousins had not been on speaking terms for months. At the same time that Da'ud was seeking tacit American support for his coup, he was also discussing a power-sharing deal with Babrak Karmal's Parcham.

A few months later, the U.S. government weakened its position further when John Connally, who had just stepped down as Secretary to the Treasury, informed the government during a visit to Kabul that America would no longer make direct loans to the country. Instead, Afghanistan should apply for funds to Iran, America's most strategic ally in the region. Connally's position reflected the prevailing Nixon Doctrine, which regarded the Shah of Iran as the main bulwark against Communism in the region, but neither President Nixon nor Connally appears to have had any idea of the long-standing rivalry that existed between Iran and Afghanistan. Prime Minister 'Abd al-Zahir had no wish to strengthen his opponents by appearing to go cap in hand to the Shah, let alone risk Iran using the provision of aid money to demand concessions over the un-resolved dispute in Sistan or influence Afghanistan's foreign policy. In the autumn of 1972 'Abd al-Zahir could take no more and stepped down. In his letter of resignation he apologized to the king for his government's failure to solve the nation's many problems, an expression of regret unprecedented in Afghan political life, but one that was long overdue.

The premiership of Musa' Shafiq and the fall of King Zahir Shah

The king was abroad at the time and postponed accepting Zahir's resig-nation until he returned from his tour of Europe. Finally, in December he appointed the Foreign Minister, Musa' Shafiq, as the new premier. Shafiq, a Shinwari and a graduate of al-Azhar, was a monarchist with links to the Islamist parties, though he was more reform-minded than Niyazi and his circle. Shafiq's cabinet included representatives of various factions includ-ing Da'udists, associates of Maiwandwal, as well as Islamists. There were also several representatives of ethnic and religious minorities, including 'Abd al-Wahid Sarabi, a Hazara who was probably a covert member of Sho'la-yi Jawed, and Muhammad Khan Jalallar, the son of an Uzbek refugee from Ferghana, who had links to Parcham.[54]

Shafiq was the most dynamic and proactive of premiers since the era of Da'ud, but the complexity of the problems his administration faced were daunting. Left-wingers and Da'udists in the cabinet knew it was only a matter of time before Da'ud attempted a coup and Shafiq's frantic attempts to stop the ship of state from sinking were probably motivated by the fact that he knew he and the king were living on borrowed time. Shafiq forced through a number of key administrative reforms that allowed better coordination of the famine crisis. In an attempt to appease the Islamists he also released a number of students affiliated to the Niyazi network. The new government had less success when it came to addressing the economic and financial crisis. By the early 1970s about 40 per cent of all Afghanistan's foreign exchange earnings was devoted to serving interest and repayments on the country's huge foreign debt. In March 1973 Shafiq requested a moratorium on repayments and rescheduling of foreign debt. The USSR promptly agreed, but the USA and European countries were far less sympathetic and even less willing to pour bad money after good.

Shafiq informed Neumann that he intended to 'correct [the] deviant trajectory of Afghan public life', a euphemism for parliamentary democracy, for Zahir Shah was seriously considering cancelling the upcoming elections, and 'cement already close ties' with the United States.[55] In order to show his good faith, Shafiq negotiated a treaty with Iran that settled the long-standing dispute over riparian rights to the waters of the Helmand, an agreement that was fiercely opposed by Maiwandwal, Da'udists and Pushtunists in the Wolusi Jirga. The Left too was incensed when it emerged that, in return for concessions over water rights, the Shah of Iran had pledged Afghanistan millions of dollars of aid. Da'ud even went as far as to condemn the treaty as treasonous. The treaty was eventually passed by a majority vote of both Houses, but Zahir Shah delayed signing it into law and was deposed before he set his seal to the treaty. In the end, the treaty was never ratified. Shafiq alienated Da'ud and supporters of Pushtunistan further by inviting Pakistan's prime minister, Zu'l-fiqar 'Ali Bhutto, to pay a state visit to Afghanistan. Unfortunately for Shafiq the visit coincided with a bloody crackdown by the Pakistan army in Baluchistan and the Northwest Frontier, which led to an influx of refugees into Afghanistan.

Relations with the USA and European nations were not helped by a series of scandals involving high-ranking members of the Afghan government. Iranian customs seized a huge consignment of Afghan heroin destined for Europe, and one of the king's close confidants, Muhammad Rahim Panjshiri, and other unnamed accomplices in the Afghan embassy

The Community Christian Church of Kabul just before its destruction by government order in February 1973. From the outset the new building was surrounded by controversy. Eight days after the construction began the minister, Rev. J. Christy Wilson, received an order from the government to stop building. Church members were also divided over the appropriateness of this new and imposing structure.

in Washington were accused of smuggling 40 kilograms (22 lb) of heroin into the United States in the diplomatic bag. Indonesia too expelled the Afghan ambassador following the discovery of machine guns in a consignment of goods addressed to the embassy in Jakarta. Relations were further strained by the expulsion of Western Christian aid workers and the destruction of the new, international Protestant church, the Community Christian Church of Kabul (CCCK). In March 1973 unnamed individuals alleged that some expatriate workers in the NOOR Blind Institute and the Medical Aid Programme (MAP) in the Hazarajat were proselytizing and importing Christian literature. It was no secret that the International Afghan Mission (IAM),[56] the umbrella organization of these programmes, was funded by foreign churches, mission organizations and Protestant Trusts; indeed when the IAM was set up in response to a specific invitation by the government in 1966, its protocol clearly stated it was a faith agency. By 1973 the IAM's various projects, particularly its ophthalmic work in the NOOR hospital,[57] had earned the widespread respect of the king, government officials and the public at large.

The accusations appear to have originated from Islamists angered at the construction of a new church in Dar al-'Aman, which was intended to replace the rented house used by the CCCK for the foreign Protestant community. The building was a grandiose affair and some *mullahs* complained that the roof of the church, in violation of Islamic tradition, was higher than the minarets of the nearby mosque. Shafiq ordered an investigation that revealed irregularities in the building consent process. The IAM became embroiled in the controversy after it emerged that the majority of the church board were IAM visa holders. Shafiq ordered the newly completed church to be demolished, but in the process of destruction the contractors, government officials and local people looted the marble from its walls and floors and most of the fittings. The government then suspended church services in the old building, but in a gesture of ecumenical solidarity Father Angelo Panigati, the Papal representative, offered the use of his chapel in the Italian Embassy instead.

The government then closed the MAP programme, nationalized NOOR and the Blind Institute, and expelled all their expatriate volunteers. The IAM was informed that the visas of its expatriate workers would not be renewed and any staff members currently abroad would not be allowed back into the country. The American Minister of the CCCK, the Reverend Dr Christy Wilson, and his wife were also declared *persona non grata*. This action was a substantial overreaction by Shafiq to a situation that ought to have been handled in a more diplomatic, low-key manner. The diplomatic fallout for the Afghan government was serious. The USA and European nations formally protested at the expulsions of their nationals, while the Western press attacked the government for its repression and lack of religious liberties. The reaction was particularly strong in the USA, for the majority of those expelled were American citizens. Furthermore, under an informal agreement with the Afghan government, the U.S. Embassy processed Wilson's visa, while the new church had been paid for by U.S.-based churches, trusts and para-church organizations.

The destruction of the KCCC and the subsequent expulsions were headline news in America's influential Christian press. The evangelist Billy Graham and other Christian leaders raised the issue with Congressmen and the White House. The State Department too came under considerable pressure to demand the Afghan government reinstate the visas, reopen MAP and the Blind School, and compensate the CCCK for the destruction of the church. The U.S. government was constrained by the Constitution's separation of church and state, but Ambassador Neumann did what he could. He and the British ambassador suggested that all IAM expatriates sign a written undertaking not to engage in proselytizing, but the organization's Director, Colonel Alan Norrish, a former British Indian army officer, informed them that many IAM members would refuse to do so on principle.[58] Shafiq, too, refused to back down and the expulsions went ahead. For President Richard Nixon, whose Republican Party relied heavily on the Evangelical and Fundamentalist vote, the incident could not have come at a worse time for he was fighting for his political life as a result of the Watergate scandal.

Having created a storm of controversy with powerful Western nations, Shafiq then proceeded to antagonize the USSR by denying a Soviet request to open a Cultural Centre in Kabul, turning down a proposal to construct more bridges across the Amu Darya and an offer to extend the Soviet railhead at Hairatan to Mazar-i Sharif. In late May 1973 Nikolai Podgorny,

Lilian Starr, Matron of the Church Missionary Society's hospital in Peshawar, dressed in Afridi costume shortly after her dramatic rescue of Molly Ellis in 1923. Five years earlier, her husband, Dr Harold Vernon Starr, had been stabbed to death by an Afridi. Up until the 1950s, missionaries were not allowed to work in Afghanistan, though many Afghans crossed the frontier to receive medical attention in mission hospitals in the Northwest Frontier and Baluchistan. After Christian organizations began operating inside Afghanistan, the security organs kept a close watch on their activities.

President of the Supreme Soviet, paid a state visit to Kabul only for Shafiq to decline the Soviet offer of joining the Asian Security Network, the USSR's equivalent of SEATO-CENTO. Shafiq's failure to toe the Soviet line was duly noted and Marxist sympathizers were given the nod by Soviet embassy officials to go ahead with the planned coup.

In June King Zahir Shah made a hastily arranged trip to Italy that was officially said to be for surgery for an eye injury, which was somewhat ironic as the government had just expelled some of the world's leading eye surgeons. In hindsight, the king's sudden departure could well have been a face-saving way of avoiding the inevitable. After an absence of more than three weeks and with no sign of the king's imminent return, at 0400 hours on 17 July 1973, Da'ud ordered his followers into action. Army units led by young Khalqi officers swiftly took control of key ministries and Radio Kabul. After a brief exchange of small arms fire in the palace, Queen Homaira, who appears to have had advance warning of the coup, ordered the royal guard to lay down their arms. Apart from a brief skirmish around the prison and traffic police headquarters at Deh Mazang, there was little resistance. Shafiq, Shah Wali Khan, General 'Abd al-Wali Khan and other members of the royal family were arrested, along with army officers, government ministers and political opponents, but no member of the royal family was injured. In all 45 soldiers and two or three policemen died in the fighting.[59]

The following morning Da'ud announced on Kabul Radio that he had acted to end the country's slide into anarchy and economic meltdown, and made it clear that the king had been deposed and would not be allowed to return. Da'ud was now President of the People's Republic of Afghanistan and the Constitution and Parliament were suspended. A few days later, following expressions of concern from Western nations that the new name implied Afghanistan was now a Soviet client state, Da'ud henceforth referred to the country as the Democratic Republic of Afghanistan.

THIRTEEN

Republicanism, Revolution and Resistance, 1973–94

One does not establish a dictatorship in order to safeguard a revolution; one makes the revolution in order to establish the dictatorship.

GEORGE ORWELL, 1984

If Fundamentalism comes to Afghanistan, war will continue for many years. Afghanistan will turn into a centre of world smuggling for narcotic drugs. Afghanistan will be turned into a centre for terrorism.

PRESIDENT NAJIB ALLAH KHAN[1]

DESPITE THE INEVITABLE RHETORIC, Da'ud's Revolution was the antithesis of the populist uprisings that were the hallmark of the French, American and Russian Revolutions. Da'ud and Na'im made a few token changes, including renouncing their royal title of *sardar*, but this failed to disguise the fact that the putsch was a military coup by disgruntled and ambitious members of the ruling dynasty. For ordinary Afghans, Da'ud was king in all but name. Da'ud's subsequent declaration that one of his chief aims was 'to rid our nation of ideological penury' is thus profoundly ironic, since he represented a monarchy that was primarily responsible for this very penury.[2]

President Da'ud's chalk-and-cheese coalition

Da'ud's Republican government was even more bizarre as it was a coalition of two irreconcilable political ideologies, Monarchism and Communism.[3] As Marxist–Leninists, the People's Democratic Party of Afghanistan (PDPA) opposed the monarchy per se and blamed the 'backwardness' of Afghanistan on its feudal system, at the apex of which stood the Muhammadzai dynasty. The ideological gulf within the coalition was exacerbated by a generation gap. Da'ud and his supporters were all in their late 50s or 60s and their vision of the state, government and national identity was rooted in Mahmud Tarzi's *Afghaniyya* and the Pushtun-Aryanism, as promoted by the Pushtu Academy and the Musahiban dynasty from the 1930s. The PDPA, on the other hand, represented a younger, newly educated generation whose membership consisted mainly of marginalized populations – Ghilzais, Hazaras, Tajiks, Uzbeks and Badakhshanis – all of whom blamed the Muhammadzai dynasty and, in some cases, Pushtuns in general for their disenfranchisement. As for Da'ud's obsession with Pushtunistan, most PDPA members, whether Parchamis or Khalqis, had little interest in the issue, other than as a way to annoy Pakistan and undermine its alliance with the USA. President Da'ud's Republican government was always a *nika mut'a*, or temporary marriage of convenience, and one that would end in a bloody divorce.

The fault lines in Da'ud's government emerged almost as soon as the shooting ceased. It took three weeks of horse-trading before President Da'ud and the PDPA could agree on a Cabinet, during which period government virtually ceased. In the end, more than half of the new ministers were PDPA party members or had strong links to Leftist movements,[4] though the leaders of the PDPA were notable by their absence from the Cabinet in an attempt to conceal the degree of Communist influence in the new government. Instead, these individuals sat on the Central Committee, the membership of which was never publicized, but Babrak Karmal, Anahita Ratebzad and Mir Akbar Khyber, the principal leaders of Parcham, were all prominent members of this committee. When Ambassador Neumann asked President Da'ud for clarification on the role of this body, Da'ud informed him that it was 'not r[e]p[ea]t not the government' but 'a group of "friends" who function as a control committee'.[5] No one in the Western diplomatic corps believed him and it was an open secret that the Central Committee was the real decision-making body.

One of the immediate problems President Da'ud had to address was the fate of the deposed king, Zahir Shah. In this respect, Da'ud had the upper hand, since the king's family as well as Shah Wali Khan and his son, General 'Abd al-Wali Khan, were under house arrest in Kabul. Da'ud offered the king a deal. In exchange for allowing his family to leave for Italy and for the king to continue to receive the revenues from his substantial estates, Zahir Shah would abdicate and undertake not to attempt to overthrow the new government. Zahir Shah tamely agreed and the day before Independence Day the king wrote a brief letter of abdication. A few days later, his family left for Italy, but Shah Wali Khan and 'Abd al-Wali Khan remained in Kabul to ensure the ex-king upheld his side of the bargain.

A month or so after the coup, President Da'ud marked Independence Day with a rambling speech in which he blamed all the country's ills on

Zahir Shah and the administrations that had followed his own resignation in 1963.[6] Da'ud then listed a swath of unrealistic and unattainable goals, including the nationalization of all major industrial, commercial, financial and social assets; a minimum wage; the 'complete emancipation of women'; the eradication of opium cultivation and the resettlement of *kuchi*s so that 'all traces of nomadic and tribal life will be eliminated'. There was to be a new flag and national anthem while 26 Sunbula (17 July), the date of Da'ud's coup, was to be a national holiday. Da'ud also announced the establishment of a committee to draft a new Constitution but made it clear that there would be no multiparty democracy in his Republic.

In an attempt to address the economic crisis, Da'ud announced the government was imposing 'protective tariffs' on cheap imports and strict controls on exchange rates and the export of hard currency. To alleviate the impact of the drought, the prices of bread, rice and other essential food-stuffs were to be fixed by the state, and shopkeepers who overcharged were threatened with fines and imprisonment. The price controls were popular but the *nanbai*s and small shopkeepers suffered since the state-imposed prices did not cover their costs and the subsidies were insufficient to make up the shortfall. As for the new, artificial exchange rate, this earned the government a great deal of hard currency, for Muhammad Khan Jalallar, the Minister of Finance, cunningly played the money markets. Foreign export companies, tourists, UN agencies and non-governmental organizations, on the other hand, were badly hit for they were obliged to buy afghanis at the official exchange rate rather than on the open market, where the rate was often more than twice that of the banks. Within a matter of months, the free market ground to a standstill.[7]

In the wake of the coup, hundreds of card-carrying PDPA members were appointed to mid-level positions in the civil service, while Khalqi army and air force officers who had supported the coup were promoted. In order to find posts for these new appointments many existing civil servants and military officers lost their jobs or were forcibly retired. Since most of the officials who were dismissed owed their position of privilege to their support of the Musahiban dynasty, their sacking undermined Da'ud's power. The Parchamis and Khalqis then proceeded to exploit their newfound power to promote their Communist ideas in schools, the University, the Teachers' Training College and the media. However, the new appointees lacked the experience of running the civil service and government departments were even more chaotic than usual. Less than three months into the Republican era, Neumann informed the State Department that President Da'ud's regime had made 'a distinctly

unfavourable impression on most observers, both foreign and international
. . . and one is hard pressed to find anyone to defend it.' As for Da'ud's
cabinet, it was 'inferior' and 'incompetent' and there was 'near paralysis
and delays in economic decision-making'.[8]

President Da'ud and u.s.-Afghan relations

Despite the government being dominated by Parchamis, Da'ud and
Na'im tried to convince Western governments that Afghanistan was
still Non-Aligned and hoped that the USA and Western nations would
quickly recognize the new regime and provide financial assistance. In
both respects they were disappointed. The USSR and India accorded the
new government diplomatic recognition almost immediately, but the
United States and NATO countries delayed until they were sure that Da'ud
was, as Neumann put it, 'master in his own house'. Na'im's argument that
American financial support would strengthen Da'ud's hand and allow
him to counteract the power of the PDPA found little sympathy with State
Department officials who were not prepared for the USA to prop up the
Republican government, let alone be played off against the USSR.[9] Da'ud's
plea for American support was not helped when his Deputy Foreign
Minister publicly declared that King Reza Shah of Iran, America's most
important ally in the region, was a 'madman who will soon share the fate
of Zahire [sic] Shah, if not worse'.[10] Reza Shah's response was to tell the
u.s. ambassador in Tehran that Afghanistan was 'nothing but trouble' and
claimed the country was turning into a 'police state under communist
control'.[11] In the end, America and the NATO countries recognized the
Republican government, but relations with Da'ud and his ministers were
strained, though publicly cordial.

Another source of tension in Afghan-American relations was President
Da'ud's resurrection of the Pushtunistan issue. Da'ud's promotion of
Pushtunistan during his time as prime minister had brought Afghanistan
to the brink of war and economic catastrophe, yet he seems to have
learnt nothing from this experience. Shortly after seizing power the state-
controlled media began a belligerent propaganda war against Pakistan
and in favour of Pushtunistan. Pakistan retaliated by reimposing restrictions on cross-border traffic and ordered a military build-up in Quetta.
When Ambassador Neumann attempted to moderate the war of words and
persuade President Da'ud to negotiate with Pakistan, Da'ud insisted as a
precondition that Pakistan agree in principle to discuss self-determination
for Pushtunistan, something that Pakistan had consistently refused to

accept. Within a matter of weeks after Da'ud's coup, Afghanistan's relations with Pakistan were once more on a knife-edge.

At the end of August 1973 Neumann, who was about to leave at the end of his tour of duty, decided to use 'shock treatment' over the state of governance and the Pushtunistan issue, since it was 'better to let a departing ambassador say some unpleasant truths than [an] incoming one'.[12] In his final official meeting with Da'ud, Neumann gave the President what he described as a 'cold shower', informing him that Washington viewed his alliance with the PDPA unfavourably and warning him that the Communists posed a threat to Afghanistan's independence and sovereignty. He reiterated America's opposition to the President's Pushtunistan policy and bluntly told him that Afghanistan risked a war with Pakistan. Da'ud, however, ignored Neumann's warnings and continued the war of words. At the end of 1973, frustrated State Department officials noted that the situation was moving 'slowly, steadily and perhaps inexorably towards confrontation'.[13]

President Da'ud's purges and the Islamist insurgency

A month or so after his meeting with Neumann, Da'ud began the first of a series of purges. His first target was dynastic rivals, members of previous administrations and supporters of the Liberal Parliament. Hashim Maiwandwal, Khan Muhammad Khan, who had been Minister of Defence in 'Etimadi's administration, and two former Chiefs of Staff of the army and air force, along with some sixty other individuals, were accused of planning a coup and arrested. The alleged ringleaders were handed over to Parchami internal security officers who beat them, tore out their fingernails and subjected them to electric shocks. The torture was too much for Maiwandwal, who died from his injuries, though officially it was announced he had committed suicide. As for Khan Muhammad Khan, Da'ud had him beaten in his presence.[14] The government laid the blame for the alleged coup on the USA and Pakistan. When challenged by the ambassadors in question, Na'im claimed the government had documentary proof for the allegation, but no such evidence was ever forthcoming. The outcome was that Afghanistan's relations with the USA and Pakistan deteriorated even further.

Da'ud exploited the coup as justification for purging Islamist critics of his government. On 5 December 1973 Radio Kabul broadcast a confession purportedly written by Khan Muhammad Khan in which he claimed the conspirators planned to 'utilize religious leaderships, military units . . . and former deputies and elders' to 'attack the government as Communists',[15] and proceeded to list a number of leading Islamists who were allegedly involved in the plot. Shortly after this announcement Maulana Habib al-Rahman, head of the Muslim Youth Organization, Maulana Faizani, Prof. Niyazi and Muhammad Sarwar Nashir, formerly governor of Qataghan and head of the Spinzar Cotton Company, were arrested along with dozens of high-ranking military and government officials.[16] Other leading Islamists, however, escaped the purge, including Sibghat Allah Mujadidi, 'Abd al-Rauf Sayyaf, Gulbudin Hikmatyar, Burhan al-Din Rabbani and a Panjshiri engineering student and friend of Hikmatyar's, Ahmad Shah Mas'ud. They fled to Peshawar where they formed an Islamist opposition to Da'ud. Following the Soviet invasion of December 1979, these men would become the most prominent leaders of the resistance.

The arrival of these political refugees provided Zu'l-fiqar 'Ali Bhutto, Pakistan's prime minister, with a major propaganda coup, which he exploited to the full to undermine Da'ud's credibility with Frontier Pushtuns and the Afghan government's Islamic credentials. Da'ud's coup and the revival of the Pushtunistan issue had come at a difficult time for Bhutto, who was engaged in a power struggle with the Pushtun-dominated National Awami League (NAL) led by 'Abd al-Ghaffar Khan's son, Khan Wali Khan. In March 1973, a few weeks before the fall of King Zahir Shah, Federal Security Forces had opened fire on a NAL rally in Rawalpindi, killing and wounding dozens of protestors. In February the following year, when the governor of the Northwest Frontier Province was assassinated in a car bomb attack, Bhutto blamed the NAL for his death and arrested Khan Wali Khan and other NAL leaders. They were tried and found guilty of treason, though on appeal the High Court acquitted them. Other leading NAL members fled across the border into Afghanistan where the government welcomed them with open arms.

In an attempt to undermine Da'ud's Republican government, Bhutto encouraged the Peshawar Islamist refugees to stage a revolt and provided them with basic military training, cash and weapons. On the second anniversary of the Republic, the Islamists planned a series of attacks on outlying provincial centres, but the uprising was poorly coordinated. Most of the agitators were arrested before they could do any harm and the rebel leaders anyway found there was little support for their revolt. The exception was in the Koh Daman, where Ahmad Shah Mas'ud's Panjshiris overran the government offices in Bazarak, Jabal Saraj, Gulbahar and Shortal. Da'ud responded by airlifting paratroopers into the region and sending tanks, heavy artillery and MiG jets to pound rebel positions. The Panjshiris fled before the onslaught but more than six hundred government troops and rebels died in the campaign, including the governor and *qazi* of Parwan province.[17] The government then publicly accused Pakistan of funding the 'saboteurs' and rounded up dozens of its political enemies. A few months later Da'ud reshuffled his cabinet, sacking several PDPA ministers and replacing them with Muhammadzais and ministers who had formerly served under Zahir Shah. A number of royalist political prisoners were released and Shah Wali Khan and 'Abd al-Wali Khan were allowed to join the ex-king in Italy. Meanwhile, in Peshawar the Islamists squabbled over whether to continue the armed struggle. Eventually Hikmatyar split from the others and set up his own militia, Hizb-i Islami, and continued the armed resistance against Da'ud's government.

The debt crisis and President Da'ud's appeal to Western and Arab nations

In November 1974 the U.S. Secretary of State, Henry Kissinger, paid a flying visit to Kabul and during a brief meeting Na'im again asserted his government's wish for closer relations with the USA, only for Kissinger to remind him that U.S.-Afghan relations could not be improved if the government continued to pursue the Pushtunistan issue. In July of the following year Na'im flew to Washington, where he had an audience with President Ford and expressed his concern about Communist influence in the military. Afghanistan, he told President Ford, did not want to be 'too close' to the USSR or 'be gripped by a small percentage of people who are in the services of a foreign power'.[18] Da'ud, Na'im and other ministers also embarked on a tour of NATO and Arab capitals. When Da'ud attended the funeral of King Faizal of Saudi Arabia, he made ostentatious show of his Islamic credentials by performing Hajj. In a subsequent visit to Iraq, he also visited the Shi'a holy sites in Najaf.

Da'ud's belated attempt to win the support of America, the Western world and pro-American Arab states to counteract the power of the PDPA was not motivated solely by political expedience, but by the unresolved economic and fiscal crisis. Afghanistan by this time was deeply in debt to the USSR to the tune of $1.5 billion as well as owing the USA substantial sums. Yet despite being barely able to repay its international debt, the government had agreed to an ambitious Seven Year Plan that was estimated to cost $3 billion. Moscow, fearing Afghanistan was about to default on its debt repayment, was only prepared to contribute $500 million to the Plan, so Da'ud hoped that Western nations and the oil-rich Gulf States might be persuaded to make up the shortfall. Yet despite much costly travel, the financial returns were minimal and even the Gulf States only pledged a few hundred million dollars. In a desperate attempt to persuade Saudi Arabia to fund the Plan, Jalallar, the Finance Minister, tactlessly told the Saudi ambassador, 'for you 1.5 billion dollars is nothing . . . you should help a [Muslim] brother', to which the envoy laughingly replied: 'God will give you wealth as well. But we will help you in other ways.'[19]

In April 1975 Da'ud travelled to Tehran and during his Republic Day speech he publicly announced the Seven Year Plan. A few days later the *Kabul Times* announced that the Shah of Iran had agreed to extend Afghanistan a $710 million line of credit, most of which would be devoted to the construction of a rail link between Kabul and Iran and a joint irrigation project on the disputed waters of the Helmand. Following Afghanistan's Planning Minister's visit to Iran in November of the same year, a further assistance package was agreed. The Iranian loan marked a shift in Afghanistan's regional relations and was a significant climbdown for President Da'ud, who had vociferously opposed attempts by previous governments to seek Iranian assistance or to settle the dispute over riparian rights. However, while President Da'ud's actions won the approval of State Department officials,[20] the Iranian credit deal never got off the ground due to the oil embargo of the Organization of the Petroleum Exporting Countries, or OPEC, and Iran's subsequent decision to double its own internal expenditure.

This was not the only concession President Da'ud made. The tours of Arab and European capitals obliged Da'ud and Na'im to face the unpleasant fact that no country supported their stance on Pushtunistan. Instead, Afghan ministers were again and again urged to negotiate with Pakistan so that Afghanistan, Iran and Pakistan could present a united front against the USSR. In the end, Da'ud's need of hard cash to keep the country and his government solvent and to pay for his Seven Year Plan took priority over his pursuit of Pushtunistan.

One of the conditions imposed by Iran on its credit agreement was that the Afghan government tone down its rhetoric about Pushtunistan and agree to unconditional negotiations with Pakistan to settle the long-standing dispute, and from the end of 1975 Afghanistan's state-controlled media began to moderate its stance on the issue. In April of the following year, when the Pakistan Red Crescent provided substantial humanitarian aid to victims of flooding and an earthquake that left more than 100,000 people homeless, the Afghan government publicly thanked Pakistan for helping fellow Muslims. As a mark of respect for the dead, Bhutto also instructed the Pakistan media to suspend its anti-Afghanistan propaganda. Da'ud took the opportunity of the thaw in relations to invite Bhutto to make a state visit to Afghanistan. When the two men met in June 1976 they struck up a rapport that dispelled some of the distrust that had existed between the two governments since 1947. In a public statement issued at the end of their meetings, both parties announced they had agreed to refrain from hostile propaganda. Bhutto accepted that there were 'political differences' between the two countries, while President Da'ud dropped the demand that Pakistan release NAL prisoners before further talks could be held over the Pushtunistan issue and accepted Bhutto's invitation to visit Islamabad. In a speech at the state banquet held in Bhutto's honour, Da'ud declared that 'on our side the door for talks and understanding is always open for reaching a final settlement regarding the prevailing political difference between the two countries'.[21] Theodore L. Eliot Jr, the new U.S Ambassador, reported to the State Department that 'after being adamant all his life on the issue of Pushtunistan, Daoud (*sic*) has given a clear signal of change of heart. We believe it improbable this issue can ever again be viewed in Afghanistan in quite the same way'.[22]

A month later, President Da'ud avoided any specific reference to Pushtunistan during his Republic Day broadcast. When Da'ud arrived in Islamabad in August he was greeted by Pushtun tribesmen, who danced all along the route of his cavalcade. The Pakistani press hailed his visit as a 'major breakthrough', while Eliot triumphantly informed the State Department that Da'ud's meeting with Bhutto had caught the 'Russians and their local adherents . . . somewhat off balance'.

Da'ud and the confrontation with the USSR and the PDPA

The growing rapprochement with Iran and Pakistan was not well received by PDPA members in the government, who accused Da'ud of betraying the Revolution. Da'ud responded by arresting the more vociferous critics and sending others into exile as ambassadors to distant countries. Da'ud's shift into the Western camp was also duly noted in Moscow. The Kremlin was particularly upset about the Iranian loan and the proposed Kabul–Tehran rail link, which, if it went ahead, would provide Afghanistan with an alternative overland route for imports and exports and a consequent loss to the USSR of transit fees and political influence. The fact that Da'ud had earlier refused a Soviet request to extend its railhead at Hairatan to Mazar-i Sharif did not help Afghan-Soviet relations either. Another source of foreign exchange for the Soviet Union was the sale of diesel, petrol and aviation fuel to Afghanistan, so when Iran subsequently agreed to sell Afghanistan millions of barrels of fuel oil at a price nearly half that charged by the USSR, the Kremlin was deeply displeased, especially as its own economy was stagnating. To add to the problems, a hike in the international spot price of gas meant Moscow had to increase the amount it paid Afghanistan for the supply of natural gas from the Jarquduq field in Shibarghan. Yet another source of tension was the Kabul Municipality's decision to level the building designed to house the Soviet Cultural Centre.

When Nikolai Podgorny, Chairman of the Presidium of the Supreme Soviet, paid a state visit to Kabul in December 1975, behind the scenes the strain in Afghan-Soviet relations was palpable. The two parties renewed the 1931 Soviet-Afghan Neutrality and Non-Aggression Treaty, but the Soviet delegation made it very clear that, according to their interpretation of the treaty, Afghanistan's northern provinces were still regarded as within their sphere of interest. When Deputy Premier Hasan Sharq informed the Soviet officials that Afghanistan was planning to use the waters of the Amu Darya and Kokcha rivers for additional irrigation, he was pointedly told to 'forget it. The Oxus waters are all being distributed in Uzbekistan and Turkmenistan . . . there are no waters left now for new distribution.'[23]

Da'ud's attempt to reduce the power of the PDPA was reflected in the new Constitution, which was published in January 1977, after nearly four years of drafting. Since there was no Parliament, Da'ud convened a Loya Jirga, packed with his loyalists, which voted the Constitution into law almost unanimously. A rambling Preamble to the text, which purported to speak on behalf of 'we, the people of Afghanistan', grandiosely declared the aim of the Constitution was to allow the Afghan people to fulfil their 'historic and human mission with trust in Almighty God and adhering to the basic principles of the sacred religion of Islam'.[24] However, the Constitution contained only a single reference to Islamic law and that was only to permit the judiciary to refer to the Hanafi legal code as a last resort, the Constitution, civil law and Presidential Decrees all being given precedence. A subsequent Civil and Criminal Code also deviated significantly from the penal provisions of the Hanafi legal code.

The Preamble included a statement that 'national life' was to be founded on 'Liberty, Truth, Justice and Peace based on the principles of Brotherhood and Equality', while the Fundamental Objectives included a pledge 'to secure democracy', eliminate exploitation 'in all its forms and manifestations' and 'respect' the UN Charter and the Universal Declaration of Human Rights. However, these resounding declarations were but a velvet glove that concealed an iron fist. One of the Constitution's stated aims was 'to ever increase the stability and consolidation of the Republican Order', declaring that it was 'the duty of all people of Afghanistan' to be loyal to the 'Republican Order' and not to harm 'the objectives of the Revolution'. As for democracy, this meant a One Party State, for the Constitution outlawed all political parties other than the state-run National Revolutionary Party (NRP). The NRP also appointed 50 per cent of the members of the Milli Jirga, the new name for the Lower House, which met for just four months each year. The creation of the NRP was a catalyst for further confrontation between President Da'ud and his Communist allies. The PDPA refused to disband, while Da'ud condemned those who refused to join the NRP as 'saboteurs'.[25] A month after the Constitution passed into law, Da'ud replaced most of the remaining PDPA members in his cabinet with Muhammadzais and former ministers.

The Moscow confrontation and the PDPA's response

When Da'ud paid a state visit to Moscow in April 1977, the Soviet leadership was determined to make sure the Afghan President knew his place and make it quite clear that the USSR was deeply dissatisfied with his government's policies. Da'ud for his part was equally determined to reaffirm Afghanistan's neutrality and independence. The clash that ensued proved disastrous not just for Da'ud but for Afghanistan and, ultimately, the USSR. In his speech at the state banquet held in his honour, President Da'ud pointedly reaffirmed Afghanistan's 'active and positive neutrality' and declared that 'the main and fundamental objectives of our policy, more than anything else, [are] the preservation of independence, sovereignty [and] national integrity' and 'non-interference in the internal affairs of others'.[26] When the two sides met in private session, Da'ud accused the PDPA of 'subversion' and told General Secretary Leonid Brezhnev to 'advise his comrades . . . to obey the new order in Afghanistan'.[27] Brezhnev responded by complaining about the increasing numbers of Western expatriates arriving in Afghanistan and noted that 'in the past . . . the Afghan government at least did not allow experts from NATO countries to be stationed in the northern parts of the country'. The Soviet Union, Brezhnev continued, 'took a grim view of these developments' and demanded Da'ud remove these foreigners for they 'were nothing more than spies bent on promoting imperialism'. Da'ud was furious: 'We will never allow you to dictate to us how to run our country and whom to employ in Afghanistan,' he retorted, 'how and where we employ the foreign experts will remain the exclusive prerogative of the Afghan state.'[28] Da'ud then rose and walked out of the meeting and despite pleas by both Soviet and Afghan officials he refused to meet with Brezhnev again.

The spat in Moscow was the last straw as far as Brezhnev was concerned and it was decided that Da'ud had to go. Soviet officials in Kabul were instructed to reconcile the warring Parcham and Khalq factions of the PDPA. Moscow then put on a show of strength; border police briefly occupied the disputed island of Urta Tagai in the Amu Darya, while Soviet military transports overflew Afghanistan without seeking prior clearance from Kabul. President Da'ud retaliated by ordering his ministers not to accept any further offers of Soviet aid and considered reducing the number of personnel in the Soviet embassy. In November Da'ud reshuffled his cabinet yet again and set up a Central Council consisting of trusted Muhammadzais. However, in the process he resurrected a long-standing family feud. Sultan Mahmud Khan Ghazi, Shah Mahmud's third son, who was head of Aryana Afghan Airlines and the Civil Aviation Authority and whose mother-in-law was a daughter of Loynab Khushdil Khan, was angry that neither he nor any of the Loynabs or Serajis were given seats on this Council. When Da'ud ignored his protests, the Ghazis and Serajis resigned from the government.

A few days later, the confrontation with the PDPA led to bloodshed when 'Ali Ahmad Khurram, the minister of planning, was assassinated. His killer, Muhammad Marjan, had gained access to the Minister in his office, where he drew a pistol and demanded he take him to President Da'ud, but once in the street Marjan shot Khurram dead. President Da'ud used the occasion of Khurram's funeral to publicly accuse Moscow of interference in Afghanistan's internal affairs and implied that the KGB were behind the assassination. Under interrogation, however, Marjan claimed to have acted in the name of the 'Islamic Revolution', but the Parchamis were probably correct when they accused Marjan of being a Khalqi. Remarkably, Marjan was not executed, and following the Taraki coup he was pardoned. He ended his days in Moscow living under an assumed name, and was described as a 'crazy, stupid person'.[29]

As tensions between Moscow and Kabul and between President Da'ud and the PDPA reached crisis point, Da'ud made one final attempt to win the support of the USA and its allies in the Arab world. In early 1978 Da'ud paid a state visit to Egypt where he praised Sadat's peace deal with Israel and signed an agreement allowing Egyptian officers to train Afghan army and police cadets. Twenty-five individuals accused of involvement in the Islamist coup of December 1973 were put on trial in February 1978 and convicted of treason. While most of the accused were sentenced to life imprisonment, Maulana Habib al-Rahman, Dr Muhammad 'Omar and Khwaja Mahfuz Mansur were condemned to death and hanged in the Deh Mazang prison. All three were respected Islamic scholars and their executions stunned and outraged many Afghans.

The assassination of Mir Akbar Khyber and the death of President Da'ud

Two months later, on 17 April, Mir Akbar Khyber, head of Parcham, was shot dead outside his house by an unknown gunman. The Kabul rumour mill claimed President Da'ud or anti-Communist members of his government were behind the assassination but Parchamis claimed Khalq's Hafiz Allah 'Amin and Nur Muhammad Taraki had ordered the shooting, while in Peshawar Hikmatyar said it was his operatives who were responsible. Whoever was behind the assassination, the PDPA used Khyber's violent death as an opportunity to demonstrate publicly their disenchantment with Da'ud's Republican experiment. As Khyber's cortège wound its way from his home in the Soviet-built Mikroyan apartment block to the Pul-i Kheshti mosque, around 15,000 people lined the streets, threw garlands of red tulips, symbolic of martyrdom, in the path of the procession, and chanted anti-American and anti-Iranian slogans.

The size of the crowds frightened Da'ud, who had grossly under-estimated both the unpopularity of his administration and the depth of support for the PDPA. Fearing the protests were the harbinger of a coup, Da'ud ordered the arrest of all the PDPA leadership. Nur Muhammad Taraki, Babrak Karmal and many others were rounded up, but Hafiz Allah 'Amin fortuitously avoided arrest. Realizing that Da'ud would probably execute all of the PDPA leadership, 'Amin sent an urgent message to Khalqi sympathizers at the Rishkhor army base and the Bagram air base, urging them to act immediately and depose Da'ud. On 27 April, the 7 of Saur in the Afghan *shamsi* calendar, the cabinet held an emergency meeting in the Presidential Palace to discuss the crisis, only for their discussions to be interrupted by gunfire, exploding shells and low-flying jet planes. For much of the day street-to-street fighting raged in the capital but by evening PDPA forces controlled most of central Kabul and had cut power and telephone links to the palace. A representative of the Revolutionary Military Council was then sent into the palace to demand the surrender of Da'ud, Na'im and his ministers, only for the ultimatum to be rejected. A battle ensued and by the morning all of Da'ud and Na'im's wives and children were either dead or mortally wounded. When Da'ud rejected a second offer of surrender, he, Na'im and his few remaining loyalists died in a hail of bullets and their corpses were later thrown in an unmarked grave. In 2008 Da'ud's body, along with the remains of sixteen members of his family, was located in a mass grave outside the Pul-i Charkhi prison and given a state funeral.

A few days later the *Kabul Times* gleefully announced Da'ud's demise with the headline, 'Remnants of Monarchy Wiped'. 'For the first time in history,' the lead article proclaimed, 'the last remnants of monarchy, tyranny, despotism and power of the dynasty of the tyrant Nadir Shah has ended.'[30] A second leader entitled 'A Glance at the Historic Crimes of the Naderi Dynasty in Afghanistan', excoriated Nadir Shah and the Musahiban dynasty in general as traitors and described him as 'the most dedicated agent of colonialism', who presided over a 'despotic and hangman state'. As for Da'ud, he was damned as a 'traitor', 'executioner' and a 'bloodthirsty' and 'egotistical' tyrant.

King Zahir Shah and Sardar Muhammad Da'ud: an appraisal

President Da'ud's death marked the end of the Musahiban dynasty and the Durrani monarchy. His reign as prime minister and president of Afghanistan epitomized the monarchy's persistent refusal to relinquish its stranglehold on power, its inability to allow ordinary citizens of Afghanistan more than a token voice in the affairs of state and the denial of fundamental civil liberties. It is hardly surprising that the younger and better educated generation were forced to seek alternatives in militant ideologies, for it seemed that violent revolution, whether Communist or Islamist in nature, was the only way to establish a more just and equitable society. Tragically, the governments that succeeded the monarchy only offered more of the same, albeit dressed in different ideological clothing.

Da'ud's Republican coup was the death blow to the Durrani monarchy, for it opened the door for Communist infiltration of the state's civil service and the military. Da'ud himself had always been a divisive figure and his attempt to turn Afghanistan into a One Party State along Ba'athist lines alienated Muhammadzais, Islamists, the PDPA, democratically minded intellectuals, and a conservative, deeply religious population that despised Communism. Da'ud and Na'im's handling of the economy and Afghanistan's foreign relations was equally inept. Their alliance with the PDPA alienated the USA, NATO, Iran and the Arab world and in the end compromised the country's neutrality, while the resurrection of Pushtunistan led to an economically costly and ultimately pointless confrontation with Pakistan.

Da'ud's attempts to purge the PDPA and shift more into the Western sphere of influence led inevitably to a showdown with the Soviet Union and his own and his family's lonely and bloody death.

Since the fall of the Taliban in 2001, much has been made of King Zahir Shah and Da'ud's secularization and move to gender equality, both by the Western media and monarchists who were restored to a measure of political power by the American intervention. Some media even tend to portray the reign of King Zahir Shah as a kind of Golden Age of democracy and social liberty, exemplified by pictures of unveiled women walking Kabul's streets in knee-length skirts. Yet this grossly overstated the actual situation. The social liberalization was confined to Kabul and a few other urban centres, in particular Mazar-i Sharif and Pul-i Khumri, and only affected a minority of young, urbanized elites and government officials. Burqa-clad women were a common sight in Kabul in the 1970s and even more so in Kandahar, Ghazni, Jalalabad and rural Afghanistan. As for the fleeting experiment in democracy, such as it was, this lasted less than a decade and the government soon reverted to its former, repressive ways after the press and independent Parliamentarians called government officials to account, exposed nepotism, corruption and incompetence and demanded equal rights for marginalized minorities.

Instead of seeking to provide the citizens of Afghanistan with basic freedoms, successive governments under Zahir Shah and President Da'ud focused on infrastructure projects. Dams and hydroelectric power stations provided limited electricity to the capital and a few urban centres and irrigated new areas in Balkh, Nangahar, Qunduz and in the Helmand–Kandahar region, while new sealed roads improved internal communications between the main cities. Rural and provincial roads remained essentially untouched and were some of the worst in Asia, while the majority of Afghanistan's predominantly rural population saw little benefit from government projects. Their primary intent anyway was to increase trade and agricultural output, and hence state revenues, rather than to alleviate poverty or raise the standard of living of ordinary Afghans. Some projects, such as the Helmand-Arghandab scheme, were more about national pride. The majority of infrastructure projects were funded by foreign aid and loans rather than from state revenues; a policy based on the assumption that when completed they would bring in substantial additional revenues to the Exchequer and end up paying for themselves. When these hopes proved to be false, the country found itself increasingly indebted to foreign banks and nations, compromising Afghanistan's neutrality. By the early 1970s Afghanistan was in default on its debt repayments and Da'ud's

Kabul's Chicken Street area of Shahr-i Nau. In the 1970s this crossroads was a popular tourist spot and its shops frequented by middle-class Afghans. Sigis Hotel was also notorious among travellers for it cheap accommodation and the easy availability of hashish and other opiates.

administration proved as inept as its predecessors when it came to solving the country's financial crisis.

The *shirkat* state-run monopolies instituted by Zabuli in the 1930s were perpetuated throughout the era of Zahir Shah and President Da'ud, though by the 1960s more small-scale private enterprises were permitted. King Zahir Shah had been an avid agriculturalist and with the help of the United Nation's Food and Agriculture Organization (FAO) new strains of seed as well as tree and vine stocks were introduced. The FAO also set up basic veterinarian services, including immunization for domestic animals, and instituted locust and pest control. One enterprising individual introduced apples and other pip fruit into the Wardak area, which soon became a major export to Pakistan.

Even so, by 1978 Afghanistan was still in the bottom five Third World nations by all indicators. It had one of the highest adult illiteracy and child mortality rates in the world; life expectancy was in the mid-40s and typhoid, hepatitis, diphtheria, measles, polio, leishmaniasis, and eye diseases such as trachoma were endemic. The government built new hospitals and schools in Kabul and provincial centres, but there was barely any health service provision in rural districts, while rural doctors and teachers were poorly trained and badly paid. As for any public health system, this was virtually non-existent in rural areas and even in the capital the service

596

was at the best poor. The majority of households in Kabul still used water from heavily polluted shallow wells or the Kabul river for drinking, cooking and ablutions, while household waste was dumped on vacant lots or in the river, where it was left to rot or be eaten by wild, *pi* dogs, which roamed the streets. The USSR may have laid Kabul's pavements, but no Afghan town had even a rudimentary waste disposal or treatment plant. Many middle-class houses had cesspits that were regularly emptied, but most people who had toilets used long drops, which discharged their effluent onto the streets. Early every morning donkey carts full of night soil could be seen heading up the Dar al-'Aman road, where it was spread on the fields and vegetable plots that fed the city's population. The government also failed to address the problem of landless sharecroppers and the indebtedness of the rural poor, absentee landlordism, nepotism, and reform of the civil service and bureaucracy. For ethno-political reasons Afghanistan was also one of the few nations in the world not to have had a nationwide census.

President Taraki and the Saur Revolution

Da'ud's death ended the brief experiment in Monarchical Republicanism and ushered in what the PDPA called 'the Glorious Saur Revolution'. This new administration too was an uneasy coalition, this time of the two rival PDPA factions, Khalq and Parcham, though Khalq was the dominant part-ner. The PDPA modelled its version of the One Party State model on that of Stalin. Nur Muhammad Taraki became the new President and Chairman of the Revolutionary Council of what was now the Democratic Republic of Afghanistan, with Babrak Karmal of Parcham as Deputy Chairman. Hafiz Allah 'Amin, another Khalqi, became foreign minister and later prime minister, while General 'Abd al-Qadir, the Khalqi army officer who had led the coup, became minister of defence. One of Taraki's first moves was to establish a new internal security agency, known by the acronym AGSA, which was later renamed KHAD.[31] It was modelled on, and supervised by, the KGB as an agency that was entrusted not just with intelligence gathering and internal security, but enforcing ideological conformity and suppressing all forms of political dissent.

Despite the new government's Marxist–Leninist credentials, Taraki tried to convince Western ambassadors and Afghans in general that his administration was neither Communist nor a puppet regime of the USSR. The USA and its allies were not fooled and, although Western nations eventually accorded diplomatic recognition to the government, there was serious concern as PDPA officials flaunted their Communist ideology:

Postal stamps issued by PDPA governments unashamedly flaunted their Communist credentials. From left to right: April 1979, a stamp to celebrate the first anniversary of the Saur Revolution shows the new red flag with its modified 'Shrine and Sheaf' motif flying from the Presidential palace; November 1985, stamp commemorating the anniversary of Lenin's death and finally this 1985 issue, commemorating the seventh anniversary of the Saur Revolution, shows Afghan and Soviet soldiers united in their fight against the *mujahidin*.

officials referred to each other as 'comrades', and the media and official communications were full of Marxist–Leninist jargon. When the new national flag was unfurled in October 1978, its background was completely red and a socialist-realist wheat sheaf replaced the monarchical wreath. In the same month Hafiz Allah 'Amin, in an article commemorating the Bolshevik Revolution, declared that 'the Saur Revolution is [a] continuation of [the] Great October Revolution'. As for President Nur Muhammad Taraki, he became the focus of a Stalinist personality cult, with state organs referring to him as the Great Leader. When Taraki's official biography was published it glorified his humble background, while his modest house in Kabul's Sher Shah Mina was turned into a shrine.[32]

A few weeks after taking power Taraki began to issue a series of decrees designed to revolutionize Afghan social life along Marxist–Leninist lines, just as those of Amir 'Aman Allah Khan had run roughshod over the traditional values of Afghans and the conservatism of rural communities. The decrees outlawed polygamy, costly dowries, usury and *girau* – an ancient system under which land or property was temporarily mortgaged to a third party in exchange for cash – and cancelled debts more than five years old without compensation. Another decree inaugurated an aggressive land redistribution policy, which included the confiscation of the estates of Muhammadzais and wealthy, absentee landlords, dividing the land into 30 *jerib* (6-hectare) blocks that were distributed to landless peasants and nomads. Workers' collectives and cooperatives were established, and a literacy drive instituted to 'educate' illiterate peasants and impart Communist ideology to the masses. The government established the country's first national census under Polish supervision, which alienated rural populations even more as young urban ideologues were sent into remote parts of the country with questionnaires that demanded detailed, personal information about family life, women, wealth and land ownership.

Taraki, encouraged by Moscow, placed heavy restrictions on the activities of Western agencies and NGOs, especially north of the Hindu Kush, and it became increasingly difficult for Americans and Europeans to obtain visas. The government increasingly recruited expatriate experts from the Soviet Union, Warsaw Pact countries and Cuba. As Moscow sought to bind Afghanistan politically, economically and financially to its interests, the Afghan government signed a series of wide-ranging treaties and agreements with the USSR and its satellite countries that encompassed everything from cultural activities to military assistance, technical cooperation and mineral exploitation.

In August 1978 the Afghan government signed an agreement with the USSR to construct a road bridge across the Amu Darya and in early December a Treaty of Friendship, Good Neighbourliness and Cooperation legitimized the USSR's role of guaranteeing Afghanistan's security, independence and territorial independence, an agreement that would later be used to justify the Soviet military intervention. Early in 1979 another series of agreements established a permanent Soviet-Afghan Commission on economic cooperation and direct Soviet involvement in economic planning. Following the Soviet invasion in December of the same year, the government of President Babrak Karmal conceded administrative control over the Wakhan Corridor and the USSR set up eavesdropping facilities to monitor the military activity in Pakistan and China.

Even if the Taraki government had come to power on the back of a popular uprising, the sweeping nature of the reforms would have met with stiff resistance. Taraki, however, like Da'ud before him, had seized power in a military coup and had no popular mandate, despite the government constantly claiming to represent 'the toiling masses'. The decrees may have stripped powerful and wealthy individuals of their land and other capital assets, but they antagonized powerful individuals, challenged Islamic values, and destroyed the symbiotic relationship between landlord and tenant, *khan* and tribe. Landlords whose land had been seized called in their tenants' debts and refused to advance them credit, seed and fertilizer, or allow them use of oxen, ploughs and tractors. Peasants who accepted grants of confiscated land lost all irrigation rights and had to either beg or buy water from their neighbours or bribe the *mirab*, and were ostracized by their community. In order to pay for seed and other costs the peasants borrowed from urban moneylenders who charged exorbitant levels of compound interest. When they were unable to make ends meet or repay their debts, they sold the land or had it seized by debt collectors. The government's confiscation of *auqaf* lands removed another traditional safety net for the rural poor, in the form of the distribution of the obligatory *zakat* tax and supererogatory alms known as *sadaqat* or *khairat*. The result was even greater hardship and some of the bitterest opponents of Afghanistan's Communist governments were the very people Marxism was meant to empower and emancipate.

Taraki's reforms were enforced at the point of a gun by a paramilitary force known as the Sarandoi, or Defenders of the Revolution, which was backed by the much-feared KHAD. These two bodies conducted a reign of terror against the 'enemies of the people'. During the eighteen months of Taraki's reign, hundreds of thousands of people were rounded up, imprisoned and tortured, and it is possible that as many as 50,000 people disappeared.[33] In Kabul's middle-class suburbs, the silence of night was punctuated by the screams of women as their menfolk were dragged from their homes and often shot dead in the street. Among those who perished during the Taraki purges were Professor Niyazi, Zia al-Mashayekh, the Hazrat of Shor Bazaar, and around a hundred members of his Mujadidi *qaum*, and Musa' Shafiq, the former prime minister. 'Abd al-Rasul Sayyaf, who had returned from exile in Pakistan, was also arrested but was released, probably because he was a distant relative of Hafiz Allah 'Amin. Sayyaf returned to Pakistan where he founded another anti-government, *jihad*ist militia, Itihad-i Islami.

Within a matter of months revolts began to break out all over the country. In the summer of 1978 there were uprisings in Nuristan, Darra-yi Suf, the Panjshir, Badakhshan and Helmand, while others voted with their feet and a flood of refugees began to pour across the Pakistan frontier, where they swelled the ranks of the Peshawar Islamist parties and the emerging Shi'a-Hazara resistance in Quetta. General Zia-ul-Haq, Pakistan's military dictator, who had deposed Bhutto in July 1977, responded to the Taraki coup by increasing financial and military assistance to the Peshawar-based Sunni Islamists. In January 1979 the first major attack by *mujahidin* occurred in Nangahar, marking the commencement of a *jihad* that would last for more than a decade.

The assassination of Ambassador Dubs and the fall of President Taraki

In February 1979 the USA became unwillingly embroiled in what now threatened to be a regional conflict. On St Valentine's Day, Adolph 'Spike' Dubs, the U.S. ambassador, was kidnapped at gunpoint and held hostage in the Kabul Hotel, a curious choice given that this hotel in downtown Kabul was full of Soviet and Eastern European diplomatic staff as well as KGB agents. When the U.S. Embassy tried to contact Hafiz Allah 'Amin, the Foreign Minister, he was conveniently unavailable and the embassy's pleas to Afghan and Soviet security forces to allow time for negotiation were ignored. Instead Afghan security forces, advised by Russian military and KGB agents, stormed the room and Dubs and all the kidnappers died in a hail of bullets.[34] The perpetrators were never identified, but the State Department rejected the Afghan government's official version, which blamed Yunus Khalis, an ally of Gulbudin Hikmatyar. The ballistic evidence suggested that Dubs had been executed – he had been shot four times in the head at close range – and U.S. officials suspected the PDPA was behind the assassination, either in a naive attempt to discredit the Islamist resistance or to force the USA and NATO powers to disengage with Afghanistan. When State Department protests to the Afghan Foreign Ministry were ignored, the U.S. dramatically reduced its humanitarian assistance and all but essential USAID and embassy personnel were withdrawn. The U.S. ambassador was not replaced, though a chargé d'affaires remained behind. A few months later President Carter gave the green light to the CIA to supply medicines and communications equipment to the Peshawar Islamists.

Meanwhile internally the uneasy alliance between Khalq and Parcham fell apart. In August 1978 President Taraki ordered the arrest of several prominent Parchami ministers, accusing them of plotting a coup. The head of Parcham, Babrak Karmal, however, evaded arrest, was given sanctuary in the Soviet embassy and a few days later quietly shipped out to Czechoslovakia. On 29 March 1979 the 17th Infantry Division in Herat mutinied and precipitated a popular uprising that led to the slaughter of hundreds of pro-government supporters, Soviet advisers and their families. President Taraki frantically telephoned the Soviet Premier, Alexei Kosygin, to plead for the intervention of Soviet ground forces to retake the city, but the request was refused.[35] Instead, Moscow airlifted weapons and heavy armour into the Shindand airbase and sent Ilyushin jets to bomb rebel positions, causing the deaths of thousands of civilians and seriously damaging the medieval quarters of Herat's old town and its Timurid monuments. It took a week for government forces to regain control of Herat and many more people were executed in the reprisals that followed. The rebel army units, commanded by a junior officer, Muhammad Isma'il Khan, withdrew into the hill country of Badghis, where they declared their support for Rabbani's Jami'at-i Islami.

A month later, on the first anniversary of the Saur Revolution, there were uprisings in the Hazarajat, Gurziwan and Badghis, and most of the central and northern highlands fell into the hands of various *mujahidin* factions. In the summer, insurgents overran district offices in Wardak, Paktika, Logar, Panjshir and Takhar, while in Kabul there were riots in Chindawal and the garrison in the Bala Hisar mutinied. As more and more rural districts were lost to the rebels, Khalqi military officers turned to Prime Minister Hafiz Allah 'Amin to step in, while Taraki and his

In April 1979 President Taraki's house in Jamal Mina, west Kabul, became a PDPA shrine. Less than six months later he had been overthrown and later suffocated by his successor Hafiz Allah 'Amin.

supporters tried to engineer 'Amin's downfall. In mid-September 1979 Taraki called Hafiz Allah 'Amin to the Presidential Palace and dismissed him, offering him an ambassadorship abroad. 'Amin refused and angrily told Taraki it was he who ought to leave the country, whereupon Taraki's guards tried, but failed, to shoot 'Amin. He fled the palace but a few hours later he returned, accompanied by Khalqi army officers, who arrested Taraki and his few remaining loyalists. A few weeks later, the Great Leader was quietly suffocated.

President Hafiz Allah 'Amin and the Soviet invasion

'Amin's coup was far from welcome in Moscow and when Brezhnev was told that Taraki, who was a personal friend, had been put to death, he damned 'Amin as 'scum'.[36] There were other reasons for the Politburo's anger. 'Amin's coup ended Soviet attempts to unite Khalq and Parcham and undermined the PDPA's wafer-thin support base. President 'Amin's subsequent actions caused even greater concern as he tried to distance his government from the USSR and repair relations with Iran, Pakistan and the USA. Some high Soviet officials were even convinced that Hafiz Allah 'Amin had been recruited by the CIA during his time at Columbia University.[37]

President 'Amin made a series of gestures in the hope of winning popular support for his administration, releasing thousands of political prisoners, denouncing Taraki as a dictator and offering the prospect of a new Constitution. He even secured a *fatwa* from a council of '*ulama*' that legitimized his government, met with Gulbudin Hikmatyar and tried to convince the public that he and his government were good Muslims. Very few were convinced by this charm offensive, nor was President 'Amin able to stem the rising tide of rebellion. Shortly after seizing power, the garrison in Rishkhor mutinied and was only suppressed after heavy fighting, while an armoured column sent to put down a revolt in Khost was almost wiped out when it was ambushed by the *mujahidin*. President 'Amin responded with another reign of terror, but all the purge did was to increase the exodus of refugees to Pakistan and Iran, which in turn provided yet more recruits for the growing Islamist insurgency.

At the end of November 1979 a high-ranking Soviet mission reported to the Politburo that the military situation in Afghanistan was now critical. According to their assessment, the Peshawar-based *mujahidin* had 40,000 men under arms while 70 per cent of the country was out of central government control. The mission concluded that without direct Soviet military intervention an Islamist takeover of Afghanistan was inevitable within

a matter of months. The prospect of a second militant Islamic government on the USSR's southern frontiers was unacceptable to Moscow, for
in April the Shah of Iran had been forced into exile and Iran was now a
Shi'a Republic ruled by Ayat Allah Khomeini. So when President 'Amin
requested limited Soviet military support against the *mujahidin*, who
had overrun Badakhshan, he unwittingly provided the Kremlin with the
justification it sought to send in the Red Army.

On 12 December 1979 Brezhnev and his inner circle met to discuss
possible military intervention in Afghanistan. Before them lay a proposal
by Babrak Karmal to depose Hafiz Allah 'Amin, which included assurances
by Karmal that he 'enjoyed the support of a significant part of Afghan Party
members and the population'. The Afghan nation, he declared, 'were only
waiting for him to show up in their country in order to act against Amin'.[38]
However, Babrak then went on to state that the coup could only be successful if it had the support of the Soviet military. Despite Marshal Orarkov,
Chief of the General Staff, and other senior military officers being absent
from the meeting, Brezhnev gave the order to mobilize the 40th Army
Corps in preparation for a full-scale intervention. When he was informed
of the decision, Marshal Orarkov tried to persuade his political masters
to revoke their decision to invade, but was curtly told to obey orders and
leave policy-making to the Politburo.[39]

A few days later a high-ranking KGB officer flew into Bagram airbase
with secret instructions to organize the assassination of Hafiz Allah 'Amin
and to prepare for the arrival of Soviet forces. Over the next few days,
Babrak Karmal and Anahita Ratebzad were flown in along with hundreds
of KGB special forces personnel, including the Muslim Battalion, which
consisted of Uzbeks, Tajiks and Turkmans dressed in Afghan army
uniforms. Several attempts to kill President 'Amin failed, however, and
Babrak Karmal and Anahita Ratebzad were flown back to Tashkent.
Meanwhile, Moscow lulled President 'Amin into a sense of false security
by informing him that the military build-up was in response to his request
for military support against the *mujahidin*.

On 23 December 1979, while the Western world was occupied with
its Christmas shopping spree, KGB units took control of Bagram and at
0400 hours on Christmas morning fleets of Antonov cargo planes began
to land at Kabul airport, where they unloaded troops, tanks and armoured
personnel carriers. The approaches and perimeter of the airport were soon
secured, while KGB agents and Soviet military officers already in Kabul
occupied key military positions and anti-aircraft defences. KGB officials
even persuaded 'Amin to allow the Muslim Brigade and KGB special units

to reinforce the perimeter defences of the Taj Beg palace, where 'Amin and his inner circle had gathered to celebrate the anniversary of the founding of the PDPA. In the north, engineers threw pontoon bridges across the Amu Darya and Soviet armoured units rolled into Mazar-i Sharif and Qunduz, where they met with only token resistance. Indeed, the only serious opposition the Soviet army faced was from the *mujahidin,* who ambushed the convoys as they passed through the Salang Pass and along the Talaqan road to Faizabad.

On the afternoon of 27 December, 'Amin's chef, who was in the pay of the KGB, poisoned the food, incapacitating President 'Amin and the rest of his party, while outside the KGB assault forces sealed off all access routes to Taj Beg. It was only when the storming party opened fire on 'Amin's Afghan guards that he realized he had been tricked. A bloody battle ensued, despite heavy losses, the KGB stormed the palace, killing 'Amin and his eight-year-old son and badly wounding his daughter. When the firing finally ended, around 150 Afghans lay dead, while most of the storming party who survived the assault were wounded.

That evening Babrak Karmal, in a broadcast from Dushanbe, announced the 'execution' of 'Amin and claimed that Soviet forces had entered Afghanistan at the invitation of the government. The following day Babrak flew to Kabul where he was installed as President. A few days later the surviving members of 'Amin's extended family were executed, along with dozens of Khalqis. On 1 January 1980 the first edition of the *Kabul Times* to be published since the invasion attacked the 'fascist' 'Amin as the 'bloodthirsty agent of American Imperialism' and a 'demagogic tyrannical dictator'. The article then justified the Soviet intervention citing Article 51 of the UN Charter and the Afghan-Soviet Mutual Defence Treaty and claimed that the USSR had intervened because Afghanistan was threatened by 'foreign aggression and intervention' (that is, Pakistan and the USA). The Orwellian nature of this declaration continued with an article entitled 'On the Threshold of Liberation', under the slogan of 'Forward towards Peace, Freedom, National Independence, Democracy, Progress and Social Justice.'[40]

Political and military fallout from the Soviet occupation

Like Britain, the Soviet Union quickly discovered that while it was relatively easy to occupy Afghanistan and place a quisling on the throne, it was quite another matter to sustain the government in power. Babrak's claim to have widespread popular support was soon shown to be a delusion and all the Soviet intervention did was precipitate a full-scale civil war and internationalize the Afghanistan crisis, turning it into a proxy war between the USSR and USA-NATO. The Soviet Union now found itself condemned to fight an unwinnable war on behalf of a government that was unsustainable.

The problems began almost as soon as the Soviet army arrived. The intervention precipitated mass desertions from the national army and millions of Afghans chose exile rather than living under occupation and a Communist regime. By the mid-1980s more than 3 million Afghan refugees were living in Pakistan, with a further 1.5 million in Iran. Hundreds of thousands more were internally displaced. As a result of this mass depopulation, between 1979 and 1991 agricultural production in Afghanistan fell 40 per cent.

In an attempt to raise a new Afghan army, the government resorted to forcible conscription but also offered substantial financial incentives for joining up. Yet despite being trained by Soviet officers, the army more often than not came off second best in its encounters with the *mujahidin*. The Red Army ended up bearing the brunt of combat, only for it too to be found wanting. As was the case with the Anglo-Indian army in the First Afghan War, the Soviet war machine was not trained for fighting a counterinsurgency but for set-piece battles in a European theatre of war. The insurgents deliberately avoided large-scale pitched battles, which they knew were unwinnable, and instead ambushed straggling, slow-moving

Digging in, Nasir Bagh refugee camp outside Peshawar. The PDPA coup and subsequent purges led to thousands of refugees fleeing to Pakistan's Northwest Frontier and Baluchistan. After the Soviet invasion this exodus became a flood. By the 1980s the Afghan refugee crisis was the largest in the world.

convoys and remote, poorly manned outposts. The Soviets responded with long-distance artillery, high-altitude bombing and strafing by helicopter gunships, and later resorted to the use of Scud missiles. In an attempt to prevent infiltration across the Pakistan frontier, Soviet planes scattered millions of anti-personnel and booby trap mines. Yet despite being relatively lightly armed and suffering a high attrition, the *mujahidin* refused to accept defeat.

Opposition to the occupation also came from citizens living within government-controlled areas. Some six weeks after the Soviet occupation, on the evening of 21 February 1980, 1 Hut in the Afghan *shamsi* calendar, and in response to *shab nama*s circulated by *mujahidin* sympathizers, hundreds of thousands of Afghans stood on their roofs and called out repeatedly *Allah hu Akbar. Mullah*s too broadcast the call from mosque loudspeakers, until the cities of Afghanistan reverberated with the traditional battle cry of Islamic armies. The following day shopkeepers in Kabul shut up their shops. Thousands of schoolchildren and students marched in protest at the Soviet occupation and tried to storm government offices. As the demonstrations showed no signs of ending, and with police and some army units refusing to fire on the unarmed demonstrators, President Karmal called in the Parcham paramilitary forces and the Soviet army, including tanks, armoured personnel carriers and helicopter gunships, which fired indiscriminately into the crowds. When the shooting finally ceased around eight hundred Afghans, including dozens of teenage girls, had been killed while hundreds more were wounded. In the purge that followed, thousands more were rounded up and executed.[41] There were further protests in the summer, but the bloody suppression of the Awal-i Hut protests forced opposition in government-controlled areas underground. Nonetheless many Afghans, even those in the government and army, continued passing information to various *mujahidin* factions.

The Soviet intervention caught the world off guard, since few Western observers believed the USSR would be foolish enough to invade Afghanistan. U.S. attention at the time was concentrated on the crisis in Tehran, where students and Revolutionary Guards had taken embassy staff hostage. Just ten days before the Soviet intervention, the U.S. Embassy in Moscow asked the Soviet Foreign Ministry for urgent clarification on the military build-up along the Afghan frontier. A few days later the CIA informed President Carter that the USSR had 'crossed a significant threshold'. However, it was only on Christmas Eve that a National Security memorandum, which dealt almost solely with the Iranian hostage crisis, mentioned briefly that a Soviet invasion of Afghanistan was 'in the offing'.[42]

The response by the USA and Western nations, however, was swift and sharp. There were the usual diplomatic protests and UN Security Council resolutions, while President Carter called General Secretary Leonid Brezhnev on the hotline and informed him that, 'neither superpower can arrogate to itself the right to displace or overturn a legally constituted government in another country by force of arms. Such a precedent is a dangerous one; it flouts all the accepted norms of international conduct.'[43] Brezhnev, though, dismissed the invasion as 'a small police action designed to restore order to a country that appealed for our assistance . . . under the provisions of our friendship treaty'. Brezhnev's inner circle, however, had underestimated the negative impact the Soviet Union's intervention would have on its international relations, not just with the USA and European countries, but also in the Middle East, Africa and Asia.

After studiously cultivating the image of a nation that supported self-determination and anti-colonialism, many developing countries now accused the USSR of acting as imperialistically as Britain, France, Germany or the USA. The USA, European and Arab countries refused to recognize the government of Babrak Karmal, withdrew their expatriate workers and cut off funding for development programmes. All but a handful of Western nationals left and most non-governmental organizations (NGOs) closed their operations. Instead, dozens of NGOs opened up offices in Peshawar, Quetta and Islamabad to meet the needs of what eventually became the worst refugee crisis of the era. The USSR therefore had to bear not only the escalating costs of its military campaign, but the burden of propping up an economy in freefall. At the height of the conflict between 15 and 20 per cent of the USSR's Gross National Product was consumed by the Afghanistan intervention. An even greater loss of face followed the decision of the USA and many Western nations to boycott the 1980 Moscow Olympics.

America, Pakistan and the Peshawar-based *mujahidin*

On Boxing Day 1979, while Soviet troops were still pouring into Afghanistan, President Carter held an emergency meeting of Pentagon, CIA and State Department officials and agreed, in principle, to fund and arm the Afghan resistance in order to prevent 'a quick, effective Soviet operation to pacify Afghanistan', since this 'would be extremely costly to our image in the region'. The objective of the operation was 'to make the operation as costly as possible for the Soviets',[44] or, as Howard Hart, head of the CIA's Islamabad operations, succinctly put it, 'raise hell . . . and kill Soviets'.[45] Whether the White House realized it or not, the USA had now stepped into Britain's shoes and the defence of the Indus-Durand Line became as crucial to America's South-Central Asia policy as it had been during the era of British rule in India. It was not simply a matter of hurting the USSR financially, politically and militarily. Many American officials considered it vital to preventing a possible Soviet invasion of Pakistan and the occupation of Karachi, which would provide a warm-water port for the Soviet navy in the Indian Ocean. Such a scenario would mean not just the break-up of Pakistan, now America's sole ally in the region following the fall of the Shah of Iran, but threaten America's oil supplies through the Persian Gulf.

This Warm Water Port theory, as it was known, was a particular favourite of Zbigniew Brzezinski, President Carter's Polish-born national security adviser. Despite the military and logistical impracticality of such an invasion, let alone the risk of war that the USSR would face since America was committed to the defence of Pakistan under the SEATO treaty, the idea was popular with Republicans, right-wing think tanks, journalists and advisers on Afghanistan. In fact, the theory was an anachronism based on the theoretical musing of Alfred Thayer Mahan (1840–1914), an American naval officer writing at a time before air power supplanted naval power as the backbone of imperial might.[46] The Warm Water Port scenario, however, provided a convenient justification for arming the *mujahidin* as well as propping up the dictatorship of Pakistan's martial law administrator, General Zia-ul-Haq, just as in the 1960s the Domino Theory was the rationale for American military intervention in Southeast Asia.

The CIA's initial priority was to decide which of the many anti-government resistance movements should receive military and financial support. The hostage crisis in Iran ruled out support for the Iranian-backed Shi'a militias, so the CIA opted to channel its military support to the Sunni Islamists in Peshawar. However, this decision posed political problems as U.S.–Pakistan relations were then at rock bottom due to the military coup of General Zia-ul-Haq and the subsequent execution of the former prime minister, Zu'l-fiqar 'Ali Bhutto, in April 1979. Zia-ul-Haq had also continued Pakistan's nuclear weapons programme despite American objections. To cap it all, a month before the Soviet invasion Islamist students from Qaid-i 'Azam University had stormed and set fire to the U.S. Embassy in Islamabad.

Support for the resistance, however, took precedence and Zia-ul-Haq came out of the political wilderness as support for his government became the linchpin of America's response to the Afghanistan crisis. Zia milked the U-turn for all it was worth, insisting that all CIA funding, weaponry and military training be channelled through the Inter-Service Intelligence (ISI), Pakistan's equivalent of the CIA. Later, when Egypt, Saudi Arabia, Britain and France joined the military campaign, they too had to agree to the same conditions. The ISI then used its position of power to channel weapons and cash to those *mujahidin* factions who were most sympathetic to Zia's and Pakistan's interests, in particular to factions with close ties with Pakistan's Jamiat Ulema-e-Islami (JUI), the Islamist party that had supported and legitimized Zia's coup.

Pakistan also exploited the supply and delivery of aid to control the Afghan resistance's political agenda and to extend its influence into Afghanistan's Pushtun belt. Later, the ISI set up training bases across the Afghan frontier to train militants for attacks on Indian-held Kashmir. The USA also rearmed the Pakistan military and when Zia-ul-Haq cancelled elections, banned political parties and Islamized Pakistan's Constitution, the USA and NATO countries made only token objections. Pakistan's economy too benefited from the millions of dollars of aid and assistance that poured in to meet the refugee crisis.

The decision to arm the Peshawar Islamist *mujahidin* was a body blow to the Muhammadzais and Afghan royalists. They expected the USA would support the return of the monarchy, especially since, in their view, monarchists were the most pro-Western and progressive party, many of whose leaders had studied in American institutions as well as in France and Germany. Zia-ul-Haq, however, had no interest in restoring the monarchy and risking a revival of the Pushtunistan issue, while the CIA regarded the royalist *mujahidin* as militarily ineffective. When the king's party called a Loya Jirga in Peshawar, in an attempt to unify the resistance in the name of Zahir Shah, the five main Sunni Islamist parties walked out and set up a rival *shura*, sidelining the royalists in the process. Many Muhammadzais eventually applied for, and were granted, asylum in North America and European countries and watched while their political enemies were armed to the teeth and feted by the leaders of the Western world.

The ISI's preferred allies were all former members of Niyazi's Muslim Brotherhood network, which in the 1960s and '70s had been responsible for violent protests against the secularizing policies of King Zahir Shah's administrations on the one hand and the PDPA on the other. These Islamist militias were supplied with a vast arsenal of Soviet-made weaponry, mostly from Egypt, as well as millions of dollars in cash, while their leaders became the spokesmen for Afghanistan's political destiny on the international stage. The bulk of the CIA arms and cash went to Gulbudin Hikmatyar's Hizb-i Islami since the ISI regarded this militia to be the most pro-Pakistani, while the CIA were convinced that Hikmatyar's men were the most effective when it came to killing Russians. Hikmatyar did indeed inflict a great deal of damage on the Soviet war machine but he was also a divisive force, for his *mujahidin* spent nearly as much time fighting turf wars with rival factions, particularly Rabbani's Jami'at-i Islami and Ahmad Shah Mas'ud's Panjshiris. As well as hijacking arms and aid convoys destined for rival factions, Hizb-i Islami was accused of being behind the disappearance or assassination of rival commanders, Afghan journalists, intellectuals, religious dissidents and foreign aid workers, including at least two American citizens. Later the U.S. State Department would list Hikmatyar as a Global Terrorist, but during the decade of Soviet occupation of Afghanistan he received in excess of $600 million in cash and arms, most of which was paid for by American taxpayers. Among the many heads of state who shook hands with Hikmatyar during the 1980s were Margaret Thatcher and Ronald Reagan, who publicly declared that Hikmatyar and the other leaders of the Peshawar Islamist parties were the 'moral equivalent' of America's Founding Fathers.

Another major recipient of CIA weapons was Yunus Khalis, a Deobandi-trained Pushtun from Nangahar who had split from Hikmatyar early in 1979 and set up his own branch of Hizb-i Islami. His deputies included Maulawi Jalal al-Din Haqqani, a Zadrani Pushtun from Khost, who would later head the Haqqani Network, and 'Abd al-Haq, a wealthy Jabbar Khel Ghilzai whose great-grandfather, Arsala Khan, had been Amir Sher 'Ali Khan's minister for foreign affairs. As well as being a noted field commander, 'Abd al-Haq was one of the few *mujahidin* commanders who attempted to unify the resistance across the ethnic and regional divide.

'Abd al-Sayyaf's Itihad-i Islami also received substantial financial and military assistance. Sayyaf, another graduate of Cairo's al-Azhar, was ideologically a Wahhabist, an ultra-radical version of Islam that was the official *mazhab* of Saudi Arabia. Sayyaf was the main beneficiary of Saudi arms and money and he spent much of his time touring Arab states raising funds and recruiting Arabs to join the *jihad*. Aided by a wealthy Yemeni-born civil engineer, 'Osama bin Laden, who was assisting the Saudi Secret Service, Sayyaf constructed an underground bunker complex across the Durand Line in Paktiya as a forward base for *mujahidin* operations. Later, in 1986, bin Laden set up his own base in Jaji tribal territory, where he surrounded himself with Arab *mujahidin* and increasingly focused on internationalizing his *jihad*, particularly against America. The rest, as the saying goes, is history.

Burhan al-Din Rabbani's Jami'at-i Islami received a smaller percentage of the military aid, even though Jami'at was the largest and most ethnically diverse of all the *mujahidin* parties. Unlike the other Peshawar-based leaders, Rabbani was not a Pushtun but a Tajik from Badakhshan, and his militia consisted mostly of Persian-speakers, Turkmans, Uzbeks, Aimaqs, Badakhshanis, Panjshiris, Heratis and a few disillusioned royalists. Since Hikmatyar regarded Jami'at in general and Ahmad Shah Mas'ud in particular as a rival, the ISI did not fund or arm Mas'ud and it was several years before the CIA woke up to the fact that Mas'ud was the most effective battlefield commander. In 1983 Mas'ud set up his own autonomous movement known as Shura-yi Nazar, the Supervisory Council, and eventually the CIA, Britain and France began to arm him directly without bothering to involve the ISI.

Very few of these Peshawar Islamist leaders had any military training, let alone combat experience. Rabbani, Sayyaf, Haqqani and Khalis were theologians while Hikmatyar's military credentials were limited to two years in Kabul's Military College. Ahmad Shah Mas'ud's father had been a colonel in the Afghan army, but Mas'ud himself had trained as an engineer. However, Mas'ud was an avid reader of military history and manuals of guerrilla warfare and used this knowledge to good effect when fighting Soviet and government forces. The lack of generalship within the *mujahidin* leadership often meant poor planning and the absence of coordination, especially in the early days, though later ISI and CIA training improved tactical planning. Furthermore, the *mujahidin* lacked heavy weaponry, in particular any effective deterrent to combat the Soviet's air supremacy. In the Gurziwan region of Faryab, some *mujahidin* used British-made Second World War Lee–Enfield rifles and at least one former *mujahid*, who was a renowned hunter and marksman, preferred his ancient, flintlock *jezail*. In Badghis, Isma'il Khan formed a camel regiment with swivel guns, while in other areas of northern Afghanistan Uzbek, Turkman and Aimaq *mujahidin* attacked Soviet armoured columns on horseback. Despite the odds being heavily stacked against them, the *mujahidin* succeeded in tying down the Soviet army in a protracted, asymmetrical war, and while foreign money and weapons made this possible, it was the courage and tenacity of ordinary Afghans that eventually forced the Soviet leadership to accept the war was unwinnable. It came, though, at a terrible cost. More than a million Afghans died as a direct or indirect consequence of the conflict, while hundreds of thousands were maimed for life by war wounds or stepping on anti-personnel mines.

As the proxy war ground on, U.S. funding for the Peshawar *mujahidin* burgeoned. President Carter initially approved a meagre $20 million for the resistance, but after Ronald Reagan became President in early 1981, the military and financial aid increased year on year. By 1983 the CIA's budget

A mine awareness poster, Khost. During the Soviet occupation millions of anti-personnel mines and booby trap devices were scattered all over the country. Thousands of *mujahidin* and civilians were killed or maimed as a result. More than 25 years after the Soviet withdrawal, Unexploded Ordinance (UXOS) continue to cause many deaths and injuries.

had risen to $325 million and by 1987 this figure had almost doubled to $630 million.[47] In contrast, in the 33 years between 1946 and 1979 the USA invested a total of $532 million in development grants and loans for civil projects in Afghanistan, or an average of $16 million per annum.[48] The CIA demanded only minimal accountability from the ISI and its Afghan clients for expenditure and the ISI's record keeping of the distribution of military equipment was almost non-existent. As far as the CIA was concerned, once the arms and cash were in the hands of ISI operators, they were no longer responsible, legally or morally, for the use to which they were put. In this way, the CIA was able to distance itself from actions by ISI clients that violated the Agency's terms of reference and U.S. law. The CIA was therefore able to deny any involvement when Afghan *mujahidin,* trained by ISI agents, attacked Indian-held Kashmir or fomented uprisings in Soviet Uzbekistan, Tajikistan and Turkmenistan. It also created a culture of impunity and corruption on an unprecedented scale, with everyone from the ISI and Pakistani government officials to *mujahidin* commanders creaming off large percentages, a culture that Afghan refugees referred to as 'the Pakistan Disease'.[49]

To raise additional funds for the war effort, commanders inside Afghanistan demanded payment from rival *mujahidin* in exchange for safe passage and, encouraged by antiquity dealers in Peshawar and Iran, they looted archaeological and heritage sites. Mas'ud initially funded his war by trading in lapis lazuli and other gemstones from the mines in Badakhshan, other commanders encouraged opium production. During the 1980s the area under poppy cultivation inside Afghanistan expanded exponentially. The raw opium was then refined in Pakistan's Tribal Territory and smuggled back through Afghanistan, Iran and the Central Asian States, eventually ending up on the European, North American and Russian black markets. Opium was openly on sale at roadside stalls outside Peshawar, while heroin addiction became an increasingly serious social problem in Pakistan's Northwest Frontier and among Afghan refugees.

The *mujahidin* and Islamization

While the CIA armed and funded the *mujahidin* resistance, little consideration was given to a post-Soviet government for it was believed that, although the *mujahidin* might tie down Soviet forces for many years, they did not have the capacity to defeat the Red Army or overthrow Babrak Karmal. The Peshawar Islamists and pro-Iranian Shi'a militias, on the other hand, had a very clear idea about the future shape of Afghanistan. All of the main militias wanted an Islamic State ruled by the *shari'a*, though there was no consensus over what this meant or what form an Islamic government might take. It was only after 1986, when it became clear the USSR was planning to withdraw, that the USA, Pakistan and UN officials tried to cobble together a government in exile, but ideological differences, personal rivalries and competition for funding failed to produce anything more than token agreement. International conferences held to discuss the Afghanistan crisis were more often than not marred by angry, personalized insults, boycotts and walkouts.

The war between the *mujahidin* and the Soviet-backed government in Kabul dragged on for a decade, yet during this time no single unifying figure emerged from the resistance movement, a statesman of the calibre of Yasser Arafat, Kemal Atatürk or Nelson Mandela, who represented the national interest rather than personal interest or one particular faction. UN, NATO and U.S. negotiators continued to cling to the belief that the ex-king Zahir Shah was such a figure, but though there was a certain degree of popular support for the return of the monarchy, all the Islamist factions opposed any role for the monarchy in a post-Communist administration. During the period of Soviet occupation, the ex-king never set foot in Pakistan, partly because the Pakistanis were not keen to host him and partly because the risk of assassination was too great.

For the *mujahidin* the *jihad* was not merely a matter of killing Russians, as the CIA planned, but it was about instilling their version of *jihad* and Islam into the hearts and minds of the populace, particularly the younger generation. Yet while being funded by the CIA and other Western nations, the political ideology espoused by these Islamists was innately opposed to the secular values of those countries. Sayyid Qutb, whose teaching had a strong influence on Rabbani, Hikmatyar, Sayyaf and Mas'ud, had penned a devastating critique of what he termed America's moral decadence and cultural 'primitiveness', portraying the USA as a Machiavellian superpower that publicly promoted peace and democracy while covertly pursuing a war against Islam.[50] While the *mujahidin* fought the Russians with American-supplied weapons and dollars, radical Islamists actively promoted an anti-American and anti-Western world view through schools, *madrasas* and mosques established in refugee camps and *mujahidin*-controlled territory. Frontier *madrasas* run by Pakistan's JUI and other radicals offered free schooling to the children of poor refugees and war orphans, while older students received scholarships to study Islam in Saudi Arabia. The *mujahidin* circulated tracts on women's deportment and warned Afghans about the moral decadence of Westerners. Islamist apologists also published tracts attacking Christianity and urged Afghans not to mix with Christians or foreigners, for fear they would be ideologically compromised by Catholic and Protestant workers who had established aid agencies in Pakistan as part of the international relief effort.

American, British, Swedish and other European aid agencies unwittingly contributed to this radicalization by funding schools inside Afghanistan, even though it was impossible for foreign advisers to monitor their curriculum. Indeed, it was difficult enough for foreigners to monitor educational activities inside the refugee camps due to access restrictions imposed by Pakistani officials and *mujahidin* commanders who controlled the camps. The University of Nebraska's Center for Afghanistan Studies even used USAID money to fund *mujahidin*-approved primary school textbooks, which included extended treaties on *jihad*, images of Kalashnikov assault rifles, tanks, grenades and graphic images of decapitation of Soviet soldiers.

While radical Islamists tried to indoctrinate the poor and displaced, middle-class Afghans who could afford to live outside the refugee camps sent their children to Pakistani schools or paid for home tutoring. In Iran, where there were no refugee camps, Afghan children attended state schools and encountered another version of revolutionary Islam, while the sons and daughters of refugees given asylum in Western countries passed through the secular North American and European school and university systems. Inside Afghanistan, meanwhile, the state indoctrinated pupils and students in Marxism and sent thousands of students to study in the USSR or Soviet bloc countries. By the time Afghan refugees began to return to their country in large numbers in 2002, a whole generation had been educated in a variety of conflicting world views and many younger people spoke Urdu better than Dari or Pushtu.

Despite the suffering, deprivation and many other problems facing the Afghan refugees, the war did have some positive aspects. For many Afghans their understanding of the wider world was broadened after generations of spatial, intellectual and cultural isolation. Television, radio, films, newspapers and the wide range of literature available in Pakistani and Iranian bookshops widened intellectual horizons, while freedom from the restraint of state censorship allowed marginalized communities to publish works in their own languages and their version of Afghan history. Hundreds of thousands of children, both boys and girls, gained literacy skills, learnt trades and skills through refugee assistance programmes, and some even gained a university education. Afghans eagerly embraced modern technology, including satellite and mobile phones, the internet and social media, while merchants set up dozens of free enterprise ventures, which were often highly profitable.

Mikhail Gorbachev and the Soviet withdrawal

As the war in Afghanistan ground on with no prospect of ending, divisions emerged within the Soviet leadership over the intervention. Brezhnev died three years after sending in the Red Army and his successors Yuri Andropov, one of the main advocates of the intervention, and Konstantin Chernenko died soon after. All these men belonged to the early generation of Communists who had been born in pre-Revolutionary Russia, but their position was increasingly being challenged by younger Party members. When Chernenko died in March 1985, Mikhail Gorbachev, the youngest member of the Politburo, became General Secretary of the Communist Party. One of his priorities was to staunch what he called the 'bleeding wound' and find a way to either win the war in Afghanistan or withdraw with honour more or less intact.[51]

By the time Gorbachev came to power, not only was the war in Afghanistan going badly, the costs were having a negative effect on the Soviet Union's economy and finances. Even more worrying were the potential social and economic repercussions from a war that was increasingly unpopular with the Soviet public. In all around 600,000 Soviet citizens served in Afghanistan and, according to official figures, by the time the last tank crossed the Amu Darya in February 1989 more than 14,000 Soviet soldiers and civilians had been killed and 50,000 wounded. Thousands more suffered from serious or permanent psychological damage, while others were addicted to hashish, opium and heroin. The harrowing accounts of returning soldiers, known as *Afghantsi*, contradicted the Soviet media's official line, which portrayed the intervention as a patriotic defence of the Motherland and an ally in the face of American and Pakistani imperialism. Instead, the veterans related how they found themselves fighting ordinary Afghans and that the foreign invader was their own country. *Afghantsi* also spoke of massacres and other war crimes committed by Soviet forces, low army morale, appalling living conditions and the harsh treatment of conscripts by Red Army officers and NCOs.[52] Soon *Afghantsi* began to openly criticize the Soviet leadership and some published their memoirs, which portrayed the Red Army's leadership in a very poor light.

Added to the concern was the fear that the accounts of the *Afghantsi* might lead to unrest among the USSR's Muslim population. During the Afghan war thousands of Turkic and Tajik peoples from the Caucasus and the Central Asian Republics, most of them with Muslim heritage, served in Afghanistan. These men understood the abuse hurled at them by villagers as well as appeals by Afghans to Muslim and ethnic solidarity. Some of the Central Asian soldiers even had distant relatives in Afghanistan, descendants of family members who had fled Imperial Russia's conquest of Turkistan, the suppression of the *basmachi* movement and Stalin's Collectivization. In the end, Moscow withdrew all Central Asian units for fear of unrest in Muslim-majority Republics.

Gorbachev gave the Soviet military eighteen months to win the war in Afghanistan, while at the same time he attempted to negotiate with the USA for a face-saving withdrawal. The Soviet generals mounted a series of major offensives but America, Saudi Arabia and NATO countries responded by pouring in more and more arms and cash and supplied key *mujahidin* commanders with ground-to-air missiles, undermining Soviet air supremacy. In an attempt to make the Afghan government more broadly based, in November 1986 President Babrak Karmal was 'persuaded' by Soviet officials to resign. He was replaced by Muhammad Najib Allah, the head of KHAD and a Ghilzai Pushtun, in the hope that his appointment might persuade war-weary *mujahidin* to lay down their arms and share power. To this end, Najib Allah instituted a programme of national reconciliation, drew up a new Constitution and called new Parliamentary elections. He even publicly renounced Marxism and did his best to convince a sceptical nation he was a good Muslim. All his efforts, however, were in vain and in the end only a handful of *mujahidin* gave up the struggle.

The Geneva Accords and the *mujahidin* reaction

Just two months after Najib Allah became president, Gorbachev accepted that a military victory in Afghanistan was impossible and ordered his chiefs of staff to plan an orderly withdrawal. Behind the scenes Diego Cordovez, the UN Special Envoy to Afghanistan, began a series of proximity talks between Pakistan and Afghanistan in an attempt to smooth the way for the Soviet departure. After months of protracted negotiations, on 14 April 1988 the governments of Pakistan and Afghanistan signed the Geneva Accords, which formalized a phased withdrawal of Soviet forces, the voluntary repatriation of Afghan refugees and principles of non-interference in each other's internal affairs.

The USA and USSR welcomed the Accords since they opened the door for lifting sanctions and the resumption of bilateral negotiations on the reduction of nuclear arsenals. The Peshawar parties, however, unanimously rejected the Accords, for though they were consulted they had not been invited to take any direct part in the talks. One cause of their anger was that the Accords indirectly legitimized the government of President Najib Allah and made no provision for the transition of power to the *mujahidin*. President Zia-ul-Haq bluntly told the Peshawar parties they should reconcile themselves to sharing power with the PDPA, while the UN Special Envoy publicly advocated the return of King Zahir Shah. The *mujahidin* retaliated by accusing Pakistan and the USA of betrayal and intensified their attempts to topple President Najib Allah. In August 1988, with the Soviet withdrawal already under way, Hizb-i Wahdat, the Iranian-backed Shi'a coalition, overran Bamiyan and a few weeks later Hikmatyar's Hizb-i Islami occupied the Kunar valley. In October a coalition of *mujahidin* tried, but failed, to cut the Kabul–Jalalabad road, but did manage to inflict heavy casualties on a government armoured column.

In February 1989, as the last Soviet troops crossed the Amu Darya, the Peshawar Sunni Islamist parties convened a *shura* and agreed to form the Afghan Interim Government (AIG). The AIG, however, did not represent the views of all the *mujahidin* factions, for Hizb-i Wahdat and other Shi'a parties, as well as royalists, intellectuals and humanitarian representatives, were excluded or boycotted the meetings. From its inception the AIG was riddled with factionalism and one outcome of its formation was a war between the Rabbani–Masʻud network on the one hand and Hikmatyar's and Khalis's Hizb-i Islami factions on the other. A month later a coalition of Pushtun *mujahidin,* encouraged by the ISI and the CIA, tried to take Jalalabad by storm, only to be defeated with the loss of more than 3,000 men, the heaviest loss of life in a single battle in the whole war. In addition, several thousand civilians died when the *mujahidin* shelled Jalalabad.

Remarkably, President Najib Allah managed to cling on to power for more than three years after the Soviet withdrawal, but only because the USSR supplied the country with everything from weapons to food and fuel. In an attempt to regain control over outlying regions, Najib Allah encouraged the formation of regional militias, guaranteeing their commanders autonomy in exchange for not fighting against the government. The most effective of these militias was commanded by ʻAbd al-Rashid Dostam, an Uzbek from Khwaja Du Koh, near Shibarghan.[53] Dostam had served as an army conscript during the era of President Daʼud and later worked in the Shibarghan gas plant, where he joined Parcham. In the autumn of 1978 he rejoined the army and proved his military prowess by retaking Sar-i Pul from the *mujahidin.* He then persuaded his Khalqi superiors to let him form an irregular Uzbek cavalry brigade and proceeded to throw Hikmatyar's Hizb-i Islami out of Darra-yi Suf. By 1989 Dostam held the rank of general and commanded the 53rd Infantry, which consisted of 20,000 Uzbeks, mostly farmers from Faryab and Jauzjan. Nicknamed *gilim jamʻ* (carpet-gatherers) by their detractors – Uzbeks are famous for their carpets – Dostam's militia earned a fearsome reputation for their reckless cavalry charges and ruthlessness.

Dostam, though, was also an astute negotiator who managed to persuade several Uzbek and Tajik commanders in the provinces of Jauzjan and Faryab to change sides by appealing to Uzbek nationalist sentiment. Among them were seven brothers and half-brothers from Maimana and Sar-i Pul known as the *pahlawan*s (wrestlers). Another *mujahidin* faction that changed sides was the Itihad-i Islami-yi Samt-i Shamal-i Afghanistan (Islamic Union of the Northern Region of Afghanistan), a pan-Turkic, neo-*basmachi* organization led by Azad Beg, a Pakistan-educated Uzbek who was a descendant of the Khan of Kokand.

Despite these defections in the north, the war in the south raged unabated. In March 1990 General Shah Nawaz Tanaʼi, Najib's Minister of Defence, cut a deal with Hikmatyar and tried to depose Najib Allah in a military coup. When the putsch failed Tanaʼi and his Khalqis fled to Peshawar, where they joined forces with Hizb-i Islami. At the end of 1990 President Najib Allah's grip on power was undermined even more by the political revolution in Moscow that led to Boris Yeltsin displacing Gorbachev. President Yeltsin had no interest in Afghanistan, and since the Soviet economy was in recession, he cut aid to the Afghan government and passed the buck to the newly independent states of Uzbekistan and Turkmenistan. They continued to supply President Najib Allah with fuel, military equipment and cash, but to a far lesser degree than Moscow had been providing. Within a matter of months, basic supplies were running out and the population of Kabul was facing starvation.

In March 1992 President Najib Allah finally agreed to a UN-brokered deal under the terms of which he would resign, leave the country and surrender power to the Afghan Interim Government. However, before the handover could take place, the situation in northern Afghanistan changed the whole political scene. In an attempt to curb Dostam's influence, President Najib Allah replaced General 'Abd al-Mo'min, the Tajik military commander of Mazar-i Sharif, with General Rasul, a Pushtun hard man who had been in charge of Kabul's notorious Pul-i Charkhi prison. When 'Abd al-Mo'min refused to step down, Dostam declared his support for him and, on the very day President Najib Allah announced his resignation, Dostam's Uzbek militia occupied Mazar-i Sharif, which they proceeded to loot. Dostam then forged an alliance with Ahmad Shah Mas'ud, Sayyid Mansur, head of the Isma'ilis of Pul-i Khumri, Hizb-i Wahdat and Isma'il Khan of Jami'at-i Islami, an alliance that went under the name of Junbesh-i Milli-i Afghanistan, the National Islamic Front of Afghanistan.

The fall of President Najib Allah Khan

The fall of Mazar-i Sharif meant President Najib Allah not only had lost control of the northern provinces, but the Afghan army was outnumbered and outgunned by Junbesh forces, for Dostam now had tanks, artillery and several military planes and helicopters under his command. The vital supply route from Uzbekistan to Kabul was cut, and the air force had to be grounded due to lack of aviation fuel. In April, when President Najib Allah tried to leave the country in accordance with the UN agreement, Dostam's Parchami allies, who controlled the Kabul airport, turned him back, so Najib Allah sought sanctuary in the offices of the UN Development Programme. Meanwhile the Parchami garrison at Bagram handed control of the airbase to Ahmad Shah Mas'ud.

Kabul was now at the mercy of Mas'ud and Dostam and the prospect of an Uzbek-Panjshiri takeover caused consternation among Khalqis, the Pushtun *mujahidin* and Pakistan's ISI. In an attempt to forestall this scenario, the Khalqi garrison in Jalalabad surrendered to a coalition of Pushtun *mujahidin*, while the ISI poured military supplies in to Hikmatyar. Mas'ud, however, refused to occupy Kabul or become head of state, for he realized that to do so would mean civil war. Instead, Mas'ud urged the Peshawar parties to set up a transitional, power-sharing agreement. Over the next two weeks the various factions of the AIG, along with a number of Khaqi officers who had defected, haggled over the formation of an administration. The outcome was the Peshawar Accord of 24 April 1992, under the terms of which the octogenarian Sibghat Allah Mujadidi, a relative of the Hazrat of Shor Bazaar, became head of an interim *shura* that would oversee the transition of power for the first two months. Professor Rabbani would then assume the Presidency for a further four months, after which a national *shura* would meet and elect a third interim government. Nationwide presidential and parliamentary elections would only take place two years after the signing of the Peshawar Accord.

The Peshawar Accord was a hastily drawn-up document that lacked specific details about the form of government. One of its many flaws was the decision to divide ministerial posts between the various Sunni factions, which created a series of autonomous, competitive power structures. Furthermore, with the exception of Rabbani and Mas'ud, all the other parties in government represented Pushtun interests. The Peshawar Accord

Herat, April 1994. Isma'il Khan's camel corps parades on the anniversary of the fall of President Najib Allah Khan and the establishment of the Islamic Republic. Note the black, white and green national flag that replaced the red one of the Communist era and the absence of the Durrani monarchy's 'shrine and sheaf' motif.

did not even mention General Dostam, nor was the main Shi'a coalition, Hizb-i Wahdat, allocated any ministerial positions. Despite pleas by the Saudis, the ISI and even 'Osama bin Laden, Gulbudin Hikmatyar refused to sign the Accord and demanded as a precondition of participation that Mas'ud be excluded from power, all Communists be purged from the army and administration and that Dostam withdraw beyond the Salang Pass. Yet despite his refusal to join the government, Hikmatyar was designated as prime minister while behind the scenes ISI officers encouraged Hikmatyar to take Kabul by storm. Even before the ink was dry on the agreement, the Peshawar Accord was doomed to failure.

Hikmatyar, supported by thousands of Arab *mujahidin*, mustered his forces at Chahar Asiyab for a final push on the capital while Khalqi sympathizers smuggled Hizb-i Islami fighters into the capital. Mas'ud and Dostam, however, got wind of Hikmatyar's plan and the day after the Peshawar Accord was signed Dostam airlifted thousands of his militia into Kabul and took control of northern and central parts of the capital. Meanwhile Mas'ud's Panjshiris rode into the capital astride tanks, where they were greeted by cheering crowds who threw garlands of flowers in their path. Three days later Sibghat Allah Mujadidi and other *shura* members flew into Kabul, where the interim government was legitimized by the presence of Pakistan's new prime minister, Nawaz Sharif, ISI officials and Turki al-Faisal, head of Saudi Arabia's intelligence service. However, the real power lay with Mas'ud and Dostam, who attacked Hikmatyar's positions a few days later and forced him back to Chahar Asiyab and Sarobi.

The *mujahidin* government and the breakdown of law and order

One of Sibghat Allah Mujadidi's first actions on returning to Kabul was to inaugurate a programme of Islamization. Afghanistan became the Islamic State of Afghanistan and all the decrees, laws and Constitutions instituted since Taraki's Saur Revolution were abrogated, while the judiciary were ordered to base all their judgements solely on Hanafi jurisprudence. A special religious court, with the power of life and death, was set up to root out all vestiges of Communism, enforce religious observance, and punish irreligious and anti-Islamic acts. Strict censorship was imposed, cinemas closed and the segregation of the sexes and veiling of women became compulsory. Overnight female presenters disappeared from TV and radio, and women teachers and civil servants were sacked. The Minister of Culture instituted a purge of 'godless' and 'anti-Islamic' publications from public libraries, schools and colleges. Later, the Supreme Court issued the 'Ordinance on the Women's Veil', which included such provisions as 'If a perfumed woman passes by a crowd of men, she is considered to be an adulteress', '[women] must not wear sound-producing garments' and '[women] must not look at strangers'.[54]

Meanwhile in Kabul and other urban centres of southern Afghanistan the rule of law broke down as thousands of heavily armed militiamen poured in. Hundreds of suspected Communist sympathizers and PDPA members were shot and their bodies left to rot at the side of the road. Infrastructure constructed during the Soviet era was pulled down or burnt: even the trams were set on fire and their cables torn down. Offices and houses were commandeered and looted, with their occupants evicted at gunpoint. Thousands of trees were felled for fuel when winter came, turning shady places such as the Mughal gardens of Bagh-i Babur into barren wastelands.

In the capital eleven separate factions occupied various parts of the city and similar situations prevailed in Kandahar, Jalalabad and other urban centres. Commanders ruled rural areas with little regard to central government, seizing revenues, imposing their own taxes and presiding over a rough justice, which routinely included torture and arbitrary execution. Travel within the urban centres as well as on the highways of southern Afghanistan was fraught with danger as armed militias set up unofficial checkpoints, searched vehicles for Communist collaborators and demanded tolls from motorists, taxis and bus and truck drivers. The Kabul–Jalalabad highway was particularly dangerous and on occasion gunmen took Hazaras and Panjshiris off buses and shot them by the roadside. Frequent turf wars between commanders made the security situation even worse.

Following the fall of Kabul thousands of refugees began to return to rural areas, where they faced the daunting task of rebuilding ruined homes, reclaiming fields that had not been ploughed for years, replanting orchards and vineyards and rehabilitating irrigation systems, while at the same time having to deal with life-threatening hazards such as mines and unexploded ordnance. Under the Rabbani government, opium production continued to rise, as did opium and heroin addiction among Afghans.[55] A major international emergency relief effort began, focused on food for work programmes, immunization, primary health care, the rehabilitation of irrigation structures and mine clearance. The aid effort was hampered by lack of funds as well as by the breakdown of law and order. During frequent outbreaks of factional fighting UN and NGO office and private homes were repeatedly looted and expatriate workers had to be hastily evacuated to Pakistan. In rural areas, commanders hijacked aid convoys and fired on

Heroin resin on sale in Tribal Territory, outside Peshawar. By the mid-1980s heroin was easily obtainable and many refugees, *mujahidin* and Pakistanis became addicted to heroin, opium and hashish.

aircraft of the UN and International Committee of the Red Cross (ICRC). In Nangahar Arab militants loyal to 'Osama bin Laden executed two UN expatriates and their Afghan colleagues in cold blood.

Within a matter of weeks of the *mujahidin* takeover, there was rampant hyperinflation and the afghani was almost worthless as the government printed more and more paper money. Soon Pakistani rupees and U.S. dollars became the currencies of preference. General Dostam later printed his own money, which the government in Kabul refused to honour. Hikmatyar added to the suffering of Kabulis by switching off the power from the Sarobi dam, lobbing rockets into the city and blockading the Kabul–Jalalabad highway, the principal supply route for the capital.

Some commanders did attempt to establish law and order and improve conditions for ordinary people. In Herat security was good under Isma'il Khan, who used the customs revenues from the Islam Qal'a border post to seal the main road between Herat and the Iranian frontier. He also linked Herat into Iran's electricity grid. Though Isma'il Khan was an Islamizer, girls' primary and secondary schools remained open in Badghis and women continued to teach. In the north, Dostam used the substantial revenues from customs duties on the Uzbekistan and Turkmenistan frontier, as well as the income from the Shibarghan and Sar-i Pul gas and oilfields and the fertilizer and power plant at Dehdadi, to redevelop the town centres of Shibarghan and Mazar-i Sharif and extend the Shibarghan gas pipeline to Mazar-i Sharif. In 1996 Dostam set up Balkh Airlines, run by British pilots with a superannuated BAC 1-11; the British stewardesses with their short dresses were a sensation. In Mazar-i Sharif and Shibarghan, Sibghat Allah Mujadidi's Islamization programme was ignored and beer and wine, imported from Uzbekistan, was openly on sale. Justice, though, was arbitrary and the *pahlawan*s had a fearful reputation for torture, imprisonment and summary execution, as well as abducting young girls and boys. Politically there were tensions within the Junbesh alliance between Tajik and Turkman affiliates of Jami'at-i Islami, Dostam's Uzbeks and his Parchami and Khalqi allies. Pushtuns loyal to Hikmatyar's Hizb-i Islami also clashed with Jami'at and Dostam's militias in Balkh, Sholgara, Maimana, Qunduz and Baghlan.

After serving his two months as interim leader, Sibghat Allah Mujadidi tried to remain in office but was prevented from doing so by Mas'ud's Panjshiris, who physically barred him from entering the President's office. President Rabbani then broke the Peshawar Accord by extending his presidency beyond the agreed four months. Hikmatyar, who still refused to come to Kabul despite being designated prime minister, responded by launching a devastating rocket attack on the capital, which led to the deaths of some 2,000 civilians and caused widespread destruction. The government retaliated by bombing Hizb-i Islami positions in Chahar Asiyab and the Logar.

At the end of December 1992 Rabbani convened a *shura*, loaded with Jami'at supporters, which voted to extend his reign as head of state. Dostam, Hizb-i Wahdat and the Pushtun Islamist parties were not invited to this assembly, while others boycotted it or walked out in protest. The *shura* precipitated another round of fighting in the capital. Dostam and Jami'at fought each other in eastern Kabul, while in the west of the city Hizb-i Wahdat and Mas'ud's Panjshiris clashed. These battles were no-holds-barred affairs with all factions firing rockets, mortars, artillery rounds and tank shells indiscriminately into residential areas. Thousands of civilians died and swaths of southern Kabul were laid waste. Hundreds of thousands of Kabulis fled the city: some headed north to the relative safety of Mazar-i Sharif, others ended up in a vast, waterless and scorpion-infested camp outside Jalalabad. Hazaras, meanwhile, made their way to Bamiyan, where they lived on the margins of the town in caves.

Following the failure of the Peshawar Accord, UN, Saudi Arabian and Pakistani officials tried to reconcile the warring factions, and in March 1993 the main *mujahidin* parties signed a second power-sharing agreement known as the Islamabad Accord. This agreement legitimized Rabbani's position as President of Afghanistan while Hikmatyar continued as prime minister with increased powers, for he alone now had the right to appoint cabinet ministers. All factions agreed to a ceasefire and a joint Defence Committee was established with the impossible mandate of merging the rival militias into a national army or disarming them, as well as to ensure that 'all the roads in Afghanistan are kept open for normal use'. The Saudis even flew the contracting parties to Mecca where they swore on the Ka'aba to uphold the Accord. In the wake of this agreement, Mas'ud voluntarily resigned as Minister of Defence and withdrew to Jabal Saraj, where he began to plan for a showdown with Hikmatyar.

The Accord led to a few months of relative calm for the capital's shell-shocked citizens, but the lawlessness on the highways was unchanged. Hikmatyar continued to refuse to come to Kabul, yet appointed government ministers and held cabinet meetings in Chahar Asiyab. Finally, in November Mas'ud mounted an unsuccessful assault on Hikmatyar's positions in an attempt to break his stranglehold on the Kabul–Jalalabad road. Taking advantage of this setback, Dostam attacked Jami'at and expelled its followers from Mazar-i Sharif and Qunduz, although he lost control of the key port and railhead at Hairatan. Dostam then forged an unlikely alliance with Hikmatyar and in January 1994 they attacked Mas'ud and

A primary school in Nasir Bagh refugee camp. Education became another battle ground during the era of the Soviet-backed governments in Kabul. Some *mujahidin*-run schools in the refugee camps and inside Afghanistan were set up primarily to instil *jihad*ist ideology in the next generation rather than to educate them.

The war-shattered ruins of Kabul's Old City as seen in spring 1996. The bitter fighting between *mujahidin* factions and General Dostam's Uzbek militia led to much of southern, western and central Kabul being destroyed and the deaths of thousands of civilians.

Jami'at in Kabul. The gamble, however, failed. When Jami'at took control of Kabul airport, Dostam withdrew beyond the Salang Pass and from this point onwards he ruled the Wilayat-i Shamal, or Northern Provinces, as virtually an independent ruler.

The factional fighting that took place from 1992 to 1994 left parts of Kabul looking like London after the Blitz. According to the ICRC, between 20,000 and 30,000 civilians died and thousands more were injured. The fighting was fuelled by ethnic and sectarian hatred and marred by atrocities including mass executions, rape, torture, looting and indiscriminate bombardment of residential areas. In some instances prisoners were burnt alive; others were locked in shipping containers and left to suffocate. The tombs of the first Mughal emperor, Zahir al-Din Babur, Amir Timur Shah, King Nadir Shah and Sultan Muhammad Tela'i were badly damaged, while 'Aman Allah Khan's palaces and state buildings in Dar al-'Aman and Paghman were gutted. The Kabul Museum was hit by mortar fire, its upper storey burnt out and many of its priceless treasures were looted.

The international community was powerless to prevent the anarchy, and since the USSR had withdrawn and the Communist government had fallen, the USA and Western countries showed little interest in the fate of Afghanistan or its government. One of the reasons for this was that in 1990 both Hikmatyar and Rabbani had declared their support for Saddam Hussein in the First Gulf War, rather than America, though the royalists

Sibghat Allah Mujadidi and Pir Gailani sent a token force of three hundred men to join the u.s.-led coalition. The Bush administration was disgusted at the *mujahid*'s ingratitude after the CIA had armed and supported the *mujahidin* during the Soviet occupation. In retaliation, the USA and NATO countries cut military and humanitarian assistance to Rabbani's government, diverting the funds to pay for the war in Iraq and the subsequent reconstruction programme. By the end of 1994 Afghanistan was yet again facing economic and political collapse, with both Afghans and foreign observers seriously wondering whether the country was about to follow in the footsteps of Yugoslavia and break up into ethnocentric mini-states.

FOURTEEN

'Between the Dragon and his Wrath',
1994–2017

Where men build on false grounds, the more they build, the greater is
the ruin.

THOMAS HOBBES, Leviathan

For us, Afghanistan is destroyed . . . It is turning to poison and not only
for us but for all others in the world . . . Maybe one day [the Americans]
will have to send hundreds of thousands of troops to deal with that. And
if they step in, they will be stuck. We have a British grave in Afghanistan.
We have a Soviet grave. And then we will have an American grave.

'ABD AL-HAQ ARSALA

BY THE SUMMER OF 1994 the chaos in Afghanistan finally convinced
Pakistan's Inter-Services Intelligence (ISI) that Gulbudin Hikmatyar
stood little chance of taking Kabul, let alone ruling Afghanistan
under Pakistan's tutelage. Yet instead of mending fences with the Rabbani
government, Pakistan regarded it as inimical to its interest and the ISI
continued to pursue the old colonial paradigm of a Pushtun solution.
The search for potential allies among the Pushtun *mujahidin* led the ISI to
Quetta where a small group of Ghilzais from Kandahar and southwestern
Afghanistan, dismayed at the lawless in their region, had banded together
and begun to take unilateral action against commanders in defence of
local populations.

The Taliban, their background and religious influences

All of these men were veterans of the *jihad* against the Soviet occupation
and had fought under the banner of one or other of the Peshawar Sunni
factions. Many of them bore the scars of war, including their leader
Mullah 'Omar, who had been badly wounded and had lost his right eye.
In an attempt to distance themselves from the *mujahidin*, whom they
believed had failed not only Afghans but Islam, the group referred to

themselves as the Taliban, for all of them had been students, or *talibs*, of various *madrasa*s in southern Afghanistan, Karachi or the Northwest Frontier Province. One *madrasa* in particular, the Darul Uloom Haqqania in Akora Khattak on the Peshawar–Attock road, played a significant part in forming the Taliban's view of Islam and the Islamic state. Its founder, Maulana 'Abd al-Haq (*c.* 1914–1988),[1] trained at the Darul Uloom at Deoband and was a *murid* of the Hajji Sahib of Turangzai, the *pir* who in 1897 and 1915 led two major Frontier revolts against British rule and was a key supporter of 'Abd al-Ghaffar Khan's Khudai Khimatgar movement. Prior to Partition 'Abd al-Haq became a founder member of the Jamiat Ulema-e-Islam (JUI).

In 1947, after Partition, 'Abd al-Haq returned to his home town of Akora Khattak where he founded the Pakistani branch of the Darul Uloom. In 1970 'Abd al-Haq was elected to Pakistan's National Assembly. After the Soviet occupation he issued a *fatwa* legitimizing the Peshawar Sunni Islamists' *jihad*, and also actively raised funds for the *mujahidin* and provided free religious tuition for war orphans and the children of impoverished refugees. As a leading member of the JUI, 'Abd al-Haq played a major role in supporting General Zia-ul-Haq's military coup and was one of the driving forces behind Zia's project to Islamize Pakistan's Constitution.

'Abd al-Haq died in 1988 and was succeeded by his son, Sami al-Haq, who promoted an even more militant vision of Islam and Islamization constructed on the concept of perpetual and obligatory *jihad*. Sami too played a leading role in Pakistan's political life as head of a splinter faction of the JUI (JUI-S) and was the principal sponsor of the bill that led to the *shari'a*ization of Pakistan's Constitution and the passing of the controversial blasphemy law. Sami's publications include virulent attacks on the Western world order, the State of Israel, Communism and coeducation. He was responsible for a *fatwa* that condemned Shi'as, Isma'ilis and Qadiyanis as non-Muslims, and called for all adult Muslims in Pakistan to be trained for *jihad*. After the Taliban's successful conquest of Afghanistan, Sami boasted that Mullah 'Omar consulted him regularly, a claim that led the Western press to misleadingly refer to him as 'The Father of the Taliban'.[2]

Many of the leaders of the Taliban had studied at 'Abd al-Haq's *madrasa* in Akora Khattak but the movement was always very much its own master. Furthermore, despite subsequent attempts by the USA and NATO to tar the Afghan Taliban with the brush of international terrorism, the movement was always a religio-nationalist movement, unlike al-Qa'ida or Daesh/ ISIS. The Taliban were essentially the latest avatar of a long-standing tradition of Pushtun resistance to domination by the state and the movement embraces traditional mysticism and millenarianism as well as *pushtunwali,* or customary law.

The Taliban, though, differed from Peshawar-based Sunni *mujahidin,* inasmuch as their model of Islam and the Islamic state was rooted in the Indian subcontinent rather than Saudi Arabian Wahhabism or Egypt's Ikhwan al-Muslimin. Furthermore, unlike Hikmatyar and Ma'sud, most of the Taliban had no secular education but were the product solely of cloistered *madrasa*s, while its leadership and supporters came from marginalized rural and nomadic tribes, Pushtuns who were at the bottom of the tribal socio-economic ladder. Mullah 'Omar's father, for example, was an impoverished sharecropper. Other Taliban were war orphans, the children of poor refugees, or *maldar* who had been reduced to poverty by the war or forced to adopt a sedentary life and eke out a precarious existence on the fringes of Baluchistan's refugee camps.

The Taliban already had strong links with Sami al-Haq and Pakistan's JUI and, since the organization was small and relatively weak militarily, the ISI believed it would be easy to manipulate the movement's political agenda to reassert Pakistan's influence in southern Afghanistan. Benazir Bhutto, who had been returned as Pakistan's prime minister in 1993, also hoped the Taliban would restore security on the Chaman–Kandahar–Herat highway and open up a potentially lucrative trade route between Pakistan, Turkmenistan and Uzbekistan. This would offer the possibility of the construction of a pipeline from Turkmenistan, which could provide Pakistan with cheap gas and oil. With the *mujahidin* in power, this trans-Asian vision was impossible, for Kandahar was divided by warring factions and commanders had established dozens of checkpoints on the Chaman–Kandahar highway, where they extracted heavy tolls and frequently looted trucks and passengers.

The Taliban and the fall of southern Afghanistan

Pakistani officials tried to negotiate safe passage for the first overland convoy only for talks to break down after the Kandahar *shura* demanded an exorbitant fee in return for safe passage. Instead the ISI began to supply the Taliban with large amounts of cash and weapons in return for a pledge they would clear the checkpoints from the main highway. On 12 October 1994 the Taliban stormed the Hizb-i Islami-held frontier post of Spin Baldak. A few weeks later a convoy of vehicles set out for Kandahar, driven by Pakistani army personnel in mufti under the leadership of an ISI colonel. When the faction that controlled Kandahar airport impounded the trucks, the ISI called in the Taliban who routed the militia, killed its commander and hung his body from a tank barrel. On 5 November Kandahar itself fell after the ISI reportedly paid Mullah Naqib, Kandahar's most powerful commander, $1.5 million not to oppose the takeover. In December, with traffic flowing unhindered on the Kandahar–Chaman highway, the first convoy of Pakistani trucks arrived in Quetta laden with Uzbek cotton.

The fall of Kandahar transformed the Taliban from a small, lightly armed militia into a major military force armed with Russian tanks, artillery, helicopters and even a few MiG jets. The ISI continued to truck in munitions and provided the Taliban with hundreds of fast-moving pickups and an almost endless supply of cash, while Sami al-Haq called on Frontier *madrasas* to send *talibs* to join the *jihad*. Within a matter of weeks, the Taliban ranks had swollen to some 20,000 volunteers. As the military balance of power in southern Afghanistan shifted, many *mujahidin* commanders and tribal leaders, including Durranis, pledged their allegiance to the Taliban. A key facilitator in this process was 'Abd al-Ahad Karzai, head of the Popalzai clan, of which the Saddozai royal line was a sept. Karzai's father had been Deputy Speaker of the National Assembly in the reign of King Zahir Shah, while his son Hamid Karzai had been Deputy Foreign Minister in the Rabbani government until Mas'ud arrested him for allegedly spying for Hikmatyar's Hizb-i Islami and the ISI. Somewhat fortuitously, Hamid Karzai escaped from jail during a particularly fierce bombardment of Kabul and fled to Quetta, where he and his father endorsed the Taliban and began to provide cash and logistical support for the movement.

Following the fall of Kandahar, Uruzgan, 'Omar's home province, and Zabul fell without a struggle and the only opposition the Taliban faced in Helmand province was from the commander at Girishk. In a bloody battle, which saw heavy losses on both sides, the Taliban were once more victorious and they followed up their victory by crossing the Helmand and attacking the Shindand airbase, only for Isma'il Khan to defeat them. A second column sent up the Ghazni highway had more success and in early February 1995 the Taliban took Maidan Shahr, the provincial capital of Wardak, from Hizb-i Islami. A week later Hikmaytar abandoned Chahar Asiyab and Pul-i 'Alam on the southern outskirts of Kabul. In a matter of five months, the Taliban had secured control of Afghanistan's main southern highway from the Helmand to the Pakistan border and from Kandahar to the outskirts of Kabul.

The sudden irruption of the Taliban caught President Rabbani and Mas'ud by surprise, although initially they hoped they could form an

The Mahipur Gorge on the modern Kabul–Jalalabad highway. The Taliban used this road on their advance on Kabul.

alliance with the movement and defeat Hikmatyar. The Taliban's military successes, however, fuelled Mullah 'Omar's conviction that he had a divine calling to rescue Afghanistan from the forces of misrule and usher in a 'true' Islamic government, a conviction reinforced by a vision he claimed to have had of the Prophet Muhammad, who had endorsed his *jihad*. So Mullah 'Omar dismissed Rabbani's offer and instead demanded his government resign and Mas'ud surrender. Instead, in March 1995 Mas'ud consolidated his control over the Afghan capital and attacked the Hizb-i Wahdat suburbs of Chindawal and Deh Mazang.

In an attempt to stave off defeat, 'Abd al-'Ali Mazari, head of Hizb-i Wahdat, cut a deal with the Taliban. In return for their military support against Mas'ud, Mazari offered to surrender a number of positions in southern Kabul to the Taliban, but his scheme backfired after rival factions within Hizb-i Wahdat rejected the deal. When the Taliban tried to occupy the posts the Hazaras opened fire, killing and wounding hundreds of Taliban. Mas'ud then overran Hizb-i Wahdat positions, during which his Panjshiris went on an orgy of killing, pillage and rape, and pushed the Taliban out of Chahar Asiyab. The Taliban responded with a sustained rocket attack on the capital, which caused hundreds more civilian deaths and yet more destruction. The unfortunate Mazari was captured by the Taliban, tortured, subjected to public humiliation and finally thrown alive from a helicopter – though the Taliban claimed he fell. His body was eventually handed over and buried in his home town of Mazar-i Sharif, where his mausoleum quickly became a major Shi'a shrine. Following Mazari's death, Hizb-i Wahdat split into three rival factions, with the party led by Sayyid Akbari, a Kabuli Qizilbash, joining forces with the Taliban.

Encouraged by Mas'ud's success, in the autumn of 1995 Isma'il Khan in Herat launched an offensive against Taliban positions on the Helmand, only for his campaign to turn into a chaotic rout. On 5 September 1995 the Taliban entered Herat almost unopposed. As for Isma'il Khan, he fled to Iran. When news of the fall of Herat broke in Kabul, a mob of around 5,000 Jami'at supporters burnt and looted the Pakistan embassy, which had recently relocated to the former mansion of the British Legation. By the time the mob had finished, Lord Curzon's grand, neoclassical edifice, designed as a statement of British wealth, power and imperial prestige, had been reduced to a blackened shell. The Taliban then went on the offensive, retaking Chahar Asiyab, overrunning Khak-i Jabbar and attacking But Khak on the outskirts of Kabul. A second Taliban column occupied the Rishkhor army base in southwest Kabul. After bitter fighting, Mas'ud eventually pushed the Taliban back, but not far enough to prevent yet another barrage of rockets descending on the already war-battered capital.

In the spring of 1996, with Afghanistan effectively partitioned into three rival governments, Mullah 'Omar sought to legitimize his position as head of not just the Taliban but of Afghanistan by calling a *shura* in Kandahar, which was attended by thousands of '*ulama*' and Talibs from both sides of the Durand Line. Following two weeks of debate, the assembly endorsed the continuation of the Taliban's *jihad,* silencing in the process more moderate voices in the movement who called for an end to the civil war and negotiations for a power-sharing agreement with Jami'at. The assembly then proclaimed Mullah 'Omar as Amir al-Mu'minin of the Islamic Emirate of Afghanistan. To reinforce his spiritual legitimacy, Amir 'Omar appeared before the assembly wrapped in the Khirqa Sharif, an action that for many of his ardent followers confirmed his mystical status. Some Taliban, though, regarded 'Omar's action as a presumption that was tantamount to sacrilege. It was as if an Italian presidential candidate had wrapped himself in the Shroud of Turin in an attempt to secure the Catholic vote. Following this dramatic gesture, Mullah ʿOmar became increasingly reclusive, living in close proximity to the relic and allowing only his most trusted advisers to be admitted to his presence.

The Taliban's unexpected military successes dealt a serious blow to Hikmatyar's military machine. Faced with political oblivion and defeat, he finally agreed to come to Kabul and share power with Rabbani and Masʿud – a decision equivalent to boarding the *Titanic* after it had struck the iceberg. In late June 1996, when Hikmatyar finally arrived in Kabul, he was greeted by another devastating barrage of rockets from the Taliban forward positions. Hikmatyar's presence in the capital, however, exacerbated the already toxic relationship between himself and Ahmad Shah Masʿud. Within a matter of weeks, the two men were at loggerheads. When in August the Taliban overran Hizb-i Islami bases in Paktiya and Paktika, Masʿud refused to send reinforcements to defend these outposts. The decision was tactically correct, since to have done so would have overstretched his resources and made Kabul vulnerable to an assault by the Taliban. Furthermore, Masʿud realized that sending thousands of heavily armed Panjshiris into the southern tribal belt would be deeply resented by Pushtun tribal leaders and inevitably lead to more defections to the Taliban. Instead, Masʿud strengthened the defences at Sarobi, Hikmatyar's last stronghold and the gateway to Kabul from the east, as well as the back door to the Panjshir and Koh Daman. Hikmatyar, however, was deeply displeased at Masʿud's decision, claiming that the Panjshiri leader was deliberately avoiding supporting Hizb-i Islami positions in an attempt to weaken his militia even further.

On 11 September 1996 Jalalabad fell to the Taliban without a fight, amid rumours that Hajji Qadir, head of the Nangahar *shura*, had agreed to surrender the town in return for several million dollars and safe passage to Pakistan. A few days later, the Taliban overran Kunar and Laghman and pushed on up the Kabul–Jalalabad highway. On 24 September they reached Sarobi where they launched a surprise night assault on the weakest section of Masʿud and Hikmatyar's front line. Hundreds of *ghazi*s volunteered to walk through the protecting minefield, blowing up the mines and themselves in the process, but in so doing they cleared a path for military vehicles and the infantry. Caught off guard, Masʿud's men fought bravely only to flee after Hikmatyar's militia turned their guns on them and joined the Taliban.

The fall of Kabul and the Taliban's Islamization programme

The fall of Sarobi created panic in Kabul for it was now a matter of hours before the Taliban reached the outskirts of the city. Fearing a bloodbath, the UN and International Committee of the Red Cross (ICRC) hastily evacuated all foreign aid workers, while Kabulis grabbed what possessions they could and fled north in fleets of buses, cars and taxis. Mas'ud, though, decided it would not be possible to defend the capital and during the night of 26/27 September he successfully withdrew his Panjshiris to Charikar. On the afternoon of 27 September the Taliban entered the capital almost unopposed. One of their first acts was to break into the United Nations Development Programme (UNDP) compound in violation of its diplomatic status, seize ex-President Najib Allah Khan and his brother and driver, whom they proceeded to torture, castrate and drag through the streets behind pickups, They were finally shot and their battered corpses hung from the traffic lights in Shahr-i Nau. After several days they were cut down, handed over to the ICRC and eventually buried in Najib's home town of Gardez. A few days later the Taliban issued death sentences *in absentia* on Dostam, Mas'ud and Rabbani.

Once in control of the capital the Taliban imposed an even more rigorous version of Islamic law than that introduced under President Rabbani and ruled Afghanistan as if it were a Frontier *madrasa*. The 'Amr b'il Ma'ruf wa Nahi 'An al-Mankar, or the Office for the Enforcement of Virtue and the Prevention of Vice, an institution originally established by Mujadidi in 1992 and which was modelled on Saudi Arabia's *Ha'yah* religious police, roamed the streets enforcing the draconian rules, forcing attendance at prayers and whipping violators of the new code. Television and music was banned, with the exception of *na'at*, or a cappella religious chants, while Radio Kabul was renamed Radio Shari'a. Most sporting pastimes were outlawed, along with the celebration of the New Year festival of Nauroz, since the Taliban deemed it un-Islamic.

Both males and females were required to conform to a strict deportment code. Adult males had to grow full beards, while trimming them was punishable by whipping. The wearing of any form of Western clothing by Muslims was banned and foreigners were forbidden to wear local dress. Inevitably, these regulations hit women the hardest. Veiling was strictly enforced and women were not allowed out of the house unless they were accompanied by a *mahram*. Girls' schools were closed, women were dismissed from the civil service and there was strict segregation between sexes. Foreign aid agencies had to make complex arrangements to comply with these *parda* regulations so that their female staff could continue working. This included separate offices, access doors and even buildings for men and women. Some female staff ended up working from home, while some of those who were laid off continued to receive their salaries. Female state employees who were dismissed because of the Taliban rules or programme closures were not so fortunate and much hardship ensued, for with the economy in tatters and rampant inflation, even basic commodities were scarce or beyond the means of ordinary people. The health sector was particularly hard hit by the segregation laws for there were very few women-only hospitals in Afghanistan and relatively few female doctors, particularly gynaecologists and obstetricians. Since male medical personnel were forbidden to see, let alone touch, a woman, it was impossible to take their pulse or temperature, let alone use a stethoscope. This led to the farcical situation of male doctors trying to diagnose a woman's condition while she sat behind a curtain and answered the medic's questions.

Tensions and confrontations between Western aid agencies and the Taliban were frequent and later became internationalized by the Feminists Majority Foundation of America, who damned the Taliban's regulations as 'gender apartheid'. In the end, several international organizations closed their programmes rather than comply with the laws on segregation. As international condemnation of the Taliban's gender policies became more and more strident, radicals on both sides of the ideological divide deliberately engineered confrontations in order to prove a point.

The social restrictions were particularly resented in Kabul but in rural communities and the Pushtun tribal belt, the gender regulations were mostly business as usual, since concealment of women and strict separation of the sexes was the norm. Furthermore, while Afghanistan's urban populations and the middle classes resented the Taliban's draconian rules and regulations, the restoration of law and order after the anarchy of the Rabbani era came as a welcome relief. The Taliban removed illegal checkpoints, though they set up their own to police the new social decrees, and travel on the highways became safe. Despite their distaste for the Taliban's gender policies, Western aid agencies found it safer and easier to deliver urgent relief supplies to impoverished rural communities. Even educated Afghans, who privately mocked the Taliban as *pa-yi luch*, or barefooted hillbillies, grudgingly admitted that security had improved and that their daughters were less at risk from the rapacity of *mujahidin* commanders – provided, of course, they conformed to the Taliban's regulations.

The loss of Kabul was a shattering blow to Jamiʿat and Masʿud. In an attempt to resist any further advances, Masʿud, Dostam and Hizb-i Wahdat settled their differences and formed a joint front against the Taliban known as the Northern Alliance. The Iranians, worried that the Taliban might extend their *jihad* into Khurasan province, smuggled Isma'il Khan back into Badghis, where he shored up Dostam's western flank. However, Dostam's position was under threat as his alliance with the *pahlawan*s was beginning to unravel, following a series of ambushes by unknown assailants on Dostam's Turkman and Uzbek allies, which culminated with the assassination of Rasul Pahlawan in June 1996.

The Taliban and the fall of the Northern Provinces and Hazarajat

Informed sources in Mazar reported that Rasul's death was an act of personal revenge by a relative of one of Rasul's bodyguards, whom he had executed, but Malik Pahlawan, Rasul's ambitious half-brother, accused Dostam of being behind the killing. In an attempt to topple Dostam, Malik turned to the Taliban in Herat for assistance. In return for agreeing not to oppose a Taliban advance through the Murghab corridor, Malik accepted $200,000 and a pledge that he would become the autonomous governor of the Wilayat-i Shamal-i Afghanistan. In May 1997 Malik lured Isma'il Khan to Maimana, where he was arrested by Taliban operatives. Malik's militia then surrounded Dostam's forces in the Maimana garrison, forced them to surrender and raised the Taliban's white flag.

Dostam at first did not believe reports that Malik had opened the door to the Taliban, but when he was told that hundreds of fast-moving pickups loaded with Taliban were heading for Shibarghan through the Dasht-i Laili, he rushed to the region to organize defences only to be betrayed by another erstwhile ally, Bashir Salangi, who controlled access to the Salang Pass. He accepted a substantial bribe from the Taliban and stood aside as they poured through the Salang Tunnel. As the militia advanced on Shibarghan and Mazar from the east and west, Dostam fled to Uzbekistan and later made his way to Turkey.

On 25 May 1997 Taliban forces rolled into Mazar, where it soon became evident that they, not Malik, were in charge. As far as the Taliban were concerned, Mazar was an even greater centre of *jahiliyya* than Kabul, for not only was it the last refuge of Parchamis and Khalqis, it was the most socially liberal urban centre in Afghanistan. The Taliban set about changing this and enforced rigorous observance of Islamic law at the point of a gun. All schools and the university were closed, rigorous *parda* was enforced and bands of Taliban went from house to house smashing televisions, videos and cassette players, pulling down satellite dishes and pouring alcohol into the ditches. The population, regardless of whether they were Shiʻa, Ismaʻili or Sunni, were then driven into the mosques to pray. But when the Taliban tried to disarm Hizb-i Wahdat Hazaras, they fought back and were joined by Malik and Dostam's militia. Trapped in the narrow alleys in an unfamiliar city, the Taliban stood no chance. Hundreds of Talibs lay dead by the time the shooting stopped, while those who survived the slaughter either surrendered or were taken prisoner. Malik then shipped most of the prisoners out to the remote Dasht-i Laili, where he executed them in cold blood and threw the bodies into a mass grave. In Mazar-i Sharif itself, Malik's men celebrated their victory by ransacking UN and NGO offices and the houses of foreign aid workers. The Taliban occupation of Mazar-i Sharif had lasted just three days.

Malik quickly regained control of most of the north while Masʻud blew up the entrance to the Salang Tunnel, cutting off the Taliban's line of retreat. The surviving Taliban fled instead to Qunduz, where they managed to beat off every attempt to dislodge them. Despite the setback, the Taliban had secured a foothold beyond the Hindu Kush. Even so, the defeat had cost the movement dear. Several thousand men had been killed, including several key commanders, and hundreds more were captured or executed. The Taliban had also abandoned hundreds of vehicles and a huge amount of military equipment. The human losses were quickly replaced since, at the urging of Sami al-Haq, *madrasas* in Pakistan sent thousands of new child soldiers across the frontier, while the ISI and the Saudi Arabian intelligence service replaced the vehicles and munitions. The Taliban defeat was also a defeat for Pakistan's military strategy in Afghanistan and a political embarrassment. Following the fall of Mazar-i Sharif, Pakistan, the United Arab Emirates and Saudi Arabia had accorded diplomatic recognition to the Taliban, though no other nation followed suit. In the clean-up after the massacre, several hundred of the dead and prisoners were found to have Pakistani passports and, according to well-informed local sources, a number had ISI and Pakistani military identity cards.

Within a matter of months the Taliban had rearmed and been reinforced. In August they were strong enough to launch a second attack on Maimana from Herat, while in the east Taliban militia in Qunduz, supported by the former Hizb-i Islami commander in Baghlan, overran Pul-i Khumri and Tashqurghan. Malik retreated and, with the Taliban closing in on Mazar-i Sharif, public demonstrations demanded the return of Dostam, and when he arrived in mid-September he was greeted by a hero's welcome. Most of Malik's militia defected and few weeks later Dostam defeated the Taliban as they tried to enter the city. Dostam then took control of Maimana and Malik Pahlawan and his half-brother Gul Pahlawan fled to Iran.

Malik's reign had been brief but it did untold damage to the delicate multi-ethnic confederacy Dostam had worked so hard to build. Malik's cold-blooded execution of Taliban prisoners and his subsequent expulsion of Pushtun *maldar* from the Maimana and Sar-i Pul regions created deep resentment among local Pushtun communities. Dostam did his best to rebuild bridges with this community, publicly condemning Malik's actions, apologizing for the massacre and allowing the remaining Taliban prisoners to return home. Dostam even asked the UN and the ICRC to conduct a war crimes investigation into the Dasht-i Laili killings. The damage, however, had been done and from this point forward the war between the Taliban and the Northern Alliance was increasingly tainted by racial hatred.

In the summer of 1998 the Taliban launched a third offensive into southern Faryab. When Qaisar fell they systematically pillaged the settlement, separated the Uzbeks and Hazaras population from local Pushtuns and executed them in the town square. In all around six hundred men, women and children died in this massacre. Dostam rushed to Maimana to try and stem the advance, only for Hizb-i Wahdat to take advantage of his absence and seize control of Mazar-i Sharif. They also attacked the Pushtun enclave of Balkh, where they went on an orgy of rape and pillage. In the east, Jami'at-i Islami's 'Ata Muhammad Nur occupied Tashqurghan. Dostam fell back on Shibarghan and the Taliban swept through Faryab, massacring thousands more Uzbeks and Hazaras. When Pushtun commanders in the Balkh area declared their support for the Taliban and attacked Dostam's forces, he fled back once more to Uzbekistan.

On 8 August 1998 the Taliban drove into Mazar-i Sharif, where they exacted terrible vengeance for the death of their comrades a year earlier. Death squads went from house to house in the Shi'a and Hazara *mahala*s, castrating the men before slitting their throats and leaving the bodies in the streets to be eaten by dogs. Those who sought sanctuary in the shrine of Shah-i Mardan were driven out at gunpoint and either killed or imprisoned. The Taliban then interdicted pilgrimage to Shah-i Mardan in the mistaken belief it was a Shi'a shrine. Arab *mujahidin*, affiliates of 'Osama bin Laden who took part in the campaign, demanded the shrine be blown up but not even the Taliban were prepared to go that far. Not only were Amir Sher 'Ali Khan and several other members of the royal family buried in its precinct, the Pushtun population held the shrine in as much veneration as the Uzbeks, Tajiks and Hazaras. Instead, Mazari's mausoleum was blown up and levelled. A band of Taliban broke into the

Darra-yi 'Ali, Bamiyan province. A sign over the graveyard of 'the most oppressed martyrs of the age', commemorating the slaughter of 25 Hazaras, mostly young men, by the Taliban.

Iranian diplomatic mission, where they shot dead eight of its members and an Iranian journalist. A further 5,000 prisoners were locked in shipping containers and dispatched to Shibarghan, Herat and Qandahar. Denied food and water, many of them died en route from thirst and suffocation. Around 2,000 people died in the Mazar-i Sharif massacre, while thousands more were slaughtered during the Taliban's rampage through Faryab and Jauzjan.[3]

The fall of the Northern Provinces made the occupation of the Hazarajat inevitable. For more than a year the Taliban had blockaded the region from the south and the population was on the edge of starvation. A month after the fall of Mazar-i Sharif, Hazara resistance collapsed. Supported by Sayyid Akbari's militia, the Taliban took Bamiyan and Yakaulang, looted and burnt the bazaars and slaughtered hundreds of Hazaras. By the end of September 1998 around 90 per cent of Afghanistan was under Taliban control. In desperation Rabbani and Mas'ud, who still held out in Badakhshan and the Panjshir, agreed to accept military aid from Russia as well as Iran and India. In the Hazarajat, Karim Khalili of Hizb-i Wahdat retreated to Darra-yi Chasht in the headwaters of the Balkh Ab, while Dostam's commanders tried to regroup in the mountain stronghold of Darra-yi Suf. The complete subjugation of Afghanistan now seemed but a matter of time.

The USA, the Taliban and 'Osama bin Laden

Pakistan urged the USA and the European Union to accord diplomatic recognition to the Taliban, claiming the militia had restored law and order in the country and that it would suppress opium cultivation. Pakistan also held out the prospect of American companies bidding for the proposed trans-Asian oil and gas pipeline. Western nations, however, were not prepared to recognize a movement that had been condemned by human rights organizations and the media for its violation of human rights, sectarian and ethnic massacres and harsh treatment of women. Iran and Uzbekistan, worried that the Taliban might attempt to invade their countries, sent reinforcements to the Afghanistan frontier, while Iran even threatened to attack Afghanistan and punish the Taliban for the deaths of its embassy staff and in defence of the country's Shi'a population.

Despite the USA not having any formal diplomatic relations with the Taliban government, UNOCAL, a California-based company that was in partnership with Saudi Arabia's Delta Oil, opened offices in Kandahar and Kabul and began to negotiate with the Taliban for the contract to build the Turkmenistan–Afghanistan–Pakistan (TAP) oil and gas pipeline. BRIDAS, an Argentinian rival, which was the preferred option of Pakistan's Prime Minister Benazir Bhutto, also set up shop in Kabul. Both the Taliban and the Turkmenistan government made the most of this rivalry to play the two competitors off against each other. In October 1995 Turkmenistan signed Memoranda of Understanding with both BRIDAS and UNOCAL. Two years later, however, UNOCAL, under the banner of CentGas, the Central Asia Gas Line Consortium, was formally registered in Turkmenistan and effectively cut BRIDAS out of any share in the pipeline project.

UNOCAL's success was due in part to its links with Saudi Arabia and employing advisers who had links at the highest level with Washington and the Taliban. They included Robert Oakley, a former U.S. Ambassador to Pakistan, an ex-member of the UN Special Mission to Afghanistan, the Director of the University of Nebraska's Center for Afghanistan Studies, and Zalmay Khalizad, a Balkh-born monarchist with American citizenship who had been an adviser to the State Department's South Asia Desk. Inside Afghanistan UNOCAL employed Hamid Karzai as their linkman with Mullah 'Omar and the Taliban inner leadership. UNOCAL gifted the Taliban computers, faxes and other office equipment and trained some of its officials. In December 1997 UNOCAL organized a tour of America for senior Taliban leaders that included a meeting with State Department officials, while the head of UNOCAL's Kandahar office allegedly kept the

CIA informed about the activities of 'Osama bin Laden, who was living in Kandahar as a guest of the Taliban and occupied the compound opposite the company.

The combined influence of Pakistan and UNOCAL was a significant factor in the State Department's lack of concern at the Taliban's takeover or its puritanical Islamic regime. Indeed, the State Department even considered reopening its embassy in Kabul. As far as Washington was concerned, the Taliban were not that bad since they had restored law and order, nor was the Taliban's harsh Islamic order seen as a problem, at least initially. After all Saudi Arabia, America's most important ally in the Muslim world, imposed even stricter gender policies and regularly beheaded adulterers in public. Following the fall of Mazar-i Sharif, Uzbekistan, Turkmenistan and Russia warned the State Department that there was a risk of a regional conflict, but Washington showed more concern about Iranian military support for Hizb-i Wahdat, Dostam and the Northern Alliance. In April 1996 Robin Raphel, President Clinton's Assistant Secretary of State, even visited Kandahar and held meetings with the Taliban leadership and publicly endorsed UNOCAL's bid for the pipeline.

A month after Raphel's visit, 'Osama bin Laden, whom the CIA had noted to be 'one of the most significant financial sponsors of Islamic terrorist activities in the world',[4] and who had been funding terrorist camps in Somalia and been expelled from Sudan, landed in Jalalabad in response to a specific invitation by Mullah 'Omar. As part of his conditions of sanctuary, bin Laden undertook not to engage in subversive actions against America or other foreign nations. A few months later CIA operatives covertly visited Mas'ud in the hope he could be persuaded to mount a snatch-and-grab operation and capture bin Laden, but Mas'ud told them he had no power or influence in Kandahar. Instead, he asked the CIA for cash and military equipment so he could regain control over Afghanistan, but his request was turned down. Mas'ud also warned his guests that the Taliban's offer of sanctuary to bin Laden risked turning Afghanistan into a centre of international terrorism. Following his fallout with the Taliban, Hamid Karzai too warned the CIA and U.S. diplomats in Islamabad about the threat posed by bin Laden, as did General Dostam. Their requests for military assistance from the USA and NATO powers however were rejected.

It was not until 1997, after Madeleine Albright became Secretary of State, that the State Department adopted a more critical approach to the Taliban, but mostly because the movement continued to provide a safe haven for 'Osama bin Laden, rather than their human rights record. In August of that year bin Laden, in breach of his promise to Mullah 'Omar, issued the first of two *fatwas* declaring war on the United States. In October, during Congressional hearings, State Department officials gave the first indications of a change in policy to the Taliban, stating that America now sought a multi-ethnic, broadly based government in Afghanistan. The following month, during a visit to a girls' school in Nasir Bagh refugee camp, Albright publicly condemned the Taliban's 'despicable treatment of women and their lack of respect for human rights'.[5] Two months later, when the UNOCAL-sponsored Taliban delegation visited the State Department, no doubt in anticipation that the USA planned to restore diplomatic relations, they were lectured on their gender policy and dismissed empty-handed.

It was not until August 1998, in the wake of al-Qaʻida's attacks on the U.S. embassies in Kenya and Tanzania, that the State Department took a harder line with the Taliban. America demanded that Mullah ʻOmar hand over bin Laden so he could stand trial and launched missile strikes on al-Qaʻida bases in Khost and Nangahar. The attacks failed to kill bin Laden but they marked the end of the rapprochement between the USA and the Taliban, while UNOCAL withdrew from Afghanistan and shelved the pipeline project. Mullah ʻOmar was now caught in the middle of a war between the USA and al-Qaʻida, unwilling to expel bin Laden but at the same time the U.S. missile strikes not only violated Afghanistan's sovereignty but were an indirect threat to the Taliban too. When Saudi Arabia demanded that the Taliban hand over bin Laden, for he was a wanted man in the Kingdom too, Mullah ʻOmar was in the process of obtaining a legal opinion from senior religious figures on the issue of bin Laden's possible expulsion, although the U.S. State Department appears to have been ignorant of this fact, or chose to ignore it. Shortly before the al-Qaʻida attacks, a delegation of senior Saudi officials had visited Kandahar in an attempt to persuade Mullah ʻOmar to extradite ʼOsama bin Laden and the two parties had established a joint commission of '*ulama*' to draw up a *fatwa* legitimizing his expulsion. In return, the Saudis had pledged hundreds of millions of dollars in aid once bin Laden was handed over or quit Afghanistan; such financial assistance was urgently needed, for the Afghan economy was in dire straits and the country was once more in the grip of famine.

ʼOsama bin Laden would have been well aware of the Saudis' activities; indeed the attacks on the U.S. embassies may well have been designed to force Mullah ʻOmar into the al-Qaʻida camp, as bin Laden gambled that the USA would damn not just him but the Taliban too for supporting terrorism. If this were the case, bin Laden's strategy was a resounding success. Mullah ʻOmar tried to bargain with America, offering to trade bin Laden's extradition for diplomatic recognition of his government and urgent food

The Greater Buddha of Bamiyan. At 55 m (180 ft) high, this image and its smaller counterpart to the east (38 m/125 ft high) dominate the Bamiyan valley, once a major Buddhist settlement that straddled two of the ancient trade routes between Kabul and the Balkh plains.

aid. Washington, however, was in no mood to negotiate and so the ground was cut from under the Saudi initiative. The usa then sponsored a series of Security Council Resolutions, which imposed travel and financial sanctions on the Taliban leadership and an arms ban, although Pakistan blatantly ignored these prohibitions.

Following the u.s. missile strikes in southern Afghanistan, several senior Taliban leaders became increasingly concerned at the movement's direction and the loss of national sovereignty to bin Laden's Arabs and Pakistan's isi. 'Abd al-Ahad Karzai and 'Abd al-Haq Arsala decided Mullah 'Omar had to be replaced and began to plan a coup, only for the isi to get wind of the plot before it could be enacted. In January 1999 'Abd al-Haq's wife and children were brutally murdered by unknown assassins as they slept in their house in Peshawar. A few months later 'Abd al-Ahad Karzai was gunned down as he left a Quetta mosque. When Hamid Karzai succeeded his father as head of the Popalzais, the Pakistani authorities informed him that they would not renew his residency visa. Hamid Karzai, though, continued his father's attempts to depose Mullah 'Omar and to create a more broadly based government, meeting with Durrani *khan*s,

The Greater Buddha after the Taliban's destruction. Ironically, this action drew international attention to these monuments and substantial funding was committed for the restoration of the two images. In the process a great deal has been learned about their construction, while mass spectrometry has revealed that they were of a much later date than originally thought. The Smaller Buddha, the first to be constructed, dates from *c.* 550 CE; the Greater Buddha from *c.* 615 CE.

former *mujahidin* commanders, and even Dostam and Mas'ud. Karzai also travelled to London and Washington to request political, financial and military support, but his appeals fell on deaf ears.

As for Mullah 'Omar, he fell increasingly under the influence of hard-liners as bin Laden's presence became a major source of income for the cash-strapped government. Eventually Arabs and radicals within his own movement persuaded Mullah 'Omar to make a series of public demonstrations of his Islamic credentials, which equally served as acts of defiance in the face of the Western nations' refusal to recognize his government and their presumed indifference to Afghanistan's plight. In March 2001 the Taliban blew up the giant statues of the Buddha in Bamiyan, overruling Mullah 'Omar's earlier declaration that they were protected historic monuments. Four months later Mullah 'Omar issued a decree banning all foreign nationals from eating pork, playing loud music, committing acts of immorality or publishing anything defamatory against the government. In August, eight foreign volunteers, including two American women, working with the faith-based relief agency Shelter Now International were arrested and accused of proselytizing. A few days later IAM and SERVE, two other Protestant agencies, were shut down and their expatriate workers also expelled.

9/11 and Operation Enduring Freedom

By the autumn of 2001 bin Laden felt he was in a strong enough position to interfere directly in Afghanistan's internal affairs. On 9 September two Tunisian al-Qaʻida operatives disguised as journalists were granted an interview with Ahmad Shah Masʻud. During their meeting they exploded a bomb concealed in a video camera, which killed themselves, Masʻud and several of his aides. It was the first, but tragically not the last, instance of a suicide bombing in Afghanistan. Two days later, on 11 September 2001, nineteen Arabs, mostly citizens of Saudi Arabia, hijacked four American passenger planes and crashed two of them into the World Trade Center in New York and a third into the Pentagon. The fourth plane, intended to attack the White House, crashed in a field after its passengers bravely fought the hijackers. In all more than 3,000 people died in the 9/11 attacks, including six Pakistani citizens, and thousands more were injured.

While smoke and flames billowed from the Pentagon, ISI and high-ranking Pakistani officials were meeting with State Department officials on the other side of the Potomac to discuss a joint operation to capture bin Laden. As they were hastily evacuated, both Pakistani and American officials witnessed at first hand the tragic consequences of their flawed Afghanistan policies. Mullah ʻOmar, too, appears to have had no inkling of either bin Laden's plot to assassinate Masʻud or his subsequent attack on American institutions. According to General Mahmud Ahmed, Director of the ISI, who flew to Kandahar a few days later, Mullah ʻOmar was terrified at the prospect of a war with America and he informed U.S. Embassy officials that the Taliban were in 'deep introspection' about what course of action to take.[6] After a second visit a week or so later, General Ahmed advised American officials 'not to act in anger' and claimed that the threat of an attack may well convince the Taliban to extradite bin Laden in order to save their own skins. General Ahmed also warned the State Department that 'if the Taliban are eliminated Afghanistan will revert to warlordism'.[7]

No one in the U.S. administration was interested in the Taliban's 'deep introspection', for amid the outrage and political fallout from the attacks on American soil, Washington was already gearing up to a massive military response and diplomacy was the first casualty. Before General Ahmed even flew to Kandahar, American officials in Islamabad informed him that 9/11 had changed everything and 'there was absolutely no inclination in Washington to enter into dialogue with the Taliban'.[8] In a speech to Congress shortly after 9/11, President George W. Bush made it clear that if the Taliban did not immediately expel bin Laden and his Arab militias and close down the terrorist bases inside Afghanistan, they would suffer the same fate as al-Qa'ida. President Bush then justified the policy of regime change by mounting a sustained attack on the Taliban's human rights record, their gender policies and Islamic credentials. When Mullah Zaeef, the Taliban ambassador to Pakistan, subsequently declared the movement would never hand over bin Laden and that the Taliban were prepared for war with the USA, his statement and similar ones by other hardliners were seen as further justification for toppling the Taliban.

Mullah 'Omar, however, was in no position to comply with America's ultimatum even if he wanted to. He knew bin Laden would not leave Afghanistan voluntarily, yet he dared not risk a war with the Arab *mujahidin*, for bin Laden controlled a heavily fortified series of deep caves at Tora Bora and if the Taliban attacked the position it would cost them dearly in terms of casualties and could end in defeat. Furthermore, while engaged with bin Laden the Northern Alliance might well take advantage of the situation to mount a counterattack. Anyway, many Taliban, especially those from Sami al-Haq's network, supported the 9/11 attacks and might refuse to fight bin Laden. Finally, Mullah 'Omar was indebted to bin Laden and his Arab *mujahidin* for their support during the Soviet occupation and the campaign against Dostam.

In an attempt to find a way out of this quandary, Mullah 'Omar called a second council of '*ulama*' in the hope that the *shura* would legitimize bin Laden's expulsion. Many of the '*ulama*' who gathered in Kandahar, however, sympathized with the radicalism of al-Qa'ida and regarded bin Laden as a Muslim hero rather than villain. In the end, all the council did was to issue a declaration of sorrow and regret for the deaths of 9/11 and offered to persuade bin Laden to leave voluntarily. The conference also called on the UN and the Organisation of Islamic Cooperation to undertake a judicial investigation into bin Laden's role in the 9/11 attacks.

Such declarations were never going to satisfy the U.S. administration. Even before the Kandahar *shura* convened, the military build-up was well underway. In early October Wendy J. Chamberlain, America's new ambassador to Pakistan, wrote to General Ahmed to ask him to inform

Mullah 'Omar that the USA would 'hold the leaders of the Taliban *personally* responsible' if they refused to comply with America's ultimatum and added that 'every pillar of the Taliban regime will be destroyed'.[9] In a secret draft memorandum, Donald Rumsfeld, Secretary of Defense, explained another motivation for the administration's policy. The Taliban government and its leadership were to be terminated as a deterrent to other states that might contemplate harbouring terrorists.[10] Chamberlain's message anyway was redundant. On the day she wrote to General Ahmed, U.S. and British missiles began pounding al-Qai'da and Taliban command and control centres in the opening gambit of an overwhelming military response known as Operation Enduring Freedom. The Taliban, whose leaders had once met with State Department officials and been wooed by UNOCAL executives, were now tarred with the same terrorist brush as al-Qa'ida. Indeed, Western politicians and the media increasingly treated these very distinct movements as two sides of the same coin. Since neither the Taliban nor any Afghan had played any part either directly or indirectly in the 9/11 terrorist attack on American soil, Mullah 'Omar had grounds to feel aggrieved, even more so since 'Osama bin Laden had broken his pledge not to conduct anti-American activities while a guest of the Taliban. The Bush administration's decision to topple the Taliban therefore radicalized the movement even further and gave the movement a new enemy that justified the perpetuation of their *jihad*.

For the beleaguered Northern Alliance, America's war with al-Qai'da and the Taliban brought these militias back from the brink of military and political extinction. Two days before 9/11 one of the movement's most effective military commanders had been assassinated and the Alliance was staring defeat in the face. Almost overnight, everything changed. The State Department's caveats about Iranian support for the Northern Alliance and Hizb-i Wahdat were shelved and America, Russia, India and Iran began to pour weapons, including tanks, into northeastern Afghanistan. Operation Enduring Freedom, however, proved to be far more complex than President Bush's famous and simplistic declaration, 'either you are with us or with the terrorists'. American Special Forces, dropped into Afghanistan to direct the bombing campaign and provide support for the campaign against the Taliban, became entangled in a world of shifting loyalties as powerful individuals manipulated the intervention to their advantage. Special Forces sent to assist Dostam, Jami'at-i Islami and Muhammad Qasim Fahim, who had succeeded Mas'ud as head of Shura-yi Nizar, were unaware that, as well as attacking the Taliban, the two men were engaged in a race to be the first to occupy Mazar-i Sharif. In southeastern Afghanistan, American troops fought alongside militias loyal to Yunus Khalis and Gulbudin Hikmatyar, individuals who were noted for their Islamic extremism and anti-Western views, and who had been accused of many war crimes. Khalis was also a personal friend of bin Laden, while the State Department would later place Hikmaytar on its list of most wanted terrorists.

America supplied cash and weapons to former *mujahidin* commanders of the Nangahar *shura* to assist in the storming of bin Laden's stronghold at Tora Bora, a complex built partly with CIA money, even though these individuals were some of the principal beneficiaries of Nangahar's vast opium trade. Having accepted the CIA cash and guns, some of these allies then took an even greater sum of money from bin Laden and let him slip across a conveniently unguarded Pakistan frontier. U.S. and British forces in Afghanistan as well as the International Security Assistance Force (ISAF), established under the Bonn Agreement of December 2001, later employed the same Pakistani Pushtun trucking mafia to supply fuel and other supplies for their military that had previously provided financial and logistical support for the Taliban's conquest of southern Afghanistan.

The other major beneficiary of the 9/11 attacks was Pakistan, and the fact that the ISI had armed and funded the Taliban and accorded the government diplomatic recognition was conveniently ignored. Pakistan once again came in from the political wilderness and became the linchpin of Operation Enduring Freedom, with American and Coalition planes over-flying Pakistan airspace, while Karachi became the main transit port for most of the American and ISAF supply. The about-turn could not have been timelier for Pakistan's latest military dictator, General Pervez Musharraf, as the country was suffering from international sanctions following its first nuclear tests in May 1998. A year later Pakistani forces backed by *jihad*ist militia had occupied Kargil on the Indian side of the Line of Control in Kashmir, which led to a brief war in which Pakistani forces were defeated and withdrew back along the Line of Control. A few months later, Prime Minister Nawaz Sharif tried to sack Pervez Musharraf, chair of the Joint Chiefs of Staff, for authorizing the Kargil expedition, only for Musharraf to stage a military coup that triggered yet more U.S. sanctions.

In the wake of the 9/11 attacks, President Musharraf realized Pakistan had little choice but to support America's War on Terror and ditch its alliance with the Taliban, at least publicly. Even so, when Musharraf's military council met to debate their response to 9/11, it took nine hours of heated discussion before the council accepted America's demands, which included unrestricted overflights of Pakistan airspace and access to ports and military facilities for the campaign in Afghanistan.[11] President

Musharraf's support for Operation Enduring Freedom reaped immediate rewards. Sanctions were lifted, Pakistan's Army and Air Force were rearmed with modern American weaponry, 3 billion dollars of the nation's foreign debt were written off and calls for a restoration of democracy waived. Economically, the country benefited from American support for an International Monetary Fund loan. Pakistan also became the main supply route for U.S. and ISAF forces in Afghanistan and saw increased demand for Pakistani goods as shopkeepers and merchants in Afghanistan restocked.

At the same time, President Musharraf was well aware that powerful factions opposed both his military regime and Pakistan's support for America's War on Terror. Many prominent Islamic leaders publicly declared their sympathy for al-Qa'ida's attacks on U.S. soil and up until 9/11 bin Laden T-shirts were openly on sale in the Peshawar and Quetta bazaars. Musharraf was therefore careful when publicly condemning the 9/11 attacks and, while he sent the army into the Federally Administered Tribal Areas to suppress al-Qa'ida and its foreign affiliates, the ISI continued to provide covert support for the Afghan Taliban, since the movement was deemed not to pose a threat to Pakistan's security. According to the Taliban themselves, the ISI not only gave them a safe haven in Quetta, but rearmed and trained them too, even though they were killing American and NATO soldiers.

The ISI undermined Operation Enduring Freedom in other ways too. When 'Abd al-Haq Arsala, the man the CIA favoured as the head of state in a post-Taliban administration, returned to Afghanistan shortly after the military campaign began, ISI officers tipped off the Taliban, who ambushed his convoy and killed 'Abd al-Haq and most of his entourage. The ISI also provided tacit protection for the most senior al-Qa'ida leaders, including 'Osama bin Laden. When American Special Forces finally tracked bin Laden down after nearly a decade of searching, he was living in a military safe house in Abbottabad, less than a mile from Pakistan's main Military Academy. Needless to say the government and military denied any knowledge of his presence.

Pakistan's Janus policy, however, eventually backfired as the very *jihad*ists the ISI had trained for operations in Indian-held Kashmir in the 1980s condemned Musharraf's support for the U.S. military campaign, and mounted a series of terrorist attacks on government and officials inside Pakistan. In 2002 an anti-Musharraf Islamist coalition, led by Sami al-Haq, gained a majority in the Northwest Frontier Assembly and in the same year the Tehrik-e-Taliban, or Pakistan Taliban, formed with the stated intention of deposing President Musharraf and setting up an Islamic state. The

Tehrik-e-Taliban attacked government buildings, churches, schools, Shi'a mosques and shrines, and assassinated prominent military officers and politicians. In the autumn of 2007 the Pakistan Taliban overran Swat and at one point came within two hours' drive of Islamabad. The Pakistan army eventually drove them out of the region, but two years later the Tehrik-e-Taliban retook most of the lost ground. A second major military campaign that lasted more than six months eventually regained control over the region but the Pakistan Taliban were far from defeated. Today they still pose a serious threat to the Pakistan government and continue to mount regular and devastating attacks, particularly in Khyber Pukhtunkhwa and Baluchistan.

In 2004 Musharraf reluctantly sent the army into Southern Waziristan to evict foreign *jihad*ists affiliated to al-Qa'ida, but the campaign met with limited success. After Barack Obama became President of the United States in February 2008 his administration, fed up with the duplicity of Pakistan's policy on Afghanistan and antiterrorism, demanded stronger action against insurgents and U.S. Special Forces and drones began to attack high-value targets on the Pakistan side of the Durand Line. In the autumn of 2009, 28,000 Pakistani troops, backed by aircraft and helicopter gunships, was once more sent into Southern Waziristan, to suppress non-Pushtun *jihad*ists. Following the Islamic Movement of Uzbekistan's (IMU) attack on Jinnah International Airport, Karachi, in June 2014, designed in part as retaliation for the Waziristan campaign, Pakistan launched another major operation aimed at eliminating the IMU, this time in Northern Waziristan. From the autumn of 2008 the Pakistan army had also conducted operations against the Tehrik-e-Taliban in Bajur and Buner districts of what was now Khyber Pukhtunkhwa. These operations, reminiscent of the Frontier Wars of the colonial era, failed to defeat the Pakistan Taliban while at the same time the Pakistan army avoided any confrontation with the Afghan Taliban and cross-border infiltration into Afghanistan continued unabated.

Pakistan's inability to defeat these militant movements, or suppress radical indigenous Islamists, has led to great suffering for ordinary Pakistanis. Since 2001 some 35,000 civilians have been killed in hundreds of terrorist attacks and thousands more injured. Among the victims have been former Prime Minister Benazir Bhutto, several provincial governors and more than 150 children of army officers who were killed when the Tehrik-e-Taliban stormed the Military School in Peshawar. President Musharraf himself was lucky to survive at least two attempts on his life. By conservative estimates, between 2005 and 2013 more than 49,000 Pakistani civilians were killed as a result of terrorist incidents, military operations or u.s. drone strikes. In 2009 alone there were 2,586 terrorist incidents, causing the deaths of 3,000 people. In 2011 the casualty rate more than doubled. By the end of 2013, more than 26,800 'terrorists' had died and in excess of 5,000 Pakistani security personnel had also been killed.[12]

The Bonn Agreement and Karzai's interim government

The Bush administration's single-minded focus on the military campaign in Afghanistan meant that the issue of the future government was low on Washington's priority list. At the end of October 2001 Rumsfeld noted in a draft memorandum that the usa should not 'agonize over post-Taliban arrangements to the point it delays success over Al-Qaida and the Taliban', since this could 'interfere with u.s. military operations and inhibit coalition freedom of action'. Rumsfeld then listed a few vague political objectives based on a simplistic understanding of Afghanistan's complex ethnic and regional politics. The primary aim when it came to a post-Taliban government, according to Rumsfeld, was 'to relieve Pashtun [sic] fears of domination by Northern Alliance (Tajik-Uzbek) tribes' and 'preserving Kabul as a capital for all Afghans, and not one dominated by the Northern Alliance', while 'the Pashtuns' were expected to declare their intention not to 'establish dominion over the entire country'. Rumsfeld suggested the usa should 'explore the value of ties with King Zahir Shah'.[13]

As the military operations got underway Colin Powell, the u.s. Secretary of State, called a hastily convened meeting of the Six Plus Two Group on Afghanistan – China, Pakistan, Tajikistan, Turkmenistan, Uzbekistan and Iran, plus the usa and Russia – urging 'speed, speed, speed!' when it came to a political solution.[14] Yet it was not until the end of November that Francesc Vendrell, the un Special Representative to Afghanistan, managed to convene a conference of the main actors in Bonn. By this time the Taliban had all but been defeated. Dostam won the race to Mazar-i Sharif, though Jami'at and Shura-yi Nizar controlled Qunduz and Badakhshan. In the west, Isma'il Khan took Herat, while Karimi Khalili occupied Bamiyan and the Hazarajat. In the south, Yunus Khalis was first to Jalalabad, only to be caught up in a gunfight with other ex-*mujahidin* commanders who demanded a share of the spoils. A similarly chaotic situation unfolded in Ghazni and Maidan Shah. Kandahar, the last urban centre to fall, fell to Gul Aga Sherzai, who had been governor of Nangahar under President Rabbani. It was Fahim's Panjshiris, though, who secured the greatest prize of all, marching into an abandoned Kabul unchallenged. By doing so he and Jami'at broke a pledge to the usa not to occupy the capital but to leave

When in November 2002 Jami'at-i Islami was restored to power, its leaders actively promoted the cult of Ahmad Shah Mas'ud. This huge painting of Mas'ud in Mazar-i Sharif, set up for the Nauroz celebrations, depicts Mas'ud walking through a field of wild tulips, a traditional symbol of martyrdom.

it demilitarized; a promise that was never going to be honoured for every commander knew that whoever took Kabul would have the upper hand when it came to the formation of a post-Taliban administration. Fahim's breach of faith was the first of many broken promises and agreements that the new administration made to the USA, UN and other coalition partners.

Vendrell was therefore faced with having to make the best of what he euphemistically called the 'new symmetry'.[15] Even before the Afghan delegates arrived in Bonn, they were fighting each other. If this were not bad enough, the conference took place during the fasting month of Ramazan. In practice, the 'new symmetry' meant that the discussions were not about negotiating a peace or inclusive government, but for the assembled Afghans to agree to a 'road map' to elections that would take place three years later. The negotiations therefore were primarily about cobbling together some sort of power-sharing agreement between the factions represented at the conference, most of whom represented the *mujahidin* militias who had been responsible for the chaos, bloodshed and misrule that had been one of the key reasons for the rise of the Taliban in the first place.

The majority of the 25 Afghans who sat around the table in Bonn represented the interests of Jami'at, Shura-yi Nizar and the Northern Alliance. A smaller faction, the Peshawar Group, were members of the Pushtun-dominated *mujahidin*. The Rome Group consisted of a handful of Western-based monarchists, mostly Muhammadzais, backed by Pir Gailani, attended at the invitation of the UN and the USA, while Afghanistan's Shi'a communities were represented by one or two delegates from Hizb-i Wahdat. Only two women and one or two independent Afghans were invited to the conference. Pakistan wanted the Taliban to have a seat at the table too, but all parties rejected this suggestion out of hand.

Except for one or two individuals, all the Afghans at the Bonn Conference represented a variety of vested and competitive interests and none could claim to represent the Afghan people as a whole, since they had not been elected. The talks were marred by heated arguments over old disputes. When the Jami'at representatives threatened to walk out, Colin Powell rang Vendrell and frantically urged him to 'keep them there; lock them up if you have to . . . If they go off, I don't know when I'll get them all back together.'[16] A compromise of sorts was eventually agreed, but despite Vendrell and Powell proclaiming the conference to be a success and the Agreement's bombastic claim to be the means to end the 'tragic conflict', and promoting 'national reconciliation' and 'respect for human rights', it was a deeply flawed document.

The Bonn Agreement was essentially a rehash of the failed Peshawar and Islamabad Accords. It too was only a provisional agreement, valid for six months, 'pending the re-establishment of permanent government institutions'.[17] After this period, a Loya Jirga would convene to elect a Transitional Government with national elections to follow in 2004. The ministries were once again divided up between the various factions represented at the Bonn Conference, with Jami'at and Shura-yi Nizar holding all the most senior cabinet positions, with Fahim as Minister of Defence. As for Dostam, the royalists and Hizb-i Wahdat, they had to be content with honorary or lower-ranking posts.

The issue of who should head the Transitional Administration was particularly contentious since Rabbani was already back in the Presidential Palace and was still officially recognized by the UN, USA and NATO countries as President of Afghanistan. Despite this the Rome Party, backed by the U.S. and UN, pushed for the reinstatement of the octogenarian ex-king Zahir Shah as head of state, a move opposed by the Northern

Alliance and the Peshawar Group. In the end, Zahir Shah was 'offered' the option of return but his representative declined to take it up, stating the king was not interested in the restoration of the monarchy. The door was therefore open for Hamid Karzai, America's preferred candidate because of his previous links with UNOCAL and the fact that as head of the Popalzai Durrani tribe he was a monarchist. However, Karzai was not the international community's first choice. Initially the USA had wanted 'Abd al-Qadir Arsala to be head of state. Qadir was a member of Yunus Khalis's Hizb-i Islami, whose brother 'Abd al-Haq had been killed by the Taliban a matter of weeks earlier. The Northern Alliance and Peshawar Group eventually grudgingly accepted Karzai as a compromise candidate since, unlike 'Abd al-Qadir, Karzai had little military clout and they knew all real power would be in their hands.

The Bonn Agreement was a hastily made deal that created an uneasy collation of unelected *mujahidin* commanders and a handful of monarchists. The preamble to the agreement even included a panegyric to the *mujahidin*, who were praised as 'champions of peace, stability and reconstruction'. The international collation then committed itself to sustain this unstable coalition in power for at least four years by the presence of the ISAF, consisting of military units from Britain, France, Germany and other NATO nations, with smaller contingents from Asian and Middle Eastern countries. The United States did not participate in ISAF, but instead it secured major military bases inside Afghanistan for operations against al-Qa'ida. Eventually, however, America was dragged into the war against an emerging anti-government insurgency.

Any hope ordinary Afghans might have had that the American intervention would exclude the *mujahidin* from power or punish individuals accused of war crimes were thus dashed. The Bonn Agreement created a 'mirage of peace',[18] an illusion of national unity that failed to address the roots of the conflict or the reasons for the collapse of governance and civil institutions in Afghanistan. This was hardly the way for the USA and Western nations to win 'hearts and minds', let alone restore the nation's shattered confidence in central government. The prospects of restoring peace and security to Afghanistan were not improved when the Bush administration refused to become involved in state-building and passed this particular buck to the interim government, the United Nations and civil society advisers and consultants. So a once-in-a-lifetime opportunity for root and branch reform of the Afghan state went begging. Any reforms that have been put into effect since about 2002 have mostly involved tinkering with a broken system, tending to reinforce embedded power brokers and extend the highly centralized state structure by creating ever more layers of bureaucracy. Rabbani was somehow persuaded to quit the Presidential Palace and Hamid Karzai moved in. Since there was no Legislature, for the next two years Karzai ruled by decree, but most of the Presidential *firmans* were ignored, or honoured in the breach, by both ordinary Afghans and cabinet ministers, many of whom were a law unto themselves. Cabinet meetings were frequently stormy affairs with Karzai and rivals from different factions openly threatening each other.

President Bush had damned the Taliban for their violation of human rights and their treatment of women, but Karzai's government was dominated by Islamists too, many of whom were wedded to the vision of a nation ruled by the *shari'a*. In order to bring 'Abd al-Sayyaf over to the government side, for example, Karzai ignored his friendship with bin Laden, his Wahhabist ideology and his role in encouraging Arab *jihad*-ists to come to Afghanistan in the first place. He even appointed one of Sayyaf's ideological allies, Fazl Hadi Shinwari, as chief justice of the Supreme Court. During his era as minister from 2002 to 2006, the octogenarian Shinwari appointed ideological allies to key positions in the justice system, even though he and many of the other appointees did not fulfil the educational criteria laid down by the 2004 Constitution.[19] Shinwari perpetuated the '*Amr b'il Ma'ruf*, endorsed Taliban-style punishments and opposed coeducation. He tacitly condoned child marriage and tried to ban women from singing on television and to outlaw cable TV. Shinwari also confirmed death sentences on journalists for alleged blasphemy and on an Afghan convert to Christianity. In many other ways he undermined the Constitution's claim to uphold international law and the United Nations' Charter on Human Rights.

The new Constitution, which became law in 2004, drew heavily on the 1964 and 1977 Constitutions and many of its clauses were almost word for word copies of these former *Qanun-i Asasi*s. Where it differed was the formal designation of Afghanistan as an Islamic state, despite objections from the USA and Western nations. Like the previous Constitutions, that of 2004 once again failed to resolve the dichotomy between the role of the Hanafi legal code and international law. The preamble yet again paid lip service to the UN Charter and the Universal Declaration of Human Rights, but the Articles themselves included statements such as, 'no law can be passed contrary to the beliefs and provisions of the sacred religion of Islam'. Article 7.15 allowed the judiciary to enforce the Hanafi legal code and/or the Shi'a version of Islamic law, which allowed judges to ignore the Constitution's 'liberal' provisions simply by declaring them un-Islamic.[20]

The cabinet itself was dominated by Jami'at and the Northern Alliance. The real power behind the throne was Marshal Fahim, Minister of Defence, and his Panjshiri militia. Karzai tried to offset his power by appointing members of his own extended family to key positions, as well as a number of former officials who had served during the reign of King Zahir Shah, many of whom had spent the last thirty years or more in exile in the USA and European countries. The UN disarmament programme, implemented shortly after the new government took power, was useful for both Karzai and Fahim since it provided an opportunity to weaken potential rivals, in particular General Dostam. In return for handing over some weapons, mostly old or out of service, commanders were compensated with government positions, tacit immunity from prosecution for human rights abuses, and the opportunity to enrich themselves from the influx of billions of dollars of foreign aid.

In 2003 Karzai acted against the two greatest threats to his own and Fahim's power. Isma'il Khan in Herat was popular but paid no revenues to the central government and used the tax and customs revenues to benefit his own region. This situation was unacceptable since the central government was almost entirely reliant on foreign aid. In August Karzai dismissed Isma'il Khan as commander of the 4th Army Corps and replaced him with a Pushtun monarchist. A few months later Karzai responded to fighting between Isma'il Khan and rival commanders by airlifting in a thousand u.s.-trained troops of the Afghan National Army (ANA) and hundreds of police, ostensibly to support Isma'il Khan. In the spring of the following year, Karzai dismissed Isma'il Khan as governor of Herat and appointed another monarchist who had previously been governor of the province during the reign of King Zahir Shah. Isma'il Khan refused to quit, so Karzai ordered the ANA and police units to depose him by force. In the street battles that followed, dozens of civilians died and United Nations and NGO offices were looted. When Karzai threatened to send in u.s. forces, Isma'il Khan agreed to come to Kabul where he was appointed to the low-ranking post of Minister of Irrigation and Power.

A few months later, probably in an attempt to appease Fahim following the fall of Isma'il Khan, Karzai appointed 'Ata Muhammad Nur of Jami'at-i Islami as governor of Balkh. Dostam too refused to relinquish power and Jami'at and Dostam's Uzbeks fought each other in the streets of Mazar-i Sharif. Dostam eventually stepped down, but he was bitter about what he regarded as an American betrayal. After all, he had been the most effective opponent of the Taliban, had worked closely with u.s. Special Forces and played a major role in defeating the Taliban in Northern

A pro-Karzai slogan on a wall in one of Herat's main streets in the lead-up to the 2004 elections. Herat though was a Jami'at-i Islami stronghold and Karzai's forcible removal of Isma'il Khan as military commander and governor created deep resentment, especially as his replacement was an old-style royalist and a Karzai loyalist.

Afghanistan after Jami'at had become bogged down in Qunduz. Karzai and Dostam's enemies, however, mounted a highly successful black propaganda campaign against him, even though many of his opponents were equally guilty of gross violations of human rights and war crimes. They even tried to blame Dostam for Malik Pahlawan's massacre of some 2,000 Taliban prisoners in the Dasht-i Laili.

Dostam instead urged the Uzbeks to vote in the upcoming presidential and parliamentary elections and then, following a failed attempt on his life, he returned to Turkey where he remained until 2009. In October 2013 he issued an unprecedented public apology 'to all who have suffered on both sides of the war',[21] the only 'warlord' to date to have made such a declaration. In 2014 Dostam supported Ashraf Ghani's successful bid for the presidency and was appointed first deputy prime minister. Two years later Dostam, now in his mid-sixties, was sent into northwestern Afghanistan where his Uzbek militia conducted successful clearance operations against Taliban and Daesh/ISIL insurgents in Faryab, Jauzjan and Sar-i Pul provinces. Not that this did him any good, for he was subsequently accused of torturing and raping a political opponent and spent six months virtually under house arrest. He eventually agreed to voluntary exile in Turkey, where he formed a new political coalition. However, he was recently allowed to return to Afghanistan. Meanwhile in his absence northern Badghis, southern Faryab and Sar-i Pul provinces have been once more overrun by anti-government insurgents, who massacred dozens of Hazaras in the Band-i Sar-i Band region of Sayyid district in August 2017. Needless to say, the provincial security forces were notable by their absence.

Karzai's appointment of royalists, including members of the Saraj and Tarzi families, was not well received by former *mujahidin* commanders. Most of these individuals had been living in North America or various European countries since the 1970s and had little understanding of the radical transformation that Afghan society had undergone in the last thirty years. Their return to Afghanistan was therefore a major culture shock but they did their best to pick up where they or their fathers had left off, only to alienate the population by their haughtiness and demand for the traditional *ta'ruf*, deference. Former *mujahidin* commanders who were dismissed as a result of these appointments openly despised such individuals who, as far as they were concerned, had lived a comfortable life abroad while they had risked everything fighting the might of the Red Army.

Karzai's attempt to turn the clock back to the 1960s was exemplified by other actions too. The 2004 Constitution restored the sheaf and shrine motif on the national flag and the Constitution reinstated the cumbersome parliamentary system of Wolusi Jirga, Meshrano Jirga and Loya Jirga. The former king, Zahir Shah, returned to Afghanistan and despite the Constitution designating Afghanistan as an Islamic Republic, it accorded him the honorary title of Baba-yi Millat, Father of the Nation. At the Loya Jirga in 2002 President Karzai unilaterally declared Zahir Shah to be the Honorary Chairman of the National Assembly, which meant he was in a position to influence the drafting of the new Constitution. When Zahir Shah died in July 2007 he was accorded a state funeral with full military honours and was buried beside his father, Nadir Shah, in his restored mausoleum on Tepe Maranjan. When the remains of President Da'ud and his family were located in a mass grave near Pul-i Charkhi, they too were given a state funeral. Even Karzai's propensity to wear the *chapan*, the long-sleeved coat worn by Uzbeks, and a *karakul* hat was a throwback to the era of Zahir Shah.

Attempts by the international community to create a more broadly based, representative government were subverted by powerful vested interests. The Loya Jirga of June 2002, which was mandated by the Bonn Agreement to elect an interim President, consisted of individuals nominated by elected provincial councils and appointees nominated by the Loya Jirga Commission: 160 seats were reserved for women, but most of these female members were nominated and not elected by popular vote. When the Loya Jirga convened some five hundred individuals, including former *mujahidin* commanders and members of Afghanistan's National Directorate of Security, turned up despite not being formally nominated or elected. After scuffles with ISAF personnel, fifty of the most powerful commanders were admitted to the sessions where they occupied the front seats of the assembly taking note of individuals who criticized the government and intimidating delegates by their presence. Around seventy delegates, disgusted at the manipulation on display, walked out and boycotted the proceedings. The Loya Jirga was then opened by Zahir Shah, even though he had no official position in government, and monarchist delegates signed a petition in favour of reinstating the ex-king as head of state. Under pressure from American and UN officials, however, the king declined the offer and his nomination was withdrawn. Rabbani, the former president, also stood down in the face of hostility from Pushtun *mujahidin* and so the Loya Jirga voted to retain Hamid Karzai as president.

Presidential elections held in 2004 were also marred by what the UN diplomatically termed 'irregularities'. Karzai was again re-elected, but only with a narrow majority and amid widespread evidence of ballot rigging, intimidation and bribery. The parliamentary and provincial elections that took place in September the following year were equally noteworthy for 'irregularities', and voter registration was so poorly policed that thousands of Afghans had no difficulty in obtaining multiple voting cards and voting in multiple locations.

The electoral system adopted after 2001 was wide open to manipulation. The UN recommended Afghanistan adopt a form of proportional representation, but President Karzai insisted on the British system of a single, non-transferable vote, or 'first past the post', while at the same time he rejected the formation of political parties. This meant that a multiplicity of individual candidates representing one party were able to stand in the same constituency: in many constituencies the ballot paper ran to several pages with voters having to choose between hundreds of names, or the logos, of candidates. Many of the 249 members who were eventually elected to the Wolusi Jirga received less than 15 per cent of the popular vote.

The credibility of the elections was further undermined by the government's failure to conduct a nationwide census, as agreed under the Bonn Agreement, the plan being deliberately stymied by the bureaucracy for ethno-political reasons. When it came to drawing up electoral boundaries, the Afghan Electoral Commission (AEC), which was controlled by Karzai loyalists, used guesstimates extrapolated from the partial census of

1979, which allowed them to manipulate electoral boundaries in favour of those factions already in power. The Hazara-Shi'a dominated provinces of Bamiyan and Deh Kundi, for example, were allocated only two seats each in the Wolusi Jirga, while Kabul province had 33 MPs. The 68 seats reserved for women were mostly filled by nominations by existing power brokers, and only a few women were actually elected by popular vote.

The outcome was that the Wolusi Jirga and Meshrano Jirga were dominated by former *mujahidin* commanders and Islamists. Despite the new electoral law specifically excluding those implicated in war crimes and human rights abuses, many members of the Wolusi Jirga either led, or belonged to, factions that were responsible for the bloodshed of the 1990s and human rights abuses during the era of King Zahir Shah or the Communist governments. Yet despite all these irregularities the United Nations, America and the international coalition legitimized the results of both the presidential and parliamentary elections. As for the census, it was not until 2016 that any actual survey commenced, and according to the United Nations Fund for Population Activities (UNFPA), a full nationwide census could take up to six years to complete. With many rural areas now out of government control, however, it is increasingly unlikely any accurate figures of the country's overall population will be forthcoming in the near future. Furthermore, due to political pressure, the census forms do not include any questions related to an individual's ethnicity or language.

The presidential and parliamentary elections of 2009/10 and 2014 took place against the backdrop of a revived insurgency by the Taliban and other anti-government factions. In many rural districts, particularly in southern Afghanistan, security was poor or in the hands of the Taliban and ballot boxes were not delivered. Threats by the Taliban and other insurgents also meant that voters stayed away in large numbers. In the first round of the 2009 presidential elections, 'Abdullah 'Abdullah, a Tajik aligned to Jami'at-i Islami, lost to Hamid Karzai by a narrow margin. A few months later a UN investigation invalidated more than a million of Karzai's votes, bringing his tally to below 50 per cent, yet Karzai still refused to step down and the AEC declared him the winner. 'Abdullah angrily condemned this decision as unconstitutional and declared the AEC to be 'illegitimate' and 'tainted', but the United Nations and the international community as a whole did nothing about the ballot rigging. Instead they persuaded 'Abdullah 'Abdullah to accept the result and not to demand a run-off. Peter Galbraith, the United Nations Deputy Special Representative to Afghanistan, accused his superior, Kai Eide, of being complicit in the electoral fraud and legitimizing a 'train wreck'.[22] As a result, Galbraith was sacked and several other key members of the United Nations Assistance Mission to Afghanistan (UNAMA) resigned in protest.

While Afghans who were able to vote eagerly embraced the rare chance to have a say in who governed them, the flaws in the electoral system, ballot rigging and the tacit acceptance of 'irregularities' by the international community undermined people's faith in Western-style democracy. Many Afghans concluded that the USA and its allies had no interest in the democratic process other than as a means to legitimize the pro-Western Karzai government. The elections therefore effectively disenfranchised the population and handed the Taliban a major propaganda coup.

The Afghan government, however, was not the only dysfunctional institution. When Kai Eide, the UN Special Representative in Afghanistan, took up his post in 2008 he noted that 'more than six years after the fall of the Taliban, the international community still lacked a clear political direction'.[23] Eide then catalogued the bitter disagreements and infighting within the UN mission and other key actors of the international coalition, including American and ISAF commanders, as well as between international actors and President Karzai. The heart of the problem was that the international coalition had conflicting agendas and priorities that were often at odds with those of Karzai and his ministers. Given the lack of a unified approach to Afghanistan's many challenges by the international community, it is hardly surprising that the Afghan administration lacked purpose, direction or accountability. Commanders and government officials adeptly exploited this infighting, playing one side off against the other, and manipulated the aid programmes and military operations for their own gain and to undermine, and even dispose of, political and personal enemies.

Operation Enduring Freedom and the Taliban resurgence

When it came to Operation Enduring Freedom, Washington was elated at how quickly the Taliban were forced from power. On 1 May 2003 Donald Rumsfeld declared during a news conference in Kabul that military operations were moving from 'major combat activity to a period of stability and stabilization' and declared Afghanistan to be 'secure'.[24] In the following year, when British troops assumed responsibility for security in Helmand province, military commanders and their political masters in London believed they were undertaking a peacekeeping mission, only to run into heavily armed and well-trained Taliban. British troops, caught unprepared, ended up fighting a bloody battle for survival that led to the death or injury of dozens of British servicemen.

Memorials to British soldiers killed in Afghanistan after 2002 in Kabul's Qabr-i Gora, or European Cemetery. These plaques are poignantly located above reclaimed and restored gravestones of British solders killed in the Second Anglo-Afghan War.

As for Rumsfeld's claim that the Taliban were no longer a military threat to the Afghan government, this came home to haunt the American administration as the Taliban rearmed and resumed their war against what they claimed was a foreign occupation. From 2004 onwards the number of American and foreign troops killed by insurgents rose year on year, peaking in 2010 with 711 deaths, of which 499 were Americans and 103 British. The following year more than 3,300 U.S. servicemen were wounded by Improvised Explosive Devices (IEDs), mostly suicide attacks and mines. By the end of 2016 American casualties had reached 2,247 dead and 20,000 wounded in action. In addition more than 1,000 troops from other nationalities had been killed. In the first five months of 2017, Afghan National defence personnel killed in action came to 2,531, with 4,238 wounded.[25] As the promised era of peace and security melted into thin air, civilian casualties too rose exponentially. According to UNAMA, between 1 January 2009 and 30 June 2016 more than 22,000 Afghan civilians died and more than 40,000 were injured. A total of 11,418 civilians were documented as having died in the conflict in 2016, the highest annual figure since UNAMA began recording civilian losses. Security incidents too were at their highest level and more than 666,000 Afghans were internally displaced as a result of the conflict, a 40 per cent increase on the previous year.[26]

Despite military commanders and politicians repeatedly stating that they do not target civilians and make every effort to avoid collateral damage, coalition forces in Afghanistan have been responsible for hundreds of civilian deaths and injuries. During the initial campaign of 2001, three times in as many weeks U.S. planes destroyed the ICRC's warehouse in Kabul, which contained vital relief supplies. British military operations in the Helmand led to some five hundred civilian deaths as well as thousands more internally displaced. In July 2008 an American missile strike in the Helmand region killed dozens of men, women and children who were attending a wedding. A few months later around a hundred more died in an attack on a family compound in 'Azizabad. In October 2015, during the battle for Qunduz, a U.S. air strike destroyed a hospital run by Médecins Sans Frontières, killing at least 42 people, including doctors, nurses and patients. Of the 8,397 casualties UNAMA documented in the first half of 2016, 61 per cent were due to insurgency activity, which means more than 3,300 Afghans died or were injured by the actions of government security forces or foreign troops. The unending war has had a devastating impact on Afghans with the Ministry of Health stating that more than 60 per cent of the population of Afghanistan suffer from war-related mental health problems.

Operation Enduring Freedom's primary objective was to degrade al-Qa'ida's ability to attack the USA and to punish and, if possible, kill 'Osama bin Laden and the al-Qa'ida leadership. Within a matter of weeks bin Laden and those al-Qa'ida forces that survived the bombing campaign had fled into Pakistan's tribal territory. Subsequent deployment of hi-tech eavesdropping and drones by the U.S. Army Intelligence and the CIA further eroded bin Laden's capability to plan major attacks on American soil, although the 2004 Madrid train bombing and the 7/7 attacks in London were inspired by al-Qa'ida and some of the perpetrators spent time in training camps in Pakistan. Yet by the time bin Laden was finally tracked down and killed, al-Qa'ida was a shadow of its former self and today it is a bit player when it comes to the world of Islamic anti-West terrorism. This victory, however, has been a pyrrhic one, for a new generation of *jihad*ists have arisen under the banner of Daesh/ISIL, a Hydra-headed movement that has a growing presence in Afghanistan as well as the Middle East. As far as Western nations are concerned, ISIL poses a far greater threat than al-Qa'ida, for hundreds of young Muslims, residents of European nations, have flocked to join the movement's war in Syria and Iraq.

President Bush's decision to oust the Taliban inevitably embroiled the American-led coalition in Afghanistan's internal affairs and marked what in military terms is called mission creep. Since there was no semblance of a national army, the U.S. military and Pentagon advisers began to train a new Afghan National Army (ANA), a programme which proved to be far more problematic than originally anticipated and one which quickly ran foul of powerful vested interests. Marshal Fahim, the Minister of Defence, wanted to rebrand his Panjshiri militia as the ANA, but Karzai rejected this plan since it put far too much power into Fahim's hands. Even so, the majority of ANA troops and its officer corps were *farsiwans* allied to Shura-yi Nizar or Jami'at, with smaller contingents of Dostam's Uzbeks and Hizb-i Wahdat's Hazaras. Relatively few Pushtuns joined up and the ethnic composition of the ANA caused resentment among those Pushtuns who had been the backbone of the army and its officer corps during the Musahiban era.

Despite millions of dollars spent on training and equipment, the ANA has not proved particularly effective at fighting insurgents and foreign troops have had little trust in their Afghan counterparts when it came to battlefield encounters. From its inception, the ANA has been plagued with large-scale desertions, absenteeism and nepotism, while many of its recruits are loyal to their militia commanders or *qaum* rather than the state. Thousands of rifles and other major items of military equipment supplied by the USA have gone missing or fallen into the hands of insurgents, and investigations have revealed that tens of thousands of individuals listed on army payrolls are either nonexistent or absent without leave. Nor were Afghan recruits used to the strict military discipline and unquestioning obedience demanded by foreign military trainers, while neither side had more than a superficial understanding of the other's culture or values. One outcome of this mutual incomprehension was the rise of so-called Green on Blue attacks, as Afghan soldiers and police turned their guns on their foreign counterparts.

Since the ANA was not fit for purpose, American, British, Canadian and other foreign forces bore the brunt of the war against a resurgent Taliban and anti-government elements, with the result that the coalition of America and its allies ended up fighting President Karzai's war rather than its own. ISAF also extended its mission into provincial capitals. When NATO took over the role of internal security in 2003, its troops too became drawn into anti-terrorist operations as well as training the ANA and the national police force. ISAF's original mandate had been to withdraw after the 2004 elections, but in the end NATO troops remained in Afghanistan for fifteen years. Despite transiting responsibility to the ANA since 2013 and the drawdown of NATO forces at the end of 2015, the Taliban remain undefeated and more than 13,000 foreign troops, including 10,000 U.S. soldiers, are still in Afghanistan under the banner of Operation Resolute Support. American advisers continue to play an active role in directing combat and advising Afghan security forces in the defence of key towns such as Qunduz. The situation, however, quickly deteriorated following the withdrawal and at the time of writing is now so serious that NATO and the USA are now sending troops back to Afghanistan. With no end in sight to the conflict, the United States and NATO seem to have effectively committed themselves to propping up the Afghan government almost indefinitely.

Coalition dual roles and reconstruction

Following the fall of the Taliban, some coalition forces assumed a dual role as both part of ISAF and as combat troops. ISAF included contingents of British and New Zealand troops in Kabul and Bamiyan, respectively, but at the same time British regiments fought the Taliban in the Helmand, while the New Zealand SAS were deployed in an anti-terrorist role and supported British anti-insurgency operations in the Helmand. To complicate matters further, ISAF was never officially a UN peacekeeping force and the soldiers did not wear the distinctive UN blue beret or have UN insignia on their vehicles. Instead, ISAF and combat troops wore the same combat fatigues and flew the same national flag. Most Afghans, government ministers, as well as the Taliban, saw no distinction between the two roles; as far as they were concerned, ISAF was never politically neutral.

ISAF and coalition forces also exceeded their mandate under the Bonn Agreement by engaging in civil reconstruction projects and by so doing unwittingly politicized the humanitarian relief effort, civilianizing the military and militarizing the civilians.[27] As ISAF established bases in provincial capitals, it set up Provincial Reconstruction Teams (PRTs), which oversaw the rehabilitation of civil infrastructure, including government offices, schools, clinics, bridges, roads and irrigation systems. The philosophy behind the PRTs derived from U.S.–NATO counterinsurgency theories known as 'hearts and minds', which sees the military's involvement in civil reconstruction as another 'weapon' in the pacification of rural communities and combating insurgencies. However, the situation in Afghanistan was very different from post-Second World War Europe, where the 'hearts and minds' policy was originally devised. Local communities had long memories of the oppression of the Soviet occupation as well as successive governments who imposed their will at the point of a gun. They therefore felt threatened and intimidated when armed foreign soldiers in full combat gear turned up in their communities, especially when they were accompanied by local officials and their heavily armed bodyguard. In such a situation informed consent, let alone dissent, was more or less impossible while communities that did accept PRT assistance risked reprisals from insurgents. The PRT assistance programme was also fundamentally at odds with the internationally agreed principles of political neutrality and not bearing arms that operate in the humanitarian sector. The neutrality of the multi-billion dollar reconstruction and aid effort that commenced after the fall of the Taliban was further compromised by the presence of foreign for-profit contractors, who employed paramilitary security firms to protect their heavily fortified compounds and escort their personnel off base.

By and large, foreign military commanders failed to understand why humanitarian agencies were so hot under the collar about what they regarded as perfectly reasonable initiatives and resented being challenged, especially by civilians, or ignored by the NGO community who, for their own safety, distanced themselves from ISAF and the PRTs. In 2009 Anders Fogh Rasmussen, Secretary General of NATO, publicly called for a 'cultural revolution' in the humanitarian effort, urging NGOs and other agencies to work closely with NATO and the PRTs, and cited as an example of this cooperation NATO's protection of World Food Programme (WFP) food convoys in Afghanistan. The WFP swiftly denied that they used NATO military escorts and Rasmussen's appeal was rejected by all major aid agencies. The damage, however, had been done. Two days after this speech the Taliban published a statement on its website denouncing the UN and NGOs as an arm of the infidel 'occupation' and 'justifying' targeting unarmed aid workers as well as foreign military.[28]

Prior to the intervention of 2001, Afghans widely respected the neutrality of humanitarian workers and the fact that they did not bear arms. Even during the troubles of the 1990s aid personnel could generally rely on safe passage through checkpoints, even though on occasion aid convoys were looted and offices and homes pillaged. During the era of President Rabbani and the Taliban only a handful of local and foreign aid workers were killed or injured. This all changed after November 2001 as the Taliban increasingly targeted NGO and UN offices and personnel, as well as hotels, hostels and restaurants frequented by foreigners. The insurgents also kidnapped, assassinated and executed dozens of foreign and Afghan humanitarian workers. Between 2001 and 2013, 325 Afghan and expatriate humanitarian workers died as a direct result of Taliban action; a further 253 were wounded and 317 kidnapped. In 2014 two Finnish IAM female staff were gunned down in a drive-by shooting in Herat, and in 2017 a woman volunteer working with Operation Mercy in Kabul was killed and her colleague abducted. At the time of writing two foreign teachers, an Australian and an American, from the American University of Kabul and at least two other foreign female aid workers are being held captive by the Taliban or kidnappers. Afghanistan is currently the most dangerous place in the world for humanitarian workers.

The accountability gap and social impact of the international intervention

The foreign intervention of 2001 created an artificial economic boom as billions of dollars of foreign aid poured into the country and thousands of foreigners arrived. The spending power of these foreigners was a godsend for Afghan traders, shopkeepers and landlords after years of rampant inflation and economic hardship. However, the boom pushed up the price of basic commodities, which hit the unemployed and the poor. Hundreds of thousands of refugees returned to Afghanistan, most of whom headed to Kabul and other urban centres in search of work, preferably with the foreign military or other agencies. The surge in the urban population led to massive hikes in house rents as the stock of habitable homes, particularly in the capital, was at a premium. As demand for housing outstripped supply, there was uncontrolled ribbon development in peri-urban areas with prime agricultural land being sold for lucrative housing developments. In the urban centres themselves, many older houses were pulled down to make way for multi-storey houses or malls. Poor people unable to afford the inflated rents ended up packed into low-cost, overcrowded hovels or living in tented settlements that sprang up in the periphery of towns. Not long after the 2001 intervention, the main streets of Kabul and other provincial capitals were full of beggars.

The government did nothing to control the urban expansion and intensification, partly because many government officials and their associates were profiting from the housing boom. Afghanistan's minimal urban infrastructure was stretched to breaking point. The streets of Kabul became gridlocked with traffic, rubbish lay uncollected in the streets and groundwater became increasingly polluted. Despite USAID's promises to restore power to the capital, for the first six years Kabul residents were fortunate if they had two hours of mains electricity a day. Instead, the population used diesel generators and burnt wood, sawdust, coal and oil. During the winter months air pollution rates in the capital and other urban centres reached critical levels and asthma, bronchitis and other lung diseases reached epidemic proportions, turning Kabul into one of the most polluted cities in the world.

Between 2002 and 2017 the United States 'obligated an estimated $714 billion for all spending – including war fighting and reconstruction – in Afghanistan over more than 15 years',[29] but most of this money has been assigned to military operations, the training of security personnel and a counter-narcotics programme. According to Oxfam only about 10 per cent of u.s. aid has been spent on humanitarian assistance, while the sum total of all international assistance after 2001 fell a long way short of that provided by the international community to other post-conflict countries. In 2008 the total of all humanitarian assistance to Afghanistan was around $7 million per day, while per capita aid averaged $57 per person, a fraction of that provided in Bosnia ($679) or East Timor ($233).[30] Furthermore, 40 per cent of all foreign aid returned to donor countries in the form of salaries for foreign consultants, aid workers, profits for private contractors and the purchase of equipment from donor nations.

In 2008 the u.s. Congress, concerned about the lack of accountability, established the Special Investigator General for Afghanistan Reconstruction (SIGAR) to audit the activities of USAID, the u.s. military and the PRTs. SIGAR's monthly and quarterly reports make grim reading as they document a litany of failures in dozens of multi-million-dollar programmes. Indeed, nearly all the programmes SIGAR has reported on to date reveal major cost blowouts, millions of dollars either frittered away on uncompleted projects or paid in advance for work that never got off the ground. Even projects that were completed suffered from shoddy workmanship and more often than not did not fulfil all the contractual requirements or conform to United States codes of compliance or best practice protocols. SIGAR repeatedly notes the lack of basic accountability or supervision by the u.s. military, USAID and its many subcontractors, as well as a culture of false invoicing and lack of even a minimal paper trail for auditing purposes.

The scale of waste and corruption documented by SIGAR runs into the millions of dollars, yet to date few Afghan or foreign contractors have been prosecuted and no u.s. military or USAID personnel have been called to account for their lack of supervision of state funds and projects. A few subcontractors have been required to hand back sums inappropriately claimed, but overall there has been little interest in enforcing accountability. Even more worrying is the fact that, despite SIGAR's damning reports, there has yet to be any fundamental shift in the paradigm adopted by u.s. military strategists in respect of the PRTs, or the cosy but compromising relationship between the u.s. military and USAID. Instead, the solution, as far as some American politicians are concerned, is to demand the disbanding of SIGAR and the sacking of its CEO.

Despite the relatively low level of international commitment to the reconstruction of civil society since 2001, there has been substantial progress in terms of rehabilitating Afghanistan's shattered infrastructure as well as in humanitarian aid. In October 2001 a major emergency relief effort, including food drops by U.S. planes, ensured there was sufficient food for most communities to make it through the winter. Shortly after Operation Enduring Freedom commenced, rain fell in the northern plain, in what many Afghans regarded as an Act of God, followed by a good coating of winter snow on the Hindu Kush. This came as a relief to the northern provinces, which had been badly hit by three years of severe drought, and most of the crops planted in the spring of 2002 reached maturity.

After 2003 the relief effort shifted to medium-term reconstruction and rehabilitation, a daunting task given the destruction of many urban centres and the complex problems facing rural communities. Thousands of homes were rebuilt, government offices rehabilitated and an intensive mine-clearing operation reclaimed vital land for agriculture. Rural development programmes played a significant role in improving facilities and agricultural output, and rehabilitating degraded irrigation canals and *karez*. There was also extensive replanting of fruit trees and vines as well as attempts to rebuild stocks of sheep, goats and cows. Health services and access to medical assistance improved and Afghanistan's rate of mother and child mortality, still among the highest in the world, has slowly decreased with the training of rural midwives and *da'is*, or traditional birth attendants.

The country's road network was repaired, major highways resurfaced and new roads constructed and improved. In Kabul and other cities many dirt streets have been surfaced, reducing the prevalence of summer dust storms, pollution and airborne diseases. However, SIGAR has noted that many of the newly rehabilitated highways are rapidly degrading due to the government's neglect of essential maintenance. The Asian Development Bank has funded the extension of the Hairatan railhead to Mazar-i Sharif, which has stimulated trade with the Central Asian Republics, Russia and China. A recently signed tripartite agreement with Iran and India offers the potential of Afghanistan using the port of Chabahar as an alternative transit port and the oil and gas pipeline project has been resurrected. Indian engineers have recently closed off the Selma Dam on the Hari Rud, but other hydroelectric power stations still work well below capacity, mostly because the equipment and generators are broken. Many dams still have obsolete machinery installed in the 1940s and '50s. Kabul is now linked

Bamiyan, graduation ceremony for rural midwives, one of many health programmes inaugurated after the regime change of 2002. Maternal and infant mortality rates in rural Afghanistan are among the highest in the world.

to the Tajikistan power grid, but this has led to protests by Hazaras, who accuse the government of deliberately not connecting the Hazarajat to the grid.

Aid delivery, however, was poorly coordinated and the reconstruction programme was skewed geographically, with Kabul, the Koh Daman and south and southeast Afghanistan receiving the lion's share of assistance. Remote provinces such as Ghur, Faryab, Sar-i Pul, Badghis, Badakhshan and Nuristan were far less well served and some communities, especially in the mountains, have still to see much benefit from the aid bonanza. The drawdown of most combat troops at the end of 2014 and the deteriorating security situation in rural districts has led to the closure of many projects, with local staff being laid off with no prospect of further employment, at least not at the salary levels paid by foreign agencies. In the wake of this drawdown and the rising insecurity in Kabul and other cities, hundreds of foreign aid personnel left the country. This in turn has led to a slump in retail sales with some shopkeepers and traders, who profited from supplying goods and services to foreign agencies, facing bankruptcy and economic hardship.

The position of women improved markedly after 2001 and new legal frameworks were established to protect women's rights, though their implementation remains problematic. The government again employed female staff and the harsh segregation imposed by the Taliban was slackened, allowing foreign aid agencies to employ women too. The Constitution reserved seats for women in the Loya Jirga, Wolusi Jirga and Meshrano Jirga, although outspoken female members have faced a barrage of verbal abuse and physical threats. Malalai Joya, an elected member of the Wolusi Jirga, was suspended indefinitely for her repeated call for ex-*mujahidin* commanders to be called to account for war crimes and crimes against humanity. The new government established a Ministry of Women's Affairs but its first minister, Sima Samar, a Shi'a Hazara from Jaghuri and long-standing advocate of women's rights, was forced to resign after she was accused of questioning the supremacy of Islamic law. In 2005 President Karzai appointed another Hazara, Dr Habiba Sarobi, as Afghanistan's first female governor.

Girls returned to school and hundreds of schools were constructed or rehabilitated, but in some remote areas *mullahs* continued to ban female education and the government was not prepared to confront them. As the insurgency has grown, the Taliban have targeted girls' schools, poisoned wells and forced the closure of rural schools by threats. Abuse of women and violations of the rights accorded to them under the 2004 Constitution have continued and are reported to be on the increase. Child and forced marriages, arbitrary divorce, wife beating, honour killing and denial of the *mahr*, the gift presented to a wife by her husband at the time of the marriage, remain unchecked. Many women still wear the full-length burqa and there is increasing concern at the number of female self-immolations. In 2012 two officials of the Department of Women's Affairs were killed in Laghman, while the lynching of Farkhunda during Nauroz celebrations in 2015, following a false allegation by a *mullah* that she had burnt a portion of the Qur'an, highlights how little progress there has been when it comes to changing embedded gender attitudes, especially among religious elites. As was the case during the reign of Zahir Shah, the greater freedom for women is confined mainly to the urban areas and the middle classes and has little impact in rural Afghanistan. Since the military drawdown, women's organizations have reported increasing attempts by conservatives to roll back gender legislation,[31] while a poll of experts commissioned by the Thomas Reuters Foundation in 2011 voted Afghanistan as the most dangerous place in the world for women.

Foreign donors have made much of the hundreds of school buildings rehabilitated or constructed since 2001 and the millions of children that now attend school. Recent surveys by the Afghanistan Research and

Evaluation Unit (AREU) and SIGAR reveal a very different picture. Many of these institutions are what are known in Pakistan as 'ghost schools', institutions that exist only on paper. Research has revealed that staff and pupil numbers in many schools are a fraction of those officially claimed in the Ministry of Education's statistics, while teachers frequently fail to turn up to class yet continue to draw their salaries. Furthermore, it is not possible to judge advances in education or literacy merely by counting the number of schools or pupils. To do so is like trying to estimate the number of literate people in a community by counting the books in the local library. Nor do government statistics reveal anything about the quality of education or teaching, let alone the availability of resources or the suitability of the curriculum or textbooks.

Afghanistan's state education and educational methodology is very poor and remains rooted in archaic practices long abandoned by educationalists in other developing countries. Rote learning remains the basis of teaching and the skill levels of teachers, from primary to tertiary level, is inadequate. In rural areas, an individual only needs a sixth grade education to qualify as a primary schoolteacher and few educators have ever studied modern teaching practice. The government continues to perpetuate a long-standing tradition in which pupils are required to complete, that is to memorize, a single textbook, per subject, per annum. The state has little control over the burgeoning private school sector, which is driven by profit rather than academic excellence, or the thousands of *madrasa*s in Afghanistan. *Mullah*s continue to resist attempts by the government to oversee their educational activities or to enforce a nationally approved curriculum and very few have any formal teaching qualification.

There has been little attempt by the government to encourage wider reading, let alone personal enquiry, experimentation or practical experience. Educational materials and resources in many rural schools are non-existent, and children and young people prefer to watch Hindi movies or spend time on social media websites or the internet to reading books. A number of NGOs now publish good reading material for children in Dari and Pushtu, and one project distributes small libraries to rural schools. Yet according to a recent USAID report, despite more than a decade of U.S. support for education, Afghan youth remain 'disenfranchised, unskilled, uneducated, neglected – and most susceptible to joining the insurgency'.[32] SIGAR too has criticized the lack of 'visibility' in the Afghan education system, noting that it is almost impossible to know what children are being taught or if these state institutions have been hijacked by radical, anti-Western *jihad*ists.

When it comes to the media, state censorship was relaxed and a host of privately funded magazines, newspapers, TV and radio stations sprung up after 2001. The internet gradually became available to most urban and peri-urban areas, and there is now a nationwide mobile phone network. This has allowed Afghans more means of expressing their views without government interference, or eavesdropping, as well as to be in touch with the wider world. Today hundreds of websites promote various aspects of Afghan culture or engage in a vigorous and frequently bad-tempered debate about politics, ethnicity and religion. The Afghan media is more robust about criticizing government officials and exposing graft, incompetence and waste, but journalists continue to face threats from powerful individuals embedded in the government as well as from insurgents. In early 2016 the Taliban claimed responsibility for a suicide bomb attack on a bus carrying the staff of Tolo TV that led to the deaths of seven staff members.

Employment opportunities improved after 2001, particularly for younger, educated Afghans who spoke some English, while the construction boom provided subsistence wages for day labourers and artisans. One group to particularly benefit from the 2001 intervention has been the Shi'a and Isma'ili Hazaras, who were traditionally at the bottom of the economic and social pecking order. During the 1980s and '90s many young Hazaras had received a good education in Iran, while the children of Isma'ilis had attended the Aga Khan's schools in Pakistan. Since they spoke reasonable English, many of them found employment as translators and 'fixers' with the foreign military, NGOs and diplomatic missions, while Hazara women were engaged as housekeepers and cleaners. The Aga Khan Development Agency (AKDA) instituted an employment training programme and the AKDA's development programmes have provided support for Isma'ili and Shi'a communities in the Hazarajat, Baghlan, Badakhshan and Kabul. Even so, there has never been enough work to go round and urban unemployment remains high among unskilled labourers. At the same time northern Afghanistan suffers from a chronic shortage of agricultural labour, since young men preferred the higher wages on offer in the cities or labouring jobs in Dubai, Iran or Pakistan.

One of the most significant reforms undertaken by the government after 2001 was the replacement of the almost worthless afghani with a new, more stable currency. Ashraf Ghani, who at the time was Minister of Finance, discouraged foreign agencies and traders from using U.S. dollars or Pakistani rupees and did his best to increase state revenues. However, one of the unfortunate side effects of the foreign aid that poured in after 2001 was that it perpetuated the culture of dependency, which began in the 1980s when the CIA and other foreign governments poured millions of dollars into the coffers of *mujahidin* commanders. The billions of dollars of foreign donors' money made it easy for President Karzai to duck the politically dangerous issue of raising taxes or calling ministers and other powerful individuals to account for misappropriating state revenues. Fifteen years after the intervention more than 70 per cent of the country's national budget consisted of foreign aid and there is no prospect of the country becoming financially self-sustaining in the medium term.[33] President Ashraf Ghani has recently attempted to address this issue, but shopkeepers in Kabul went on strike when he raised taxes in 2016. Ghani has been more successful in increasing revenues from the provinces and customs duties, but even so the International Monetary Fund estimates the government is running a current account deficit of $6.7 billion, equivalent to 36.6 per cent of GDP.[34]

The crisis of corruption

While many Afghans struggle to make ends meet, high-ranking government officials have become wealthy beyond their wildest dreams, skimming off large percentages from aid money, illegally annexing state land for housing developments, and giving contracts for development projects to for-profit aid agencies and companies set up by family members. Others have been less subtle and made a great deal of money by accepting bribes, nepotism or by threats and extortion. When it became evident that the USA and its allies were not prepared to demand accountability, officials became even more blatant and greedy. Well-connected individuals would regularly fly to Dubai with suitcases stuffed full of dollars, while customs officials stood by and did nothing. Belated calls by the United Nations and other international actors to curb corruption were ignored by President Karzai, until corruption became so much a part of government culture that it was institutionalized. The CIA did little to discourage this activity by allegedly handing suitcases full of cash to President Karzai, which he used as a slush fund to buy tribal loyalties.

In 2012 Mahmud Karzai, President Karzai's elder brother, was implicated in one of the most spectacular corruption scandals Afghanistan has known to date. Following an independent audit of the New Kabul Bank's accounts it emerged that its directors, of which Mahmud Karzai was one, had loaned each others' families around 1 billion dollars of mostly American taxpayers' money from funds designated to pay the salaries of security personnel and civil servants. The money instead was spent on purchasing prime real estate in Dubai, building luxury houses in Kabul and funding the directors' lavish lifestyle. In all some 5 billion dollars of the bank's funds had been diverted into private, offshore bank accounts. Several of the bank's executives were eventually tried and a few imprisoned, but only 10 per cent of the embezzled funds were ever recovered. Mahmud Karzai was never prosecuted and President Karzai rejected international calls for independent oversight of the bank and reform of the banking sector.

Corruption on such an industrial scale not only adversely affected the nation's parlous financial position but diverted funds designated for development projects into the pockets of Afghanistan's power elites. According to a recent UN survey, Afghans pay $3.9 billion annually in bribes, backhanders and sweeteners to government officials, with the average payment in excess of $200, or roughly four months' average wage. Such a level of bribery has a major impact on attempts to reduce poverty and fuels disillusionment with not only the government but its international backers, for it seems to Afghans that foreign donors have turned a blind eye to the blatant corruption. It is not surprising that Transparency International ranks Afghanistan as one of the most corrupt nations on earth.

The cash bonanza had other unfortunate consequences, with some ministers claiming Afghanistan was the next Dubai. This fantasy was fuelled by a report by the United States Geological Survey, which valued Afghanistan's untapped mineral resources at between 1 and 3 trillion dollars. Government officials were fond of musing about how they would spend this treasure trove, but there was a distinct lack of realism about how to transform this survey into hard cash. As early as 1888, Carl Griesbach noted Afghanistan's potential mineral wealth, an evaluation confirmed by American and Soviet surveys in the twentieth century. By 2001 little had been done to exploit these resources commercially, for Afghanistan lacked the infrastructure and technical expertise, while the government was hamstrung by its loyalty to the will of Amir 'Abd al-Rahman Khan, in which he told his heirs not to surrender the country's mineral rights or exploitation to foreign countries or companies. Furthermore, as one USAID official noted, it would take the U.S. government 'a hundred years to build the necessary infrastructure and fulfil training requirements to completely develop Afghanistan's extractive industries'.[35] What mining operations do take place are pick-and-shovel affairs and are controlled by government ministers, commanders and other powerful individuals who pocket the revenues. None of these individuals have any intention of surrendering control of these lucrative revenue streams to the state, let alone foreign multinationals.

Despite the logistical and technical challenges, the government has signed a series of mining contracts with local and international companies in a process marred by corruption and bribery. In 2007 the China Metallurgical Group Corporation (MCC) was awarded the contract to extract copper from the Mes Ainak mine in the Logar in return for annual royalties that were less than 10 per cent of estimated annual returns. Later the minister of mines was forced to resign after he was accused of taking a multimillion-dollar backhander from MCC. In 2015 the government cited Mes Ainak royalties in its income stream for the ten-year Economic Self-reliance Plan, but seven years after MCC signed the contract, mining operations had yet to commence. Mes Ainak today is a major infiltration route for the Taliban and the whole area is increasingly insecure, despite the presence of a garrison of 1,500 ANA soldiers. Given the lack of security and Taliban threats against the mining company, any extraction will probably be delayed for several years, if not abandoned completely. This has not prevented the government serving eviction orders on six villages in the Mes Ainak area, without offering compensation or providing alternative locations for new settlements. Not unexpectedly, the communities have refused to budge and are now doubtless covertly assisting local insurgents in order to preserve their lands, homes and livelihood. To date the only benefit of the Mes Ainak mining project has been the spectacular discovery of the largest Gandharan Buddhist site ever found in Afghanistan. French and Afghan archaeologists are now racing against time to excavate and document scores of religious structures scattered over a large area before they are bulldozed into extinction.

The crisis of opium production

Another significant failure of the 2001 intervention was the USA's inability to suppress the cultivation of opium and marijuana despite the occasional deployment of U.S. troops and drones to destroy opium-refining facilities. Opium production had continued to rise under the Taliban, though in the final year of their reign they did eradicate most of the opium crop. Once the new government took power, production once more took off. USAID and its subcontractors battled to reduce opium cultivation in the Helmand, Kandahar and Nangahar by introducing cash crops and small-scale industries, and opening international markets for dried fruit, while the Danish Committee for Aid to Afghan Refugees (DACAAR) has experimented with growing saffron. However, no alternative cash crop can match the returns per hectare realized from opium cultivation. Furthermore, government officials, commanders and tribal leaders have a vested interest in maintaining the production since many of them benefit directly or indirectly from this multimillion-dollar harvest.

According to the United Nations Office on Drugs and Crime (UNODC), in 2001, the last year of the Taliban government, 8,000 hectares were under opium production. A year later this had increased almost tenfold to 74,000 hectares and by 2007 the figure had more than doubled to 193,000 hectares. By 2014 the area under opium cultivation had reached 224,000 hectares with an estimated potential crop of 6,400 tons of raw opium, or 90 per cent of the world's illicit heroin. Farmers in the Helmand have recently obtained faster-growing varieties of seed from China and are openly relishing the prospect of three opium crops a year. The Taliban, too, benefit substantially from the opium crop by taxing opium production and acting as middlemen for drug barons. Drug addiction is now at epidemic proportions in Afghanistan, Pakistan and Iran with around 1.6 million Afghans, 6.7 million Pakistanis and 1.3 million Iranians addicted to heroin or other opiates, yet Afghanistan and Pakistan have only a few drug treatment centres and hardly any specialist medical staff to treat addicts.[36]

The many failures of the 2001 American intervention are an indictment of its counterinsurgency strategy and the regime change policy instituted by the Bush administration. America and NATO also pursued a similar policy in their subsequent interventions in Iraq, Syria and, to an extent, in Libya. If there is any lesson to be learned from Afghanistan after 2001 and subsequent interventions in the Middle East, it is that bombing and attempting to oust unpleasant and unfriendly regimes from power, without giving serious thought to the composition of civil government, state building and the strengthening of civil society, creates more problems than it solves. It is like trying to contain the tidal wave after blowing up the reservoir, or driving a car after disconnecting the steering wheel. 'Regime change' has failed the people of Afghanistan, Iraq, Syria and Libya inasmuch as it has not brought peace or security to these countries and has provided little more than a veneer of democratic institutions, with real government in the hands of unaccountable militia leaders and Islamist factions. All this has led to is perpetual insecurity, the rise of militant anti-Western Islamist movements, the undermining of civil society, rampant corruption and mass displacement.

The failure of stabilization, civil and military

The 2001 intervention in Afghanistan significantly failed to bring political stability or restore security. The civil war has not only continued but has worsened, and for many Afghans the conflict now seems to be endless as well as irresolvable. Despite more than 100,000 foreign troops and billions of dollars of military assistance from the world's most powerful nations, the Taliban and a plethora of other insurgent groups pose an increasing threat to the government and are even more radicalized than they were prior to September 2001. The best the Pentagon planners can now hope for is that the government will hold on to the areas it currently controls. Or, as John F. Sopko, Inspector General of SIGAR, remarked shortly after President Donald Trump took office, 'We may be defining success as the absence of failure.'[37]

Viewed from August 2017, even this scenario is looking over-optimistic. The Taliban are the de facto government in many rural districts and are continuing to make substantial gains, not only in the Helmand and southern provinces but in central and northern Afghanistan too. The Taliban, supported by foreign *jihad*ists, have twice overrun the city of Qunduz and many settlements in southern Faryab, Sar-i Pul and northern Badghis are out of government control, while Daesh has mounted a series of attacks in Jaujan Ghur and Nangahar. In Helmand province Musa Qal'a has changed hands several times and Lashkargah, Girishk and other towns are virtually under siege. The Taliban too have mounted a series of attacks in Ghazni, Logar and Nangahar. In the spring of 2014 an al-Jazeera journalist filmed Taliban and local insurgents walking freely in the streets of Charkh in the Logar within sight of the ANA garrison, less than an hour's drive from Kabul.

In late 2016 Taliban suicide bombers even infiltrated the Bagram air base and killed two U.S. soldiers and two American contractors. In the spring of 2017 the Taliban killed at least 140 Afghan soldiers in the army base in Mazar-i Sharif. Suicide attacks and car bombs are now almost a weekly occurrence in Kabul, despite the capital being the most militarized city in Afghanistan. In June 2017 a massive truck bomb exploded in Kabul's Shahr-i Nau, killing around 150 people and devastating the area around the German, Iranian and Turkish embassies. Since 2016 attacks by insurgents have also been marked by massacres, especially of Hazaras and Shi'as. At the time of writing insurgents control around 30 per cent of Afghanistan's rural districts, with another 11 per cent listed as 'contested'.[38]

The record of the ANA and the police in countering insurgents' attacks is poor, to say the least. When the Taliban overran Qunduz in September 2015, the ANA and local police fled, leaving former *mujahidin* commanders to defend their settlements as best they could. In 2016 the Taliban stormed a Hazara garrison in the Behsud district of Wardak, killing, mutilating and beheading the defenders, while the ANA failed to respond to their frantic calls for help. ISIL, not to be outdone, has claimed responsibility for the bombing of Shi'a mosques in Kabul and Herat. The failure of the ANA and other state security organs to contain the insurgency has led two former Jami'at commanders, 'Ata Muhammad Nur and Isma'il Khan, to threaten to reactivate their militias. Dostam too is actively attempting to form some sort of military-political alliance with former Jami'at and Shi'a leaders. As for ordinary Afghans, they are voting with their feet. Next to Syrians, Afghans are the largest contingent of boat people arriving on the shores of Mediterranean Europe.

In 2001 President Bush damned the Taliban as terrorists and ruled out any negotiations with Mullah 'Omar, but fifteen years later the United States, the United Nations and other international actors are actively encouraging President Ghani to negotiate with these same terrorists in an increasingly desperate attempt to end the war. In the autumn of 2016 President Ghani signed an armistice with Gulbudin Hikmatyar and his Hizb-i Islami militia, and in April the following year he and his militia returned to the Kabul area. Despite almost overnight having been listed as a global terrorist, Hikmatyar was removed by the UN and the USA from the list and he is now presumably exempt from any attempt to call him to account for alleged war crimes. One wonders how long it will be before Hikmatyar is once more a government minister. His rehabilitation has outraged many Afghans, who have not forgotten his refusal to join the government of President Rabbani, the rocket attacks on Kabul and the many abuses carried out by Hizb-i Islami in the 1980s and '90s.

Politically the problems of governance in Afghanistan have never been resolved. The 2004 Constitution effectively pits the Executive against the Legislature and in the process revisits the power struggles of the 1960s and '70s. Since the Wolusi Jirga has little say in Executive affairs, they exercise what powers they have, refusing to confirm President Ghani's ministerial nominees and rejecting his budget. President Ghani has simply ignored them and told his ministers to continue to carry out their duties as normal in defiance of the Constitution. President Ghani's recent attempt to replace 'Ata Muhammad Nur as governor of Balkh, and the effective exile of General Dostam, has further increased tensions between himself and Jami'at, and between the President and 'Abdullah 'Abdullah, Afghanistan's Chief Executive Officer and Ghani's unwanted power-sharing partner. Financially the government is still unable to raise sufficient revenue to pay the wages of civil servants or security services. Afghanistan has reverted to a rentier state, with the United States and NATO now providing the 'money from God'. According to the World Bank, Afghanistan's financial dependency will continue well beyond 2030. The USA and NATO thus faces the same dilemma as the British did in the First Afghan War, summed up by John F. Sopko of SIGAR as, 'withdraw, and the democratic government may well fall. Stay, and continue what we have been doing and we may be faced with . . . a stalemate'.[39]

Sooner or later American and European taxpayers and politicians will tire of pouring money into the bottomless pit and walk away. When this happens, it is anyone's guess what will occur. It is unclear what the international community's response will be in the event of the collapse of central authority or if the Taliban manage, for example, to take control of major cities or threaten to take Kabul itself. One suspects that there is no action plan for such a scenario. President Donald Trump in this respect is hardly the right man for cool, calm and objective planning. Six months into the most dysfunctional American presidency of the post-war era, all the White House seems to be offering is more of the same, sending back troops to Afghanistan in an attempt to defeat the insurgents militarily. In so doing, President Trump and his advisers have shown they have learnt nothing from the failure of the military surge implemented by his predecessor, President Obama, or from the Soviet one under President Gorbachev.

Furthermore, sending back more NATO forces will not solve the problem of Afghanistan's governance, corruption or the dysfunctional relationship between the Executive and Legislative branches of the state, let alone end the insurgency. Indeed, it may even make matters worse. As one Taliban official remarked to an American diplomat in 2007, 'You have all the clocks, but we have all the time'.[40] President Trump also risks undermining his already declining popularity with his own political support base if more American soldiers die or are maimed for life. The stark fact is that the government of Afghanistan, as currently constituted, is unsustainable since it only survives by being propped up financially and militarily by foreign powers, and the country's Constitution and governmental structures are fundamentally flawed. One also wonders how much appetite NATO's European members have for re-engaging militarily in Afghanistan. Britain, the main partner of the USA when it came to combat operations in Afghanistan, will hardly want to become embroiled again, given the high losses its troops suffered, the recent financial crisis, and the cost and complexity of leaving the European Union. Even with additional military support, President Ghani faces a challenge of Herculean proportions and there is little optimism among Afghans or informed observers that the ageing and sick president is able to meet such challenges. Indeed one wonders if anyone is capable of doing so.

Ordinary Afghans meanwhile have to try and live their lives as best they can in a country beset by insecurity, a dysfunctional government and a seemingly endless and irresolvable civil war. The only political solution offered by the international community boils down to a power-sharing agreement with the Taliban, Hikmatyar and other radical Islamic *jihad*ists. For Afghans, especially Shi'as, Hazaras, Uzbeks and women, such a coalition is even more frightening than the continuation of the insurgency. Rather than solving Afghanistan's problems this is more a council of despair.

This is hardly the future Afghans anticipated when the United States and its allies intervened in October 2001, nor is it one they deserve. Today all inhabitants of Afghanistan under the age of forty have known nothing but war, displacement and the social and economic insecurity that is an inevitable consequence of conflict. Unlike the foreign military, international advisers and aid personnel, Afghans do not have the luxury of withdrawing to California, Geneva, the Home Counties or a beach in New Zealand unless, of course, they risk their lives at the hands of people smugglers – something that thousands of desperate Afghans are increasingly prepared to do. So while American and NATO politicians, military strategists, academics and the Western press engage in post-conflict heart-searching about what went wrong with the Afghanistan 'experiment' and whether it was worth the cost in cash and lives, it is Afghans who have to face the consequences of a foreign intervention poorly conceived and badly executed. For Afghans and Afghanistan, Enduring Freedom remains a very distant dream.

Conclusion

THE EMERGENCE OF AFGHANISTAN as a nation state and its survival is a remarkable story given the tumultuous nature of the country's political life and the fact that, as defined by its present colonial frontiers, it lacks historical validity or cohesiveness. Afghanistan is the product of a series of fortuitous circumstances precipitated initially by the break-up of the Safavid, Mughal and Uzbek empires and the conquests of Nadir Quli Khan Afshar, and subsequently perpetuated and sustained by the rise of British and Russian power in India and Central Asia, respectively. Under British tutelage, the rump of the kingdom founded by Ahmad Shah Durrani, which was on the verge of collapse, was redefined and its frontiers reorientated, creating a nation state that bore little resemblance to the tribal belt known as Afghanistan in the pre-colonial era, or to historic, pre-colonial geopolitical frontiers. The outcome was a political entity that was unstable and riddled with factionalism, both within the ruling dynasty and society as a whole.

Imperial and Afghan nationalist-monarchist discourse claims the foundation of modern Afghanistan began with the 'election' of Ahmad Shah Durrani in Kandahar in 1747 and has tended to emphasize the Afghanness, or Pushtunness, of the dynasty. This narrative ignores key historic factors that gave rise to this Durrani dynasty, while glossing over the uncomfortable fact that the 'Abdali tribe and its dynasties were essentially persianate. The alliance with Safavid Persia was arguably the key element that facilitated the rise of both the Hotaki and Saddozai kingdoms, an alliance that came about in part because urbanized 'Abdalis in Kandahar, though referred to as Afghan, spoke a local dialect of *farsi*. Indeed, more than likely the ethnogenesis of the 'Abdali tribe derived from the Persian-speaking peoples of medieval Ghur and Gharchistan.

The Saddozai alliance with the Shi'a Safavid monarchy of Persia was due to a power struggle between Mughal India and Safavid Persia for control of the key frontier town of Kandahar. This same geopolitical rivalry gave rise to an internal conflict between Barakzai and Saddozai for the headship of the 'Abdali tribe, a rivalry perpetuated under the dynasty founded by Ahmad Shah Durrani and which played a significant part in undermining the stability of the kingdom. The long-standing feud within the Saddozai clan between the Khudakka Khel and Sarmast Khel, itself in part the outcome of the Safavid–Mughal power struggle, played into Ahmad Shah's hands, but at the same time contributed to his dynasty's ultimate demise.

Ahmad Shah's debt to Persia, though, went much deeper. It was under Nadir Shah Afshar that he and the 'Abdalis rose to military prominence, while it was Nadir Shah who provided the 'Abdalis with modern military training and arms as well as opening the door for Ahmad Shah to raise his own regiment of loyal *ghazi*s. Taqi Beg Shirazi's decision to join forces with Ahmad Shah, and his subsequent advocacy that persuaded the Qizilbash garrisons of Kandahar and Kabul not to oppose the Saddozai coup, allowed Ahmad Shah to secure control of these two key frontier posts without a fight. At the same time, Ahmad Shah acquired a substantial, battle-hardened force of non-Afghan troops whom he used to offset challenges from his own kin and tribe. The influence of these Shi'a Qizilbash *ghulam*s eventually went well beyond their military capabilities and, like the Ottoman Janissaries, the Qizilbash played a significant role in determining the succession, while the marriage alliances between the Jawanshir and descendants of Hajji Jamal Khan Barakzai reinforced their political power base.

Another forgotten element in the emergence of Ahmad Shah's dynasty is the importance of Multan. This sophisticated Mughal city in northern India had a profound influence on the Saddozais – indeed the Sultans of Herat were culturally more Multani than they were Herati or indeed Afghan. Ahmad Shah himself was born and brought up here and his court, and that of his successors, reflected the Mughal and Indian influence in a number of ways. Ahmad Shah's personal spiritual adviser was a *fakir* from Lahore, Saddozai court protocols were modelled on that of the Mughals and the Safvids; and many court officials bore Turkic titles. Furthermore, the conquests of the Hotaki dynasty and of Ahmad Shah meant that many of the sons and daughters born into the ruling families and tribal elites were the offspring of Hindu, Persian, Qizilbash, Mughal, Kafir and even Armenian mothers.

Even before his death, Ahmad Shah's empire was imploding, primarily because his campaigns were really opportunistic looting expeditions on a vast scale, justified by a veneer of religious legitimacy. Ahmad Shah's relentless pursuit of conquest was done at the expense of stable government and he failed to established functional and enduring state institutions, but left the administration of his *diwan*, or bureaucracy, to the Qizilbash and farmed out revenue-raising to the highest bidder. He also created a privileged Durrani elite, who were effectively tax-exempt. The Durrani empire itself lacked political coherence and was undermined by internal feuds and cultural and ideological alienation between the conquerors and the conquered. Rather than establishing an enduring kingdom, Ahmad Shah's legacy was a kingdom riddled with competitive power structures that on occasion rendered it ungovernable. The instability was exacerbated by an ideological struggle between the crown and Islamists, which first raised its head in the wake of Timur Shah's death and would later act as a brake on political, social and educational reform.

When the Saddozai dynasty was finally swept aside by the Muhammadzais they inherited the structural flaws of their predecessors. Amir Dost Muhammad Khan was more 'hands on' when it came to the administration of justice, but by placing all power in the hands of members of his own clan he created a kingdom akin to an Arab sheikhdom, run more as a family enterprise than a nation state. The Muhammadzais too were plagued by sibling rivalry and, as with the Saddozais, the country was often plunged into civil war. The country itself remained fiscally non-viable and lacked anything approaching an effective army. Externally, Afghanistan's political stability and territorial integrity was threatened by Persia, Bukhara and the Sikhs, and subsequently by Russia and Britain. By 1838 the rump of the Durrani kingdom was increasingly beleaguered. The war with the Sikhs was all but lost and Peshawar was now a Sikh possession, though still governed by Amir Dost Muhammad Khan's half-brothers. What territory was left was divided into semi-independent, rival fiefdoms: Herat, Kandahar and Kabul. North of the Hindu Kush, the Chahar Wilayat, Balkh, Qataghan and Badakhshan were beyond the Amir's jurisdiction.

Just as it seemed the surrounding kingdoms were about to sweep aside what little remained of Ahmad Shah's kingdom, Britain became embroiled in the Machiavellian world of Afghan dynastic, tribal and religious politics. In 1808–9 the Elphinstone Mission avoided being dragged into the dynastic struggle between Shah Shuja' and Shah Mahmud. After the fall of Shah Shuja' and the defeat of Napoleon, the East India Company relied on its treaty arrangements with the Sikhs and Persia to provide the necessary buffer against possible invasion by France or Russia. As for the rulers of Afghanistan, they were left to their own devices. This arrangement was arguably the best solution as far as the defence of India's northern frontier was concerned.

From 1830 onwards, however, there was a major shift in British policy towards what was known at the time as the Cis-Indus states, which led to a far more interventionist approach. Yet this new policy was not due to any direct or imminent military threat to India from the Amir, Dost Muhammad Khan, from Persia, Bukhara or any European power. As for the presumed Russian threat to India, this was grossly exaggerated. Rather, the policy was based on highly speculative presumptions about Russian and Persian intentions and theoretical scenarios thought up by imperially minded politicians and armchair theorists in London. Yet despite this, Lord Ellenborough adopted an aggressive and intrusive policy in the Cis-Indus states, despite strong objections from the Governor General and his Council about their potentially negative impact. Despite Ellenborough's Central Asian policy being based on a misunderstanding of Afghan politics and the region's military geography, the Ellenborough Doctrine became the foundation stone of what later became known as the Forward Policy and the Great Game.

Britain therefore became increasingly entangled in the internal affairs of Afghanistan and eventually had to choose between its treaty with the Sikhs and better relations with Afghanistan. In the end the attempt to bind the Amir to Britain's imperial bandwagon backfired, in part because of the choice of inexperienced and highly ambitious young imperialists such as Burnes, as well as incompetent diplomacy and poor military leadership. The outcome was the most disastrous British attempt at regime change in the nineteenth century. A century and a half later, during the Soviet invasion of Afghanistan of the 1980s, Lord Ellenborough's Indus policy was revisited, revived and revamped as the Warm Water Port scenario in order to justify American military support of the *mujahidin*.

It is therefore profoundly ironic that the British military intervention in the First Anglo-Afghan War actually saved the Muhammadzai dynasty from political oblivion and the kingdom of Afghanistan from collapse. From being a remote and unruly kingdom, from the mid-1840s onwards Afghanistan increasingly became the keystone of Britain's Defence of India policy. In the wake of the disaster of 1841–2 and the subsequent collapse of the Sikh kingdom, Britain made the best of a bad job and attempted to control Afghanistan's external and internal relations by proxy. Successive Amirs were tied to British interests by treaties, cash subsidies and regular shipments of modern military equipment, an arrangement that was far less costly in terms of men and money than outright annexation. It is no wonder that courtiers referred to the British subsidy as 'the Money from God', for the Anglo-Afghan relationship provided the hard cash and weapons the Muhammadzais needed to defeat their enemies. Britain also tacitly encouraged and ultimately legitimized the expansion of the Durrani kingdom to the banks of the Amu Darya. This dramatic reversal of Afghanistan's fortunes must have seemed almost miraculous to government officials in Kabul, especially since the provider of this bounty was the very nation that had invaded and deposed Amir Dost Muhammad Khan a few years earlier.

Britain's Afghanistan policy during the colonial era continued to be confused and vacillated between intervention and disengagement, depending on which administration was in power in London. On occasion the British were held hostage by the Amirs on the one hand, and by the ideologies and vested interests of imperialist politicians and military theorists on the other. Britain's Afghanistan policy was also increasingly tainted by assumptions about Britain's innate cultural, racial and religious superiority and its civilizing mission, ideas derived from Ptolemaic myths about Alexander the Great's conquest of Asia as well as an Orientalist vision of Islam and Islamic civilization. Steeped as British administrators and planners were in classical history, British strategists regarded rivers, particularly the Indus and the 'Oxus', as Central Asia's Rubicons. Like many other assumptions on which the Defence of India policy was constructed, this was a fallacy, for historically it was mountain chains, or rather passes and watersheds, that traditionally formed the northern frontiers of India and Central Asia. Even today watersheds and ridgelines still determine community boundaries as well as water and grazing rights.

Yet despite many strategic, political and moral ambiguities, the British government could claim its Central Asian policy succeeded, since Russian influence and the threat of invasion were deterred. Afghanistan therefore fulfilled its colonial function as a buffer state, but it was touch and go. Following the annexation of Samarkand and Bukhara in the late 1860s, Russia pushed the boundaries, literally, as far as it dared. Had the Tsar called Britain's bluff and occupied Herat or Afghan Turkistan, British military strategists knew there was little they could do to prevent such a move, given the logistical nightmare this involved. It was also privately accepted that the Afghan army, despite all the cash and military equipment Britain had supplied, would offer only token resistance.

Britain's involvement in Afghanistan was not due to any sense of paternalistic altruism or an innate interest in the welfare of the people ruled by the Amirs, but merely seen as the best way to serve Britain's own geopolitical interests. In many ways this has been the story of all European interventions to date, as Afghans have found themselves unwittingly caught up in wider conflicts in which they are often just bit players. The cost of these European ventures, however, has been immense suffering and social dislocation for the inhabitants of the country. In Britain's case, it provided the Amirs with the necessary cash and weapons they needed to impose their will on a reluctant and often recalcitrant people, and was indirectly responsible for the suffering inflicted on many peoples, including the Pushtuns whose interests the dynasty claimed to represent.

Afghanistan's population was never consulted about these policies, nor were its peoples given a choice as to which nation they wished to be citizens of. Instead, they were obliged to live in a kingdom with which many had no historical or ethnic connection, under a government that denied them representation and was essentially hostile to their interests, and ruled by a dynasty they regarded as alien. By the time British surveyors had completed their demarcation of the nation state of Afghanistan, it bore little resemblance to the original Afghanistan of the Mughal and Safavid era. Indeed, in yet another irony, the modern state did not even include all of the original Afghanistan, for the Pushtun tribal belt ended up being partitioned between Afghanistan and India (and subsequently Pakistan), a situation that created unresolved tensions between the rulers of Afghanistan and its southern neighbour.

While the nation state of Afghanistan was legitimized by Britain, Russia and other European powers, its social, religious and governmental structures bore only a superficial resemblance to European institutions and remained rooted in archaic, feudal models that served the interests of one particular clan, ethnicity and Islamic *mazhab*. This situation has remained more or less the same to this day, for despite numerous political upheavals, revolutions and constitutions, Afghanistan is still governed by tribal and religious cliques with a vested interest in excluding others from the seat of power. Nor is there much interest in the enfranchisement of the population as a whole.

Afghanistan's survival against all the odds is due primarily to the fact that none of the surrounding powers were prepared to risk outright annexation, for the experience of two Anglo-Afghan Wars made it apparent to St Petersburg and London that to do so would lead to a long, costly and unwinnable war. It is a lesson that Western nations have yet to take to heart: to date every European military intervention in Afghanistan has failed to achieve its objectives, and more often than not has made matters worse and created yet more instability. This in turn emphasizes the essential stupidity of pursuing a military solution to the 'problem of Afghanistan', or revisiting the colonial strategies of the nineteenth century.

In this respect, the present u.s.–nato intervention is no different to that of the early British or Soviet military occupations, though it is now the United States of America, primarily, that provides the Money from God. Afghanistan has reverted to its rentier-state status and remains incapable, or unwilling, to become self-sustaining financially or militarily. Once again the citizens of Afghanistan find themselves unwittingly entangled in events beyond their control and condemned to what increasingly looks like an endless civil war. Despite all the efforts of the world's greatest military powers and billions of dollars of military aid, Afghanistan and its government once more teeters on the brink of collapse. Yet the international community's solution to the problem is more of the same: send back the troops to fight the government's battles, keep paying the country's bills and turn a blind eye to rampant corruption, military and governmental incompetence and electoral fraud.

The historic culture of reliance on foreign subsidies, loans and military aid meant that successive Afghan administrations have had little incentive to reform state institutions, and created a sense of dependency and entitlement. Furthermore, the subsidies indirectly supported entrenched tribal and religious self-interest, fuelled nepotism and sustained the patronage system and 'old boy' networks. The Afghan government's solution to social upheaval, meanwhile, remains the same as it has always been: resort to military suppression and centralize power in the hands of the few.

To one degree or another European solutions to the 'problem of Afghanistan' have been backward-looking too, and have usually ended in failure. In the First Anglo-Afghan War Britain tried and failed to restore the discredited Saddozai monarchy. On the back of this military catastrophe, Dost Muhammad Khan and his son, Wazir Akbar Khan, whom Britain had roundly condemned in the Simla Declaration, returned to power as national heroes. The Second Anglo-Afghan War was more successful in terms of regime change, but while the army of occupation survived by the skin of its teeth, the intervention was a moral defeat for Britain. General Roberts's brutal repressions created yet more anti-British sentiment and played a part in the development of an emerging nationalist discourse and the creation of national icons such as Mushk-i 'Alam, Malalai and the Battle of Maiwand. The British decision to recognize 'Abd al-Rahman Khan as Amir, rather than one of Sher 'Ali Khan's sons, led to the peoples of Afghanistan having to endure two decades of the most tyrannical ruler to date. Despite many British officials privately expressing their concern about Britain's abnegation of its 'Christian duty' and moral conscience, Britain's Afghanistan policy, rooted as it was in the dogma that Britain's strategic interest took precedence over any negative impact it might have on ordinary Afghans, meant that the Viceroy did little more than write an occasional mild rebuke.

The Soviet intervention of 1979–89 was arguably the only attempt by a European power to transform the state and governance in Afghanistan. This too in part was backward-looking, for like Amir 'Abd al-Rahman, whose role model was Tsar Peter the Great, the Soviet Union attempted to impose its vision by brute force. Yet instead of creating a united Socialist and secular state, the intervention sparked a civil war, which is still raging, and dragged Afghanistan back into a neo-Great Game. In response, the USA assumed the mantle of the former imperial power and, drawing heavily on the nineteenth-century policies of the Great Game, revived paranoia about a Russian invasion of the Indus. The outcome was that the Soviet Union ended up with a hostile, Islamic state on its southern frontier, backed by the regional powers allied to the USA and NATO.

As for the *mujahidin* government that emerged after the fall of the Communist regime, their idea of government and the state was even more backward-looking, rooted as it was, and still is, in an idealized Islamic theocracy conceived more than a thousand years ago. Pakistan, too, failed to impose its proxies, the Taliban, on the country. Mullah 'Omar's decision to provide a safe haven for bin Laden ended in the fall of the Taliban and the de facto restoration of the Durrani monarchy in the form of a Popalzai president. Subsequently, successive Afghan administrations revived the Pushtunistan dispute by formally rejecting the Durand Line. Furthermore, by arming radical anti-European Islamist groups, Pakistan's Inter-Service Intelligence agency opened the door for militant *jihad*ists to gain a foothold in the region, which created an Islamist insurgency that now aims to topple Pakistan's ruling elites.

The U.S. support for the *mujahidin* in the 1980s and '90s indirectly contributed to American military intervention in 2001 and regime change. Like all previous European military interventions, U.S. involvement was fuelled by internal political pressures and self-interest, in particular the need to avenge al-Qa'ida's attacks on American soil and appease outraged American citizens, especially Republican voters. When it came to addressing the structural problems that had given rise to the instability and civil war in Afghanistan or the underlying causes of anti-American Arab terrorism, such considerations were near the bottom of America's Afghanistan agenda. Like the British colonial administration before them, the Bush, Obama and Trump presidencies distanced themselves from anything more than token nation building and instead pursued the chimera of a military solution.

The oil and water government that resulted after 2001, with a Durrani Pushtun monarchist Executive and an Islamist, predominantly Turco-Tajik, military and Legislature, was hardly the solution to Afghanistan's historically dysfunctional government. However, as far as the international community was concerned this arrangement was a quick, if dirty, solution to establishing a pro-Western government, which was legitimized subsequently by flawed elections. Yet despite the international community's decision to restore the Durrani supremacy, in the mistaken belief that only a Pushtun head of state could unite the country, the main opposition to both President Karzai and President Ghazni's administrations has come from Pushtuns.

Despite more than two centuries of European involvement and engagement in Afghanistan, very few lessons seem to have been learned. European, American and United Nations politicians, military strategists and 'specialists', as well as Afghan government officials, still cling to discredited imperial models. Like all previous European interventions, the latest attempt by Western powers to put Humpty Dumpty back together again has failed in terms of its original objectives. Perhaps more seriously, it has let down the Afghan people they claimed to be liberating and the promised era of peace, stability and inclusiveness is as elusive as ever. Today the presence of foreign troops increasingly looks like part of the problem, rather than part of the solution.

When it comes to the internal history of the Afghan monarchy, this too is hardly a happy tale. From the very earliest days, the heirs of Saddu Khan fought each other for the right of succession; infighting which continued unabated long after the Saddozai dynasty had been overthrown. It is rare in Afghanistan's history for a reigning monarch to die of natural causes while in office. Amir 'Abd al-Rahman Khan in 1901 was the last ruler to do so (though it was rumoured even he had been poisoned) until President Hamid Karzai stepped down in 2014. In the intervening century or so, every other head of state has been forced out of office in various ways. Some were toppled as a consequence of revolts, coups or foreign interventions; others were assassinated, executed or died during military coups. Until the election of President Karzai in 2004, no Afghan head of state could claim to have even a semblance of a popular mandate to govern. Rather than representing the nation, its peoples and ethnicities, Afghanistan's kings and presidents have ruled on behalf of a small clique, be they Monarchist, Communist or Islamist.

Afghans, though, may argue that at least during the heyday of European colonialism their country, unlike some Muslim countries, remained a free nation. Yet this freedom was limited and came at a heavy price. Britain, after all, controlled Afghanistan's foreign policy, had a strong say in who ruled the country, paid the government's bills and armed its military. Frequent revolts and revolutions however consumed much of the country's scarce resources and as a consequence British subsidies failed to benefit ordinary people. After independence the government continued to rely on foreign subsidies in the form of loans, which were spent on prestigious infrastructure programmes, such as the Helmand Valley Irrigation Scheme, that failed to deliver the anticipated fiscal benefits, or on white elephant projects such as Amir 'Aman Allah Khan's new capital of Dar al-'Aman.

Britain's closed-door policy of the nineteenth century, backed by heavy government censorship, also denied Afghans contact with the outside world until relatively recently. The state's policies of mass relocations, seizures of land and private assets, as well as the unreformed nature of Afghanistan's feudal agrarian system, corruption, nepotism, oppression and government ineptitude, have all contributed to Afghanistan's poverty. The country has one of the worst track records in the world when it comes to literacy, educational standards, social welfare and health. Afghanistan remains an essentially pre-industrial society that failed to benefit from the technological or social benefits of colonial administrations, such as sealed roads, railways and electricity, and a public health system.

In the early twentieth century Afghan monarchists, led by Mahmud Tarzi and his Young Afghans, attempted to impose some form of national identity that would bind the nation together. Yet the model he and his ideological heirs embraced was derived from European ideals that were the antecedents of the secular, ethnocentric nationalism of the Young Turks and Mustafa Kemal. Such a model was unsuited to Afghanistan's multi-cultural and multi-ethnic society and divided more than it united. Under the influence of revolutionary Indian nationalists, the Wish Zalmiyan and German National Socialism, Tarzi's *Afghaniyya* mutated into a concept of Pushtun supremacy heavily influenced by Nazi Aryanism. Despite the inappropriateness of this ethnocentric model, Muhammadzais and mon-archists still cling to this model of Pushtun nationalism as justification for the Durrani claim to the divine right to rule Afghanistan. This posi-tion was and is still tacitly endorsed by many American, United Nations, European and Pakistani politicians, even as they attempt to incorporate other ethnicities and religious factions into the political process. Yet all ethnocentric nationalism, by its very nature, promotes minority interests and is exclusive rather than inclusive.

Another problem is that the various state-sponsored ideas of nation-alism that have been mooted since the late nineteenth century have been rooted in European models. 'Abd al-Rahman Khan's vision of national unity was based on the despotism of Peter the Great of Russia, Tarzi's *Afghaniyya* was Turkism with a turban rather than a fez, while Da'ud's and the Pushtun Academy's idea of Pushtunness was an Afghan version of German Aryanism. The Communists attempted to impose their European secular model of national identity based on Marx and Lenin, while President Rabbani and the Taliban tried to re-Islamize a nation based on political theologies evolved by north Indian, Egyptian and Arab radicals.

Since the era of Amir 'Abd al-Rahman Khan, successive governments, reformers and modernizers have blamed Islamist or reactionary tribal leaders, or both, for the failure of their attempts to reform the nation. However, the government itself bears much of the responsibility. Successive administrations of every ilk have proved incompetent when it comes to running a government and the Executive, while deploying the rhetoric of an inclusive society, has fought tooth and nail to maintain its stranglehold on power. Successive constitutions have reinforced this autocracy and lack of accountability, while establishing a parliamentary system that is both unrepresentative and designed more as a rubber stamp for the Executive's plans and legislation. The result has been a power struggle between the two Estates, which remains unresolved to this day and has rendered effective government impotent.

Change has always been a top-down affair in Afghanistan, imposed by a ruling elite who have little interest in winning popular support for their initiatives, let alone govern on a basis of consensus. The outcome has been either too little or too much. Administrations that have attempted to impose their Westernizing, secular world view by fiat have inevitably sparked a backlash that usually ends in rebellion and the fall of the government. This has then led to a reversion to the status quo, which makes any reform even more fraught with difficulty.

Islamists attempt to unify the nation by their appeal to Islam, only for the imposition of their interpretation of Islamic law to create more dissonance than harmony, for their radical political philosophy is fundamentally divisive. Rather than a vision of state and society modelled on the inclusiveness of the Mughals or the Ottomans, they have embraced the polarizing dogmas of the Muslim Brotherhood, Wahhabism and other radical elements that undermine the foundation of traditional Muslim society. On occasion their political philosophies verge on sectarianism, since their assumption is that any Muslim who does not share their vision of Islamic society and the Islamic state needs to be re-Islamized or is an apostate. Needless to say, this blinkered world view does not sit well with ordinary Afghans, who are generally tolerant of differences and contemptuous of movements that demean their deeply held faith and discount more than a millennium of Islamic civilization and Muslim heritage.

Islamists, too, lack consensus as to what constitutes an Islamic state and society and have gone to war with each other again and again despite all of them claiming to share the same political and religious values. In the 1990s the Taliban's main enemies in Afghanistan, after all, were *mujahidin* parties founded on the political philosophies of Islamizers such as Sayyid Qutb and 'Abd al-Wahhab. These forms of Islamic radicalism furthermore exacerbate differences between Sunni, as well as between Sunni and Shi'a. Since most of Afghanistan's Shi'as are Hazaras, this has fuelled ethnic violence too. Indeed, one of the hallmarks of the era of *mujahidin* resistance to the Soviet occupation and the Taliban was the increasing polarization of regional and ethnolinguistic differences. These tensions, of course, already existed under the monarchy, though they were suppressed, yet the leaders of the various Islamist parties by and large failed to unify the opposition, even though most of those who fought against the Soviet occupation did so, in part at least, in defence of their faith. As for the Islamist governments that took power following the fall of the Communist government, these were the most fractious and dysfunctional administrations since the era of the Saddozai sultanate of Herat.

Successive governments have attempted some kind of synthesis between the Islamic and European legal systems only to create a dichotomy that affirms both. Since European and Islamic law are essentially at odds over, for example, the issue of women's rights, gender equality, the role of the judiciary and the function of the justice system, this is one more strand of conflict that has undermined stable government. Attempts by Amir 'Aman Allah Khan and the Musahiban dynasty at establishing a *modus vivendi* with Islamizing networks quickly broke down under the weight of its own contradictions and contributed to the fall of the Durrani dynasty. Today Islamists control the political and ideological agenda. With NATO and the UN anxious for militias such as Hikmatyar's Hizb-i Islami and the Taliban to join the so-called peace process, Afghans can look forward to yet more Islamization rather than less.

The outcome of these various attempts to unify the country has been mostly counterproductive with the gap between the government and the governed becoming wider as the years pass. The majority of Afghanistan's population care very little about central government's impositions and ordinary people have evolved mechanisms that have allowed them to survive the vicissitudes of insecurity and the vacillations of their leaders.

Indeed, given the history of their country, the resilience of ordinary Afghans is remarkable, even extraordinary. At grass-roots level there is a far greater sense of cooperation than there is in the country's dysfunctional government. Afghans too have their own idea of what it means to be a citizen of Afghanistan and most of the time they manage to negotiate their way through life without interference by the state. Cooperation, after all, is essential for both rural and urban communities, since individuals have to work together and share the same resources as neighbours who may well be from other ethnicities. *Hamsayagi*, neighbourliness, or literally 'sharing the same shade', which goes hand-in-hand with Afghanistan's deeply rooted culture of hospitability, even to complete strangers and non-Muslims, has been a significant cultural bond that has sustained communities and created a sense of identity which runs much deeper that any state-imposed nationalism.

Another glue that binds communities together is the village assembly, or *shura,* and the tribal *jirga,* institutions rooted in practices that are both ancient and well understood. These forums have been central to the survival of civil society at the subnational level. Throughout the troubles of the past decades they have continued to function in spite of the lack of effective central government. While some community assemblies have been hijacked by commanders and militia leaders – *shura*s set up by aid agencies to manage development programmes are often a case in point – the traditional assembly is a consensus-based system where neighbours are allowed to vent their frustrations and grievances, debate important local issues and negotiate compromise settlements or seek arbitration. More often than not, the issues are resolved without recourse to provincial government officials.

Broadcasts by the BBC World Service, Voice of America and other foreign media have aided the development of a national consciousness far more than any Afghan government. The BBC Persian Service is listened to avidly even in the remotest corners of Afghanistan, places where Afghan national radio, TV or newspapers cannot reach. Wider access to reading material, modern education and more recently smartphones and the internet have all contributed to a growing sense of national identity at grass-roots level. Since the 1970s millions of Afghans have lived as exiles, refugees or migrant labourers in Iran, Pakistan, the Gulf States, Western Europe, North America and Australasia, an experience which has shattered their cultural and ideological isolation. Today millions of expatriate Afghans live cheek by jowl not just with Afghans of different ethnicities and creeds, but Muslims from other countries and foreigners who are Christian,

Hindu, Buddhist or secular atheists. Many have married non-Muslim Europeans and their children are educated in Western, secular schools and universities. These encounters, particularly among the younger generation, have broadened Afghans' understanding not only of their own identity, but of 'the other'.

Afghanistan emerged from the collapse of three great empires. Despite not being a coherent, historical entity it has somehow survived the vicissitudes of the colonial and post-colonial eras. Its history is a troubled one with the struggle for identity, stability and good governance still unresolved. The jury is still out as to whether Afghanistan in its present form will survive or if it will revert to rival, self-governing fiefdoms once foreign funding and military support is withdrawn. One can only wish Afghans well, for they deserve better than to be condemned to perpetual insecurity and uncertainty.

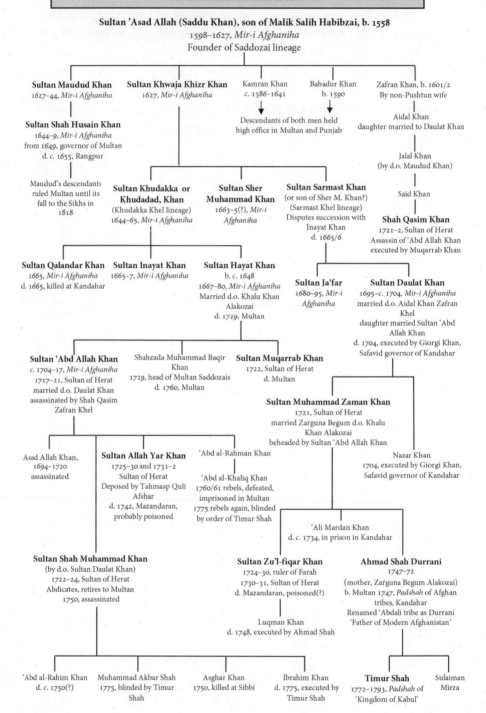

CHART 1: Lineage of Saddozai Sultans and *Mir-i Afghanihas*, 1558–1747
Holders of titles indicated in **bold**

Sultan 'Asad Allah (Saddu Khan), son of Malik Salih Habibzai, b. 1558
1598–1627, *Mir-i Afghaniha*
Founder of Saddozai lineage

Sultan Maudud Khan
1627–44, *Mir-i Afghaniha*

Sultan Khwaja Khizr Khan
1627, *Mir-i Afghaniha*

Kamran Khan
c. 1586–1641

Bahadur Khan
b. 1590

Zafran Khan, b. 1601/2
By non-Pushtun wife

Descendants of both men held
high office in Multan and Punjab

Sultan Shah Husain Khan
1644–9, *Mir-i Afghaniha*
from 1649, governor of Multan
d. *c.* 1655, Rangpur

Aidal Khan
daughter married to Daulat Khan

Jalal Khan
(by d.o. Maudud Khan)

Maudud's descendants
ruled Multan until its
fall to the Sikhs in
1818

**Sultan Khudakka or
Khudadad, Khan**
(Khudakka Khel lineage)
1644–65, *Mir-i Afghaniha*

**Sultan Sher
Muhammad Khan**
1663–5(?), *Mir-i
Afghaniha*

Sultan Sarmast Khan
(or son of Sher M. Khan?)
(Sarmast Khel lineage)
Disputes succession with
Inayat Khan
d. 1665/6

Said Khan

Shah Qasim Khan
1721–2, Sultan of Herat
Assassin of 'Abd Allah Khan
executed by Muqarrab Khan

Sultan Qalandar Khan
1665, *Mir-i Afghaniha*
d. 1665, killed at Kandahar

Sultan Inayat Khan
1665–7, *Mir-i Afghaniha*

Sultan Hayat Khan
b. *c.* 1648
1667–80, *Mir-i Afghaniha*
Married d.o. Khalu Khan
Alakozai
d. 1729, Multan

Sultan Ja'far
1680–95, *Mir-i
Afghaniha*

Sultan Daulat Khan
1695–*c.* 1704, *Mir-i Afghaniha*
married d.o. Aidal Khan Zafran
Khel
daughter married Sultan 'Abd
Allah Khan
d. 1704, executed by Giorgi Khan,
Safavid governor of Kandahar

Sultan 'Abd Allah Khan
c. 1704–17, *Mir-i Afghaniha*
1717–21, Sultan of Herat
married d.o. Daulat Khan
assassinated by Shah Qasim
Zafran Khel

Shahzada Muhammad Baqir
Khan
1729, head of Multan Saddozais
d. 1760, Multan

Sultan Muqarrab Khan
1722, Sultan of Herat
d. Multan

Sultan Muhammad Zaman Khan
1721, Sultan of Herat
married Zarguna Begum d.o. Khalu
Khan Alakozai
beheaded by Sultan 'Abd Allah Khan

Asad Allah Khan,
1694–1720
assassinated

Sultan Allah Yar Khan
1725–30 and 1731–2
Sultan of Herat
Deposed by Tahmasp Quli
Afshar
d. 1742, Mazandaran,
probably poisoned

'Abd al-Rahman Khan

'Abd al-Khaliq Khan
1760/61 rebels, defeated,
imprisoned in Multan
1775 rebels again, blinded
by order of Timur Shah

Nazar Khan
1704, executed by Giorgi Khan,
Safavid governor of Kandahar

'Ali Mardan Khan
d. *c.* 1734, in prison in Kandahar

Sultan Shah Muhammad Khan
(by d.o. Sultan Daulat Khan)
1722–24, Sultan of Herat
Abdicates, retires to Multan
1750, assassinated

Sultan Zu'l-fiqar Khan
1724–30, ruler of Farah
1730–31, Sultan of Herat
d. Mazandaran, poisoned(?)

Ahmad Shah Durrani
1747–72
(mother, Zarguna Begum Alakozai)
b. Multan 1747, *Padshah* of Afghan
tribes, Kandahar
Renamed 'Abdali tribe as Durrani
'Father of Modern Afghanistan'

Luqman Khan
d. 1748, executed by Ahmad Shah

'Abd al-Rahim Khan
d. *c.* 1750(?)

Muhammad Akbar Shah
1775, blinded by Timur
Shah

Asghar Khan
1750, killed at Sibbi

Ibrahim Khan
d. 1775, executed by
Timur Shah

Timur Shah
1772–1793, *Padshah* of
'Kingdom of Kabul'

Sulaiman
Mirza

Key: d. = died; c. = *circa* (about); b. = born; d.o. = daughter of; s.o. = son of

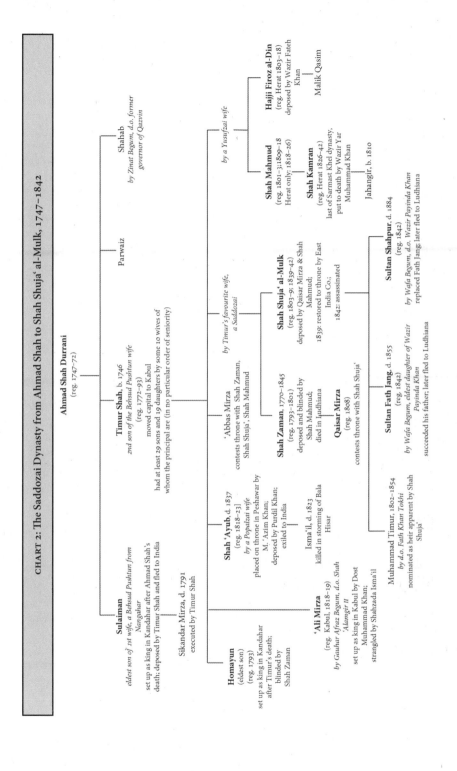

CHART 2: The Saddozai Dynasty from Ahmad Shah to Shah Shuja' al-Mulk, 1747–1842

Ahmad Shah Durrani
(reg. 1747–72)

Sulaiman
eldest son of 1st wife, a Behsud Pushtun from Nangahar
set up as king in Kandahar after Ahmad Shah's death; deposed by Timur Shah and fled to India

Sikandar Mirza, d. 1791
executed by Timur Shah

Timur Shah, b. 1746
2nd son of the Behsud Pushtun wife
(reg. 1772–93)
moved capital to Kabul
had at least 29 sons and 19 daughters by some 10 wives of whom the principal are (in no particular order of seniority)

Parwaiz

Shahab
by Zinat Begum, d.o. former governor of Qazvin

by Timur's favourite wife, a Saddozai

'Abbas Mirza
contests throne with Shah Zaman, Shah Shuja', Shah Mahmud

Homayun
(eldest son)
(reg. 1793)
set up as king in Kandahar after Timur's death; blinded by Shah Zaman

Shah 'Ayub, d. 1837
(reg. 1818–23]
by a Popalzai wife
placed on throne in Peshawar by M. 'Azim Khan; deposed by Purdil Khan; exiled to India

Isma'il, d. 1823
killed in storming of Bala Hisar

'Ali Mirza
(reg. Kabul, 1818–19)
by Gauhar Afraz Begum, d.o. Shah 'Alamgir II
set up as king in Kabul by Dost Muhammad Khan; strangled by Shahzada Isma'il

Shah Zaman, 1770–1845
(reg. 1793–1801)
deposed and blinded by Shah Mahmud; died in Judhiana

Qaisar Mirza
(reg. 1808)
contests throne with Shah Shuja'

Shah Shuja' al-Mulk
(reg. 1803–9; 1839–42)
deposed by Qaisar Mirza & Shah Mahmud;
1839: restored to throne by East India Co.;
1842: assassinated

Muhammad Timur, 1802–1854
by d.o. Fath Khan Tokhi
nominated as heir apparent by Shah Shuja'

Sultan Fath Jang, d. 1855
(reg. 1842)
by Wafa Begum, eldest daughter of Wazir Payinda Khan
succeeded his father; later fled to Ludhiana

Sultan Shahpur, d. 1884
(reg. 1842)
by Wafa Begum, d.o. Wazir Payinda Khan
replaced Fath Jang; later fled to Ludhiana

by a Yusufzai wife

Shah Mahmud
(reg. 1801–3; 1809–18
Herat only: 1818–26)

Shah Kamran
(reg. Herat 1826–42)
last of Sarmast Khel dynasty, put to death by Wazir Yar Muhammad Khan

Jahangir, b. 1810

Hajji Firoz al-Din
(reg. Herat 1803–18)
deposed by Wazir Fateh Khan

Malik Qasim

699

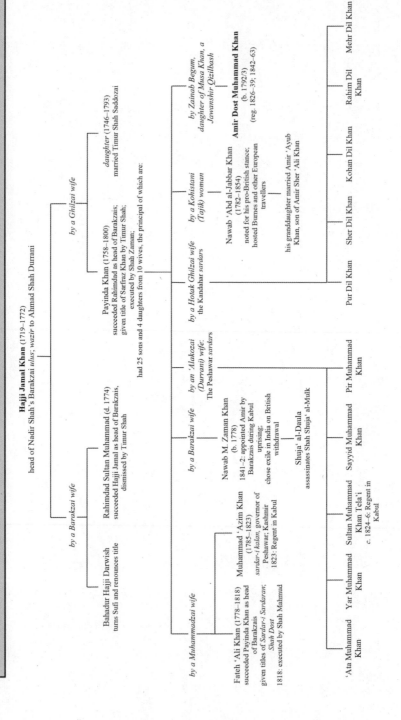

CHART 3: Principal Descendants of Hajji Jamal Khan Barakzai down to Amir Dost Muhammad Khan, 1772–1863

Hajji Jamal Khan (1719–1772)
head of Nadir Shah's Barakzai *ulus*; *wazir* to Ahmad Shah Durrani

by a Barakzai wife

Bahadur Hajji Darwish
turns Sufi and renounces title

Rahimdad Sultan Muhammad (d. 1774)
succeeded Hajji Jamal as head of Barakzais,
dismissed by Timur Shah

by a Ghilzai wife

Payinda Khan (1758–1800)
succeeded Rahimdad as head of Barakzais;
given title of Sarfraz Khan by Timur Shah;
executed by Shah Zaman;
had 25 sons and 4 daughters from 10 wives, the principal of which are:

daughter (1746–1793)
married Timur Shah Saddozai

by a Muhammadzai wife

Fateh 'Ali Khan (1778–1818)
succeeded Payinda Khan as head
of Barakzais
given titles of *Sardar-i Sardaran*;
Shah Dost
1818: executed by Shah Mahmud

Muhammad 'Azim Khan
(1785–1823)
sardar-i kalan, governor of
Peshawar; Kashmir
1823: Regent in Kabul

by a Barakzai wife
The Peshawar *sardars*

*by an 'Alakozai
(Durrani) wife:*

Nawab M. Zaman Khan
(b. 1778)
1841–2: appointed Amir by
Barakzais during Kabul
uprising;
chose exile in India on British
withdrawal

Shuja' al-Daula
assassinates Shah Shuja' al-Mulk

by a Hotak Ghilzai wife
the Kandahar *sardars*

*by a Kohistani
(Tajik) woman*

Nawab 'Abd al-Jabbar Khan
(1782–1854)
noted for his pro-British stance;
hosted Burnes and other European
travellers

his granddaughter married Amir 'Ayub
Khan, son of Amir Sher 'Ali Khan

*by Zainab Begum,
daughter of Musa Khan, a
Jawanshir Qizilbash*

Amir Dost Muhammad Khan
(b. 1792/3)
(reg. 1826–39; 1842–63)

'Ata Muhammad
Khan

Yar Muhammad
Khan

Sultan Muhammad
Khan Tela'i
c. 1824–6: Regent in
Kabul

Sayyid Muhammad
Khan

Pir Muhammad
Khan

Pur Dil Khan

Sher Dil Khan

Kohan Dil Khan

Rahim Dil
Khan

Rahim Dil Khan

Mehr Dil Khan

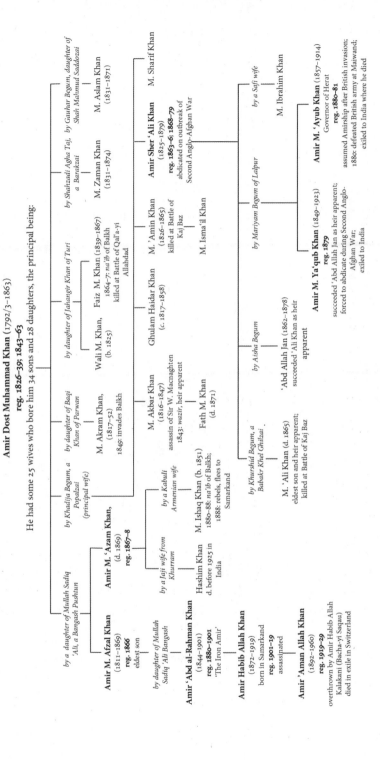

CHART 4: Principal Descdendants of Amir Dost Muhammad Khan

Amir Dost Muhammad Khan (1792/3–1863)
reg. 1826–39; 1843–63
He had some 25 wives who bore him 34 sons and 28 daughters, the principal being:

by a daughter of Mullah Sadiq 'Ali, a Bangash Pushtun

Amir M. Afzal Khan
(1811–1869)
reg. 1866
eldest son

by daughter of Mullah Sadiq 'Ali Bangash

Amir 'Abd al-Rahman Khan
(1844–1901)
reg. 1880–1901
'The Iron Amir'

Amir Habib Allah Khan
(1872–1919)
born in Samarkand
reg. 1901–19
assassinated

Amir 'Aman Allah Khan
(1892–1960)
reg. 1919–29
overthrown by Amir Habib Allah Kalakani (Bacha-yi Saqau) died in exile in Switzerland

by Khadija Begum, a Popalzai (principal wife)

Amir M. 'Azam Khan,
(d. 1869)
reg. 1867–8

by a Taji wife from Khurram

Hashim Khan
d. before 1925 in India

by a Kabuli Armenian wife

M. Ishaq Khan (b. 1851)
1880–88: na'ib of Balkh; 1888: rebels, flees to Samarkand

by daughter of Baqi Khan of Parwan

M. Akram Khan,
(1817–52)
1849: invades Balkh

M. Akbar Khan,
(1816–1847)
assassin of Sir W. Macnaghten
1843: wazir, heir apparent

Fath M. Khan
(d. 1871)

by Khurshid Begum, a Babakr Khel Ghilzai .

M. 'Ali Khan (d. 1865)
eldest son and heir apparent;
killed at Battle of Kaj Baz

by daughter of Jahangir Khan of Turi

Wali M. Khan,
(b. 1825)

Faiz M. Khan (1839–1867)
1864–7: na'ib of Balkh
killed at Battle of Qal'a-yi Allahdad

Ghulam Haidar Khan
(c. 1817–1858)

M. 'Amin Khan
(1826–1865)
killed at Battle of
Kaj Baz

M. Isma'il Khan

by Aisha Begum

'Abd Allah Jan (1862–1878)
succeeded 'Ali Khan as heir
apparent

by Shahzadi Agha Taj, a Barakzai

M. Zaman Khan
(1831–1874)

by Gauhar Begum, daughter of Shah Mahmud Saddozai

M. Aslam Khan
(1831–1871)

Amir Sher 'Ali Khan
(1825–1879)
reg. 1865–6; 1868–79
abdicated on outbreak of
Second Anglo-Afghan War

M. Sharif Khan

by Mariyam Begum of Lalpur

Amir M. Ya'qub Khan (1849–1923)
reg. 1879
succeeded 'Abd Allah Jan as heir apparent;
forced to abdicate during Second Anglo-
Afghan War;
exiled to India

by a Safi wife

M. Ibrahim Khan

Amir M. 'Ayub Khan (1857–1914)
Governor of Herat
reg. 1880–81
assumed Amirship after British invasion;
1880: defeated British army at Maiwand;
exiled to India where he died

701

CHART 5: The Muhammadzais: Dynastic Relationships of the Siraj, Musahiban and Tarzi families

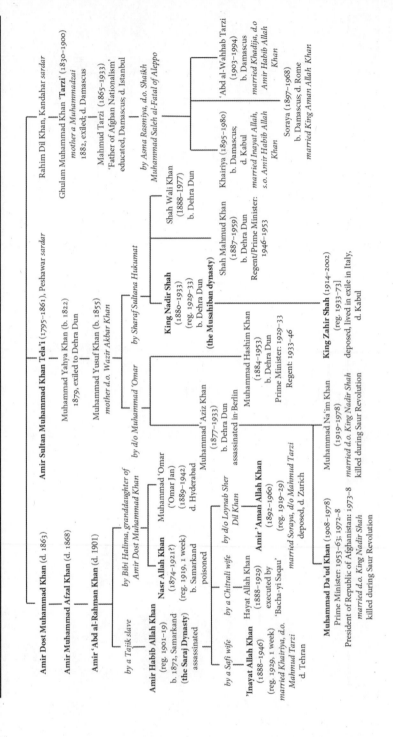

GLOSSARY

āb (colloquially *au*) water, river, stream

'ādat (a) customary law; (b) tradition

afghānī a unit of currency introduced by 'Aman Allah Khan in 1925. Originally 100 *pūls* = 1 *afghānī*; 20 *afghānīs* = 1 *'amānī*. After 2002 a new *afghānī* was introduced without any smaller value coins

'ahd treaty, covenant, agreement

akālī The Immortals, an elite Sikh regiment

ākhūnd, ākhūndzāda a religious leader or theologian

amīr (a) (military) head of a Muslim state (b) a Chingizid provincial governor (c) head of a militia

Amīr al-Mu'minīn Commander of the Faithful. The title of the Four Rightly Guided Caliphs who Sunnis recognized as the successors of Muhammad. Subsequently the title was assumed by the Ottoman Sultans, the Manghit Khans of Bukhara and Amir Dost Muhammad Khan

arg fortress, citadel

'Āshūrā the Shi'a festival held on 10th Muharram that commemorates the martyrdom of Imam Husain

atālīq literally, father-like: a title given to the tutors of Chinggisid princes and rulers of provinces; an adviser to a prince or governor

bābā (a) father (b) a term of respect used by a younger to an older man (c) head of a Sufi Order

badal exchange, or reciprocity, especially in relation to revenge and the pursuit of vendetta

ba'it oath of loyalty, submission or allegiance

baniya (Anglo-Indian, *banyan*) a trader, moneylender or banker, usually Hindu or Sikh

baqa' wa fana' negation and subsisting: the goal of Sufism in which the self is negated by sensing the unity of the Divine essence

baraka charisma; the spiritual power believed to pervade relics, shrines and spiritual leaders

bātin in Sufism the inner or esoteric meaning of Islamic teaching and reality

bēg (a) lord, or high-ranking individual (b) any wealthy individual

bēglar bēgī a rank equivalent to provincial governor

bēgum the title of women of the royal household

bid‘a innovation, heresy; a term applied to reforms or theologies that do not concur with Qur’anic doctrine and Islamic law

burqa the full body covering, tent-like veil worn by women in Afghanistan

buzkashī a Turco-Mongolian game involving horsemen competing to place the decapitated carcass of a calf or goat in a goal circle

chādur literally, curtain; in Afghanistan the tent-like cloak worn by women

chahār four

chahār bāgh a formal Persian garden divided into four quarters, particularly associated with the Timurid and Mughal periods

chahār sū the traditional Central Asian bazaar in which four roads meet in a central market square

Chahār Wilāyat The Four Provinces, the term historically applied to the alliance of four city-states: Maimana, Andkhui, Shibarghan and Sar-i Pul

Chahār Yār The ‘Four Friends’, a term commonly applied by Sunnis to the first four Caliphs

chapan a long-sleeved coat or cloak, usually made of silk, traditionally worn by Uzbeks

chapandāz horsemen who participated in *buzkashī*

chars cannabis resin, hashish

chauk the central area, or crossroads, in a bazaar

chaukīdār watchman, guard

chehel forty

chehela khāna a cell or cave where a Sufi performs the forty-day fast and retreat

chūl (a) loess dunes (b) peripheral, non-irrigated land

crore 100 *lakh*s, or 10 million

Dār al-Harb Abode, House, or Door of War: countries that are either at war with a Muslim state or regions where Muslims are not free to practise their religion

Dār al-Islām Abode, House or Door of Islam: countries and regions ruled by Islamic law and/or whose ruler is a Muslim

darbār (Anglo-Indian *durbar*) an assembly of the royal court, or ceremonial gathering

darra valley

darwīsh dervish, a Sufi ascetic who has taken a vow of poverty

daryā river

dasht (a) desert, wilderness (b) uncultivated wasteland

daulat (a) country, kingdom or government (b) wealth

deh village, settlement

dhimmī non-Muslim, member of a religious minority living under an Islamic government

dīwān bēgī chief fiscal officer

dusteh a military division, regiment

falāqa the bastinado, a torture in which the soles of the victim are repeatedly beaten

faqīr literally, poor or impoverished (a) a term applied to itinerant mystics, cf. English fakir (b) the lowest rank of Sufi initiation

farāmūsh khāna literally Forgotten or Forgetful House, the term used for Masonic Lodges *farangī* (a) literally, a Frank (b) a pejorative term for all Europeans

fard/farz a religious duty that Muslims are required to perform

farmān a royal, or imperial decree

fārsīwān a native Persian-speaker of Afghanistan

fātīha (a) first chapter of the Qur'an (b) funeral prayer service

fatwā a legal opinion or pronouncement

ghairat honour; in Pushtu tribal society this is a pro-active, jealous protection of *qaum* honour, especially women

ghāzī (a) a title adopted by those who have fought in a *jihād* (b) Ahmad Shah Durrani's royal guard

ghulām (a) slave (b) military levies conscripted into an army by virtue of conquest

ghulām khāna the royal guard of the Saddozai monarchs

gilīm hand-woven rug that has no pile

girau a customary system of lease, mortgage or pawning

gurdwārā a Sikh place of worship

hadith The Traditions, a corpus of texts that include accounts and anecdotes of the life, actions and sayings of Muhammad and which form a key textual authority for the Islamic legal code

hāfiz a title used for an individual who has memorized the Qur'an

hājj pilgrimage, particularly to Mecca

hajjī a person who has performed the *hājj*

hākim (a) governor, commander (b) judge, magistrate

hakīm (a) physician, herbalist (b) a learned person, philosopher

halāl actions and foods that under Islamic law are lawful, permitted or ritually clean

haram actions and foods that under Islamic law are forbidden, sinful or ritually unclean

haram sarāi the harem, or secluded women's quarter

hawāla the informal system of financial exchange and brokerage

hawelī (a) a north Indian walled courtyard house, the abode of wealthy merchants and the aristocracy (b) colloquially (*aulī*) any enclosed courtyard

Hazhda Nāhr Eighteen Canals, the name given to the irrigation network of the Balkh river basin

hazrat a title accorded in Islam to prophets, caliphs, kings and high-ranking Sufi *pīrs*

hijra (a) migration, emigration for religious reasons, especially the migration of Muhammad from Mecca to Medina (b) the Islamic lunar calendar

hisar citadel, fortress

hizb political party

hukumat-i a'lā a sub-provincial district under the Musahiban dynasty

hundī a letter of credit or bill of exchange

'Īd an Islamic religious festival

imām (a) prayer leader in a mosque (b) the title Shi'as give to the descendants of 'Ali b. Abi Talib who they claim had the right to leadership of the Muslim community

inqilāb revolution

ishān a high-ranking Sufi *pīr*

Islāmiyat the study of traditional Islamic subjects, including Qur'an, *Hadith* and *Tafsir* (Commentaries)

Isma'īlī The branch of Shi'ism that recognized seven, not twelve, Imams

istiqbāl formal welcome, greeting or reception

'izzat honour, respect, esteem

jāgīr a hereditary estate

jāhilīyya literally, ignorance or paganism, the term used to describe Arabia prior to Islam. Modern Islamists often use this for any non-Islamic legal system and civilization

janda bālā the banner, or flagstaff raising ceremony, part of the Nauroz festival in Mazar-i Sharif

jashn a secular festival or National Day

jawānmard hero, warrior, in particular one who upholds the ancient Persian code of chivalry or *jawānmardī*

jezail a long-barrelled, muzzle-loading flintlock rifle, which was the traditional weapon of the Afghan tribes

jezailchī a musketeer

jīgha an imperial plume or aigrette

jihād literally, struggle (in the way of God), hence Holy War

jinn cf. English genie; powerful, supernatural beings who in Islamic and popular tradition are made of fire

jirga a Pushtun clan or tribal assembly

jizya the capitation tax imposed under Islamic law on non-Muslims

jūī irrigation canal, ditch

kāfir (a) a generic Islamic term for an idolater (b) the name of the former polytheistic people of southeast Afghanistan, now known as Nuristan

kalāntar (a) mayor or magistrate (b) head of a military or civil region

kalima see under *shahāda*

karakul (Turkic *qarāqul*) (a) the skins of young lambs (some aborted while still foetuses) (b) the Central Asian breed of sheep from which the wool derives

kārēz a subterranean irrigation system

kha'lat an ornamented robe bestowed by rulers as a mark of favour or honour

khairāt supererogatory charitable giving, especially to the poor

khālsā a Sikh militaristic Order

khān (a) tribal leader amongst Pushtuns (b) a honorific title accorded to important individuals

khāna house

khānagāh a Sufi meeting house

kharwār a donkey-load: in modern Afghanistan the Kabuli *kharwār* is equivalent to 80 *sēr* (567.2 kg). The Mazar-i Sharif *kharwār* is twice as much as its Kabuli equivalent (1,134.4 kg). The Herati *kharwār* is equivalent to 100 *mann* (Anglo-Indian *maund*) or 3,000 kg

khēl Pushtun clan, sept, lineage

khirqa a cloak or mantle worn by Sufi adepts, prophets and other major Islamic figures *khutba* the sermon delivered at Friday prayers, during which the name of the reigning sovereign is mentioned

khwāja; khōja (a) saint, holy man (b) Sufi teacher or head of a Sufi sub-order

kōh mountain, hill

kōhistān (a) a mountainous region (b) a region of Parwan province in the mouth of the Panjshir

kōtal mountain pass

kōtwāl (a) an individual in charge of a fort (b) mayor-magistrate; the individual responsible for maintaining security in a town and supervising prisoners and jails

kūchī (a) nomad (in Afghanistan the term is usually applied to the semi-nomadic Durrani and Ghilzai tribes); (b) a migrant

kufr blasphemy, unbelief

lakh 100,000

lalmī non-irrigated land usually planted with spring wheat

landai a Pushtun epigram consisting of two lines of poetry

langar khāna Sufi retreat or place where free food is distributed to pilgrims

laqab (a) by-name or nickname (which usually refers to the individual's trade or a physical/personality characteristic) (b) pseudonym

lashkar army, a military division

Lōya Jirga Grand (Tribal) Assembly, Afghanistan's national consultative assembly established in the early twentieth century

madrasa Islamic school; seminary

mahala a city precinct, quarter, district or suburb

Mahdī the 'Guided One' who, in Sunni eschatology, will return at the end of the age to rid the world of evil. In Shi'a theology the Mahdi is the Twelfth Imam who is believed not to have died but is hidden, or in occultation, until the end of the world

mahram a close male relative who escorts adult females who leave the family home

majlis assembly, meeting, gathering, council

māl property, possessions, particularly herds of domestic animals

malang (a) a shrine attendant (b) an itinerant mendicant

māldār (a) nomadic or semi-nomadic Pushtuns (b) a rich person or anyone with substantial possessions

malik (a) village head (b) a tribal or clan representative appointed by government; (c) a king or regal title

mansabdār a rank of nobility under the Mughals. There were varying degrees within the *mansabdārī* system that covered both military and civil office

mashrūta constitution

mashrūtīyya constitutional

maulawī (*maulvī, maulānā*) title accorded to Sunni religious scholars who have attained a high level of Islamic knowledge

mazār a shrine mausoleum

mazhab (a) a school of Islamic jurisprudence (b) sect (c) religion (in popular usage)

mehmān nawāzī hospitality

mehmāndārī formal hospitality accorded to a visitor or ambassador by a host, or *mehmāndār*

mēla (a) festival (b) picnic

melamastia Pushtun tradition of hospitality to guests, visitors and strangers

Meshrānō Jirga House of Elders, the Upper House in Afghanistan's parliamentary system

millat nation

milli national

minbar the lectern, or pulpit, found in major mosques from which the *imam* recites prayers, gives a sermon, or reads out decrees

mīr (a) prince, lord (a) governor (a) chief

mīrāb water bailiff, water master

mīrzā (a) prince or noble (b) writer, scribe

muftī high-ranking Islamic scholar qualified to issue *fatwās*

muhājir (plural, *muhājirīn*) (a) Muslims who chose exile rather than live under a non-Muslim government by undertaking *hijra*, or emigration; (b) a refugee

Muharram (a) the first month of the Islamic, Hijra, lunar year (b) the Shi'a festival held from the 1st to 10th of this month

mujāhid (plural, *mujāhidīn*) a person who fights, or has fought, in a *jihād*

mujtahid in Shi'a Islam, the highest authority on Islamic law

mukhlis a term applied to an affiliate of a Sufi *pīr* whose leader has pledged devotion on behalf of the clan or tribe. Unlike a *murīd*, a *mukhlis* is not obligated to undergo personal initiation into the Order or practice *zikr*, instead he venerates the *pir*, pays tithes and performs pilgrimage to the shrines of the Order. In Afghanistan *mukhlis* is particularly applied to followers of the Qadiriyya Order

mullah (Persian, *mullā*) religious teacher, legalist

munshī scribe, clerk, writer

murīd initiate of a Sufi Order

murshid Sufi guide or teacher who instructs the initiate (*murīd*) in the mystic path

Mustūfī al-Mulk Auditor General, Chief Financial Officer

mutawallī guardian and administrator of a shrine and its endowments or *waqf*

nā'ib deputy governor

namāz the formal, ritual prayers performed five times a day

nān flat bread, the staple food of Afghanistan

nanawātai Pushtun tradition of sanctuary even to rebels, foreigners or one's enemies who seek protection

nānbāī baker

nang in Pushtun society, proactive defence of honour

nāqel (plural, *nāqelīn*) settler, colonist

naqīb a senior religious teacher in the Chingizid system

Naurōz Persian New Year, which in Afghanistan commences on 1 Hamal or the spring equinox (21 March in a non-leap year, 20 March in a leap year)

nawāb (Anglo-English, *nabob*) – title bestowed by the Mughals on autonomous Muslim rulers *nazrāna* (a) annual payment made by subordinate rulers to the overlord or sovereign power (b) gifts made by, and to, individuals of equal or superior rank

niyat intention, in Islam this is essential for the right performance of religious obligations and deeds

pādshāh king, monarch

parda term used in Afghanistan for the veiling or concealment of women

pau unit of weight, which in Kabul is equivalent to 0.975 lb or 443 g

pīr head of a Sufi Order or sub-order

pōstīn a sheepskin coat

Pushtūnwalī/Pukhtūnwalī Pushtun customary, law and code of honour

qadamgāh literally, a footprint (a) a relic shrine (b) any holy place where a *pīr* or other holy person has performed a miracle or passed through

qāfila trade caravan

qal'a (a) fort, castle (b) a fortified, high-walled compound

qālīn hand-knotted pile carpet

qānūn law, legal code, regulation

qānūn-i asāsī foundational law, constitution

qaum extended family or clan

qāzī Islamic judge

qisās the right, under Islamic law, of reciprocal retaliation

ra'īs (a) president, or principal (b) mayor

Ramazān (*Ramadān*) (a) ninth month of the Hijra year (b) the fast that takes place during this month

rasm wa rawāj custom and usage

rasūl prophet, apostle

rōshanfikr term applied to Westernizing reformers, intellectuals and/or Rationalists

rūd river, riverbed

sadāqāt alms or charitable donations

sadhu Hindu or Sikh holy man, ascetic, occasionally used pejoratively for heterodox Muslim mystics

safēd white

sāl year

salāt ritual prayers performed by Muslims five times daily

sangar breastwork; a shallow trench protected by a stone or compacted mud parapet

sarāi (a) an inn, wayfarer's lodge (b) a walled and gated compound for the storage of goods and animals

sardār (a) commander, general (b) military head of tribal levy (c) a royal title adopted by the princes of the Muhammadzai dynasty

sardār-i sardārān (a) chief of the *sardārs* (b) commander-in-chief

sawāb religious merit

sayyid honorific title used by those who claim descent from the prophet Muhammad

shab nāma night, or secret, letter

shāh king, sovereign, monarch

shahāda witness, testimony, in particular the fundamental confession of
 Islamic faith, *kalima*, or word: 'There is no God but Allah and Muhummad
 is the Messenger (or Apostle) of Allah'

shahīd (a) witness (b) martyr

shahr town, city

shāhzāda prince

shaikh in Afghanistan, a spiritual leader, usually associated with a shrine or Sufi
 Order

shamshīra sword or cutlass

shamsī Afghan solar year

sharī'a Islamic canon law

sharīf (a) noble, honoured (b) a honorific title (for example, Sharif of Mecca)

Shī'a generic name for the followers of the Twelve Imams

shirk the sin of associating individual or other beings as equal to God, hence
 idolatry

shūrā (a) religious council (b) community council

silsila (a) genealogical tree (b) the chain of authority of Sufi *pīrs* and Orders

sipāh salār general, military governor, supreme commander

sīyāh black

sōwār cavalry soldier

stūpa Buddhist reliquary

sūbadār (a) Mughal title for a governor of a *sūbah*, or province (b) a sepoy rank
 in the British Indian army, equivalent to lieutenant

sūfī devotee of an Islamic mystical Order

sultān king, emperor, monarch

sunna the Traditions, sayings and teaching attributed to Muhammad

surkh red

tagāb (colloquially, *tagau*) valley or river system

takhalus pen name

takht-i rawān palanquin, sedan chair

tālib (plural *tālibān*) a student of a religious seminary, or *madrasa*

tangi gorge, deep-sided valley

tarīqa a Sufi Order

ta'wīz charm or amulet consisting often of a Qur'anic verse, or on occasion
 relics or dust from a shrine

tazkira identity card or document

tepa hill, mound, knoll

tōmān gold coin used in Safavid and Qajar Persia

'ulamā' (singular, *'alīm*) Senior Islamic jurists

ulus (*wulus*) originally the Turco-Mongolian word for people, but subsequently
 applied to a tribal confederacy or a clan-based military division

'umma the community, commonwealth or 'nation' of all Muslims

'ushr Islamic agricultural tax paid at the rate of 10 per cent for irrigated and 5
 per cent for non-irrigated or hand-irrigated land

vihāra Buddhist monastery

wafādār loyal, faithful, trusty, a title conferred by the Mughals on certain
 Multani Saddozais

wakīl (a) tribal representative (b) agent (c) parliamentary representative (d) a British native news writer

walī (a) saint, 'intercessor', often referred to as a 'friend of God' (b) an individual who is said to possess the ability to perform wonders (*karāmāt*)

wālī deputy, governor, viceroy

waqf (plural *auqāf*) religious endowments, gifts and property

watan (a) region of birth (b) Fatherland (c) country or nation

wazīr (a) viceroy, governor-general (b) an Afghan government minister

wilāyat province governed by a *wālī*

Wolusī Jirga Assembly of the People, Afghanistan's Lower House of Parliament established under the 1963 Constitution

wulswāl head of sub-provincial district (*wulswālī*) in Afghanistan

wulswālī sub-provincial district in Afghanistan

zāhir in Sufi terminology the exoteric, material or external practices and teachings of Islam

zakāt Islamic wealth tax paid annually on assets and herds, reckoned at 2.5 per cent

zanāna the women's quarters, seraglio, harem

zikr literally, remembrance (of God); the term used for Sufi chants, either silent (mental) or spoken

ziyārat shrine

A NOTE ON SOURCES

In order to keep the text to a manageable length, endnote references are limited to key published works, quoted material, journal and magazine articles, unpublished records and online sources. The Bibliography at the rear includes many of the standard works as well as Persian sources. For the early history of the Saddozais, I have drawn on studies by Pakistani and Indian scholars, some of which are not readily available outside of the subcontinent. In such cases I have included these sources both in References and in the Bibliography. The online Royal Ark genealogical website gives extensive details of the complex interrelatedness of the Saddozai and Barakzai lineages (www.royalark.net). For the biographies of individual actors, readers should also consult Ludwig W. Adamec's various historical and biographical dictionaries.

The Political and Secret Department records of the India Office Library and Records, part of the British Library's Asia and Africa Collection, are an invaluable and still underutilized resource. The main sources are listed in Leslie Hall, *A Brief Guide to the Sources for the Study of Afghanistan in the India Office Records* (London, 1981). Primary material from the India Office Records (IOL) that I have drawn on include: *Political and Secret Department Records*, L/P&S series; *Proceedings, Bengal Secret Consultations*, P/BEN/CON; *Military Department Records*, L/MIL/17; Mss Eur, which contains the personal papers and diaries of many British officials and travellers; and *Records of the British Legation in Kabul, 1923–1948*, R/12. Many of British Legation and Foreign Office Records from the early twentieth century have now been published: see Anita L. P. Burdett, ed., *Afghanistan Strategic Intelligence: British Records, 1919–1970*, 4 vols (Cambridge, 2008). References to my earlier book, *The 'Ancient Supremacy': Bukhara, Afghanistan and the Battle for Balkh, 1731–1901* (Leiden, Cologne and New York, 1996) will provide the reader with more specific reports in the IOL. I have also drawn on material in the Peshawar Record Office.

The online records of the U.S. State Department's Office of the Historian (https://history.state.gov and https://uwdc.library.wisc.edu) and WikiLeaks's *Plus D Cables* provided a wealth of information about the internal workings of the Afghan government and U.S. policy after the end of the Second World War. Copies of the *Kabul Times* and *Kabul New Times*, the main English daily newspaper published in Afghanistan, as well as many other historic publications in Dari and Pushtu, can be accessed from: The Arthur Paul Collection at the University of Nebraska-Omaha's Digital Commons (http://digitalcommons.unl.edu/afghanuno); the University of New York's Afghanistan Digital Library (http://afghanistandl.nyu.ed); and the University of Arizona Libraries Digital

Collections (http://content.library.arizona.edu). Several former Afghan ministers and journalists have recently published autobiographies that provide new insights into the inner workings of government during the reign of Zahir Shah, President Da'ud and the Communist governments.

The online *Encyclopaedia Iranica* (www.iranicaonline.org) is an essential first point of reference for anyone serious about studying the region and I have referred extensively to its many authoritative articles. For the situation post-2001 the publications of the Afghanistan Research and Evaluation Unit (AREU, http://areu.org.af) and Afghanistan Analysts Network (AAN, www.afghanistan-analysts.org) are another invaluable resource.

REFERENCES

Introduction

1 Jadwiga Pstrusinska, 'Afghanistan 1989 in Sociolinguistic Perspective', *Central Asian Survey Incidental Papers*, no. 7 (October 1990).

2 Thomas J. Barfield, *The Central Asian Arabs of Afghanistan* (Austin, TX, 1981).

3 For the debate about the Mongol origins of Hazaras, see Elizabeth E. Bacon, *Obok: A Study of Social Structure in Eurasia* (New York, 1958); G. K. Dulling, *The Hazaragi Dialect of Afghan Persian* (London, 1973); H. F. Schurmann, *The Mongols of Afghanistan* (The Hague, 1962). The historian Faiz Muhammad Katib, author of the *Serāj al-Tawārīkh* (Kabul, 1331–3 s./1913–15), was a Hazara and included Hazara vocabulary in his work.

4 I differ somewhat from the system employed by Raphy Favre and Gholam Monowar Kamal, *Watershed Atlas of Afghanistan* (Kabul, 2004).

5 Rafi Samizai, *Islamic Architecture in Herat* (Kabul, 1981); Bernard O'Kane, *Timurid Architecture in Khurasan* (Costa Mesa, CA, 1987).

6 For the issue of the Silk Road, see Warwick Ball, *The Gates of Asia: The Eurasian Steppe and the Limits of Europe* (London, 2015), pp. 108–32.

7 For Sufism in Afghanistan, see Nile Green, ed., *Afghanistan's Islam: From Conversion to the Taliban* (Oakland, CA, 2016), particularly Parts 1 and 2; Asta Olesen, *Islam and Politics in Afghanistan* (Richmond, Surrey, 1996); Bo Utas, 'Notes on Afghan Sufi Orders and Khanaqahs', *Afghanistan Journal* [Graz], 7 (1980), pp. 60–67.

8 For studies on women in Afghanistan, see Isabelle Delloye, *Women of Afghanistan*, trans. Marjolijn de Jager (St Paul, MN, 2003); Hafizullah Emadi, *Politics of Development and Women in Afghanistan* (New York, 1993); Benedicte Grima, *The Performance of Emotion among Paxtun Women* (Austin, TX, 1992); Sarah Safdar, *Kinship and Marriage in Pukhtoon Society* (Lahore, 1997).

9 See *The Customary Laws of Afghanistan*, International Legal Foundation, September 2004, www.usip.org; *Afghanistan: Blood feuds, traditional law (pushtunwali) and traditional conflict resolution* (Oslo, 2011), www.landinfo.no.

10 Arezou Azad, *Sacred Landscape in Medieval Afghanistan: Revisiting the Fadā'il-i Balkh* (Oxford, 2013), pp. 143–4; Margaret Smith, *Rabi'a: The Life and work of Rabi'a and other Women Mystics in Islam* (Oxford, 1994).

11 Farid al-'Attar, *Muslim Saints and Mystics: Episodes from the Tadhkirat*

*al-Auliya*ʿ, trans. A. J. Arberry [1966] (London, New York and Ontario, 1990), pp. 39–51.

12 See Veronica Doubleday, *Three Women of Herat* (London, 1988); Malalai Joya, *Raising my Voice* (London, Sydney and Auckland, 2009); Jenny Nordberg, *The Underground Girls of Kabul* (London, 2014); Annemarie Schimmel, *My Soul is a Woman: The Feminine in Islam* (New York and London, 1997).

13 For *badal*, see Grima, *The Performance of Emotion*, pp. 70–79; for *ghairat*, see Nasifa Shah, *Honour and Violence: Gender, Power and Law in Southern Pakistan* (Oxford and New York, 2016), pp. 40–43.

14 Alfred Lord Tennyson, *In Memoriam*.

1 Afghan Sultanates, 1260–1732

1 Umar Kamal Khan, *Rise of the Saddozais and the Emancipation of Afghans* (Multan, 1999), my translation of the Persian text at p. 35, n. 2.

2 Unless stated otherwise all dates are CE. *Hijra* dates (Islamic religious/lunar calendar) are given as H. (for example, 1150 H.) and Afghan/Persian solar dates with S. (for example, 1355 S.).

3 *Hudūd al-ʿĀlam, 'The Regions of the World', a Persian Geography, 372 AH–982 AH*, trans. V. Minorsky, E.J.W. Gibb Memorial New Series, XI, 2nd edn (London, 1970), pp. 111–12, 347 n. 22; C. E. Bosworth, *The Ghaznavids: Their Empire in Afghanistan and Eastern India, 994–1040*, 1st Indian edn (New Delhi, 1992), pp. 35–6, 109, 205–6.

4 W. Vogelsang, *The Afghans* (London and Malden, MA, 2002), pp. 168–9; L. Lockhart, *The Fall of the Safawid Dynasty and the Afghan Occupation of Persia* (Cambridge, 1958), pp. 80–82.

5 C. E. Bosworth, 'The Development of Persian Culture under the Early Ghaznavids', in *The Medieval History of Iran, Afghanistan and Central Asia* (London, 1977), XVIII, p. 35.

6 Bosworth, *The Ghaznavids*, pp. 98–115.

7 Ibn Battuta, *Selections from the Travels of Ibn Battuta, 1325–1354*, trans. and ed. H.A.R. Gibb [1929] (Lahore, 1985), p. 178.

8 Maulana Minhaj al-Din Juzjani, *Tabāqāt-i Nāsirī: A General History of the Muhammadan Dynasties of Asia including Hindustan from AH 194 (810 AD) to AH 658 (1260 AD)*, trans. and ed. Maj. H. G. Raverty [1881] (New Delhi, 1970), vol. II, pp. 852–3.

9 Muhammad Akbar Rahim, *History of the Afghans in India, AD 154–631* (Karachi, 1961), pp. 30–31.

10 Ibid., p. 54.

11 Ibid., pp. 30–38; my translation of the Persian text at n. 3, p. 38. In Islamic tradition *Dajal* is a semi-human figure covered in red hair, one-eyed and corpulent. The term is often used for barbarians or ugly, coarse people.

12 Zahir al-Din Babur, *Babur-Nama*, trans. Annette S. Beveridge [1922] (Lahore, 1979), pp. 331, 341.

13 Rahim, *Afghans in India*, pp. 248–55; Niccolao Manucci, *Storia do Mogor, or Mogul India, 1653–1708*, trans. William Irvine (London, 1907), vol. I, p. 147.

14 See Tariq Ahmed, *Religio-political Ferment in the N. W. Frontier during the Mughal Period: The Raushaniya Movement* (Delhi, 1982).

15 Jahangir, *The Tuzukh-i-Jahangiri, or Memoirs of Jahangir*, trans. Alexander Rogers, ed. Annette S. Beveridge [1909–15] (Delhi, 2006), vol. I, p. 89.

16 Rahman Baba, *The Nightingale of Peshawar: Selections from Rahman Baba*, trans. Jens Enevoldsen (Peshawar, 1993), p. 7.

17 Khwaja Neamat Ullah, *History of the Afghans translated from the Persian of Neamet Ullah*, trans. Bernard Dorn [1829] (New York, 1969), pp. 38–42; Mountstuart Elphinstone, *An Account of the Kingdom of Caubul*, 2nd edn [1839] (Karachi, 1972), vol. II, pp. 95–6.

18 Muhammad Hayat Khan, *Afghanistan and its Inhabitants, translated from the 'Hayat-i-Afghani' of Muhamad Hayat Khan*, trans. Henry Priestley [1874] (Lahore, 1999), p. 57; Khan, *Rise of the Saddozais*, p. 33.

19 Due to intermarriage, usually with first cousins, Afghans would commonly have several kith-kin relationships to other members of the clan or tribe, both by birth and marriage. The suffix *–zai*, as in Muhammad*zai*, means 'born of' (cf. the Scottish Mc or Mac).

20 *Hayat-i-Afghani*, p. 58, says Saddu's father was 'Omar. I have followed Khan, *Rise of the Saddozais*, and the online Durrani genealogy: www.4dw.net/royalark.

21 Elphinstone, *Kingdom of Caubul*, vol. I, pp. 215, 222–6; vol. II, p. 41.

22 *Makhzan-i Afghani*, p. 64; Elphinstone, *Kingdom of Caubul*, vol. II, p. 96.

23 Olaf Caroe, *The Pathans, 550 BC–AD 1957* (Karachi, 1958), p. 224.

24 Ibid., p. 252; Elphinstone, *Kingdom of Caubul*, vol. II, p. 133.

25 Muhammad Jamil Hanifi, 'Editing the Past, Colonial Productions of Hegemony through the "Loya Jerga" in Afghanistan', *Iranian Studies*, XXXVI/2 (June 2004), p. 297.

26 Ina B. McCabe, *The Shah's Silk for Europe's Silver: Eurasian Trade of the Julfa Armenians in Safavid Iran and India (1530–1750)* (Atlanta, GA, 1999), pp. 24–5, 142–5, 166, 292.

27 François Bernier, *Travels in the Mogul Empire, A.D. 1656–1668*, ed. Vincent A. Smith [1934] (Delhi, 1992), p. 184.

28 C. E. Luard and H. Hosten, ed. and trans., *Travels of Fray Sebastian Manrique, 1629–1643* (Oxford, 1927), vol. II, pp. 260–62.

29 Elphinstone, *Kingdom of Caubul*, vol. II, p. 132.

30 *Tuzukh-i-Jahangiri*, vol. II, p. 240.

31 Ibid., vol. II, pp. 240, 248; Rahim, *Afghans in India*, pp. 279–80.

32 Ganda Singh, *Ahmad Shah Durrani*, 2nd edn (Lahore, 1981), p. 2; Khan, *Rise of the Saddozais*, pp. 61–3; *Hayat-i-Afghani*, p. 59.

33 Khan, *Rise of the Saddozais*, p. 71.

34 Luard, *Travels of Manrique*, vol. II, pp. 221–2.

35 *Hayat-i-Afghani*, p. 59.

36 Some sources say he was the son of Sher Muhammad Khan.

37 Khan, *Rise of the Saddozais*, pp. 96–101.

38 *Hayat-i-Afghani*, p. 63.

39 J. P. Ferrier, *History of the Afghans* (London, 1858), pp. 35–6. Ferrier claims it was his grandson 'Asad Allah Khan who was raped, but 'Asad Allah was born after Hayat Khan fled to Multan.

40 Khan, *Rise of the Saddozais*, p. 118.

41 *The Chronicle of Petros di Sarkis Gilantez*, ed. and trans. C. O. Minasian (Lisbon, 1959), p. 19.

42 Ibid., p. 11.

43 For translations of the correspondence of 'Abd Allah Khan and Hayat Khan, see Khan, *Rise of the Saddozais*, pp. 154–6.

44 Ibid., p. 167, translated from the Persian text.

45 Ibid., pp. 200–205.

46 For the full terms of the treaty, see ibid., p. 232.

47 Caroe, *The Pathans*, p. 252.

2 Nadir Shah and the Afghans, 1732–47

1 Olaf Caroe, *The Pathans, 550 BC–AD 1957* (Karachi, 1958), p. 250.

2 See M. Axworthy, *The Sword of Persia: Nadir Shah, from Tribal Warrior to Conquering Tyrant* (London and New York, 2006); L. Lockhart, *Nadir Shah: A Critical Study* (London, 1938).

3 Ludwig Adamec, *Historical and Political Gazetteer of Afghanistan*, vol. V: *Kandahar and South-central Afghanistan* (Graz, 1980), pp. 509–12.

4 Vesta Sarkhosh Curtis, *Persian Myths* (London, 1993), p. 32.

5 Axworthy, *Sword of Persia*, pp. 211–12.

6 The Four Aimaq tribes are: Firozkohi, Jamshidi, Sunni Hazaras and Taimani. A fifth tribe, the Timuri, is often confused and conflated with the Taimani. For an account of the Chahar Aimaq tribes, see Government of India, *Records of the Intelligence Party of the Afghan Boundary Commission*, vol. IV: *Reports on the Tribes* (Simla, 1891), pp. 43–276.

7 For the Balkh campaign, see Axworthy, *Sword of Persia*, pp. 191–2, 218–21; Jonathan L. Lee, *The 'Ancient Supremacy': Bukhara, Afghanistan and the Battle for Balkh, 1732–1901* (Leiden, 1966), pp. 63–72; Robert D. McChesney, *Waqf in Central Asia* (Princeton, NJ, 1958), pp. 198–216.

8 Literally 'donkey load'. A *kharwar* differs from region to region but the author probably uses the Persian *kharwar*, which is equivalent to around 300 kg.

9 Muhammad Kazim, *Nāma-yi 'Ālam-ārā'-yi Nādirī* (Moscow, 1962–6), vol. III, fols 91b–100a; McChesney, *Waqf*, pp. 204–11.

10 McChesney, *Waqf*, p. 43; Lee, *The 'Ancient Supremacy'*, pp. 18–19, 24 and nn. 19, 24, 35.

11 Père Louis Bazin, 'Mémoires sur les dernières années du règne de Thamas Kouli-Kan', *Lettres édifiantes et curieuses écrites de missions étrangères*, ed. C. Le Gobier and J. B. Du Holde (Paris, 1780), vol. VI, p. 304; for Nadir's last years, see Axworthy, *Sword of Persia*, chaps 10 and 11.

12 I have mostly followed Bazin's eyewitness account of Nadir Shah's assassination.

13 Edward G. Browne, *A Literary History of Persia*, vol. IV: *Modern Times, 1500–1924* [1924] (Cambridge, 1969), p. 137.

14 Ibid.

15 Munshi Mahmud ibn Ibrahim al-Jami al-Husaini, *Tārīkh-i Ahmad Shāhī* [1974] (Peshawar, 2001), fol. 17.

16 Mountstuart Elphinstone, *An Account of the Kingdom of Caubul*, 2nd edn [1839] (Karachi, 1972), vol. II, p. 247.

17 Umar Kamal Khan, *Rise of Saddozais and Emancipation of Afghans* (Multan, 1999), pp. 314–17.

18 Ganda Singh, *Ahmad Shah Durrani: Father of Modern Afghanistan* [1959] (Lahore, 1981); Khan, *Rise of Saddozais*, p. 321, n. 41.

19 Al-Husaini, *Tārīkh-i Ahmad Shāhī*, fols 17–18.

20 Elphinstone, *Kingdom of Caubul*, vol. II, p. 281; George Forster, *A Journey from Bengal to England through the Northern Part of India, Kashmire, Afghanistan, and Persia etc.*, 2nd edn (London, 1808), vol. II, p. 95.

21 Abu'l-Hasan ibn Amin Gulistana, 'The End of Nadir Shah, being Extracts from the *Mujmal al-Tawārīkh*', trans. Jadunath Sarkar, *Modern Review*, XLV/5 (May 1929), pp. 533–6.

22 Singh, *Ahmad Shah*, p. 29; Khan, *Rise of Saddozais*, p. 320, says the treasure was only 30 *lakh*, or 3 million rupees, but even this was a substantial sum of money.

23 For an image of the Sher-i Surkh shrine, see Mildred Caudill, *Helmand-Arghandab Valley: Yesterday, Today, Tomorrow* (Lashkargah, 1969), p. 6.

24 Mir Gholam Mohammad Ghobar, *Ahmad Shāh Bābā-yi Afghān* (Kabul, 1322 s./1943).

25 Louis Dupree, *Afghanistan*, 2nd edn (Princeton, NJ, 1978), p. 333n.

26 See 'Aziz al-Din Wakili Popalzai, *Tārīkh-i Khirqa-yi Sharīfa Qandhār* (Kabul, 1367 s./1989–90); McChesney, *Waqf*, pp. 222–7.

27 Sultan Mahomed Khan, *The Life of Abdur Rahman Amir of Afghanistan* [1900] (Karachi, 1980), vol. II, pp. 216–17.

28 Ibid., vol. II, pp. 215–16.

29 Faiz Muhammad Katib, *Sarāj al-Tawārīkh* (Kabul, 1333 s./1914–15), vol. I, pp. 9–10.

30 Ghobar, *Ahmad Shāh*, p. 88, claims that Sabir Shah was the son of a certain Ustad Lahori, though he cites no sources.

31 Singh, *Ahmad Shah*, p. 27, n. 5.

32 See Nile Green, *Islam and the Army in Colonial India* (Cambridge, New York and Melbourne, 2009).

33 Singh, *Ahmad Shah*, pp. 27–8.

34 Muhammad Jamil Hanifi, 'Editing the Past: Colonial Production of Hegemony through the "Loya Jerga" in Afghanistan', *Iranian Studies*, XXXVII/2 (June 2004), pp. 296–322.

35 Elphinstone, *Kingdom of Caubul*, vol. I, p. 95; Khan, *Life of Abdur Rahman*, vol. II, p. 499.

3 Ahmad Shah and the Durrani Empire, 1747–72

1 Mountstuart Elphinstone, *An Account of the Kingdom of Caubul* [1839] (Karachi, 1972), vol. I, p. 233.

2 See Ganda Singh, *Ahmad Shah Durrani* [1959] (Lahore, 1981), pp. 347–56; Elphinstone, *Kingdom of Caubul*, vol. I, pp. 210–35, 332–3.

3 Elphinstone, *Kingdom of Caubul*, vol. I, p. 229.

4 'Notes by Mountstuart Elphinstone on the History, People and Geography of Afghanistan and Central Asia, 1808–9', British Library (BL), Asia and Africa Collection: India Office Library and Records (IOR), *Papers of Mountstuart Elphinstone*, Mss Eur. F88/377, fol. 230.

5 Singh, *Ahmad Shah*, pp. 45–6.

6 Mesrob J. Seth, *Armenians in India* [1943] (New Delhi, 1992), p. 207. See also H. Heras, 'The Jesuits in Afghanistan', *New Review* (16 February 1935), pp. 139–53; Jonathan L. Lee, 'The Armenians of Kabul and Afghanistan', in *Cairo to Kabul: Afghan and Islamic Studies Presented to Ralph Pinder-Wilson*, ed. Warwick Ball and Leonard Harrow (London, 2002), pp. 157–62; Edward Maclagan, *The Jesuits and the Great Mogul* (London, 1932), pp. 36, 133, 193, 319–22; C. H. Payne, trans., *Jahangir and the Jesuits . . . from the Relations of Father Fernão Guerreiro, S. J.* [1930] (New Delhi, 1997), pp. 24–5.

7 Singh, *Ahmad Shah*, pp. 258, 358, calls him Shah Nazir, but his tombstone gives his name as Shah Nazar Khan, see Seth, *Armenians in India*, pp. 115–19. The date of the cannon's casting is found in the *abjad*, or numerical value, of the gun's Persian dedication.

8 *Haweli* are the walled and gated compounds of wealthy merchants and courtiers.

9 For the Afghan-Baluch Treaty, see Singh, *Ahmad Shah*, p. 214.

10 For Shah Wali Allah, see Aziz Ahmad, *Studies in Islamic Culture in the Indian Environment* (Oxford, 1964), pp. 201–8; Wm. Theodore de Barry, ed., *Sources of Indian Tradition*, 5th edn (New York and London, 1970), vol. I, pp. 448–54; Olivier Roy, *Islam and Resistance in Afghanistan*, 2nd edn (Cambridge and New York, 1990), pp. 55–6.

11 Singh, *Ahmad Shah*, p. 295; Sarbaland was a Bahadur Khel Saddozai.

12 Ibid., p. 296.

13 Ibid., pp. 128–30; John Malcolm, *The History of Persia from the Most Early Period to the Present Time*, new edn (London, 1829), vol. II, pp. 59, 64–6.

14 Singh, *Ahmad Shah*, p. 93; J. P. Ferrier, *History of the Afghans* (London, 1858), p. 79.

15 See Robert D. McChesney, *Waqf in Central Asia* (Princeton, NJ, 1973), pp. 198–200; Jonathan L. Lee, *The 'Ancient Supremacy': Bukhara, Afghanistan and the Battle for Balkh, 1732–1901* (Leiden, 1996), pp. 72–91.

16 See Warwick Ball, *Archaeological Gazetteer of Afghanistan* (Paris, 1981), vol. I, pp. 91–2.

17 The citadel of Aqcha was levelled in the 1940s; see Rudolf Stuckert, *Erinnerungen an Afghanistan, 1940–1946* (Liestal, 1994), pp. 99–100.

18 See 'Report of Ghulam Sarwar, Native agent of the Hon. East India Co., on Special Mission to the Country of Shah Zemaun, 1793–1795', BL, Asia and Africa Collection: IOR, *Proceedings, Bengal Secret Consultations, 1797*, P/BEN/CON/41.

19 Singh, *Ahmad Shah*, p. 71, citing the *Tārīkh-i Ahmad Shāhī*; Elphinstone, *Kingdom of Caubul*, vol. II, p. 288, who erroneously dates this revolt to later in Ahmad Shah's reign.

20 Singh, *Ahmad Shah*, pp. 268–70, 325; Singh says 'Abd al-Khaliq was executed, but he reappears in Timur Shah's reign.

21 Ibid., pp. 270–72. Singh claims the land was gifted voluntarily.

22 Ibid., pp. 32, 34; Munshi Mahmud al-Husaini, *Tārīkh-i Ahmad Shāhī* [1974] (Peshawar, 2001), fols 20–26; 'Aziz al-Din Wakili Popalzai, *Ahmad Shāh* (Kabul, 1359 s./1980), vol. I, pp. 54–9.

23 Ferrier, *History of the Afghans*, pp. 73–4.

24 Elphinstone, *Kingdom of Caubul*, vol. II, p. 297.

25 Singh, *Ahmad Shah*, p. 215.

26 Ibid., p. 268.

27 Mohammed 'Ali, *A New Guide to Afghanistan* (Kabul, 1958), p. 147.

28 Ahmad 'Ali Kohzad, *Men and Events through 18th and 19th Century Afghanistan* (Kabul, 1972), p. 1.

29 Olaf Caroe, *The Pathans, 550 BC–AD 1957* (Karachi, 1958), p. 259.

30 W. K. Fraser-Tytler, *Afghanistan: A Study of Political Developments in Central and Southern Asia*, 3rd edn (Oxford, 1967), pp. 64–5; see also M. Jamil Hanifi, 'Editing the Past: Colonial Production of Hegemony through the "Loya Jerga" in Afghanistan', *Iranian Studies*, XXXVII/2 (June 2004), pp. 296–322.

31 Louis Dupree, *Afghanistan*, 2nd edn (Princeton, NJ, 1978), p. 340.

4 Fragmentation: Timur Shah and his Successors, 1772–1824

1 Ganda Singh, *Ahmad Shah Durrani*, 2nd edn (Lahore, 1981), p. 325.

2 Arthur Conolly, *A Journey to the North of India, Overland from England through Russia, Persia, and Affghaunistaun* [1838] (New Delhi, 2001), vol. II, p. 261.

3 Mountstuart Elphinstone, *An Account of the Kingdom of Caubul* [1839] (Karachi, 1972), vol. II, pp. 300–301; J. P. Ferrier, *Caravan Journeys and Wanderings in Persia, Afghanistan, Turkistan, and Baloochistan* (London, 1857), p. 97; Singh, *Ahmad Shah*, p. 387.

4 See Brig. C. W. Woodburn, *The Bala Hissar of Kabul: Revealing a Fortress-palace in Afghanistan* (Chatham, 2009).

5 For Timur Shah and Zaman Shah's administration, see 'Report of Ghulam Sarwar, Native Agent of the Hon. East India Co., on Special Mission to the Country of Shah Zemaun, 1793–1795', British Library, Asia and Africa Collection: India Office Library and Records (IOR), *Proceedings, Bengal Secret Consultations, 1797*, P/BEN/CON/41, fol. 89a.

6 Elphinstone, *Kingdom of Caubul*, vol. II, p. 301.

7 Ibid., p. 303.

8 Arsala is sometimes referred to as Arsalan Khan. For his revolt, see Christine Noelle, *State and Tribe in Nineteenth-century Afghanistan: The Reign of Dost Muhammad Khan (1826–1863)* (Abingdon, 1997), p. 165, and n. 188, p. 332, which lists numerous sources for this revolt; Ashiq Muhammad Khan Durrani, 'The Last Phase of Muslim Rule in Multan, 1753–1818', PhD thesis, University of Multan, n. d., pp. 141–50; Elphinstone, *Kingdom of Caubul*, vol. II, pp. 302–3, who places this conspiracy after the revolt of 'Abd al-Khaliq Khan; J. P. Ferrier, *History of the Afghans* (London, 1858), p. 102; Singh, *Ahmad Shah*, p. 338; P. Sykes, *A History of Afghanistan* [1940] (New Delhi, 1981), vol. I, p. 370.

9 Elphinstone, *Kingdom of Caubul*, vol. II, p. 303.

10 Ferrier claims Timur ordered the execution of one in every three Peshawaris as reprisals, but this is not corroborated by any other source and is probably a fabrication.

11 *Report of Ghulam Sarwar*, fol. 125b.

12 Ibid., fols 124b–125a; Elphinstone, *Kingdom of Caubul*, vol. II, pp. 305–6; Ferrier, *History of the Afghans*, pp. 100–101; Jonathan L. Lee, *The 'Ancient Supremacy': Bukhara, Afghanistan and the Battle for Balkh, 1732–1901* (Leiden, 1996), pp. 93–4.

13 Elphinstone, *Kingdom of Caubul*, vol. II, p. 198.

14 Conolly, *A Journey to the North of India*, vol. II, pp. 261–3; Elphinstone, *Kingdom of Caubul*, vol. II, p. 307–8; Ferrier, *History of the Afghans*, pp. 109–11; Singh, *Ahmad Shah*, pp. 338–9.

15 Elphinstone, *Kingdom of Caubul*, vol. II, pp. 308–9.

16 For Saddozai Herat, see David Charles Champagne, 'The Afghan-Iranian Conflict over Herat Province and European Intervention, 1796–1863: A Reinterpretation', PhD thesis, University of Texas, 1981, fols 49–51.

17 Elphinstone, *Kingdom of Caubul*, vol. I, p. 56; vol. II, p. 316.

18 Durrani, 'The Last Phase of Muslim Rule in Multan', fol. 115 and footnote, 162; Faiz Muhammad Katib, *Serāj al-Tawārīkh* (Kabul, 1331–3 s./1913–15), vol. I, p. 59; *Report of Ghulam Sarwar*, fol. 109b.

19 See Ferrier, *History of the Afghans*, p. 122; Mohan Lal, *Life of the Amir Dost Muhammad Khan of Kabul* [1846] (New Delhi, 2004), vol. I, pp. 17–18.

20 For *Mukhtar al-Daula*, Sher Muhammad Khan Bamizai, see Conolly, *A Journey to the North of India*, vol. II, pp. 266–7; Elphinstone, *Kingdom of Caubul*, vol. II, pp. 334–8; Ferrier, *History of the Afghans*, pp. 132–4; Lal, *Life of the Amir*, vol. I, pp. 36–7; Charles Masson, *Narrative of Various Journeys in Balochistan, Afghanistan, the Panjab, & Kalât* [1842] (Delhi, 1997) vol. III, pp. 40–42; Noelle, *State and Tribe*, pp. 26–7, 278–9; George Passman Tate, *The Kingdom of Afghanistan: A Historical Sketch* (Bombay, 1910), pp. 98, 101, 103, 128.

21 Elphinstone, *Kingdom of Caubul*, vol. II, pp. 335–6.

22 For Ashiqan wa Arifan, see Nancy Hatch Dupree, *A Historical Guide to Kabul* (Kabul, 1972), pp. 152–3; Muhammad Ibrahim Khalil, *Mazārāt-i Shāhr-i Kābul* (Kabul, 1339 s./1960), pp. 107–29; Bruce Wannell and Khadeem Hussain, *Kabul Elite Burials: A Wounded Heritage* (Kabul, 2003), pp. 36–105.

23 For Khwaja Khanji, see Masson, *Narrative of Various Journeys*, vol. III, pp. 22–6; Noelle, *State and Tribe*, pp. 15, 27, 52, 278–9.

24 Elphinstone, *Kingdom of Caubul*, vol. II, p. 338.

25 John William Kaye, *The Life and Correspondence of Sir John Malcolm* (London, 1856), vol. I, p. 399.

26 See Amitas Das, *Defending British India against Napoleon: The Foreign Policy of Governor General Lord Minto, 1807–13* (Martlesham, Suffolk, 2016).

27 Elphinstone, *Kingdom of Caubul*, vol. II, pp. 347–8; Champagne, 'The Afghan-Iranian Conflict', p. 71; Lee, *The 'Ancient Supremacy'*, pp. 110–11.

28 Elphinstone, *Kingdom of Caubul*, vol. I, pp. 84–5.

29 Ibid., vol. I, p. 67.

30 Benjamin D. Hopkins, *The Making of Modern Afghanistan* (Cambridge, 2008); Martin J. Bayly, *Taming the Imperial Imagination: Colonial Knowledge, International Relations, and the Anglo-Afghan Encounter, 1808–1878* (Cambridge, 2016).

31 Jonathan Lee, 'The Elphinstone Mission, the "Kingdom of Caubul" and the Turkic World', unpublished conference paper presented to 'Mountstuart Elphinstone and the Historical Foundations of Afghan Studies: Reframing Colonial Knowledge of the Indo-Persian World in the Post-colonial Era', London, 6 November 2015.

32 Elphinstone, *Kingdom of Caubul*, vol. II, p. 182.

33 The date 1745 refers to the Jacobite Rising of Charles Stuart, or Bonnie Prince Charlie.

34 Elphinstone also failed to mention the Irish Rebellion of 1798 or the civil unrest in England created by Pitt's suspension of habeas corpus in the wake of the French Revolution.

35 Elphinstone, *Kingdom of Caubul*, vol. I, pp. 82–3.

36 The *mutawalli* administered the *waqf* of three shrines: Sakhi Saheli Sarkar, Sah Anyat Wali and Dhani Mai Sahiba.

37 Elphinstone, *Kingdom of Caubul*, vol. I, p. 88.

38 Ferrier, *History of the Afghans*, p. 138.

39 Conolly, *A Journey to the North of India*, vol. II, p. 289.

40 Alexander Burnes, *Travels into Bukhara, being the Account of a Journey from India to Cabool, Tartary and Persia, etc., 1831–33* [1834] (New Delhi and Madras, 1992), vol. II, p. 312.

41 Masson, *Narrative of Various Journeys*, vol. III, p. 46.

42 Ibid., p. 48; Lal, *Life of the Amir*, vol. I, p. 114.

43 The sources for events in Balkh at this era are few and far between, which makes dating of the Bukhara reconquest of Balkh difficult to determine.

44 For Ishan Nabib and Ishan Uruq, see Lee, *The 'Ancient Supremacy'*, pp. 119–22, and nn. 95–6.

45 The *akali*s, or Immortals, all swore an oath never to surrender or retreat.

46 Phula Singh's father had been killed in the Wadda Ghalughara massacre, while Phula died in the Battle of Nawshera. The Sikhs regard Phula Singh as one of their greatest saint-heroes.

5 Afghanistan and the Indus Frontier, 1824–39

1 Trevelyan's report quoted in Malcolm Yapp, *Strategies of British India* (Oxford, 1980), p. 209.

2 For Hajji Khan Kakar, see Charles Masson, *Narrative of Various Journeys in Balochistan, Afghanistan, the Panjab, & Kalât* [1842] (Delhi, 1997), vol. II, pp. 292–3 and vol. III, pp. 72–3; G. T. Vigne, *A Personal Narrative of a Visit to Ghuzni, Kabul, and Afghanistan* [1840] (New Delhi and Chennai, 2004), pp. 316, 326–33.

3 Masson, *Narrative of Various Journeys*, vol. III, p. 75.

4 George de Lacy Evans, *On the Designs of Russia* (London, 1828) and *On*

the Practicability of an Invasion of British India (London, 1829); Edward M. Spiers, *Radical General: Sir George de Lacy Evans, 1787–1870* (Manchester, 1983).

5 Edward Law Ellenborough, *A Political Diary*, vol. II: *1828–1830* (London, 1881), pp. 82, 104–6, 124.

6 Richard Cobden, *Political Writings*, 2nd edn (London, 1868), vol. I, p. 46.

7 Yapp, *Strategies of British India*, p. 201.

8 J. A. Norris, *The First Afghan War, 1838–1842* (Cambridge, 1967), p. 43.

9 For the Indus survey, see Alexander Burnes, *Travels into Bokhara: Being the Account of a Journey from India to Cabool, Tartary, and Persia; also, Narrative of a Voyage on the Indus, from the Sea to Lahore* [1834] (New Delhi and Madras, 1992), vol. II, pp. 193–309; for Burnes's biography, see James Hunt, *Bokhara Burnes* (London, 1969).

10 Metcalfe's words quoted in Norris, *First Afghan War*, p. 45.

11 Arthur Conolly, *Journey to the North of India, Overland from England through Russia, Persia, and Affghaunistaun*, 2nd edn, 2 vols [1838] (New Delhi, 2001); for his biography, see John William Kaye, *Lives of the Indian Officers* (London, 1867), vol. II, pp. 67–144.

12 William Moorcroft and George Trebeck, *Travels in the Himalayan Provinces of Hindustan and the Panjab . . . from 1819 to 1825* [1841] (Karachi, 1979); Gary Alder, *Beyond Bokhara: The Life of William Moorcroft, Asian Explorer and Pioneer Veterinary Surgeon, 1767–1825* (London, 1985).

13 Edward Stirling, *The Journals of Edward Stirling in Persia and Afghanistan, 1828–1829*, ed. Jonathan L. Lee (Naples, 1991); Edward Stirling, *Some Considerations on the Political State of the Intermediate Countries between Persia and India with Reference to the Project of Russia Marching an Army through them* (London, 1835), pp. ii–v.

14 Yapp, *Strategies of British India*, p. 209.

15 Joseph Wolff, *Researches and Missionary Labours among the Jews, Mohammedans and other Sects* (Philadelphia, PA, 1837).

16 Burnes, *Travels into Bokhara*, vol. II, p. 343.

17 Ibid., vol. I, pp. 189–229; vol. II, p. 353.

18 Ibid., vol. I, p. 205.

19 Ibid., vol. II, p. 381.

20 Ibid., vol. II, p. 344.

21 Ibid., vol. II, pp. 330–33.

22 Major D'Arcy Todd, 'Observations on the Military Memoir of Captain Burnes on Afghanistan', 2 July 1837, British Library (BL), Asia and Africa Collection: India Office Library and Records (IOR), *Secret Letters and Enclosures from Persia*, L/P&S/144, fols 420–63.

23 For Masson in Kabul, see Masson, *Narrative of Various Journeys*, vols II and III; for his biography, see Gordon Whitteridge, *Charles Masson of Afghanistan: Explorer, Archaeologist, Numismatist and Intelligence Agent* (Warminster, Wilts, 1986).

24 Masson, *Narrative of Various Journeys*, vol. III, p. 493.

25 Ibid., vol. II, pp. 295–323; Christine Noelle, *State and Tribe in Nineteenth-century Afghanistan: The Reign of Dost Muhammad Khan (1826–1863)*

(Abingdon, 1977), pp. 32–6.

26 Masson, *Narrative of Various Journeys*, vol. II, p. 302.

27 Mohan Lal, *Life of the Amir Dost Mohammad Khan of Kabul* [1846] (New Delhi and Chennai, 2004), vol. I, p. 158.

28 Masson, *Narrative of Various Journeys*, vol. III, pp. 325–6; Yapp, *Strategies of British India*, pp. 14–15.

29 Masson, *Narrative of Various Journeys*, vol. III, p. 307.

30 Ibid., vol. III, p. 310.

31 Ibid., pp. 329–32.

32 Ibid., p. 332.

33 Ibid., p. 334.

34 Josiah Harlan, *A Memoir of India and Avghanistaun* [1842] (Philadelphia, PA, 2005); Frank E. Ross, ed., *Central Asia: Personal Narrative of General Josiah Harlan, 1823–1841* (London, 1939); for his biography, see Ben Macintyre, *Josiah the Great: The True Story of the Man who would be King* (London, 2004).

35 Melvin M. Kessler, *Ivan Viktorovich Vitkevich, 1806–1839* (Washington, DC, 1960).

36 Lal, *Life of the Amir*, vol. I, p. 248.

37 Ibid., pp. 250–52; Norris, *First Afghan War*, pp. 92–3.

38 Yapp, *Strategies of British India*, p. 223.

39 Masson, *Narrative of Various Journeys*, vol. III, pp. 384–91.

40 Norris, *First Afghan War*, pp. 98–9.

41 Yapp, *Strategies of British India*, p. 232.

42 Lal, *Life of the Amir*, vol. I, p. 259.

43 Norris, *First Afghan War*, p. 122.

44 Lal, *Life of the Amir*, vol. I, p. 259.

45 David Charles Champagne, 'The Afghan-Iranian Conflict over Herat Province and European Intervention, 1796–1863: A Reinterpretation', PhD thesis, University of Texas, 1981, fols 174, 148.

46 For Asaf al-Daula's campaign, see Jonathan L. Lee, *The 'Ancient Supremacy': Bukhara, Afghanistan and the Battle for Balkh, 1732–1901* (Leiden, Cologne and New York, 1996), pp. 149–58; Faiz Muhammad Katib, *Serāj al-Tawārikh* (Kabul, 1331–3 s./1913–15), vol. I, pp. 132–4.

47 For Eldred Pottinger, see Maud Diver, *The Hero of Herat: A Frontier Biography in a Romantic Form* (London, 1912); Kaye, *Lives of the Indian Officers*, vol. II, pp. 145–208; George Pottinger, *The Afghan Connection: The Extraordinary Adventures of Major Eldred Pottinger* (Edinburgh, 1983).

48 Lal, *Life of the Amir*, vol. I, p. 260; Yapp, *Strategies of British India*, pp. 146–7.

49 Norris, *First Afghan War*, p. 133.

50 Ibid., p. 153.

51 Lal, *Life of the Amir*, vol. I, p. 344.

52 John William Kaye, *History of the War in Afghanistan* (London, 1874), vol. I, p. 209n; see also Louis Dupree, *Afghanistan*, 2nd edn (Princeton, NJ, 1978), p. 374 n. 9, where he discusses alternative versions of Vitkevitch's reception and his subsequent suicide.

53 Whitteridge, *Charles Masson*, p. 152.

54 Auckland's dispatch quoted in Norris, *First Afghan War*, pp. 163–4, 168.

55 Ken McNaughton, 'Sir William Hay Macnaghten and the First Afghan War', www.clanmacnaughton.net, accessed 9 October 2017.

56 Masson, *Narrative of Various Journeys*, vol. II, pp. 452–4, 493; Rev. G. H. Gleig, *Sale's Brigade in Afghanistan, with an Account of the Seizure and Defence of Jellalabad* [1846] (Uckfield, 2004), pp. 73–4; Whitteridge, *Charles Masson*, pp. 144–5.

57 Masson, *Narrative of Various Journeys*, vol. III, p. 495.

58 Kaye, *Lives of the Indian Officers*, vol. II, p. 41.

59 Burnes's letter (now lost) quoted in John William Kaye, *History of the War in Afghanistan*, 2 vols [1851] (Delhi, 1999), vol. I, p. 352n; *aut Caesar aut nullus* was the motto of Cesare Borgia.

60 For the Tripartite Treaty, see ibid., vol. I, pp. 319–33; Norris, *First Afghan War*, pp. 188–9.

61 Champagne, 'The Afghan-Iranian Conflict over Herat Province', p. 198.

62 For the Simla Declaration, see Kaye, *History of the War in Afghanistan*, vol. I, pp. 355–9.

63 Ibid., p. 363n.

64 For the British government's response to the war, see Norris, *First Afghan War*, pp. 207–30; Yapp, *Strategies of British India*, pp. 278–303.

65 Macnaghten's words quoted in Norris, *First Afghan War*, p. 249.

66 Kaye, *History*, vol. I, p. 383.

67 Robert A. Huttenback, *British Relations with Sind, 1799–1843: An Anatomy of Imperialism* (Berkeley, CA, and London, 1962), p. 49.

68 Norris, *First Afghan War*, pp. 263–4.

69 Macnaghten's words quoted in Kaye, *History*, vol. I, p. 423.

70 Lal, *Life of the Amir*, vol. II, p. 211.

71 Ibid., vol. II, p. 226.

72 Ibid., vol. II, pp. 273–8; Shahamat 'Ali, *The Sikhs and Afghans in Connexion [sic] with India and Persia* [1847] (New York, 2005), pp. 305–15.

73 Lal, *Life of the Amir*, vol. II, pp. 235–6.

74 *Cucumis colocynthis* is the bitter cucumber or bitter apple.

6 The Death of the 'Great Experiment', 1839–43

For the quotation the 'Great Experiment' used in the title of this chapter, see John Russell Colvin on the Indus policy, in J. A. Norris, *The First Afghan War, 1838–1842* (Cambridge, 1967), p. 361.

1 John William Kaye, *History of the War in Afghanistan* [1851] (Delhi, 1999), vol. II, pp. 142; this phrase was omitted in subsequent editions.

2 Mohan Lal, *Life of the Amir Dost Mohammad Khan of Kabul* [1846] (New Delhi and Chennai, 2004), vol. II, p. 313.

3 Ibid., pp. 318–24.

4 Malcolm E. Yapp, 'Disturbances in Western Afghanistan, 1839–41', *Bulletin of the School of Oriental and African Studies*, XXVI (1963), pp. 288–313.

5 For the situation in Turkistan and Bamiyan, see J. H. Stocqueler, *Memorials of Affghanistan, 1838–1842* [1843] (Peshawar, 1969), pp. 85–95; J. L. Lee, *The*

'Ancient Supremacy': Bukhara, Afghanistan and the Battle for Balkh, 1732–1901 (Leiden, Cologne and New York, 1996), pp. 163–78.

6 Kaye, History, vol. II, pp. 550–51.

7 Hobhouse's report quoted in Norris, The First Afghan War, p. 314.

8 Lal, Life of the Amir, vol. II, p. 344; Colin Mackenzie, Storms and Sunshine of a Soldier's Life (Edinburgh, 1884), vol. I, p. 179.

9 James Atkinson, The Expedition into Affghanistan [sic]: Notes and Sketches Descriptive of the Country [1842] (Uckfield, 2004), p. 354.

10 'Abd al-Karim 'Alawi, Muhābarāt-i Kābul wa Kandhār (Kanpoor, 1264 s./1866), pp. 47–9. I am grateful to Sayyid Reza Huseini for pointing out this reference.

11 Macnaghten's dispatch quoted in Kaye, History, vol. I, p. 561.

12 James Atkinson, Sketches in Afghaunistan (London, 1842), plate 18.

13 Lal, Life of the Amir, vol. II, p. 456.

14 Quoted in Kaye, History, vol. I, p. 551.

15 Ellenborough's comment quoted in ibid., vol. I, pp. 567–8.

16 Ellenborough's dispatch quoted in Norris, First Afghan War, p. 405.

17 Auckland's dispatch quoted in ibid., p. 338.

18 Quoted in Kaye, History, vol. I, p. 609.

19 Todd's report quoted in Malcolm Yapp, Strategies of British India (Oxford, 1980), p. 365.

20 Macnaghten's report quoted in Kaye, History, vol. I, pp. 602–3.

21 Macnaghten's report quoted in ibid., pp. 594–5.

22 Quoted in ibid., p. 549.

23 See M. Yapp, 'The Revolutions of 1841–2 in Afghanistan', Bulletin of the School of Oriental and African Studies, XXVII (1964), pp. 338–44.

24 Lal, Life of the Amir, vol. II, pp. 384–5.

25 J. Greenwood, Narrative of the Late Victorious Campaign in Afghanistan under General Pollock [1884] (Uckfield, 2004), p. 202.

26 For Charikar, see John Colpoys Haughton, Char-ee-kar and Service there with the 4th Goorkha Regiment (London, 1879).

27 Lal, Life of the Amir, vol. II, p. 416.

28 Ibid., pp. 393–9.

29 Ibid., p. 407.

30 Quoted in Lady Florentine Sale, A Journal of the Disasters in Affghanistan, 1841–2 [1843] (Lahore, 1999), p. 170.

31 Kaye, History, vol. II, p. 281. In subsequent editions of Kaye's history, large sections of Macnaghten's report and other private papers were culled, see ibid. (Delhi, 1999), pp. 128–9.

32 Ibid.

33 Mackenzie, Storms and Sunshine of a Soldier's Life, vol. I, p. 241.

34 Lal, Life of the Amir, vol. II, p. 421.

35 The account of Macnaghten's assassination is taken from Mackenzie's eyewitness account, see Mackenzie, Storms and Sunshine of a Soldier's Life, vol. I, pp. 238–49.

36 For events after the British withdrawal, see Lal, Life of the Amir, vol. II, pp. 436–53; Yapp, 'Revolutions of 1841–2', pp. 350–64.

37 Lt Vincent Eyre, *The Military Operations at Cabul* [1843] (Stroud, Glos., 2005), p. 310.

38 See Lt G. A. Croly's sketch, 'Khoord Caubel Pass, 1842', National Army Museum, London, NAM-1966-10-19-1.

39 Charles Rathbone Low, *Life and Correspondence of Field Marshal Sir George Pollock* [1873] (Uckfield, 2000?), p. 389.

40 Lal, *Life of the Amir*, vol. II, p. 452.

41 Atkinson, *Expedition into Affghanistan*, pp. 273–4.

42 See Lt G. A. Croly's sketch 'The Sacking of the Great Bazaar of Cabul, 1842', National Army Museum, London, NAM-1966-10-15-1; Atkinson, *Sketches in Afghanistan* (London, 1842), plate 19; Reginald C. W. Mitford, *To Cabul with the Cavalry Brigade* (London, 1880), p. 89. The painting by 'Abd al-Ghafur Breshna entitled *The Char-Chatta Bazaar of Kabul* was composed in 1932.

43 Maulana Hamid Kashmiri, *Akbar Nāma* (Kabul, 1330 s./1951). Sections of his history are quoted in William Dalrymple, *Return of a King: The Battle for Afghanistan* (London, New Delhi and New York, 2013); see also Lutz Rzehak, 'Remembering the Taliban', in *The Taliban and the Crisis of Afghanistan*, ed. Robert D. Crews and Amin Tarzi (Cambridge, MA, and London, 2008), p. 205.

44 Yapp, *Strategies of British India*, p. 453.

45 J. A. Morris, *The First Afghan War, 1838–1842* (Cambridge, 1967), p. 418.

46 Norris, *First Afghan War*, pp. 387–8.

47 Kaye, *History*, vol. II, p. 647.

48 *Afghanistan (Expenses of Military Operations) – Resolution*, 9 December 1878, hansard.millbanksystems.com.

49 Yapp, *Strategies of British India*, p. 445.

7 The Pursuit of 'Scientific Frontiers', 1843–79

1 Christine Noelle, *State and Tribe in Nineteenth-century Afghanistan: The Reign of Dost Muhammad Khan (1826–1863)* (Abingdon, 1977), pp. 198–205.

2 For the campaigns in Balkh, see Jonathan L. Lee, *The 'Ancient Supremacy': Bukhara, Afghanistan and the Battle for Balkh, 1732–1901* (Leiden, Cologne and New York, 1996).

3 Ibid., pp. 451–2.

4 Futteh Muhammad Khan, 'Narrative of a Journey through Toorkistan, 1855', British Library (BL), Asia and Africa Collection: India Office Library and Records (IOR), *Secret Correspondence and Enclosures with India, 1756–1874*, L/P&S/5/225, no. 59, encl. 11.

5 'Minute by Lord Dalhousie', 14 January 1856, IOR, L/P&S/5/2263, fol. 625; Lee, *The 'Ancient Supremacy'*, pp. 244–5.

6 Major H. B. Lumsden, *The Mission to Kandahar* (Calcutta, 1860).

7 Lee, *The 'Ancient Supremacy'*, p. 270.

8 Charles Allen, *Soldier Sahibs: The Men who made the North-west Frontier*, 2nd edn (London, 2000), pp. 281–2.

9 David Charles Champagne, 'The Afghan-Iranian Conflict over Herat

Province and European Intervention, 1796–1863: A Reinterpretation,
PhD thesis, University of Texas, 1981, fols 431–5, 488.

10 Lee, *The 'Ancient Supremacy'*, p. 312, where I incorrectly locate the battle site
near Khinjan.

11 Ibid., pp. 313–31; Sultan Mahomed Khan, *Life of Abdur Rahman Khan* [1901]
(Karachi, 1980), vol. I, pp. 91–7.

12 Sir Henry Rawlinson, 'Memorandum on the Frontier of Affghanistan',
20 July 1868; *Umballa Papers*, 2 vols, IOR, *Political and Secret Department
Library*, L/P&S/20/B17/A; George Douglas Hamilton Campbell, Duke of
Argyll, *The Afghan Question from 1841–1878* (London, 1879), pp. 26–9.

13 Rawlinson, 'Memorandum'.

14 Argyll, *Afghan Question*, pp. 40–41.

15 Ibid., p. 42.

16 Faiz Muhammad Katib, *Serāj al-Tawārīkh* (Kabul, 1331–33 s./1913–15), vol. II,
p. 307.

17 Nikki R. Keddie, *Sayyid Jamal al-Din al-Afghani: A Political Biography*
(Edinburgh, 1985). Afghan nationalists erroneously claim al-Afghani
was born in Asadabad in Kunar. He died in Turkey, but in 1944 his body
was exhumed and reinterred outside Kabul University and a monument
constructed over the grave.

18 Ibid., p. 41.

19 Argyll, *Afghan Question*, p. 5.

20 Ibid., p. 36.

21 Edward C. Moulton, *Lord Northbrook's Indian Administration, 1872–1876*
(London, 1968), p. 227.

22 See Katib, *Sarāj al-Tawārīkh*, vol. II, pp. 314–17. This official history was
written nearly fifty years after the Umballa Conference and reflects an
emerging, anti-British nationalist discourse in relation to this event and
the build-up to the Second Anglo-Afghan War.

23 Moulton, *Lord Northbrook's Indian Administration*, pp. 230–31.

24 Argyll, *Afghan Question*, p. 7.

25 Moulton, *Lord Northbrook's Indian Administration*, p. 234.

26 Ibid., p. 241.

27 Ibid., p. 241.

28 Ibid., pp. 243–4.

29 Ibid., p. 246.

30 Ibid., p. 247.

31 Lady Betty Balfour, *The History of Lord Lytton's Indian Administration, 1876
to 1880: Compiled from Letters and Official Papers* (London, New York and
Bombay, 1899), p. 44.

32 John Martineau, *The Life and Correspondence of Sir Bartle Frere* (London,
1895), vol. II, pp. 147.

33 Ibid., p. 148.

34 Balfour, *History of Lord Lytton*, pp. 45, 88–93.

35 G. R. Elsmie, *Thirty-five Years in the Punjab, 1858–1893* [1908]
(Lahore, 2001), pp. 234–5.

36 Balfour, *History of Lord Lytton*, pp. 60, 244.

37 Ibid., pp. 31–3.

38 Ibid., p. 60.

39 Ibid., pp. 61–3.

40 Ibid., p. 105.

41 Quoted in Vartan Gregorian, *The Emergence of Modern Afghanistan: Politics of Reform and Modernization, 1880–1946* (Stanford, CA, 1969), p. 112.

42 Balfour, *History of Lord Lytton*, p. 154.

43 See ibid., pp. 136–54, for Lytton's memorandum on Afghanistan and quotations from it.

44 Ibid., p. 147.

45 Ibid., pp. 152–3.

46 Dwight E. Lee, 'A Turkish Mission to Afghanistan, 1877', *Journal of Modern History*, XIII/3 (1941), pp. 335–56; S. Tanvir Wasti, 'The 1877 Ottoman Mission to Afghanistan', *Middle Eastern Studies*, XXX/4 (1994), pp. 956–62.

47 Gregorian, *Emergence of Modern Afghanistan*, p. 113.

48 Charles Marvin, trans., *Colonel Grodekoff's Ride from Samarcand to Herat* (London, 1880).

49 Balfour, *History of Lord Lytton*, p. 265.

50 Ibid., pp. 292–4.

51 Katib, *Sarāj al-Tawārīkh*, vol. II, p. 342.

52 *Punch*, 30 November 1878; *The Times*, 21 November 1878.

53 For example, Muhammad Hassan Kakar, *A Political and Diplomatic History of Afghanistan, 1863–1901* (Leiden, 2006), pp. 15–20.

8 'Reducing the Disorderly People', 1879–1901

1 'Accessories to a crime', in B. Robson, ed., *Roberts in India: The Military Papers of Field Marshal Lord Roberts, 1876–1893* (Stroud, Glos., and Dover, NH, 1993), p. 120.

2 Lady Betty Balfour, *The History of Lord Lytton's Indian Administration, 1876 to 1880: Compiled from Letters and Official Papers* (London, New York and Bombay, 1899), pp. 330–34.

3 William Trousdale, ed., *War in Afghanistan, 1879–80: The Personal Diary of Major General Sir Charles Metcalfe MacGregor* (Detroit, MI, 1985), p. 104. For views of the British Residency, see C. W. Woodburn, *The Bala Hissar of Kabul: Revealing a Fortress-palace in Afghanistan* (Chatham, 2009), figs 35–41, pp. 28–30.

4 Balfour, *History of Lord Lytton*, pp. 344, 348.

5 Ibid., p. 349.

6 Faiz Muhammad Katib, *Serāj al-Tawārīkh* (Kabul, 1331–3 s./1913–15), vol. II, p. 351.

7 Balfour, *History of Lord Lytton*, p. 354.

8 Afghan and Indian accounts on the Residency siege include those by 'Ali Hasan Jawanshir, Sardar Kajir Khan, a son of Payinda Khan, and 'Timoos', one of the few Guides to survive the massacre; for sources, see Jonathan L. Lee, *The 'Ancient Supremacy': Bukhara, Afghanistan and the Battle for Balkh, 1732–1901* (Leiden, Cologne and New York, 1996), p. 385, n. 114. For

other accounts, see Demetrius C. Boulger, *India in the Nineteenth Century* (London, 1901), p. 283; Archibald Forbes, *The Afghan Wars, 1839–1842 and 1878–80* (London, 1892), pp. 184–6; Howard Hensman, *The Afghan War of 1879–1880* [1881] (Lahore, 1999), pp. 3–4, 112; Sultan Mahomed Khan, *The Life of Abdur Rahman Amir of Afghanistan* [1900] (Karachi, Oxford and New York, 1980), vol. I, p. 152.

9 Balfour, *History of Lord Lytton*, pp. 358–9.

10 For 'Aisha's conspiracy, see, Katib, *Serāj al-Tawārīkh*, vol. II, pp. 352–4; Khan, *Life of Abdur Rahman*, vol. I, p. 152; Boulger, *India in the Nineteenth Century*, p. 283; Hensman, *Afghan War of 1879–1880*, p. 112.

11 Robson, ed., *Roberts in India*, pp. 119–21; the emphases are Lytton's.

12 Trousdale, ed., *War in Afghanistan*, p. 101.

13 Robson, ed., *Roberts in India*, p. 157.

14 Ibid., p. 145.

15 John Alfred Gray, *My Residence at the Court of the Amir* [1895] (London, 1987), p. 209.

16 Balfour, *History of Lord Lytton*, p. 408.

17 Sultan Muhammad Khan, *The Life of Abdur Rahman*, p. 192.

18 Balfour, *History of Lord Lytton*, p. 414.

19 M. Hassan Kakar, *Afghanistan: A Study in International Political Developments, 1880–1896* (Kabul, 1971), p. 56.

20 Ibid., pp. 63–4, n. 1.

21 For the Amir's reply to Landsdowne's letter, see Lee, *The 'Ancient Supremacy'*, appendix ix, p. 648.

22 Frank A. Martin, *Under the Absolute Amir* [1907] (Lahore, 1998), p. 102.

23 Angus Hamilton, *Afghanistan* (Boston, MA, and Tokyo, 1910), p. 227.

24 Government of India, *Records of the Intelligence Party of the Afghan Boundary Commission*, 5 vols (Simla, 1888–91).

25 See Lee, *The 'Ancient Supremacy'*, pp. 480–529.

26 For the Amir's illness, see Jonathan Lee, 'Abd al-Rahman Khan and the "Maraz ul-mulūk"', *Journal of the Royal Asiatic Society*, 3rd ser., I/2 (July 1991), pp. 209–42.

27 For the Turkistan Atrocities, see Lee, *The 'Ancient Supremacy'*, pp. 543–77, Appendix IX, pp. 637–44, where the Kabul *wakil*'s, Warburton's and Griesbach's reports are reproduced.

28 Carl Ludolph Griesbach, 'Memorandum of the Disposal of the Turkistan Prisoners by the Amir', 13 August 1889, British Library (BL), Africa and Asia Collection: India Office Library and Records (IOR), *Political and Secret Letters from India*, 1889, L/P&S/7/48, fols 327–52.

29 General Sir Fredrick Roberts, 'Memorandum', 22 May 1885, IOR, *Political and Secret Letters from India*, L/P&S/7/64, fol. 30 (p. 14); Lee, *The 'Ancient Supremacy'*, pp. 466–7.

30 See, for example, Khan, *Life of Abdur Rahman*, vol. I, p. 272; vol. II, pp. 252–7.

31 For Landsdowne's letter to the Amir, see Lee, *The 'Ancient Supremacy'*, Appendix IX, pp. 644–5.

32 For the Amer's reply to Landsdowne's letter, see ibid., Appendix IX, pp. 645–7.

33 Ibid., pp. 570–71.

34 For the Hazara Wars, see Sayed Askar Mousavi, *The Hazaras of Afghanistan: An Historical, Cultural, Economic and Political Study* (Richmond, Surrey, 1998), pp. 111–31; Lilias Hamilton, *A Vizier's Daughter: Tales of the Hazara Wars* (London, 1900), a novel about the repressions based on Hamilton's experience living in Afghanistan at the time; Husain 'Ali Yazdani, *Sahnahā-yi Khunīnī az Tārikh-i Tashayyu' dar Afghānistān az 1250 ta 1320* (Mashhad, 1991).

35 Ludwig W. Adamec, *Historical Dictionary of Afghanistan* (Metuchen, NJ, and London, 1991), p. 9.

36 The Shah of Persia's letter quoted in Lee, *The 'Ancient Supremacy'*, pp. 581–2.

37 M. Hassan Kakar, *A Political and Diplomatic History of Afghanistan, 1863–1901* (Leiden, 2006), pp. 177–92.

38 See ibid., pp. 178–83, for the controversy surrounding the Durand Agreement and frontier. See also Kakar, *Afghanistan: A Study*, pp. 110–13; Louis Dupree, *Afghanistan*, 2nd edn (Princeton, NJ, 1978), pp. 426–8; J.R.V. Prescott, *Map of Mainland Asia by Treaty* (Melbourne, 1975), pp. 177–211; Prescott's chapter includes copies of the treaty and related official correspondence.

39 See Ahmad Shayeq Qaseem, 'Pak-Afghan Relations: The Durand Line Issue', *Institute of Policy Studies, Special Issue on Afghanistan*, 2008, www.ips.org.pk.

40 Khan, *Life of Abdur Rahman Khan*, vol. II, p. 164.

41 Ibid., p. 212.

42 However, in May 2016 the Iranian, Afghan and Indian governments signed a tripartite agreement that gave Afghanistan transit rights to the Iranian port of Chabahar in the Gulf of Oman.

43 For the text of Anglo-Afghan Agreement, 12 November 1893, see Prescott, *Map of Mainland Asia*, pp. 187–8.

44 For the Kafirs, see, George Scott Robertson, *The Kafirs of the Hindu Kush* [1896] (Lahore, 1995); Max Klimberg, *The Kafirs of the Hindu Kush: Art and Society of the Waigal and Ashkun Kafirs*, 2 vols (Wiesbaden, 1999).

45 Surgeon-Major A. Heahy, 'Confidential Medical Note on Shahzada Nasrullah Khan and his followers whilst in England', 17 October 1895, BL, IOR, *Political and Secret Letters from India*, L/P&S/7/84.

46 Khan, *Life of Abdur Rahman Khan*, vol. II, pp. 163.

47 Ibid.; Amir 'Abd al-Rahman Khan, *Tāj al-Tawārīkh*, 2 vols (Kabul, 1900).

48 See May Schinasi, *Kaboul, 1773–1948* (Naples, 2008), pp. 71–102; trans. as *Kabul: A History, 1773–1948* (Leiden, 2016), pp. 56–88.

9 Reform and Repression, 1901–19

1 Marjorie Jewett Bell, ed., *An American Engineer in Afghanistan* [1948] (Kabul, 2004), p. 222.

2 For the Tarzis, see Mahmud Tarzi, *Reminiscences: A Short History of an Era (1869–1881)*, trans. and ed. Wahid Tarzi (New York, 1988); May Schinasi, *Afghanistan at the Beginning of the Twentieth Century: Nationalism and*

Journalism in Afghanistan, a Study of the Serâj ul-akhbâr (1911–1918)
(Naples, 1979).

3 For al-Afghani, see Nikki R. Keddie, *Sayyid Jamāl ad-Dīn al-Afghānī:
A Political Biography* (Berkeley, CA, and Los Angeles, 1972).

4 See Mohammad Masoom Kotak, 'Afghan Shahghasis', trans. Zaki Hotak,
2008, www. hotakonline.com, accessed 18 October 2017.

5 Nile Green, 'The Trans-border Traffic of Afghan Modernism: Afghanistan
and the Indian "Urdusphere"', *Comparative Studies in Society and History*,
LIII/3 (July 2011), pp. 479–508.

6 Christopher M. Wyatt, *Afghanistan and the Defence of Empire*
(London and New York, 2011), p. 43.

7 For Dobbs and Dane mission, see ibid.

8 Ernest Thornton and Annie Thornton, *Leaves from an Afghan Scrapbook*
(London, 1910).

9 Dorothe Sommer, *Freemasonry in the Ottoman Empire: A History of the
Fraternity and its Influence in Syria and the Levant* (London and New York,
2015).

10 Bell, *An American Engineer*, p. 257.

11 Dr Abdul Ghani, *A Review of the Political Situation in Central Asia* [1921]
(Lahore, 1980), p. 37. For the Mashruta Conspiracy, see also Senzil Nawid,
*Religious Response to Social Change in Afghanistan, 1919–29: King Aman-
Allah and the Afghan Ulama* (Costa Mesa, CA, 1999), pp. 36–7; Ghulam
Haidar Hakim, *An Appeal to the Muslim Brethren of the Punjab and India*
(Lahore, 1914); S. Fida Yunus, *Afghanistan: A Political History*, vol. I: *The
Afghans and the Rise and Fall of the Afghan Dynasties and Rulers* (Peshawar,
2006), pp. 479–95.

12 Followers of the Jam'iyat-i Sir-i Milli also referred to themselves as Jan
Nisaran-i Millat, Devotees, literally Life Scatterers, of the Nation. It is
unclear exactly what the relationship was between these various factions.

13 For a list of those implicated in the Mashruta Conspiracy, see Yunus,
Afghanistan, vol. I, pp. 481–3.

14 James M. Caron, 'Cultural Histories of Pasthun Nationalism, Public
Participation, and Social Inequality in Monarchic Afghanistan, 1905–1960',
PhD thesis, University of Pennsylvania, 2011, January 2009, fols 22–46.

15 Ursula Sims-Williams, 'The Afghan Newspaper "Sirāj al-Akhbār"', *British
Society for Middle Eastern Studies*, VII/2 (1980), pp. 118–22.

16 For British correspondence on the Mashruta Conspiracy, see Kew, National
Archives (NA), FO 371–782, fols 191–224.

17 Sayyid Iftikhar-ud-din Fakir, 'Final Report by the Late British Agent
at Kabul, 1907–1910', 19 September 1910, NA, FO 371–1213, p. 35.

18 Afzal Nasiri and Marie Khalili, eds, *Memoirs of Khalilullah Khalili:
An Afghan Philosopher Poet* ([Woodbridge, VA], 2013), pp. 16–18.

19 Bell, *An American Engineer*, p. 215.

20 Ibid., p. 228.

21 For the *Seraj al-Akhbar*, see Schinasi, *Afghanistan at the Beginning of
the Twentieth Century*; Sims-Williams, 'The Afghan Newspaper "Sirāj
al-Akhbār"'.

22 Romila Thapar, 'The Theory of Aryan Race and India: History and Politics',
   Social Scientist, XXIV/1–3 (1996), pp. 3–29.

23 For the Pushtunistan Manifesto, see Paul S. Jones, *Afghanistan Venture*
   (San Antonio, TX, 1956), pp. 433–41.

24 Schinasi, *Afghanistan at the Beginning of the Twentieth Century*, p. 219;
   Vartan Gregorian, *The Emergence of Modern Afghanistan: Politics of Reform
   and Modernization, 1880–1946* (Stanford, CA, 1969), p. 182.

25 Sims-Williams, 'The Afghan Newspaper "Sirāj al-Akhbār"', pp. 120–21.

26 Ludwig W. Adamec, *Afghanistan's Foreign Affairs to the Mid-twentieth
   Century* (Tucson, AZ, 1974), pp. 27–41; Werner Otto von Hentig, *Meine
   Diplomatenfahrt ins verschlossene Land* (Berlin, 1918).

27 Oskar von Niedermayer, *Afghanistan* (Leipzig, 1924); Emil Rybitschka,
   Im gottgegebenen Afghanistan als Gäste des Emirs (Leipzig, 1927).

10 Dreams Melted into Air, 1919–29

The title of this chapter is suggested by Prospero's words in William
Shakespeare, *The Tempest*, Act IV, scene I.

1 Leon B. Poullada, *Reform and Rebellion in Afghanistan, 1919–1929*
   (Ithaca, NY, 1973), p. 121.

2 See Anne Baker and Sir Ronald Ivelaw-Chapman, *Wings over Kabul:
   The First Airlift* (London, 1975), p. 43.

3 Afzal Nasiri and Marie Khalili, *Memoirs of Khalilullah Khalili: An Afghan
   Philosopher Poet* (Manassas, VA, 2013), p. 27; Fayz Muhammad Katib, *Kabul
   under Siege: Fayz Muhammad's Account of the 1929 Uprising*, trans. and ed.
   R. D. McChesney (Princeton, NJ, 1999), p. 92.

4 Nasiri and Khalili, *Memoirs of Khalilullah*, pp. 23–4.

5 'Amir Amanullah Khan to His Excellency the Viceroy', 3 March 1919, in
   Afghanistan Strategic Intelligence, 1919–1970, ed. A. Burdett (Cambridge,
   2008), vol. I, pp. 91–3.

6 Amir Habib Allah Khan's letter quoted in P. Sykes, *A History of Afghanistan*
   [1940] (New Delhi, 1981), vol. II, p. 265.

7 Ibid., p. 268.

8 W. K. Fraser-Tytler, *Afghanistan: A Study of Political Developments in
   Central and Southern Asia*, 3rd edn (Oxford, 1967), p. 196.

9 General Staff of India, *The Third Afghan War 1919, Official Account* [1926]
   (Uckfield, n.d.), pp. 16–22.

10 'Diary of the N.W. Frontier Province Intelligence Bureau', week ending
   2 March 1922, in *Afghanistan Strategic Intelligence*, vol. I, p. 342.

11 Ludwig W. Adamec, *Afghanistan, 1900–1923: A Diplomatic History*
   (Berkeley, CA, 1967), pp. 113–14.

12 Sardar Shah Wali Khan, *My Memoirs* (Kabul, 1970), pp. 7–26.

13 Personal communications from various Afghans.

14 Khan, *My Memoirs*, pp. 23–6; Vartan Gregorian, *The Emergence of Modern
   Afghanistan: Politics of Reform and Modernization, 1880–1946* (Stanford, CA,
   1969), p. 230.

15 General Staff of India, *Third Afghan War*, p. 128.

16 G. N. Molesworth, *Afghanistan, 1919: An Account of Operations in the Third Afghan War* (Bombay and New York, 1962), p. vii.

17 For the negotiations following the Third Anglo-Afghan War, see Adamec, *Afghanistan, 1900–1923*, pp. 118–66.

18 Grant to Foreign Secretary of India, 4 August 1919, Kew, National Archives (NA), FO 371–3991, fols 128–9.

19 Chelmsford's dispatch quoted in Adamec, *Afghanistan, 1900–1923*, p. 129.

20 For Sir Hamilton Grant's letter see Sykes, *A History of Afghanistan*, vol. II, Appendix F, p. 359.

21 Viceroy to Grant, 5 August 1919, NA, CAB 24–86, fol. 501.

22 Adamec, *Afghanistan, 1900–1923*, pp. 163–4.

23 Ibid., p. 154.

24 Ibid., pp. 155–6.

25 Lenin's letter to the Amir quoted in Fazal-ur-Rahman, *The Basmachi Movement in Soviet Central Asia* (Peshawar, 1985), p. 131.

26 Ibid., p. 95; H. B. Paksoy, '"Basmachi": Turkistan National Liberation Movement, 1916–1930s', in *Modern Encyclopedia of Religions in Russia and the Soviet Union* (Gulf Breeze, FL, 1991), vol. IV, pp. 5–20; available at http://vlib.iue.it, accessed 20 October 2017.

27 Poullada, *Reform and Rebellion in Afghanistan*, p. 226.

28 Adeeb Khalid, *The Politics of Muslim Cultural Reform: Jadidism in Central Asia* (Berkeley, CA, 1998). *Jadid* in Persian means 'new', 'modern'.

29 Senzil Nawid, *Religious Response to Social Change in Afghanistan, 1919–29: King Aman-Allah and the Afghan Ulama* (Costa Mesa, CA, 1999), p. 71 and Appendix J (1).

30 Abdullaev Kamoludin, 'Central Asian Émigrés in Afghanistan: First Wave (1920–1931)', *Central Asia Monitor*, I/4–5 (1994); William S. Ritter, 'Revolt in the Mountains: Fuzail Maksum and the Occupation of Garm, Spring 1929', *Journal of Contemporary History*, XXV (1990), p. 551.

31 Sorab K. H. Katrak, *Through Amanullah's Afghanistan* (Karachi, 1929), p. 52.

32 Robert Byron, *The Road to Oxiana* [1937] (London, 2004), pp. 368–70.

33 Nancy Howland Washburne, ed., *The Afghan Diaries of Captain George Felix Howland, 1935–1936* (McKinney, TX, 2008), p. 105.

34 For the plans of Dar al-'Aman, see May Schinasi, *Kaboul, 1773–1948* (Naples, 2008).

35 That is, *Regulatory Decree of the Fundamental Laws of the Exalted State of Afghanistan*; see Nawid, *Religious Response to Social Change*, p. 79. Poullada, *Reform and Rebellion*, pp. 70–79, 93, 99.

36 Quoted in Nawid, *Religious Response to Social Change*, pp. 80–81.

37 Lilian A. Starr, *Tales of Tirah and Lesser Tibet* (London, 1923), pp. 163–247.

38 For the Loya Jirga, see Nawid, *Religious Response to Social Change*, pp. 106–13.

39 Ibid., p. 109.

40 May Schinasi, 'Italie-Afghanistan, 1921–1941, part 2: De l'affaire Piperno à l'évacuation de 1929', *Annali, Istituto Universitario Orientale di Napoli*, L/2 (1990), pp. 177–216.

41 Emil Trinkler, *Through the Heart of Afghanistan* (London, 1928), pp. 202–4.

42 Quoted in Gregorian, *Emergence of Modern Afghanistan*, p. 256.

43 The Amir was out of the country from December 1927 to July 1928.

44 Ludwig W. Adamec, *Afghanistan's Foreign Affairs to the Mid-twentieth Century* (Tucson, AZ, 1974), p. 119.

45 Ibid., p. 127.

46 Roland Wild, *Amanullah, ex-King of Afghanistan* (London, 1932), p. 167.

47 Ibid., p. 100.

48 Quoted in Poullada, *Reform and Rebellion in Afghanistan*, p. 169.

49 Nawid, *Religious Response to Social Change*, p. 149.

50 Quoted in Gregorian, *Emergence of Modern Afghanistan*, p. 259.

51 According to a secret file in the Peshawar Record Office, British officials gifted Nur al-Mashayekh land and a shop in Peshawar 'as a very special case' and 'under very secret policy'. The report notes that 'in view of our relations . . . it is desirable that Hazrat Nurul Mashaiikh (*sic*) should be treated with special consideration', *Memorandum*, 6 and 23 March 1953; Political Secretary to HE the Governor NWFP to Scrtry to Govt. of Pakistan, Ministry of Foreign Affairs and C.W. Relations, Karachi, 11 April 1953, B Proceedings, Foreign Punjab Govt., Civil Secretariat NWFP (Home Medical), Previous Deptt. F.F. Political Civil Secretariat NWFP, Grant of Land to Hazrat of Shor Bazaar in Peshawar, S(eries) no. 1795, bundle 65 (1950).

52 Asta Olesen, *Islam and Politics in Afghanistan* (Richmond, Surrey, 1996), pp. 147–8. According to Katib, *Kabul under Siege*, p. 115, Qazi 'Abd al-Rahman was not executed until after the fall of 'Aman Allah Khan.

53 Olesen, *Islam and Politics*, pp. 150–53.

54 *Saqau* is the Dari colloquial form of *saqab*. Bacha-yi Saqau was the disparaging title used by his royalist enemies after 1930, for water carriers were at the bottom of the social ladder. Habib Allah Kalakani's relatives, however, claim he inherited this title from his father, who carried water to Afghan troops in the Second Anglo-Afghan War.

55 See Nawid, *Religious Response to Social Change*, p. 164; Katib, *Kabul under Siege*; Shah Agha Mujadidi, *Amīr Habīb Allāh* (Peshawar?, n.d.). The so-called autobiography of Bacha-yi Saqau, *My Life from Brigand to King* (London, 1936) is a fiction authored by Sardar Iqbal 'Ali Shah. For the India Office's extensive secret file on Ikbal Shah's activities see British Library, Africa and Asia Collection: India Office Library and Records, *Departmental Papers: Political and Secret Separate (Subject) Files, 1902–1931*, L/P&S/10/806.

56 Katib, *Kabul under Siege*, p. 34.

57 Nawid, *Religious Response to Social Change*, p. 165.

58 See Baker and Ivelaw-Chapman, *Wings over Kabul*.

59 Nadir Khan's declaration quoted in Gregorian, *Emergence of Modern Afghanistan*, p. 290.

60 Khan, *My Memoirs*, p. 47.

61 Humphrey's comment quoted in Adamec, *Afghanistan's Foreign Affairs*, p. 176.

62 Humphrey's report quoted in Baker and Ivelaw-Chapman, *Wings over Kabul*, p. 43.

63 A. E. Housman, 'Into my heart on air that kills', *A Shropshire Lad* (1896).
64 Mariam Ghani and Ashraf Ghani, 'Palace of Abandoned Dreams', in
    Afghanistan: A Lexicon, 100 Notes – 100 Thoughts (Berlin, 2012).

11 Backs to the Future, 1929–33

 1 Ben James, *The Secret Kingdom: An Afghan Journey* (New York, 1934),
    p. 276.
 2 For Katib's journal of his time under Amir Habib Allah Kalakani, see Faiz
    Muhammad Katib, *Kabul under Siege: Fayz Muhammad's Account of the
    1929 Uprising*, trans. and ed. R. D. McChesney (Princeton, NJ, 1999).
 3 James, *Secret Kingdom*, pp. 266–9; Khaled Siddiq Charkhi, *From
    My Memories: Memoirs of Political Imprisonment from Childhood in
    Afghanistan*, 2nd edn (Bloomington, IN, 2010), pp. 8–11; Percy Sykes,
    A History of Afghanistan [1940] (New Delhi, 1981), vol. II, pp. 321–2.
 4 In particular 'Ali Ikbal Shah's account in *My Life from Brigand to King*
    (London, 1936).
 5 See Katib, *Kabul under Siege*, p. 279; Charkhi, *From My Memories*, p. 10;
    Leon B. Poullada, *Reform and Rebellion in Afghanistan, 1919–1929* (Ithaca,
    NY, 1973), p. 195, citing a cable from the Viceroy to Secretary of State for
    India, 4 November 1919; Shah Wali Khan, *My Memoirs* (Kabul, 1970), p. 115;
    Sykes, *History of Afghanistan*, vol. II, pp. 321–2.
 6 Ludwig W. Adamec, *Afghanistan's Foreign Affairs to the Mid-twentieth
    Century* (Tucson, AZ, 1974), p. 183.
 7 Shah Wali Khan, *My Memoirs*, p. 115.
 8 Nancy Tapper, *Bartered Brides, Politics, Gender and Marriage in an Afghan
    Tribal Society* (Cambridge, 1991), p. 34.
 9 William S. Ritter, 'Revolt in the Mountains: Fuzail Maksum and the
    Occupation of Garm, Spring 1929', *Journal of Contemporary History*, XXV/4
    (1990), pp. 547–80.
10 William S. Ritter, 'The Final Phase in the Liquidation of Anti-Soviet
    Resistance in Tadzhikistan: Ibrahim Bek and the Basmachi, 1924–31', *Soviet
    Studies*, XXXVII/4 (1985), pp. 484–93.
11 Senzil Nawid, *Religious Response to Social Change in Afghanistan, 1919–29:
    King Aman-Allah and the Afghan Ulama* (Costa Mesa, CA, 1999), pp. 184–5.
12 That is, Enjoining Conformity to God's Law.
13 M. Nazif Shahrani, 'Local Knowledge of Islam and Social Discourse in
    Afghanistan and Turkistan in the Modern Period', in *Turko-Persia in
    Historical Perspective*, ed. Robert L. Canfield (Cambridge, 1991), pp. 170–88.
14 *Nejat* means salvation; *istiqlal* is independence.
15 Asta Olesen, *Islam and Politics in Afghanistan* (Richmond, Surrey, 1996),
    p. 181.
16 For Zabuli and the Afghan economy, see Vartan Gregorian, *The Emergence
    of Modern Afghanistan: Politics of Reform and Modernization, 1880–1946*
    (Stanford, CA, 1969), pp. 314–20, 361–70; Maxwell J. Fry, *The Afghan
    Economy* (Leiden, 1974); Sara Koplik, *A Political and Economic History
    of the Jews of Afghanistan* (Leiden, 2015), pp. 114–36.

17 Louis Dupree, *Afghanistan* (Princeton, NJ, 1978), pp. 471, 474.
18 See Koplik, *Political and Economic History*, chapters 4–6 in particular.
19 Jehanzeb Khalili, *Mujahideen Movement in Malakand and Mohmand Agencies (1900–1940)*, ed. M. Y. Effendi (Peshawar, 2000).
20 Charkhi, *From My Memories*, pp. 4–15.
21 Adamec, *Afghanistan's Foreign Affairs*, pp. 192–3.
22 Charkhi, *From My Memories*, p. 10.
23 W. K. Fraser-Tytler, *Afghanistan: A Study of Political Developments in Central and Southern Asia*, 3rd edn (Oxford, 1967), pp. 239–40.
24 Ibid., p. 241; Charkhi, *From My Memories*, pp. 1, 3, 15, has 26 November.
25 For Muhammad Gul Khan Mohmand, see James M. Caron, 'Cultural Histories of Pasthun Nationalism, Public Participation, and Social Inequality in Monarchic Afghanistan, 1905–1960', PhD thesis, University of Pennsylvania, 2009, fols 79–138; Thomas Ruttig, *Afghanistan's Early Reformists*, Afghan Analysts Network (Kabul, April 2011).
26 Caron, 'Cultural Histories of Pasthun Nationalism', fol. 105.
27 M. Gul Khan Mohmand's poem (in English translation) quoted ibid., fol. 88.
28 Translation of Riktin's interview with Sabir Shah Sabir, 1998, quoted ibid., fol. 88.
29 Edward Hunter, *The Past Present: An Account of Life in Afghanistan Today* (London, 1959), p. 345.
30 Charkhi, *From My Memories*, has 26 November.
31 Nancy Howland Washburne, *The Afghan Diaries of Captain George Felix Howland, 1935–1936* (McKinney, TX, 2008), pp. 43–4.
32 Fraser-Tytler, *Afghanistan*, p. 243; Ronald M. S. Morrison, 'H. M. Mohammad Nadir Shah-i Ghazi of Afghanistan', *Journal of the Royal Asiatic Society*, XXI/1 (1934), pp. 170–75; see also Sykes, *A History of Afghanistan*, vol. II, p. 328.

12 A House Divided, 1933–73

1 Nancy Howland Washburne, *The Afghan Diaries of Captain George Felix Howland, 1935–1936* (McKinney, TX, 2008), pp. 143–4.
2 Ernest F. Fox, *Travels in Afghanistan, 1937–1938* (New York, 1943).
3 Albert Herrlich, *Land des Lichtes: Deutsche Kundfahrt zu unbekannten Völkern im Hindukusch* (Munich, 1938).
4 See photograph in *Official Report of the XIth Olympic Games Berlin, 1936* (Berlin, 1973), vol. I, facing p. 547.
5 Milan Hauner, 'One Man against the Empire: The Fakir of Ipi and the British in Central Asia on the Eve of, and during, the Second World War', *Journal of Contemporary History*, XVI/1 (1981), pp. 183–212, available at www.khyber.org, accessed 24 October 2017.
6 W. K. Fraser-Tytler, *Afghanistan: A Study of Political Developments in Central and Southern Asia*, 3rd edn (Oxford, 1967), p. 267.
7 Afzal Nasiri and Marie Khalili, eds, *Memoirs of Khalilullah Khalili: An Afghan Philosopher Poet* (Manassas, VA, 2013), p. 223.

8 Ibid., pp. 230–32; 'Engert to U.S. Secretary of State', Kabul, 24 May 1943, in *United States Department of State, Foreign Relations of the United States Diplomatic Papers* (henceforth FRUS), 1943, vol. IV, 'Documents on South Asia', pp. 35–6, https://uwdc.library.wisc.edu.

9 Vartan Gregorian, *The Emergence of Modern Afghanistan: Politics of Reform and Modernization, 1880–1946* (Stanford, CA, 1969), pp. 346–7; Mohammad 'Ali, *A Cultural History of Afghanistan* (Kabul, 1964), chaps 2–3.

10 Rudolf Stuckert, *Errinerungen an Afghanistan 1940–1946: aus dem Tagebuch eines Schweizer Architekten* (Liestal, 1994). Stuckert did not approve of the widespread destruction and sketched some of the towns and fortifications that were destroyed.

11 Andrew Wilson, *North from Kabul* (London, 1961), p. 84; see also Robert Byron, *The Road to Oxiana* [1937] (London, 1981), p. 240.

12 Wilson, *North from Kabul*, p. 89; Rosita Forbes, *Forbidden Road: Kabul to Samarkand* (London, 1937), p. 113.

13 'Ali, *A Cultural History of Afghanistan*, pp. 19–20; Mohammad 'Ali, *A New Guide to Afghanistan*, 3rd edn (Kabul, 1959), pp. 224–5.

14 See Pierre Centlivres, *Un bazar d'Asie Centrale: Forme et organisation du bazar de Tâshqurghân (Afghanistan)* (Wiesbaden, 1972).

15 Personal observations and photographic archive; the gates of the Shibarghan citadel were reused in a local house.

16 'Engert to Secretary of State', Kabul, 27 January 1943, FRUS, 1943, vol. IV, p. 20.

17 See Shah Mahmood Miakhel, 'Human Security and the Rule of Law, Afghanistan's Experience', in *The Rule of Law in Afghanistan: Missing in Inaction*, ed. Whit Mason (Cambridge, 2011), pp. 84–96.

18 See 'Ghazi Mir Zaman Khan', www.zamanifamily.org.

19 Sayed Askar Mousavi, *The Hazaras of Afghanistan: An Historical, Cultural, Economic and Political Study* (Richmond, Surrey, 1998), p. 163.

20 'Discussion with Afghanistan Concerning Afghan Requests for Financial Assistance and Provision of Military Equipment, etc.', 7 January 1948, FRUS, 1948, vol. V/1, 'Documents on South Asia', pp. 492–4, https://uwdc.library.wisc.edu.

21 'Memorandum of Conversation by Mr. Richard S. Leach', 8 December 1948, FRUS, 1948, vol. V/1, pp. 491–2.

22 For the Helmand Valley scheme, see Mildred Caudill, *Helmand-Arghandab Valley: Yesterday, Today, Tomorrow* (Lashkargah, 1969); Nick Cullather, 'Damming Afghanistan: Modernization in a Buffer State', *Journal of American History*, LXXXIX/2 (2002), pp. 512–37; Louis Dupree, *Afghanistan*, 2nd edn (Princeton, NJ, 1978), pp. 499–507; Edward Hunter, *The Past Present: A Year in Afghanistan* (London, 1959), chaps 4–5; Aloys Arthur Michel, *The Kabul, Kunduz, and Helmand Valleys and the National Economy of Afghanistan* (Washington, DC, 1959), pp. 148–64; USGS/USAID, *Geology, Water, and Wind in the Lower Helmand Basin, Southern Afghanistan*, Scientific Investigation Report, 2006-5182.

23 Arnold J. Toynbee, *Between Oxus and Jumna* (Oxford, 1961), p. 67.

24 Tudor Engineering Company, *Report on the Development of the Helmand Valley, Afghanistan* (Washington, DC, 1956).

25 Donald N. Wilber, *Afghanistan: Its People, its Society, its Culture* (New Haven, CT, 1962), p. 239.

26 Amin Saikal, *Modern Afghanistan: A History of Struggle and Survival* (London and New York, 2004), p. 107.

27 Nasiri and Khalili, eds, *Memoirs of Khalilullah Khalili*, pp. 434–9.

28 See M. Halim Tanwir, *Afghanistan: History, Diplomacy and Journalism* (Bloomington, IN, 2012), vol. I, pp. 171–4; Dupree, *Afghanistan*, p. 495.

29 The date of the Balkhi coup is uncertain: Nasiri and Khalili, eds, *Memoirs of Khalilullah Khalili*, pp. 450–55, gives no date; Gilles Dorronsoro, *Revolution Unending: Afghanistan, 1979 to the Present* (New York, 2005), p. 55, n. 85, has 1946; Tanwir, *Afghanistan*, vol. I, pp. 174–5, implies it was in the autumn of 1951. I have followed Hafizullah Emadi, *Dynamics of Political Development in Afghanistan: The British, Russian, and American Invasions* (New York and London, 2010).

30 Daveen Gartenstein-Ross and Tara Vassefi, 'The Forgotten History of Afghanistan-Pakistan Relations', *Yale Journal of International Affairs*, VII/1 (2012), pp. 38–45, available at http://yalejournal.org, accessed 24 October 2017.

31 Arnold Fletcher, *Afghanistan: Highway of Conquest* (Ithaca, NY, 1965), p. 253.

32 Hasan Ali Shah Kafri, *Indo-Afghan Relations (1949–1962)* (New Delhi, 1976), p. 64, and Appendix I.

33 Hunter, *The Past Present*, p. 346.

34 The SEATO Treaty is also known as the Manila Pact, CENTO as the Baghdad Pact. For texts of these agreements, see *The Avalon Project: Documents in Law, History and Diplomacy*, http://avalon.law.yale.edu/, accessed 24 October 2017.

35 'Ward to Department of State, Afghan Agitation Regarding Pushtunistan', Kabul, 21 July 1953; 'Memorandum of Conversation by the Officer in Charge of Pakistan-Afghanistan Affairs (Thatcher)', Washington, DC, 18 September 1954, *FRUS*, 1952–1954, vol. XI/2, 'Africa and South Asia', nos 846, 859, https://history.state.gov.

36 'Ward to Department of State', Kabul, 2 December 1954, *FRUS*, 1952–1954, vol. XI/2, no. 874.

37 For the Soviet aide-memoire and the Afghan government response, see 'Horner to Department of State', Kabul, 9 September 1952 (2 telegrams), and 'Secretary of State to Embassy in Kabul', Washington, DC, 12 September 1952 and sequential correspondence, *FRUS* 1952–1954, vol. XI/2, nos 882–91. For the quote ending 'recent history', see 'The Charge d'Affairs (Horner) to the Department of State', 9 September 1952, FRUS, XI/2, no. 883.

38 Dupree, *Afghanistan*, p. 522.

39 Wilson, *North from Kabul*, p. 134.

40 M. Husain Kakar, *Afghanistan: The Soviet Invasion and the Afghan Response, 1979–1982* (Berkeley, CA, and London, 1995), p. 53.

41 'Revision of Constitution', *Kabul Times*, 1 April 1963, p. 2; 'Us and Democracy', *Kabul Times*, 2 April 1963, p. 3, http://digitalcommons. unomaha.edu.

42 For the text of the Constitution of 1964, see http://digitalcommons.unl.edu.

43 For a summary of Leftist parties in Afghanistan, see Thomas Ruttig, *Islamists, Leftists – and a Void in the Center: Afghanistan's Political Parties and Where They Come from (1902–2006)* (Konrad Adenauer Stiftung, 2006), available at www.kas.de, accessed 24 October 2017.

44 *Kabul Times*, 25–8 October 1965; Dupree, *Afghanistan*, pp. 590–97.

45 'Neumann to Assistant Secretary of State for Near and South Asian Affairs', Kabul, 29 December 1970, FRUS, 1969–1976, vol. E-7, 'Documents on South Asia', no. 337, https://history.state.gov.

46 Dupree, *Afghanistan*, p. 618.

47 'Memorandum of Conversation, The President's Conversation with Afghan Prime Minister Maiwandwal', Washington, DC, 28 March 1967, FRUS, 1964–1968, vol. XXV, 'Documents on South Asia', no. 539, https://history.state.gov.

48 'How the CIA Turns Foreign Students into Traitors', *Ramparts*, 5 (April 1967), pp. 22–4.

49 'Telegram from the Embassy in Afghanistan to Department of State', 28 April 1967, FRUS, 1964–1968, vol. XXV, no. 542.

50 Dupree, *Afghanistan*, p. 622.

51 'Intelligence Note', Washington, DC, 29 July 1971, FRUS, 1969–1976, vol. E-7, 'Documents on South Asia', no. 339, https://history.state.gov.

52 'Telegram from the Embassy in Afghanistan to the Department of State', 12 February 1972, FRUS, 1969–1976, vol. E-7, no. 355.

53 'Telegram from the Embassy in Afghanistan to Department of State', 3 March 1972, FRUS, 1969–1976, vol. E-7, no. 359.

54 Muhammad Khan Jalallar, *Rumi Tomato: Autobiography of an Afghan Minister*, ed. Babur Rashidzada (Create Space self-publishing, 2011).

55 'Embassy in Afghanistan to Department of State', 16 January 1973, FRUS, 1969–1976, vol. E-8, 'Documents on South Asia', no. 1, https://history.state.gov.

56 The IAM was later renamed International Assistance Mission.

57 NOOR is an acronym for the National Organization for Ophthalmic Rehabilitation. *Nur* is also the Persian word for light.

58 For the expulsions and the destruction of KCCC, see *Plus D Cables*, 1973, https://wikileaks.org.

59 'Meeting with President Da'ud', 23 July 1973, *Plus D Cables*, 1973.

13 Republicanism, Revolution and Resistance, 1973–94

1 President Najib Allah Khan's remarks quoted in Steve Coll, *Ghost Wars* (London, New York and Toronto, 2005), p. 235.

2 'Presidential Address, Republic Day Speech', *Kabul Times*, 10 July 1975, http://content.library.arizona.edu.

3 See 'Telegram, Embassy in Afghanistan to Department of State', 17 September 1973, *United States Department of State, Foreign Relations of the United States* (henceforth FRUS), 1969–1976, vol. E-8, 'Documents on South Asia', no. 8, https://history.state.gov.

4 Hafizullah Emadi, *Dynamics of Political Development in Afghanistan: The British, Russian, and American Invasions* (New York and London, 2010), p. 89.

5 'Kabul Embassy to State Department, Meeting with President Da'ud', 22 July 1973, *Plus D cables*, https://wikileaks.org.
6 'Presidential Address, Republic Day Speech', *Kabul Times*, 10 July 1975.
7 For Da'ud's fiscal manipulations, see Muhammad Khan Jalallar, *Rumi Tomato: Autobiography of an Afghan Minister*, ed. Babur Rashidzada (Create Space self-publishing, 2011), Chapter Eight.
8 'Evaluation of Da'ud's Government and Comments on Pushtunistan Policy', 29 August 1973; 'Republican Government after Three Months: an Assessment', 22 October 1973, *Plus D Cables*, https://wikileaks.org.
9 'Telegram, Embassy in Afghanistan to State Department', 17 September 1973; see also ibid., 17 and 30 July 1973, *FRUS*, 1969–1976, vol. E-8, nos 4, 5.
10 'Evaluation of Da'ud's Government', 29 August 1973.
11 'Audience with the Shah', 2 October 1973, *Plus D Cables*, https://wikileaks.org.
12 'Evaluation of Da'ud's Government', 29 August 1973.
13 'Pakistan-Afghanistan, Three Ways to Confrontation', 5 November 1973, *FRUS*, 1969–1976, vol. E-8, no. 9.
14 See 'Arrests of Prominent Civilian and Military Leaders and Rumors of Abortive Coup Attempt', 21 September 1973; 'Afghanistan: More on Alleged Coup Attempt', 24 September 1973, *Plus D Cables*, https://wikileaks.org; 'Death of Former Prime Minister Mohammad Hashim Maiwandal', 16 October 1973, *CIA (FOIA) Collection*, www.foia.cia.gov.
15 'Confessions of September Coup Plotters Broadcast on Radio Afghanistan', 7 December 1973, *Plus D Cables*, https://wikileaks.org.
16 See Dr M. Halim Tanwir, *Afghanistan: History, Diplomacy and Journalism* (Bloomington, IN, 2010), vol. I, pp. 253–8.
17 'Reactions to the Panjsher Clash', 1 August 1975, *Plus D Cables*, https://wikileaks.org.
18 'Memorandum of Conversation', 1 July 1976, *FRUS*, 1969–1976, vol. E-8, no. 26.
19 Jalallar, *Rumi Tomato*, p. 148.
20 'Year-end Afghan External Assessment', 13 December 1975, *Plus D Cables*, https://wikileaks.org.
21 'Afghanistan has no other wish but friendship, brotherhood with Pak Nation', *Kabul Times*, 12 June 1976.
22 'Embassy in Afghanistan to Department of State', 19 June 1976, *FRUS*, 1969–1979, vol. E-8, no. 22.
23 Jalallar, *Rumi Tomato*, p. 174.
24 For English text of the 1977 Constitution, see http://afghantranslation.checchiconsulting.com, accessed 27 October 2017.
25 'Eliot to Secretary of State', 13 April 1977, *Plus D Cables*, https://wikileaks.org
26 'President Da'ud's Speech', *Kabul Times*, 14 April 1977.
27 Jalallar, *Rumi Tomato*, p. 185.
28 Abdul Samad Ghaus, *The Fall of Afghanistan: An Insider's Account* (Washington, DC, 1988), pp. 179–80.
29 Tanwir, *Afghanistan*, vol. I, p. 267.
30 *Kabul Times*, 4 May 1978.

31 AGSA stands for the Pushtu, *Da Afghanistan da Gato de Satalo Adara*,
    the Afghanistan Interests Protection Service; KHAD is the acronym for
    Khidmat-i Etla'at-i Daulati, State Intelligence Service.
32 David B. Edwards, *Before Taliban: Genealogies of the Afghan Jihad*
    (Berkeley, CA, 2002), pp. 32–45.
33 Afghanistan Justice Project, *Casting Shadows: War Crimes and Crimes
    against Humanity, 1978–2001* (Kabul, 2006), http://afghanistanjusticeproject.
    org; Kate Cark, 'Death List Published: Families of Disappeared End a
    30 Year Wait for News', 26 September 2013, Afghan Analysts Network,
    www.afghanistan-analysts.org.
34 Chris Sibilla, 'The Assassination of Ambassador Spike Dubs – Kabul, 1979',
    Moments in U.S. Diplomatic History, Association for Diplomatic Studies and
    Training, http://adst.org.
35 M. Hassan Kakar, *Afghanistan: The Soviet Invasion and the Afghan Response,
    1979–1982* (Berkeley, CA, and London, 1995), pp. 321–6.
36 Alexander A. Lyakhovskiy, 'Inside the Soviet Invasion of Afghanistan and
    the Seizure of Kabul, December 1979', trans. Gary Goldberg and Artemy
    Kalinovsky, in *Cold War International History Project,* Working Paper 51,
    January 2007, p. 17, www.wilsoncenter.org.
37 Coll, *Ghost Wars*, pp. 47–8.
38 Lyakhovskiy, 'Inside the Soviet Invasion', p. 13.
39 Ibid.
40 *Kabul Times*, 1 January 1979, http://digitalcommons.unl.edu.
41 Kakar, *Afghanistan: The Soviet Invasion*, pp. 110–23.
42 'Message from the President's Deputy Assistant for National Security Affairs
    (Aaron) to President Carter', 24 December 1979, FRUS, 1977–1980, vol. VI,
    no. 243, 'Soviet Union'.
43 For a summary of President Carter's hotline call to Leonid Brezhnev and
    his reply on 29 December 1979, see FRUS, 1977–1980, vol. VI, no. 248,
    'Editor's Note'.
44 'Summary of Conclusions of a Special Coordinating Committee Meeting',
    26 December 1979, FRUS, 1977–1980, vol. VI, no. 245.
45 Coll, *Ghost Wars*, p. 55.
46 Alfred Thayer Mahan, *The Problem of Asia and Its Effect upon International
    Policies* (Boston, MA, 1900).
47 Coll, *Ghost Wars*, p. 151; Joe Stark, 'The CIA in Afghanistan: "The Good
    War"', *Middle East Report*, 141 (July–August 1986), pp. 12–13.
48 Leon B. Poullada, 'The Failure of American Diplomacy in Afghanistan',
    World Affairs, CXLV/3 (1982/3), pp. 230–52.
49 Personal conversations with Afghan refugees in Peshawar.
50 Sayyid Qutb, 'The Scale of Human Values' (1951), in *America in an Arab
    Mirror: Images of America in Arabic Travel Literature, an Anthology, 1895–
    1995*, ed. Kamal Abel-Malek (New York, 2000), pp. 9–28.
51 Rafael Reuveny and Aseem Prakah, 'The Afghanistan War and the
    Breakdown of the Soviet Union', *Review of International Studies*, XXV (1999),
    pp. 693–708.
52 Svetlana Alexevich, *Zinky Boys: Soviet Voices from a Forgotten War,*

trans. Julia and Robin Whitby (London, 1992); Oleg Yermakov, *Afghan Tales: Stories from Russia's Vietnam*, trans. Marc Romano (New York, 1993).

53 Brian G. Williams, *The Last Warlord: The Life and Legend of Dostum, the Afghan Warrior who Led the u.s. Special Forces to Topple the Taliban Regime* (Chicago, IL, 2013).

54 From text of the decree in the author's personal archive.

55 United Nations Office on Drugs and Crime, *The Opium Economy in Afghanistan: An International Problem* (New York, 2003).

14 Between the Dragon and his Wrath, 1994–2017

The title of this chapter comes from Lear's warning to Kent, 'Come not between the dragon and his wrath', in William Shakespeare, *King Lear*, Act I, scene i.

1 Not to be confused with 'Abd al-Haq Arsala.

2 For example, Maria Golovnina and Sheree Sardar, 'Pakistani "Father of Taliban" keeps watch over loyal disciples', 15 September 2013, www.reuters. com.

3 Human Rights Watch, *Afghanistan: The Massacre in Mazar-i Sharif*, vol. X, no. 7 (C), November 1998, www.hrw.org.

4 *The Osama bin Laden File*, National Security Archive Electronic Briefing Book 343, http://nsarchive.gwu.edu.

5 'Albright Lambasts Taliban over Treatment of Women', *Chicago Tribune*, 19 November 1997.

6 'Deputy Secretary Armitage-Mahmoud phone call', 18 September 2001, National Security Archives, *New Documents Detail America's Strategic Response to 9/11* (henceforth NSA, *New Documents, 9/11*), no. 9, http:// nsarchive.gwu.edu.

7 'Embassy in Islamabad to Secretary of State', 23 September 2001, NSA, *New Documents, 9/11*, no. 8, http://nsarchive.gwu.edu.

8 'Embassy in Islamabad to Secretary of State; Musharraf, we are with you in your action plan in Afghanistan', 13 September 2001, NSA, *New Documents, 9/11*, no. 4, http://nsarchive.gwu.edu.

9 'Armstrong to Chamberlain, Message to Taliban', 7 October 2001, NSA, *New Documents, 9/11*, no. 16, http://nsarchive.gwu.edu.

10 'Rumsfeld to Feith, u.s. Strategy in Afghanistan', 16 October 2001, NSA, *New Documents, 9/11*, no. 18, http://nsarchive.gwu.edu.

11 For the list of u.s. demands see 'Deputy Secretary Armitage's Meeting with General Mahmoud: actions and support expected in the fight against Terrorism', 14 September 2001, NSA, *New Documents, 9/11*, no. 5, http://nsarchive.gwu.edu.

12 Physicians for Social Responsibly, *Body Count, Casualty Figures after 10 Years of the 'War on Terror', Iraq, Afghanistan, Pakistan* (Washington, DC, Berlin and Ottawa, March 2015); Bureau of Investigative Journalism, *Drone Warfare, The Bush Years: Pakistan Strikes, 2004–2009*, www.thebureauinvestigates.com.

13 Donald Rumsfeld to Douglas Feith, U.S. *Strategy in Afghanistan*, National Security Council, 16 October 2001.

14 'Interview: Colin Powell', PBS *Frontline*, 7 June 2002, available at www.pbs.org.

15 Francesc Vendrell, 'A Decade of Mistakes', *Foreign Policy*, 3 December 2011, http://foreignpolicy.com.

16 'Interview: Colin Powell', PBS *Frontline*, 7 June 2002.

17 For the text of the Bonn Agreement, see 'Agreement on Provisional Arrangements in Afghanistan pending the re-establishment of Permanent Government Institutions', www.un.org.

18 Chris Johnson and Jolyon Leslie, *Afghanistan: The Mirage of Peace* (London and New York, 2004).

19 See Kara Jensen, 'Obstacles to Accessing the State Justice System in Rural Afghanistan', *Indiana Journal of Global Legal Studies*, XVIII/2 (summer 2011), www.repository.law.indiana.edu.

20 For the text of the 2004 Constitution, see www.afghan-web.com.

21 For Dostam's role in the U.S. campaign of 2001 and the black propaganda campaign, see Brian Glyn Williams, *The Last Warlord: The Life and Legend of Dostum* (Chicago, IL, 2013), pp. 225–73.

22 Peter W. Galbraith, 'UN isn't addressing Fraud in Afghan Election', *Washington Post*, 4 October 2009, www.washingtonpost.com.

23 Kai Eide, *Power Struggle over Afghanistan* (New York, 2012), p. 21.

24 Rumsfeld's press conference can be viewed at www.youtube.com.

25 Special Inspector General for Afghanistan Reconstruction (SIGAR), *High-risk List, Afghanistan*, 2016, www.sigar.mil.

26 UNAMA, *Afghanistan: Record Level of Civilian Casualties Sustained in the First Half of 2016*, http://unama.unmissions.org; SIGAR, 'Reprioritizing Afghanistan Reconstruction', *Quarterly Report to the United States Congress*, 30 April 2017, www.sigar.mil, pp. 1–13; Neta C. Crawford, *War-related Death, Injury and Displacement in Afghanistan and Pakistan, 2001–2014*, Watson Institute for International and Public Affairs, 22 May 2015, http://watson.brown.edu.

27 See Sarah Sewall, 'Introduction to the University of Chicago Press Edition: A Radical Field Manual', in *The U.S. Army/Marine Corps Counterinsurgency Field Manual* (Chicago, IL, 2007), pp. xxvi–xxxii.

28 Eide, *Power Struggle over Afghanistan*, p. 236.

29 SIGAR, *36th (July 2017) Quarterly Report to Congress*, www.sigar.mil.

30 Figures vary considerably, see Curt Tarnoff, *Afghanistan: U.S. Foreign Assistance*, CRS Report for Congress, 12 August 2010, www.fas.org; Matt Waldman, *Falling Short: Aid Effectiveness in Afghanistan*, ACBAR Advocacy Series, March 2008, www.oxfam.org.

31 International Crisis Group, *Women and Conflict in Afghanistan* (Brussels, 2014).

32 USAID Office of the Inspector General, *Audit of USAID/Afghanistan's Skills Training for Afghan Youth Project*, February 2012, p. 1, https://oig.usaid.gov.

33 Aureo de Toledo Gomes, 'Statebuilding and the Politics of Budgeting in Afghanistan', *Journal of Intervention and State Building*, 6 July 2017, https://dopi.

34 Ibid.; SIGAR, April 2017, 'Reprioritizing Afghanistan Reconstruction', www.sigar.mil.

35 SIGAR, 'Afghanistan's Mineral, Oil, and Gas Industries: Unless U.S. Agencies Act Soon to Sustain Investments, $488 Million in Funding is at Risk', *SIGAR 15-55 Audit Report*, April 2015, www.sigar.mil.

36 Figures for drug addicts in these countries vary greatly. See Lionel Beehner, *Afghanistan's Role in Iran's Drug Problem*, 13 September 2006; Brian Morales, *Afghanistan National Drug Use Survey 2012*, International Society of Substance Use Professionals (ISSUP), 20 October 2016, www.issup.net; Council on Foreign Relations, www.cfr.org; UNODC, *World Drug Report*, 2017, www.unodc.org.

37 John F. Sopko, 'The Fifteen Year Experiment: An Update on the Afghanistan Reconstruction Effort', presented to the Centre for International Policy Studies and the Fragile States Network, University of Ottawa, 5 April 2017, www.sigar.mil.

38 SIGAR, *35th (April 2017) Quarterly Report to Congress*, 1 May 2017; SIGAR, *High-risk List, Afghanistan*, 2016, www.sigar.mil.

39 Sopko, 'The Fifteen Year Experiment', p. 10.

40 'American Embassy in Kabul to Secretary of State, Washington', 7 February 2007, NSA, *New Documents, 9/11*, no. 25, http://nsarchive.gwu.edu.

SELECT BIBLIOGRAPHY

Adamec, Ludwig W., *Afghanistan, 1900–1923: A Diplomatic History* (Berkeley, CA, 1967)

—, *Afghanistan's Foreign Affairs to the Mid-twentieth Century* (Tucson, AZ, 1974)

—, *Historical Dictionary of Afghanistan* (Metuchen, NJ, and London, 1991)

Ahmed, Tariq, *Religio-political Ferment in the N. W. Frontier during the Mughal Period: The Raushaniya Movement* (Delhi, 1982)

Alexevich, Svetlana, *Zinky Boys: Soviet Voices from a Forgotten War*, trans. Julia and Robin Whitby (London, 1992)

'Ali, Mohammad, *A Cultural History of Afghanistan* (Kabul, 1964)

'Ali, Shahamat, *The Sikhs and Afghans in connexion* [*sic*] *with India and Persia* [1847] (New York, 2005)

Arnold, Anthony, *Afghanistan's Two Party Communism, Parcham and Khalq* (Stanford, CA, 1983)

Atkinson, James, *The Expedition into Affghanistan* [*sic*]*: Notes and Sketches Descriptive of the Country* [1842] (Uckfield, 2004)

Axworthy, M., *The Sword of Persia: Nadir Shah, from Tribal Warrior to Conquering Tyrant* (London and New York, 2006)

Azad, Arezou, *Sacred Landscape in Medieval Afghanistan: Revisiting the Fadā'il-i Balkh* (Oxford, 2013)

Ball, Warwick, *The Monuments of Afghanistan: History, Archaeology and Architecture* (London and New York, 2008)

—, *Towards One World: Ancient Persia and the West* (London, 2010)

—, *The Gates of Asia: The Eurasian Steppe and the Limits of Europe* (London, 2015)

Bayly, Martin J., *Taming the Imperial Imagination: Colonial Knowledge, International Relations, and the Anglo-Afghan Encounter, 1808–1878* (Cambridge, 2016)

Bell, Marjorie Jewett, ed., *An American Engineer in Afghanistan* [1948] (Kabul, 2004)

Bosworth, C. E., *The Ghaznavids: Their Empire in Afghanistan and Eastern India, 994–1040*, 1st Indian edn (New Delhi, 1992)

Burdett, A., ed., *Afghanistan Strategic Intelligence, 1919–1970*, 4 vols (Cambridge, 2008)

Burnes, Alexander, *Travels into Bukhara, being the Account of a Journey from India to Cabool, Tartary and Persia, etc., 1831–33*, 3 vols [1834] (New Delhi and Madras, 1992)

Byron, Robert, *The Road to Oxiana* [1937] (London, 1981)

Caroe, Olaf, *The Pathans, 550 BC–AD 1957* (Karachi, 1958)

Charkhi, Khaled Siddiq, *From My Memories: Memoirs of Political Imprisonment from Childhood in Afghanistan*, 2nd edn (Bloomington, IN, 2010)

Coll, Steve, *Ghost Wars* (London, New York and Toronto, 2005)

Conolly, Arthur, *Journey to the North of India, Overland from England through Russia, Persia, and Affghaunistaun* [*sic*], 2nd edn, 2 vols [1838] (New Delhi, 2001)

Cunningham, J. D., *History of the Sikhs* [1849] (Delhi, 1997)

Dalrymple, William, *Return of a King: The Battle for Afghanistan* (London, New Delhi and New York, 2013)

Delloye, Isabelle, *Women of Afghanistan*, trans. Marjolijn de Jager (St Paul, MN, 2003)

Doubleday, Veronica, *Three Women of Herat* (London, 1988)

Dupree, Louis, *Afghanistan*, 2nd edn (Princeton, NJ, 1978)

Dupree, Nancy Hatch, *A Historical Guide to Afghanistan* (Kabul, 1977)

Edwardes, Michael, *Playing the Great Game: A Victorian Cold War* (London, 1975)

Edwards, David B., *Before Taliban: Genealogies of the Afghan Jihad* (Berkeley, CA, 2002)

Eide, Kai, *Power Struggle over Afghanistan* (New York, 2012)

Elphinstone, Mountstuart, *An Account of the Kingdom of Caubul*, 2nd edn, 2 vols [1839] (Karachi, 1972)

Emadi, Hafizullah, *Politics of Development and Women in Afghanistan* (New York, 1993)

—, *Culture and Customs of Afghanistan* (Westport, CT, 2005)

—, *Dynamics of Political Development in Afghanistan: The British, Russian, and American Invasions* (New York and London, 2010)

Eyre, Vincent, *The Military Operations at Cabul* [1843] (Stroud, Glos., 2005)

Ferrier, J. P., *History of the Afghans* (London, 1858)

Fletcher, Arnold, *Afghanistan: Highway of Conquest* (Ithaca, NY, 1965)

Foltz, R. C., *Mughal India and Central Asia* (Oxford, 1998)

Forbes, Archibald, *The Afghan Wars, 1839–1842 and 1878–80* (London, 1892)

Forster, George, *A Journey from Bengal to England through the Northern Part of India, Kashmire, Afghanistan, and Persia etc.*, 2nd edn, 2 vols (London, 1808)

Fox, Ernest F., *Travels in Afghanistan, 1937–1938* (New York, 1943)

Fraser-Tytler, W. K., *Afghanistan: A Study of Political Developments in Central and Southern Asia*, 3rd edn (Oxford, 1967)

Fry, Maxwell J., *The Afghan Economy* (Leiden, 1974)

General Staff of India, *The Third Afghan War, 1919, Official Account* [1926] (Uckfield, n.d.)

Ghani, Abdul, *A Review of the Political Situation in Central Asia* [1921] (Lahore, 1980)

Ghaus, Abdul Samad, *The Fall of Afghanistan: An Insider's Account* (Washington, DC, 1988)

Gleig, Rev. G. H., *Sale's Brigade in Afghanistan, with an Account of the Seizure and Defence of Jellalabad* [1846] (Uckfield, 2004)

Gommans, Jos J. L., *The Rise of the Indo-Afghan Empire, c. 1710–1780*
(Leiden, 1995)

Goodson, Larry P., *Afghanistan's Endless War, State Failure, Regional Politics and the Rise of the Taliban* (Seattle, WA, and London, 2001)

Government of India, *Official History of Operations on the N. W. Frontier of India, 1920–35*, parts 1–3 [1945] (Uckfield, 2004)

Gray, John Alfred, *My Residence at the Court of the Amir* [1895] (London, 1987)

Green, Nile, ed., *Afghanistan's Islam: From Conversion to the Taliban* (Oakland, CA, 2016)

Greenwood, Lieutenant [Joseph], *Narrative of the Late Victorious Campaign under General Pollock* [1844] (Uckfield, 2004)

Gregorian, Vartan, *The Emergence of Modern Afghanistan: Politics of Reform and Modernization, 1880–1946* (Stanford, CA, 1969)

Hamilton, Angus, *Afghanistan* (Boston, MA, and Tokyo, 1910)

Hanifi, Shah Mahmoud, *Connecting Histories in Afghanistan: Market Relations and State Formation on a Colonial Frontier* (Stanford, CA, 2011)

Harlan, Josiah, *A Memoir of India and Avghanistaun* (Philadelphia, 1842)

Hensman, Howard, *The Afghan War of 1879–1880* [1881] (Lahore, 1999)

Hopkins, Benjamin D., *The Making of Modern Afghanistan* (Cambridge, 2008)

Hunter, Edward, *The Past Present: An Account of Life in Afghanistan Today* (London, 1959)

Jafri, Hasan 'Ali Shah, *Indo-Afghan Relations, 1947–1967* (New Delhi, 1976)

Jalallar, Muhammad Khan, *Rumi Tomato: Autobiography of an Afghan Minister* (Create Space self-publishing, 2001)

James, Ben, *The Secret Kingdom: An Afghan Journey* (New York, 1934)

Johnson, Chris, and Jolyon Leslie, *Afghanistan: The Mirage of Peace* (London and New York, 2004)

Jones, Paul S., *Afghanistan Venture* (San Antonio, TX, 1956)

Kakar, M. Hassan, *Afghanistan: A Study in International Political Developments, 1880–1896* (Kabul, 1971)

——, *Afghanistan: The Soviet Invasion and the Afghan Response, 1979–1982* (Berkeley, CA, and London, 1995)

——, *A Political and Diplomatic History of Afghanistan, 1863–1901* (Leiden, 2006)

Katrak, Sohrab K. H., *Through Amanullah's Afghanistan* (Karachi, 1929)

Kaye, John William, *Lives of the Indian Officers*, 2 vols (London, 1867)

——, *History of the War in Afghanistan*, 2 vols [1851] (Delhi, 1999)

Kessler, Melvin M., *Ivan Viktorovich Vitkevich, 1806–1839* (Washington, DC, 1960)

Khalid, Adeeb, *The Politics of Muslim Cultural Reform: Jadidism in Central Asia* [1998] (Karachi, 2000)

Khalili, Jehanzeb, *Mujahideen Movement in Malakand and Mohmand Agencies (1900–1940)*, ed. M. Y. Effendi (Peshawar, 2000)

Khan, Shah Wali, *My Memoirs* (Kabul, 1970)

Khan, Sultan Mahomed, *The Life of Abdur Rahman Amir of Afghanistan*, 2 vols [1900] (Karachi, Oxford and New York, 1980)

Khan, Umar Kamal, *Rise of Saddozais and Emancipation of Afghans* (Multan, 1999)

Klimberg, Max, *The Kafirs of the Hindu Kush: Art and Society of the Waigal and Ashkun Kafirs*, 2 vols (Wiesbaden, 1999)

Kohzad, A. A., *Men and Events through 18th and 19th Century Afghanistan* (Kabul, 1972)

Koplik, Sara, *A Political and Economic History of the Jews of Afghanistan* (Leiden and Boston, MA, 2015)

Lal, Mohan, *Life of the Amir Dost Muhammad Khan of Kabul*, 2 vols [1846] (New Delhi, 2004)

—, *Travels in the Panjab, Afghanistan and Turkistan, to Balk, Bokhara and Herat* [1846] (Boston, MA, 2005)

Lee, Jonathan L., *The 'Ancient Supremacy': Bukhara, Afghanistan and the Battle for Balkh, 1732–1901* (Leiden, Cologne and New York, 1996)

—, *Amazing Wonders of Afghanistan* (Kabul, 2014)

Lockhart, L., *Nadir Shah: A Critical Study* (London, 1938)

—, *The Fall of the Safawid Dynasty and the Afghan Occupation of Persia* (Cambridge, 1958)

Lowen, A., and Josette McMichael, eds, *Images of Afghanistan* (Karachi, Oxford and New York, 2010)

McCabe, Ina Baghdiantz, *The Shah's Silk for Europe's Silver: Eurasian Trade of the Julfa Armenians in Safavid Iran and India (1530–1750)* (Atlanta, GA, 1999)

McChesney, Robert D., *Waqf in Central Asia* (Princeton, NJ, 1985)

Macintyre, Ben, *Josiah the Great: The True Story of the Man who would be King* (London, 2004)

Maley, William, *Fundamentalism Reborn? Afghanistan and the Taliban* (Lahore, 1998)

—, *The Foreign Policy of the Taliban* (New York, 1999)

Mango, Andrew, *Atatürk* (London, 1999)

Martin, Frank A., *Under the Absolute Amir* [1907] (Lahore, 1998)

Marwat, Fazal-ur-Rahim Khan, *The Basmachi Movement in Soviet Central Asia* (Peshawar, 1969)

Masson, Charles, *Narrative of Various Journeys in Balochistan, Afghanistan, the Panjab, & Kalât*, 3 vols [1842] (Delhi, 1997)

Mason, Whit, ed., *The Rule of Law in Afghanistan: Missing in Inaction* (Cambridge, New York and Melbourne, 2011)

Mills, H. Woosnam, *The Pathan Revolt in North West India* [1897] (Lahore, 1996)

Minault, Gail, *The Khilafat Movement: Religious Symbolism and Political Mobilization in India* (New York, 1982)

Moorcroft, William, and George Trebeck, *Travels in the Himalayan Provinces of Hindustan and the Punjab from 1819 to 1825*, 2 vols [1841] (Karachi, 1979)

Moulton, Edward C., *Lord Northbrook's Indian Administration* (London, 1968)

Mousavi, Sayed Askar, *The Hazaras of Afghanistan: An Historical, Cultural, Economic and Political Study* (Richmond, Surrey, 1998)

Nasiri, Afzal, and Marie Khalili, eds, *Memoirs of Khalilullah Khalili: An Afghan Philosopher Poet* (Manassas, VA, 2013)

Nawid, Senzil, *Religious Response to Social Change in Afghanistan, 1919–29: King Aman-Allah and the Afghan Ulama* (Costa Mesa, CA, 1999)

Noelle, Christine, *State and Tribe in Nineteenth-century Afghanistan: The Reign of Dost Muhammad Khan (1826–1863)* (Abingdon, 1977)

Noelle-Karimi, C. Schetter, and R. Schlagintweit, eds, *Afghanistan: A Country without a State?* (Linz, 2002)

Norris, J. A., *The First Afghan War, 1838–1842* (Cambridge, 1967)

Olesen, Asta, *Islam and Politics in Afghanistan* (Richmond, Surrey, 1996)

Pottinger, George, *The Afghan Connection: The Extraordinary Adventures of Major Eldred Pottinger* (Edinburgh, 1983)

Poullada, Leon B., *Reform and Rebellion in Afghanistan, 1919–1929* (Ithaca, NY, 1973)

Pstrusinska, Jadwiga, 'Afghanistan 1989 in Sociolinguist Perspective', *Central Asian Survey*, Incidental Papers, no. 7 (1990)

Rahim, M. Akbar, *History of the Afghans in India, AD 1545–1631* (Karachi, 1961)

Rashid, Ahmed, *Taliban: Islam, Oil and the New Game in Central Asia* (London and New York, 2002)

—, *Descent into Chaos: Pakistan, Afghanistan and the Threat to Global Security* (London, 2009)

Rawlinson, Maj. Gen. Sir Henry, *England and Russia in the East* (London, 1875)

Robertson, George Scott, *The Kafirs of the Hindu Kush* [1896] (Lahore, 1995)

Robson, B., ed., *Roberts in India: The Military Papers of Field Marshal Lord Roberts, 1876–1893* (Stroud, Glos., and Dover, NH, 1993)

Ross, F. E., ed., *Central Asia: Personal Narrative of General Josiah Harlan, 1823–1841* (London, 1939)

Roy, O., *Islam and Resistance in Afghanistan*, 2nd edn (Cambridge and New York, 1990)

Rubin, Barnett R., *The Fragmentation of Afghanistan*, imprint (New Haven, CT, 1995)

—, *The Search for Peace in Afghanistan: From Buffer State to Failed State* (New Haven, CT, and London, 1995)

Saikal, Amin, *Modern Afghanistan: A History of Struggle and Survival* (London and New York, 2004)

Sale, Lady Florentia, *A Journal of the Disasters in Affghanistan, 1841–2* [1843] (Lahore, 1999)

Schinasi, May, *Afghanistan at the Beginning of the Twentieth Century: Nationalism and Journalism in Afghanistan, a Study of the Serâj ul-akhbâr (1911–1918)* (Naples, 1979)

—, *Kaboul, 1773–1948* (Naples, 2008)

Scott-Moncrieff, Maj. Gen. Sir George Kenneth, *Canals and Campaigns: An Engineer Officer in India, 1877–1885* (London, 1987)

Simpson, St John, *Afghanistan: A Cultural History* (London, 2012)

Singh, Ganda, *Ahmad Shah Durrani*, 2nd edn (Lahore, 1981)

Skrine, F. H., and E. D. Ross, *The Heart of Asia* (London, 1899)

Stocqueler, J. H., *Memorials of Affghanistan, 1838–1842* [1843] (Peshawar, 1969)

Sykes, P., *A History of Afghanistan*, 2 vols [1940] (New Delhi, 1981)

Tanwir, Dr M. Halim, *Afghanistan: History, Diplomacy and Journalism*, 2 vols (Bloomington, IN, 2012)

Tarzi, Mahmud, *Reminiscences: A Short History of an Era (1869–1881)*, trans. and ed. Wahid Tarzi (New York, 1998)

Tate, George Passman, *The Kingdom of Afghanistan: A Historical Sketch* (Bombay, 1910)

Thomas, Lowell, *Beyond the Khyber Pass* [1925] (Lahore, 1998)

Thornton, Ernest, and Annie Thornton, *Leaves from an Afghan Scrapbook* (London, 1910)

Trinkler, Emil, *Through the Heart of Afghanistan* (London, 1928)

Trousdale, William, ed., *War in Afghanistan, 1879–80: The Personal Diary of Major General Sir Charles Metcalfe MacGregor* (Detroit, MI, 1985)

Vogelsang, W., *The Afghans* (London and Malden, MA, 2002)

Washburne, Nancy Howland, ed., *The Afghan Diaries of Captain George Felix Howland, 1935–1936* (McKinney, TX, 2008)

Whitteridge, Gordon, *Charles Masson of Afghanistan: Explorer, Archaeologist, Numismatist and Intelligence Agent* (Warminster, Wilts, 1986)

Wilber, Donald N., *Afghanistan: Its People, its Society, its Culture* (New Haven, CT, 1962)

Wild, Roland, *Amanullah, ex-king of Afghanistan* (London, 1932)

Williams, Brian Glyn, *The Last Warlord: The Life and Legend of Dostum* (Chicago, IL, 2013)

Wilson, Andrew, *North from Kabul* (London, 1961)

Wolff, Rev. Joseph, *Researches and Missionary Labours* (Philadelphia, 1837)

—, *Narrative of a Mission to Bokhara* (London, 1848)

Woodburn, Brig. C. W., *The Bala Hissar of Kabul: Revealing a Fortress-palace in Afghanistan* (Chatham, 2009)

Wyatt, Christopher M., *Afghanistan and the Defence of Empire: Diplomacy and Strategy during the Great Game* (London and New York, 2011)

Yapp, Malcolm, *Strategies of British India* (Oxford, 1980)

—, *The Making of the Modern Near East, 1792–1923* (Harlow, New York and Tokyo, 1987)

Yate, A. C., *England and Russia Face to Face in Asia, Travels with the Afghan Boundary Commission* (London, 1887)

Yate, C. E., *Northern Afghanistan* (London, 1888)

—, *Khurasan and Sistan* (London, 1900)

Yermakov, Oleg, *Afghan Tales: Stories from Russia's Vietnam*, trans. Marc Romano (New York, 1993)

Zahab, Mariam Abou, and Olivier Roy, *Islamist Networks: The Afghan-Pakistan Connection* (London, 2004)

Persian and other oriental sources

Ahmad, Tasneem, *Tārīkh-i-Akbarī of Muhammad ʿArīf Qandhārī* (Delhi, 1993)

Babur, Zahir al-Din, *Bābur-Nāma*, trans. and ed. Annette S. Beveridge [1922] (Lahore, 1979)

Begam, Gul-Badan, *The History of Humayun, the Humāyūn-Nāma*, trans. and ed. A. Beveridge [1902] (Delhi, 2006)

Farhang, Mir M. Sadiq, *Afghānistān dar panj qarn-i ākhir*, 3 vols (Kabul, 1373 s./1994)

Ghorbar, Mir Gholam Mohammad, *Ahmad Shāh Bābā-yi Afghān* (Kabul, 1322 s./1943)

Gulistana, Abu'l-Hasan ibn Amin, 'The End of Nadir Shah, being Extracts from the Mujmal al-Tawārīkh', trans. Jadunath Sarkar, *Modern Review*, XLV/5 (May 1929), pp. 533–6

al-Husaini, Munshi Mahmud ibn Ibrahim al-Jami, *Tārīkh-i Ahmad Shāhī* [1974] (Peshawar, 2001)

Katib, Faiz Muhammad, *Serāj al-Tawārīkh*, 3 vols (Kabul 1331–3 s./1913–15)

——, *Kabul under Siege: Fayz Muhammad's Account of the 1929 Uprising*, trans. and ed. R. D. McChesney (Princeton, NJ, 1999)

Kazim, Muhammad, *Nāma-yi 'Ālam-ārā-yi Nādirī*, 3 vols (Moscow, 1962–6)

Khan, Amir 'Abd al-Rahman, *Tāj al-Tawārīkh*, 2 vols [1900] (Peshawar, 1994/5)

Khan, Hayat M., *Afghanistan and its Inhabitants, translated from the Hayāt-i-Afghānī*, trans. Henry Priestley [1874] (Lahore, 1999)

Mujadidi, Shah Agha, *Amīr Habīb Allah* (Peshawar?, n.d.)

Neamat Ullah, Khwaja, *History of the Afghans translated from the Persian of Neamet Ullah*, trans. Bernard Dorn [1829] (New York, 1969)

Popalzai, 'Aziz al-Din Wakili, *Ahmad Shāh*, vol. I (Kabul, 1359 s./1980)

Records, manuscripts and unpublished theses

Caron, James M., 'Cultural Histories of Pasthun Nationalism, Public Participation, and Social Inequality in Monarchic Afghanistan, 1905–1960', PhD thesis, University of Pennsylvania, 2009

Champagne, David Charles, 'The Afghan-Iranian Conflict over Herat Province and European Intervention, 1796–1863: A Reinterpretation', PhD thesis, University of Texas, 1981

Durand, H. M., 'Diary of the Afghanistan Mission, 1893', British Library, Asia and Africa Collection, India Office Library and Records (IOL), Durand Papers, Eur. Mss D 727/5

Durrani, Ashiq Muhammad Khan, 'The Last Phase of Muslim Rule in Multan', unpublished (?) PhD thesis, University of Multan, n.d.

Hamilton, Lilias, 'The Power that Walks in Darkness', Wellcome Institute for the History of Medicine, PP/HAM/A.21

Jawan Shir, Rasikh, 'Nationalism in Afghanistan: Colonial Knowledge, Education, Symbols and the Junket Tour of Amanullah Khan, 1901–1929', MA thesis, James Madison University, 2012

Lee, Jonathan L., 'The New Year's Festivals and the Shrine of 'Ali ibn Abi Talib at Mazar-i Sharif, Afghanistan', PhD thesis, Department of Religious Studies, University of Leeds, 1998

Masson, Charles, 'Journals', British Library, IOR, Eur. Mss E.163

'Report of Ghulam Sarwar, Native agent of the Hon. East India Co., on Special Mission to the Country of Shah Zemaun, 1793–1795', IOR, Proceedings, Bengal Secret Consultations (1797), P/BEN/CON/41

ACKNOWLEDGEMENTS

I am indebted to many individuals who have assisted me in various ways with the research and writing of this book. I owe a particular debt to those many Afghans who, over the past forty or more years since I first visited their country, have contributed to my knowledge of Afghanistan, told me their stories and challenged many of my preconceptions. I am also thankful to the many people who have generously accommodated me and facilitated my work during my visits to Afghanistan, Pakistan, Uzbekistan and Tajikistan, as well as those who have hosted me during my research in the UK.

Profs Jamil Hanifi, Shah Mahmoud Hanifi and Said Reza Huseini provided me with comments on various aspects of this study and references to Persian sources. Shah Mahmoud Hanifi also reviewed the book and made some helpful and incisive comments. Dr Christopher Wyatt, Research Fellow at the Institute of Conflict, Cooperation and Security, University of Birmingham, helped with a number of British Foreign Office reports as well as reviewing the book, making a number of factual and typographical corrections. I am also thankful for my many conversations with Dr Wyatt over the past two decades around British imperial policy in Afghanistan. Bruce Wannell kindly checked, corrected and commented on the glossary of foreign terms and Warwick Ball FSA generously granted me the use of some of his archival images and has encouraged the completion of this work.

Others who have contributed in various ways include: Dr Arezu Azad of the University of Birmingham, and the Balkh Archaeological and Cultural Heritage group at the Oriental Institute, Oxford; Paul Bucherer-Dietschi of the Bibliotheca Afghanica; William Dalrymple; Dr Nancy Dupree of the Afghan Study Centre, Kabul University; Jolyon Leslie of the Afghan Cultural Heritage Consulting Organization; Dr Arley Loewen; May Schinasi; Brigadier C. W. ('Bill') Woodburn RE; and William Trousdale, Emeritus Curator of the Smithsonian Institute. Thanks too is due to Sebastian Ballard, my cartographer, who has done a superb job.

Like many, I am indebted to the late Ralph Pinder-Wilson FSA, former Director of the British Institute of Afghan Studies, and Prof. Edmund Bosworth, both of whom encouraged my studies for many years and whose deaths are a great loss to Afghan, Islamic and Middle Eastern Studies. Yolande Carter, my 93-year-old mother-in-law, deserves a medal for proofreading successive drafts and redrafts of this book. I cannot begin to express my thankfulness to my wife, Kathy, for her constant encouragement to persist with this and other projects when on occasion I have despaired that it would never be completed.

PHOTO ACKNOWLEDGEMENTS

The author and the publishers wish to express their thanks to the below sources of illustrative material and/or permission to reproduce it.

Author's Collection: pp. 15, 18, 21, 25, 27, 32, 36, 37, 40, 41, 48, 53, 58, 62, 71, 82, 92, 97, 98, 99, 108, 119, 120, 132, 133, 135, 145, 146, 152, 157, 166, 180, 189, 197, 199, 200, 202, 210, 216, 224, 238, 248, 271, 274, 275, 277, 286, 311, 313, 321, 324, 329, 331, 347, 365, 369, 377, 381, 389, 391, 399, 403, 407, 409, 413, 420, 428, 438, 445, 456, 458, 466, 471, 472, 477, 495, 504, 506, 516, 520, 528, 536, 538, 542, 547, 548, 551, 555, 558, 577, 579, 596, 598, 602, 606, 613, 621, 624, 626, 627, 633, 641, 645, 646, 654, 659, 664; Copyright © Warwick Ball, by kind permission: pp. 67, 89, 182, 519, 544; © Sebastian Ballard (2018): pp. 11, 50, 186, 243; Copyright © the Breshna family, reproduced by kind permission: p. 112; Kathy Carter-Lee: p. 672; Courtesy of the Council of the National Army Museum, London: pp. 294, 301; Courtesy of John Weedy: pp. 104, 483, 486; copyright © the family of J. Christy Wilson, reproduced with kind permission: p. 577.

INDEX

To alphabetize Arabic names, those beginning with 'Abd al- are alphabetized under the element following the particle, unless 'Abd is related grammatically to the follow name; those beginning with al- are alphabetized under the element following the particle, while those beginning with Abu, bin or Ibn are alphabetized under these elements.

Persian names ending in Khan are alphabetized under the preceding element. Where two preceding elements are grammatically linked, they are alphabetized by the first element of the compound: for example, Rahim Dil Khan, not Rahim, Dil Khan.